THE LETTERS OF
A. BRONSON ALCOTT

Edited by
RICHARD L. HERRNSTADT

THE ALCOTT LETTERS take one back to a graceful and enviable time that is a valued part of our American heritage, the New England period of Alcott, Emerson, and Thoreau. The parental guidance and encouragement, the gracious manners, and the lively intellectual achievement are here delineated in this collection of all available extant letters written by the father of Louisa May Alcott.

The value of Alcott's correspondence as a resource collection lies in his generous descriptions of nineteenth-century New England life, with emphasis on the transcendentalist intellectual community. Enthusiastically engaged in many activities, Alcott was involved in the movements of the time and came into contact with many prominent individuals. His letters describe such subjects as the life of a Yankee peddler; passenger life aboard ship to England; England in the early 1840's; the widespread nineteenth-century interest in communal living; health movements; the struggle for women's rights; the Concord School of Philosophy; and philosophical trends in America. His acquaintances and correspondents include such figures as Emerson, Thoreau, Agassiz, Julia Ward Howe, Carlyle, Whitman, and Horace Greeley. ▶

The letters illustrate the kinds of incidents and ideas and the sources of satisfaction that were influential in Alcott's life. While past impressions of Alcott often have emphasized the failures occurring early in his career, the letters reveal the comparative success he enjoyed in his later years. Taken together, they reveal the flavor of much of Alcott's life in a direct, intimate, and complete way—confirming part of the present estimate of the man, while providing some new impressions and correcting some of the existing distortions. They tell a story that is not one of failures, but rather of an original thinker whose ideas gained a significant degree of acceptance in the later years of his life.

The Letters of
A. BRONSON ALCOTT

The Letters of
A. Bronson Alcott

Edited by
Richard L. Herrnstadt

The Iowa State University Press, Ames, Iowa

RICHARD L. HERRNSTADT is professor of English and chairman of Freshman English, Iowa State University. He holds the Ph.D. degree from the University of Maryland and the M.S. and B.S. degrees from the University of Wisconsin.

FRONTISPIECE: Portrait of Alcott by Winckler (1877). *(Courtesy Concord Free Public Library)*

© 1969 The Iowa State University Press, Ames, Iowa 50010. All rights reserved. Composed and printed by The Iowa State University Press. FIRST EDITION, 1969. Standard Book Number: 8138-0087-0. Library of Congress Catalog Card Number: 76-76209.

FOR HELEN

CONTENTS

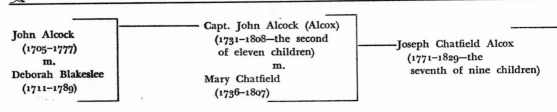

John Alcock
(1705–1777)
m.
Deborah Blakeslee
(1711–1789)

Capt. John Alcock (Alcox)
(1731–1808—the second
of eleven children)
m.
Mary Chatfield
(1736–1807)

Joseph Chatfield Alcox
(1771–1829—the
seventh of nine children)

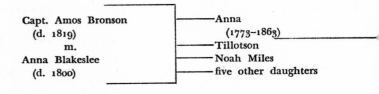

Capt. Amos Bronson
(d. 1819)
m.
Anna Blakeslee
(d. 1800)

Anna
(1773–1863)
Tillotson
Noah Miles
five other daughters

Joseph May
(1760–1841)
m.
Dorothy Sewall
(1788–1825)

The principal sources of this genealogy are Samuel Orcutt, *History of the Town of Wolcott (Connecticut) from 1731 to 1874* (Waterbury, Conn., 1874); *A Genealogy of the Descendants of John May* (Boston, 1878).

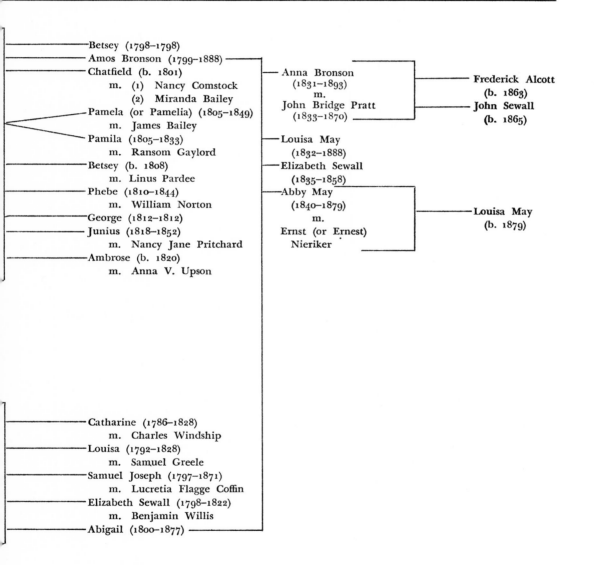

Betsey (1798–1798)

Amos Bronson (1799–1888) ——

Chatfield (b. 1801)
    m. (1) Nancy Comstock
       (2) Miranda Bailey

Pamela (or Pamelia) (1805–1849)
    m. James Bailey

Pamila (1805–1833)
    m. Ransom Gaylord

Betsey (b. 1808)
    m. Linus Pardee

Phebe (1810–1844)
    m. William Norton

George (1812–1812)

Junius (1818–1852)
    m. Nancy Jane Pritchard

Ambrose (b. 1820)
    m. Anna V. Upson

Anna Bronson
(1831–1893)
m.
John Bridge Pratt
(1833–1870) ——

Louisa May
(1832–1888)

Elizabeth Sewall
(1835–1858)

Abby May
(1840–1879)
m.
Ernst (or Ernest)
Nieriker

Frederick Alcott
(b. 1863)

John Sewall
(b. 1865)

Louisa May
(b. 1879)

Catharine (1786–1828)
    m. Charles Windship

Louisa (1792–1828)
    m. Samuel Greele

Samuel Joseph (1797–1871)
    m. Lucretia Flagge Coffin

Elizabeth Sewall (1798–1822)
    m. Benjamin Willis

Abigail (1800–1877) ——

ILLUSTRATIONS

PREFACE

But for letters the best of our life would hardly survive the mood and the moment. Prompted by so lively a sentiment as friendship, we commit to our leaves what we should not have spoken. To begin with "Dear Friend" is in itself an address which clothes our epistle in a rhetoric the most select and choice. We cannot write it without considering its fitness and taxing our conscience in the matter. 'Tis coming to the confessional, leaving nothing in reserve that falls gracefully into words. A lifelong correspondence were a biography of the correspondents. Preserve your letters till time define their value. Some secret charm forbids committing them to the flame; the dews of the morning may sparkle there still, and remind one of his earlier Eden. . . . Letters . . . better represent life than any form in literature.
(A. Bronson Alcott, CONCORD DAYS, pp. 123–24)

AMONG THE 126 MS VOLUMES in a collection on deposit in the Harvard College Library are about thirty-seven volumes of the correspondence of Bronson Alcott. The material is bound chronologically and contains what must be a fair share of the letters written *to* Alcott. Those MS volumes also contain a large number of letters written by Alcott; for Alcott had early acquired the habit of making copies of and preserving letters he wrote to other people, although most of the letters to members of his family (many written while he was away from home) undoubtedly are originals.

The present volume is the first attempt to collect all extant Alcott letters.[1] Only a relative handful have been reproduced previously—and few of those have been quoted in full. Some letters appear in Franklin B. Sanborn

---

[1] I have seen a summary of the letters in the Alcott-Harris Collection in the Concord Free Public Library. For a list of those letters, see Appendix B.

and William T. Harris, *A. Bronson Alcott: His Life and Philosophy* (Boston, 1893), 2 vols.; a number of letters from Alcott to his daughters when they were young children have been quoted by Jessie Bonstelle and Marian deForest in their *Little Women Letters from the House of Alcott* (Boston, 1914); some early letters have been quoted in part in the notes in Sanborn's edition (Boston, 1887) of Alcott's autobiographical poem, *New Connecticut* (see Appendix A); and occasional letters and/or parts of letters may be found in other printed sources.

The major source of the letters in this present edition is the Harvard College Library collection—already mentioned—referred to herein as the Alcott-Pratt Collection. (Microfilm copies of the Alcott-Pratt Collection have been retained in the Concord Free Public Library.) Letters were also discovered in a number of other places. Chief among these are the Fruitlands Museums in Harvard, Massachusetts, which has over fifty items, including a number of Alcott's letters to Mary E. Stearns; the Abernethy Library at Middlebury College, which has the originals of forty of Alcott's letters to Ellen A. Chandler; other collections in the Harvard College Library; the New York Public Library; and the Clifton Waller Barrett Library at the University of Virginia. Alcott's letters to Georgiana Hemingway Cook are in the Flavius Josephus Cook Papers in the Duke University Library. Other collections containing fewer Alcott letters are noted elsewhere in the list of acknowledgments.

My work has been made possible primarily by the kindness of the late Frederic Wolsey Pratt, Bronson Alcott's great-grandson, and formerly owner of the Alcott manuscripts now housed in the Harvard College Library. Both Mr. and Mrs. Pratt gave me permission for the use of Alcott's letters, as well as permission to make photocopies of the letters, which greatly facilitated my work.

For permission to make use of Alcott letters in their collections, I am indebted to the Abernethy Library at Middlebury College; the American Antiquarian Society; Mrs. Adele A. Bachman, South Orange, New Jersey; the Boston Public Library; the Boston University Libraries; the Brown University Library, for material in the Harris Collection of American Poetry and Plays; the Cincinnati Historical Society; the Clifton Waller Barrett Library at the University of Virginia; the Concord Antiquarian Society; John L. Cooley; the Cornell University Library; the Dartmouth College Library; the Detroit Public Library, for material in the Burton Historical Collection; the Duke University Library; the Friends Historical Society of Swarthmore College; the Fruitlands Museums; the Harvard College Library; the Haverford College Library, for a letter in the Charles Roberts Autograph Collection; the Historical Society of Pennsylvania; the University of Illinois Library; the Iowa State Department of History and Archives; the Library of Congress; the Library of the Chicago Historical Society; the

Lilly Library at Indiana University; the Louisa May Alcott Memorial Association; the Massachusetts Historical Society; the Minneapolis Public Library; the New York Historical Society; the New York Public Library, for material in the Berg Collection and in the Manuscript Division (Astor, Lenox, and Tilden Foundations); the Pattee Library at Pennsylvania State University, for a letter in the Pennsylvania Historical Collections; the Tanner Library at Illinois College, for a letter in the Beecher Family Letters; the Vassar College Library; the Wellesley College Library; the Yale University Library.

Very special thanks are due Professor Carl Bode of the University of Maryland for his advice while this work has been in progress. I also wish to express my appreciation to the following persons: Dr. William Henry Harrison, Director of the Fruitlands Museums, both for permission to use the letters in that collection and for his many suggestions; Professor Leonard Lutwack of the University of Maryland; Professors David K. Bruner, Robert B. Orlovich, and Norris W. Yates of Iowa State University; Professor Ethel Seybold of Illinois College; Mr. George Goodspeed of Concord, Massachusetts; Mrs. Ednah Henry of Ames, Iowa, who did the bulk of the typing for me; the librarians at the Concord Free Public Library who helped make my work there so pleasant; Mrs. Marcia E. Moss of the Concord Free Public Library, who was kind enough to arrange for some of the illustrations used in this edition; and the librarians at Iowa State University.

I particularly wish to note my gratitude to Professor Albert L. Walker of Iowa State University and to his wife, Jav, for their considerable help during the time this edition has been in progress.

A grant from the Iowa State University Research Foundation has made possible the publication of this edition.

Finally, I am especially grateful to my family for their patience and understanding—and particularly to my wife, Helen, for that and for the countless hours she spent proofreading the manuscript with me.

R. L. H.

INTRODUCTION

T͟H͟E͟ ͟L͟E͟T͟T͟E͟R͟S͟ ͟O͟F͟ B͟R͟O͟N͟S͟O͟N͟ A͟L͟C͟O͟T͟T͟ are brought together primarily for two reasons. First, they are intended as a resource collection to be used as one means of understanding a number of aspects of nineteenth-century life with an emphasis on the intellectual community. A glance through the collection will show that Alcott engaged in many activities, that he was interested in any number of movements and came in contact with any number of prominent people. Among other things, the letters describe, in varying degrees of completeness, the life of a Yankee peddler (Letter 20–1 and Appendix A);[1] educational movements of the time; passenger life aboard ship to England (Letters 42–5 and 42–6); one American's view of England of the early 1840's (Letters 42–7 to 42–16); the widespread nineteenth-century interest in communal living; health movements, particularly water cures and vegetarianism; the struggle for women's rights (see especially Letters 69–20 and 69–41); the Concord School of Philosophy (letters for 1879, 1880); philosophical trends in America. Alcott had more than a passing interest in these and many other matters of which, the letters show, he was knowledgeable in more than a superficial way. A list of his acquaintances and correspondents would be indeed extensive, but in mentioning a few at random, one would include Emerson, Thoreau, Agassiz, the Channings, Julia Ward Howe, Franklin B. Sanborn—actually, just about all the leading intellectual figures of New England—and Carlyle, Whitman, Henry Barnard, Horace Greeley, A. R. Spofford, Millard Fillmore, Isaac Hecker, and Mary Baker Eddy.

The use of Alcott's correspondence as a resource collection will be dealt with indirectly in the main body of this introduction; to realize it fully and fairly one must look at the letters themselves.

A second major reason for bringing these letters together is that they are one aspect of Alcott's own life that has not been examined earlier. They add substantially to the picture of Alcott and confirm much that has been previously recorded about him. They reveal the flavor of much of his life in a direct, intimate, and complete way. Most important, perhaps, the letters help to correct impressions of the man and his experience which

---

[1] The letters in this collection are numbered consecutively beginning with each year. The first two digits indicate the year; the last digit(s) the number of the letter. Hence, 20–1 would mean 1820, Letter 1.

have been based too heavily upon the failures which occurred during roughly the first half of his career. The two biographies of Alcott are concerned mainly with the first fifty years of his life.[2] On the other hand, most of the extant letters written by Alcott are concerned with his later years and the comparative success he then enjoyed—a success which is generally overlooked.

My purpose in this introduction, then, is to illustrate directly the second significance of the letters by summarizing some of the more important material contained in them. In that way it is shown how the letters confirm part of the present estimate of the man and how they provide some new impressions and correct some of the existing distortions.

Since I am trying to show how the letters are important for an overall view of Alcott from the beginning to the end of his career, the discussion of the letters is largely chronological. No attempt is made to provide the completeness that would be required in a biography, and many of the events in Alcott's long life, including some major ones, have been glossed over or simply omitted.[3] What follows illustrates the kinds of incident, the kinds of idea, and the sources of satisfaction which the letters show to have been influential during Alcott's life and which, taken together, convey the nature of the man. In that way may be seen, for example, the development of Alcott's views on education, the scope of his acquaintance with other people and the regard in which he was held by some of them, his religious attitudes, and his final assessment of communal living—in short, the effects that earlier events had upon later attitudes. (It may be observed that the story is not one of failure, but of a kind of moral certainty or innocence—a quality more rare today but enviable in any day.)

I have also attempted in this introduction a summary of the more general impressions which arise from the letters, impressions which really amount to a somewhat different perspective on Alcott.

1

BRONSON ALCOTT LIVED for eighty-eight years—from 1799 to 1888. He was born and reared in the environs of Wolcott, Connecticut, a short distance from Waterbury, and attended the local school. The land is poor and even today the area is sparsely settled.

Frequent hints, especially in later letters, reveal the life Alcott lived in those very early days, but none of the letters contains a detailed exposition of that life. Perhaps the best source of information concerning Alcott's youth is his autobiographical poem, *New Connecticut* (1881), and the copious notes to that work, particularly as added to by Sanborn in an edition published in 1887. That and the supplemental material in Odell Shepard's

---

[2] Odell Shepard in his *Pedlar's Progress* (Boston, 1937) devotes about 450 of 522 pages to that portion of Alcott's life. The proportion is about the same in F. B. Sanborn's *A. Bronson Alcott* (Boston, 1893).
[3] The introductory material presented is taken almost exclusively from the letters. Any other material is included mainly for reasons of continuity.

Pedlar's Progress provide a quite satisfactory outline of the routine of Alcott's youth.

The letters quoted or listed in the present collection do not begin, however, until Alcott had reached early manhood. When he was seventeen he set out on the first of several peddling expeditions to Virginia and the Carolinas in company with first a cousin, William Andrus Alcott, and later his brother Chatfield. The first trip was a moderate financial success, but the next four were disastrous. Alcott wound up his career as a peddler with a $420 deficit. In many respects the financial problem here illustrated was to recur throughout much of his life.

The earliest extant Alcott letter (Letter 20–1) is dated January 24, 1820, and is written from Norfolk, Virginia, to his parents in Wolcott.[4] The letter, interestingly, displays the same optimism that was to remain with Alcott with but rare, brief exceptions throughout his life. He wrote that he and Chatfield "have been very successful in business, notwithstanding the dulness & hardness of the times. . . ." They hoped to earn some $200 in eight or nine months in the South. Alcott also showed an interest in his work for other reasons: "I take much pleasure in travelling, & in conve[rsing] with the Virginians, in observing their different habits, manners, & customs, &c & I am conscious that it is of great advantage to me in many points of [view.]"

On two occasions, Alcott's motive for travelling South was not so much the promise of the money to be made from peddling, but to secure a position as a teacher in the Carolinas. Although unsuccessful in obtaining a teaching position in the South, Alcott seems to have retained that "professional" ambition. His own formal schooling had been, of course, rather limited, but Bronson and William Alcott had early begun the practice of criticizing each other's compositions, employing the medium of the formal letter. The criticism (as undoubtedly the compositions) displayed a pretentiousness and formality, an immaturity, that is amusing but engaging. Note, for example, the following: "In commencing the present correspondence, our motives it is believed are mutually understood; and in its continuance the exercise of candor to each others [*sic*] opinions, it is hoped will be scrupulously regarded. We write to benefit each other: let us then be plain & familiar" (Letter 24–1).

There was an awareness in the cousins that they were different from their Wolcott contemporaries: "While many, perhaps most, of our youthful associates are still groping their way through the mists of ignorance, to the attainment of wealth, or to the gratification of their passions: the Great Author of Good has raised us from the grovelling herd, and illuminated our minds, if it be but feebly, with the beams of knowledge" (Letter 26–1).

By 1825, however, Alcott was happily employed teaching school in Cheshire, Connecticut (he had already taught briefly in Wolcott and Bristol), and apparently enjoyed some measure of success for a short while:

---

[4] Portions of other letters written from the South, during these years, to his parents, to Chatfield, or to William Alcott are quoted in the notes to *New Connecticut*, and present a sometimes quite detailed account of the way of life of a not too typical Yankee peddler. See Appendix A for a list of those letters.

God, in his goodness, has placed me, though unworthy, in a sphere in which I can with his assistance be useful—can benefit a few of my fellow-travellers, young and inexperienced in the world, by example and instruction, and endeavour to lead them to usefulness and happiness. I am incompetent, vastly incompetent to the task. But I am not to desert my rising charge. They are daily gaining upon my affection, & esteem, and with many, their course is laudable, & I am encouraged. Success beyond my expectations has thus far crowned my efforts—and my prospects are, on the whole flattering. The confidence of parents is extended to a greater extent than I deserve. The greatest difficulty in the way is *number*. About 70 daily attend—In addition to the branches of instruction usually taught in this school, Arithmetick, Grammar and Geography are attended to—and I have about 30 who write. The most systematick arrangement of time and exercises, you will readily perceive, to be indispensably necessary to successful instruction, among so many. But this I do not pretend to. Of course exertions must be much limited in result: None can be extensively benefitted. And my fondness for speculations perhaps limits the extent of instruction. (Letter 26–1)

Again, "I have been encouraged in Cheshire to a much greater extent than I expected . . ." (Letter 26–2).

Counting too much, perhaps, on the warmth of his welcome in Cheshire, Alcott began to make changes in the physical aspect of the school (desks with backs, slates, classroom decorations), as well as to introduce advanced teaching methods designed to impress his students with the practical application of each subject. However, it takes little to make people wary of the reformer, and Alcott was forced to discontinue his school in 1827 when the enrollment diminished, although he wrote to his brother Chatfield that "The school in Cheshire has been discontinued at my choice. I thought best to leave there for various reasons; although a greater part of the Villagers were very desirous that I should continue at the rate named . . . ($27. per month) . . ." (Letter 27–1).

In the same letter Alcott wrote that opportunities beckoned in both Hartford and New Haven. During his employment in Cheshire (and for a short period after in Bristol again) Alcott had gained some reputation among those people in his native state who were interested in educational reform. Among them was Samuel Joseph May, who then lived in Brooklyn, Connecticut, where there was founded "a society for the improvement of common schools."[5] Alcott and May became lifelong friends. At this time, also, Alcott met Samuel May's sister Abigail whom he was to marry in 1830. Undoubtedly it was the Mays who suggested that Alcott visit Boston.

Alcott planned "to go to Boston . . . to visit Schools, and collect information—to be gone about a month" (Letter 27–1). Once there, however, he was made captive by persons interested in advancing the cause of education, by the sermons of the noted Unitarians, and by the promise of a three-month appointment as teacher of an infant school, which was

[5] Dorothy McCuskey, *Bronson Alcott, Teacher* (New York, 1940), p. 28.

opened in June 1828. Alcott left that position in October and in the same month opened what was to be a successful school of his own.

In May, 1830, Bronson Alcott married Abigail May (Letter 30–1)—a marriage that was to last happily through many trials for forty-seven years. The couple moved to Germantown, Pennsylvania, in December, where Alcott was to conduct a school with William Russell, Alcott to handle the younger children. They remained in Pennsylvania until 1834, first in Germantown and then in Philadelphia, despite the failure of the school to supply Alcott with enough students (Letter 33–1). Two of their four daughters (Anna and Louisa) were born in Germantown. Alcott wrote to his mother from there in 1832: We are very pleasantly situated here on many accounts, and I should not leave, did not greater inducements urge me: this is not quite the place for me—and, I believe, I shall ultimately find my way back to my own, and Abba's friends, in Boston. *That* is the place for me, and where the place is there I must go" (Letter 32–1).

By this time, and despite his failure in Germantown, Alcott's educational theories were pretty well formed. Hoping to find patrons for a school in Philadelphia, Alcott wrote early in 1833 to Roberts Vaux:

> It is my wish to operate chiefly on the characters of those committed to my care—to form and mature habits of accurate thought—pure feeling, and correct action—to fit the mind for the acquisition of knowledge, and inspire the heart with the love of virtue, and pursuit of excellence.—The results which I aim at producing, cannot, of course, be rendered immediately obvious, but will be, I trust, satisfactory and permanent in the end.—
>
> If a few children, between the ages of four and ten years, could be collected from those parents who would enter with an intelligent interest into my purposes, and wait with the necessary patience for the production of results, I should highly prize the opportunity thus offered for making known my views on early education. Twenty five or thirty children, at the rate of $15. per quarter, would enable me to commence a sch[ool] for this purpose. (Letter 33–1)

However, the students were not forthcoming, at least not in sufficient numbers; and by the fall of 1834, Alcott was back in Boston and had opened his famed Temple School which was to run, at first with a good deal of success, until 1839. His educational techniques were original and far advanced of his time (and even of our time, for that matter). The following excerpt from a letter to Elizabeth Peabody indicates well the level of the subject matter Alcott presented to his students, aged three to twelve:

> In the discharge of my duties as a teacher . . . I have found few works to aid me. I have been thrown mostly on my own resources, to create from circumstances, and the ideal of my own mind, the material for the intellectual and spiritual nurture of children. Of the few works that have become established favorites with my scholars, works containing thoughts to which they recur with delight, and which awaken, as it were, a brood of other thoughts in their minds, I can only recollect

the Bible, Pilgrim's Progress, The Fairy Queen, . . . Coleridge's Poems, Wordsworth's Poems, Milton's Paradise Lost, Quarles' Emblems. . . . It is from these books that I generally read; for, although imagination is acknowledged to be the shaping power of the soul; and, when rightly nurtured by meditation and observation, she clothes the spirit in the chaste and beautiful robes of truth, how seldom is it cultivated among us! I seldom hear any one speak of cultivating this faculty. And yet if there is any fact settled by the history of our race, it is, that imagination has been the guiding energy of light and life to humanity. For what is genius but this faculty in its most vivid action? And genius has shaped the institutions of society in all past ages. We need schools not for the inculcation of knowledge, merely, but for the development of genius. Genius is the peculiar attribute of soul. It is the soul, indeed, in full and harmonious play; and no instruction deserves the name, that does not quicken this its essential life, and fit it for representation in literature, art, or philosophy. (Letter 34–1)

Perhaps the most surprising thing about Alcott's methods is that they apparently worked (if one can rely at all on the observations in Elizabeth Palmer Peabody's *Record of a School*).[6] Further, the letters seem to confirm Dorothy McCuskey's judgment that the school commanded some respect. It was attended by children of some of the most influential families in Boston.

In late 1836 and early 1837 Bronson Alcott published in two volumes his first book, *Conversations with Children on the Gospels;* and the storm broke. Alcott felt that what he was doing belonged properly to the field of education, but Boston felt the "book was religious and heretical to the very core."[7] So severe was the reaction to Alcott's book that enrollment rapidly lessened. Even as early as February, 1837, Alcott wrote to Lemuel Shaw asking if he would object to an increase in the tuition to twenty-five dollars a quarter (Letter 37–1), since he by then had only twenty-five pupils remaining. By May the number was down to ten (Letter 37–3). The last straw insofar as Boston was concerned was the admission of a black child to the school. When Alcott refused to dismiss her, he lost his few remaining pupils.

Toward the end of this period Alcott first became acquainted with the method of holding Conversations[8] in parlors for pay. In March, 1839, he wrote to his mother in Wolcott, Connecticut: "I have a few children, as pupils, at present, but how long I shall have them, I do not know. . . . But I am living rather by *Talking* now, than by my School: and shall be able, by and by, I think, to live in this way entirely. I meet circles of thirty, forty, fifty, or more, persons, for ten or twelve evenings, and hold conversation, on great subjects, with them. These circles I have in Boston, and also in the neighboring towns" (Letter 39–2). Some twenty years were to pass,

[6] *Record of a School: Exemplifying the General Principles of Spiritual Culture* (Boston, 1835), pp. 16–17.
[7] McCuskey, p. 99.
[8] Alcott always capitalized the word when referring to these gatherings, a practice referred to in Shepard, *Pedlar's Progress*, p. 174, *n.* 1.

however, before Alcott's Conversations were to pay significant financial dividends. But elsewhere in the letter just quoted he wrote that he was filled with hope and the realization that his poverty would ultimately prove a meaningful experience. On December 28, 1839, he wrote again:

> You ask me what I am about now. I reply, still at my old trade, *hoping,* which has thus far given food, shelter, raiment, and a few warm friends, who cherish me and mine in this time of need. And not in this adopted city only, but over the seas. Several encouraging letters have come to me from friends in England, who appear to take that interest in my labors which my countrymen have not yet shown. . . . But all is indefinite just now. God has some task allotted and waiting for me, and will employ me in his service in his own time, with wages proportionate to my deserts. (Sanborn, I, 299)

One of the "warm friends" was Emerson. They had first met in 1835; that Alcott confided to Emerson his trials and hopes during this time of difficulty is made clear in Letter 37–8. The same letter indicates Alcott's growing concern over what to do for a living, since even by late in 1837 the failure of his school appeared certain. The prospect of having Emerson as a neighbor was apparently a primary influence on the Alcotts' moving to Concord on April 1, 1840. On April 6, Alcott wrote to Samuel J. May:

> Again I have planted myself, and am seeking to extend my roots into the soil of the earth, if perchance it shall prove more genial than hitherto, and ripen my fruits for the sustenance of others. I sow again in hope, and if not made partaker of the same while in this earthly tabernacle, know full well that my harvest shall come in in due season, and there shall be bread and fullness in the land. I seem, at times, to have been an impatient husbandman, misauguring the signs of the spring time, and to have scattered my seed even during the wintry season. . . .
>
> I feel yet the more assured of the fitness of my present position than ever, to fulfil the great ends of life. I have now abrogated all claims to moral and spiritual teaching. I place myself in peaceful relations to the soil. . . . My little cottage lies low and humble in the bosom of nature, under the sky of God: and I would ornament its walls, and its acres, by honour and independence. My chief regret is that in gaining Emerson, I lose you . . . (Letter 40–2)

The letters Alcott had begun to receive from admiring educational reformers in England culminated in his visiting them in 1842. Inasmuch as Alcott's Journals for this period have not survived, the letters he wrote between the date of his departure from Boston on May 8 and his return to Concord on October 21 (especially his letters to Mrs. Alcott, which are largely copied from his Journal entries), provide us with the most detailed surviving account of his journey. Alcott won a complete acceptance by the educational reformers who had extended the invitation to him and who had named a school Alcott House and patterned it after Alcott's theories.

He liked them, but was disappointed with England: "I have no love of England, nor England's sons nor daughters. There is here no repose, nor gentleness, nor grace—strife and violence mar all things, all men . . ." (Letter 42–15). Worthy of note is Alcott's complete disenchantment with Emerson's friend Thomas Carlyle:

> I rode to Chelsea and passed an hour with Carlyle. . . . It must have been a dark hour with him. He seemed impatient of all interruption: faithless quite in all social reforms. His wit was sombre, severe, hopeless, his every merriment had madness in it; his humour was tragic even to tears . . . nor could the rich mellowness of his voice . . . hide from me the restless melancholy, the memory feeding on Hope, the decease of all prophesy in the grave of history, wherein with his hero whom he was seeking to disinter, himself was descending—a giant mastered by the spirit of his time. . . . We had desultory talk, but none gave me pleasure. The man is sick; he needs rest . . . (Letter 42–11)

Several weeks later he visited Carlyle a second time: "I have seen . . . Carlyle again, *but we quarrelled outright,* and I shall not see him again" (Letter 42–15). But those letters (42–5 to 42–16) describing Alcott's trip really need to be read in full.

Alcott was disillusioned by his failure with educational reforms in this country. That disillusionment plus the warmth of his reception in England, seemed to lead inevitably to the disastrous communal-living experiment at Fruitlands in 1843. Alcott returned from England with two friends, Henry Wright and Charles Lane (Letter 42–7, *nn.* 1, 2), and they immediately began to make plans for the "ideal" community (see Letters 42–16 and 42–17).[9]

The history of Fruitlands is too well known to report in detail here; and the extant Alcott letters of that time are few in number and shed little new light on the matter. It should be said, however, that Fruitlands *was* every bit the failure it has always been pictured as being, and that Alcott suffered then the keenest disappointment of his life and a temporary loss of faith in the world he lived in. But it was a temporary loss of faith and Alcott did learn from the experience.

The failure was a disappointment, but one must remember that the time from the inception of the plan in England to the disintegration of the Fruitlands community was only a year and a half—and Bronson Alcott lived a long life. It may well be that this particular phase of Alcott's life has been overly publicized in the popular picture of the man. Louisa May Alcott's "Transcendental Wild Oats," delightful as that sketch is, has been of no help in achieving an objective view of her father.

Following the abortive Fruitlands episode the Alcotts returned to Concord, where they lived until they moved to Boston in 1848. The extant letters written during this period of residence in Concord are mostly to Anna and are concerned mainly with family matters. Those written after

---

[9] Henry Wright did not become a member of the Fruitlands Community.

the family's removal to Boston show Alcott trying more and more to earn a living by his Conversations; they also show him as one of the organizers of the short-lived Town and Country Club. Generally, though, the ten years following Fruitlands seem to have been relatively quiet ones.

2

IN EDNAH DOW CHENEY's *Louisa May Alcott: Her Life, Letters, and Journals,* we find the following oft-cited account by Louisa of Alcott's return from his first trip West, in the winter of 1853–54:

> In February Father came home. Paid his way, but no more. A dramatic scene when he arrived in the night. We were waked by hearing the bell. Mother flew down, crying "My husband!" We rushed after, and five white figures embraced the half-frozen wanderer who came in hungry, tired, cold, and disappointed, but smiling bravely and as serene as ever. We fed and warmed and brooded over him, longing to ask if he had made any money; but no one did till little May said, after he had told all the pleasant things, "Well, did people pay you?" Then, with a queer look, he opened his pocket-book and showed one dollar, saying with a smile that made our eyes fill, "Only that! My overcoat was stolen, and I had to buy a shawl. Many promises were not kept, and travelling is costly; but I have opened the way, and another year shall do better."[10]

Letters written by Bronson Alcott reveal a different, albeit less dramatic, picture of that first tour West.

On August 10, 1853, Alcott wrote to his wife: "The West, I am told, has most hospitable ears, and likes a free fair thought, as our Eastern people, I am compelled to affirm, do not always and to the issues. At any rate I am disposed to ascertain these matters for my self. . . . Such an expedition should pay and more than pay its own expenses. But it were safest, I suppose, to be in funds to the amount of expenses, at starting" (Letter 53–2). Accordingly, November found him in Cincinnati where he was enthusiastically received. He delivered a course of six Conversations. Among the company were what Alcott might have called the "best minds" of the city. On November 22, he wrote to his daughter Anna, who was teaching school in Syracuse, "as the attendance has been large at Boston prices, (3 dolls the ticket) there must be $200, if not 250 (expenses of the Room not included) . . . for me; $100 of which I shall send (by Adam's Express, very safe and insured) to your mother, at once" (Letter 53–6). On November 29, he sent home $150. There were still many debts, but the West was seemingly a promising source of income. From Cincinnati, he journeyed to Cleveland with high hopes, only to be disappointed, though there were some returns, and he sent another twenty-five dollars from

[10] Boston, 1890, pp. 69–70.

Syracuse in time for Christmas (Letter 53–12).[11] Louisa's story is, then, at least not complete. Most important to Alcott at the time was that the journey provided him with renewed hope that he could make a living by his Conversations: "It looks now as if aid and comfort were lodged about this tongue somewhere, and the West were putting some little faith in its cunning" (Letter 54–1).

But there yet remained trying times ahead before financial and intellectual security was to be a reality. In October of 1856, leaving his debt-ridden family in near poverty in Walpole, New Hampshire, Bronson Alcott left for New York City to give some Conversations. An additional purpose for the trip was the hope of finding a suitable situation for the relocation of his family. The many long letters Alcott wrote to his wife from New York (Letters 56–9 to 57–4) provide a most complete record of his stay in that city; and, in addition, they give the reader an excellent picture of several aspects of life in New York at that time. He planned to be gone only a month, but was warmly and well received and remained until spring, although he made a visit home over the Christmas holidays. The monetary returns from the visit were small, especially considering the length of time he was in that city; but the letters show that he met many people prominent in intellectual circles. He frequently saw Samuel Longfellow, then a Unitarian minister in Brooklyn; met Walt Whitman (see especially Letter 56–16) whom he recognized as indeed an important figure in American literature and life; renewed his acquaintance with George Ripley, and through him met Horace Greeley. Among others, he met Albert Brisbane, Arnold Buffum (one of the founders of the American Anti-Slavery Society), Anne Charlotte Lynch Botta, Alice and Phoebe Cary, Judge Grimke and his daughters, Caroline Kirkland, Catherine Sedgwick, and Charles Robinson, and he saw again Isaac Hecker, who earlier had been involved with the Fruitlands community. He became acquainted with people from the medical, literary, ministerial, political, and journalistic worlds.

While in New York, Alcott did receive some tentative offers: an invitation from R. T. Trall to manage a water-cure establishment in Connecticut (Letter 56–15); the half-promise of an offer from a former student of Alcott's, a well-to-do Swedenborgian minister, of a home and position in Orange, New Jersey (Letter 56–22); and a proposal to join a Fourieristic community, the Raritan Bay Union—Mrs. Alcott to serve as matron and Bronson Alcott to serve as teacher and gardener. Regarding the last of these, Alcott wrote to his wife: "I have no doubt as to our being serviceable in many ways, and of great advantage to the enterprise; but where all is yet crude and unsettled, perhaps it would be risking too much" (Letter 56–12). Apparently Alcott had learned something from his Fruitlands experience.

As was usual with his tours, Alcott's plans were uncertain, depending upon the whims of acquaintances who sometimes issued invitations and

---

[11] David Mead, in his "Some Ohio Conversations of Amos Bronson Alcott," *NEQ*, XXII (September, 1949), 360, 361, gives Alcott's earnings on the tour as follows: Cincinnati, $209; Cleveland, $50; Syracuse, $25—for a total of $284.

then did not keep their promises. Following his commitments in New York City he had intended to go to Philadelphia and then to Cincinnati, but, typically, the plans never materialized (Letter 57–3).

Instead, he went, in March (1857), to New Haven. He expected a cool reception there, and on March 11, wrote to his wife in Walpole that the family would be unhappy in that stronghold of orthodoxy: "I think we should find ourselves out of place here, surrounded by influences against which yourself and the girls would rebel forthwith" (Letter 57–7). However, Alcott did find that some of the faculty and students at Yale were interested in him, and he was invited to give a course of six Conversations.

Although the winter's work had not been overly remunerative, Alcott had made some money and began again to have hope of freeing himself from debt. On April 29, he wrote from Boston: "I hope to come free of debt here, & able to square accounts with all in Walpole for the spring and summer. Let us hope, and take the autumn in season to secure the winter quarters for the family somewhere here in these parts" (Letter 57–12). In May, though, in an unusually pessimistic letter to his brother Ambrose, he wrote: "My own receipts for the season have fallen far short of our family expenses. . . . But people I find, are quite ready to hear, yet slow to pay much for the hearing of what I have to say to them. I must wait for my turn to be served, and patiently. . . . Poverty is never chosen by any of us, and has its trials often and many. I have had the full benefits of these from the first, and expect the same continued to me to the end of life" (Letter 57–13).

Nevertheless, in August, Bronson Alcott journeyed to Boston and vicinity to look for a permanent home for his family. He indicated clearly his wishes to his wife: "For me *Concord* seems the spot for us to plant ourselves, and bear the harvests home" (Letter 57–17). Indeed, Concord was the one place the Alcotts had always seemed to think of as "home." The letters show there was some hesitancy on the part of the rest of the family, for they still owed money to people in Concord. But Alcott was insistent: "I am minded to take the reins a little more firmly in hand, and think you may rely upon me for supports of labour and money in the years to come" (Letter 57–21). A few days later, with financial help from friends, they purchased (for $950) "Orchard House" in Concord, which was to remain the family homestead for the next twenty-five years.[12]

That November (1857), Alcott again set his face westward with high hopes. He wrote home from Rochester, a month later: "I shall glean something to plant us a little more firmly in the friendly soil of Concord, let us hope and believe, meanwhile. There is prospect of finding in these flourishing Bushes and pocketing honestly some golden handfulls [*sic*]: here in this city 50 dollars; 75 in that, in another 100, 200, it may be, in another; and, if no more than 30s or 40s. in some, we can beat the bush for the slender winnings, and esteem it luck in these pinching times" (Letter 57–33). On January 1, however, he wrote from Cleveland: "Hard times

[12] For details of the transaction see Letters 57–22 to 57–25.

and no money for me, or very little. But I hope to send soon a ten or twenty from my gleanings, if not something more" (Letter 58–1). Still, he looked hopefully to Cincinnati which had so handsomely rewarded his services a few years earlier. Shortly after his arrival in that city, though, he was called home by the illness of his daughter Elizabeth, who died in March.[13] Yet, as always, Alcott could rely on his essentially optimistic nature. He had written: "Nor will my winter be wasted if I shall have paid my court to good people, and my expenses, no more" (Letter 58–1).

For once Alcott was at least partially correct in his judgment; if nothing else, he had paid his court and by the end of 1858 was again in the West. His travels this time were more remunerative and carried him farther from home: to Chicago and St. Louis, the latter at the invitation of William Torrey Harris, then a young public school teacher devoted to philosophy (see Letters 57–38 and 58–14). (Harris, as a student at Yale, had first met Alcott at one of Alcott's Conversations in New Haven in March of 1857.)

3

By 1860, Alcott was being asked to lecture to various reform organizations. In politely declining an invitation to address an abolitionist convention, he wrote to James Redpath that it has not "been my habit, of late years, to speak at public meetings often, and from choice. What pleased me better to meet private companies, with the fullest advantages of conversation and comparison" (Letter 60–10). The passage of two or three years was to change that attitude, and though he was always to prefer the Conversation as the most effective method of reaching people, he did begin to speak frequently before more public assemblages. In a letter to Daniel Ricketson, Alcott wrote: "Lately it has seemed as if the call had come for me to speak, not in parlours alone and privately, but from public platforms and pulpits . . ." (Letter 65–1). The deference shown him by such men as James Redpath, Harris, and other young correspondents was flattering, and, more important, gave him the faith in his own abilities he sorely needed. The number of these young correspondents was increasing and Alcott was always most gratified to hear from them and to help them. In 1863, he wrote to a Miss Powell: "Be assured your interest in us this way honors us; for I have always esteemed the faiths of young persons the highest honors their elders can receive" (Letter 63–12).

Early in 1866 Alcott went again to St. Louis, this time with a firm pledge of $200 for a course of Conversations (Letter 65–29, n. 2). A letter to Mrs. Alcott tells of Alcott's high estimate of St. Louis:

I esteem it fortunate for me to be here at this time. The men who invited me are Powers and Influences in this city: the Peace brings pro-

[13] One possible reason for the delay of success for Alcott in the West was that his tours were cut short on at least four other occasions: once to bid farewell to Louisa and May who were sailing for Europe; once because of financial depression; once by the illness of Mrs. Alcott; and once when Anna was seriously ill with pneumonia.

digious questions and issues before the minds of all men; Nor have I found anywhere more profound treatment in the true American spirit, than these men exhibit. It is suggestive and powerfully stimulating to look at life and affairs, through the perspective of their clear logic. I am persuaded that if Philosophy has found a home in modern times, 'tis here in this New New England, and that St. Louis is stealing past Boston and Concord even. The freedom and grasp of Genius, the force and speed of thinking, the practical tact in dealing with men and business transactions, which these students of the pure ideas, have to show, all this is as unexpected as it is convincing. Eastern men, slow to believe in things originating elsewhere, might profit by a visit out here. The possibilities of this wondrous West are infinite, and the thoughts rise naturally out of all limitations into the freest expansion. (Letter 66–7)

Alcott's expansiveness was repaid in kind, for, he wrote to his wife, "they accept me beyond all expectation, and I must run home soon, if I will escape apotheosis" (Letter 66–9). Back in Concord by the middle of March, Alcott wrote to Louisa, in France: "You will be pleased to learn that it [his 'six weeks journeyings'] proved most successful, and in the money way remunerative" (Letter 66–11).

A letter in July of the same year (1866) shows Alcott encouraging Harris in the latter's plans for the *Journal of Speculative Philosophy,* the first number of which appeared in 1867: "What you write about the desirableness of having a Speculative Journal, I also feel as strongly as yourself, and wish the thing might be. There is a class of thought most important to be circulated among the few thinkers we have, for which we have as yet no organ . . ." (Letter 66–18). The inception of that periodical elicited from Alcott a statement of his hopes for an American philosophy, one that would clearly outshine the likes of "Carlyle, Mill & Co." (Letter 68–3). He was willing to admit those hopes might not come to pass during his own lifetime, but he was confident he could hasten their realization.

Alcott had been reluctant to take pen in hand ever since Emerson had dissuaded him from publishing *Psyche* some thirty years earlier. By 1867, however, he was willing to try again. Accordingly, in 1868, *Tablets* was published, his first book since *Conversations with Children on the Gospels.* Letters written during the fall of 1868 indicate the book was favorably reviewed, and by November all but three hundred copies had been sold.[14] Perhaps as important is Alcott's acknowledgment, in a letter to Sanborn, that he would "be very well content, if the book please and edify the few choice readers who owe its author good will and know how to excuse its literary blemishes: a popular fame, I do not expect" (Letter 68–29).

Yet Alcott's fame, although not essentially a literary fame, did continue on the increase—especially in the West. In 1869, he wrote to Harris: "I find it stimulating and invigorating, this eager and curious West. Unlike our East, which is mostly content with a dainty nibble at my things, the

[14] For a description of Alcott's seeing the book through publication and its reception see Letters 68–24 ff.

western people like a bold bait, and bite hard and ask for more of that sort"
(Letter 69–62).

A man of some reputation by 1869, Alcott seemed to have achieved a
more stable kind of self-confidence than was characteristic of his earlier
years. He expressed himself less formally. The letters are more impromptu.
He was, in short, surer of his place in the world of men and ideas. Letters
to such persons as William Oldham, who had been involved in Alcott
House in England when Alcott visited there, show that he could look upon
the misfortunes of earlier ventures with a new-found calmness: "Those
old times and experiences have now grown *historical,* and begin to live
again in memory. . . . *The Ham*[15] and *Fruitlands Fellowships* will deserve
a place in the history of these times. . . . My life has since been rather
rich and fruitful of satisfactions, and my Journals are ample. It is true that
I have not *planted a Paradise outside,* as I once dreamed of doing, but rather
cultivated the one already planted *inside,* and grown a little pleasant fruit,
still good to taste and promising future crops of satisfactions" (Letter 69–18).
Alcott had come to realize that "men and women are yet *too individual*
to affiliate readily in any new social attempts . . ." (Letter 75–28). "The
family is *the unit* around which all social endeavors should organize, if we
would succeed in educating men for the true ends of existence" (Letter
75–17). All sorts of people, many of them influential, wrote asking for his
advice or for a statement of his beliefs on any number of issues he was
close to.

Mrs. Howe wrote in 1869 asking Alcott's views on the suffrage issue,
and Alcott responded (Letter 69–41) with a lengthy outline of a plan of
action, *only* after clearly indicating that women must themselves decide
how to seek equal rights, not men, who should merely carry out Woman's
plans. The theme is repeated on several occasions. For example, in a
letter to Elizabeth Cady Stanton, Alcott wrote: "Woman complements and
perfects man, and she is last taking her fit place abreast of him to perfect
herself. You will not, I am sure, think me indifferent then to her welfare
if I cherish the conviction that she is helping herself to secure her place in
a better spirit and manner than any we can suggest or devise, and that it
becomes us to take, rather than proffer Consels [*sic*], readily waiting to
learn her wishes and aims, as she has so long and so patiently deferred to
us" (Letter 69–20). Alcott arranged his tour of that year (1869) so he could
attend the Suffrage Convention in Cleveland in November (Letter 69–61).
That he had always held the highest opinion of Woman and her intellectual
capabilities is amply illustrated by the extent and character of his correspondence with Ednah Dow Cheney, Mary Stearns, Mary Newbury
Adams, and Ellen Chandler.

On a number of occasions Alcott was asked for material concerning
vegetarian societies (about which he had always kept himself informed)
and for his own dietary principles. He was a strict vegetarian. In a letter
(79–86) written when he was eighty years old he stated with real certainty

---

[15] Alcott House was located at Ham Common, Surrey.

that his perfect health was the result of his having forsworn animal food some fifty years earlier (and at one time that had included milk and eggs). Fruits, he asserted, were the best of all foods; then, in descending order, grains (though he never ate pastries); green vegetables; roots. He would drink water and cocoa; tea, coffee, and alcoholic beverages but seldom. The result of such a regimen was, he claimed, a heightening of the ideal and spiritual nature of man.

By the late 1870's Alcott was answering letters of inquiry concerning his religious beliefs and denying suggestions in other letters that he had been converted to religious orthodoxy. The basis of the charge of orthodoxy may have been in part his speaking from the pulpits of many religious sects, something Alcott was quite proud of: "I have . . . been favored with frequent opportunities to speak in pulpits and on platforms during the season, and find a hearty response from religionists of all denominations. This is to me a happier fortune than were I favored with the acceptance of only one or two of the sects only" (Letter 78–26). He was, he wrote in other letters, trying to bring the various sects together. He regarded himself as a member of the "Church Universal," as distinct from the "Church Individual." He came to sympathize less with Unitarianism; he asserted he never had been a Pantheist, for although he did not view God as anthropomorphic (God might be "apprehended," but never fully "comprehended"), he believed man as a person must necessarily view God as a "person," not as a "thing," an abstraction; and although he had been classed as a Transcendentalist, that school of thought, he claimed, had never fully satisfied him. He was, he claimed, a believer in a "pure Personal Mind" (see especially Letters 79–46 and 79–51).

In the 1870's Alcott's career reached its peak. Many young men paid him tribute and he returned the compliment: "Great and greatly to be praised is *this* country, and the more *because it is run by young men*. What were progress without them" (Letter 73–1). He met with the Harvard Divinity School students. In April 1875 he acknowledged his election as an honorary member of the Phi Beta Kappa Chapter Alpha of Massachusetts (Letter 75–4), a distinction for a man who had never been to college.

He published three more books in those later years, and *Concord Days* (1872) enjoyed a moderate success for a book of the sort Alcott wrote, quickly running through at least three printings (Letter 73–5).

His tours to the West came to include an ever larger area.[16] They became more exhausting as the rewards, spiritual and financial, increased. He could ask for and get twenty dollars for a single lecture at Amherst College (Letter 78–53). In 1879, the Concord Summer School of Philosophy was inaugurated with Alcott as "Dean." The importance to Alcott of the enterprise may be judged by the extent of his correspondence for that year. It was the final and (as far as Alcott was concerned) the crowning success of his long career. The winter of 1881–82 saw Alcott's last tour of the

---

[16] His later tours included many cities, large and small, in Ohio, Michigan, Illinois, Iowa; and he visited other states as well.

West. It was the most extensive one he ever made, the most arduous, and the most successful.

4

THANKS TO EARLY FAILURES, many of his own making, and thanks to the poverty which had become a matter of course to the Alcott family, and thanks to his utopian schemes (of which Fruitlands is the most extreme example), and thanks to the legend created in the popular imagination by Louisa and some of her biographers, Alcott more often than not has appeared to the student of New England Transcendentalism as a "tedious archangel"—somewhat of an errant fool. He is, to judge from his letters, a weightier figure. His literary attainments are slight (though some of his poetry is not at all bad). But he did have his influence, even at the time of his failures; and especially after they belonged to the past, he was looked upon in many circles as a man of some stature. His ideas were on occasion impractical, but even Alcott did not deny that they were impractical for his time and place. The knowing individualist will normally be aware of the ill-fatedness of his dreams. What may have led Alcott into trouble was that, unlike many individualists, he often felt the need to practice his ideas with or in the company of other people. Further, he had a family of four children whom he had at least to try to provide for.

That Alcott did in later years become rather widely known over a large area of the country is often overlooked, and is a point adequately demonstrated in his letters. He was a prime mover in a number of organizations; and many others which he did not as actively support sought his name and his words. Educationally, he remained an original thinker.

Since success did not come to him early he seems to be more the dreamer than he probably was (though "dreamers," merely as such, are important). Alcott, however, actually tried to put his ideas into practice. Perhaps that was a mistake insofar as material "success" was concerned; yet the innate optimism, the moral certainty regarded by many simply as an indication of Alcott's naïveté, may well have been the trait that sustained Alcott through early trials and helped him to a later success in which his ideas became widely enough known to gain a significant degree of acceptance.

These opinions are not an attempt to excuse Alcott's eccentricities, but rather to explain some of them through the somewhat different perspective provided by his letters. The sources of the popular misconceptions are obvious: (1) the legend created by Louisa May Alcott and some of her biographers; (2) an overemphasis of the failure at Fruitlands; (3) a failure to look at the whole of Alcott's career and the consequent emphasis on the obvious failures Alcott suffered during roughly the first half of his life; (4) his being a reformer in a world not ready for reform and a man who persisted in practicing uncompromisingly what he preached, sometimes in an unpolitic and impractical way.

Finally, the letters underscore two other factors which should not be overlooked in forming a rounded estimate of the man: first, Alcott was a self-educated man, lacking during his formative years many of the advantages of, for example, Thoreau and Emerson, and as a result his social maturity came late; and second, the life of the Alcott family, although at times hard, was essentially quite happy.

Editorial Practices

I. Textual

A list of the procedures used in editing the text of the letters follows. Other procedures employed but not noted below should become evident to readers of the letters. Special editorial problems are clarified in the footnotes or in the text of the letters.

A. Unless otherwise noted, all letters are from the Collection owned by Mrs. Frederic Wolsey Pratt and on deposit in the Houghton Library, Harvard University (microfilm copies are retained in the Concord Free Public Library). Letters from other sources—including other collections in the Houghton Library—are identified in the footnotes following the letter. Where I have located the original of a letter a copy of which is in the Alcott-Pratt Collection in the Houghton Library, I use the original and note the existence of the copy. Generally speaking, the differences between the originals and the copies are minor.

B. In the MS. volumes in the Alcott-Pratt Collection, an occasional letter has been bound out of correct order. In those cases the letter is placed in proper chronological order without notation.

C. Where two or more letters for a given date appear, the practice is as follows:

1. Letters in the Alcott-Pratt Collection are placed first and in the order Alcott arranged them. However, when internal evidence from the letters shows clearly that the letters were written in a different order, they are rearranged accordingly.

2. Letters from other sources are placed after those from the Alcott-Pratt Collection, and are arranged alphabetically by addressee with letters to unknown addressees placed last.

D. When the date of a letter differs from the day of the week indicated, the day of the week is assumed to be correct, the date incorrect. Wherever the day of the week is given, the date has been checked and a note made of any inconsistency.

E. Mechanics:

General Note: Occasionally Alcott has omitted necessary punctuation, or he has used wrong punctuation (for example, a period instead of a question mark or vice versa). In these instances the material is reproduced as in the original MS. and no note made of the error. However, some obvious careless errors in punctuation are silently corrected for the sake of clarity and readability.

1. *Periods and commas:* It is frequently difficult to distinguish between periods and commas in the MS., and at times Alcott has seemed to use one where the other is called for. Again, I attempt to duplicate the MS.

When commas or periods appear to be directly under quotation marks they are placed inside the quotation marks. Otherwise, they are reproduced as in the MS.

2. *Quotation marks:* Alcott did not always remember to open or close or reopen quotes. A double quote may be used to open and a single quote to close, or the other way around. All quotation marks are reproduced as in the MS. and no note is made of inconsistencies in their use by Alcott.

3. *Dashes:* Alcott frequently used other punctuation with dashes or parentheses, especially the comma. This punctuation appears as in the MS., and without notation.

4. *Colons and semicolons:* It is generally difficult to distinguish between the colons and semicolons in the MS. I base the decisions here on what seemed to be Alcott's practice in other letters of his written at the time.

5. *Apostrophes:* Alcott, as often as not, used the apostrophe incorrectly (after an *s* rather than before or vice versa), or he omitted the apostrophe when one was clearly called for or vice versa. These marks are reproduced as they appear in the MS. In a few early letters the comma was used instead of the apostrophe (e.g., o,clock).

6. *Italics:* Alcott's underlining sometimes was or was not broken between words; sometimes he underlined part of a word only; sometimes he double-underlined. I merely italicize the word or words and do not attempt to reproduce the peculiarities of Alcott's underlinings and flourishes.

7. *Abbreviation:* Alcott's common style of abbreviation was to use superior letters with a period or comma under them. In these cases, the superior letters are brought down to the line and followed by a period or a comma. Abbreviations are copied as they appear in the MS. No period is printed if Alcott used no period; the period may or may not be omitted following certain abbreviations (e.g., Mr., Mrs, St Louis). Incorrect abbreviations are reproduced without notation.

8. *Use of capitals:* In some cases it is difficult to distinguish capitals from lowercase letters. An attempt is made to be consistent. *S* is the most difficult letter to so distinguish; *C, I, O,* and *T* are also frequently difficult to so distinguish.

9. *Spelling:* Obsolete, archaic, variant, or reformed spellings are not noted by a [*sic*] (e.g., intire, despatch, surprize). Unusual spellings have been verified by *Webster's International Dictionary,* Unabridged, Second Edition.

Alcott generally misspelled certain words: "complement" for "compliment," "audiance," "Missisippi." All misspellings are noted by a [*sic*].

Some words are sometimes written clearly as two words, other times as one word, still other times they are hyphenated (e.g., to day, today, to-day, with out, my self). In each instance I attempt to reproduce the word as it appears in the MS.

In later letters especially it is difficult to determine whether a final *s* was intended.

When the misspellings were quite obviously careless ones, or when words were scrawled, they are corrected without notation.

F. Editorial Notation:

1. Words or phrases which were erased in the MS. are omitted even though frequently those words can still be read. Words or phrases which were crossed out in MS. are included when they can still be read, and appear between double vertical bars.

2. Where a guess has been made as to a word, it is indicated by a question mark in brackets: [?]. But where the reading is reasonably sure, no note is made.

3. An illegible word(s) is indicated thus: [word] [2 words]. The same mark is used where a word or words are hidden by the binding of a volume or the seal of the letter, or where the MS. is blotted or worn. Where the MS. is torn, missing material is indicated thus: [torn]. Brackets about a word or part of a word or a mark of punctuation indicate that material is obscured in one of the ways noted above (except see G, 2, below), but that a reasonable guess may be made as to what is obscured.

4. [p. o.] means the preceding matter (usually a word or a phrase) has been crossed out in pencil by Alcott, probably some time after the letter was originally written. All such material appears between double vertical bars. [p. in] means the preceding word only has been added by Alcott, unless special note is made, e.g. [2 p. in], which means two words penciled in. Some lengthier comments concerning [p. in] or [p. o.] matter appear in footnotes.

G. Miscellaneous.

1. Some obvious carelessnesses of Alcott, such as the insertion of a word in the wrong place by means of a caret, are corrected without notation.

2. In a few places a word or phrase may have been accidentally omitted by Alcott. When the intention seemed obvious, the missing element is interpolated, but only when it seems necessary to serve the interests of clarity. Otherwise, the material is reproduced as in the MS. When it seems necessary, a [*sic*] is used.

3. Datelines, when they consisted of more than one line in MS., are brought together into one line by means of vertical rules. A single space appears between the complimentary close and the signature.

4. Postscripts are placed at the end of the letter even though they may have appeared elsewhere in the MS.

5. Double hyphens have been converted to the conventional single hyphen.

II. Footnoting

The footnotes accompanying the letters are, necessarily, selective. To identify every person or place or thing referred to by Alcott would be an almost endless task. When someone or something seemed of genuine im-

Introduction

portance to Alcott and to his career, an identification is attempted, except that well-known matters are generally not annotated. Where the reference seems of lesser value to the picture of Alcott developed by the letters or of relative unimportance, it is not annotated. In addition, persons are generally not considered in the annotations when they are amply identified by the letters themselves or when they may be identified in standard reference works such as the *DAB*.

R. L. H.

SHORT TITLES USED IN THE FOOTNOTES

Alcott, *Journals*—Odell Shepard, ed., *The Journals of Bronson Alcott* (Boston, 1938).

Bonstelle and deForest—Jessie Bonstelle and Marian deForest, eds., *Little Women Letters from the House of Alcott* (Boston, 1914).

Cheney—Ednah Dow Cheney, ed., *Louisa May Alcott, Her Life, Letters, and Journals* (Boston, 1890).

Rusk, *Emerson Letters*—Ralph L. Rusk, ed., *The Letters of Ralph Waldo Emerson* (New York, 1939), 6 vols.

Sanborn, *A. Bronson Alcott*—Franklin B. Sanborn and William Torrey Harris, *A. Bronson Alcott: His Life and Philosophy* (Boston, 1893), 2 vols.

Shepard—Odell Shepard, *Pedlar's Progress: The Life of Bronson Alcott* (Boston, 1937).

Thomas Lewis photograph of Alcott in his study
(Lewis's Stereoscopic Series of the late 1800's).
(Courtesy Concord Free Public Library)

PART ONE

㊗

1820–1828

[to Mr. and Mrs. Joseph Chatfield Alcox, Wolcott, Conn.][2]

Norfolk 24th January 1820.

Dear Parents—

We have received your letter dated the 28th December, the perusal of which gave us much pleasure.[3] To hear that you were well, that you were successful in your business, & enjoying the comforts resulting from your labor & industry, in circumstances affluent enough to preclude the idea of complaining, were subjects which heightened our pleasure in the extreme. With satisfaction we exulted in your prosperity,—with joy we felicitated you as the objects of the Almighty's pleasure & protection, & while our Prayers ascended to the "Throne of Grace," for your continued prosperity, our own thanks were not forgotten, to, "The Author of Good Gifts." for the full portion of "Health & Prosperity"—which we enjoy.—To that Author of Good may our Thanks ever be offered, without dissimulation or insincerity.

We have been very successful in business, notwithstanding the dulness & hardness of the times, & have traded as much, & sold at as good advantage, as we ever anticipated. Should we be prospered during the season, as we have been since we commenced pedling, we shall make a good winters work of it I am confident. We hope to do better hereafter,—as we have but just begun, & Chat—altogether is unacquainted with Pedling. He does well, & will I think make a very good hand at the business, before we return. He sells nearly ‖ half ‖ as much as I do, & at about the same profits. Our Articles afford escclusive [*sic*] of Expenses ⅓rd or 33⅓ per cent profit, consequently in selling $100. we clear $33⅓. The last Trip which we made, we went out together, we were gone just 2 weeks. I sold $100. worth of property, & Chatfield about $50.—We get our property of Allyn,[4] as cheap as Ranney used to let me have it.—Chatfield left Norfolk last week I shall follow him within a few days.—I am cal[cu]lating on keeping him in the country, while I come to Norfolk to buy Goods [a]s he cannot be of any service to me here, & our Board costs us but very little in the country, and 3, dols a week in Norfolk, by this means he will be earning something continually.—

With our 2 Trunks in our Hands, "toating" them by our sides we travel through the country, entering the Rich & poor mans house alike, exposing & offering our Articles for sale.—Father & mother, how do you think we Look? Like

2 Awkward, poor, unpolished, dissipated, Homespun, begging, tugging, Yankee pedlars, think you? No. This is not the case with your sons.—By people of Breeding & respectability, they are treated with, politeness & gentility. and if they are sometimes treated with contempt by the low vulgar class of the com[munity,] it is then not worth minding—For my part I can make pedling in Virginia a[s] respectable as any other business—I take much pleasure in travelling, & in conve[rsing] with the Virginians, in observing their different habits, manners, & customs, &c & I am conscious that it is of great advantage to me in many points of [view.]

Yes, dear parents, we make the business, not only respectab[le] but lucrative, & so long as mankind are unprejudiced against Industry, Perseverance, Honesty, & Integrity, they well consider the person, who with those qualities on his side, let him pursue whatever calling he may, ‖ I say ‖ that per[son] strictly adhering to those principles will be respected by them, however, humiliat[ed] & contemptible he may appear to the Silken sons of Pride and dissipation.—

It was out of my own voluntary choice that I left Home,[5] & most willi[ngly] too, & for what?—

"To conduce too my own & Parents good,
"Was why I left my home;
"To make their cares, and burdens less,
"And try to help them some.—
"T,was [sic] my own choice to earn them cash,
"And get them free from debt;
"Before that I am twenty one,
"It will be done, I,ll [sic] bet.—"
"My Parents, they have done for me
"What I can never do for them,
"If I can help them when they need,
"They,ll [sic] thank me when ther,e [sic] done.—"
"My chief delight therefore shall be,
"To earn them all I can;
"Not quite a year, it will be, before that I am
"My own man.—"

200 dollars, owed by a Farmer, who has no other means of accumulating that Sum, than by the cultivation of a Farm of 80 Acres, & when the times are extremely dull, & the cultivation to be chiefly done by the owner who is over 45 years of age, & considera[bly] debilitated: is a great Sum.—If that parent has 2 Sons, who can earn him but very little during the winter season, at home & can by running a little risk by going 5 or 60[o] miles from Home earn him in 8 or 9 months with prosperity on their side, that $2,[oo,] it would be considered by most as managing business the best way—Dont you think so Father?—[6]

[1] Portions of this letter appear in Sanborn, *A. Bronson Alcott*, I, 31–33.
[2] Bronson Alcott's parents. The family name had been Alcocke, altered to Alcox, and by Bronson and William A. to Alcott.
[3] Chatfield Alcott, b. 1801, accompanied Bronson Alcott on this the latter's second peddling expedition to the South.
[4] J. J. Allen, a "Yankee" living in Norfolk who supplied peddlers (see Shepard, *Pedlar's Progress*, p. 48).
[5] Wolcott, Connecticut, Alcott's birthplace.
[6] The letter breaks off at this point.

LETTER 24–1[1]

[to William Andrus Alcott][2]

[Wolcott? *ca.* 1824 or earlier]

Sir, Mankind wish to be considered reasonable beings. To their opinions a respectful deference is due, since such opinions unsupported by reason, affect not its conclusions in investigating truth. The neglect of this, is a tacit assumption that their opinions are inconclusive; and an open violation of the laws of candor. Every liberal mind knows by experience the effect, which the exercise of this disposition has upon its feelings. We regard with complacency, those, who in their associations with us, are disposed to treat our opinions with ingenuousness. Nor is such a disposition inconsistent with a laudable independence. Whatever concessions may seemingly be made to the opinions of others, our own opinion, may still be retained. In a world of minds so very different in their views; a rigid adherence to our own, would prevent the acquisition of truth, and evince the highest degree of arrogance. Social as our nature is, the great Author of our Existence made it susceptible of pleasure, in our intercourse with each other. In a great measure, a mutual dependence obtains amongst us. To preserve a disposition which affords us so many satisfactions, is surely no inconsiderable attainment: it deserves our sedulous attention; our consistent endeavor. Whatever is calculated to win the esteem of our fellow men, and render our intercourse with them engaging, is agreeable to the God of Love himself: it is making a proper use of those faculties, with which his goodness endowed us.

In commencing the present correspondence, our motives it is believed are mutually understood; and in its continuance the exercise of candor to each others opinions, it is hoped will be scrupulously regarded. We write to benefit each other: let us then be plain & familiar.

In presenting your performance for examination,[3] you could not reasonably, in return, expect a critical analysis of its character. And in submitting to your inspection the following remarks, no such pretentions [*sic*] are assumed. I am no *Critic*: I understand neither Russell, nor Blair. My *opinion* only is given: its variance from Truth your judgement will discern; and your candor excuse.

No definite explanation, of the manner in which you wished your piece treated, occurred at the time I received it. My usual desultory manner will be pursued, in 'picking it to pieces.'

To commence:

'By peace &c.' This period is perspicuous: the collocation and choice of words is judicious, and exhibited to the best advantage ‖ in their disposition. ‖ It is distinguished by clearness, unity, and strength. The synonyms are properly applied. The style is nervous, and approaches to neatness. This sentence would suffer by transposition.

'For if the wicked &c.' This, and the following period, are exposed to some objections. The parenthesis and the injudicious choice of the word '*consolation*', as synonymous with '*peace*', or '*rest,*' destroy the unity of the sentence; render it ambiguous, and consequently weaken its strength. In every sentence some person or thing is generally the governing word: *this* or its synonyms should if possible be continued through it, especially if it is definitive, or explanatory. The obscurity of this sentence might be removed by omitting the parenthesis, and the adverb '*how,*" as superfluous; and by inserting 'peace,' or '*tranquillity*' in the place of '*consolation.*' In the short sentence following, '*the*' instead of *our,* would have been better. My views with regard to the use of *I, me,* & *our,* in certain cases, you are already acquainted with. The third and fourth periods in this paragraph, are well arranged, & unexceptionable.

The remainder of the paragraph is objectionable. The first period is verbose: the ideas might have been expressed in fewer words; & the sentence would have been clearer had the affirmation been *direct—'In truth,'* in the second period might have been omitted. In the place of *'it', 'this place* would have rendered the sentence clearer.—The commencement of the third sentence is obscure—*What wretch?—'To follow a road'* and to *'dare the laws,'* are common, but elliptical & inadequate expressions.—In the fourth period *'their'* is superfluous.—The next sentence is harsh: the quotation is not well connected with what precedes it, and the turn in the sentence is abrupt. The sentences now under consideration are defective in clearness and unity. The style is loose and feeble. 'But with far &c.' The adjective *"greatest"* should have been in the *com. degree.* I should omit *'hope'.* ‖ It is uncertain whether the writer intended. that the greater ‖ The relative should have been inserted in this sentence. In its present arrangement the sense is indefinite. The use of the pronoun 'we' in this sentence might have been avoid[ed.]

These two sentences are unexceptionable.

The arrangement of this sentence destroys its harmony: it is too abruptly introduced. Perhaps the Exclamation is ill timed.

'In every age &c.' This is a good sentence. It is perspicuous & clear; has unity & strength. The style is neat and nervous. If it be defective, the terms *'ranks and conditions'* are too nearly synonymous to be copulatively connected. —The first member of the next sentence, ‖ sentence ‖ is abrupt, and inelegant, in its termination. The metaphor is common; & the style diffuse.—The following sentence is the worst in the piece: It is too prolix: the arrangement is clumsy and labored, and the style too diffuse and feeble. It might be much improved.

'The Warrior & statesman &c.' The definite article should have preceded *'statesman.'* Contrary to rhetorical rules, figurative and plain language are here jumbled together. This sentence should have continued as it commenced; the figure of Metonomy [*sic*] continued, or the whole been plain language. Unity, and beauty would then have been preserved. *'Pursuit of folly'* is not a clear expression. The latter word of the Exclamation should have been plural. This sentence is musical.

'To squander years,' might be objected to as a faulty expression. The arrangement of this sentence might be improved. The metaphor is common.

This is clear & harmonious. Of the same character are the two following sentences, except the occurrence of the word *'ransack'* which destroys the harmony of the one in which it stands: *search* would have been better. The illustration and application of the text in this instance, is forcible and clear. The three preceding sentences are well arranged & perspicuous.

'The doctrine &c.' This is clear and concise.—It is followed by the most harmonious and beautiful sentence in the piece: it is somewhat figurative.—The three following periods are emphatic, and concise. The arrangement and phraseology of this paragraph is good in general. With the exception of the last sentence, which is too abruptly introduced, it is characterised [*sic*] by strength, harmony & neatness.

This sentence might be improved: the form of expression might be more condensed; and the exclamation omitted. The pronoun *'this'* occurs too frequently in this paragraph, and its antecedents are too indefinite. The writer appears fond of using 'this.'

These two sentences are concise, but obscure.

'*Son and daughter of Adam*', is an expression somewhat antiquated. I should prefer '*the text.*'

Surely *this* is &c. &c. &c. *What* is?_____The transition is too abrupt.

This sentence is quite figurative, harmonious & elegant; & the antithesis is happily applied.—It is followed by a concise, simple, & neat sentence_____

The metaphor in this sentence is far-fetched and obscure. Figures are multiplied too much, in this place.—The remaining sentence is picturesque, harmonious & elegant. The figures are well chosen, and are the best which occur in the piece. I am much pleased with this sentence.

The first sentence of the last paragraph is unexceptionable—The second is figurative, well arranged and elegant. The climax is forcible & smooth, graceful & flowing. If '*which shall*' was not repeated at the commencement of the third and fourth ‖ paragraph ‖ members of the climax, perhaps it would be improved.— The adverb '*only,*' in its present collocation conveys a meaning which was not probably intended. A little reflection will show the error.—The piece closes too abruptly.

The style of the piece *in general* is diffuse, and plain. In some instances it is neat, & sometimes elegant. No attempts seem to be made in the florid. It is sometimes concise, and nervous, & characterised [*sic*] by a degree of strength. It sometimes too is dry, harsh, & obscure. No errors are discovered in Orthography or Syntax.

Thus, I have looked over your piece, and expressed my opinion of its merits, and its demerits. But it is *my* opinion *only;* and as such you will regard it. To pretend to have done justice to your performance, would be arrogance. I have decided on its character with impartiality, and now present you with the result. You will *perhaps* be disappointed upon reading ‖ this ‖ it, *possibly* offended. Trusting however to your usual candor & forbearance, I have ventured to submit it to your inspection—I shall add no excuses for delaying *so long,* to return your favors; but can in some measure anticipate your exclamation, when you shall have received and perused this—"*The mountain has labored, & brought forth a— mouse.*"

---

[1] Unaddressed and unsigned. Identified by Sanborn, *A. Bronson Alcott*, I, 17, as "probably about 1824"; but the material and the tone of the letter indicate it was probably written earlier.

[2] A cousin of Bronson Alcott, William Andrus Alcott (1798–1859), became a noted educator and doctor of medicine.

[3] At this time, each cousin evidently made a practice of having the other criticize his compositions.

[to Chatfield Alcott, Paris, N.Y.][1]
To Mr. Chatfield Alcott
Paris, New York

Cheshire[2] June 15. 1825.

Dear Brother—

I should have written to you before this time. You have perhaps concluded that I have forgotten you, or at least, am so much interested in studies, that you have no place in my mind. It is true, I am interested, entertained, & pleased; but still this affords no excuse for neglecting my Friends. Nor shall they be neglected or forgotten—I sit down with pleasure to converse with you. By the date of this you will perceive where I am, & from thence conclude how I am employed. I came to Cheshire soon after my school closed, & have been here most of the time— a few weeks absence only in obtaining Subscribers & establishing agencies for Churchman's Magazine.[3] My health is daily improving, & I have the pleasing prospect before me of again enjoying my former health & cheerfulness. I have the command of nearly all my time—The writing does not take up but about 2 hours in a day—the remaining time I have at my own disposal. Aunt however finds many little errands & notions for me which take up some of my time. It is now 4. weeks since I was in Wolcott, our people were then *well*. I have heard nothing particularly from them since. If any thing material had happened in the family I should probably have heard, as I see Uncle Bradley every week. Father enjoyed himself as he usually does when I was at home—a boy of Truman Sanfords had then come to work with him a few days expecting to continue through the summer, if he suited. I have not yet heard whether he stays or not. The necessity of having some one to help Father perhaps might be questioned; on the whole I think it best. He has been used to have some one to help him, & even if a hired boy should not do a great deal the circumstances of having him for company, & his seeming to do something, would have a tendency to cheer Father's spirits. You well know his hypochrondrical [*sic*] turn and that he needs some one to cheer him ‖ spirits ‖. Circumstances at this time of the family tend to work on his feelings. His Family are now many of them leaving him, at least, 4 of us, and this would have a tendency to make any Father of a large family feel in some degree lonesome. Mankind, are social beings, and those ties which link a family together, which have been strengthening for 20 years or more, & drawn more closely together, must give feelings to Parents of which you & I can form but faint conceptions. His pecuniary situation too is by no means calculated to produce contentment. Ill health added to these, & old age advancing, which always tends to produce gloomy reflectio[ns] are to be considered when we think of our Father.—Our Mother ought not to be forgott[en.] It is natural for children to love & respect their parents—it is their duty & particularly, th[e] [torn] situation which a mother holds in her family, ‖ is calculated to produce ‖ inspires this affection. We, *dear brother,* have a kind & affectionate *mother*—a mother who has not had the returns from us (on my part at least) that her virtues demanded. She has done a great deal of good in our family—she has been *a mother* indeed to us. In the humble sphere in which she has moved, she has been the means of doing a good deal—Tho. her talents are humble, & her means limited—She has exemplified the maxim, which you & I & every one else, should endeavour to do—viz—"*To do all the good (which our means afforded)* ‖ *we could* ‖ *& as little hurt.*"

You will undoubtedly reccollect [sic], with what seeming reluctance I parted with you—believe me, 'twas real. I know not why, but I never parted with you with more, not even when in a destitute situation in a Southern country, the circumstances of which, you may well reccollect [sic]. When I beheld you in the enjoyment of fine health—& promising hopes, with the world before you, & reflected that before I should see you again an important decision with regard to your future condition in life would probably be formed, & that on that condition your own & perhaps the welfare of the Family depended, how could I part with you with indifference. Trusting however to your prudence & judgement, & thinking it for the best that you should leave us, I was unwilling to detain you—I trust you will remember us, & pardon the errors of an unworthy, though affectionate Brother, who perhaps has been, & still is too fond of obtruding his advice upon your notice. Be assured Dear Brother I wish you well. I heartily desire & ardently pray for your happiness & prosperity. I hope you will consider your opportunity, and reccollect [sic] that life is not to be measured by its number of days, but by the *good* which is done in it—From your letter I conclude you are pleasantly situated; & enjoy yourself in the family of Mr. Hotchkiss. You have as many advantages probably as you could expect, in a situation like yours—I hope you are thankful for them, & that you will endeavour to deserve them.

So far as I can judge by the appearance of the season in this vicinity, (for I have not been a mile from Uncles in 3 or 4 weeks) it is forward and promising. Contrasted however with your Grass & Wheat fields, perhaps it would not be so—Cherries a[re] now ripe with us—The weather has been remarkably hot for 4 days past—The thermometer standing at nearly 100 degrees on the 12 ult—which is higher than it has risen for several years—You will not expect me to be very particular in regard to the weather, season &c. I reflect so little on these things & make so few observations, that if I were to enter into a detail of them I should be dependent on others for the information.

My information in like manner is limited in regard to Wolcott. Uncle Bradley has just informed me that it is a general time of health in Wolcott at this time. With regard to your acquaintances there I will endeavour to give you the best information of which I am possessed—I have just recd. by Uncle Bradley a Letter from Wm. A. who is at his Fathers pursuing his studies, and writes me he is in good health. Harry Plumb. & Bailey are pedling yet for aught I know to the contrary. Willes Peck lives with *Mr.* Hough. with respect to the Female world you know, I am silent. I have made enquiries with regard to our southern acquaintances but do not learn that any of them have returned.—

Nothing worth relating has transpired since you left us, that would be interesting to you that I think of.—I am in fact growing too negligent with regards to these things. I am on the whole enjoying life, for what is there to hinder me? It is true I have some dull days, but who does not? Even yourself, healthy and apparently happy as you are, are not I conclude, without them.—

Uncle's[4] family are [p. in] well. Isaac you probably knew is in N. York City.—Give my respects to Denison, Johnson, & Addison—My thanks ought again to be repeated to Mr. Blakelee's Family[5] for their kindness to me when I was in Paris. I should be happy to hear from Denison by Letter. I wish he would write to me.—I shall go home about the first of July life being spared.—

The Magazine is in successful operation—having about *800* Subscribers, & will probably have *1000* (Thousand).—You wrote to have me send you the Columbian Regr. I should have so done, but for the want of Cash. I had it not on hand—To supply the place of it I have sent you "Churchman's Magazine"—thinking you will be pleased to take it. Perhaps you will not always obtain them early, but I shall send them so soon as I get them—monthly—If you, & Cousins Denison Johnson & Addison, live near each other, I wish you would give them an opportunity to read them. You will thus have an opportunity of hearing from me monthly—Avail yourself of a private opportunity should one offer of writing to me, if not, write by mail. I would not wish you to defer writing—waiting for a private conveyance. I am anxious to hear from you.—

Your affectionate Brother.
Amos B. Alcott

Mr. Chatfield Alcott
The length of this Letter, & the value of time, has induced me to ‖ perform ‖ write it but indifferently
P.S.—I have paid Father the Int. for one Year—nearly.

[1] In central New York State, about twenty miles southwest of Utica.
[2] Alcott taught school at Cheshire, Connecticut, for two years, 1825–27.
[3] Published at New Haven (?). Alcott helped edit the periodical during the spring and summer of 1825, and evidently did some writing for it.
[4] Rev. Tillotson Bronson, headmaster of the Cheshire Academy until his death during the time Alcott taught at the common school in Cheshire. He was Anna Bronson Alcox's brother.
[5] Probably a relative of the Alcotts. Bronson Alcott's maternal grandmother was Anna Blakeslee of Plymouth, Connecticut; a paternal great grandmother was Deborah Blakeslee of New Haven.

LETTER 25–2

[to Joseph C. Alcox, Wolcott]
Mr. Joseph C. Alcox
Wolcott

Friday Noon Dec. 15–1825[1]

Dear Parents—
I am in fine health and spirits, and proceed in the management and instruction of my School equal to my expectations. I make it my business chiefly—The bundle, by Mr. Bradley is recd. and by his return I send you another—Permit me to repeat my thanks to you for your goodness to me from infancy—It is my anxious wish that I may deserve your continued regards—and be able to return some of your attentions—*some* I say—*all* I cannot expect to—the solicitude and care of my younger years can never be returned—Uncle's family are well—My excursion at Thanksgiving was beneficial both to my health and spirits. I know not how soon I shall repeat it—perhaps in 4, or 5—weeks—Parents are apparently pleased with the mode of instruction which I have adopted, and with the progress of their children, ‖ in Sciences ‖—How much reason have I to be thankful to the Creator for his goodness to me—Four years ago where was I? The reflection should excite me to the best improvement of every faculty which I possess—that his goodness and guidance may be continued to me—We have Dr. Parents no cause for repining but for rejoicing. Let us then *do whatsoever our hand findeth to do, with all our might.*

Yours affectionately
A. B. Alcox

To amuse Junius & Ambrose,[2] some soap-suds, to blow bubbles with a pipe might be made—Such little folks want amusement. They should be gratified.— You are good boys I suppose Ambrose & Junius & go to school to learn

[1] Almost certainly written from Cheshire, Connecticut. Friday was December 16.
[2] The two youngest of Anna and Joseph Alcox's children: Junius, b. 1819; Ambrose, b. 1820.

LETTER 26–1

[to William A. Alcott, New Haven, Conn.]

Cheshire Jan. 3 A.M. 1826

Dear Friend—

Journeying on, through this inhospitable region to another—perhaps a more congenial—clime, how benevolently has our Creator formed our hearts to the susceptibility of friendship and social intercourse, that the rigours of our climate, and the toils of our journey may be sweetened, by the company and kind attentions of our kindred and friends!—And to bring forth those dispositions into exercise, how kindly has he made us dependent upon each other! By the interchange of numberless charities || to each other ||, how has he rendered us awake to the emotions of gratitude, affection, and sympathy! And to crown all, || he || has taught us, in his Word, the modes whereby those best emotions of our nature, may be brought forth into complete and successful exercise, and directed to their proper objects. In the highest sphere of animated existence, with which our senses are conversant, and claiming, through his condescension and goodness, the greatest portion of his regards, we, my friend, find ourselves placed—actors on the same stage, at the same time, and travelling to the same country.—To that country may our course ever be shaped, our efforts ever || be || directed. God in his goodness has thus far marked our course with his guidance, that, by experience, we might learn wisdom. Even from the commencement of our existence, his guiding and merciful hand appears. To call forth our young sympathies and affections, our juvenile efforts and recreations were together—to ripen them into friendship, we have been mutual sharers of adversity and of prosperity—to keep us from the contagion of vicious example, our first years were shaped in a retired and humble situation—and to touch our hearts with a sense of the wants, and condition of our fellow beings, our understandings have been, in some degree, enlightened, and our efforts, though feebly, directed *to become doers of good.* While many, perhaps most, of our youthful associates are still groping their way through the mists of ignorance, to the attainment of wealth, or to the gratification of their passions: the Great Author of Good has raised us from the grovelling herd, and illuminated our minds, if it be but feebly, with the beams of knowledge. Or, if we still grovel, he has given us a desire to arise and shake ourselves from the dust with which we are surrounded—from the mire in which we are immersed. Our language is not perhaps that *"all is well."* The great field of exertion, lying sterile and uncultivated, prompts, now when the time for action has arrived, to unceasing labour. Though humble individuals, like ourselves, can effect but little, still that little, if on the side of virtue, and done from a pure motive & *with all our might,* shall meet its reward. Cast into the great *treasury* of collective

9

effort, our individual *mite* shall form an integral part. The rich and great may cast in their accumulated sums: ours may be *more, than they all* shall contribute, in the sight of him who measures not by amount, but by motive. Our one, or two talents may be used—may *gain other two.* What more, or greater encouragements do we want, than are offered, to prompt to virtuous action? If eye cannot see, nor ear hear, nor the heart of man conceive the superlative excellence and happiness of the reward, promised to virtuous action, what regard will stimulate the grovelling mind to the production of pious effort? The government of our Creator involves the system of rewards, and punishments, to stimulate us, by associating happiness with virtue, and misery with vice, to avoid the one and obtain the other. In submitting to this government consists our wisdom, as well as our happiness. If we, my friend, have on the whole, turned our course to the paths of happiness, if we have fixed our eye on the summit of the hill of virtue, and are directing our course thitherward, how grateful ought we to be, that the God of all grace has thus turned our thoughts, from other foundations, based on the sand, to that whose existence is stable and permanent! Let us then ascend together. If our Great Author should continue our lives, how much can we aid, comfort, and benefit each other, in the various scenes of prosperity and adversity through which we may be called to pass, on our ascending journey. O that we may never relax our efforts, reverse our steps, or alienate our affections in our course! By dependence on the God of our salvation, and trusting in the merits of the Redeemer, we shall ultimately reach the summit of the ascent. Nor is the journey tedious. Surrounded by numerous friends and connexions, with whom to interchange the numerous charities of friendship, and benevolence, our path will be pleasant and interesting, scattered with roses, and ‖ blooming with ‖ passing through fields, blooming with verdure and beauty. Imagination paints ‖ it out ‖ the scene in rain. The original view, is veiled from her eye by the curtains of heaven.

Commencing our course of action, how much do we need, how ardently should we seek, for the guidance of the Spirit of Grace, in the application of our powers, both bodily and mental, to noble, and elevated, and useful objects. We have but one life to live. That, at most, will be short. On our conduct during this period our immortal, and best interests are involved. Nor are we only *ourselves* concerned in the event. The future happiness, or misery, of others may be influenced by the course of action we pursue, in this state of existence. Consequences, eternal and unchanging, may depend upon our conduct—In *the great business of doing good*, let us then more emulously engage—Let us improve our talent—Let us glorify our Author, our Benefactor, and Friend—Let us endeavour not to *be weary in well-doing.* Our fellow-men are before us—Can we assist them? Do they need assistance? Do they want enlightening—their pains and ills removed—the means to effect these pointed out? And can individual exertion do nothing? Though much of its power may be left, for the want of union, shall benevolence and [h]um[an]ity look calmly on, without raising her hand and voice in the great work? Howard—Boo[r?]have—and Dwight have answered. And though we cannot hope to shine with that lustre, are they unworthy of our imitation; or should we aim at ‖ a ‖ less perfect models? We *might* be active. We *might* do something. Virtue is both active, and passive.—And in that part of existence which we now fill, is ‖ the ‖ *action* expected by our Creator, as well as by our fellow-men.

God, in his goodness, has placed me, though unworthy, in a sphere in which

I can with his assistance be useful—can benefit a few of my fellow-travellers, young and inexperienced in the world, by example and instruction, and endeavour to lead them to usefulness and happiness. I am incompetent, vastly incompetent to the ‖ charge ‖ task. But I am not to desert my rising charge. They are daily gaining upon my affection, & esteem, and with many, their course is laudable, & I am encouraged. Success beyond my expectations has thus far crowned my efforts—and my prospects are, on the whole flattering. The confidence of parents is extended to a greater extent than I deserve. The greatest difficulty in the way is *number.* About 70 daily attend—In addition to the branches of instruction usually taught in this school, Arithmetick, Grammar and Geography are attended to—and I have about 30 who write. The most systematick arrangement of time and exercises, you will readily perceive, to be indispensably necessary to successful instruction, among so many. But this I do not pretend to. Of course exertions must be much limited in result: None can be extensively benefitted. And my fondness for speculations perhaps limits the extent of instruction. From this description, your conclusion, that I am necessarily busy, will be just—'tis just what I want—'tis time the *chains* were broken, that Indolence might no longer reign.—On this subject—my friend—you will perhaps, having read the above paragraph, justly exclaim *"Vanity."* I shall need your indulgence in this, as well as on a recent occasion—while in N. Haven. On the subject of Education you will perhaps justly call me enthusiastick. *I* should perhaps endeavour to make it out self-complacence. I feel the want of science in the business of instruction, but am on the whole encouraged by the prospects before me of obtaining a degree of it, and of the visible improvement of mind, mostly in the use of words to express ideas. I get but little time to read, two hours of each evening being devoted to Writing for the *"Magazine",* and *"Science the handmaid of Religion."* During this time however I have the opportunity of being instructed by the matter which I am transcribing. I can usually avail myself of the conversation of a *Superiour* for half an hour or more daily—this you well know ought not to be neglected.—My situation is on the whole pleasant—I value it—and I think justly.—Ambition, sometimes however when I think of *New-Haven* sets up her crest. But she is not very troublesome. Should we put her down entirely?—

Few incidents have occurred in the retired circle of my observation since I last saw you to afford common place topics for conversation or correspondence. To such I find I am becoming indifferent. You will therefore excuse the want of interest & entertainment which such subjects are supposed to give to correspondence. To me they are dry and uninteresting. I turn from them with disgust. But perhaps the objects with which my thoughts are occupied may not produce the like effect on others—not however entirely so to the person to whom this letter is addressed. The object of letters should be to stimulate, animate, instruct, and to a certain extent amuse—but amusement should not be the sole object. Some useful end should be included in all our efforts. Letter writing as well as every thing. Indeed, I think Letterwriting ‖ g ‖ opens a channel of extensive importance and usefulness. The means may not answer the end—the peculiar taste of the person to whom it is addressed may be misunderstood—and no valuable end subserved—To those who are aware of the effect of a letter from one whom they esteem upon their mind, especially from one whose train of thought is analogous to their, the reflection is pleasant. While the feelings of men are so much influenced by external objects no one can receive a letter from a friend with indifference.

Last week I went up to Wolcott—heard nothing worth relating—I conclude you have heard from home since I was there.—Your people were well—I arrived in Cheshire on the morning that I left *New Haven* at half past eight—in season— I was on the whole benefitted by the excursion in point of health—and certainly much interested.—Your roommates[1]—Messrs. *Cowles, & Stoughton* deserve ‖ my ‖ my regards—for their hospitality and attentions during my visit. An excursion of this kind lasts me about a month, for *stimulus*—From the retired habits which I am inclined to follow—from the little round of action of each day—the mind loves occasionally to escape, and turn her attention from mental, to external objects. Those excursions afford fine instances and opportunities. But I fear I am growing tedious, and perverting the end for which I had hoped to write.

Yours, sincerely,
A. B. Alcott

[1] At medical school.

LETTER 26–2

[to Chatfield Alcott, Paris, N.Y.]

Cheshire Ct. | Feb. 14

Mr. Chatfield Alcott
   Paris, New York
   At 'Paris Furnace'

Cheshire Feb. 13–1826

Dear Brother—

Your's of the 20. ult. January, addressed to us collectively I have just had the happiness of reading. I had expected a line from you for several months, supposing the delay was caused by your being unsettled in business. Your letter now informs of your business and prospects. You have certainly great reason to be thankful to the great Author of Good for the measure of health, happiness, and contentment which you enjoy. A sense of this goodness is undoubtedly felt, by you, and your efforts directed to promote the good of your fellowmen, and the glory of your God, in which the great business of life consists. In the situation in which you are now placed you can render yourself very useful by attending to the wants, consulting the feelings, and annexing the many comforts to the lives of those who call upon you. We all, in some way or another, can be *doers of good*. And as it is your province, for a while at least, to be employed among your fellow travellers you no doubt will do your part to conduce to their comfort and convenience.—If you are living with the man whom I think you are, Deacon_____[1] he is a worthy and pious employer. When I was in Paris I rode with him to Bridgewater[2] and a Village on the Great Western Turnpike, and had considerable conversation with him. I hope you have been fortunate to be employed by him, for I formed a very favourable opinion of him, and heard him well spoken of by others.—I reccollect [*sic*] the appearance of the village at the Furnace very well—especially the Schoolhouse.—It is a neat—pleasant, and no doubt lively place. You are undoubtedly very busy—and have company in abundance with which to associate, and such as you like, gay—serious—old—young—learned and illiterate. A fine chance to study Human Nature. I hope you improve it.

I still continue in Cheshire—and have now kept School in this place near four months—My school is large amounting to about 70 daily—My health is however pretty good for me, and I have yet met with little difficulty. We are pursuing nearly the same course that was pursued in Bristol last winter—I have been encouraged in Cheshire to a much greater extent than I expected—and can probably continue in School through the summer if I choose. I board at Uncle's—

People in Wolcott are I believe in general well. It is now three weeks since I was there. Your friend *Harry* Plumb you perhaps knew was teaching the school in which you spent last winter—Albert R. Potter—the one by his Father's—Cyrus Upson—on the Hill—Clark Bronson—Woodtick—and Thomas Upson in our district. Rev. M. Clark from Waterbury is likewise keeping a private School in Town—& has about 20—scholars. Pamela[3] wrote me last week that she was going.

Father's family were well three weeks since—Father himself is uncommonly well—and the little boys attend school—and keep our honoured parents company by their chatter now in their declining years—They now want company—I go up about one in four weeks, and they seem to be very much pleased—almost as much as when you and I used to come home from the South. The satisfaction of seeing their children *doing well,* as they are pleased to call it renders their lives comparatively pleasant. I hope Dr. Brother we shall never by our conduct diminish this pleasure—but increase it—The time for action with us is come, let us then be busy—*And never weary in well doing*—but endeavour to gild the evening days of our parents with protecting and assiduous care.

Pamila has been truly unfortunate. She has been the mother of two interesting girls—but they are now no more—they were dead at their birth.—Her husband was almost inconsolable—she was very patient—She merits much—and has a husband whose best efforts are used to make her happy—In the meek and patient virtues she much resembles our [torn] [m]other, to whom we Dr. Brother are so much indebted. We know not how much our characters have been formed and shaped by her instructions—O let us never forget her.

Wm. A. Alcott is attending the Medical Lectures in N–Haven ‖. and ‖, preparing himself for usefulness in life. And shall you & I never be roused to action—or if we act shall *sordid pelf* be our object—No—let us act from better motives—money shall not be our aim. We want not wealth—we only want a competency—this with proper exertion we are sure of—In the mean while let us be industriously employed in some laudable course of action—improving our talent, with contentment in the humble sphere in which providence may place us contributing our mite to the great Treasury of human effort and trusting, through the merits of the Redeemer, to obtain an entrance into that abode of joy ‖ and ‖ unspeakable and full of glory, in another State of existence. We have great encouragements. The reward is beyond our conceptions. Of The faithfulness of the great Rewarder we [torn]. O let us then Dr. Brother *Work while our day lasts—Whatsoever our hand findeth to do let us do it with all our might,* and may God by his grace aid us in the discharge of every duty, and guide us to peace & happiness.

I hope to see you next fall—You will treat me with attention if I will call at your Tavern? But this must not be—I must wait for you. Why don't you write to me? Let us be more social—I shall expect a Letter—my respects to Cousin

13

Denison & Addison—and the good people of Paris with whom I am acquainted—
Your affectionate Brother

A. B. Alcott

(P.S. —The ‖ April ‖ March No. of the *Magazine* closes the year. Shall I continue
them another year?—Write to me if you please._____

¹ Deacon H. (see Sanborn, *A. Bronson Alcott,* I, 72 *n.*) Sanborn also quotes a portion of this
letter.
² A few miles southwest of Paris, New York.
³ Pamela and Pamila were Bronson Alcott's twin sisters, b. 1805.

LETTER 27–1

[to Chatfield Alcott, New Hartford, N.Y.]
Mr. Chatfield Alcott
New-Hartford.¹
(Oneida County)
New-York.

Wolcott, 18. July 1827.

Dear Brother, and Sister:
    Your letter dated June 28.th came to hand in due season. It was received
last Wednesday (July, 13.) The gratifying intelligence which it brings to us, is
the more increased, because it was unexpected. Your present connexion in marriage had never for once entered my mind. Permit me to wish you both, much
happiness. As soon as may be consistent with your concerns, will you make us a
Visit in *Connecticut?*
    I have gratifying intelligence to offer you in return. The family are all in
health and prosperity, with one exception, and that depending more upon too
great an amount of care and exertion than real ill health, or unpromising prospects. I mean Father. His health is very imperfect. The sole care of his own
concerns devolves too much upon him. With growing age and infirmities, his
life is not made to possess that comfort and quietude, which are so universally
sought and which belong to the declining period of life. Let us hope however,
that a few years more, will enable us to make that provision fo[r] him, as well as
our mother, to which they are entitled, that [their] latter days may be days of
enjoyment, in the attentions and resp[ect]ability of their children. Notwithstanding the labour and cares which fall upon our parents, they appear on the whole
cheerful. They pursue their daily employments with a degree of contentment, as
much so perhaps as could be expected from people of their age, and infirmities.
Mother has assistance a part of the time, from Betsey or Phebe.² Father, with
what he hires occasionally, does his work himself. Labour is however high, and
labourers scarce. It is with difficulty that he can obtain that which the urgency
of the present busy season demands. He has been disappointed in having labour
for half the time during harvest. He says he lives now upon *Faith* for the completion of his work.
    Crops of all kinds are this season abundant—The quantity of grass in par-
ticular. *Rie, Corn, Oats, Flax,* are uncommonly good at present. Fruit is likewise
plenty, and excellent in prospect. Indeed the bounties of *Nature,* seem to be

14

distributed to us with a liberal, and unsparing hand. Gratitude commands an appropriate use of them.

You will perceive, with Father's present cares and labours,—it will be very difficult for him to make you a visit. If possible however he intends coming to see you. But you must not be disappointed if he does not. Mother expects to come with him.

Brother *Ransom's*[3] Family were well the last we heard from them. Pamila had a son the 3rd of the present months. Ransom talks of visiting your part of the world in autumn. Perhaps he may not however. You are acquainted with the state of his affairs—that it is difficult for him to dispose of his property under existing circumstances—that it is likewise against his interest to stay. I have always thought he would do much better to get away from the place of his old home. His property well disposed of, and located elsewhere, would doubtless be much to his advantage.

Should Father come out to see you, I hope you will devise some arrangement in regard to his property, which will be for his interest as well as yours. You know my mind. I ‖ hope ‖ trust you will give this subject a very attentive consideration. Our own interest, as well as our parents, are concerned in it, as you well know. May it not be hoped, that your usual good judgement, and arrangement will be used in this case?

Pamela and *James* were married on the 30.th, May last, and began keeping house in three weeks afterward. They reside with *The Deacon,* James having taken his Father's farm and having the whole superintendence. Pamela was home yesterday, and in good spirits. She says I must tell you she does not blame you for not staying a week longer, when business of so much importance, and interest was calling you away. She wishes you would be less *forgetful,* desiring to know your Ladies name, which by the way, as well as your marriage you ‖ had ‖ seem almost to have *forgotten.* As you observe, *a little more explanation* would, she says, be very well received. When shall we have it—in your next letter? Or do you intend to leave us in the dark untill [sic] we shall come and ascertain for ourselves? (*James* means to come and see you in autumn.)

I did not think you able to keep a secret, so long, and so completely, as now appears. Do you belong to the Fraternity of Masons?

I will now give you some notice of my little affairs. The school in Cheshire has been discontinued at my choice. I thought best to leave there for various reasons;[4] although a greater part of the Villagers were very desirous that I should continue at the rate named while you were here ($27. per month) But I wished to avail myself of opportunities for visiting schools, seeing individuals taking an interest in them, extending my acquaintances and information, and finding a place for the winter. I have accordingly visited various places since the school was discontinued, which was in June, and am at present flattered by the prospects which are before me. Great interest is taken in the subject of Education in various places which I have visited, and especially in Hartford. In this place there is a very favourable opportunity offered, which I shall perhaps secure. There is likewise a chance very favourable in New–Haven. In a pecuniary point of view these opportunities exceed my expectations. From 3. to 400 Dolls a year. The continuance of my present good health, will I think enable me to avail myself of a situation at one of the above places—or perhaps in Cheshire, where my expectations are good in point of salary something like $200. per. annum.

I am expecting to go to Boston in a few days to visit Schools, and collect information—to be gone about a month. Thus you see what my mind is occupied about. Yours, no doubt is equally absorbed in your domestick, and social, and agricultural concerns. How soon the time may come when it may be my happiness to enjoy the results connected with an union like yours is at present uncertain. Doubtless I am losing a part of those endearments which sweeten the cup of domestick enjoyment, and render life desirable. But rigid regard to the welfare of that person with whom a connexion might be formed, forbids my present attempt. In the mean time permit to wish you much happiness, both of mind and body, and to [words] in [word] be myself.

Your affectionate Brother
Amos B. Alcott.

Chatfield Alcott &
_____ Alcott.

with their Parents & Friends. If you see Denison or Addison, tell them their people are well. Aunt Sylvia intends visiting them in the fall, unless *they* should come to Connecticut. She is anxiously waiting for a Letter from them.

A letter from you will be expected immediately after the [rece]ption of this. Now do not disappoint us. James, & Ransom are both waiting to hear from you.

¹ A few miles southwest of Utica.
² Bronson Alcott's sisters: Betsey, b. 1808; Phebe, b. 1810.
³ Pamila's husband.
⁴ Alcott left Cheshire toward the end of June. Enrollment had fallen off because of objections by parents to Alcott's advanced methods of teaching. The Episcopal Church decided to reopen the Cheshire Academy (evidently closed after the death of Alcott's uncle, Tillotson Bronson). Further, a second common school was started by way of competition on May 21.

LETTER 28–1¹

[to Abigail May, Boston]

[Boston, July 17, 1828]

You will place me under still deeper obligations by mentioning my proposed school to your friend Miss Savage, and ascertaining her views about it. Certainly I should esteem myself especially fortunate in receiving the assistance of so accomplished a lady. But must I relinquish the pleasing anticipation awakened a year since, while visiting Brooklyn, of *your* assistance? I must acquiesce if your decision is irrevocable. But I shall hope that you will sometimes visit my little circle in Salem Street.² I thought I caught a glimpse of you in that vicinity the other day. Shall I add that only my diffidence prevented me from accosting you there?

¹ Reprinted here as it appears in Sanborn, *A. Bronson Alcott*, I, 117. In transcribing letters, Sanborn frequently altered the wording and/or the punctuation.
² For a discussion of the infant school Alcott ran at Salem Street, Boston, see Dorothy McCuskey, *Bronson Alcott, Teacher* (New York, 1940), Chap. III, esp. pp. 45–49.

PART TWO

1830–1839

[to Samuel E. Sewall, Boston]

[Boston, May 20, 1830]

Mr. Saml. E. Sewall,
 Milton Place.
Dr. Sir,
 Permit me to ask the favour of your calling at Col. May's at 4. o,clock pre-
cisely, on Sunday afternoon next, to accompany me, and my friend Miss. May to
King's Chapel.[2]

With esteem,
 A. B. Alcott.

Thursday, May 20.
 112. Franklin St./

[1] MS. owned by the Houghton Library, Harvard University.
[2] Miss Abigail May married A. Bronson Alcott on the Sunday mentioned, May 23, 1830, at
King's Chapel, Boston. Colonel Joseph May was her father; Samuel E. Sewall, her cousin.

[to Roberts Vaux,[2] Philadelphia]

Boston, 27—July. 1830—

Dear Sir,
 I have delayed answering your very generous favor of the 14. ult. until this
time, that I might inform you of the disposition which I have concluded to make
of the Essay about which you speak in terms of so high commendation—[3] It is to
me most gratifying to find in one so well qualified to judge as yourself on subjects
involving the highest and dearest interests of our race, that sympathy and encouragement which is expressed in your letter.—
 I have thought best to publish the Essay in the Christian Examiner—one of
our most liberal periodicals—and after its appearance in that form, to have a few
hundred copies struck off, for more individual distribution. This can be done at

a trifling expense; and, in the carefulness of our Booksellers here, about what they publish, seems all that I can venture to do. The 'Examiner' will appear on the first day of Sep. and the Essay in the form of a Pamphlet can come out in a week or two after.[4]—Any advices, or suggestions respecting it; or assistance by way of circulating it, will be gratefully recd by

Yours Sincerely, &
with great respect
A. B. Alcott

[1] MS. owned by the Historical Society of Pennsylvania.

[2] Roberts Vaux "was at this time President of the School Board in Philadelphia, and of the Pennsylvania Society for the promotion of Public Schools." (Sanborn, *A. Bronson Alcott*, I, 154, n.)

[3] Alcott had submitted (though he did not win) an essay for a one hundred dollar prize offered by the School Board in Philadelphia. For a portion of Vaux's letter of July 14, 1830, see Sanborn, *A. Bronson Alcott*, I, 153–54,

[4] The pamphlet appeared as *Observations on the Principles and Methods of Infant Instruction* (Boston, 1830).

LETTER 32–1[1]

[to Mrs. Anna Alcott (Joseph Alcox), Wolcott, Conn.]

Germantown[2] November 29th. 1832

Dear Mother,

This is the 29th of November—you will of course remember it as my birthday. I am 33 years of age—my life is, at most, half measured, and I have but to fix my thoughts on that better part which is yet to come. It is better, at any rate, to hope that the future will bring more substantial happiness than the past—though, in my own case, I feel that the past, full of varied experience as it has been, has also been full of instruction—and instruction too of the most effective kind—from which I have profited, though often at the sacrifice of present desires and purposes. It is true, I believe, that the trials and experiences of life, much more than books and formal teaching, impart to us our best and most effective lessons. *It is in the school of Experience that we are taught almost all we know.—* Should my life be as chequered with vicissitude in the future, as it has been in the past, I shall, therefore, have more cause for gratitude than complaint, since I shall have the means of obtaining the best of instruction from the changes of life. I know not that I would have had the past different from what it has been, if I could—it has done everything for me; and I will not complain. *All is well to those who believe so.*

But, besides reflections on my life and experience—this is, *the birth of a second daughter on my own birth-day.*[3] She is a very fine, fat, little creature, much larger than Anna was at birth, with a firm constitution for building up a fine character, which, I trust, we shall do our part to accomplish.—Abba is doing well thus far. She has suffered a good deal during the summer, but has been unusually cheerful amid the cares and anxieties of life, and of her situation. There are few, I believe, more interested in home than she is—more devoted to their families— She lives and moves and breathes for her family alone.—Such, as you are aware, was the companion which I wished to secure to myself; and such, have I, indeed, found. I hope she may be spared to bless those whom Providence has given me. Little Anna, now 20 months old,[4] is remarkably well, active, and intelligent. She has passed through the usual complaints of children during the first year, or 18 months of life, and has a large stock of health and strength for future trials. Her heart and mind develope beautifully—she is full of affection and intelligence—of freshness and activity, and begins to talk a few words intelligibly. We think she has the *mother's heart,* and the *father's mind;* time, if she lives, will prove.

I know you must long much to see her—a[nd] must have been greatly disappointed at my no[t] visiting you last August—but you have still the pleasure in reserve. We shall probably leave Germantown in the Spring wither for Philadelphia or Boston, and shall then endeavour to visit you. We are very pleasantly situated here on many accounts, and I should not leave, did not greater inducements urge me: this is not quite the place for me—and, I believe, I shall ultimately find my way back to my own, and Abba's friends, in Boston. *That* is the place for me, and where the place is there I must go.—I have a strong desire, at times, to make my home with you; but this is not, I believe, the thing—I can be happier and more useful elsewhere. Abba has planned of passing the next summer with you; but this might be disagreeable to you on some accounts, and 'tis too early to decide.

I should enjoy a few months residence in Wolcott, very much.—I have heard nothing from Chatfield and friends, since I last wrote you.—Henry Kenece[?] I did not see, being absent from home when he called. I am glad the money was of so much use to you.—Love to brothers & sisters—

Your affec. Son.
A. Bronson Alcott.

Mrs. Anna Alcott
   Wolcott
      Connecticut.

[1] MS. owned by the Houghton Library, Harvard University.
[2] Alcott left Boston for Philadelphia and Germantown in December, 1830. He taught school in Germantown from February 18, 1831, to late in the winter of 1833, when he moved to Philadelphia where he remained until his return to Boston in the fall of 1834.
[3] Louisa May Alcott.
[4] Anna Bronson Alcott, the eldest daughter, had been born March 16, 1831.

LETTER 32-2[1]

[to Colonel Joseph May, Boston?]

Germantown, Nov. 29, 1832.

Dear Sir,—

It is with great pleasure that I announce to you the *birth of a second daughter.* She was born at half-past 12 this morning, on my birthday (33), and is a very fine healthful child, much more so than Anna was at birth,—has a fine foundation for health and energy of character. Abba is very comfortable, and will soon be restored to the discharge of those domestic and maternal duties in which she takes so much delight, and in the performance of which she furnishes so excellent a model for imitation. Those only who have seen her in those relations, much as there is in her general character to admire and esteem, can form a true estimate of her personal worth and uncommon devotion of heart. She was formed for domestic sentiment rather than the gaze and heartlessness of what is falsely called "society." Abba inclines to call the babe *Louisa May,*—a name to her full of every association connected with amiable benevolence and exalted worth. I hope *its present possessor* may rise to equal attainment, and deserve a place in the estimation of society.

With Abba's and Anna's and Louisa's regards, allow me to assure you of the sincerity with which I am

Yours,
A. Bronson Alcott.

[1] Reprinted from Cheney, pp. 14–15.

LETTER 33–1[1]

[to Roberts Vaux, Philadelphia]

Germantown, January 10–1833.

Dear Sir,

My object in addressing you, at this time, is to ask your opinion in reference to the probable success of an endeavour to establish a school for children in your city. This request I make with the more confidence from the knowledge of the interest felt by yourself in general education, and the favour with which I believe you have regarded my own views and efforts. A personal interview would have been more desirable, but I have heretofore failed of seeing you.

The issue of our experiment in education, undertaken at the invitation and sustained during its earlier stages of progress chiefly through the zeal and liberality of our mutual friend, now deceased, has proved wholly inadequate to the consummation of our ultimate purposes of establishing a seminary for the diffucion of generous views on the subject of education. The death of Mr. Haines[2] not only modified our original plans, but rendered some change in my own relations to instruction, necessary—The encouragement given to the labours of Mr. Russell[3] is sufficient to induce him to remain in Germantown. My own endeavours have met with less patronage. But I feel unwilling to return to New-England without expressing my desire to make trial of my views on the minds of a few children in your city—fraught as I deem them to be, with genial influence on the juvenile being.

It is my wish to operate chiefly on the characters of those committed to my care—to form and mature habits of accurate thought—pure feeling, and correct action—to fit the mind for the acquisition of knowledge, and inspire the heart with the love of virtue, and pursuit of excellence.—The results which I aim at producing, cannot, of course, be rendered immediately obvious, but will be, I trust, satisfactory and permanent in the end.—

If a few children, between the ages of four and ten years, could be collected from those parents who would enter with an intelligent interest into my purposes, and wait with the necessary patience for the production of results, I should highly prize the opportunity thus offered for making known my views on early education. Twenty five or thirty children, at the rate of $15. per quarter, would enable me to commence a sch[ool] for this purpose.

These views and purposes I offer to y[ou] as an individual intimately acquainted w[ith] the relations of education, and the views and wants expressed by parents, in your city,—and whose opinion in reference to the practicability of the plan now hinted at, would be of more service to me than that of any other person.

Yours,
With great respect,
A. Bronson Alcott.

Roberts Vaux Esqr.
Philadelphia

[1] MS. owned by the Historical Society of Pennsylvania.
[2] Reuben Haines of Germantown, a Quaker, at whose invitation Alcott and William Russell went to that area to teach. He died in October, 1831.
[3] A good sketch of William Russell is to be found in McCuskey, *Bronson Alcott, Teacher*, pp. 64–68.

LETTER 34–1[1]

[to Elizabeth Palmer Peabody, Boston]

[Boston, before September, 1834?][2]

" 'Emblems,' (to quote Mr. Alcott's own words in a letter to myself,) 'I have found to be extremely attractive and instructive to children. I could not teach without them. My own mind would suffer, were it not fed upon ideas in this form; and spiritual instruction cannot be imparted so well by any other means. The universal spirit flows into nature, whether material or human, through these media; and sense and imagination are the faculties that receive the divine stream —the one from without, and the other from within—and pour it upon the soul. The manner of Jesus and of Plato is authority, were any needed on this subject, to show what the mind requires in order to be quickened and renewed. *"Without a parable*, spake he not unto them." Neither should the teacher of spiritual truth now-a-days. From neglecting this mode of instruction, we have shorn the young mind of its beams. We have made it prosaic, literal, worldly. We have stripped truth naked, and sent her cold into the world, instead of allowing her to clothe herself with the beautiful associations in which she presents herself in infancy and childhood.' "

"In one of Mr. Alcott's letters, from which I have already quoted, he says, 'To form a library, suited to the wants of the young, from modern works, would be impossible. We have few, very few, that nurture the spiritual life. A dozen volumes would include all that are of a quickening and sustaining power. On subjects of mere fancy, and of the understanding, we have many; but these too often tend to dissipate the wants of the young, and materialize their spirits. I have been seeking works for my purpose for the last ten years, and my library is still scanty; yet within this period, hundreds of volumes have been contributed to our juvenile literature.

" 'Indeed, modern works, whether for children or adults, are greatly deficient both in depth and purity of sentiment: they seldom contain original or striking views of the nature of man, and of the institutions which spring from his volition. There is a dearth of thought and sterility of sentiment among us. Literature, art, philosophy, life, are without freshness, ideality, verity, and spirit.

" 'But the works of some of the more ancient writers are of a more vivid and spiritual character. They are not however to be found in our book stores. Seldom do we see a copy even of Spencer [sic], Jeremy Taylor and Dr. Henry More, to say nothing of other writers of a highly spiritual character, whose names are not so familiar. The age of spiritualism seems to be past, and few are the representations of that age which have come down to us; they are generally only to be found in the libraries of collectors, who value them for their scarcity, or peculiarities of exterior, rather than for their intrinsic merit. In truth, we have fallen so far below the high standard of these authors, both in thought and style, that we do not appreciate their transcendent power. We do not rise to the apprehension of their beauties of language, their richness and profoundness of thought, their delicacy and humanity of sentiment. We are less of metaphysicians than they; i.e. we know less of man; we have less faith in humanity. How affluent are those deep-thoughted minds! How full of wisdom and love! Their thoughts flow from the heart; they are clear, strong, quickening, effective; unlike the sterile notions of modern minds. Open any of these works, and you are upon a deep, rich, fresh thought, clad in imagery all a-glow with life; you feel you are at once in communion with a great spirit; your spiritual faculties are quickening into being, and asserting their prerogative of insight. You are charmed into reflection. But I do not at this moment think of any writers, since the days of Milton, excepting Coleridge and Wordsworth, whose works require a serene and thoughtful spirit, in order to be understood. Most works since this date, require little thought; they want depth, freshness; the meaning is on the surface; and the charm, if there be any, is no deeper than the fancy: the imagination is not called into life; the thoughts are carried creepingly along the earth, and often lost amid the low and uncleanly things of sense and custom.

" 'In the discharge of my duties as a teacher, therefore, I have found few works to aid me. I have been thrown mostly on my own resources, to create from circumstances, and the ideal of my own mind, the material for the intellectual and spiritual nurture of children. Of the few works that have become established favorites with my scholars, works containing thoughts to which they recur with delight, and which awaken, as it were, a brood of other thoughts in their minds, I can only recollect the Bible, Pilgrim's Progress, The Fairy Queen, Krummacher's Parables—English Translation and Edition, The Story without an End, Coleridge's Poems, Wordsworth's Poems, Milton's Paradise Lost, Quarles' Emblems.[3]

" 'I have this day sent to England for Bunyan and Spencer [sic], as fine copies cannot be procured in this country; and I wish I had added Quarles. It is from these books that I generally read; for, although imagination is acknowledged to be the shaping power of the soul; and, when rightly nurtured by meditation and observation, she clothes the spirit in the chaste and beautiful robes of truth, how seldom is it cultivated among us! I seldom hear any one speak of cultivating this faculty. And yet if there is any fact settled by the history of our race, it is, that imagination has been the guiding energy of light and life to humanity. For what is genius but this faculty in its most vivid action? and genius has shaped the institutions of society in all past ages. We need schools not for the inculcation of knowledge, merely, but for the development of genius. Genius is the peculiar attribute of soul. It is the soul, indeed, in full and harmonious play; and no instruction deserves the name, that does not quicken this its essential life, and fit it for representation in literature, art, or philosophy.' "

[1] The text is quoted from Elizabeth Palmer Peabody, *Record of a School: Exemplifying the General Principles of Spiritual Culture* (Boston, 1835), pp. 9–10, 15–17. Second and third editions appeared in 1836 and 1874; the text of the letter varies in each edition.

[2] Alcott opened his Temple School—named for its location at the Masonic Temple, Tremont Street, Boston—in September, 1834.

[3] "Light & Horton have in contemplation, to publish a series of books of a more spiritual character for children, than has yet been attempted. This will include Shoberl's translation of Krummacher, (for the American translation falsifies, as well as abridges the original;) Pilgrim's Progress, prepared by Mr. Alcott, for children; Story without an End; Quarles Emblems; and Pictures of Thought, which is a work Mr. Alcott already has in manuscript, and which will probably be the first of the series" (Elizabeth Peabody's note).

LETTER 35–1[1]

[to Lemuel Shaw, Boston][2]

Temple March 1 1835

Mr. Shaw to A. Bronson Alcott Dr
For Instruction of Lemuel from Dec 1 1834 to March 1 1835 - - - 15.00
1 Copy of Lee's Spelling Book - - - - - - - - - - - - - 12
Stationery - - - - - - - - - - - - - - - - - - 50
$15.62

Received Payment

A. Bronson Alcott

[1] MS. owned by the Massachusetts Historical Society.

[2] Lemuel Shaw (1781–1861), a noted lawyer, member of the Massachusetts legislature, and Chief Justice of the Massachusetts Supreme Court from 1830 to 1860. In 1847, his daughter, Elizabeth, married Herman Melville. His son attended Alcott's school.

LETTER 35–2[1]

[to Emma Savage, Eastport, Maine][2]

Boston August 5 1835.

My dear Emma,
Your letter has just been handed to me. I had been expecting to hear from you, and feared that I should miss you entirely, as I am on the point of setting out for Connecticut to spend a few weeks with my mother taking Anna with me. But I have now heard from you, and shall enjoy another letter, should you incline to write to me, while in Wolcott where my mother resides. Write me, do, while I am there.
You seem to have met with not a few adventures on your way to Eastport; all of which, I presume are put into your Journal. The scenery, and goingson, of the country, must afford you great pleasure, and fill your imagination with images

that will never grow dim and be wholly forgotten. (We city-people can hardly be aware how much we lose by living almost all our lifelong amid brick-walls, and walking about on stone pavements, instead of being surrounded by the beautiful works of nature, the green trees, and uneven fields, the murmuring brooks, joyful living creatures, and all the natural things of the country. You must enjoy them I know; and this enjoyment will be the best preparation for the studies of the school when you return. Your mind will be freshened, and filled with images, for the hours of thought and acquisition; and your feelings receive an impulse that will carry you on for a long time. I mean to go and enjoy this communion with the Outward myself, and Anna requires the same privilege. Nature is a Book which every body likes to peruse, and of which they never grow tired.

I closed school on Wednesday last—just a week ago. A few of the scholars left, before the close of the quarter to go into the country. I am glad to learn that most of them return to begin the next quarter. We shall have a very interesting time, I think. I have a good deal planned out for thought and study; and shall be disappointed if the children are not deeply interested in it. Robert— Gustavus—Edward[—]Dexter, may possibly leave us; but they all expressed their deep unwillingness to do so, and yield to the wishes of their parents, who have ideas regarding their education into which, as yet, they cannot fully enter. There is much you know in early life that we cannot fully understand, yet believe, and perform.—I shall like to see your Journal when you return. I hope your journeyings and visits will be pleasant to you. Nothing was more interesting to me when young, than to travel and look around me. And how much good it did me.

My regards to your sister, whose company must add greatly to your pleasure. Anna unites with me in kind remembrances, and expressions of affection.

A. Bronson Alcott.

For
Miss Emma Savage

---

[1] MS. owned by the Fruitlands and Wayside Museums.
[2] A student of Alcott's at the Temple School, daughter of James Savage of Boston. The family was evidently spending the summer, or part of it, in southeastern Maine.

LETTER 35–3[1]

[to Lemuel Shaw, Boston]

[Boston, November 28, 1835]

Mr. Shaw to A. Bronson Alcott Dr.

For instruction of Lemuel - - - - - - - - - - - - - - -	$15.00.
" Elements of [word] - - - - - - - - - - - - - -	.50
" Woodbridges Geography & Atlas - - - - - - - - -	1.00
" Blank Books & Stationary [sic] - - - - - - - - - -	.75
" Latin, Grammar & Reader - - - - - - - - - - -	.75

18.00

Rec. Payment

A. Bronson Alcott.

Masonic Temple Nov. 1835.
1835 From Sep. 1 to Nov. 1, 28.

[1] MS. owned by the Massachusetts Historical Society.

LETTER 36–1[1]

[to Lemuel Shaw, Boston]

Temple No. 7. [Boston] February 1836.

Mr. Lemuel Shaw to A. Bronson Alcott Dr.

1835

Nov. 29	For instruction of Lemuel - - - - - - - - -	$15.00
Feb. 19	" Blank Books and Stationary [sic] - - - - - -	1.00
1836		*16.00*

Received Payment

A. Bronson Alcott

[1] MS. owned by the Massachusetts Historical Society.

LETTER 36–2[1]

[to Lemuel Shaw, Boston]

Boston May 14. 1836

Mr. Shaw to A. Bronson Alcott Dr

For instruction and discipline of Lemuel from Feb. 28 to date - -	$15.00
Blank Book & Stationary [sic] - - - - - - - - - - -	1.00

16.00

Received Payment

A. Bronson Alcott

(Temple No. 7.)

[1] MS. owned by the Massachusetts Historical Society.

LETTER 36–3[1]

[to Mrs. Anna Alcott, Wolcott, Conn.]

[Boston, June 6, 1836]

My memory lingers fondly about my early home. As years multiply and the cares and duties of life press, the more am I reminded of my early days, when as a son and brother I dwelt under the same roof with you—and him who has gone hence. In this new relation of father, I seem to be living out his life; in my children I seem to see myself as a child, fondly delighting in his and your approval. My children, calling for their mother, recall the time when I was wont to come to you, with that beautiful name on my lips,—sure of your smiling upon me and taking me to your heart. And when my little ones need correction,—for what children do not sometimes, even the best?—then I think of my father's earnest manner with me, as I stood before him, perhaps conscience-stricken and acknowledging my fault. I have been trying to remember when you had cause to reprimand or correct me, but I have no such recollection. You are associated in my heart with kindness, forbearance long, sympathy for me ever; for when others wronged me, it was grateful to have your encouraging look, your approving word. I was diffident,—you never mortified me; I was quiet,—you never excited me; I loved my books,—you encouraged me to read, and stored my mind with knowledge. You helped me when I needed help, were glad at any success of mine, never frowned upon me when I failed. You knew my love for neatness of appearance, my sense of the beautiful,—and you cherished it. These things I have not forgotten, and love now to tell you so. I am sure that I owe not a little of my serenity of mind, equanimity of disposition, hope and trust in the future, which is my usual habit, to you. Preachers I have had, teachers a few, trials and vicissitudes,—I have failed in much, have been schooled into resignation by all (you know all this, when in my ill health and despondency I seemed useless and insignificant in the world); yet no preaching, teaching, or trial, or despondency brought me more abundant benefit, none such abiding joy, as the recollection of your affectionate encouragement while my character was forming. I pray that my own life may never disgrace yours, and that while cherishing my children, I may exercise those graces which were called forth first by your parental solicitude and pains unrequited.

[1] Reprinted from Sanborn, *A. Bronson Alcott*, I, 19–21.

LETTER 36–4[1]

[to Lemuel Shaw, Boston]

[Boston, June 26, 1836?]

Mr. Alcott regrets the necessity that leads him to anticipate the favour of Mr. Shaw's bill, but hopes that it will be quite as convenient to meet it at this time, as any other.
Temple, 26 June.

[1] MS. owned by the Fruitlands and Wayside Museums.

LETTER 36–5[1]

[to Lemuel Shaw, Boston]

[Boston, June 27, 1836?]

Mr. Shaw will perceive that where five or six weeks' holiday are given in August & Sept. one of the quarters must, of course, be shortened. The present quarter is so by two weeks—from May 22. to July 29. being just ten weeks. June 27

[1] MS. owned by the Fruitlands and Wayside Museums.

LETTER 36–6[1]

[to Lemuel Shaw, Boston]

[Boston, July 23, 1836]

Mr. Shaw to A Bronson Alcott Dr.

For instruction of Lemuel during the Summer Term - - - - - - $15.00
Books and Stationary [sic] - - - - - - - - - - - - - 1.00

16.00

Boston July 23, 1836

Received Payment

A. Bronson Alcott.

26 Front Street

[1] MS. owned by the Massachusetts Historical Society.

[Letter to Mrs. A. Bronson Alcott, Boston; from Wolcott, Conn., August 7, 1836.]

LETTER 36–7[1]

[to Mrs. A. Bronson Alcott, Boston]

Wolcott August 12th 1836 | Friday Morning.

My dear Abba,

Anna begins this letter with the revealings of her heart.[2] Let me take up the song and disclose my own.—I must go back to *Sunday* last—the date of my letter to you. Anna attended Church with me. We heard a sermon in the morning from Rev. Mr. Clark of Cheshire. Our good *church* folks thought it very good, but it would be difficult to tell what it was about. There was not a glimmering of an Idea in it. But it slipt off very glibly. Mr. Vail preached in the afternoon on *"being straightened."* His sermon was a living exemplification of his text. He was "straightened" in *thought, speech,* and *effect.*—But I cannot feel a disposition to deal harshly with the well-meant endeavours of my kind. I grieve that so much endeavour should be wasted—and both minister and people suffer for lack of knowledge. Verily, priests and prophets are wanting to go among us, and declare the simple truths, which are well nigh lost sight of, amid an unmeaning jargon of words and phrases. Yet *Human Nature* is an *Inspired Nature,* and we may yet hope—for in this very striving after Ideas—encumbered as it is by all manner of Verbiage—by superstitions, and traditions—the spiritual Instinct reveals itself: and Hope shines forth to irradiate the path of the simple and the pure. Man is *wise* even in his ignorance—*strong* even in his weakness—for God works in him, and makes even his folly and his imbecility to praise him. My townsmen despite their blindness, walk as erect, and see as clearly, as the more favored sons of the city. The Image of God shines forth from under the rustic gaberdine, of the swain, with a lustre not less significant, than from the tinselled vestments of the citizen, and God *eyeth* both alike. *It is dimmed in* each[3]

[1] MS. owned by the Houghton Library, Harvard University.
[2] Alcott's letter is preceded by a note from Anna to her mother.
[3] The letter breaks off at this point. Probably only the closing and signature are missing.

LETTER 36–8[1]

[to Miss Sophia A. Peabody,[2] Salem, Mass.]
Miss Sophia A. Peabody
    Salem
       Mass.   Boston August 23 1836
Dear Friend
    I have just returned from my mother's, and find your two letters waiting for me. I have read them with a double-sentiment.—The interest which you express in my Thoughts, and their influence over you, I can explain in no other way than as arising from similarity of temperament and of taste—heightened exceedingly by an instinctive tendency—almost preternatural—to reverence whatever approaches, either in Spirit or Form, your standard of the Ideal.—Of minds of this class, it is impious to ask for tempered expressions. They admire. They marvel. They love. These are the Law of their Being, and to refuse them the Homage of this spiritual Oneness with the objects of their regard, is Death!
    Their words have a significance borrowed from their inmost being; and are to be interpreted, not by ordinary and popular acceptation, but by the genius of the individual that utters them. These have a significance of their own. They commune not with words but in spite of them. Ordinary minds mistake them. For they cannot be revealed through the illusory medium of words. *Psyche* telleth not all her Heart to *Hermes* for Hermes maketh nought—nor apprehendeth aught—save *Language.* Sentiments and Ideas belong exclusively to Psyche, and she giveth them to whomsoever she listeth.
    You inquire whether portions of *"Psyche"* are to be copied for the press. Mr Emerson has not returned the Ms.[3] But should I find any thing left, (after his revisions) worthy of attention, I will send it to you. You are very good to propose such favours.
    I send you some numbers of the "Reformer". Among others, is the one containing Mr. Brownson's[4] Notice of the "Story without an End".[5] The alle-

gories which you copied while with us are also among them.—I read your allegory to Mr. Brownson, who was interested in it, and took it for the Reformer. It is a beautiful thing, and will be useful. Mr. Brownson spends this week with his family. I am preparing for the Institute which meets on Thursday of this week— and also for the opening of the School.

We shall expect to see you her[e] in October. Meanwhile write me as of[ten] as you feel inclined. I will sometimes write in return. I would often, were I at all given to the practice, and did I feel that my letters could give pleasure. My mind flows not freely and simply in an Epistle.

                          Very truly,
                            Yours,
                          A. Bronson Alcott

Yours of Aug 20 has just reached me. I am sorry to hear you speak so doubt-fully concerning your visit in Oct. Yet I *hope* you will come. I have read Car-lyle's Schiller. You re-utter my conceptions at the time. You are very kind to propose copying the *'Young Christ'*. The original is a borrowed one, and a copy would be useful.* I had sent your allegory to Mr. B. before your letter reached me. Will it be less useful in Elizabeth's paper? I hope she will carry her purpose into execution. Such a periodical is extensively wanted.

                          A. B A

Aug 24—
* Copy it just as it is—size of the copy of 'School Room'.

¹ MS. in Berg Collection, New York Public Library.
² Sophia Amelia Peabody (1809–71) occasionally assisted her sister, Elizabeth Palmer Peabody, in Alcott's Temple School. She married Nathaniel Hawthorne on July 9, 1842.
³ At Emerson's suggestion *Psyche* was not published. Portions of it have been printed in Kenneth Walter Cameron, *Emerson the Essayist* (Raleigh, N.C., 1945), II, 101–25.
⁴ Orestes Brownson (1803–76).
⁵ Friedrich Wilhelm Carové, *Story Without an End,* trans. Sara Austin (Boston and New York, 1836). Contains a Preface and Key to the Emblems, by A. Bronson Alcott.

LETTER 36–9¹

[To Sophia A. Peabody, Salem, Mass.]
Miss Sophia A. Peabody
    Salem   Boston Sep. 12 1836
        Mass.
Dear Friend

Your letter, with one from Elizabeth,² reached me on Saturday. I was glad to hear from you again—for I find my thoughts often dwelling on you, and linger-ing around the pleasant hours of your late visit. The sympathy of spirits is the Heart's *undersong,* and its warblings are heard, oft in the still quiet hours of solitude and meditative thought, as it were the soft voices of celestial quires. Music reaches us from the distance, amid all the discordant noises of the *External.*

Your remarks on De Maistre have interested me in the Book. Mr. Brownson takes it to-day, and I shall have the interesting passages from him. If you have passages transcribed that will interest, send them in your next packet—with whatever else you incline. And if you have a Copy of the "Valley of Quietude", will you send it likewise. B. B. Thacher is preparing a "Boston Book",[3] and has taken a fancy to that Improvisation, from the name. I gave him the "Invocation to a Child," yet he wishes to see the allegory before he decides upon inserting it. The Book is nearly through the press, and he waits for something from some persons. He wants something from Elizabeth, and have you nothing for him? I was under the impression that you preserved portions of the "Valley", and intended to recall and write out the remainder at your leisure. Now don't attempt this because Mr. Thacher wants it; but simply tell me as soon as convenient how much of the allegory is preserved, and send, if you can, some thing from Elizabeth.

Have you seen Mr. Emerson's *"Nature"*? If you have not, let me send you a copy on Saturday. It is a Divine Poem on the External. It is just to your taste; and you will not be the less pleased that in it he alludes to your friend, most kindly.[4] It reminds me more of Sampson Reed's "Growth of the mind" than any work of modern date. But it is unlike any other work—a beautiful Idyl. I send you Mr. Brownson's notice of it. Yet *Nature* is not the best critic of "Nature". Spirit can alone do it justice. Mr. B. gave us two splendid discourses yesterday. Surely, this man is a terror to pseudo-ministers and would-be philosophers. He is one of our most eloquent preachers. His doctrine is with power. He grapples with the highest matter and deepest wants of our being, and spreads these before the reason, as with a light from heaven. Our small men must retreat, awe-struck and confounded, from h[is] presence. When Jupiter thunders, the demi[gods] affrighted, hide their heads!—Mr. B. will write to you soon.

Eliz. is absent I suppose. Will you assure her that nothing definite will be done regarding the "Record of Conversations"[5] till I have seen her. There will be no difficulty in arranging the matter to which she refers.—My school opens favorably. I am expecting an assistant this week[6]—the arrangement will, however, be temporary, as I have *Miss Thaxter* of Hingham in view.[7]

With great regard
A. Bronson Alcott

Your Antinants[?] is coloured—shall I send it on Saturday, and how? I am obliged to you for proposing to copy the "Infant Christ'—but defer sending it at present. If the Conversations are printed in two volumes, I shall have this as the frontispiece to the 2nd. vol. It will then remain in its present size.—Write me when the *God* invites.

A.B.A.

---

[1] MS. in Berg Collection, New York Public Library.
[2] Elizabeth Palmer Peabody.
[3] Benjamin Bussey Thatcher, ed., *The Boston Book* (Boston, 1837).
[4] Emerson's *Nature* was first advertised for sale in Boston on September 9, 1836—see Ralph L. Rusk, *The Life of Ralph Waldo Emerson* (New York, 1949), p. 240. Alcott had finished reading the published *Nature* on September 11. Regarding the reference to Alcott in Emerson's essay, see Alcott, *Journals*, p. 78 and 78, *n.* 3.
[5] Alcott's forthcoming *Conversations with Children on the Gospels*, the first volume of which appeared in 1836, the second in 1837.
[6] During the summer Elizabeth Peabody had left her job as assistant to Alcott. Margaret Fuller succeeded her for a short period.
[7] Anna Thaxter. Hingham is a short distance southeast of Boston on Massachusetts Bay.

LETTER 36–10[1]

[to Lemuel Shaw, Boston]

[Boston, October 15, 1836]

Mr. Shaw to A. Bronson Alcott Dr.

For board of Lemuel from Sep 14. three weeks, @4 - - - - - - - - - *12.00*

Received payment

A. B. Alcott
per W. L. Gerrish

Boston October 15. 1836.

[1] MS. owned by the Massachusetts Historical Society.

LETTER 37–1[1]

[to Lemuel Shaw, Boston]

[Boston, February 18, 1837]

Dear Sir,

As the Spring term of my school opens on Monday next, and some additional encouragement is indispensible in order to meet the unavoidable expenses of the same, permit me to inquire your views as to the expediency of raising the terms of tuition to $25 a quarter;[2] and whether in case such addition were made, the patronage which you have heretofore extended to this enterprise will be continued.

Very respectfully
A. Bronson Alcott

Temple No 7
Feb 18.

[1] MS. owned by the Massachusetts Historical Society.
[2] Alcott had been charging $15 a quarter, but enrollment had fallen off drastically—to twenty-five pupils.

LETTER 37–2[1]

[to Ralph Waldo Emerson, Concord]

Boston May 9 1837

My dear Sir,

I shall see you early next week—on Monday or Tuesday I think. For some time I have been looking forward to this visit. I have much to say to you. And, to find some one whose ear you can command, but for a moment, during these times of frivolous and blinding action, is no small pleasure. A man intent on realities, shall scarce find sympathy, much less apprehension, from the busy and anxious seekers after shows and shadows, with which our time abounds. Doubtless you feel this, with all the thoughtful & earnest among us. At no time have I felt it more. Yesterday I saw our friend Ripley,[2] who seemed to be burdened in the same way. He proposes to resume our meetings. As Mr. Hedge is in town, and purposes to spend some weeks, why should we not? Mr. Francis inquired about them with interest when I saw him a few days since; and there are others who would join us. I see no reason to delay our meeting a single week—especially since those who were first to close, are now first to propose the renewal of our interviews.[3] We will talk this matter over when I see you.

Mr. Fuller writes me in deep disappointment at the possibility of losing your discourse at the opening of the institution.[4] He says you must come—The friends of the school are expecting you—Mrs Farley and Hale desire much to hear you &c. He begs me to say my best words to persuade you to be with them. I hope you will incline your ear to this petition. It is a good moment to say a good word for the soul; and none can do this more worthily or acceptably than yourself. I should feel honored by the occasion; and our friend Miss. Fuller feel herself honored also.[5]

Shall I see Mr. Hedge at your house? I wish much to become acquainted with him. He interests me more than most men of our time. I shall be with you on Monday—Perhaps he would join us on Tuesday, and then we should have a day at least in common. I know not where I am to see him under circumstances so favorable. With you I should find his value I fancy; and should I be unfortunate (as I am wont) your friendly apprehension might set all to rights. I hope I shall see him during this week somewhere.

I heard of you last week from a friend who is staying with Mr. Francis—Miss Thaxter. She was deeply pleased with your sermon; and, in her note, says many fine things of you. I hope you found her out. She is one of the descern[ing] of the time.

Very truly,
Your friend,
A. Bronson Alcott.

Rev. R. Waldo Emerson,
Concord,
Mass.

[1] MS. owned by the Fruitlands and Wayside Museums.

[2] George Ripley (1802–80), leader in the Brook Farm experiment and later literary critic for the New York *Tribune*.

[3] Alcott here refers to the Symposium which first met at George Ripley's on September 19, 1836. The nucleus of this "club" consisted of Alcott, Emerson, Ripley, Convers Francis, Frederic Henry Hedge, and James Freeman Clarke.

[4] Hiram Fuller opened a school in Providence, Rhode Island, patterned after Alcott's Temple School. Emerson *did* deliver the dedicatory address on June 10, 1837.

[5] Margaret Fuller had left Alcott's school in December, 1836, to assist Hiram Fuller with his school.

LETTER 37–3[1]

[to Ralph Waldo Emerson, Concord]

Boston May 24 1837

Dear Sir,

Monday of next week (29 ult) is named as the time of our proposed meeting. Mr. Ripley desired me to apprize you of the time and place. We meet at his house in the afternoon as usual. So you will be there of course prepared to give us free and bold speech as usual: Mr. R. Spoke of adding Robbins and Dwight to the number, and Stetson may be present.[2] Let us meet and see what can be done or devised.

I had an agreeable evening with Mr. Francis. He seems quite free. It is pleasant to talk with him. He is apprehensive and casts no doubts in your way. In the Spiritual Horologe he is an admirable balance-wheel to keep all movements in fit order. Such men are most useful. He spoke kindly of you. And seemed pleased with the idea of resuming the Conversations. He will be with us on Monday next.

I opened school on Monday with 10 pupils. These are all I fancy that this good and wise city intend to lend me during this quarter. So I have made up my mind to walk to and fro, and do for these whatsoever I may, waiting for light as this may be vouchsafed. Bread comes quite as easily ‖ and with less anxiety ‖ in this way as in any other. And so for the present I shall continue to teach. Possibly at some day, I may take the benefit of your suggestion, and turn this matter over to the hands.

Very truly,
Your friend,
A. Bronson Alcott,

Rev R. Waldo Emerson,
Concord
Mass.

[1] MS. owned by the Houghton Library, Harvard University.
[2] S. D. Robbins, John S. Dwight, Caleb Stetson.

LETTER 37–4[1]

[to Ralph Waldo Emerson, Concord]

Boston June 6. 1837.

Dear Sir,

Not only on my own, but account of Mr Fuller[2] and friends, do I please myself with the hope of hearing your good word, on occasion of a good purpose. And yet, you must needs let special and local topics slide into broad and general insight into things & principles. For such, the world suffers.—Would you believe it? I wasted last week foolishly, and scandalously, at these glorifying and glorified anniversaries.[3] And no! to the world if it seek life or soundness from these. Quacks! Quackery! Poor sick, infirm, lunatic Humanity. And these know nothing of the regimen that restores sanity and soundness. Holiness! Holiness! the man of Nazareth hath it; but not these. Now; dose! dosing! and the Patient special, half conscious of misplaced faith, dies, faintly uttering "Physician heal thyself:" Still the same results: arms, legs, with sundry faculties meant for Gods worthiest works at their service, do flourish most dextrously in the light of Gods blessed day-time, if perchance his kingdom shall be forestalled and taken by violence.

And yet, I attended to some profit withal. For, to see the straights of Humanity, as well as fullness[?], is somewhat. A sage observer perceives, under all this hammer and sword play, primal and irresistible instincts, which do ever strive consciously or blindly, to compass the Possible. There yet lingers in all souls a belief in the possible perfectibility of outward and secular interests. And hence finite organs and instruments, are developed into some show, at least, of dexterity: the legs and arms work for somewhat. But open the eyes above them to perceive the occasions for securing the Onward and Divine, and then shall the infinite faculties be sharpened, and the soul use them worthily. Behold a Heaven! But the eye of this age is holden: it apprehends not times, nor organs nor instruments, nor shall, till some, standing in its midst, preach the true Gospel of the Kingdom and restore it to sight.

I intend accompanying you to Providence. I suppose you will reach Boston on Friday in season for the cars in the afternoon—4 or 5. oclock is the latest hour I believe. Please call on me at No 3. Temple place if you pass that way before 1 P.M. or, should you miss, a word dropped at Munroe's[4] would enable us to act in concert. Yet better: a word from your "Sanctum sanctorum" at Concord, would shed light, meanwhile,

whereby, I might discern the more
vividly the aspects of "Psyche",
with whom I am much
in love at this moment.
Most truly,
A. Bronson Alcott.

Rev. R. Waldo Emerson,
Concord
Ms.

---

[1] MS. owned by the Library of Congress.
[2] Hiram Fuller.
[3] A reference to the practice adopted by a number of organizations of holding their annual meetings in and about Boston during the same week in the spring. For a list of the meetings Alcott attended during the Anniversaries of 1837, see Shepard, *Pedlar's Progress*, p. 280.
[4] James Munroe, Boston publisher, who had published *Record of a School* and *Conversations with Children on the Gospels*, 2 vols. (Boston, 1836, 1837).

LETTER 37–5[1]

[to Ralph Waldo Emerson, Concord]
Cottage Place [Boston] | July 25. [1837]

Dear Sir,
I am just up from a severe indisposition and find myself extremely weak and shiftless. I hear that you are regaining your former strength; and hope the de-

mand upon your corporeal nature will enable you to compass the P.B.K.[?] without detriment.[2] Shall see you soon.

Very Truly,
A. Bronson Alcott.

Rev. R. W. Emerson.
Concord.
Mass

[1] MS. owned by the Houghton Library, Harvard University.
[2] Emerson delivered his Phi Beta Kappa address, "The American Scholar," on August 31, 1837.

LETTER 37–6[1]

[to Mrs. A. Bronson Alcott, Boston]

South Scituate, July 28, 1837.

My Dear,—

I write a word, just to tell you how well I am; for truly, since I began to breathe this sweet country air, drink this pure water, and taste of my good hostess's wheaten loaf, I entertain the pleasing hope of returning a somewhat comelier specimen of the man Adam than when I left you last. Let me assure you that I sleep soundly, have a good appetite, enjoy conversation, and am getting strong again. Wine, though prescribed, I now eschew, and tea is distasteful. No further need of resorting to the comforting little bottle that you and mother put into my trunk, so womanly. Then for exercise, we ride or walk daily, threading the lanes, edging the river shores, sitting under the shade or bathing, as the time favors. I rise refreshed,—the fine morning breeze intruding at my window, which, like Christian Pilgrim's, opens to the sunrise. Here, too, for company, besides your good brother's household, I have fallen upon a young disciple, a Mr. Tilden, ship carpenter, but emulous of becoming a preacher of the Carpenter's son's Gospel, a sensible man and likely to honor his profession. This afternoon Mr. Sewall is expected, and in the evening the Sunday-school teachers meet in your brother's study. Next week I purpose accompanying him to Plymouth, and on my way home to stop a day at Hingham with the advocate of the Prussian system of instruction, and while there meet Saint Anna. My love to mother, and tell Psyche and the other two[2] that I hope to see them at the cottage by Friday or Saturday of next week at farthest. Mr. May wishes you were here; so do I, and the little ones. I am more and more for the country. Write soon, and in the mean while take this little assurance of the affection of your

A.B.A.

[1] Reprinted from Sanborn, *A. Bronson Alcott*, I, 230–31.
[2] "His three daughters" (Sanborn's note).

LETTER 37–7[1]

[to Ralph Waldo Emerson, Concord]

Boston Oct. 6, 1837.

Dear Sir,

I venture to enclose my Bill for Hillman's[2] tuition during the present quarter; trusting that my needs, (which now stare me in the face somewhat more grimly than in times past) will be my excuse for troubling you with such intrusion, in advance. The Bill is, as usual, $25: and, if convenient to you to remit this sum by mail, I will transmit a receipt for the same.

Health now fine: school amounts to a chance for a little quiddling for me; yet which, by the bye [sic], shall [word] yield me the tub and crust of Diogenes. But—patience—sun-light shall dissipate these clouds in God's own time.

Very Truly,
Your friend,
A. Bronson Alcott.

Rev. R. Waldo Emerson,
    Concord
        Mass.

[1] MS. owned by the Houghton Library, Harvard University.
[2] Hillman B. Sampson, the son of a late friend of Emerson's (see Rusk, *Emerson Letters*, II, 28).

LETTER 37–8[1]

[to Ralph Waldo Emerson, Concord]

[Boston, October 9, 1837]

Dear Sir,

Thanks for your favour. Amidst my present fortunes it was quite a favour and bestowed in needful season. For here I am, quiddle, quiddle, day in and out, (Sunday excepted) on half a dozen souls. And how soon the wise, in their plenitude, shall shine brighter favour, time alone shall show. Meanwhile I am safe in tub, with corn, rain, sunshine, lampshine, and fireshine. But how long these shall be vouchsafed, the oracle, as yet saith not—sundry ill omens instead. For tub, grumbleth, "thou yieldest no rent, and standest in great danger, sirrah, of ejectment with all they tublings streetwise. Cistern cock rageth, "thou shalt not quench thirst, delinquent, for thou dost not pay for thy tank. Corn cleaveth to the hand of clutching seller, and churlishly crieth, 'not for thee nor thine, shirk, thou. Showest no hard hand. Sun even threatens to withdraw his face, and saith, Offender, I will duly honour thee with peep at grated window sometime soon. And ‖ lamp ‖ fire smouldereth, lublard [sic], thou dost not ply thy saw dextrously, and art in disgrace with the woodman. And lamp saith, flickeringly, no shine for thee, niggard, thou feedest me not. Destitute! thou has nought available about thee. And so moonshine in pity befriends, saying, this is fit emblem, of thy wan, leaden, profitless shine; thou shall eat moonbeams to thy fill, what else doth the age proffer thee?

And yet amidst all this parley,—these omens—methinks, the true soul-lovers shall needs, in some sort, find subsistence. Submit, utters Instinct, be brave, faithful, so shall thou not hunger nor thirst. Feed on thy deeds. Hope in thy purpose. Shall not principle house thee, and truth light they dwelling. The wide world thou shall not possess; nor things thereof, wouldst thou chasten thy jewels for it, or these? Care thou more to be a world-upholder, than world-holder, so thou shalt not fear thy ground plot; all is safe in thy hand, solid under thy foot: aim thou rather to be rich in rents of honour, and deeds of glory. Perchance thy farm is sown already, and dost thou not sing harvest home when thou wilt. Beside[s] this cunning in thy soul, hast thou not yet some reserve in thy fingers; brave then thy fortune, and bear thee nobly.

And thus, doth this soul of mine, beset with such hindrance—such quid-dlings,—such omens, seek self insight and drink life and light from God, not world-spoiled. An Idea of this same soul, hath fed and housed me amidst such hours of destitution, and doth still. I have decked it after mine own fashion; it hath the manners of my choice circle, and now would make fale to my age. I lay to it, go forth my bantling, sing thy best song in the ear of thy time; per-chance thou shalt find favour; and if thou dost, by hap-hazard, bring ought of corn or vine, in thy left hand, God be praised. Take passport then, my Psyche, and run on thy errand.

> Very truly,
> Your friend,
> A. Bronson Alcott.

Cottage Place
   Oct 9. 1837.
Revd R. Waldo Emerson
   Concord.
     Mass.

[1] MS. owned by the Houghton Library, Harvard University. This letter needs to be read in light of the difficulties which had beset Alcott. Reaction in Boston to the *Conversations with Children on the Gospels,* was of such a nature that the successful Temple School lost nearly all its pupils. In addition, Alcott suffered a good deal of personal abuse and was in debt.

LETTER 37–9[1]

[to Ralph Waldo Emerson, Concord]
           26 Trout Street. | [Boston] 19. Novr. [1837?]
Dear Sir,

   I send, addressed to you, the Bill for Hillman's tuition, for one quarter; and also for Sophia's[2] board,—which, if I rightly understand the last arrangement, was fixed at $2.50 per quarter.

> With deep regard,
> A. Bronson Alcott

Revd. R. W. Emerson
   Concord.

[1] MS. owned by the Houghton Library, Harvard University.
[2] Sophia Brown, Emerson's niece.

LETTER 37–10[1]

[to Anna, Boston]

[Boston, December 24, 1837]

For Anna.
1837

To my Daughter Anna.

A longer time ago than you can understand, a beautiful Babe was born. Angels sang at his birth. And stars shone brightly. Shepherds watched their flocks by their light. The Babe was laid in his Manger—cradle. And harmless oxen fed by his side. There was no room for him nor for his mother in the Inn, as she journeyed from her own home.

This Babe was born at this time of the year. His name is Jesus. And he is also called Christ. This is his birth night. And we call it Christ-mas, after him.

I write you this little note as a Christmas Gift, and hope my little Girl will remember the birth night of Jesus, think how beautiful he was, and try to shine in lovely actions as he did. God never had a child that pleased him so well. Be like a kind sister of his, and so please your Father, who loves you very much.

Christmas Eve.
  Dec. 24. 1837.

From your
Father.

[1] MS. owned by the Houghton Library, Harvard University. This letter has been printed in Bonstelle and deForest, pp. 66–67.

LETTER 37–11

[to Elizabeth, Boston]

[Boston, December 24, 1837]

For Elisabeth.
1837

[drawing][1]
Elizabeth and Father

Christmas Eve
  Dec. 24. 1837.

[1] Here appears a drawing of Elizabeth on her father's lap. The words "Elizabeth and Father" serve as a caption for the drawing.

LETTER 38–1[1]

[to Emma Savage, Boston]

[Boston, April 4, 1838]

Mr. Alcott's thanks to his friend and former pupil, Emma, for the expression of her interest, in the useful present of yesterday—the more valued from being wrought with her own hands. Hereafter the gentle graces of the giver, will be associated with the quiet pursuits of his own household and study; and recal hours of studies and disciplines, than which none of his professional life, are more pleasing.

Mr A. adds his profound regard for those, with whom it has been his privilege to cooperate, in the formation of the character of his friend: and trusts that neither shall have cause of sorrow, as they follow her course into the more serious duties of life.

Temple
Wednesday, April 4.
1838.

For
Emma
Temple Mall

[1] MS. owned by the Fruitlands and Wayside Museums.

LETTER 38–2[1]

[to Mrs. James Savage, Boston]

Temple | June 24. [1838?]

Nothing could be more grateful to the feelings of Mr Alcott, than the interest expressed by Mrs. Savage in the anniversary of his little daughter' [sic] birth-day;[2] and the manner in which she has conveyed it.

Birth, to all pure and simple souls, is a joyous holiday, full of fresh and fair associations. And no eras of life are more befitting expressions of sentiment. Mr. A. hopes that the day is near, when life shall deem it not only a pleasure but privilege, to refresh its affections, and inspire its love, at the full fountain of the heart of childhood!

Mrs. Savage
Temple Place

[1] MS. owned by the Fruitlands and Wayside Museums.
[2] Elizabeth Sewall Alcott, b. June 24, 1835.

[Letter to Mrs. Anna Alcott (Mrs. Joseph Alcox), Oriskany Falls, N.Y.; from Boston, October, 1838.]

LETTER 38–3[1]

[to Convers Francis, Watertown, Mass.][2]
Beach Street No 6 | [Boston] Dec 9—[1838?]
Dear Sir,

At our last meeting,[3] we adjourned to meet at my house on Wednesday next. I hope nothing will hinder you from meeting with us. The children of Light must needs have concert to dispel the darkness which ever blinds the eye of the ages. These are too few in our day; and Wisdom shall suffer loss by the absence of a single member of her shining Circle. Hope you will come early.

Very Truly
Yours,
A. Bronson Alcott.

Rev. Dr. Francis
Watertown

[1] MS. owned by the Boston Public Library.
[2] Convers Francis (1795–1863). A graduate of Harvard College and the Divinity School, he was at this time pastor of the First Church in Watertown. Though he early tended toward transcendentalist thought, he (according to Perry Miller) "soon retreated into conformity."
[3] Of the Symposium.

LETTER 39–1

[to Anna, Boston]
[Boston, March 15, 1839]
For Anna
1839

My dear daughter
Anna,

This is your birth-day. You have now lived eight years with your Father and Mother; six years with your loving sister Louisa, and almost four years with your sweet little sister Elizabeth. Your Father knows how much you love him, and your mother, and your sisters too, and wants to have you love them still more dearly; so that you will never give them pain by any thing you wish, or say, or do: but bear pain, and disappointment, without impatience or complaining. He wants to see his little girl kind and gentle, and sweet-tempered; as fragran[t] as the flowers in spring time, and as beautiful as they are when the dew glitters on them in the morning dawn. Do you want to know how you can be so beautiful and so sweet? It is easy. Only try, with all your resolution, to mind what that silent teacher in your breast says to you; that is all.

A birth day is a good time to begin to live anew: throwing away the old habits, as you would old clothes, and never putting them on again. Begin, my daughter, today, and when your next birth-day shall come, how glad you will be that you made the resolution. Resolution makes all things new. It will make you a new girl; so that when your Father and Mother, your sisters, and friends, look upon you, they shall see how beautiful and good a little girl you are, and try to be so too; for good people make every one good that sees them.

I looked at the bookstores for a book for you; but I did not find any that I thought would please you; so I write you this letter instead.

From your Father.

Friday evening.
    March 15. 1839

Written to be given to Anna to morrow at breakfast.

Anna Bronson Alcott,
    at Breakfast,
in the Parlour, March 16. 1839.
    being her Eighth Birth-day.
    No 6. Beach Street.

LETTER 39–2[1]

[to Mrs. Anna Alcott, Wolcott, Conn.]

Boston March 18. 1839.

Dear Mother,

It seemed good to behold your painstaking hand writing once more, and read that you and those about you were all well and prosperous. It had been a long time since I had heard a word from you. I wrote to you sometime in October, I think, while you were with Chatfield at the West;[2] and Abba wrote also I believe. I wish I could come and sit with you in the "South Room," where so many of my hours of study have been passed, and tell you what I have to say. But this I cannot do just now. But I fancy you sitting there in your rocking chair, in your cleanest, whitest, Sunday cap, and spectacles well polished, reading, or perhaps talking with Phebe about your children, declaring that they are the kindest best children that ever a mother had, and wondering why it is so. For this very clear reason, that they have one of the kindest and best of mothers: that is reason enough, and no cause of wonder. I hope you will come and prove us. In the midst of our destitution,—and this can never be greater than when you were last with us—we shall show the truth and reality of our love for you; and *this* is all to you. Abba will write you about it. I should love dearly to have you with us again, and the children's pleasure would be unfeigned. In May or June we shall have made our summer arrangements and then can let you know all about them. I have a few children, as pupils, at present, but how long I shall have them, I do not know. They come to my house daily, and are with me from 9 till 12, and from 3 till 5.[3] But I am living rather by *Talking* now, than by my School: and shall be able, by and by, I think, to live in this way entirely.[4] I meet circles of thirty, forty, fifty, or more, persons, for ten or twelve evenings, and hold conversation, on great subjects, with them. These circles I have in Boston, and also in the neighboring towns. I think you would enjoy such meeting greatly: for you love society as well as I do, or any of the Brownson's, who are dear lovers of it. Only think now of your bashful, silent, boy, who could hardly look any one in the face, getting to be bold all at once, and going about to talk, and make talk! It is quite strange, as strange to me, as to you, I dare say. But we know not what we are growing up for; and do just the contrary thing that we think we shall, quite often.

I am full of hope, and every thing looks encouraging. As to money, that you know, is one of the last of my anxieties. I have many friends, and am making more daily, and have only to be true to my principles, to get not only a useful name, but bread, and shelter, and raiment. A few years more, and I shall reap even these quite secondary rewards, and be above want. And this experience of penury, meanwhile, will have been a good, rather than an evil. So you see, I am still the same Hoper that I have always been. Hope crowned me while I was following the plow on the barren and rocky fields of that same farm on which you now dwell, and Hope will never desert me either on this or the other side of the grave. I fancy that I was quickened and born in Hope, and Hope in the form of a kind and smiling mother, nursed me, rocked my cradle, and encouraged my aspirations, while, ‖ a youth ‖ I was the child and the youth, seeking life and light amidst the scenes of my native hills. Those visits to libraries; those scribblings on the floor; those hours given to reading and study, at night or noon, or rainy-day, and even those solitary wanderings over southern lands, were this same Hope seeking to realize its highest objects. My grandfather was a Hoper; my mother inherited the old sentiment, and my father fell a martyr to it—witness that same farm, which you speak of selling. I have a double port[ion] of the sentiment, and thank God that it is my hap[py] inheritance. All right and title to the little farm I quit—sell it if you can, and put the money in your pocket, and take the good of it while you live in this world. And, as you say in your letter,—you shall live with me yet.

But here I am at the end of my sheet. Dr. Alcott takes this.[5] I seldom see him now. He is one of the bees, always making honey; too busy to stop a moment with a drone like myself. I *hope* he will fill the Hive, and supply the world with other than wasps hoardings upon which it has fed for ages. Success to all that is good in this honey-making buzz of his. By and by, the young bees will swarm, and find other Queens in spite of all this din of tin pans and kettles.

Love to all.

Your grateful Son,
A. Bronson Alcott.

PS. Abba has told you, I suppose, if not, she will, that a young Hoper is on his way into the midst of us, and, before I write again, will be a cradled Babe with a name. His sisters will jump with joy. I say *He,* because I am to have a Boy according to the Promise. Strange that Grief should bear him to me, is it not?[6]

Mrs. Anna Alcott
    Wolcott
      Conn.

---

[1] This letter appears as Alcott copied it into his Journals, with differences of style and punctuation (Alcott, *Journals,* pp. 117–19). That copy is dated March 17.

[2] I.e., Oriskany Falls, New York, about fifteen miles southwest of Utica.

[3] Alcott continued his school at his home, No. 6 Beach Street, Boston, from June, 1838, until June 22, 1839.

[4] Alcott had given his first Conversations late in 1838, at Hingham, Massachusetts. In 1839,

he began to give Conversations as a principal means of subsistence, but not until late in his life was it to become a really successful financial venture.
⁵ William A. Alcott.
⁶ A boy *was* born on April 7th, but lived only a few hours.

LETTER 39–3[1]

[to Louisa, Boston]

[Boston, November 29, 1839]

For Louisa
1839.

My Daughter,

You are Seven years old to day, and your Father is forty. You have learned a great many things, since you have lived in a Body, about things going on around you, and within you. You know how to think, how to resolve, how to love and how to obey. You feel your CONSCIENCE, and have no real pleasure unless you obey it. You cannot love yourself, or any one else, when you do not mind its Commandments. It asks you always to BE GOOD, and bears, O how gently! how patiently! with all endeavours to hate, and treat it cruelly. How kindly it bears with you all the while! How sweetly it whispers Happiness in your HEART when you Obey its soft words. How it smiles upon you, and makes you Glad when you Resolve to Obey it! How terrible its Punishments! It is GOD trying in your SOUL to keep you always Good.

You begin, my dear daughter, another year this morning. Your Father, your Mother, and Sisters, with your little friends, show their love on this your Birth-Day, by giving you this BOX: Open it, and take what is in it; and the best wishes of

Your Father.

Beach Street,
Friday Morning, Nov. 29. 183[9]

For/
Louisa May Alcott
No 6 Beach Street.

[1] MS. in Alcott House, Concord, Massachusetts; quoted in Bonstelle and deForest, pp. 83–84.

LETTER 39–4[1]

[to Anna, Boston]

[Boston, December 24, 1839]

For Anna
1839

You were once pleased, my daughter, with a little note which I wrote you on Christmas Eve concerning the Birth of Jesus.[2] I am now going to write a few words about your own Birth.

Mother and I had no child. We wanted one—a little girl just like you: and

43

we thought how you would look, and waited a good while for you to come, so that we might see you and have you for our own. At last you came. We felt so happy that joy stood in our eyes. You looked just as we wanted to have you. You were dressed in a pretty little white frock, and Father took you in his arms every day, and we loved you very much. Your large bright eyes looked lovingly into ours, and you soon learned to love and know us. When you were a few weeks old you smiled on us. We lived then in Germantown. It is now more than eight years since this happened, but I sometimes see the same look and the same smile on your face, and feel that my daughter is yet good and pure. O keep it there, my daughter, and never lose it.

Your
Father.

Christmas Eve
  Beach Street.
    Dec 24. 1839.

[1] MS. owned by the Houghton Library, Harvard University; quoted in Bonstelle and deForest, pp. 68–70.
  [2] See Letter 37–10.

LETTER 39–5[1]

[to Mrs. Anna Alcott, Oriskany Falls, N.Y.]

[Boston, December 28, 1839]

Dear Mother,—

I have suffered too many months to pass by without an expression of my love and interest in yourself and in those with whom you dwell. We passed the summer at Scituate, near Mr. May, and late in September returned to our former Boston dwelling in Beach Street. We were all much benefited by the change of air and scenery. As I have no school now, and am much at home, the children pass an hour or two daily with me at their lessons. They are all well and thriving.

You may ask what I am about now. I reply, still at my old trade, *hoping*, which has thus far given food, shelter, raiment, and a few warm friends, who cherish me and mine in this time of need. And not in this my adopted city only, but over the seas. Several encouraging letters have come to me from friends in England, who appear to take that interest in my labors which my countrymen have not yet shown. Commendatory notices of my books have appeared in the London journals, and they wish to reprint my "Record of a School" in that city. My wife declares that I shall cross the water to find the sympathy and appreciation denied me at home; and I may. But all is indefinite just now. God has some task allotted and waiting for me, and will employ me in his service in his own time, with wages proportionate to my deserts. Nor am I an idler even now. I have Sunday evening conversations at my house, and I meet circles during the week elsewhere. They are attended by parents, students of divinity, ministers, and many young persons, to the number of fifty or more. It is a pleasant and edifying mode of teaching. Dr. Alcott is living some miles out of the city, and making books as fast as ever. Your good friend Mrs. Shaw[2] remembers you with pleasure. A few evenings ago she took tea with us, and inquired if you still kept your diary. I must leave space for my wife.

Affectionately your son,
A. Bronson Alcott.

[1] Quoted in Sanborn, *A. Bronson Alcott*, I, 299–300.
[2] The "wife of Lemuel Shaw, afterward Chief Justice of Massachusetts" (Sanborn's note).

LETTER 39–6[1]

[to Louisa, Cambridge, Mass.]

[Boston, December ? 1839]

For Louisa.

1839.

My Dear Little Girl,

Father hopes you are well and happy. Mother will soon be well enough we hope for you to come home. Anna has gone to Dr. Winship's. She rode out in the Omnibus this morning. Elizabeth is at Grandpa's.[2] Father saw her this morning. She played on the Piano and was very happy.

You want to see us all I know. And we want to see you very much. Be a good Girl and try to do as they tell you. You shall see us all in a few days.

You was never away from home so long before. It has given you some new feelings.

I have printed this Note. I hope you can read it all yourself.

Good Bye
From FATHER.

Saturday

11. o Clock

in the School Room.

1840 [*sic*]

(For
Louisa May Alcott
Cambridge.)

[1] MS. in Alcott House, Concord, Massachusetts; quoted in part in Bonstelle and deForest, pp. 81–82.
[2] Col. Joseph May.

PART THREE

✠

1840–1841

[to Anna, Boston]

[Boston, March 16, 1840]

For Anna.
1840
My dear daughter,
With this morning's dawn, opens a New Year of your life on Earth. Nine years ago you were sent, a sweet Babe, into this world, a joy and a hope to your Father and Mother. After a while, through many smiles and some few tears, you learned to lisp the names of Father and Mother, and to make them feel how near and dear you were to their hearts whenever you pronounced their names. Now you are a still dearer object of love and hope to them as your soul buds and blossoms under their eye. They watch the flower as it grows in the garden of life, and beside its sisters, scents the air with its fragrance, and delights the eye by its colours. Soon they will look not only for fragrance and beauty, but for ripening, and, at last, ripe fruit also. May it be the fruit of goodness: may its leaves never wither; its flowers never fade, its fragrance never cease; but may it flourish in perpetual beauty, and be transplanted, in due time in to the Garden of God, whose plants are ever green, and bloom alway, the amaranth of Heaven, the pride and care of angels. Thus speaks your father to you, on this your birth-morn—

Monday March 16 1840.
Beach Street.
Boston.

---

[1] Quoted in Bonstelle and deForest, pp. 70–72.

LETTER 40–2[1]

[to Samuel J. May,[2] Boston]

Concord April 6 1840[3]

Dear Brother,

Again I have planted myself, and am seeking to extend my roots into the soil of the earth, if perchance it shall prove more genial than hitherto, and ripen my fruits for the sustenance of others. I sow again in hope, and if not made partaker of the same while in this earthly tabernacle, know full well that my harvest shall come in in due season, and there shall be bread and fullness in the land. I seem, at times, to have been an impatient husbandman, misauguring the signs of the spring time, and to have scattered my seed even during the wintry season: small chance of its germinating while yet the churlish winds career through the heavens, and the snow and the frosts yet cover the fields. Let me wait my season in faith & patience: for it shall come.

I feel yet the more assured of the fitness of my present position than ever, to fulfil the great ends of life. I have now abrogated all claims to moral and spiritual teaching. I place myself in peaceful relations to the soil—as a husbandman intent in aiding its increase—and ‖ am ‖ seem no longer hostile to ‖ things as they are ‖ [p. o.] the powers that be [4 p. in]. My little cottage lies low and humble in the bosom of nature, under the sky of God: and I would ornament its walls, and its acres, by honour and independence. My chief regret is that in gaining Emerson, I lose you; were you near us, life would be greener, and many social delights which we shall now miss, would be ours. But I feel that Fortune will, one day, be more kindly to us all: those whom the Great Heart unites shall not be sundered: alway; and so I ejaculate as of old, Patience! Submission! Peace!

We had a most fortunate day for leaving the city: a part of our goods followed us, and the remainder come on to-morrow. We staid the first night at the Middlesex Hotel: And entered our cottage early Wednesday morning. It pleases both housewife and little ones: and the neighborhood enjoys the highest reputation ‖ both ‖ for courtesy kindness ‖ and ‖ probity. My garden and Acre are rich in promise; and, if I can draw with temperance on the stock of strength that yet remains within these shoulder-blades and shackle-bones, I see an independence made out to my household. Debts, I will pay in all honour whensoever I may.

I regret chiefly that your wonted generosity, must for the present, be so slimly requited. Last autumn, the result could not be foreseen; and I am aware of [torn] means of which I could avail, to release or part[ially] relieve you from the obligation. Be assured, that I am not insensible to these favours of friends. I wish, sometimes that God had witheld [sic] some portion of the gifts with which he has blessed me, that so I might dwell in closer sympathy with the outward interests, and enter with a keener delight into the secular labours of men. O' it is the hardest of all trials to be sundered from your kind, and tread the solitudes of life without the sweet and approving voice of a brothers' approval. But then God wills, in his own divine order, and to the faithful vouchsafes his own, though the face of mankind be averted in scorn, or frown in rebuke.

I should enjoy your Eulogium on the just and noble Fallen: but must wait to read it in print.—Abba is as energetic and heroic as in her best days; And we both ‖ as ‖ feel truly grateful for the kind and timely sympathy of Father. without which we might have been straitened even amidst the assistance proffered by other friends. I repeat it—his attentions were most grateful to us; and let me add your own also.

Most truly
A. Bronson Alcott.

Rev. Samuel J. May
(Care of Col Joseph May)
Boston

Ap. 6. 1840:

[1] A portion of this letter is printed in Sanborn, *A. Bronson Alcott,* I, 307–8.
[2] Alcott's brother-in-law. They first met while Alcott was teaching school in Connecticut and Samuel May was living at Brooklyn, Connecticut. It was there Alcott first met his future wife.
[3] The Alcotts moved into the Hosmer Cottage in Concord on April 1.

LETTER 40–3

[to Mrs. Anna Alcott, Oriskany Falls, N.Y.][1]

Concord June 21st. 1840.[2]

Dear Mother,

I write from my little cottage in Concord, (18 miles from Boston) into which we moved on the first of April last, ‖ and ‖ to find much happiness by this change from the city to the country. I cultivate a garden and ‖ a ‖ field,—in all about an acre and three quarters—, and find constant occupation on this my small farm: my vegetables look finely at this time. I shall raise more than a supply for my family. Abba does all her work and the children all go to School in the village close by, and we are free to do all that farmers and farmers' wives find necessary in managing a household. I labour all the while out of doors in fair weather, and in foul take to my book and pen, or some work in my little shop with tools, after the old fashion. We are all in perfect health: more active pursuits than are possible in the city are all to our advantage.

I left Boston, finding that the people were not ready to support a man who ‖ like myself ‖ would reform not only their children but themselves, ‖ by my teaching and life ‖. They ‖ did not like ‖ disliked one who attempted so much and went at once to his work in good earnest. But I shall hope to convince some of them by and by, not only by the great sacrifice which I have been driven to make in relinquishing public teaching at present, but by this very pursuit of gardening in which I am now engaged. I do not purpose to spend many years in this way, but ‖ shall ‖ hope to return to my teaching again ‖ in school ‖ when the public have opened their eyes a little to what I can do for them. I meet circles frequently for conversation on the most important subjects, and draw many persons particularly young men and women to my house. and my influence begins to be felt some not only in this country, but also in England. Some persons there are interested in my life and opinions, and but a few days since, I received a letter giving some account of a school conducted in like spirit ‖ of my principles ‖, and called the *"Alcott School.*[3] Indeed, I feel assured that after long and patient waiting, I ‖ shall ‖ may attain the great ends of all my labours.

Some of the wisest and best people are beginning to approve and adopt the great principles so ennobling and so dear to me.

I am within a mile of my friend Emerson, who continues to feel all the interest in my purposes of former days. He is a great blessing to me. We hope by united labours to leave the world some better than we found it.

You will observe the drawing of our Cottage, which we call *Concordia*.[4] I wish you were one of its inmates: and trust the time is near when if we remain, you will behold it with your own eyes. How are all the brothers and sisters? They are all near you now I conclude. I always think with pleasure of visiting you and them; but know not when this is to be. My love to all of them. I leave space for Abba to add a word.

Ever Yours
A. Bronson Alcott

[1] The letter is addressed to his mother, care of Chatfield Alcott.
[2] The postmark reads "Concord, June 16."
[3] Since September 4, 1837, Alcott had been in correspondence with James Pierrepont Greaves, William Oldham, and John A. Heraud, in England. The school was located at Ham Common, Surrey.
[4] At the top of the first page of the letter is a careful pen and ink drawing of the Hosmer Cottage.

LETTER 40–4[1]

[to Louisa, Boston][2]

Cottage,[3] Sunday, June 21st | 1840.

My Dear Louisa,

We all miss the noisy little girl who used to make house and garden, barn and field ring with her footsteps, and even the hens and chickens seem to miss her too. Right glad would Father and Mother, Anna and Elisabeth, and all the little mates at School, and Miss Russell, the House Play-room, Dolls, Hoop, Garden, Flowers, Fields, Woods and Brooks, all be to see and answer the voice and footsteps, the eye and hand, of their little companion. But yet all make themselves happy and beautiful without her; all seem to say, "Be Good, little Miss, while away from us, and when we meet again, we shall love and please one another all the more; we find how much we love now we are separated."

I wished you here very much on the morning when the Hen left her nest and came proudly down with six little chickens, every one knowing how to walk, fly, eat and drink almost as well as its own mother; to day (Sunday) they all came to the house and took their breakfast from their nice little feeding trough; you would have enjoyed the sight very much. But this and many other pleasures all wait for you when you return. Be good, kind, gentle, while you are away, step lightly, and speak soft, about the house; Grandpa loves quiet, as well as your sober Father, and other grown people.

Elisabeth says often, "Oh I wish I could see Louisa, when will she come home, mother." And another feels so too. who is it?

Your
Father.

I forgot to write how much *Kit* missed you.

[1] MS. in Alcott House, Concord, Massachusetts; quoted in Bonstelle and deForest, pp. 85–87.
[2] Louisa was visiting her grandfather, Col. Joseph May.
[3] The Hosmer cottage, in Concord.

LETTER 40–5[1]

[to Elizabeth, Concord]

[Concord, June 24, 1840]

For Elisabeth.
1840.
I I I I I Years.
onetwothreefourfive
Birth-Day.
in the
Cottage.

My very dear little girl,

You make me very happy every time I look at your smiling pleasant face— and you make me very sorry every time I see your face look cross and unpleasant. You are now five years old. You can keep your little face pleasant all the time, if you will try, and be happy yourself, and make every body else happy too. Father wants to have his little girl happy all the time. He hopes her little friends and her presents and plays will make her happy to-day; and this little note too. Last birth-day, you were in Beach Street in the great City, now you are at your little cottage in the country where all is pretty and pleasant, and you have fields and woods, and brooks and flowers to please my little Queen, and keep her eyes, and ears, and hands and tongue and feet, all busy. This little note is from

FATHER,

who loves his little girl very much, and knows that she loves him very dearly.

Play, play,
All the day,
Jump and run,
Every one,
Full of fun.
All take
A piece of cake
For my sake.

For
Elisabeth S. Alcott
at the Table
on her Birth-Day.
Concordia June 24, 1840

[1] MS. owned by the Houghton Library, Harvard University; quoted in Bonstelle and deForest, pp. 92–94.

LETTER 40–6[1]

[to Samuel J. May, Boston?]

29 July 1840 | (Concordia.)

Dear Brother,

I was sorry to miss seeing you at Lexington, and Abba was disappointed that she could not present, with her own hands, the quiet little lady who entered our household at dawn on Sunday.[2] But you will come again and salute her for yourself. Providence it seems, decrees to us daughters of Love instead of sons of Light. We joyfully acquiesce in this dispensation and hopefully rear Women for the new order of things. Both Mother and Babe are well.

You left just before I reached Prof Pierces.[3] He spoke with interest of you, and the young Women were encouraged by your words. I discoursed nearly three hours with them on the spirit and doctrine of the Faith. They gave eye and ear, and seemed to bear testimony in their hearts to the Hope set before them. I did not expect to kindle an abiding enthusiasm in their bosoms at a single interview. But the time draws near when these doctrines shall find favour and renovate all our modes of culture. Every where the young and hopeful embrace them with joy, and they shall quicken and exalt the life of a coming generation. Already they illuminate a noble Future.

I have spent several days in the harvest fields, and find an unexpected elasticity and vigour. Now is the prime of haying and tomorrow I enter the meadows with my neighbours. Labour is, indeed sweet, nor is that a severe, but beneficent decree, which sends man into the fields to earn his Bread in the sweat of his face. Labour invests man with a primeval dignity. Sloth is the tempter that beguiles him of innocence, and casts him out of Paradise, an idler in the wastes of the world. Let no man deem himself a servant of the divine Husbandman unless he labour in his vineyards for the wages of Peace. Alas! the broad world is full of idlers; the fields are all barren; men are hungry and there is no corn. The wheat lies unsought in the Heavenly Granaries, and men sow and harvest but tares. Gaunt is the Age; even as the seeds man winnows the chaff from the wheat, shall the winds of Reform, blow this Vanity away.

But my daughter waits and the berries for our hands: and I must draw my Georgic to a close, yet not without adding my regards to your wife, and the affections of

Your Brother
A. Bronson Alcott.

[1] A portion of this letter is printed in Sanborn, *A. Bronson Alcott*, I, 323.
[2] Abigail May Alcott was born July 26. Sanborn (I, 308) incorrectly gives the date as July 28, 1840.
[3] He apparently ran a state normal school in Lexington, Massachusetts. The first one in the country, it was later moved to Framingham.

LETTER 40–7[1]

[to Mr. Sewall, Boston?]
July 1840

[Concord] Wednesday 29 July

Dear Sir,

I am glad to relieve your surprize at our long silence, by the intelligence that a fourth daughter was born to us at dawn on Sunday last. I should have given you earlier information of the happy fact, had I not expected to meet Mr May at Lexington yesterday, or seen him at our cottage. Mother and child are well, and nurse makes us all as comfortable as nurses are wont. I hope you are quite well. My garden—and field would welcome you most cordially, as would all at the cottage, to Concordia. Abba will write in a day or two and direct concerning the means of replacing an absent figure in our family group. We wish the grandfather would furnish a commanding addition also. Please say to our Pet, that her unseen sister is very fair, and will look at her with great joy when she returns, as will all others in the little cottage which she left six long weeks ago.
Regards to Louisa G.

Very truly
Yours
A. Bronson Alcott

[1] MS. in the Clifton Waller Barrett Library, University of Virginia.

LETTER 40–8

[to Samuel J. May, South Scituate, Mass.]

August 10th. 1840. | Concordia.

My Brother,

Enclosed is the paper sent in yours of the 4th. signed according to your instructions. This affair was present to my thought while you were with us, but I was silent expecting you would speak about it. I fear you have suffered from this generosity. But I knew not how to prevent it. This world's wisdom is too subtle for me; I am an inapt student of its lore. What God does not teach I would not know. Surely there is no wisdom other than Virtue, no Prudence beside Obedience. To these all else shall be added. Let these proffer a discipline how austere; bring reverses how many, open solitudes how vast. It is my trial, that my course sanctioned alike by conscience, and the examples of the good of all Past Time, receives a commendation so faint from my contemporaries, and by most is deemed hostile to the Laws of God and Man. But every day, yea, every hour, brings a serene and peaceful sense of the divine approval, and strengthens the assurance that if principles noble and exalted like mine have not yet achieved their triumphs in the world, it is because of the obstacles which beset them in order to prove their might. Sweet and grateful as would be the sympathy of my Brothers who name the name of Reform and gain the ears of the people, yet sweeter and more grateful is the reflection that I have withstood these temptations which beguile the love of her allegiance to God, and find in the solitary verdict of my own heart, a joy that the multitude can neither give nor take away. The time of Public Favor has not come. A public worthy of the Principles which I befriend must first be created, ere sympathy can be received without guilt[?]. The Saints are popular in Heaven alone: on Earth they are held in low esteem: God even is here least popular of all Beings, and finds but a chosen few who earn his favor alway by losing that of the multitude. The true man will [word] his Age, its approval, its awards; yea, his own affections even unless he worship godlike attributes alone, which unite him in sweet and enduring friendship with Justice, with Valor, and Love. Whoso loves Father or Mother, Wife or Child, House or Lands, Pleasures or Honours, or Life, more than these, is an Idolater, worshipping in the courts of Sense[?]. This life is death: evermore is he breathing his last, yet cannot die.

Brownson's late word on "the Laboring Classes" has provoked no small stir in our midst. This man is too imposing a Reality to be skipped by the world; he will play a part in the work of Reform, and have a name in history. Men of like fierce independence are God's chosen ministers of good to mankind. A revolution of all Human affairs is now in progress; we are in its midst; the issue we cannot doubt; but the crises are not without alarm: Brownson has sounded a note which must ring through out the Land, in which that of Garrison[1] will for a time be lost. For Slavery and war are but branches of the Tree whose root is selfishness, whose trunk is property, whose fruit is gold. Planted by Beelzebub it shall be rooted up. Let us prepare for the conflict, it may come on the morrow.

The mother and Babes are all well. Louisa has returned, and Mrs Blake has left us. The cares of the household are too great for the anxious housewife, but she meets them with a resolution that gives me great joy. In a state of things more equitable than the present, she shall have her reward, with the army of those who now murmur against the oppressions of m[an.]

Truly
Your Brother
A. Bronson Alcott

To
    S. J. May
        South Scituate
    * What of dialling? do you discern the hour of the universe on our Famous Time Piece?[2]

---

[1] William Lloyd Garrison, whom Alcott had first met in 1830.
[2] A reference to the *Dial*, the first issue of which appeared in July, 1840.

LETTER 40–9[1]

[to Louisa, Concord]

[Concord, November 29, 1840]

For Louisa.
1840

Two Passions strong divide our Life
Meek gentle Love, or boisterous Strife.[2]

on her eighth birthday, Nov. 29th. From her father

[1] MS. owned by the Houghton Library, Harvard University; quoted in Bonstelle and deForest, p. 87.
[2] Below is pasted a card showing a figure playing a harp and another holding a spear. The first figure is labelled "Love—Music   the second "Anger—Arrow
Concord";   Discord."

LETTER 40–10[1]

[to Anna, Concord]

[Concord, December 24, 1840]

For Anna.
1840

Beauty or Duty;
which
loves Anna best?
a
Question
from her
Father;
Christmas-Eve
Dec. 1840
Concordia.

For
Anna.

[1] MS. owned by the Houghton Library, Harvard University; quoted in Bonstelle and deForest, p. 73.

LETTER 40–11[1]

[to Louisa, Concord]

[Concord, December 24, 1840]

For Louisa.
1840

Louisa loves,—
What?
(Softly)
FUN.
Have some then,
Father
says.

Christmas Eve Dec 1840
Concordia.

[1] MS. in Alcott House, Concord, Massachusetts; quoted in Bonstelle and deForest, p. 74.

LETTER 40–12[1]

[to May, Concord]

[Concord, December 24? 1840]

For Abba
1840

For
Abba

Babe fair,
Pretty hair
Bright eye,
Deep sigh,
Sweet lip,
Feet slip,
Handsome hand,
Strut grand,
Happy smile,
Time beguile,
All I ween,
Concordias Queen.

[1] MS. owned by the Houghton Library, Harvard University; quoted in Bonstelle and deForest, p. 75.

LETTER 41–1

[to Anna, Boston]

Concordia | Thursday Eve 14th. May | 1841[1]

My daughter,

How seems the great City to you, with its nice men and women, and pale, prim children; its dullness and confinement? And how, now, the little Cottage under the hill, with its spaces, for racing, loud speaking, and all the freedom to do as you would whensoever you steppe[d] over its threshold? Homesick, are you! We[ll,] 'twill do you some good—'twill show you the difference between places and people; between being Home-sick, and sick of home, and bring you back with your love all new, and your friends too. I miss you; but baby misses you more, though Louisa's ready arms support her long, within doors and out; in garden and street; to barn and bridge; but still the little sweet wants you again, I know.

To-day, I planted some peas and other garden vegetables the sun showing his face to us after veiling it so long. In a few days, the Earth will tell her joy and thankfulness by growing tokens, as we do even now all, by grateful looks and gentler words—soul-shine within; as sun-shine without.

Elisabeth hastes daily to school; Louisa plies her hands nimbly with her Mother, or flies like a bird over the garden, and field; Mother's economies all prosper well; and that silent man with a pen, complains no more of noise! Concord it now is! Two make peace; three ring discord. But peace and love should sometimes be tried to see what they are worth; and patience thrives most (they say) if its trials are not too great for the tender Heart. You are likely, my daughter, to have your share, and will reap, not anger, I trust, but meekness therefrom.

Be gentle and docile; (look [torn] that word in your dictionary) while [torn] your friends; simple and frank [torn] your words and behaviour; suffer [torn] to tempt you, by entreaty, nor yourself, from your feeling of Duty; say, Yes, or No, not to please others, but your own Conscience; and when you return to your Home, your eye and manner will tell the story of your Fidelity to us all.

Thus writes
Your Father.

Write us soon.
To
   Anna Bronson Alcott
    at Mr Sewalls
     Boston

[1] Thursday was May 13.

LETTER 41–2[1]

[to Junius S. Alcott, Oriskany Falls, N.Y.]

Concord 28th September 1841.

Dear Brother,

I have deferred writing till I should be able to speak definitely concerning my residence for the coming autumn and winter. This is now determined. I shall defer my removal from this place till spring, and await the indications of Providence meanwhile. My brother S. J. May wishes me to live nearer him and offers me a ‖ fine ‖ House, and farm with many other advantages. But I do not feel ready to accept them now. I wish to remain free. My friends in Providence[2] urge me to live with them, and ‖ are ‖ will build ‖ ing ‖ a Cottage for me, if I will dwell in it. I hesitate in this matter. The step I shall take now is one of vital importance, and its consequences of deepest interest to myself and family— to my future freedom and influence. I shall take time to consider.

And now having settled my place of residence, I desire you to come and live with me, as you promised almost when with us last. I think we can make it agreeable to you, and I assure you t'will be most grateful to us. The children desire it greatly. You will find a good deal of time for thought and reading: and we can write and converse at our pleasure. You will be near those who understand and appreciate your character and opinions. Indeed, I see not how you can fail of passing a profitable and agreeable winter, and when spring opens, you will join us in the new enterprise upon which we shall then enter. I need not tell you how great is the Hope you inspired by the little intercourse we had during your visit. These things are not told in words. Come and live with me, and those who will soon be drawn around us, and let us become more and more one in purpose, thought and deed—brothers in life, and workers together in the great Reforms of our Day. Mother shall come whenever she will. Her presence and word will ever be sweet to us.

I feel that the period of destitution is full passing over ‖ with ‖ me and mine. Persons, here and there, are taking us kindly by the hand, and, without complaints and misjudgements, ministering of their love, their confidence, their respect and substance to our needs. We are just beginning to reap of fruits sown long ago in misapprehension and neglect, but which we have cherished in love and hope, looking forward with an assurance of harvest. A little while and we shall ‖ inquire and ‖ I trust be anxious no more for the Bread to sustain, and the Raiment to clothe us. We shall enter into the Fraternity of Kind and faithful Hearts, and all wants shall be supplied.

Last week, I attended a Convention of Non-Resistants in Boston, where much was said, and more implied than said, in great questions of Reform. I left with the conviction deepened that a few years will bring changes in the opinions and institutions of our time of which few now dream. All things are coming to Judgement; and there is nothing deemed true and sacred now that shall pass this time, unharmed: all things are doomed: the eye of Justice searches the Hearts of men, and the secrets of all Evils and Wrongs are made known to all men. Another Convention sits ‖ in October ‖, when questions of yet graver moment are to be discussed, and measures bolder even than any before proposed. A band of valiant souls is gathering for ‖ the work of ‖ conflicts with the hosts of ancient and honorable Errors and Sins—these shall assuredly overthrow the Idols now standing in our High Places, and do somewhat to restore the worship of the True and living God in the Hearts of men. I would be of and with these in their work.

I sent some of you a copy or two of "The Plain Speaker,"[3] a week or two since—a better number ‖ than ‖ too than any which had preceded it. The editors, C. A. Greene, and W. M. Chace, (young men) were here last week. Abba and the Babe left this morning to make them a visit of a day or two at Providence where they reside, and where we may go in the spring. I spent a week with them lately to my great content. They would joy in you. And one day you shall know them.

Give my love to mother, and all my kindred near you. Chatfield and Ambrose would give me great pleasure if they would write.

I shall look for you at Concordia: but write me first.

Yours affectionately,
A. Bronson Alcott.

Junius S. Alcott
Oriskany Falls
New York

[1] A portion of this letter with textual differences is printed in Sanborn, *A. Bronson Alcott*, I, 324–25.
[2] Christopher A. Greene and William M. Chace.
[3] A short-lived newspaper published in Providence, Rhode Island. The first extant number was January 30, 1841, and the last was in December, 1841.

LETTER 41–3

[to Anna, Louisa, and Elizabeth Alcott, Concord]

[Concord, December 24, 1841]

For All.
(Dec 25. 1841)

My daughters,

This is the Birth Night of one of the best of men ever born into this world. He was a good and wise Child, and grew into a good and wise man, living for the good of those who lived with him, and going about to make men wise and happy as himself. He was a friend of children and like them was innocent and pure in his thoughts and feelings. He wanted them to keep their ‖ their ‖ innocency and not give it up to any of the things that tempt it away. He did not give himself to the indulgence of his appetites or passions, but governed himself in all things. He ruled his own spirit: he obeyed his Conscience, and did not know what it was to feel sorry for having done wrong. He was happy in the knowledge of having done right. I suppose his father and mother loved him very much, and so did all good people. But when he became a man, he could not be happy without trying to make every body better. But then, as now, the people who were not good disliked to have him try to make them better, and they told false things about him, and he was slain to gratify their bad feelings. But the things he said and did they could not kill; his friends wrote them down, and they have given pleasure to a great many people since, and you may read and be made better by them yourselves. I have his Life you know, and you can read nothing better than this to help you in all resolutions of being good. Read it—think of it—strive to be good—and to make others good also. And be ready like him to bear unkindness, and to suffer for doing right. To feel and do so will be keeping his Birth day in the truest way, and continuing to do so will make you a Christian, that is, a person like Jesus, and all your days will be Christmas days—your life holy and good like his.

I give each of you a pencil ‖ case ‖ as a token of my love, and trust that you will use it in recording thoughts and feelings and actions that shall be pleasing to your own hearts, to your parents and to Him who is wiser and better than Father or Mother or Friends whom you love—who is the parent and friend of all men and wom[en] and children and creatures in the world and in heaven.

Your Father.

Christmas Eve.
  Dec. 1841
    Concordia.

           For   Anna Bronson
                Louisa May   Alcott.
                Elisabeth Sewall

                      Concordia
                      Fireside

PART FOUR

✠

1842

[to ?]

[Concord, January 1, 1842]

Dear Sir,

You will find the terms at which the Temple is held, by reference to Emerson's letter written on the sheet containing the balc.[2] These are $22 a day, including the evening, and he has engaged it for our use. So let us have the hall forthwith.

The New Year comes in bravely—the herald of brave deeds during its passage.

Very truly
yours,
A. Bronson Alcott.

Concordia Jan 1st
1842

[1] MS. owned by the Boston Public Library.
[2] "balance"?

[to Elizabeth, Concord]

Concord, Cottage, | February 2nd. | 1842.

My Dear Elisabeth,

You give me much pleasure by your still, quiet, manners, and your desire to do things, without asking impatiently and selfishly, for others to help you without trying first to help yourself. Trying is doing; Doing is but trying: try then always and you will do; and every one loves to help those who try. I will print a little sentance [sic] for you, in large letters, and you who have already found it so easy to do things for yourself will, I dare say remember it, and follow it to—

This is it—
    "Try first; and then ask; and try patiently till you have tried
your best; and you will not need to ask at all."
                Trying is the only
                    Schoolmaster
                        whose
                    Scholars
                        always
                            succeed.
                    Your Father

Cottage
    Feb 2.
For Elisabeth

¹ MS. owned by the Houghton Library, Harvard University; quoted in Bonstelle and deForest, pp. 94–95.

LETTER 42–3¹

[to Junius S. Alcott, Oriskany Falls, N.Y.]

                                        Concord 19 February 1842.
Dear Brother
    I have deferred writing till I should have some definite intelligence to communicate of my plans and prospects. As I now have some light on these matters it is fit that you should have the earliest possible benefit of it, as your own movements may be affected by mine; and, moreover, as there has been an implied understanding of our dwelling together, if so desirable a society could in any way be promoted by ourselves. And I have all along been pleased with the idea of having you in my family. And now it is quite practicable and desirable to have you with us, and the more since I am to be absent awhile—till October or November at least. And if mother will come we shall all be the better pleased—Abba and the children will have more Society, and I shall dwell with greater pleasure on you as inmates of my family during my absence. Here are my wife and children, my house, library, friends, garden, (and acre if you desire it) all at your profit or service, and you can read, meditate, labour or converse, as you shall incline—and mother shall do likewise. The garden and few family chores will all minister to your health and content, and my good wife is humane and social, and other friends there are, whom you would soon love and appreciate. These are some of the benefits; but I do not intend to flatter you hither, desirable as it may be to me and my family. There may be reasons in your mind which shall deter you and if there be, you have but frankly to say so, and we shall understand the matter at once.—Now there is but *one* circumstance to mar my pleasure, and that is *my own absence*. I had dwelt with great hope and promised myself true satisfaction in the fraternal intercourse which would then be ours, and felt how good, how needful, indeed, the influence of a soul ‖ fresh and ‖ glowing with the pure and holy light and love of a serene and earnest piety, on my own mind and character. And the Idea had been sweet and re-

freshing to me. And I know that I am sometime to enjoy it, if not now; and so wait in the like trust and hope for it.

And now you will partake, I am sure, of my own feeling when I tell you that I purpose visiting my friends in England; and intend leaving on the first or early in April.[2] I have little to do at this moment in my own country, every avenue to honest and worthy employment is closed against me, and so I seek sympathy, and possibly business in a foreign land. These Englishmen have manifested a true interest in my objects, and I seek them with hope—sure of their friendship and aid. ‖ And ‖ I go *honoured* the more by the neglect of my own countrymen. No, not quite thus—a few there are a worthy few—who promote this object, and provide ‖ the ‖ means ‖ of my ‖ to carry me across the waters and supply my needs while absent. And my family are left sure of all needful supplies. And so I go forth again upon my mission in the world, free and unconfined no longer.

The winter is gone. I have passed some days in the woods wielding my axe: but the time has been less hopeful to me than during any former period of my chequered life. The *Bible Convention* meets soon. You will wish to be at it. And I shall ‖ leave ‖ embark immediately after for England, meaning to sail direct for London. Write *immediately,* as we wish to make every necessary arrangement in season. Love to all at Oriskany.

Your brother,
A. Bronson Alcott.

[1] Quoted in part in Sanborn, *A. Bronson Alcott,* I, 330–31.
[2] Alcott sailed from Boston on May 8, 1842, aboard the *Rosalind* (see Letters 42–5 and 42–6). The financial arrangements for the trip were made and guaranteed by Emerson, who felt the journey might help Alcott again "find" his place in the world.

LETTER 42–4[1]

[to Anna, Concord]

[Concord, March 16, 1842]

For Anna
(1842)
A Fathers Gift
to his
Daughter,
on her
Eleventh Birth Day.
Concordia
16th March
1842.

My dear daughter,

This is your eleventh birth-day. And as I have heretofore addressed a few words to you on these interesting occasions, I will not depart from my former custom now.

And, my daughter, what shall I say to you? Shall I say something to please or to instruct you—to flatter or benefit you. I know you dislike being pleased unless the pleasure make you better, and you dislike all flattery. And you know too that your father never gave you a word of flattery in his life. So there remains for you the true and sweet pleasure of being instructed and benefitted by words of love and the deepest regard for your improvement in all that shall make more happy in yourself and beautiful to others. And so I shall speak plainly to you of yourself, and of my desire for your improvement in several important things.

First—Your manners. Try to be more gentle. You like gentle people and every one is more agreeable as ‖ they ‖ he cultivates this habit. None can be agreeable who are destitute of it. And how shall you become more gentle? Only by governing your passions, and cherishing your love to every one who is near you. Love is gentle: Hate is violent. Love is well-mannered: Selfishness is rude and vulgar. Love gives sweet tones to the voice, and makes the countenance lovely. Love then and grow fair and agreeable.

Second. Be Patient. This one of the most difficult things to every one, old or young. But it is also one of the greatest things. And this comes of *Love* too. Love is patient: it bears; it suffers long; it is kind; it is beautiful: it makes us like angels. Patience is, indeed, angelic; it is the gate that opens into the House of Happiness. Open it, my daughter, and enter in and take all your sisters in with you.

Third. Be Resolute. Shake off all sluggishness, and follow your Conscience as fast as your feelings, your thoughts, your eye, your hand, your foot, will carry you. Hate all excuses: almost always, these are lies. Be *quick* in your obedience: delay is a laggard, who never gets up with himself, and loses the company of conscience always. Resolution is the ladder to Happiness. Resolve and be a wise and happy girl.

Fourth. Be diligent. Put your heart into all you do: and fix your thoughts on your doings. Halfness is almost as bad as nothing: be whole then in all you do and say.

But I am saying a great deal, and will stop now with the hope of meeting you on the 16. March 1843 (the good God sparing us till then) a gentler, a meeker, more determined, and diligent girl.

Concordia
16 March
1842

Your friend
and
Father.

For
Anna Bronson Alcott.

[1] MS. owned by the Houghton Library, Harvard University; quoted in Bonstelle and deForest, pp. 76–80.

[to Mrs. A. Bronson Alcott, Concord]

Boston | Saturday Eveg May 7 1842.

Dear,

To morrow we sail—early if the winds favour. All my things are on board; my two trunks standing closely under my berth: your fine loaves are in the steward's store-room, with the ‖ pot ‖ jar of apple sauce, which came safely, and the apples and crackers are accessible at any moment. My passage is paid: the ten sovreigns [sic] are in my red pocket book, with the Bill of Exchange for Twenty pounds on Baring Brothers & Co. and various little sundries are in my trunks. So you see I am cared ‖ for ‖, and provided for.

The passengers are seven in number. Mr. Mackintosh and wife, Dr. Walker's son of Charlston [sic], Mr Lyford and Mr Sampson of Boston, and myself. I have seen none of them yet. Mackintosh is a son of Sir James Mackintosh, and married a daughter of Nathan Appleton. I have heard Emerson speak of him, and believe they have met sometimes. We shall meet (if possible) during our confinement aboard: and possibly find intercourse mutually agreeable, if not on my own, on Emerson's credit. More than ever as I leave this friend do I feel the more deeply the worth of this friendship; it is the highest prize (but one) in Life's Lottery in which I have been the lucky, taking the great ones—a wife, whose worth I am living to appreciate the more and more, and this unparalleled friend.

And now I am leaving them for a short time, and others whom I am learning to value (but whose kindness I might not have but for this absence)—friends here whom I have met yesterday and to day & friends whom I have left behind. I sometimes feel as if this voy[age] was meant to ‖ bring me from my wanderings and ‖ show me what I had not dared to believe that there were those who knew and loved me indeed! and so reclaimed me from the injustice of that bigotry into which I was fast falling. I shall bless God for the benefit.

I have thought much of you and the children since I left you. No, I have not left you while I think of you. Now be of good cheer—I know you will try.— It is a noble sacrifice which you have made the greatest I know—for my sake, and I feel how poor is my regard in return. You will be, you are, rewarded for it, and your reward will grow the sweeter to you daily as you acquiesced in the event that separates us for this little while to unite us the more when we meet. That event will be to us like a second nuptial eve—a wedding a festival[?] spousal rather, in which ‖ (not parent now [words] and heartless) but ‖ [p. o.] our own children shall partake of the sweet sacredness of our Joy. Till then, till thus we meet, (if God so willeth) Adieu.

Adieu my children till I ‖ meet ‖ see your faces once again in the retreats of Concord‖ ia ‖: and you, too, my great and hopeful brother,[1] whose friendship I am just beginning to taste, as we part adieu my friends, once more.

Sunday Morg 6 oclock. A refreshing nights rest—& the like blessing to your powers dear!—Last ev'ng Garrison called with letters of introduction to G Thompson Dr. Bowring Elizabeth Pease Mr. Ashurst and to Mr and Mrs More at whose Boarding House Americans often stop. He was all urbanity and most ready to serve me having walked in from Cambridgeport on purpose—I go on board at 8 this morg if the wind favors, shall soon leave these shores.

A morning Kiss to Abba (Mother and Child)[2] and greeting to the little ones.
from Father.

Morton Place.

Mrs. A. Bronson Alcott
Concord
Mass.

[1] During Bronson Alcott's absence, his brother Junius stayed with the family.
[2] Abigail May Alcott, the youngest daughter, was sometimes called "Abba" (as was her mother), sometimes "Abby," but later on "May."

LETTER 42–6[1]

[to Mrs. A. Bronson Alcott, Concord]
Ship Rosalind, English Channel. | 31st May 1842 4 oclock Morning.
Dearest,
I rise from a sweet vigilant night-time passed with you—one of many such since I left you. No. I have not left you; you have been my companion and compan[y] all the way, and have grown more and more precious to me, as the winds wafted us together across the seas. And most propitious of breezes bravest of ships, this Rosalind. Here no[w] lie, in this faerie water, on this breezy May morning, in full light of the British Isles. w[ithin] two days distance of London, and but twenty two from land to land, and this without reefing a sail, nor scarcely an adverse wind during all our passage. Fortunate man! selectest of ships. But that Atlantic queasiness I did not escape during the first days, still it left me a most vigorous appetite, and the Cottage Bread kept sweet and good till devoured. It lasted a week or ten days; the applesauce some days longer, with the stewards scalding and sugar[ing,] and an apple or two remains in prime condition in my Wallet at my Berth's head. Apples I shall henceforth and always recommend to all my friends who may try this Brine. Mine were most grateful at all times, and a treat to my fellow p[assengers.] with potatoes, which were most excellent in kind and admirably dressed, hot veg[etables] I f[ed] very well.—I have had no settled love of writing and so my Diary has little of interest for you. But I will send you a few minutes [torn] it; they may give continuity to your thoughts about me, and serve as a [torn] for your memory.
"Sunday 8—Embarked at 11. Am, and left the wharf, immediately. In two or three hours the land faded from sight. Before night I betook myself to my Berth, and looked over my letters of introduction. (Emerson's to Carlyle you saw.)[2] Garrison has behaved as nobly by me in his way as Emerson. I will copy one of his—the letter introducing me to Dr. Bowring—for the eye of my admirable wife.[3] (Copy)

"Boston May 8. 1842.
"Esteemed Friend, You will not require of me an apology for introducing to you an esteemed friend of mine, the bearer of this, (A. Bronson Alcott of Concord, near Boston,) for I am sure you will greatly admire the sweetness of his spirit the independence and originality of his mind, and the libera[lity] of his

soul, as he cannot fail to admire those noble traits of charact[er] which endear you to a most extensive circle of friends and acquaintan[ces.] [torn] Mr. Alcott is a true man in the Anti-Slavery and Peace Questions—an enlightened and warm-hearted philanthropist—a resolute and an uncompromising foe of priest craft, bigotry and sectarianism, under every guise a Reformer who is for laying the axe at the root of the tree, and not for pruning its branches—and a philosopher who is determined to think for himself. Though not harmonizing with him in all his speculations, religious, metaphysical and social yet I hold him in high esteem for the purity of his life, for the many virtues which adorn his character, and for the rare moral courage which he has displayed in giving utterance to "heretical" doctrines and unpopular thoughts. He is the bosom friend of Ralph Waldo Emerson, and both are well known to Thomas Carlyle. I have no doubt that his intercourse with the free, educated, reformatory minds with which he will probably come in contact on your side of the Atlantic, will be mutually instructive and delightful. May his visit be greatly blessed to the promotion of "peace on earth, and good will to men," and to the demolition of all those national and geographical distinctions and prejudices, which alienate and curse our race! I write in great haste, &c. &c.

	With great respect, I remain,
Dr. John Bowring M.P.	Your admiring friend
London.	Wm. Lloyd Garrison."

[torn] [prop]itious gales till Sunday 15. Off Banks of Newfoundland, becalmed. Stately [torn] iceberg, from Labrador probably, passed near us.—Reading "Wordsworth's "Excursion." This, with the Essay on Epitaphs and the Ode on Childhood are favorites [of m]ine.[4] Some of the characters in the Excursion have much in common with experiences of mine: the likeness is closer than I was aware, and the sentiments of the Wanderer seemed but repetitions of my own.—17—Had a spirited conversation on deck after tea on Reform. My doctrines were at first taken as pleasing fables, but grounds of fact were yielded me by little and little and before we closed I succeeding in taking firm and vigorous root in the solid terra firma of reality.—Macintosh seems quite a frank and tolerant Scot. Yet an advocate of property and of the established order. I like him very well, we have pleasant talks now and then. He knows several persons in whom I am interested, and his wife is a good natured and social, woman[.] 27—Reading Emersons Essays. Divine poems these, having the exalting effect of poesy on the mind. 'Tis like the fragrance of woods and fields, so sylvan, so balmy. Delicious those improvisations on Love and Friendship—reviving all my ties at Concordia. Again, am I a youth; and after long wanderings in the solitary wilds of thought, I am a denizen of the realms of Affection—a dweller in the courts of humanity.

> T'was once in Love's young morn of Babes I dreamed,
> And gentle mats my rural cot to grace,
> Where freed from fear, and strife, and carking cares,
> Contentment, peace, and mutual love should reign,
> Religion, taste, the genius of my haunt.
> Nor hath that dream, nor passed away nor gone,
> Yet doth the vision stay, nor will it go;
> Still are my babes, and mate, and cottage all,

> The cherished idols of my constant thought,
> And day by day my plighted vows renew.

28   Fair and strong gales still favor us. I have admirable company [torn] own thoughts in the seclusion of my stateroom. I am at home. And how [torn] few days absence transfigures, exalts, idealizes the holiest experiences—humaniz [torn] friends. As yonder needle at my ship's helm, ‖ inclines ‖ so doth the heart of friend, in all the latitudes of life's drifting interests, incline with constancy to the hearts it loves. Ah there is a mysterious sentiment, surpassingly humane and tender in this alliance of husband and wife. Now, my love mate, do I feel the sweetness of your regards, the preciousness of your love, and accuse myself again of inconstancy almost in leaving you for this little while even. But even now this short absence has invested our quiet cottage, our babes, ourselves, with a new and holier charm, broken the sorcerers' rod of custom, and woven the sweet charities of Home all anew. And we shall each bless this separation, and find again that intercourse which was ours in the prime and innocency of our espousals. Am I not thine, dear woman; and art thou not mine; and what shall bereave us of each others trust. You did but resign me for a little while to prove how inseperably we were one. And I did but leave you to find that I could not depart from your embrace.

29.   My child, that little one, usurps my thought. And here is a little ditty for [torn]

For Abba

> The naughty wind, naughty wind blew,
> Blew papa over the Sea:
> Now goody wind, goody wind blow,
> And bring papa back to me.

30—We are in the English Channel. A waterman with provisions came on board: several others in sight. It seemed like meeting neighbors to see these bluff, hardy persons, and hear them speak in their rude brogues, as he took his place in the circle we made around him.—Another boatman in the afternoon, from the Eng. shore. Made land.—I took my berth late, but sleep forsook me. Troops of gentlest, fairest, sublimest thoughts usurped my brain all night, I slept not, but was planting Edens—fabling of worlds—building kingdoms and men—taking the hands of friends and lovers—of wife and babes. So at 4, it being light and a most magnificent morning, I arose to write.

31st.   Becalmed almost, but delightful weather. The English shore appears indistinctly in the distance—passing the Isle of Wight. Visited again by God's Genius, and wrote much during the day—the air of Britain inspiring my thought.—June 1st. Near Brighton, two hours ride to London, and hope to send this ashore by Macintosh in season for the Liverpool packet of the 4th.—Those little girls are often in my thoughts. Tell them, dear, of Father's love, and also of their promise to behave well during his absence. A great deal of regard to Junius, and the hope of hearing soon from you, dearest, dearer never than at this hour to

> Your devoted husband,
> A. Bronson Alcott.

Is mother with you? If so all love to her. And add my regards to that unparalled [*sic*] *friend* whose proud ship sends me across these waters. Farewell now, my friends, farewell.

A. B. A.

Mrs. A. Bronson Alcott,
    Concord
        Mass.
    United States.

---

[1] Portions of this letter are torn; hence the frequent use of brackets about words or parts of words guessed at. Where [torn] appears a word is missing and no guess has been made.
[2] See Rusk, *Emerson Letters*, III, 49.
[3] Dr. John Bowring, M.P. The following copy of the letter from Garrison appears with slight differences of punctuation and with part of a sentence intentionally omitted, in Shepard's *Pedlar's Progress*, p. 304
[4] The first eight lines of Stanza 5 of "Ode: Intimations of Immortality from Recollections of Early Childhood," beginning "Our birth is but a sleep and a forgetting," is probably the one piece of poetry most frequently alluded to and quoted by Alcott.

LETTER 42–7

[to Mrs. A. Bronson Alcott, Concord]
Alcott House, Ham Common, Surry [*sic*], | 12 June 1842.

Dearest,

A week's stay in this abode of divine purposes and loveliest charities, has quite restored me to a good degree of health and vivacity, so that I shall make my addresses to the good and wise of the great-metropolis to morrow, where I stopped but a day on my way to this hamlet. I wrote you from the English Channel ten days ago, and so the Steamer bearing my letter must be nearing your shores by this time. My letter was a transcript mostly of my Journal at sea, and I will continue my extract of passages from the same since I left the Rosalind.

"Sunday 5 June. Took passage in a small boat from Deal for Dover, the winds adverse to our ascending the Thames. After passing along the shore for an hour or two, we reached Dover, passed examination at the Customs, and took lodgings at the King's Head, where we slept. Dover is one of the Cinque ports, and the great thoroughfare to the Continent. The coast of France is quite visible across the straits, and steamers pass in an hour or two from Dover to Calais. It is a fortified town and almost hidden under the hills which rise in the background, on the brow of which is the Castle commanding the Harbour on the south and east; and on the west overlooking the town are the Heights, bristling with Soldiers who reside in its bowels below. We ascended the Heights this morning (June 6) by means of a subterranean shaft, and had a commanding view of the harbour, and surrounding country for many miles. After breakfasting, we took passage in the steamer for London, sailing swiftly through the Downs, stopping at several places to take in passengers, and also as we ascended the Thames. We reached London Bridge, in the very heart of the city, at 5 P.M. Here Mrs Mackintosh took a hackney coach for Gower Street, and the cabman drove us (Walker and Lyford), at once to the London Coffee House, Ludgate Street, near St. Pauls. After taking some refreshment, I walked around St. Pauls, and then down through Temple Bar, Charing Cross and the Strand, and back to my lodgings to bed. ‖ Time has [word] its influence to deepen the impression of ‖ St Pauls is a commanding structure, overwrought with ornament, and built by Sir Christopher Wren. But I found myself transmuting the material into the spiritual architecture instantly, and St Paul, with the other apostles, seemed to me to emblem the fortunes which their doctrines have had in the world. There they stand above the din and smoke of the town, their voices spent ere they reach the multitude below; their sublime inspirations all hardened into dogmas and rituals,—their prophet a mystery—even to the few who tread the aisles within— effigies and echoes of the Everlasting word—Christendom mortar and stone—its Christ a Ghost and its Priests ossified at the heart. London seems a rare union of the costly, elegant, magnificent, with the useful convenient and plain. Every thing I see implies great resource and is executed in a finished style: all is solid, substantial, for comfort and use. But all is for the body; all seems body.)

Tuesday 7   Presented my bill of Exchange this morning at Baring Brothers and Co. Bishops gate Street, and called on Charles Lane[1] at the office of the London Mercantile Price Currant I found him at his desk. Most cordial was our meeting. He invited me to accompany him to Alcott House, where he resides: and where we arrived in the afternoon. Here we found Mr and Mrs Wright,[2] with their coadjutors and pupils—a circle in which I found myself ‖ quite ‖ at home, all being ‖ quite ‖ familiar with my purposes and thoughts, and all receiving me with a ‖ deep and ‖ serene and quiet joy. It seemed, indeed, like returning home after an absence of a few days, so familiar, companionable, was all about me." (I had not dreamed even of ‖ the ‖ finding this oneness in all things—particularly with Mr Wright, ‖ the first man and only man whom I have found to see and know me even as I am seen and known by myself ‖. He is a younger disciple of the same Eternal Verity which I have loved and served so long. ‖ He is not yet thirty years of age, but is possessed by a wisdom and Love possesses a wisdom and Love incarnate in no man, save Mr Lane, that I have ever met ‖. You have never seen his like, so deep, serene, so clear, so true and so good. I now understand the instinct that sent me across the waves—it was to enjoy this spiritual communion, this concord of will and of Ideal—this concert of Thought and Act. His school is a most refreshing and happy place—the children are mostly under twelve years of age, and his art and method of education simple and natural. It seems like [torn] being again in the Temple, save that a wiser wisdom directs, and lovelier love presides over its order and teachings. It is a purer version of the same scripture a brighter revelation of the same Divine Idea in thought and act. He seems, from what I gather, to be held in high estimation by the thinking class, and is on terms of intimacy with the best and wisest people of the kingdom. I feel that our purpose is one, and that we might become cooperators in the work of carrying the same to its ultimate issues, whether here or in America, a few months will disclose. Himself and friends command many resources for such an enterprize, and are desirous of uniting with us in its prosecution. They have the most select and rare library I have seen, including most of the books which we have sought with so ill success on ‖ the other ‖ one side of the water.) Mr. Greaves[3] was the soul of the circle—a prophet of whom the world heard nothing, but who it seems has quickened much of the thought now current in the most intellectual circles of the kingdom. He was acquainted with every man of deep *character* in England, and many both in Germany and Switzerland; and Strauss, the author of the Life of Christ, which has shaken the faith of the Old World and is now exciting ‖ alarm ‖ interest in the new, was a pupil of || his, when || Mr Greaves when he held conversations in one of the colleges of Germany, after leaving Pestalozzi. A most remarkable man—nobody remained the same after meeting him. He was the Prophet of the deepest affirmative Truths, and no man ever sounded his depths. The Best of the New in the Monthly magazine was a transcript of his Idea, and Lane, the deepest, sharpest, intellect I have ever met, was converted from infidelity by him. He read and wrote much, chiefly in the manner of Coleridge, with pen in hand in the form of notes on the text of his author. But, like Behmen and Swedenborg, neither his thoughts nor writings were for the popular mind. His favorite [torn] were the chosen illuminated minds of all time, and with them he was familiar. This influence was not unlike that of Jesus, and his friends cherish his name with a like affection. (I was not permitted to see him with these eyes, but am not bereft by his departure of his presence and society. I write these lines, while sitting on the couch from where he was borne to the village cemetery, and on the table where was wont to delineate his mystic thoughts. He was buried from Alcott House in March || last, || breathing his last at the very hour when the Divinity moved me to visit this charmed spot. By the documents I send herewith, you will learn much of the spirit and doings of the circle he left, and for the rest you must wait in patience, till I rejoin you at Concordia, or meet you here with your little ones. Junius would realize his Ideal with these people, finding his brothers in the earth, || and the || [p. o.] our [p. in] children companions for whom they have long sighed. Mrs Wright seems a most happy, sensible and affectionate person, devoted to the interests of her husband and the great ends of the school. She is not yet a mother, but extends a mothers care over the thirty or more children of the household: and directs also in the culinary department, having several assistants in these matters. Scarcely an item in these || household, or || domestic arrangements, that has been discussed with us, but is here in operation and practically carried out. The living as simpler even than ours.)

"(June 10.   Walked this morning with Mr Wright to Hampton Court, built by Wolsey, and the residence of the former kings of England. Here we saw some ancient tapestries and paintings, but we were too intent on diviner architectures and lymnings [sic], to bestow our eyes on these royal || apartments. || baubles.)

(June 11.   Sunday. Many persons from London were at the school, Mr Wright having a service of reading, singing and conversation. I read the children a Parable from Krummacher with paraphrase and conversational episodes interspersed, and Mr Wright gave a lesson in worship, not unlike mine in the Temple. To morrow I return to the city, and find Carlyle and others whose names are familiar to me.) I shall remain in London some weeks, and wait letters from you. Write me full and true. and Junius must add his word, and the little girls theirs too, in their own very thoughts and with their veriest little hands. I am full of tender and hopeful thoughts about you all, and now your faces and tongues would please me more than any thing else. I left home and you, as I now feel, to find how dear you were to me—how sweet a spot was home. Have patience, and a little while will assemble us again; and make the spot beautiful meanwhile by being so yourselves, and so when we meet our joy will be the more || beautiful || [p. o.] delightful [p. in], and our intercourse the more sweet. Tell me about your school, and Bessy about home and Abba, and be good and gentle, and mindful, and kind, as so your mothers cares will be lightened, and father's absence made the less wearisome to her, and that sweet and approving voice in your hearts will make you happy all day long, and you will see Fathers face smiling in upon yours whenever you think of him. So good night to ye all, my children, and pleasant dreams, but sing first the little ditty which I sent you for Abba, and kiss mother, and then one another for me. Good night; I shall go to bed soon, and kiss God for mother and you all, again good night.—

Tell me all about yourself, dear; the act of communicating will be a sweet intercourse between us. I am now so related to my brothers here that I should feel this my home could I see yourself and children, and || those those || two trans atlantic brothers of mine, Junius and || Waldo || Emerson, who yet has a counterpart here in Charles Lane—a man whom Emerson would feel as rich as in || Thomas || Carlyle—whose hand I have to take tomorrow and whose face I thus see for the first time.

(This journey, I see already, is to be of great present as well as prospective importance to us all, and we shall be reaping its fruits for years to come in the new hopes it inspires, and the substantial goods it shall give us. England is in advance of America in the province of thought and action wherein I have dwelt so long, and with so little company to cheer me in my work. Presently we shall make to ourselves a public, and if I || bring || take some of these workers home with me, and we can find room and helpers there, let Time and its noblest births thank my friend E. who favored and cherished my || visit || purpose, and gave me to these shores to gather us together.)—Be sure to read all I send you, and then let Emerson read. I think the parcel will be a glad surprize to him. I shall write to him when I have seen Carlyle. And I wish him to remember my Dial. And to send along with that || some || six copies of the same, addressed to H. G. Wright, Alcott House, Ham Common, Surry [sic]. They will come I suppose through Mr Greene, the agent in London. Mr Wright has the names of the subscribers for it, and will transmit payment on my return. The friends of the Dial think that thirty copies at least will be wanted to supply the demand on this side of the water, and it might be well to transmit this number in advance. I shall have contributions [torn] send || also of || [p. o.] papers of which we ought to be proud.—But I am near the end of my sheet, and have yet every thing to say but this one thing I || have time and space to || must add, the assurance of my love, deepened by absence, and becoming day by day the more living in the Breast of

Your Husband
A.B.A.

Mrs. A. Bronson Alcott
    Concord
        Mass
    United States

---

[1] Charles Lane (1800–70), editor of commercial periodicals, reformer, vegetarian.
The best material on Alcott's English sympathizers is to be found in an unpublished paper by William Henry Harland, "Bronson Alcott's English Friends," owned by the Fruitlands and Wayside Museums.
[2] Henry Gardiner Wright (1814–46).
[3] James Pierrepont Greaves (1777–1842), merchant and educational reformer.

LETTER 42–8

[to Mrs. A. Bronson Alcott, Concord]

London Queen Street Place | 17 June 1842

Dear

I wrote you from Alcott House, Ham, on the 12th. but my letter does not leave the Post Office till this evening for Liverpool and so I add further of my movements and purposes. Mr Wright came to town with me, and I took my present lodgings for a few days until I should recruit myself a little, and make some repairs of ‖ my ‖ raiment. I have now made my purchases, and am ready to call on the few persons who reside in town. But the attractions at Ham may yet draw me thither again to spend Sunday next and a day or two, in which case I shall not see Carlyle, Heraud, Marston, and the rest, till some time in the coming week. I shall soon thereafter draw my plans for the future a little, and take lodgings at the West End. (But I shall not remain long, I am sure, in the City. My senses are all pained by the din and huddle about me. Every body looks bestial and ferocious, and the voice and manners, the very build and gait of the men and women I meet, no less than their opinions and institutions, betray the injuries inflicted on the human sentiments and affections. Every Englishman is a fortification—‖ he is ‖ organized of blood, ‖ and ‖ he believes in the necessity of spilling it. The warlike element seems wrought into his ‖ very ‖ constitution, and reappears in the temper and genius of the institutions which he promotes and loves. I have seen little as yet of the serenity, gentleness and meekness which mark the refined and peaceful soul. The barbarity within is too obvious, in no repose, no harmony, no tenderness; but all is strife and unrest. But this I say of the town; the country when I shall make acquaintance with it, may report more humanely of itself and tenants.)—

(I said I was drawn towards Ham. But the attraction is chiefly moral. The place in itself is most beautiful, ‖ the ground classic ‖ classical indeed, being near Richmond, and Twickenham—near the dwellings of Thompson and Pope and Sheridan and Walpole—but these have no charm for me: it is the poets and statesmen of the Hamlet, the life and literature which these shall inspire, the genius that is dawning on Britain, that most interests me. Both the school and the men were a glad surprize. I had dreamed long and indulged in many fables about them as you well know, but the dream and the fable were alike real, and I am now here to give the interpretation and the moral. Henceforth I am no more solitary and without kindred in the worl[d,] for I have found a man who can divine ‖ the depths of ‖ the mystery of life, and touch the heart of childhood to the holiest issues. Mr Wright has more genius for education than any man I have seen: and not of children alone, but he possesses the rare art of reaching men and women. What I have dreamed and stammered, and preached and prayed about so long, is in him clear, definite; it is life, influence, reality. I wish you to come within the sphere of his magnetism: and to the children his influence would supply the need you most feel. And I flatter myself that I shall bring him with me on my return. He cherishes hopes of making our land the place of his grand experiment in human culture, and of proving to others the worth of the Divine Idea that now fills and exalts him.—But time will determine for us, and unite us in spirit, wherever our scene of action, whether associated in person or separate from each other. It is much to have seen him, a reason worthy, indeed, for crossing the waters.)

I am waiting to hear from you with some impatience. We have never before been separated so long. I think much of you. I am with you often and the Cottage and its inmates seem beautiful and dear to me. I know not how it is, but it seems sometimes as if absence was, indeed, the best of society—as if I knew and most loved my friends when away, their portraits seem so fair as I draw them on the canvas of memory. It may be that a man is too near while in his own family to see and draw the same as it is: that he must be hold it in the lights of time and distance, and so its lineaments shall appear to him, || and || idealized in the hues of his affections. The heart will not paint unless her colours are mixed and softened in Beauty. I hope, dearest, to bring [torn] me the painting I draw and dwell thereafter in the beauty of lights.

Tell me particularly about yourself—You will make me the more unhappy by reserve. Those secular and family matters now revolve more immediately upon you: let me know your burdens, and what shall most lighten them. Junius will do his best to assist you, and you have great resources in yourself. Cherish Hope: Brighter days are dawning on us—are, indeed, risen—to me || at least || assuredly[?] here in this East, and shall appear soon on your horizon. Love and sacrifice like yours *cannot* baulk their possessor. Whatsoever the loving heart yields, it shall find again; yea, find always in yielding: not until we yield all, do we find peace in the joy that all is ours. Ourself alone is hindrance to felicity.—I fancy by this time my letter from the English Channel is in your hands. This, with the one from Ham, and the parcel of books addressed to Miss Peabody, leaves soon for Liverpool, and will reach you in ten or twelve days if the winds favor. I should have told you to pay the postage on yours to me in Boston, otherwise I may not get them. Uncle Sewall will do it for you.—How is my Baby? I need not ask—God keeps the Innocents always under his eye, and they shall joy in his smile. Kiss the little Queen on the brow, the mouth and cheek, for me. Tell Lizzy to wear her sweetest smile all the time: tell Louisa to run her fleetest step to serve her mother and sisters: and Anna to let all her large eyes mean show itself in her tone and manners to all. And || tell || [p. o.] reassure [p. in] Abba, the elder, || that || [p. o.] of [p. in] my love.

A B A

Mrs A Bronson [Alcott]
    Concord
        Massachusetts
    United States.

LETTER 42–9

[to Junius S. Alcott, Concord]

Alcott House June 30 1842.

My Dear Brother

I am made happy in these trans atlantic friends, not in myself alone, but for your sake also, since I find so much that reminds me of yourself, and have pleasure in the prospect of your better acquaintance with them. They are brothers to me already. They cherish like purposes with ourselves, and dwell in the presence of that light which shines upon us. Ham is home to me; and the return here after a few days spent in London, is like the quietude of our own Concordia after a tedious jaunt to the metropolis of N-England. Already am I knit to these friends by ties which cannot be sundered, and must take them along with me to America, or else remain here with them. But I flatter myself that I shall bring them to our shores. They are ill-placed here in this oppressed realm. It is not in Old, but in the New England, that God's Garden is to be planted, and the fruits matured for the sustenance of the swarming nations. The world's hope is in us, and we must take our work greatly in hand, deeply at heart, and satisfy this desire. I see more clearly every day that this thing of which we have dreamed so long, must be set about in good earnest, nor can I have rest or pleasure till it be thus undertaken. My visit here is most timely. Mr Greaves on whom our friends leaned for support has just been withdrawn from them, and the ties that bound them to England are all loosened, and they can never transplant themselves so well to a more fertile soil. Providentially I was directed hither; what the end shall be does not yet appear. But a few months will determine. Next week we have a meeting of those who are waiting for a new order of things, and this new plantation in America is the topic among others for discourse. I would not scatter so lavishly in hope as to reap mortification and defeat, but am assured that this promise which haunts me ever, and has so long painted the sky of my future, shall not deceive me, my hope setting in darkness. The heart's visions shall all be realized; this prophet never speaks falsely. I will hope ever even against all hope, for only in hope is the reality of life: and doubt is the grave wherein the precious interests of the soul are buried.[1]

> Hope is the sower, saith the quickening beam,
> This I affirm and reap my brightest dream.

I sent you by the steamer of the 18. a parcel of tracts and papers which you will find, if you have not already, at Miss Peabodys. There will be a trifle to pay on it, I suppose. but it is worth all it will cost. By this of the 4th.[2] I transmit a second parcel quite as valuable as the former one, and shall continue to send as documents come to hand. I have journeyed but little as yet. Places do not attract me. I seek persons rather but have not found many of these. I shall not go gadding after reputations: the one or two I have met were || most || empty enough,—and I have no inclination to seek echoes again. Carlyle, Heraud,—let them speak—'tis all sounding brass, the tinkling cymbal's empty note, and I am ashamed of myself for turning aside to give a moments ear to their voice. But the fool must purchase whatsoever of wit he may have, and I have paid full price for my own small modicum, and would cheat no foolish gazer by hiding my chagrin from him. But here is one man nevertheless whom I do purpose to see, and this no quack, nor popular gazing stock, but a true and sincere man, so much as there is of him—and this is Mr Owen[3]—the poet who writes in brick and clay, in gardens and green fields, and is a believer in the comforts and humanities of life and would give these in abundance to all men. Britain already owns his influence and shall feel him the more, as the years pass by. True, he has no religion to give to mankind, but he has that which the popular religion witholds [sic], and must wrest the Sceptre from her Queen ere long. Better, far worthier of Carlyle to give himself to the life of this better, this greater than Cromwell, and [torn] honor to the living, instead of disinterring the ghastly dead [torn] the gaze of his contemporaries. But the dead must ever garnish the sepulchres of the dead, and what is the living Owen to the deceased historian.

What success have you with your garden? and how prosper your manu-
scripts? and what fills the hours in your rural retreat? I shall have much to tell
you and more, I hope, to Be to you on my return. But you are in Being yourself,
and so can offer to spare me, ‖ and all my intelligence ‖ very well. Write me
soon, and tell me much of your self, and add much of that beloved wife and
babes, to whom you are both husband and father during my sojourn in foreign
and distant lands. But I must leave you now to discourse awhile with them. I
know you will be all that is kind and helpful to them, and that they must love
and serve you in return. In a few days, I shall resume my place again, and prove
the more worthy of the trust I hope, from the new lights that absence casts over
it. Adieu, my brother, may the hours ripen your fruits and our friendship
mellow with our years into all the sweetness of that relation which is ours. Turn
now your most radient face upon me, and let me behold the serenity that is
playing over it, and let the inmates of that retreat full rejoice in it, and see not
only the love that it portrays, but the reflex also of his who is far away, and
must needs smile through the brother's countenance on those whom he now
illuminates in thought. Farewell.

A. Bronson Alcott

Junius S. Alcott
    Concord
        Massachusetts
    United States.

[1] This paragraph is the first concrete indication of the forthcoming Fruitlands community.
[2] The date is confirmed by the postmark.
[3] Robert Owen (1771–1858). The first infant school in Great Britain was begun at Owen's instigation. That plus his experiments in communal living no doubt appealed greatly to Alcott, although Fruitlands was planned on a far less materialistic basis than were the Owenite communities.

[Letters to Ripley, Parker, and Whitmarsh; from Alcott House, England, June 29 and/or 30, 1842.]

LETTER 42–10[1]

[to William A. Alcott, Dedham, Mass.]

Alcott House, Ham Common, Surrey, June 30, 1842.
I avail myself of this earliest opportunity for sending you a small parcel of
such tracts as have come to hand, during the short time that I have been on the
Island,—some of which I think will interest you, and all of them serve to gratify
curiosity, if not to feed the understanding. I am now at Alcott House, which is
ten miles from London; where I find the principles of human culture, which
have so long interested me, carried into practical operation by wise and devoted
friends of education. The school was opened five years ago[2] and has been thus
far quite successful. It consists of thirty or more children, mostly under twelve
years, and some of them not more than three years of age,—all fed and lodged at

the House. The strictest temperance is observed in diet and regimen. Plain bread with vegetables and fruits is their food, and water their only drink.

They bathe always before their morning lesson, and have exercises in the play-grounds, which are ample, besides cultivating the gardens of the institution. They seem very happy, and not less in the school-room than elsewhere.

Mr. Wright has more genius for teaching than any person I have before seen; his method and temper are admirable, and all parties, from assistants, of which there are several, to the youngest child, delight in his presence and influence. He impersonates and realizes my own idea of an educator, and is the first person whom I have met that has entered into this divine art of inspiring the human clay, and moulding it into the stature and image of divinity. I am already knit to him by more than human ties, and must take him with me to America, as a coadjutor in our high vocation, or else remain with him here. But I hope to effect the first.

Britain, with all her resource and talent, is not the scene for the education of humanity: her spirit is hostile to human welfare, and her institutions averse to the largest liberty of the soul. Nor should an enterprise of such moment be endangered by the revolutions to which all things are here exposed, and which threaten, as I think, the speedy downfall of the realm.[3] Our freer, but yet far from freed land is the asylum, if asylum there be, for the hope of man: and there, if anywhere, is that second Eden to be planted, in which the divine seed is to bruise the head of Evil, and restore Man to his rightful communion with God, in the Paradise of Good,—whereinto neither the knowledge of Death nor Sin shall enter; but Life and Immortality shall then come to light, and man pluck wisdom from the tree of life alway.

The Healthian is edited here by Mr. Wright and Mr. Lane, and they are contributors to almost every reform journal in the kingdom. They are not ignorant of our labors in the United States; almost every work of any value I find in the library at Alcott House,—your own works, those of Mr. Graham[4]—besides foreign authors not to be found with us. I shall bring with me many works, both ancient and modern, on my return to America.

I have traversed the island but little as yet. We have a general meeting here of the friends of reform next week [July 6, 1842]; and soon after I purpose visiting Mr. Owen at Tytherly, where he is establishing a community. I find that he is more felt than any other man in England; and although his reforms are quite partial and secondary, and fail utterly of feeding the religious instincts of man, and aim only at improving his outward circumstances; yet all this is good as far as it goes, and most needful in this oppressed and starving land; so that to many he comes as a saviour from want and dependence, and is the harbinger of that spiritual Messias whose advent is near, and whose coming shall unloose the heavy burdens, and let oppressed humanity go free. The same state and conditions must be secured in our own country, or we too must fall to pieces, and add to the long catalogue of the world's disappointments. But our reforms are deepening year by year, and presently we shall reach the great heart of the social and physical body, and learn whence health and healing come.

I have not yet seen Miss Goeris[?] but hope to, if possible. My regards to your good wife, and confidence that you will not fail to visit Concord during my absence. My wife deserves a visit from you,—do not disappoint either of us. I shall hear from you with pleasure. Address me at Alcott House, etc. Parcels will reach me through James Munroe, sent to John Green or Wiley & Putnam, London.

Truly your friend,
A. Bronson Alcott.

[1] Reprinted from Franklin B. Sanborn, *Bronson Alcott at Alcott House, England, and Fruitlands, New England (1842–1844)* (Cedar Rapids, Iowa, 1908), pp. 15–19.
[2] "Really not until July, 1838, as Mr. Harland shows in his accurate monograph. A lease was first taken of the property by Wright, and then the lease purchased by his friends above named. It opened with twelve pupils" (Sanborn's note).
[3] "This was a gloomy anticipation then, and for some years, common" (Sanborn's note).
[4] "Dr. Graham was a vegetarian" (Sanborn's note).

LETTER 42–11

[to Mrs. A. Bronson Alcott, Concord]

Alcott House 2nd July 1842
My Dear,

Will you believe me—not one whisper from those lips of yours has yet fallen on my ear since I left you. But you must have written I am sure and your word will find me. Meanwhile I shall strive to find you by copying a passage now and then from the Diary of my seeings and doings, with present comments and addenda on the text. I wrote you last, if I remember, from Queen Street in London, and will resume my copyings from thence.

London June 18—Called on Hugh Dougherty a disciple of Fourier and editor of The London Phalanx. I gave him a collection of our tracts and papers. He was ‖ much ‖ [p. o.] pleased to see me, and we had much conversation chiefly on communities. He spoke with great interest of the success of associations in France, and particularly of the establishment of Wm.[?] Young who purchased a few years since a large estate in that ‖ country ‖ kingdom and was prosperous in his enterprize. I gave him some account of similar attempts in the U.S. and referred him to the tracts which I had brought him for particulars. He spoke of Emerson with great delight, and desired to know all I could tell him of the new order of things with us. I like him quite well. He is a hearty Irishman, has travelled in the continent where he became acquainted with Fourier, and brought his principles to England a few years ago. Though of sanguine temper, he is a friend of temperate measures, and would carry his points with cautious prudence and wise moderation. I shall see him again in a few days.—Passed the evening with J. A. Heraud and Francis Barham. Heraud is much the person I fancied him, receptive, kindly, rhetorical, not original, and owes his present position to these qualities mostly. He was under large intellectual obligations to Mr Greaves, and still borrows largely from him and Coleridge. The fine writing in the Monthly Magazine is ‖ mostly ‖ Greaves and others in Herauds coat.[1] Barham is an Irishman of a certain nervous fire and grit, but still a book-monger, and dealing little with original ideas.—19.—Evening—I had an hour with ‖ Mr ‖ Wilkinson ‖ who is ‖ a disciple of Swedenbourg and discerner of original doctrines. I met him at Heraud's where we discussed at large the merits of Swedenbourg. I said he was not the prophet of a religion, but the interpreter ‖ merely ‖ of the science of Nature ‖, and ‖ was not the founder of a Church any more than was Bacon or Milton. He was a man of intellect ‖ he ‖ had no religious character: there was nothing in him for the moral principles: nothing epic, and he must ‖ [word] away [word] at best ‖ take his place, not with the Gods, but demigods, of the New Olympus.—20—Heraud read a Lecture before a Literary Institution on the Influence of Continental Philosophy on England. He dealt largely in the logomachies of Kant and Coleridge scarce[ly] descending to the apprehensions of his audiance [*sic*], who were really very much more tender of the speaker than we should have been in Boston. He had little or nothing of his own to give them.—21—I rode to Camden Town, and saw ‖ Mr ‖ Harwood, who lectures weekly, on Sundays, at the Beaumont Institution in London. I found him reading the Dial, which he had just seen for the first time. He was pleased at seeing me, and had ‖ a great ‖ many questions to put concerning friends of the New Ideas in N. England, and of Emerson particularly, whose "Orations" and "Nature" I gave him. He invited me to pass the coming Sunday with him which I promised to do, and returned with ‖ Mr ‖ Lane to *Alcott House* which I make my home while in the island.—"22—I had a good deal of Conversation with Mr Lane on the "Newness," as he terms it, and with particular reference to the soil and conditions needful for the germination and growth of this divine seed, and whether it were better to plant the same in England or America. He is one with myself in preserving the latter, and ready to unite in any enterprize which is worthy of this divine end: in this preference Mr Wright also concurred.—23rd—Walked to Kingston upon Thames, with ‖ Mr ‖ Lane & ‖ Mr ‖ Wright to a meeting for assessing Parish Rates held in Kingston Church, the Vicar of which served as Chairman. A better occasion I could not have desired for gaining insight into the practical workings of the Established Church. Dissenters of all names, including, socialists and chartists, made their protest against the oppressions and extortions to which these rates gave rise, while the supporters were ready with their pleas of loyalty and usage to urge the highest tax. The elements of disunion are ripe, I perceive, at the very vitals of the realm, and it must ere long decease, nor Church nor State having a remaining drug to prolong its decrepit existence. 24—America has been our topic all day. Really, it seems the ‖ promise of the ‖ [p. o.] world's promise as I behold its giant proportions, and amplitude of resource, its free and fearless tread, amidst the nations. 25—I rode to Chelsea and passed an hour with Carlyle. Ah me! Saul amongst the prophets! It must have been a dark hour with him. He seemed impatient of all interruption: faithless quite in all social reforms. His wit was sombre, severe, hopeless, his every merriment had madness in it; his humour was tragic even to tears: there lay smouldering in him a whole French Revolution—a Cromwellian Rebellion[;] nor could the rich mellowness of his voice, deepened as it was, and made more musical by his broad northern accent, hide from me the restless melancholy, the memory feeding on Hope, the decease of all prophesy in the grave of history, wherein with his hero whom he was seeking to disinter, himself was descending—a giant mastered by the spirit of his time. I told him the dead only dealt with the dead—that the living breathed only with the living—and that the spirit of the past waked by the historian, darkened ever on him like a ghost, to haunt him by night and by day, till it blotted the sweet light of heaven, crept coldly around the charities and human [word] of the heart, and bore him at last to the sepulchres of the dead. We had desultory talk, but none gave me pleasure. The man is sick; he needs rest; he must get that Book off his brain before he can find his better self,[2] and prophesy wisely to his contemporaries. I know his ailment: I know its cure. (Emerson will sadden when you tell him what I write, but here is another of the thousand confirmations to the suicide of the pen in which literature abounds. Let us provoke the divine afflatus by godlike deeds, and these shall report as with tongues of flame of the Omnipresent Being to all men and all times.—I shall call again soon, and hope to find[?] him[?] exempt from his brain, ‖ and ‖ disposed for discourse ‖ then ‖ on living men and things.—26—Sunday. I heard a discourse from ‖ Mr ‖ Harwood, at Mile End in the Beaumont Institution, and passed the afternoon and evening with him at Camden Town where he resides. His doctrine was fine and enforced in a simple and vigorous style, with a warm and humane eloquence. Some hundred or more persons were present to hear him. He read a simple hymn; singing followed, with an accompanyment [sic] on the organ; then extracts from Confucius, Seneca and John; then a short address to the Benignant spire of the Universe, and he then closed with his lecture on the Changes in the individual life of man, one of a course on the Vicissitudes which happen[?] to all terrestrial things. You will find an account of the Institution in the parcel addressed to brother Junius. I gave him ‖ quite a full ‖ some account of our domestic experience, particularly our reform in diet and regimen, in which both himself and his wife, a good simple Englishwoman, seemed deeply interested, as they had never heard of like wonders before.—27—Heraud read his lecture on the Influence of Continental Philosophy on America, in which, after losing himself and his audiance [sic], who applauded him ‖ quite ‖ often for his success in this particular, he pounced most lovingly on Mr A. Bronson Alcott, who, he informed them, was at that moment in their presence, having crossed the Atlantic, as the representative of the Emersonean Idea at the Transcendental court in England; and he then alluded to the labours of Mr Alcott as an Educator, quoted largely from his "Conversations with Children," and closed by his assurance that he would be welcomed on the English shores. Emerson and Brownson and Ripley were treated less vividly, but were represented as adepts in the same school.—I leave you to your readier wits to rid me of the company into which I had fallen unawares.—28—I returned with ‖ Mr ‖ Wright to Alcott House, having made arrangements with the bookseller, for facilitating the distribution of the Dial in England.—29 and 30[—]At Alcott House discussing Cosmogenies and sundries pertaining there[to,] and writing also to Emerson, Parker, Ripley, Whitmarsh, Dr. Alcott, Br[other] Junius and last, though not least ‖ when the heart speak the ‖ to your own dear self, and those babes about you, whose presence steal daily into my light.[3]

July 1st. You will inquire how I am—a right woman question, and in this instance a wifes—and therefore the most connubial of answers shall be given. Well, dear, I was never better, nor know of but one thing to make me better still—the light of your smile and that of the little ones around you. But I shall seek this in practical earnest soon, and then adieu to old Care and melancholy—to Inaction and Dreams. We will marry them off and transport them as culprits to make the best of each other ‖ at ‖ to Botany Bay or elsewhere: and rid of them once for all, we will enter as denizens of the Kingdom of Trust and Repose ministers of Humanist Ideas and lovingest Deeds—our Children ends[?], and not the offspring of Abstraction nor Haste.—Then will we make beautiful the Idea of Family, and blossom anew in the Garden of Love. 2nd. I hope you will keep me apprized of your domestic affairs the state of your finances, if such department there be in the new order of the family—what befalls that Boston

Estate matter—and everything else that interests you, whether pleasurably or painfully. We shall be well rid of those old embarrassments and harassments too, I trust, and a dear bought, but yet most valuable estate or no state they have been—even of more worth vastly than all they have cost us—since they have purchased for us independence of the world's good name, and that inward peace that springs from self-integrity alone. They have given us an Estate in our own characters which thieves cannot steal nor moth nor rust corrupt, and which, if we husband aright shall descend a precious inheritance of benefits and gifts and graces in the characters of our children. God be praised not less for the seeming adversities than the successes of his Providence, and man forgiven for his short-sightedness in seeking to ‖ arrest the causes of ‖ chaffer with Heaven's Beneficent almoner.—The little girls all—how are the budding maids? I am proud of their natures, so deep and rich, so full of promise, so imperv[ious] to surrounding evils. See them obey the divine law within, [torn] wrench their powers rudely from their centres—tis the still small voice and the persuasive accent, the reverential love, that wins to the performance of Duty. I bless God too for their strength of self-protection, and know that we cannot tempt them wholly from their adherence to the Duty within. Let us be faithful ourselves and these little ones shall be kept in their celestial orbits, and shed light on all around, suns to ourselves and one another; as Love beholds its own image in the eye of love, and is the light which it sees.—I mean to write next steamer to Anna and Louisa Elisabeth and Abba, and tell them a little about such of my seeings and doings as may interest them. Meanwhile, dear, Be as happy as love and hope can make you, and rest assured that this foreign visit of mine, though it bereft us for a little while of each others presence, and our children of their rightful benefits, shall prove a ‖ most beneficent ‖ Bequest of Blessings to us all, and the good pass to our kindred and friends and even to the country that gave us birth; but first let me kiss the lip of Her who first kindled me into that sweeter and holier birth the gentler and fragrant life of Love—and last let me embrace all those Charities and Humanities, their types and symbols too which now move around you, in those little maids, those graces and lives[?], in that Concordium, which my constant Fancy now portrays, and into which my Heart yearns again to enter—But, verily, I am already in its midst and so need but dash aside my pen.

Lovingly yours and ever.
A. Bronson Alcott

Mrs. A. Bronson Alcott
   Concord
      Massachusetts
   United States

---

[1] John Abraham Heraud (1799–1887), poet and dramatist, edited the *Monthly Magazine* from 1839–42.

[2] Carlyle was working on *Oliver Cromwell's Letters and Speeches* (London, 1845).

[3] Evidently Alcott began the present letter to his family, as well as the following letter, to Emerson, on June 29 or 30.

LETTER 42–12[1]

[to Ralph Waldo Emerson, Concord]

Alcott House, Ham Common, Surrey, | 2nd July 1842

My dear friend,

Herewith I send you a small parcel of tracts and a MS paper or two, which if worthy may serve the readers of the Dial. The writers care little about them and will be quite as well pleased if you cast their papers aside. Presently we shall be richer in our contributions. The Dial, I am pleased to find, is quite an Oracle here, and needs but a little aid, by way of advertisements and notices in the public Journals to become sufficiently famous. Green and Putnam are quite ready to receive and distribute the numbers, but alike complain of not receiving them, and so missing the sale of many copies. They advise advertisements and notices, and only await your orders to give the Book a fair chance with the Public here. Two or three Pounds, or even thirty shillings, if no more were ventured, they say would do the thing for it. These Englishmen, sellers and buyers of our wares, seem all friendly. I have made a happy acquaintance with some, and am daily adding to my list of friends. Carlyle I have seen for a short hour or two, but he was not in his happiest mood, nor am I yet clear whether even that shall take greatly with me. But I shall see in a day or two. Heraud I have seen, too, and with less pleasure even. These men of letters are all ridden by the hag Melancholy or the dragon Need, and so lose the serenity and fragrancy of ‖ high and ‖ creative Hope. I am not here inhaling the breath of the words or gardens of N. England, much less of Concordia. They pay homage to the dead rather than the living: losing themselves in empty logomachies, or wasting the costly gifts of genius in adorning the sepulchres of the dead. But from this, I exempt the inmates of Alcott House. Lane and Wright are living men and live in the world of the living—piercing keenly the core of things around them, and feeding on the sweetness of the present hour—the heralds of a happier era in life and letters. I have been here a good time, since I stepped into this Kingdom, and feel quite at home with the friends here. They cherish like thoughts and designs, and work after my own methods. I shall be rich in their friendship, and breathe a voiceless gratitude to the friends who favored my visit to their threshold: and yet richer, if they shall return with me to ‖ the threshold of ‖ my friends threshold in America. Bear with me this once, Emerson; I am now gone silent.—Here is a plan of Herauds. I copy it for your eye—whether you will bestow a thought upon it or not. A publisher he says is pledged to take all pecuniary risks, and the best of the new lights here will contribute. I suppose it would further the interests of the Dial, and if yourself and Carlyle should favor the scheme, would take instantly with the better public both English and American. I shall name it to Carlyle: and will you tell me what you think of it.—Sterling was in London a few days ago, but we missed each other. I called at his fathers in Chelsea very near Carlyle's, and saw his beautiful boy, whom the kind grandma brought me, as a picture she said of the father, and a portrait for the eye of Emerson's friend. But that ‖ Titular ‖ Journal of Heraud's—"The Old and the New a Quarterly Organ of the Philosophic Mind in Europe and America: Contributors—

Payment to Contributors from 8 to 20 guineas per sheet (large double fools-cap) It is desirable that contributors should assist the first 2 numbers as much as possible.— —add Charles Lane & H. G. Wright to this list.

European	*American*
T. Carlyle	R. W. Emerson
John Sterling	A. B. Alcott
J. A. Heraud	S. M. Fuller
F. Barham	Theo. Parker
J. W. Marston	F. H. Hedge
Hugh Dougherty &c.	Geo. Ripley &c.

We have a public meeting next week at Alcott House for the discussion of the Needs of the Time and the Means of their supply. The New Plantation, whether it shall take root in America or Eng[land] will come in, I suppose, for entertainment by us. The[re a]re some fine materials here in men and books—almo[st] every mystic author has place in the library of Mr. Greaves—a man too majestic for the all[?] on which he was cast, but whom we shall yet know and honor. Like Coleridge he wrought in a hidden and subtle way; germinating in the characters whom he won; and like him a Conversationist, and annotator on the Books he perused. I have looked into his M.S.S. and read also many of his Notes. Mr Lane will edit his Life and Writings.—Whether I shall visit Words-worth, or journey at all, remains a possibility. I am not bent on doing so.—The Bill at Barings was duly honored, and I have yet 12 Sovereigns in my purse. I find living very expensive and must practice the wisest economy in every respect. Clothing I have—and at less cost than I expected. Keep me within limits in this—the world is mine at all costs, but these have no value at the Royal Mint. I am doing very well just now.—I shall look for the New Dial by the next steamer. If you desire me to advertise, write your own and send it along, and the booksellers here should be supplied. Mr Wright has subscribers names for 6 copies—20 at least should be sent for this market.—

Of course I may hear by the return steamer. I have written to Ripley and Parker and sent them tracts also. Tell me to slacken, if I send you what you care not for.

Affectionately Yours
A. Bronson Alcott.

Ralph Waldo Emerson
Concord
Massachusetts
United States

[1] MS. owned by the University of Illinois Library.

LETTER 42–13

[to Anna, Louisa, Elizabeth, and May Alcott, Concord]

For All.
(1842)

Alcott House, Friday, 15. July 1842.

My dear Girls,

I think of you all every day and desire to see you all again; Anna, with her beauty-loving eyes and sweet visions of graceful motions and golden hues and all fair and mystic shows and shapes—Louisa, with her quick and ready senses, her agile limbs, and boundless curiosity; her penetrating mind and tear shedding heart alive to all moving breathing things—Elisabeth, with her quiet-loving disposition and serene thoughts her happy gentleness and deep contentment, self-centred in the depths of her affections—and last, but yet dearest too, in her frolick joys and impetuous griefs, the little Abba with her fast falling footsteps, her sagacious eye and auburn locks and word-forming tongue with ready lips to help—and Mother too (for how can I think of you without being reminded of her) whose unsleeping love and pains-taking hands provide for you comforts and pleasant things, and is your hope and stay, and now more near and important to you, while I am taken from your eyes—All and each of you I have in my mind; daily I see you in my thoughts, and as I lay myself on my pillow at night, or awake from sleep in the morning, or walk in these fields and Parks or streets, or ride in coaches, or swim in boats the Thames, or sit alone, or talk with friends, I have you near, sometimes one of you alone, sometimes all, and your Uncle Junius too, with that soft and gentle voice, and lowly air, and blushing cheek of his; nor can the tumbling waters hide my group of loves from my eyes, the little Cottage there behind the Elm, the garden round, strawberry-red, or arbored vines, or fragrant pea, or climbing bean, or waving leaves of corn, or rasberry [sic] ripe, or boughs of apples near, or melon creepers far; or corn-barn play house by; or street or bridge, or winding stream; or busy school with Ann and Lo their lessons loved and got (by heart not rote) and Lizzy too with little Ab, in parlours, study, chambers, lawn, with needle, book, or pen, or hand in hand with sister dear, or lisping letters for her little lips; or feeding her with bread or cream; or helping Ma to wash the clothes or bake the wheaten loaves; or holding pleasant talk the while of Pa, a long way off across the seas and wondering where he is and why he went away and stays so long, and sighing deep and saying sad, "Oh never will he come, so long it seems," and Ma and Baby sighing too; and Pa. across the separating waters joining in the sigh and answering low from Mother's loving breast, "He'll meet you soon, the while love one another more, the more you love the sooner will he come—Love is the wave that brings him back to those he loves. He left us, dear, to show us how we loved and what a sweet and tender thing it is, and how it makes us all and every thing, more lovely, sweet and fair, and is the very best of friends—the Friend whose friendship none can lose and happy be—and now that friend of Father takes good care, he took him safe across the tumbling sea, he loves him well, and loves us all, he'll bring him safe, and with him bring his brothers ‖ that has ‖ found in Queen Victoria's isle, and never leave us more: and we'll all wait the happy hour: had he not gone we n'er should known the pleasure of his coming home:" And so you see, my gentle girls I cannot leave you quite; though far my body is away, my mind is near, and all the while I see and hear and taste and touch and think and feel your very selves—the Life that lives in all you are and say and do—the Mind, the Heart, the Soul—the God that dwells in you, in which you dwell—your breath, your pulse, your sight, your voice, your taste, your touch your smell—all that comes through your every sense, and makes you little growing shapes, and seen and known to all around. And now be loving little girls and grow more fair with every day, and when I come to see my Garden plot, then shall my flowers all blooming, scent the fields around my lot, and I shall joy in every scent they lend, in every tint and form they wear. So now, my dears, adieu; again

Your Father's fond Adieu.

For/

     Anna Bronson Alcott
     Louisa May Alcott
     Elisabeth Sewall Alcott
          and
     Abba May Alcott
       at
       Concordia Cottage
        U.S.

Let Mother read this with you and talk long and sweetly with her about what is in it; and then kiss her all, and each other, and then her all again for Fathers' sake.

LETTER 42–14

[to Mrs. A. Bronson Alcott, Concord]

Alcott House, Ham, Surrey, | 16. July 1842.

Dear,

The steamers follow each other so speedily that scarcely have I dispatched my last before other favors are due. But what else more pleasing! I wrote you from hence on the 2nd ult., and my letters are just now finding you. How I envy these epistolary rivals of mine! But I will yet magnanimously befriend them and do whatsoever I may to further their suit. To-morrow is near, and will bestow your favors lavishly I hope—the mail from Liverpool then reaches [me] here, and it will be so unlike you, dearest, to keep me longer in suspense, for not a word has yet reached me from across the seas, and it is now more than two months since I left you. But to-morrow is at hand when I shall discourse with yourself and the little ones again, and so I will copy my Diary from the latest dates for you to day. Your loving kindness will breathe life and significance into the dead scroll of mine.

"Sunday 3 July.—I met this morning with a circle of Swedenborg [torn] seceding from the orthodox body, and holding Sunday meetings for reading and interpreting the Christian Scriptures according to Swedenbourg. I hoped something of these schismatics, but they were perplexed by their master's images and void of the charities and humanities, dreamers all, dreaming of dreams. They asked me to speak on the day's reading, which I did, and met them again in the evening at the house of their leader for further discourse.—4. Monday

Visited Westminster Abbey. Prayers were being chanted with responses from the choir as I entered. The service is imposing but derives its interest from historical associations altogether. It is a spectacle merely; there is no worship in it—a pantomimic ritual—a masked show. Here are the tombs of the English Kings—of Mary and Elisabeth and Henry the VII—their effigies repose on the mausoleums which enclose their relics—the dead aping the dead. Here too is the Poets' Corner, an [torn] Goldsmith and Ben Johnson [sic] [torn] workmanship, with other names known to fame. But all seemed ignoble to me, and the Abbey with its Gothic architectures, its cloisters and tombs, its chapels and aisles but an eulogium on the desecrated genius of man—a monument of his fallen greatness.—From the Abbey I went to the Royal Academy, but saw portraits only of honored sanguinary Britons, of the pride and folly of England. The statuary was best, but the subjects were chiefly busts of royalty, of the nobility and gentry, and had no attraction for me. My eye is pained, my thought revolts at portraits and originals, and I sigh to be given back to the land of my birth.—In the evening I met several persons to consider the means of Promoting Health and Chastity, and gave them an account of the progress of Temperance in N-England, and of our own domestic experience particularly.—5. Tuesday. Saw George Thompson at a meeting of Delegates from all parts of the Realm to discuss the Corn Laws and devise measures for the relief of the People. Statements were made of the distresses of the working classes, most appalling to hear, and a petition was drawn for asking Parliament instant attention and relief. But the Delegates have little or no [torn] of finding favor, and have extreme measures, I believe, in reserve. Blood is to be spilled, and not on questions of policy, but of life—the growling hungering multitude will bear their wrongs no longer. I passed the night at Carlyle's, but we sped no better than at first. Work! work! is with him both motto and creed; but tis all toil of the brain—a draught on the memory—a sacrifice of the living to the dead, instead of devotion to living Humanity and a taste of her ennobling hopes. Ah! wo is me! My brothers all are sold to the dark spirit of Time; no man hopes aught of himself or of another; the golden chain of Love is snapped asunder, and each sits now sullenly apart, weaving a chaplet of despondency for his own brow, or else rushes madly into the embraces of another—a refugee from himself.—[W]ednesday 6.—I returned to Alcott House, where I met some of the freest men in [the] Kingdom. The conversation was lively and impressive. Reform in [torn] its aspects [torn] soci[al], political, religious, indivdu[al] &[?] the doings of the meetings recommended for the press (copies of which I enclose for circulation in N. England.)—This visit of mine now promises a harvest of good to us all. I shall glean valuable informations to serve us: the Dial will be made known and more widely circulated here; possibly a new Journal created, supported by contributors from both countries; the Healthian[1] circulated in N. England; valuable Books collected; definite and friendly relations instituted between disciples of the "Newness" on both sides of the waters: and I hope to import living minds into N. England to plant there the new state of things.—7 to 10—Discussing our plantation in N. England.—Monday 11—I saw Geo. Thompson again at the Corn-Law Convention, Westminster, and obtained an admission into the House of ‖ Lords ‖ Peers. Lord Brougham brought forward his motion for raising a committee to inquire into the present national distress, and supported his motion in a speech of great energy and eloquence. But the motion was lost. He stood nearly alone—a young Lord and Marquis only supporting him, by speech, and but a s[mall] minority, (as you will see by the Report which I send) in his favor [torn] Thompson I have seen but little; he is busy on the Corn-Laws, and I [torn] divert him from them. He urged me to speak in the meeting, but I insiste[d] it were better for his cause to let me remain silent, and he let me off. (Send Garrison the papers when you have read them from me; I would write, but shall not have time by this steamer.) 12 Tuesday. I left Emerson's Letter to Miss Martineau[2] with a friend of hers in Regent's Park, and then visited St. Paul's Cathedral. This is a grand structure— a monument to the artist, Sir Christopher Wren, and of the age in which he lived. It is a triumph of human genius over ‖ the ‖ material elements. Here are statues of Howard and Dr Johnson, with numerous effigies of sanguinary warriors in whose ‖ fame ‖ prowess and fame England so delights—desecrating her noblest cathedral by making it the receptacle of these bloodstained priests [torn] view from the top of the great dome commands all London, its suburbs and the surrounding country for many miles—a huge den this ‖ is ‖ truly, wherein Beelzebub whelps, and the roar of whose voice reverberates throughout the whole civilized world. But the reign of the Beast is near its end, and London with its greedy glories, its cruelties and its Enormities—its thrones and hierarchies lording it over the souls and bodies of men, shall become the footstool of a nobler race of Kings.—" But I must here close my copyings for the present. And now let me add a word of my present intents, more interesting to you than all else. I mean soon to return. I have attained the end of my visit. I shall not spend a moment gadding after and gaping at the many shadows of men with which this island abounds—I shall bring the living along with me, Lane and Wright, when I come—at least such is now the plan. But I must remain a few weeks longer to complete these smaller matters; and so continue to write me till September. I am in the best of health. All love to the little ones, to brother Junius; and not the less to yourself. Adieu now, dearest, and write me soon.[3]

[Word(s)] for Emerson to whom all and [word(s)] friendship and joy with me in the new mines I have here opened.

I wrote you by the last steamer (Liverpool, July 5.) long and double. I [word(s)] to say, but find I can say nothing [word(s)]—and have lost my tongue too. [word(s)] excuse this, from

Yours ever
A.

Mrs. A. Bronson Alcott
   Concord
      Massachusetts
   U. States.

---

[1] A short-lived periodical edited by the inmates of Alcott House, England. Only fourteen numbers were issued, during 1842 and 1843.

[2] Harriet Martineau (1802–76). She wrote some uncomplimentary things about Alcott's Temple School, which she had visited on a trip to America (see Harriet Martineau, *Society in America* [New York, London, 1837], II, 277–79). On her return to England she related the details of Alcott's school to James P. Greaves, and it was her account which awakened an interest in Alcott on the part of Greaves and his disciples in England.

[3] The signature has been torn off. In the following postscript some words in the first two lines are concealed by the binding of the volume in which the letter is contained. Some words in the final paragraph of the postscript are obscured by the postmark.

LETTER 42–15

[to Mrs. A. Bronson Alcott, Concord]

Alcott House 2nd August 1842

Joy to you, dearest, and to myself no less. I have finished my work here, and await now the return of the Packet to embark for Boston. I have done much for ourselves and for the wellbeing of those dear to us; and shall return with the hopes and promises of earlier years, and with friends and coadjutors in the work that God sent me forth to do.[1] Mr Wright will either accompany me now, or else defer his coming till spring, and then join us at Concordia, with his wife and Babe (now but two weeks ‖ of age ‖ [p. o.] old [p. in] and Mr Lane will follow soon.[2] This, on second thoughts seemed best. It gives time to make all needful arrangements on either side of the waters, and to enter upon our work under the best advantages. That first of all wants which we felt so long— some one to assist us in the care and culture of our Children—is now most providentially met—Mr Wright is an accomplished educator, in love with his vocation, and finds in it full scope for his Genius. He looks with pleasure and hope to his union with us, ‖ and will begin his labours on our own Children, who serve as the nucleus of the ‖ [p. o.] new institution. I admire the simplicity of our plan. It takes materials already given: it demands nothing of the public, nor is in the least dependent thereon for support; it makes no pretensions to the unbelieving; but with the divinest of all problems solve a work which neither kings nor priests, legislators nor philosophers, empires nor states, have yet solved for mankind—goes quickly to the demonstration in the simplest of manners, and with certainty of success. It needs no costly apparatus, no expensive outlays; its apparatus and its resources are the gifts and graces of its subjects; and squandering nothing on costly lusts, on vain-glorious aims, it secures not only an independence of the world, but a competency of substantial goods, and makes obvious to all, the sublimity of worldly indigence. I have done a noble deed, dearest, and you will share my joy as none other in human form can do; for now is my life's aim to be realized and that too in harmony with all your own most cherished desires. I waited long for the man to come who should take an interest like mine in the demonstration of the true culture; I sought him amidst my own country men; for a time I postponed my own work, and despaired almost of my Hope; but now from this darkness that well-nigh swept my Sun from the heavens, rises my Genius again ‖ from ‖ in this East, and I return to my own land to dwell in its rising light. It was a divine Instinct that sent me hither, and an instinct divine now bids me to return. My thoughts are all Occidental now, and I shall not find rest till I tread that land again and give myself to those ministries which are ours. I am not at peace in this Lion's Den, ‖ amidst beasts of prey ‖ [p. o.]. I would dwell in quiet with husbandmen; repose in gardens and tread fields unstained with blood. I have no love of England, nor England's sons nor daughters. There is here no repose, nor gentleness, nor grace—strife and violence mar all things, all men: Hercules stands at every corner with sanguinary club, grim, ‖ beastly ‖ [p. o.], in iron mail, and neither by day or by night is there exemption from the grasp of the Destroyer. I will not turn on my heel to see another man ‖ (Beast I meant) ‖ [p. o.] and the women are tragic all. (Mrs Carlyle, Fox, Heraud, and all ‖ now ‖) tears of sorrow, they mourn even in their joys—

Of hope, the Hours are Bereft; and the breeze
Murmurs in grief along its vital tides;—

and my Queen at Concordia is a Hymn of Faith to me when I behold these
doleful daughters of Britain. Enough of them—I know of a fair Heart that
shall smile on me once more, and her smile shall be to me as in love's young
morning, even in this my noon.—I would copy passages from my Diary, but tis
so lifeless to me—I sent you by last Steamer the ghost of my goings and doings—I
will come this time myself and make verbal report.—Your letters were most
grateful—I read them sitting [p. in] at the Anti Corn Law Conference, but myself was not there. You were in a sweet, hopeful, mood, and wrote from experiences akin to my own of the teachings of separation. Dearest! This few months
Divorce is the sacrement of our Espousals—this Absence an Invitation of Guests
to our Wedding—that meeting the Bridal Ring at our Reunion—those Children
our chaplet of Loves.—I am here much of the time. We have a great deal to
say and to foresay. I cannot tell you all about it now. I have done not
a little for us all—but cannot sound my own praises—let Time blazon them,
‖ herself ‖. I know not what I have done—it has been Time fulfilled and I am
happy in it.—I trust you have got my letters. I have written by every Steamer,
and sent parcels to yourself, to Emerson, Parker, Ripley, &c. &c. Owen I have
seen, and Fox and Morgan and O'Connell—and Carlyle again, *but we quarrelled
outright*, and I shall see him not again. Greatness abides not here: her Home
is in the Clouds, save when she descends on the meadows or treads the groves—
‖ of Concordia ‖. I will take the hand of that Deity with a warmer love, a
nobler hope, on my return from this far sojourn amidst ‖ the ‖ Satyrs and
Sorcerers.—Yesterda[y] saw "the Dial" at Greens' and read it with truest delight.
That [torn] of Thoreau's is worthy of Isaac Walton himself, and the woods
[torn] of Concord are classic now. Something else I saw that pleased me, but
[torn] has skipped aside at this moment. I have many things in reserve for the
Dial, and sent a paper of Hermes Trismegistus and a Report of ou[r] Sayings
and Doings at Alcott House, with sundry other things to Emerson, in [torn] my
parcel to you.—Thank the little girls for their affectionate letters. I have read
them many times, and shall read them many more, before I read their own dear
faces. How is my little one? Dear Girls, I shall be with you again soon, and so
patience shall be introducing us meanwhile, a surly fellow you will say, and
much of a laggard too, but you may be sure of him nevertheless. Silence for
B.J.[3]—a long, divine, mystic silence. I read his Prayer in the Dial here in this
prayerless land, and felt there was piety again on the Earth, the rumors of
which had reached the ears of Englishmen even. And not less absolute is this
sentiment in my own country—Ah! Prayer and Prophesy are olden things, but
the Hope of the Renewed ones is making them contemporaries and friends, and
the Old and the New shall reappear in the eternal Present.—I am expecting letters from half a dozen of you by this steamer which is due at this moment. I
may be detained here till after the 20th, but if your letters reach me now, I shall
sail immediately. I must be about my Father's Business, and this is now on the
other side of the waters.—I am now setting off for London to make arrangements
for my passage, and learn when I am to sail. Good by to you, now, dearest—God
will protect us, and unite us in lovelier ties, and so I resign myself again to the

winds and waves, which shall bear me soon to your Arms, in the Circle of our Loves.

A. Bronson Alcott.

(yours and Emerson of the 10th & 11th inst just received.—

London
Augst 3d

Mrs A. Bronson Alcott
Concord
Massachusetts
United States.

---

[1] It would seem that Emerson's hopes that the trip to England would act as a restorative to Alcott's spirits were fulfilled, at least for the time being.

[2] Wright did accompany Alcott, leaving his wife and child in England. Lane, with his son, also accompanied Alcott.

[3] "Brother Junius." Junius Alcott contributed a Prayer to the *Dial*, Vol. III, p. 80.

LETTER 42–16

[to Mrs. A. Bronson Alcott, Concord]

Alcott House, Ham Common, Surrey. | 16th. August 1842

My dear,

I have copied passages from my Diary from which you will learn of my doings and goings since my last, and these I enclose herewith. When I wrote you last, I purposed sailing immediately, and was about engaging my passage, but I have deemed it desirable, on further thoughts, to remain a little longer here. Many persons are becoming interested in our purposes—letters are coming to me daily from various parts of the Kingdom—and my friends at Alcott House desire me to stay till we can see more clearly into the future of our designs. And, besides, I have hopes now that Mr Lane and his little boy will return with me. He has relinquished the editorial charge of the "Price Current",[1] and hopes to dispose of his affairs in season to take passage with me in September. The School is now in operation, but will be discontinued if he determine to accompany me: And Mr and Mrs Wright would go at once, but for the Babe, whose welfare the mother fears to risk by a sea-passage. Mr Wright has a brother too who is unwilling to stay behind; And his sister, now in Germany, at a Pestalozzian Institution there, is expected here early in September, with Mr Bennett—a friend and patron of her and of Mr Greaves [torn] inclining to resist N. England. He is [torn] retired from the China trade, and interested in the New Ideas. Lately he reprinted "Emerson's Man the Reformer," and has circulated it widely both here and in Germany. Miss Wright is governess to his children, for whose benefit he visited Germany. I have heard from him and shall meet him with hope. He was an intimate friend of Mr Greaves, and holds his possessions for public good— [torn] agrarian in sentiment and waiting only for objects worthy of his ideas with whom to share them. Miss Parsons too, (of whom I speak in my Diary) inclines to unite with us, and may come along also. Her brother was here yesterday and told me she would write me her mind at length soon. She is engaged now in educating a few children as day pupils, but is impatient of the restraints imposed on her by the popular usages and opinions here. I like her very well. She is grave, sincere, aspiring—desirous of becoming an Educator, and quite sensible of the utter emptiness of professions at present, not only in education, but all things. She would be a most useful and accomplished inmate of our circle in Concord, or wheresoever we may fix our residence. I please myself with the design of taking a House, with adequate grounds, including orchards and gardens, private rooms being given to each member of our [torn] and the parties living together according to their in [torn] I do not instance a dwell [torn] moment, suited in all respects to our purpose; but doubtless one could be found or *created* for us. Ten or twelve persons would make our household at first, and others might come in as seemed desirable. Ourselves, Mr and Mrs Wright, Mr Lane and son, and if we add Mr Wright Jr. and Miss Parsons, we have a circle at once.² Perhaps Mr Davis³ and the Greens,⁴ would unite with us. But I incline to the simplest arrangements. Almost every human being is disqualified now for such an enterprize—scarce one (of all our friends even) is emancipated from the bonds of self, and made free in the freedom of love. || having overcome themselves and the world ||. And of the free can we alone hope any thing worthy of themselves or of the Idea we love. Mr Palmer, Davis, Greene and wife, Chace, and perhaps Whiting too, will someday make members of our fraternity; And I am not without hopes of inspiring Emerson, and others of our dwellers in Concord and near, of the feasibility of our life and living. Wright and Lane are unlike any persons of his acquaintance. They must impress him most favorably. He will see that they are all in earnest, that they know whereof we speak, and are proceeding to the practice at once. Henceforth I am no more alone—a solitary believer (in that little village) in the reality of Hope—deferred it is true till the heart became sick, and Hope had well nigh fled. But I have passed this winter of my discontent—long and dreary as it was, and longest, Dearest, dreariest, to yourself—saddened by the sadness that crept over the brows whereon Hope had alway written her prophecies. But now cometh the spring and summer of Hope, and casteth the melancholy seasons behind and there in the caves of memory let them hide themselves forever from the sweet light of day—blotting it no more in darkness. The sun shall rise fair over the hills, with promise on his wings: nor set more in despair—The dews shall bathe our feet as we tread the gardens, and purity attend [torn] at the fountains and pluck the [torn] Emerson's letter came to hand with yours. He would have me write of Carlyle. I cannot—I can write of none. I am not in the writing mood, and my friends must bear with me, if they are expecting letters. To brother Samuel,⁵ Miss Thaxter, and others, I believe letters were promised, but I have nothing now for them. I can write only to *you*, and speak only of the realization of this Dream; And *you* are almost the only one, in the wide world, to whom it is grateful—almost the only one who deems it possible. Of literature, of literary men—the ghosts and shadows of the Everliving, everlasting Word—I have no call to write just now. I would gratify my friends, all of whom seem the dearer to me as I live in the life of my thought, but, alas! how few of them take this dearest of all Friends at heart! But I shall soon be with them—be with yourself again, and that Brother too, and those Little ones. I go first into Derbyshire—visit a few places—add some valuable Books to my collection—authors whom Emerson will value—And then leave with my [torn] of hope of men and women—of Books and M.S.S.—for that [torn] for the taste of Promise in Co[ncord.]

For My little Girls,
Dears!

I wrote you a letter and enclosed it in my last to your Mother, both of which are now with you in your little Cottage, I dare say. I am sure it gave you all pleasure, as your pretty letters did me. I read them very often: they make me seem with you, and I talk with you. At the top of this letter you will see a sketch of *Alcott House,* where I stay, when I am not in London, or journeying. But I am here most of the time. It is another Home—another Concordia; And my friends here are almost like dear mother and yourselves to me: yet I wish much to be with you and her again, and shall be soon: The Good God—our Best Friend—will bring us together again to love one another more than ever. Mrs Wright has a dear little Baby—a month old now—one day you shall see it. I hope you have good times with Uncle Junius, and are happy. Mr Wright will come to help Father teach you, and perhaps Miss Parsons too; and we shall have a happy Family then, if we are all good people.—Love that little *Daughter Abba* of mine, and that good *woman* her namesake of mine too, and each other— for your Father loves them and you all very much, and hopes to bring some friends along with him for you to love too. A Kiss to Abba, to mother, and one another for [torn]

Y[our] [Fa]ther

Your letters by the [word], with Emerson's, just reached. Thank all busy in arrangement for Concord tomorrow for [word]

[1] The London *Mercantile Price Current.*
[2] Of the group, only Henry Wright and Charles Lane and his son, William, went to America. And Wright never participated in the Fruitlands project.
[3] Thomas Davis of Providence.
[4] Christopher A. Greene of Providence, who did become a member of the Fruitlands community.
[5] Samuel J. May.

LETTER 42–17[1]

[to Junius Alcott, Oriskany Falls, N.Y.]

Concord 28 November 1842

Dear Brother,

We were most glad in receiving your letter. It made us happy in the intelligence of your short journey, your reunion with mother (to whom you seem so very important) and the welfare of our mutual friends, our kindred all, at Oriskany. I parted with you with sincerest grief, yet from the depths of my reluctance there was, and is now, an assurance of joyful reunion when each of us are more in states to profit by a more lively and undisturbed intercourse. Such a time and state will come to us. Meanwhile let us fulfil the duties assigned us apart, and get the good from them which they proffer.

You are constant to your trusts; I must be to mine. Mother needs you, you are a second Amos to her—more now to her than Amos the first can well be. Thank Heaven that we are ministers of Good to any of our fellow beings; I thank Heaven for so constant a brother; I bless God for so kind a Mother, and only wish that it were in my power to be nearer them while I stay in time.

You give good accounts of every body in Oriskany. I am glad that Mother is so well for her. She will be still better now that you are with her. With Chatfield and wife, I can feel, but there is a voice in bereavements of this nature that issues from deeper depths than human sympathies: 'tis well to listen and learn its moral. There is no livelier preacher than this: better were it that man should hold his peace in its presence.

We are tenants still of the Cottage. I know not how long we shall remain here. The Lincoln Farm still seems desirable and we may take up our abode there this very autumn. Some few preliminaries are first to be settled, and then we shall have light on our future doings. Our English friends are with us, and ready to unite in this Household. Robbins from Chelsea is coming on Tuesday next to see us, and to visit the Farm, and it looks now, as if we should take the place: ourselves, Lane, Wright, Robbins and wife, Greene and wife making our present family. We shall see. Thos Davis, Mr. May, Emerson are disposed to aid us, and let us do the best we can. So we stand, so we are trying to move: in God's own time move we shall, and *to stand* is perhaps the swiftest movement now: so few there are who do stand watchful, ready to take their own duties in hand, and execute them from the heart. Who now is shod and vigilant for God?

I am just now very much taken up with my family. Much is to be done for them. You know how much: You have had them in charge. And let me again express my sense of all your kindness and providence to and for them during my late absence. You have your reward; it is not for me to give or take this from you. The coming years shall reveal the burden of our relations to each other, of yours to my family. You were sent and came here for some high end. The children all send their love: little Abba talks of you often. I have always felt the love and remembrance of children the truest compliment that could be paid me. I hope I shall always deserve and win this grateful testimony. My kindest regards to Mother and all our kindred at Oriskany. I would that I knew and could see them better and oftener. Adieu, now, my good brother.

A. Bronson Alcott.

**We have a public Conversation next Sunday in Boston. Your Gifts we shall send for to morrow—thank you heartily.

---

[1] Alcott had returned from England on October 21.

LETTER 42–18[1]

[to Louisa, Concord]

[Concord, November 29, 1842]

For Louisa.
(1842)

My Daughter,

This is your birth-day: you are ten years of age to day. I sought admidst my papers for some pretty picture to place at the top of this note, but I did not find any thing that seemed at all expressive of my interest in your well-being, or well-doing, and so this note comes to you without any such emblem. Let me say, my honest little girl, that I have had you often in my mind during my separation from you and your devoted mother, and well meaning sisters, while on the sea, or the land, and now that I have returned to be with you and them again, meeting you daily at fire-side, at table, at study, and in your walks and amusements, in conversation and in silence being daily with you. I would have you feel my presence and be the happier, and better that I am here. I want, most of all things, to be a kindly influence on you, helping you to guide and govern your heart, keeping it in a state of sweet and loving peacefulness, so that you may feel how good and kind is that Love which lives always in our breasts, and which we may always feel, if we will keep the passions all in stillness and give up ourselves entirely to its soft desires. I live, my dear daughter, to be good and do good to all, and especially to you and your mother and sister[s.] Will you not let me do you all the good that I would? And do you not know that I can do you little or none, unless you are disposed to let me; unless you give me your affections, incline your ears, and earnestly desire to become daily bett[er] and wiser, more kind, gentle, loving, diligent, heedful, serene. The good Spirit comes into the Breasts of the meek and loveful to abide long; anger, discontent, impatience, evil appetites, greedy wants, complainings, ill-speakings, idlenesses, heedlessness, rude behaviour, and all such, these drive it away, or grieve it so that it leaves the poor misguided soul to live in its own obstinate, perverse, proud, discomfort; which is the very *Pain* [?] *of Sin,* and is in the *Bible* called the worm that never dies, the gnawing worm, the sting of *Conscience* while the pleasures of love and goodness, are beyond all description—a peacefulness that passes all understanding. I pray that my daughter may know much of the last, and little of the first of these feelings. I shall try every day to help her to the knowledge and love of this good *Spirit.* I shall be with her, and as she and her sisters come more and more into the presance [*sic*] of this spirit, shall we become a family more closely united in loves that can never sunder us from each other.

Thus your

Father

in Hope and Love

on your

Birth day.

Concordia
>   Nov 29
>   1842

[1] MS. in Alcott House, Concord, Mass.; quoted in Bonstelle and deForest, pp. 88–91.

LETTER 42–19[1]

[to Edmund Quincy, Dedham, Mass.]

Concord 24 Dec 1842

Dear Sir,

My friend Mr Wright from England delivers a lecture in Boston on Tuesday evening next, and will, I dare say, repeat the same before any company you may draw to hear in your village.[2] His topic is Education practically considered. It will afford me pleasure to learn of your giving him a hearing on this deeply interesting subject, which he treats with ability and from considerable experience.

I am very Truly,
Yours,
A. Bronson Alcott.

Edmund Quincy
  Dedham
    Mass.

[1] MS. owned by the Boston Public Library.
[2] Henry Wright gave a number of lectures while in America, without attaining any real popularity.

LETTER 42–20[1]

[to Junius Alcott, Oriskany Falls, N.Y.]

[Concord, December 26, 1842]

Mr Junius S Alcott
  Oriskany Falls
    New York
26/12/42.

My Brother,

For so you seem to me in consanguinity of Spirit, and I would have yo[u] near me, a dweller under the same roof, a sitter by the same hearth-place, my worker beside me, i[n] the fields of Humanity. But God wills you from us for a little while to restore you to us again, a reaper and garnerer of ripe experiences. Come to us again as soon as Divinity can spare you, though it should be but for a season. We need you quite as much as you need u[s,] there are so few made wise by inner illuminations, and we are so indigent of outwa[rd] goods and gifts that every new-made man is a Godsend truly. Our enterprize is begotten in poverty, but is yet rich in hope, and like every divine seed must be cherished and kept alive in faith, till it spring up into ripeness. My country men are too faithless yet, and but for England I were alone. Mr Lane will purchase a farm as soon as the snow melts, and we intend fixing ourselves for a demonstration of a truer life under more favorable conditions. Such a Home we hope to obtain not far from Concord. I shall take charge of the agricultural and educational departments, assist too in household labours, and carry forward the literary work with Mr Lane, as far as I have time. It remains to be seen whether Mr Wright will unite with us. Abba is in some respects quite unequal, but in others very potent as you know. She is visiting in Boston with Louisa now, and may be from home some weeks. She needs recreation. I hope distance and absence from Home and cares will restore her. I pass much time now with the children and am very happy both in present and prospect. Spring will open new and most noble labours for me, and I am ready, nor "can I bate[?] a jot of heart or hope, but steer I must right onward."—

We are well, Apples and flour safe in our cellar and pantry. Write. Charles Lane is near to me, and now I have the best substitute for yourself at [my] fireside. Give my love to mot[her and] kindred all near you. If you were [here I] should set you to making a case for our vols of Books. But thanks for your inte[rest] and skill without such article.

Ever yours
A. B. [Alcott]

¹ MS. owned by the Fruitlands and Wayside Museums.

PART FIVE

✠

1843-1844

LETTER 43-1

[to Anna, Louisa, Elizabeth, and May Alcott, Concord]

[Concord, February 1, 1843]

For All

(1843)

My Children,

I will show you what is beautiful, beautiful, indeed—surpassing all other things in beauty—; and more lovely and more to be desired than every thing upon which the eye can rest, ‖ or the ‖ the heart ‖ can ‖ caress, or the tongue ‖ express ‖ can utter. It is more fair than all the gems on the brows of ‖ the ‖ Kings and Queens ‖ of the earth ‖; more precious than ‖ the ‖ all treasures of gold and silver and costly stones in the bowels of the earth; brighter than the stars in the firmament; dearer than life itself; and that for which the world and all its glories was made; for which life itself is given, with all its comforts, delights, and duties—for which man, and woman, and child, were furnished and sent into the body, and set to work in it, *with* ‖ it ‖, and *by* it, on the world and on men and things—on things, and on each other—and which is the happiest work of the Holiest Fathers Mind and hands—his divinest action—

It is a pure and happy; a kind and loving family—a house where peace and joy, and gentle ‖ ness and ‖ quiet, abide always, and from which sounds of content, and voices of confiding love, alone ascend—around whose hearth gather serene and loveful countenances; where every hand is quick to help, every foot swift to serve, every eye to catch the wishes, and every ear, the wants of the other;—where every day is a long and well-gotten lesson—a Benefactor that fills Time's glass with more than golden or silvern sands, ‖ that ‖ enriching all with the precious gifts of heavenly love and wisdom—and patient resignation, and steady trust in that Good and generous Power that sends Health and Hope and Peace; and binds all ‖ those ‖ Hearts, as one fresh and growing garland, around the brow of undying Love. This is the Jewel—the Pearl of priceless cost.

The Heavens above, the Earth beneath, can witness nothing more glorious than this—nor can one cover, nor the other support, a more comely Building than such a Home. 'Tis a Holy Spot—a consecrated Hearth—a temple wherein to God himself enters and there abides with his angels. 'Tis Heaven and Earth in substance—that, indeed, of which the blue vault above, and the broad world around, are but vanishing and nothingless shadows.—Come then, my Children and abide in this imperishable mansion which I would prepare for you. Clutch not at the vain and aiery vapour—dwell in peace in the serene blue ether!

Feb 1—   Your Ascended Father,
    Cottage   Your Present Friend, and
    Concordia   Careful Provider.[1]
To
    The Young Inmates of the Cottage
        ....while supping around
            Its Hearth.

[1] This letter indicates that Charles Lane's later attempt to get Alcott to break his ties with his family for the sake of the Fruitlands Community would be to no avail.

LETTER 43-2

[to Anna, Concord]

[Concord, February 3, 1843]

For Anna
(1843)

Concord [p. in]
My very dear daughter,
        Anna,
    Shall I tell you how much pleasure you give me by your well meant, and by no means ineffectual endeavours to improve yourself, and to aid in improving your sisters and your friend William[1] in goodness and knowledge, your kindness and gentleness at [p. in] sometimes, your patience and care at othertimes; the thoughtful love that leads you to help your Father and Mother in the cares of the household, and of your little inmates of our cottage, during this winter season when we are all brought near to each other, and have to do many things near, which we could better do separate and with more room and ampler means of doing them.[2] Our cot is small, and our best and only way is to make small our wants, to have few, and these so simple that they can all be supplied without pain or cost to any one. You are growing fast into a woman—I trust into a woman both in mind and body—and you can do more for your sisters' good, than even your father or mother, because you are more with them than ourselves, and they catch your thoughts, and words, and actions, and feelings, and will become what you are, in a great many ways, that you can hardly believe now. Go on my daughter, in your good resolutions, your kind manners and give me yet deeper content by your conduct. We are all now striving to do all we can for each other: we shall all be helped by the good and all provident Helper, and if we deserve better things, these will be given us.
    Our lessons in the school room—in the parlour—at the table—our music, dancing, eating, drinking, working, playing, all are helps or hindrances to our improvement.

The Cottage never seemed to me in a more lively and improving state than just now.

Your Father,

Cottage 3rd Feby. 1843
For
    Anna Bronson Alcott
        at Concordia Cottage.

¹ Charles Lane's son.
² Wright and Lane and his son were living with the Alcotts, so that there were nine people in the small house.

LETTER 43–3[1]

[to Parker Pillsbury,[2] Concord, N.H.]

[Concord, February 14, 1843]

Dear Sir,

I leave the supervision of the oven and the pot,[3] to assure you of the pleasure which the perusal of your epistle has given me, and to add my gratulations of hope in the spiritual triumphs already yours, and your desire to meet manfully those which await you. It is not a little for a man to find his own eyes; much, indeed, to use them willingly, vigilantly, verily, when found; and but a man or two in an age ever comes to this privilege of being a visionist and seer of eternal verities; the multitude dreaming, in the depths of their own darkness, only of unsubstantiated shadows.—I have cherished many auguries of better things from the more manly and clear-sighted of N. Hampshire and Vermont, and predict the noblest deeds from their wisdom and valour. Reformers they now are; they will ere long grow into reformed men, and reap in their own characters the seeds they have sown broadcast over the land. My friend, Lane, you will perceive, has boldly sketched the doctrine of human regeneration in the preceding sentences; and I please myself with the hope that the readers of your "Herald", will find much to approve in the effusions of his fluent and profound pen. Reform leap jubilant over those hills, that the Day of Freedom is come already.—Address us according to your inclinations: one or other ‖ of us ‖ Janus will reply, as best he may, to your inquiries.—My confidence to the valiant editor of the "Herald of Freedom", and trust in yourself, whom, I doubt not, I shall see in the coming campaign.

A. Bronson Alcott.

Cottage, 14 Feb. 1843.

¹ MS. owned by the New York State Historical Society.
² Parker Pillsbury (1809–98). A staunch abolitionist and advocate of woman's rights, he was active in various anti-slavery societies and edited the *National Anti-Slavery Standard* for a few months in 1866. At the time of this letter he was editor of the *Herald of Freedom*, a weekly newspaper published in Concord, New Hampshire, from 1835 to 1846.
    Pillsbury visited Fruitlands in September, 1843, during the time Alcott and Lane were on a trip to Providence, New York City, and Connecticut.
    Alcott's letter to Pillsbury is preceded by a seven-page letter written by Charles Lane "to the Herald of Freedom, Reform and Reformers."
³ Alcott prepared most of the meals for the inmates of the Cottage during the winter of 1842–43.

LETTER 43-4[1]

[to   ?   ][2]

February 15. 1843

Concord, Mass.

Dear Friend:

In reply to your letter of the 12th, I have to say that as until the snow leaves the ground clear, the Family cannot so much as look for a locality (which then may not readily be found), it seems premature to talk of the conditions on which any association may be formed.

Nevertheless, as human progress is a universally interesting subject, I have much pleasure in communicating with you on the question of the general conditions most conducive to that end.

I have no belief in associations of human beings for the purpose of making themselves happy by means of improved outward arrangements alone, as the fountains of happiness are within, and are opened to us as we are preharmonized or consociated with the Universal Spirit. This is the one condition needful for happy association amongst men. And this condition is attained by the surrender of all individual or selfish gratification—a complete willingness to be moulded by Divinity. This, as men now are, of course involves self-renunciation and retrenchment; and in enumerating the hindrances which debar us from happiness, we shall be drawn to consider, in the first place, ourselves; and to entertain practically the question, Are we prepared for the giving up all, and taking refuge in Love as an unfailing Providence? A faith and reliance as large as this seems needful to insure us against disappointment. The entrance to Paradise is still through the strait gate and narrow way of self-denial. Eden's avenue is yet guarded by the fiery-sworded cherubim, and humility and charity are the credentials for admission. Unless well armed with valor and patience, we must continue in the old and much-trodden broad way, and take share of the penalties paid by all who walk thereon.

The conditions for one are conditions for all. Hence there can be no parley with the tempter, no private pleas for self-indulgence, no leaning on the broken reed of circumstances.

It is not for us to prescribe conditions; these are prescribed on our natures, our state of being—and the best we can do, if disqualified, is either to attain an amended character, or to relinquish all hopes of securing felicity.

Our purposes, as far as we know them at present, are briefly these:

First, to obtain the free use of a spot of land adequate by our own labor to our support; including, of course, a convenient plain house, and offices, wood-lot, garden, and orchard.

Secondly, to live independently of foreign aids by being sufficiently elevated to procure all articles for subsistence in the productions of the spot, under a regimen of healthful labor and recreation; with benignity towards all creatures, human and inferior; with beauty and refinement in all economies; and the purest charity throughout our demeanor.

Should this kind of life attract parties towards us—individuals of like aims and issues—that state of being itself determines the law of association; and the particular mode may be spoken of more definitely as individual cases may arise; but, in no case, could inferior ends compromise the principles laid down.

Doubtless such a household, with our library, our services and manner of life, may attract young men and women, possibly also families with children, desirous of access to the channels and fountain of wisdom and purity; and we are not without hope that Providence will use us progressively for beneficial effects in the great work of human regeneration, and the restoration of the highest life on earth.

With the humane wish that yourself and little ones may be led to confide in providential Love,

I am, dear friend, very truly yours,

A. Bronson Alcott.

[1] Reprinted from Rev. Walter Elliott, *The Life of Father Hecker*, 2nd ed. (New York, 1894), pp. 78–79. The letter is quoted in part in Clara Endicott Sears, *Bronson Alcott's Fruitlands* (Boston and New York, 1915), pp. 12–13.

[2] ". . . addressed to . . . one of his [Father Hecker's] most-valued Brook Farm associates" (Rev. Elliott's note). Miss Sears states (p. 12) that the letter was written to Isaac T. Hecker.

LETTER 43–5

[to Elizabeth, Concord]

Concord 6, March 1843

For Elisabeth.
(1843)
Father, Mother.
[torn] other.
[torn][1]
Especially, Father.

Cottage
March 6

[1] An uneven portion of the letter has been torn out.

LETTER 43–6[1]

[to Junius S. Alcott, Oriskany Falls, N.Y.]

[Concord, March 7, 1843]

I hope that the little cash I have collected from my London toils will suffice to redeem a small spot on the planet, that we may rightly use for the right owner. I would very much prefer a small example of true life to a large society in false and selfish harmony. Please put your best worldly thoughts to the subject, and favor me with your view as to how and where we could best lay out $1,800 or $2,000 in land, with orchard, wood and house. Some of the land must be now fit for the spade, as we desire to give all animals their freedom. We feel it desirable to keep within the range of Mind and Letters; or rather, to keep refinement within our range; that we may be the means of improving or of reproving it, without being injured by it.

Our mutual friend, Mr. Lane, has detailed so minutely and fully our present vocations and intents, that nothing remains for me to add, but my pleasure in all he has written, and to repeat my earnest hope that Providence may include yourself, with all your fine gifts and graces, in the circle of our family. Your own sense of rectitude must plant or transplant you, according to its interior and superior dictates; and to it I submit the decision. . . Our Mother must not be deserted; if she feels you needful, and prefers to remain in Oriskany with you—then so let it be. We shall dwell together some day. I would that she might join us also—on a visit at least, if she declines making her home with us.

We are all waiting to see the earth (under the snow), and select our spot—a convenient house, orchards and fields—and begin to plant for our own sustenance. Great improvements have blessed my labors for the companion and children, during the winter. Mr. Lane is a most potent and friendly coadjutor, and will meet your idea of a man.

[1] Reprinted from Franklin B. Sanborn, *Bronson Alcott at Alcott House, England, and Fruitlands, New England (1842–1844)*, pp. 50, 51–52.

LETTER 43–7

[to Anna, Concord]

Concord, 16. April | 1843

For Anna.
(1843)

My daughter,

Your pretty present of a place mark for my Books gave me that pleasure which every affectionate act of yours always yields me. It is a fit token of your regard for a fathers' tastes, and an apt symbol of || the affection of || a daughters' interest in like pursuits. It is neatly wrought and delicately imagined, and as delicately conveyed to me. Be assured that I shall prize it, and that it will serve to remind me in my readings not only of a daughters kindred tastes but of her skill [word] in handling the needle—of domestic gifts and graces that so fitly adorn the womanly character, and prepare her for the discharge of her social duties. I need not add, what your discernment has already divined the assurance of my hopes in the integrity and steadiness of your character, and the rewards which these shall bring to yourself and those who know you, as you come more and more into the future opening upon you. My daughter, upon you it devolves to sustain, by the virtues of your own cherishing, the hopes and interests your father has so long espoused and amidst many hindrances, endeavoured to carry into actual life—hopes and interests, which are yours by birth right, by inheritance, and the elections of your own heart. Sully not either your nature or name—the inherent love of justice and the kind humanities of blood which descend to you from your mother, or whatsoever of pure and good may run in your veins from || your father || [p. o.] another [p. in]. A career of noblest usefulness awaits you—you are favored above || the || [p. o.] many [p. in] daughters of men; fewer hindrances and temptations beset you from within and without, and according to your genius and position in the spiritual state, should be your faithfulness and

101

energy in the duties laid upon you. A few years will transfer you into new ‖ and most ‖ [p. o.] responsibilities, scenes and states, and make ‖ large ‖ [p. o.] demands upon your gifts and graces. Assiduously cultivate them; ornament your mind and heart with pure manners, cherish every divine trait of your being, and be all that the love and confidence of a Father can desire or portray. dear Anna, I am yours in the depths of a serene and confiding affection, which more by silence than speech, through acts than words, would [p. in] manifest‖ s ‖ [p. o.] its constant and abiding presence.
Concordia 16 April 1843.
For
  Anna Bronson Alcott
      Concordia

LETTER 43–8[1]

[to Junius S. Alcott, Oriskany Falls, N.Y.]
                    Fruitlands, Harvard, (Mass) June 18 1843.
Dear Brother,
    I begin my letter, as you see, with dating from Harvard, not Concord, from Fruitlands, the name we give to the spot we now occupy, and which we design to use for divine ends in future. The Estate is within 2 miles of the village of Harvard, and less than one mile of Still River hamlet. It contains nearly 100 acres all arable land, easily cultivated, and finely adapted to the culture of grains, herbs, roots, and fruit. About 15 acres are in wood, of oak, maple, walnut, chestnut, some pine, and the timber is very thrifty, and quite sufficient for fuel,[2] and building. There is already some fruit; apples, cherries and peaches, and the intervales and hillslopes offer most favorable scites for orchards. The meadows are prolific; and the uplands bring good crops of wheat, maize, and other useful crops. ‖ The whole can be irrigated by ‖ [p. o.] There are many [3 p. in] springs which descend from the uplands into the fields and meadows and pass off into the Still River which flows on the West of us into the Nashua. We are within sight of the Shaker Families in Shirley; a couple of miles distant across the Stream.—We have just completed the planting and pruning. About 3 acres of corn are now nearly ready for the hoe; we have about 2 acres in potatoes; 1 in beans; and are preparing an acre or two more for barley, carrots, turnips, beans; and have commenced ploughing for winter wheat and rie. Of oats, we have an acre of spring rie about 2 acres to harvest in their seasons.—The buildings [torn] a two story dwelling house, a large barn and cow-house, with a small barn in the intervale being ill-placed, unsightly, and inconvenient, we have not redeemed for our future use: we are to inhabit the first, and store our crops in the second during the present season; when they are all to be removed by the owner from the estate, unless we are determined to convert them into the new cottages which we purpose to build in the margin of the wood, as soon as we can—within the present season we hope.—For the land $1800 was paid, and we would put as much into cottages—perhaps even more. The spot deserves all that we design in

the way of ornament architectural, and agricultur[al?] and will reward us for ‖ our taste ‖ any outlay of taste, industry, and love. There is a living fountain, from which we may derive water for all household uses, for drink, cooking, bathing &c, and which may easily be carried to any apartment of our dwellings, and to the gardens, and pass thence into the rich peat lands near by to the river. We are planning a dam, not far from this Spring, by which we ‖ can ‖ [p. o.] hope to [p. in] gain a head of water of two or three feet, for mechanical uses. The place is quite remote from the busy haunts and thoroughfares of trade; it lies in a sequestered dell, and is reached by private lanes on either side. We are thus protected from the invasion of the ruder secular world, and enjoy the quietude ‖ and ‖ of a dignified independence. The neighbours seem thus far quite kindly disposed; and what may be a glad surprize to you, especially to Chatfield and his wife, is that Mr Egarton, a brother, I believe of Mrs Bailey, is with in sight of us, and but a single farm divided his lands from those on which we dwell. He spoke of their visiting him when they were in Mass, a few years ago. I cannot but think this neighborhood will have some other attractions to you ‖ all ‖ now then heretofore, and we shall look for some of you to see us in autumn. There is land enough to support ‖ two ‖ [p. o.] many [p. in] persons, and facilities for almost every worthy object of desire that outward advantages can offer. We shall find many benefits in some near intimacy. I wish you would all think seriously of it, and write us in time concerning your purposes.—The place is paid for: and our next enterprize of an outward nature is fit buildings: Your talent, skill, and cooperation will serve us, yourselves and posterity.

There are now with us, beside Mr Lane and his boy, a Mr Larned,[3] lately from Mr Ripley's community, Abram[4] whom you know, (and a most efficient soul he is;) a Mr Bower,[5] a year since from England, and known to Mr. Lane; and a man working [torn] wages on the farm. The latter, boards and lodges at a neighbours. Several other persons are expected soon. Greene and his wife have not yet come. We shall have as many seekers as we deserve, and laborers and love for them all—Dyer[6] remains on his native mountains a little while longer. He visits us in autumn whether to remain time will prove. We are all in the most hopeful health and spirits, I am as busy as I can well be. The farm, orchard, children, library, press, public, repairs, building &c, give me abundant care: I should have added truest delight. This dell is the canvas on which I will paint a picture (Divinity prospering the design, and adding the means)—a worthy picture for mankind. My friend Lane, blessed of the like influence, shall be a not unapt coadjutor in the humane work.

My visit gave me renewed hopes of you all. It does one good to see the faces of his kindred.[7] Much love to Mother;—regard to your newly-given companion; and the greatest confidence in the integrity of those brothers and sisters near you.

Write me soon. Chatfield will not I am sure, go silent now. I shall hear from you with hope and delight

Your kindred brother
A. Bronson Alcott

J. S. Alcott

Junius S Alcott
Oriskany Falls
New-York

[1] MS. owned by the Fruitlands and Wayside Museums.
[2] Amended in pencil to read "*but* quite *in*sufficient for fuel." The tone of the letter indicates the penciled change was effected at a later date.
[3] Samuel Larned of Providence.
[4] Abram Wood. "The transcendentalism of this last individual showed itself chiefly in insisting upon twisting his name hind side before and calling himself 'Wood Abram.' As this he was always known at Fruitlands." Sears, *Bronson Alcott's Fruitlands*, p. 21.
[5] Samuel Bower of Andover, Massachusetts.
[6] Benjamin Dyer of Braintree, Vermont.
[7] Alcott had visited his mother at Oriskany Falls shortly before his move to Fruitlands.

LETTER 43–9[1]

[to Elizabeth, Fruitlands, Harvard, Mass.]

[Fruitlands, Harvard, Mass., June 24, 1843]

Ode to Elisabeth

On her Birth Day at Fruitlands,
June 24, 1843.

Here in the Grove
With those we love,
In the cool shade
Near mead & glade
With clover tints oerlaid,
Ahaunt that God—ourselves—have made;
The Trees among
With leaves oe'r hung,
On sylvan plat,
On forest mat,
By meadow sweet
We take our seat,
Whilst all around
Outswells the sound
Our happy hearts repeat.
The wood and dell
Our joy to tell
The morning air
Our peace to share
Flows by us cool
A balmy school
The sun his fires
His kindled ires
Not yet inspires
In midnoon blaze
His scorching rays;
But all is soft, & calm, and clear,
And all breathes peace around us here.

II

Works, wake, harmonious swell
Along the deep sequestered dell,
Along the grass and brake,
And where the cattle slake
Their thirst; where glides
Adown the sloping sides,
    In ceaseless fret,
    The wizard rivulet:
And let the springing maize
Join in the violin's note
In hymning forth our praise
From every jubilant throat,
Our holiest joy to raise.

III

Father's here
And Mother dear,
And sisters' all
The short & tall;
And father's friends
Whom Britian [*sic*] lends[2]
To noblest human ends,
With younger arm
From "Brooklet Farm";
_____ But absent now,
        At yonder plow
        With cleaving share
Upturning to the vital air
The unyielding soil,
        The sober Son of hardy toil.

IV

Hither we all repair
Our hope and love to bear,
        To celebrate
        In rustic state,
Mid'st this refulgent whole
The joyful advent of an angel soul,
That, twice four years ago
Our mundane life to know,
Descended from the upper skies
A presence to our very eyes,
And now before us stands
And asketh at our bounteous hands
Some tokens of our zeal
In her celestial weal—

Before us stands displayed
In raiment of a maid,
Unstained and pure her soul
As when she left the Whole
That doth this marvellous scene unrol [*sic*]
And day by day doth preach
The Gospels meant for each
That on this solid sphere
Designed for mortals were.

V.

Then take our tokens all
From Great to Small;
   take all & make them thine;
‖ And ‖ Closer that nobler treasure keep
That in your Heart doth sleep.
Mind what the spirit saith
And plight thereto thy faith
My very dear Elisabeth:
Nor let the enemy reap
The heavenly harvest from that field divin[e]
   Nor tares permit to grow
   Nor hate nor wo,
In the pure soil God's grace itself would so[on][?] sow
Bud, bloom, and ripen all the day
And be a flower that none shall pluck away
A rose in Fruitlands quiet dell,
A Child intent in doing well;
Devote, secluded from all sin
Fragrant without, & fair within,
A plant matured in Gods device,
An Amaranth in Paradise.

Fruitlands 24. June 1843.

---

[1] This birthday ode to Elizabeth is also quoted, with minor changes, in Sears, *Bronson Alcott's Fruitlands*, pp. 94–97.
[2] Lane and Wright.

[Letter to Chatfield Alcott, Oriskany Falls, N.Y.; from Fruitlands, before August 4, 1843.]

LETTER 43-10

[to Chatfield Alcott, Oriskany Falls, N.Y.]

Fruitlands, Harvard, 4. August 1843

Dear Brother

My last letter was chiefly given, I believe, to the subject of our settlement in a Family, and to some of the earlier details of our doings here. I am still deeply interested in these family arrangements and a good deal has been done by us, during the short time we have been here, to improve the lands, in growing crops for winter use and in preparing for yet more extensive and varied operations in the spring. Our crops are promising: the corn, potatoes, beans, melons, oats, rye, buckwheat, &c are abundant, and promise a ready reward for our labour. The hay has yielded us a profitable crop, and not a spire of it has been injured by the rains. Our early harvest is all stored; and the ploughing for winter and spring grains and roots is in a state of forwardness. We have ploughed in some acres of fine clover as a sweet manure for our garden plants in spring, and are putting the estate in order as fast as our men and means will allow.

Our family has numbered 15 or 16 members during a part of the season; but is smaller by three or four persons at present, when we have less need of assistance. The care and burden of the work, falls on Abba and myself. It is most agreeable to me, and had Abba like assistance in the household department, she would have been less busied with manifold duties. But her assiduity has been constant, and her courage equal to these pressing labours. She has been in remarkable health, and continues, with the assistance of the little girls, and such help as I can give, to do all the work needful for our comfort within doors. We have so simplified our mode of living in many particulars, that but a small time is required in comparison with the usual methods, and we all feel the more comfortable and independent, by the change, to say nothing of the moral and religious benefits we experience; and we are daily making improvements in all practical ways. I wish you were one of us, one with us, in these benefits. And I cannot readily yield the hope which my late visit but served to quicken, of your becoming inmates of our Family, and coworkers with us in this good enterprize. You are riper for it than most of those who linger yet in the beaten ways of worldly business, and have had invitations from superiour sources to unite your estates, your family with ours. I am sure you will be with us sooner or later. Yourself and companion are worthy of nobler things than those which claim the ambition of the multitude. I am the more desirous of seeing you now, because a prospect opens, more inviting than I expected, of our entering sooner into the realization of our hopes, by the occupancy, (and that immediately) of a most desirable Estate in Leominster, but 10 miles from us. An exchange of our means here needs but to be effected, and for this time is permitted us. This Estate contains 150 acres; of 50 or more of which are as valuable as any lands in the county of Worcester, and the woodlands are very thrifty and ample. There is an abundance of fruits of all kinds: the buildings are spacious; the mansion house—very commodious, and the grounds beautifully disposed, both for use and profit. A water privilege is found on the place, and another just by, which in past times has been used, but is now superseded by mills in another quarter. Either of these would serve our purposes. The place was improved some twenty years ago by an opulent gentleman who invested large sums in fences, trees for use and ornament, and who made it at the time, the richest and most desirable residence in the vicinity. The fruits of his labour and taste still remain; indeed, are just ripening to maturity; the orchards, are in their prime; the fences are mostly in good repair; the timber is thriving, the meadows, are productive; the arable fields are enriched, and the dwelling house and barns, are in very good repair. It is within two miles of the Village, & the rail road depot is to come within a mile of the house. We obtain the whole for about $5000. Two thousand we pay by exchange of this property here in Harvard; as much more we can have from a *Mr Palmer,*[1] who is interested in our plans, and who holds estates near us, and unites with us in the purchase. The other thousand comes from Mrs Alcott's family. This for the present transaction. But I desire a better: and that is this— I would that you should put your means, or a part of them into this estate, including of course the water privileges, and come and abide with us. We hope to be on the estate soon, and then it would be our wish to have you and your family take possession of the house in common, as we could find most desirable. Junius and his wife and mother and Ambrose and Betsey (if she will) should be with us also. Of Junius, indeed, I am most sure. Now, I wish you to take this matter into serious consideration at once, and so arrange your affairs as to pay us an early visit, and let us settle the important points at once. Come and see us; view the Estate, judge of our designs, and see if you are not commanded to be with us. Give up your present, for a superiour employment, as we talked when I was with you. Your good wife and brother, are ready I trust to move with you. Let us do something worthy of our selves and the gifts we inherit. Your wife will be near her relations here, your children, yourself, and kindred, in company and condition, superiour to any into which you are likely [to] enter for ‖ the ‖ your improvement and well-being. ‖ of your ‖ I do no[t] see how you can resist or refuse this important chance for bettering all your fortunes, secular and moral. But I will not press the matter. Write me, or indite for Junius to write, your thoughts and decisions about this matter. We shall not doubt of your coming to visit us: and shall look for you. Will Junius and his wife come also. They should be with us: they should not stay from advantages of the kind we have in store for them and yourselves. Decide this matter as its importance demands.

I have nothing so important to communicate as this, and add only my affectionate desire of beholding your faces soon to remain as inmates of the Family, and coworkers for the same divine ends.

A. Bronson Alcott

Tell me about Mother.

I esteem the water privileges most valuable for our purposes. Yourself, Junius, and Ambrose, Linus too, if he chooses, would find ready employment and fine facilities for your mechanical skill, and ready exchange for your work. I consider the benefits of company especially for your children's education above all price. But no more. Write me soon. Don't fail.

Aug 9— A.B.A.

We are all going now to see the place. Palmer is here.

Aug. 10—

Mr. Chatfield Alcott
Oriskany Falls
New-York.

[1] Joseph Palmer, who became a member of the Fruitlands Community and bought the place when the experiment failed. A good sketch of him is to be found in Sears, *Bronson Alcott's Fruitlands*, pp. 53–67.

LETTER 43–11

[to Anna, Boston]

Sunday Novr [26] 1843

For Anna
1843
Fruitlands

Dear Anna,

I miss your presence from our Family Circle, and wish you heartily again with us. And by your letters I learn that you as heartily desire to be an inmate of our house, humble and out of the way as it is, and simple as are our household thoughts and ways. Come home to us as soon as you will. Your visit will be a lesson to you, and I doubt not you will derive the good it was meant to teach you. The show and bustle of the great town seems less grateful to your simple tastes than the quiet plainness of our rural retreat: we have enjoyments that neither gold nor silver can give and employments that can neither soil our hands nor taint our thoughts, with impure aims or urge to unworthy deeds. Beautiful, indeed, and as comely to Heavens' eye, as to the sight of man, is a pure and Holy Family, whose inmates are united in a serene and lively love, and whose hands and hearts are alike servants of a gentle and all-[word] affection. The sun shines not on a lovelier scene; nor can all the gaudy glories of the town, its arts, amusements, its pleasures and shows, add lustre to its beauty, or give charm to its enjoyments[,] or send elegance and peace to its thresholds. Only the rustic beauties of field and dell, of woods and fountains[,] of gardens and orchards, are fit ornaments, and worthy accompanyments [sic] of such simple persons; only in such scenes and the employments to which they prompt, is the abode of truest love and purest content.

> "I roamed the world around,
> For Home and Friend I sought;
> All spots, all climes, surveyed—
> Man, woman, maid—
> Beauty terrestrial I found;
> Estates and men were bought;
> Friends, gifts were won:
> But whereso'er I sent,
> Where'er th' refulgent sun
> His glories cast,
> Oe'r cities vast,
> Oe'r desarts [sic] waste,
> On man or continent,
> To me came meek Content,
> My constant habitant,
> In humblest cot,
> Midst orchard plot,
> Where, with familiar friends
> I dwelt to holiest ends,
> And tenures free are given
> By love divine and Heaven."

All things remain as when you left us. But all manner of plans are drawn for our residence and way of living in the future. Providence will overrule all our schemes for good; so that whether we stay *Here,* or go *There,* matters little. You are just opening to an interest in our outward welfare; may you be warmed also to a living regard for our inward blessedness. Nature may appear cold, and her countenance wear frowns to the faithless, but to the loving she smiles always. Even so, though the winter is coming, and the mountain-tops are hoar in the distance. Come, you, my daughter, and drink of the lively warmth of our hearthstone while this yet remains to us.—Mother desires me to leave space for her, and so I will withdraw, for the moments that separate us, and leave you to her kindlings of love and words of intelligence.

Your Father.

To
  Anna Bronson Alcott
    in Boston

[Letter to Junius S. Alcott, Oriskany Falls, N.Y.; from Fruitlands, November, 1843.]

LETTER 44–1

[to Anna]

Still River, 16 March 1844

With a Poem, and Daguerreotype
Likeness.

(Poem lost)[?]

My earliest born!
On this Birth morn,
A little Poem I'll read to thee,
Thine own, with his Biography,
Sketched swiftly from the elden Past
That hath us both oer cast,
And holds us in its Vast,
And is the dark mysterious Page
Of Life's terrestrial Age;
Where [word] by Hand divine
Appear ourselves in line
And in deeper signatures,
Our Spiritual miniatures:
Painted by the Eternal Sun
As he along doth run;

Behold thy Father's face
As erst twas lightly cast
Within this framed space
By distant limner's taste.

And take it with thee keep
Till he shall fall asleep.

Harvard 16 March
1844

LETTER 44–2[1]

[to Junius S. Alcott, Oriskany Falls, N.Y.]

Still River, Harvard, Mass. 15-June | 1844

Dear Brother,

I must not suffer another day to pass, without assuring you of my remembrance. Lately, indeed, you have been much in my thoughts, and I have not seldom fancied you on your way to see us here in Mass: frequently I have fancied || seen || you alighting at our humble door, and my hand extended to grasp yours. I desire greatly to see you now. For I am all alone again; and you seem the sole person in the wide world, designed as a faithful coadjutor—a lover of the Excellent and willing to join in the attainment of the same day by day, with the constancy of a true lover. Is there no possibility of our meeting soon? I have been on the point of setting out to visit you, (perhaps remain with you a little while,) several times; but my family detains me yet. I am doing little, beside planting and dressing my garden. We came here in April, and purpose remaining till autumn. Where I am to go next does not appear. Lane left me, and joined the Shakers nearby, where he now is.[2] And "Fruitlands, our former place, is in their care || care of the Shakers ||. So we found another residence where we are, for the time being. I am unwilling to join any of the Communities in Mass—they aim at little, and are but new phases of the Spirit of Old Society. I must have something better, and of vastly nobler aim, than these. Sometimes I think of the West, as the scite for a True Family settlement, such as I cherish; and you are || one if not || my main Hope and stay in such an enterprize. I fancy Chatfield is disposed too, with his family, by this time, for something better than his present condition yields him. You too, have had *much* experience since I saw you;—what do you purpose for the coming years? Write me at once. I should have written you long ago, but have lived on from week to week, hoping to have something positive to tell you, and || now || here it is, June, and you have waited since November last, without getting a word from me. And now I have nothing but Hopes and wishes to impart; but I must hear from you at once.

|| Abba || [p. o.] My wife [2 p. in] is well, and all the children. A little income—her support nearly—falls to her from her Fathers' Estate.[3] But she will bind her interests with mine, I trust, and rely on something more sure and worthy than Boston Gold;—asserting a true and brave independence by adherence to the la[w] of Justice, and the labors of self-support. We shall see.

Can't you visit us soon? yourself or Chatfield. You may be sure of our joy at beholding your faces. How is dear Mother? will she not come; or are we too unsettled for her love of quiet and comfort. But we shall see each other soon. My regards to your good companion, and all my friends there.

Your brother
A Bronson Alcott

Write me at once, do. Yesterday Emerson was here; and Abram has just come with, a little Book which he has just published entitled "My First and last Book," he has one fo[r you b]ut knows not how to get it to you. Goodby—
Monday 17—

Harvard Mas,
    June 17

Junius S. Alcott
  Oriskany Falls
    New York

---

¹ MS. owned by the Fruitlands and Wayside Museums.
² Lane and his son left Fruitlands on January 7, 1844. The Alcotts left about a week later.
³ Col. Joseph May had died in 1841.

LETTER 44–3

[to Elizabeth, Still River, Harvard, Mass.]
                    At Mr Lovejoy's, Still River, | Harvard, June 24th. 1844.
My very dear Elisabeth,
    I have always given you some little present of gifts and notes on your Birth days. Last Year we celebrated this day, you remember with pleasure I dare say, at Fruitlands. Then I wrote a little Ode for you, and all of us were very happy in the grove, and gave you our little gifts. To day we celebrate it in a different way. I have no verses now for you, but this little note, with a pretty China Cameo of "Love", which I brought from England. The Cameo will be a handsome toy to have a place among your nicely arranged treasures, and remind you of your Fathers' pleasure in your quiet, neat, and orderly ways, and help to make you more so, as you grow older, and other toys of furniture, and cares of housewifery, and of living things, are entrusted to you.
    Sweet hopes your Father has of you, my quiet and thoughtful Child. Surely, nothing on your part shall disappoint him. You are nine Years of age: a few more years will bring you to be a woman. Continue to use your mind faithfully: study to be kind, gentle, diligent, obedient, and thus enjoy the praise of your own dutiful Heart, and you need not then regard the Praise or Blame of others. Sweet are the words of an approving Conscience, and beloved of God and all good people, are the obedient and gentle Children in all the Families on the Earth. May my dear Elisabeth ever hear its soft whispers in her Heart, loving all that is pure and good.
    I hope you will enjoy the company of your friends on this Birth day. Kind Mother has done much to make the time pleasant to you, and your sisters have been busy to minister to your joy. And now, as I write, dear Anna brings me a useful gift to present you, lest I should chance be unfurnished, or forget to do

as all your friends delight in doing; so I present it with my other gift—the Beautiful and the Useful together.—

From your hopeful
Father.

For
  Elisabeth S. Alcott.

LETTER 44-4

[to Mrs. A. Bronson Alcott, Still River, Harvard, Mass.]

Oriskany Falls, N.Y. July [19] 1844

Dear,

You will be glad to hear of our[1] arrival here, and learn what we are purposing for the days to come. We had a most quiet and expeditious journey. Leaving Worcester at 6 oclock we reached Springfield and were comfortably disposed in adjoining chambers at the American ‖ Hotel ‖ House before 9, where we slept, and set off at 7 in the morning (—Tuesday), crossed the Hudson at Albany at noon, and reached Utica at sunset. There being no stage till some time the next day, we ‖ were ‖ set off immediately ‖ disposed ‖ for Oriskany, in a private carriage, and reached Chatfields the same day, not however till all were in bed. We saw Chatfield and his wife a little while, and, somewhat wearyed [sic], sought rest. On coming to Breakfast the next morning we found the brothers and sisters all ‖ there ‖ present, and Mother among the rest. All were well, (saving the usual abatements of complaints ‖ of low spirits ‖ & ailments) and glad to see us. Mother returned a few weeks since from Pamela's who came to Oriskany with her, and left, after a short visit, in good spirits. Mother seems even more lively than I expected to find her: but has her usual turns of depression. She was not purposing to visit us this Summer, but reserved the pleasure till we ‖ were ‖ are more settled. Wednesday she invited me to take a little ride with her, and we had a most cozy time, chatting incessantly all the way, the horse having as comfortable a time of it, as ourselves, for he took his own way and speed all to himself, walking most gravely all the while up and down the slopes about the little ‖ business and ‖ busy village of Oriskany. She means to spend her "last days," as she calls, them with us, and hopes much from your kind and healing influences. I catch now and then the same benignant smile and gentle tone, that were the joy of my childhood and the encouragement of my Youth. May her last days be as calm and serene, as the memory of these to me now in the prime of my manhood. I think she will incline to remain with Chatfield at present.

Junius and his wife had just returned from Wolcott. He left home with a design to visit us, but heard, while at Phebe's whose husband returned from Oriskany, while he was in Wolcott, of our fortunes at Fruitlands, and so did not extend his journey into Massachusetts. He is about leaving this place: whether for Massachusetts or elsewhere is yet undetermined. On Monday we purpose setting off for Skaneateles,[2] and Marengo, to be gone five or six days. At the latter place are a few persons whose plans deeply interest me, and whose principles are so akin to those dear to me, that I feel strongly disposed to know more of them. The Estate on which they are living is about 60 miles from Oriskany and 10 or 15 from Skaneateles. I may be well to cast my eye on the deeds and designs of these persons while I am so near.—Anna is lively and happy, I believe, but she shall speak for herself.—All love to the daughters and wife left in Still River.—You shall hear from us again soon; when I hope to have more of interest to communicate.

A. Bronson Alcott

Oriskany Falls NY
July 19th
Mrs Abba Alcott
  Still River, Harvard,
    Mass.

¹ Anna accompanied her father.
² The Skaneateles Community, led by John A. Collins, was started in 1843. It was located in Mottville, Onondaga County, New York.

LETTER 44–5

[to Junius S. Alcott, Wolcott, Conn.]

Concord 28 October 1844.

Dear Brother,

Yours of 14th Sept from Wolcott found me in the midst of arrangements for moving to this place, and I delayed writing, in answer, till we should be disposed for the coming winter, and some further insight, if possible, be obtained of our future disposal and endeavours. Immediately on my return from Oriskany, I set about looking for places adapted to our purpose, or which might be made to serve us, within the neighborhood of Boston and Concord; feeling a deeper conviction than before, that I am best fitted to act on men and things in Massachusetts, although I might easily be drawn into my native State if assured of the company and objects which I desire to secure and promote. Even our early friend Dr. Alcott might be drawn into some good enterprize and cooperate happily with us. But I feel || even || more strongly than when I saw you last, that there are very few, if any, persons, ready to unite fully with us, in the ends and measures we cherish; and that yourself and my family, are the only associates with which I am to be favored at present. If we perform wisely our parts, Providence will send us worthy company in due time. A few are looking on with hopeful interest, and need the braver hope and surer hands of some one or two, whom they love and trust, to engage in the good life. Jewett, of Haverhill, a practical handicraftsman, ingenious and wise like yourself in the useful arts, a cabinet maker at present, is very desirous of entering into truer relations, and seems better fitted than most to this end. His wife is ready also for this change. I visited him a few weeks since and am expecting him here soon. He will assist in the purchase of an Estate, or build on one, as shall be deemed best. He has a little property; and but himself, wife, and one child, to provide for. Henry Thoreau, is interested in || the || our simple plan of life, and might, at times, be one of our house and field mates. Emerson has offered to buy me a few acres and build me a plain house and Mr May and others desire to aid in placing us

114

on the soil, free of rents and landlords. I hope to obtain space and dwellings for several families by these means. I cannot consent to live solely for one family: I would stand in neighborly relations to several, and interpose an internal check to all selfish and narrow interests: institute a union and communion of families, instead of *drawing aside within the precincts of one's own acres and kindred by blood.*

There are several places within a mile or two of Edmund Hosmers,[1] (half of whose house we occupy till an estate is found,) that might serve us very well; some with buildings; but the best without. And, for myself, I prefer to build after a better model, than accept the ill constructed and inconvenient tenements which deform our landscape, and offend by their unsightliness. You, too, if I remember, prefer to build; and you will need all your means for a house, without taking part for the purchase of land: Put it on the Estate purchased with Emerson's generosity, and let us have no show of deeds or dollars in the matter. With the $12 or 1500 there are at command, soil may be obtained and foothold for us all. I want, more than I express, your company and cooperation, and see now no hindrance of a secular nature, to hold us apart. Now seems the time to bring matters which have long been lagging shiftlessly behind to a decision. I hope it is ‖ neither ‖ your purpose to visit me this autumn. Come soon, and bring that faithful spouse of yours, and see with your own eyes what there is here for you. If Wolcott is not the place for you, then Concord, or wherever I may settle, unquestionably is. Come and let us determine this very important question. The Rail roads bring you within a mile of us, and you ‖ can ‖ can come, by Meridan,[2] nearly the whole distance, cheaply, and swiftly by steam, or in your horse and wagon in a couple of days. We were speaking yesterday of you, when Edmund Hosmer expressed his deep respect, and added, "that you were the only person whom he had seen fitted alike by natural and spiritual gifts to abide with me." Good brother, tis, verily, so: Providentially we are Brothers by Nature and Grace.

What you say of Phebe is saddening: faithful soul, with as soft and tender a heart as beat ever in a womans breast, she is releaved [sic] from the sufferings that toil and unrequited affection imposed: a blessed exchange for her, and a righteous discipline of the partner, (if indeed he was such ‖ save ‖ in any thing but a participation in the avails of her trials) You will see that her children are taken care of. I have sometimes harbored the idea of taking orphans, as the readiest means of bringing up worthy members of the true Church and State. Possibly, Betsey and hers might be subjects of our regard.

How seem your days in the factory: and how likes your companion the company she finds in her new neighborhood. I shall be anxious to hear from you soon: write me, or come yourselves along at once. Mother writes me, that she expects Ambrose to return to Oriskany; and I should not be surprised at her venturing this way again with him.

Anna returned greatly impressed by her Western journey. She begs Uncle Junius and Aunt Jane[3] to come and live in Concord near us. There is a beautiful spot on Walden Pond, half a mile from us, of 11 acres clearing, and 4 of wood which Emerson will give me, and build a house on it: the land is thinnish, but would yield garden crops and fruits, with some cultivation: it needs enriching by forest leaves, muck, of which there are plenty at hand. The Hallowell place nearly opposite the bridge close by the Cliffs is for sale—30 acres cultivated, and wood lots near—$1000; another estate in sight of the Emersons, of 20 acres with a thrifty young orchard, and wood lot—$1200. Small places of 10 acres, with houses, near the village cost about the same sums.—one of 5 acres for $500.

Anna commences going to school in the village to day. Emerson has just published a second Book of Essays. I keep much at home, busy in domestic duties. Lane is writing letters to England on Shakerism. I have not seen him since my return from the West.

Your Brother A Bronson Alcott.

My wife presses you visiting us this autumn if you possibly can. She desires to know your companion, and has much to say about your dwelling near us. If you cannot come soon let me know. My business during the winter mont[hs] will be determined by *your movements* in so[me] measure.[4]

Junius S Alcott

Wolcott

Connecticut.

[1] A Concord farmer and a cousin of the Hosmer family whose Cottage the Alcotts had rented before going to Fruitlands.

[2] Meriden, Connecticut.

[3] Junius' wife.

[4] This letter would seem to indicate that despite the period of extreme mental depression Alcott went through following the failure at Fruitlands, he had not abandoned his hopes for some sort of communal living.

PART SIX

⚓

1845–1848

[to Junius S. Alcott, Wolcott, Conn.]

[Concord] Thursday Morning, 2nd. January, | 1845.

My very Brother,

Yours of Dec. 1st was duly recd. and its contents very grateful to me. I know not how it is, but your sympathy and company seem almost needful to sustain my hopes and cheerfulness in the solitudes to which I am driven. But I yet know that I must not trust too hopefully even in these, since our reliance is on higher and nearer Powers than Persons; and success comes of Divine succours. Our friends are endeavouring to plant us here in Concord; and this wish of theirs is perhaps the clearest purpose of Providence yet made known to us, and so is to be accepted.[1] Close by Emerson's, under the brow of the Hill, lies a very pretty spot—the Boston Road running between the House and the fertile field of 8 acres, every rod of which is adapted to gardening, and lies warmly to the sunny south. The house is a convenient structure, and with some additions and repairs would serve two families, being two stories, with large parlours and chambers. There is a woodhouse, and a Shop—the latter, with a little cost, may be converted into a good cottage house, as roomy as your Oriskany tenement. There are a few Fruit trees || are || beginning to bear. Emerson will give the 8 acres, in trust to us, for all such as desire to come upon a free soil, and to occupy and till the earth un- molested by loads of land or men—tax-gatherers, usurers, and other oppressors of freemen. There is land not quite sufficient for the support of several families; and I will not abide in a House set apart for myself and family alone. The law of Love opens arms and doors to our spiritual kindreds nor selfishly appropriates the gifts offered to these related by ties of blood only. Two families may live comfortably in the House, and another in the Shop. $3 or 400 will put the build- ings in good repair; or move the Barn to a more suitable foundation, and put us all in a good way to begin our endeavor. The whole will cost about $1400 (build- ings and land—9 acres—) and, if you could lend us your skill, the repairs would not add greatly to this amount. Think of it: come as soon as you can: immedi- ately, if possible, and look and decide for yourself. April, and the labours of the Garden, will soon be here. Your devoted companion should visit and know us better. We are learning to live righteously, and all injoy health, with freedom from debt and servitude. Emerson, Thoreau &c are busy as usual. I regret my inability to return the $12. to Mother before, and send them enclosed herein to you, not knowing whether Mother is in Wolcott or at Oriskany. Do as you think safest and best about getting the money to her if she is still in N-York. Perhaps she will incline to come to Massachusetts in the Spring: undoubtedly, if you come here to abide. I desire this above all things, and 'tis Abba's fervent wish. Perhaps some of Phebe's children might find homes with us. There are several persons who would like to live near, or with us. I believe Providence is providing a *Home* for a Company of pure and true persons. You will be ready, I am assured to enjoy it with us. If you prefer to build yourself a cottage on the 8 acres, there is a fine scite, and as generous soil as any in Concord; free to your occupancy and use. $500 will build you a neat dwelling. Write me directly; and tell me when you will visit us. My regards to all in Wolcott. Tell me about Ambrose; will he like Massachusetts? Write me (if you will) how your affairs stand. I trust you are fast relieving yourself from debts and the evils of the same. Can I aid you in any way? We begin the year with the comforting assurance of freedom from all secular thraldom. And are releasing ourselves, I humbly hope, from every yoke of oppressive indulgence

> Faithfully Your Brother
> A. Bronson Alcott.

Junius S. Alcott
    Wolcott
        Connecticut

---

[1] Alcott here refers to "Hillside" to which place they moved on April 1. The money for its purchase ($1,350) came in part from the estate of Col. Joseph May and in part from Emerson. In 1852, Nathaniel Hawthorne bought the property for $1,500 and renamed it "The Wayside."

LETTER 45–2

[to Junius S. Alcott, Wolcott, Conn.]

Concord 28th January 1845.

Dear Brother,

I wrote to you on the first of this month,[1] enclosing $12 for mother, thinking she might have returned with Ambrose and be with you. A few days ago, we received a letter from Oriskany, informing us of her continuance there, and of her ill health, and low spirits. She feels the absence of her children; and will rejoin us, if possible, I doubt not, as soon as the Spring opens, to smile on her journey eastward. Whether she will incline to come to Concord, depends, I fancy, on the prospect of your settling here with us. She seems to cling, with fondness and hope to you. And I please myself, in turn, with the promise that our words may soon become deeds, and yourself and mother, join us in the family life, so grateful to us all. There seems nothing to hinder a settlement of this kind: nothing, at least, of an outward and secular nature; and our fitness for fellowship can only be proved by actual trial. Providence human and divine, has freed us, and a little estate, at one and the same hour, and it seems fit for us to occupy these ‖ gifts ‖ gardens of the soil and the soul, for the growth and ornament of both, as worthy laborers in the service of Justice and Love.

Since I wrote you, the little spot near Emersons has been freed for our occupancy: and I see no foothold so unencumbered, on the whole, as these acres. I must wait,—an idler,—long, and perplexed with manifold considerations,—with still mixed conditions, or accept these premises, with all their drawbacks and difficulties, yet affording a field, if not of free and fair, yet *less* foul play, than is given to others: than most of my contemporaries indeed, are ready ‖ and ‖ or willing to occupy. It is a little pittance, but we should be ashamed to accept the exclusive use of it, and appropriate even the small inheritance to ourselves alone —confessing our poverty by such covetousness.—Come and look at it as soon as you can answer past demands and mortgages on your gifts and chattels. We purpose to move on the first of April. The House needs some repairs; a very little cost of labor and time will render it very convenient for two families. The apartments are large and distinct: private and sacred as we please to make them. The land is esteemed very fertile and lies handsomely along the road—affording fine scite for gardens and orchards: 8 acres will serve us well, if we do our part well by it: and the shop invites us to the exercise of whatsoever manual gifts may be ours. I shall wait to see or hear from you soon. It is quite unlikely that others will unite with us, especially at first. Few, perhaps not a solitary soul, is ready for such an enterprize; How far we are ourselves remains to be proved to us by actual trial. If a Holy Family is beyond us, we may, at least, exclude much that annoys and renders uncomely the Households on which we cast our eyes wheresoever we turn—on the world around us. To aim at simplicity and purity, amidst the ‖ extravagant ‖ [p. o.] profusion [p. in] and ‖ show ‖ [p. o.] corruption [p. in] every where about us, and none the less amidst indigence and rags, is, in itself, the noblest and most needful lesson we can teach our fellows.

> "Some great estates provide, but do not breed
> A mastering mind; so both are lost thereby;
> Or else they breed them tender, make them need
> All that they leave; this is flat poverty"

I am waiting for spring to open upon us. We abide at Hosmers. I read a little; help about the house: and try to reconcile my present idleness and solitude with my intentions and deserts. But the ways of God, are less clear to me, at times, than at former periods of my human life. Such a disproportion between my desires and deeds! ‖ such a withering of the members[?]: ‖ such a distance between the Heart and Hand! Surely it is Faith alone that can restore soundness to the whole Being: Faith that shall strengthen and renovate the Soul, and give energy and adroitness to the feeble Body. There is no company like the sweet presence of a noble purpose; no face so smiling as the beam of our Hearts through the simple deeds of a sincere and constant Love. Henceforth let the Gospel for us be preached from ‖ the lips of ‖ our fingers tips, and the sublimity of the Hand proclaimed to the busy-idle world!

Your Brother,
A. Bronson Alcott.

Junius S. Alcott
Wolcott
Connecticut.

¹ The preceding letter, 45–1, is dated January 2.

LETTER 45–3

[to Anna, Concord]

at Ed. Hosmers | Concord.

> Deny thyself, take up thy cross,
> Nor fear that thou shalt suffer loss;
> Nought can to thee be given,
> Unless thou yieldest Earth for Heaven.

March 16. 1845
Concord

Will my daughter, Anna, accept [this] Portfolio, as a neat dispository for [her] Papers. Her father gladly encourages every [in]dication of a love or habit of Order and [neat]ness, and would avail himself of all occasions [word?] inspire and cherish these graces of womanhood. [A] most fit occasion is this, your 14th Birth day: [May] it be a day of brave resolutions, as well as [word] amenities and congratulations. And to [word] you in so good a work, let me name a few [thin]gs, as the subjects of your prayers and trials—

Contentment with your lot in life:
Meek and gentle behaviour amidst all trials:
Constant watchfulness of yourself.
Surrender of your will to the commands of God's
    Spirit in your Conscience:
Putting all Wrong and Slavery far from you.
Self-Denial:
    These to begin with, relying on the aid of the Spirit ever ready to assist the faithful:

From Your Father.

LETTER 45–4

[to Junius S. Alcott, Wolcott, Conn.]

Concord April 6. 1845 | (Sunday)

Dear Junius,

We are now on the "Glebe" and expecting the pleasure of your becoming an early guest in the new mansion. But I take a moment to day to press our former invitation again. I would not hurry you, I know I cannot if I would: you will take your own fair time, nor be moved by any brother in the flesh. We have your promise of a visit, and wish to apprize you of our earnest desires to behold your face again. Spring already greens upon us, and the lands before our door will soon ask for all my skill, and will be grateful no less, for the tillage of other hands beside my own. There are six acres of fertile soil, and easy of tillage. I cannot dress the whole to advantage, and shall enjoy your company from day to day beside me in the field. There is enough, and to spare, for ourselves, & one or two beside. And there is present room for us in the Mansion House: and tenements near on sale, or rent, (if you will still commit these || social || civil sins). I wish you were here to advise concerning some repairs necessary to be made on the buildings. The carpenter begins in a few days and will soon give us still more room and accommodation.

Mr Jewett writes of visiting us: I am daily expecting him. I wish you may meet here and remain with us. It seems most desirable to me, and I persuade myself that it is to be. But am yet content to wait till the Wise God decree for us all: if concert fail us *here* there *is* a union, beyond times and changes, await-ing us: we are sure of our friends' presence in the life of the Spirit.

Abba is hoping to welcome yourself and wife; and Mother's comfort is never out of mind when she thinks of you. We have invited her to come and abide with us. If you were settled here, all doubts would cease; we know she would soon be with us, unless infirmities of age forbid her journeying. We have not heard from her lately: but you will inform us when you arrive; till then

devotedly your Brother
A.B.A.

Junius Alcott
   Wolcott
      Connecticut.

LETTER 45–5

[to Elizabeth, Concord]

Hillside, Concord, 24 June 1845.
My very dear Elisabeth,

Your dear little Head is so full of loving and quiet stillness, that I will not disturb its calm thoughtfulnes by any words of graver Wisdom: And so let me furnish your Feet with a neat covering, in which your footsteps may be as light as your gentle Heart, and swift as your Obedience. So take these from your Father, on this your Tenth Birth-Day.

Glebe. 24 June 1845.
Concord.

P.S. I hope the Shoes will fit your ready Feet, as nicely as does your still little Head the shape of your Mind.

LETTER 45–6

[to Junius S. Alcott, Wolcott, Conn.]

Concord 27 July 1845. | (Sunday)
To Junius S. Alcott,
My very dear Brother,

I have had you much in mind lately, and begin to be a little impatient to see you and yours on the spot which seems ‖ now ‖ destined to be our common haunt. In your last, you write of coming to us as soon as your child will bear the journey with safety and the mother risk herself abroad. I wish it may be soon. It seems most desirable to have you near and with me. There are so many things to be done which two can so much better dispose of, and I need your company, not less than your skill and counsel. I am still busy as ever a man need be. My garden has kept me hard at work, and the carpenters have made and are still making large and daily drafts on my time and thoughts. The repairs are going forward, and we hope to have comfortable rooms to offer you when you arrive. I have had the shop set at the end of the House, and it is now being partitioned and done off into several convenient rooms, making a neat house of itself. If you like it, we wish you to occupy it, and if you prefer to build there are fine spots adjoining on which you may set your cottage, residing for the time in this end of our dwelling. The House is large enough for us all. I have also moved the Barn to a better place, and am having it repaired for storing our crops, all of which look unusually promising. The improvements I am making render the Estate much more seemly, and vastly more easy of tillage, beside the greater convenience in-doors and about them. We shall be furnished with all that is needful in houses and lands. I trust you are fast bringing your affairs to adjustment, and will come free of incumbrance. Do, if possible, arrange all your business, and join us with the little you have, at such command as to benefit you in the readiest way. Land, you will not have to buy, here is enough for us all, and of the best quality, and you can build you a house or not build one just as you choose.

Mr Jewett || has bought || intends buying the lot adjoining for building a house and shop. He || has || will dispose|| d || of his effects in Haverhill and purposes to join us as soon as his buildings here can be erected: so you will not need be at the expense of a separate shop: he is a cabinet maker, and skillful in wood, like yourself; one shop will serve us all. We are expecting him to spend a few days with us in making necessary preparations for building and removal. Miss Ford is now with us, and a most useful aid in the house, and care of the Children.

I thought I would just write these particulars, and apprize you of our expectations of seeing you soon, and of abiding with us. All things now await your arrival amongst us.[1] We are all well, and very busy.

With regards to your wife and child,

I am, Your Brother,
A. Bronson Alcott.

Mr. Junius S. Alcott
Wolcott
Connecticut

[1] There is no evidence that Junius visited the Alcotts in Concord at this time.

LETTER 45–7[1]

[to Junius S. Alcott, Wolcott, Conn.]

Concord, August 1845

Our repairs indoors are now nearly complete, and fencing, levelling and underpinning are in daily progress. The garden is now luxuriant and yields abundantly of melons, corn, squashes, beets, tomatoes, beans, carrots, turnips, and your favorite oyster-plant, which we are waiting for you to show us how to prepare for the table. This week I am designing to sow some rye: the buckwheat is now fast ripening for our winter cakes: twelve or fourteen bushels of spring grain are awaiting the flail. Everything has prospered with our garden and improvements: I cannot pronounce like thrift in the human glebes and tenements. There is more of peace, I may say, and of faith and patience. But the house and inmates consecrated to the Spirit, and blest in union throughout, in every temper and design,—we yet hope for these. Who is he that has attained this hope?

¹ Reprinted from Sanborn, *Bronson Alcott at Alcott House, England, and Fruitlands, New England (1842–1844)*, pp. 94–95.

LETTER 46–1

[to Thomas Davis, Providence, R. I.]

Concord 2 Jan 1846

Yesterday served me greatly beyond my deservings. It brought some token of my friends' interest in me, or what I best aim to be; and made me unselfishly happy at finding myself in the thoughts of good people for the moment. But I am not informed just now of the means whereby to serve these friends and discharge my debt of Benefits: and so I fain receive from the Alms-basket of Charity without shame.¹ Doubtless the Great Task master will make plain my way, if, meanwhile, I steadfastly abide in Patience, and am faithful to the trusts of the current Hour, whether of [word] [wr]ought or of humble toil. Yet ‖ it is hard ‖ tis a weary work to be untasked, or doomed to put forth ‖ half ‖ [p. o.] a [word] of [3 p. in] our strength in idle refrainings when the deed we would, we may not yet do. Yet so it must sometimes be.

>   "   God doth not need
> Either man's work or his own gifts: who best
> Bear his mild yoke they serve him best; his state
> Is Kingly: thousands at his bidding speed
> And post oer land and ocean without rest:
> They also serve who only stand and wait."

And yet nothing seems more imperative at this hour than Action of some sort—and prevailing Action. The Time is pregnant with Revolution. Change is lurks [p. in] written on Human Affairs. And the Benignant Power is pledged to deliver us from all Ills with least harm for the conservation of the worlds. Our refuge, as in past commotions, is doubtless in that unshaken Virtue which brings Victory home.

>   though new Rebellions raise
> Their Hydra heads and the false North displays
> Her broken league to imp their serpent wings
>   O yet a nobler task awaits our Hand

> (For what can War but endless War still breed)
> Till Truth and Right from Violence be freed,
> And Public Faith cleared from the shameful brand
> Of Public Fraud. In vain doth Valour bleed
> Where Avarice and Rapine share the Land."

Our tasks are coming. God help us to be ready to assume them, and bear ourselves manfully to the Victory. Vain all our toil, unworthy [word] of [p. in] the very air we breathe, unless we standfast by the Birthright of our Freedom, and prevail, not for ourselves alone, but for the multitudes of coming time. The Reformation is yet incomplete. What the German Protestants began, and the Puritans of England, Old and New, so valiantly prosecuted, is now given as our task to carry onward to its final issues. Freedom in Church and State they partially won for us [p. in], but to these are we still bondmen, so long as the right of Private Judgement is not ours, and our Persons Character [p. in] and Families can be violated on any plea whatsoever. For this, for the defence of this inalienable right, has the Foresight of Providence, been training the Abolitionists, and now—even at this same Hour—is the trial of their faith. Will these fail us amidst the social infidelity. Let each answer for himself on peril of his own and children's liberties.

> With much regard
> I am Your friend
> A. Bronson Alcott.

¹ Alcott's copy of this letter is preceded by the following note: "Thomas Davis of Providence sends me Twenty five Dollars the last of the hundred which I had received from him since Jany. last."
Alcott evidently owed a great deal to the kindness of Davis. For material concerning a fund for the support of Alcott begun by Emerson some years later and to which Thomas Davis contributed, see Rusk, *Emerson Letters*, IV, 511–12; V, 159–60.

LETTER 46-2

[to Charles Lane, New York City]

Concord Jan 1846

My Dear Friend,

Could my small doings give you the least satisfaction I should despatch this sheet with great joy. But sharing the Idlers' fate I am not I suppose to be quite exempt from its inheritance of Poverty and Shame. Inaptitude is an Alms house quite palpable and real, it seems, to some of us Moderns. What, indeed, can fill us and spare us from Ignominy, but fit and Prevailing Endeavour: Yet for this even, the Wise God enjoins Patient waiting (in Heroic unprofitableness sometimes) till the task is given.

I have had some faithful readings, during these January days—all of Carlyle including his translations—all of Goethe that came within my reach—and am feeling for the first time, my great debt to these wisest of modern men. My Diary is, I am gratified in seeing, a somewhat clearer transcript of Life than formerly. I have found refreshment, too, in Conversing with some little Children who pass the day in my study—Besides, I visited last week the town Schools and am encouraged to repeat my calls. Just now there is begotten in me the liveliest sense of my right and duty of Teaching again—a School for Teachers with an Experimental department of Children, seems the broadest sphere for the noblest activity. The Actual Human world seems quite uninviting, and I see not how it will willingly yield its trusts into my hands, for this end, yet some ten or twenty years devotion to a score or two of young souls, would please me vastly: and I cannot but feel that what I so earnestly desire, will come in some wise way and time. One conscious of gifts desires place and work in this great Business of Life. And with such Powers as Emerson and Caryle already at work sweeping the dust of Cant, and the cinders of Unbelief from the doors of this Century we may actually get a little room soon for earnest and effectual doing. It remains for some of us to second and carry forward this majestic Enterprize for instructing the Nations. A still more immediate and intenser world culture is inevitable;—a deeper and broader working through Individuals and the World at large, in edifying the Character of Mankind.

What a noble Book this last of Carlyles for the study of modern man.[1] I know not if a more commanding word has been spoken by Mortal since Cromwell's time. It is counsel for all men. All my past reading seems languid and pale beside these strenuous and flashing thoughts of Carlyle. It comes quite opportunely too. Cromwell and his Time are admirable studies for us, fierce Republicans as we are; and may help us to see the vast difference between Royal Self-Rule and a Government of Brutes and Clowns. His time is a Glass of ours. Our Country is no less charged with Revolt, no less luxuriant the crop of Unbelief. Sorcery and Confusions dire, shooting forth in the Social Hotbed. Our fortunes too seem fearfully forecast in those of the English Commonwealth. What Luther, Cromwell, and the N. England Puritans won for us, has been surrendered already, and there remains for us, (what is even now apparent to all wise men) but to fall assunder. With the recovery and rise of these Principles in Majestic Souls, we may predict the fall of our social Evils—present institutions must [word], superseded by living men, and speedier and more trustworthy servants. Flame, Lightning, do our Business even now, and soon the nimbler and safelier Couriers of Intuition and Enthusiasm (Godsent) shall dispatch our Thinking and Ruling.

Emerson has just finished his course of Lectures in Boston; and is much in demand at Lyceums in the neighboring towns. I have heard none of these Lectures, and have read reports of ‖ but ‖ two or three. Fine Heads of Representative Men, he has chosen—Plato, Montaigne, Shakespeare, Swedenborg, Napoleon, Goethe: with these, and Carlyle's masterly Portraits, the Young World can scan its own Possibilities and kindle its Ambition. Emerson will read these Lectures to the Concord Lyceum, and Thoreau has a Lecture on Carlyle. I have scarce seen Emerson since these Heads were before him; we meet indeed less frequently than I can well account for.

I have little or nothing of the ephemeral to report. Books, Pen, Children, task me idly these brief winter days. The beams of a friend's countenance glance kindly on me, from near and far, now and then, bringing pleasing reflections of the yellow autumn, glowing summer, and mild spring time of communion: and, amidst these rigours, I wish ‖ quite ‖ often for the closer intimacy around my solitary fireside. And if these, the most precious of Human Satisfactions are not permitted, it must be of some ill-desert and undoing: for Comforts thus eminent are not inmates of every Inn by the way side. The Comforter enters only through the doors of the Private Heart into the Private House to gladden the Family

Circle: and admits the pure and upright alone into the Chambers of Intimacy. Of such Benefits it is not my happiness to partake in full measure: my thrift falls far short of my importunity; the Great Society, the lofty Intercourse, is yet the blessed privilege of solitude and self-companionship.

Miss Ford spends the morning here with the Children, and dines usually with us, giving the afternoon to Mrs Alcott. I have desired her detention here during the coming summer, but no worthy task awaits her hands. It seems not quite possible to bring the elements of Life into concord. Human Beings are yet too feeble to come near each other.

Mrs A and Anna are spending a week or two in Boston. I have scarcely been absent, even in thought, during these months. As the spring advances, I may venture abroad a little into the Actual World. I have thought some of looking at Mr Pierce, and his neophytes at Newton; and even of C. A. Greene at the Bridgewater School. A few days intercourse with these young persons would be refreshing to me I dare say. I desire to call on G. B. Emerson[2] in Boston also. It will be possible soon to have a little Teaching in this world of ours.

It gives me pleasure to hear of your opportunities of Communion with Superiour Persons and Public, both quite needful to Health and Felicity of Being —to Human Being at least.

Express my regard to those of your circle by whom I am known:—to Miss Fuller particularly, whom I wish it were my lot to see much oftener: for of women, I know of none, who fills a place more worthily. Most are quite out of place, if, indeed, there be place yet for them in the eye or heart of mankind.

Shall I hear from you again—Our tasks, though long delayed, and for a while quite miscellaneous, are becoming somewhat individual and distinctly visible. As the Patience in waiting for the call of the Great Taskmaster, so the Perpetuity, the Prevalence, and Felicity of the work.

Very truly
Yours
A. Bronson Alcott

to
    Charles Lane.

C. Richmond writes me Jan 22. from Enfield, Conn. having joined the Family there, and seems happy in his new Habiliments.[3] He speaks of yourself and hopes to hear from you.

Charles Lane
Care of Marcus Spring Esqr
   52 Pine Street
      New-York City

---

[1] *Oliver Cromwell's Letters and Speeches* (London, 1845).
[2] George Barrell Emerson, second cousin of Ralph Waldo Emerson.
[3] A reference to the Shaker settlement located about twelve miles south of Springfield, Massachusetts, and about five miles northeast of the town of Enfield.

LETTER 46–3

[to Samuel J. May, Syracuse]

[Concord, October 4, 1846]

In this closing sentiment of Abba's Epistle, I can most readily unite, and if not with her emphatic climax, with all her sincerity and good feeling.[1] Your visit was a pleasure to me, and I hoped to have entertained our guest again, for a night at least; if no longer. But kindness, which in the Old Saxon sense meant Nature, or Naturalness, or better still, perhaps, companionableness, always affects your friends, and if we had you not, others had, and all the delights of the hours. Poor Abba had a day of desolation in consequence, so confidently has she announced your passing a night with us again; And in this business concerning the Land your presence would have been as it is, and without impediments. Mr Moore sends you, by his son, his Note, drawn on the most favorable terms that I could negotiate, and such as, I hope, will find acceptance with yourself. I shall find ways to pay the $15 or 20 besides the sum he hopes from you, and shall put my hands to that Slope and Hill-top; with swiftest and richest income of expectations. So fine a canvass deserves a fair picture, and as you incline to give me this great pleasure of putting my hands to the design, I can do no less than repay your goodness by my happiest treatment of it. Come and see for yourself a year hence, and take your first ocular dividend of opulence and Beauty. If not then, a second instalment is yours at the end of a second twelvemonth. I had given to the foreground, a pretty feature, while you were in Boston and about it; It was a fair Bower, rising so softly from amidst the locusts, and giving a tempting glimpse of its shapeliness from house and road side. It had been decorated by the Sister and nieces to meet the eyes of their expected guests, as a scene from fairy land itself. Its Gothic colums, doors and windows, latticed of willow osiers, and its animated seats woven of hazel rods on a warp of locust, hung gaily in festoons of evergreens, and were spread with soft plush coverings of delicate moss. It was, I verily believe, (and is now, with its light gables, and serpentine rustic fence, and inviting approach,) worth coming to see. But when you do come, it will have added to itself a fleece of the cleanest neatest thatch of straw, and so be complete. I defer the working of this canopy till the season of threshing, and winter be past. Just now, I am sleeplessly busy on a Garden House, the Design of which invites my eye, yet more charmingly than the Arbour. But I will spare you another elaborate description, drawn as you will fancy, I suspect, from Fancy, and wait your beholding the Reality. Such Primitive occupations are most absorbing and elevating. And, indeed, such must and deserve fitly to be sweetly contentful. Planting and Building are the prime of Humane Creations. And I may add Needlework and Spinning as inclusive of more richly endowed fingers, and the Blossom and Bower of the Family Eden. It is not alone needful to the fullness of Blessedness that Man should Occupy or Hold his gifts and Estates, but he must Himself Be occupied and Holden by Creative Ideas and Blooming Affections, that so he may be swiftly and blissfully driven, from an animating Enthusiasm, to the busiest and never wearying toils; sleep but slipping the tools softly from the members, to woo the Artist mind from the realm of mixed Deeds to that of Pure Designs in the Originating Heaven within. Painful and desolate, as the Exiles lot, are the lives of those who abide alway in the Obscure and Incomplete, the Alien sphere of mere Handiworks without admission to the world, native, and the Soul's Birth Place, where is Clearness serene, and Comeliness complete. Ah me! the Home-remembering, the Patri-loyal Heart sighs long and waileth piteously in these Sorrow fraught Breasts, for its own dear Country and its domestic mates. "Occupy! occupy, till I, this Descending Comforter, Come", is the Inmost Injunction of the Spirit to the Sense ridden Humanity. Happy are all they, my Brother, who find their Joy in their Earthly Task, and to whom there is neither Day nor Night of Work.

I close with expressions of regard for all the members of your family, and of yourself

A. Bronson Alcott.

Monday Morning—I find Rev Mr Moore goes by Philadelphia and not by you at Syracuse, and so send this by Mail. Mr Moore, the Landholder, says draw a Note for $75. payable at a years' end, and the Deed shall be sent to you, or await your order. You will write me soon.

A.B.A.

Mr Moore desires me to request that his Son may witness the Papers, if the Terms answer, and that these, with your advices or comments, be transmitted to him by mail. Should you find it impossible to comply, I must incur a like obligation from some of the good friends to me and mine. The Owner of the World, and of man's Gifts, will devise a way of executing this Deed of Trust, and of facilitating my Desires and aims upon a precious pile of dust and pebbles so close to my Brain and fingers Ends.

NB. Abba rejoices exceedingly in this my lengthend line to you.

Revd Samuel J. May
  Syracuse
    New-York

---

[1] Alcott's letter is in the nature of a postscript to a letter from Mrs. Alcott to her brother. Her letter had closed as follows: "Mr. Alcott wishes to add a few lines. My love to all, write when you can—and believe me never nearer, never more gratefully."

LETTER 47–1

[to Anna, Concord]

Wednesday Night | Feb. 1847 | Hillside.

Dear Anna,

Your Note was the first thing I saw this morning, when I came in to make my study fire: and I was glad to find, all I knew, of your earnest desire to help us in these times of trial, confirmed in your own handwriting. You wish me to tell you what you can do to lighten your mother's cares, and give your father a still deeper enjoyment in yourself, and your sisters. I wish I could tell you all I feel about these duties you owe to others and yourself. But Life is a lesson we best learn and almost solely too, by *living*. The Conscience within is the best, and, in the end, the only Counseller [*sic*]: and we suffer and inflict suffering unless we obey this inner monitor. By this are we taught, encouraged, rewarded, discouraged and punished, no less. I can only say, secure all the time you can each day. Tis that first of all duties ‖ the ‖ Self-improvement, to which end life, and the world, and your friends are all given. I think I speak truly when I say that you wish this most of all things, and so you are earnest and persevering about your music and languages, which are improvements of your mind, and may be ornaments of your Heart, and Character. Next to these, turn your thoughts to aid your sisters through the day, by all the thoughtful kindness, and timely help you can lend them. Don't mind what they say or do to you; but what you say and do to them. You will help your Mother most by helping them all you can; and gain not only the approval of your own mind which is the first thing to have, but of theirs and ours:—Get all the day the Light of the World offers you—that is All-days, and so rise early, and listen to yourself, that is, your Mind, for that alone is your abiding Self, all else will perish, and vanish away. As for me, and my thoughts—Great is my Peace, if in going at night to my Pillow, I have the sense of having earned my faculties, or limbs even, by thinking One Thought, speaking one word, doing one deed, that my task master approves, or the nearest or remotest Person or Time shall adopt, repeat, or enjoy.—

Dear Anna, this from your thoughtful, yet careful-minded Father.
For the rest, our friend Henry[1] shall answer and explain in the Lecture you hear this evening.

[1] Henry Thoreau.

LETTER 47–2

[to Mrs. Anna Alcott, Oriskany Falls, N.Y.]

Concord, June 13th. 1847.

Dear Mother,

You have just cause to inquire the reasons of my very long silence. A much longer time has passed since I have had communication by letter than since we have been separated by distance, as we have been these last years. The blame is all mine, for I have now received two or more letters from yourself, and as many from Junius, since I wrote you. But you cannot suppose me forgetful of you and yours during this very long interval. I have had your serene countenance quite often present in thought, and found myself as often wondering by what un-expected mischance it was, that Mother and son, who had each cherished for years ‖ an ‖ so lively hope of abiding under the same roof should be cast so wide asunder, and hold intercourse with each other so seldom, and that so brief and unsatisfactory. But on second thoughts it seems less strange to me, and if I am not reconciled to the privation, I submit with a patience that becomes as in-evitable, as the imposition. And when I think of it, it becomes by no means clear to me, that your happiness would be increased by living with us: there is so much in our modes of thinking and living at wide variance from all your customs and inclinations, which have gained strength, and become as second natures to you, with the years of a long life. There would be no generosity in inviting you to our threshold, if there were not within a greater share of comfort and support for both body and mind, than you have found with others of your children. A change in many respects has lately taken place with us, and all in your favor, so that our daily entertainments and occupations would minister much more to your diversion and delight, to your health and ‖ peace ‖ repose, than would have been possible to you during some past years of extreme austerity and almost of positive want. If you came to spend some time with us, life would doubtless take many agreeable colours, from our quiet and some what busy days. We are a private circle, see but few people, and seldom leave the house and garden to find our pleasures and duties. House wifery, gardening, and instruction give our hands and minds a daily pressure of cares, and the days pass with their burdens of business, not wholly without charm, and profit. I delight in the improvement of the place and find already many proofs of skill, comfort, and taste, in my handiworks. I sometimes think of the delight these would give yourself, and Junius would find great satisfaction in my rustic arbours, and garden houses, my alleys, lawns, and orchards, and the many tokens of ‖ my ‖ our industry. Perhaps he will bring you to see us; and as he will not live in Massachusetts himself, will do a better thing, even, leave you in it, and go back to his turning and inventing unless he like mine, (the latter I mean) without you. There is a rail road all the way, and the cost is trifling for a man with a productive pair of hands like his. Think of it. You could spend the summer here, at least, and, if I should defer my visit to England till next spring,[1] perhaps you would stop here through the winter till then. I have not full occupation during the snowy months, and may seek some either in England, or Boston.—Anna takes charge now of her sisters Elisabeth and Abba, with Mr Emersons two little girls, and a boy now living with us, Edward May, from Boston, who make her quite a pretty school. She is busy with this, and her Music, French, and German, and bids fair to become an efficient and excellent woman. Louisa is spending the summer with a friend near Boston, and is full of talent and character: She needs years to reveal her gifts.—Tell Junius that Lane has returned to Alcott House in England; Emerson is busy in writing as ever; Thoreau lives a hermit by Walden Pond, and has a Book in press,[2] and the rest of Concord shall remain unspoken of. Dr. Alcott, is, I suppose, in Connecticut. But I must reserve a place for Abbas few bold strokes, and with remembrance to all kinsfolk about you, am

Your Faithful Son,
A. Bronson Alcott.

Mrs Anna Alcott
(care of Junius S. Alcott)
   Oriskany Falls,
     New York.

[1] A trip Alcott did not make.
[2] *A Week on the Concord and Merrimack Rivers.* The book, however, was not published until May, 1849.

LETTER 47–3

[to Anna, Walpole, N.H.][1]

Concord 28. Novr 1847.

My dear Anna,

   How could you fancy there could be the least condescension on my part in writing to you? It is quite otherwise with me, I assure you, and but for much business, and some hindrances at times set apart for yourself, you should have had proofs of my remembrances and thoughts of you, before. Sunday, you know, is my freest day of the seven; and but for Ellery Channing's call a fortnight since, and, Henry Thoreau's last Sunday, you would have had a word from me. And now that I have closed my pretty arbour for the winter, I shall have a little more command of the Days, for you and others, and hope to communicate of such thoughts and things, as may entertain, if not instruct you, from time to time. And it will afford me pleasure if you will sometimes do the same by me. There will be some things about which you will most easily and properly communicate with me; nor can any thing give me greater delight than to find some freer and fuller intercourse than has yet been made possible to us, either by the pen or discourse. Perhaps this absence of yours may be a means of such closer intimacy, if we use it as we may. There is no better discipline for the mind, than epistolary correspondence, nor a finer accomplishment, especially for a young lady, than an aptness in writing of her experiences to her friends. I trust you will avail yourself of this fine privilege, and so reap not only the delight, but the profit it gives. And if you should take a little more pains with your hand-writing, as well as the expression of your letters, so much the greater will be your own, and our satisfaction in these productions. It is but a few days since that I came across some letters and journals of yours, and the proofs of your taste and neatness, at the early period these were written, gave both your mother and myself, great delight. Your handwriting was graceful then, and elegant even. Now gratify us, sometimes, dear Anna, in this way. You will not fancy us as prizing the costume more than the thought, I know: for nonsense is none the worse, but even the better nonsense, by a little care bestowed on the dressing. The little girls delight in adorning very uncomely dolls, in pretty finery, and if you happen by chance or otherwise, in any company,—as at visiting or at Church —you cannot well miss seeing very insignificant faces, in very fine apparel. And as a lover of your mind, it will afford me as true a joy, to see your thoughts in comely raiment, as your person; nor have you any cause to disparage either of these. A good education, indeed, is but a finer clothing of mind and person in simple manners and fair thoughts.—But here I am interrupted by Hosmer, the carpenter, who comes to talk about repairs, and tells us he is coming to morrow to begin; and so when you arrive the Old House will have doffed its shabby garb, and you too shall leave behind, as much of yours, as you can meanwhile cast off.

Your affectionate
Father.
A.B.A.

[1] Anna had gone to Walpole to teach school, living with Mrs. Alcott's relatives, the Wellses.

LETTER 47–4

[to Anna, Walpole, N.H.]

[Concord] 29 Novr. Monday, 1847

Dear Anna

This has been a busy day with us. The carpenters have just begun their work for us; and the painter and Walldraper has been here to survey the rooms and the house at large; and the woodsawyers have been active at the woodpile; and, ‖ most ‖ more important for you ‖ know ‖ than all these things, it has been my own and Louisa's Birthday—the Papa 48, and the daughter 15 years of age. The Mamma and sisters have been doing their best to please and serve us, by their little gifts, and we have just rec'd them in the School Room after supper, and given ours in return. Louisa will tell you all about it, I suppose—as such news from home you will joyfully devour, I am sure.—I meant, dear Anna, that this letter should have reached you tomorrow night, as you will be expecting something from us, but you will not have it till Wednesday,—48 Years—that is being old you will fancy, but my affection for the absent as well as the present members of our little Family, partakes not, I am persuaded of *Time,* but is both older and younger than dates, lasting as the unbeginning, unending mind, from which it proceeds, and the imperishable qualities it cherishes and admires in the characters of its inmates.

Receive these words, my daughter, as a Father's Birthday gift, to whom the knowledge of your happiness, in yourself and the friends you have found, gives much content.—7. oclock Monday Eve.—[1]

[1] Unsigned.

LETTER 47–5

[to Anna, Walpole, N.H.]

Hillside, Friday. 3 o.clock P.M. | December 10th | 1847

Dear Anna,

Elisabeth has just left us, to pass some time with Miss Robie in Boston. Your Mother, Louisa and Abby have ‖ just ‖ [p. o.] now [p. in] returned from the "Station," (whither they were driven by Mr Kendall) with tearful eyes, and a sadness at the heart; And little Abby declares there is no pleasure now for her, "in this old ugly house." The house is indeed shorn of some of its attractions, now that the pure little maid is gone whose gentle assiduities to all its inmates were so uninterrupted and so sweet. But she will reap advantages from the change and we shall learn the more of her worth. The Good God will protect so much goodness ‖ of Soul ‖, wherever it may abide; nor can she fail to find sources of happiness in any employments that may be given her. Families must swarm sometime, and it is well for her, and yourself too, perhaps, to seek fields of richer thyme than grows about the Old Hive, and fall to honey-making for yourselves, since all true and lasting enjoyment must be sipped from the cup by our own exertions alone. I well remember the time of leaving my humble home, at the age of twelve years, and the strength which but a few months absence gave to my youthful character. So it will be with yourself, and with Elisabeth, I doubt not. No Home was ever quite sufficient for the Mind of a Child, and but few for the Heart and Hand. But yet knowing this, as I do, and feeling the truth of it every day more and more, I am not quite reconciled to that necessity which sends two of my daughters so soon from our threshold into the houses of comparative strangers. And did I not know of that wealth of self resource and of self enjoyment, of which none can bereave the Heart of Youth—that sense of forth coming satisfactions—that defence of Innocency, which is ever cast about, and in whose aid, the young confide, I should not yield even to this dispensation, I fear, with a becoming Piety. My good Mother used to say,—and it ‖ it ‖ seemed a heart sentiment of hers as well as a word on her lips—"Tis for the Best." And such seems the confidence of youth: I might go further, perhaps, and say, that all trust in the necessary and Providential, is youthfulness of Soul, and that Piety itself is faith in and resignation to the Inevitable. For if there is a good Being at the Head of Affairs, then all that happens must be, *in the end,* of least harm, and so, best for us mortals in this shiftless state of ‖ our own ‖ existence, wherein much that we design and do, is, from our blindness or wilfulness, hostile to our welfare here; but shall somehow, in a way at present inscrutable to us, be overruled to our final advantage.—

But I had no thought, dear Anna, of filling my note with a Sermon to you: Perhaps you will find it as dull and unsuitable to the heart of a happy maiden, as are most, but, for a fathers' sake give it a [word] ear than I fear you have ever lent the Parson: so good by, which means you know, "God be with ye,"—a truth I have never questioned ‖ with ‖ as regards any absent daughters.

Your Father.

For Anna
   at Walpole.

LETTER 48–1

[to Anna, Walpole, N.H.]

[Concord] February 1st. 1848.

Dear Anna,

So it seems I am to have never a letter from you. Well, if some natural inclination does not move you, there is no sufficient reason for writing: as only those things are good and pleasurable which are inly prompted, and inspire a like pleasure in those for whom they are meant: and it is a good rule in manners to feel before you venture on such sacred expressions as speech and action. I am not in the least concerned about the demeanor of diffident people. It is oftentimes a promising omen of all that is graceful and becoming, especially in youth, especially in women. A certain diffidence belongs, indeed, to refinement, and distinguishes it from whatsoever is vulgar and unbecoming so fine a creature as maid, man, or woman. It is the mark of gentility, which is but good sense, spoken or acted in natural words, tones, and looks. Fine manners are the ornaments of fine souls, and seem the fit study of young People.

Now if you have nothing to say to me, please think not of writing to me—it would be ill manners, and unworthy affectation in you. It would be like speaking, because another wished [torn], with never a sentiment or a thought in your poor mind and Heart to utter. No, No. Be sincere. Strive to be all you would be, and so take consel [sic] of your Heart and conscience, and your way to speech and writing, and conversation will become plain to you. A youth of Silence is quite often the liveliest converse with one's self. Speech and ease of manner will come as the fruit of such years. But there must be thought all this time: as there is neither grace nor loveliness without this refiner of manners.

133

—But my paper bids me cut short this little Essay on manners and diffidence; which I will, having given it [torn] the readiest excuse I know of, for your hesitating to write a thought or a wish now and then to

Your absent "Papa[."]

Miss Anna Bronson Alcott
> Walpole

Let me tell you that I read all your letters, and see not why some portions of them were not addressed to myself, as whatsoever interests you, reveals your mi[n]d and character, which [word] [word] I must[?] wish[?] to [words]

LETTER 48–2

[to Sylvester Graham,[1] Northampton, Mass.]

Concord 12 April 1848.

Dear Sir

This gratifying assurance of our own readiness to comply with the wishes of our friends at Ham, I shall transmit to them at once, with my own best wishes for its furtherance and that the best advantages may be given it. The Enterprize looks quite fair to me now, and I am persuaded must yield lasting benefits to yourself and to that needy English Nation, so steadfast and strong when once convinced of a good thing. And if you can still teach, and as eloquently persuade, as once, when I was privileged to listen, the victory is all your own. The Present invitation appears too very auspicious. Lane and Associates are favorably known to their countrymen; they have been first to print and spread your own, and kindred Ideas; they will give their advocate a reception every way worthy the cause he pleads, and can best place him before his rightful auditors, and report his doings in their Journal. So all is open for you to meet and teach them and the English People. But before you go, let me hope to see you here in Concord. For besides the pleasure it would give me personally to see you here, and the free interchange of sentiments I should so much enjoy, there are many things much better said in your ear, concerning England and our English friends, than written of, yet which it might be well for you to know before your departure. I would gladly visit you were that possible. But it is not. Do you not some times come to Boston? We are but an hour's ride from that City, and our Village has attractions many and rare, to a philosopher and Humanitarian like yourself. In Mrs Alcott, too, you are sure of finding a living friend and disciple, to give you a cordial welcome. She is now in Boston making inquiries of Dr. Kitteridge concerning the Water Cure Institution at Waterford,[2] Mr Farrar being desirous of her services in that Establishment, and but for family cares, and the difficulties of removal, would join him there.

Your candour invites me to speak fully and freely of my self, but that field is so vast, and so indefinite withal, that I must not venture yet awhile to invade the silence and speak of what I must falsify if I speak at all. Were you near me, such revelation would ‖ would ‖ doubtless come simply and not unworthily in conversation, but my pen is no Sibyl and at best defames. Of this I am assured, however, that each fine soul earnestly at work on the Idea that haunts him day by day, is the nurse and saviour of mankind. I may add the reason of their continuance: and the interest I have in yourself as one of that company of the Elect of Heaven.

A. Bronson Alcott.

Dr S. Graham.

[1] Sylvester Graham, a vegetarian. Alcott had known him for some years.
[2] Waterford, Maine, about fifty miles northwest of Portland.

LETTER 48-3

[to Anna, Walpole, N.H.]

Thursday Evg. 13th | April 1848.

Dear Anna,

Your letter, for days mislaid, has just come to light, and I improve this evening hour in blotting a few thoughts for your form-loving Eye, and would gladly awaken, if I could, fair and dear images in your Heart. Our household Goddess is flown from us for a few days to the City, and so I have the house and the maids ‖ alone ‖ [p. o.] to myself [2 p. in] the while. On Saturday she will return to us again, and as our Purchaser decides on postponing a settlement here for the present, we shall pass another Summer in our wonted nest, awaiting some coming time for flight to the towns or mountains, as the Fates decree. By some chance as yet unforeseen we may some or all of us drift even to Waterford hills, but that seems less likely[1] to be our destiny as we now read the dark page. Eliza went along to the City, and perhaps as far as Springfield to visit the Stearns there, and Dr. Woodward on the way. But—but—the poor girl's prison no human hand can open: the doors are barred by inexorable destiny, to which Omnipotent Love has alone the Key. Pity, and her gentle handmaids, Kindness and Long-Suffering, can alone alleviate her Earthly lot.

The manner in which you speak of the School encourages me to believe in your final success. Believe that you can teach and rule these little ones, and you will prosper in your labours. *All things are possible to the earnest and steadfast heart;* and these, if I read my daughter's Genius, are constitutionally hers. Faith in yourself is the hand of Power, the sceptre of the gentlest and wisest rule; and your very *diffidence* about which you blush and quake in secret, is no hindrance but a help to you, coming to check impatience and a long list of teacher's infirmities. Bashfulness is a virtue of the self-reverent; think what were a maiden incapable of this blushing interiour grace. I have always admired a blushing boy, seeing in him the budding beauties of every civility: but few can dispense with this ornament and maintain integrity of body or mind. It is a Conscience animating and enlivening the flesh, kindling the flame of reverence in the very cheek, the eye, the manners and motions of the limbs, and softening the voice into the tremulous movements of music.

Soft moves the maid with lovely Sense,
Victim and Queen of diffidence.

Your Plan of Teaching drawing deserves trial, and I beg you to follow it out, & on your own account. The faithful teacher finds himself the pupil whom he most benefits. Teaching has been the College at which some of the rarest minds have been graduated. I was glad to learn of your intention to study.

Please remember it every day. And by study, I mean, *business done in the mind* —thinking—only that is study. Refresh yourself every day with a little French or German, as regularly as you go to the bath or to breakfast. And write me an elegant letter every month.

Affectionately Papa

¹ Originally read "quite unlikely," but was changed in pencil.

LETTER 48–4

[to Charles Lane, Ham, England]

Concord 16. April 1848.

Dear friend,

Yours of March 2nd. came duly to hand, and I made haste to dispatch the inquiry contained therein to Mr Graham, whose reply I copy at length.—

"I certainly am not only 'inclined,' but very desirous to go to England on the mission you propose. I have for some time past, watched the movements on the other side of the water in respect to the great reform in which I have been so many years engaged, and I have been encouraged and delighted to see the intelligence and zeal which are engaged in the same cause in England, and my heart has yearned to be with them, and participate in their labours and joys. And I hail it as an omen of good to the cause of human progress and melioration, that there is an effective wish and a willingness to make the attempt to get me over there to cooperate with the Philanthropists of the mother country. The question which Mr Lane puts to you and which you reiterate to me, is 'What would it cost to bring S. Graham over here to lecture a year?—Now friend Alcott how can I answer this question? I have no notion of what it would cost to get me across the Atlantic and back, nor what it would cost to sustain me a year in England. Whatever the sum may be, *it* would be requisite for such an undertaking. If our friends in England take me over there, they must take me from my home with empty pockets, and defray my *necessary* expenses till they have returned me to my home. If they can do no better by me than to return me to my home with empty pockets, as empty as when they take me away, then let it be so. Howbeit I could do much better than that, in a pecuniary respect, by laboring in America. But if I go to England it will not be for the money I can get, but for the good I can do.—The only answer I can give to Mr Lane's question, therefore is, that it would cost at least as much as my necessary expenses would be, and as much more as the good people of England were willing to give me. All I shall stipulate for as a *sine qua non* is my necessary expenses from my home to my home. Should I go, however, I should like to take my little son with me, for company and my contentment, and for improvement, and I should hope to be able to visit some portions of Europe besides England before I returned; but these I do not include or comprise in my *sine qua non*."

I have written to Mr Graham, since his letter was received, and assured him of my intention of forwarding his reply to yourself, with hope that he might visit you on the good errand he carries in his heart. The Enterprize looks fair and the best advantages should be given it. Mr G. is the man for yourselves and for England. Should further service of mine be useful in any way to the further-ance this design I shall privileged [sic] and disposed to give them. If you wish to communicate directly with him, address him at Northampton where he resides.

You appear hungry for some of our trans-atlantic "gossip." But I am in the way of tasting little of this ‖ confectionary ‖ here in my retreat, passing for the most part studious days, meeting my daughters awhile in the morning, and en-joying an afternoons walk, with Thoreau or Channing, both of whom are occu-pied all their mornings in studyes [sic] also. I have seen more of them than for-merly during these months, one or other passing an evening at my room once a week or sometimes oftener. Thoreau has a Book nearly off his hands, which we think admirable,[1] and Channing's mornings yield Poetic lines, which are fast growing into another and third Volume of Poems. These, my townsmen, are both wise men, and live to perform earnest and faithful work, which men as eager and clear seeing shall one day discern and approve.

Parker and Channing (W. H.) are busily occupied, and to very good purpose in Boston. I heard them the other day for the first time, and thought the teaching every way superior to any thing else there. Parker speaks to the largest audiance [sic] in the City; and Channing draws to him many of the best people there. Gar-rison and Co. are still vigorously at work, scenting out the sins of our Republic and as fierce in their denunciations as ever. Admirable Harriers these, and run down game for us all, nor do they at all weary in the sport. This French affair now absorbs every thing American, and wonderfully invigorates and emboldens every member of the Freeman's League, here and elsewhere: the nations already sympathize electrically, and we may not predict the vast Revolutions and Reforms already in progress. It is already "too late" not only for Kings, but for most else that now impedes man's steps to Imperial Self-Rule: the Imperial Man will arrive at last. England, when once aroused, is likeliest to stride forwards, and maintain her position in advance of the Nations, for she has the animal[?] Basis for[?] unprecedented Moral and Social Achievements, and she steps with the force of Fate, and has a steadfast will of her own. By and by she will uprise & Be. Of America no lover of his country will wish to speak, and silence can no longer hide his shame. The Hope of nations has become the scorn of Freemen the world over.

Emerson, I learn, has been at Ham, and is now at Chapman's in London. We take a personal share in his success with your countrymen, and England is the dearer to us all on his account. The fruits will ripen in all the coming years. —Thoreau tells me your "Dials' were forwarded by Munroe & Co to Chapman, and have been acknowledged by him in letters to Munroe.

A copy of your "Truth-Tester" came to me last autumn, I have just sent it to Farrar & Kittredge at Waterford. Farrar has lately invited Mrs Alcott to take charge of the household affairs at the Water Cure over which he presides, and she inclines to go there. Possib[ly] it may draw me along some day, with yet freer scope for some ampler teachings than the Country has yet supplied. But Concord detains me as yet. Nor can I engage in any thing that leaves part or parts of me behind.

Anna is now engaged in teaching at Walpole N. Hampshire where a cousin of hers resides. She bears yourself gratefully in mind, and often speaks of accompanying me some day to Alcott House. A like vagary I [*sic*] sometimes possesses me for a moment. It only needs for me to know of any sphere, *out* of my thought, to fly into and eagerly assume its duties forthwith. Unless the [word] Quarterly Review were better have you any claim upon the work.

Your friend,
A. Bronson Alcott

¹ *A Week on the Concord and Merrimack Rivers.*

LETTER 48–5

[to Anna, Walpole, N.H.]

[Concord] May-day Evening | 1848.

Dear Anna,

I have this afternoon ploughed my garden, and begin to think a little of my Summer's labours, which will take me, as heretofore, from my Book and pen to the spade and rake, to finishing the garden houses here, and at ‖ Mr ‖ Emerson's. These things will give me health, and pleasing occupation. Some day, I yet allow my self to hope, will furnish tasks still more agreeable, and for the want of which good fortune, the hours yield me but ‖ a ‖ stinted fruits. Yet all complaints are ‖ most ‖ [p. o.] so [p. in] unbecoming, and of no avail. We poor beggars are never quite content, nor know what we want.—But I did not intend to preach thus far in my letter. I meant to signify the pleasure your long epistle gave me. It made me very happy. I was glad to learn from your own handwriting that you found satisfaction in your little circle, and seemed intent on doing all you could for its improvement. The School will do more for the mistress than for her pupils, and this is what interests me most in it. Pray devote yourself to this pleasing charge, and so reap the rewards which faithfulness always yields her votaries. Your plan of teaching Geography is admirable. Pestalozzi taught in that way, and so have some of the best teachers since his day. You will find every invention of your own far better than every other. And originality in teaching is ‖ one ‖ the rarest of gifts.—I am glad you adopt *persuasion,* and succeed with it. Take time with your children, and you will gain time with them in the end. You have but few, and so can command ‖ time ‖ [p. o.] this [p. in] to pursue your own methods. Write me from time to time month to month [3 p. in] about difficulties, if such beset you. I shall most joyfully help you if I can. But you will need little help while you are so earnest, and ready to help yourself. Nothing would give me greater pleasure than to find in you the *Genius and devotion of a Teacher*—gifts and a vocation second to none in the world—Your mother will tell you of her decision to go to Waterford, & Louisa & Elisabeth all they feel about the separation of these family ties for a few months. But it seems best, and we try to feel right about it. So there will be only three of us here in this Homestead,—we will ‖ try ‖ endeavour to find occupation, and happy days. The mail is lively, and so may be our pens—and there is a certain charm about letters that nearness does not give us—or not always—at best. Write us when you have things to say & I trust many letters will chronicle this absence of yours, from your affectionate

Father.

LETTER 48–6

[to Anna, Walpole, N.H.]

[Concord] Thursday Evg. 11. May | 1848.

My dear Anna,

I have just delivered your letter, addressed to your mother and Louisa, safe ‖ into ‖ into the hands of the latter; for the first, with the little Abby, is by this time far away on the mountains of Maine; and only this remnant of the six of us remains behind. This separation breeds unwonted sensations, and calls forth what of fortitude and courage there lies within us all. But dispersion of families is at sometimes inevitable; and must come soon to us, by occasions of sorrow or of joy;—by marriage, by calamity, by disappearance from the Scene in sad earnest at last. It is well to meet it with heroic front, and to set each to the performance of his task with a steadfast heart. I honour the good Mother for this brave deed of hers, purchased at the cost of so many enjoyments, taking her from those whom she loves and has served so well, and whom she still loves and serves in the pains of absence. All Saints and Angels will accompany and bless the dear woman in her ministrations at the Pool. Would that some Power as propitious might task my Gifts, and fill my hands too with work and my table with bread. But 'tis not thus with me and I submit to the decrees of fate, till times and men discover and use me, as I would be used. "They also serve who only stand & wait."

Your mother left us but yesterday, so we have had but a single night and a day of the Change. Elisabeth and Louisa will write you, if they can, how it seems—three of us here in our new solitude. They will enjoy your letters more than ever, nor can you omit writing the more frequently to them. Your letters make us all happy, you seem so happy yourself. Write often to us; and oftener now to your Mother. Every word of yours will be grateful, and a solace ‖ to her ‖ her heart, and I beg of you to take pains to spare her poor eyes, by the plainness and accuracy of your writing. Of defects of spelling I come in for a large share; as you were my pupil please spare the master also.

I am glad to hear of the reception of your parcel and of your great joy at its safe arrival. Greet ‖ my ‖ these glad Eyes soon with samples of the budget you most prize; and a thousand blessings on your own fair Eyes, which, if I mistake not, rule the little School.

Affectionately,
Your Father.

Anna.

[Letter to Mrs. A. Bronson Alcott, Waterford, Maine; from Concord, May 16, 1848.]

[to Anna, Walpole, N.H.]

[Concord] Tuesday Evg 16th. May | 1848

Dear Anna,

The same mail which gave us yours, brought a letter from Waterford, at which place the travellers alighted on Thursday the day after leaving us, here in Concord. Mother writes us briefly and promises particulars when she becomes a little rested from the Journey and has had time to look about ‖ her, ‖ [p. o.] and see what is expected of her, and what she finds herself equal to perform at the Cure. She "was taken into a neatly furnished room," she writes—"a parlour, with red cotton and white muslin curtains, a handsome piano, on which Abba and Eliza have been thrumming ever since; we sat down to a neat supper of a bowl of applesauce and various kinds of bread, and simple cake; We are all very weary and shall soon find our rests, in one large room with three single beds. To morrow, if I have any strength to rise, I shall begin operations. I find Mr Turner[?] very busy, and two women were taking care of the Infirmary, in which I found two patients, one very sick. All seems very unsettled waiting I suppose, ‖ I suppose, ‖ for me to give the finishing touch to the arrangements. You must let me know as soon as you hear from Anna, and tell me how you are—what you do."

I have just written a long letter; and Louisa and Elisabeth have written also; and the dear woman will hear all about us; and I must add yet more, and something of writing to you, before the letter goes off to-morrow with yours to me of this morning.

It was ‖ a ‖ neatly written, and clearly conceived, and I noticed but one or two errors in spelling[.] The order you describe so minutely shows good judgement and a knowledge of the minds of Children, who hate sameness every day; and will yet do the same things every day with love, if disposed a little differently. But your plan of having few studies in each day, and of insisting on faithfulness in these, is better, and you spread out your various subjects through the week, and so win their Minds[.] I think of nothing to suggest to you by way of amendment of your plan. It pleases me, and it proves to me you have some of the requisites of a good Teacher. I shall be glad, if the Genius is found in you for this Art—this Art of Arts. Arithmetic you must wait a little upon; it will come to you, as your mind matures, and you strive to give yourself to thinking. The German and French come duly ‖ to you ‖ [p. o.] and you will have the accomplishment of the tongues with a little pain, and your usual perseverance. We are quite still and busy here in the House. L. & E. will tell you how life runs with them. Write to your Mother, and as often as you please, to your

Affectionate Father.

Anna.

LETTER 48–8

[to Charles Lane, Ham, England]

Concord ‖ 29 ‖ 30. May | 1848.

Dear friend,

Henry Clapp of Lynn already known of you as an able lecturer in Popular Reform brings this to you. He visits you at this time of Revolutions as a friend of popular rights, and from what I know of his temper and abilities promises useful services. It was my hope to have seen him here a day in Concord under the best advantages for conversation, but in the preoccupations and haste of embarking it came not so far. And he leaves with claims on your hospitality and good fellowship. I trust you will meet and to mutual advantage while he is in England.

I have had your Enterprise at Ham often in mind lately, and have felt desirous of learning from yourself particulars of your modes of working, and the bearing late events have on your thoughts and endeavours. Private education seems almost impossible to us just now while the Eye and Ear are fixed intently on Church and State, and this vast-world-culture is going forward with majestic stride, and in such an unprecedented way. The Private impulses, interests, and ideas of individuals coming before the Eye in the Affairs of the Nations, and Revolutions[?] and Universities in which People and [word] are educating to serve each other. The populations of Europe and of N. America seem intent on the lesson, and one feels at times impatient at the delays and wishes it would come to some results forthwith. In my eagerness to work, and behold my doings, I still please myself with drafts of Institutions, and some Ham, or Hoff, or Yverden,[1] some Fruitlands or Temple that was, rises fair and possible to the mind, and I taste the cup of childhood again. It was in times of Revolution that Pestalozzi was most active, and some Switzer, some son of Germany, or of Italy, may yet arrive to us, driven from his country, as was Greaves from England, that the names of both may be honored in a worthy successor, and education become possible once more. The students of Berlin, the disciples of Schelling, the readers of Fichte and Richter, of Goethe, and of Carlyle, of Emerson even, are already the patrons of the New Academy.—

Emerson by this must have returned from France to his London Lectures. His acceptance with the British People is as creditable to them as honorable to himself. You will see him frequently of course. And shall you send me nothing by him on his return. Sutton's Book[2]—I am curious to see, and still more wishing to see the man himself. Chapman wants a Journal common to contributors from both sides of the sea, and Emerson has written over to us about it. The Concordonians are not quite content it seems with that *Boston Massachusetts Quarterly Review*,[3] and would have a better or none. Ellery Channing wrote from my room lately a proposition to edit a better for Chapman, and we set down as contributors Emerson, Thoreau, Channing, Newcomb, Alcott, on our side, with Froude, Clough, Sutton, Lane, and some Oxonians whom Emerson writes of on yours.

I wrote you April 16. and sent S. Graham's proposals to visit England and lecture. He awaits your answer.

I have had a busy winter, at book and pen, and am here now with Louisa & Elisabeth as housemates, Mrs Alcott and Abby being at Waterford in Maine and Anna in N. Hampshire, teaching School. Mrs A writes in admirable spirits, and is charged with hope and business to the [word]. She will be there during the summer, if no longer. Her services are invaluable there.—I have just ‖ to ‖ recd a Book from W. Scott of Edinburgh—a Poem on *"The Year of the World."*[4] Get it quick, and read it. I send a news paper or two. I have had bound lately a few copies of the "Conversations on the Gospels" & would exchange for Eng. Books.

Ever Yours
A. Bronson Alcott

Chas. Lane
    Ham, England

[1] Hoff, may be a reference to the institution at Hofwyl near Berne, Switzerland, founded by Fellenberg, and which sought to combine education with manual labor.
    Yverden, Switzerland, was the site of Pestalozzi's school (1806–25).
[2] Henry S. Sutton, *Evangel of Love* (1847).
[3] *Massachusetts Quarterly Review* (December, 1847–September, 1850).
[4] William Bell Scott (1812–92). *The Year of the World* appeared in 1846.

LETTER 48–9

[to Anna, Walpole, N.H.]

[Concord] Tuesday Morning | 6 June | 1848.

Dear Anna,
    Your letter came in this morning just before we had break-fast, and Louisa has laid your words to her and Elisabeth on my desk for me to read; so that I am able to know how you pass your time both in school and out of it. All I read gives a very agreeable notion of you and your doings. You seem to be busy and happy. The meeting to read French pleases me; and the accounts you write about your own studies, and your ways of managing the School, afford me great satisfaction. You are learning more than you know. The book of useful knowledge is good reading for you. The German you are learning will be invaluable to you. French I suppose you read already without much difficulty. It is instructive to have several names for the same things, as each name helps us to know the things and see them in various and pleasing lights. Every word is a portrait or voicing of some thing in the mind, or in the world of people and things around us. So the languages are rightly called the tongues.
    Your strictness or decision in the management of the scholars is admirable. With that all else takes care of itself almost. All children need is something to hold them steady and keep them where they will go, if they can have but a little help at the right moment: that is the encouragement they need and almost all. You cannot drag them safely, but they must go willingly or no good comes of it, and always harm. Make things, *externally,* as agreeable as you can; wait patiently and excuse much to weakness; set an example of activity on your own part before the unwilling, and connect pleasure with every earnest endeavour, and you will have done your part. Nobody does any thing well if there be no love for the thing set about. If that child you speak of who wills not to study, or obey you; nor cares for punishments, will scarcely[?] be made to *care for, or will to* study and obey, by harsh or merely compulsive means. *Neglect for a day or two* is sometimes a very good stimulant to exertion. If the books are taken

away, and she is not permitted to engage in the exercises with her mates, good might come of it, and that would help show her the matter better perhaps than any thing else. But you must judge for yourself.

About Waterford every thing is quite unsettled, and it is safest to let things come to a little more clearness before we can speak much about it. I send Mother's last letter; by which you will see that while there is *hope* about it there is *doubt* also. A few months will determine for us. In August you will be with us, if not in July, I suppose. Elisabeth is enjoying her music. You are good to help her.

Goodmorning
Father.

LETTER 48–10

[to Anna, Walpole, N.H.]

Concord, | Tuesday Morning, | 19. June. | 1848.[1]

Yes, dear Anna, close your School, as you propose, and bring your Cousin[2] to pass the night, if she will no longer time, with us, as she returns to Boston. No other arrangement could please us so well. Louisa wishes it beyond all things, Elisabeth wishes it, and now that your Mother is away, it becomes almost needful to us, to have you, her best substitute, with us here, both for company and the honor of housekeeping, for though Louisa leave nothing undone, and Elisabeth is the tidiest of house maids, there is yet need of your sharp eyes, and indefatigable hands to make the mothers place good[?] to us, or seem ‖ to be ‖ so. I am very glad you can come, and have it in your heart to be with us again.—

Bring Mother's letter: and I will put it with the comely volume which has accumulated since she was at Waterford, and then, here at home, you shall have the pleasure of reading the whole from first to last all to yourself. I suspect my self as your Rival in this matter of letters, but we will not have any ill-will towards each other; our correspondent has Love enough for us both, and loves no less in silence than in speech; in one, or many letters.

You say you will come in three weeks. This will be early in July—that is close at hand, but the time will seem long, now you are waiting for its arrival, so I will send Mother's last letter for your solace, (if it shall prove such,) meanwhile. The Mamma has had *Long Letters* to write, as you will see, what Papa has written the daughter must guess. Read, *it is for you, and only you to read.*

Write us when you will come so that I may be at the depot.

Good bye till I
see you.
Papa

[1] Tuesday was June 20.
[2] Lizzie Wells, Mrs. Alcott's niece, with whose parents Anna stayed while teaching school at Walpole.

LETTER 48–11

[to Anna, Walpole, N.H.]

[Concord] Friday 23 June, 1848.

Your mother has written that she would like Louisa's company and services at Waterford; and the eager girl will now fly as soon as opportunity and speed shall favor, to answer that much desired invitation, even though she lose the next cherished expectation of greeting a sister's arrival here in Concord, at our threshold. But it will be some solace to your disappointment at not finding her here, that she is a comfort to a mother, whom you would bless; and that not many weeks can intervene between her leaving us, and our union ‖ again ‖ here or elsewhere, as a family again. Perhaps you will return before she leaves, and you will have some few days together. I wish it may be so: write us soon and tell us the day you purpose to come. We shall be right glad to see you again! and the more that you left us with purposes so creditable to us and yourself, and which you have honored, as I have reason to believe, by your conduct in services during your absence. Come, and be mistress of yourself and sisters, and a pleasure to your father here at home. Bring all the letters.

Elisabeth is very faithful to her music. She will rejoice in your interest in this, and other studies. She passes some hours every day in the little room beside mine at her desk and books. Your company will be an encouragement to her mind and heart.—

I need not remind you of your obligations to your kind hosts—Mr & Mrs Wells—your own heart, and the intimacy between yourself, and the love you bear, Mrs W. will teach you, (better than I can express,) the manner of your gratitude. Some little hearts there are too who have words and wishes to be remembered by you; and whom you leave with affection. Please add to this my sense of the kindness of our friend to yourself and the good will of your Father.

Anna.

LETTER 48–12

[to Elizabeth, Concord]

[Concord, June 24, 1848]

Dear Elisabeth,

I must write you a little note on this birth day morning, just to give you these little presents, and my love for all the best there is in your mind and manners, and to give my best wishes, also, for your future welfare and improvement.

From your Father.

June 24. 1848.
    Concord.

LETTER 48–13

[to Elizabeth, Boston]

[Concord] Sunday Afternoon, | September 3.—1848

Dear E—

I am unwilling this little pacquet should go from us, without my own little note to you, along with Mothers and sisters' big and bigger letters. I was pleased to see you leave home which you love so much, so cheerfully, and though I miss you every meal, and especially every breakfasting, am quite willing to have you look a little at the great town, and towns folk, and find how you like them, with your own dear eyes, and for yourself.

You have never left home before without taking the best of it along with you: some one or more of us has always accompanied you, and I shall not be at all surprized to learn of your not finding the home enjoyments, so dear to you, even with your kind friends in town. But Home-sickness, if it come to you, is easily cured, home is so near, and you are free to invite the swift steam-steed to bear you to our thresholds. I left home for the first time to spend a month* when about your age, and so long a month was there never before, nor has since been, and my courage failed me, and I was glad to return to the familiar places and delights at the long four weeks end, unashamed. But you have more courage, and more love, perhaps, ‖ at the ‖ withal than I had, and so will brave out your week or more with your accustomed fortitude, hiding your feelings in silence, quite likely, as you are sometimes wont. But come or stay, we shall all love you, and such as you forever, dear E.—

To day, you have been to Church in town I fancy, and that is an event quite new to you. How did it seem?—the spacious Church, the courtly people, the gowned Priest; the service of prayer and praise; the pealing anthem, and the pealing bells? Beautiful, most beautiful, where sincere devotion leads, ‖ and love ‖ and homage of the All-Beautiful prompts! Write to us about it, for I hear you will write to-morrow. Little Abby has written out her *Loneliness* in her little Note to you, and will count the days of your absence till it is ended.— We have all had a quiet day. This morning I gathered the apples, and saved some fine golden Porters' for you, which are sent along with other tokens of our regard ‖ for you ‖ [p. o.]; your kind friends will share these with you: and I will persuade my self that when you leave them to come to us, you will leave much love and regard behind you. I desire that you may find as happy a home as theirs, whenever you shall leave ours. Present Uncle the fairest Porter; spread the table in your tidyest [sic] manner for Miss Robie, and be your own best self all the time of your stay, which I, for my part, desire may not be long.

* at Dr. Bronson's in Cheshire Conn [6 p. in]

Your affectionate
Father.

For
     Elisabeth
          in Boston

LETTER 48–14[1]

[to Louisa, Hopedale]

Boston Nov [29] 1848

My dear Louisa, at Hopedale,

Our Birth days arrive again today—"Forty Nine" years to the Father, and to the daughter comes the celebrated "Sixteen." May they be years of harvest to us, those upon which we now enter—

Fruits and flowers
Crop't from hours,
To virtue given,
Thrifty for Heaven.

With this prayer and sentiment I send along my Circular for the Conversations, which promise to open under the best advantages of place, time and company. If you were here, the spectacle, if nothing more, might please your own curious eyes once in a week, ‖ and could not displease easily. ‖ Anna means to find some corner, and become invisible to overhear the talk, and laugh at our wise nonsense. I wish we may all be as diffident and unpretend[ing] as this sister of yours, and so escape the terrors of meeting. Come home before we weary of one another, and see how wise we all are there together.

I am pleased to hear good tidings of you. I read your letter and find you give lively accounts of yourself. Serve your friends to the best of your skill, and come and see us here in these snug quarters, suburban four that we are, when you can be spared fro[m] the cottage and the dale. I shal[l] dart that way again sometime this winter possibly.

Rememember [sic] me to the good people, whom I think of with respec[t] and hope to see again soon.

Your affectionate Father.

Dedham Street 29. Nov. 1848.

[1] MS. in the Clifton Waller Barrett Library, University of Virginia.

PART SEVEN

⚹

1849–1852

Boston, Feb. 20, 1849

Dear Sir,

I send you, herewith, the names of a select company of gentlemen, esteemed as deserving of better acquaintance, and disposed for closer fellowship of Thought and Endeavor, who are hereby invited to assemble at No. 12, West-street, on Tuesday, the 20th of March next, to discuss the Advantages of organizing a Club or College, for the study and diffusion of the Ideas and Tendencies proper to the Nineteenth Century; and to concert measures, if deemed desirable, for promoting the ends of good fellowship.

The Company will meet at 10, A.M. Your presence is respectfully claimed by

Yours truly,

A. Bronson Alcott.

Rooms 12, West-street.

Names.

R. Waldo **Emerson**
William Lloyd Garrison
Theodore Parker
William Henry Channing
A. Bronson Alcott
Wendell Phillips
Thomas T. Stone
F. Henry Hedge
Samuel G. Howe
J. Freeman Clarke
Edmund Quincy
John W. Browne
J. Elliot Cabot
T. Starr King
J. Russell Lowell
Samuel G. Ward

Caleb Stetson
George P. Bradford
Adin Ballou
Jones Very
William F. Channing
Elizur Wright
Stephen S. Foster
Charles C. Shackford
Emanuel Scherb
E. P. Clarke
Samuel D. Robbins
Joshua Melroy
J. T. Fisher
Oliver Johnson
O. B. Frothingham
C. K. Whipple

147

John L. Weisse
Edwin P. Whipple
T. Wentworth Higginson
Parker Pillsbury
Henry D. Thoreau
Henry I. Bowditch
Henry C. Wright
John S. Dwight
Francis Jackson
W. Ellery Channing
William B. Greene

Samuel Johnson
James N. Buffum
William H. Knapp
Samuel May, jun.
Otis Clapp
J. M. Spear
Charles Spear
W. R. Alger
Edward Bangs
R. F. Walcott
A. D. Mayo

¹ MS. owned by the Boston Public Library. The printed form letter (and list of people to whom it was sent) proposes a club subsequently named the Town and Country Club. The letter (with minor differences of punctuation) is quoted in Sanborn, *A. Bronson Alcott*, II, 461; and the list, II, 459–60, *n.* The letter and list are also quoted in Walter Harding and Carl Bode, eds., *The Correspondence of Henry David Thoreau* (New York, 1958), pp. 239–40. The minutes and other records of that relatively short-lived club are among the Alcott papers in the Houghton Library, Harvard University. They have been printed in Kenneth Walter Cameron, "Emerson, Thoreau, and the Town and Country Club," *Emerson Society Quarterly*, No. 8 (1957), 2–17.

LETTER 49–2¹

[to James Russell Lowell, Cambridge, Mass.]

12 Wall Street² | March 22, 1849

Dear Sir,

The New Club meets at my Rooms on Tuesday morning next at 10 oclock and holds through the Day and evening. Meet with us then if you can. I was sorry to hear of that unlucky cause which witheld [*sic*] you from on [*sic*] yesterday. But come and take your Place and part in the Parliament of next week.

I am reading the "Poetry of the Seventeenth Century" to my company here and in Salem, and have to express many thanks to the instinct that led ‖ my hands ‖ me to the Library and yourself where so many fruits and flowers awaited me.

Hoping to see you on Tuesday,

I am,
truly yours
A. Bronson Alcott

J. Russell Lowell
Elmwood

¹ From a typescript made from a MS. in the Whelpley Collection, Cincinnati Historical Society.
² The Alcotts moved to Dedham Street, Boston, in November, 1848; and Alcott also rented rooms (for Conversations) at 12 *West* Street, Boston. The error is probably in the typescript.

LETTER 49–3[1]

[to Samuel Longfellow]

12. West Street, Boston, | 21. April, 1849.

Dear Sir,

A monthly meeting of "The Town and Country Club," will be holden at Rooms No. 12. West Street, on Wednesday 2nd May next, at 10. o,clock A.M. R. W. Emerson will read a Paper, and important matters will come before the Meeting.

Hoping to see you on that occasion and to add your name to our list of subscribers,

I am,

Respectfully Yours,
A. Bronson Alcott

Rev. Sam. Longfellow.

[1] MS. owned by the Abernethy Library, Middlebury College.

LETTER 49–4

[to Mrs. Anna Alcott, Oriskany Falls, N.Y.]

Boston, April 22nd 1849.

Dear Mother,

I have thought often and much of you lately, and was about writing to you when your letter came to me a few days ago. I was glad to hear of your good health and the many comforts you are able to enjoy at your advanced age, as unexpected to yourself, I am, inclined to believe, as they are to me when I remember your discomforts of some few years ago. I have tried to reccollect [sic] your age, but am unable to do so; whether it is 80 and more years or not I cannot tell. But if old in years, your letter breathes of youth and freshness of soul, and I was glad to have it in my hands, and be made to feel, as I read, the ties that bind mother and son to each other, though silence and distance may seem to sever and separate them. For what you say, in your letter, I have always felt to be true, *"that one Mind may be conveyed to two friends,"* and *"that there is no time when those who love each other are deprived of each others' company"* which I take to be the surest evidence we have, (and is in itself an *experience* of the Spiritual Society and family enjoyments which we call, *Heaven*. As we are *Spirits in Bodies,* so we communicate with the Spirits in our own, or friends' Bodies, as we seek to become pure—which is but another name for being spiritual: And the stupidity of which so many complain, is but another name for the Sensuality in which they indulge; *unbelief* in Spiritual things being but that blindness which they have brought on themselves, that renders them unable to see their own Souls or Spirits: Our Bodies are somewhat like looking glasses, clear and reflecting the figures of our Souls to our eyes, as we coat the glass with the quicksilver of Purity; or dimming and distorting features of our souls, as we speck the foiling behind the glass with impurity, and sin. *"If the light that is within us be darkness how great is that darkness!"* And to the clear-minded all is Spiritual, as to the foul-minded all in material and impure. So we abide in the worlds we create, and invite into the private parlours of our own Hearts, company like ourselves. ‖ and ‖ Our Prevailing desires and ruling thoughts are but the keys that open the doors, and the compliments that welcome our guests, into our inner apartments. Spirits, good or evil, angels or devils, come in and sit with us, and depart from us, at our bidding, and we are known of all who take note of us, by the company we keep, as by that we shun. Nor can any have friends indeed, till they have first made friends of the Soul that inhabits and entertains, for good or ill, the Body they call their own, and which is its friend, or foe, as they love or hate in their Hearts.

Of these things we may have more or less knowledge and belief, as we have experienced the life of our Souls.—A. J. Davis'[1] Books are very good for many people; they will help them out of some of the old perplexities in which so many are cast by the perverted teachings of former times, and so will do good. I should think them very good correctives of the Sensualism and Infidelity of our day, and helps to the better understanding of the Bible, and of the laws and duties of Life. I read them, and have had some correspondence with Davis lately by letter. Here in Boston we have much of the same and similar thinking, which will come to some useful ends before long.—But I must not enter into these matters now.

You will see that we are living now in Boston. We came here last November, and shall [p. in] continue in the City during the summer. I have been much occupied in my *"Conversations,"* both in this city and Salem; and am purposing to give courses in other places during the spring and summer. They interest me, and seem to please and instruct others. I have *"Readings"* also at my Rooms, No. 12. West Street.—Lately I have been interested in getting up a Club, which we call *"The Town and Country Club,"* which is to meet monthly the Quarterly for the discussion of the great questions that now divide the minds of men: and which we hope to see a little more clearly into if we can. Emerson, Channing, Parker, Hawthorne, and others, to the number of 100, or more, of the leading minds of our time, are members, and I am to have charge of the Rooms and act as Secretary of the Club. This will give me a house and home in Boston, and bring most of the active Persons in the Reforms to my doors. It promises well. We shall live during the Summer in Temple Place, near the Masonic Temple where I had my School.

We are all well. Anna is teaching School in Roxbury, and passes her Sundays at home. Louisa is living in the family of Mr S. E. Sewall, a few miles from us. Elisabeth and Abba attend school in the City: and "Abba," the larger, is "City Missionary to the Poor and Perishing in her neighborhood—and has been useful to an extent beyond my powers of describing. Her house has been the haunt of hundreds, coming to ask[?], and to leave comforted. I must leave her to tell you her own story.—Pamela is released: & I have reason to believe has entered upon wider labors of love, for which she was prepared. She was a good woman, I may truly say, although I saw her not after she became a wife and mother. I remember her as an affectionate, ‖ high ‖ devoted sister, and the domestic qualities she possessed must have made her a true wife and tender mother. I shall not be able to write to her husband now, as I know not his residence.

Thus we pass on and off the stage of existence. Of the sisters only Betsey survives—lives to be near you, and see the translation to a purer sphere: so Providence supplies a daughter's breast upon which the mother may sink into her last sleep. The Sons yet remain, and all, but this older one, near and to be seen of you, and see you in their circle. I may not behold your *human* face again: but serene in my heart beams a countenance that I have never lost sight of, and which from the dawn of memory has rejoined[?] me and blessed me; which shall beam upon me, as I too cast off the darkness, and rise into the light of that Day wherein it abides.—Heaven is near to us bot[h.]

Love to all. If Junius or Chatfield would write—will they not favor us with a line?

Dear Mother,
Your affectionate Son
A. Bronson Alcott.

[1] Andrew Jackson Davis of Poughkeepsie, New York.

LETTER 49–5

[to Louisa and May, Hopedale? Mass.]
Temple Place [Boston] | Sunday 17[?] June | '49
Dear Girls,

I had no chance to write a word in the letter of last week, and will make some amends in the dispatches of to day. Your letters left you well and happy; may this find you so. It is good for you to be absent sometimes from us, and you could not have had a finer season chosen for you; this leafy June, and in that pleasing country where you are with so much freedom, and yet with cares on your mind and hands that vary your pleasures, and leave you the satisfactions of serving the friends who invited you to their house and its keeping. I know you will do your best to be a wise and faithful and tidy mistress of the mansion. And Abby will find her old country delights, with her former playmate; and the numerous friends the lively Child cannot fail to make in the village, in the fields, brooks, hills and skies of Leicester. It will do her good, and yourself too, after the cramped and unvaried life you both were doomed to pass in Dedham Street, without choice of associates; and occupations that gave no colour to your days. The airs, and woods, and waters, and skies, you now enjoy, will flow into you, and be borne off in your mind and heart to the City.

The Common is looking very beautifully. We enjoy it at all hours, but most in the morning, when we get a walk, and again in the evening. There is more company in the afternoo[n] than at other times; but the fountain and the foliage are more refreshing than the most observed of observers: and our walk before breakfast, and after the bath, is the best meal of the day. Anna and Elisabeth are beginning to taste and find how good it is for mind and body. It was meant that the whole season should be put into us, as it is into a flower; and its virtues should reappear in us, as the sun colours the peach, and mellows the pulp of the plum and apple.

<pre>
                    Forth from ourselves

                    We may not stir,
                             of the world
                    Ere, Nature is
                    Were
                    Our Pensioner.
</pre>

I am hoping for good times at Fall River. I go on Tuesday to pass Wednesday, and have two Conversations, and a sail to Mount Hope.

My love to you both; And wish for many pleasures to enjoy and speak of when you return to us again.

Your Father.

LETTER 49–6

[to Mrs. A. Bronson Alcott, Boston]

Concord, Mass. | Monday Morning | 17. Sep. 1849

My dear,

A man, beset as I am just now, with the felicity of some half score of guardians, and th[e] airs[?], company and the rest of what this Village has to offer him, must needs die outright, or come soon to life again, and the taking of a man's part in affairs once again. And I have the happiness of informing the senders of so many things for an invalid's comfort, in the shape of clean, well-aired and neatly disposed linens and sundries of Peaches and Apples and Cakes too, that this last good piece of fortune—restoration from the dead—is likely to prove mine; And to intimate further, that when you come, lady, we will go see Fruitlands, if you please, where *A man once lived,* instead of Mt. Auburn, where, perchance the same man, shall find a resting place some half century hence; For I am, within the last days and without much bathing or company, but by muc[h] walking, and my landlady and her daughters care of me, become almost freed of that boding cough, and sleep without seeing goblins, or stumblings over the plac[es] of the dead: and am myself almost again; altogether so in Hope, and wait for som[e] ten days or a fortnight more to justify my Prospects, an[d] dispatch me to town, to be all the more careful, (may we trust?) of this brittle implement, dust-moulded, and not[?] the same thereafter with some discretion, getting a wise lesson from this adventure, if not a wise Book off the brain[?] to see, and to be shown, for our summer's devotion.

I hope you will not fail to see yourself have a days' respite from the City and its drudgeries (as you intimate) now while you may, out here with me, and see the Cottage, and "Hillside," and if you incline, as I shall, take a look at Fruitlands, by way of a reminiscence. Come, and leave that Poor Self, and the Poor creatures you enrich, for one clear day, before the winter's campaign opens to us both; and Miss Ford will come, too, perhaps; for Sarah[1] will be glad to see her, as I am always, and enjoy in Person rather than by epistle; for of the last, I am persuaded few if any care so much about, or care to read, as the living Person.

Such tidy, punctual, housewifery as I enjoy (here under these Elms) and salutary quiet, are benefits, for which my good guardian, always having me best cared for from the very cradle, shall be praised with a life long thankfulness of Heart and thought.—Nature and Nature's almsgivings conspiring still to serve me—the[?] incapable of anxiety and doubt. Providence as we best call this care-taking, practices a foresight, a kind of long-logic, much like a womans, and quite beyond our Poor comprehensions. It was *your own* pains taking of a humble damsel, some half dozen years since, that gives me now in the cares of that same maiden, and her mother's well wishes for the daughter's benefactors, a home, and chamber of quiet delights, that never my spouse, with all her formidable loves, & prompt and sleepless carefulness could secure to me, and find for herself. Great is quiet, and great is strife: and the strife for quiet is the pleading for the Rest to be won some day.

But here I am, and it is almost 9, and I am at the end of these sheets—Abbas careful little billet came, Lizzies did not come, and I leave her, and the rest, to write when they can. I am glad to hear of the fair Prospects at South End, and will return *whole* at a fortnights end to see: and enjoy with the rest. Sarah goes to the City tomorrow, when I shall complete my letter.

Affectionately A.B.A.

Concord, 6. o'Clock 17. Sep. | Monday Aftern. | 1849.

Henry and I have bathed since 5 P.M. near the Indian Fishing Place, where lay the Boat Undine[?], and I am just from Supper, to add something to my morning's note for Sarah to bear to you by the earliest train to morrow, at 6. On looking for my linen, there is nothing to send I find, for she has undertaken to spare all carriage of this sort. Nor will you need give a thought to the matter for some days to come. Anna's carefully disposed box of collars, the stockings and the rest, will serve me for a week or more.

I am taking life here most agreeably. I rise at 6. (called punctually by S—) at half past 6 we breakfast, and I walk afterwards till 9. am in my chamber—the East one—till half past 12. when we dine; and return to my studies, leaving usually at 4 for another walk till half Past 5, when we take supper, and I get to bed not far from 8. I have shunned the evening damps, and have come but once from Emerson's after dusk.

The old haunts, by the Hallowel road, across the river Bridge by the Wil-lows—up the rail-way to the factories Barretts Hill—I have been once to Walden with Emerson, and once along the River meadows by Mrs Ripleys—these, are my resorts thus far: and to the Village and Station, but I shall find others during the coming fortnight[.]

I have seen scarce nobody only Thoreau and Emerson, nor shall, I suppose, while here. Elisabeths letter to Cary was delivered by Lydia Hosmer who goes daily to Miss Whitings.

I hear that S. D. Robbins of Chelsea will buy Channings Place: to ours, I have not yet strolled, but will when you come if you like.

I shall hope to see you some day soon: meanwhile, love and benedictions,

153

and contents, nameless and many, at 1. Temple Place; and at Washington and Groton Streets, when any or all chance that way.

Affectionately, A.B.A.

¹ Sarah Hosmer. Alcott stayed at her mother's house while in Concord, where he went to recuperate from a tiring summer.

LETTER 49–7[1]

[to James Russell Lowell, Cambridge, Mass.]

15. Tremont Row,[2] | 18 December 1849.

Dear Sir,

'The Town & Country Club," you will bear in mind, expects the reading of a Paper from yourself at the Quarterly Meeting on the 3rd. January 1850. We shall take it most kindly, if you will indulge us on that occasion; and may we venture to hope for such entertainments as the muse alone can bring?—A Poem were indeed a celebration worthy of the names and Objects of the Society. Do not let the occasion slip.

Miss Bremer[3] has been with you I hear. I am yet to see her, and with much hope.

Truly yours
A. Bronson Alcott

¹ MS. owned by the Houghton Library, Harvard University.
² In Boston, where the Town and Country Club had taken rooms.
³ Fredrika Bremer, who was travelling in America. See Adolph B. Benson, ed., *America of the Fifties: Letters of Fredrika Bremer* (New York, 1924).

LETTER 50–1[1]

[Boston, March 4, 1850]

Town and Country Club.

Henry Giles, Esq.[2] will read a paper before the TOWN AND COUNTRY CLUB, at the Rooms, NO. 15, Tremont Row, on Thursday, 7th March, at half-past three o'clock, P.M. A Committee will report upon the precuniary condition and prospects of the Club, and recommend a plan for re-organization.

A full attendance of members is requested.

A. BRONSON ALCOTT,

Boston, March 4, 1850.   *Corresponding Secretary*

¹ MS. owned by the Houghton Library, Harvard University. The item is a printed announcement and includes a membership list which has not been reproduced herein. For a list of persons invited to the organizational meeting on March 20, 1849, see Letter 49–1. For lists of members, see Cameron, "Emerson, Thoreau, and the Town and Country Club," pp. 15–17.
² Well known as a lecturer.

LETTER 50–2

[to Mrs. Anna Alcott, Oriskany Falls, N.Y.]

Boston, 28 April, 1850.

Dear Mother,

Your long and carefully written letter, dated February 10th. has lain before me till this time unanswered, but was far from being unheeded; the prospect of seeing you here with us once more was too pleasing to permit this, and I was desirous, besides, of knowing what our own family arrangements were to be; that I might invite you, and brother Chatfield and family, into comfortable quarters during your stay with us, which, I trust, will be as long as you incline to remain guests of ours. We are now at home and well all of us, and living at No 88. Corner of Atkinson and Purchase Streets, where you must come from the Depot near by when you arrive in our city.

I am very glad that you incline to visit us just now, while I am engaged in collecting every thing that I can lay hold of respecting our Family History, about which you know more than any body else.

And I wish you would rummage faithfully, if your eyes still serve you, all the papers that you may have in possession; such as letters from your children: any of Father's M.S.S. Papers, (no matter what these may be) deeds, account Books, written Prayers, (for I remember some of the last which he kept in a little red box under his chest-till) and if Chatfield has any MSS. of his, or books, or other documents, I should like much to see these, also. You, too, must have many letters, by this time, in your keeping, from your children, and some perhaps, from your own brothers and sisters; and if your own *"Journal"* that I used to ‖ see ‖ [word] the [word] of in the Old Oaken Chest, up stairs, and *"the Dilworth's Spelling Book,"* have been saved till now, let me have sight of them again; also, the Family Bible, and any books remaining of the few that used to lie on the red shelf in the Old house. But of the last, I remember only *"Bunyan's Grace Abounding to the Chief of Sinners,"* and the Almanacs. Don't fail to bring your own Diary, the one you kept when you were with us at Cottage Place in 1837. I shall want this; and every thing you can recollect beside of the times of my earliest childhood and youth, and all you can remember of your own and father's childhood, and your grandparents. I hope to find you able to recal much for me of Uncle Tillotson, and if you have any of his printed sermons, or other documents concerning him, bring them along also: or of Uncle Amos or Noah. These things are becoming of unexpected interest to me just now, and I am covetous of such informations. Chatfield must have many reminiscences of our early days, and of the era of pedling particularly, which will render intercourse all the more interesting at this time. I have written many letters both to him and to Junius, from time to time, and should esteem it a great privilege to see them now; If they value these letters, I would return them again. Any M.S.S. they may have of mine, or of the days gone by, would serve me well, and give me pleasure to recover. Dr. Alcott has a good many which I am to see in a few days. He lives within an hours ride of us, and is the only one of our name known to me in these parts.

We have had less communication for this last year than ever before. Junius has not written, nor have I heard often from you. I find, on looking over my files of letters, but one from Chatfield, nor have I a single line from any of my

155

sisters, now all gone but one of the four, that I knew and enjoyed during my boyhood and youth.

My love to Betsey and family, and to all members of the Oriskany group. We shall expect you during all of May, and wait with pleasure the hope of taking your ‖ by the ‖ hands.

Affectionately
A. Bronson Alcott.

Mrs Anna Alcott
Oriskany Falls
New York.

LETTER 50–3

[to Anna, Lenox, Mass.]

Sunday 30 June, 1850 | 88 Atkinson Street.[1]

Dear Anna,

You shall have a word from me along with your sister's parcel, which leaves to-morrow.—I wish you would reconcile your calling a little with your fancy, I have a clear sense of your duties, & so a contented mind.[2] But you have, it seems, an admirable & strong sense of what seems becoming & best to be done, & a patient resolution to carry it out, ‖ quite ‖ against your inclinations & all that is most charming to your Eye & Heart. That is your Castle to detain you prisoner, ([word] a little disposed to flee sometimes,) on the mountains far away from the City ‖ & ‖ its inmates & all most ‖ so ‖ pleasing to you. I respect, & love you for your disinterestedness, & sympathize with you in all that would bring you back to us again. Let Time decide for us, & you shall perform the tasks meanwhile that fall to you; & your last letter breathes a little more of contentment I see.—Yesterday, Orson, the wild-man, shaved himself, the first time, for three weeks back, & is getting a little civil, & to be seen again;[3] and is in the mood now of writing the name, 'Father,' affectionately at the close of his note. Goodbye, dear daughter dear.

Miss Anna Bronson Alcott
Lenox

[1] The house of Mrs. Alcott's relatives, the Mays, in Boston, where the Alcotts spent the summers of 1849 and 1850.
[2] In her Journal for July, 1850, Louisa wrote, "Anna is gone to L. after the varioloid. She is to help Mrs. _____ with her baby." (Cheney, p. 62.)
[3] Alcott had been ill with smallpox and unable to shave. See Letter 50–5.

LETTER 50–4[1]

[to Ednah Dow Littlehale,[2] Gloucester, Mass.]

Boston 29 August 1850 | 88. Atkinson Street.

My dear Miss Littlehale,

Yesterday's criticism of yours on Carlyle, or rather on my criticism on him, seemed, as I read, very just & becoming for a wise woman to take on our heathen, whom none may accept & justify but from Jewry & the Sinai mount: nor from these fully with the later law & prophets in his hands.—And yet it has seemed to me, sometimes, from his side of the world, as if this foolish race of ours, were wishing to escape, not from its Sins, but from its Judgments; and were quite willing that some body or another should swing for the Laws sake. But it is always the Other one—never this One, or the moiety of him in each man's mind & memory. It is mercy for myself, mostly; misery & minder of thyself; and—"the devil take *thee for me.*" Indeed, there goes so much of God's grace into the sentiment of Mercy, that few, if any, have come so fully into it as to see how any man can be saved without some *Otherism* or another; letting Satan have a little length of tether, meanwhile, "to fetch up" the sinner, as the boys say, by falling foul of his own foolishness, to get some sense out of his prone experiences. So it is. "Tis good Lord, and good Devil, too, if we knew it. But it takes a good man to find out the Divine Secrets, as it does a bad one, the Demonic; and to thank the last as dearly as the first for his doings on him, also. I, for one, should like well to speak with the Saint whom the devil has never *d – – – –d* a little bit (according to Miss Bremer's faith) by daring him to the proof of his integrity, sometime. Evidently, the devil is a busy-body, and we might Christen him rightly enough, Imp and Impertinent;—here now in our way, as we fancied: then, "Presto," soon, we find 'tis ourselves in his way, instead; and, like Bunyan's Apollion, he withstands unspectorally[?]. to show us our own figure, & to shove us clean back into the way of Salvation, if we will let him have that happiness. A good man should never blunder too seriously. He gets the better of Baalzebub & Bedlam both, by humouring his sulks a little, and rather boldly too; and has reason to be most thankful for the scarlets always, when he comes to himself again. Good flowers forth from evil: the orthodox Quarles has it, that

"The common way to Heaven's by Hell,"—

and, possibly, it has been almost as bad as that. Is it that the Devil is a disguised Friend of ours? And are we to bless Baalzebub, Blame, Brimstone, & Co. devoutly; bless, & but curse, these most excellent friends of ours mistaken mostly for foes by the foolish, but yet, for need of which, the good Lord will not issue his mittimus, seeing the thousand years lack some centuries of accomplishment to bring the world out of ‖ the ‖ said companies service, & dissolve the same as useless; dooms day being done up fairfuly[?] and forever?—

But of Carlyle, we say it is not Best, only better a little with him, than with some, he is a Hebrew heathen—no man,—coming far short of ‖ the B ‖ Christ's Beatitudes. I pity the man whom the Fates have frozen so: formidable, frightful, relentless; stooping[?] to the horses, like tomorrow's sunshine in Leverett Street, screening never the Saint in the soul's soul from the sinner outside of it, whence penitence would "turn off," presently, of its own accord, if he would wait a little for the soft whispers to muffle the moment's madness for the poor lunatic, born with defect of love & the lights.

The laws—the Laws; majestic, mighty, in their exactions of Mercy—the cloked and not the bared thunders—but mean and murderous otherwise—

"Who breaks a fly upon a wheel,
Himself the ponderous axe shall feel.

On the whole, Carlyle has cast himself, "full many a league," beyond the nether-most comforts: is no Christian, properly; or at best a Calvinistic Minotaur: a mixed monster; say, British-Alexandrine-Jew; hardly the St Thomas of the Latter day Scriptures, being more incredulous than was him of old, of martyrdoms that have no substantial breadth of body to show for themselves. 'Tis a dire[?] drinking, as dreneking[?] deep in the Lethes: not ‖ any ‖ some

> "draught restorative
> Forth willing from the depths of his own soul"

You are coming to Town soon & to see me. Come, & welcome!—The Pedler Boy stole away yesterday just before your letter came in to get a little time, I fancy; & ripening, into his crude credulous brain, before he ventures forth, the school-master, as he next shows himself before folks about the Year 1827. The Summer is passing into Autumn ripe, & I am soon to have a taste of the last, for a fortnight or so, in Concord; & please myself with the hope of seeing you at the Poet's Place, while I am there at work on the Summer House.[3] "Aunt Vitty" I have heard of, & once saw at the Chardon Street Gasconades in 1840, or thereabouts. And Miss Hunt shall come & teach me, too, if she will. I hope to see her sometime, at least, if she cares for it.

I am having fair days: the Haven is handsome alike by sunlight and by moon-light, from my window; and my majestic mystic is seen by me every morning—I meet no body else in the Common, at my hour.

> Memories many of yourself, sister,
> and Miss Walker, & pleasant ones:
> and, were I the unforgettable,
> I should be yours, forever,
> A. Bronson Alcott.

Miss E. D. Littlehale.
Gloucester.

[1] MS. owned by the Massachusetts Historical Society.
[2] Afterward, Mrs. Ednah Dow Cheney.
[3] Built by Alcott for Emerson.

LETTER 50–5

[to   Chatfield Alcott, Oriskany Falls, N.Y.]
Boston September 16, 1850. | 88 Atkinson Street
Dear Brother,

I have been thinking of you, and of my friends at Oriskany a good deal lately; and suppose, from some hints dropped in the letters we received from you last February, that you were intending to visit us, and are still meaning to come this way, soon. I hope you are coming, for I wish to see you here, and dear mother, very much; and write now chiefly for information from you whether you are com-ing, or not, and when we may expect you, if you are. We are all quite well, and at home, and shall be most happy to entertain you, and those you may bring with you, at No 88 Atkinson Street, where we are purposing to pass the winter.[1] My wife tells me that she wrote to you about our sickness in June last, and you may be waiting to hear further from us before you venture this way. But we are all very well now, and there is no danger from us, or any one here. The girls had the viraloid[2] very slightly; my wife a little severely; but mine was the old-fashioned small-pox, and kept me in the house a couple of months, yet leaves me unpitted, and I am as well now as before I had it. I could not shave myself for a month, and looked frightful enough—like the wild man, Orson, of the woods, in the story of Valentine & Orson, which we read when boys. But I had a good appetite all the time, and kept the doctor out of the house, and so got well without medicines of any kind, and am left speckled a little in the face, and shall not get a fair skin on again for some weeks to come, perhaps. I suppose my wife had it first but where she got it she does not know. Now I want you should write to us immediately on receiving this letter whether you are coming to see us, or not, or if you do not write, then Junius, or some one of you. And if you are not coming, I shall hope to visit you sometime in October, before I begin my "Conversations' here for the season. I am intending to go by way of Wolcott, and Waterbury, and to be gone a fortnight or more from home. But if you are coming and Mother with you, I shall defer my visit. I cannot hope to see mother many times more, and fear I may miss seeing her at all, sometimes; though she wrote last in good hope and spirits, and may survive some of us now living. I am now fifty years of age, and as old, wanting only [p. in] a few years, as our Father was when he left us; and you are come close upon your half century now. Junius & Ambrose might be sons, ‖ of ours ‖ rather than brothers, of ours. Junius has not written me for a long time: and I find but one letter from you, since the days of pedling. Lately, I have been writing about our Southern Adventures, and earlier than these times and should like to read the story to you, and the rest—mother & Betsey—right well. Remember to bring all the letters and papers about these & later times, when you come. I hope Mother is well enough to undertake the journey. My love to her,—and kind remembrances of yourself, wife, and the ‖ others of you ‖ rest, at Oriskany. I shall hope to see you soon.

Your brother
A. Bronson Alcott.

Mr. Chatfield Alcott.

[1] Instead, the Alcotts moved to 50 High Street, Boston.
[2] "varioloid."

LETTER 50–6

[to Junius S. Alcott, Oriskany Falls, N.Y.]

Boston 7 December 1850 | (50 High Street.)

Dear Brother,

I was sorry to leave Oriskany in such haste, and to miss seeing you for the conversations which I had promised myself while on this visit. I thought to have seen and passed Sunday with you and Ambrose at Chatfields. But it happened otherwise, and I must wait to renew our intercourse when you come this way in the Spring. I saw Chatfield and family a good deal, and am glad to have had this opportunity of renewing our acquaintance, and of indulging in many remembrances of early days. It was an agreeable visit and I shall remember it with pleasure.

We passed a night at Clinton with cousin Denison, and family.[1] I found him a very good and sensible man, and saw many of his parishioners at his house in the evening at a sewing circle. I like him, and his wife very well. I did not see his son: the daughter seemed a pleasing girl. He is evidently a useful man, and much beloved by his people.

We reached Albany at 3 P.M, next day, and stopped at the Merchants' Hotel. I did not recover my lost trunk of papers, but entertain some hope of finding it. We staid over night, and left early on Saturday morning by rail; dined at Springfield, and the carriage set us safely down at 50 High Street, between 6 and 7 in the evening. Mother was very lively all the way, and came with little fatigue. My wife and girls were glad to see, and have her an inmate of ours again. She is quite busy now beside me with her needle, and seems cheerful, social as ever, and contented. The weather has not been favorable for going out, but she has been once to see the Fountain on the Common, walking all the way without difficulty. I trust that she has a comfortable winter before her for a lady of 77.

We are all quite well. My wife is very busy about the "Help"; and the girls are all very helpful and industrious. I hope your wife is recovering to resume the care of her little family. Will you write me sometimes. You seem to be in prosperous business, and I think of you now with hope. So much ingenuity must yield its rewards in due time.

Chatfields losses are heavy, but he can bear them better than most men, and redeem himself sooner. He promised to send me a newspaper notice of the flood, and the losers by it. I found Ambrose's "Waterbury American" among my things when I got home.

Love to all.
A. Bronson Alcott

Mother says. "I am well & contented. The woodfire in my chamber, where I sew and sleep, is very agreeable to my feelings. Abby sits with me when she can, and it seems like home in the house here. The food [word] me as yet.—Write soon.

[1] Rev. Denison Alcott.

LETTER 51–1

[to Denison Alcott, Clinton, N.Y.]

Boston 29th April, 1851.

Dear Cousin,

Yesterday came your letter to hand, which I had scarcely finished reading when in came our Cousin Hiram Bronson upon us, and passed the evening, much to our gratification, as he brought good news from our common friends in Ohio whom he has left behind some fortnight's time back in good health, as he told us. He inquires particularly about yourself, and the Oriskany cousins, but doubted whether he should have time to stop on his way to pass even a night with any of you:—busy merchantman, and gold-gatherer as he clearly is, and prosperous, too, in his business. He seemed intelligent, enterprising, and is a fair sample of the class of Western traders. He told us a good deal about his affairs, and leaves for home to day, by way of N. York City.

You are purposing to visit us, I am well pleased to learn, and we shall take it for granted, that you come, at once, from the Depot, where you will be left, to No 50 High Street, which is but a little way from the Station, and any hackman will bring you, baggage and all, for 25 cts to my door, or direct you to us, if you have only your valice [sic] or carpet bag along, and prefer to walk. My wife and daughters will be glad to see you, and I shall take special pleasure in serving you in any way lying within my power. Bowdoin Square and Church are not far from my house, and you will be here during Anniversary Week, when the religious world is all in town, and talking its best, for humanity and Christendom. I hope to see a good deal of you, and show you a good deal besides of our city and its men. We shall look out for you about the 15th May.

My mother is still with us, and is quite well: an example of cheerful, quiet industry, and a comfort to us all An old age like hers is beautiful, and a just reward for the life she has lived. Hiram tells me that your mother was unusually hale and as smart as ever when he left Medina.[1] Our mothers are good women, and gave us more than we know. I remember with pleasure my visit for a night, and your attentions. My regards to your wife, and daughter, both of whom I should esteem it a privilege to be acquainted with.

Very truly
Your Cousin
A. Bronson Alcott

Rev. Denison Alcott.

[1] In Ohio.

LETTER 51–2[1]

[to Ednah D. Littlehale, Boston]

[Boston, September 11, 1851]

Ednah D. Littlehale
    Bowdoin Street
       Boston.

My dear Miss Littlehale,

Here is a basket of "Hillside" Fruits. Be so good as to take, taste, and, on some of these current Ambrosial mornings, come yourself with leisure to tell us how you like it.

Lately, that is, yesterday and this morning, I have been earlier by half an hour in the Park than formerly—but to discover as I think that the little hale birds of our aviary, dip their plumes in a rosier dawn, than some of us of the paler and more sluggish wing can safely emulate.

Yours ever,

And, moreover, heartily obliged, to day, by certain wardrobes of comforting friendships that bid fair to survive, as they surpass, the coming winter's snows in whiteness. **Many thanks.**

A. Bronson Alcott

50 High Street
11th. September 1851.

¹ MS. owned by the Fruitlands and Wayside Museums.

LETTER 51-3

[to Mrs. Anna Alcott, Oriskany Falls, N.Y.]

Boston 19th October, 1851

Dear Mother,

Your letter date 20th July, last, I meant to have answered, at once, but Abby dispatched an answer before I knew any thing of it, leaving me in your debt, and since that time we have heard nothing of your welfare. Then you were recovering, you told us, from the effects of your unlucky fall. I trust you are fairly afoot again, and at your customary journeyings from son to son's houses;—a matter of health and cheerfulness to you. If it is not so, and you are yet confined to chairs and chambers, pray write and let us know more than you have told us of the damages you received, and of your present condition. Old people are not so easily mended as young ones; but then I am unable to think of you as one of the old; you have been so active and sprightly during these old years past and passing. So the home laid and unsuspected stair-way, proved less safe for your conduct from story to story, it seems, than the firm, and, as you feared, perilous Rail track, which yet took you from High Street to Oriskany and set you down safe and sound at your friends door, despite of age, and all your apprehensions, to be cast down the treacherous stairs afterwards.

There is nothing of special interest to communicate. Life runs off the reel very much after the old sort: Abby charged with a confusing business below; Anna going daily to meet her little School at Jamaica Plains; Louisa having the care of some children from ten till two in Beacon Street; Elisabeth doing the housework, and Abby, the younger, going to school to Mr. Blake, the gentleman who came sometimes to see me, you may remember, last winter. So all are busy, and, I may add, profitably engaged. And, now, that I begin to kindle my fires again, I am reminded of a certain handsome, cheerful, ready-to-talk, venerable, and lady like (even to the cap and spectacles) piece of chimney corner furniture missing, that once adorned my chamber, when a mother was with me. I often think of those days, and blame myself for being so much less companionable than became a son; but habit held the pen, and still holds, and must, I suppose, to the last. I am poor company enough.—Cousin Hiram Bronson was here with his daughter three weeks ago, and gave good accounts of all our friends in Medina. Aunt Sylvia had gone to pass the winter in Wolcott, and was as lively as ever. Helen, the daughter, had been at school in New Haven, and seemed intelligent and lady-like.—Dr William & family are well.—Yesterday Theodore Parker told her [sic] he had received a letter from Junius, lately, asking for Books. Miserable brother that I am to send you and him so few things from this East of Wisdom. But I will do better in future. Regard to all: with hopes of hearing from you soon.

> Your affectionate Son
> A. Bronson Alcott.

[to Sarah Helen Whitman, Providence, R.I.]

Boston 4. Feby 1852.

My dear Madam,

You will like I am sure to know my friend Ellery Channing, who has been reading us here lately some very sensible and highly amusing "Lectures on Society", and will like to repeat his readings to your-self and friends in Providence; in which purpose I bespeak your sympathy and countenance. I have written also to Mr Hedge and Mr Davis, introducing the poet to their regards, and through them and yourself as I hope to the right minded of your City.

Sometime soon—in March perhaps, I may venture into your neighbourhood again, when I hope to see and know more of you and yours than has been mine to know during these last months.

> Very truly, Yours,
> A. Bronson Alcott.

[1] MS. in the Harris Collection of Poetry and Plays, Brown University Library. Addressee identified by the library.

LETTER 52–2

[to Mrs. A. Bronson Alcott and daughters, Boston]

Spindle Hill, Monday | July 5th 1852.

Dear Wife and Children,

Saturday brought me your letter, and I take a moment now, before I leave for Plymouth[1] to visit my Mother's birthplace and my grandfather's tomb, to write a line to apprize you of my doings and designings for the week past and current, with the hope of hearing yet once more from you before I leave these hills for Boston, and yourselves. I have now seen many old friends, and townspeople: having walked in most of the by ways, and passed nights under the humble roof of cousins too many to enumerate. To day, I am for Plymouth, and purpose to be here again on Sunday next, to meet my friends and neighbours ‖ again ‖ here, or at the meeting house on the Hill. Yesterday, I was at Church there, and they came—the little company of Spindle Hill—nearly every one of my name remaining here, with many others of my former neighbours and acquaintances—to the School House near Mrs Obed's where I addressed them for a couple of hours, and we had a good time of it; from 5 P.M till 7.—A little plain and profitable preaching, the minister, Mr Beach, being present and took part in the Conversation. Here, too, is a field for missionary labor, and we shall Cousin some while we stay, for the Lord's pleasure as well as our own.

Please favor me with another of your epistles on Saturday when our weekly mail comes in from Waterbury: the girls adding their words to the message.

In haste, for Plymouth, on this fair, clear, delicious, morning, and with much love to the citizens of the dusty town, the inmates of our dwelling in High St, particularly.

A. B. Alcott.

Plymouth, Tuesday. 6.

Direct to Hartford where I am to be on Sunday next, and a few days after.

Plymouth, Tuesday 6. 3. P.M. Please to direct to Hartford, Conn, where I am to be on Sunday the 17th with A. J. Davis.—

A.B.A.

Mrs. A. Bronson Alcott,
    50 High Street,
        Boston,
            Mass.

¹ In Connecticut, near Wolcott.

PART EIGHT

1853-1854

LETTER 53-1

[to Thomas Wentworth Higginson, Worcester, Mass.]

Boston[1] 30 March 1853.

Dear Sir,

You inquire about terms in the matter of Conversations. To which I have to say—usually just what the parties wanting such please to give. At Haverhill for a course given since my return from the West, I had Fifty dollars good; the like sum for five evenings I am to have from Lynn presently. Your friends at Worcester shall follow suit if they will for a like sum they making every arrangement and letting me know when all is quite ready. Let them be in parlours, if you please, and follow as fast as may be on each other: say three in a week, if practicable.

Last Sunday I was at Emersons and found the sage in fine spirits: on Monday Thoreau read me parts of "The Walden Life" which you will be pleased to learn is now printing for us, and its publick.[2]

Hoping to see you soon and yours wit[h] advantages for discourse, I am, meanwhile,

Cordially yours
A. Bronson Alcott.

[1] In October, 1852, the Alcotts had moved to 20 Pinckney Street.
[2] *Walden* was not published until August 8, 1854.

LETTER 53–2

[to Mrs. A. Bronson Alcott, Syracuse]

Boston 10 August 1853.

My Dear Wife/

Your letters are come to hand and find us much as you left us,—very comfortable and very busy here. Elisabeth's part comes off to the quietest perfection in whole and detail; the apartments all [word] their tidy mistress whose housekeeping throughout, for ought I can see, vies favorably with that of the absent Matron alike in neatness promptitude and efficiency, to the credit of her teacher, and comfort of guests. So please spare all anxieties and spend the century, if you can, with the friends whose hospitalities you are gone from us to embosom.[1] Will do you and them good: and is the thriftiest diet for such as you now that you are fallen once again upon the banquet.—An orchard of like sort and luxuriance, somewhere east or west, would please us all; so Syracuse and Plymouth may cast lots for the choice if they will.—East or West—? Now I am not surprised at the attractions of that new luxuriant country for you; nor shall doubt for a moment the quickening influences which a residence amidst such stirring and energetic forces as prevail at the West, would exert on us all, were we once transplanted and our boots[?] had a little season to spread and find the pieces[?] proper for us. Nor is the commercial character of the population an obstacle perhaps. Society is every where commercial. Commerce is fast becoming the Missionary of human melioration, feeding still deeper and more cordial needs of soul and body, to the softening and subjugation of the merely superficial and base. And we must mix, it seems, here in the social and spiritual, as in the secular, before we can mellow and ripen the human fruits. Heaven itself, if we must credit saints, and sinners alike in all foregone times, practices a like chymistry resting (they say) on a stratum of sulpher and lies, which our crimes alone render discernable and safe for us to tread.

Last Sunday I was at Emersons. And we had a long and lofty morning in the study the rain pouring outside also. Towards night the windows[?] closed overhead, and we walked to Walden and back to supper. Family matters got a more hospitable treatment from us both than has usually happened, and some clouds seemed to pass off the sun, as we threaded the mud and puddles in the highway. The Conversations—and, if the thing could be compassed, a fair trial of the same along the Canal towns—say Syracuse, Rochester, Buffalo, Cleaveland [sic], Cincinnati,—this was deemed the best thing for the coming autumnal months; and to further which purpose, he pledged my ticket to Cincinnati. So if you and the girls shall think favorably, we shall try to find some decent outfit of clothes, &c. and, sometime in September, set our face upon that enterprize. The West, I am told, has most hospitable ears, and likes a free fair thought, as our Eastern people, I am compelled to affirm, do not always and to the issues. At any rate, I am disposed to ascertain these matters for my self, if it can be made quite feasible. Such an expedition should pay and more than pay its own expenses. But it were safest, I suppose, to be in funds to the amount of expenses, at starting. Please think of it, and if you deem best, consult Mr May, with whom, should it be taken, I ‖ should ‖ hope to have opportunity to ‖ take possession of his confidence once again, and the affections of earlier [word]. ‖ see at leisure. ‖ These journeys far and long from first to last, are frightful and [word] us to all [word]. But the great Heart brings us all home and together some day again. ‖

Elisabeth and Sam. G.[2] enclose their words also. I shall see Abby to morrow morning again, and write soon to Walpole and Leicester[3] whose mails, I suspect, favor the West, these days and not this Hill of ours so often. My regards to friends in Syracuse: I wish to write once again before you leave: and am looking to hear from you by Saturday certainly.

Affectionately Yours
A.B.A.

[1] Mrs. Alcott was visiting her brother, Samuel J. May, a Unitarian minister now in Syracuse.
[2] Probably Samuel Greele, Mrs. Alcott's brother-in-law.
[3] Anna was, apparently, again in Walpole, New Hampshire; Louisa was working as a domestic servant in Leicester, Massachusetts.

LETTER 53-3

[to Mrs. A. Bronson Alcott, Boston]

Syracuse 30 October [1853] | Sunday.

My dear/

All's well, and prospects brighten as the journey lengthens westwards of which and sundries, full accounts shall be mailed for you and ours as soon as the refugee finds himself fairly housed and defined in Cincinnati. And it looks now as if this might happen as early as Saturday next, or on the Monday following, as there came last evening to Mr. May from W. H. Channing a letter enclosing the telegraphic enquiry from Mr Spofford,[1] (to whom Emerson has written) *"Is Mr Alcott in Rochester and can he come here next week,"* date *"28,th Cincinnati."* So I shall post forwards ‖ from here ‖ by Wednesday, after visiting Gerrit Smith with Mr May, ‖ and ‖ first meeting the proper people here, stopping at the cities for a train or a night as I proceed: At Rochester, Buffalo, Cleveland; leaving Medina and the cousining to be looked after when duties are fairly done for, and the spoils are won. I can take those ‖ all the ‖ more leisurely on my way homeward: Also my mother and the visit I mean for her. She being just now 22 miles from Oriskany with Betsey, as I found on reaching Chatfield's on Thursday last, to find only himself and family there, Ambrose and his having moved three weeks since to Southington in Connecticut: and Chatfield thinking hard of quitting for *somewhere* he knows not well where, soon—perhaps it may chance to be Massachusetts and as neighbours of ours. I had an agreeable visit—staid from Thursday noon till Saturday morning, and met some of his neighbours at the School house on Friday evening preceding, who gave good heed, and ask for more of the same on my return to their village—Temperance, Woman's rights Spiritualism, &c. all which I am ready to serve to them according to my ability. And now for Anna and her kind friends here.[2] The child confesses to some home fondnesses and the solitudes of the days here, but says she is getting accustomed to it a little, and means to study German with the Professor (whom I have met and like very well) in right good earnest. Yet I foresee that she will never let me leave her here behind on my return East. Her ways are not those of her kind entertainers and it is not so easy from them to meet.—Anna seems in good spirits however, and improved in health. Yesterday we had a pleasant walk along the path over the hill and back almost to the bridge city ward; and

167

we shall get others before I leave. Mr May promises me a Class on my return; and I am to attend a meeting this afternoon at the City Hall, of the different religious persuasions for discussing the Authority of the Scriptures, and shall speak perhaps, but cannot say just now. We shall see and you shall hear (if we can tell you), next time.—

I am going to Church now, and shall only add, what you will like to know, that thus far our means have been ample; and if we shall not return with Golden ‖ there can be no ‖ abundance the disappointment, ‖ since treasures of that sort will ‖ only instruct us all in the act of *preferring the last sometimes to first*, according to the good Nazarene's doctrine of waiting and serving.

Much love to all, and more from these parts soon.

A. Bronson Alcott.

[1] Ainsworth Rand Spofford (1825–1908). At the time of Alcott's first visit to Cincinnati he was a bookseller and publisher. He later became (1864) librarian-in-chief of Congress.
[2] Shortly before Alcott left on this first western tour of his, Anna had gone to Syracuse to teach.

LETTER 53–4

[to Mrs. A. Bronson Alcott, Boston]
Cincinnati, 12 November 1853. | 96 Fourth Street.

Dear Wife
and Daughters three,

You are waiting as I for my part have been for the letters. But now that I am here and so sumptuously lodged and cared for, and your kind remembrances, enclosed by the ardent Anna's hands with hers, too, have overtaken me,—preceded me I should say;—after "Conversation the First," is become a thing of Yesterday, fairly off the tongue's tip, and pronounced a great success—a victory for all time to come, and the presage of greater—(so the partial friends declare in my scarce believing ears)—I shall discharge the grateful duty of making yourselves partakers of its first fruits. You will remember my doubts as to any adaptedness of mine to this wild population and will share the surprise at the results. Last evening was a decided stroke, and I am to follow on Tuesday and so on Friday evenings—two Conversations a week till the promised Six are all given. This you see will detain me here for three weeks to come and I am to go to Dayton 60 miles, for a Conversation or more the while, so you must address me at Cincinnati, 96 Fourth Street, Care of Truman[?] and Spofford Booksellers," all the coming fortnight. This Mr Spofford is an important person here and has taken our Interest greatly at heart to the printing of tickets, distributing the same, engaging the Room, and all this in the most gentlemanly and generous manner possible. I am to dine with him to morrow, and see Mrs Perkins (Wm. H. Channing's cousin's[1] widow) and other members of the elect. I have seen many persons already, Judge Stallo, who called on the first evening after my arrival, and at whose house I have been since by invitation, Rev. Mr Livermore

(Unitarian) Mr Green, Mr Uncer, (Fisher's friend) Dr. Rolker Mrs Ernst, to whom Mr May gave me letters, and others. You will rejoice to hear that about 100 tickets at Boston prices are disposed of, and some for single evenings also. Next week I will send particulars, and some spoils for your comfort during these present and coming days. And, prospects are good for Cleveland, for Buffalo, Rochester and Syracuse on my return Eastwards at all which places I passed a night, and left advertisements in the hands of my entertainers. Mr Channing was especially desirous of having the Conversations under the best advantages, and was every way friendly as he must be to things of the sort. At Buffalo I saw Mrs Williams and husband, Hon Mr Tracy, of whom Margaret Fuller speaks you remember perhaps in her "Summer on the Lakes." And I slept at Rev. Mr Hosmers. Mrs H. inquired kindly of you having known you at Duxbury. At Cleveland I saw Mrs Vaughan, and heard Sallie Holly lecture; also saw Chapin (Fisher's partner), I had letters to Mrs Severance from Mr May but did not see the lady. On Friday 4 I reached Medina and passed the following Saturday and Sunday with my kindred there, having a Conversation at Cousin Hiram's on Sunday evening. His wife, (Helen's mother) seemed vastly pleased with her Boston Cousin, and is a sensible though sad woman. I am to see them all again and shall have more to write hereafter.

I have reserved the fairest news till the last, and this will be to you the Comforter. Emerson it seems had written to several persons, and among others to Mrs Dr Wilson, a lady of great excellence here, an artist, also the mother of accomplished daughters, to whose hospitalities I am owing all that wealth and taste and the kindest interest can bestow: a large chamber, fire, a simple yet elegant table, and her daughter's attractions, the eldest having been at G. B. Emerson's School, and knows the best Boston people. Mrs Wilson has taken a bust of R.W.E., || an excellent likeness, || [p. o.] and is besides her Art, a true mother and a very superiour woman. I tell her some excellent things of my excellent wife whose virtues are of the stamp to inspire the admiration of my partial hostess. Dr. W. is one of the few silent sensible men whom one meets with sometimes and respects for their amiable reserves and quiet ways. And here I am to stay, poor unworthy me, and glean pleasures till I leave for the East and the harvests there awaiting my return. Your affectionate note, made me so ashamed of myself: for who is worthy of all the love and devotedness that ensouls the creature we call woman: and what man has fathomed the fair fountains of a wife's loves. Am I mistaken in believing the wifeless, the poorest of the poor; and that Wisdom is but foolishness till it has wooed and won Affection to his embrace. || Fountains! ||—Conversation 2nd. is on *The Fountains,* and I will here indicate to your eye those following. Better, the entire series, (as I gave up my "New England Representative Minds," and called the Course

Human Life.

Con.	I.	*Chaos.*	Con.	IV.	*The Seminary*
"	II.	*The Fountains*	"	V.	*The Mart*
"	III.	*Paradise*	"	VI.	*The Altar.*

I may add many presentiments of fairer skies for the wife and daughters, whom Providence spares for yet serener softer services, and the palms of deserved victories. Hope is the holdfast; so please remember, my desponding ones, (if any maid or matron of my name there chance to be in this plight) that Fate frightens only the Hopeless; and that absent Husbands and Father's sometimes love most when they write of every thing else besides. Yet I will venture to subscribe, nevertheless, in good flowing flourish, as others, and as affectionately,

Ever Yours and inseparable.

A.B.A.

To my Wife and ours.

¹"James Perkins": a marginal note in Alcott's hand.

[Letter to Anna, Syracuse; from Cincinnati, November 12, 1853.]

LETTER 53-5

[to Anna, Syracuse]

Cincinnati, 16th November 1853. | Wednesday, Afternoon.

Dear Anna,

I wrote on Saturday last and now a few lines this morning just to say that last evening's Conversation was again very well attended, and though less animated (on my part) than the first, was not profitless nor unacceptable to the company. I am engaged for four evenings more—Thursday & Saturday of this, and Monday and Wednesday of next week: and shall leave for Cleveland by Friday following or Saturday, to pass a week or more and talk in that City. And you must address me there if you write later than Monday next. I shall look for letters from you, and hope to hear, not only from Yourself but from your mother, while here. Yours, enclosing hers, is all I have heard since I left home.—I hope you are now quite in favor with German and Professor also, and making good progress. Pray how are your ears? and have you done any thing for them yet? I shall be quite disappointed, and who knows but I may look sour for once on the most dutiful of daughters, if she fail to hear quick as once, when I come. So please, if you have not, set bravely about it at once, and be yourself again with hearing as nimble as your own heart is swift to love and serve your friend. I hope to have a pleasant fortnight or so with you and your housemates on my return, and something at heart for you, as good as you can give in its kind. But we will wait and see. Here is Cleveland, perhaps Buffalo, and Rochester, a week or more in each, and then I am to be with you. Meanwhile, health, spirits for your lessons and every thing you please to undertake. I suppose you hear often from home, and so are quite familiar with all going forward at 20 Pinckney Street. Why not send the letters along with your own to the traveller for his comfort also? I am thus far tenderly cared for, and have only prospects the fairest before me. But there are some faces at the East that meet me not, and I shall be quite ready to face the sun any day, and journey back into the Light of its countenance.

Thus far all prospers, and these autumn and winter months bid fair to ripen some golden fruits for us all: so good bye, and a letter from you soon, if you please to please

Your affectionate Father.

Miss Anna Bronson Alcott,
    Syracuse.

Enclosed are 5 dolls, for which you are too modest to ask but must not be to take and use for your little expenses.

LETTER 53–6

[to Anna, Syracuse]

Cincinnati, 22nd November 1853 | 96 Fourth Street.
/Tuesday Afternoon/

Dear Anna,

You will be glad to hear that my engagements here are very nearly completed; my Fifth Conversation is on Wednesday evening (to morrow) and the Sixth and last on Saturday following. And my hope is to leave here for Cleveland on Monday, at which place I shall be within day's ride of Syracuse and yourself. But must linger a little on my way eastwards and postpone for some weeks to come the pleasure of meeting you there. Besides the most hospitable entertainment here at 96, where I am domesticated and quite at home, I am seeing many people and feel quite at ease for one so bashful and disinclined to see company. On Sunday evening I am to meet "the Young Men's Literary Club," and so close my first visit to this Cincinnati of the West.

Yesterday brought letters from home and glad tidings of health and many comforts at 20 Pinckney Street. They had received my letter giving accounts of the good favor shown "the Philosopher' (I think you call him by that sounding name) and seemed a little crazed at his reception. Yr. Mother writes; "The long || desired || looked for much desired letter greeted our glad eyes this morning; (17) never was penny paid for so much treasure—the picture seemed to locate you,[1] the prospects seemed to gladden us beyond happiness: the former with its forest of spires, its fleet of steamers, and its broad beautiful river, that its inhabitants must be of the kind that could hear and love the prophet's things— and as we read on to find you were in a cozy home, where art, and hospitality and beauty were all in mates. It is too good to believe. Enjoy it (dear) all you can, and fear no charge of recreancy to your own humble home. Hours like these are sacred spots in our memory's history, and it is sweet to know that there are such places and people on the Earth. Thank God you are among them, &c. &c." Again, "We are having more cheerful letters from Anna, and Uncle is doing all possible things for her comfort and benefit. Do write to her and send her a picture like ours, and if in sight dot the houses or street where you are. Mr Wheeler continues very pleasant and kind, Abby very good and studious, Lizzy is quite recovered, Louisa very busy with her School. I have allowed no despair to dim the cheerful duties of the day, but must confess I never labored to so little purpose." &c. Then Louisa—"I consider the Western folks sensible, wide-awake people, who know what's good and are willing to pay for it; so in Abby's words I sincerely "wish you good luck."—We were in a high state of rapture when your letter arrived, for we began to think you had left the flesh: and mother mourned her lost spouse with exceeding sorrow: and there was no horrid accident that she did not fear had happened to you. And it was a joyful burst of news to find you well, happy, and flourishing. The house was of course in an uproar, and even the quiet "disciple" vented her feelings in a shout, and joined me in my dance of joy. How nice it seems to know you are being taken such good care of, and among such kind thoughtful friends. I consider Mrs Wilson and her daughters very wise praise-worthy females, and feel a great respect for them, which will continue as long as they make Plato happy and comfortable. I send my blessing to them all." And she describes, in her lively vein the present condition of the Pathetic family. &c. Lizzie too remembers me in a line—thinks "Anna is very good about writing" and wishes "we heard oftener from the dear father" yet thinks him "though very busy not forgetful of us." Now I have copied this for you, because I read the originals and shall again and wish to have them by me. I suppose you are in weekly receipts of intelligence from the family, and shall value any little thing of the sort you may send along. I would write oftener and more, but am seeing something or somebody all the while, and what with Conversations to meditate, and company, and this and that, find neither leisure nor mind to discharge my debts to these amiable correspondents. Besides, letters were never mine to write, and I defer to the last perhaps from the sense of the Gifts not mine. Bear with me, and sometime you shall have it all. And if I can, I will copy my little Diary and send it to you.—Last Wednesday (16) I wrote you, enclosing *Five dollars,* which I trust is in your keeping and comfort before this time. Please write and tell me whether you have received the same. I have enquired nothing concerning receipts for the Conversations here, but shall have the same at the Close (Saturday) and as the attendance has been large at Boston prices, (3 dolls the ticket) there must be $200, if not 250 (expenses of the Room not included) in Mr Spofford's hands for me; $100 of which I shall send (by Adam's Express, very safe and insured) to your mother, at once. And never came Gold more beautifully and benignantly into a poor man's palm than this. So let us maintain our faith and the courage that conquers.—I shall write soon again.—As for the kind company who are showering fast so many benefits on the gentlest of maids, thank them for yourself, and for

Your Affectionate Father, and
Good Friend no less.

Mrs E. Oakes Smith is here, and lectures this evening. I passed this forenoon with her, and go with Mrs Wilson to her lecture.—

A.B.A.

Miss Anna Bronson Alcott
   Syracuse

---

[1] A picture of Cincinnati as viewed from across the river was on the letterhead of Letter 53-4, as well as the present letter.

LETTER 53-7

[to Mrs. A. Bronson Alcott, Boston]
     Cincinnati 23rd November 1853 | 96 Fourth Street | Wednesday
My very Dear. Wife,
     Yours, enclosing kindest remembrances from sundry inmates at No 20 and all most grateful to have, but reached me yesterday and found me too far gone in meditations for the evening's Conversations, engagements, calls &c, to leave

me free as I wished to discharge my epistolary debts to yourself and them: Nor am I in a plight much more propitious to day. Conversation the Fifth (inviting the State with its confessions all into the brain) awaiting such treatment as *this evening's sitting* shall chance to give it at our moods. But I must not defer to a less favorable hour what the present moment permits, since tomorrow and Friday's engagements and then Saturday and Saturday evening's Conversation, (the Sixth and last) promise nothing better. And then I am engaged to meet *"The Young Men's Literary Club,"* on Sunday evening following, which completes my present doings here in this generous City, leaving me quite free to take Monday's train for Cleveland to be some 200 miles nearer my partial friends at the East. But I shall write once again from this place; And as all receipts will have come to hand by Monday, I shall then negotiate here through Mr Spofford a draft for $100 or 150 on one of the Boston Banks, from whence my scarce believing comforter shall draw, if she will, that sum of solid support for all and sundry inmates of her household, with no thanks to the poor sorry sender, whose idling hands and tongue have brought so little and so seldom into her treasury of benefits hitherto. I wish it were millions and as opulent as her generosities have been for these long years past to me and mine. And am sure we shall value the little treasure all the more for the slowness of its coming. Never fell golden showerlet into friendlier lap; and all fables are henceforth quite believable let us hope handsomer far than fairest facts; and quite competent to keep house, for a month if no longer, at 20 Pinckney Street even. In my next, you shall have fuller particulars, and the—Draft. As to the disposition of the same please use your own good judgment and I shall be all the more content. Some $200 (perhaps 250), will come to me from the Cincinnati—if the larger sum, I shall send you more. Prospects are fair, I learn, at Cleveland; and the Cities along the great thoroughfare owe us good will and good gold, also. Expenses can be but trifling, and I hope to make further remittances, as I pass Eastward.

Never was poor philosopher more kindly cared for than yours here at Mrs Wilsons. I begin indeed to accuse my hostess of sundry quite indisputable dispositions to fret almost to the spoiling, and threaten outright quarrelling if she persist in that indignity. The good lady has conceived the best opinions of yourself, and is most curious to learn all I can tell her. I wish you may meet some time and I may have the good fortune to be present at the interview: for I am not sure which is the better at scandal—I mean, of course, of fine ladies, fine gentlemen, and the follies and wickedness of fashionable society, of which she knows a great deal: And is from all I can learn, *the Woman* of the City. Will you care to hear of my little doings here in the way of seeing people? A word then. I dined of a Sunday with Mrs James Perkins where I met Judge James, the scholar of the place, Mr Cranch, brother of Christopher C. Mr. Jo. Longworth, the great wine grower of the West, Mr Elliot, brother of Mrs Perkins, and Mr Spofford, at whose house at Walnut Hills, near Lane Seminary, I have slept twice, and there met the Blackwells, one of whom is the physician, as you know; also several persons, attendants of the Conversations. Then I have attended a lecture of Dr Muzzy's and visited him at his house at Mount Auburn; also taken tea and passed the evening at Mr Greens, where I met Rev. Mr Livermore, Dr. Rolker, Mr. Elliot, and many ladies. And last Saturday I crossed the river Ohio with Mrs Wilson, Mr Davies Wilson her son, a graduate of Harvard College, Mr Page, student in theology, Miss Gay from Hingham, teacher in the Cincinnati Highschool, Miss Stetson, Miss Vose—and passed the forenoon in

Kentucky which lies opposite—the little towns of Newport and Covington sleeping still on its banks. The day was warm and most like April in N. England, and the prospect from Covington Hill very fine, the City and Suburbs, the river, steamers and all beneath us in the defile, with the coal smoke and passing clouds, from which the atmosphere has not been free during the last fortnight: nor is there any sign of fair winter as yet. I am oppressed with the languour [sic] of this climate, and should breathe gladly of our hyperborean air for this evening's inspiration. Ask Abby to find us on her Map, and you will see the difference in latitude and forget sundries left behind for colder climates. Yet if it will relieve you to know (perhaps Anna forgot to mention it,) I found one of my night garments at Chatfields, and so am as well provided as you could wish. Mrs Wilson has all my washing done and nobody but yourself could care better for your friend's comfort even to bathing, and all else.—I am to write personally to dear Louisa and Elisabeth, kind children, and Abby must give the proper description of *"the ring"* in her letter, which is my remembrance of the sprightly maid for this present.—Your letters were very acceptable, more so than I shall confess at the close of this. You shall address me for the coming fortnight at Cleveland, Ohio. Mr Spofford will remail and send any thing coming after my leaving here. I have written twice to Anna since I came to this city. Grateful remembrances to Mr Wheeler for his kindness to the family (also his verses sent and the best affections of

Your Husband's memories.[1,2]

[1] The letterhead contains a picture of "Walnut Street, Above Fifth." On the top half of p. 2 of this letter is the following in Alcott's hand:
"See in the picture, on the left, at the Corner, the Apollo Buildings in which are the Conversation rooms, (entrance from Walnut,) in the 3d story, and very well furnished with chairs; seating, if necessary, some 200 persons. About 150 have attended, sometimes 100 of an evening: and thus far quite spirited. To-night, I am to have Cassius Clay, the Kentuckian, and Mrs. Elis. Oakes Smith who is lecturing here. But Lucy Stone won all hearts, and this in the Bloomer too.—"
[2] It is apparent from the foregoing letter, that Alcott held his Conversations before and circulated among some of the "best" people in Cincinnati (many of them readily identifiable in the *DAB*). Such was evidently true of his visits to other cities and on other tours.

LETTER 53-8

[to Mrs. A. Bronson Alcott, Boston]
Cincinnati, 29 November 1853 | 96 Front Street. | (Tuesday)
My Dear,

Within you shall find a draft on Willis and Co. for One Hundred and Fifty dollars payable to you at their Office, or should you prefer to draw the same from any of the Boston Banks the paper is good to you to that amount at these also. You will first endorse your name "Mrs Abby Alcott" across the back to make it payable. And if you have doubts, please call on Mr Sewall who will give you the proper advice, perhaps do the business for you at the Bank or at Hamiltons. I never enclosed treasure of the sort with like pleasure to the mails before, and wish the comforts it may purchase may be equal to the satisfactions with which it has been earned. You should have had these avails earlier had they come earlier to hand. My engagements here were completed on Saturday evening, and the money paid to me late on Monday that is yesterday. On receiving the sum I sent you forthwith a telegraphic dispatch, which I suppose reached you on Monday evening sometime, announcing that I had mailed the Draft, obtained for me by Mr Spofford, and which will reach you herein,—say, Friday next—and distribute its benefits to yours and ours during these days of thanksgivings.

To-morrow I am to leave for Cleveland where a good circle awaits Conversations, and where I shall be for ten days or a fortnight, perhaps longer. Please let me hear from you at once on your reception of the Draft. As to the distribution of this little sum, I shall wish you to use your own good judgment and I shall be best satisfied. If I have any suggestion to make it is that "the teeth" should pay for themselves out of their earnings, but this they can do as well perhaps a month hence as just now, when you may need all and more than I have sent you for the pressing necessities. They owe $25 only, and Dr M. can wait according to agreement made at first. *All of my Debts proper may lie and must, till I return to see to them,* so please leave them aside, and apply the money to the settlement of household claims, which I hope are not beyond partial reduction and the leaving of some comforts for yourself, by the small sum now sent. Hereafter we may reasonably trust that fortune's favors will flow the more freely into our possession. Let us hope and have the benefits of that persuasion at least. The West may have annual showers, golden harvests even, for such poor pensioners as ourselves, and something to celebrate philosopher's birth days withal, as they come round for the years to come.[1]

Last Sunday evening I met the "Young Men's Club," and was much gratified at the freshness and freedom of the members, of whom some thirty or more were present. It was worth coming West to enjoy. The evening was given to Conversation on our favorite themes and passed quite pleasantly. Most of the company had been attendants at the Apollo Rooms and so we got forwards as acquaintances can with ease and profit. It is refreshing to find here a faith in the East, in such influences as Emerson, Parker, Garrison, and men of their Class, and tells the story for this West. Half a century hence and we shall have the fruits.

Anna has written me hopefully and sent letters of yours, Elisabeths and Abby's, along also. It seemed so domestic to read all these home things here in my comfortable chambers. I am to write to the girls all, when I get away from this pressure of company. I hope to do so at Cleveland, yet fear the pen will never serve me as I wish. And wife and children are doomed to open so-called letters to read only of poor commonplaces of narrative and sentiment. Had yourself, had Anna or Louisa, my materials for Correspondence here, how happy should I be to peruse the letters you would write from them. But poor philosopher all flowering at the lip, is so barren and disappointing in all ways else and writes with shame if he write at all.—

This evening I am to take tea with Mrs Wilson at Mr William Green's, and meet Prof. Mitchell, the Astronomer & Author of "the Orbs of Heaven", also Mr Thomas [p. in] Corwin, ‖ of Kentucky ‖ [p. o.] Cassius Clay I have met, and he has attended one or more evenings at the Apollo.

My next shall be from Cleveland.

Kindest regards to Mr. Wheeler, to the Girls, (including Cora[?] & Lizzie) and many inexpressible affections for yourself,

From Your Husband and friend.

A.B.A.

Mrs Abby May Alcott
20 Pinckney Street
—Mr Fisher has just called coming by way of New York City.

¹ Alcott's letter (enclosing the draft) is dated on his birthday.

LETTER 53–9

[to Mrs. A. Bronson Alcott, Boston]

Medina, 4. December 1853 | (28 Miles from Cleveland.)

My dear/

I am here spending Sunday with Uncle Noah¹ and Cousins. And shall return to Cleveland to begin my Conversations there on Wednesday Evening coming: Mrs Hiram Bronson going in with me to attend the same. There is prospect of a good company and good fruits. Mr Chapin to whom I had letters, has taken this interest kindly at heart, and we shall have something to speak of for you in my next. I left Cincinnati last Wednesday (30) passed Thursday and Friday there, meeting a little party on Friday evening at Mr Chapins—Mr and Mrs Vaughan Mr & Mrs George Bradburn, Drs Tulle and Gatchell, Mr & Mrs Severance &c. and came out here yesterday.—Your letter, announcing the receipt of my "telegraphic despatch" came to hand just as I was stepping into the stage to come out here. And I take this earliest moment to answer. Concerning the *poor paltry tax Bill*, I called on the Assessors, as you may remember, and had the Lecturer's assessment (of 3 dolls and something more) abated, as you will find endorsed on ‖ my tax ‖ the bill, which is among my papers in the Book Closet; just where, I cannot say, but you can find it if there, and for peace, if not justice sake, please pay: there may be some little costs, but the whole cannot be the 5.30 sent you for bill.—As to the House Tax of 30.50. that is to be paid by Mr Rice according to agreement, and you are not to know any thing of it. We were to pay the water tax for the first year, which I have done, to Mr Rice; and the 350, and no more, for the two years following. So you see how the matter stands and will act accordingly. The Draft for 150 dolls on Hamilton is now, I trust safely arrived, and cashed, to your comfort. It is too small a sum to meet the many demands coming in at this season, but you will divide and distribute the same, as you best can, and I hope to send further remittances as I come Eastwards. Something ‖ at ‖ from Cleveland, ‖ at ‖ Buffalo, Rochester, and then at Syracuse at all which places I am to pass, a fortnight or more, I suppose, and so make a rather longer winters stay from you and ours than was at first thought of. Yet if there are harvests here in this West even in this winter season we will remain to reap the same, and return to enjoy while the summer sun shines for us in the East.—

You write feelingly and justly of Brother C. and I am happy that he has a sister and I a wife who carries a heart of courage and of consolation in her bosom for the faithful and the wronged everywhere.—Give C. my sympathies if he is still with you. and the Girls' letters: also Mr Wheeler to whom give my thanks for all his kindness to yourself and family during my absence.—

I am encouraged by all you write: as I am by Anna and Elisabeth's reviving spirits, for which the spring and its prospects will do more let us hope. I purpose returning by way of New York City and Raritan Bay, but cannot yet say confidently.

Nothing can exceed the kindness and respect shown alike to the person and doctrines of your friend, here in this hospitable West—save always the like from yourselves, the wife and daughters of many dear memories & hopes.

Let me hear from you soon at Cleveland.

Affectionately.
A.B.A.

---

[1] Noah Bronson, Alcott's uncle on his mother's side.

LETTER 53-10

[to Mrs. A. Bronson Alcott, Boston]

Cleveland, O. 11. Dec. 1853.

My dear/

I wrote last Sunday from Medina from which place I returned here late on Wednesday to give Conversation the First, and, (what was more to me) to get letters several and seasonably too,—One from your sovreign [sic] self, one from laughing Louisa, a daguerreotype of its kind, another from fair Anna (which I send) & enclosing yours of Nov 29; and all filled with the most cordial expressions of regard for unsuspected virtues lately come to light and exercise in some Absentee, (who may remain nameless) with Alleluias &c. &c. quite surprising, yet not altogether uncalled for nor unpleasing to read of here in this wild world of the west. Louisa's touches are so picturesque that I have sent her letter along with yours for Anna's enjoyment, and may Heaven's blessings rest on Mother, maids, and all they intend of Good to present and absent objects alike and forever.

I came in from Medina just in time for our first meeting here. Second and third are now among past experiences, the rest promised are following fast on Monday, Wednesday, and Thursday evenings of this week; so I shall hope to leave here for Buffalo on Friday or Saturday, to be there a week or so (if they wish it) and thence on to Rochester. As Mr Channing is to be absent for a fortnight at Washington City, I may go direct to Syracuse, and return to meet him and his friends afterwards for some Conversations in R. You will read in Anna's fair sheets what prospects await us at Syracuse.

Here I am meeting some very select sensible people, and having fair success—about which more in my next. Cleveland is an Eastern City in manners and opinions, and reminds me of New Haven, from which place and from Connecticut parts, the population is derived. Here I have met several old acquaintance, among which are John A Foote, son of Gov. Foote of Cheshire, and whose wife, wife's sisters & his brother, were formerly pupils of mine at

Cheshire, and whom I am to meet tomorrow at his house. And I dine to day with G. Bradburn at Mrs Severances,[1] to whom S.J.M. gave me letters, and whom I like exceedingly. Mr and Mrs Vaughan I have seen, also many more, and to good ends.

The Chapins where I am staying are good people & ‖ most ‖ sensible, and as hospitable as any good wife could desire to her absent friend. Besides the weather here is like September, so mild and hospitable, ‖ that it were ‖ as a woman's breath. I shall gladly learn any particulars of your affairs during these winter days of Tax bill, Rents, &c. Is the boarding adventure to prove *a losing interest?* If it is dismiss at once. Far better are tenantless chambers and fewer trenchers, than dinners served and to be paid for by serving afterwards. But you will take due time and decide providently this and the rest.

All things look hopeful to the hopefully disposed. I am Eastwards slowly along,—too slowly—yet not unwilling to linger the while snatching some scanty Comforts on the road for the coming spring, and short is the time at longest, that restores all to the loved Home once more.

Address me next at Buffalo.

May the Best be yours, and ours in all times

Ever Your Husband
Affectionately
A.B.A.

[1] Caroline Severance, wife of Theodoric C. Severance, a Cleveland banker.

LETTER 53–11

[to Mrs. A. Bronson Alcott, Boston]

Cleveland 15th. December, 1853.

My dear,

I gave my last Conversation here last evening and am to leave sometime tomorrow for Buffalo, from which place I shall soon write, unless it should happen to me to pass on to Rochester, it may be to Syracuse even, and have Conversations before they are ready for the same at Buffalo. Here the company has been quite select, mostly friends, and we have had pleasant evenings together, as if it had been at Salem or Medford. And though more private and un-ambitious they have been quite as pleasing and more profitable perhaps than the course at Cincinnati, which from all accounts were esteemed ‖ as ‖ [p. o.] popular and entertaining. I sent you in my last some notice of them by Rev. Mr. Livermore of Cincinnati, whom I have mentioned in my former letters.—As to receipts they happen to fall short of those of the former city, yet shall help to keep us merry as well as comfortable the coming Christmas and following Holidays, and be thankful withal for the smallest benefits. Presently you shall have some substantial evidences of profits and the fuller histories.

This evening I am to take tea with an old acquaintance, Hon. John A. Foote, formerly of Cheshire, Conn. and whose wife and sister were pupils of mine, also a brother of his wife's, at the Cheshire School. It is a family party, and will doubtless remind of the Schoolmaster's times—very pleasing to recal, and all the more under these circumstances.

I am seeing a good deal of George Bradburn and wife who are friends of Mrs. Hildreth,[1] and of ours also. They are now staying at Mr. Severances, at whose house I often pass a morning or an evening and see other people somewhat less formally than at the Conversations. You remember Mrs Hildreth has rooms in Tremont Row Jomenken[?], and will be pleased to see you. Mrs. Bradburn writes often, and has taken an interest in these Cleveland visits, so it may be agreeable to you to call as well on her part as your own. Besides we are her debtors already.

I am making a short stay here, and shall leave, as I said above, tomorrow, to sleep at Buffalo. As you may readily imagine this traveller's life is not for such as I am, but the evenings and preparations for the same—and the fruits—render it not without attraction, and I am reconciled for the while, since so many years of the student's satisfaction have preceeded [sic], and perhaps ripened the sort of entertainments that people are not unwilling to exchange for the gold that warms and cheers during days of cloud and frost. And certain summer months are stealing along for certain good people whom I am seeing seldomer just now than I could desire. So pray for a little patience, and the said[?] months, and the rest, if you and yours please.—

Yesterday came your letters, Abby's and yours—and I read that all is well with you. Tax, rents, &c. are all easy I infer from your silence of the same.

Mrs Hiram Bronson is come to town and attends the Conversations. I have written to Anna and to Mother and just mailed the same.

I shall hear next from you at Buffalo, unless I pass through to Rochester or Syracuse.

To Louisa, Elisabeth, and Abby much love, and many promises of answers to their letters.

Meanwhile I am
faithfully, Your Husband,
A. B. A.—

[1] Caroline Neagus Hildreth, an artist who had done a good portrait of Alcott, in crayons, in 1851. Her husband was Richard Hildreth, a writer and lawyer. Perhaps best known of his works are an antislavery novel, *The Slave; or Memoirs of Archy Moore* (1836); and *The History of the United States of America* (1849–52).

LETTER 53–12

[to Mrs. A. Bronson Alcott, Boston]

Syracuse 18. December | 1853.
My dear,

You will be no less surprised than I am to find myself here and with the promise of spending the Holidays with Anna—the friends at Buffalo celebrating their "New England" on the 22nd. and Mr Channing to be absent from Rochester preaching at the Capital for a fortnight to come. So I hope to give my 'Conversations' here meanwhile, returning afterwards to meet engagements at these cities. I was at Buffalo but for a night, yet saw Mr Williams, Mayor

Wadsworth, Dr. Hosmer, Mr Cameron,—all most desirous of having Conversations and mentioning others of their friends, amongst which are Ex President Fillmore and daughter—So all looks hopeful for us at that place. And Mr Channing has good hopes and good people also for the same thing at Rochester. All January is thus bespoken, and the visit to Oriskany, (and perhaps to Raritan Bay) to be made before I am to see you at home. But we shall await the guidance of events and return accordingly.—

Anna seems quite content, and may return with me—visiting mother on the way.

I shall hope to get more time while here to think of home, and of home duties, and shall like to hear as often and as fully of yourself and prospects as you may please to communicate. About boarders—I fancy, you will find rather losses than gains, and agree with me after this fair trial, that it is a hard way to pay rents at such costs of perplexities. [I suppose Mr. W_____ will scarcely care to remain, and shall wish, *on the whole*, it may be so.] The rest are slowly leaving one by one, and so that matter is coming to and end of itself.

I think how much of yourself and of Elisabeth has gone into this and former endeavors—Anna and Louisa too—and the slow profits—the swift expenditures, I may say, of Life's fairest energies—of incomes seemingly lost or worse than wasted—Yet there is somewhere compensation for the sacrifice, doubtless, and an end—the times of reward to come to us all. Let us not believe otherwise, and perish of Unbelieving as do Infidels. To Elisabeth, to Louisa, many acknowledgements for letters, and respects for their devotion to the family interests. I owe some answers to correspondents which I wish I may send while here—Abby's sprightly letter among the first. And then yourself—But I will not confess lest I shall not repent and forsake the old sins.

The weather has been vernal. No snow till last night, and to day it is falling fast, and growing cold. I bless Heaven there is warmth for us all. And having come to have "a little run of Providence" (Comforts, as you call them) just now, (the Cleveland shower being only less copious than that of Cincinnati) I can only bless, and take courage for the future.

My regards to Mr. W.—

faithfully, Your Husband
A.B.A—

Christmas shall not pass without *further acknowledgements* from us. Annas long confessions &c. must compensate for my most meager sheets this time as before.—But you shall anticipate the Christmas partly, by a day or two, and so I enclose $25,—less by half than I meant it should be this time

---

LETTER 53–13

[to Mrs. A. Bronson Alcott, Boston]

Syracuse 22nd. December 1853.

My dear,

By last Monday's mail I sent you enclosed in bills $25, also a letter from Anna. And followed the same by a telegraphic despatch, announcing the coming monies—all which and sundry, is come faithfully to heart and hand, and is, I am not permitted to doubt, quite willing to keep Christmas and the New Years according to your wishes, though the senders may not be present at the merry-making, as sendees and themselves do all desire. Yet the remnant East will manage kindly to make good the occasions without us. 'Tis the first, I think, on which all have not been present since Children were ours to name. I wish you may enjoy without sadness and celebrate the Epiphany as becomes good cheerful Christians, without shadow or shame to mar the festival. As for me—you see I am providentially favored—since Anna is a sort of sunny snug home for the Refugee, who can keep Christmas and endless Holidays, as you know full well, in hospitalities such as hers—if indeed they are not the more properly speaking, fair extensions of yourself to an absent vagabond of yours. So it seems, ‖ as the case may be, ‖ I am the more favored beneficiary and you but spare of your alms from the feast of fondness dispensing to the remnant West ‖ of its ‖ some crumbs of Comfort also.

Anna's little parcel contains some little gifts for you. And thus I distribute mine;

To "Mother"	1.	The gold piece.
Louisa	2.	The Thimble
Elisabeth	3.	The Sewing Bird
Abby	4.	The Gold Cross.

I wish the Gifts may please and profit also. So a merry Christmas "in a crystal draught" at supper, for

A.B.A.

LETTER 53–14

[to Mrs. A. Bronson Alcott, Boston]

Dec. | Monday 26. Syracuse | 1853

My dear,

To Anna's full sheets of Narrative and sentiment one little line, just to say that we are enjoying here together these Holidays, and with fairest prospects ahead.—This evening there is to be a meeting for Conversation at Mr May's Vestry, to be followed by others on Wednesday and Saturday evenings unless I shall be called to Buffalo to begin my Course there sometime this week, of which there is present probability; and in which case I am to give the same here after my return. Mr May seems interested in promoting our interests here, thinks there will be some forty or fifty attendants and a good service done by the meetings. He announced the same to his Congregation last evening, and will do all that is becoming: so here as at former places and times all is auspicious of the best.

I trust the Christmas Parcel came timely to hand, and is just the thing for all. We were glad to get yours by Mr May, and thankful for the remembrances.

The snows are now falling and the weather is cold. But I am getting days of discourse with S.J.M.[1] and have readings to fill the hours profitably. Still home-studies and companions were the more desirable, as in seasons past. I wish you may find comforts and contentments all in the charmed circle.

Your Buffalo letter has not reached me but I shall get it perhaps to day.

The Rochester Conversations will follow those at Buffalo, and bring me some fortnights time nearer home and its contentments. Meanwhile, as heretofore,

Cordially Your Husband
A.B.A.

Tell Abby, her pocket penstand serves me well, and that this and all my letters are dipped therefrom. Love and progress to her, and all the sisters also.

Mrs. Abby May Alcott.
20 Pinckney Street.

¹ Samuel J. May.

LETTER 54–1

[to Mrs. A. Bronson Alcott, Boston]

Syracuse 15 Jan. 1854

My dear/

My long stay here with Anna and the excellent of this house and place ‖ comes to ‖ ends for the present with all its midwinter satisfactions. And I leave for Rochester to morrow, where I am to be for the ten days or fortnight to come, as Mr Channing, who has just returned from Washington City, shall arrange for me. This, I believe, will close my series of Western teachings for this season, and leave me free to set my face homeward thereafter.

Anna intends to be ready as I pass, and visit Oriskany with me on our way home. So sometime about February 1st. you may look for our arrival, and all that our union implies. I, for my part, shall enjoy all the more *for these sometime very tedious days between my evenings, and the irksomeness of unsuitable company not seldom.* There is a certain handsomeness about home figures and manners that only absence can best reveal, they say, and I suspect myself to be at moments if not forever, a convert to that fair faith.

We have had five Conversations here and found good favour. My season was not so propitious for the sages as some other, but there was good company and select, and all was very good. I have seen fewer people privately than I wished, but 'tis not the habit, I am told, nor has been from the beginning, to call on Philosophers, a class every where not a little dangerous if not embarrassing to encounter particularly in one's house, and at tea.

I wrote you about debts. And add that it shall be my first business to settle fully the same on my return. Aunt Davenport's gift gives us with Emerson's $1000 to be invested, and from which we shall receive a little annual income to help along. The rest, with what I may bring, will pay all debts, and fit us for future fortunes.

It looks now as if aid and comfort were lodged about this tongue somewhere, and the West were ‖ finding ‖ putting some little faith in its cunning. The season shall prove it and us according to the merits of each and all. Nor has this three months been without hopeful significance. I have had some good hours with Sam. and to profitable ends.

Poor Abba, I am sorry for the teeth pangs, but doubt your cure proposed, (as [word]?)

Love and lover's good to all.

Please address me here and let Anna transmit to me.

Very dearly, Yours
A.B.A.

Preserve the [word] and advertisements

LETTER 54–2

[to Mrs. Anna Alcott, Oriskany Falls, N.Y.]

Boston 13 July 1854 | 20 Pinckney Street.

Dear Mother,

I address you at Oriskany rather than at Southington,[1] presuming that you would have written from the latter place had you left Oriskany and informed us of your present residence.—It is now some months since we have heard any thing from you; nothing at all since January last, I believe, when I left you at Chatfields, on my return from the West. I hope and trust that you are quite well now, and shall wait to hear from you soon, to know where you will pass your coming autumn and winter months, whether with Chatfield, Betsey, or Ambrose, and whatsoever you may communicate about yourself and prospects. Are you able to undertake the journey to Connecticut, or to Boston—for we shall expect to see you here, if you get as far as Connecticut, and shall let you know more about it in due time. So please write soon and say just how you wish it to be.— We are all quite well. Anna has been at Syracuse since June 15, and writes often. She said she should write to you, and I hope she has written before this and told you all about how pleasantly she is living there. And she will be glad to get a letter from you. She came home to us a few weeks after my return in January last, and Louisa and she had the School here together till she left, a month since, and returned to Syracuse. The School was a pleasant one of some dozen or fourteen little children, and the profits to all worth naming, they, the teachers, getting good experiences, and the children, a good share of elementary learning,—besides || and we all share in || the money coming in to the Family for their services: about 80 dollars a quarter. Abby still goes to school, and is a good scholar they say. But she is to have a vacation now of the month of August, and needs it to recruit for the winter studies. Elisabeth helps her mother about the house, and is now taking lessons in music besides for a quarter.—Louisa has closed her school till October, when Anna hopes to return to help her again as before. We have said nothing about Chatfield's Abby May, because we found she is older than the age permitted at the City schools, and because we have thought Chatfield might come this way before long himself and see how things look here.—Will he visit us this summer?

I have been rather busy since I returned. I have been to Haverhill, to Plymouth,[2] and Worcester where I had Conversations, and very good company.

Sometime in October, I shall be going West again, if nothing happens to prevent or alter my present intentions, and shall see you, going or returning.

I was at Dr. William Alcotts and passed a day lately. They are all well, and about going to pass a little while at Wolcott. If you are at Southington you will see them doubtless.—

My wife is very well and desires much love as do the children all.

Ever your affectionate Son
A. Bronson Alcott.

¹ A few miles east of Wolcott, Connecticut.
² In Massachusetts, where Alcott visited Benjamin Marston Watson.

LETTER 54–3¹

[to Mrs. A. Bronson Alcott, Boston]
Plymouth 21, September 1854. | Thursday morning

My dear/

We have been looking out for you here at Hillside all since Tuesday, and if you don't come before, shall now expect you on Saturday certainly, to spend Sunday and as much longer as you can spare from the remnant of us still staying at No. 20. Pinckney, which with Master Joseph, the Collegian,² might ‖ stay ‖ [p. o.] abide [p. in] safely there, one would say, and resignedly, [comma p. in] till such time on Monday as you could return to their eyes and comfort, if you felt you must so soon. So come down by the early train if you can, and we can have Saturday and all Sunday for this charming place and our [p. in] hospitable host, and all that both have at heart for us and ours. I very much wish you to see the place and them, and discuss at leisure, orchard and cottage comforts, and whatsoever advantages the Old Colony has in store for the family. Watson himself, is worth the journey, and then his kindly wife, (so pleasing to our children's memories) and Madame Watson, from whom the prudent son seems to have got not a few of his virtues, ‖ and ‖ [p. o.] then [p. in] the children and natural as well as cultivated charms of this little Paradise, to say nothing of the pleasure you will give us all, will abundantly reward your coming: and we shall be here together—a happiness that has rarely happened to us away from home, not since our jaunt to Wolcott in the year, '30, I believe. I really think you will come and find the means to come as women can. "The Orchard" is a beauty; and you may have any quantity of apples and of speculation there under the russets golden, or To[l]lman³ sweetings, porters, or greenings, you please, or can desire, build cottages or castles in the grove, and the like, endlessly, with such bases for them all as the Phillips, Frothingham. (Davenport, I meant,) Emerson, and perhaps Tho. Davis'.⁴

Solid good-will, and Watson's nurseries, shall warrant. A dream of this sort is not the idlest we have dreamed, separately or together, since the rosy Brooklyne days; and old people, they say, are all the more given to put faith in some of their early dreams, if not for themselves for their children none the less, and all the more believable and believingly then‖ . ‖ [p. o.-p. in material is illegible] By the way, I am getting anxious and dream about Anna,⁵ and shall write after seeing and consulting with you about the maiden; and meanwhile I hope you have advised, strongly insisting on her returning with Louisa and pretty soon too. That climate is unfriendly to such as she, and we must have her near us, as I think you will agree with me. New England for our sort, and Plymouth—or—Concord:—unless the powers unitedly insist on the metropolis and keep us there for the safer and surer ends. We shall see and know presently, and so setttle [*sic*] and for something of a[?] long twelvemonth and more, I doubt not.

As for me—I am having never busier or more satisfactory days, and here have already accomplished the best part of my work, and put "Year 1849" into some shapely readable form, for referance [*sic*] now or hereafter of yours or mine, or any who chances to care for us and ours. Yesterday we "picked up apples" Watson and I, gathering 30 bushels and more, and had a good time of it. The weather is ambrosial. Romona's harvest hour. I read or walk with the children before breakfast, and have the day uninterruptedly to myself, in my pleasant chamber looking out upon *Duke Marston's*[6] dominions, all unfenced the cultivated and the wild, as is their owner's princely heart; and happy should I be had I something of the like, of both kinds to bestow on the most generous of wives and faithful of women. So till Saturday at the Station, I rest[?].

Ever yours, and gratefully.
A. B. A.—with a kiss for

Elisabeth—and Abby and my best love through yourself therby [*sic*].

[1] Quoted (with minor differences) in Sanborn, *A. Bronson Alcott*, II, 480–82.
[2] Joseph May, Mrs. Alcott's nephew, at that time a student at Cambridge.
[3] The bracketed "l" is p. in.
[4] Thomas Davis of Providence, Rhode Island.
[5] Anna was at Syracuse, New York, teaching school.
[6] Benjamin Marston Watson, whom Alcott was visiting, was generally referred to by his middle name.

LETTER 54-4

[to Mrs. A. Bronson Alcott, Boston]

Hillside, Plymouth, | Wednesday 3. October 1854.[1]

My dear/

I am staying here in these parts against time, and the fronting of quarter non payments of rent bills, and sundries besides, to say nothing of Louisa's return and opening of her School, without being there at No. 20 with its mistress and landlady now, as best beseems at the Head or near the place where Heads are wont to be wanted in Houses and family affairs, but as, in this particular instance, Heart is Head manager and very capable to do without such shifts as I; as, moreover, I am not wholly out of place away and in this mansion, and, as, third and last, Henry Thoreau is to be here surveying and to read something to a circle of Watson's neighbours on Sunday next, and so into the week, they have persuaded me somewhat against my sense of duty to you and the Girls, to remain and see him back to Boston sometime in the week, by Wednesday say, or Thursday at farthest, I should think; and you may then expect me, if you have or can get to send the $1.50, which should have brought you here last week to see our Orchard in its burden of Gold, (but now all shone, and cannot, alas! be seen of you or tasted I fear,) N.B. 1,12 for road ticket, and 37½ for hack to bring me and my copied reams to your board again. So here in a ponderous long drawn two page sentence of a report is the story of my doings [word] and excuses awaiting your candour and such answer as you may return at your convenience. As to linen &c. I have every thing, shall bring home and all unworn some of your careful ironings, and so present my self to you, as I left, in fair saint's wardrobe, a grace, not disgrace, to the wifely washerwoman's arts and pains-takings. So send me nothing of the kind, if there remain to send any thing, which I doubt. And J. O. Wattles[?] may wait for his response till I come, good Enthusiast and Company.

Here as Watson has said nothing of Conversations, I take it such are not desired by any number of the Puritans, and so shall have nothing the less for New York, from whence we are expecting letters every mail with promise, if not pledge, of better luck for us all these hard times. I hope so. For I have now done a good summer's work on the whole, and can go pedling a little again in the distant parts during these coming winter months, *and, perhaps, of want.*

I hope Louisa brings good news of herself, and ditto of Anna, whose concern for us rather than for herself, I fear, has prompted her to stay behind, and to bring less of Anna for the more of service-money, when she comes a month hence. Good girl, good girls, and true, I may say, all with a sort of filial providence in their hearts, nor yet without some craft in their hands, and heads too. We have reason to be thankful and take in our live-estate since it yields so fair an income whatever else may [be] said of it.

I wish you and Elisabeth, (Abba has had hers) were breathing the gales of these orchards and rosegardens, scented with the owner's hospitalities and favors, and not those of cark and chambers—but—you too shall have the pleasures and rewards and "the good well done "and faithful," and the cares which are comforts too.—Courage and the girls! and to[?] whom my love, and to yourself, and a return by Thursday next probably.

A.B.A.—and some flowers

from my breakfast plate the gift of the Duchess.[2]

[1] Wednesday was October 4.
[2] Mrs. Watson.

PART NINE

⚹

1855–1856

LETTER 55–1

[to Bronson Brothers, Publishers, Waterbury, Conn.]

Boston 16 March 1855.

Messrs. Bronson, Brothers,
    Publishers,

I send, herewith, to your care, my contribution, such as it is, to your advertised book on "Ancient-Waterbury," in which, besides ‖ the ‖ [p. o.] a [p. in] general, I have,[1] also as you will perceive, some personal interest. ‖ also ‖ [p. o.] Waterbury is my native place—that part of it now called Wolcott. ‖ and certainly ‖ [p. o.] Also [p. in] the name, which I bear, in common with yourselves, has undoubted claims upon any history of the early times—the Bronsons having been highly respectable from the first settlement, and contributors in their way, to the making of the town what it has been and is now. Not to speak here of those of the name of whom I know less. I may ‖ name ‖ [p. o.] mention [p. in] Dr Tillotson Bronson who was born and bred in the place, and was for several years rector of the Episcopal Church there [p. in] and very widely known for his character and attainments: his ancestors, moreover, on his mother's side, the *Blakeslee's,* were among its early founders and inhabitants. The editor will doubtless see that due note of their services and connexions is taken in his book: and I have enclosed some minutes to this end, which may chance fill the break in his collections.

As to the Family whose genealogy I herewith transmit, it may best speak for itself. The name is perhaps more common in Wolcott, and has been from the first, than any other.—Spindle Hill where the first settler, *John Alcock,* planted himself,—in 1731. being still in possession of his descendents, who yet [p. in] seem for the most part[2] to inherit something of his skill, also, in husbandry and handicrafts, to feed and man your busy borough, after their peculiar ways and manners, converting ancient Farmingbury into Modern Waterbury.

Please see that this communication, with the accompanying parcel, find its

187

way to the editor's hands, and that I have an early sight of your volume when it comes out, and oblige,

Yours, gentlemen,
Very respectfully,
Amos Bronson Alcott

No 20 Pinckney Street,
 Boston.

¹ Comma p. o.
² "for the most part" p. in.

LETTER 55–2

[to Hiram Bronson, Medina, Ohio]

Walpole¹ 27 August 1855

Dear Cousin,
    Two months' time is enough, you will say, in which to answer a friends' letter: and ‖ quite an ‖ [p. o.] a large [2 p. in] allowance even [p. in] for such a slow correspondent as myself. But I was absent when your letter came, and our moving to this place to spend the summer with a brother-in-law of my wife, Benjamin Willis, followed my return from Connecticut, where I saw the editors and publishers of the Book on Ancient Waterbury, and gave your name and Uncle Noah's ‖ names ‖ and address, and urged inserting your Fathers' portrait, which all seemed disposed to favour. They mean to make a valuable Book, for which there are good materials, and a sufficient and interested editor, Dr. Henry Bronson of Yale College Faculty, and a native of the town. I have sent him a full genealogy of *Alcocke,* from the first settler *John* who came to Waterbury in 1731. to the present descendents, and of his ancestors who came in 1660 to New Haven from Boston: the first of the name came over with Winthrop in 1630. How much of this they will print I cannot say, but something, and that is a point gained for us all.
    As to the Bronsons, a name so prominent in the history of the town, they mean to do them full justice, and your father, ‖ and my uncle ‖, is rather the most commanding name in that highly respectable family: ‖ and ‖ unless it be grandfather's ‖ hardly less than his son, Tillotson ‖, while Noah divides his good name and services with your town and the place of his nativity. I have sent what little I had of the Genealogy, from John Bronson of Farmington 1644. to grandfather's children: but this is but a lifeless genealogy, and unfortunately I have nothing else. Grandfather died in 1819.² and I saw him but seldom when he came to Spindle Hill to bring us apples from the early tree in the meadow, or when on a visit to him at Jerico.³ Very venerable and very sensible, I remember him, exceedingly fond of theology in which, I have heard your father say, he was more than a match in argument, for the best of the clergy. a good Churchman, too and whose services to the Church were very great, certainly when he gave it one of its chief ornaments and faithful adherents, his son, your father. Grandmother I never saw, as she died 3. Dec. 1800,⁴ ‖ a few days ‖ [p. o.] year [p. in] after I was born. But I have heard my mother tell of her

enterprise and pertinacity, and all of us have heard many times of her *weaving Tilly through Yale College*.[5] Uncle Noah has this and much more in his memory, and nobody can relate it in a more interesting way than he can. I trust it is all written, and sent, for the memoir; if it is not, pray get him to tell, and you shall write: there could be nothing finer in the way of anecdote, and reminiscences for those times.

Uncle I scarce ever saw, and nearly all the acquaintances I had with him, was while I lived with you, a shy and silent young man, wishing but unable to be sociable, and to know many things. He was busy with the Churchman's Magazine, and had the academy in his thoughts, and I with my school. So that nothing memorable remains with me about his early life. But his handsome form, and genial manner and dispositions abide with me; and I was present at his bedside, and saw him depart. There are his Poems, from which passages might be extracted, from "the Retrospect—" particularly; and then there are Dr. Noble's Discourse, and Dr. Beardsley's Address containing biographical matters. I gave memoranda of these last to the editor of the Book and you must send the Profile, if there is nothing more any thing that resembles his face commanding, and yet serene presence.—I tried to get at the Christ Church Records in Boston but the Rector, was out of town. I called several times unsuccessfully: when I return I will try again.—The Book will not go to press, I was told, till January 1856, so there is yet time to have all ready. *You* are *the natural* biographer or Charles, (whom I should meet with great pleasure,) and Uncle Noah comes in for his part also.

Tell him I have found nothing more concerning the Blakeslees. There is no name in the Boston Records. It first occurs in this country as far as I can ascertain at North Haven 1670. Ebenezer Blackesee[?] being one of the original proprietors and settlers of that town, as you read in Barber's Collections.[6] Nor have I been able to visit Col. Thayer of Weymouth as I half promised, when I was at Medina. Then I had a future journey to Cincinnati and the West, and a visit to Medina, in prospect: but it is deferred. and now I have another voyage to England before me; perhaps this fall, or if not in the spring. So I may be your way before I go. I wish I may be. Aunt Sylvia and the cousins are all well I hope. Remember me kindly to all, and to your sisters, ‖ whom I wish all ‖ affectionately

Myself and family are all well. I heard her[?] [word]

Truly yours, Cousin,

A. Bronson Alcott.

Heard from my mother
who is well and the [word]
there, at Oriskany Falls.

[1] Walpole, New Hampshire, on the Connecticut River in the southwest part of the state. The Alcotts lived there in a rent-free house for a little over two years.
[2] Captain Amos Bronson.
[3] A few miles from Wolcott.
[4] Anna Blakeslee Bronson.
[5] Rev. Tillotson Bronson.
[6] John Warner Barber, *Connecticut Historical Collection* (New Haven, 1836).

LETTER 55–3[1]

[to Louisa, Boston]

Walpole, Tuesday, | 27th Nov. 1855.

Dear Louisa,

I am unwilling the family Parcel should be sealed and sent, without enclosing some slight token of my remembrance, and interest in your present fortunes and indeavours [sic].—As regards Your Book it can afford to wait and be all the richer and more seasonable for the Christmas of '56. and so you may spare any regrets about it now. Meanwhile, you have the range of City Entertainments and Services, for any spoils for works of Truth or Fiction, you may care to indulge in, together with the full stores gathered from a maiden's chequred [sic] experiences, of 23.—whose birth day comes twined annually with mine, and making me 56. on this 29 of the month, and all too dull and prosy to be very interesting to the livelier scion luxuriating in town, far away from my little chamber of reminiscences here. But as the sere stems regoice [sic] and pride themselves in the bloom and fragrence [sic] of the branches and flowers they still claim as theirs, by bith-right [sic] and paternity, so thy Childs' courage and spirit,—yours, and Annas too—are daily prides and satisfactions to me. And, never doubting the mother principles that nourish the roots of your purposes and performances, I rest assured that fruits must succed [sic], and be all the more mellow and mature, from their vigorous growth, and the hard seasoning they have had, from their beginnings the fairest and best fruits grow, not in the blandest climes, but in those attempered of sun and shower, of heat and cold; and these *Alcott plants*, have had a pretty fair chance to prove, and put forth, their virtues, and, I doubt not, will come to something presently, to justify the trials, moral and social, through which they have passed. The years are showing us, and shall show. As for me, I could not have asked better means of training— though not just what, in my ignorance I should have asked, and have sometimes demurred at, for the time, along my half century and six, and now can only wish the Grace had been mine, to have made the most of it, for myself and mine, as it passed.—

Heaven bless you, my child, in all your good intentions, and shield you from any others, if such are yours, at any time, and make you rich in every [word], || any || talent, it has bestowed, to bless, also

Your father, and friend.

[1] MS. in the Clifton Waller Barrett Library, University of Virginia.

LETTER 56–1[1]

[to Louisa, Boston]

Walpole 31 March, 1856.

Dear Louisa,

I am glad you are urging Anna to come at once to Walpole and have the benefits of *Home* for a few weeks before she goes to Boston, and to the excitements of your Play, which will come soon enough for her if it is not brought out till May. I have written begging her to come this way and so has your mother. She needs the rest and opportunity to recruit herself here after so much fatigue and false feeding: and, if I may judge from the Effigy you sent the other day, and which is now on my mantel piece, you are needing a similar privilege, yet seem bent on making as long a stay from good bread and fine air and early hours, as you can with any grace about you. I wish you sisters, after a little fellowship in the city—(if *Anna* comes that way or goes down to meet you) *would come home together, and pass a little while with us.* Anna to get strong again, and you to get leisure for your writing, and with the summer before you to mature some **plan** for the coming winter's enterprizes—permitting us all to have some interest **in** the same as we wish to have. There is no need of your remaining away. *Our bills are all met here in Walpole.* Anna's little earnings shall be hers to help her forwards, and you both need *leisure and rest,* which you cannot get away from home. Now think of all this, my brave Child, and generous, and make up your mind to have it so; and let us have the pleasure of your company over again, here in our solitudes: *Your mother wept when she read of your thinking of staying for the summer,* and is far from well since her return from Lynn.

Write me, will you not, and say you will come to her, and

Your Father Also.

Miss Louisa M. Alcott.

¹ MS. in the Clifton Waller Barrett Library, University of Virginia.

LETTER 56–2

[to Mrs. A. Bronson Alcott, Walpole, N.H.]

Worcester, Saturday Morning | 26 April 1856. | (At Mr. Blakes.)¹

My dear wife

I came here yesterday from Dr. Alcott's with whom I passed Thursday Night, leaving Boston at 5 after dining with Louisa at Mr Bonds, and reading Anna's letter, just received, saying she will be in Boston in a few days, as early as Saturday next, or the beginning of the week following I imagine. So we shall all meet there and, *"Play and Conversations"* over, come home together; such is our hope at present. All goes prosperously thus far. Louisa appears discreetly, and takes her good fortunes in a becoming spirit, just as you could have wished.² We walked in from Mr Bond's and called on Mrs Severance, with whom I have since passed a night, Mrs Hildreth occupying a part of the same house, while her husband is in the Tribune Office in New York city. We visited also the Atheneum together, and saw Mrs Hildreth again at her Rooms, where I am to have my Conversations, as you will see by the Circular and Cards, herein sent. Tuesday evening, 22nd. I met a pleasant company at Mrs Dall's³—Dr Wm. Channing Mr and Mrs Severance, Mrs Hildreth, Mr Fisher, and others. Dr. Channing has taken the Conversation to heart made all the necessary arrangements, and there is every hope of a good company for me, not very numerous, to be sure, but cordial, and of good quality: 75 persons perhaps or more—about 60 tickets having been taken on Thursday when I left town. My company at Manchester was receptive and kindly. We had three meetings on Sunday, and met on Mon-

191

day Tuesday and Wednesday evenings following: there were some 50 persons in attendance steadily, and Mr. Johnson's hospitalities were of the true sort. The $25. dolls he gave me, was *"good money"*, he said, and they must have more soon; for more money and as good. So I shall run across again sometime at their call, while the peas are blossoming, and the garden can spare me for a week or so.—Here, I am to meet Higgenson's Congregation on Sunday afternoon, (to morrow) and pu[r]pose returning to Boston sometime on Monday to be ready for Tuesday Evenings company.—The Bonds were cordial and communicative: and so were the Windships. Hamilton I have not seen. Woodman invites me to dine next Thursday at "Parkers' Hotel," with Agassiz[4] and Emerson. The last I have not seen yet: nor can I well stop at Concord with the Girls on our way home. I run up and pass next Sunday, May 4th. with him. It will be as late as the 10. or 15 before we return to High St. and summer quarters. Please inform me of yourselves soon. I shall be at Mr. Sewalls,—at Melrose—Mr. Bonds, and distributively for the time. The farmers are just turning their earliest furrows here; and beginning to plant their gardens. I shall not fall behind them nor your wishes, heaven favoring us all.

Mrs Hildreth will gladly instruct Abby,[5] and is finishing the picture for us to bring when we come. Now Heaven bless you till then; and bestow a Summer of satisfactions on the family unitedly.

Yours ever
A.B.A.

[1] Harrison Gray Otis Blake—later, editor of Thoreau's Journals.
[2] Louisa's first book, *Flower Fables*, was published late in 1854 and was rather successful.
[3] Caroline H. Dall.
[4] Louis Agassiz (1807–73).
[5] In drawing.

[to Mrs. Anna Alcott, Oriskany Falls, N.Y.; from Walpole, N.H., before August 5, 1856.]

LETTER 56–3

[to Mrs. Anna Alcott, New Haven, Conn.]

Walpole, N.H. 5. August | 1856.

Dear Mother,

Your letter dated at New-Haven with brother Ambrose's, written on the same sheet, reached me in due course of mail, and informs me of what I had written but a few days before to learn of your health and present whereabouts. It was addressed to you at Oriskany, but as failing of finding you there, may have been sent along and come to hand at Ambrose's, where I am greatly pleased to know you are now, and so well, and so much nearer Wolcott, and Walpole. It was no small matter for a woman of your age to undertake the journey, and required all your earlier courage and independence, which, it seems, brought you safe and sound, to your son's door; and prompts you to extend your jaunt to Wolcott and Plymouth Homesteads, and the familiar spots, and friendly faces, still surviving, of former years. I am strongly tempted to join you there, and accompany you in this jaunt to the places and friends you will visit after so long an absence. How pleasant it will be to see again the old haunts and the old neighbors there, *with you*: to revive memories which those places and people would recall in us both;—in mother and son!—Now please write to me, as soon as you get this, and let me know *where* you are, whether at Ambrose's, or at Wolcott, and *when* I shall meet you, for such a pleasant reunion. If I can, I will come, as I am planning a little journey that way sometime this autumn, and can perhaps accommodate my movements to suit yours. You will stay about those parts some weeks, at least; and I take it for granted you do not purpose to return to Oriskany, but remain with Ambrose or with us. But that will appear and arrange itself when I see you, as I shall, either at Wolcott, or New-Haven soon. Write and tell me of your plans and wishes. I can leave home early in September; perhaps late in this month:—but let me hear from you meanwhile, as I have said.

We are all well: the girls are all at home. My garden promises ‖ well ‖ [p. o.] fruits [p. in], and prospects are of the old sort—a good share of comfort, at the cost of some labour and dependence.—But much to be grateful for; and no thing in the way of complaints to speak of.—

Give my regards to Ambrose and family, with those of my wife, and take to yourself, our united and

Affectionate remembrances,—
A. Bronson Alcott.

Brother *Ambrose* will send this to Wolcott, or Plymouth, if mother has gone there—

A.B.A.

LETTER 56–4

[to Mrs. Anna Alcott, Wolcott, Conn.]

Walpole, New Hampshire, | 14th August, 1856.

Dear Mother,

I have just taken from our Post Office, and read, a letter from Ambrose, mailed at New Haven on the 12th and answering one from me addressed to you *there,* and dated the 5th which, Ambrose writes me, will reach you at Wolcott on Saturday next, the 16th. and come to hand, I suppose, with this; also my letter sent to you at Oriskany, and remailed to New-Haven from thence to you. I am glad to know of your being once more in Wolcott, and shall meet you there, or at Plymouth, sometime in September early, say by the 10th or thereabouts, if I can reach you so soon. But you must write, *next week* if you can, and tell me *where you are to be for the coming month,* so that I may find you without mistake. I wish to go about with you to all the old haunts, and see such of our kindred, and friends, and neighbours, face to face, as remain to be visited. I can spend a week or two in those familiar places, and live with you in the past for the time. Besides objects and persons in *Wolcott,* we must visit *Plymouth* and *Waterbury* together, and compare our remembrances once again of early and ancestral times and places. It will be an unexpected pleasure to me; nor will I have it saddened by the presumption of its being the last I may enjoy with you on these wonted spots. We will meet, and make the most of our experiences thereon. Nor shall we willingly permit your too wide separation again from your old homes.—I am going on to New-York, and, perhaps, as far as Philadelphia, *on my lecturing tour,* to be absent for a month or two from home, and shall see you again in Connecticut, on my way back, when we will see whether you wish to come and pass the winter here with us, or delay your coming till next spring, when I shall perhaps be that way again. But you will write *and be particular to tell me when and where, I shall find you.* It will be easier to get a horse and chaise for our jaunt, in Plymouth perhaps, than in Wolcott, and the rails run so near *Terryville,* I could stop at my pleasure, and we could take a chaise there.— But you shall plan and let me know. With regards to old friends in those parts, I am. Your faithful son,

A. Bronson Alcott.

LETTER 56–5

[to Mrs. Anna Alcott, Wolcott, Conn.]

Walpole, N.H. Sep 2nd 1856.

Dear Mother,

I am sorry to hear of your illness, and low spirits, but trust the rest you are taking there with your old friends and neighbours with the breathing of the fine air of those hills will soon restore you to yourself, and fit you to enjoy with me the rides I am hoping to take with you to see the old places and people. I find I shall not reach *Wolcott* till after the 20.th of this month, and it may be it will be as late as the 25 before I shall see you. I leave home on the 12:—shall be in *Fitchburg;* perhaps, [p. in] *Worcester* and *Hartford*—each place some days, so that I shall not get to Wolcott or Plymouth till *late in the month.* I mean to spend a week with you, and then go on to *New Haven* and *New-York* where I am engaged to have *Conversations;* also in other places. You will see my *Circular* on the opposite leaf[1]—Now, dear mother, get well rested from your fatigues, and let me see you as much as possible when I come. We are all well. My wife and girls send much love to you to make you feel better: add that also of

Your affectionate Son,
A. Bronson Alcott.

[1] The Circular follows:

CONVERSATIONS

Mr. Alcott wishes to converse on his favorite themes, during the current Lecture season, in some of the New-England cities and towns; also in New York and Philadelphia, if practicable.

He promises five Conversations on
PRIVATE LIFE;
ITS GENIUS, OPPORTUNITIES, AND INFLUENCES.
Considered under the general heads of

CONVERSATION I	DESCENT.
CONVERSATION II	HOME.
CONVERSATION III	HEALTH.
CONVERSATION IV	PURSUITS.
CONVERSATION V	VICTORIES.

The discussions, it will be perceived, are suited to select companies, and invite the protection of the parlour, and the presence of ladies particularly.

TERMS accommodated to the interest and ability of the parties.

WALPOLE, N. H., Aug. 20, 1856.

LETTER 56-6

[to Mrs. A. Bronson Alcott and daughters, Walpole, N.H.]

Terryville, Plymouth, Ct. | September 20, 1856.

My dear Wife,

and daughters,

I find my self here sooner, by some days, than I had planned at Walpole: Mr Tilden and friends, releasing me for Worcester on Monday, and Blake and Brown, with whom I dined, commending me on my journey the same day at 4. P.M. to Hartford city. I slept at *"The Trumbell House"*, called on Hon. Henry Barnard next morning: at 10 took the train, and reached Waterbury to dine. In the afternoon, I walked to Wolcott, sending along my trunk, and slept at Mrs. Obed Alcott's. Finding my mother had passed through to Gaylords the day before, I visited the Homestead and Cousins, for a beginning, and slept at Johnson Alcotts on Wednesday night. Thursday morning (yesterday)[1] he brought me up here—I find mother a good deal fatigued by her recent journeyings and visitings, but finding good rest here with her nephew, my sister ‖ Phebe's ‖ Pamilas' eldest son, as you know. I have just returned from a little ride with her, which she has greatly enjoyed; and, if her strength and spirits favor, we shall ‖ ride ‖ [p. o.] again drive [2 p. in] on Saturday to her birth place at *Riverside*, 5 miles from here, and pass the night with some old friends of hers in the neighbourhood.—Next week we go together to Wolcott, and Waterbury, returning here by Wednesday or Thursday; ‖ and ‖ giving me time to reach New-Haven by Saturday; where I shall pass some days, and to which place you shall send your letters, till advised otherwise by me.

Mother inclines to return with me, yet may remain with Ambrose for the winter. She will stay here a few weeks, and meet me at Ambrose's on my return from New-York City. If you know of any objection other than we have considered together to her spending the winter at Walpole, write and let me be advised in season. She needs company and kindness, rest and quiet, and these we seem to have, and ready to bestow on her, as our choicest gifts. I do not press, but leave her to choose for herself. Her days must be few, at best, and I must hasten to pay my debts.

All looks propitious now, and has thus far: I am $20 the lighter for having that sum added to itself since I started, and Blake and Brown propose Conversations in Worcester on my return.

Mr. Barnard of Hartford wishes to accompany me also, for memoirs and materials for *"The History of Education"* which he is writing. Dr. Alcott preceded me in Wolcott, so I missed seeing him there.

Mother sends her love and wishes you would write to her, here.—Her cap was just the thing.—Also Ransom Gaylord sends his remembrances to Anna whom he saw at Oriskany. I shall hope to hear from you at New Haven, care of Ambrose Alcott.

Ever Yours
A. Bronson Alcott.

---

¹ Thursday was September 18, and the letter is dated September 20.

LETTER 56–7

[to Mrs. Anna Alcott]

New Haven, September 27. 1856. | (Saturday.)

Dear Mother,

My stay in Waterbury was short, and I reached Ambrose's on Thursday, to find them all well and expecting your coming along with me.—The family you were troubled about has left, and the rooms are clear now of the children you spoke of. Ambrose's wife will write to you in a few days. They seem to be awaiting another visit from you and your own choice of spending the winter with them, or of accompanying me to Walpole, on my return from New York. A few weeks will determine for us all. I trust the quiet you are getting at Edward's will do something to restore your spirits, and render you able to go home with me in November, if you choose.

I shall pass Sunday here in New-Haven, and perhaps longer. Yesterday, I saw Dr. Taylor, and Professor Silliman, of Yale College, and am to meet some of the other professors to-day. It looks now as if I might have some Conversations here: I shall know by Monday next.

This evening I am hoping to have letters from home. If I get any thing of importance to you, I will write again || to you ||, before I leave New-Haven. Ambrose has letters from Abby May, and aunt Bayley, also my letter addressed to you at Oriskany. They hoped to have some private chance of sending them to you; but keep them now for your coming. Chatfield had been at home from Oswego, but had returned there. The letters are dated August 3.—

Ambrose and family are well. I sleep here, breakfast and take supper; but get a bite for dinner in the city.

I have seen Dr. Bronson, and the publishers of the Waterbury Book, which will hardly be published before next spring. They want your son's likeness for it; but I doubt about giving it.

Ambrose and wife send much love, and hope to see you here soon.

My kind remembrances to Edward and wife for all their hospitalities to me, and yourself.

Affectionately,
Your Son,
Amos Bronson Alcott.

LETTER 56–8

[to **Mrs. A. Bronson Alcott**, Walpole, N.H.]

New Haven September 30th 1856.

My Dear,

I reached this city on Thursday last, and your yetters came to hand on Saturday. My stay in Plymouth was shortened a little, as I found mother soon wearied of the rides, nor did she incline to accompany me to Wolcott or Water-bury, as I had promised myself she would: her journey from Oriskany and the meeting of her old friends and neighbours here becoming irksome and even painful to her, wearied and age stricken as she is. I left her at Edward Gaylords —where she hopes to recruit her spirits for returning hither in the course of a week or two, and where I am to meet her on my return fom New York home-wards. I almost fear to *t*ake her along to Walpole, since, after what has lately transpired, there appears to be less prospect than ever of a home there for any of us. But we shall see the more clearly into the darkness, a month hence, and take the proper steps toward finding some fixed abode, if any such felicity await the wanderers. It were the safer under such uncertainties impending for her to stay with Ambrose here till the spring. Yet, if she should set her heart strongly on returning with me, I shall gladly bring her along to Walpole to take the chances with the rest. She has not many years to give her children, and it seems so good to have her for the little time with us. She will never return to Betsey's, the only one of her children now left in York state; Chatfield and ‖ family ‖ [p. o.] son [p. in] having gone to Wisconsin, and will probably settle there sometime [p. in].

Professor Norton has done the fit thing for me here in this city. I called on him on Friday, the day after my arrival, was invited to tea, and he took me to see Drs. Taylor and Silliman of Yale College, in the evening. Saturday forenoon, I spent in the College Library; met Prof Norton again at his house after dinner, and made appointments to see Dr. Bacon, and Prof Porter on Monday.—Dr. Bronson, editor of "the Waterbury Book," also the publisher, Bronson, both of Waterbury,—the first Professor in the Medical College here,—I had seen on Fri-day. Sunday, my brother accompanied me to hear Dr. Bacon at the Church of my ancestors on the Green: and we walked together to see Spindle Hill in the far distance from the top of East-Rock, with a view of the Sound, and the environs of this fair city of elms and steeples.

Monday, I called on Dr. Bacon, and found him exceedingly affable and communicative. He spoke of Kanzas and Fremont as a Priest and a Patriot should, and I wished we had some of his spirit in Massachusetts, (from which we have never departed, except for the little time, and shall soon return, shall we not?) I met Prof. Porter afterwards, who took me to see the Trumbell Gallery of Paintings, and the Cabinet, said to be richest in mineral specimens of any in the Country: also met President Woolsey, and Prof. Fisher, at the College.

Prof Porter,—he is Prof of Moral Philosophy—has taken my "Conversations" into favour, and hopes to have a circle for me here on my return from New York. Mrs. Norton also seemed kindly disposed toward the same. She is a highly intelligent and practically energetic person—and a good friend to insist in one's purposes: a friend of Freedom and wishes to vote for Fremont. She is very active just now in serving Kanzas, having formed a Ladies Sewing Circle here for the suffering Free States men and women and children.

I shall leave here today or to morrow for New-York, hoping to talk in Brooklyn and Jersey City before meeting Dr. Bellows[1] and friends. I would have gone first to Newport but for the distance and uncertainty. I can venture there a month hence the more safely after the profits of the Metropolis are cropped and in hand. Nor shall I fail of seeing Mr. Furness[2] and Philadelphia, if the thing is found practicable. We shall see.—These debts, and W_____s must be discharged, as soon as possible, this very autumn—certainly, by the spring coming —and we will take less of others, and earn more for ourselves,—may it be competence entire, and honorable independence of every body. I would engage myself here in a Clock factory at a dollar and a half a day, if I saw it necessary, and stick to handiwork till the end of me: and may do it yet. I could put a clock together with the best of them, and am going this afternoon to look inside of the workshops to reconnoitre in prospect. Duty is always a prompt pay-master and overpays besides.

Your full letter and particulars reached me here and was read on Saturday evening. I shall heed all your wise counsels, and come to you as heavily freighted with comforting considerations as I can. Much love to the girls: they shall address me at New-York City when they write. Abby shall hear concerning Mrs. Hildreth in my next. Tell Anna to keep up good spirits—her day is coming with the rest of the ministrants.

I will write on my arrival in New-York, and await letters from you then.

Faithfully Yours.

A. Bronson Alcott.

[1] Henry Whitney Bellows (1814–82) of Walpole, N.H., and New York City. Alcott saw him frequently on this present trip, and he did a lot to further Alcott's activities in New York.
[2] William Henry Furness.

LETTER 56–9

[to Mrs. A. Bronson Alcott, Walpole, N.H.]

New York, International Hotel, | October 4th 1856. | Saturday.

My dear,

I wrote on *Tuesday* morning last and mailed to you at N-Haven. I was at the New Haven Clock Factory, also called on Prof. Fisher of Yale College, same day, and had a good time. He is preacher to the undergraduates, and a young man of fair talents and free Spirit. I think the way is open for some Conversations in the Elm City on my return homewards, perhaps.

Wednesday, Oct 1. This morning brought me letters from you. Louisa's prospects gave me good hopes. Let me know further as matters ripen. We may as well take for granted the golden success, and thank the gods and Germantown, for so much called after our names. I hope to be a Spectator of her triumphs fairly soon.

I left New Haven at 9. and reached here about 1. to take rooms and dine. —This House is kept on the Foreign Plan. You take rooms by the day, and your meals in the Saloon, or at the Common Table, as you like. I pay four York shillings for mine, and get all I want in the Saloon, for two shillings more by the plate, and as two meals serves me very well, I live cheaply for about one dollar a day, and elegantly besides. The Hotel is central on Broadway, and near the frequented haunts of life and letters. I am well pleased and shall perhaps remain here while I stay in the city. Washing is done in the house, and your two shillings includes your newspaper, and single independence at your meal whenever you call for it. After dinner, I crossed to Brooklyn and spent the evening with Longfellow[1] and friends. He will promote some meetings for me on that side of the River.—and I am to dine with him on Monday next, and talk in the evening, for a beginning.—

Thursday 2. Never was there a morning brighter: and I crossed over to Jersey City and had an hour with A [T?]rottingham at his own house. He will attend my Conversations here in town, and bring along his friends. Returning I called at the Tribune office where I met Ripley, Dance and Hildreth: Greeley had gone to Pennsylvania, for Fremont and the elections. Abby will be glad to learn of Mrs Hildreths coming next month to New York: Nor is there any chance, I fear, for Louisas "Elves" with the Harpers. Mr. Ripley gave us no hope. But she can afford to wait, with her betters: her book will keep.—Also I called on Dr. Bellows, and found him all I wished. He showed me his study, his Church, his house, which is an appendage to the Church, and all of the costliest workmanship, the pattern his own.—All Souls' Church, Catholic, and we hope for the [word] liberty and humanity. The Study is highly ornamented, and will seat perhaps *fifty* persons as many as he wishes for the inauguration, as he pleases to compliment our first meetings. Same evening, came Drs. Osgood & Farley, Mr Longfellow and Frothingham, and set *Thursday evening next*, the 9th for our first Conversatio[ns.] The company he persists shall be very select and the best advantages given that the City affords. He talks greatly and promises magnificent results, seeming to see and seize fast what he has in prospect. I must do my part becomingly, and you shall hear ‖ how ‖ more ‖ soon ‖ after our first trial of the wits of Gotham.

Yesterday, I called on Dr. Chapin,[2] (who is to [be] one of our Company) and found him affable and communicative. I was at the Bookstores also. Fear not, I buy nothing, nor shall, till debts and the _____s are wiped clear out of mind and memory. Thank you for the *Channing* and *Cheney notices*. How great the contrast in the couples!—Will Anna write and Elisabeth: all—my love to the four. When does Louisa leave? and how is my Garden? and the moods—? Write me, dearest, and tell me all.

A. Bronson Alcott.

[1] Samuel Longfellow (1819–92), Unitarian minister, younger brother of Henry Wadsworth Longfellow, and one of the group of "transcendentalists."
[2] Edwin Hubbell Chapin.

LETTER 56–10

[to Mrs. A. Bronson Alcott, Walpole, N.H.]
New York City | International Hotel | October 10th. 1865.
My dear,

Saturday 4. Mailing my letter to you of that date. I crossed to Brooklyn, and passed some hours with Walt. Whitman the Poet, author of "the Leaves of

Grass," of which he gave me a copy of the new edition, just published, and containing a characteristic letter of his in answer to Emersons, printed some time since in "the Tribune." I am well rewarded for finding this extraordinary man, and shall see more of him before I leave N.Y.

Sunday 5.[1] I hear Dr. Bellows at his Church, and Dr. Chapin in the evening, and find this city is graced with ministers of the good word not less than ours. Chapin's Church was filled to overflowing and many stood for want of seats.

Monday 6. To Brooklyn and dine with Longfellow. Evening, company comes and we have a good Conservation, Dr. Bush, Swedenborgean, and others taking parts. Monday evening next, 13—I meet them again.—

Tuesday 7. Today, at Gowan's Antique Bookstore. Also met Wm. Chace and Edward Palmer. Chace is here as "Secretary of the National Republican Committee" and doing good service for Fremont. Palmer is married and living at the Raritan Bay Community[2] where I shall see more of him and his.

Wednesday 8. At the Astor Library. P.M. meet Isaac Hecker, now a Father of the Religious Order of Redemptioners, and an Enthusiast as when we knew him at Fruitlands: now devoted Romanism, and is Mrs. George Ripley's Confessor. He seemed much pleased to see me, took me over the House, and into the Church, and introduced me to Father's Walworth and Deshon, both young men and devotees like himself; also spoke of you and of the Fruitlands experiences with interest. Lane, he saw, he tells me, about two years since in London. He was there a clerk in the Bank of England.—

Thursday 9. At Dr. Tralls'[3] Water Cure and Hydropathic Medical College where I dine, and engage to meet the Professors students and Patients for Conversation on *Health and Temperance,* on Tuesday evening next. 14 . .—Here, meet your *Miss Pellelt*[?] of Syracuse, since been to California, to Nicaragua, and now on her way to Chicago in the service of Kanzas. She remembers you, and brother Samuel with much interest and regard: and had seen Anna. She is a graduate of Oberlin College and is full of energy and courage.

Thursday 9.—Evening, hold my first Conversation in Dr. Bellows' Library. I left my hotel early and took tea with the Dr. and wife. Company came, and the Conversation, opened with some complementary [sic] words on "his friend, the Plato of our time. Father of transcendentalism in this Country, and friend of Emerson. &c. &c. all which was taken in good Faith seemingly by the fine company invited —Dr. and Mrs. Osgood, Mrs Kirkland, the authoress, Mr. and Mrs. Botta, (Mrs B. was Miss Anna Leach the artist, whom I had met formerly at Providence,) Drs. Hitchcock and Smith, besides many good persons, many women, whose names I forget, numbering 40 or more. The evening was pronounced a success. I thought it moderately good, and so leaving room and appetite for the better things to come. The talk ran far onto 11. oclock: and we meet again on Thursday evening. 16. for further trial Drs. Bellows and Osgood, Mrs Kirkland and Botta supported our theme, in tune, very handsomely: so I am now fairly launched and hope to swim gallantly to the havens[?], on coming evenings. The thing is new and strange here, but must go, and gain praise to itself for this once and hereafter, if all will have it so. I suspect the Dr. and Co. will get as good as they bargained for, and some better, if I may say so. But of this more presently.—

Friday 10. This morning get a letter from Marcus Spring inviting me to come and pass Sunday at Raritan Bay, and give some Conversations there. I am well pleased at this opportunity of meeting him so, and his friends: and am about leaving here at 4. this afternoon, to return for my Conversation at Brooklyn on Monday next, when I hope to get letters from you: nothing has reached me here since I came to the city. Write and let me know all there is to be written of yourself and the girls. I find the value of home and privileges more and more as I leave them behind. I may get to Philadelphia and perhaps Newport. Tenney's[?] son[?] is lately married and lives in Newport, and Calvert is there.— Now goodbye, and may Heaven bring us soon together in a home of our own. To each of the girls a reminder, and many from

Yours ever, A.B.A.

[1] Here, as in a number of other letters, Alcott copied his daily doings for (or from) his Journals.

[2] A Fourierist Phalanx begun in 1853 at "Eagleswood (the estate of Marcus Spring on Raritan Bay about a mile west of the center of Perth Amboy, and now within its city limits), Middlesex County, New Jersey." Arthur Eugene Bestor, *Backwoods Utopias* (Philadelphia, 1950), p. 240.

[3] Russell Thacher Trall, M.D. (1812–77).

LETTER 56–11

[to Mrs. A. Bronson Alcott, Walpole, N.H.]

New York City | Taylor's International Hotel | 17. October, 1856.
My dear,

I am in for company and engaged for a week now to come—all which yourself and the girls, will be pleased to hear—This afternoon I go to pass Saturday and Sunday at "the Raritan Bay Union," and talk three evenings, meeting Mr. Weld and his school on Sunday morning; the assembled company in the evenings during my stay. On Monday, 20. I am to return to meet Mr. Longfellow and friends at Brooklyn:—Tuesday evening I discuss Health and Temperance at Dr. Tralls institution: Wednesday evening, I meet George Ripley, the painter Lawrence and other company at Mrs Botta's: Thursday evening comes Conversation the 3rd. at Dr. Bellows, and I am to go to Mr Springs on the following Friday for other sessions. So much in prospect to come. You shall have the retrospect now.
Friday 10. Just a week since, I wrote to you of my doings up to date. And I have since mailed some newspapers to you.
Saturday 11. At Gowans Antique Bookstore again finding some spoils for my collections—"*Hermes Trismegistus*," and some of my lost Books of 1843 at Albany. 3. P.M., I take the boat for Perth-Amboy, and reach Mr. Springs, to supper: attend a dance in the evening, where I meet Mr Weld,[1] Miss. Grimke, Judge Grimke, Mrs. W.'s brother, from Ohio, Ed. Palmer and wife; and the rest of the unionists young and old: Arnold Buffum, Mrs. Springs Father, also used to come often to see us you may remember when we were living in Philadelphia— Rebecca Black, Mr Reed formerly of Hopedale &c. Miss. Peabody has gone to Philadelphia to pass the winter. I stay with Mr. Spring, who lives in his own house apart from the Common Buildings, and whose || well quiet || unobtrusive good sense pleases me || greatly || well. They have imported many admirable English Comforts into their elegant hospitalities, from their foreign travelling experiences, and I have never perhaps found so much household ease and accommodation, in any family before. German Governess at Dr. Bellows in Walpole who you liked so much lives with them. Mrs. Spring is a lively, communicative,

well disposed, woman, and good company. She has known very good people, and talks interestingly of her friends and foreign travels She told me many things about Margaret Fuller Ossoli, and husband, Miss. Bremer, and others whom we know.—The Springs have three children—a son, now just coming of age, and designing to be an artist, and two daughters, much younger.

Sunday 12. At 10. I meet the company all, and discourse on *Worship.* P.M. walk with "Marcus," "Rebecca" riding on horseback and taking us through the grounds, the Park, by many winding ways, and pointing out the rustic seats placed here and there under the oaks, by her directions: also leading us over the fields and pastures to the commanding points. It is a magnificent estate of about 300 acres lying on the Raritan Bay, about one mile from Perth Amboy: and reminds me of the Southern Plantations, reached as it is, by a private road, and gates opening into lanes, the frame house and barns, on the river side as you approach the Family Mansion of Mr. Spring, and the costly Community Buildings, a sketch of which I will send you in my next, with other particulars and considerations.—In the evening, I met the Children, thirty or more: afterwards discourse on Private Life with the Elect of the place till 11.

Monday 13. I take the morning boat and walk the International at 12: finding letters, enclosing venerable tokens of love and remembrance from yourself: with pleasing addresses from all the girls, and all taken so gladly to my room, read there, and taken also to heart. At my first leisure they shall have answers for their pains and kindness, such as I can bestow. Louisa must write to me from Boston when she is once fairly there and settled at boardings. Evening: I meet my circle at Brooklyn and discourse effectually on *Private Life,* the women taking good parts.

Tuesday 14. Call on Rev. Dr. Osgood, also on Mr. and Mrs Botta: and discourse with Dr. Tralls' party on Health and Temper[ance] in the evening. The doctrines seemed new to most of them,—patients, pupils and professors; very taking too, and I was invited to speak again the next evening. You would laugh to see what a Dr. of Divinity and of Physic, I am taken to be here with these neophytes, *Dr. Alcott,* every where in both acceptances: Dr. Bellows introducing me thus to the brilliant company at his rooms, Platonic Dr. A. in contradistinction from the Physiologic ‖ of the ‖ namesake, always understood.

Wednesday 15. To-day call on Mr. Allan and look at his choice collection of antique Books—the rarest I have ever seen "Withers' Emblems, 1635, folio. "Pilgrims Progress," 1796, the edition I read when a boy. Dibdin's Bibliomania, 2 vols. illustrated. Missels richly illuminated and embossed. &c. &c.—forgetting time and space the while. Mr Allan is a Scotchman, and has devoted a fortune and a long life to his passion for books. His daughter keeps his house, and shares his tastes and hospitalities, offering me cakes and wine, and leaving me to myself amidst the books, her father being confined for the day in his chamber, I did not see him, but sent up my card of thanks for the privilege and pleasure he had given me.—In the evening, I met the same eager and receptive party at Dr. Tralls, and discoursed again on *Health and Virtue* from 7. till 10. The Dr. invites me to take board and lodgings with him during my stay in the city. Perhaps I shall do so on my return from Mr. Spring's next Monday: But, you shall address me here at *"the International* Hotel," till I intimate otherwise.

Thursday 16. I call on A. J. Davis and wife, and find them very glad to see me. I think I may meet Mr D. and friends for some Conversations before I leave the city: Also S. P. Andrews, Brisbane, Hugh Doherty, and others of that company of socialists.—It is best for me to trace things to the source and origin—Free Love or Foul, with the rest. Fred. Cabot is here. I have seen him for a moment at the Fowlers, Phrenologists in Broadway[.]

Last evening came "*Conversation* the Second, *on Home,*" at Dr. B.s. The company was the same, and the theme inspiring. We had a good time the women venturing into the depths and helping us most handsomely. All said good things, and the meeting was voted a success. I will give the names of the company hereafter.

I am waiting to hear from Dr. Furness and Mr. Calvert.

At Dr. Tralls the other evening, I met a young Englishman from Baltimore where he is connected with the public press—a vegetarian, and fond of good things, who thinks he has a company for me there; and will write on his return, and let me know. He left yesterday, so I may go as far South as Baltimore before I return to Walpole.—You give good accounts of the garden.

I am hoping to save something from this professional work of mine to pa[y] off old scores all round; I wish there may be wherewith to carry us through the winter, *and move us in the spring;* but we shall see out of all in due time. If mother can be comfortable at Ambrose's I shall prefer her staying there for the present. But she may have set her heart on us, and so must be indulged if she has.

The weather has been exceedingly fine, with only one or two chilly days here.

Now, dear, accept my thanks for all your affectionate remembrances of me and mine—for yourself, moreover, and the good girls you have given me—all precious and priceless to

Yours and theirs ever,
A.B.A.

[1] Theodore Dwight Weld, who married Angelina Grimke.

LETTER 56–12

[to Mrs. A. Bronson Alcott, Walpole, N.H.]
New York City, International Hotel | 21st October, 1856.
My dear,

I returned here yesterday from "Eaglewood,"[1] where I passed Saturday and Sunday, meeting the company on Friday evening for Conversation, also on the morning and evening of the following days, and the children in the afternoon; Mr. Weld being disposed to promote as much acquaintance with them as the time permitted, and to gain any advantages and hints suggested by our interviews and methods. My visit was every way agreeable to me, and seems to have given pleasure to all parties. Our meetings on Sunday were well attended and the Conversation profitable and spirited: Mr. and Mrs. Spring, the Welds, Sarah Grimke, James G. Burney and wife, Mr. Cutler, assistant of Mr. Welds, Miss. Virginia Vaughan, from Cincinnati, and a friend of the Wilsons, Arnold Buffum, Dr. Redfield, the physiognomist, Edward Palmer and wife; the children, some thirty or more, and all intelligent and attentive, and making our audiences worthy of our themes, "Home and Housekeeping, Marriage and Culture." Mr. Barker from Providence, Fred. Cabot, and Macdaniel[?] and wife from New York City spent the Sunday there, and helped us in the discussions. The Community is abandoned, the school having taken its place, and the hope now is to invite purchasers hither onto the Estate, and to form a pleasant neighbourhood, around the School. The Union Buildings are spacious, as you may see, the grounds are already under good improvement, and there seems to be laid the foundations of a good institution of Education. Mr. Weld, I find exceedingly liberal in his views; very able, Fatherly, beloved by his pupils, and of an earnest, devoted mind; executive and practical in all his purposes, a man to suceed in his undertakings. Of Mrs. Weld, I saw less, and should hope less. You may judge a little, from her persistency in "the Bloomer movemen[t,"] and her making it a matter of conscience and duty.

Herself and sister alone wear it here, Mrs. Spring and the women generally dressing plainly, if not elegantly. The Springs live in the fine Mansion you see in the picture, and have their own ways and manners. I like them pretty well, especially "Marcus." The population is miscellaneous, and there is not a little of the individualism, dissent, and antagonism, incident to the coming together of so many people. Something was said both by Mr. Weld and Mr. Spring of our taking parts in the enterprise. Yourself as Matron, and I as teacher and gardener, but I question whether they are able to make it worth our acceptance even should the vote be in our favor, of which, as regards myself, there is some doubt. Then agues and fevers prevail here sometimes, as in all the district surrounding New York City for many miles. I have no doubt as to our being serviceable in many ways, and of great advantage to the enterprise; but where all is yet crude and unsettled, perhaps it would be risking too much. Mr. Spring is the mainstay, and may withdraw at any moment from it, if the chances seem doubtful. He is unwilling to make pledges, but wishes to sell building lots, and plant a good neighbourhood around him. I have confidence in his goodness, and humanity, and doubt not of his wishing to serve us to the extent of his ability. He is generous, prudent, and every way a man, and a gentleman. I shall see and speak with him more fully and confidentially on my next visit to Eaglewood. Mr. Weld told me much of himself in a walk we took together on Sunday afternoon: also made many inquiries about our purposes and means of subsistence: all which I freely answered, and shall further entertain when I see him again. Possibly something may come of it for us and the girls by next spring.

I wish I had something to spare from my receipts for Louisa and Abby, But these have been inconsiderable as yet. Mr. Spring gave me Twenty dollars from the Unionists—something to help me along here and away a fortnight hence, and Dr. Bellows will redeem all promises and more, I doubt not. You shall have me, or something next best, in all good time. Your letter awaited me here on my arrival yesterday, full of friendliness for husband, and Kanzas, in which I take the pride of a husband and patriot, and read the first page to my evening circle last night at Brooklyn. The Country will be spared for woman's sake. and Kanzas freed. I rejoice heartily in you and the girls; and the Kanzas women, shall yet send their thanks to their kind benefactor—the women of Walpole.—I dine this afternoon at 6 with Albert Brisbane, Doherty, and A. J. Davis:—and am to talk again at Dr. Trall's in the evening: To morrow evening I am to be at Mr. Bottas. The weather is delightful. My washing comes in to day—three dozen pieces at a dollar a dozen. Write me the details of the days. I mailed you a double letter and newspapers on Friday last. Caress the good girls for me, and keep up hope till I come to your own embrace.

A.B.A.

[1] Alcott seems generally to have omitted the s from "Eagleswood."

Letter 56–13

[to Mrs. A. Bronson Alcott, Walpole, N.H.]

[New York City] Saturday, 3 p.m. | October 25–1856.

My dear,

The porter has just brought my trunk here to this College,[1] and I am shown my apartment, comfortably neat and clean, where I am made welcome and to stay while I [p. in] remain‖ing ‖ [p. o.] in this City. This evening, I meet patients, students and professors again for further discussion of Health and Temperance, the company professing to have been pleased and instructed at our previous meetings, and wishing more of the same sort. So I am housed and fed for the time on good honest terms, to the saving of further expenditure of my little means, at the sumptuous "International" where I have had the best entertainment, and for very reasonable considerations certainly. Nothing can be better in the way of comfort, elegance and cheapness than this princely establishment, said to be surpassed by none in England or on the Continent. Imagine three hundred persons dining at once in the spacious saloons; families at their tables, or single occupants apart, and alone, like myself, gentlemanly service at your call, and the newspapers also. For two or three York shillings you may have all you care for of good eatables: I have not gone beyond that, and have done nicely on my one and sixpence more than once. Mr Barker, of Providence, our good friend and benefactor breakfasted once with me, and *Taylor* has [p. in] honored me with a sitting, and his best iced creams for complements [sic].

I wrote you on Tuesday last, and this morning got your letters of the 23.—giving me the best accounts of home and its inmates. My weekly mail from the mountains never disappoints me, bringing as it does tidings of trust and triumphs from those I love, to drown the tumult and roar of this Babylon. I shall glean every information for you concerning the *"Eaglewood matters"* when I visit there again on Saturday next, and you shall have the earliest account of my views and impressions, on my return to the city. Monday next, I am to meet Mr. Furness who preaches for Longfellow tomorrow at Brooklyn; and we hope to have him at our Conversation there on Tuesday Evening. In my next, you will find whether I am to go as far as Philadelphia or not during this jaunt from home.

6. pm. after writing to you, I dined with Brisbane at his house, where I met Doherty, A. J. Davis and wife, Macdaniel[?] and others, and discussed "Fourier," and Freedom till 10, with hopeful results. "The Freelovers" were present, several of them, and I trust were profited, if not amended, by the venerable doctrines delivered over the grapes, cakes and wines of the vintage of '25 and '37; yet which our host's importunities did not prevail with the philosopher to taste.—Wednesday. 22. I visit Gowan's and other bookstores, and the Tribune office where I have some good talk with George Ripley. In the evening, I meet him and his

205

wife at Prof Bottas: here find the painter Lawrence, son of Sir Thomas, and get on so well, that he invites me to meet him at his studio, and see his pictures: besides many to whom I was not introduced. There were many of my circle at Dr Bs': many women, among them a fair Tennessean whose name I forget. I had a good half hour with Mrs. Ripley, who celebrated [word] while her Religion, and with deep earnestness, inviting me to meet her at ‖ the ‖ St Catharine's Convent to witness the veiling of a nun, which I gladly accepted quite disposed to see the spectacle.—Miss Sedgwick[2] was of the party, also Dr. Pierce and wife, a very brilliant and sensible French lady with whom I had a good time. It was 11 and after when I reached my Hotel.

Thursday 23. Half past 10. I find Mrs Ripley at the Convent, and myself the only gentleman present to see the show—I shall need more space to describe it and will reserve the same for Louisa, when I get the moment to tell of this, and of the virtues of thes[e] Sisters of Mercy to which the noviciate was admitted. I dined afterwards with the Vicar General, the Archbishop's representative at the Ceremony, and some dozen of sleek Fathers' and priests, the nuns serving us at table.—Evening I meet my company at Dr. B's. the discourse unusually fine and flowing, and my part quite acceptable to the Muse and all the graces present, if I may credit the complements [*sic*] afterwards.

Friday 24. Call on Lawrence and see his pictures. He has just completed a fine head of *Calvert,* also of *Bryant:* and is the man to do *Emerson.* I saw also his sketch of *Carlyle.*—In the evening, I am at Brisbanes again, and talk on the *Genesis:* Davis and wife, Wm. Green (Lane's friend) Doherty, Cabot are there.—

I will write you again next week. Hope the news-papers and Lizzy's music came to hand safely.

Goodbye, and love and benedictions.

A.B.A.

[1] Dr. Trall's water-cure establishment, 15 Laight Street, New York City.
[2] Margaret Sedgwick.

LETTER 56–14

[to Mrs. A. Bronson Alcott, Walpole, N.H.]
New York City, | 15 Laight Street. | November 1st. 1856. | Saturday.
My Dear,

Yesterday came your letters—Elisabeth's affectionate remembrance, with your own, and bearing good news from you all—the little garden's harvest in, Louisas' prospects for the winter, and the common interest of the family in *"the Itinerary"* of its correspondent, mailed thitherward from week to week,—some leaves from which I now copy and dispatch to the waiters and kind respondents there.—

Saturday 25. Oct. I wrote you last from this house, where I met a good company in the evening, and discussed Health and Temperance. Dr. Hayes, students, and patients, boarders, and others, taking parts. A good deal was said on Diet, especially on the importance of *Fruits,* and the superiority of these to the Roots, which, I am sorry to find, are the mainstays here, as in all of the Graham Houses, I know, or hear of anywhere.

Sunday 26. This morning hear Harris, the Spiritualist, and Poetizer of some florid rhymes, entitled "The Epic of the Starry Heavens", professedly dictated by Spirits, and celebrating the Spheres in verse. There was a good congregation to hear, and the preacher was earnest and impulsively eloquent. I spoke with him, and am to meet him and his friends some evening next week for comparing notes and queries a little. In the evening, I heard Dr. Cheever on slavery.

Monday 27. I met Dr. Furness and walked with him to the Jersey Ferry on his way home. He is in hopes of collecting a circle for me of his friends for some Conversations, and will write next week, after the Elections have given us our President. Dr. Bellows is seeking to give me a private interview with Col. Fremont, and you shall hear the results in due time. Also met Horace Greeley at the Tribune offices, and am to spend Sunday 9th with him at his *Farm* on the Hudson, some thirty miles out of the City. It was good to see his honest face, and hearty welcome. I shall accompany him up the river on Saturday next. Call afterwards on Prof. Botta. Mrs Botta invites me to breakfast with her on Friday morning. Evening, I meet the women of the Cure, in Dr. Hayes' Rooms, and speak of Chastity and Women's sphere and victories. This interview was very agreeable to all parties. Dr. Hayes and myself were the only gentlemen present. We talked from 7½ till 10, and unreservedly.

Tuesday 28. Call on Dr. Chapin, also on Lawrence, the painter. P.M. Converse with the patients, and inmates of the House. Evening, I hear Gov. Robinson[1] of Kanzas and *N.P. Banks,*[2] address the multitudes at Brooklyn. You will find some account of the meeting in the "Tribunes" I send with this.

Wednesday 29. See Dr. Bellows. Afternoon, I pass at the Anatomical Museum, and see the best wax models of the Human Body, exhibiting its organs and functions in health, also diseased—a sight I could not have witnessed elsewhere, innocently and to profit. I pass the evening at Dr. Johnsons' discussing spiritualism, and the Genesis, with the Dr. and his friends.

Thursday 30. At the Bookstores, and find something for my readings,—"Newton's Return to Nature", The Book which converted Shelley, the poet, to the School of Pyth[ag]oras.—Our third Conversation at Dr. B's. this evening: [word] was very spirited, varied, and broad—the company numerous, and well pleased, (as I learned) Lawren[ce,] the painter, Prof Mitchell, from Cincinnati, and others attended. Drs. Bellows and Osgood behaved handsomely, an[d] the meetings are becoming favorites with the circle. Nex[t] Thursday evening closes the course.

Friday 31. I breakfast at 9. with Mr & Mrs Botta[,] and meet Chas. Brace there. Mr. B. has ju[st] returned from Sweden and Denmark, and will publish a book of travels. I am to see *some places* in this City with him, on my return from "Eaglewood" where I go to pass Sunday. P.M. Meet G. Ripley at the Tribune office. Evening, I have a letter from Ambrose, telling me of my mother's return to his house and that she is still feeble.—

I shall be here through next week, and will write on my return from Eaglewood, and again after visiting Greeley. *Thoreau* is at Mr Spring's surveying the Estate. I leave at 3. p.m.—all goes prosperously: if I take Newport on my way, it must be December before I return to you, and yours. Blessings rest on you all

A.B.A.

[1] Charles Robinson (1818–94), the leader of the conservative free-soilers in Kansas.
[2] Nathaniel Prentiss Banks (1816–94), at the time a member of the House of Representatives from Massachusetts.

LETTER 56–15

[to Mrs. A. Bronson Alcott, Walpole, N.H.]

New York City | 7th November 1856, | Friday.

My Dear,

I met my company for the fifth time last evening at Dr. Bellows'; and dine with him next Tuesday to discuss the considerations and the fruits. Our interviews have been pleasant, and profitable, I am persuaded, to the parties generally. Also promise good things and times for us to come. This morning came a letter from Dr. Furness inviting me to Philadelphia as Mrs. Morrison's Guest while I stay in the City. It is good news, and pleasant to yourself and the girls, as it is to me. I send you his letter, wishing heartily it were possible for you to share with me the hospitalities I shall partake solely on your account. I may first visit Newport &, perhaps Providence also: be here again at the Womans Convention on the 25th. and reach Philadelphia early in December. Or, I may stop a week or two in New Haven on my way from Providence. So yourself and girls are left, for aught I can see, to the Philosophers dreams till sometime about the Christmas and New Year, for any tasting of the good things he hopes to bring along to grace the glad festival of reunion around the hearthstone of glad hearts. Here my reception has been cordial, and all I could have wished. Dr. Bellows and Osgood, Mrs Botta, (who gives me a party, the first of her season meetings, this evening,) Mr Longfellow, and now Mrs Manning, Margaret Fullers' friend, at whose hospitable home in Brooklyn I am staying when I am not here for the night—these are some of the good people to be named and remembered. In this house, I am kindly lodged and boarded too for the consideration of discussing the virtues of the porridge and porringers with the listening inmates. The women are all mine of course.

This evening comes Henry Thoreau from Eagleswood, and we accompany Horace Greeley to morrow early to pass the Sunday at his Farm in the Country.— Monday evening, I meet my Brooklyn Class for the last time: and dine, as I said, with Dr. Bellows on Tuesday. If I come in from Greeley's on Sunday, I meet some friends at Mrs Mannings in the evening.

The Springs would like to have us at Eagleswood, but do not dare to urge it. Grave considerations and many, are involved in that venture, all which I must reserve till we meet.—Dr. Trall has a *"Water Cure Establishment"* at *Meriden,* near Wolcott. He wishes to rent the premises to some one who shall conduct the Cure on Vegetarian principles, and will himself take some part in the concern. I am talking with him about it, and shall find whether it offers any thing for us or not, and will write you in due time.—

I am going to call on Mrs Hildreth today. I hope Abby's little parcel came safe and is acceptable. I sent you some "Tribunes" at the same time.

During the week of the Convention, I shall ask for a *Conversation.* If I see Mrs Davis at Providence, we can arrange the matter to good advantage perhaps.

Your letters are gladly opened and read by me. Continue to tell me all about yourselves and let me give my poor returns for so much love and excellence called by the tender names of wife and daughters.

Ever Yours and Theirs,

A.B.A.

LETTER 56–16

[to Mrs. A. Bronson Alcott, Walpole, N.H.]

[New York City, November 13, 1856]

Diary.

Saturday 1st. November.
                    1856.

I write letters home, sending some pretty drawing Cards to Abby; and Yesterday and to day's "Tribune" Newspapers.

5. P.M take the boat "Thomas Hunt" for Perth Amboy: arrive at Eagleswood to dine with Thoreau at Mr. Springs, where I sleep. Thoreau is here surveying "the Eagleswood Estate".

Sunday 2.—This morning see Edward Palmer at the Union Buildings. He tells me that my friend Barker of Providence offers me a building lot at Eaglewood if I will come here to reside. We walk over the domain and look at scites for gardens and cottages. At 10 ½ we meet at the Union Hall and discuss Liberty and Responsibility to good effect: Mr and Mrs Weld, the Springs, Mr Reed, Dr. Redfield, Thoreau, Mr Cutler, and others taking parts in the Conversation. After dinner, take a walk with Mr. Weld, and talk of the present condition and prospects of the Union and School. He waits to see whether they can maintain themselves and win the public favour: wishes myself and family were here but dares not recommend our coming under the circumstances. The present season will determine matters.—Returning, I have some conversation with Mrs. Weld who expressed freely her doubts of the final success of the enterprize and dissuaded our coming for the present. Company at Mr. Spring's at supper, and flowing talk. Evening, Thoreau reads his lecture on Walking to the whole company, and interests all. It was the first and only walk any one had ever taken, and a signal success.—I discuss Eaglewood as a residence with Mr. and Mrs. Spring till late bed time. They also speak cautiously, and approve waiting a little.

Monday 3. Return by the early morning boat to Dr. Tralls, and dine. Mr. Hill, of the "Tribune" comes up with me. I see George Ripley, at the Tribune Office: Greeley, also, who invites myself and Thoreau to accompany him on Saturday next to his Farm at West Chester some thirty-five miles from the City. This afternoon, converse with students and patients at the Cure, when I find myself esteemed the best Doctor under the sun, if not Esculapius, the very God of Healing to soul and body both.

Evening. I meet Longfellows company at his study in the Brooklyn Atheneum, and we talk of Health till 10. I accompany Mr. and Mrs Manning to their house on Clinton Avenue, where I pass the night, and am invited to stay, coming and going, as I list. They are excellent persons, prized by all who know them, by Margaret Fuller, particularly, who made their house her home for a time. Mrs. M. is one of the Saints, whose face is a firmament of lights, and good to see. I shall be with them all I can be while in these parts: thanking Heaven [word] [word].

Tuesday 4. Converse all the morning with Mrs Manning and sister inlaw on Woman's rights and conditions.—Return to Dr Tralls, and meet the company there in the evening: we have a spirited conversation on the Gifts of Healing, the students and Professors assisting. Much interest was excited and expressed, as if the Angel had descended into the Pool and troubled the waters to salutary issues.

Wednesday 5. Election returns, but against us: Four years hence, all for us, and a commanding victory.—I read news at "The International": also look at Appleton's collection of Antique Books, and find "Bishop Berkeleys Sirus," containing within the same cover also "The Life of Dr. Mead, and a rare pamphlet, entitled, "Lucian sine[?] Concubitu. London, 1750.—Dine at Dr. Ts, afterwards walk to the Fulton Ferry and cross over to Brooklyn to sup with the Mannings. Mrs M. and her friend, Mrs Kimball return with me to Dr. Johnsons in the City, where we meet A. J. Davis and wife. Doherty, Mr and Mrs Brisbane, Dr. Wilson, with many more, and talk about Spiritualism till 11. oclock. I return with my friends and sleep at Mrs. Mannings.

Thursday 6. After breakfast, I walk to the ferry and cross: dine at the International and have further talk with the patients and women at the Cure. I meet my company at Dr. Bellows in the evening for the last time, and preach very well from my Chair on *the Victories* from 8. till 11. Dr. B. and friends complementing [*sic*] the priest and prophet, to his more than content.

Friday 7. This morning brings me a letter from Dr. Furness, inviting me to Philadelphia and some Conversations there, with his friends. I write and mail letters to my wife.—Find Mr Richards at the Tribune office. He invites me to come out and see him and his Idiots at Harlem, and gives me "an Illustrated account of his School for Imbeciles," which I shall send home. Evening. I am at Mrs. Bottas and meet Lawrence and wife, Dr. Anderson, Prof Hackley of the Geological School, Misses Margaret and Kate Sedgwick, Mr. Chas. Brace, Mrs Brace, &c. &c—a pleasing company.—Henry Thoreau arrives from Eagleswood and sees Swinton, a wise young Scotchman, & Walt Whitman's friend, at my room; he, Thoreau, declining to accompany me to Mrs Botta's parlours, as invited by her. He sleeps at the Cure.

Saturday 8. We find Greeley at the Harlem Station Office, and ride with him to his Farm, where we pass the day and return to sleep in the city, Greeley coming in with us—Alice Carey, the authoress, accompanying us also.

Sunday 9. We breakfast at Savery's Hotel where we slept, afterwards cross the ferry to Brooklyn, and hear Ward Beecher at the Plymouth Church. It was a spectacle, and himself *the preacher,* if preacher there be anywhere now in pulpits. His auditors had to weep, had to laugh, under his potent magnetism, while his doctrine of Justice to all men, bond and free, was grand, and fairly home on all of the North, as of the South. House, aisles, entries, galleries, all were crowded, and the praise, the prayers the baptism of the babes, a whole dozen of them, were select and impressive. Thoreau called it Pagan, but I pronounced it Good, very good, the best I had witnessed for many a day, and hopeful for the coming time.— After the preaching, we walk to Mrs Manning's and dine. Here we find Mrs. Tyndale,[1] from Philadelphia, a sort of Saintly Walrus of a woman, stuffed with goodness to the full, and spread wide "full many a road" abroad: taking the slaves, the Magdelen's [*sic*] part, and eloquent for Love and Justice, as yourself when provoked to the debates. Miss. Margaret Sedgwick was there also, curious to see Thoreau. After dinner, we called on Walt Whitman, Thoreau and I, but finding him out, we got all we could from his Mother, a stately, sensible matron, believing absolutely in Walter, and telling us how good he was, and how wise, when a boy, and how his four brothers, and two sisters, loved him, and still take counsel of the great man he is grown to be. We engaged to call again early in the morning, when she said Walt would be glad to see us. The talk was earnest at Mrs Mannings in the evening.—Thoreau, the Welds, celebrating the wild, Mrs Tyndale, the Human, your philosophic Half, the divine, while others of the company joined in the sport. We slept at Mrs Mannings.

Monday 10. Mrs Tyndale goes with us to see Walt—Walt the Satyr, the Bacchus, the very God Pan, and here as we found, or as I did, to my admiring surprise, bodily, boldly, standing before us—the complement your Modern Pantheon to be sure. We met with him for two hours, and much to our delight, leaving Mrs. T. to have him all to herself. She wished to see him longer: He, promising to call on me at the International tomorrow at 10 in morning, and there have the rest of it. I leave Thoreau, to call on Longfellow, who pays me twelve dollars, for my evenings with his friends, and promises something more. I dine at Taylors in the City. Send home "The Tribune" of this morning, containing a list of this season's Lectures.

Evening. I call on Mrs Hildreth, also on Drs. Gray and Warner and talk till 12 midnight, on Goblins and Spiritualism. The Drs. wish me to meet a party of Spiritualists on Friday evening, and compare notes further. I sleep at the International.

Tuesday 11. At Fowler's where I meet Mr. Baner who invites me meet his friends for some Conversations at his House sometime early in the next week.— Whitman fails to call at his hour, and I miss seeing him at Taylor's. At 4. P.M. I dine with Dr. Bellows. He speaks well of the Conversations, and thinks favorably of an advertised Course here, which he will favour also, and pays me $50. of the 75. the sum of receipts for the Course at his Library.—I talk in the evening, at the Cure, and to good purpose, on Purity, our company being interested, as I learn, in the doctrine and methods of the Dr.

Wednesday 12. Get letters from my wife and Abby. Abby going to Boston soon, and Louisa being there, and her play to come out soon. It will do her, and especially, Anna, so much good, such pleasure will flood the sisters, at any the least success. I wish I may be there and yourself, and mild Lizzy to see and celebrate the spectacle in that city of victories[?].—Meet Greeley who will advertize in the Tribune if I say so, and give me a paragraph also. Calvert writes hopelessly of Newport, so I shall not venture in that direction just now.—I write to Tenney asking some sound of civility concerning my Dials. It would be just the thing for spending money now, and enable me to send the more to you soon.

Thursday 13. I copy my Diary to my wife and girls, to send forthwith by this day's mail—and shall write, if I have time, of prospects and purposes, to send along also. This evening, I go with Dr. Bellows to a Kanzas Meeting at Mrs Sinclairs where Ward Beecher is to be: and am to meet a party of gentlemen, tomorrow evening for Conversation at Dr. Bs: also go to Dr. Gray's on Saturday evening to meet the Spiritualists.—

Thursday 12 oclock Meridian.
—Dr. Bellows will send his "Christian Inquirer" newspaper to you.
Enclosed is my letter of today's date, and $50.00 sent by "Adams' Express

November, 13. 1856.
You will have to pay something to the Expressman for carriage from Boston, to which place all is paid. I wish it were more—twice fifty, three times, four

times fifty, that I had to send, but this trifle will help a little, and I shall have something more, I doubt not, presently, for you. Please write on receipt of this.

Ever Yours,

A.B.A.

¹ Sarah Tyndale. The identification by Odell Shepard seems to be in error (see Alcott, *Journals*, p. 289, *n*.).

LETTER 56–17

[to Mrs. A. Bronson Alcott, Walpole, N.H.]

New York City | 13th November. 1856.

/$50.00. enclosed./

My dear,

Yours of Sunday last, and the preceding, both came swiftly to hand, the last enclosing Abby's pretty note, her declarations of thanks and pleasure in the New-York present of drawing Cards, and her pleasing prospects for the winter's pursuits and pleasures, near Louisa, and the cities entertainments. I am well pleased to hear, also, that all things move in such good keeping with yourself, and the remnant which lingers unwillingly with you there amidst the hills, awaiting, and for Anna, the [word] especially, a more congenial residence and home. I trust the wish and the waiting, shall come to fruition in good season, to each and every member of our household. Mr. Wells, I am glad to learn is recovering: also that our little river town has found a Pastor for the folds on its banks, and $\frac{meadows}{pastures}$¹ green. I doubt not of Mr. Hales getting more from you in the interview you speak of, than did the congregation from his part in the services.—and he was the man for you to speak with about abused and bleeding Kanzas. Give my regards to Mr Lathrop, and say for me, that, failing at any time of theme or text, he need but call on my very Unbiblical, yet Christian, Commentator, for the same.—I must write to Louisa now pretty soon, and express my hopes and complements [sic].—About affairs: how for wood, water, and the accounts at Edwin Wells, and Brittons? I think you will incline to deal with the last always, if he have the things you want. I shall settle all accounts with E as soon as I can. Let us pay all dues, and have the satisfaction of consum[ing] free groceries, and wearing the free man's wardrobes hereafter. He is a kindly man, but his politics taste rank from an honest man's trenches. I must preach free Coin from free pockets sufficient to square the accounts, and thank heaven from the jubilee from democracy.

And prospects brighten. Here are the $75. from the Bellows' godsend;—the Brooklyn and the 5 dollar evenings here to come off with Mr Banes[?]: for the travelling and hotel expenses—the Furness avails in Philadelphia,—I know not how little or much—Then, should I venture here a public course, something is to be hoped beyond the expenses of Parlour or hall, for honest wives and daughters benefit, for discharging debts all round. I may find it advantageous to stay here for a week or two to come. I am here at the Cure free of any cost, but only an evening's talk when I can spare one, and am a sort of divine doctor regarded of the inmates, the women all, and the best of the men: and can stay till I disgrace my calling, i.e. till I please to go. Then besides, Mr Richards wishes me to spend a day or two with him: and I may run up to Ambrose's and see mother for a comfort and a change, before I leave for Philadelphia. Mrs Greeley, too, who comes to the City presently, wishes to gather a little company for me at her house to talk out the private themes fairly and to good account.

Yet I shall endeavour to [word] into my haven, and seek my Comforter at the earliest moment: I hope as early as Christmas and the New Year. Meanwhile, I have the gift of newspapers and journals to send into the solitudes at High St.—"the Tribune" sometimes; "the Water Cure and Life Illustrated," journals monthly: and the Letters from week to week, and the cities where we[?] sojourn for the time.

Dr. Trall's Meriden Establishment is unfurnished with the fixtures for the cure: He thinks 4[?]oo dollars would put it in good order for a beginning, and he will rent or sell the furniture for housekeeping, as we choose, about 900. dols with this, or 700. without: the profits, if the whole were it well managed, would be something like $1,500, or 2000, a year. We should need a man for the farm, and three or four servants to conduct the Cure: and he will help us at the start to medical advice.—I am willing to enquire, and give the matter every advantage to show what it can promise, and make good to us

Dear Anna, must have a month or so in the City, this winter, if the thought is practicable. I think of her, and shall think often, and the more deeply, if I go to Germantown, her birthplace, and early Paradise. God prosper the maid— our first born, of the blessed eyes, and great heart, so full, so fair, the prime and flush of the confiding wife and noble woman from whose Bosom she flowered into life: or all one[?], and the rest of hers and mine, all graces rest and reign.

A.B.A.

Address me *here* for the present. Abby [word] [word]

---

[1] In the MS. "meadows" appears above "pastures."

LETTER 56–18

[to Mrs. A. Bronson Alcott, Walpole, N.H.]

New York City | 15. November 1856.

My dear,

Yesterday, after dispatching letters to you by Mail and Express, enclosing the first fruits of my Conversations here [$50.00][1] I called on Lucy Stone, now Blackwell, as you know, where I dined; and met the sisters, Drs. Elisabeth and Emily Blackwell—Dr. Maria Zakrzewska, a Polish young lady, also Madame Blackwell, formerly my hostess at Cincinnati, and a hearty English woman of the broadest hospitalities. I spent the afternoon discussing woman powers and possibilities, and staid talking through supper and onto 7. the hour at which I was due at Dr. Grays, where I met a select company of Spiritualists, sensible, learned, and curious, and passed my two hours with them, by appointment: Then at half-Past 9. to Dr. Bellows, at whose elegant Library Room, were assembled the members of "The Sketch Club," artists, scholars, and gentlemen of high respectability—Appleton, the great N. York Bookseller, Dr. Chapin, Judge Verplanck, Gray and Lawrence, painters, Dr. Osgood, Henry Tuckerman, Drs. Anderson and Stone,—some thirty in all. It was a pleasing spectacle. Dr. B. enjoyed the entertainment, and played his part to perfection. Thursday evening before, he made an admirable speech for Kanzas at a Parlour gathering at Mrs. Sinclairs where I was, and heard good things said besides by Colfax, M. C.[2] from Illinois, Messrs Fry, and Horace Greeley. It was gotten up by the ladies, and the admission tickets—at 50 cts—brought Kanzas some Hundred and twenty five dollars. Next Monday, the ladies meet to arrange for another meeting, when I am to give them "A Conversation," as my Kanzas contribution. Also Lucy Stone wishes me to follow the Woman's Convention here, with an *evenings talk on Woman*, at Dr. Wellington's parlours, where I may stop after a week or so, while I linger here in the city. Higginson, Wendell Phillips, and brother Saml. J. are expected.—Then, besides, Lucy has planned a Course for me, to begin next Wednesday at her house. So I shall be here, it seems now, for a fortnight to come.—Dr. Gray and the Spiritualists wish more; and this evening I am to talk at Dr. Taylor's Water Cure to his patients. He tells me, that he once had a consultation with you on the subject at Dr. Kitteridge's in Boston.

I send enclosed, the Blackwells' "Circula[r] for the Hospital for Women and Children." Who knows but that we may find places in it as Professor and matron—the girls, assistants?

The money, ($50,) will, I trust, reach you safely to day and be a comfort to keep Thanksgiving with. Freight and carriage are all paid, and I have *Adam's receipt* for the same.—The weather here is sunny and delicious.—My love to you all, and a blessing.

A. Bronson Alcott.

[1] The brackets are Alcott's.
[2] Member of Congress.

[Letter to Ambrose Alcott, New Haven, Conn.; from New York City, November 21 (or earlier), 1856.]

[Letter to Louisa, Boston; from New York City, November 21, 1856.]

LETTER 56–19

[to Mrs. Anna Alcott, New Haven, Conn.]

New York City, | November 22nd. 1856.

Dear Mother,

Yesterday, I mailed to you a newspaper, "the New York Tribune", also one to Ambrose, both of which will reach you to day, or perhaps they came to hand last evening. I wrote to Ambrose the other day in answer to his note concerning you, which I suppose reached him at once. I was glad to hear of your return to his house, because I think you feel more at home there than you do any where else in these parts, and are the most comfortable. My wife writes that she sent you a letter of encouragement and kindness lately. I hope it did you good. I had letters from her the day before yesterday when all were well at Walpole. Louisa had gone to Boston to spend the winter: she was at boardings there, and engaged with her pen, writing for the Journals and expecting "her Play" to be brought out sometime this winter. Abby had left, also, a few days before, to live with my wife's friend, Mrs. George Bond, and take lessons in Drawing, of which you remember, she is very fond, and has more than ordinary skill, as an artist. So there remains my wife, Anna, and Elisabeth, to keep the house together there in Walpole. And when I am to rejoin them there appears yet a good deal uncertain. Here, in New-York City, I have engagements to keep me for a fortnight longer: then, I am expected in Philadelphia, where I shall be for the three or four weeks following: so that I can hardly hope to reach New-Haven till sometime in January. But I may come before.—I hope you are gaining in strength of mind and body, and so getting some share of comfort out of your days. I shall be glad to hear from you here, if you are able and disposed to write a few lines about yourself. You need but to put *my name, and New York City,* on the outside, and your letter will reach me, as I call at the Post Office every day.

I am having good times here, and unexpected success. The weather is still mild and agreeable, as if it were October, and the Indian Summer, Give my regards to Ambrose and wife and the little ones; and take a good deal for yourself, as but a poor return for all you are, and have been, to—

Your eldest Son,

A. B. Alcott.

LETTER 56-20[1]

[to J. B. Johnson, Manchester, Mass.?]

New York City, | 22nd November, 1856.

Dear Sir,

Yours of the 10th has just reached me here, where I have been engaged professionally for the last month; and shall remain for a fortnight to come: then I go to Philadelphia for three weeks or more to meet Mr. Furness and his friends for a Course. It will be sometime in January at best before I can return to Walpole, and come to Manchester as you wish. I shall be very ready to come, and will advise you of the earliest day when I can do so.

Here, I am having a wide survey, and a fair success, having met a good company at Rev. Dr. Bellows, and at Brooklyn, and we have a "Kanzas Evening" next week.

With regards to your friends, and with pleasing memories of evenings in your family,

I remain,

Very truly, Yours,

A. Bronson Alcott.

J. B. Johnson Esqr.

[1] MS. owned by the Houghton Library, Harvard University.

[Letter to Louisa, Boston; from New York City, November 26, 1856.]

LETTER 56–21

[to Mrs. A. Bronson Alcott, Walpole, N.H.]
New York City. | 27. November. 1856. | Wednesday.[1]

My dear,

Your letter came with good news, and kind complements [*sic*] from all. I rejoice and am thankful for the gifts and prospects; and have just written this morning, to Louisa, of some of my recent experiences here, sending also the remembrances suggested by you in your last, for the Birth day,[2] also a Gift to Abby, who is dazzled as little maids before have been, by any thing from the grand Metropolis where I happen to be anchored for the time being, and perhaps for the fortnight longer. The Woman's Convention is setting now, and, last evening, Wendell Phillips said admirable things to a good company. To day, Higginson speaks, Mrs Mott, Wasson, and Mrs. Rose.[3] Saml J. sends word, "he cannot come." Tomorrow evening, we have a meeting at Dr. Wellingtons.—Mr. Beall[?] and I breakfast together early, and go out to see Richards and the Idiots at Harlem, returning in season for the evening at Dr. Ws. I have seen Mrs. Mott, and several of the Women, who are here at the Convention and shall see them to better advantage again to morrow evening. You shall have the report afterwards, and more fully.

I have written an account of my recent breakfast at Dr. Bellows with Ward Beecher and Fanny Kemble—to Louisa, which she will get on her birth-day, and send you, of course.[4] Dr. B. is now gone West, and tells me he shall be in Walpole next Sunday, and will call and see you. Thank him heartily for all his unexpected hospitalities to me, his introductions to the persons here whom I most wished to see, and the more especially, at his house and table.

I am having the freedom of the City and seeing every person and thing I care for, under the best advantages. Next week, I hope to see Emerson here also and some new company.

As to Mother, and her coming to Walpole, that is set aside now by the lateness of my return, and other contingences. If we remain, she may venture along perhaps in the spring.—The weather here is delightful; and all goes prosperously thus far with the Missionary. Love to Anna and Elisabeth, who shall have each a letter soon.

Ever Yours,
and affectionately,
A. B. A.

Mrs. A. B. Alcott.

[1] Wednesday was November 26.
[2] Louisa's birthday, November 29.
[3] Thomas Wentworth Higginson, Lucretia Mott, David Atwood Wasson, Ernestine Rose.
[4] For an account of that affair (in the absence of the mentioned letter), see Alcott, *Journals*, pp. 292–93. For a shorter account, see Letter 56–23.

LETTER 56-22

[to Mrs. A. Bronson Alcott, Walpole, N.H.]

New York City, | 6th December, 1856. | (Saturday)

My dear,

I have yours of Saturday last, with Elisabeth and Anna's pretty Postscripts, and must report some further adventures and personal experiences to day.— And, first—do you remember the openeyed student, Barrett of 1838 and 9, who used to walk in from Cambridge to my Conversations in Beach Street, with Dwight, Bartlett, and others of the Class?—Well, he is now a Swedenborgian preacher here in the city, and has a country seat at Orange, N.J., about 12 miles out, and with him and his family, I have been passing the time from Monday last till yesterday and have pleasant things to tell of him and them. Some few years ago he came into possession of a good estate, by the rise of land in Chicago, to which place he had been led, seeking a competence, and quite unexpectedly to himself, finding riches and abundance, and now he comes here to plant himself and enjoy his gains, in a sensible and humane way, with such good neighbours as he may attract to his neighbourhood. Lately, he has purchased a tract of land there in Orange, some 200 acres or so, and is having it plotted for building lots. The Appletons booksellers Carter's, and gentlemen of good estate and standing, are purchasing villa scites, with the purpose of building soon. Lowell Mason is there; also a Mr. Hashall[?] from Mass. the owner of a tract of 500 acres adjoining, and already laid out, some eight or ten houses to be built on it the coming summer. The Estates are beautifully situated on the Eastern slope of the Orange Hills, wooded with fine forest and commanding a view of the spires of New York City, also of the Hackensack river, and Newark, of the Raritan, and Staten Island shores, in the distance. About half way up the slope, are orchards already in bearing, and the mountain is moist with living springs of good water. Mr. B. intends building himself in the spring. Yesterday, we walked over the tract, and he pointed out the scite of his house and grounds: the park, lodge on the Cliff: the garden, and pleasant walks, through the shrubbery. *We* too are to have a lot, if we will come and occupy, and, (so says my benefactor,) a house; presently and other comforts, and I am to superintend the laying out, build the summer houses, the lodge, plant and advize, for my part. It is a generous offer, too much so, if not something romantic withal, to count upon and trust for the bread and board, but he, and she, are both in good earnest about it, and quite reliable people. I like them very well. They have a family of four children, and know how to keep house, and bring them up as Christians should.—Tis something for us to think of, meanwhile, and may come to something by and by. I am to go out again soon, and meet his neighbours, for some Conversations. He is a fair-minded, trustworthy man, and author also, of some good books, which he gave me: also promises me the whole of Swedenborgs writings—a large library in all, of some thirty volumes or more. He wrote my name, besides, in "Vaughan's Hours with the Mystics," a work very valuable, and all the more prized by me for the givers sake. Mr. B. remembers his evenings in Beach Street, and Emerson. I am to have comfort in him, I daresay, and yourself too and the rest of us.

Last evening, came off my Second Conversation, at Dr. Wellingtons, and grandly too. || There were as many as || forty persons, perhaps fifty present, and the talk ran deep and strong on Home and its delights. Drs. Wilson, Hall,

Haddock, Johnson, Dunning, Wellington, A. J. Davis and wife, Mrs Rose, and husband, and some brilliant women took parts in the theme. I am to meet them again on Monday evening next: again on Friday following, and close the course on Monday the 15th.—"The Spiritualists" are getting me a company, and it looks as if I might meet them before going to Philadelphia. This evening, I am to be at Mrs Botta's Saturday Night Party, where I am to meet Mrs A. J. Downing—Miss Bremer's friend, and Mrs N. P. Willis. I think it possible I may be invited to Newburg, and perhaps Troy, on the River Hudson. I shall be here for a week or ten days to come, and shall keep you advized of my movements. Letters are brought to my table by the private carrier of this House if directed to me here. Dr. Trall is very generous and friendly. I gave the House another talk last week, and feel quite easy here, to the saving of much expense if I were stopping at the Hotels. I still see gentlemen sometimes at "the International", and take a meal, for variety there.

I have heard nothing from Louisa, but trust she is happily engaged, and received my letters and the little box by Mr. Higginson who left here direct for Boston on the 27th. I hope the pins pleased, and Abby had "the chosen second choice."—

About the wood, you must do as you think best. I have no clear notion of the sum of my receipts here. People will hear readily enough, and pay *something* therefor: but I am thus far unable to tell how much, or how little. I hope to have a little to send you before I leave for Philadelphia.

The weather has been pleasant till within the last few days: no snow yet, but wintry today.—I suppose there is already snow with you.

I send "Putnam," for December, containing "Emerson's Monograph to Mr. Hoar," like all his things, concise and characteristic of the writer.—I believe he is to be here sometime this month.

To-morrow, I purpose going across and hearing Prof Bush at the Atheneum in Brooklyn. I may pass the night with Mr. Manning, and see Longfellow.

It seems a long while since I said low words at parting, and I shall turn my face homewards at the earliest practicable moment. It looks as if it must be January sometime before I can reach you fairly without leaving the present calls unhonored. But you are in better hands, and can wait for poor unworthy vagrants, better than any good wife, I happen to know.

I have not seen Dr. Bellows since his return from Walpole. I trust you said, and *said your say* in his bland presence, as women will.

To Anna and Elisabeth much love, and thanks for their pretty notes of remembrance.—

> Ever your husband, and
> Friend.
> A. B. A.

LETTER 56-23

[to Mrs. A. Bronson Alcott, Walpole, N.H.]

New York City, | 10th December, 1856. | Wednesday

My dear,

I mailed letters to you on Saturday last, and again Yesterday, also the "Tribune and Times newspapers. This morning, brings me yours of the 8th. with Anna's and Abby's enclosed from the reading of which I turn to copy the Diary" of the last weeks for the three deserted women—the mother, wife and daughters of the dreary wilds of Walpole. My jaunt to Orange explains my not writing to you during my stay there, and your anxiety and disappointment at my silence.—I forget the date of my last transcripts, and shall begin copying at a venture from notes of my seeings sayings and doings here in this Babylonia of the West.

Diary.

November.

Thursday, 20th Swinton comes and we cross to Brooklyn and see Walt. Whitman—the Satyr. We dine and converse freely with the God, who invites us into his study, and entertains us becomingly. I felt amply paid for my visit, and brought home clusters of spoils for future use. We return and take an ice-cream at Taylor's. Swinton is an earnest talented Scotchman, and has high aims in view. He wishes to report some of my Conversations thinking thus to make a good book. I find letters from home acknowledging the receipt of the 50 dollars. I sleep at Dr. Tralls.

Friday 21. I write to Louisa, also to brother Ambrose, and send newspapers to my wife. P.M. See Lucy Stone, Drs. Taylor and Wellington, Mrs. Hildreth, Dr. Johnson, also, call on Mrs Oakes Smith and A. J. Davis. In the evening, I meet company at Dr. Blackwells, and discourse on Life and Genesis till 10. The Blackwells, Mrs Hildreth, Dr. Wellington and friends, Davis and wife, the Sedgwicks, Miss Pritchard, from Concord, Swinton, and many more attend. Again sleep at Dr. Tralls.

Saturday 22. Write to my mother at New Haven. See Dr. Bellows at the office of "the Christian Inquirer, newspaper. Call on Dr. Wellington, and dine with Dr. Bellows at 5—Dr. B. invites me to breakfast with him at 10. on Monday. Call on Alice Cary who tells me she has gathered a circle for me including Horace Greeley and friends, to meet me after the Holidays. I pass the evening with Dr. Curtiss and sleep there.

Sunday 23. I breakfast with Dr. C.—and hear Mr. Barrett at the Swedenborgian Chapel. See him afterwards, and engage to visit him at Orange N.J. where he resides. Dine with Dr. Johnson, and accompany him to the Spiritualist Conference at Dodworth Hall, where I meet some of the leading persons of the persuasion. I sup with Dr. Wellington, and pass the evening at the Sedgwicks. 9th St. Here meet Mr. Sedgwick and daughters, Miss Howland, and pass an agreeable evening. Mr. S. is a gentleman of high standing, and of the old School, reminding me of Father May. He repeated his invitation again and again, "Come and see us, Sir, Come and see us Sir, Come again Sir; good night, Sir; good night; Come again Sir: good night, Dr. Sir, Good, night." A tall, portly, gentleman, the cousin, I believe, of the late Theordore, whom Dr. Bellows buried, and relation of the S. of Syracuse. Perhaps Anna knows all about them. Again sleep at Dr. Curtiss. He reads me the story of his strange experiences, too long to report here, and very singular. Dr. C. is a very remark-able man, and one of the most skilful of the profession.

Monday 24. I get letters from home, and hopeful. Breakfast at Dr. Bellows, with Ward Beecher and Fanny Kemble; also Mrs Kirkland, Charles Brace and wife, and the brother of Mrs Brace. The breakfast was sumptuous, and Mrs Kemble, an[d] Beecher the more stimulating || than the || viands [I have written to Louisa all about this breakfast and the guests][1] Afterwards call on Lucy Stone; also on Mrs. Botta, where I meet the petite enthusiast German Artist, Mrs. Dessell. wh[o] praises so Louisa, whom she had met lately a[t] Mrs Reed's in Boston, and makes me blush to tears for the soft colours in which her fancy paints my promising Child, and all deserved. Mrs. Botta will write to Mrs. N. P. Willis proposing some Conversations for me at Newburg. At 4. P.M. I dine with Mrs. Kirkland, and have a good talk on American Life and Culture. Mrs. K. will go to Eagleswood next summer[.] She is the author of "Westward Ho," and has seen more of Life, and taken it more [word] than most women. I had a good deal to tell of my wife and daughters, and made a good story of it.— In the evening I am at Dr. Wellingtons and meet the leaders of the Women's Convention, Mrs. Mott, Mrs Rose, Miss Anthony, Mrs Jones, Mrs Davis,[2] and the rest. I sleep at Dr. Tralls.

Tuesday 26.[3] I write to Louisa about my Breakfast yesterday.—P.M. at the Tribune Office, where I meet Greeley and Fry, editors, and have some talk on the Times and editing. Greeley is as simple in his greatness as a Child, and a sound, sensible, good man: perhaps the most influential power just now in the whole Country.—I am at the Woman's Convention in the evening, and hear Mrs. Jones, and Wendell Phillips. Both speak admirably, and to good effect. The Convention is well attended, and bids fair to make an impression on the public mind. Yet is far too popular and political to suit and enlist such as I am in its measures. But it is aiming at the good things, and needs the favor of all good friends.

Wednesday 27. I write to my wife, and mail reports of the Convention. In the evening I hear Higginson, Mrs Rose, Mrs Mott, and Lucy Stone. Also send my letter and gifts by Higginson to Louisa and Abby.

Thursday 28. I breakfast with Brace and we go out to Richards Idiot School at Harlem, where I dine, and discuss Culture and Genesis, with Richards, who is the father of Dr. Howe's Institution, at South Boston, and knows more about Idiot Training than any body I have met. I think I could do what I have not seen done with these *Imbeciles,* also with the *Geniuses;* knowing something of the Causes and conditions of both, not intimated yet, nor suspected, || by any one yet || at the root and seminal origin of Intelligence and strength. I return and pass the evening at Dr. Wellingtons', where I met a large company chiefly of progressive friends, Mrs. Rose, Mrs. Farnham, Miss Beebe, &c. &c. some 200, or so, being of the party. I had a good time, and enjoyed the evening. I sleep at Dr. Curtiss again.

Friday 28. I breakfast at the International, and call on Mrs. Rose with whom I dine. She is the daughter of a Jewish Rabbi, and has a story to tell unlike any thing I have heard before of Persecution from Jew and Christian alike, and is a Heroine, and an Israelite in deed || and spirit || without compro-mise or guile. She told me more of Jewry and her people's faith than I knew before, recounting her own adventures with tears in her eyes, till I wept from sympathy at the wrongs and courage of my noble Jewess, whom, I pitied, and almost loved besides. Swinton comes, and we sup together at Taylors'. I tell him my adventures, to which he listens with a greedy ear, and asks for more.

Saturday 29. I am 57. today, and far younger than at 47—thanks to time and a family—a wife and daughters to divide my days with Ideas, and hold me fast to both worlds in turn. I call on Lucy Stone to learn more of her Conversations. She sends me to Mrs. D_____ . G_____ who surprizes me with words never before spoken to me by a woman. _____ I defend myself, and flee to sup with Dr. Wellington, and talk afterwards with the inmates at Dr. Trall's, where I sleep and dream [torn]

Sunday 30th. I get letters from my wife, Anna and Elisabeth. Attend the Spiritualists Meeting at Dodworth Hall: afterwards see Mr. Barrett, and promise to visit him at Orange very soon. At Dr. Wellington's and arrange for continuing the Conversations at his rooms. I see Mr Poor, and others, during the day. Sleep at the International and dream of the Syren again, as on the night before.—

December

Monday 1. I see Swinton, Wyman, Mrs Rose, A. J. Davis, and others. In the evening Converse at Dr. Wellington's on *Descent,* some forty persons attend, and we have hospitable and flowing discourse: we open at 8. and continue to talk till 11.—I get a note from Mrs. Oakes Smith regretting she cannot come.

Tuesday 2. I take an early train for Orange, arrive at 9 and pass the day with Mr. Barrett and family."—

[⁴This visit and prospects, I have detailed at length and fully in my recent letters; also put you in possession of all I know regarding my future movements. I am to be here at least for a fortnight to come. Mr. Furness, you remember, thinks about midwinter the best time for me in Philadelphia—that is—sometime in January. Had I the money to spend honestly, I should be tempted strongly to run for a fortnights holiday with wife and girls, and may run thitherward as it is. The coming fortnight will determine for me, and you too, and we shall see what is to be, and how the Fates dispose our Fortunes. Should I be invited to Troy, or to Newburg, it might chance to seem the shortest cut to Brotherly[?] Love to take Walpole on the route, and the precious human traits[?] it embraces, and which await embracing. I should not wonder at any such estimates myself, nor will you.—

The weather till within a few days has been mild and genial, but is to-day sour pinching and sullen, as are the hospitalities of some I could name to you, and not the most distant of Zones neither, as we all know very well. I shall do my best to find the more friendly clime, and the means of moving, at the earliest spring available.

My receipts have been moderate thus far, Dr. Wellington's Circle should give me something handsome: and the Spiritualists are able; the heads and movers of the proposed Class, among the rich men of the City: Drs. Gray, Warner, Wilson, Johnson, having a very large practice and are professionally respected. I should like to send home the avails, and shall as far as I can, and get to Philadelphia with a few dollars. At Mrs Morrisons, I shall be free of expense and can do without a full purse. Perhaps I shall find it necessary to recruit a little my wardrobe; and to feel as a gentleman likes in gentleman's company. But I shall need very little: and mean to pay and not make debts this winters-sojourn. A pair of shoes, pants, and hat, are about all I need, and even these I can manage to do without, and shall, if my receipts come short.

I have not heard any thing direct from Louisa. Abby writes gaily. Pray take good care and advize her wisely about her health. The Bonds is a famous infirmary, and I dread the infection. Don't meddle with too many "Pathys," nor let her meddle, nor any miserable Aunties[?], tho'[?] Saints, and King's Chapel communicants, or Church of the Disciples besides.

I trust Anna and Elisabeth are good girls, and keep the rules. It is so respectable to be well, and truly sane and sweet. Anna['s] note was a comforter, and Lizzy's silence ditto. Embrace the maidens for me, and take good care of them, and of yourself,

for Your Husband's Sake.
A. B. A.

P.S.

Address me here at Dr. Trall's till otherwise advised.—

<hr>

¹ The brackets are Alcott's.
² Paulina W. Davis.
³ Tuesday was November 25. The dates of the following two entries are also incorrect.
⁴ The brackets are Alcott's. He neglected to close them.

<hr>

LETTER 56–24

[to Mrs. A. Bronson Alcott, Walpole, N.H.]

New-York City | 12th December, 1856.

My dear,

Yesterday it was arranged for me to meet my Spiritualists here, and I am to open my Course on Monday evening next, the 15th. and to give them five Conversations on Monday and Saturday evenings following. This will close the Year, and release me for Philadelphia, or Walpole, as the intervening weeks may determine for me. I have a Conversation this evening at Dr. Wellingtons, and again on Tuesday evening next; and am engaged for Sunday coming at Mrs. Mannings in Brooklyn, to meet a circle of her friends, for the afternoon and evening, as a beginning of something, she thinks, for Sunday entertainments. The mighty Mrs. Tyndale, already known to you, is staying with her, and is to be of the company, also, the Sedgwicks. I wish we may have a good time and initiate edifying things for the company.

Wednesday last, I met Conway,¹ the young Virginia priest, here at the "International." He is settled at Cincinnati now, and returns there in a few days, taking Boston and Concord on his way homeward, spending Sunday next with Emerson. He speaks of a Class for me at Cincinnati, and thinks I must come out in January some time, but will arrange the matter with my good friend Spofford, his parishioner, and let me know, pretty soon. I would not mind another jaunt to the West; it pays well in hospitalities to soul and body, as you know very well; but I must first come home and partake of yours, in my best outfit, for the expedition. It looks now as if I might fulfil my engagements here also, in Philadelphia, and return to you by the middle of January perhaps— run, presently, across to Manchester for a week or so; see Louisa and Abby in Boston then, or return that way now,—and be free for Cincinnati and the West, for February and the early spring months. But I cannot tell. I trust we are not to be drift-wood always in this sweeping stream, and shall have an eye to some haven, if there be such, for our little family raft, be it on the shores of Eastern or Western waters. I told you of my writing to Abby, I believe; and shall hear from her and Louisa presently, I doubt not. May they have health and great success.

Yesterday we had a pouring rain all day. This morning is fair and friendly as the face of loving woman, cloudless and kind. I suppose Anna is diffused, mother, wife, and daughters two, in the genial element and wafted cityward and hither through the windows of my chamber, falling softly, blandly, upon the sheet, as I write. It is very certain, such is my faith, at any rate—that women weave the silken solar rays,—if not the luminary itself; and the moon is all their own as we know.

I think I shall be at Mr. Poors after Monday next; but you shall address me here at Dr. Tralls.—I am trying to spare your borrowing the Newspapers of your Neighbours, and send from time to time.

Affectionately
A. B. A.

¹ Moncure Daniel Conway (1832–1907).

LETTER 56–25

[to Mrs. A. Bronson Alcott, Walpole, N.H.]

New York, 16th Dec. 1856. | Tuesday afternoon.

My dear,

Having an hour to myself—here at my room, and before my evenings' engagement at Mrs. Shoars', I shall just transcribe and send further notes from my Diary, and post myself fairly to the present hour and day.

"*Thursday 11. Dec.* This morning see Dr. Johnson, who informs me his friends have arranged to meet me at Dr. Gray's for some Conversations, the first to be given next Monday evening: the company are mostly spiritualists, several are professional gentlemen, and is to consist of thirty persons, or so, and meets for discussing my favorite themes. This will detain me here for a fortnight longer.—I see Dr. Wellington; dine at Taylors, where I find Conway, who invites me to come to Cincinnati pretty soon, and will make distinct propositions to that effect on his return there, and let me know. Sometime in February he thinks a good time.

Friday 12. Write to my wife, also to Dr. Furness. The weather is delightful, and I walk for a couple of hours in the Park. Meet Walt. Whitman, and take him to Taylor's where we dine, and discuss America and social institutions. Find him very knowing, and as docile as sagacious, very good company withal, and a man to see again.

Evening, I talk professionally at Dr. Wellingtons on *the Calling.* Here I meet the brilliant Mrs. Shoar and sisters, and engage to pass Tuesday evening (tonight) at her house in Lamertine Place: also to be at Dr. Curtiss' on Wednesday (tomorrow) Evening.

Saturday 13. This morning write to my mother, who is still at New Haven.

223

I call at Dr. Bellows, and get a letter from Louisa who writes in good hope from Boston. This[?] letter has lain some days at Dr. Bs waiting for me to call.— Swinton comes and we walk up Broadway to Grace[?] Church and back to my rooms.

I am at Laura Keene's theatre this evening, and see her in "Second Love," and 'Young New York". Here is the fashionable resort, and her parts were done with spirit and grace, and the entertainment was pleasing: but *Anna* would have played as ‖ better ‖ well, and Louisa can write ‖ far better than either of the ‖ as good plays ‖ than ‖ as either of the two. I send the playbills for the evening. The theatre is new, and highly [word] throughout.

Sunday 14. Cross to Brooklyn and pass the day with the Mannings. The rain made our company less numerous, but the conversation was very good in the evening: and we sat late.

Monday 15. I return early this morning, and dine with Dr. Wellington; talk with his people all the afternoon and sup there.—Meet my Class of Spiritualists this evening, and have a good reception. I find the company highly intelligent and meeting in good faith to hear *"the Drs. opinions."* Prof Nelefes[?], Drs. Wiesan[?], Gray, Warren[?], Wellington, Toboson[?], Judge Edmonds, besides other gentlemen and some ladies are of this circle. I sleep at Dr. Wellingtons.

Tuesday 16. Talk with the inmates at Dr. Ws. awhile this forenoon: dine at Taylor's, and write this, and shall mail it on my way to Mrs. Shoars, where I am to take tea, and perhaps, pass a week.—But tis getting dark, and I can only add much love, and my hope of finding a letter awaiting me below.

Ever yours
A.B.A.

LETTER 56–26

[to Mrs. A. Bronson Alcott, Walpole, N.H.]

New-York City | 19th December, 1856. | Friday morning.

My dear,

Yours of the 14th came to hand on Wednesday. On Tuesday I sent you some Diary notes to date. To day, I add something further concerning my past doings and future plans as far as made clear to me now. I wish to pass the New-Year with you; and, as my engagements here close on the 29th (Monday) (unless I shall meet Alice Cary's[1] party which may detain me a few days over that time) I can reach home, January 1st. to open the year with wife and daughters as a good husband and true should do. Then, I can run away for a week presently to Manchester, if they wish, perhaps, take Boston and Louisa, for a few days, on my return, and be ready for Cincinnati, or Philadelphia, as the parties shall make ready for me. As to the last place, I have heard nothing from Mr. Furness, but shall doubtless before I leave. After midwinter, you may remember, was his choice. I might even take him and friends on my way home from Cincinnati sometime in February or later. Thus, you see, some little uncertainty hangs about my plans and movements just now. But if I can arrange to be with you for a fortnight or three weeks in January, I shall do my best to bring it about. I wish to be *"at home"* then especially. And ‖ if I can ‖ to bring *the most wherewith to pay debts.* My wardrobe needs repairs, which only wife's and daughter's love can best put in order. For a new suit, I can try my old friend, Tolman of Boston. I owe him something on the old account, which my Manchester receipts shall pay, so all my present earnings can go to discharge the January debts about which you write.—The Spiritualists are to pay me $50.00. for my course; I am to have $30 from Dr. Wellington's company; and as much, or more, from Alice Cary's if I stay so that I hope to bring home a clean 100. for the Walpole obligations, besides being with you to put things in trim for the future. But I may fall something short of this sum: my expenses here are inconsiderable, and I can reach you in a day for a little over 5 dollars. I have slept a night at Mr. Poor's, and they wish me to take my meals with them: Dr. Wellington, and Mrs. Manning extend the like hospitalities. And here at Dr. Tralls, I have bed and board, so long as I choose to avail myself of them: Two York shillings,[2] or two and sixpence, gives me a dinner, if I care for any thing a little extra nice; at "Taylors," where, also, I can take a friend for a Conversation and a meal sometimes.

I am learning a great deal of New-York, and of the extremes of society here: my two months' survey has given me rich and varied spoils. I am the wiser and better man for all I have seen and heard in the wide range I have taken. Perhaps I feel myself better acquainted with Life here than in Boston. My opportunities ‖ here ‖ have been ample, and I have availed of them to the fullest extent. My profession brings me advantages of intimacy unsurpassed not even by any priest or doctor, if indeed, I am not honored with the confidences proper to both, in all that pertains to the mysteries of Life. The title of Dr. seems no longer strange, nor, as things go, altogether insignificant or misapplied I may believe.

Wednesday evening, I was at Dr. Curtiss, and met Horace Greeley, Mrs Greeley, Alice Cary, Mr. and Mrs. Oliver Johnson, Dr. Wellington, and others. We discussed the old themes of Home, and had *"a soso"* time of it: Greeley taking his nap the while as ‖ is ‖ his custom is, whether in private companies or at Church. I told him of Anna's diffidence in not introducing herself at Bellows Falls,[3] and of Bell Peck's[?] enthusiasms, which pleased the simple hearted President-Maker, and Editor of the Nation's Mind to [word?].

Tuesday evening, I passed with Mrs. Shoar, and her three sisters, their husband's also, at her house in Lamertine Place. It was a family Party invited to meet "the Dr." professionally, and we had a profitable talk on Private Life.— On leaving Mr. Shoar put his $5. bill into my hand with a delicate silence, and a kind good nigh[t] from his wife at the door.—

I am to meet Dr. Wellington's company this evening, and close my course there. On Sunday and Sunday evening I am to be at Mrs. Mannings in Brooklyn, and meet the Spiritualists again on Monday evening next.—

The weather is wintry cold, but no snow yet. I mail the newspapers, and much love to all. Please write me once again. I shall advize you of my time of leaving, north or south, as may be.

Ever Yours,
A.B.A.

[1] Alcott generally spelled her name "Car*ey*" (see Letter 56–16). All subsequent instances of this have been corrected.
[2] A York shilling was worth 12½ cents.
[3] In Vermont, a few miles from Walpole.

1855–1856

LETTER 56–27

[to Mrs. A. Bronson Alcott, Walpole, N.H.]

New-York 24th Dec. 1856.

My dear,

My engagements here, for the present, close on Monday next, and I shall take the morning train, on Tuesday, the 30th. via. New Haven and Springfield, and be with you and the girls at 6 the same evening. I can spend three weeks or more in New-Hampshire, at home for the most part, going to Manchester, and perhaps to Boston, during the time. But I shall gladly sit again around my own hearthstone and partake of the home delights, after these months of absence.

Mr. Furness writes to have me come to Philadelphia any time after the middle of January. And here Conversations are not to be thought of while the Holidays last. So I may honestly leave and take mine with you. Alice Cary and friends have all arranged for me—a good company, Mr. Greeley, the Sedgwicks, Miss Hayward, Mr and Mrs. Field, Mrs. Cleveland, and others. They wish me to meet them on my transit to Philadelphia; and with advantages of an advertisement in the way of notice from Dr. Bellows and Mr. Greeley in "the Inquirer and Tribune" newspapers. We shall have a good time and make pleasant acquaintance, I doubt not.—

I wrote you last *Friday, the 19.* and mailed some newspapers for Walpole. In the evening I talked at Dr. Wellingtons.

Saturday 20. I called on Alice Cary, also on Mrs. Rose, with whom I supped and passed the evening. She is the Jewess of whom I gave you some account in a former letter, and is a very remarkable woman.

Sunday—I hear Judge Edmonds at the Spiritualists' Hall, and cross afterwards to Brooklyn, and dine with Mr. Manning. In the evening, we have a select company, Browne, the sculptor, and wife, Miss Tappan, sister of Caroline Sturgis' husband, Mr Longfellow, Maxwell, Oliver Johnson and Mrs. Johnson, Mrs. Parmelee, and many more. The mood was propitious, and the conversation flowing and lively, portraits of Parker, Garrison, Margaret Fuller, Emerson, Fanny Kemble, Walt. Whitman, Ward Beecher, were done surprisingly, and to great acceptance. Next Sunday evening, I am to be at Mrs Manning's again—and hope to meet Beecher before I leave the city. The Mannings are greatly respected here. Mr. M. is a merchant and friend of Wm. H. Channing. I think myself fortunate in making their acquaintance.

Monday. I called on Longfellow, and returned to the City, where I met Swinton, the Scotchman, and Locke. We sup together at Taylors', and they accompany me to Dr. Gray's, where I meet my Spiritualist friends, for our second Conversation: the seven doctors being present and partaking as before.—This evening the first snow falls here: the weather wild and wintry.—

Tuesday, 25. I breakfast at Taylor's, and call afterwards on Alice Cary, also on Mrs Greeley, and Dr. Johnson, the last, as you may remember, a pupil of mine, and a very worthy man. Mrs. Greeley had a great deal to tell me of her children, and seemed making propositions to me, by implications, to take charge of them, for an hour or so, daily. I said nothing would please me more than the meeting of a little class for Conversation: and talked for an hour with hers, and read them stories much to their delight, and the mothers too—

This evening, I am to meet my Class again at Dr. Gray's, also on Friday, and Monday evenings. To-morrow night, the students invite me to meet them here for a parlour Conversation; and on Sunday and Sunday evening, I am to be, as I said before, at Mrs. Mannings in Brooklyn. And on Tuesday, early, I leave here for yourself and the New-Year.—

I may write again on Friday, and expect something from you before I leave. With this, I mail some Newspapers, and a great deal of hope.

I need not add of affectionate
remembrances, and regards to
Wife and daughters, dear.
A. B. A.

P.S. I cannot say what sum I may be able to bring from my receipts, $50. certainly, and I hope $75. Sufficient, I trust, to make all easy, for the present, at Walpole; and Manchester shall give me an outfit, for finding the rest to square accounts all round in March or before. Here and in Philadelphia, and Cincinnati, if I go there, should be enough for the balance of our debts. But wait till I come.

LETTER 56–28

[to Mrs. A. Bronson Alcott, Walpole, N.H.]

New York, 27 December 1856. | Saturday.

My dear,

I wrote on Wednesday and sent newspapers, also to Louisa: and got letters from yourself and Anna on Thursday, Christmas. I add something further of my times here since, and shall follow fast to speak the sequel and the rest, in person on Tuesday coming, the 30th.—

Wednesday 24—I write to my wife, also to Louisa: at the Tribune office awhile afterwards. Evening, at Dr. Gray's discussing the Genesis, incarnation and Regimen, with my set of Spiritualists. They behave handsomely and know better than almost any company I have met before, the canons of Conversation. Most are masters, and all students of the better spiritualism, and are getting some of my best things in the magnetic way, as befits and renders pleasing and profitable, all human communions. I am well pleased in having met them thus professionally, and to good ends[.] We talk from 8 till 11 and after. I sleep at Dr. Tralls.—

Thursday 25. Christmas. I get letters from home: my wife and Anna writing affectionately as usual. I am surprised, on looking at my tablets, to find I have been here in this city now three months almost, and more than three and a half months, from home: Left Walpo[le] 13th. September, & reached New York October 1st. I have had busy days, and gleaned a great deal from this Broadway of the sown tares with the wheat. For here men sleep, as no where else besides. The dire[?] sleep, and here the Enemy is busied all the long night in scattering broadcast the noxious evils, huge giant, and of rankest growths: nor can the foul fields be cleansed save by fire unquenchable consuming the chast.—

Swinton comes—the handsome Scotchman, intent on spoils for his Book of Conversations—and we call at Bixby's Hotel on Tillman, the chemist and inventor. We three dine at Taylors. And I give a Christmas Conversation in the evening to the students of the College, which comes off pleasantly: Drs. Trall, and Beach, the Eclectic, and Father of the Botanic School of Medicine, are present. Dr. Beach has done good service in preparing a work on the properties of Herbs in which he has embalmed the skills of the old [word] wines,[1] having taken the knowledge from their life[?] or from the Indians, also from culling the old Herbals, for his Pharmacopia. Our little man, Edward Palmer, graduated from his College here in the City, and, I think, laid[?] in his house, for a time, *perhaps* as an assistant [word] and got his "doctorate" so,

Friday 26. The morning clear, soft, sunny, and the snow nearly melted from the pavements of this broad thoroughfare—swarming with life and restlessness: florid with filth, sin, and the fascination of Beauty and the Beast.—I call on Alice Cary and leave tickets for Conversations, also on Mrs. Poor. Then visit the Egyptian Antiquities, Dr. Abbotts' Collection on Broadway, and pass some hours looking at these relics of Antiquity—taken from tombs and buried Cities of Egypt, and the East, the Sacred [word], mummies, sphynxs [*sic*], household vessels and ornaments, chariots, papyrii, &c. ar[e] older than Solomon, and wondrous to see live in proximity, to the very heart, of this sovreign [*sic*] Sodom.—I dine at Taylors', and in the evening, meet a brilliant company at Dr. Nissons[?], many women [word] doctors as before, Gray, Warner[?], Toboson[?], Prof. Mapes, and we have a great Evening on the Chaos, and Cosmos flowing forth therefrom. I get to my room and to bed here to hear the midnight bell ring me to sleep.

Saturday 27—(today.) I write this morning readvertising my wife and girls of my coming on Tuesday: [word] and also[?] permitting.

I shall breakfast at Taylors on my way to Mr. Manning's where I am to meet company tomorrow afternoon and evening: return to the city on Monday, for my last setting with the Spiritualists in the evening at Dr. Grays: then to sleep, and wake for Walpole and the [word] three in the Lane[?]. I shall see mother on my return here late in January. It would only tantalize to call and go forwards without her next morning. She is more at home at Ambrose's, than she could be where I am not steadily; an[d] had best stay where she is for the winter at least.—I shall find a nest somewhere for us all and occupation, I doubt no[t,] during my travels. Chicago offers Dr. Chapin $10,000, to settle there: double the salary of any minister in the U. States. I am undecided whether to be dubbed D.D. or M.D: shall own grandly to both, without fear or flinching I imagine, and put out my shingle in ‖ brass ‖ gold and bronze, somewhere between this and the Year '60.—

Now good hope all three, till I am with you, for a fortnights' bybye, and the endless [word] attending; and the New Years.—

Ever yours
A.B.A.

---

[1] Probably a variant spelling of "vines."

PART TEN

&

1857

LETTER 57–1

[to Mrs. A. Bronson Alcott, Walpole, N.H.]

New York,[1] 81. St. Marks' Place | 12th February, 1857.
My dear,

A hasty line to you now, simply advizing you of my punctual arrival here at this hospitable house,—and of some informations about my future movements. We reached New York about 6, and I came here at Mr. Poors from the Station direct: the amiable hostess spreading the board for me, to the biscuits and shells, as kind housewives know how. and my chamber was warm and every way comfortable: and it seems settled that here I am to stay and partake while I am in the City, and am really very content to have it so.

Yesterday, I called on Alice Cary and Mrs Dietz to find them waiting for me, and all ready for our meeting, the first of the five being appointed for Tuesday evening next. Mrs. Dietz is Teacher of a Young Ladies School, a friend of Dr. Bellows, and speaks hopefully of our Interviews. She is an accomplished, energetic person, and brings some of her young women, as auditors, if not partakers; all which looks fair and for the good ends.

Dr. Bellows, I found had gone to Providence. I saw, the son, and told him the good things, and recent,—about Walpole. The letter there, I found is from New Haven. A Mr. Sheldon of Yale College, inviting me to come and meet himself and friends at my convenience: and shall do so on my return from Philadelphia. I am to be here for a fortnight certainly.

The snow is gone, and the streets clear. Yesterday was chilly and so is today. The Bendell[?] murder still fills the newspapers, and is all the talk.

I mailed some "Tribunes" for you yesterday, and more to day.

Emerson lectures here, this evening. Mrs. Poor is going with me to hear, and invite him to meet some friends here to morrow night—Mr. and Mrs Manning from Brooklyn and others. I shall find him to day, if I learn where he stops.

My cold is gone, and you sorrowing three shall sorrow no more of it, or other ails.

Address me here at
    81 St. Mark's Place
and await the fuller accounts next week.

Affectionately
A. B. A.

---

¹ Alcott, as planned, *had* gone to Walpole for a few weeks and then returned to New York City.

LETTER 57–2

[to Mrs. A. Bronson Alcott, Walpole, N.H.]
81. St. Mark's Place. | New-York, 18th Feb. 1857.

My dear,

Your very admirable, and very admiring epistle, came straight to hand. Many thanks to you, most excellent friend, for its cordialities, and its confidences. I wish there were some better returns for so much, than the poor "Transcripts" which I am about mailing to you now. But trifles are made important sometimes by being seen through the distance, and by kindly hearts.

Thursday 12th. I wrote to you some account of my journey, and of prospects here. I was expecting to hear Emerson in the evening, and hoped to find him, for a word, at some of the Hotels: but he did not arrive in the City till just in time, for his reading. I had called on his brother, William, also at the Metropolitan, St. Nicholas, and Astor House.—Mrs. Poor accompanied me, and we got a front seat at the lecture, finding there Marcus Spring, Swinton, Sam. Longfellow, Livermore—now Editor of "the Christian Inquirer," with some other acquaintances. The Lecture was sparkling in parts, but more didactic than usual. It was well received, and was very good. I spoke with Emerson, and made an appointment for 11. at the Astor House.—

Friday 13th. Call at 11 and find Emerson. He is just come from Cincinnati, and a lecturing tour at the West. He saw Conway, Mrs. Wilson and others of our mutual acquaintances; took tea, he tells me, at Sam. J. May's, on his way, and had to cross the Hudson River with his valise only along, on account of the ice. His baggage was refused, and left behind. It was a little skiff in which he embarked, and, like Caesar, swimmingly, with his Commentaries in his teeth. We had a good two hours or so in which to compare Notes and experiences. He seemed much gratified with my little sayings and doings here, also with the prospects. I think I must content myself with Philadelphia, New-Haven, and perhaps Boston, for this season's avails: to make a three month's Tour next autumn and winter when all will have ripened into a broader and better success. Yet if Conway presses, I will go for a month or more, and make the most of the luck. Emerson has seen Walt. Whitman, and values him much as I do. This evening, he lectures at Jersey City, and will leave tomorrow morning early for Boston, and Concord.—

I am at the Tribune Office where I see George Ripley: also at Appleton's

Bookstore for an hour. Mr. and Mrs. Manning, are at Mr Poors in the evening, also Fred Cabot and Mr. and Mrs. Hildreth. Mrs. H. means to make the picture the more what you wished, but suspects she has not improved it. If you have the inspiration for it, please write and tell her what she has done. It will gratify, and bring some good returns.—

Saturday 14. I call on Swinton, and leave "the Way to Paradise," of which he promises me an abstract, and the best passages. He talks of the Book of Conversations. I think him rather the best talented Boswell who has volunteered his services so, and it may not be wholly amiss to give him the full swing, and see what comes of it. I dine with him,—his Scotch-Irish wife and bouncing boys— all hearty and handsome, as could be desired.

We call on *Stephen Pearl Andrews,* the Frisky Free Lover, and Sire of Sodom—the frankest sinner I have seen as yet,—of whose Agapemone, his Aspaseus, and the rest, I here forbear the pen—and blush.—

Sunday 15. I hear Dr. Osgood at his Church. He asks me to spend tomorrow evening with him. Have some talk with Mr. Poor, and find him a very good hearted and worthy person; free, friendly, and full of sound sense. The family are united and seem to enjoy my staying here. Mrs Poor is radiant with affections for her husband; the true woman, considerate and devoted mother. I am an honored guest, on the best of terms with all—parents and children. My room is spacious, the linens sweet, gas when I choose to put the match to it, marble wash-bowl, towels renewed every morning, a commodious closet, Couch, bureau, table, and french bedstead, all elegant and handsome, as eye could wish. Then the bread is excellent, the cheese: my host and hostess being half converted to their guest's doctrines, and the children curious to hear, and begin to do better. —Miss Agnes and Master Henry, fair blondes, and fit subjects for the finer diets. There are two children besides:—Eva, about three, and a babe just beginning to walk a little.

I hear Dr. Bellows at his Church this evening.

Monday 16. I call on Dr. Bellows and find him friendly and communicative, as if I had him in my own study at Walpole. He inquired about his townspeople, of you, and of Anna's Masquerade and the young folks on the Hampshire hills. He is to address the Players and public here, on "the Stage," sometime in March he thinks, and read me passages from Fanny Kemble's letters to him on that subject. I wish Anna could hear her Readings in Boston. Perhaps Louisa will contrive to get admission to them. George Bond was here yesterday, and tells me good things of her and of Abby too. I saw him at Dr. Bellow's Sunday evening meeting, and sent remembrances to the girls. He was to leave early this morning for Boston.—

Also call on Dr. Johnson, and am at Tunison and Reeves', also at Gowan's bookstores awhile.—

Evening. At Dr. Osgood's. Sible,[1] Librarian of Harvard College is there, young Badger, a promising lawyer, and Mr _____ agent of Horace Mann's College at Yellow Springs, Ohio. Mrs. Poor goes with me.

Tuesday 17. I have letters from home promptly brought to the door by the penny postman. Call on Alice Cary and Mrs Dietz and learn that all is arranged for me for this evening at Miss Carys. They hope to gather a good company, and some gold for the gathering: tickets they put at $2.50. for the course, or 50 cents, for an evening. I am to have Tuesday and Friday evenings and give them five Conversations. This holds me fast here, as you will see by your almanac till

March 3rd., and gives me that month for Philadelphia and New Haven engagements.

I am at Mr. Poor's Office, near the Tribune Buildings, also at Mr Manning's place of business in Courtland Street. I am to meet Company at Mr. M's some evening this week, at Brooklyn.—

I dine at Taylors and return to Mr Poors.

Evening. 8. oclock, find a large but miscellaneous company at Alice Carys and talk till near 11. The spectacle is novel to most of them, but they seem taken with it, and hopeful of the coming evenings. Nearly all were strangers to me: Dr. Curtiss, Dr. Hallock, the Cary's, Mrs Dietz, Mrs. Cleveland—Horace Greeley's sister, and Mr. Poor, who accompanied me, were all I knew. If they care to come and pay money for it, yourself and girls will thank them, I doubt not, for the gold if not for the discernment, and take your share of the benefits to pay honest debts with. There were as many as thirty five or forty person in all— women two thirds of them at least, and with the due curiosity of the sex. I have four evenings more with them.

The weather has been dull for the last days; fog and mud—and Broadway a perfect spatter. To day, 'tis clear, sunny, and inviting. I am quite well, and shall preach all the better for this gift. To the girls, their father's remembrances, and write soon to your

A.B.A.

Mrs. A. Bronson Alcott.
Walpole.

¹ John L. Sibley.

[Letter to Mrs. A. Bronson Alcott, Walpole, N.H.; from New York City, February 20, 1857.]

[Letter to Louisa, Boston; from New York City, February 21, 1857.]

[Letter to Anna, Walpole, N.H.; from New York City, February 22, 1857.]

LETTER 57–3

[to Mrs. A. Bronson Alcott, Walpole, N.H.]

81. St. Mark's Place, N.Y. | 26 February 1857.

My dear,

I mailed a letter to Anna last Monday, and the newspapers daily since that time to you. Same day came your letter, also a note from Mr. Furness advising the postponement of the Conversations till next season. "The Motts and the Davises, (Lucretia Mott's children), whom I expected to be among the persons who would be interested," he writes, "in the conversations, go very early, in a few weeks, into the country. Mrs Morrison herself also goes, into the country with a venerable cousin of hers, and should we have an early Spring as the weatherwisest predict, may be away from the city at an early day. Upon the whole, he adds, as the winter is so far spent, the season for parlor comforts and conversations, I think it will be better than coming now, to devote next winter to us. When you come I want you and all of us to have a time of it. You must have two or three circles here and spend as long a time in Philadelphia as you have spent in New-York. The two or three weeks you propose to give us, will be just time enough for you to be misunderstood. It will be better to wait for a larger opportunity."—So I shall leave here on Wednesday next for New-Haven, where I may pass a week or fortnight and talk, if desired. Mr. Sheldon was earnest about a course there when he wrote to me; and it will not be too late for his friends now. I can see Mother too, Ambrose, and family at the same time.

To-morrow evening and Tuesday evening next, close my engagements here— This last, my late gleanings over the winter's fields, yet quite worth the labour. I am seeing and saying to good purposes, present and future. Nor is there question of coming harvests here whenever I shall come again.

I have not been to Brooklyn yet. I shall be there over Sunday, and at the Mannings' Sunday evening to meet a little company.

Yesterday, I passed at the Astor Library. To day, I am to call on Rowse,[1] the painter, who spent sometime at Concord, and is thought a good deal of here for his portraits. I am also to see Mrs. Goodman, Mr. Cheney's sister, and Mr Green, an artist, and friend of hers.

Louisa's visit must be a comfort to you. Is she still at home—if home it may be miscalled—and with Anna and Elisabeth. Together you will fashion a home for us, no doubt, and I will come soon to assist about it.

Had I best take Boston and suburbs, Abby too, on my way to Walpole? I should like to stop a day or two in Worcester, also in Concord. But I shall hear from you to morrow or Saturday,—by Monday, certainly. And you may address me hereafter at New-Haven. I shall write as soon as I get there and find how long I am to stay. Meanwhile as voluminous reflexions on Mystics— yours, and not yours,—as you please to indulge in and send to your Pietist, Quietist, Theurgist, or any thing of that quality: as many Hours with them as you will, since they shall be hours with your philosophic "Well beloved," also, as Mrs. Hildreth's picture of that worthy.

I wrote Louisa and sent my letter to care of Mr. Reed. If she is still with you, may I not have something from her, with the rest. I enclose "Webb's Critic on Medea" for Anna

The weather is spring like, as if the birds were already here; and for Elisabeth's Sake.—

Affectionately.
A. B. A.

Shall I go to England with Hamilton? I fear my courage would fail on leaving all behind.

---

[1] Samuel Worcester Rowse.

[Letter to Ambrose Alcott, New Haven, Conn.; from New York City, February, 1857.]

[to Mrs. A. Bronson Alcott, Walpole, N.H.]

81. St. Mark's Place, N-York. | 2nd. March, 1857.

My Dear,

Your prime parcel has this moment come to hand. My good hostess has hers, and, if this snowstorm abates, I shall myself deliver the graceful complement [sic] you have conceived and sent, to the other, sometime to-day. Meanwhile, some further Transcripts posting me to date.

Friday 20. I write again to my wife, and mail the Newspapers. 'Tis rainy, and Broadway a slough of Despond to the pagan pilgrims, and helplessly. Evening. Mr. Poor accompanies me to the Conversation at Alice Cary's. We talk on Home.

Saturday 21. I write to Louisa, and mail newspapers: also at the Tribune Office afterwards.

At Wallack's, and see Miss. Matilda Heron in "Medea," this evening. Mr. Poor goes with me. The play is exciting, yet enjoyable with all its appalling accompanyments [sic]. I wished Anna with me, and my family, yet the Spectacle of the Sacrifice would have been too much for my wife, and the tenderhearted Elisabeth, suggesting events too vividly, perhaps, of home experiences, and the Courage of Principle. I had "Fruitlands" before me, and Ideas there celebrated and played oft to the applauding snows—the tragedy of ox-team and drifting Family wailing their woes to the wintry winds. You shall imagine the Sequel, and the rest.

Sunday 22. I am at the Spiritualists' meeting this forenoon. P.M. write to Anna about Miss Heron's Medea. Evening, I talk on Theism at Mrs. Clevelands.

Monday 23. Mail my letter and the Newspapers. Have a good day at Tunison and Reeve's bookstore, where I find "Dr. Henry More's Philosophical Poems," "Des Cartes Philosophy," and "Baldwin's Wisdom of Antiquity." Whether the privilege of writing "A.B.A." on their title pages shall be mine, this tongue must testify, and so I wait to see.

I have a letter from Dr. Furness postponing the Conversations till next Season. Also hear from my wife, who writes hopefully, and of Louisas being with her at Walpole for a few days.

Tuesday 24. I write to Tenney about my unpaid for Dials. At Appleton's bookstore where I meet Prof. Botta.

Evening. I talk prosily on Health at Miss Cary's.

Wednesday 25. Call on Olmstead, the Genealogist, and Rowse, the Crayonist, but miss seeing them.

P.M. at the Astor Library, and look over Baptista Porta's Physiognomy, 1623: and Magea Naturalis, 1650.

Thursday 26. Write to my wife, and enclose "Webb's Critique on Matilda Heron," for Anna. At Baillaire's Scientific Bookstore, also, at the Swedenborg Societies' printing and publishing House in Astor Place. Call again and find Rowse, whose portraits please me, for their fineness and delicacy. He has taken Henry Thoreau, but made a gentleman of him, which is no improvement plainly on Silenus; "gentle boy" though there be in the whistle of him some where, and apparent in the memory—, after he leaves the parlour often.

Friday 27. Again read at the Astor Library. Also at Putnam's, Wiley's, and Norton's, Publishing Houses. Meet Dana of the Tribune, who tells me of his

"Book of Household Poetry," being choice selections from the English wells un-defiled, and should be a good book for Family Readings. He will print now very soon.—I dine at Taylor's with George Copway, who tells me about his Indi-ans, their prospects and habits.

Evening, a good company at Alice Cary's, and some good things said on the Callings. Mrs Field, the brilliant French governess once, and the little pastille painter, Mrs. Dessell, Louisa's amiable admirer, are present. Mrs. Field's broken French accent, and naivete, gracing all she said—she conversing, as accomplished French ladies can so well.—

Saturday 28. I call on Olmstead, also on Mrs. Cleveland. She wishes me to stay and meet a few ladies friends of hers, and is to let me know on Tuesday, to-morrow evening, at Miss. Carys. Mrs. Cleveland is in good earnest, and if she finds any amiable fanatics to join her for three or four evenings, I may remain till Saturday next, and meet them meanwhile. But her brother Greeley's only son, a boy of great promise, is just gone with croup, cannot survive to see and be seen of his Father fast hastening from the far West, only to find his poor crazed wife and agued little daughter, wailing over the perished promise of his Heart. His cup is full: The Tribune's son is laid low: I pity him great Child as he is, and without a successor now.

I dine again at Taylors—and have a pleasant evening of personal reminis-cences with my host and hostess. Mrs. P. is interested in my Schools, and so I give her "The Record", and Louisas "Fables" to Miss. Alice, of the marvellous eyes, meaning more than she knows, or can tell any one to advantage.

March.

Sunday 1. This morning, I hear Harris, the Christian Spiritualist, and see how little his temperament has done for him—a protest against Christianity almost, and the gentle Spiritualism it pretends. He preached scandalously about Scandal and fiercely for Charity, tearing her seemly mantle all into unsightly shreds. Opium was the sinner, I suspect, with coffee and company, as holds with these lunatics and infatuates, for the most part, here, and elsewhere. Afternoon, I have more of the same, calling itself pagan, and honestly, at the other meeting: S. P. Andrews, speaking, and other adepts of his Agapemone—men,—but of womenkind all sat silent and seemed confused as they should be. In the evening, I hear Chapin at his Church on the Martyr Spirit of former and present times—the martyrs of domestic life—women and children particularly. The audiance [sic] was large, || and attentive || the preaching effective, as the contribution for the widows' and children's benefit, proved afterwards. A great many clerks and young women were present to hear, and take the doctrine to heart: and the con-gregation seemed generally attentive and touched.

Monday 2nd. The Tribune's Son died yesterday morning, and is buried to day. Whether the Father has arrived, I have not learned.—This event will de-termine for me as to the Conversations here: and I shall leave for New Haven sometime on Wesdnesday to reach Ambrose's to sleep. I have written him to let him know of my coming, and shall write you, by Friday from thence or Saturday.

"The Tribune and Times" Newspapers keep you well posted from mail to mail. I have sent them to you regularly, and hope to feel able to subscribe for the "Semi weekly Tribune," before I leave New York.

Mrs. Manning has been too unwell for company and conversations, so I shall not visit them as was purposed. Nor have I found the time for going to Orange, as I intended. Our thoughts seem tending Boston-ward, and so let them have free chance to run and be glorified, if they can be. I fancy you will write your wish to have me cast my eyes about there, as I come on my way to Walpole. How soon that may be I cannot say. Perhaps a week, possibly, a fortnight for New Haven; and April at farthest, must bring me home, or to find where home is, and surroundings for a little future.

My letter of the 26th has reached you of course with the extract from Mr. Furness' letter. Address me next at New Haven.

Excuse my prosing thus at length about my nothings here. It takes women, and wives, as I have cause to know, to write good letters.

Ever Yours,
A.B.A.

Cordially to the girls.

[Letter to Mrs. A. Bronson Alcott, Walpole, N.H.; from New York City, March 4, 1857.]

LETTER 57–5

[to Ambrose Alcott, New Haven]

New-York March 5th 1857. | Thursday.

Dear Brother,

I shall not go from here to Philadelphia as I expected to do when I wrote some days ago, but shall come at once to New Haven, and may be there to-morrow or Saturday afternoon:—by the middle of next week certainly, to pass some days with you, and, if it is convenient, at your house. I am sorry to hear of mother's condition. The coming Spring with its opportunities of out-door exercise, and fair weather will do something, I trust, to relieve, and restore her to her feet, and the wonted cheerfulness. If I can promote her to her good old ways and spirits, I shall be very glad, and will do my best to that end. I may be with you for a week or more. I had letters from home lately: they were all well.

Your letter came straight to hand. If you write on Sunday, I shall get your letter before I leave here. To-day is fair and sunny here in the city.

With love to Mother, and regards to your wife.

Your Brother,
A. Bronson Alcott.

LETTER 57–6

[to Mrs. A. Bronson Alcott, Walpole, N.H.]

New Haven 8th March 1857.

My Dear,

I left New-York last Friday, and reached here forthwith to sleep at my brothers. They are quite well and expecting me to stay with them while I remain in New-Haven. I find mother confined to the house, as she has been for some weeks past, and much of her time she spends in bed. She has not escaped her old complaints, but has a good appetite, and needs fair weather and opportunities for stirring abroad to restore something of her former serenity and cheerfulness. I doubt whether she can reach us. Age and confusions of mind have overtaken her, and she may pass into the Unseen at any moment. She yet cherishes the hope of visiting us sometime, but it seems quite improbable. The ride is too long and tedious for her remaining strength, even if our home were fixed in Boston or its neighborhood. She is well cared for here, and, much as it would minister to her comfort, and our satisfaction, to have it otherwise, 'tis best that she remain here. Ambrose's wife's sister lives with them, and has done since Mother came last autumn. If my poor receipts shall warrant my contributing something for their kind care and trouble I shall so gladly do the best I can, and wish it were more.

Yesterday, I called on Mr. Sheldon, and found him a believer in Mr. Alcott, and the possibility of a select hearing for him here—the best minds consenting. I am to see him again to morrow, and learn whether his enthusiasm finds fair honest backers to the Course of Five Conversations to be given, at once, three or four of them during the present week. I wish it may prove all he anticipates, and yield golden fruits for all parties concerned. So I may be here for some eight or ten days to come. There are worthy people here with whom intercourse will be agreeable, and introductory to future opportunities. Mr. Sheldon is the master spirit, as, I learn, from all quarters: has done good service in past seasons by inviting Emerson, Parker, Phillips, & co. to lecture here to the staid Puritans, and means to carry the doctrines, he says, quite home and clean through, winding up with Mr. Alcott. Thus I am to have full swing and the best entertainment. Presently you shall have more about it, or nothing.

I have seen Dr. Bronson whose "Book on Ancient Waterbury," is nearly ready for the press. I have also called on Dr. Beardsley of the Episcopal Church, and author of a History of the Cheshire Academy in which he has given a sketch of my Uncle Dr. Tillotson Bronson, its founder and principal for many years.

This morning (Sunday) I heard Dr. Storrs' of Brooklyn, N. Y. He preached at the First Church on the Green, Dr. Bacon's. There seemed to be a good deal of life responding from the well-filled, well-dressed, pews, to the better orthodoxy than I was wont to hear in my earlier days. Here is an expanding Puritanism; and there a broad Episcopacy: a tolerant Unitarianism, a Spiritualism gathering up all extremes of Skepticism and of Superstition, every where; and we wait for the fusion and results. For me, and such as me, (if such there be) the single sight, the sovereign [sic] independence, meanwhile, with the best opportunities of mingling intellectually, spiritually, with all and saying whatsoever is to be said, for their edifying of all in the Central Truths underying the Sects and sophistries of our time—The conversion of the Mind to the duties of Life here and hereafter.

And a good Conversation implies, as it is, indeed, a Conversion, and a Gospel, to the partakers.

Yesterday, I mailed here for you, some Tribunes, the Times, with a New Haven newspaper. I am expecting letters by to-morrows' mail (4. oclock) and shall write again by Tuesday if I go to Boston without Conversing here.—To-day is sunny, and there is a sharp Puritanical air abroad, and as blue as it is nipping.

Yet, I am

Yours, ever and affectionately,

A. B. A.

LETTER 57–7

[to Mrs. A. Bronson Alcott, Walpole, N.H.]

New Haven 11th March, 1857.

My Dear,

This evening I meet my Company of some thirty or more persons; Profs. Porter, Fisher and Norton of Yale College are promised, a few students also, and some accomplished women. I am doubtful as to other meetings just now, Mr. Sheldon thinking an autumn circle will be every way the better and more profitable all round. Still this evening may chance to be so very promising as to invite the other four, and detain me here till into next week. I have met Dr. Bacon, Mr. Day, Librarian of the Young Men's Association, and other gentlemen, and shall find it agreeable to remain. But it seems the more probable that Thursday, to morrow, will find me in my way,—whether for Walpole straightways, or through Worcester and Boston, I am undecided. I think we should find ourselves out of place here, surrounded by influences against which yourself and the girls would rebel forthwith. Yet I am making all inquiries as if the thing were a possibility and shall bring the necessary information along with me.

Mother is less composed to day. I slept last night at Mr. Barnes where Mr. Sheldon boards, and shall accept the like hospitalities for to night. Mr. Sheldon is a bachelor, and much respected here. I have twice dined with him, and shall again to day. He is a lawyer: a good republican, and takes an active part in the Kanzas difficulties.

I shall be with you soon, even if I take Boston and Concord on my route home. And if I remain here over Sunday will write to you for Monday's mail. Your letter reached me on Monday. Keep up your spirits: the unseen ways and means are often the best and most efficient. We have spring—the summer and even autumn for range, and prospect. I will do my part, and when was the time, my steadfast friend and companion failed of hers?

Affectionately

A. B. A.

Love to the Girls also.

LETTER 57–8

[to Mrs. A. Bronson Alcott, Walpole, N.H.]

New Haven 13 March 1857. | Friday.

My Dear,

Contrary to prospects when I wrote you last Wednesday, I am to be here for a week or so; say till next Thursday. I have had two Conversations—the first on Wednesday and again last evening, and am invited to give four more, on Saturday, Monday, Tuesday, and Wednesday evenings' coming: Prof. Bailey, Mr. Brown, Mr. Sheldon, and some of the more thoughtful, the bright boys, of the College, professing an unexpected interest, and their unwillingness to wait for the rest till autumn. I find a curiosity and an earnestness, which make it pleasant to communicate with this expectant company, and shall deem my longer stay here well advised and profitable to all parties. Yale is no exception to other Colleges, of young minds seeking Professors under difficulties, and surprised when something of that sort turns up; oftenest, it is beginning to be suspected, in shape of some travelling lecturer, or, as here now, in the complaisant Converser, who they are finding carries the candid divinities along with him, offering them a taste on their own terms and times; accommodating very, and gracious even to the free gift of his best such as it is. Our two evenings have been pleasant and acceptable. New-Haven, if a bigoted, is nevertheless a virtuous city, contrasting so favorably with New York, if it does not with Boston even. Their faith, and hence their health, seems less sapped and more vigorous, with all its superstitions and deferences to the old traditions. But I may be overpartial to my native people and state, with which I have so little in common now, scarce nothing abiding with me, save my mother's transplanted gifts and graces: A Puritan of kindlier faith, and, (excuse the egotism), of fuller bloom and the mellower fruitage.—

I have your letter of the 8th. and shall take its suggestions to heart while staying here. If we could house our affections as cheaply as we can our bodies here in this city, I should be clear as to our future residence; but that "drowsy Depot" you hate so, is more tolerable far and friendly than the rigours of orthodox landlords and College civilities would be to the proud spirited dame, and free hearted daughters, whom I call mine; I prize too highly to transplant out of their native soil, suddenly, or from any straights yet overtaking them, or Theirs, ever,

and affectionately
A.B.A.

Address me here till I leave.
I shall write again in a day or two.

[Letter to Mrs. A. Bronson Alcott, Walpole, N.H.; from New Bedford? Mass., April 4, 1857.]

LETTER 57-9

[to Mrs. A. Bronson Alcott, Walpole, N.H.]

Woodlawn, New-Bedford. | 7th April, 1857.

My Dear,

My Saturday's notes and prospects will have found you by today's Mail, and shall be followed by some furtherances of the same this fair morning from the seat of our hospitable friend Ricketson; who, more than any person I have known in parlance and manners, reminds me of the complaisant and kindly brother inlaw of yours, the late Dr. Windship, as also in his complexion of sentiment and features, sprightly, critical and conscientious in his way, and generous almost to extravagance: a man of fortune, which, to the Drs. trial, *He* was not, and his fellows' disadvantage and loss. Woodlawn is three miles from New-Bedford, and is a neat, plain, place, suited to its owner's comforts and tastes, fashioned and furnished as it is, by himself, with abundant means at his command—a sort of drap-draped Estate and surroundings, all in keeping with its Quaker occupant and designer. There is a houseful of life also, and lawns of loving kindliness within; my hostess and her sunny daughters the freshest of flowing hearts. Thoreau is here and a partaker of all with me; Channing also passed the Sunday, and seemed saner, & sounder than heretofore when Hillside and its inmates knew him and his caprices untold, if not unendurable. Mrs. Ricketson and daughters alone of women here as far as I learn, have touched his desolate heart, and held him to solace in their charities. No one knows where he sleeps in the city or dines: or finds any thing of his in "The Mercury" he edits, and to which for three or more days of the week he devotes his wits without finding them as far as he or his readers can discover. He comes forth from his den to spend the intervals at Woodlawn with his kind friends: sits with Ricketson in his Shanty enjoying his pipe, or strolls with him through the old fields, solitary and sad-seeming through the jocund companionship around him the jubilance of the spring season,—through his own jokes more than all else besides—too fated to weep, or dissolve the frosts of more than forty winters' of Sorrows—wooing the snows forever.—I know not whether he is the more solitary than others; no more so perhaps than Thoreau, whom Nature would marry if he would once consent to the nuptials; but the cold coy Boy will not listen it seems, still Adam ‖ still ‖ aloof naming his beasts and birds, his earliest flowers and friends; feeling, yet not finding himself alone without his Eve building from his side to animate and humanize the wilderness of his Paradise which without woman is solitary and desolate —the unbreasted Sphynx, weather- and way-sore, and a peril.—For Nature, unless wooed and won through the womanly love, is ever the fanged Dragon to snap up the mortal man or woman drawn toward her by the brute affections, these never solving life's riddles.—But of this Gemini—of Thoreau and Channing—for this present, more than enough of them and their significance here for you.

I dined on Saturday with the Arnolds, and again on Sunday after hearing Mrs. Howland at the Friends' meeting. They offer their spacious drawing rooms for the Conversations, and their invitations are sent out for our first gathering on Thursday evening coming—some sixty and more—the best families—the Roach's, Morgans, Rodman's, &c. are to compose our Company. Mr. Weiss[1] is taking the earnest part with our friend Ricketson, and now my wits must fulfil expectations if they can. Saturday following, then Monday, Wednesday and Friday of next week—these evenings open and so close my engagements here for the present, *profitably* let us hope to all parties concerned. May Beck in Boston and his Company find the like furtherance.

Garrison and Pillsbury have been here, also Elihu Burrett and Warren Benton, lecturing. Richard H. Dana, the elder, is expected soon on a visit to the Arnolds; so may have to honor us with his presence in the drawing rooms on our evenings. Ben. Rodman has called here at Woodlawn to see me, but I was in town at the time and missed him—Boreas[?], Old[?]. Sunday evening, I was at Dr. Wilder's, where I met Swasy, formerly of Brooklyn, and Longfellow's friend, —now living at Nantucket and wishing me to visit him there and talk sometime next autumn. He tells me Emerson was there last week and read three lectures —Miss Mitchell, the astronomer, lives on the Island. The women, I hear, are sensible and able-bodied: independent islanders for three fourths of the year or more from their husbands, who are whalers and at sea—as[?] from the Continent and Massachusetts men and women. Sherbe has sometimes spoken of these people, with the hope of my seeing them professionally also as he has more than once.

As to houses about Boston—the Sewalls assured me three weeks or so would find more to be rented and the better choices for us, than just now. I shall time every enquiry then, and make all surveys till our points are carried. I hear as yet nothing from you, nor mother. You shall address me here till the last of next week—"Care of Daniel Ricketson, Esqr." Every morning the Carriage goes to town, and brings the letters. You shall hear again after our first Conversation of Thursday coming.

Ricketson is active, eager—the most mobile, mercurial of men, and carries his ends always—the compliments and the Conversations of course.—

Much love to my Maids, and [word] months or more waiting to their mother, the friend, and faithful wife, of her

A.B.A.

¹ John Weiss (1818–79).

LETTER 57–10

[to Mrs. A. Bronson Alcott, Walpole, N.H.]
New Bedford, Monday Noon, | 13th April, 1857.

I am just come out here to Woodlawn from the City where I slept last night, having heard Mr Weiss at his Church yesterday and dined with him afterwards, also addressed the children of his Sunday School after dinner, and successfully. Then I took tea at Mr. Lindseys where I saw some pictures—a "Joseph's Temptation" piece by some one of the Masters, perhaps by Titian, and quite worth the seeing. Mrs. Lindsey is of the Sedgwick family a niece I think of Katharine, the novelist, and a pleasing person to know. Fanny Kemble has been her guest. She told me a good deal about this remarkable visitor of hers, and among the rest, mentioned Dr. Bellows and the breakfast of which you have had full reports. I had much to say of Ellery Channing whom her husband employs as Editor of "The Mercury" Newspaper here, and a friend of the poet engaged. They are excellent people, and comprehend the melancholy man to make their house a hospitable home for him whenever he will avail himself of the offering.

I staid at Joseph Ricketsons—Daniel's brothers—and he drove me out here this morning. Thoreau has taken my host away to the Middleborough Pond for the day, but brings him home to supper, and this evening's Conversation at Charles W. Morgans in town.

Saturday evening at Mrs. Arnold's brought a larger Company together than on Thursday evening: there must have been eighty at least: the rooms were crowded, and the Conversation met with general approval. This evening I am to treat of Health and Temperance, and try my auditors again. They say less than I could wish, but hear well—all which is helpful, and encouraging. 'Tis the best company I have ever met.

Miss Weston is here, and tells me all about her sister Mrs Chapman who lives now at Weymouth.

I have no letters from you—none by today's mail, and am growing a little anxious. Have your letters missed? Pray write and relieve me. I shall leave on Saturday morning for Boston. You will get this on Wednesday.

Affectionately
A.B.A.

—Nothing from mother has reached me here.—

LETTER 57–11

[to Mrs. A. Bronson Alcott, Walpole, N.H.]
Melrose, 19th April 1857. | Sunday, at Mr. Sewalls.

My Dear,

I came out here last evening and am spending the Sunday with cousin Sam. and his girls. Mrs. Roby is still in town, but comes out here sometime next week with Mary and Fanny, Louisa is going to keep house for Thomas while his girls are away; and this will take me there to sleep and for a meal sometimes while I am in these parts. Mrs. Bond also invites me to Roxbury and the hospitalities of her house. I shall find Abby there to morrow and perhaps pass the night with them. I dined yesterday at Mrs. Reed's with Louisa, and we may go over there together. Abby is in delectable favor, I learn, with herself and her art, as she is with her Teacher, Mrs. Murdock, and all the Bonds'. I mean to see her at her easel in school and talk with Mrs. M. of the promising pupil's performances and prospects.—Louisa, and I are to seek some shelter for the family genius—one and all—in that neighbourhood, besides,—and intend devoting this week to the search for the suitable place for *it and them*. Mr. Sewall thinks $200. or 250. will give us a comfortable house (including my garden of course) within walking distance of the city attractions. We will make thorough surveys, and I shall come within a week or two, and report in person. Meanwhile I am invited to meet some good people at Greenwood, and shall be there, I think, next Sunday: Mr. Locke being from home to-day, but is to return by Tuesday or Wednesday. I shall know more of the prospects of Conversations in the City by to-morrow or next day: and, from what I hear, a course seems probable and to be given under every advantage of place and company. You shall hear further when I know more.

New-Bedford has outdone the cities in its hospitalities to the Ideas I am commissioned to celebrate—giving them and their Indicator, the flower of their houses, and their costliest drawing rooms, with the largest liberty and full swing, for five sittings. This my last, is also my best work, and a victory very memorable. I am invited to meet the same company again at a suitable interval, and have the rest of it all; and for the present service I am paid the pleasure, and by Mr. Weiss $75. besides. It looks now as if we could move freely, unincumbered of debt, or nearly so, with some prospects ahead for the family and its support. I shall add as largely such advantages as may open to me here before I see you. If we have the King's Chapel assistance all will go smoothly with us for some time to come certainly.

I copy a paragraph or two for your encouragement from the last "North American: also send My host Ricketson's salutation to "Madame and Mada-moisells [sic]" to feed their reflected fames meanwhile.—

Your letters reached me last Wednesday.

Ever Yours
A.B.A.

LETTER 57–12

[to Mrs. A. Bronson Alcott, Walpole, N.H.]

Boston 29th April, 1857. | Wednesday.

My Dear,

I have had a confused week here in the city, at Melrose, Greenwood, and Jamaica Plain, since I wrote you last: Fanny's funeral, a Sunday's talk at Mr. Locke's, and Abby's preparations for returning home; with inquiries for houses in the suburbs, seeing friends miscellaneously from day to day, and dinings with the philosophers once at Parker's, have done up my week for me, as you may conceive without the details. Your letters have come to hand with the mountain news meanwhile, and all seems very passable, if not hopeful now. Abby brings you this, and I will follow with myself and the rest sometime next week, or early in the following, if I ‖ call ‖ [p. o.] pause [p. in] for a Sunday at Concord, on my return. Some Conversations are arranged for me here. I give my first on Friday Evening at Dr. Wm. F. Channing's, and a second and third on the following Tuesday and Friday evenings. The company is to be select, and limited to some thirty or thirty five persons—these I am told—Starr King, Alger, Freeman Clarke, and sister, J. W. Browne, J. A. Andrew, Mrs. Howe, Sam. Ward, Russell Lowell, Sherbe, Longfellow, &c—the women included, as the best of the opportunity—Abby May, Emma Rogers, & Martha Kuhn among others. Woodman has behaved handsomely about it, and we have good hopes of the ‖ same ‖ occasion. Mr. Emerson and Ellen will come once or more certainly.

Then, I have an engagement for this evening at Cambridge: Sherbe's Lecture comes to morrow evening, and I may go to Worcester for the Sunday coming and see Higginson.

Abby has acquitted herself here to the surprise of all her friends; and takes along the tokens of her Genius to delight her mother and sisters. 'Tis a hopeful work: the likeness is perfect, and shall adorn our parlours wherever we find ourselves in times to come.

As to houses:—we have seen some in Roxbury, Jamaica Plain, Cambridgeport; rents about $200. or 250.—But under the circumstances, it seems the part of prudence to wait a little. Prospects are opening on all sides for me, and the responsibilities are falling where they should do for the comfort of all concerned. I shall be in season for the Garden, and there is a jaunt to Vermont, if we will, to be taken during the summer.—I hope to come free of debt here, & able to square accounts with all in Walpole for the spring and summer. Let us hope, and take the autumn in season to secure the winter quarters for the family somewhere here in these parts.—Elisabeth must walk now, ‖ and bathe ‖ or ride [2 p. in] daily.[1] But I will come and see to these matters in a few days. To her and Anna much love, as to yourself, and ever, from—A.B.A.

[1] Elizabeth had contracted scarlet fever in May, 1856, from which she never recovered, developing, probably, rheumatic fever.

LETTER 57–13

[to Ambrose Alcott, New Haven, Conn.]

Walpole, N.H. May, 13th, 1857.

Dear Brother,

I returned yesterday from New-Bedford, Worcester, and Boston, having held Conversations at these cities. Louisa came with me, and Abby preceded us a few days. And now we are all together again for the Summer. We are pretty well. Elisabeth gains we hope [2 p. in] from the effects of last spring's scarlet fever as fast as could be expected. I think some [p. in] of taking her and her mother with me to spend a fortnight in Vermont soon after my planting is done. Our Season here is late and cold. My Garden is but just ploughed, and my seeds are still out of the ground. There is good prospect of fruit in these parts, I am told, and a productive season generally.

My wife tells me she wrote to you lately while I was from home, and I have just read your answer. I am sorry to hear of the straits you speak of, and of mother's protracted debility and confinement. You write of her reviving a little. I wish the warm Spring days so slow in coming, may do their part in restoring her to herself, and enable her to enjoy them and her friends again. I was sorry to hurry from your house so fast, and from her. But I did not see how my stay could promote her comfort very greatly. I trust you are now moved, and find yourselves better placed than at your house on Bishop Street. You have my good wishes as regards your business plans also. My own receipts for the season have fallen far short of our family expenses, or I should have something to send to relieve you of some of your burdens. But people, I find, are quite ready to hear, yet slow to pay much for the hearing of what I have to say to them. I must wait for my turn to be served, and patiently. Meanwhile, of such avails as come to hand, you must have something, be it ever so little. I am invited to talk with the friends of Benjamin W. Dyer now living in Randolph, Vermont, and may get some dollars out of them for mother and yourself possibly. You shall hear again from me soon. And you will write presently, let me hope, and more fully of mother's condition, as of your own affairs particularly.

Your wife must feel the want of her sisters' help about mother and the children. Poverty is never chosen by any of us, and has its trials often and many. I have had the full benefits of these from the first, and expect the same continued to me to the end of life. But 'tis too much for most people, and breaks them down often.

If you see Mr. Sheldon, or others of the New-Haven friends, speak to them of me. My stay in your city was not without some pleasantness, and I shall stop again on my way to Philadelphia next autumn, if I pass your city. [last clause p. in]

Read this to mother, if she can hear it.

Hoping for the best for yourself and family, I remain

Affectionately Your Brother,
A. Bronson Alcott.

Mr Ambrose Alcott,
New Haven.

LETTER 57-14[1]

[to Daniel Ricketson, New Bedford, Mass.]

Walpole, N.H. 13th May, 1857

My Friend,

I take an early moment simply to apprise you and yours of my return here, with my daughter Louisa, on Monday last, having passed the Sunday at Concord with Emerson. Thoreau I did not see, but only Sanborn and Mrs. Ripley at Emerson's on Sunday evening.

The Concord College had the best place in our thoughts for the time, as had some farms adjoining Emerson's and awaiting good purchasors. We settled it in our plans for yourself, and you have but to take the train and make it good at your earliest convenience. I think wise men and excellent women have no right to live elsewhere for the coming half century; so please be of my mind, and get the titles forthwith.

I had a pleasant company for three evenings at Dr. W. F. Channings in Boston, Whipple, Mrs. Howe, and Emerson were of the party. I enclose an admission card as an intimation of our topics of discourse.

My wife received, and has thanked you as good wives can, for your praise of her husband in the New Bedford Mercury: a duplicate also reached me to Emerson's address, while I was at his house. I have by me a note from you, besides, from which my wife had taken the sum enclosed, as somebody's contribution to the evening, in New Bedford.

It will give me great pleasure to see you and family sometime again and renew the friendship so favorably begun.

Truly yours,
A. Bronson Alcott.

To

    Daniel Ricketson, Esq.
    Woodlawn, New Bedford.

¹ From a typescript owned by the Houghton Library, Harvard University.

LETTER 57–15

[to Mrs. A. Bronson Alcott, Boston, Mass.]

Walpole, 3rd August | 1857. Monday noon,

My dear,

I have just risen from the Table, where, assembled all to hear with expectant hearts, I read your letter which I had just brought from the office, for once anticipating the news by reading along the lane, and so fronting with happy countenance the circle of guests about me. It brings good news indeed, dear Elisabeth is safe, and we trust still comfortable as invalids can be, in the chambers and hospitalities of her namesakes,¹ and her mother's presence. I thank the Benignant powers for so much, and for the Hopes we cherish, moreover, in the salutary Sea, and the change of scene. All is well to the good and the Gentle: they inheriting the whole earth as do the meek, and the Heaven beside. "Lizzy's Journal shall tell us of her days, and the rest from your flowing, full pen on Thursday. Her Winchendon billet came straight and relieved us of anxiety for the rest of the route. It is copied into my "Journal" for Saturday and there stands a cherished memorial of that day's experiences, and we all slept sweetly to wake thereafter to this mornings as yesterday's works. Anna has told all about us since you left: except to celebrate her own praises as a pains taking tidy housekeeper to which she is devoted. All nice and right within—Grandmother cheerful wrote a half sheet letter yesterday, and confesses to returning spirits.²

Dear Elisabeth, use all your discretion, and come soon the ruddy maiden to your mountain home, and those who love you more than [word].

I shall write presently at large

Ever Yours
A. B. A.

¹ The Sewalls.
² Alcott's mother had come in July to visit them, remaining until November.

LETTER 57–16

[to Mrs. A. Bronson Alcott, Swampscott, Mass.]¹

Walpole. 8th August | 1 P.M. Saturday.

My dear,

We have your letter of Tuesday, and the good prospects for Elisabeth at Mrs. Phillips, where you will accompany her today, perhaps, by Monday next certainly. And we shall expect letters by Wednesday, if not before. All seems propitious thus far; and to the good and faithful good hopes are ever realized in the good time. Tell us the sequel soon: we are all much with you, and your dependant charge.

Here the days pass quietly and have their compensations. Anna is the assiduous house keeper, and keeps her Guests in the best humour with her table and chambers. I find her consulting the Books, and her bread and cakes are excellent whether mixed in the orthodox way or not. Such order and tidiness it does one good to witness. All the private virtues and accomplishments are embosomed in this modest maiden, and await their times.—Grandmother dines at Mr. Wells to day. She is so-so—but on the gain very obviously, and begins to own it.—

This morning came Miss King, and the girls and young Holland,—whom I like rather,—have had a sitting in the ravine and have just returned to dinner—

The garden sends its respects, and is in the best of keeping, luxuriant beyond all expression: yields in cucumbers, squashes, &c in profusion.

To dear Elisabeth, my love, and to yourself.

A. B. A.²

¹ A resort town on Massachusetts Bay, thirteen miles northeast of Boston.
² Pasted near the bottom of the sheet is the following newspaper clipping: "Nathaniel Tucker, who retired from mercantile li[fe] in Boston 40 years ago, and has since lived [torn] Bellows Falls, died there last Sunday at the [the remainder of the notice has been cut out]."

[Letter to Mrs. A. Bronson Alcott and Elizabeth, Swampscott, Mass.; from Walpole, N.H., August 13, 1857.]

LETTER 57–17

[to Mrs. A. Bronson Alcott, Swampscott, Mass.]

[Walpole, N.H.] Saturday 15th. August | 1857.

My dear,

I wrote on Thursday, also to Elisabeth, dating Friday by mistake, mailing to Swampscott as you advised; and yesterday the Girls Anna and Louisa wrote also: their letters being come fairly to hand, and read of you, and your charge by this time, I doubt not. I have just come from a little walk with mother— proposed by herself, to the Town House, just now the centre of fair hopes for the young folks, and there we [2 p. in] saw the scenery, now being painted for the

247

coming Village Entertainments, particulars of which you will be certain of having from Anna—the prima donna, as they transpire. The maiden herself, Abby, as one of the Artist' Committee, Hatty Door and Russell Bellows, were there; also C. Titus painting away on some Kitchen scene. Mother is a little *so-so* today, but enjoyed the walk, and came back to her sewing, feeling—she admitted—some better for it. She improves from week to week, and has fewer troubles past and coming to speak of—Old Age always omitted in her list of discomforts.—Last Sunday she accompanied me to Church, and had a good time. She walks, bathes, and seems taking the best means for regaining cheerfulness and herself.—When she feels poorly she comes and sits with me, and thinks she feels the better for the visit. Her sleep is sound, and her appetite pretty good, though she is unwilling to say so. I think she feels your absence, and kindly nursing.

Our housekeeping conducts itself neatly under the alternate weeks' admin-istration, serving us to the old comforts and bountifully, at bed and board. The absent matron would plume herself admiringly, to see how tidily and punctually all things are managed, by her serene substitutes—the newly initiated house-maids two, and who contrive to see company proudly and visit besides—the Artist maiden playing her part handsomely, in these last hinted hospitalities. The morning walks are taken also, and Holland is welcomed as an Innocent should be. He ventures into my study now and then, and takes affectionately as he can what soever I may have for him. We have had some talks besides in the Garden, and he has read some of the good things recommended from my books. I wish he may justify the Title of *Divine* to which he aspires.—

So far, before the summons to dinner_____

1 P.M. Just from the P. Office with yesterday's letter of yours, and renewed thanks for dear Elisabeth's brightening prospects. May the Sea, and Sovreign [*sic*] Hope's catholicon, save and restore. Three weeks of shore life, and a fourth with Aunt Caroline, another in and about Boston—must heal these wounds, or salve them so that our mountains can do the rest: or, what were better far some *Haunt* nearer persons and scenes endeared to us, or made memorable, by their familiarity hitherto. For me *Concord* seems the spot for us to plant ourselves, and bear the harvests home. But let us take the time and prudence due so great, so decisive, a step: and have all Boston and Suburbs as the field of our choice; making the family interest one and indissoluble if we can.

> Some sweet sequestered spot,
> Orchards' and gardens' plot,
> Wild woodlands, fountain,
> Dell'd near snug mountain,
> Children within, fair friends,
> To operate serenest ends,
> Our tenure's sure, and given
> In trust, for present Heaven.

Of our little spot here now in its luxuriance and opulence:—shelled beans and new potatoes today—with cucum-bers from a bed of concealed abundance. The tall corn, rich in promise, with the embracing beans, of the Indian's favorite dish; and your baptised tomatoes hiding the trellis, now loaded with fruit for your return. I wish it may be ere the frosts have laid these glories low. The Vines veil the ground every where, yellow already and green with the set fruits—never so munificent under my hands before. The beets too, and ditto the sage; the scarlet runners of your hopeful planting, now peeping in at the Artists window to be noticed of art.—

As to myself and occupations now—Have had *"The Tablets"* under revision, and some gleams of a Book sometime. Then Mr.s Barnard and Russell,[1] are to come presently for the *"Memoir:"* He writes saying I may expect him after the 20, and about that date. They will stay where _____?

A thousand hopes for E. S. A. many wishes for her welfare, and return, with her mother to

Ever Yours and hers
A. B. A.

Mrs. Abby May Alcott,
Swampscott.

[1] Henry Barnard and William Russell.

LETTER 57–18

[to Mrs. A. Bronson Alcott, Swampscott, Mass.]

Sunday morning | 23 Aug. 1857. | Walpole, N.H.

My dear,

I cannot open my "Tablets," and my morning's work, without first saluting my Absentees—"Health, Hope and peace, be theirs, be yours, and the good news for *us* tomorrow! Your last letter made *me* anxious, but the sisters read the hopefuller, and we wait for the confirmations. Friday brought nothing, nor Yesterday's mails, so we look forwards a little impatient for the 12. or 4. oclock of tomorrow. The girls, also mother, interpret your silence for the best;—please Heaven and here, it may prove so, and the ill omens be mine and mine only. And I remembered some dates—revived my old fancy of the periodicity of diseases, and especially the *lunar:* there the salt air and the sail in the boat—a long one, it seemed, for so frail and feeble a body,—solved the cough. Perhaps caught so from the cold and exposures of the sea. Dr. Newell's opinions seem sane & sagacious, and I rather approve, than doubt his prescriptions for E. Hippocrates says, "The more you nourish a diseased body the worse you make it," and Hahnemann repeats the aphorism approvingly. Strength *and flesh* should come in company, and stay; not the strength, ‖ which ‖ only oftentimes not the patients, but the meats and stimulants super imposed and feeding on the strength to exhaust and waste both presently. Yet E's regimen was not much amiss for the time perhaps, and provoked her sluggish forces to a healthier activity. I trust all is going if not best, then *not worst* with the dear patient, whose life and future are so precious to us, and herself.—Her letter was trustful and sweet as she ever must be and is. Write me particulars, for the facts are significant, and to Idealists doubly so, manifoldly.

I have waited for further intelligence expecting to hear on Friday, and should have written by the return mail, then, or yesterday, but nothing came, and I must write my poor anxieties and pains now. Anna, Louisa, and Abby I believe, have written during the week.—All goes quietly here, and agreeably: our housekeepers, the friendly competitors for the interweek's praises, and each getting them unanimously. To-morrow takes Louisa to task again, and on Tuesday night comes off the first play at the Town House: They will tell you all presently, and E. shall not miss any thing if she reads as they describe. *Grandma* is *cheerful* and busy as she *can* be, and rather more busy, from rising till bed-time. This morning she got the breakfast nice, and smiled over it afterwards. It rains, or she would have gone to church today.—Mr. Barnard writes he will not come, his children are sick, and Russell will fail therefore, and the girls get relief. Our Garden! its fruitfulness tongue fails to tell. Succotash coming this week; and *your tomatoes* will kill you with fruit when you come.

My wife and child,
farewell,
A. B. A.

LETTER 57–19

[to Anna, Louisa, May, and Mrs. Anna Alcott, Walpole, N.H.]
Swampscott, | Thursday Morning | 27. Aug. 1857.

My dear girls,
    and grandmother,

I reached Mr. Sewall's a little before 9, and found Thomas and Mary just returned from Lynn. They had passed the day with your mother and Elisabeth, and so brought me the [p. in] latest news. all of which was so favorable,—or *so not unfavorable,*[1] I should say—that I slept at ease for the night. Yesterday at ½ past 7, I took the train and was here at Mrs. Phillips before half past 8. your mother saluting me at the foot of the stairs, and dear Lizzy, who was already up and dressed for the day, came following fast after her. My first impression on seeing the dear Child again after three weeks or more, was that she was slightly thinner, her countenance paler perhaps and more elongated, but that she was on the whole looking not for the worse. She was pleasant and, for her, communicative, all day, entering into our plans for herself and the family with interest and spirit. She had a pretty good day sitting downstairs till noon almost, and in her chamber with us pleasantly. All the Walpole news &c. was discussed after reading our Sunday's letters which only came in after my arrival. About 6 came Dr. Newell and made some further examinations discovering, he tells us, *nothing organic,*[2] and puts his hopes of our patients restoration in a gently stimulating diet, tender nursing, and Time. Yet the case *is a critical one* and there is also a darkside to the prospect. The cough was slight all day, and perhaps no more than irritation from the last day's extreme cold here, and the dampness. The examination made Lizzy a good deal nervous, and she had a return of the old pains from wind for a half hour or so: but became quieted presently and had a good night, sleeping till after daybreak soundly. As I write she is scarcely awake, but will rise before long for the day, she said. To morrow, we intend returning to Thomas Sewall's where your mother will be with Lizzy for the present, and where you must direct your letters. I hope to go to Providence by Saturday, or Monday. The plans must have a week or fortnights time to ripen. Your mother is well, and energetic and hopeful on the whole, of Lizzy and the future. Tell us of the play last night, and Friday's when it comes off. The day is fair and mellow, and let us hope all will be well with us.

Your father and son
A.B.A.

¹ The underlining and comma are p. in.
² The underlining is p. in.

LETTER 57-20

[to Anna, Walpole, N.H.]

Boston, 11 o,clock, Friday 28 Aug. [p. in] 1857. | at Mr. Sewalls.
My dear Anna,—

I mailed a letter from Swampscott yesterday morning, which will reach you sometime to-day, and make you acquainted with the state of persons and affairs up to date. 'Tis manifest that Elisabeth has gained very little from the Sea-airs,— I wish I could add my conviction—had lost nothing from her three weeks stay at Swampscott. She may have lost nothing of strength, but has gained nothing in flesh, and caught something of a cough, yet this may prove but the effect of the raw damp air upon her sensitive lungs, and pass presently off, and harmless. Yet I wish it were not there to get seated and prove the omen of coming troubles. But for the cough, I should not see any change for the worse since she left Walpole, unless a slight wasting of flesh—if indeed she had this to lose then. She had ‖ none of this, or of ‖ neither flesh nor strength to spare, and the Eye falling upon her wasted form scarcely dares to hope for her continuance long. Yet her countenance is full of hope when she is not distressed, and we wonder why we should venture to fear or doubt: so like herself, so gentle, confiding, and pleasant is our patient.

We left Mrs. Phillips at 9 this morning, and reached here about 10—Lizzy bearing the ride without any alarming fatigue, and is now sleeping quietly in Mrs Robys chamber, while I write. She chose this rather than Fanny's room, and is to occupy it with her mother while she stays in town. It rained while we were coming and still does. She is more protected here than at the seaside, and more private. Let us hope some weeks of quiet and good nursing will add hope to hope, and place her on the convalescence list unmistakably. Your mother is now disposed to be hopeful, and if devotion to a child can save and heal Lizzy is ours for the Years to come.

I shall leave for Providence perhaps to morrow. Mr. Sewall, your mother fancies has something in his mind for us, which our stay here with him may disclose. He has offered the gift of a lot in Malden about 8 miles out, if we will build a house on it. Perhaps we shall go out and see it: and, if the funds for building can be got of Mr. Barker or Mr Davis, shall think it worth considering. It is about two miles this side of Melrose, and Mr Samuel Sewalls. But the Roxbury, Brooklyne, and even *city places,* shall have their chances; nor do I omit Concord from the possible scites of our future home.—

Write us by Monday's mail if not before. Comfort to Grandmother, [word] love to her and all.—

Your father.

Lizzy, waking, says add my love to all.

Letter 57–21

[to Anna, Louisa, and May, Walpole, N.H.]

Boston, September 9. | 1857.
Tuesday 11. A.m.

Dear Girls,

I have just come in from Concord, where I spent Sunday and Yesterday, discussing family plans with Emerson, and seeing places. Houses can be rented there from $75, to 150, a year: not much room for the smaller sum, nor many comforts, but for the larger, we can find good quarters, and for $200, the best the little town affords. There is a snug little cottage on the road to the Barrett Place, near the stone bridge—the rooms are small, but there [are] six or more, water inside, and a [woo]dshed. This may be had for $90 [or] 100. Mr. Frost's house is for sale [word] $3,500: and Mrs. Goodenow, now [a] widow, may rent hers. But I [have] engaged nothing yet.

The Watts' place, near Emersons may [word] for something like $2000: about [word] acres including the fields by the road, [word] orchard of thirty or more trees, [word] garden land, and woodlands over [the] hill. The house will need some [repai]rs to make it habitable. Mr [Emer]son will take one field adjoining [his] for $600. But this Estate does [not] look inviting to me, and is more [word] and costly than we should purchase. Our repairs would swell the cost to $2000 or more, and then would not be what we want.

I looked at the Moore place adjoining Hillside, under the Elms and butternuts, embowered in a thrifty apple orchard of forty and more trees, all in bearing, the apple crop averaging $30, per, ann, and double that sum in the fruitful seasons. I can have five or ten acres of woodland behind the house. There is an excellent well of water, and a dry celler. The House is old, but still habitable, and with some repairs might do till our means enabled us to make it what we want. All this I can have for $950. dollars: 500 of which can come from Mr. Emerson's Hillside. The rest I will get from Mr Davis Mr Barker. Uncle Sam perhaps will like to add a little, and so leave your mother's investments untouched, and our income of the last years reduced but $30. or so. I will pay the Concord debts from the avails of my Winter's Conversations—the whole amount is not more than $100, as I shall manage it. And we can live in snug quarters, and humble ways, for a little while. Means for repairs will come if we show the disposition to make the most of a little, and so help ourselves to that. The Estate would soon become valuable with my improvements, and a handsome Home for us all. Nothing like it can be found for the money near the City, and we are too poor to pay so much for what is after all, neither bread nor meat. Presently, you may have a boarder or two, if you choose, at four and five dollars a week. But Mrs. Thoreau says there is no profit in it at the present high prices.

I am minded to take the reins a little more firmly in hand, and think you may rely upon me for supports of labour and money in the years to come. And I am fitly placed[?] so, and shall command the respects of your mother's connexions, and the family all the more favours they may have in their hearts to bestow. The garden and orchard will be yielding their incomes of fruits and occupations. Nor do I see where can be found society or advantages better for us, for yourselves during the coming years, than Classic Concord affords. Sanborn's School brings agreeable young persons to town; and, as for me, you need not one word of argument or persuasion, to convince you that tis the home for me. I will press nothing, but only state frankly my views, and preferences. Will you do the same, and let us abide the result.—I can do more for you, and for myself, from the Concord position, than any known to me, and think you can help yourselves as well, I fancy better, than elsewhere under all circumstances. Let me be the central figure of the Group, and try our family fortunes so, for a little time. I cannot have forfeited the respect and confidence of any friend; or if so unfortunate, please give me my last chance of redeeming my goodsense and discretion in their eyes. Your mother's benefactors will not think the less of her or of yourselves.

I am going to talk with Saml. Sewall about our affairs, after dinner, and shall not rest till some place is rented or purchased in good deed. Write me your considered judgments for my guidance in this matter.

I find Elisabeth has overdone a little, and is less hopeful to-day. But Dr. G.[1] is assured, and pronounces her fairly convalescent, awaiting time and tender care— take good heart my children, and we will soon praise God in a home of health competence and peace.

Let the beans be, and the squashes,—unless frost threatens—as they are. Ask Mr. Smith or some one about them. Nothing else can harm.—How for wood? Mr Howland will bring some if you need, and Burns can saw and split it. I must remain a little and linger here. Love to dear Mother and Sympathy.

Your Father

---

[1] Christian F. Geist. Alcott generally spelled his name "Gheist."

LETTER 57-22

[to Anna, Louisa, and May, Walpole, N.H.]

Boston 16th September | 1857. | (Tuesday Afternoon.)[1]

Dear Girls,

I am just come in from Concord, where I passed Sunday again and Yesterday: and have laid aside your last letters in which you describe the state of things at home up to last Monday. I have mother's full letter also. You are wishing to have me with you now, and may expect to see me presently: perhaps sometime next week, but I cannot say on what day I may come. Meanwhile pick the squashes, if you fear frost, and put them in the piazza, and cover them at night. You may harvest the beans also. Gather melons ‖ you pick ‖ as you need them for eating, and the corn. Nothing can suffer much till I come: the potatoes are as well in the ground, the beets and the roots generally. We shall have a good supply for the winter's use, and I will come in time to save all.

I feel encouraged about dear Elisabeth, though I am slow to expect any sudden restoration. Dr. Gheist has done much for her since he took her under his kindly care, and continues his promise of healing the dear patient in the reasonable time. I trust he may, not doubt in the least save when the distressed moments come. But these occur not so often, and her symptoms are less and less alarming, her sufferings being all mitigated by his prescriptions. Yet you must wait a while to find the sister fair and florid you once had and knew. She has ridden out today with her mother, and bore the ride without any great fatigue. I found her sleeping when I returned, and have just had some pleasant talk with her on Concord and our present plans. She wishes to go to Concord with her mother next week or ‖ the ‖ week after: and will I think if we go there to live, which seems to be the most feasible plan for us, and the only one that can be carried, if we leave Walpole this fall. I do not find any house suitable for us to be rented there. Mrs. Goodenough does not rent hers nor sell, and Mr Frost's is too costly.

I can have the Moore Place including the Orchard and woodlands behind— 10 acres, with the buildings—for $950. $500 or a little more perhaps will repair them,—so the carpenter's say—and, with my labour taste and skill we can have as pretty a place as there is in Concord, and worth $2000 to any purchaser. The bargain is not closed; but I am to give an answer on Monday next. Mr. Emersons $500, and Thomas Davis' pledges and Mr. Barker's pay for the place. Mr Emerson making all secure. Mr. Wigglesworth is ready to use a part of the Davenport legacy for repairs. And to morrow Emerson sees Mr Sewall to make everything straight, if we purchase. This takes but 27 dollars from your mother's income; and gives us a house, wood for one or two fires, and more fruit than we can consume. There are now not less than 20 barrels of winter apples, which will be ours if we buy. Sanborn's School is flourishing. I spoke with him about Abby's draw[ing.] She can take lessons in drawing without any thing else, also in musick: and so can Lizzy.—Dr. Folger gave a lecture yesterday to the School which I heard. Sanborn is much loved and respected. Marston Watson and wife are visiting Emerson. Watson is high[ly] pleased with my Place, and will se[nd] peach, plum trees, grapes, and flowers to any extent.—

Your mother is anxious, and divided in mind about Concord. I sha[ll] write again soon. Love to all.—

Your Father

9. oclock, Wednesday Morning. Lizzy had a good night and is bright and beautiful and speaks of Concord with pleasure. I think her improved a good deal, but not free from danger: a week or two will prove the Drs. assurances.

A.B.A.

---

[1] Tuesday was September 15.

LETTER 57-23

[to Anna, Louisa, and May, Walpole, N.H.]
Boston September 17th | 1857. | Thursday noon.
Dear Girls,

Your letters of yesterday have just come to hand, and just in time to arrest your mother's return with Elisabeth to Walpole on Saturday coming. Dr. Gheist had been consulted and given his assent to Elisabeth's leaving him: but your urgent pleas have so far modified her decision as to prepare the way for their going to Concord instead, on Saturday perhaps, or Monday next, when I am to decide matters with Mr. Moore, the particulars of which I wrote to you on Tuesday. Mr. Emerson was in town and saw Mr. Sewall yesterday about the place in Concord. They settled all the particulars of the purchase, and the Estate is ours, if we say so, and at once. Mr. E. is security for the $400 pledged to me by Messrs Davis and Barker to be paid in within four or five years, Mr Moore waiting so long for that sum. I think we may as well have the deeds drawn and call the place ours forthwith. Henry Thoreau is ready to survey it: and all necessary repairs can be completed by the first of November. Meanwhile your mother and Elisabeth can stay at Hillside for 4. or 5. dollars a week, or return for the time to Walpole as may seem best on the whole || and ||. The cost will be no more; perhaps not so much and your mother would feel better satisfied she says, and Lizzy be more comfortable, at home. Yet I have no doubt of our finding ourselves comfortable in the smaller house, which needs only scrubbing and some little papering perhaps to be quite habitable, for all but Elisabeth, if we thought so. But she might remain at Mr. Peabody's close by, and your mother be near her and all parties the while. We shall have the apples at any rate: and if we stay in Walpole till April, the 50 dollars rent which the present tenants pay for the houses. They would like to stay till then. If we should conclude to come straight home then I should take mother presently if she inclined to go West with me to sister Betsey's, and make my lecturing tour in those parts at once. I should hope to get wherewith to pay off the Concord debts, and move us there in the spring, deferring the repairs till sometime in March next. The Davenport and Easter monies come in about that time, and the Walpole debts can be paid from our quarterly income which is made only about 7 dollars less by the purchase of the place. Then there are some apples to sell for the present straits But this last plan keeps you all winter in Walpole, which you cannot think of with any patience, it seems.

If we move the last of October, there will be something due more than we can settle in Walpole, but that I can manage, as I can the Concord debts from my own earnings during the winter. Our groceries we can get at Chaffee's[?], and pay for [p. in] quarterly, without running much in debt for the first in Concord. I can take care of these matters if you will trust me for once a little, and give you a good home there in two or three years, all our own. I cannot but think your mother's reluctances will be somewhat overcome and soften by the time and the experiment, as well as yours. We purpose leaving early in the week for one place or the other.

Good bye,
Father

LETTER 57–24

[to Anna, Louisa, and May, Walpole, N.H.]

Boston 20th September | 1857. | Sunday.

Dear Girls,

I wrote you on Friday last,[1] and particularly concerning our plans for Concord and the winter. Yesterday, your mother went up and saw the place, likes it very well, but thinks it best to rent the cottage near the Barrett place for the winter if we can have it, or some house near the village, and move down forthwith. The repairs can proceed if we choose at once, or the present tenants may remain till Spring, paying their rent to us for the time, and the apples can be gathered for our winters supply. This plan has some important advantages as it gives us time to take every thing without haste or indiscretion. We can move, add something to our little means during the autumn and winter months, and be all the more able to make the needful repairs at "The Orchard" when the spring opens. And I think will suit best all round.

I shall go to Concord to morrow, and complete the purchase also find a house for the family during the winter. $75 or 100 will pay the rent at most and our place will yield us some thing meanwhile to pay it with. So much you may take as already settled, and proceed to act accordingly. I shall be some days in Concord making ready. Your mother and Elisabeth intend coming up by Friday next or Saturday, and I shall be with you as soon as all the necessary arrangements are completed,—by Saturday next, or early in the week after probably. They will go to Nat. Peabody's to stay while we move, and make all ready for them at the rented house.

Elisabeth still needs the tenderest care and will for the months to come. All depends on the choicest adaptations of food as regards quality and quantity, and good nursing. The least mistake prostrates and pains her, and costs days and nights of suffering. Still she is visibly better in spite of all relapses, and will recover herself in a reasonable time if the Dr. and our senses are honest and trustworthy in the matter. But it will be like a resurrection from the dead, and despite many doubts and anxieties. I am all the more desirous of our coming again together that your mother may find some respite from her long and pains taking cares. She needs rest and the comforts of children and home. Every one is kind and disposed to relieve, but none can take a mother's place in this office of watching and succou[r] of the sick.

We have written to Uncle Samue[l] about our plans, and hope to have some aid in the way of leaving Walp[ole] honorably, and returning creditably [to] Concord for a residence. Every thing promises fair up to this present writing and opens forth good prospects ahead. You will write to me at Concord, an[d] do *not* address to the care of R. W. E. but to me A. B. A. I shall stay mos[t] likely at Mr. Thoreaus for the time. I have nothing to add concerning the Garden but shall come to uproot a[nd] leave all Walpole recollections behin[d.] Make all due preparations as if we were to leave early in October or before[.] Remember me to mother, and take my love and blessings meanwhile.

Your Father.

[1] The preceding Letter 57–23.

LETTER 57-25

[to Mrs. A. Bronson Alcott, Boston]

Concord, 23 September | 1857. | At Emersons.

My dear,

Thus far all is propitious for us. "The Orchard" is surveyed and Thoreau promises to give us the plot fair and finished to the acres and rods, all lined and bounded, to morrow. The tenants occupying the larger house wish to remain till the Spring, they say, and Garfield agrees to pay his six months rent—his five months, as we shall agree, in advance,—$15 dollars,—Harris will pay the like sum also in advance monthly, for the same time; and would like to help pick the apples. Garfield has a team and will move us from the depot, if we wish him to serve us so. Mullet, I am advised, is shiftless, and might as well budge[?] at once. The small house might be very convenient as a store room for any furniture we might not have use for at our winter quarters.—I have three houses awaiting your inspection here, The Wheeler cottage, which is neat and comfortable in itself, but too remote from the village perhaps; then there is a comely house opposite the Universalist Church, roomy enough, another family occupying a part of it, which you might find inconvenient, and annoying;—also one half of the old fashioned Wheeler house, near the Depot: 40 dolls, for the six months. You can see and judge for yourself when you come. The Peabody's are expecting you: but don't hurry till Elisabeth can come up safely, and pleasantly to herself. I can stay here at Emerson's till Monday or Tuesday, if needs require, and we shall have time to move down at once. Three days at Walpole are as good as three weeks for moving off handsomely.

Here are the girls letters—all pertinent and in good understanding, as you will read. Write me of your decisions at once, and let me get your letter by Thursday. A kiss for my precious patient, and much love to my wife.

A.B.A.

LETTER 57-26

[to Anna, Louisa, and May, Walpole, N.H.]

Concord 24th September | 1857. | at Emersons.

Dear Girls,

Your letters came to hand yesterday, and were remailed forthwith to your mother, who will get them today. You feel right about Concord and moving down here at once; in which view your mother agrees with you, and comes up on Friday or Saturday to Hillside with Elisabeth where they will stay till we move into our winter quarters here in the village, and await the repairs which cannot be hurried to advantage. I have three tenements in my eye, one of which we shall rent for five or six months at about $40. for that time: the cottage, namely, near the Barrett place, the Old Wheeler House near the Depot, and a house near the Universalist Church, all comfortable, and affording snug winter quarters for the family. Your mother will choose for herself when she comes up from Boston. And I shall leave at once, on Saturday possibly, certainly early in next week, for Walpole, hoping to move down immediately. Three or four days are as good as so many weeks to move in. Meanwhile we shall hear from Uncle Sam, to whom your mother and my self have written of the purchase here and of our plans. I trust we shall be able to pay debts all round, and to leave Walpole and come handsomely into Concord with honour, and a free future before us. Thus far all is propitious for us. I left Elisabeth mending on Monday and wishing to come up here to meet you all. Dr. Gheist consents, and all looks well for her recovery in due time.—The present tenants wish to remain at "The Orchard" till Spring, and are to pay rents in advance. Mr. Moore estimates the apple crop at 20 barrels or more. and some are choice winter fruit. If you write on Sunday address us here at Concord.

Your Father.

[to Mrs. A. Bronson Alcott, Concord; from Walpole, N.H., September 29, 1857.]

LETTER 57–27

[to Mrs. A. Bronson Alcott, Concord]
Walpole, N.H. 30th Sepr. | 1857.

My dear,

We are far advanced in packing and mean to leave, Abby and I, in the morning train of Friday to reach Concord at noon, or after a little: the girls with mother following us in the next train: otherwise there will be another unpleasant night for them to pass with Hannah, and a desolate house; the furniture gone, and no comforts for mother. If Abby and I reach the depot in good time, we shall be able to see some furniture taken to the house; the beds at least, and we shall *all* be at hand to make ready for the Sunday. Our things will go to the Station here all Thursday, and be packed forthwith, to leave here a little before us on Friday morning and arrive about the same time at Concord. I think Garfield should be ready there with his team on Friday afternoon to carry some of our things to the house. If we must sleep out of our own house for a night, "the Middlesex," is near and convenient. But I think we can have rooms ready by the evening for the girls and Mother. The Garden is mostly harvested, and *Helden* is to move us. I have packed the books, and the girls will complete the rest in good time for him. As yet nothing from Syracuse, but I shall hear to morrow, unless the draft is mailed to S. E. S.[1] direct at Boston.

I wrote you last night and mailed this morning. If you send by N. Peabody to Boston on Thursday morning I may get your letter perhaps by the afternoon mail.

Should any thing delay our coming down on Friday, I will endeavour to apprize you in season. One of the Miss Peabody's will perhaps oblige you by calling at the Concord P. Office for letters.

The girls are gone to Hatty Doors this Evening. Grandmother is knitting, and talks of going to see Betsey with me this autumn.

Lizzy is not out of my thoughts any moment. Be careful of yourself, dear Child, soon you will see us all together again, if our good hopes and plan prevail.—Ever Yours,

and Your Mothers.
A. B. A.

¹ Samuel E. Sewall.

LETTER 57-28

[to Benjamin Marston Watson, Plymouth, Mass.]

Concord 10th October | 1857.

Dear Sir,

"The Orchard" is ours and my family are here now in a rented house awaiting our repairs in the Spring. Elisabeth is comfortable, and we hope convalescent. She has just returned from a pleasant ride, and is hopeful of herself. She has pleasant memories of School days with your wife, to whom she sends her regards.

We are having sunny days to ripen the apple crop. I am to gather mine next week.

I wish to leave home for the West early in November, and enclose my Circular of the coming Winter's work.¹

Cordially, Yours,
A. Bronson Alcott.

To Benjamin M. Watson,
Plymouth.

¹ The circular (printed at Concord, October, 1857) announces Alcott's proposed tour of the West and Philadelphia. The general topic is "New-England Life; Its Genius, Impulses, and Institutions." The Course of Conversations consists of, "I. The Household, II. Planting, III. The Press, IV. The Lecture, V. The Conversation."

LETTER 57-29

[to Mrs. A. Bronson Alcott, Concord]

Syracuse, 16th Nov. 1857. | Monday.

My dear,

Fair prospects to this date, and a comforting history for you and yours since we left Concord on Wednesday last, all which you shall have now, and the particulars. First, of our journey, and of mother. At Lancaster, Mr. Russell got into the cars, and rode with us to Worcester, showing kindly attentions to mother, getting her tea and cakes at the station. We reached Springfield about 7, and refreshed ourselves from our basket, mother taking her cup of tea there while we paused for an hour, and then drove onwards arriving at Albany at 11, and taking beds at the Delaven House for the night. She slept well, and was ready for the Utica train at 7 in the morning: breakfasting from our basket again before we took the cars. At St, Johnsville where we halted for 10 minutes, I found some substantial cakes for her which with cheese and apples served us a good lunch. We reached Utica about 12. Here she took a cup of tea, and I saw her safely seated in the stage for Betsey's[1] at 3. P.M. and in good spirits. She seemed quite content to make the rest of her journey with the company inside the coach, and I left her there to go cheerfully on her way.

At 3. came the train going West and took me on to Syracuse, and brother Sam's, to supper. I found him a good deal worn down, and preparing to leave home on Monday for Glen-Haven where he is to spend some three or four weeks. Joseph is there still and improving.

Friday 13.—I dine with Mr. Mills[2] and find him a very sensible & thoughtful person, reads Carlyle and Emerson discriminatingly, and believes much in Mr. Alcott. He preaches for Mr. May during his stay at Glen Haven. In the evening Mr. Mills came, and discussed the matter of Conversations here with brother Sam.

Saturday 14. Dr. Wilbur sends his carriage with a note inviting me to dine with him. I ride to Mrs Sedgwick's and see her for half an hour; She wishes to have the Conversations under the best advantages, and promises to see the right people forthwith. So Mr. Mills leaves ‖ the ‖ the whole to her, and brother Sams management. I found Dr. Wilbur exceedingly cordial and communicative: saw the Idiots, to some of whom I was introduced as "Anna's Father," and the Dr. pointed out to me her favorites, also the room in which she taught. He spoke tenderly of her, dwelt particularly on her goodness, her devotion, and success in winning the love of every one who knew her at the Institution. Miss Holden came over to see me almost as soon as I arrived at Mr. Mays, with her love and many inquiries and enthusiastic words about her dear friend Anna. And Mrs Wilbur's praises were not spared at dinner. On Mrs Sedgwick, I found Anna had made a deep impression also, and her children came in to inquire, and hear, about their good mistress. Mr. Sedgwick was particular in his inquiries also. Nor was Elisabeth's welfare forgotten by all those sympathizing acquaintances of Annas.—Dr. Wilbur sent me back in his carriage, and I pass the evening discussing family matters with brother Sam. He feels right about the purchase and thinks the move well advised. I shall hope to meet all demands before I come home: nor need make further now, with the good prospects of recruiting my scanty means from my receipts here for the three evenings I am to talk. It cost us 24. Dolls for passages, and so leaves me very little. The prospects are fair for my Conversations, however, and for abundant means of going Westwards for richer spoils. James Richardson is settled at Rochester. I have written to him, also sent forwards to Mrs Drury at Canandagua, Emerson's note with my Circular and designs on those cities.[3]—Conway is expected here to lecture, and I may see him before I leave.

Sunday 15. Mr. May preaches in the morning, and announces from his pulpit the Conversations, commending them to his people, in good earnest, and properly. P.M. I attend the Free discussion meeting with Mr. Mills where I speak, and Mr. M. gives notice of the Conversations here also.

In the evening, many friends come in to see the Minister, and wish him health, and a speedy return from the Water Cure. He is spent for want of rest and goes there to recruit on Dr. Jackson's regimen, and such leisure as he can secure him.

Monday 16. He leaves at 9. and I see Mrs. Sedgwick. We are to have three Evenings—*Thursday* the 19. at *Mrs. Wilkinsons* drawing rooms. Friday evening following, at Mrs.

Dr. Drurys and on Saturday evening at *Mrs. Leavenworth's.* Anna will tell you all about them, and I shall send other names of my Company when I have met them. Mrs. Sedgwick thinks we may have as many as fifty persons, and speaks most hopefully of the party. I will send my Advertisement in my next. *The Household—Business,* and *Conversation,* are our topics, and our company is the best there is here.

I am here on the best of terms with Mrs May, Charlotte, and Bonny. Have a comfortable chamber, and nothing wanting. Last evening Mrs. Calvin and Marion were here, and invited me to take tea with them this evening. and meet Mrs. Sedgwick again. I am going: Also, to Dr. Wilder's some day this week. I think I may leave for Canandagua on Monday next or Tuesday, and Shall expect letters from you before that time.

If I have good fishing here you shall have some samples of luck by my next writing.

Keep me informed of every matter pertaining *to your welfare.* And let me hear weekly if you can command the leisure from your imposed cares. Elisabeth's condition you cannot fail to state. To her, and all, much love.

Ever Yours,
A.B.A.

---

[1] At Oriskany Falls, New York.
[2] Charles D. B. Mills.
[3] Emily Mervine Drury. For Emerson's letter to her, see Rusk, *Emerson Letters,* V, 88–89. Alcott regularly misspelled "Canandaigua."

[to Mrs. Anna Alcott, Oriskany Falls, N.Y.; from Syracuse, between November 13 and 20, 1857.]

LETTER 57–30

[to Mrs. A. Bronson Alcott, Concord]

Syracuse, N.Y. | 20th November, | 1857.

I wrote last Monday and dispatched some careless notes of our journey to Utica, and of my arrival here, and prospects for some Evenings with the Syracusians. Mrs. Sedgwick has made good her assurances thus far, and brought together in spite of the pouring rain and the darkness, a fine company last evening at Mrs. Hamilton Whites, where we made acquaintance with each other, if not with our theme, and a hopeful beginning. A good many women graced the circle and || some || [p. o.] contributed to the entertainment some [p. in] by taking parts in the Conversation:—Mrs. Davis, Mrs Judson, Mrs. McCarty, Mrs. Sedgwick, and some others. A good many more were detained at home by the storm. But this day is fair, sunny, and promises us a favorable evening, and a full gathering to night at Dr. Clarys. I think the company may number forty persons, or more; and trust we may have a profitable and reasonable time. Mrs. Sedgwick took me home in her carriage, and expressed pleasure for herself and her friends in this introductory Interview. It should have been better on so fine a theme, but the fault was mine that it was not, since every one came with kindly Sympathies in the theme and good expectations. I had so much better things to say than were spoken that it seemed all commonplace and unworthy || enough; very || yet agreeable gossip and pastime for the two hours Sitting. I hope for the free deliverances and the memorable on these coming opportunities. Mrs. May and Miss. Coffin are intending to accompany me this evening and tomorrow. My party is, I learn, composed of the very best people here and comes rightly together under Mrs. Sedgwicks leadings. She is a general favorite, and has shown a true woman's discretion about bringing the right persons together. Mr. Mills came with Pres. Green, and both took parts in last evenings discussions.—Last Wednesday I took tea with him and his friend at Mills' house. This is Beriah Green, once President of Oneida College at Whitesborough, where he now resides: a sensible man, of sixty years or more, a friend of Gerret Smiths, and brother Sams, an Abolitionist,—independent—a little pragmatic, perhaps, and crotchety; but we compared notes with || out much || [p. o.] some [p. in] differences, yet liked each other very well.

Anna promised and so will write: and the Invalid shall add her fortnight's gain, if she can, in the pounds avoirdupois and ounces exact, by the inevitable standard. Hoping for the good tidings from the family group, and that soon, I remain Yours, and

Theirs ever,
A.B.A.

LETTER 57-31

[to Anna, Concord]

Syracuse 21st November, | 1857. | Saturday Morning.

Dear Anna,

Your letter and your mothers have just reached me, and have had the best of reading here in your Uncle's warm, comfortable, tidy, Study, where I am passing these days quietly, and, for most of the hours, by myself, as Scholars' love to do: Mrs. May and Charlotte keeping the house, and having things all in their own chosen manners, and times. Their hospitality to me in all my quiet ways and wishes is unwearied, considerate, punctual, and free: warm water for mornings bathing and shaving, clean chamber appointments, excellent bread and abundant butter within your reach, apples at every meal, and as much leisure as you choose, or conversation, when you will. You shall complete the picture of comforts,—yourself and your mother together—and leave me in the kind hands of your kindred for the present, and till I fall gladly again into your own to increase our stores of outward comforts, if I may add nothing better to the family goods and gains.—

Your letters bear to me good tidings. Now, let us believe, the propitious future is taking root to blossom presently, and afford shelter, shade, sun, sod, fruitage for the waiters. Your plays are a pleasure to you—The Lyceum, and now the Church Spectacle, promises delight, and entertainment; and Elisabeth's prospects are clearly[?], it seems, all yourself, or any of us can reasonably anticipate. Then I am relieved in knowing there is wood sawed to order, split and piled dry and accessible, with kindlings of pine, and shavings as you need them: a friendly grocer and handy: neighbourly Hosmers to thank; and some of our fair apple-crop stored for winters use in our cellar—myself and mother transported here on the avails of that productive orchard of ours.—I will see to the admission tickets to the Lyceum and send the money as soon as it comes to hand. This evening closes my course here, and, if possible, you shall get some thing—(I cannot say whether little or more, till the receipts come in)—by Tuesday's mails. Very likely Mr. Emerson will give tickets to his Lecture for that evening

The weather has been unfavorable for the former evenings' attendance here, —yet the rooms were filled at Mrs Whites, and last night at Mrs. Clary's;—between thirty and forty persons, I judge,—and some others were detained, I learn, by the darkness and the distance. Last evening, was of the better sort; the fluent mood came on, and streamed steadily from 8 till 10½, none venturing any words, and all the expressive silent consents. I wish we may swim in the same soundless serene sea to-night at Mrs. Judsons. 'Tis strengthening to recover the Gifts of speech and the insights, after a long and anxious spring and summer of distracting cares.—I am all the easier and abler from this morning's intelligence. For, with your letter, came also one from Richardson inviting me to come at once to Rochester and talk; a most respectful note from Mrs. Drury, who is now at Utica, but goes to spend the winter with her sister in Buffalo, to whose house she invites me, and hopes to give me a good company there, on her return, a fortnight hence. With Emerson's note to Mr. Tracy,[1] Dr. Hosmers' interest, and hers, we may hope for some results. Meanwhile I shall write to Mrs. Drury, and advise her of my wishes and movements.

"May I beg of you," she writes, "to tell me of your plans, so that I may know if there be any possibility of meeting you. I am greatly indebted to Mr. Emerson for his kind mention of me, and his good intentions in seeking to procure for me so great a privilege and happiness. I can think of nothing more desirable than to hear you discuss the subjects named in the Circular in the presence of a company who are worthy to listen."

Conway has not appeared yet, nor written to me. But his silence means "come",—I so construe it,—and shall pass on to Cincinnati, stopping at Rochester, at Buffalo perhaps, and at Cleveland as I go Westwards. December late or Mid winter even, may chance to be the more propitious for me and favors the fulfilment of any engagements (and the avails) on my way as they come. I shall be guided by circumstances.

You have no cause for any anxiety—yourself or mother—about your Uncle Sam. His parishioners, seeing him worn from preaching and his family trials, kindly send him to spend some weeks with Joseph, and get leisure, rest, and the benefit of the water cure, if he cares to avail himself of this last advantage. Rest is the one thing needful for him; but the Sewall and May ingredients seem hostile to each other and refuse to mix and caress atomically, so there is neither rest nor repose for the unfortunates, only tribulation and anguish to the end.— I mean to have some quiet talk with Dr. Jackson, who comes up this afternoon from Glen Haven, and learn something helpful to Elisabeth if he has any information for us. Of one thing I am certain already: she must use water—warm water even—with great discretion now in her present enfeebled state, having no heat to spare in too frequent bathing; and be sure she never bathes in cold water, or before going to bed. The beef tea experiment she need not repeat.—Keep yourself warm, my Child, take fresh air as you can safely, ride rather than walk at present, keep the good watch and consult your experiences about your food, and sleep, and occupations, and, more than all else, encourage good hopes, esteeming yourself gaining as your spirits waken and your interest in life and the little things becomes more active and freshens from week to week. I do not say, day by day. You will have ebbs and languors, and little discouragements, but the months will measure gain, to you, if not in flesh just yet or weight, in comfort and slow mitigation of the old troubles; the cure working itself out for you in the reasonable manner and time. Not to lose is great gain, and the pledge of restoration. So be a good Child and get well in the best way.—And write me, sometimes about your day's occupations and any thing you care to communicate. But be careful about using your eyes, or any of your poor senses, rashly or too long at once. Take care of the draughts of air, and practice your usual caution in every thing. I shall write to you now and then, and have you much in mind.

I hope Louisa will better conditions by any change she may propose and carry out. Clapp is uncertain, but so are any others she may deal with in these times. I don't relish *"the Governess"* in proud people's palaces for any child of mine. There is no better blood nor more noble, to pride upon in any family in Boston into which she may enter or serve, than flows in her own veins and holds itself to the old nobilities still. She must have her way, as all of that folk before her have had, and take the chances. I respect her for the impulse. I have her Book to bring when I come.

Abby must tell me something of herself and studies presently. I wish she may find all she wishes in the drawing School. She has made a hopeful beginning and all depends on herself to make the promise good.

I may run up to Oswego and see my brother on Monday, but cannot say. A night and morning is time enough with him, and I can return for the Rochester train on Tuesday. If you write again after you get this, as you will of course, direct to *"The care of Rev. James Richardson at Rochester N.Y.* I shall be there some days, and shall advize you of my movements from thence. The best of prospects await and attend me: and the fruits be yours, prays

Your absent Father.

To my daughter,
    Anna Bronson Alcott.
      Concord, Mass.

P.S. I have omitted my impressions from visiting the Asylum, and must tell you about it in my next.—

---

[1] Albert H. Tracy of Buffalo. In a letter of January 13, 1857, Emerson mentions "Mr Tracy who is almost as rare a talker as Mr Alcott." (See Rusk, *Emerson Letters,* V, 53.)

[to Mrs. A. Bronson Alcott, Concord; from Rochester, N.Y., November 25, 1857.]

LETTER 57–32

[to Mrs. A. Bronson Alcott, Concord]

26th November, 1857. | Rochester, N.Y.

My Dear,

Yesterday letters and today verses. These will reach you after "Thanksgiving Day," but cannot come too late for confiding Hearts. Faith takes on its complexions from Temperament in its hues even of melancholy and despair. May all be lightsome, genial, and fair in all apartments, in all Hearts in our house, stablished in Concord in spirit as in place, and a Thanksgiving Ode.

Here we have a clear sky and searching cold and snow. Our Company is listed numerously, I am told, for Monday Evening next, and prospects are good for a good beginning of our sittings. Wednesday and Thursday evenings will close them. And I wish to pass on to Buffalo, and Mrs. Drury on Saturday following.

Meanwhile, some letters from you and the weekly bulletin of the family creed.—You shall hear from your wanderer, and often, while he pauses here.

Last evening I was in the city, and saw many people.

Then on Wednesday, I breakfasted with young Morton and Green Smith, his pupil,—Gerret's son,—at Mrs. Sedgwicks. They came over from Peterborough to hear Chapin on Tuesday evening at the Institute, and left by the afternoon train. Morton wishes me to take Mr. Smith's on my way home from he West, and I may.

I am expecting letters from Mrs. Drury and from Richardson, today or tomorrow: and shall drive West by Tuesday certainly or Wednesday of next week. John is expected home from New York to-morrow. Mrs May has good accounts of her husband and Joseph. Dr. Jackson is expected here to morrow and is to lecture in Mr May's Church on Sunday evening. So I shall meet the Hydropathist and measure him for myself. Also, I am expecting letters, and shall be till they come, by every mail. It takes three days or more for them to come by way of Boston, as they must,—where there is more or less delay,—and some carelessness here at this delivery, I am told. But you are sure nevertheless; and good news is good, though late, and bad is converted into good oftentimes by the suspense.

I left home, never so hurriedly and confused as this last time, and wait for the separation and the distance to restore the light and solve our perplexities. Time is the sovereign [sic] ointment, and heals at last.—I have written to Mother, and hope to hear from her or Betsey before I leave here.

The Orchard is ours, and you are mine, Ever and affectionately,

A.B.A.

Mrs. Abby M. Alcott,
Concord.

Lead Thou me On!

I.

"Send kindly Light amid the encircling gloom
And lead me on!
The Night is dark, and I am far from home
Lead Thou me on!
Keep Thou my feet: I do not ask to see
The distant scene; one step enough for me.

II.

I was not ever thus; nor prayed that Thou
    Shouldst lead *me* on!
I loved to choose and see my path; but now
    Lead Thou me on!
I loved day's dazzling light and, spite of fears,
Pride ruled my will; remember not past years.

III.

So long thy power hath blessed me, surely still
    'Twill lead me on
Through dreary doubt, through pain & sorrow till
    The Night be gone,
And with the morn those angel faces smile
Which I have loved long since and lost awhile!"[1]

Rochester, N.Y. 26th November,
1857

[1] John Henry Newman's "The Pillar of the Cloud," with some changes in wording and punctuation.

LETTER 57–33

[to Mrs. A. Bronson Alcott, Concord]

Rochester 1. December | 1857.

My Dear,

You have by this time my letters of Nov. 25 and 26, with the news to dates. Yours of the 24 came to hand and gladdened me by the comforting intelligence on the 27th And now 'tis time I heard from you again, as I shall presently and again, before I leave here for Buffalo and the West. I have written to Mrs. Drury, who returns about this time and makes ready our party at Buffalo. I purpose reaching there by Monday or Tuesday next. Letters of Thursday or Friday's date will come to hand here before I leave on Tuesday coming.

All goes fairly here. I am seeing the best people—Lawyer Danforth of the Boston family, his wife a cousin of Mrs. Henry Longfellow; Judge Warner, at whose Villa I took tea on Sunday with Mrs. Richardson; Mrs. Collins, &c. This evening I am to meet Judge Selden and wife at Mr Danforths. Mrs. Selden is interested in the Conversations and promotes them eagerly. I hear her spoken of as sensible and accomplished, the person of all others to serve us to the best there is here.

The first families are from Puritan Connecticut mostly, and slow to praise hastily the new things. And here Conversations are a novelty, and come scented moreover with the Concord fragrance which it may prove hazardous for the Saints to breathe so freely in Drawing Room and from evening to evening. So our party must be select and less numerous. We are to have three evenings:

Wednesday	to	morrow	*Health.*
Friday	—	—	*Housekeeping.*
Saturday	—	—	*Company.*

Mr. Danforth seems intent on having those only who belong rightly to our party, and is a good manager. So I must do my part to ensure content and success, and you shall have our accounts in my next of these matters.

These things require a little time. I am moving slowly, as you see, and confidently westwards. It will be January, and the New-Year, before I can reach Cincinnati, if I pause at Buffalo and Cleveland, as I should like. Then, for that City and Chicago, all January, to bring me home in February sometime—for a short sally soon Philadelphia, perhaps, and a stop in New-Haven for a day or so on my way to planting and repairs in the Spring. I shall glean something to plant us a little more firmly in the friendly soil of Concord, let us hope and believe, meanwhile. There is prospect of finding in these flourishing Bushes and pocketing honestly some golden handfulls [sic]: here in this city 50 dollars; 75 in that, in another 100, 200, it may be, in another; and, if no more than 30s or 40s. in some, we can beat the bush for the slender winnings, and esteem it luck in these pinching times. It will be something to swell our little income and pay honest debts with in Concord and elsewhere. And, now, I wish yourself and girls were less anxious and restless about what comes to the balance fairly and squarely at last. Content is good weight always and provident of all needs, necessary and lasting.

We have keen cold winds here from the Lake, and rain almost every day. There has been snow but it is gone and left us muddy roads, and wet side walks in the City. Yesterday I was at the Atheneum while reading newspapers: also at the Corinthian Hall, and the bookstores. If you have not had the reading of the "Atlantic Monthly" for December, I can send you mine. My Conversations are advertised in the Rochester papers for this day, which I shall get this evening as I go to Mr. Danforth's where I sleep to night.

I trust you kept Thanksgiving thankfully. Lizzy shall tell me about her admirable pastries: and Anna of Sanborns and the plays.

I might reasonably expect a word from the Authoress and Artist, by this time, and shall soon have the pleasure of breaking their seals, shall I not, proud pair?

Tell me how Dr. Jackson's opinions please you, and Dear Lizzy. I shall hear *particulars* always gladly, *not sadly now*. As soon as may be, dispense with the pellets and powders, and find the strength that can feed itself and increase on the virgin substances—the social influences—friendly food for body and soul.

Farewell all, and

Yours the great Contentments.

Yours faithfully

A. B. A.

Mrs. Abby M. Alcott,
    Concord.

[to Mrs. A. Bronson Alcott, Concord; from Rochester, N.Y., December 4, 1857.]

LETTER 57–34

[to Mrs. A. Bronson Alcott, Concord]

Rochester, 8th December | 1857. | Tuesday.

My Dear,

Yours of Friday last reached me yesterday. I am made glad by its contents, and so go Westwards on my way with the freer spirits. I think I shall leave here sometime to morrow.

My Course of three closed on Saturday evening. The company was select, appreciative, thinking in their hearts the good things were spoken from evening to evening. Mr. Danforth has behaved as became the friend of the East and of Eastern Ideas. I dined at his House on Sunday, and shall meet him again to day to receive *"Your interest* in the matter.[1]

Last evening I met Richardson's people—a party of 70 or more,—at the Union and Republican Newspaper. It promised well, and I meet them again this evening—Channing was here once, you may remember: also your nephew, F. W. Holland, whom I hear spoken of with respect by good people.

I shall be in Buffalo for a week or more, if things go as I hope for me in that City. If not the Symposeum[2] we could wish, then something respectable very, with say, Mrs. Drury, Mr. Tracy, Ex President Fillmore, and Dr. Hosmer, as members of our circle.

You shall direct your letters to me there, Care of nobody. I prefer to call for them at the P. Office.

Yesterday the weather was sunny, the first fair day since my coming here. To day is clear also, and I am to dine with Judge Warner, at his Norman Villa two miles out of town, and come in to the Conversation at Mr. Elder's, where I slept Sunday night.

'Tis a month since I left you and must or may be another before I set my face Eastwards. I may stop a week at Detroit, and another at Albany.

My letters of Friday last with newspapers must have come to your hands. Continue to write often and fully as in your last.

Ever Yours,
A. B. A.

Mrs. Abby Alcott,
    Concord.

[1] The receipts from the Course of Conversations.
[2] Alcott generally spelled the word in this manner.

LETTER 57–35

[to Mrs. A. Bronson Alcott, Concord]

Buffalo, 14th December, | 1857. | Monday.

My Dear,

My last letter was dated at Rochester and mailed for Concord on the 8 [torn] Tuesday. On that evening and Wednesday following I had Conversations. I heard Starr King's Lecture on Thursday evening, and slept at the house of Mr. Prindle in the city after it. I reached here about 2 P.M on Friday and took lodgings at the American House. This morning, I left there, and am at Mrs. Lyon's Boarding House where Martha Hosmer and husband, Mr. Harlowe, are staying. Mrs. H. arrived from the East on Saturday and brings good news,—the last I have had—from you and the girls. Here, in comfortable quarters, and on reasonable terms, I am to stay till Saturday, and perhaps over till Monday.

Mr. Tracy has taken my designs very kindly to heart, and seems disposed to give the Conversations the best advantages of place and company. He offers his drawing rooms, and invites his friends to come in. 'Tis settled that we have three Evenings.—Wednesday, Thursday and Friday. Mr. Fillmore is to be of the party. Dr. Hosmer takes the matter heartily, also, and will bring some of his best people. I dined at his house yesterday. To day, he took me to see Rev. Dr. Thompson, Dr. West, Principal of a flourishing young ladies Seminary here, and others of his acquaintance. He seems to be an influential || and || person in the city. I find him || one of the most || [p. o.] genial and friendly, || of men || [p. o.]. I was at his Church yesterday forenoon and again in the evening. Mrs. Hosmer and sister inquired about you, remembering earlier and Duxbury days.

I think we may have a circle of select sensible persons, and some profitable evenings. Those whom I have seen have spoken with interest of the Conversations and seem fitted to enjoy them. Eastern Men of Culture take rank as *Magi* || in the estimation of all cultivated citizens || [p. o.] here, || in || the East, || where || [p. o.] and [p. in] Starry Concord rays forth Auroras of Promise to multitudes.

I have spent an evening with Mr. Tracy. He reads Emerson, and admires the blending of genius and common sense in our philosopher. But Compte and the Frenchmen, I judge, are the greater favorites with him and his. He is a man of great much [p. in] acuteness and persistency: of a sceptical habit, logical: || and || reminds me a good deal [3 p. in] of Jefferson both in cast of features and thinking. I asked him, if he had been told of the resemblance, and he said, never till the day before by Healy, who is here painting the Expresident for Congress, and with whom he has dined at Mr. Fillmores Saturday, he took me there. It was after dinner, and we found this genial gentlemanly person in his study, where we sat, discussing Slavery and Kanzas, for a couple of hours. Tracy is a democrat, I am sorry to find, but larger than his party a good deal. The Expresident was candid, conservative, and fearful of consequences. He is sincere in his timidities, I am persuaded, and conscientiously adheres to the Union. I tried to make plain the indebtedness of the Country to Abolitionists and the place they must take in the history of Freedom. Of the parts taken by us, president and Committee of Vigilance, once in Court Square, nothing was said by either, though something significant may have been suggested by my praises of the Rescuers. Mr. Hosmer tells me that he the Expresident [2 p. in] was anxious to meet brother Sam. and regretted he had not seen him when here lately.

Our themes here are the same as at Rochester.

> *Health.*
> *Housekeeping,* and
> *Company.*

You shall hear further how far we prosper with our Buffalo company. I shall write again by Friday or Saturday: and shall leave for Cleveland, certainly by Monday. Meanwhile my letters, now on the way,—nothing since 5th December —must come to hand. I am anxious to hear. Your last letter brought agreeable news. Lizzy must replenish her Spirits by all good helps: flesh and weight will come—it may be so slowly and imperceptibly as to tell nothing to the senses ‖ and ‖ or the scales for some time—but she must not expect Nature to rally from such a shock forthwith to bring the health she so desires. Pray let me know just how she is, *and how she Behaves by Night and by day.* I can excuse every thing. Only she must take the part of painstaker about herself, and not defeat the helps and hopes of careful nurses and kindred, by any imprudences of hers. I will not talk for [erasure]—my precious patient, but come home to see to it, eye to eye, if she will not mind me otherwise.

It may be well for you to look in upon our tenants at "The Orchard" and see if there be waste of matters &c there. Have you wood, and other household comforts? I hear of Anna's praises even out here so far the trumpets have sounded them. Miss Heron is here, and plays to night in *Medea.* She came to "The American House" just before I left it. I may see her to morrow night.

The weather has been "Indian" for the last three days.

Yours
with much love
A.B.A.

Mrs. Abby Alcott.

LETTER 57–36

[to Mrs. A. Bronson Alcott, Concord]

Buffalo, 18 December | 1857. | Friday.

My Dear,

Your full particular letter of Sunday, with Elisabeths choice little bulletin of herself, came yesterday to reassure and forward me to Cleveland to morrow. There I may be for the week to come, and you shall address me there till otherwise advised.

Here, I have had very good company and an agreeable evening, and am fairly advertised for something better on my return eastwards. Mr. Tracy and Dr. Hosmer take the matter in hand heartily, and mean to give the next Course some advantages found not easy to secure to this first experiment. So the better things await us. Mrs. Drury, who is a daughter, it seems, of Commodore Medwin, is still at Utica with her father; the Sturgen family are there also, but they return here after Christmas. She is much interested and will promote our circle and success.

Also at Rochester, I am invited to pause and talk with a larger party which Mr. Danforth promises to make ready for me: and a worthy citizen, Mr. Prindle, at whose house I slept a night, asks me to stay with him while I am in that city. At Cleveland, I hope to find my friend, John A. Foote, formerly of Cheshire, also Horace, his brother, and a favorite pupil of mine. They are sons of the late [2 p. in] Gov. Foote, and very hospitable people. Mrs. Foote was a pupil of mine also. I please myself with having a good time with them and their city. Medina is about twenty miles distant. I am undecided as to visiting my friends there. It will be Christmas and New-Year's day, so I may ride over and spend a little while with Uncle Noah, and the cousins.

You have written to mother, but do not write of having heard any thing from her. Nor have I. But she will write presently, I doubt not, of her condition, and of Sister Betsey. Chatfield, to whom I wrote from Syracuse, does not respond. Nor have I heard further from brother Sam. Have you written to him since he has been at Glen Haven? He will like to hear from you.

I am made comfortable in every comfort, the traveller need desire. The washer-woman brings in my two and a half dozen before I leave in the morning.— I have added some collars and pocket hand kerchiefs, since I left home.

The weather has been delightful for the week past. There is fair sun, and a cloudless sky. Yesterday strolled about the city, and along the shore of Erie Lake. 'Tis a pity I am not going to the Niagara falls, but may on my way homewards from Chicago & Detroit.

I wrote at length and mailed to you last Monday. May Heaven's blessings rest on you and ours.

Affectionately
A. B. A.

LETTER 57–37

[to Mrs. A. Bronson Alcott, Concord]

Buffalo 19th December | 1857. | Saturday—
My Dear,

Good luck attends good ladies and whatsoever they espouse heartily, be it person or purpose. And so Mrs. Drury, good lady, arrives last night, and arrests her fugitive from taking the rails today as he had purposed for Cleveland: she gathering her company for him forthwith. Fillmore, Tracy, Dr. and Mrs. Hosmer, Rev. Dr. Thompson, Dr. West and lady, Mr. Putnam, and others of our first party joining hers, to make a good company for Monday Tuesday and Wednesday evening of next week. We meet at Dr. Flints. Dr. F. is professor in the Medical School here, and a noble person to see. He is from the East somewhere, and Mrs. Flint is from Boston. I was at her house last evening, and found her very sensible and agreeable. She knew some of the old families and yours among the rest:—your father, Mrs. Carey, Perrin May, Dr. Freeman, Dr. Greenwood. Sarah, her daughter, and a most lovely girl, was at the Sedgwick's school at Lenox—with Ellen Emerson and thinks much of her, as does Mrs F. of Mr. Emerson.—Let us hope for fair evenings and the great discourse.

I am well pleased with my quarters here at Mrs Lyons, where I have every comfort, a good chamber, and fire when I wish one, unexceptionable table, and ready service. I shall be here now till Thursday or Friday, and will write again meanwhile. My last left here yesterday. Then I was purposing to go to Cleveland to day, and so wrote as you will see.—I may turn homewards from Cincinnati, stopping for a week or so at Rochester, and perhaps at Albany. 'Tis plain this will be a fair advertising tour, and something more, if the Cities West prove as friendly to me as those I have passed. We shall see and report from station to station.—I may pass the Holidays at Medina.

Has Abby gone to Boston? Anna, dear, has fallen into silence lately. But Sanborn and the Show are absorbing, and shall acquit my merry maid of any seeming sad neglects for this time. Your accounts of all are very comforting; so full and particular, and hopeful withal. Christmas and the New-Year must add their best and appropriate assurances. Let me know the state of family affairs as soon as may be,—and your wishes. This wide West must yet do its part in payment of some debts: let us hope the clear quittance by Spring. But spring must determine for us as it may.—

To-morrow, I am to address Dr. Hosmer's Sunday School, and see some of his people in the evening.

With my prayers for dear Lizzy, and sisters, I am

Yours faithfully,
A.B.A.

Harris[1] letter forwarded by you, has just come to hand, and may take me to *St. Louis* before I return to you.

Mrs. Abby Alcott,
Concord.

[1] William Torrey Harris (1835–1909). Harris first met Alcott while a student at Yale College, and beginning with the letter here referred to was to become a most important factor in Alcott's career. He was Superintendent of Schools in St. Louis; founder and editor of the *Journal of Speculative Philosophy;* active in the Concord School of Philosophy; and, later, United States Commissioner of Education. For a biography of him, see Kurt F. Leidecker, *Yankee Teacher: The Life of William Torrey Harris* (New York, 1946).

[to Louisa, Concord; from Buffalo, N.Y., December 21, 1857.]

LETTER 57–38[1]

[to William Torrey Harris, St. Louis]

Buffalo 22nd December | 1857.

Dear Sir,

Your letter dated Nov. 26th. has just reached me here. The stranger who kindly waited upon me at the New Haven Station, and expressed an interest in my thoughts and Conversations there, I distinctly remember, and am well pleased to hear from again, out of the West, so friendly to free and formidable thinking, to the daring designs of widest scope—American throughout in spirit and deed. I am spending a season in these wild parts, pausing a little at the cities, going out and returning—to Cleveland presently, and from thence to Cincinnati sometime in January. If the way were fairly opened for me, as you and your friends—the young men you speak of in your letter, have thought of sometimes, I might perhaps extend my jaunt as far as St. Louis, and spend some weeks, before my return to the East. If you think it might be compassed with profit to the parties concerned, and will signify your wishes in the matter, please address the same to me by letter to Cincinnati and I will reply. I shall be there as early as the 5 or 7—of January and stay some three weeks or more, after which I can pass on to St. Louis, if you wish me to come. I enclose a Circular of some topics for discourse, but others may please better, and can be adopted according to place and company.

As to books, "Jamblichus"[2] you must order from England. "The Dial", I can furnish, all but two numbers, which are scarcer, and not to be had. There are four Volumes of it.

The Orphic Discussions I must not open, so near the ‖ close ‖ end of my sheet. If I should venture into your neighbourhood, we might hope these would find the hospitable entertainment, and the full treatment.

Please present my regards to your Companions, and take my expression of good hope in them and yourself.

Very cordially
Yours
A. Bronson Alcott.

[1] From a copy, in Alcott's hand, in the Alcott-Pratt Collection. The original is in the Alcott-Harris Collection in the Concord Free Public Library (see Appendix B).
[2] Jamblichus' *Life of Pythagoras*.

LETTER 57-39

[to Mrs. A. Bronson Alcott, Concord]

Cleveland, Ohio | 27th December 1857. | Sunday.

My Dear,

I left Buffalo last Thursday, and slept at the house of Horace Hitchcock where I am staying while I tarry in Cleveland. Mr. Hitchcock remembers pleasant days passed as a child by him at the Cheshire School, and seems gratified, if not proud, of entertaining his Teacher and friend, whom he has followed, strange to say, through "Dials," and other reporters of progress or otherwise, up to the present moment. His hospitalities are unstinted and his house a pleasant home for me. His brother in-law, Mr. Foote, is now gone to Connecticut, so I shall not see him.

I went immediately to the *Post Office* but there was nothing, no, for me: nor have any letters come to hand since your last, dated 13th. December. ‖ since which time I have ‖ I wrote to you on the 14th. and again on the 17th. to Louisa on the 21st., and Mr. Harris letter with your P.S. came to hand on the 19th. I begin to suspect your letters may be lying for me at Buffalo. You will of course write me at once, and relieve me of the anxieties of suspense. Christmas has passed, and, I trust, brought merriments, without stint, sadness or sorrows, to the family and friends. Let me hear the particulars—household doings, the Dickens' entertainments, and the village varieties. I pray dear Lizzy may have been able to participate, in some sort, and to be merry with the rest of you.

I am to be here for a few days. Mr. Chapin remembers our evenings when I was here before, and is doing his best for gathering a suitable company for me. George Bradburn is here, also Mrs. B. and assisting him. There is good hope of some thirty persons or more, and we wish to meet on Monday, Tuesday and Wednesday evenings. I think I may leave here for Cincinnati, by Friday or Saturday. The roads are so bad and the staging to Medina, that I hesitate venturing that way. I can do so returning, and have my time the more at command. No 'tis almost midwinter and I am not yet ready to face Eastwards, as I wished and hoped by this time. Still Cincinnati, Chicago, St Louis, are far South and West of me, and perhaps to be visited, one, or all of them, before I shall find myself journeying homeward. Here I am and so far now, and may as well make the circuit, perhaps, and the bold adventure, while it is feasible, and promises spoils. I can tell better about it when I have tryed [*sic*] Cincinnati after the New-Year of '58.—These backwoodsmen are a hearty, yet heady, and blunt bearing people, seeming to take me kindly enough, for a wonder, and to like me rather well. So I shall make the most of it, of them and of their good-nature, for your sakes, as for theirs.

Pleasant weather, with a slight snow, but not wintry. Direct to Cincinnati.

To the five, one and all, the Season's fair complements [*sic*], with Much Love and Hope,

A.B.A.

PART ELEVEN

✠

1858–1859

[to Mrs. A. Bronson Alcott, Concord]

Cleveland, Ohio, 1 January | 1858.

My Dear,

I am here most comfortably housed and hospitably cared for by my Cheshire pupil, a successful merchant now and respectable citizen. His kindness and his good wife's welcome, render my stay an enjoyment here in these fast parts where most ears are closed to me, and the gains are slow and sorry as yet. I shall leave here on Monday and sleep same night in Cincinnati where letters from home must await me. I sent to Buffalo and got yours and Annas' of the 21 and 22. and yesterday brought me another of the 27th. It was long to wait. But the contents have removed some anxieties, and shall speed me the less unwillingly toward the City of the West. You give me particulars, Anna also, and my precious patient herself. Her notes of business, of coverlets of hexagonal seam, of good friends kindnesses, all fairly written by the pale figures yet firmly, were comforting to her father's eyes. I beg she have discretion given her to ford this lake of dangers and come safely to the terra firma again. Temperance, Temperance, and wise moderation: select, simple, steadfast in the best things, and avoidance of the dainties. Madame Hoar's sympathetic recipe is good forever and safe. The kindly care, simple food regularly taken, neither too much, nor too sparingly, fresh air, and as much exercise as the strength permits: Add thereto, the cordials and elixirs of company, occupation, and cheerful hope.—I shall try to see Dr. Jackson again on my way homewards. And if meanwhile yourself or Lizzy think best to consult Dr. Geist further, send for him to come up and prescribe. I don't think of any suitable book for her hearing read just now. Caution the maid about being up of nights, sewing or on worse mischiefs bent. She risks all on such enterprizes, and is too weak to venture so. Dr. Jackson sends his patients to bed at 9. and keeps them there snug and safe till 5. He insists, persists in this, as in other essentials, and heals. I am glad to hear of brother Sam's improvement under his treatment.

To morrow evening closes my engagement here. We have had two sittings: not many but sensible people, and fair success. Next week I will report progress from the Metropolis witherwards I have been creeping so tardily. But I was advertising my self at these intermediate places along, and stablishing Committees of one or more for coming seasons. Nor must I return till the ways are surveyed, and my work is done. I have written to Harris and hope to hear from him while in Cincinnati. Hard times and no money for me, or very little. But I hope to send soon a ten or twenty from my gleanings, if not something more. Once in Cincinnati and seeing definitely how it is going there, I can find what sum I may safely spare and reserve ample means beside for future adventures. Nor will my winter be wasted if I shall have paid my court to good people, and my expenses, no more. I may not distrust Cincinnati.

Davis, the impertinent, to beg your custom so and impose it then, and now importune you for money. He shall be the last man to get a farthing, and have that till he begs no more. And I shall take care to seal safe the letters. Pay Collier his rent in full, and if the money does not hold out, to Hastings and Everett all you can on accounts. Possibly some bills may be sent down from Walpole, but I shall see to that matter. Let me know our obligations as soon as you have the sum. Are we not as well off or better than we have been at the New-Year aforetimes? Spring must better further let us believe and bring about. The girls are popular, busy, and contented. If the cup of blessings does not overflow it is far from empty; nor are we forbidden to taste of the fountains of joy and hope. I shall write again soon.

Here is a scant return for your ample sheets, and a dull report of myself. Next to Dear Lizzy you are oftenest in my thoughts, as I wander wide from you and home. To God be thanks for all you have been and are to Yours ever

A. B. A.

Also thanks to Anna for her full letters. From the others something recently?

LETTER 58–2

[to Mrs. A. Bronson Alcott, Concord]

Cincinnati 7th January 1858.

My Dear,

I have your letters. Yours, Louisa's, Abbys, Anna's, all so full and particular. They came yesterday. May the New Year's pleasures ripen into blessings and stores of comforts. There is Hope to-day, nor may we distrust tomorrow's good designs for us all. This move seems not so bad that plants us again in historic grounds, with prospects of coming springs and summers spent together in our "Orchard Home". The girls may go and come ‖ when called ‖ as opportunity offers. I wish Abby may have a pleasant visit. Louisa's turn will come presently and Anna's too if they have patience and faith to wait a little.

Your visit to the City, though it shall be for only a day, will refresh and encourage you. You will see good friends, and perhaps the best and most servicable [sic] of all just now, Dr. Geist. Yet I wish he might see his patient rather and judge from sight, if he will, and Elisabeth consents. Fair hopes, the cheerful views, the amplest draughts of these, and the cordial of good spirits—these—every day and always—the potent pellets to lay the ghosts and rout the goblin troop of miseries.

I left Cleveland last Monday. It was Christmas and New Year's Holidays, but I was willing to wait there for the ten days. And they wish me to stop and give them three evenings more on my return homewards. Perhaps I may: and again at Syracuse and Albany. But I shall not venture further West, I think, unless invited by Harris, which looks unlikely in these pressing times.

Here three evenings are proposed for Monday Tuesday and Thursday of next week. They are to be advertised, and Conway is to notice them from his pulpit on Sunday. He and Spofford are busy in the matter. They can promise nothing very brilliant as might have happened in rosier times, but yet something worth having, and good as far it can go just now.

Last evening I took tea at Dr. Wilsons. She, Mrs. W, you remember, as my kind hostess when I was here before. She leaves in a few days to visit her daughter Cary, now Mrs. Allan, residing at Richmond, Virginia. I am sorry to find her troubled and anxious about her son, now an invalid, and perhaps never to recover from his epilepsies.

I am taken and to stay while in the city at Mr William Greenes. Mr. Greene is one of the most respectable citizens and takes pride and pleasure in entertaining Eastern company. He is from Rhode Island.

I wish to send some money to you but must not yet. You shall hear from me soon when I have particulars, and I will tell you where to direct your letters next.

Heaven preserve you and yours

prays

Your Husband.

Mrs. Abby M. Alcott.

P.S.   If you write before Wednesday the 13. I think it will reach me here as I may not leave Cincinnati till Monday the 18. for the East.

LETTER 58–3

[to Mrs. A. Bronson Alcott, Concord]

Cincinnati, January 9th | 1858. | Saturday.

My Dear,

Yours dated 4th January has just reached me here. And I add now to mine of the 7th on its way to you, that I purpose leaving here on Friday early and to reach Syracuse to spend Sunday there, and to be with you by Tuesday following —the 19. Tis in vain to press my interests further West just now, and while my thoughts are so constantly with you and yours. I may be detained some days later but shall not feel free to make further engagements in these parts.

My work is advertised here for Monday, Tuesday and Thursday evenings, 12—13 and 15—as you will see by the Card and Notices enclosed.[1] The prospects are fair for a select company. This evening, I meet "The Young Men's Literary Club": To morrow dine with Spofford and see Judge James, Mrs Perkins, Mr. Cranch and others invited. I have met Dr. Rolker and Stallo pleasantly.

Conway will advertise me to his congregation to morrow.

—

Tuesday P.M. | 13th.

—   Meanwhile, since writing the foregoing and not sending, Anna's letter enclosing the Drs. has come to hasten my return.[2] But I find I cannot reach you sooner than Tuesday sometime of next week. And must wait, either at Cleveland —where I have an engagement for Friday, Saturday and Sunday evenings—or at

Syracuse as I purposed at first—to ride onwards on Monday reaching Boston late in the Night.—

I give my third Conversation on Thursday evening, and shall leave, as I said, early on Friday for Cleveland to spend the Sunday there.

Last evening's company was select as promised, and a success. Many of my former guests were present, Mrs. Wilson and son Davis, Dr. Rolker, Mr and Mrs Greene,—my kind entertainers—Mr and Mrs Flagg and many more. Spofford and Conway behave handsomely in the matter and are bent on making the most of it. My numbers are about fifty and of these many ladies. To-night I am to speak on *"Hearts,"* and their *promises.*

My letter will not reach you till Monday possibly, and Tuesday I hope to be with you all. Whisper dear memories to my feeble shadow and pale: I shall see and say the rest and precious very soon.

My sympathies are with you all.

A. B. A.

¹ Monday, Tuesday, and Thursday were January 11, 12, and 14.
² An entry in Louisa's Journal, for January, reads, "Lizzie much worse; Dr. G. says there is no hope." (See Cheney, p. 96.)

LETTER 58–4

[to Mrs. A. Bronson Alcott, Concord]

Cleveland, Sunday | 17 January 1858

My Dear,

I shall so fast follow in person that I would not write a word, did I not fear you must wonder anxiously about the delay, adding thereby the needless to the necessary sorrows. Behold me thus far on my way homewards and here staying restlessly. Yet to reach you in person, if the roads prove faithful to their trust late on Friday evening, unless failing to connect at Worcester, I may have to sleep in Boston, and come up early on Saturday. I am detained contrary to assurances here by three days' time. Friday evening last, Saturday and Sunday were to have been mine but I find now 'tis Monday, Tuesday and Wednesday of this week. I have my through ticket and shall take Thursday morning's train, impatient as I am to be at home, and beside my Child. May every encouragement gladden her chamber, and hers the cheerful hours. Anna's note makes me anxious, nor is she long absent from my thoughts whether by day or by night.

Cincinnati served me handsomely again. I gave them three evenings which they liked they said, and pressed me for a fourth, which I added. All were good, and this last very good, so excellent the company said they must have more of the sort in autumn. So Conway and Spofford will make all ready and let me know.

Here Bradburn has made sure of the right persons and promises fair things. I am at Hitchcocks. To day attended Church piously, and am to pass this evening with Bradburn the Pagan, at his house. Mr Foote has returned.

No snow yet, but for the last week mild weather in Cincinnati.

To Elisabeth dear memories and sweet hours till I see her, with love and sympathies to the rest.

Your ever and entirely
A. B. A.

Mrs. A. May Alcott.
No letters from you since the 6th. Spofford will remail to me here.

LETTER 58–5[1]

[to Ainsworth R. Spofford, Cincinnati]

Concord 25th Jan. 1858.

Dear Sir,

I reached home on Saturday last to find my family comfortable; my daughter Elisabeth, though feeble very, still better than I expected to find her and hopeful of recovery.

Bradburn's company at Cleveland was very good and came to take the good parts for the three evenings.

This morning's mail brings me the "Cincinnati Daily Enquirer Newspaper containing the paragraphs on "Mr. Alcott's Conversations." or Echoes of Emerson; and so rather good bad praises of him.

We crossed Walden yesterday, Emerson, his children and myself, the ice being solid and supporting to the Idealists' feet as he glided across and struck into the woodpaths on the opposite shore. Last evening I saw Thoreau, who is trenchant and masterly as ever. He had been reading some papers in Drawing rooms to a good company lately at Lynn.

I enclose the overplus of money, with my thanks to yourself and friends for their interest in our hasty evening's performances. I am to go to Lynn and New Bedford presently.

The weather is mild and sunny today and the fields have the air and port of spring.

Very cordially
Yours,
A. Bronson Alcott.

A. R. Spofford Esqr
  Cincinnati.

[1] MS. owned by the Library of Congress.

LETTER 58–6

[to William Russell, Lancaster, Mass.]

Concord 10th Feb. 1858.

Dear Sir,

Yours of the 8th has just come to hand. It finds me but returned from my jaunt into the West a few days ago, and with some engagements to meet pres-

279

ently in the Eastern cities. Among them is the prospect of meeting a Class in New-Haven sometime within the present month, and, if I shall pass through Lancaster[1] going or returning I will pause for a day or two at your house, and we will then review some of our past times together, along with those portions of mine which belong properly to Mr. Barnard's Journal. I shall be quite pleased to do so: and will bring the necessary papers when I come.

The West has been generous considering the pressure on men's fortunes for the last months. I was at Syracuse, Rochester, Buffalo, Cleveland, and Cincinnati, a fortnight or thereabout at these cities all, and met select and agreeable companies in most of them. I am invited to New-Haven by Prof Bailey of Yale College, and a former pupil of yours, he tells me. I will write and let you know when I can come to Lancaster.

Elisabeth continues to be comfortable.[2] The other members of my family are well. Abby is now for a month in Boston with her kinsfolk.

You are very kind to write particulars of yours: to all of your children and to Mrs Russell my regards with Mrs Alcotts.

Cordially,
Your friend.
A. Bronson Alcott

Mr. William Russell
    Lancaster.

[1] About twenty miles west of Concord.
[2] Elizabeth died on March 14.

LETTER 58–7[1]

[to Elizabeth Oakes Smith, New York City]

Concord, | 4th March, 1858.

Dear Mrs. Oak [sic] Smith,

My daughter Louisa, has some stories by her, which she would like to see printed in some of the magazines. But feeling diffident of offering them herself, she asks me to propose them for your reading (and acceptance she hopes) if you shall think it worth the while, and will take the trouble to write saying whether she may send you a sample. I think them excellent, and shall be pleased and proud to find they suit you.

We are now settled in Concord beside Emerson and Hawthorne.

My family are well, with the exception of our third child Elisabeth, about whose recovery from a long illness we are all anxious just now.

With good hopes for your Magazine,[2]

I am,
Cordially Yours
A. Bronson Alcott.

Mrs. E. Oak [sic] Smith
    N.Y.

[1] MS. in the Clifton Waller Barrett Library, University of Virginia.
[2] *Emerson's Magazine and Putnam's Monthly.* For a brief account of this periodical, see Frank Luther Mott, *A History of American Magazines, 1850–1865* (Cambridge, Mass., 1938), pp. 448–51.

LETTER 58-8

[to Charles A. Dana]

Concord, Mass, | 4. November, 1858.

Dear Sir,

I have to thank you for the Book of Poetry which came yesterday, and is adopted by my wife and daughters as a delightful inmate and profitable companion of our Household.[1] I find most of my favorites in the collection, and think the Public will confess to being largely your debtor for your painstaking. Many of the poems will be new and a surprize to the readers.

If convenient, may I ask of you to correct the mistake of residence as regards myself in your list of Lecturers. I am settled here in Concord, Mass, but you printed me at Walpole, N.H. It is a small matter, but may prevent future mistakes.

Yours, obliged,
A. Bronson Alcott.

[1] Charles A. Dana, comp. *The Household Book of Poetry.*

LETTER 58-9

[to Mrs. Anna Alcott, Oriskany Falls, N.Y.]

Concord, Mass. | November. 25th. 1858.

Dear Mother,

We have heard nothing from you since last February; Then you wrote us one of your good letters, and sister Betsey added her welcome Postscript of particulars. I have written once since certainly, and now write again; hoping to hear of your present welfare, and especially as regards your health and Spirits. I wish you may be enjoying the good old age you have reached, to find the satisfactions your busy life-long endeavours deserve. Are you free from the old troubles now, and in peaceful possession of your Mind. I trust you are, and still active about your works of industry and pains-taking for others. If I can possibly take Betsey's on my way out West this season, I shall come in sometime upon you all—and see for myself how you are. But you will write or Betsey for you soon, and let us hear about yourselves. Then if I take my trunk I shall bring along the *"Waterbury Book,"* and we will talk over together those early times. There is a good deal about the planting of Buckshill, Spindle Hill, of the *Welton's, Warner's,* and *Alcocks.* Also about Plymouth, the Bronsons and Blakeslees. You can tell me of many matters attended to in the history, and so live over the old times again. There is a Genealogy of the Principal Families—Ours, on both sides, and pretty full. How Uncle Noah will enjoy the Book.

I mean to leave home some day in next week, and may be gone two months going as far West as Chicago and St. Louis, and stopping at the chief cities to talk ten days or a fortnight in a place—beginning at Albany perhaps.

We are all well. Louisa and Abby are to spend the winter in Boston. Louisa has been there some weeks, and Abby left us yesterday. Louisa writes for the Magazines, and Abby takes lessons in drawing. My wife and Anna keep house while I am absent. We have had a busy time since last March repairing our house and putting things in order about the place. It is now comfortable and we like it. I wish your visit could have happened at a more favorable time for us all.—We picked 35 barrels of apples this fall, and our garden was fruitful. Another season I can give more exclusively to out-door improvements.

I hope you are well and prosperous. Write soon. My wife and girls will be glad to hear from you all during my absence. They send their regards, to which let me add mine,

with the love of
Your Son,
A. Bronson Alcott.

Mrs. Anna Alcott.

LETTER 58–10

[to Mrs. A. Bronson Alcott, Concord]

Syracuse December 4th 1858.

My dear,

I have just reached here and dined, having passed yesterday in Albany. Dr. Sprague was gone to New-York, and Mayo was from home lecturing. Mrs. M. gave me the hospitable reception, offered her ample parlours, and seemed heartily interested in having some Conversations on my return. She has no doubt that a small company can be gathered for me in Albany.

Here, on comparing prospects a little with your brother, I find matters look hopefully. He has made a list of some sixty persons, and I am to see Mrs. Davis this evening to learn more about matters. As Mr. May is to be at Peterborough on Monday and Tuesday of next week, I am in doubt whether to pause a few days, or pass on, and discourse here on my return. I think I shall leave on Monday for Rochester and may reach Buffalo to sleep. If I find Mr. Danforth at home we can arrange forthwith for Rochester. I intend reaching Chicago by Saturday certainly, to which place you shall address your letters.

Your brother seems about as you last saw him in Concord. He means to leave early in January for Europe. Joseph is expected and his father waits to see him. He was improving by the last accounts from Paris. Bonny is here tall and personable to look upon. He is improving the fine sliding this afternoon. Charlotte and baby seem nicely. Mrs. May appears well, and Charlotte the elder spread us one of her simple dinners.—I shall write again before I leave on Monday or Tuesday, with something more to communicate. Every thing bids fair thus far and encouraging for this Western tour.

In Boston, Abby was not sure of staying long, I found, and seemed a little disappointed about her chances. I saw her at Mr. Sargents. She is looking stately and handsome. Mrs Cheney has her interests at heart and so has Miss. Peabody.

Louisa bore herself proudly and gave me great pleasure. We had a walk together on the Common with Alice[?]. I took a story to the Union, but did not find "Clapp" to speak with him about her for his Paper. Mr. S. E. Sewall was very kind, and willingly gave me the Ten dollars for expenses. He thought himself and Mrs. S. might visit you and spend a night sometime soon. It will give you much pleasure, I know, to see and entertain them.

My passage to Chicago was $26.00. I shall have wherewith to stop for arrangements at the cities as I go West. My wallet leaves me independent of porters, and I like the convenience of this simple outfit. Presently I hope to add an article or two if necessary.

There is sleighing here, but the weather is not cold.

Heaven spare and give you peace.

Ever Yours
A. Bronson Alcott.

Mrs. Abby Alcott
Concord

LETTER 58-11

[to Mrs. A. Bronson Alcott, Concord]

Chicago, Illinois, 11th December, | 1858.

My dear,

I wrote from Syracuse, Saturday 4th. Sunday was rainy. I read Barnard's Journal and other things in your brother's Library, which I had alone all the morning. There was but one Service at the Church, so I had something of the Minister in the afternoon and evening awhile: Then called on Mrs. Davis and staid till 10. or later. She was expecting first copies of her Book just published by Ticknor and Fields, "The Life and Times of Sir Philip Sydney." I found her wishing some Conversations, and believing much in Mr. Alcott. She had been in Boston lately and seen Fields, Whipple, and others of that set, had dined at Fields, there met Abby May, and her brothers at Dorchester. She was sensible and kindly disposed as one could desire to Eastern thoughts and New-England people. I think we may see her sometime in Concord a guest for a day or so.—I saw nobody in Syracuse. The weather was impropitious, and your brother anxious about himself and his family. We thought of going to Peterborough on Monday, but he refrained on account of his wife's unwillingness and some re-lapse seemingly of hers into the old malady. I should not be surprized if he found it difficult to reconcile her to his absence, and should postpone his visit across the Seas finally. His courage seemed failing, and Joe's condition may determine his future movements.—Mr. Fish of Cortland, formerly of Hopedale; also Mr. Lee of Auburn, dined with us on Monday. Mr. Lee is a Universalist minister, and wishes me to meet a company of his friends at Auburn on my return Eastwards.—

At 3 P.M (Monday) I left for Rochester slept at the Osburn Home, and saw Danforth, Prindle, and Bronson on Tuesday. Danforth thought we might have some evenings on my way East, and will write and let me know whether to stop or not. Mr. Bronson, an enterprizing merchant here, and of our family, asked me to be his guest. Mrs. Bronson, his wife, is an intelligent person, given to good thinking and good works. I was at the house last winter and liked her very well.

283

Richardson was about leaving for good, himself and family; the society broken up, rent asunder by spiritualism, abolition, and Jamic's[?] fatuities.

At 12. I took the train for Buffalo. Spent the evening with Dr. Warner. Slept at his house, and breakfasted on Wednesday. Dr. W. was born and bred within a mile of Spindle Hill. He knew all about us. He was glad to see me, entertained me hospitably, and hopes to have a good company ready to meet me on my way home. It looked as if it might be so. Dr. Warner is in good practice and repute here in Buffalo. His wife is a western woman, (the daughter of an early settler in the wild lands whereon the city stands now.) and an agreeable person to know. A Mr. and Mrs. Howland from New-Bedford some thirty years ago, passed the evening with us.—I left for Detroit by the Chicago Express train, passing across the Lower Canada country, reaching Detroit Ferry after dark, and taking supper in the Boat as we crossed. As I took the lower route, I missed seeing the Falls; we rode on all night through Kalamazoo and the smaller towns, reaching Chicago at 1. oclock on Thursday to dine late at the Tremont House. I would have stopped and seen Mr. Mumford at Detroit, but for his absence at the East during the winter.—

Wiley greeted me heartily at his Banking House, and presently went for his friend Mr. Noyes, who took me to his house where I found Mrs. N. a handsome woman, with a bright babe, her firstborn, and a brother of Mr. N.—all taking me kindly in keeping and member of the family circle. Here I am to stay while in this city. We discussed the Conversations—ways and means therefor—all the evening, and fixed upon three evenings for next week certainly, with one or more, if trial warrants for the week following, which will bring us close upon the holidays and the New Year. Yesterday, Sam. Greeley[1] dined with us, and invited me to take tea and pass the evening at his house. He takes an active part in promoting my interests here, and the Gains for you.—Particulars in my next.—

To-morrow, Sunday, I am to speak with the children of the Sunday Schools, Mr. Noyes', and Ministry to the Poor. Mr. Noyes urges me to preach for him, but I must defer to the Parlour, and the accustomed teachings. His Drawing rooms are large, & will seat a hundred persons comfortably. They speak of a good company, and are in earnest about the matter.

I found Sam. and his family, hearty and agreeable, staid all evening, talked about house, and house repairs, yourself and girls, largely, and he accompanied me back to Mr. Noyes. He speaks of prosperities here, has a good house, is much respected, I judge, and an efficient man for the West. He has prospects of city street-paving, which he hopes to make lucrative, and thinks Alfred Wilkinson, may join him, with a capital at command, to undertake heavy contracts and carry them out effectually. His wife was cordial and pleasant. There are two children, boys, and of the May type decisively. She has a sister here married and living next neighbour. Sam. told stories of his father, and repeated some of your best ones of Fruitlands and the heroic periods of our history. The Clarkes, I have not seen, but shall next week and some Eastern people. I have not called on the Hosmers: have seen Mr. Barty, former minister at Framingham and Lowell, and now out here as Librarian of the Chicago Historical Society.

I am in health and spirits with promise of agreeable days here for the coming fortnight. My room is comfortable: an open grate, next best to the fireplace and billets, so you may think of me in my element, and blazing, or about blazing professionally in the due time athwart[?] the West. I don't mean the setting, but the rising Light, of course, and Aurora of the Eastern Sky.

The weather is cold and the winds raw and piercing for Lake Michigan. There is no snow. Tis a wide spread city of the Plain, with costly blocks of marble and freestone, open squares without houses or improvements of any sort, prairies grounds, & uneven streets, stretching straight for miles in the distance, and all the growth of a night: 125000 inhabitants and doubling its population every five years.

7. PM. Mrs. Noyes brings in your brother's letter which I enclose. I shall expect something from you by Monday or the middle of next week.—All's well.

Much love to dear Anna, and regards to the good John. I think of you daily. God preserve and keep you and yours safe and sound forever.

Ever Yours,
and affectionately,
A. B. A.—

Mrs. Abby Alcott.
Concord.

¹ Samuel Greele.

LETTER 58–12

[to Mrs. A. Bronson Alcott, Concord]

Chicago, Illinois, Dec. 16. 1858.

My Dear,/

Your letters of 7 and 10, with Anna's Village Chronicle, came to hand on the 11 and 14. For all these pleasant things they contain—thanks, thanks, and the wish for more in due time. I wish I might give as good as I get. But cannot. Yet you shall have the best I have from my Diary.

On Saturday the 11th. I wrote to you, and on the 14th mailed a newspaper. Sunday. Mr. Noyes announced my Conversations to his Congregation, and I addressed the Sunday Schools. Monday. I see Wiley¹ and Sam Greele. They conclude tis best to have the Conversations at the Hall of the Young Men's Association: three Conversations on Tuesday, Friday, and Monday evenings, and to advertise them in the newspapers, with Emerson's commendations from the New Cyclopedia.² *Tuesday evening.* A good company, but not numerous, the snow falling fast. Yet we have a good time and a most hopeful beginning. We shall have many more to-night, as, from what I learn, our first evening was thought delightful. Sam. Greele expressed himself greatly pleased, as did his friends who came. *Wednesday evening.* Mr. Noyes' Parlours were filled, it being the Sociable. The Clarkes were here, Sam. and his wife. Next Wednesday evening is to be mine for Conversation, and the entertainments.

Thursday, (Yesterday) Horace Greeley dined with us. In the evening he read a good lecture on "Great Men." I think he may come to the Conversation this evening. Miss Willis from Portland dined with us. She is a niece of Ben's, and knew a good deal about our family. She is an agreeable girl, and sensible also.

Mr. Noyes presses me to preach for him next Sunday evening. But I defer in preference to the select company to be at his house on Wednesday evening. He is a strong man and makes his mark on men. I admire his handsome, kindly wife, and enjoy my quarters here for the time greatly. I shall stay till Thursday certainly, and may pass the Christmas here. I have written to Harris at St. Louis, and hope to hear from him by Monday, if not before. You shall address me here to the care of Mr. Noyes.

Our expectations are moderate. Every body is pinched for money out here, and you know my things are not of the most substantial seeming. Yet we shall glean something as we go, and have a profitable season, let us hope, and take generously.

My Engagements close on Wednesday. You may expect to hear from me again and particularly by New-Year's day, if not before.

This is but a word, and a poor word enough. I enclose another newspaper notice.

To all, my love and benediction.

A.B.A.

Mrs. A. Alcott.
  Concord

¹ Benjamin B. Wiley.
² Emerson wrote the sketch of Alcott in the *New American Cyclopaedia* (1858).

LETTER 58–13

[to Louisa, Boston]

Chicago, Ill. Decbr 23rd. 1858.

Dear Louisa/
  Your mother and Anna have been good about writing since I left them three weeks since, and have kept me advised of their welfare, and yours up to the last dates. Yesterday's mail brought me full letters from them; village chronicles, city news, and things pleasant to hear of about yourself and Abby.—I have just written and sent them a part of the first fruits of the season's gleanings.

My company here has been agreeable. I gave them three evenings. My wish is to leave now on Friday for St. Louis. Mr. Harris has written that all is ready for me to begin in January. It will be as late as the 20th. before I can turn my face East and homewards. I think there is little doubt but I shall pause at Cincinnati, Buffalo, Auburn, Syracuse, and Albany—a week or longer for Conversation, on my route to Concord.

Mr. Noyes' friends are invited for this evening at his house. To-morrow Dr. Holland lectures before the Young Men's Association.—Every body is preparing for the Holidays, so there are no evenings for the Eastern Magus till Christmas Eve, if there be any till after the New-Year, and he waits, to wonder, and worship at strange shrines, and private hearths meanwhile.

Abby and yourself are fortunate. I hope you are all ready to run up and warm the House of Seven Gables and as many fire places. Your mother writes that she is expecting you. I wish you the Merry Christmas and the fair prospects to open the New Year. Make your stay as long as possible; and the house joyous to its inmates all.

These long intervals between companies, at strange firesides, and far away, could not have been chosen. But they have many compensations, and come presently to an admission into spring and the garden.

I have seen Sam. Greele: have been at his house, once to tea: and once to an evening party. His friends were there and the talk ran far on to midnight. He has promised your mother his children's pictures. They are handsome. I have seen Mrs Greele but slightly. They are to be here again this evening, I believe.

Mr. Wiley has done his best to get me a good company. So has Mr. Noyes, at whose house I have every comfort you could pray for. Mrs. Noyes is a lovely woman, and her baby boy a sage to behold.

I hope your cares lighten as you come daily to them. I take pride in your enterprize and Courage. And Abby's good fortunes are to bear fruits, I dout not.

Much love and joy in you, and the promises for both.

Your Father.

to Miss. Louisa May Alcott
  at T. R. Sewall's, Boston.

LETTER 58–14

[to Anna, Concord]

Chicago, Ill. 25th Dec. 1858. | Christmas.

Dear Anna,

I am a favored person and blessed every way, save in this separation from the home circle to-day. For yesterday came Letters from your sisters, and I had yours and your mothers of the 16th in hand: and so am posted fairly up to date. I fancy you all merry-making by the firesides under the Gables, and making it pleasant as innocent hearts can wish. My little contribution may come too late perhaps, yet I meant it should reach you by this night's mail, if not before. And so add its tithe of comfort and thankfulness. I could not send earlier. The gift is small, but 'tis the most our friends here could command under the circumstances. It will serve us all as far it goes, and get our hearty thanks I am sure.

I have done here, and await Mr. Harris return from Connecticut to leave for St. Louis. Every thing is so agreeable, that I have concluded to stay over till Monday, and begin my Conversations sometime in the first week of the New-Year. Mr. Harris writes hopefully and has made arrangements for me at St. Louis.

Last evening, Mr. Noyes had his Christmas Tree and festival for the Children. Most of his parishioners came—presents were distributed—with music, dancing, cake and Conversation. Sam. Greele and wife, the Clarke's were there. To-morrow I am to take tea with them at Sams.

I have spoken with Sam. about your friend John.[1] He thinks he may have need of his services in the Spring, and will have him in mind meanwhile. Sam. is a candidate for City Surveyor, and if elected in March will have a good deal of work on his hands. He is greatly respected here, and prosperous, though doing little just now. Did I tell you that Alfred W. thought of joining Sam. in this street business and moving out here sometime? And if John should come to assist them, we should all feel less reluctance at the thought of your leaving us, if you could make up your kind heart to such cruelties. I am glad you find every thing so agreeable this winter. Give my best regards to your friend with my thanks for his considerate cares for you and your mother during my absence.

I think I shall pause homewards at Cincinnati, Buffalo, Auburn, Syracuse, and Albany.

The weather here is clear, cold, but we have no snow.—'Tis rather tedious, this roughing it out here so long, and for the slender gains, withal. But the Spring and Garden, and the home-pleasures are coming, with the harvest of returns.

You are very dear, my Child, and a pleasure, to
Your Father.

Miss. Anna B. Alcott.

---

¹ Anna had become engaged to John Pratt of Concord, on April 7.

LETTER 58–15

[to Mrs. A. Bronson Alcott, Concord]
Chicago, Ill. 27 Dec 1858. | 4. P.M Monday.

My dear/

I leave at 10 this evening for St. Louis. I am to ride all night and reach there to morrow. Harris writes that he is to return from Connecticut on New-Year's day, and that all is arranged for my Conversations forthwith. So by this time next week you may expect to hear further of our reception and proceedings in that City. Here, I have waited over Christmas and am so far on towards the end of the holidays when people may have times and a hearing to give to me. I have found wherewithal, and something to fill these Passover days: have been to Sam. Greeley's since I wrote and taken a pleasant tea there, and passed an evening with Mr. and Mrs. Wm. Clarke, Mr. Larned, Sam's brother in-law, and other friends. Yesterday, I addressed the S. School again.—This morning Mr. Clarke called with an invitation to meet Mr. Ogden the great man of the place, this evening—but I am off for St. Louis, and so decline, of course.

I have had letters from Anna, Louisa, and Abby, and have answered them. My letter to Anna I mailed yesterday, I had written to Louisa on Tuesday last the 23. and shall take an early opportunity to write again after I reach St. Louis. Christmas is now passed and become a memory, I trust. 'Tis an agreeable one to all. Did my little Gift reach you at supper? I wish it may not have been a damper on your pleasures and prospects. It was the most and best there was to send, and in keeping with our humble fortunes. And should other cities have no more for us, we will accept the pittance thankfully. Blessed be *something* to those who have so long waited for *nothing*.

I have made some hearty friends here and doubt not a coming season may yield an income of gains for all parties. The Clarkes are a slow, but sure people, as you know, when once yours; and Sam G. owes all the hearty good will he has to his good aunt, if not to her philosopher, and his Ideal surveys. As he has not put the pictures you asked for into my hands, I have not reminded him of them.

Mr. and Mrs. Noyes have made me comfortable. My washing has come in, so He is presentable;—as near so at least, as becomes the bearer of the Good tidings to all peoples who will have them.

I shall write on my arrival at Saint Louis, and set my face towards you as soon as may be from this West.

"East, West,
Home is best."
Yours, Meanwhile, and ever,
A.B.A.

Mrs A. B. Alcott.

LETTER 59-1

[to Mrs. A. Bronson Alcott, Concord]

St. Louis, Missouri, 1st. January | 1859.

My Dear,

The last thing I did before leaving Chicago on Monday was to mail a letter to you. I had written to Anna on the 25th (Christmas,) and on the 23rd. to Louisa. I reached here late on Tuesday, taking room and supper at the Planter's Hotel. There was nothing at the P. Office for me, though I inquired in Mr. Harris name, thinking you might have addressed to his care. Finding Harris had not returned from Connecticut, and would not be here till Saturday, (today) I found the residence of Mrs. Gage, with whom I dined, Wednesday, and at whose house I am staying, with every comfort which the freest hospitality and spacious apartments can afford. Judge Gage's Mansion is about two miles from the Court House, and commands a view of the City proper, the spreading Missisippi,[1] levee, its steamers, [word] the banks on the Illinois side, with the prairies and woods, the distance stretching far as eye can reach—I have a chamber and fire side privileges as at Chicago. The family are kind-hearted & strongly [word]. A son and daughter have been at Horace Mann's College at Yellow Springs, and have opinions of their own to speak of and defend if need be. Another son is partner of his fathers in the Iron Foundry Business. Judge Gage is from Ohio where he held office, but now gives his time and thoughts to his concerns principally. He is something of a free-soiler a man of large and generous views generally, very sociable and easy in his disposition and manners, and so we get along cozily enough. In person he reminds me of Dr. Alcott, being tall, but with a good head, not unlike George Bradburns. Mrs. Gage has fewer of the strong-minded woman's weaknesses than most of the set I have seen, and seems a fit companion for Mrs Severance, her old friend and admirer. She regrets exceedingly the mischance of not seeing yourself and Mr. Emerson, last autumn. I think you would like her well, and am sure she would like my wife, for the many traits of strength and courage which you have in common. Her domestic trials have been many, and she tells her private story with much simplicity and natural eloquence. Her visit east seems to have been profitable. I find she saw men and things with eyes of her own. I think Emerson would have been gratified by her good sense, her courage, and catholicity. I have told her of his coming twice to meet her at our house, and how significant is a favor of this sort from him.

She took me yesterday to see Dr. Eliot, and some friends of his, about the prospects for Conversations here. We found the Dr. very well disposed and ready to help about it. Also the Principal of the Teachers' Seminary, Mr. Pennell, brother of Miss.[?] Prof Pennell of Antioch College. We met some teachers of the High Schools, and friends of Mr. Harris. They seemed pleased and thought we might gather a good company, have a grand time of it. Harris, I learn, is known here as a young student of eminent promise, devoted to philosophy and letters. He has refused a Professorship in the College[2] here as interfering with his leisure and independence. He brings home with him to day from Connecticut, a wife:[3] having made *"the flying visit,"* he wrote to me of, to meet his bride, and be married. I believe he is from some of the towns about Hartford. Miss Gage tells me they go to house-keeping, and that I am to be their guest. If they reach here in season, I may see them this evening. They are to live nearer the centre of things than where I am staying for the time. Miss. Gage is a member of a philosophy Class consisting of a dozen or more. Mr Harris is of the number. It is taught by a German, well known here, the head and centre of a little company of thinkers, who meet for sympathy and discussion Sundays, morning and evening. How I am to like them I cannot yet say. Tis this circle who have taken the fancy, I infer, to invite me out hither. They know something, it seems, of Emerson and *Eastern* lights generally,—a little of Carlyle and Goethe, of Cousin and Kant, as representatives of the free thinking of the Century. The teacher, Mr. Brokmeyer,[4] I understand, is fairly posted on all matters of philosophy at home and abroad.

It must take a week or more to gather our company and make a beginning. I wish I may get away for Cincinnati by the 20th. but cannot say. Prospects are fair for a good time here and you shall hear further in a few days ‖ from us ‖.

Andrew Jackson Davis and O. A. Brownson are advertised for lectures. Davis and wife got into the cars at one of the stations on my route from Chicago, and rode with me to Alton junction. They are known to the Gage's and will be in St. Louis next week. I shall see more of them while I am here and other Spiritualists.

I think much of home, and just now, and to-day, of the New-Year's affairs. As to settlements, there will be not much in hand to balance accounts. Fifty dollars is the most that I know of, unless the brave Louisa add something from her hard earnings to help out of straits. Hastings has no reason to expect more than fifty at most:—I named *forty dollars,* as the least,—and with that he should be content for the present. Tuttle, if possible, should have *fifteen,* but there is no pledge of that certainly. He gets his quarter a cord for waiting longer, and that is a bribe you know to such as he. I shall have something to send,—I wish it may be much,—before many weeks, if things go well with me here:—and at Cincinnati. The cities, if not good for their $50. each, will disappoint me. They should yield us double that sum, beside expenses—Cincinnati, Buffa[lo,] Auburn, Syracuse and Albany, I am counting. And if I choose to take the trains by way of New-York, there is—that city, Brooklyn,—perha[ps] New Haven—and Worcester,—all good for small gains, on my route homewards. Write me particularly, and soon. I shall get your letters when Mr Harris arrives, as, not finding any thing at the P. Office addressed to me, I take it for granted you have sent to his care, and so shall [word] to send till I advise otherwise.

The weather is almost vernal: some frost at night, but sunny days; with nothing but mud and smoke to mar the walking or prospects at presen[t.]

A happy New-Year, and many to you, and the remnant left us.

Affectionately,

A. B. A.

Mrs. A. B. Alcott.

[1] Alcott regularly misspelled "Mississippi."

[2] Washington University. Harris, incidentally, had left Yale in his junior year.

[3] Sarah Tully Bugbee. They were married on December 27, at Providence, R.I.

[4] Henry Conrad Brokmeyer. For an account of Alcott's relationship with Brokmeyer, see Henry A. Pochmann, *New England Transcendentalism and St. Louis Hegelianism* (Philadelphia, 1948), Ch. 11.

LETTER 59–2

[to May, Boston]

St. Louis, Missouri, January, 2nd. | 1859.

My dear Abby,

I have pleasant news, today, from your mother about the Christmas spending, Louisa's visit, and yourself. I am sure yours was an agreeable party also at Mr. Sewalls: and could your mother and sisters have been with you and your kind friends, it would have left nothing to desire. Thank Mary, Miss Robie and Mr. Sewall for me.

Your mother writes, "Abby is being promoted and goes into the "last room" next week for Crayons." I am very glad to hear as much. I have never doubted of your finding the shortest ways to the art you so love and live for. Yesterday, I met a Miss Stetson, a teacher of drawing out here, and a graduate of the School of Design of which she spoke with praise and enthusiasm. Remember me to Mrs Cheney, with many thanks for her interest in your pursuits, and the good part she has taken for you with Mr. Tuckerman. He is one of my boys, you know, and so honours his teacher. I shall be pleased to hear further of your pleasure and progress. Your letter came just as I was leaving Chicago.

I wrote yesterday to your mother, giving full particulars of prospects in St. Louis. Mr. Harris is expected from the East to-day with his bride, and I hear I am to be his guest for the rest of my stay here. I think we may have a good company. The people please me. Miss. Mary, daughter of Judge Gage, and about your age, or a little older, and a graduate of Horace Mann's College, is a sensible young woman, and very agreeable. She has told me about matters and things there. Her mother interests me as the friend of Mrs. Severance. I have a chamber, fire, and privacy, when I care for it; and Judge Gage is good company.

The weather is delightful. The Missisippi [*sic*] winds about the City, and from my windows, I see its shores on the Illinois side, the wilderness beyond: with steamers passing and repassing all the time. We have no snow and at noon it seems like spring.

Make the most of your privileges, my busy Child, for our sakes, and the kind friends who serve you so disinterestedly.

I shall be here for a fortnight. To Louisa much love and pride.

Affectionately,
Your father.

Miss. Abby May Alcott.

LETTER 59–3

[to Mrs. A. Bronson Alcott, Concord]

St. Louis, Missouri, 6th January, 1859.

My dear,

Harris has returned with his young wife; He called his friends about him last night, some thirty of them, and chief amongst them the learned German Brokmeyer, a graduate of Brown University, and a Kantian. It was a Class-meeting, and we had a lively discussion preliminary to some Conversations chiefly for taking our themes at advantage and in good earnest. There were several teachers present and every one seemed interested. Every thing promises fair for a good attendance. Harris is plainly a leading intelligence, and the centre of a thoughtful circle of young persons chiefly teachers. I think I shall like him. His wife is from R. Island. She comes from some town near Providence, and seems to have adventured something as a Boston maiden did once upon her philosopher without counting the costs. I shall have opportunities of becoming acquainted with her soon. Several young women, not present at this introductory meeting, are coming, I learn.—Dr. Eliot waits, I suspect a little to find how the winds blow. But a Universalist minister, Dr. Weever called yesterday at Mrs. Gage's, and offered his vestry for our meetings, said he would come himself, and bring as many of his friends as he could persuade to come with him. I think we may have Five evenings. Mrs. Gage and her daughter Mary, are busy and believing.—A notice was to have appeared in to-day's paper. It will come to morrow. I will send you one forthwith, also particulars of progress next[?] week.

Chelmondley [sic] has not appeared in these parts. I wish he may, and if he fails of finding me here, I doubt not, we may meet at Cincinnati or some of the cities Eastwards. I should be sorry to miss him. What he seeks I cannot surmize, unless it be to persuade me to accompany him to the West Indies and perhaps home with him to England. Ask Thoreau about him, and send me the particulars.[1]

Anna's descriptive letter was next best to being with you and a partaker of the Christmas times. 'Twas good also to read the notes from Louisa and Abby. The interest of the Sewalls' and Miss Robie in their comfort and struggles for independence, makes me grateful. I wish we may find suitable returns. Let us claim fairly some dividends from our Apple-crop annually henceforth as theirs and against all others. I am glad you sent the barrel of marketable Baldwins.—But you have said not a word of the other Apples, though I believe you promised to assort them all before this time, and tell me how they keep and hold out; also about the celler. Your fire-places, and sundry household comforts and discomforts that housewives affect and experience since Eve's bridal.—The day of

Annual Settlements and reckonings has come round. So you will have occasion to look into matters a little and report presently. Our Creditors must wait till I have something for them, and if any call, tell them so, and that I shall not return without something. All so understand it.

I have written to Abby. Her letter with Louisas reached me last Monday enclosed in Annas.—It takes three days from Boston to St. Louis, and oftener four days for letters to reach me from Concord.—Days for writing home, I improve, all to the best advantage possible. I continue here at Mrs. Gages with every comfort. You shall hear from me soon again.—Direct to "A. Bronson Alcott."—

Friday morning. 7. The *Notice* has come to hand and is herewith enclosed, with its printer's blundering lines, &c.—To the Gentle Anna and friend love and regards.

Faithfully
A. B. A.

Mrs. Abby M. Alcott.

---

[1] For Thomas Cholmondeley's whereabouts at this time, see F. B. Sanborn, ed., *Familiar Letters of Henry David Thoreau* (Boston and New York, 1895), pp. 397–99; also, Walter Harding and Carl Bode, eds., *The Correspondence of Henry David Thoreau* (New York, 1958), pp. 528–29, 536, 540.

LETTER 59–4

[to Mrs. A. Bronson Alcott, Concord]

St. Louis 17th January, 1859.

My Dear,

I have yours of the 8th January left unfinished by yourself, and sent off by Anna with the intelligence of your illness and the Drs. assurances of your speedy recovery. I trust her statements, and expect soon to have them confirmed by your own assurances and signature. Pray write or dictate and let me know how it is with you in every particular.—I had heard nothing till yesterday since yours of the 3rd. Louisa's came at the same time, with pleasant accounts of her city experiences.—Louisa Wigglesworth's withdraw[al] and pretext need not surprise us.—Mr. Noyes wrote from Chicago and apprized me of Mr. Willard's check and of Wiley's sending it to you. About Hastings and the rest, I infer all is right for the present, and may so stand till you hear from me further.

My engagements are closed here, and I leave for Cincinnati to morrow. This evening I meet Harris and friends at Professor Watters to discuss the matter of organizing "The Missisippi [sic] Club." It is to consist of the more thoughtful persons of this city, some thirty ‖ and is designed for their improvement. ‖ the members to contribute a sum annually sufficient to have the best things from the ripest minds of New-England to be given them in the shape of lectures and Conversations. Emerson, Parker, are to come, and Mr. Alcott is to open the course next year with his Conversations. It is a good design and deserves to be carried out broadly and prosper.—Besides the four evenings, I have given others to select companies, and found these interviews very agreeable. I passed a night four miles out at the house of Mr. Bland a cultivated gentleman from Virginia and a lawyer of some reputation here. I have also met A. J. Davis and wife at the house of a Mr. Tilly brother of the present Mayor of St. Louis. My visit bids fair to prepare for something better in coming seasons. Tonight, I shall have the money receipts whatever they may be from this first experiment on the faith and intelligence of the people. Dr. Eliot sent his son, but I have not seen him, the father.

We have had dark, drizzly days, and fathomless mud. But yesterday and to day skies and streets were and are better. The snow is gone and it is more like March than January days.

I have come out to Judge Gage's to write and take my wallet into the city. Mrs Gage has returned my clothes clean and in order for Cincinnati. She has also done some mending. So I am not without being cared for kindly, and shall leave in good time for new conquests.

I hope the good Anna is not overdoing herself with the cares of the heart and housekeeping. She writes in spirits, though "wishing her sisters were at home to take the gloom out of the dismal days. Yet gets on very well she says with "the dear Comfort," who has taken the family "under his fatherly care." Thank him for all his kindness to both mother and daugh[ter.] Cannot Mr. pumpmaker put the pump in order for you? Anna writes the stoves do well [and] there is wood for the present, if not water. I wish I were with you to see to the comforts of the invalid, and warm her heart as well as chamb[er.]

Direct to Cincinnati. I shall be there on Wednesday.

May health and peace be yours, my friend and help mate.

Ever Yours,
A. B. A.

Abby M. Alcott

LETTER 59–5

[to Mrs. A. Bronson Alcott, Concord]

Cincinnati, Ohio, | 20th Jan. 1859.

My dear,

A hasty note this morning just to announce my arrival here yesterday, from St. Louis, and a sound night's rest at Conway's, whose guest I am to be while I am in Cincinnati. Spofford and he have arranged four evenings, three for next week and the fourth on Monday of following. They speak hopefully and are doing their best for a large gathering under the best advantages of place and advertisement.—I will write soon and say what comes of it for you and the parties concerned.

Meanwhile I send enclosed a draft for *Thirty five dollars*, the most I can safely spare from the avails of our St. Louis adventure, too scanty by far for our needs, ‖ but ‖ [p. o.] yet [p. in] something for the present straits and to be thankful for nevertheless. *Fifty* at Chicago and *the same* at St. Louis. Cincinnati promises a larger harvest: and if the intermediate cities shall do their little parts, our sheaf may yield, if not abundance, the means at least of comfort and freedom from the pressing debts of anxiety and dependence. I must take time ‖ , and ‖ [p. o.] to [p. in] return with the honour in ‖ my ‖ hand for you and all claimants besides.—

294

I wait to hear of your health and am anxious. Write me soon all the particulars, or if you cannot, let Anna. I am in the best of health, and have escaped agues and the colds of the season. A pleasant sun, to-day, and dry streets. I am to see Spofford, and may pass the night at his house two miles out at Walnut Hills.

May Cordial Hope restore, and health be yours, prays

Your friend
and husband.
A. B. A.

I wrote last Monday (17)th from St. Louis and trust my letter comes to hand to day if it failed to reach you last night. [all in pencil]

LETTER 59–6

[to Mrs. A. Bronson Alcott, Concord]

Cincinnati, Ohio, | 21st January, 1859.

My Dear,/

Yesterday, I mailed Spofford's draft to your order for *Thirty Five Dollars,* for which Cheney will pay to you the amount in Concord money,—good as far as it goes to discharge our debts to Tuttle, perhaps Messer, in part, or others to whom you think best to deal the little sum. I shall have something more to send soon, if the Cincinnatians favor me with their company for a few evenings to make good their interest on former opportunities when the like was offered. Spofford is the person of all others to bring a good company together, and see justice done all round, as you know from past adventures. He brought me out to his house at *Walnut Hills* where I slept last night, and where I am spending this day, while he makes arrangements for the Conversations in the City. Yesterday I dined with Conway and wrote to you from his house. I passed the forenoon and Thursday night, and am to return there on Saturday, tomorrow, or Sunday evening, to stay through next week and into the following. Unless something detains me here, I shall leave for *Cleveland* by Wednesday 5th. February. I may take *Medina* on my route and give two or three days to Uncle Noah and the Cousins. But I shall hasten eastwards as fast as this business of ours will dismiss us from city to city. 'Tis tedious and the gains scanty enough; still the profits are not to be estimated as yet by us, or by any one of this generation, thoughtful as it is, yet not much given to forecasting the future. Every where here in this wide West, I find earnest men and women, seeking faith if they have lost it, or stablishing themselves as they may in the little they have chanced to keep. They have tried many things and come to nought, or next to it. The old teachings have no validity. They fail to get answers from the lecturers, and are seeking teachers who can serve their needs in some sort. Emerson, Parker, Beecher, the Atlantic Monthly, they believe in—and very little else. And they wish to have these without the accompaniments of Lecture committees and mammoth gatherings of frivolous and stupid people at Lyceums and Library Associations. They are finding how to help themselves to what they want by forming Clubs, and getting the men they want to come out and meet with them, face to face; men to whom they may put their questions and from whom they get the final answers. I hope to live to see the *Symposeum* and institution, or if *I* shall not, a coming generation will suit, and the part of its planters. If Parker shall pass onward presently, there remains the seed he has scattered to spring up and bring forth fruits in due season; or if it were not his part so much to sow as clear the grounds, he has done good service, and may pass to his rewards. The papers speak of his sailing for the West Indies. May he sail to salubrious climes and find the health he seeks. Beecher remains at his post, and Emerson—strong, healthful, and health-giving for a little while to come—Seminaries of new men and times.

You have had cold days, the newspapers say, in New England. 22°. below Zero at Concord. I hope you have found the warmest chamber, and sunny nooks for an invalid's comfort and solace during the frosts and snows outside. Kind Anna has done her best to dissolve them, I am sure, and if she fails, I shall distrust Providence and scout the sun from the heavens as impostors. Let me hear from you soon, and from Anna.

Ever Yours and affectionately
A.B.A.

Mrs. Abby Alcott.

LETTER 59–7

[to Mrs. A. Bronson Alcott, Concord]

Cincinnati 30th January, 1859.

My dear,

I have yours of last Sunday, Louisa's also and yours of the 20th. They bring assurances of your convalescence and steady amendment. I trust no haste or inadvertance of yours will postpone your recovery. As nothing but necessity delays my hastening to your side to do what I might for your comfort and restoration. It was good and true in Louisa to come up and cure you so kindly and so soon. And relieve Anna from solicitude and cares too pressing and prostrating. I feel grateful to the dear Providence whose daughters are so near and so swift to minister to the afflicted and the feeble. Your account of yourself, and the girls' confirmation of your statements, leads me to trust that all is well as could be hoped under the circumstances, and that I shall find you as well or better than I left you. As to household matters and perplexities, you have pretty fairly and fully described them in these last letters. I am not without some assurances of mending and unravelling the coil [a?] little when I come. 'Tis a handsomer mode of begging for the needful supplies, per[haps] than any within my sphere,—this of [word] wandering thus far from one's fireside and chambers, to sit solitary often and strange in stranger's houses and companies to which one feels drawn by sympathies he is sometimes ashamed to own, and yet is fated to admit. *Here,* I have another evening to give to-morrow night, and shall leave early on Tuesday for Cleveland. I may stop there for three or four days, and possibly for a week. I hope to hear from Dr. Robinson before I leave this city. I have written to Dr. Warner, and think it likely he will have made ready for me in Buffalo. Then, if I pause to talk at Auburn, Syracuse, and Albany it must be March sometime before I can reach you.—Thus far, the gains are pitiful enough. But I will hope for the better luck and loaf, as I journey homewards. And when you shall have heard the story of the Cities fairly from ‖ the seer's ‖ [p. o.] one's [p. in] lips, may perhaps [p. in] find some softer accents of forbearance, for their scant contributions of rations to his unsuspected kindred in the flesh. Yet it seems but a slow "justifying of Wisdom's Children," this begging of ‖ both ‖ [p. o.] a hearing and of bread, and getting neither for the pains.—Who knows but Chelmondly [sic] has something to make our hearts glad in keeping for us?—

I have been at Mrs. Wilsons, also at Mr. Greenes, and taken tea. To-day heard Conway, and dined at Mr. Gs. Every body is gracious and kind. And the Young Men's Reading Room, to which I have free access, is one of the best furnished on the Continent. The doings of the Boston [word] Celebration are fair and worthy, Emerson's and Lowell's parts particularly.

If I stop any time at Cleveland I will write again from thence. Direct till you hear to the contrary and after to-day, to Buffalo. I fear I shall not go by Medina.

Ever Yours,

A.B.A.

Monday, P.M. 31. Just read Anna's full letter of 26th.

[Letter to Mrs. A. Bronson Alcott and Anna, Concord; from Cleveland, February 6, 1859.]

LETTER 59–8

[to Louisa, Boston]

Cleveland, Ohio, | 7th February 1858 [sic].

Dear Louisa,

Yesterday I wrote to your mother and Anna. And you shall have a word today. I came here last Wednesday, and am staying at Mr. Pratt's. His daughters have been at Concord in times past, and know you and your sisters very well. They have pleasant recollections of your plays, and say they had parts in the Christmas performances. I find they value John Pratt exceedingly and think him worthy of Anna, whose virtues they greatly prize, and think the pair are meant for each other. Anna writes me that you are of the same persuasion and that your fortnight's visit has converted you entirely to her own convictions about him. I think we all feel under great obligations to him for his thoughtful kindness and care of your mother and sister during my absence. I hope he is finding agreeable occupation in town.

From all you tell me of yourself and Abba, I fancy you are enjoying your friends and the city. I believe I have written to you once if not twice and to Abby also. Your letters are pleasant and playful. They are comforting and I cannot have too many, nor hear too frequently from you. Letters from home and the Eastern papers are the chief pleasures of your Missionary during these months of absence: the Post Office and Reading Rooms, his first blessings. It is a week since I have heard from home, but expect letters at Buffalo on reaching there day after tomorrow.

I have had two Conversations here the first on Saturday and again last evening, and am to have a third to morrow night. The company is earnest and enquiring. About 40 persons have come, and some additions are expected for the next evening. Something has been said of my giving them three evenings more. If I should do so I cannot reach Buffalo till Monday. I suppose I am to be there for a week or so. Dr. Warner wishes to gather a circle for me, and is doing his best to bring it about. I think I may pause a little at Syracuse, Auburn and Albany, on my way home. It will be March before I can return.

Cincinnati was too busy and indifferent to be very hospitable or generous this time. But we will remember past years and refrain from calling hard names these hard times. I shall have something to show for the three months begging, and must make up my face to say *"thankee"* if such grace is left me. The profits should have been three times what they will be at most, to mak[e] all as we meant to have it in the spring.

I am glad you take things so bravely. It encourages your Mother under her trials, and ‖ takes off ‖ ligh[tens] the load with which she is so burdened. The past year has changed the aspects of life to us all. I pray we may be equal to meet whatsoever the future shall send of weal or no. Much love and a deal of hope in yourself and Abby of whom I hear hopeful things. To your kind entert[ainers] and cousins and Miss Robie my regard[s and] thanks.

Affectionately
Your Father

Miss Louisa M. Alcott,
    Boston.
Friday Evening, Grace Greenwood read her Lecture here on "Joan of Arc" and to night Bayard Taylor reads on "[word]."

LETTER 59–9

[to Mrs. A. Bronson Alcott, Concord]
Cleveland, Ohio, | 13th February 1859.
My dear,

I close my engagements here to day, and shall leave to morrow for Buffalo. Dr. Warner has written and invited me to his house, but speaks doubtfully about gathering any numbers of the right sort to make it worth my while to pause for Conversations as I go Eastwards. I think I shall stop for a night to see for myself, get my letters from you and pass on to Auburn where there is a Mr. Lee, a Universalist minister, and who wished me to take his little city on my way home. I met him at your brother Sam's on my way out. He thought there would be a few of his neighbours who would enjoy some evenings, and said he would make ready for me. So I shall hope to find it as he wished, and may be there through next week. I shall pass Monday night in Buffalo and reach Auburn sometime on Tuesday. My next point will be at Syracuse, where, if Mrs. Davis and the rest of the good friends make a party, I may spend the week following. I think you had best address me at Syracuse after to-day.

I am detained here longer than I thought I should be when I wrote last. My company wanted three evenings more, and a Sunday meeting. Tis a city of Churches of the true Connecticut Puritan order; many of the first families are from New-Haven, and still cling to the Orthodox faith they brought from the East. I have my meeting at 3 P.M. today. Dr. Atkinson, Mr. Pratt, and others of our company have made all ready, and we shall see what can be said for the hungry folk who may come together if they may chance get a few crumbs of the famishing. Here is a field for planting a Church. Since Mayo, now at Albany, was here, there has been no teaching for the few, and they take eagerly such things as chance may cast before them. Chapin, I have not seen: Hitchcock and Foote but once. I shall not go out to see friends at Medina. It is 27 miles and by stage on a hard road. I have not the time for it.

I first came upon cold weather here and chill winter. 'Tis good sleighing now to-day, and has snowed every day since I have been here. The winds are piercing from the Lake and more searching than Boston Easterlies. Thus far I have proved cold and cough proof, and hope to escape sound and sane from the maladies of the season—and the West. This has been a tedious tour, but shall yield something for the pains of absence to us all.

I shall send you a check for most of my little gettings here as soon as I get them and can safely mail to you from Buffalo or Auburn. Have you got some newspapers since last Sunday? I wrote on Tuesday to Louisa and sent her a newspaper containing a notice. I have had nothing from you since I came here but shall expect letters awaiting my arrival at Buffalo to-morrow.

I think much of you, and of your recovery. Pray write me particulars. I shall soon be with you, and our complements—the prides and hopes of our house and hearts.

Faithfully
A.B.A.

Mrs. Abby Alcott,
    Concord.

//P.S. *Buffalo, Tuesday morg, Feb. 15th.* I came here yesterday and got yours of the 3rd. enclosing Louisas addressed to Dr. Warner's care. I may leave at 3 today for Auburn Yet Dr. W. thinks we may have three evenings. I have called and found nothing at the P.O. direct to Syracuse for a week to come. Enclosed is a check for *$30.—thirty dollars.*

LETTER 59–10

[to Mrs. A. Bronson Alcott, Concord]

New Haven February 28th. 1859.

My dear,

I reached here last Friday, and am stopping at Prof. Baileys. I staid over a train and took tea with the Russell's at Lancaster. Mr. and Mrs. R. were from home; Mr. R. in New-York City, and Mrs. R. at New Britain with Frank. I passed the night at Blakes, and left early on Friday for Hartford. There I saw Mr. Barnard for an hour in his chamber, and took the late evening train for New-Haven. Prof. and Mrs. Bailey received me kindly, and here I am to stay while I remain in this city. I find them cordial, genial, and am at ease in their house. Yesterday we found Prof. Fisher at the College Chapel. The Faculty with their families attend here in prime Puritan fashion, having seats in the Galleries, and the Students, now near five hundred, occupy‖ ing ‖ the basement floor below.

Last evening some of my former company were here, friends of Prof. Bailey, students and graduates. 'Tis proposed to have three meetings; to-night, to-morrow evening, and the last on Thursday. The party will be small, but the persons are earnest and thoughtful; some of them a little enthusiastic, as young Boardman, Harris' friend, and a musician of good promise. Sheldon too, my former helper, is much interested. I shall have a pleasant visit, and something, a trifle, to show for it.

I may take Waterbury on my route back: Perhaps leave on Friday and get to Boston to spend Sunday, unless I should pause at Worcester.—Thoreau left Blake's last Thursday morning. He read two lectures in B.'s parlours, and won many praises from his auditors. Mr. B. as true and devoted as ever. I liked Mrs. B. finding much more than I suspected was there.

This afternoon I am to see Dr. Bronson. Brother Ambrose was here last evening, and I took tea at his house yesterday. They have just buried their little girl, a child of three years. Ambrose is in a fair business. Mother writes from Betsey's that she is very well, as are my sister's family.

To-day is sunny, and the air fresh and native.

affectionately,
A.B.A.

LETTER 59–11

[to Samuel E. Sewall, Boston]

Concord, 5th March, 1859.

Mr. Sewall,
    Dear Sir/
The House debts are as follows—

To Prescott for lumber, lime, &c—	$197.10
" Smith for doors, sashes, & painting,	" 90.13
" Benjamin for masonry—	" 36.00
" Derby Brothers, for nails locks & fixings	18.61
" Messer for joinery—	21.00
" Moore for team-work—	17.00
	380.00

Debt for woodlot— 445.00

For payment Nathan Brooks has my note secured by R. W. Emerson, payable in four years from date, October 31. 1857.

Interest on this is paid for 1857,8.

Hon. Thomas Davis of Providence pledges $25. for four years, annually.— $100.

And Joseph Barker of the same place pledges $25. for three years— 75.

175.00

The preceding is the Sum of the whole debt on the Estate, also pledges in part payment of the same. Mr. Davis may add something to his annual contribution.

Yours, greatly obliged,
A. Bronson Alcott.

Samuel E. Sewall, Esq.
   Boston.

[Letter to Mrs. Anna Alcott, West Edmeston? N.Y.; from Concord, April 4, 1859.]

LETTER 59–12

[to Mrs. A. Bronson Alcott, Boston]

Concord April 11th 1859.

My Dear,

Life is full of compensations, so say the philosophers, and to make good the saying, comes the last of them, and I think, if not the wisest, very wise, certainly, and entertaining, Thoreau, to pass the afternoon and drink tea with Anna and myself, without you. And spend an hour after, talking delightfully. I having struck work, and passed all day with Anna in the East room, to recruit after my months intemperances. Tis an ancient doctrine this of self-denial; and abstinence from the strong draughts that set us mortals reeling, is still hard for saints and poets, who have in all times been too spilling[?] of the same in their immoderations—taking the Kingdom by force. So I have only tippling a little yesterday and to-day, and am getting sane and sound seeing Anna and serving myself to a milder nectar and ambrosia in quite human fashion, and at Puritan times: breakfasting, dining and supping together. Besides pleasant family talk, and I making thicker covers for my papers, while the rain and some sleet was moistening and whitening our prospects outside. Altogether a very agreeable day of it, two days of it.

But it has kept you in doors and perhaps unwillingly, I fear, unless you had the good luck to use yesterday, so bright and sociable, and so fit to see old friends in, in one's native City. I doubt not yourself and girls had a good time together. You are from home so seldom, I wish you may make the most of your visit, now you are fairly launched abroad on that sea of associations, to return into our little Islet, refreshed in Heart and strengthened, from your short, sail seawards and back here. Can you spare a train's time and ride out and see Mrs. Dr. Alcott? I wish you may. But I shall take her house on my way, I think, when I go next to Boston. My "Waterbury" has not come to night and so I get nothing further from those parts concerning him, or his remains.[1]

We shall wish to see you home again, but beg you to see, and *be seen of* your good friends and admirers for the reasonable time. To Louisa and Abby

301

sisters, love and remembrance, also to your and their kind entertainers, the Sewalls and Miss Robie.

Affectionately, A.B.A.

Mrs. Alcott, Boston.

---

[1] William Andrus Alcott died on March 29, 1859, and was buried at Newton, Massachusetts, near Auburndale, where he had spent his last years.

LETTER 59–13

[to Mrs. Anna Alcott, West Edmeston, N.Y.][1]

Concord September 23. 1859.

Dear Mother,

Your last letter to us is dated March 20th. last. And I have written once, if not twice to you since we received it. I write now to inform you of Uncle Noah's death at Medina on the 7th of this month. I had a letter yesterday from Cousin Isaac Bronson in which he says "Our Uncle was 92 years of age last June. He had been unwell all Summer of a heart-affection, cancer in his eye and trouble from the gravel. Yet he was about the house and farm until within four days of his death.' My impression is that more of history and of facts which took place within 70 years died with him than of any man west of the Allegany [sic] mountains since I have resided here. He had "a letter he writes from your mother about two months since and the letter has been lost so that we do not know where to direct a letter giving your mother notice of his death. If you get this note just answer it. Hiram's wife is in the Insane Hospital. My Sisters are tolerably well."—

So all are gone of the family of twelve, but yourself, and you have reached the age of 86 by my reckoning. I hope you may survive years to come and that I may see you again and again.

By my family Register of deaths,

Grandfather died	at	88
Grandmother	"	68
Aunt Lucy	"	
Aunt Phebe	"	83
Aunt Zerah	"	73
Uncle Tilly	"	65
Uncle Noah	"	92
Uncle Amos	"	56
—	—	
Aunt Sarah	"	
Aunt Sylvia	79.	

A long-lived family certainly. My grandfather's Family did not live so long generally.

Grandfather Alcock	was		77
Grandmother	"	"	71
Aunt Lydia	"	"	75
Uncle Solomon	"	"	59

Uncle Samuel	"	"	49
Uncle John	"	"	73
My Father	"	"	58
Uncle Isaac	"	"	40
Uncle Mark	"	"	73.

We are all well. The girls are all with us and have been during the Summe[r.] Louisa may pass the winter again in Boston. Abby is busy with her drawing. Our house is now very comfortable, and the season has given me time for making many improvements on the grounds. We shall have a good many apples: Last year 40 barrels, nearly as many this year.

I doubt whether I shall be out West during the coming winter. If I come near you I will try to see you.

I wish you would write a word when you get this and tell us about yourself and Sister Betsey. I have nothing from Chatfield. Ambrose and family were all well when I saw them last spring. My regards to Betsey and family.

Your Son
A. B. Alcott

¹ About twenty-five miles south of Utica.

[Letter to Seymour Bronson? Hingham, Mass.; from Concord, September 23 or 24, 1859.]

LETTER 59–14

[to Isaac Bronson, Medina, Ohio]

Concord, September, 24th 1859.

Dear Cousin,

The news of Uncle Noah's death comes not unexpected, since at his advanced age one may drop away at any moment of time. Yet he came of a stock very tenacious of life, as appears from our family records, and had reached an age beyond any of his generation in the family.

Grandfather Bronson died at	88
Grandmother was	— 68
Aunt Lucy "	—
Aunt Phebe "	— 83
Aunt Zerah "	— 73
Your Father "	— 65
Uncle Noah "	— 92
Uncle Amos "	— 56
My Mother survives at	— 86
Aunt Sarah died at	—
Aunt Sylvia " "	— 79.

It was my hope to have seen him again, before he passed away, but I found it difficult in the circumstances to pause on my ways West and visit my friends at Medina. But I shall cherish pleasing memories of him, and of the entertaining hours spent under his roof in Ohio, so full of early reminiscences, so abounding in anecdote, telling his stories so well, and himself such good company; that I missed seeing yourself and sisters, as I wished. But if I come into your neighbour-hood again, I hope to make some ame[nds] for it.

I have written to my Mother, who is living at this time with my Sister Betsey at West Edmeston near Utica, New York, also to Cousin Seymour at Hingham, informing them of his decease. Col. Thayer, has been dead for a year or two I believe. I know so little of Uncle's connexion with the Weymouth road, that I could say nothing of interest to the general reader. But I should like to see some notice of him in the Waterbury American; some account of his char-acter, his enterprize and public spirit a native of Old Waterbury. I shall look for something from you; his descent, age and decease, if nothing more. I am glad the "History" came out to interest him in his last days. How much of life and event he might have imparted had he been at the editors' elbow when compiling the history of times of his childhood and till he moved to Ohio.—As it is, I find frequent traces of him in the narrative. The Book is one of the liveliest of the many Town Histories published during the ten years past, and is alike creditable to Ancient Waterbury and its Historian. You have detected some mistakes in "Our Genealogies," doubtless, but nothing serious.

You write very little concerning yourself and sisters; nor of Hiram and Aunt Betsey. Sad to hear of Hiram's wife, but sadder perhaps to have it as it must have been before that infliction. If I were a trustworthy correspondent, I might ask for particulars of yourselves and of my old acquaintances near you, the Weltons, Atkins, cousins Addison and Seth Alcott, if not others from these parts. I am always pleased to hear, but not swift to write in return as I could wish.

Mother was well when I last heard from her. She writes us frequently, and [word] she is able to be about yet and enjoy herself. She was out here two years ago, and passed a summer with us. Dr. William Alcott died last March at Auburndale 12 miles from us.

My family are all well, and with us. Three daughters, Louisa, the second, spends her winters in Boston. She writes prettily for the Magazines. Abby, the young[est] has taken to drawing in crayon. Anna expects to be married presently to a young Merchant of Boston.

We have a pretty place here, and I need not say how pleased we should all be to see you and sisters.

To them, to Aunt, and other cousins my remembrance.

Yours cousin.
Amos Bronson Alcott

LETTER 59–15

[to Abby W. May, Boston]

Concord October 31st | 1859.

Miss. Abby May,

I shall enjoy any such privilege as you propose to me of reading Plato with your friends. And if you will arrange your plans and let me know of them, I will see if I can suit your wishes in the several particulars.

I think your preference for the Apology wise. I know of no piece of antiquity to which a few hours may be given with prospects of greater benefit, || and || if taken along with advantages of opportunity for comment on the Text.

I shall feel myself highly privileged, if I may further your good purpose in such ways as I can.

The circle will be the more hopeful if the company have sympathies in common, and are known to each other. Nor must it be too large for free interchange of sentiments.

I am seldom in Boston lately. But, if you think best, I will endeavour to see you, at such time as you shall name. And it may be desirable that all shall be made plain and satisfactory at first—the coming month leaves me free of any engagements for Conversations at a distance.

My family are all very well. Anna goes to Boston to day, and bears this to you.

> Very truly
> Your friend,
> A. Bronson Alcott.

Miss. Abby W. May,
Boston.

LETTER 59–16

[to Daniel Ricketson, New Bedford, Mass.]

Concord November 6th 1859.

Dear Sir,

Your book on the History of New-Bedford reached me through the Post Office a day or two since, and I have found time to give it a hasty perusal.[1] Like all memorials of the old time it has a pleasing interest, and I have to thank you for the pains you have taken to revive and make replete again for us so much of the past history of your growing city. Books of this sort are becoming more and more important and valuable as parts of the veritable records of men and times venerable and historical. I have before me an octavo of 500 pages, by Henry Bronson, Professor at Yale College, on the History of my native town, Waterbury, Connecticut: with an appendix of Biography and Genealogy: and one of the many of those true histories, like yours, that one reads with pleasure and improvement.

I was not aware of being so near the homestead and grave of a worthy ancestor, when at your house, and while we stood in the old burying ground at Acushnet. You were kind enough to turn a leaf at the page of your book where you speak of him.

Rev. Samuel Hunt, the first minister at that place, was from Plymouth. He was the eldest son of Capt. Ephraim Hunt who came with his father Enoch Hunt from Titenden in the Parish of Lee about two miles from Wendover in the County of Buckinhamshire, 35 miles W.N.W. from London. His mother was Joanna second daughter of Dr. John Alcock, of Roxbury whose Mother was the sister of Rev. Thomas Hookers of Hartford, Conn. and wife of George Alcock of Roxbury, John Eliot's first deacon of the first Church in Roxbury. Rev.

Zechariah Whitman of Hull married his (Rev Samuel's) aunt Sarah sister of his mother. He graduated at Harvard College in 1720. His father was one of his Majesties Justices at Boston in 1700. also a representative to the General Court in 1689 and 1691, and a captain of the militia. Barber, says in his Hist. Coll of Mass. "The territory comprising the town of Ashfield, Franklin County, Mass. was granted to Capt. Ephraim Hunt of Plymouth, as a compensation for services rendered in the Canada Expedition of 1690. It was actually conveyed to his heirs forty six years afterwards, and was settled by a few families in 1742. It was incorporated as a town in 1764: survives to that time it went by the name of *Huntstown* from the name of its original proprietor."

I hear your son has been in Concord but I failed of seeing him, as I did yourself when you were here sometime since.

Channing is in town, I believe, though I never meet him lately. Thoreau has just come back from reading a revolutionary Lecture on John Browne of Ossawatomee [*sic*], a hero and Martyr after his own heart and style. It was received here by our Concord folks with great favor, and he won praise for it also at Worcester.[2] I wish the towns might become his auditors throughout the states and country.

Sometime I shall wish to meet your friends again at New-Bedford. I remember with pleasure my kind host and family when I was there. We shall be pleased to see you at our house and now that we have Wasson[3] for townsman and neighbour added to our numbers, hope to draw frequent visitors.

Remember me to your wife and family kindly.

Your friend, and servant,
A. Bronson Alcott.

Danl. Ricketson,
N. Bedford.

---

[1] *The History of New Bedford, Bristol County, Massachusetts* (New Bedford, 1858).
[2] Thoreau's address, "A Plea for Captain John Brown," was delivered at Concord on October 30, 1859. According to Alcott's *Journals*, p. 320, the lecture was to be given at Worcester on November 7.
[3] David A. Wasson (1823-88). For a detailed sketch of him, see Frank Preston Stearns, *Sketches from Concord and Appledore* (New York, 1895), pp. 134-79.

LETTER 59-17

[to William Russell, Lancaster, Mass.]

Concord December 31st 1859.

My dear Friend,

My thanks for your letter and the parcel which came yesterday. The Head is a good likeness, and takes its place in my collection, associating yourself with the spirit of persons and times pleasant to recall. I value it. And regret that we have met so seldom since the dissolution of a partnership too brilliant perhaps in purpose and prospect for any but successors of ours to enjoy and make fairly their own.

The sketches, too, which the young enthusiast dreamed[?] and closed his eyes upon too soon. They have a sadly pleasing interest. I remember the ardent boy, the devotee of Ideas, and their worshipper in persons and things. I fancy his was the Platonic vision the faculty divine, seeking to show itself, and would have done so, had he been privileged to haunt some longer the shows of nature, and taken his time to steal the scents of colours and ‖ shows ‖ form. One accomplishment, and the rarest, he had certainly, the diffident sense and good faith in Persons: gifts and graces significant always, and pledges of true manliness in their owner. Not the least of his Teachers' victories is this of winning a heart so affectionate and so pure as his. I know you will bear with me in this tribute to the talents and worth of your son.

You tell us particularly of yourself and family. We are always pleased to hear from and of them, and trust the old sympathy still survives between us all. I wish we could make an occasion, and bring the families together sometime.

We are all very well. Mrs. Alcott enjoys something of her usual vigor of thought and action. Louisa is busy just now writing a Book (though that is a secret) and Abby devotes herself to drawing with an artists persistency and zeal. She has several pupils now, and lately has added to the list, Mrs. Horace Manns boys Horace and George. The family are living at Hawthornes place, next door to ours. And Mrs. Mann is wishing to build a house on our street, in the spring. Anna is in Boston. She was up at Christmas and happy.

As for me, I am at home and taking the comfort of it. For the last two and three seasons, I have been absent, the two last at the West, and the one before in New York City Conversing. 'Tis good to be here and busy, though it should come to no more than posting one's accounts a little as leisure and mood favor. So many things had fallen loose and behind hand with me. Then the Schools afford an agreeable variety of occupation, as I am to make monthly visits to them,[1] and we have besides Sunday Evening meetings at the School-houses round which have proved acceptable and been well attended thus far.

As to the Institute of Teachers meetings. Our people are not indifferent exactly but negligent rather about School matters, and though they might like to have the meetings, are not yet disposed as they should to bestir themselves in their behalf. I think our teachers would promote them heartily and attend. Better if you would come and speak to them sometime and prepare us all for the favor. And I should gladly make the occasion and all ready for you. and then we might talk over our own matters at leisure and at length.

The chances seem still to be against us, and Dr. Barnard. Had I the time and talent for the work, something might be done by me to help it forwards, and to your hands a little. But these are not mine, nor likely to be. So it will fall to some believer if it is done ever, or attempted. I must not doubt of their being matter deserving and serviceable to high ends. Yet the spirit of it transfuses so, and so transcends the letter of [word] that it cannot be seized bodily and held forth to the commonsense of the common mind. Still I like to think of someone's trying his chances at finding the significance of what has seemed so good and fair. And were you once here, and bent on beginning something of that sort, doubtless I should ‖ be ‖ hasten ‖ ready ‖ to spread the scrolls before you at any length and to the end.

Our year dies out coldly grand, and snowy to eyes that have owned their sixty winters. I have forgotten your age. I was 60 last 29 November. ‖ Doubtless the ‖ I must think years have fuller blessings in store for us. And ‖ I like to believe they will ‖ promise spare us the endless misery of surviving our early and life cherished dreams.

Mrs Alcott desires her remembrance to Mrs Russell and your children. She hopes the ways may bring you here to share the hospitalities such as they are of our pleasant home.

Most cordially
Yours
A. Bronson Alcott

Mr. William Russell.

[1] Alcott had become Superintendent of the Concord Schools in May, 1859.

PART TWELVE

✠

1860–1862

LETTER 60–1[1]

[to Mary Elizabeth Preston Stearns,[2] Medford, Mass.]

Concord 13 January 1860.

My dear Mrs. Stearns,

A righteous life is always a Throne of Pure Power in the world, and a good biography of it, the greatest of privileges to study and enjoy. You have sent me a Book of this rare sort,—and for which you have my hearty thanks—; written as it is by a disciple of the martyred Truths he celebrates so ably, and in fast colours of admiration and love of their defender. So now we have added to our Saints' calendar and library henceforth, "The Life and Epistles of St. John, the Just."

Moreover you have added cause for joy in your part of it, the prompted chapter of his early life; a piece of work done in a style of English unsurpassed, and for which we shall give praises due and thanks beside to young Henry of your household, whose hospitalities your illustrious guest thus hastened to repay.

A great act ennobles us all, and casts its lustre on the humblest fortunes and scenes whereon it falls. And so I must covet my chance share in the largeness of the glory, since our Eyes first opened on the same cold landscape and not many miles apart—I being a few months the earlier spectator of the bleak Puritan hills adown whose slopes herds and flocks did feed, and from whence went forth the shepherd-boy to smite in his maturity of strength, the Goliath of the Philistines.

"Twas the boldest stroke for freedom struck by any of the Mayflowers' men, brushing aside the old superstitions of union where none was, and cementing a republic of loyal hearts in the martyr's blood.

> "Tis vain to flee till gentle mercy show
> Her better eye; the farther off we go,
> The swing of justice deals the mightier blow."

I am slow in my acknowledgments. But I have not yet had the book to read through, it finds so many rivals for the chances, and chiefest amongst them, him of the highest Claims and first, Sanborn, who has this snowy morning and before breakfast, just returned it with a revolutionary smile of exceeding hearty approval.

The Austrian dungeons are not opened yet for their hunted victims, though there be hints of celebate [sic] scissors that such search is threatened in good

309

families not far off. I have no doubts of our women proving themselves good resolute Romans when the Crisis comes.

Again thanking you for your kind thoughts of us, and with cordial remembrances of hours passed under your republican roof.

I am Yours, and obliged greatly,
A. Bronson Alcott.

Mrs. Mary E. Stearns,
    Medford.

¹ MS. owned by the Fruitlands and Wayside Museums.
² The wife of George Luther Stearns, a successful businessman and a leader in the anti-slavery movement. For material on them, see Frank Preston Stearns, The Life and Public Services of George Luther Stearns (Philadelphia, 1907).

LETTER 60–2

[to Mrs. Anna Alcott, West Edmeston, N.Y.]

Concord, April, 12th 1860.

Dear Mother,

You wrote us a full particular letter at New Year's, and we have owed you an answer so long. I have been meaning to write from day to day, but have been unusually busy with the Schools since the Year came in, and have delayed it till now. But our Report is just printed, and I have some time to think of the old folks, and first of you, as the first and oldest, and the Mother of me, and my brothers and sisters. I am rejoiced to read of your being so well now in your 86th. year, and still so able to be about, and so busy. Few people are as favored as you are in these particulars or make so good a use of their privileges as you are doing. One hundred garments is a great many for fingers as old as yours to make in a year, to say nothing of the eight pairs of Stockings which you say you have knit, beside. Then to have the use of your mind and to sleep well, are great blessings. I am thankful for them: and can only wish they may continue to the end of your days, and that these may be many more, and as usefully spent as the former ones. We often speak of your visiting us, and wish it might be. Linus and Betsey are kind and like to have you with them, as we know: and so should we. Still it does not seem as if you could venture again upon so long a journey: and we have not proposed your coming. Our house is very comfortable, and we are all well. Anna expects to be married in June. She has been engaged for almost two years, and will go to Boston to live. Her husband is in an Insurance Office there and is a very worthy young man; I suppose you must remember him, as he was often at our house when you were with us in Concord. His name is John Pratt, and his parents live near us. We hope Mr May of Syracuse will be here to marry them. Louisa is at home, and has been through the winter. She writes for the Magazines. The "Atlantic Monthly" paid her $50. for her last story, called, "Love and Self Love." Abby is busy with drawing and moulding. Her health is much better. My wife is in Boston this week. She means to write to you soon. She is full of Anna's expected marriage just now; and is as energetic and busy as ever. I have been at home through the winter and interested in the Schools, visiting them every month. I send you a copy of my

Report. It may please you, and Betsey, and her family. The Supervision of the Schools has been pleasant: and I have the care of them for the coming year also. I hope you will like Louisa's "Children's Song," printed in the account of the Exhibition of the Schools. The "Shepherd," is Rev. Mr. Reynolds; "Father of the Vines," is Mr. Bull who raises the "Concord Grape[";] Mr. Thoreau is the "Hermit of Walden"; "the Novel[?] of the pines" is Mr. Emerson, and "The Friend["] is the Superintendent—your son.

I wish I could send you "the Waterbury Book["] but cannot. Chatfield never writes to us. I have a letter once in a while from Isaac Bronson.

The girls all send their love to you, and Sister Betsey's family: to which I add mine.

We shall be pleased to hear from you.

A. Bronson Alcott

LETTER 60–3

[to Anna, Chelsea, Mass.]

Wednesday Afternoon, | May, 23rd. 1860.

My dear Anna,

Never a sunnier day embosomed a sadder one; or embraced a lovelier occasion![1] It was all grace and becomingness, the company, the spectacle, the ceremony, the season; and to me, pleased as I was made and surprised by its fitness, and so honored: still so sadly pleasing, and covering emotions that I may not yet describe. By and by, I hope to make them familiar, and, for my own peace of mind, get reconciled to your absence, since now it must be. Nor would we dare restore you now, if we could to the old standing.

May the auspicious omens attend your choice, and all coming choices. In my heart of hearts, I wish you all happiness, and of that preciousness of which the Good are alone privileged to taste, without harm. I am sure you deserve such, and believe they are in store, and abundantly, for you and yours.

We are all the richer—and I was about to add all Concord—for the events of to day.

Your parting memento has already found its place. And I add this apology for myself to ‖ your ‖ the parcel going to you in your trunk.

If I can come out and see you next week, I will, as I may be in Boston for a day or so.

Uncle Sam. has gone to take tea with Elisabeth Hoar, and Abby has just returned from a ride with Bonny: while your Mother is resting. Regards to your excellent husband.—

Your Father.

Anna.

---

[1] Anna's marriage to John Pratt. The wedding was officiated by Samuel J. May.

LETTER 60–4

[to Mrs. Anna Alcott, Oriskany Falls? N.Y.]

Concord, June 3. 1860.

Dear Mother,

I wrote to you on the 8th of April last,[1] and sent you my School Report. These were addressed to you in care of Linus at West Edmeston, and may be there for you. It was a full letter of family particulars; and an answer to yours of January. I hope you will get it. Since then some things of interest have taken place here about which my wife will inform you at length and particularly. I am glad you are so well, and enjoy yourself.

I am expecting to be in Syracuse sometime during the autumn, and, if I am, shall certainly see you; and if you wish to come this way then, and are able to venture upon so long a journey, will try to arrange for bringing you home with me. Think of it during the summer, and prepare for it, as I think we might make you comfortable now, and offer you a good home with us. And write us meanwhile and often how you are and feel about coming. Our house is pleasant and I wish you were here this fine morning to see how beautiful it is, even without Anna who has found one of her own, and gone from us.

My regards to all our relations [and] friends out West.—

Your Son.
A.B.A.

[1] Letter 60–2, dated April 12.

LETTER 60–5

[to Anna, Chelsea, Mass.]

Concord, June 4th 1860[1] | Sunday.

Dear Anna,

It was my purpose to spend some part of this pleasant Sunday with yourself and husband at your other home in Chelsea. Besides yourselves, I thought the Anniversaries would offer pleasing inducements to come to the city, and pass a night or two. But as I read of their sayings and doings from day to day reported in the newspapers, it seemed a little questionable whether there was much going forwards for me, and Friday and then Saturday came to leave me without the necessity of determining the matter. So I am still here, and without the pleasure of meeting you and yours, or of hearing your Uncle at the Music Hall to day. I am disappointed and, from your mother's account, fear you will be. But I shall take the earliest opportunity of seeing you. And it may chance to be the more profitable, as well as agreeable, for the postponement. For indeed, I feel too insig[nif]icant and inadequate to meet such felicity as yours, unprepared and too soon. It is a manifold experience, very precious very holy, and deliciously tender and human: and though I am not perhaps the poorest and profanest of men, nor all unworthy of kindred to sentiments of such friendship, I shall not be quite equal to speak or face them, as I wish. They are good for silence and to keep. Bye and bye the voice will come and the suitable words, and the fair honors.

Your letters prove your happiness, and your mother's report confirms all. Let my few words mean more than many: and more possibly than you can yet know. I am glad that you open upon the Future as the flower to the sun, and that Experience so confirms your hopes. You deserve so much, and may you long enjoy it. We miss you, but another very dear to you shares you, and that is the law of Love and goodness evermore. Our home is the happier from our assurance of your happiness, and that a friend can be more to a wife than all friends beside.

dear Anna, Yours, & his for your sake.

Your Father.

¹ Sunday was June 3.

LETTER 60–6

[to Betsey Pardee, West Edmeston, N.Y.]

Concord, June 5th 1860.

Dear Sister Betsey,

We had a letter from mother a few days ago dated at Madison, in which she writes that she had heard nothing from us for a good while. I wrote to her last April and addressed my letter to your husband's care, thinking she would get it from you. But it seems she has not: and so I judge it never reached you. Along with my letter, I sent one of my School Reports, thinking it might interest her and yourselves, and let you know something of what we are doing here in Concord. Mother writes in good health and spirits, is busy as ever, she says, with her needle, and has the use of her eyes at the age of 87. How well she bears her age, and how few infirmities she has!

But I am sorry to hear of your lame hand. You have been so active and industrious the loss must be a trial to you. Do you use any remedies for getting the use of it again? Are your children all well, and your husband? We hear of you from time to time by mothers letters, but not so often and fully as we should like. Will you write sometimes? I hear Chatfield has been lately at the Falls,¹ and Mother saw him there. I suppose he came also to see you. He never writes to us.

I think I may be in Syracuse sometime during the autumn, and shall then try to see you: and if mother wishes, and is able to take the journey, shall bring her home with me. My wife has written to ask her to come if she gets a chance before then. We should like to have her with us, and think she would be happy here in our family. We are well. Anna was married on the 24th [sic] May, and has gone to housekeeping at Chelsea near Boston. My wife has just returned from making her a short visit. She is very happy and has a worthy husband who is in good circumstances, and loves her very much. Louisa and Abby are with us. Louisa writes for the Magazines, and is paid handsomely for her stories. Do you ever see "the Atlantic Monthly." If you do read the story entitled "*Love and Self Love:* it is hers. Perhaps some of your neighbors take the "Atlantic." Abby

313

is busy with Drawing and has a few Scholars who come in once a week and take lessons of her. My wife is very well, and does her own work, as I do mine. We have a pretty place here, and enjoy it. I am busy with my Garden and the Town Schools, eleven in all, which I visit once a month. I have been Superintendent of them for the last year and am at present. I hope my *"Report*["] will come to hand: and am sorry I have not another to send you if it fails[.]

Remember me kindly to all your family.

Your brother,
Amos B Alcott.

¹ I.e., Oriskany Falls.

LETTER 60–7

[to Anna, Chelsea, Mass.]

Concord June 10th 1860.

Dear Anna,

I hope you have now made sure of getting your letters punctually at your Post Office. A week's delay defeats the best ends of correspondence, and comes to nothing. I do'nt wonder you felt lonely a little and foreboded much. We had written full and all of us, and I mailed your letters just before going in to the Temperance Meeting on Sunday, so that you should have the earliest words on Monday. It will be better now, and I shall like to write often, and hope I may. You give us some particulars about Mr. Parker, and Uncle Sam's discourse that we had not had before. It must have been a touching occasion to the friends of the deceased, and impressive. I have seen but a short report of the discourse. Mr Emerson was here on Friday Evening, and told me he had just received Mr. Clarke's. If you find one or both, and have opportunity, please send them to us.

I may be in town next Sunday at the services at the Music Hall,¹ and shall see you at your snug little home, admired so much by all that have seen it, and its inmates to grace the apartments. I am glad your Uncle and Geo. B. Emerson came to admire—Happy pair and deserving!—

Last Monday, I visited the North Quarter School, and dined and passed the afternoon, with Mr. and Mrs. Bridge, at Mr. Pratts. We had much talk, and general agreement all round. Very sensible and worthy people on whom Life has not been wasted: and good company for you and yours. I like them very well and shall see more of them in my visits to you.

I am very busy now with grounds garden and the Schools. Sanborn has invited me to meet his: and I have my first interview next Tuesday. Many thanks for your long letter, and much love to you and yours.

Your Father.

¹ The commemoration services for Theodore Parker, who had died May 10, 1860. Alcott did not attend.

LETTER 60–8

[to Samuel J. May, Syracuse]

Concord August 24th 1860.

Dear Brother,

I think favorably of Sanborn and of his School. Tis not all one desires, but as good as any in these parts, and in important particulars perhaps better than any. He promotes good feelings, gentlemanly manners, and wholesome sports and recreations. I believe he aims to be strict and kind in his discipline and intercourse. I have not often been in his School: my impressions are derived from the part he has taken as School Committee Man, and at our Sunday Evening lectures and Teacher's Meetings. He is much liked by parents, and pupils. I have reason to think his teaching to be scholarly and thorough. Mr. Emerson and Judge Hoar speak well of his literary acquirements, and have children under his care. I think you need not hesitate about committing George E. to him. Indeed, I know of no School about which I could safely say as much in its praise. And if we can serve you and your son in any way, you may be sure of the pleasure it will afford us. We shall esteem it a privilege to have him as an inmate of our family, and under our supervision.

My wife will add further particulars.

Yours truly,
A. Bronson Alcott.

LETTER 60–9[1]

[to Robert Montgomery Smith Jackson, Cresson, Penn.]

Concord, August 25th[2] 1860.

Dear Sir,

I owe you my hearty thanks for the gift of your Book on "The "Mountain. I have read it—parts of it more than once—with satisfaction and pride: its doctrines are so sound and wholesome, and so pertinent and admirable for the strong sense and conservative tone underlying the contents. I breathe freely and long as I read, and scent the sovreign [sic] airs once more, and so have glimpses often of Paradise Restored. I wish the book may find continents of readers and converts.—The first Parts I read a year since in Thoreaus' copy. I think I value the second Parts most. 'Tis so rare to light upon any Speculations grounded in Nature and practically embosoming her Spirit, that a thoughtful person takes hope and comfort in any surprise of the sort. I fully appreciate and endorse your faith in the Mountain. I find, moreover, that you have had free intimacy with the great Masters of Mind and Body in past times.—

I hope the "Atlantic Monthly" is to speak the good word for you. Emerson will see that it does. My neighbour Hawthorne is now reading your Book admiringly: And Thoreau, who has been busy with Monadnoc, for the last ten days, tells me he shall acknowledge your gift presently.

Wishing the success you deserve in your humane undertaking, and the leisure and strength to complete your Promised "Atlas" for us.

I am

truly Yours,

A. Bronson Alcott.

Dr. Jackson

[1] MS. owned by the Pennsylvania Historical Collections, Pattee Library, Pennsylvania State University. The text of this letter has been reproduced with detailed annotation (though with some differences in transcription) in Émile A. Freniere, "The Mountain Comes to Concord: Two New Letters from Alcott and Thoreau," *Thoreau Society Bulletin*, Bulletin 75 (Spring 1961), 2–3.
[2] The envelope is postmarked the 24th.

LETTER 60–10

[to Mrs. A. Bronson Alcott, Syracuse]

Concord, October, 29th 1860.

My dear,

I meant to have written yesterday (Sunday) but one thing and another took up all day and the evening; And now I come to my pen after the day's rounds to the Schools and with very little to write of the week's burden since you left us. You are so seldom from home, and enjoy so keenly these perspectives of distance that it were a great kindness on our parts, to write often and particularly of the days as they pass.—As to the house and housekeeping, under the supervision and charge of the girls, we have reason to be satisfied. They seem to have profited by past lessons and experiences, if not born to the act. A clean tidy sleight of hand and eye that keeps rooms neat, & suited to the ends of a house. Then our meals have been only slightly different from those we praise every day under your pains taking administrations. They gave me some excellent bread at supper to night, and the applesauce and cocoa were admir[able.] So you may be quite at rest as regards these common comforts. And I am saving one of the tall bottles of your beer for a working day about the grounds. We have set the strawberries along the path by the tomato row; and shall improve a fair day in making your rose Garden on the Terrace behind the house. I hope to make some other transplantings before your return and wish I may find time and pleasant days to build the piles of lumber into handsome additions of some sort and useful. Next week I suppose, I am to see to transplanting the evergreens about *Hawthorne's* grounds, and I hope to set some on ours also. The chimneys are finished at the house, and the plastering is going forwards fast. Should we have pleasant days for the coming three weeks, we can add many ornaments to our quiet landscape and salute the Spring with new beauties. Certainly if the odious old barn will walk out of sight meanwhile and open the prospect in that direction. So much for the little world I inhabit these days with its round of plans and pursuits—designs and dreams.

I see by the placards that Charles Sumner is to open our Lyceum Course next week. Then we have town meeting and *elections*—I shall finish my school rounds to-morrow, and mean to harvest the beets, parsnips and turnips by Saturday. Mr. Bigelow is to take a barrel of the winter sweetings to morrow, and Adkins the fruit seller on the Milldam wants a barrel also.

Our house was thronged with very genteel young gentlemen having no particular errand all yesterday afternoon, one or two of the like calling in the evening. Abby may be silent on this score, but will tell you doubtless about the pink of a party she extemporized here on Friday evening. The highfliers, Maggie and she, are fairly bewitched, and rather the largest partakers of the planet, just now.

I trust you are enjoying the hospitalities of that hearty people, and am sure of your adding largely to the pleasures of all you shall meet. Tell us soon about yourself and your good entertainers, to all of whom my regards.

Ever Yours,
A.B.A.

To Mrs. Alcott at Syracuse, NY.

LETTER 60–11

[to James Redpath, Boston]

Concord November, 19th 1860.

Mr. Redpath
Dear Sir,

I have delayed replying to your invitation to attend a Convention called by yourself and friends to meet at Boston on the 3 of December, for the purpose of discussing the Evils of slavery and the right methods of abolishing it from our Republic. And for the reason chiefly that I was not sure of having any thing to propose adequate to the subject, the company, and occasion. Nor has it been my habit, of late years, to speak at public meetings often, and from choice. What pleased me better to meet private companies, with the fullest advantages of conversation and comparison. But my interest in your objects, so far as I have any intimations from a glance at your Circular, from what Sanborn tells me, as well as from my hope in yourself, will incline me to attend your conference. I cannot now promise to speak. But I hope to enjoy the privilege of listening to the suggestions and counsels of those who are entitled to be heard on that occasion, ‖ and will gladly offer their matured thoughts and measures ‖. It is good to know that young men are disposed to undertake something and to give the prehearing to all sides at the outset. Certainly 'tis time, this courtesy and hospitality were given to the views of earnest and humane minds; since good must come of it, alike to freemen and slaves.

Very truly yours,
A. Bronson Alcott.

James Redpath

LETTER 60–12

[to Mrs. Anna Alcott, West Edmeston, N.Y.]

Concord, December 30th. 1860

My dear Mother,

Your full and particular letter of the 25th of November reached me on my Birth day—the 29th—as you intended it should. It gave us all pleasure to hear of your good health, good spirits, and great activity, at your advanced age. Very few of your years are favored as you are with unimpaired faculties, and the privilege of making the days pass pleasantly away in useful occupations. It is the fit sequel to a life of good wishes and good deeds like yours, and, I doubt not, a kind Providence intends to bestow these blessings on you to its very close. It would give us, as I know it would you, an added pleasure, if you could be with us; and that hope we trust is to be realized yet. I meant to have had you with us this winter, and still think I may go to Syracuse, and so bring you home with me. But there is some uncertainty about my going there, and if I should go I should not leave here till March perhaps. But I will write and let you know. If you should have a good chance to come on with any one meanwhile pray come at once. We have a chamber ready for you, and know of no person who has better right to occupy and enjoy it.

You will like to hear something about us. We are now but three:—Anna is living at East Boston, and we are expecting her and husband on Monday, tomorrow, to spend the New-Year with us—myself wife and Louisa. Abby is making a visit at Syracuse, and may pass the winter there. We are all very well and comfortable. Louisa is busy writing stories, for which she is well paid—the Atlantic Monthly giving her from $50. to 75 and 100. for her story, according to the number of pages it makes. "Love and Self Love," "The Modern Cinderella," are the names of her last. I wish I could send them to you. They are much liked by many readers of that popular Magazine and do her great credit. She has a Book nearly ready which she hopes to have printed if any publisher will take it. She is not wanting in Talent and Character. I see nothing to prevent her becoming a favorite with the public, as she becomes generally known. Her mother hopes good things of her,—in which hope her father certainly joins. Anna is very happy with her husband, who is an excellent young man and in good business. You know how much we think of Anna, and can judge of her husband, when I tell you that we think him worthy of so good a woman for wife as she is. May they live long to deserve and enjoy one another.

My wife often wishes she had your company these wintry days. I wish she had for your sake as well as her own: for I too should have more of you than I have had at any time past when you have been with us. We are better placed now and can take life to better advantage. Our house is comfortable in winter, and the place a picture all summer: then we have good neighbours, and a pleasant town to live in,—good health, employment, and I trust, thankful hearts, for so much. I certainly find full and agreeable occupation the year round My garden during the season of out door service; my Schools and studies at all times; —some proofs of not living wholly in vain. We had fewer apples this year than last: but a good garden. The Schools which I visit every month are prosperous. I also give lectures on Sunday evenings at the several School houses, and meet the Teachers and school Committee often, for discussing the whole matter of education. The Report, a copy of which I sent you, has been largely read and liked, and I am beginning to think of another for the present year. I am reading "Pilgrim's Progress" to the Children in all the Schools. Mr. Russell who married Mr. Wood's daughter, is writing an account of my Schools in Bristol, Cheshire, Germantown, Philadelphia and Boston. But I will not speak longer of myself.

I have heard nothing from any one in Wolcott, or at the West. Give my love and remembrances to Sister Betsey, her husband & family. If I go West, I shall see you all. My wife and Louisa desire to be remembered kindly to all.

dear mother, Yours inseparably
Amos

LETTER 61–1

[to Anna]

New Year's Morning | 1861.
My dear Anna

Herewith receive this Book. "Faithful Forever."[1] It is the simplest and sweetest celebration of the Friendship in whose pleasures you and Yours so largely partake and so richly deserve. May it survive many coming New Year's days as fresh and fair as this, and conduct you beyond all times and dates—yours and his forever.

Your Father.
Anna and John.

[1] Coventry Patmore's *Faithful Forever* (1860).

LETTER 61–2

[to May, Syracuse]

Concord, | Monday Morning | 10th February, 1861.[1]
Dear May,

I most gladly obey my Child's commands, since they are mine also; the thought of my not having written a word since the New-Year came in persecuting my memory day by day for the last month, and yet I have postponed the pleasure to pleasure's present till now, and the winter is almost past into the coming spring time to bring its flowers, and you to us again: meanwhile I have been treated the hearing of your letters coming to us, week after week, giving the rosiest accounts of your pleasures and pursuits among that stirring folk, and in your private Asylum. From all which, I infer that you are usefully employed and pleasantly, to the satisfaction of your friends, and your appealing pupils.

As to your teaching the drawing and articulation, I should say:—

Try to strike their senses strongly by boldness and distinctness of voice and stroke of pencil, and by lively gestu[res] and Conversation aided by all the Fancy you can command of images drawn from familiar objects and ever[yday.] Call them one by one before the Black board, and set each at trying his hand at the same stroke, kindly encouraging, and seeing no failures to critizise [*sic*]: their Eyes and ears will do that best, you commending Success heartily and winning *will* and *work* at once. If you can get "Philbrick's Tablets"—I think they must be in some of the city Schools—ask Uncle Sam—you will have just what you want for the Articulation and Drawing, and the Cards are simple and proper for all beginners; very well suited to your classes. I am pleased to know of your trying to teach well, and doubt not of your success. Write me further particulars presently. and remember me to your kind friend and your Pupils' benefactor, Dr. Wilbur. I hope to see and know more of him and his plans sometime. Possibly I may be in Syracuse in April coming after our Concord Schools are fairly examined and reported.

I am having a busy winter and enjoying uninterruptedly my writing and thinking beside your mother here before our parlour fire, days in and days out, since January first; and with something good to show for my Season's work. Louisa has occasionally appeared at the supper table to vary a little the round of work, by dashes of wit and amusement, for us chimney-corners ancients. Your mother appears very hopeful, only sick a day now and then, when she forgets how young she is at 60, and what promises her children are!—I closed my Conversations last Saturday with some eclat: Very good for Concord. Louisa and your mother send you all proper news.

Your Father.

¹ Monday was February 11.

LETTER 61-3

[to William Russell, Lancaster, Mass.]

Concord April 2nd. 1861

My dear friend,

Now that my Annual School Report is fairly and "Respectfully Submitted"; approved moreover by the Committee yesterday, and a sovereign snow-storm blocks the town indoors to-day insisting upon a general family reading of it, for better or for worse as the case may be—I have a moment at command for thanking you for your kindly notice of the schoolmaster's endeavours in times past, and, as an appendix to which and continuation of them up to the present time, I transmit herewith these images and accounts of our Concord Schools. The pamphlet has been hustled into paragraph and type, under every impediment of pressure, amidst examinations that must be had before they could be described, and but a weeks' time or a little more allowed us for composing large parts of the text and the printing of the thousand copies of it, for delivery at our town meeting yesterday. The portraits were mostly drawn at the Printing office, and only seen but once by me in proof: you will find many provoking errors of course, and excuse us if you can under the circumstances, though our schoolmaster can hardly hope to escape hearing charges of shiftless spelling and composition, from his readers. It would gratify me if our Genial Professor would run through the pages and mark them in pencil for us, as I know they cannot elude the eye of his logic or good taste or skill in the composition of our tongue. Then we shall be so far advanced in comparing notes when we meet; which must be at the earliest moment—I wish it may be,—if not at my house—before the meeting of the Institute at Acton next week, or sometime while it is in session certainly. If I knew the days of your being in attendance I could meet you there: and perhaps you could come down and pass a night or a Sunday preceding or following, if not while the Institute is in session. I should hope it may be so, and then we may touch up and dismiss our schoolmaster to Mr. Barnard's acceptance. I have been too [word] to copy in the extracts in their places, and shall wait your selections. Mr. Barnard has sent me his Journal for April. I have heard nothing otherwise from him, and imagine we shall be in season for the July number.

Mr [word] has sent me his Prospectus of the Institutes meetings. It would please me to have an opportunity for showing something of our Schools at some time during the sittings.

We are all very well, and hear happy news from Anna and Abby from week to week. Our cordial regards to all members of your family. If no other arrangement can be made, I will try to suit your convenience in visiting you at Lancaster. I wish this may find you in time to let me hear from you before Saturday coming in reply.

Truly Yours,
A. Bronson Alcott.

Prof. Russell.

LETTER 61–4

[to May, Syracuse]

Concord, April | 12th 1860.[1]

I send along with the more excellent articles for a young Lady's outfit (though not a non-essential as the School Committee and Superintendent consider) a copy of their Report, commending it to the perusal of the young Miss for her Father's sake: She may find suggestions as she reads to serve the needs of the little company she meets daily, and so glean a double benefit. I send copies also to Dr Wilbur and Mr. Mills. Your Uncle Sam. has one already. If you should wish for more to give to any friend of yours, I can send copies. I hope you will like it. I have corrected numerous errors made in the haste of Printing.

The town still gives me the charge of its Schools, and seems well pleased with my past services. Mr. Shepard's School acquitted itself to admiration last night: full particulars of which you will get from our domestic reporters, who will give you the last news in full.

I am gratified to hear that you are liking every thing so affectionately and are liked so admirably by every body. It seems you are making friends, and are useful to a needy class of unfortunate children: You may learn from them a great deal more than you can teach them. I know you will do well whatever you undertake, and are not much given to undertakings into which you cannot throw your own earnestness and enthusiasm. Do your best to attain "The Best" and that

Excellency is yours of necessity.—I must wait I am told till August to see you here in our quiet home—now just budding and cropping out into its spring green already with its promises; its temptations to leave studies and partake of its beauties.

On page 16 of the Report you will read of our "Concord Book," which we hope to get out for the coming Christmas and New Year. It is to be illustrated. How "the Orchard" would like to see itself in a pretty little tasteful vignette just under the compilers name in the Title page: if you agree please come home in time to take the Sketch for the Engraver. Remembrances to Dr. W. and your kind friends, with your father's

Love.

May.

---

¹ Alcott must have meant "1861." According to Louisa's Journal, May was in Concord in April of 1860 and went to Syracuse to teach in December (see Cheney, pp. 120, 123).

LETTER 61–5

[to Mrs. Anna Alcott, West Edmeston? N.Y.]

[Concord, August, 1861?]

Dear Mother,

I blame myself for letting so long time pass without writing to you. Your last letter is dated January 1st, and I fear you have had no answer. There is no excuse for such negligence. But though I have not written, I have thought of you meanwhile, and think I sent you one of my School Reports, which I hope reached you. I am busy in doors this summer: the sprain having kept me from my gardening, but I am about, and shall be strong again soon. The girls are all at home now. Anna spending August with us. We are well, and thankful for so many comforts and enjoyments.

I hope you have recovered from your illness. Louisa has been waiting almost since the year came in for her money, that she might send some to you. We wish it were more and that you were able to make the journey here, and live with us. If you feel that you can, write to us, and some way will open to have you come safely. I often think how pleasant it would be to have you with us again, and that you would enjoy being one of our family now in your old age. I have heard nothing from Chatfield or Ambrose lately.

It is possible I may be out in your neighborhood sometime during the coming autumn or winter. If I am, I shall come and see you.

My remembrance to all.
‖ Yours, ‖ With love and duty,
Amos.

LETTER 61–6

[to Anna, East Boston]

Concord, Monday Eve, | Sepr. 23rd 1861.

Dear Anna,

You are very kind in copying from your History the paragraphs concerning Dr. Tillotson, thinking my uncle Dr. Bronson had his name from being some relation of his. He was only a son and namesake of the Church, no relation otherwise. At the time of "Tillys" birth, my Grandfather (from whom I am named) had just become an Episcopalian, and being an admirer of the Archbishop, he named my uncle after him. And I find many traits of mind and disposition that entitle him to his name—for he too "was good-tempered and much beloved in private life," and they looked some alike. You may remember the Archbishops portrait in our Collection. My uncle's style of writing also resembled his in its simple plainness and directness and but for his wife (a second one) he too would have been a Bishop. He was a man of the Priestly cast, as tall and personable as your Grandfather May, and wore his small[?] clothes till the last. He died in 1826 at Cheshire. Most of the Episcopal clergymen were educate[d] under his care at the Academ[y] there, which was a College in every thing but the name. You do not of course rememb[er] ever being in Cheshire with us when you were a Child.—

I am glad you promise to come and pass a day or more with us in October, when you may have more Genealogy if you wish it. Come up to stay as long as you can. You are daily in my thoughts. I wish you could be in my sight. But we can wait a little for that happiness.

I am having busy day, and harvesting our little crop at leisure minutes. I think we have cause for thankfulness in health and many Comforts: and, let me add, fo[r] your dutiful remembrance. My great respect to your husb[and.]

Ever Your,

Father.

Mrs. Anna B. Pratt.
East-Boston.

LETTER 61–7

[to George B. Emerson]

Concord Novr. 20th 1861

Dear Sir

I have received your Note enclosing the Check for One Hundred dollars from the King's Chapel Vestry, whose generosities ‖ value ‖ are greatly enhanced by the ‖ kind generous ‖ hands which convey the gift to myself and family as well as by the venerable name and ‖ associations ‖ memories with which it is associated. Will you please to communicate to the Vestry our thankful acknowledgements, ‖ of the Gift ‖ and believe in [2 words] and Yours

Greatly obliged
A. Bronson Alcott

George B. Emerson.

LETTER 61–8

[to Mrs. Anna Alcott, West Edmeston? N.Y.]

Concord, November 29th 1861.

Dear Mother,

I am 62 years of age this day, and you were 87 last June. If you live till next September you will then be as old as Grandfather Bronson was when he died. May you live till then, and years longer, and enjoy your health and faculties till the last, as, by your last letter, you tell us you are enjoying them. These are the chief privileges of age, and you deserve them in all their fulness. I wish it were in my power to add every comfort, and, among the rest, that of a home, if you wished one, with us. Nor is there any thing in the way, but the difficulties of the long journey to one of your years. And these might doubtless be overcome, had you some one to accompany you on the route. I feel, and so does my wife, that we could do a good deal for you were you with us, and we often express our hope that circumstances favor your coming, while it is among the possible things. I thought I might be in Syracuse sometime during the winter months or next spring, but the war has made this a doubtful matter, and will keep me about home for the present. I wish you would write and tell us how you feel about coming.

Louisa and Abby are now at home and will be with us most likely during the winter. Anna is living at East Boston, but visits us very often. She is wishing to pass next summer with us. She is very happy with her husband, who is a very worthy man, and thinks every thing of his wife. He is in a very good business. Abby gives lessons in drawing to Mr. Sanborn's scholars here in Concord. Louisa writes stories still and assists her mother about housekeeping. Just now all are sewing and knitting for Capt. Prescotts' company of soldiers, who leave to morrow for Fort-Warren in Boston Bay, to take good care of the Rebel Commissioners Slidell and Mason, during the winter. We are all in the best of health, and find ourselves very comfortable here in our large house. I have the Schools to visit once a month, and meet a few good people as often on Sunday at Greenwood about 14 miles from Concord. It is a kind of Church, and a little parish of earnest seekers for what they do not find in the other Churches. Next time, I am to meet their children and talk with them. I find these meetings pleasant and shall continue them so long as these friends wish me to give them the Sundays.—

I have not heard from Ambrose since I wrote to you. I hope you have, and from Chatfield. These war times pinch us all, and are likely to touch us more closely as the war continues. But we can afford to pay any sum of cuffering [sic] for the freedom of the slave, and for our own independence. You write that you have seen two-wars before this one which, I trust, is to give us a Country without a slave, and a Republic founded on Justice for all men.

You give us particular account of Betsey and her family. I wish it were possible for her and her husband to visit us. My children have known too little of my sister and family. They have never seen any member of ‖ them ‖ it, and have met Chatfield and Ambrose but once I think. Pamela and Pamila they never saw. Anna remembers Phebe.

Mrs. Dr. Alcott is living still at Auburndale about ten miles from us. William has just graduated from Williams College. His Uncle George G. Alcott is living at Church Hollow in Plymouth and his grandmother (Mrs. Obed Alcott) lives with her son there. William is a bright young man, and wishes to teach School. He writes that his sister Phebe is with them.

My regards to Linus and family.

I send you three dollars, the gift of your friend Mrs. Shaw of Boston.

Ever your affectionate Son

Amos

LETTER 61–9

[to Anna and John Pratt, East Boston]

Concord Dec. 1st 1861.

My kind Children,

You have sent me a touching birth-day Gift and tender notes for which you have my thanks. Now and henceforth my five are associated in characteristic ways, and speak from the Portrait that glances so meekly from the wall of our parlour, as if the dear Original were restored to my eyes and present as in days past. Abby has done her part admirably, and you yours. I wish I may do mine by you, as fitly and deserve as worthy a place in your remembrance.

I had many good wishes for you, and saw some suitable tokens at Stacy's which suitable considerations only staid my hand from appropriating and sending to you, as a slight return for your most endeared remembrance of my birth-day. Come up at Christmas, and take them then. It is virtuous to think of friends at such times. And so I tried to be good all day, writing at length to my dear ancient mother, (enclosing a little gift from her friend Mrs. Shaw) and spending the evening with my old friend, Miss Abby May[1] beside our kindly flame while Louisa and Abby were at Mrs. Anna Whiting's party.

And now before I put on my cozy new-gloves to go for the news, let me thank you again, good Children, for your remembrances and regards, and beg your taking mine as return for what you are, and promise to your friend and

Father.

For John and Anna.

[1] Abby W. May, Mrs. Alcott's cousin.

LETTER 62–1

[to William Russell, Lancaster, Mass.]

Concord January 20th 1862.

My Dear Friend,

Yours came to reassure me of your being at home again, and of your re-membrance of us. I was very happy to open your note and to read it. And wish most heartily that I may have the privilege of spending a day or so with you in recalling the pleasures of earlier days, and their hopeful purposes; some of which we are at least beginning to realize, if not in person, by proxy;—and so may esteem them ours, and thank the Powers, who hasten forwards the world's progress against every hindrance, whether of stupidity, or of misguided enthusiasm, to the great and good issues. If our civil troubles cannot now be avoided, we may not doubt that our States, whether these[?] shall maintain their integrity or not, shall come out of ‖ them ‖ the conflict, the better by a century or so, for for the schooling they knew not how to give themselves without this humbling disaster. For us, for you, and such, as you have persisted in being and doing, their remains [2 words] but to continue the good work of preparing for the peace which, come when it shall. [word] understanding, and in which nations, as individuals, must be planted fast, and deeply rooted, safe from accidents, and sure of their future. Had we a day together, we might draw the portrait of that time, which must bring body and feature and colour, such as enthusiasts delight in, to our dreams.

I am busy now, and delightfully so, engaged as I am in recovering some of these sky-pictures before they fade from these Skies and dissolve away. My Report is written: only waits for some touches, the last days of our school term, can supply to me. It must be shorter than our last, as our people must pay for their war—and behaved so generously last year by their Superintendent, and the schools of the town.

I have passed an afternoon lately with G. B. Emerson, and found him cordial, even more—affectionate, and full of assurances that surprised and strengthened me. There was no measure to his praises and commendations. And I gave him some glimpses of my plans and hopes. Had he been made Secretary of the Board, the Golden Age of Culture had come to us, to you, and your friend also. I hope to meet him often and again hereafter.

We are very well at home, Abby and wife with me. Louisa's school promises good fruits and encourages her much.[1] She is staying with James T. Fields, the publisher, whose wife—Miss Adams, daughter of Dr. Adams, is cousin to Mrs. Alcott.

Your accounts of your family gratify us. Remember me, and us to them. I must try to come and see you during the winter, or sometime in spring.

Ever yours
A. Bronson Alcott.

William Russell.

[1] Louisa conducted a kindergarten in Boston, against her own wishes, from January to May, 1862.

LETTER 62–2

[to Daniel Ricketson, New Bedford, Mass.]
Concord ‖ January ‖ February | 10th 1862.
Dear Friend,

You may not have been informed of the state of Henry's health this winter, and will be sorry to hear that he grows feebler day by day, and is evidently failing and fading from our sight. He gets some sleep, has a pretty good appetite, reads at intervals, takes notes of his readings, and likes to see his friends, conversing however with some difficulty as his voice partakes of his general debility.

We had thought this oldest inhabitant of our planet would have chosen to stay and see it fairly dismissed into the Chaos out of which he has brought so many precious jewels, gifts to friends to mankind generally, and a diadem for fames[?] for[?] coming followers[?]—forgetful of his claims to the honors—before he chose simply to withdraw from the places and times he has adorned by his [word]. But his work is nearly done for us here, and our woods and fields seem sorrowing, though not in sombre but in the robes of white most becoming the purity and probity that they have known so long and are soon to miss. There has been none such since Pliny, and it will be long before there comes his like:— the most knowing and wonderful worthy of his time.

I write at the suggestion of his sister, who thought his friend would like to be informed of his condition.

Ever yours,
A. Bronson Alcott

Daniel Ricketson
New Bedford

LETTER 62–3

[to Cynthia Dunbar Thoreau, Concord]

[Concord, May 19? 1862]

Mrs Thoreau,

You are very attentive to Henry's bequest in sending me, by fit hands,[1] the rare and wise books, which, in his last thoughtful hours, he deemed his friend worthy of inheriting. As every thought of his was a virtue, I shall prize these books the more on his account, and think tenderly of the giver whenever I open them. These volumes are from his choice library. They came to him honorably and are only older in time, but not in wisdom than his own writings. That he has left so much of his essence behind him: of his life, which he said
—"has been the poem I could have writ,
But I could not both live and utter it"
is a great happiness to his friends, and partly compensates for his laying aside his sun so soon. None living, had a better right to hold it. Nor do I think of a cotemporary who accomplished so much in so short a time as he has, whether we regard the weight of matter, or wealth of thought. We may be sure of his being read and prized by coming times, and the place and time pertaining to him, will be forever and sweeter for his presence. For as [word] which are cut down with the morning dew upon them, do, for a long while after, retain their fragrancy, so the good actions of a wise man perfume his mind and leave a rich scent behind them; so that his memory is, as it were, watered with these essences, and owes its flourishing to them.

Though I address this note to the mother, the sister is in my thoughts, also, as I write.

For Henry's sake,
as for yours,
your obliged friend.
A. Bronson Alcott

[1] Emerson.

LETTER 62–4

[Mrs. Anna Alcott, Oriskany Falls, N.Y.]

Concord September 1. 1862

Dear Mother.

I am uncertain as to whether your last letter has been answered. And write to answer if it has not been. You told us that you were about going to stay a little while at Oriskany Falls, with Chatfield's son who lives in his Fathers' house there. I believe you have not written to us since you spoke of going there. We shall be glad to hear from you whenever you are pleased to write to us and still better pleased if it were easy for you to come and live with us at Concord. Anna is now with us. But she is going to housekeeping in Boston, and leaves us next week. She is well. Louisa and Abby are with us. Abby teaches Drawing in Mr. Sanborn's School in the village. And Louisa is as active as ever with her pen. They both intend being with us during the winter. My wife is in the best of health, and often wishes you were here to advise with her about family matters. Our Garden has been productive, and we have an abundant apple-crop, fruit being good in these parts.

William, Dr. Alcott's son, now 25 years of age, and a very sensible young man, passed a day with us last week. His mother and sister are living at Newton about ten miles from Concord, and the same distance from Boston. He tells us they are well. His grandmother is living at Plymouth Hollow, with his uncle Garry, who has let the old Homestead at Spindle Hill. Widow Eldad lives at the old place, and Almon and Jed are where they have been. Uncle James Alcott and wife are both dead, as I suppose you have heard. I hope to see Wolcott again, and wish you could accompany me.

I see by the Waterbury American that the draft for men for the Army is to be made on the third of this month[.] 22 men are wanted from Wolcott. How it is in York State, I have not learned[.] I suppose Ambrose comes within the age. I have written to him, and hope to hear from him. He cannot leave his wife and family very well. Chatfield and I are too old to be of service. He has sons, or one certainly[.] I have none to help bring this unholy strife to an end, and free white and black from their long servitude. My wife and daughters send their love and kind remembrances, also their regards to my nephew.

Your son,
A. B. Alcott

LETTER 62–5

[to Chatfield Alcott, Oswego, N.Y.]

Concord September 1st 1862

Dear Brother,

How happens it that we have written so seldom, or not at all to one another, for these last years. Indeed, I have not a single letter of yours, I find, in my collection, and you cannot have many of mine. I wish you would write, if it were only to tell me something about your health and business, and as much about the times as you chose. Mother wrote a few weeks ago, that she was going to be at

Oriskany Falls with your Son, who was living in your house, married I think she said[,] and that I should address her there for the present. I have written to her to-day, and my letter will go forward with this to you, to morrow.

These war-times not only call for thought, but for action. You and I are less fitted to serve the Country in the field than you[ng] men. Nor have I any Sons to serve as you have. Ambrose is liable drafted, I believe. The draft comes on the third of this month in Connecticut. Wolcott is to furnish its 21. men, almost as many as we send from Concord. I shall be curious to learn who goes from the little town, and have asked Ambrose to inform me, when he knows.

William, Dr. Alcott's son, now about 25 years of age, and a sensible young man, passed a day with us last week. His mother and sister live about 10 miles from us in the town of Newton. His grand mother lives with her son Garry at Plymouth Hollow. So the Old homesteads at Spindle Hill have gone into strange hands. I hope to see them again sometime, and wish we could look at them together. Will you not come East sometime? I yet hope to have mother with us, if she is able to come so far at her advanced age. My family are all well. Anna, the eldest is married, about going to housekeeping in Boston. We are pleasantly situated here, and all busy. Louisa and Abby are with us. We shall be most glad to see you and your wife at any time.

I send one of my School Reports, for Mr. Sheldon, superintendent of the Schools in Oswego, and whose labors for Education I greatly respect. Call and give it to him yourself.

My wife and daughters send regards to you and yours.

Your Brother
A. B. Alcott

Mr. Chatfield Alcott

Letter 62–6

[to Anna]

[Concord, September 1, 1862] | (Pilgrim's Progress.)

Dear Anna,

This Book, associated with delightful memories of your childhood and youth, I now present to you, as a gift from

Your Father.

Concord September 1, 1862

Letter 62–7

[to Mrs. A. Bronson Alcott, Chelsea, Mass.]

Saturday Morning | Sepr 21st 1862

My Dear,

Sanborn proposes to drive me down to Medford, if the day prove fair to-morrow, and Harry Stearns took our message to his mother last night.[1] If I do not go with Sanborn, then I shall leave early on Monday, (as we planned) do my errands in the city, and come to Chelsea sometime in the afternoon. The girls see no reason why I may not spend the night, and come up on Tuesday. They are proving their skill in house keeping, every thing thus far going smoothly and neatly. Thinking to hear from you they have not written. Nor have we had any intimations of you since you left. I trust the new house and its occupants have kept your heart and hands busy. And I know that you will leave nothing undone within your power to make it and them cozy and comfortable. I wish I had an estate as ample as they deserve to offer them. Yet they are richer than most I know in each other, and can better afford to live with a little

"How fruitful may the smallest circle grow
If we the secret of its culture know,"

says Goethe.

I saw fair fruits at the Fair on Thursday, and heard a poor oration. Though the day was fair, the time was sad, ominous of days of evil. What can one do but[t] read the news and weep at our victories even.—To Anna and John much esteem, and to yourself.

A.B.A.

¹ Henry L. Stearns, eldest son of Mary and George Stearns.

LETTER 62–8

[to Thomas Davis, Providence, R.I.]

Concord October 13th | 1862.

Dear Sir,

On the last of this month, I am to make payments on my place. These will nearly discharge my debt, if I can command the sums pledged to me for this purpose. It is unnecessary perhaps to remind my friends of my obligations except as to the time of their becoming due, though these times of ours derange every ones affairs more or less, and render business uncertain. But we may hope for the better now that their cause has been touched, and the country is awakened to a clearer perception of the evils we are suffering.

I trust we shall now strike blows that will tell, and bring terms that righteous men and true patriots can accept.

I read the other day of the death of your brother inlaw, William Chace. The part he had taken in human affairs is associated in my mind with much that is noble and worthy of a wise man, and leads to regrets that he should have left us when so much wanted by his country.

Shall we not see you and Mrs. Davis here sometime. It must be some years since you were here, and I wish you may come this way. My wife would be glad to see you, as would your friends here.

Truly Yours,
A. Bronson Alcott.

Hon. Thos. Davis

LETTER 62–9

[to Mrs. Anna Alcott, West Edmeston? N.Y.]

Concord, November 30th 1862

Dear Mother,

Your letter with the likeness came yesterday, on my birth-day as you intended it should. I was glad to have it, and my wife had it put at once into a pretty frame in which it now stands and looks benignantly forth from the mantel piece. A goodlooking body certainly for a Spirit that has numbered near ninety human years. You could ‖ not ‖ not have sent us a more acceptable birth-day gift, or more encouraging accounts of yourself. I wish you may enjoy the remainder of your years as peacefully and usefully as the past. Thank you for the letter and the gift. And my wife shall tell you the rest. With remembrances to all,

Your Son,

A. B. A.

LETTER 62–10

[to Thomas Davis, Providence, R.I.]

Concord December 31st 1862

Dear Friend.

Yours came to hand this day and in season to meet the season's demands. Thank you for it, and for your timely generosities heretofore. I wish I may find wherewith to reward you, if not in kind in some equivalent as good.

I am tempted by your invitation to visit you. And may do so sometime during this winter. A good house with a good man in it, and its builder are always worth seeing, and I value them as highly as any one can, especially in times like ours. It would give me pleasure to meet my friends in your city also.

Yours truly,

A. Bronson Alcott

Hon. Thomas Davis.

PART THIRTEEN

✳

1863

LETTER 63–1

[to William Lloyd Garrison, Jr.]

Concord, January 5th 1863.

Dear Sir,

Here are the Dials you enquired about the other evening. Numbers 2 3 5 and 14 are wanting to complete the set of 4 vols. They were published originally at 75 cts the number. They now bring 1 dollar at the bookshops though full sets cannot be obtained there—and you shall have the numbers here enclosed at that price. Burnham may have numbers 2 and 3: 7 and 14 are very scarce, and you must take your chance for getting them to complete your set.

I am happy to add the Book to your library. Tis a hopeful sign that young men are taking to reading the books of [2 words] to which it belongs, and of which it is the earliest and liveliest representative.

Wishing to become better acquainted with you and your kindred, and hoping we shall see you here sometime,

I am
Truly Yours
A. Bronson Alcott.

Wm. L. Garrison Jr

LETTER 63–2

[to Anna, Chelsea, Mass.]

Concord, Jan. 25th 1863.

Dear Anna,

It will be comforting to you and your husband to know that Louisa is here at home again, though much enfeebled by her sickness and the long journey.[1] She was hardly able to come away, but came through with courage, and less harm than I anticipated. We left Washington at 6½ P.M. on Thursday and reached Boston yesterday hoping to take the four oclock train for Concord. But missing this, by a few minutes, we went to Thomas Sewall's and passed the night.

Louisa was faint and overcome by the long ride, but much better in the morning. Miss Stevenson came to see her, and met us again at the station at 4. P.M. We reached home safely, and Louisa was communicative, and though much spent, seemed far better than I feared. To day, Dr. Bartlett has seen her, and thinks, that with quiet and good nursing she will be up again before long. Her trouble is sore throat, with fever at times. She sleeps more or less, and talks at times in her usual lively way.

I beg you will not be alarmed about her. For though it may be that she will need time to recover her strength, the Drs. all say there is nothing against her getting well.

It was most fortunate for her that I went to her as I did. Every thing was against her at the Hospital. And the Dr. advised her leaving before her strength was wasted by delay. I decided to bring her away as soon as I saw her though she thought it ignominious to depart her post, and persisted at first in staying longer. But made up her mind to leave on Monday or Tuesday, as we should have done but for the storm.—I have much to tell you about the journey, people &c. but must defer all till I come out and see you, which I hope to do soon. If not sometime this week, then on Monday of next, when I am to give my first Conversation in Boston. Your mother begs room to add a word.

Affectionately,
Your Father.

---

[1] After serving for about six weeks as a nurse in the hospital at Georgetown, D.C., Louisa had come down with typhoid fever, and her father had gone to Washington to bring her home.

LETTER 63–3

[to Anna, Chelsea, Mass.]

[Concord] | Tuesday, [January] 27th 63.

Dear Anna,

Louisa has had a quiet day, sleeping some, and her fever seems abating a little. She does not talk much, but inclines to be let mostly alone, loving to have your mother, Abby or myself in her chamber, and asks questions occasionally about things passing. To-day she enquired about letters from you, read the newspaper account of Mrs. Ropes death,[1] and spoke of events at the Hospital. It was a long journey we made and required all her strength and cour[age] to come through. She has but just got over the effort, and must need some weeks of tender nursing and all her patience to recover from the fatigue and the disease. Dr. Bartlett pronounces every thing hopeful about her case, and wonders she is not more exhausted by the journey than he finds her. We may be thankful that it is made, and that she is out of the dangers of that infected place here at home, and so likely to be well again.

Your mother is freed from her past anxieties, and things take their accustomed course here with us, in good part, again. Should any thing fall out to the contrary, you shall be at once informed. *This* has been the most comfortable day she has had since her return.

If it does not storm badly, I hope to see you to-morrow. And you shall hear from her, or about her, whether I see you or not.

I am now going to the P. Office, and hope to get something from you to read to her.

Affectionately
Your Father

Your mother is resting from last nights watching. Regards to your husband.
A.B.A.

[1] Mrs. Ropes, of Boston, had served in the same hospital as Louisa and had died there of typhoid fever.

LETTER 63–4

[to Anna, Chelsea, Mass.]
Concord, January 29th 1863

Dear Anna,

I was sorry to see you for so short a time yesterday, and to hurry away, leaving you on the side walk for my seat in the Car. I had time to get yesterdays papers at the Station, and found Louisa resting comfortably on my return. She had a somewhat restless night, but is quiet and conversable to-day. The Dr. pronounced her, if no better, not worse, when he saw her at 9 this morning, and assured us that there was nothing as yet to prevent her recovery. I have been with her much of the time to day. She asked me to sit near her bedside, and tell her the adventures of our fearful journey home, the same which I related yesterday to you—and enjoyed the story, laughing over the plot and catastrophe, as if it were a tale of her imagining.

The oranges were a treat to her sore throat, which is slightly better. She dreads the fever fits which come twice in the twenty four hours, and leave her perplexed and exhausted. But sleep follows to refresh her wasted spirits and give intervals of comparative ease. We hope the fever has not many days more to run. When this leaves her, then she may steadily recruit her strength and be herself again. Abby is now sitting with her, and your mother is getting rest after the half-nights watching. Her anxiety has given place to the better feelings of hope and assurance, so that she is willing to rest, and go about her housekeeping with something like cheerfulness.

Louisa spoke of hoping to be able to write a few lines to you to-morrow. I hope she will be.

I shall look for the Transcripts by Saturday's mail, and if your husband has time to drop me a word about the advertisement[1] I will thank him.
Your Father.

4. o clock P.M. Thursday.

PS. Enclosed is mothers note which I should have given you yesterday

[1] Of Alcott's forthcoming Conversations in Boston.

LETTER 63–5

[to Anna, Chelsea, Mass.]

Friday 4 P.M. | 30th Jan. 1863.

Dear Anna.

According to promise I send you to-days bulletin of Louisa's condition. She has had a day of less quiet than she had yesterday: was restless, and flighty through the night, with shorter intervals of connected conversation, the fever running higher than on any preceding day since she was taken. Dr. B. speaks hopefully of her recovery still. We take turns about watching and manage to get some sleep every night. Your mother thinks Mr. Pratt may be willing to pass Monday night in the house, in case of necessity so that I may hold my first Conversation.

Abba has gone to find a woman to do the housework, since Louisa will need tender and constant care for some weeks to come.

The "Journal and Liberator" advertise my Conversations, and I am expecting the "Transcripts" by to night's mail.

Thanks to your husband.

I may not go down on Monday till the 6½ train, but will meet you at 10 at Mr. Sewalls office.

Your Father.

LETTER 63–6

[to Anna, Chelsea, Mass.]

Concord, Wednesday [February 4, 1863] 3. P.M.

Dear Anna.

On my return from Boston yesterday, I found Louisa much as I left her on Monday. And to-day she is more comfortable than she has been at any time since her return. The fever appears to have about run its course. Sweet sleep, and less disturbed, has come at last. She begins to ask impatiently for food; has taken her beef-tea more than once, and Dr. B. said this morning on leaving that he "should not come again till to-morrow." We trust the main perils are past, and that her recovery dates from this hour, though it will need careful nursing for some weeks to restore her strength and right-mindedness. Your mother thinks you may perhaps accompany me home next Tuesday, if nothing goes amiss meanwhile. She begins to ask about the events of the last weeks, and to converse a little. And we think it will be comforting to her to have you beside her by that time.

My Conversations opened hopefully Company not numerous; some having gone to hear Murdock read on that evening, who will attend, I doubt not, hereafter. Mr. Dudley put $40 into my hand for the twenty Season tickets which he had sold to his friends.

As Mr. G. B. Emerson was not there, I am ignorant of his success in that way: or of receipts for the single evening.

R. W. Emerson is expected home next Saturday, and we may have him at our next. Conway promises a notice in this week's "Commonwealth."[1] Your mother is writing to Uncle Sam; and delighting in her woman "Mary."

Let me see you somewhere on Monday or Tuesday.

Your Father.

[1] Moncure Conway and Franklin B. Sanborn had assumed the editorship of the *Commonwealth,* an anti-slavery journal, the first number of which had appeared on September 6, 1862.

LETTER 63–7[1]

Concord February 28th 1863.

Town of Concord Dr. to A. B. Alcott.

To services as Superintendent of the Schools for the year 1862–'63———$100.00.

Received Payment,

A. Bronson Alcott.

[1] MS. owned by the Concord Antiquarian Society.

LETTER 63–8

[to Mrs. Anna Alcott, West Edmeston, N.Y.]

Concord March 25. 1863.

Dear Mother,

You will like to hear from us again, and I write now that I may send you what I am sure you will look upon with pleasure—the picture of your oldest boy, though he shows snowy locks and is seated in a grandfatherish manner in his arm chair comfortably enough. To you, his mother, he may look no older than 17 and remind you perhaps of earlier days. It is thought a good likeness,—and I send it at once. It was taken but last week, and I have just brought it home, with others, then taken in Boston. I wish I could send you a larger one, which is also good, and intended for framing. Yours and mine are now facing one another in our Family Album, containing those of our girls and other relations.

Did I write to you about Louisa's being brought home from Washington where she had been to nurse in the Army Hospital? I am not sure whether I did. But am glad to tell you that she is up and about the house again, though weak and feeble yet from the effects of the typhoid fever which she caught, and which ran its course of thirty days, and made us all anxious, as you may imagine about her. That was our contribution to the war and one we should not have made willingly had we known the danger and the sacrifices. The rest of us are well. Abby ‖ is ‖ has been at home this winter, and Anna is still at Chelsea expecting soon to be a mother. My wife will write to you in due time about her. I have just closed a course of ten Conversations in Boston which were well attended. Remember me and my family to Sister Betsey and hers.

Your Son
A. Bronson Alcott.

LETTER 63–9

[to Anna, Chelsea, Mass.]

[Concord] Monday Evening, | March 30th. 63.

Dear Anna,

And now a happy mother, with her first born at her breast, and prospects of indescribable satisfactions to make good the dreams of past years,—the fullness of bliss.[1] I can add nothing to your fullness of life by words. Yet cannot be silent on the joyous advent that brings your mother to share in your pleasures for a day, if no longer. I, too, must come and see how my first-born bears herself with hers. And a husband-father beside her. You had chosen otherwise, as did those who chose another, not you. Yet got a better than they chose, had their prayers been answered bodily. Boys are blessings too. I asked for one, at least. And had I been told I must wait till my girl should bear me one, three and thirty years after my first disappointment—glad as I was to have her—I should doubtless have thought it a hard joke. But so it was; and now if he shall inheri[t] his parents' graces, his grandfather will be doub[le] blest—nor has waited a minute too long: so name him by the fairest name, taking ample time to choos[e.] You cannot chance amiss, and will please him, and your father

Affectionately.

The young mother.

[1] Frederick Alcott Pratt was born March 28, 1863.

LETTER 63–10

[to Sophia Hawthorne, Concord]

[Concord, April 10, 1863]

Dear Mrs. Hawthorne

Thanks for the restored shade. It is as beautiful as it will be useful. Certainly nothing could be more scholarly. I shall set it in the centre of my Study Table, and associate the givers with the Arts and Graces whose radiance they have contrived to mellow for my pleasure.

When next in the city I will see if I can find a picture worthy of the acceptance of Rose and Mr. Hawthorne.

Truly Yours,
A. Bronson Alcott

Friday Morning
   April 10th 1863.

LETTER 63–11

[to Mrs. A. Bronson Alcott, Chelsea, Mass.]

Concord April 24th | 1863.

My Dear,

Louisa's things came this morning early, and every piece is now in its place. We all think it suitable and tasteful. Chestnut too is cheaper and as durable— though Abby was a little disappointed when she found the fancier ‖ Walnut ‖ painted was not to ornament the Spinster's chamber.—Your (and my) room Our room,—I meant dutifully to say—now prides itself in the added ornaments of the bureaus and mirrors, worktable, pictures &c. and waits your arrival to take pride in it and praise it also. Then Abby has begun and hopes to finish the papering of the dining room to morrow. It will be neat and handsome—good enough to receive the ancients—the veteran sideboard now set on firm feet— included. Indeed we are getting up into the higher ranks, and our house only waits for its matron to be completely furnished. We think the paper chaste and of the right tints. I dont see how you could have done better. So you see we are pleased, and forgive Leslie[?] and one another for past presumptions.

Louisa brings proper accounts of Ma, Grandma and baby. I shall want to see the little ‖ gentleman ‖ fumbler when he has found out where he is, and who is who, which lesson in the transcendental metaphysics, he must be very eager about feeling and seeing and sucking out just now. I hear his mother is very amiable in his discipline, has opinions about his welfare, as becomes her, in advance of his grandmothers, hers belonging to antiquity, and for the rising generation obsolete and unsuitable. As to a name suppose you ask him to wait till he can speak and tell you his wishes about his proper ancestries, which one of the[m] he represents and ‖ wishes ‖ chooses to be named after. That would be a very sensible thing for a daughter of the Father of the new mankind to do. Think of it.

Meals all punctual and nothing amiss. The rhapsodist chanting yet. I shall send Anna and John "the Commonwealth" tomorrow.

Ever Yours.

A.B.A.

LETTER 63–12

[to Miss Powell, Ghent, N.Y.]

Concord April 24th 1863.

Dear Miss. Powell

Your note revived pleasant memories of yourself, and good people with whom I had associated you. Be assured your interest in us this way honors us; for I have always esteemed the faiths of young persons the highest honors their elders can receive. When you come East again I hope to see more of you. Not- withstanding ‖ the ‖ our national calamity, there has been a good deal to en- courage and interest during the last months. There is freedom and a country apparent, if not established in the persuasions of the best people, where alone they can be and survive threatened evils. I find our young people feeling right about it. Mrsrs. [sic] Conway and Sanborn are doing something in the right ways, and others following.

I trust you read their "Commonwealth," and like it. Lest you should not, I send a copy of the last, with the School Reports, which I am pleased to find yourself and Brooklyn friend care for.

If you have thoughts asking[?] associates[?], write sometimes. It will always gratify me to receive and hospitably entertain them.

Truly yours.
A. Bronson Alcott.

LETTER 63-13

[to David A. Wasson]

Concord April 24th 1863.

Dear friend,

I am detained unexpectedly at home this week, by my wife's visit to worship her first and only grandson, at Chelsea, and as I am not [word] as yet on what day of this week or next, she may return, I fear I must postpone my visit to Worcester till perhaps week after next, or later. I am sorry for I had fancied some good hours with you and your friends. That pleasure I still hope to make good.

Your methods of thought and style of writing have interested me lately, and I want to talk with you about both. The sonnets in "the Commonwealth" were a surprise to us here Emerson has found even more than he hoped, and that was much, for you are to be told that he believes absolutely in your gifts. Don't think me speaking beyond measure when I say, these are the first sonnets any American has written, that remind one of Shakespeare. Your matter is high and the treatment worthy of it. Their sweetness and melody are beyond praise. About the Essays on Personality—there is neither time nor space to add a word here and now. You are dealing with the [word], and divine much to my mind.

I must see you when that can be.

Most truly yours
A. Bronson Alcott

Mr. Wasson

LETTER 63-14

[to Mrs. A. Bronson Alcott, Chelsea, Mass.]

[Concord] Thursday Evening | 30th April 1863.

My Dear,

Louisa has given her version of affairs, and I add a word. Our house papering and painting drags, but promises to go forwards now. So if you should not return till Tuesday of next week, all will be done, we hope. The girls seem bent on having it, and every thing else, in the best order for your approval: and though they dont say so, I suspect they secretly hope you will stay over Sunday, and not be here in the hurry and worry of matters. I see no reason why you should not stay,—certainly if you can serve Anna, who, I know, will keep you as long as she can. And you can be of so much to her now. On the whole, stay and enjoy her, and ‖ hers ‖ your grandson, a few days longer.—John will miss you too.

The weather has been very spring-like for a few days past. Mr. Moore engaged to plough our garden, but must needs sell his horses just when I expected the ploughing to be done. But Conner has partly promised to do it tomorrow. And as soon as that is done, I plant some early peas and potatoes; though not many of my neighbors have planted yet.—

Carney has cut some of the wood, and is to do the rest. I believe Mrs. Hawthorne has got him for a few days now. But I think I shall undertake less gardening this season.

I hope "the Commonwealth" suits John and Anna. Sanborn tells me John has subscribed for it. S. E. Sewall says 'tis the best paper in New England.

Parker comes to-morrow, and *Beecher* next week. I am told *"the Club" paper* of last week, has been read and much praised.

Can you manage to get the two pictures at Masury's that were to be touched up for Emerson and Hawthorne? And if you go or send for them, ask him to do two more. I dont see how I can well not give one to Channing, and Mr. Russell. Tell Anna she shall have one with the hand where she puts hers.

The Girls really manage to keep house, and do a great deal of work besides. The Girl in caps[?] takes better care of her sire, than he fears she does of herself, though she has not appeared the worse. You will testify to her good works when [you] see how they praise her here in these gates.—

Is not this the longest time yo[u] have been from us, for several y[ears.]

Love to the *three in one.*

Ever Yours,
A.B.A.

LETTER 63–15

[to Mrs. A. Bronson Alcott, Chelsea, Mass.]

[Concord] Friday Noon. | May Day, 1863.

My Dear,

I committed to Adam's Express a box from Louisa containing flowers and letters for you, which I trust you will get this afternoon. This morning came your letter saying you thought of staying over till Tuesday of next week, and giving the best grandmotherly accounts of all your pets, which we were glad to receive. You will see from our notes that you are doing just as we wished, that is, keep yourself out of a general revolution of dust kicking &c. here at Hillside. Tuesday is to find all in spandy fine order and ready for the Mistress to return and admire. The painting is going forwards to-day, and the papering follows as soon as paint will dry. I think these revolutionists have made as little havock [*sic*] with the Ancients as could have been expected considering their lineage and breeding: on the whole, reformed upon the old settled order.

The day is delightful: the lawn grassy and your birds melodious in the grove.

If you can stop down as far as Masury's, nearly opposite William's and Everett's on Washington Street, ‖ not far from Hollis[?] ‖ and get the pictures, for Emerson and Hawthorne I shall be glad, and, if all seems accommodating, let them do one for Channing and one for Mr. Russell, in the same way.

Wasson writes for me to come to Worcester, next week, or the beginning of the week following. If I can do the early planting and the Schools in time, I will try to spend the Sunday after next with him.

I am pleased to find that Anna hopes to be with us in June: baby of course, and papa on Sundays.

Much love.

A.B.A.

I enclose $1.00. and wish it 1000. wer[e.]

LETTER 63–16[1]

[to William T. Harris, St. Louis]

Concord June 4th 1863.

Dear Sir,

I have read the critique on Kant you sent me the other day. The metaphysical ability displayed in hunting out errors, and complementing the deficiencies of the Father of modern Transcendentalism, I think should have a freer scope, and address quite another class of thinkers than those to whom you have submitted your conclusions. I shall be glad to see ‖ the ‖ paper you allude to, and if you will send it to me, I will see that it has a chance for other judgments than mine.—If it shall prove suited to "Sanborns' Commonwealth newspaper", we hope you will consent to ‖ have ‖ his printing it therein, for our New-England readers. And if you have other things like it, or concerning the ‖ the ‖ times, that you would care to print, I doubt not he will gladly find place for them. Indeed, I had mentioned your name to him before your letter came, and advised his seeking your correspondence for his paper. It is but just started but promises good things. Lest he should not have sent you a copy I mail one to you with this.

Yours truly

A. Bronson Alcott

[1] From a copy, in Alcott's hand, in the Alcott-Pratt Collection. The original is in the Alcott-Harris Collection in the Concord Free Public Library (see Appendix B).

LETTER 63–17

[to Mrs. Anna Alcott, West Edmeston, N.Y.]

Concord June 24th 1863

Dear Mother,

Your letter came to day telling us that you are 90 years old. It is a good while to live and you have seen and done a good many things in your time, beginning your life there by the river-side; moving to the little neighborhood where your children were born and grew up to marry and move in their turn to begin life for themselves most of them far away, and you to follow them and leave all behind. It seems as if I had lived long, but you have seen 27 years more than I have, and I can hardly reach your term at most, though I should like to see these disastrous civil troubles settled, and my children having a free chance in a free country, before I leave them for a little while. I think I may say that the prospect for us was never more promising since we made a family. All of us are in the best of health, and busy; Anna's boy thriving, herself a happy wife and mother, Louisa just beginning to be known as a lively writer, her stories and sketches coming into Notice and winning much favor. I send you her account of herself while at Georgetown, and a story of hers is to appear in the Atlantic monthly for August, some verses also; besides a tale in a New York Magazine. She is busy and intends to devote herself to her pen. Abby too is full of life and promise, has a drawing pupil, and is trying moulding in plaster lately. My wife is encouraged by all this prosperity, and lives in her family mostly as mothers and wives will. I am occupied with gardening, writing, Conversing occasionally, and Superintending the Schools. I met good companies in Boston for ten evenings during January and March. Lately I have printed some things in our "Commonwealth," which is edited by our town's man Mr. Sanborn. Louisa is also a contributor.

But I have little room for enquiring about your own welfare. I wish I could visit you with my wife. I trust your eresypilas [sic] is but temporary. Remember me kindly to Betsey and family. Ransom's letter shows him to be a worthy son of his mother.

Yours ever,
Amos

LETTER 63–18

[to Samuel Gray Ward]

Concord June 28th 1863.

Mr. Sam. G. Ward,

Please pay to the bearer Mr. John B. Pratt, the sum now due me on the "Alcott Fund", and oblige, Yours

A. Bronson Alcott.

July 3. Recd. from Mr. Ward by Mr Pratt, $108.75.

LETTER 63–19

[to Mrs. A. Bronson Alcott, Chelsea, Mass.]

Concord June 29th. 1863

My dear.

All's well. Yesterday was a quiet day, and this forenoon I was at Sleepy Hollow, am to be there again to meet Suretta[?] this afternoon, and arrange about the lot. We must wait for rain to sod and finish the spot. I am glad it is to be done. It has laid accusingly on my mind for the years past. We shall no longer reproach ourselves for the seeming negligence.

I hope to see you and our Grandson on Friday. The boy of course cannot come yet without his mother, and the father cannot escape following fast after the two.

Before you come can you call at Masury's and get the four pictures that I am to have touched for me.

I have enclosed the order on Mr. Ward for John to take to him if he can. You will see Sam. Sewall yourself, doubtless.

Our house is hardly ours without its hostess. It will be doubly so with her and the guests she brings.

Ever Yours,
A.B.A.

Louisa will write tomorro[w.]

LETTER 63–20

[to E. Bronson Cooke, Waterbury, Conn.]

Concord July 10 1863.

E. Bronson Cooke Esqr.
Dear Sir,

I am pleased to find that my daughter's "Sketches have found discerning readers in my Native State, and in my native town especially. It may afford you gratification to know that your estimate of their literary merits, their humor and humanity have found appreciation from the best sources. They are to be printed in a more readable form with some additions for Hospital and Army reading. I shall be glad to send a copy of the book when it comes out to yourself and the Widow of Capt. Bronson of whose funeral we lately had an account in your Paper. Accompanying this, I send the numbers of the "Commonwealth" containing the Sketches.[1]

My daughter has recovered from the Hospital fever she brought home, and we have the prospect before us of visiting Waterbury and Wolcott sometime, if not during this summer, then perhaps in the autumn. She has not been in those parts since she was a Child, and knows little of your thriving city, and of Spindle Hill, the Homeste[ad] of her ancestors, than by family report.

Yours truly
A. Bronson Alcott

¹ *Hospital Sketches,* published in book form by James Redpath in August, 1863.

LETTER 63–21

[to ?]

Concord July 20th 1863

Dear Sir,

I have had your father's books done up for some days intending to return them with my thanks to you at Cambridge in person on Commencement day. As I could not be present then, I now send them by Express with many apologies for keeping them so long, though I spoke of returning them when your father was last at my house and he kindly begged me to retain longer if I had not completed making some extracts from them. This was but one of many kindnesses of which I have been the recipient from time to time since I first knew him. He loved to lend books and knew better than most what they contained. Let me express to the son the many obligations I am under to him.

The last time I saw [word] was at a Conversation of mine in Boston, and think he did not go out much after that.

He was one of the few persons whom I always met with the certainty of having delightful intercourse, and his company, as his books wer[e] always open to all.

Very truly yours
A B Alcott

LETTER 63–22

[to Anna, Chelsea, Mass.]

Concord July 26th | 1863.

Dear Anna,

This war comes nearer and quite home to us here at the North to try our patriotism and principles: comes to you and yours. Nor do I doubt will find you equal to the trial whatsoever this proves to be. We looked for letters by last night's mail, thinking you would be swift to let us know the final decision if it has been pronounced. Pray write as soon as you know.

I spent an hour yesterday with Frederick, who is with the Conscripts here in Camp on the Cattle Show grounds. He thinks they may be ordered on Monday, to morrow, to Long Island where they report to the Government and await further orders. He hopes to get his discharge from the Government Surgeon. I wish he may, as he seems unable to stand the fatigues of the soldier. His wife is feeling much about his going as you may conceive, feeble as she is, and almost alone here in New England.

But war is heartless, and respects none—not wives nor babes even.

Abby takes this as she goes for the recreation she needs, and hopes to find at Clarke's Island.[1] I am glad she goes. She will meet good people, and vary the scene for a fortnight at least.

Things look fair for us here and we hope nothing is to darken your fair future; and what can, while your husband is brave, and your boy smiles?

Affectionately,
Your Father

[1] Clark Island, Maine?

LETTER 63–23

[to James Redpath, Boston]

Concord July 27th | 1863.

Mr. Redpath
Dear Sir,

I return by Mr. Sanborn my hearty thanks for the copy of your elegant edition of Phillips Speeches[1] which he brought me, yesterday, as a gift from you. Tis a solid and superb Book. And you have done no small service to the cause of freedom and of nationality in publishing such a body of history and of eloquence at this time. It better deserves the study of statesmen, patriots and philanthropists than any book likely to appear during the war—which it does so much to explain, and bring to the righteous close, for the [word]—of the country; and its true friends.

The portrait is characteristic, though for myself, that of the orator standing as he speaks would have pleased me better. I am glad to learn the book‖ s ‖ finds such ready sale.

Very truly
Yours
A. Bronson Alcott.

Mr. Redpath.

[1] Wendell Phillips, *Speeches, Lectures, and Letters.*

LETTER 63–24

[to Mrs. A. Bronson Alcott, Chelsea, Mass.]

[Concord, July 31? 1863] | Friday Evening.

My dear,

You feel right about matters, and have done what I was about asking you to do—i.e.—write to G. B. Emerson yourself, as the natural Petitioner, and gifted besides with that humane eloquence which Christian George is likely to be touched by. It was the proper thing be done at this time, and he is the man to help us. I trust help will come of it.

As to Fields, tis plain his contributor is of an ancient race, and far too slow and starless to sail in Atlantic Seas. If he opens any little Parlor Archapelegos [sic] for us to sport in, after this damage done, let us forgive and forget.

All goes smoothly here these fine autumn days. And if you have any thing to detain you over Sunday, stay and do it. Anna can count another day as hers, and we can wait.

I send some of our apples, and if I could gather only the ripest ones from the clusters, would add a few grapes, which are ripening fast though none are fairly ripe and sweet yet.

The potatoes are all in the cellar, and good. Also the hops, mint and sage, in your chamber awaiting your return.

Love to Anna, and much comfort in her new house.

Ever Yours
A.B.A.

LETTER 63–25

[to Betsey and Linus Pardee, West Edmeston, N.Y.]
Concord August 6th 1863.

Dear Brother and Sister,

Your letter came yesterday. What you write about mother's condition is not surprising when we consider her extreme age, 90, as I learn from my Family Record, on the 20th. of June last,—an age none of us are likely to reach, and beyond which only one of her long-lived family, Uncle Noah, lived, he being 92. She has outlived her five sisters, being now the last of a good family.

I have always felt how much we all owed to her; how, in our quiet home, quiet reigned because of her presence in it, and how her influence was felt for good throughout the rural neighborhood into which she brought so many excellent qualities of heart, good sen[se] so much to soften and sweeten the rudeness of that district. She had best of influence over our father who, among all his brothers, all of whom I very well remember, appears to have been the superior man. He left us just when a father feels the deeper interest in his children from their then beginning to take their parts in life and Reward him for his painstakings on their account. He was a good man, with all the plain virtues and few of the vices,—faults I should have said,—of the district where he was born, where he lived and died. I had never suspected my strong resemblance to him in features till seeing a copy of a medallion head of me for the first time the other day.[1] It seemed so like him, and revived all my impressions of his face, though he has been dead this 34 Years, last 3rd of April.

Were it not so large, I would send an impression by mail to you. I wish it were easy for me to bring one in person, for mother's eye, as well as yours. I fear it will be almost impossible for me to leave home just now. Abby is away. There is only my wife and Louisa here. Still if my coming is necessary I must try to come. Let me know from week to week how mother is.

I do not address this to ‖ you ‖ her personally but to you, and leave it for ‖ her ‖ you to read any parts of it to her you think proper.

I trust the final change will be a peaceful one. My love and lasting thanks to her for all she has been to me and the rest of us. In the run of nature we must take the journey too before long. I am 63, and you, Betsey, are 55. I believe your husband is about your own age.

If mother is able, and disposed to write, or dictate through any of you, any words or wishes, I will reply to her at once.

We are all well and send our tender regards to you and yours.

Your Brother,
A. Bronson Alcott.

[1] The work of Seth Cheney, *ca.* 1854.

LETTER 63–26

[to W. A. Wellman]

Concord Aug. 7th 1863.

Dear Sir,

In reply to your note of yesterday's date, asking to add my name to Gov. Andrews' Committee's Call for raising funds for recruiting colored soldiers, I hasten to say that if it will serve the good cause in the least, I shall be most happy to give it, with any personal services it may imply in consequence. Certainly it behooves every good citizen to take the black man's part by rendering him every facility for uniting his fortunes with the white man's, in this struggle for the freedom of the races, and in which he has so good a right to claim his share of the sacrifices and rewards of victory.

Whatever duties belong to me I shall be happy to know and discharge according to my ability.

Respectfully,
A. Bronson Alcott.

Mr. W. A. Wellman.
Sec. Commy.

LETTER 63–27

[to E. Bronson Cooke, Waterbury, Conn.]

Concord Aug. 30th *1863*.

E. B. Cooke, Esqr.
Dear Sir,

Knowing your interest in whatever relates to the personal history of Waterbury and of the surrounding towns, I send you the following, for insertion in "the American."

Died at West Edmeston N.Y. August 27th. Mrs. Anna Bronson Alcott, widow of the late Joseph Chatfield Alcott of Wolcott, and daughter of Capt. Amos Bronson of Plymouth, Conn. Mrs. Alcott was the last of a long-lived family. She having reached the advanced age of 90 years, and her brother Judge Bronson of Medina, Ohio, lived to be 92: Several of her sisters were over 70, and her father died at 88. Mrs. Alcott was a sister of Dr. Tillotson Bronson, Rector of St. John's Church, Waterbury, and Principal of Cheshire Episcopal Academy, in which, for nearly a quarter of a century, were educated the Clergy of that denomination here in New England, and from different States of the Union. She was a woman of great good sense, sweetness of disposition, industry, and engaging manners. On her 90th birth day she wrote, without spectacles, to her son, and kept a Journal during most of her long life, which she enjoyed, with but slight interruptions of illness, till the last. She valued the Church in which she was educated, and of which she was a member ‖ of ‖ at the time of her death, which took place at the house of her daughter Mrs. Pardee.

My daughter asks your acceptance of the accompanying copy of her "Hospital Sketches," in which you expressed so discriminating an interest.

If convenient will you mail half a dozen copies of "The Waterbury," containing the Obituary to Concord, Mass. and oblige,

Yours, respectfully
A. Bronson Alcott.

LETTER 63–28

[to Isaac and Rebecca Bronson, Medina, Ohio]

Concord, Mass. | September 20th 1863.

Dear Cousins,

You will not be surprised to learn of my mother's death, a notice of which I send you in the accompanying newspaper. She died at the house of my Sister Betsey Pardee, with whom she had lived since she left my house here in Concord in the autumn of 1857. Her health had been slowly declining, my sister writes, since she left us, though she seemed cheerful, and up to almost the last few days of her life, she was occupied as usual in thoughts and labors for her kindred. It was her custom to write to her children often; I have letters of hers, written at intervals of two or three months during the last seven years, and I presume to say most of her children received them as often. Of all your father's sisters, I have thought she partook most of the sweetness of disposition and calm thoughtfulness by which he was distinguished, and which made them both so engaging in their intercourse with every one. I do not remember our grandmother, but can recal similar traits and graces in our grandfather's behavior. I often wish, and all the more deeply now that my mother is no longer here to illustrate the good family from which she descended, those who still bear it, were nearer to me that we might dwell ‖ together and ‖ on the many virtues and gifts of our ancestors. But it has fallen otherwise, and I have had too little intercommunication with the widely scattered members, to keep me acquainted with their fortunes. Yourselves and Uncle Noah's family only remain, I believe, in Ohio. I have heard nothing from any of you for some years. It would give me much pleasu[re] to read here in Concord a letter from any one of you cousins. I hope Charles has not suffered in his fortunes [word?] faith from our civil troubles.

My regards to him and all. Anna Bronson, my eldest daughter is married and has a son, five months old. Louisa and Abby are with us. I wish I could send[?] so far Louisas "Sketches."

> Affectionately Your
> Cousin
> A. Bronson Alcott

Isaac & Rebecca Bronson, Medina, Ohio.

LETTER 63-29

[to W. E. Sheldon,[1] West Newton, Mass.]

Concord October 20th 1863.

Mr. Sheldon,
Dear Sir,

I shall gladly attend your Teachers' Association and speak on the subject you name in your note, yesterday received. All the other subjects on your Programme are most deserving of discussion, the two last especially.

And, should you not secure any one to lecture at 3½ P.M. on Tuesday, why not continue the discussion of "What is the next step to be taken by Educators to secure the highest interests of Education in the Commonwealth?"—as this, more than any question on your list, opens the whole doctrine and duty of Human Culture, and deserves time and scope for its proper entertainment. Indeed, I think it most deserving an entire lecture to itself. Nor is that on "the means of securing Loyalty and Patriotism" scarcely less deserving of the amplest consideration of teachers legislators and citizens.

> I am
> respectfully Yours,
> A. Bronson Alcott.

W. E. Sheldon,
West Newton.
Mass.

[1] Sheldon was president of the Massachusetts Teachers' Association and had written Alcott enclosing a program notice of a meeting on October 23.

LETTER 63-30

[to Alfred and Sarah Bicknell, Boston]

Concord October 20th 1863

Mr and Mrs Bicknell,

It is proper that I should acknowledge your note, and express to you the pleasure its reading affords me, on finding that any sympathies shown or manner of mine touched you in the least in the hours of your sorrow.[1] I shall cherish the rembrance of the confidence which led you to ask my presence on that occasion with heartfelt satisfaction. So tender a wound only time and good sense can heal. I read in your letter the clear assurance that you are equal to the event that unfits so many for the duties and delights of living—regarding it not as an affliction alone, but the bearer of blessings you know not how rich. Tis much to have lived thus into the significance of life, and so found its imperishable essence.

I know not that words of mine can add to solace to your bereavement, or render its lessons the more edifying or impressive.

I pray you to consider me

Your Friend.
A. Bronson Alcott.

¹ Their daughter had died of diphtheria a few days before and Alcott had attended the funeral at their request.

LETTER 63–31

[to Anna, Chelsea, Mass.]

Concord October 23rd 1863.

Dear Anna,

I have put up for your use a b[ar]rel of our best Baldwins, large and sound and good for winter. Also a small barrel of varieties,—Baldwins of a second quality at the bottom, then some winter Sweetings, and, atop of these, a few Northern Spies and golden pippins, go[od] for eating now. They are all good. I could send you none that were not: and [torn] to let me know when these are gone that I may send you more. Apples are almost the only thing we have to give yo[u] but our love, and wish you to have your winters supply from our Orchard, which yields an a[bu]ndance. I have them all picked but not all in barrels: Sanborn has had his four, and Mr. Benjamin his four barrels. I have put seven into our cellar, and shall have ten or twelve to sell, I judge. Little Freddy will take to his fruit presently, and shall have all he wants. All well this frosty morning. With prospect of a fine sunny day.

Love [to] Freddy, and regards to you and yours,

Your Father.

PART FOURTEEN

✠

1864–1865

LETTER 64–1[1]

[to Mary E. Stearns, Medford, Mass.]

Concord, February 7th 1864.

I have, my good friend, Mrs. Stearns, inscribed, on the sheets you sent me, some tribute to the character and services of the heroic Leader of the Nation's Leaders, the Father of that Independence which, we trust, the Country may soon celebrate with honor to itself and justice practically rendered to men of all races. These paragraphs you will Perceive, have been printed in the Commonwealth, and I would not have copied them for your Album, had I found any thing new in memory or imagination better suited to clothe my reverent appreciation of the bravery and magnanimity of the incomparable man they aim at celebrating. I am happy however in having contributed these,—all unworthy as they seem,— since I have nothing better, to your Collection. They go into the best company and keeping, and to you more, than any one, belongs the honor of making them yours, since in your hospitable apartments, the Virtues they sing and speak, were earliest entertained, and from thence went forth to the victory and the ascension.

I should have sent the sheets at once, had I not hoped to have the pleasure of bringing them, and seeing yourself and Maj. Stearns, long before this. I trust that pleasure will fall to me during the summer, if not before, when you shall have become more equal to seeing your friends.

Louisa has copied the verses you asked for, and hopes to know you better, that she may thank the friend who bestows her kindnesses on one near and dear to her Let me add my thanks to hers.

Shall we not see yourself and the Major, sometime here in Concord?
With cordial remembrances,

Believe me
your friend,
A. Bronson Alcott.

Mrs. Mary E. Stearns
Medford

---

[1] MS. owned by the Lilly Library, Indiana University.

LETTER 64-2

[to Mrs. A. Bronson Alcott, Chelsea, Mass.]

[Concord] Sunday 14th Feb. 1864.

My dear,

You will like a word from me by this time, since you have had none for some days. All runs smoothly, and now that so many of our debts are fairly settled, Louisa again adoing as she desires, Abby happy, and Anna improving, I see not why you and I should not take counsel of our hopes, finding them better advisers than our fears, and very much more comforting.

The coal bill is paid $17. Stewart $10. and pants ordered, and as I do not find shoes and rubbers here to suit me, I may come down some day this week, dine with you, see Fields[1] and Redpath, get my shoes, and return to sleep. It will be some fair day towards the end of the week, I think. Next week come School Examinations.

Meanwhile Currey, having been paid $10. is sawing and splitting the wood for us. It will be good economy as well as a great comfort to have a load of good seasoned oak to burn with[?] the birch and pine, as our last years' stock is about gone.

We miss you, but you must stay with Anna as long as she needs you. I hope to find her eyes better. It is a great comfort to her to have you with her, as well as a blessing that you are able to nurse her now.—And the boy too is so well. May nothing happen to him! Regards to John, and much love to all

Yours Ever

A. B. A.

PS. Abbey desires me to add that she will come down Wednesday morning, and come out to Chelsea after lecture.

[1] James T. Fields.

LETTER 64-3

[to Mrs. A. Bronson Alcott, Chelsea, Mass.]

Concord Feb. 19th 1864.

My Dear,

Abby came home with much to tell us about herself, all highly favorable, and most encouraging. It will be something to think about and hold her active and in spirits during the summer, besides proving whatsoever gifts she may have to be cultivated further.[1] I am heartily glad as I know you are and Anna.

I left you not without sadness, as well for yourself as Anna. You were troubled alike with a cold and anxiety, and though you said little, you felt and thought the more. Pray take care of yourself, and add nothing more to the causes that now oppress and dispirit. I am not assured by Abby that either you or Anna are really any more encouraged about things. Anna tried to seem hopeful when I was there, and if any thing more than another can aid in raising her health and spirits, 'tis the prospect of coming *home;* for that word is life and happiness, as it ever has been to her. How much she has suffered from being no longer one of the circle in the same sense she was once—more than we knew; and then it was so like her to be silent so long about it. She must come and you with her as soon as she is able, and fair days have come. It is fortunate that we can make it so pleasant to her and her family: I wish they were here now.

The weather is cold, but we crowd about the fire, all about one in the dining room, and keep busy.—

Are you sure all is being done for Anna that art can divine? She must have relief in her eyes and head. I feel very much for her. I was sorry not to see John. Ask him if Anna's Photographs taken by Masury were paid for, as I shall see him on Wednesday; and you and Anna too.

Ever Yours, A.B.A.

Kiss my boy for me.

---

[1] An entry in Louisa's Journals for February, 1864 (see Cheney, p. 156) reads, "Mrs. S. takes a great fancy to May; sends her flowers, offers to pay for her to go to the new Art School, and arranges everything delightfully for her."

LETTER 64–4

[to Seymour? Bronson? Hingham, Mass.]

Concord March 9th 1864.

Dear Cousin,

Yours informing me of your Father's decease came to me this morning. It has been some years since I had the pleasure of seeing him, and I have often regretted that distance, and your Village lying wide of my route of travel, has separated us. Besides, I am not often farther from home than Boston and then with less time to spare than I could desire. It was my hope to have visited Hingham long before this.—Your father and family particularly. There were many things to make such a visit desirable. For though your Father left Conn. some fifteen or twenty Years before I came into these parts in 1827, there were family circumstances and traits in which we had a common interest, and I enjoyed his companionable manners and strong intelligence perceiving much that reminded me of our grandfather Bronson, and uncle Tillotson. His mother, my aunt Phebe, I remember as a lively lady. My mother thought her the most gifted of the sisters, Aunt Sylvia the Blakely, Sally the gayest; the elder aunts I never saw. In disposition, your father, resembled my mother, sweetness mingled with good sense, saints by nature and grace. I know not how it happened "the Commonwealth" of last September containing a notice of my mother's decease, failed to reach you. I enclose the notice now.

Be assured of my regards and remembrance. Will you not come up and see us this summer? Anna and her babe are with us, and Louisa is at home. My wife and Abby will take it as a special favor. Remember me to your brothers and sisters. Next time I am in the city, I will try to find you.

Your aff. Cousin
A. Bronson Alcott

1864–1865

LETTER 64–5

[to W. M. Fernald, Boston?]

Concord March 30th 1864.

Dear Sir,

Thursday 14th. of April will suit me very well. And, if advertised, let it be for, *"The Significance of Sex and Complexions."* I wish I may bring to the treatment of a theme so delicate, so delightful ‖ and divine ‖, the spirit and modesty to make it worthy of the women who may come to hear.

Yours truly,

A. Bronson Alcott.[1]

Rev. W. M. Fernald

---

[1] Alcott's letter is an answer to a request (dated March 15) for him to speak before the Ladies Physiological Institute.

LETTER 64–6[1]

[to Mary E. and George L. Stearns, Medford, Mass.]

Concord April 15th 1864.

Esteemed Friends,

On returning yesterday from an absence of several days from home, I found your note enclosing your contribution in aid of my Plan of meeting the people and speaking to them on the Ideas and issues, the dangers and Duties of the Hour. I thank you most heartily for your confidence and the generous contribution. And before I take my first steps feel inclined to have further conversation and counsel. I shall be in the City on Monday next, and, if I know you will be at home, would come out and pass the night, seeing Phillips meanwhile. I have seen Dr. Clarke,[2] Dr. Bartol,[3] Geo. B. Emerson, and all favor our plans.

Truly Yours

A Bronson Alcott

Mr. and Mrs. Stearns

---

[1] MS. owned by the Fruitlands and Wayside Museums.
[2] James Freeman Clarke (1810–88).
[3] Cyrus Augustus Bartol (1813–1900).

LETTER 64–7

[to the Fraternity of the Twenty-eighth Congregational Society, Boston]

Concord. May 25th 1864.

To the Standing Committee
of the Twenty Eight Society.

I shall most gladly avail myself of your kind invitation to be present at your "Social Festival," and hope to bring one or more of my daughters with me.

Yours truly
A. Bronson Alcott.

Standing Com

LETTER 64–8

[to A. P. Wace, Worcester? Mass.]

Concord, May 31th 1864.

Dear Sir,

I purpose to be in your city sometime on Saturday next, (June 4th.) and shall gladly spend Sunday and perhaps Monday. Any arrangements for speaking on Sunday or Sunday evening that you may make, will be acceptable to me. And I will stay with Mr. Brown or Mr. Goddard, as may be most convenient. Should have no objection to preach for Mr. Richardson a part of Sunday!

Yours, truly.
A. Bronson Alcott

A. P. Wace, Esq.

[Letter to Mr. Calthrop, Marblehead, Mass.; from Worcester, June 8, 1864.]

LETTER 64–9

[to Mrs. A. Bronson Alcott, Concord]

Worcester June 8th. 1864.

My Dear,

All well thus far with the traveller, who, considering the opportunities nearer home, decides, this morning, to postpone his jaunt to Conn. and attend to the claims of Mass. I go to the State Reform School at Westborough to day, to-morrow stop and see the Normal School at Framingham Friday go to Boston, and, if Calthrop writes in answer to mine of this morning, for me to preach for him on Sunday, I shall go down to Marblehead on Saturday and spend a day or more with the Englishmen, visiting Schools and perhaps having a Conversation or two, and may go on from thence to Amesbury and see Whittier. If I do not go to Marblehead on Saturday, but am preferred for the Sunday after, I think

I shall go to Plymouth, and stay a few days with Watson: See Lowell, Norton, Longfellow, the Cambridge students, on my return to you my garden, and Freddie,—of whom Anna writes encouragingly. And I wish you would drop me the latest account you have, so that I shall get it on Saturday as I pass through Boston. I will call at the P. Office for it. Anna's pious feeling that she "does not need the trial of losing Freddie," will spare him to her, let us hope; if Doctors' skill and her own embracing arms fail, though the prayers of the Child's friends were else unavailing.

Did Louisa tell you of the compliment bestowed on her by Miss Cheney's cousin at the Fraternity Festival? If she did not, I must. The Good lady sought an introduction through the father, addressing her admiration in this grand style: "Mr. Alcott is a great man, but his daughter Miss Louisa is greater"—It would have been the proudest of compliments had the mother come in for her full share also. Indeed, every where I am coming into importance in these old years, through that rising young lady; people here speaking with enthusiasm of her Genius—"The Father of Miss. Alcott," honored as never before.

I send you a newspaper notice of my visits to the Schools. We have had two evening Conversations,—the first good. And yesterday I dined with Mr. Richardson, the Beecher of the Pulpit here.

Affectionately
A.B.A.

LETTER 64–10

[to Mrs. A. Bronson Alcott, Concord]

Plymouth, June 12th. 1864.

My Dear,

I date, as you see, from Watsons where I am to be till Wednesday morning, visiting the Schools to-day, and having a Conversation to-morrow evening. I purpose stopping at the Bridgewater Normal School on my way to Boston, and think I shall reach home sometime on Friday to be at the Fair; though I may not, but go to Marblehead to preach for Calthrop on Sunday. I got the letters, but failed of finding Mr. Slack, who had left the city. I have written him this morning.

I left Worcester on Monday morning last, had the day and evening with the children of the School at Westborough, some 400 of them, and am to go over from Concord some Sunday and speak to them again. Mr. and Mrs. Allen made many kind enquiries about yourself and the girls. Thursday, I visited the Normal School at Framingham, passed the day in the several departments, and spoke to the young Ladies in the evening. Here are near 200, preparing to be teachers, some of them very bright, and beautiful to see and talk with. I enjoyed my visit greatly; and hope to attend the Celebration on the first of July. Yourself, or one of the girls, should accompany me, to bring your brother to Concord, else some idolater, will appropriate the good man and you lose him. On Friday, I came to the Severances, in season to see Seymour and Miss. Powell leave for her home in New York. I was in Mr. Allen's School all the morning, and met the Reading Club in the evening. I reached Boston on Saturday, and got your letters: left part of the contents of my Carpet-bag at Mr. Sewalls, saw John, who confirmed all you had written about Freddie's teething victories, and came down here, where all is pleasant and kindly as one can desire. The place has put forth the planters designs surprisingly since I saw it eight years ago, and is, indeed, a Paradise of fragrance and quietude. I think it the perfection of a Home. Here are all the trees of wood domestic and foreign, ‖ here ‖ tastefully grouped, flowers of every hue, and a family of good natures to cultivate and enjoy them. Yesterday, we were at the Island and Uncle Edward returned and passed the night with us. I do not wonder at May's delights here with the place and people. Mrs. Martin sent her regards to "the young lady", my daughter."

The morning is charming, as I write, and I am ever yours, with love to all.

A.B.A.

Letter 64–11

[to Charles W. Slack, Boston]

Plymouth June 12, 1864.

Dear Sir,

Your letter came too late to be answered earlier, and I had arranged with Mr. Calthrop meanwhile for Sunday the 19th besides ‖ arr ‖engagements ahead for the month of June. I regret that it so happens, as I wish to speak to your Fraternity, and trust we may be more fortunate in days to come.

Truly yours,
A. Bronson Alcott

Charles W. Slack Esqr
Boston.

Letter 64–12[1]

[to Oliver Wendell Holmes, Boston]

Concord August 7th 1864.

Dear Sir,

I must not attempt in this note of acknowledgment of your Book of Poems, to tell the pleasure my readings of most of its pages have given me. Let me hope some opportunity for dwelling on the varied beauties sparkling all over these leaves, the subtlety, the sense, the melody—may occur before long. Besides, three days were insufficient for doing any justice to a Volume of the solidity and size of yours.

I may say, however, that "The Chambered Nautilus, Contentment, The Deacon's Masterpiece," and other pieces not named by you in your note, as "The Ploughman, To my Companions, Daily Trials, The Old Man's Dreams," several of the Patriotic pieces, to say nothing of fine lines in others, had been known and admired by me. The Pictures from Occasional Poems, the Vignettes, Agnes, were all new to me. And I think they show most happily what I most value in your Poetic vein, the gift of flowing melody, I would say warbling, if it did not degrade a little. My ear is always charmed, my eye delighted with the surprising transitions, the sprightly imagery, the fit epithets.

Your publishers too have done us all a favor in giving you to us in such tasteful attire.

As to the questions of Fate free-will, the Genesis, I am accustomed to look to the Poets rather than metaphysicians for solution. And we will, if you please, dip a little into those depths when I have the pleasure of meeting you again

With thanks for your beautiful Book,

I am,

with much respect

Your,

A. Bronson Alcott.

¹ MS. owned by the Library of Congress. A copy, in Alcott's hand, in the Alcott-Pratt Collection is dated August 4.

LETTER 64–13

[to Anna, Chelsea, Mass.]

Concord Sep 10th 1864.

Dear Anna,

I have opened, as you will see, my correspondence with Freddie as well as his mother, and hope and trust that both will speed happily and long for both and all. I was glad to hear so good accounts of him and of yourself, your host and hostess, boardings, and neighbors. That long pebbly avenue for your riding and walking must be very pleasant for you. I wish it reached Concord, and we could see the little cortege in the distance, as it parades day by day. I need not tell you and John how much I miss the little man, and how pleasant is the memory of him. I shall ever esteem it one of the privileges of the Spring of '64, and all through the summer, that I was permitted to enjoy his delightful company, and to contribute my little moments' delight in return for all he was and promised to me and mine. Do write us all about his sayings and doings. Your plan of keeping a Diary is a happy thought, and I wish it may give all his pretty things, as well as your. One who writes as well as you do, may well write all the time.

Regards to John, and ‖ the rest ‖ all of the ‖ Brotherhood ‖ three.

Your Father.

P.S.. Freddies letters will be delivered to him from mammas lips, and become so much the sweeter.

[Letter to Frederick Pratt, Chelsea, Mass.; from Concord, September 10, 1864.]

LETTER 64–14

[to Rebecca Sprogell Gould, Boston]

[Concord, October 1, 1864]

Mr. and Miss Alcott will gladly avail themselves of Mrs. Gould's kind invitation to partake of her feast of Grapes at No. 80 Pinckney Street on Wednesday evening next.[1]

Concord October 1st 1864.

to,

Mrs. T. R. Gould.

[1] The letter is unsigned.

LETTER 64–15

[to Julia Ward Howe, Boston]

[Concord, November 14, 1864]

Dear Mrs Howe,

I am asked by your daughter, Miss Julia, for my contribution to your Seaman's Paper.[1] I wish I had something suited to the place and occasion. And for lack of such, must beg you to receive, as the best I can commend at this moment, the verses herewith enclosed, though printed sometime since in the "Boston Commonwealth." Should you find them worth filling some corner of your sheet, I shall be [p. in] the less ashamed of having offered them to the courtly contribution of wit and Charity which the Sailor is so generously receiving ‖ for ‖ at the hands of England Old and New, the Nation at large.

Very truly yours,

A. Bronson Alcott.

Concord Nov 14th 1864.

[1] The *Boatswain's Whistle* (published for the National Sailors' Fair), of which Julia Ward Howe was the editor. For a brief discussion, see Laura E. Richards and Maud Howe Elliot, *Julia Ward Howe* (Boston and New York, 1916), I, 210–11.

LETTER 64–16[1]

[to Mary E. Stearns, Medford, Mass.]

Concord Novr 27th 1864.

Dear Mrs. Stearns,

I could only send my message instead of my note by Frank, concerning the Dials about which you made enquiries. There are four numbers wanting to complete the set. And for the twelve committed to Frank's charge, I must ask the $15.00 offered for them by Mr. Greene, a friend of Henry Thoreau's who writes from Michigan and will take his chance for completing the series, as others must. I was unwilling to part with these till I learned your wishes. They are the last I have, and cannot pass into better hands than those of the friend for whom you desire them.

Yes, you will return overspilling with satisfaction from your Sunday evenings draught at the Poets' fount. Is'nt it auspicious for us that His Sundays have Come around again, and the Metropolis is eager to hear?[2]

Then you will make me glad if thinking favorably of distributing, in the way we talked about, the little token yourself and friend Phillips approved.

I hope to be at your hospitable home, sometime soon, and speak of this, and the winter's plans with you and your estimable husband.

Very truly
Your friend,
A. Bronson Alcott

Mrs. Mary E. Stearns
Medford.

[1] MS. owned by the Fruitlands and Wayside Museums. A copy, in Alcott's hand, is in the Alcott-Pratt Collection.
[2] A series of six Sunday evening lectures by Emerson. For details, see Rusk, *Emerson Letters,* V, 389, *n.*

LETTER 64–17

[to Samuel Johnson, Salem, Mass.]

Concord Novr. 28th 1864.

Dear Sir,

Your telegram only reached me at 5. P.M., having been arrested at Waltham, and sent from there by mail, the wires from Concord being out of order. So the best I could do under, the circumstances, was to despatch a hasty word, (saying I would come) by the evening mail.

But lest you should not [p. in] be fairly advised, I write again explaining the matter more distinctly. And if any thing need be returned by yourself please answer at once. I shall be pleased to speak to your congregation, and may [p. in] ‖ shall ‖ [p. o.] spend ‖ the evening of ‖ Saturday night at Mrs. Stearns in Medford, taking the horse cars on Sunday morning for Lynn.

Shall I not see you, or have you an engagement that takes you away?

Very truly yours
A. Bronson Alcott

Rev. Samuel Johnson
Salem

LETTER 64–18

[to Samuel Johnson, Salem, Mass.]

Concord Dec. 9 1864.

Dear Sir,

Yours came to hand last night, and was duly honored at our Bank, today.

So I have good reasons to be content with your own and peoples' kind interest.

Sunday evening's meeting was especially agreeable. You have not been speaking to listless ears for these last years. It was good to find so many earnest persons, and so receptive: Good to meet among them old friends too.

Then my host, I had never met on terms so pleasant before, and my hostess was all kindness and good sense.

'Tis a pity that Shackford must leave a people and city, he has served so well and so long. There are few abler men, very few as thoughtful and vigilant, in any of our New England cities.

Thanking you for the opportunity of knowing your people, I am

Very truly yours,
A Bronson Alcott

Rev. Samuel Johnson.

LETTER 64–19[1]

[to Mary E. Stearns, Medford, Mass.]

Concord Dec. 17th 1864

Dear Mrs. Stearns,

Instead of naming our Surprise Book to Fields, who could have kept our secret hardly, I went at once to the headman of the University Press,[2] and now send you his general estimates.

He thinks he can give us an imprint with initial letters, tinted paper, cloth bindings (like Weiss' Discourse) for a dollar the volume. In extra cloth, ornamentation, with the Photographed head, two dollars. The engraved medallion, calf bindings, three dollars the copy. Can put it to press sometime in January, ensure secrecy, wishes to serve us, Emerson being a favorite of his, and deserving the best his art can bestow on him in type and ornaments. Any devices of wreath, letters, seals, he executes himself, superintends work at all stages, and give the best at the cheapest rates.

Now wishing the best and considering the cost, perhaps you will advise printing fewer copies than we talked of, thus making our Gift the more choice and elegant. Besides one may spend less or more on bindings, having secured the fair text to his eye. Then if you are as successful as we hoped, the new Profile will add to its elegance.

These being the Printer's estimates hastily given, I beg of you to drop our design at once, if they transcend your largest expectations greatly, and we will trust our little tribute to more propitious times, to more munificent hands it cannot be than yours certainly, and I shall always consider it as done. Yesterday I looked it over, and felt the more willing to wait longer.

My kind regards to Mr. Stearns. My list of names is nearly completed and shall be sent soon.

Ever Yours, and the more for my last visit.

A. Bronson Alcott[3]

[1] MS. owned by the Fruitlands and Wayside Museums. A copy, in Alcott's hand, is in the Alcott-Pratt Collection.
[2] Mr. Welch—named in the copy in the Alcott-Pratt Collection.
[3] This is the first in a series of letters concerning the book (*Emerson*) written by Alcott and privately printed at the expense of Mrs. Stearns. The book was given to Emerson as a birthday gift in 1865.

LETTER 64–20[1]

[to G. C. Hickok, Boston]

Concord, Dec. 24, 1864.

Dear Sir

I reached home last night, and today have looked into my Dials. In the parcel I send you, you will find all the numbers I have, and you might get the others to complete the set as you can. Perhaps Burnham may have the numbers wanting. I have added the Aesthetic Papers,[2] and a School Report or two of mine.

For the whole, you may leave with my daughter, Mrs. Pratt, $12.00.

You will find good reading in them for these wintry days.

And when the Spring opens we shall expect to see you here in Concord.

Very truly yours,
A. Bronson Alcott

Mr. G. C. Hickok
Boston

[1] MS. owned by Mr. John L. Cooley, who kindly provided me with a typescript.
[2] A journal edited by Elizabeth Peabody, only one number (May, 1849) of which appeared.

LETTER 65–1

[to Daniel Ricketson, New Bedford, Mass.]

Concord February 12 | 1865.

Dear Friend

Many thanks for your kind thoughts of me and mine. And especially of my daughter's story.[1] Your own and daughter's hearty words about its spirit and influence gave us pleasure. The book has provoked much criticism, has been widely read, and is winning an acceptance with discerning readers, as surprising to its author as 'tis encouraging.

Immediately after your letter came to hand, I hastened to read it to the Thoreaus. What you say of Henry was most grateful to them. Miss Sophia desired me to say that but for press of cares, your letters would not have been left so long unacknowledged and unanswered. She has been busily engaged in overlooking her brother's Papers, copying some, reading proof sheets of the books of

Cape Cod and *the Letters,* finding no moment for correspondence. Besides, her mother's infirmity has been an additional and constant call upon hands and heart.

Henry Letters are to appear soon, and will increase his fame. You will be pleased to learn that there remains matter for a book or two of *Politics,* one or more of *Morals,* and several volumes of *Field and Table Talk* choice reading all, and to be finished sometime.

You speak of the spring of 57. and of having *"passed through many experiences since."* Happy man to have known changes at your age! I trust the keys of life are in your keeping now.

Lately it has seemed as if the call had come for me to speak, not ‖ from ‖ in parlours alone and privately, but from public platforms and pulpits: as if our ripest thinkers and best men's utterances needed to be followed out into clearness, to be complemented in Ass[ocia]tions of a *Personal God, a vital theology,* answering to the claims of our revolutionary time. Neither *James, Bushnell, Bucher*[?], *Phillips, Emerson,* quite content me, and yet these if any, have good words to speak and the gifts for speaking eloquently. You may have noticed in the Boston Papers our advertisement of some Sunday Eveng Lectures to be given by these and others. I have my chance too, and gave my word last Sunday Eveng, by way of an opening. Have been also at Lynn and Haverhill speaking lately. Certainly men had teaching badly enough when any words of mine can help them. Yet I would fain believe that, not I, but the spirit, the Person, sometimes speaks, to receive[?] and spare[?].

Come and see me and let us talk over the good matters again.

With pleasant memories of your [word], I remain Your

friend
A.B.Alcott

Dan¹. Ricketson.

¹ Louisa's *Moods,* published in December, 1864.

LETTER 65–2

[to Henry James, Sr., Boston]

Concord Feb. 15th 1865.

Dear Sir,

I was in the city last Tuesday, and am sorry not to have seen you about the Sunday Evening Lecture. But I saw Mr. Fitz, who told me you were ready to speak then and that he should advertise you in good time.

It was my intention to call at your house again, but many errands about town left me no time.

Mr Manning was out. But he will doubtless be ready for the next evening, and Phillips will follow. Emerson owes our plan his good will, and, I hope, will help us. I had Monday Evening with him. He had just returned from the West, and was in good spirits. We discussed the matter of *Personal Theism.* He said his last Lecture in the Boston Course, had been shaped more to his thought in his Western readings, and seemed now better suited to the needs of the Times.

I was glad of the opportunity to find your sons so fast for the new and True.

To day, I have looked into your Book, and am surprised to find how strong it is. Perhaps less of Biblicism than I find would have suited me better. But with this drawback upon its spirit, I have read nothing so able lately, and so eloquent.

Very truly yours
A. Bronson Alcott

Henry James, Esq.

LETTER 65–3[1]

[to E. L. Hammond]

Concord March 1 1865.

Dear Sir,

Your flattering note of the 26th has just reached me. And I hasten to say that it will give me pleasure to visit your place at such time as shall be most desired by your Society. Please name the earliest day as I am wishing to journey in your part of the state, and might arrange my route accordingly.

The Pamphlet you sent interests me. Such Free Societies organizing facilities for teaching and influencing our people in the towns and cities, are in keeping with the free spirit of our time, supplying a want already beginning to be felt throughout New-England. You have made a fair beginning, and one, I am sure that will be imitated far and wide.

It may interest you to learn that our Boston Sunday Evening Lectures promise well. Henry James gave the last on English and American Ideals. I gave one on American Religion, and speak again next Sunday evening on The Religious Views and Issues of our Time. Wendell Phillips, Rev. Mr Manning, we hope Dr. Bushnell and Mr. Emerson, will follow.

Questions are arising that must be discussed in the spirit of widest thought and broadest hospitality.

Very truly
Yours,
A. Bronson Alcott.

Mr. E. L. Hammond.

[1] MS. owned by the Fruitlands and Wayside Museums. A copy, in Alcott's hand, is in the Alcott-Pratt Collection.

LETTER 65–4[1]

[to Mary E. Stearns, Medford, Mass.]

Concord March 17th 1865.

Dear Mrs Stearns,

I purpose to be in Cambridge on Tuesday next. And should the forenoon be fair, perhaps you will ride over, and we can arrange all with the Printers. The cars reach Porter's at about ½ past 9. and I will wait there a little while on the look out for you. Or, if any other arrangement suits your convenience, please write meanwhile informing me of your wishes.

What you write of the New Head is hopeful certainly.

The printers say they can give us the book by the time we wish it, but will like to begin their work at once. The M.S. is already in their hands.

Hoping fair Spring days, birds, flowers, friends, and your own fresh heart, may speedily revive and restore, and looking forward to the pleasure of seeing you soon,

> I am Yours
> faithfully,
> A. Bronson Alcott

Mrs. Mary E. Stearns.

[1] MS. owned by the Fruitlands and Wayside Museums.

LETTER 65–5[1]

[to John Weiss]

Concord March 17. 1865

Dear Sir,

Mr. Manning lectures next Sunday Evening. And I shall depend upon you for the Sunday Evening following, March 26th. Please send your Subject as early as Thursday preceding, to John C. Haynes, 277 Washington Street. He will see that you are advertised in the city papers.

Johnson is ready to speak April 2nd. after him, we hope Phillips.

> Very truly
> Yours,
> A. Bronson Alcott

Rev. John Weiss.

[1] MS. owned by the American Antiquarian Society, Worcester, Mass.

LETTER 65–6[1]

[to Mary E. Stearns, Medford, Mass.]

Concord March 22nd 1865.

Dear Mrs Stearns,

It seems my note of last Friday[2] did not reach you in season for our meeting at Cambridge on Tuesday. But, aside from my pleasure in seeing you there, and the refreshment of your ride, I know not that we could have furthered much the work on our Book. Every thing is now in the best plight for the printing, and nothing is to be done without your knowledge. Proofs of page, paper, ornaments,

&c, are promised by Friday of next week, when I hope to be at the Printing Office, and if you will ride over, we can see them together. The New Head must be ready for inspection also, and we can leave our last instructions with the Printers.

On Friday next I leave for Worcester with Emerson, shall hear his lecture in the evening, and go forwards to Florence (near Northampton) where I am to speak on Sunday, perhaps on Monday also.

I brought home Yerrington's Report yesterday of my Lecture on The Religious Tendencies of our time, and find it better than I knew.

Wasson is invited to settle by Parker's Congregation, and goes a delegate, I hear, to the New York Convention,[3] which comes the first week in April. Our Parish, I doubt not, will send its representative.

I am happy to hear of your improving health and spirits.

Truly Yours,
A. Bronson Alcott.

[1] MS. owned by the Fruitlands and Wayside Museums. A copy, in Alcott's hand, is in the Alcott-Pratt Collection.
[2] See Letter 65-4.
[3] The National Unitarian Convention.

LETTER 65-7[1]

[to Mary E. Stearns, Medford, Mass.]

Concord April 3rd. 1865. | Sunday.[2]

Dear Mrs Stearns,

But for the rain and Mr. Stearns illness, I should have ventured to come out last Friday. But it seemed better to wait until you signified your wishes. So I took another look in at the University Press and found our matter in a state of forwardness—samples of paper, type, initial letter, all awaiting my inspection. Yet the Printer thought he might improve on these and have something ready to show us a week hence, and persuaded me to wait, there being time enough, he said, to give us the book early in May.

Should you drive that way, you might stay your carriage at the door, and ask Mr. Welch to show you his work, taking any suggestions of yours.

I called at Black's but he had sent the impression to you.

To morrow, I am off for New York, expecting to join Wasson at Worcester, and we go on together to the Convention. The Free Congregational Society at Florence, where I passed Sunday last, send me as their delegate. If not admitted, we shall question the *Liberal* name the Convention has taken, and may rightly plead for Christendom's enlargement.

Shall hope to see you and Maj. Stearns immediately on my return late in the week, or all through the next.

Your note left him mending and you nursing. I shall hope to find you both better and able to see

Your obliged friend and servant
A. Bronson Alcott.

Mrs. Stearns,
P.S. Phillips lectured here, and passed Thursday forenoon with us.

[1] MS. owned by the Fruitlands and Wayside Museums. A copy, in Alcott's hand, is in the Alcott-Pratt Collection.
[2] Sunday was April 2.

LETTER 65-8

[to Mrs. A. Bronson Alcott, Concord]

New Haven April 8th, 1865.

My dear,

You see I am here and facing homewards. Leave for Waterbury at 10. intending to pass Sunday at Wolcott, and move on by Monday. You may expect me in all next week. I may be a day in Hartford, perhaps visit the schools at New Britain and Westfield, also stay over a train at Springfield.

I found Wasson and the Worcester delegates had planned to leave by the 7 oclock train on Monday, and so took passage with them, Rev Mr. Shippin, Mr Wace, Wasson and myself. We reached New York early Tuesday morning took quarters at St Nicholas breakfast, and went to ‖ the convention ‖ see each his friends. I to Brooklyn and had a pleasant two hours with Longfellow, finding we were thinking and feeling much alike about Convention matters. In the evening Dr. Clarke gave his discourse. 'Twas Catholic in spirit, recommending sympathy and union on the broadest grounds, and made a favorable impression. Wednesday morning the Convention met. Burleigh[?] appeared with our Credentials which were put with the rest into the hands of the Committee and we took our seats in the Convention with the delegates. I send you Reports of the doings, of *my speech* among the rest. Wasson made a good speech. Dr. Clarke appeared to great advantage and but for his liberal course we should have lost the day. But as it is have gained a step at least: our side made a good issue, and maintained it handsomely, both in temper and argument.

I am glad I came: have met many good men, and seen with eyes how things are. Mr Brooks of Newport asked me to preach for him soon. Ames also of Albany and to these places I am to go during this month.

Brother Sam was there. He took dinner with me at my quarters once and seemed pretty well. Will be our way in May.

The Festival was a grand affair. Gov. Andrews speech magnificent. Read it in the Reports.

Brother Ambrose is pleasantly placed here and in good business. Mrs A. has a little babe just five weeks old. George a boy of 13. and studious.

Ever yours. AB.A.

P.S. Wm. H. Channing spoke in terms of high praise of Ls book. I trust she will consider well about the Charleston[?] plan.

LETTER 65–9[1]

[to Mary E. Stearns, Medford, Mass.]

Concord April 27th 1865.

Dear Mrs. Stearns,

I am just home from Albany, where I found some earnest excellent people, and had an agreeable visit.

To morrow I am to leave for Newport, Mr Brooks having invited me to speak there next Sunday. 'Twas my wish to have had an hour with you at Medford to-day. But find I must delay my planting to do so, and will try to come out on my way home from Newport some day next week. By that time our Printing will be done, and I can bring along the proofs for your approval. The new head, I trust, will also be ready.

We are having vernal days here, and fair prospects for ourselves, let us believe for the Republic also.

Ever Yours.
A. Bronson Alcott.

Mrs. Stearns.

[1] MS. owned by the Fruitlands and Wayside Museums. A copy, in Alcott's hand, is in the Alcott-Pratt Collection.

LETTER 65–10

[to Clara W. Adams, Chicago]

Concord May 20th 1865.

Mrs Adams,

Herewith please receive these few autographs for your Fair, with the best wishes for its success,

from yours,
Most respectfully.
A. Bronson Alcott.

Mrs. Clara W. Adams.
Chicago.

LETTER 65–11

[to Lidian Emerson, Concord]

[Concord, May 25, 1865]

Dear Mrs Emerson,

I remember with pleasure an evenings' Conversation with you over the manuscript which a friend has since put into type for the eye of a few friends of hers. Of the six copies bound, may I ask your acceptance of this one.

The photograph you will recognise [*sic*] as taken from Mr Gould's bust in Gore Hall, Cambridge.

Wishing the text were as befitting its subject as are its ornaments.

Believe me
with much regard
Yours,
A. Bronson Alcott

Concord May 25th 1865.
Mrs. Emerson.

LETTER 65–12[1]

[to Mary E. Stearns, Medford, Mass.]

Concord May 30 | 1865

Dear Mrs. Stearns,

It happens that I have not chanced to meet Emerson since our Birthday Gift was left at his door. But from what May learned on Sunday Evening from Mr and Mrs E. I judge we have escaped the displeasure of the Divinity, and won his forbearance if not good will toward the tokens of our friendship,—worship, I was about to write, but did not as you see, paganly.

I had not the courage to come nearer than to address myself to Mrs E. who writes me a most complimentary note of thanks in which she says, "I am delighted with the photograph. Mr Goulds' bust is the best likeness of Mr Emerson extant."

I believe we think the same, and are happy that it came in our straits to grace ‖ the ‖ as frontispiece.

Fair Book! to my partial eyes were the text worthy of its ornaments.

Fair friend! may I add, who seconded so gracefully the wish to see it in print. Many thanks for the kindness, not forgetting the pair whose generosities seem inexhaustable [*sic*].

I have kept the surprise for Mrs. Alcott till her return from Annas, not caring to risk so much by Express.

I fear I am too busied about garden and trellis works to leave these for the anniversaries, or for you even.

Can't you ride this way one of these leafy fine days coming?

Ever yours,
A. B. A

Mrs. Stearns.

---

[1] MS. owned by the Fruitlands and Wayside Museums. A copy, in Alcott's hand, is in the Alcott-Pratt Collection.

LETTER 65–13[1]

[to Mary E. Stearns, Medford, Mass.]

[Concord] Wednesday Morning | May 31. [1865]

Bear with this long delay please, since it brings what we have [been] waiting to learn and rewards for the waiting. For just as my Yesterday's note was about being despatched, Emerson himself came to say how gratified he was with the Gift and its manner of bestowing—A Token too costly to be trusted long outside of its casket" as costly, with other complements [sic], showing his sincere pleasure in it, assuring us that he feels as we could wish. The only hint dropped as qualifying his delight, was the blazonry of name on the cover. And should other copies get into bindings, I think a copy in calf, with gilt edgings and leaves, (not *carmine*,) without his name outside, would suit better. If you agree, he shall have one sometime. But I am asking too much where so much has already been bestowed and shall be quite content to wait a little.

Again let me say, how pleased he seemed with the photograph, about which he was curious to learn the history, as also the name of the lady whose taste had touched the leaves with so much beauty. At tea last evening, Mrs Emerson again expressed to me her admiration of the Gift, and the lady's name. Emerson read me his lecture on Character as lately revised, and which I hope Fields will dare print, though it should suppress Atlantic, editor and Churchmen all, by its searching criticism.

I hope this lovely morning finds you equal to taste it off without pains of any kind.

Yours faithfully,
A. B. A.

[1] MS. owned by the Fruitlands and Wayside Museums. A copy, in Alcott's hand, is in the Alcott-Pratt Collection.

LETTER 65–14

[to ?]

Concord June 12 1865.

Dear Sir,

I have copied at your request my few notes about the Philadephia Association of Teachers and its Journal of Instruction. I wish they were fuller, more definite and satisfactory. But such as they are they are at your service to be printed as they are or abridged, or not printed at all, as you shall determine. My recollections are slight as to other details and doings of that time and city. Nor do I know had I the time to spare, that much could be added to what I now send. Mr. Russell might give you something more, and correct perhaps in some particulars my notes. I regret to learn that your Journal draws so near its close. It is a monumental work; and will serve the future historian of Education to the materials of what has been done in our country with much also [word].

I need not be ashamed to say that it will afford me an old mans pleasure to read his own Epitaph in your November No. If you print it give us all of it for which you can possibly find room, and perhaps the subject may plead that having waited till the last, he shall be shown up in all ragged glory to his contemporaries.

I was sorry to miss you when in your city. Can you not take Concord again on your way ‖ to ‖ East.

Yours [word][1]

[1] The letter is unsigned.

LETTER 65–15

[to Richard Randolph, Philadelphia]

Concord June 12th 1865.

Dear Sir,

I owe you more apologies than I can well make for detaining your paper on Conversation so long in my keeping, and this, too, without acknowledging its reception, or writing to you about it. But, frankly speaking, I was somewhat embarrassed as doubting what were Civil and Free in me to do about it. So in my hesitancy I allowed it to pass into a friends hands, thinking his judgment might aid mine, and he but returned it the other day feeling as I did that you would not like to see it in print. The verse also came with the like feeling after his careful reading. I hope there was no breach of confidence in all this. Nor am I willing to trust your paper to the mail till I learn whether you wish it sent as directed by yourself, or to your present place of residence. I wait to hear.

Such a piece of legal logic seems better suited [to] have ‖ to find ‖ found its place in Blackstone, than in any [word] work known to me. It is too subtle and formal for any popular use, and the verses are best kept for private perusal. As you challenge my criticism, I have frankly given it.

If I ever come to Philadelphia be sure I shall seek you, and press my many thanks for your confidence and generosity, and as some return hope to send you a little book before long.

Your friend.
A.B.Alcott

R. Randolph.

LETTER 65–16[1]

[to Mary E. Stearns, Medford, Mass.]

Concord June 12th 1865.

Dear Mrs Stearns,

Mrs. Alcott but returned late last week to receive your gift, and sends her note of thanks for that, and the golden Gift that makes the giving possible. I am tempted in spite of modesty to write your name on the fair chocolate leaf of a possible Copy to come into my hands sometime, and ask your acceptance of this given Gift, half persuaded it would have some added value in your partial eyes.

Really it is a pretty thing to look at, and too costly to be wasted on any but

371

the deserving. I have good reason to know that the Emersons prize it: and have had the more frequent visits from the Poet and the more charming Conversations than for a long time before it fell under his eyes.

Shall I infer that you are about riding this way. As I hear not a word. All the better and the health that brings you into our neighborhood.

These are good times to live in, and days lately that make life a luxury.

Yours Thankfully,
A. Bronson Alcott

Mrs Stearns.

[1] MS. owned by the Fruitlands and Wayside Museums.

LETTER 65–17[1]

[to William T. Harris, St. Louis]

Concord July 12th 1865.

Dear Sir,

I shall be at home all this month and free to see you at any time most convenient to yourself. And, when once here, shall hope to detain you till we shall have compared notes on Nature man and Mind to the end. Emerson is to be at some College—Williamstown I believe it is—for a day, but at home I believe during the month otherwise. Sanborn too you may like to see while here.

Come straight to my house, and let me return your kind hospitalities in my way. My wife and daughters will be glad to see you, and should you come before the 20th, you may see Louisa, who is to leave then for Germany.

I am very happy in the prospect of seeing you at this important moment and learn how you look at men and the country.

Very truly
Yours,
A. Bronson Alcott.

Wm. T. Harris Esqr.

[1] From a copy, in Alcott's hand, in the Alcott-Pratt Collection. The original is in the Alcott-Harris Collection in the Concord Free Public Library (see Appendix B).

LETTER 65–18[1]

[to Mary E. Stearns, Medford, Mass.]

Concord July 21st 1865.

Dear Mrs Stearns,

I have been expecting to see you here now for the three last weeks, looking for your carriage to pass this road and before my gate. But as yet have had no glimpse of it or of yourself,—only Frank's[2] message that you were coming, and that the Poet's Present was in the binders hands with copies for me. Since then Mrs. Emerson has been here and told Mrs. A. of its having reached his hand and eye, praising all parties. I suppose you have had ere this his proper acknowledgements, and that our way is free to offer our Gift to his friends and ours. I shall be grateful for any copies you may choose to send me. George Bradford has been here, and Elisabeth Hoar, both admiring and doubtless wishing to call copies theirs. I would like also to give copies to Mr William Emerson, and Miss Sophia Thoreau; Besides Mr. Sanborn deserves one, and Mr. Ripley. Then near and far are rightful owners, to whom it would give me pleasure to send copies. If you cannot come and see us, and my summer works, indoors and out, will it suit you to send the parcel by Express? I am to be at home, and sorry not to be free to leave just yet.

You will be pleased to learn that Louisa has gone to Germany. She sailed on the China last Tuesday, and is now fairly on the waves, East-faced and full of hopeful expectations. She may be gone a year. May leaves on Monday with the Emersons' for Monadnock for a week's excursion.

Health to you, and a ride this way soon.

A.B.A.

[1] MS. owned by the Fruitlands and Wayside Museums.
[2] Frank Preston Stearns, younger son of Mary E. and George L. Stearns.

LETTER 65–19

[to Samuel Gray Ward, Boston?]

Mr S. G. Ward.
Concord August 3 1865
Sir,

Mr Emerson informs me that you have monies in your hands from the Trust Fund, and wish to pay the same to me at once.[1] Please hand the sum whatever it may be to the bearer Mr John B. Pratt, and take his receipt.

Respectfully,
A. Bronson Alcott.

[1] Concerning the "Trust Fund" set up for Alcott, see Rusk, *Emerson Letters*, V, 159–60.

LETTER 65–20[1]

[to George L. Stearns, Medford, Mass.]
Concord August 4th 1865.
Dear Sir,

I am sorry that I cannot conveniently join your party on Saturday and meet the Chief Justice for discussing the great national issues of this eventful hour. I trust your other invited guests will find themselves free to sit at your hospitable board, and am sure the countries good name, the nations needs, will receive the best entertainment from your distinguished company with which I should have esteemed it a high honor to have sat.

We all remember your visit with much satisfaction, and hope it may be repeated soon. Give us the whole day next time, if you please. The morning for conversation and prophesy always as for business.

Very truly
Your friend.
A. Bronson Alcott

George L. Stearns Esqr.

[1] MS. owned by the Fruitlands and Wayside Museums. A copy, in Alcott's hand, is in the Alcott-Pratt Collection.

LETTER 65–21[1]

[to Mary E. Stearns, Medford, Mass.]

Concord August 23 1865

Dear Mrs Stearns,

Your note of the 6th came to hand yesterday. Meanwhile came also yours of the 17th in which you speak of riding to see us this week. Monday we looked for you, and again today. But must wait till tomorrow when you will surely come. Come early and let us have the fair morning together. I have Channing and Holmes notes of acknowledgment for our Booklet to read to you, and shall hope to hear the notes of some of your receivers of the Gift. Channing's pleas were irresistable and he took three copies to England. The rest are nearly distributed. When you come we will consider the claims of some not yet honored.

Since you were here, Mr. Harris has come and gone. Mr. May left us yesterday, and Anna and the boys have paid their visit. My Leaves have had large accessions, Phillips begins to take shape, and you shall add the last touches if you will. Last evening the Poet was here, and I read a few leaves of it to him.

The shovels are busy about the foundations of the additions, and all looks propitious.

May intends to bring you tomorrow, and Mrs. A. will look for you early.

Very truly
Your friend
A. B. Alcott.

[1] MS. owned by the Fruitlands and Wayside Museums.

LETTER 65–22[1]

[to Mary E. Stearns, Medford, Mass.]

Concord Sep. 8 1865.

Dear Mrs Stearns,

The day must have looked unpropitious for your ride, though it seemed fair to us, and Mr Stearn's assurance that you would come led us to wait dinner till it was plain you had declined setting out. It was a disappointment to May, who in her mother's absence had spread her plain repast, and only waited your presence to make all as she had wished. Mr. Stearns, beside his only kindly contribution of information, added a fresh basket of peaches and all went otherwise pleasantly. Week has followed week with promises and now another is to be added, but you will come when you can, and I must wait patiently. Meanwhile, I send for your reading some notes from receivers of our Book. (And you shall return them when you come. Whittier has none from me, and you shall send him one, if you like. Channing begged so hard for a Copy or two, that I gave them to him.

Mr. Stearns and I have arranged about the money matter we talked about: and by the time you come the carpenters will have something to show for his and your kindness to us and ours.

The Leaves are all waiting for you.

Yours ever.
A. B. Alcott.

Mrs. Stearns.

¹ MS. owned by the Fruitlands and Wayside Museums.

LETTER 65–23

[to Editors of the *Nation*, New York City]

Concord Sep 11th 1865.

Dear Sir,

Your note of 10th July has lain by me unanswered for the good reason, that I had nothing suitable for your Paper, and was questioning whether I might promise anything in future. I fear it will be as in times past, and must respectfully ask of you not to look to me for contributions.

Yours respectfully,
A. Bronson Alcott.

Editors of the "Nation".

LETTER 65–24¹

[to George L. Stearns, Medford, Mass.]

Concord September 11th 1865

Dear Friend

I return here with in my note for the loan you have so kindly favored me with, adding my thanks for the same. Next time come up, I think there will be something to show you beside rude timbers and unfinished rooms.

Next week, Thursday is our Annual Cattle Show and a crowded day in the village, which Mrs. Stearns may not care to encounter. Still any day will suit us that suits her convenience, and we shall look for her with hope no longer delayed.

Very truly Yours
A. Bronson Alcott.

George L. Stearns Esqr.

¹ MS. owned by the Fruitlands and Wayside Museums.

LETTER 65–25

[to Seth Hunt, Northampton, Mass.]

Concord October 3rd 1865.

Dear Sir,

Your note has just reached me, and I hasten to say, that I will speak for your Society next Sunday, leaving here on Saturday in time to reach Northampton by one of the Springfield up River trains, the station master here telling me the Worcester train connects at Springfield in due time to make Northampton sometime on Saturday late. If not so, please write in time for me to leave here earlier.

My subject for Sunday morning will be:
Religion considered as a sentiment and an idea.

In the evening:
Health and Temperance

Very truly
Yours,
A. Bronson Alcott.

Seth Hunt, Esqr.
Northampton.

LETTER 65–26¹

[to Mary E. Stearns, Medford, Mass.]

Concord October 22nd 1865.

Dear Friend,

All Phillip's friends must thank him for the noble eloquence of last Tuesday evening, and I am pleased to learn that yourself and Emerson, chiefest of these, were there to listen. How fortunate for the country that it has One Voice, at least, to warn it of danger and suggest the remedy, which political parties, statesmen, priests, are ever slow to learn, slower to apply—justice to all men, to the helpless, and downtrodden especially.

Thank Heaven, not for Presidents whether middleman or martyrs; not for the wonderful war setting the nation wondering at its new position, its deeds and opportunities, but rather for the man that faces the facts, and warns it of the dangers of abusing its victories and fortunes: thank heaven for Him. I wish the country may take the warning in time to arrest the impending woes: before it embark in this wicked design of killing the black man because he is proving himself more the man than the white. You see I too have caught the strain of that evening from the spirit of your indignant note. 'Tis patriotic, and good company to frequent.

I hear Mr. Stearns has met the President,[2] and takes hope yet of him and of his policy. May none of us be deceived at last.

Every copy of our little Gift Book has gone from me to deserving persons. But others plead, and our little edition would be exhausted were but a portion of these given a copy. Whittier has none, Furness none, Longfellow none. Lowell shall have none, were the edition a million; think of that paper of his on Thoreau in last no. of the "N. American," and call him E's friend afterwards!

Pity that Miss Edith did not add yours to the number of her costly bridal gifts![3] I was so sure of yours coming that I relinquished my pleasure to the better giver of gifts. But she does not lose it, I trust, though it come later to hand from yourself.

Channing took three Copies to England, and you write that Longfellow had as many, or more. I regret with you that Brooks got none.

Our repairs hold me fast, though I was a Sunday at Florence where Emerson is to-day, and Sanborn goes early in November. Emerson has been reading his six Boston lectures to orthodox Amherst. Ride this way soon, please.

Ever Yours,
A.B.A.

[1] MS. owned by the Fruitlands and Wayside Museums. A copy of only a portion of the letter, in Alcott's hand, is in the Alcott-Pratt Collection.
[2] Andrew Johnson.
[3] Emerson's daughter Edith married William H. Forbes on October 3, 1865.

LETTER 65–27[1]

[to Louisa, Vevey, Switzerland]

Concord November 29th 1865.

Dear Louisa,

I cannot hesitate about dating my letter on this memorable day for both of us, you reaching your 33rd birth day, and I my 66th. So let me discharge as I best can some part of my large debt to you for your lively Letters, which, like Photographic pictures, portray the persons and things you see. Your powers of description never showed to better advantage, and I am charmed every time I hear the letters read: let me add, too, proud of the pair of eyes that note, the Genius that draws so skilfully. Was it for this that you went across the seas! The weekly event is the reading of the newly arrived epistle, and not ours only. The letters, sheet after sheet are listened to, as May posts[?] away to Elisabeth Hoar, Martha Bartlett, the Emersons, and the rest. I wish Italy may have the good fortune to receive the faithful painter, for if you succeed with her monuments of art, as you have done with the Rhine scenery, we shall have another taking tourists' book. Yet, if you can visit but one country, let it be England rather, and try your hand on that Old Isle of Ancestries, its arts, institutions, people. That flight across it from Liverpool to London, is one of your richest pictures, and makes me covet more from the same painter. You will visit at the most favorable season if you cross over from the Continent in the spring: a glance at France is enough. and Paris is France. Then Conway owes you much good will. He will be proud to serve you. Wm. H. Channing, too. Find Conway first *at Warren Farm*[?], *Wimbledon, London.* and you are put at once into communication with the persons you wish most to see. The places you can visit without introduction. Pray make the most of your opportunities. There are Carlyle, Tennison [*sic*], why not see them too, along with the cathedrals and Museums. Great men, like natural objects or works of art, are not to be slighted when one is in their neighborhood. You need not be diffident. Your claims are as good as any American lady of your age. and you know how to press them modestly. Besides, Pictures of distinguished persons abide long in the fancy and memory: And Carlyle surely offers a subject for you to try your hand at. I wish you may meet Dr. Chapman, too, editor of the Westminster Review, and former friend of Greaves and the Bennetts. I suppose you will avoid Lane.

If you remain in Switzerland you are safe from Cholera.

I was pleased to read of your winning the game at good manners with Col. Polk and Sett[?]. The Sanborn's came to tea last evening and to hear your letters read. There was not time to finish, so we are all invited to tea with them, and they hear about the interview at the dinner Party.

I have written about the repairs, and have nothing more to add, save that these all await your approving eyes. The autumn has been charming. I have hardly thought of indoor pursuits, busied as I have been and still am out of doors. Harris has written that a good company awaits me at St. Louis. If I go, twill not be till January. and stop along the route. But 'tis a long and dreary undertaking, and must offer good money inducements to tempt me from home. I hope to meet engagements here in New England also. Of our lecturers, we have had Curtiss and Higginson at the Lyceum, and are to have Phillips and James along with the popular voices.

Channing is here *Maying* as Poets will at all seasons.

Anna, John and boys are to spend Thanksgiving, (Dec. 7) here, if the days are fair. Were the wanderer to be with us our cup would overflow.

Blessings attend you ever, and the Careful Guides return you safe in good time, prays

Your affectionate
Father.

Dec. 12. Noon. Anna is about leaving, and I close with impress of Freddys hand and little red. scribble.[2] Health be with you and safe return.—

---

[1] MS. in The Clifton Waller Barrett Library, University of Virginia.
[2] The first and last pages of the letter are marked with a scribbling in red pencil, by Frederick Pratt, who was not yet three years old.

LETTER 65–28[1]

[to Louisa, Vevey, Switzerland]

Concord December 17th 1865. | Sunday P.M.

Dear Louisa,

Our debt to you should have been more amply and far more punctually paid than it has been, and by myself especially, who have been afar in strange lands, and should call to mind the strange sweetness that any tokens of remembrance from those we love, derive from absence. Tis plain from the confessions of your last letter, as from the tone of your former ones, that Nature, though clothed with all the attractions of Alpine scenery, your company sparkling with the novelties that national traits offer, yourself abroad in Switzerland and with prospects of seeing Italy France England, before your return—that with all these dreams enjoyed or promised soon to be, you are still much with us here in our humble home, and finding that Nature thus imposing, landscape thus lovely, people thus interesting, are strange still, unsatisfying, and that Our Home is in our affections,—the geography of Persons rather, not of Natures.

"Nature befriends us not
Nor hearthside hath to spare
In all her ample plot.'

Perhaps the old religions were right in calling homesickness the truest test of our virtue and sign of our capacity for immortal friendships.

Your letters are all charming, and the more so, from this undertone of suppressed melancholy, which by the way is older than Alps, the appenines upon which you are perhaps almost looking now—Old as Nature herself. The Spaniard that take[?] dashed in spite of the Saxon, into the elements of your temperament. and you may be near Ancient Home after all. Yet I advise wintering in Switzerland, if you have not left. For though the Cholera finds those only who breed it; and you may be as safe in its neighborhood as any one, yet *those Hospital adventures once,*[2] and now the *nurse's cares,* may predispose you to take it. If plants are poisonous, so are persons: and *touch* who may! You may be the healing magnetist, but depend upon it virtue goes from you with every stroke of the hand, and yourself become the patient at last. Beware of the Sorcerer though he tickle your fancy with saintly names, and your own kind heart play the Sorceress, too, by you. What were all the glories of the Continent to you, if you return the invalid unable to celebrate them in charming story? Yet we owe the invalid you take such pains for all that humanity can reasonably claim. We refuse services only which humanity may not ask of the humblest for money, or even for love, were that supposable.

The views you sent in your birth day letter, fix your boarding house and relations to the city and surroundings. Besides these, we have a larger picture of the town lent us by Elisabeth Hoar, so we can follow up and down the slopes and at some distance. Your visit to Chillon and description of of [*sic*] the Prison, is as good for the romancer as for the poet, and this with the legend the best matereal [*sic*] for a story by the former. Dont name your writing "poor scribble,' write away about whatever interests you: all is delightful to me, and will be so suggestive to you on your return. May you have the health, leisure, comforts, as you have the Genius to shape them into fair volumes, for the wider circle of readers.

We have had snow. but now the ground is bare, the weather cold, and winter cannot be far off. Our house is comfortable. and the Post office brings new comforts from over seas, spite of winds and waves, not every week to be sure, but as often as we have right to expect. I hope to write you oftener, now that I have resumed the pen inside, and winter occupations. If I go to St. Louis it will not be till January. Anna's visit was a great happiness. On Thursday your mother goes to spend a week or two. Now health and all satisfactions to my dear daughter prays her hopeful

Father.

¹ MS. in The Clifton Waller Barrett Library, University of Virginia.
² See Cheney, pp. 137–49; also Letters 63–2 through 63–6.

LETTER 65–29¹

[to William T. Harris, St. Louis]

Concord December 31st 1865.

Dear Sir,

I had hoped to have written, Yes, and in January, in response to your note of invitation to converse in St. Louis. The thoughtful circle of persons whose names you give, the interest shown by them in one's [word], offer strong temptations to set forth trustfully west, without further considerations alike indespensable [sic] to his passage. A month's time out of the scholars thrifty season is much to give, especially when his indoor pursuits are delightfully rewarding, and can be had without the dreary fatigues and chances of winter travelling. If some of the cities on the route offered like inducements ‖ with ‖ as to a hearing and good coin, one might take the rails with good cheer. But as yet such assurances are wanting along the way. Such being the case, I think I must have the pledge of double the sum you name, from your city, to [word] my leaving home for so long a distance.² If that can be made sure, I will promise to be with you as soon after the New Year opens, as feast and frolic ‖ will allow ‖ consent to entertain ‖ for ‖ the [word] matters, trusting for chance favors along going and returning.

If you deem it practicable to have a larger and more popular course, I will undertake to meet that & your phil. ‖ and ‖ also spending a fortnight with you. I regret not having better terms to offer you.

Very truly
Yours,
A.B.Alcott

W. T. Harris

¹ From a copy, in Alcott's hand, in the Alcott-Pratt Collection. The original, dated December 3, is in the Alcott-Harris Collection in the Concord Free Public Library (see Appendix B).
² Harris, acting for the St. Louis Philosophical Society, had pledged $100, but met Alcott's terms of $200.

PART FIFTEEN

1866

LETTER 66–1

[to Franklin B. Sanborn]

F. B. Sanborn Esqr.
    Resident Secretary of
The American Social Science Association.

Concord January 12th 1866.

Dear Sir,

Your letter informing me of my being made an honorary member of your Association, is before me. I esteem it an honor, indeed, and a privilege, to be associated with so many friends of man and students of whatsoever shall promote his welfare.

And in returning, through you, my thanks for this mark of respect and confidence, allow me to assure the Association of the pleasure it will afford me to partake in its labors, and to express my hope that the complement [sic] it has conferred, may prove something more than an empty name.

Respectfully,
    A. Bronson Alcott.

LETTER 66–2[1]

[to William T. Harris, St. Louis]

Concord Jan 15th 1866.

Dear Sir,

I have heard nothing from you since my writing, Dec. 3rd and have concluded that my letter failed of finding you: and write now to repeat my strong desire of meeting the rare circle of minds to which you invite me. Nothing could be more pleasing or promising, and cannot resist the pleasure and profit which such fellowship proffers for any secondary considerations. I am not sure but that there was a pledge on my part given to meet you on the terms named in your letter, though, if I remember rightly, these were contingent on finding like opportunities along the route. Pray do not think me dishonoring the faith and false to the name of philosophy, if remembering how remote are its rewards, and how inevitable are bodily needs meanwhile. If you fail to find a circle of persons outside of yours, caring for my things, then let me come and take the most you can contribute. I feel honored by the high claims you make upon my thoughts, and wish I may be able to meet them. Write me at once, and let me know the state of matters, also whether February will suit as well as earlier.

Mr. Emerson has gone West, but cannot come to St. Louis, till late in February. If written to by the proper officers, I think he might lecture in your city.

I am reading Stirling's Hegel greedily.[2]

Yours truly,
A. Bronson Alcott.

Wm. T. Harris,
    St. Louis

[1] From a copy, in Alcott's hand, in the Alcott-Pratt Collection. The original is in the Alcott-Harris Collection in the Concord Free Public Library (see Appendix B).
[2] James H. Stirling, *The Secret of Hegel* (London, 1865).

[Letter to William Russell, Lancaster, Mass.; from Concord, January 16, 1866.]

LETTER 66–3[1]

[to Benjamin B. Wiley, Chicago]

Concord January 17th 1866.

Dear Sir,

I am to be at St. Louis early in February, and should yourself and friends favor my coming to Chicago, I would like very well to meet them, for some four or five evenings. If, on consulting them, this seems feasible, and desirable, and you will write informing me of prospects, or better, definite results, I shall esteem it a favor. It would give me great pleasure to visit your thriving city, see yourself, Mr. Collier,[2] and others of your friends.

I am invited to meet a select company at St. Louis, where I am to spend a fortnight. Perhaps you can write definitely before I leave home: if not address me there.

Besides meeting circles for Conversations, I am wishing to speak to larger audiences [sic], where the way is open, and have lately spoken at Lyceums, and occasionally from the pulpit.

As to terms, make these agreeable to yourselves. If a free parlor were opened to us, the cost of meeting would be spared, and the profit, as the pleasure, greatly enhanced.

Mr Emerson is lecturing at various places far West, and is to be from home till the middle of next month.

The Thoreau's are as well as usual. I have just been reading Henry's Letters to yourself, Hecker and Chelmondeley [sic], and wish all may find place in a second edition.

Please remember me to Miss Waterman, also to Mr. Collier.
The Sanborn's and Channing are well.

Yours truly,
A. Bronson Alcott.

¹ MS. in the Berg Collection, New York Public Library. A copy, in Alcott's hand, is in the Alcott-Pratt Collection.

² Robert Laird Collier. A note distinguishing him from Robert Collyer is in Rusk, *Emerson Letters*, VI, 190, *n*.

LETTER 66–4

[to Samuel Johnson, Salem, Mass.]

Concord January 17 1866.

Dear Sir,

I have just read the December and January numbers of the Radical.¹ How fresh and hopeful it is, and how promising its list of contributors superior in thought, as in live scholarship, ‖ to that of other Journals ‖, and its theme the theme of themes. I like, too, the natural basis upon which it exists. Let ‖ me ‖ us consider it American; free [word], humane, and breathing the breath of the everliving spirit.—Tell me more about its purposes and prospects if you have the time to write about it. I have only seen Wasson and he praised it properly. I observe too the Examiner and other Unitarian organs speak respectfully about it. May we hope that Clarke and Hedge are coming to the Fountains, or must they, too, dip their pitchers from the distant tanks, with Bushnell and the rest.

I trust you intend presently to publish your lectures on the orientals, and give us some deeper insight into the Books of the Spirit. Your present discussion in the Radical are opening the way for them.

I am tempted to try some paragraphs of mine. But hesitate about it, lest the good name and prospects of the Radical suffer in consequence.

What say you to some Conversations with your friends at Lynn. It would give me pleasure to meet them again, for two or three evenings at least, after my return from St. Louis, where I am invited to meet a score of Hegelians and unfold my world to them[.] I suppose I am to converse also at Chicago, Cincinnati, and Cleveland, preaching also where the way is open to me. I leave here early in February, to be gone about a month.

If you think favorably of the Lynn adventure, and your friends, I shall esteem it a favor if you will write.

Perhaps I shall see you at the Antislavery Meetings next week.

Yours truly,
A. Bronson Alcott.

Rev. Samuel Johnson
    Salem.

¹ A journal published and edited in Boston (1865–72) by Sidney Henry Morse. Alcott became a frequent contributor.

LETTER 66–5

[to Henry W. Longfellow]

Concord | January 27th 1866.

Dear Sir,

May I ask your acceptance of this little book on Emerson. 'Tis but a trifle: but where so much is due to the Gifts and Graces of a good man, one may perhaps be pardoned for proffering his small share of respect and admiration, thus privately.

The generous lady, to whose taste, the volume owes its chief attractions, and by whose kindness it stands thus fairly in type, will be gratified, with myself, if it find acceptance in your eyes.

With respect,
A. Bronson Alcott.

Henry W. Longfellow.

LETTER 66–6[1]

[to Hannah Robie, Boston]

Concord February 2nd

Many thanks, my kind friend, for your favor by the hands of Mr. Sewall. It will lighten my heart all the way Westwards and home again: besides enabling me to bring home so much the more solid comfort to those who are already so largely indebted to your timely generosities in times past, and speak of you always with love.

I have tried, when in the City, to find a night to go out with Mr. Sewall and spend at his house, and hope to do so soon after my return from the West. It is some time since I have been there.

To Mr. Sewall, Mary and Louisa my regards.

Yours truly,
A. Bronson Alcott

Miss Hannah Robie.

P.S. I leave this evening, and expect to pass Sunday with Mr. May at Syracuse.

[1] MS. owned by the Massachusetts Historical Society.

[Letter to Mrs. A. Bronson Alcott, Concord; from St. Louis, February 12, 1866.]

[to Mrs. A. Bronson Alcott, Concord]

St. Louis February 20th 1866.

My Dear,

Yours, enclosing Anna's, and mailed to me here by your brother, came to hand last Wednesday. And my engagements have been so pressing from day to day, that I have not found the moment to write since then. But now this fair fresh morning finds me free to shed some ink on these sheets.

And first of Louisa. I am encouraged by what you wrote Perhaps all is now done on this side to bring relief: the Welds themselves feeling rightly and ready to do the right thing.[1] Your brother too promising his aid. I shall await your news and doings with anxiety, and may hear possibly from you before I despatch this. Before I leave this city I intend writing to Louisa.

On the 12th, I think it was, I wrote to you about prospects and proceedings here. Since then I have been seeing various persons privately, have met the Philosophical Society three times, spent a morning in Harris' School, another at the Normal School, have had three Conversations, and dined with Profs. Howison and Tweed of the Washington University. Tonight I am to meet the Conversational circle again. On Thursday evening, am invited to a social party of literary gentlemen, Professors and distinguished citizens. The Spiritualists have expressed a wish to have me speak for them sometime before I leave; and talk of opening some parlor for a Conversation or two.

I enclose some newspaper notices which may interest you.

I think I may stay over into next week, and if I get letters from Collyer, favoring my going round by Chicago, shall leave perhaps by Wednesday next, for that place. So you shall direct to me here, and letters may be sent after me. Direct to the care of—William T. Harris, Salisbury between 9 [p. in] and 10 [p. in] Streets, otherwise your letters may miss, or be delayed.

I esteem it fortunate for me to be here at this time. The men who invited me are Powers and Influences in this city: the Peace brings prodigious questions and issues before the minds of all men; Nor have I found anywhere more profound treatment in the true American spirit, than these men exhibit. It is suggestive and powerfully stimulating to look at life and affairs, through the perspective of their clear logic. I am persuaded that if Philosophy has found a home in modern times, 'tis here in this New New England, and that St. Louis is stealing past Boston and Concord even. The freedom and grasp of Genius, the force and speed of thinking, the practical tact in dealing with men and business transactions, which these students of the pure ideas, have to show, all this is as unexpected as it is convincing. Eastern men, slow to believe in things originating elsewhere, might profit by a visit out here. The possibilities of this wondrous West are infinite, and the thoughts rise naturally out of all limitations into the freest expansion. Think of a city that can claim—what I fear Cambridge with Aggasiz [sic] and University cannot—two masters of Hegel and Schelling, one of Swedenborg, and one of LaPlace [sic] another of Goethe, another of Oken. Then the Mr. Childs, whose funeral I attended yesterday, was a mind of promise in his calling, and master of the art of Education. I send a short notice of him. I am sorry that I reached here too late to meet him, in his school.

We have had three days of dismal weather, very cold, searching to the very bones and marrow, but now it is mild as April. Think of me, as very comfortable, very much flattered by my reception here, and sanguine as to coming results. You shall hear from me again soon. Mr. Channing's words were not sound altogether. I shall look for letters from you every day.

Ever Yours,
A.B.A.

---

[1] Louisa had gone to Europe as a nurse for Mr. Weld's invalid daughter.

LETTER 66–8

[to Mrs. A. Bronson Alcott, Concord]

St. Louis February 26th 1866.

My Dear,

It seems I am to pass this week here, having engagements for every evening. The Conversations are winning favor from evening to evening; my company numbers good people and we work smoothly together. There is talk of a Lecture on New England considered in its relations to the West. I am hesitating, but think I shall venture. My friends assure me of a good audiance [sic].

Since I wrote last, I have met Chancellor Chauvenet of Washington University, Profs. Tafel, Tweed, Howison, Pennel; and am invited to the College Reunion on Thursday Evening, where I shall see the literary and social celebrities of the city.

Last evening, we took tea at Mrs Allens, sister of Maj. General Pope. Here were the General, his brother in law, Mr. Yeatman, President of the Western Sanitary Association, Mrs. Pope and sister. Genl. Pope succeeded McClellan, you may remember, in the command of the Army of the Potomac. A man of affability, frank, fearless, blending gentleness with strength, uttering not a sentiment that Wendell Phillips would not applaud. He talked more like a New Englander than most whom I meet at the East, and we liked each other very well. His sister Mrs Allen also shared his views, and Miss Allen, about May's age, thought and spoke like a true American. Mr. Yeatman is a native of Kentucky, has been a Slave holder, is now a conservative Abolitionist, and most agreeable man. Emerson, he told me, was his guest when here some years ago. The Pope family is from Virginia. I retain distinct reccollections [sic] of their ancient estate situated on York river, and the evening here seemed to revive all the vivid associations of my youthful days while travelling in those parts. Their present mansion is about a mile from Harris'. It stands on a bold ridge commanding a broad view of the Missisippi [sic], spreading South, and the opposite bank in Illinois; Louisa would draw a picture of it that would delight you.

I wished yourself and May could have been present at the hearing of some of Beethoven's Sonatas played by a German lady yesterday afternoon. Mrs S. was educated in Germany, and lives a few doors from Mr. Harris. It was a Select company, all Germans save Harris and I. Dr. Tafel, the Prussian Consul, a son of the poet Herwig.[1] Wine and cake came in at interludes || to the music ||, a Professor accompanying Mrs S. on his violin. It was kind in them thus to strive to entertain one on whom the art, I fear, was lost, but the party was a study, and the spectacle, I was told, one that may be witnessed throughout all Germany of a Sunday afternoon. I wish I could describe it properly; ‖ and the ‖ Kaufman's[2] picture too of Columbus debating his theory of the Earth's rotundity with the monks, which I saw at the Mercantile Library Rooms.

Tomorrow evening, I am to meet the Teacher's of the Public Schools. Wednesday evening, I have a Conversation, at the house of Maj Easton [p. in] one of Dr. Eliots congregation, where I may meet the Dr. I spoke yesterday to the Spiritualists, and may meet them again for a Conversation. We have Sunday sessions of the Society of Philosophers, who surprise me with their dialectic ability and force of thought. My visit promises good fruits.

Collyer discourages my coming to Chicago, at present. He writes. "I hope, when I get my new Church and Parsonage, to have things in better trim, and then be able to arrange such a matter as this as easily as one of my own Services." A Mr. Hough whom I met at Syracuse invites me to stop at Rochester on my way home. I think Monday next will be as early as I can hope to turn my face eastwards. I shall hope to have a weeks stay at Cincinnati and Cleveland, which will take me into the middle of March.

Pray what led May to suppose that Mr. Emerson was expected here? Mr. E's letter has just reached Harris who will write in explanation.

Many thanks to Channing for his kind helpfulness; and write me all particulars about yourself.

Ever yours,
A.B.A.

[1] George Herwegh.
[2] Angelika Kauffman.

LETTER 66–9

[to Mrs. A. Bronson Alcott, Concord]

St. Louis March 1st 1866.
My Dear,

To-morrow evening completes my engagements here, and I shall take Monday's train for Cincinnati, at which place I shall stay over a train, at least, and may remain a week. I have just written to Judge Tafts, and shall perhaps find a company gathered for me. You shall hear from me soon about the matter.

I have good reasons for staying so long. My reception has been most flattering. I have met many good persons, seen a good deal of Western life here, and shall cherish agreeable memories of my visit.

Yesterday, I dined with the Chancellor, Prof. Tafel, Dr. Strothene[?] at the house of a friend of Genl. Hitchcocks—a very agreeable party. We were shown the General's library of rare mystic books. The ladies of the house spoke with admiration of his genial qualities. There he makes his home when not away on military duties.

You will see by the card enclosed that I am to speak of New England Men. The Conversation is private, a good company having been gathered for that evening. I have abandoned the thought of a public lecture. These restless thinkers are inexorable critics, jealous of the East, though unwilling to admit any thing of the kind. One must have a care of his speech in their company. To my surprise, however, they accept me beyond all expectation, and I must run home soon, if I will escape apotheosis. They are ‖ curious ‖ eager to fall upon Emerson and Phillips as ‖ great ‖ [p. o.] high [p. in] Game, holding other New Englanders at the lower mark. I must run the gantlet of their fierce ‖ stabbing ‖ [p. o.] logic, and come out of the encounter, as I best can.

The spring opens here to depress the spirits instead of refreshment. Such weight I am not wont to carry, and but for the stimulus of conversation, I should wilt, like a leaf and shrivel. Otherwise, I am very well: as I go East this will [word].

I have just reread your letters. All seems good and hopeful which makes me glad. I shall ride into the city after dinner, hoping to find news from you. Your last was dated, Feb. 14. since which time, I have written once, before this. Address your next to the care of Alphonso Taft Esqr. Cincinnati.

Mr. Harris has received two letters from Emerson explaining the matter of the Lectures. He has freed himself from the Hall engaged for Emerson: and hopes another season to have a good understanding: Emerson and Phillips ‖ bring ‖ to be invited to speak in the Theo cantile[?] course.

It looks now as if this tour of mine, though nothing should be gleaned along the road East, would prove reasonably remunerative. Keep me informed of your state and prospects, and think of me as wheeling homeward. I must not omit my love to May, Anna and hers. My thanks to Mr. Channing for his kind care of you in my absence.

Again and Ever Yours,
A.B.A.

[Letter to Mrs. A. Bronson Alcott, Concord; from Cincinnati, March 7, 1866.]

LETTER 66–10

[to Mrs. A. Bronson Alcott, Concord]

Walnut Hills | Cincinnati March 10th 1866.

My Dear,

I wrote to you last Wednesday (the 7th) and now add a word, just to say that no letters have yet reached me here, and that I purpose to leave on Tuesday next for Cleveland. To morrow, I am to speak in the City.

The Conversation on Thursday evening was thought a success, and another is proposed for Monday evening. Today, I am to visit Mr. Longworth, son of the famous Nicholas, the grape grower of the West. His villa adjoins Mr. Harrison's where I am staying. He was at the Conversation, wishes to show me his pictures of which he has a rare collection. I have seldom met ‖ a ‖ so rare a son of Adam, a sort of Henry Thoreau in his love of nature, and with as little ‖ of ‖ pretension as any man I have ‖ met ‖ seen. His conversation is entertaining, and if something wild[?], shows a man of simplicity and common sense. I expect to like him right well, and may find him the typical man of the West, of the class who, as he says, are *"to Ohioize the East;"* and very good it were for us to be helped in that way. You would take to these free western folk. || and might show them there is some freedom and abandon possible. || I cannot wonder at the Conway's thinking Concord an[1] || dull || [p. o.] exclusive place, going, as they did, from the free society of this city, and of Walnut Hills especially. I wish I may speak the free acceptable word to morrow.

Next Sunday, Sam. Johnson is to speak and Wasson is expected in April. I think I see, in this growing intercommunication between East and West, the promise of good things. It was my wish to see Stallo, but he is sick, and I may fail. Judges Tafts and Hoadley, seem able men.

The weather today is lovely. I am somewhat recovered from that three weeks siege at St. Louis. Sleep and the lavish comforts of this house, are a Paradise of delights to a spent veteran, after talking seven nights in the week, and resting none; besides meeting everybody[?] and any how, all day. But I have come out of the trial, and am now || very well || [p. o.]. better. [p. in]

Pray let me hear something on reaching Syracuse. Tis too long to be left thus in the dark, and not like you at all. I will borrow no trouble. Had there been trouble with you, you would have informed me, and I must think your letters have miscarried, though I have kept you informed of my doings and movements. By this time, you must have intelligences about Louisa. It was my purpose to have written to her, but there was so much uncertainty about her movements that I have deferred till my return. I hope to be with you as early as the 20th but may be later. Your hopes bid fair to be met about this tour. But I must not [word] it now. All seems open for the coming season.—I hope the [word] remembers you.

Ever Yours
A.B. Alcott

[1] The "n" has been p. in.

LETTER 66–11

[to Louisa, Nice, France]

Concord March 18, 1866.

Dear Louisa,

The sheet upon which I am tracing these lines, has made the tour of the West with me, and now lies before me awaiting what I had no moment to commit to it, during my six weeks Journeyings and from which I returned yesterday. You will be pleased to learn that it proved most successful, and in the money way remunerative. I saw many good people, held high discourse in numerous companies, and opened the door for like opportunities on coming seasons. The Great West is a wild wondrous country, and it will be well worth your while, after reenriching[?] yourself from the Fatigues of your foreign Journeyings, to accompany me another season into those, parts where nature and men alike ask the eyes and fun of an || consummate || artist like yourself. It would interest you greatly, and there are many persons, in the cities, to whom you are already well known by your books, and who would esteem it an honor to meet and entertain you in their homes.

But we are too anxious to see you safely across the family threshold, to dwell upon your leaving it soon. Yet we wish you to get all you can before setting your face homewards. It is a great relief to me to learn that you are soon to be freed from those exhausting duties, in the discharge of which you have proved so faithful. I wish you may come out safely and return refreshed from your journey. Arrangements are nearly completed for sending your Bill of Exchange for $400. and your Uncle Sam, with whom I passed last Thursday evening at his home in Syracuse, assured me that you should have $100 from him; which sum will be sent to you after you reach London if you say so.

I am going to Boston on Thursday to see the business completed for you; shall see Sam. Sewall, the Welds, and shall write you again soon, so that you shall not long wait in suspense. Sanborn is to take tea with us this evening. I shall ask him to write at once to Conway about your coming to London. Through him, we trust, every facility will be opened to you for seeing what you desire in England. You have Conway's address, and can post a note from your hotel, and he will meet you there. When I know you are in London, I can also put you in the way of meetings. Four hundred dollars will serve you some months; the other hundred will be good to have as you are about leaving the Island. Once with Conway you will feel supported, and Mrs. C. is a woman to prize above price. The Harrisons, at whose home in Cincinnati, I spent a week, spoke in admiring terms of her kindness of heart. And, if I remember rightly, you found out her excellent qualities, while the Conways were here.

I am to bring up Anna and my boys on Saturday to spend Freddy's birthday here with us.

I suppose your mother will write of that wicked West "using me fairly up," ‖ or foully ‖ [p. o.]. But a little of that rare comfort which she knows so well to administer, will soon restore me. I find all prosperous, debts never less,—next to nothing—spring opening auspiciously, yourself provided for in a way unexpected. Now, my noble daughter, take care of your health, see all you can, and come home to tell us, what ‖ in ‖ [p. o.] out of [2 p. in] your lively letters, remains to be told.

The doors are opened wide for the freest exercise of your good Gifts, fame, if you must have it, and a world wide influence. Permit me to claim you in my name, and for your sex and country.

Your affectionate Father.

Miss. Louisa May Alcott.
    at Nice, France.

LETTER 66–12

[to Louisa, Nice, France]

Concord 25th March 1866.

Dear Louisa,

I wrote at length last week on my return from the West. Meanwhile, I have been in Boston and arranged the matter of Exchange for you. So when you reach London, you will call on Baring Brothers, for the letter containing your Bill addressed to you at London. It is for £60 sterling, and is to be paid to you by Messrs M[?]c. Calmont & Co. London. You will endorse your name on the back, and thus get the money. When you want more, another bill for £20 shall be sent you. You will write to us at once on reaching London.

Yesterday I called on the Welds at their house in Boston. They had just received your letter saying that Dr. Weld was daily expected to determine your future movements. Mrs Weld spoke in terms of grateful regard of your devotion to her daughter, your assurance that you should not leave her till a companion was supplied, and Mr. Weld said he had written to have your salary paid as you desired. I understand your passage home is to be paid by him, leaving so much of your salary as you have not already expended, for your travelling where you please. It has been a great satisfaction for me to send you so much, and that it [p. in] is ours to spare and yours to spend as you need. Mr. Sewall's note enclosed will explain the transaction. I hope Conway will prove all you desire on your arrival in England.

It is important that we should be apprised of your movements as early as possible, so that our letters may be directed rightly. Mrs. Weld thought Anna would return to Swaalbach, and that you would go at once to Paris. I am impatient to have you left free to follow where your inclination leads. France doubtless has its attractions, and you will wish to see all your time allows of the French capital. I wish you may be fortunate in falling in with a suitable travelling companion. Mr. Weld said to me, "Miss Alcott can easily pay all her travelling expenses by contributing to some newspapers." "Yes, I replied, and perhaps may!" besides making a Book sometime". Ah! Yes that she may, rejoined he, adding that he had been pleased with her "Hospital Sketches." Sanborn has written to Conway about your visiting London. Tilton of "The Independent," to whom I wrote last week, has not answered, but doubtless will. That is a good paper and pays well, only you will take care not to meddle with the religion of its readers.

I had a pleasant visit at Annas, all well there. Also spent a night at Melrose, and saw Phillips to talk about The West: dined too with Wasson for whom I am to speak the first Sunday in May.

Spring is near. I hope to complete the house repairs, and improvements about the grounds, making all worthy of your arrival.

Praying for your pleasure and safety. I am

Your affectionate Father.

Miss Louisa May Alcott,
    at Nice France.

LETTER 66–13

[to Benjamin Marston Watson, Plymouth, Mass.]

Concord March 26th 1866.

Dear Friend,

On returning Saturday from Boston,—having dined with Morton at the Parker House, and heard glowing accounts from his lips of your new seed

House,—I found on my study table a sweet scented parcel, which, I judge, must have come from yourself, as the pretty papers have the labels of the "Old Colony Nursery and Seed Establishment," and none but the hands that plucked these, could have sent the coveted ‖ seeds ‖ [p. o.] sorts [p. in]—Sweet Basil, Caraway, Dill, Anise, Sage, Thyme; and the choice ‖ seeds ‖ kinds for early planting too. Not every gentleman's garden is thus supplied from Evelyn's, and I shall plant in thanks on the choicest soil I have for them; doubting nothing of harvesting a fertile crop in the season. Moreover [p. in] i["I" p.o.; "i" p. in]t pleases my fancy to think of my friend as the disseminator of the Classic herbs and shrubs, and gives good hope of the future of our country, now that peace favors a return to the rural arts and occupations. The seed house will be an argument, if I needed any, to bring me to Hillside, to see for myself this improvement on the spot, to whose every touch ‖ hus ‖ I have not been indifferent, since I first became a visitor of its tasteful host and hostess.

Besides I have pleasant things to tell of my visit to the wild wondrous West and see not how this can be done justice but beside the Hillside hearthstone—the happiest contrast I can con[ceive] to all that I so lately saw—a country where every one is loaded[?], and drives straight at his task, with a desperate grasp which we can hardly imagine in our easier mode of living and doing.

If you *would* ever come here I could[?] swear[?], by Evelyn, the gentleman, that I would not stir a step to see you anywhere but inside my threshold. But you never will pay your debts thus magnanimously, and so I consent to stoop to the complements [*sic*] and my friend's cheer—sometime.

Ever Yours
A. Bronson Alcott

B. M. Watson Esqr.
Hillside.

[Letter to William T. Harris, St. Louis; from Concord, April 17, 1866. Noted in Letter 66–14, below. See also Appendix B.]

LETTER 66–14

[to A. E. Kroeger, St. Louis]

Concord April 18th. 1866

Dear Sir,

In my letter, mailed yesterday to Mr. Harris, written hastily, I forgot to speak of the pleasure your notice of my visit to your City, gave me and my friends here. And it may interest you, in turn, to read Sanborn's notice of Your Society, printed in last weeks' "Commonwealth," both of which, I trust, you have seen. Morse, editor of the Radical, passed last Sunday with me, and intends, he tells me, under the head of *"Movements"* to give reprints of these papers in the May number. Your article, he said would also appear in that or the June issue. He speaks hopefully about the prospects of his Journal, and appears to be greatly encouraged by the new accessions of strength from your circle. Howison's papers he will also print soon. And Emerson has promised Verses. I have urged upon Harris the task of getting from Brockmeyer the letters promised on *Faust,* and wish you would second my plea in your persuasive way. Emerson is interested in Brockmeyer; thinks highly of the literary art shown in the Poem of the *Foggy Night,* and has good hopes of the author's *poetic genius* especially. Goethe, too, has been his Master, and he is curious to learn if any student has things new to show him about the Olympian. Could Brockmeyer trace the thoughts uttered in the Conversation at Harris'. The papers would be an acquisition to our literature. I have asked Harris, too, for his Eulogy on Childs, of which he has given me the points in his late letter. It would be instructive reading, good to print in the Radical, which, under the head, *Religion,* embraces the whole circle of human interests. I trust you will continue *your* contributions to it.

If I am not much mistaken, your circle of thinkers are to find high place in American letters, rooted as you are deep in richest grounds of German philosophy, and to bear in fit time original fruits.—The excitement, long and continued, of my intercourse with ‖ them ‖ you, proved too intense, but I am recovering from the stroke, and shall know how to parry, should I visit you again, which, I need not say, I shall gladly do if desired.

If we have a Conference here in May, for comparing notes, as is now thought of, St. Louis should not fail of sending its representative. Did I not hear some whisper, from yourself or Mrs. Kroeger, of your visiting New England this summer? You come to Concord, of course, and to my house. I have pleasant memories of your household. Pray remember me to your genial wife whose open countenance is now before me.

Very truly yours
A. Bronson Alcott

LETTER 66–15[1]

[to William T. Harris, St. Louis]

Concord June 3rd 1866.

Dear Friend,

I must not hold you longer in suspense about the disposition of your paper sent by mail to me some weeks since. I read the same with satisfaction, submitted it to Sanborn who agreed with me that the North American should have the chance of enriching its pages with good solid paragraphs of sound philosophical criticism, and the article has accordingly been ‖ sub ‖committed to the editors, who will report their decision in due time to us. I wish they may have the discernment to give the same to their readers in the October number. If they are found faithless the Radical will gladly print it. Do you say, in that case, Part I. may precede Part IIi.d.[?], and make two articles, or one continued in two numbers?—Morse is now in Cincinnati, to be there for another Sunday. We have delayed the Conference, I named to you, for good reasons. Johnson (whose new Church at Lynn is to be dedicated this week) did not care for holding it; Weiss was in Cincinnati, Frothingham did not respond, and so Emerson and myself had it at my room—seeing how *individual the priests still are.* Perhaps next autumn will open the ways for the true concert; || and || philosophers are careless of time and space, you know, and so can wait, meanwhile. Your paper on "the Philosophical Society," is to come, I infer, by Brokmeyer,[1] who, Sanborn tells me, is to be in Boston this week, where I shall hope to meet him; and bring him to Concord. I hope your article will reach in season for the July Radical, which I hear is now far advanced in the printing. I shall see that Brokmeyer fulfils his promises about "the Faust Letters."

It may interest you to learn that Stirling is a candidate for the chair of Philosophy in Glasgow College, Scotland, and that Emerson has written a letter to the Faculty commending his Book on "Hegels' Secret." We shall be glad to hear of any Professor of Hegel in any college. Stirling, it seems, is a countryman of Carlyle's, and has lately met him.

I shall await your Eulogy on Childs, and indeed, anything of yours, with hope: Most of all your "Introduction to Hegel." Now the eyes of these *Atheneans* are on your designs, I see not how you can sleep or defer rushing into type long. It will be good when it comes.

With Brokmeyer, I am expecting good interviews here at my house and at Emersons. Give my greetings to the members of your Society. I have to thank Prof Howison for copies of his Verses on Lincoln, and you one to Emerson, the other to Sanborn.

Very truly yours
A. Bronson Alcott.

Wm. T. Harris.
     St. Louis.

[1] From a copy, in Alcott's hand, in the Alcott-Pratt Collection. The original is in the Alcott-Harris Collection in the Concord Free Public Library (see Appendix B).
[2] In Letter 66–14, Alcott spells the name Brockmeyer. Either spelling, apparently, is correct.

[Letter to David A. Wasson; from Concord? before June 8, 1866.]

LETTER 66–16

[to Parker Fraternity, Boston]

Concord July 9th. 1866.

To the Com. of Parker Fraternity.
Gentlemen,

You honor me with an invitation to your Annual Pic Nic, July 11th, at Walden Water.

It will give me pleasure to meet so many friends of freedom and ideas as, I know will be gathered under your banners, and, unless extreme heat shall prevent, I will endeavour to attend. The place, associated as it is, with classic names, seems the fitting spot for your meeting.

Very respectfully,
A. Bronson Alcott.

LETTER 66–17[1]

[to William T. Harris, St. Louis]

Wm. T. Harris
   Secretary of
The St Louis Phi Society.

Concord July 15th 1866.

Dear Sir,

   Your letter advising me of my being made an Auxiliary of your Society is before me.

   Allow me in reply, to express through you to the President, my grateful sense of this complement [sic] of respect, the confidence with which I am honored, the [word] thus opened of comparing views with friends of free thought at St Louis, and withal to asure them of my wish to promote in ways most [word] the [word] interest[s] [word] which these unite to further and secure.

Very respectfully
A. Bronson Alcott.

[1] From a copy, in Alcott's hand, in the Alcott-Pratt Collection. The original is in the Alcott-Harris Collection in the Concord Free Public Library (see Appendix B).

LETTER 66–18

[to William T. Harris, St. Louis]

Dear Friend,

Concord July 17th 1866.

   Your letter came duly to hand, and Sanborn has shown me yours to him. In these, we are informed of being elected "Auxiliaries" of your Philosophical Society. Please accept my sense of the confidence thus extended to me, and the assurance of my wish to serve you in such ways as I am able. You will have in Sanborn a valuable correspondent. Your estimate of Stirling's Book accords essentially with mine. I was very glad to know about it, having been asked repeatedly by persons curious about the St. Louis thinkers, what they thought of it. I have no doubts as to your giving us as ‖ better than ‖ good as his, and justifying your claims to the name of philosophical critic.

   What you write about the desirableness of having a Speculative Journal, I also feel as strongly as yourself, and wish the thing might be. There is a class of thought most important to be circulated among the few thinkers we have, for which we have as yet no organ: the Radical is very good in its way, but does not serve our speculative needs; nor is it likely to command the full strength of the country. We need space and time, scope and Volume, such as a Quarterly allows: and if Emerson, James, Cabot, Wasson, will join the men of the West,— yourself, Stallo, Goddard, Brockmeyer, Kroeger, Howison, I think, we should open with fair prospects of longevity. When we come West, let us consider the matter together; meanwhile using the Radical, as advertisement.

   I have not seen Morse since I sent your Constitution. He wrote, wishing to be informed "if there was not something to accompany it." and seeming to doubt about the propriety of printing it alone, perhaps expecting your account of my visit as a sufficient reason.

I hope your health is now restored. Yet cannot trust it long in hands and head, dealing this terribly with it. Atkinson, of the Technological School, promises to spend a day with me, when I hope to interest him in your schools and teachers. He had printed some remarks of mine about you in the "Mass. Teacher", which he now edits. I would send you Mills article on Fichte in Christian Examiner, did I not suppose you would see it.

Yours truly
A. Bronson Alcott

WmT. Harris

LETTER 66–19

[to Sidney H. Morse, Boston]

Concord July 17 1866.

Dear Sir,

I was expecting to meet you at Walden on Wednesday, but was called suddenly to attend a funeral on that afternoon. If you have a day at command, come up and spend it here, and tell me about your plans and periodical. I send another sheaf of "Tablets," which you may print in the August number, if you have space, or they may wait.[1]

I have written to Harris about printing the paper on the Constitution of the Phi Society. He promised some thing to accompany it, but he has been sick, he writes, and will presently inform you about printing it.

Yours truly
A. Bronson Alcott

Mr. Morse.

[1] The earlier "Tablets" appeared in the *Radical* for May, 1866; the present material appeared in the November, 1866, number.

[Letter to Mrs. A. Bronson Alcott, Concord; from Syracuse, November 24, 1866.]

LETTER 66–20

[to Mrs. A. Bronson Alcott, Concord]

St. Louis November 30th 1866.

My Dear,

I dispatched a line from Syracuse along with a word from your brother, relieving you from anxiety about him. This was on Saturday. Sunday he had no services. I dined at the Sedgwicks, and Mr. Mills spent the evening at your brothers, staying late. We thought it best to postpone Conversations till my return. Monday morning I spent in High School. Mr. May riding there with me and going about his social errands till dinner. Taking the afternoon train I stopped, and took supper with Mr. Hough at Rochester. He hoped to have a little company ready for me on my way homewards. Mr. Holland he thought distrustful of the New Divinity and indisposed towards introducing his people to the friend of the Radical. I was told that some of them preferred the son's preaching and would like to have more of it.

I left Rochester at 11: took a sleeping car at Buffalo, had some hours of comfortable sleep, and reached Cleveland about 8 Tuesday morning. Wiley on his way west, and promised to write from Chicago about prospects there, before I leave this city. It was 7. in the evening, when we reached Cincinnati. I slept at the Spencer House. On Wednesday called on Mr. Harris[on,] Mr. Hooper, & Judge Stallo. Wasson had gone East on Sunday night, still anxious about his family, after the newspaper accounts of the robbery &c. Samuel Longfellow was expected to speak for them for a Sunday or two. If he should not be able to stay longer, I am to stop on my way home, and give them a Sunday. Wass[on's] services seemed valued highly by those who spoke to me about his preaching.

At 8.P.M. I took the rail again, riding all night, and reaching [here] at 2.P.M. yesterday. Thursday I rode to Kroegers' at once. My trunk was immedia[tely] sent for, and I am to be his guest, for a part of my stay at least. You already know, it was my hope to enjoy the hospitalities of his house. Mrs. Kroeger is a broad faced, kindly Englishwoman, and knows how to entertain ancients like myself. So all is good as it can be care[?].

In the evening, Kroeger took me to the ‖ opera ‖ [p. o.] concert [p. in] where I found Harris and wife, and enjoyed the mysteries of Mendelssohn and Beethoven to the extent of my uninstructed ear. I enclose the "programme." How I wished you and the girls beside me. The Performers were German and the audience largely so. It was amazing and served to make palpable the wonders of music. Harris indulged in some remarkable criticisms, ‖ showing how a philosopher can *feel* as well as *think*. ‖ [p. o.].

This afternoon, I am to visit with Kroeger, Shaw's "Botanical Garden" five miles out, and meet some of the philosophers to arrange about our meetings, this evening.

The day is soft and sunny, like October. The little trouble in the throat mending. I abstain from tasting the turbid Missisippi [sic] waters, finding the Rhine wines palatable. I hope to escape the ills of last season's experiences here.

You shall hear further from me soon. Impressions are favorable now, and by Monday I shall have something definite to give you. All I know as yet, beyond this evening, is, that I am to meet the "Society," in full, on Sunday next.

I trust you are finding some respite from the long weary days of pain and restlessness of the last two months. As you regain the use of your eye the former satisfactions come again. Pray be prudent and take care of exposures. Louisa is an arsenal of powers, if you will but cal[l] them forth to your assistance. I hope the blaze of her Genius is kindled with that of her chamber-fire. Words to May presently.

Express my thanks to Mr. Channing for his true interest in your comfort, and readiness to give you so much of his time.

Ever Yours affectionately,
A. B. A.

LETTER 66–21

[to Mrs. A. Bronson Alcott, Concord]

St. Louis December 3rd 1866.

My Dear,

I wrote hastily last Friday of my arrival here, and gave some account of my journey out, with intimations of my work for the fortnight coming. Today, I spend quietly in my chamber and add a word further.

'Tis arranged that I am to meet the Philosophical Society four times. Yesterday came our first sitting, the second comes on Wednesday, then on Sunday and Wednesday next, the rest. To morrow evening, I give the first of four Parlor Conversations: Friday evening of this, Tuesday and Thursday evenings of next week, the remaining three. Meanwhile, I am invited to address the Association of City Teachers, and visit the Schools. I thus hope to complete my work here in time to leave by the 14th. Beyond this date all is indefinite. If my present health and spirits hold good, I shall gladly accept opportunities for speaking or conversing that open on my way East. Thus far I have found myself equal to the new demands, and mean so to husband my stock of strength as to escape last season's penalties. This city is now healthy, the weather pleasant, and bids fair for the time of my stay. I find my host and hostess wanting in nothing that kindness and hospitality can supply. So please sit at rest about my personal comforts —at least while I stay in this house—nor otherwise, if I spend a few days at Mr. Homers' where I found comfortable quarters last spring. Yet I shall not disguise the fact that a deal of *"roughing"* enters into the luxury of this Western life. ‖ Still there is ‖ The substance of comfort is served out nevertheless with a hearty good will and genuine kindliness. I cannot fail to remark however, that here, as in older countries, the women pay the dearest prices for all good that is going. It may interest you to learn that one of my topics is "Woman," about whom the philosophers here along with common men, I suspect, as every where, need enlightening. I wish I may be equal to my theme and the occasion. Perhaps the women are even more eager to hear what men can say of them than the men can be to speak it. I suspect that my work this time lies chiefly outside of the circle of philosophers. Not that they are deficint [sic] in good services within the sphere of pure thinking, or useful doing. I wish I had found ‖ as ‖ like able and earnest work among the young men of New England: enthusiasm as vigorous, devotion to thought as untiring. These young students have adventurous aims, broad views, nor are they all their zeal, at all deficint [sic] in practical sense and ability. I still think highly of their purposes and plans, and believe they have a great future before them, some as translators some as authors, others as professors and teachers. Certainly they stand well, most of them, with their townsmen here.

I have left room to say how gladly I shall hear of your recoverd strength and spirits, and shall hope to see, as soon as your eyes allow, your own account of yourself and family matters. I trust this is not to be a long jaunt of mine, and that I am to be with you again soon. It will add greatly to our satisfactions if it shall also prove remunerative, which as yet I have no reasons for doubting. None but the thinker can know the full measure of woes the worldling ignorantly inflicts on him whose pursuits transcend ‖ alike his ‖ popular conception and sympathy.

Love to Author and artist.[1]
Ever affectionately

A. B. A.

[1] Louisa and May.

LETTER 66–22

[to Mrs. A. Bronson Alcott, Concord]

St. Louis December 10th 1866.

My Dear,

I came out to Mr. Harris' yesterday and have spent the forenoon in his school. This evening I have a Conversation, another on Wednesday evening, which closes my engagements here, and I purpose leaving on Thursday (13th). Whether I go to Chicago I do not yet know, but expect a letter from Wiley about that matter. I have had very agreeable interviews with friends here, and stood the climate thus far with out special detriment. My throat is some better, and the colder days since Friday last, have given some elasticity of spirit. But I shall not wish staying beyond the time named. And it is quite likely that you may find me with you again by the 20th.

Your letters of 27th Novr. and Dec. 2nd came to hand by due course of mail. I am sorry to hear that your eye heals so slowly. Are you doing all that can be done for it. Louisa writes that you have ridden out, and that your general health is improving. It must have been a great happiness to have had Anna and the boys with you at Thanksgiving. Anna wrote a most encouraging account of herself. Freddy's picture was a surprise, and gets a look from me every day. May's care for the Effigy is characteristic. I am glad to learn that her services are in demand, and that Louisa has seen actual greenbacks for hers. I shall bring as large a count as I can, and hope to open the New Year with out pressing embarrassments. How thoughtful it was in your brother to ensure me from the risks of travel. I shall probably pass some days with him on my return. Sam Greele's misfortune must be felt deeply by his new-wife. Her grandfather's condition can be of little consequence to her, or any one else. Mr. Hough writes that his friends would be glad to have me stop at Rochester. I think I may pass a day or so there to advantage.

‖ About ‖ As to my visits out here this season and the last. I am now fully persuaded that good results are coming. These are earnest men with whose thoughts and prospects I find much in common. I have nowhere met with a reception so hearty and acceptable. I am in possession of their future plans, and have good hopes of them. The matter for the first number of their "*Journal of Speculative Philosophy,* is already arranged and must attract thoughtful men every where. Harris is in correspondence with the deeper thinkers, ‖ appears to be growing in public estimation, ‖ is himself the chiefest of metaphysicans [sic], and cannot well fail of making a Journal worthy its name. The first number is to be issued sometime in January 1867.

399

I wrote to you on the 3rd and hope to have letters before I leave here. Any addressed to care of Mr. Harris, can be sent after me. 'Tis probable I may stop a Sunday, as I may have written, in Cincinnati, but as yet I have no word from that place.

You have not mentioned Mr. Channing in your former letters. I trust you are having his good company often during my absence.

Though finding many satisfactions in this intercourse with persons abroad, I begin to suspect that home is the proper place for me, and find this journeying is not the most desirable exercise to one of my age and habits.

Ever Yours
faithfully
A.B.A.

Send Freddy Grandpas' thanks
for his blooming picture.

LETTER 66–23

[to Mrs. A. Bronson Alcott, Concord]

St. Louis December 13th 1866.

My Dear,

It was my intention to have left this morning for Cincinnati. But the Conversations have found such good favor, that I am invited to stay till Friday evening next, (Tomorrow) and give a "fifth". So I shall hope to take Saturday's train for the East. A touch of cold during the last days, has given spring to the feelings, and I have recovered something of eastern elasticity of spirits. Our two last Conversations have been greatly improved in consequence. The Company has increased and our evenings have proved satisfactory to all. To morrow evening, I am to speak of the *"East and West"*—. I find my auditors disposed to hear, ready to question, generally in earnest, and, on the whole, good to have. Thus far, all our interviews have been successful. I have been honored with the presence of many elderly ladies and gentlemen to dignify and ornament our discussions.—My engagements with the Philosophers are now [p. in] closed.

I spent Tuesday evening at Mrs. Beverly Allen's three miles out of the city. The family is from Virginia, connected with the Scopes, and other F. F.s, but retaining ‖ nothing but ‖ [p. o.] the good traits of that old aristocracy. We discussed anti-slavery—free suffrage, woman's-rights, as freely as if all were New Englanders[.] The young ladies were specially intelligent and free-speaking, and the old-grandmother, near 80, still good company. Mr. and Mrs. Harris, Prof Howison and wife, went out with us. I wished Louisa had been of the company. Mr. Yeaton, Mrs. Allen's, brother in law, and formerly President of the Western Freedman's Association, is now in Boston, to promote Miss Hosmer's design for the National Lincoln Monument ‖ , and ‖ [p. o.]. He may visit Concord. He knows Emerson, and was very attentive to me last spring. I hope you will see him. He is a bland gentleman; in personal appearance, reminding me of Samuel May of Boston. One of the young ladies gave me the enclosed photograph of the Negro woman whose contribution of five dollars, first suggested the Lincoln Monument.

Since I wrote last, I have visited the Normal School under the charge of Miss

Brackett, who has just returned from visiting the Prussian Schools. I hear that several letters of hers were published in the Commonwealth. This paper is read here and valued. Yesterday I was pleased to find an extract from Louisas' Sketches for the Independent. I shall look for ‖ some ‖ [p. o.] others [p. in] sent before I left home. Tilton, the editor, is out West, lecturing. Emerson and Phillips are to be here, I believe sometime in January. Much interest is expressed by all I meet about hearing them. Phillips is sure of an ovation, and must make a profound impression on the multitude.

I am expecting to meet Judge Holmes, author of the new Book on Shakespear. I hear he is to be at my Conversation to morrow evening.

I have every comfort here at Kroeger's, even to Rhine wines, warm chamber, and attentive service. On the whole, find myself better than when I left home. I hope to hear from you before I leave: nothing has reached me since Anna's and yours of Dec. 2nd. Pray write—if not permitted yourself, then by daughterly hands.

Every thing at present looks auspicious as to my tour.

Much love to you
and Yours.
A. B. A.

Direct hereafter to care of S. J. May.
Syracuse.

PART SIXTEEN

1867-1868

LETTER 67-1

[to Mary A. Whitaker, Chicago]

Concord Feb 7 1867

Dear Mrs Whitaker,

I have received the papers you sent me and your letters asking attention to your New Spiritual Republic, and should have replied before this, had I not been confined to my chamber since New Years day with a painful rheumatism which allowed me but little sleep by night or thought by day. Now I am partially relieved and find, on looking into your Journal, much that interests me along with a good deal that does not commend itself to my religion or good sense. But this shall not blind my eyes to the really strong claims of your paper upon the public attention. It is far more acceptable to me, ‖ than ‖ as I am sure it will be to earnest and openeyed minds every where—than are the other spiritual journals which I have chanced to see. And in its department of *Social Reform* must do much good. I have read Mr. Loveland's contributions with acceptance, especially, and could wish that spiritualism had always shown a spirit as religious and catholic, as free from sensualism and intolerance.

It has long been my persuasion that out of this maelstrom of mixed forces, good and bad, a purer faith would sometime emerge and shape itself for us. Americans [word] here, if any where, religion is to plant itself and spread far and wide.—Were I in the way of contributing by pen you should hav[e] a word. But it would please me better to have the pleasure of meeting your friends, and those of the Republic, in the parlor, and there talk out my world in free Conversations. I had some hopes of visiting Chicago on my recent tour West, but it was not found feasible to do so.

My daughters are now home.

With regards and good wishes
I am truly yours
A Bronson Alcott

Mrs Mary A. Whitaker.

LETTER 67–2

[to Charles D. B. Mills, Syracuse]

Concord February 20th 1867.

Dear Friend,

I have been through Jamblichus's Life of Pythagoras, (I forget whether you possess a copy) Diogenes Laertius lives of the Philosophers," for the information you ask for. Also, dipped a little into Grote's History of Greece, when at a bookstore last Monday, but find nothing definite concerning the continuance of the Pythagorean School. Grote thinks the Alexandrian or Neo-Platonists, were not Pythagoreans, but revived the traits of the School only. It is certain they had much in common; and that Plato must have been familiar with "the Master's" main doctrines, if he was not his disciple, transmitting his spirit and, to some extent, his methods of thinking, down to Proclus, Plotinus, and the rest. Any one conversant with the history of thought, must perceive that the Germs of all modern philosophy are properly speaking Pythagorean, and that specula- tive theology is deeply tinged with its essence. One shall find the best of our "New Testament" intimated, if not expressed, in these Pythagorean and Platonic Books. Taston Martys,[1] as you know, has much to say on this subject.

Perhaps we might claim for our modern Transcendentalism German, and American, little more than a following forth into the manifold relations of life and nature, the central truths and ideas of the Samian Sage. I consider him the *only Educator* the world has known. We are yet far from treating the human being with any thing like the skill which history shows was his, and wait for the first ‖ intimation ‖ hint of an institution for training youth into the principles and victories of a divinely human life.

Christianity seems to have drawn the minds of the generations away from practical efforts of this sort—deserting *humanity* while professing to cherish and strengthen it for this life.

I wish I had something more to offer you, and am glad that you are about giving us some account of the great Educator. Besides the books I have named I have none that give us any light. There is an English translation of *Ritter* which I read some years ago.

It may interest you to know that I gave the fourth Lecture of the Sunday Evening Course in Boston, last Sunday—subject—*Modern Religion.* Also, that a Conference held at Bartol's, of *Radicals,* proved that something like concert was possible.

I am up and about again after a months' confinement.

Very truly yours
A. Bronson Alcott

C. B. D. Mills.[2]

---

[1] Tassin, a Maurist monk?
[2] Alcott has reversed the second and third initials of Mills' name.

LETTER 67–3

[to Henry Batchelder, Hilliston, Mass.]

Concord Feb. 27th 1867.

Dear Sir,

You honor me with your confidence in a delicate matter, and one in which time and events must give the counsel you ask, rather than persons. Especially in your case, where religious persuasions interpose themselves, and words can have but little influence. Much, I should say must depend upon your friends temperament and natural dispositions. If inclined to enthusiasm, the victim of moods, if of a devout turn, & the sport[?] of feeling, rather than of reason, I suppose the priests have the advantage. Still these fervors of revivals are usually short lived, and good sense comes to the aid of their victims shortly. I could wish this might happen for you—certainly if the young lady of your choice is worthy of you. Perhaps you will conclude disappointment to hear your grief and mortification, meanwhile, awaiting the issue with patience and magnanimity. I take you to be strong in thought and above being yourself seduced from convictions even by the tender temptation that has befallen you.

If you choose, write to me again, as I take ‖ it ‖ kindly this mark of your confidence. I hope my reply will not seem cold.

Very truly Yours,
A. Bronson Alcott.

Mr. Henry Batchelder,
Hilliston Ms

LETTER 67–4

[to Seth Hunt, Northampton, Mass.]

Concord March 7[?]th 1867

Dear Sir,

I will speak for your People on the 17th My Subjects will be
‖ *Education* and ‖
Modern Religious Instrumentalities

You shall arrange the order ‖ of these ‖ as you think best. I shall wish to speak to the Children of the Sunday School also.

Being a little tender after my long siege of rheumatism, I must be careful of exposure. Shall I come to your house? And will the road connexions suit for Saturday? I can leave here by either the Worcester or Fitchburg routes.

Very truly
Yours
A. Bronson Alcott.

Seth Hunt
Northampton

LETTER 67–5

[to Mary E. Stearns, Medford, Mass.]

Concord April 13th 1867.

Dear Mrs. Stearns,

How could one speak words to cleave away the clouds of a great sorrow?[1] May the night and consoling sleep have done what words could not. "Time we say "brings roses.' rather, and better say, the roses are [word] only upon which tears of sorrow are shed, and the deeds[?] of eternity have fallen. Kneeling before and dropping roses into the tomb of the beloved, is there a fairer symbol of one's superiority to Time and Sorrow. Your friend, Parsons said to me there, "Death is the one universal fact."—"Except life," I added, and he accepted. And now, my stricken friend, on looking at that, and the array of Immortality yesterday bearing the laurels for crowning the Life Immortal, the testimonial speech and yet more the silence of that solemn hour and company, it seems a beautiful dream, no part of measured time, but of immeasurable, and the apotheosis of the dear Friend you had won, and would not withold [sic] from heavenly honors and spheres of nobler labor. How gratefully || to || on the ear fell the accents of a good man's virtues and career. Ah! my friend, you were the favored one, in having your Friend so long, and a friend to speak worthily of him, there and then! Maj Stearns is sure of immortality and seldom has any won its rewards in any time, so modestly. I think his a new type of character that only New England could have ripened into flower and fruitage. You shall not find his like. I said to Emerson here is a hero of a foreign style: ideal in its downrightness of realism, and a match for the mightiest, and but for whom we had perhaps missed a Harpers' Ferry martyr, and a free Republic. Yes, my friend, your sorrow has cleared away, and the weeks and months shall reconcile you to your future.—

With sympathy for your sons solitude for[?] a little, believe me,

Ever Yours and Theirs
A.B.A.

[1] George L. Stearns had died of pneumonia in New York City on April 9, 1867.

LETTER 67–6

[Mrs. Frances D. Gage, St. Louis?]

Concord April 14 1867

Dear Mrs Gage,

Your Book of Poems came to hand some days ago, for which you have my thanks. Mrs Alcott wishes me to add hers and to say that as soon as her sight is restored, she hopes to be able to read and enjoy the verses beyond the pleasure the few of them she has heard read have given her—as their kindly spirit and brave tone interest her. I recognized here and there a verse which I had the pleasure of hearing from your own lips when at your hospitable home at St Louis some years since, and am glad that you have contributed your strains to swell the melodies of life, private or national, that we have lived during these years of sad experiences—but now becoming hopeful and to be consummated, we trust, in a perfect joy for the races of all hues and conditions.

I was interested in what you told us of yourself and family. And read of your continued good works from time in "The Anti-Slavery Standard.

My family are near ‖ and ‖ or with us here at Concord, giving in pride and happiness, Louisa had been disabled for some time, since she returned from Europe, but is recovering strength and spirits for future works. May, the youngest, is busy with her [word] and sketching. Anna the eldest has two pretty boys[1] and lives at ‖ Chelsea ‖ East Boston.

Yours, with much esteem,
A. Bronson Alcott

Mrs. Frances D. Gage.

---

[1] The second was named John Sewall Pratt.

Letter 67–7[1]

[to William T. Harris, St. Louis]

Concord May 12th 1867

Dear Friend,

Your Journal of Speculative Philosophy more than answers my expectations, both in thought, style, type, and the rest.[2] Your part contents me especially —the Introduction, the Speculative, invite and satisfy. And "The Herbert Spencer," shows the masterly criticism that should command it to thinkers, whether agreeing or disagreeing with its judgments. I wish it may provoke criticism in reply, though I do not care to see you stooping from your ideal Olympus to wage war with any clique of opinion here or any where. But wish you to hold on your high road of thought and let the Atlantics or transatlantics have their say as they choose. It will not amount to much, and you have better work on hand than to prick ear or ‖ pen ‖ quill at them.—I was pleased to find the "Notes on Raphael's Transfiguration,["] showing how works of art might be [word]. Emerson was highly pleased with your criticism and returned with increased respect for the ability of your "Society." I trust you made the most of him while he was with you. He regrets not having met Kroeger and Brockmeyer. He thinks you are made "Superintendent of the Schools." I wish for their benefit it ‖ is ‖ [p. o.] be [p. in] so, but trust nothing will take you from your high calling of Philosopher. I am glad Kroeger has found publishers for "Fichte."[3] Martlings paper is good reading.[4] Brockmeyers "Faust" must not be further postponed, nor Howisons thought. I shall hope to hear as your plans open and prospects.

I have had two months of work on my "Tablets." They stand now under the heads of I Speculative[,] II Practical, III. Biographical, with an Introduction on "The Times."

I go next Monday week to a meeting for forming a *Free Religious Club,*"[5] and shall take your Journal. Abbot[6] is interested in this movement, and should be in yourself and Journal. Emerson gives the fourteenth Lecture in the Sunday Evening Radical Course, to-morrow night.

I am partially restored, though much reduced in strength.

Truly Yours,
A. Bronson Alcott.

Wm. T. Harris.

[1] From a copy, in Alcott's hand, in the Alcott-Pratt Collection. The original is in the Alcott-Harris Collection in the Concord Free Public Library (see Appendix B).
[2] The date of the first number is generally given as January, 1867, but it appeared later than that.
[3] The first number of the *Journal of Speculative Philosophy* contains a translation by A. E. Kroeger, "Introduction to Fichte's Science of Knowledge."
[4] James A. Martling's translation of Bénard's "Analytical and Critical Essay upon the Aesthetics of Hegel."
[5] Also called the Radical Club, the group continued meeting until 1880. See Letter 67–8.
[6] Francis E. Abbot.

LETTER 67–8[1]

[to Mary E. Stearns, Medford, Mass.]

Concord, May 21st. 1867.

Dear Mrs. Stearns,

Next week being Anniversary week in Boston, I am to be in the City for a day or two, and, if agreeable to you, should enjoy spending a night, and as much of a day as you might desire, at your hospitable home. Among other topics that might interest, beside the *One* sacred in the memory of yourself and family, as of so many of the excellent of these States, I have a MS. Volume, upon which I have been engaged during these last crippled months,[2] and parts of which it would give me great pleasure to read to you, for comfort it might chance, and for your criticism especially, before I commit the papers to the printers hands. I know it is planting season with you, as with Nature, but have thought you might like some recreations, literary, moral, philosophic, to vary your days. I should not come earlier than Wednesday and it might be later in the week to suit your convenience.

I was at a meeting of the *New Radical Religious Club* yesterday at Mr. Sargeants'[3] and found it profitable and promising good things. Mr. Towne who was there and who told he was to dine with you, has doubtless told you about it. As women are to take place and part in the discussions, which are private and conversational, I have wished we may have the benefit of your presence and thoughts, and shall hope to enjoy the pleasure of your accompanying me at our next meeting, June 17th. at Mr. Sargeants.

We are all getting up and about again.

Yours with great
Esteem
A. B. Alcott.

Mrs. Stearns.

[1] MS. owned by the Fruitlands and Wayside Museums.
[2] *Tablets*, published late in 1868.
[3] John T. Sargent.

[to John Weiss]

Concord June 30th 1867

Dear Sir,

We shall hope to see you and Miss Swett early on Tuesday to spend the day and dine with us. If you come by rail there is a morning train arriving here at 8½. if later at 12.

If at Waltham at 8. you will reach us at half past 8. and will find a coach at the station to bring you to my door.

Meanwhile, I shall see Emerson and take pains that he shall not miss you.

Yours fraternally
A. Bronson Alcott.

Rev. John Weiss.

[Letter to Seth Hunt, Northampton, Mass.; from Concord, June 30, 1867.]

LETTER 67–10[1]

[to Mary E. Stearns, Medford, Mass.]

Concord July 14th 1867.

Dr. Mrs Stearns

I am happy to learn by your late note of your improved health, and trust spirits too,—so much is implied in the phrase of the enjoyableness of life, and which wanting, life were not. Even if there be sadness mingled in the cup, is it the less enjoyable, and good to taste? Evil and only evil are they who drink sorrows only from the fountains of Good. How can any sip sadness from the sunshine of days like this?

"He is not gone being gone, where'er thou art,
He leaves in thee his watchful eyes, in thee his loving heart."

As to the superservicable [sic] young Divine we are all not without instinctive advisement. And but for the touch of religious mysticism which I detect behind his courage, liberality and intelligence, I cannot suppose he would much interest me even at this time of Promise. Very clearly behind in the background are seen figures coming forwards to fill the places that history will remember. Thus far, tradition gives the planting of Religions to the Gods alone.

When you feel equal to a day's Conversation and free to enjoy it, be so kind as to let us know.

We are mostly freed from the winter's ails, Louisa having been at Gloucester for some days and is enjoying the sea.

Very Cordially and ever,
Yours
A. Bronson Alcott

Mrs. Mary Stearns.

[1] MS. owned by the Fruitlands and Wayside Museums. A copy, in Alcott's hand, is in the Alcott-Pratt Collection.

LETTER 67–11

[to Sidney H. Morse, Boston]

Concord Aug 5th 1867.

Dear Sir,

Can you give me a day or part of one soon; the sooner the better, this week would please me best? If you can, please write, and name any day but Thursday, when I have an engagement. I can hardly hope to see you here at my house. Yet if you give me a day, I shall forbear finding you in Boston, and secure a longer interview. I am your debtor for more *Tablets,* and wish to consult you about printing first in your Journal. My collection runs to the length of a good sized volume which I will publish in some form soon, if publishers' favor. Meanwhile, selections might be made for "the Radical," if you liked to print such.

The August number, I have just read with pleasure and pride, and cannot doubt about its acceptance by a growing public.

I am to see Weiss and Wasson soon.

Yours truly
A. Bronson Alcott.

S. H. Morse,
Editor of Radical

LETTER 67–12[1]

[to William T. Harris, St. Louis]

Concord August 5th 1867.

Dear Friend,

Prof. Davidson wishes me to send his translation of "Schelling's Idealism" for insertion in your Journal, if you think it deserves a place. In the August no. of the Radical you will find an Article on "Kleanthes" written also by him. Enclosed is a note accompanying the translation. He has been here once or twice lately, having relinquished his professorship in the British College at London, Canada. He thinks of journeying West, and may find you at St. Louis. Emerson speaks highly of his scholarship and culture. I believe he designs to give himself to literary pursuits hereafter.

The Second No. of your Journal came to hand some weeks since, and lately a parcel of your "Prospectus," for which I am finding readers. Mr. Geo. P. Bradford a good friend of Emersons, a teacher now at Newport, R.I. told me he should like to subscribe[,] and I gave your address. I shall take copies of your Prospectus to our Club Meeting ‖ next week in Boston ‖ in August. I hear good words about the Journal from all—Emerson, Sanborn, Wasson, Weiss; and Abbot writes in a note, to me "Some of the articles in Mr. Harris Journal of Spec.' Phil. are quite Able, and I trust the enterprize will succeed. The influence of Hegel is evidently deeply felt by most of the writers. I look for an American Philosophy as I do for an American Religion—perhaps not in my day, though I believe I can do something for it if I live."

Your second no. I thought, an improvement on the first. I looked in it for your contributions, and find these instructive reading. The "Notes on Lycidas" were a surprise. Sanborn tells me that Miss. Brackett[2] is to be here this week for a day, when I shall be sure to see her. I read in the Commonwealth that she takes two young Ladies' West to teach in *your* schools. Do your duties as Superintendent absorb all your time? I hope philosophy may not suffer in consequence.

My *Tablets* have found place and arrangement in a Bookform, which I should like to print soon. Would my last chapter on *Genesis* || would publish not || be out of || keeping and || place in your Journal? and when you are making up the papers for the fourth no, perhaps you will like this, as one of them. I *might* like to have it appear about that time.

Weiss and Wasson are expected here on Thursday to spend the day.

Yours truly,
A. Bronson Alcott.

Mr. W. T. Harris

[1] From a copy, in Alcott's hand, in the Alcott-Pratt Collection. The original, *dated August 6,* is in the Alcott-Harris Collection in the Concord Free Public Library (see Appendix B).
[2] Anna C. Brackett, who wrote the "Notes on Milton's Lycidas."

LETTER 67–13

[to Thomas Davidson]

Concord Aug. 7th 1867.

Dear Sir,

At your request, I have mailed your translation of Schelling to Mr. Harris; and have written him concerning yourself and translation. "The Kleanthes" he will read in "the Radical".

Last evening, Emerson was here. He spoke in terms of praise of the Kleanthes, and wishes to see you when you are next in town. Can you not come up again soon and spend a day?

Very truly yours
A. Bronson Alcott.

Prof. Davidson

LETTER 67–14

[to Sidney H. Morse, Boston]

Concord August 8th 1867.

Dear Sir,

Come up on Thursday, and by the 7'30 Express, so that we may have a long day. If not then, your next chance is 11,—which brings you here at 12. m.

The last no. of the Radical is excellent. Emerson speaks in terms of praise of "The Kleanthes," and we owe you thanks for your Cambridge Theology paper.

Yesterday Wasson and Weiss were here, and we talked long on theological education and religious Reform.

Yours truly
A. Bronson Alcott.

S. H. Morse.

LETTER 67–15

[to William T. Harris, St. Louis]

Concord Aug 23rd 1867

Dear Friend,

I send by Miss Brackett a paper on *"Genesis"* for your Journal if you think it deserves a place. At first, I thought of sending my *"Notes on Philosophers"*, but find them so brief and unfinished that I withold [*sic*] them for the present. "The Plato's Ideal State" I copied from Sewalls' book on Plato—the title of which I do not recall. The tone, I remember, was less English than usual.

Shall you publish the other numbers of Vol. Ist before January? Miss. Brackett thought you would. She tells me you are busy on your translation of Hegel, doing your stint regularly day by day. The Journal must not think of stopping while it has interested so many, and is gaining a good philosophical reputation. I have wished not to prejudice its reception by its favoring openly any [word] like mine, while honestly believing I had something deserving of place, and American in spirit, if not in origin.

Write and let me know your time of publishing the numbers.

I am expecting to learn more about *Philosophia Harrisia* from Miss Brackett, who dines with Sanborn to day, and is to be at my house afterw[ards.]

Truly yours
A. B. Alcott.

W. T. Harris.

LETTER 67–16

[to Lucy Stone, New York City]

Concord Sep. 13th 1867

Dear Madam,

I have not been able to see Mr. Emerson till yesterday since receiving your note. He declined giving his signature to your Appeal, saying he would write his objections: taking your P.O. address, at New York City. Having none myself, I gladly sign it, assured that woman is soon to have her place in the State with every right of the citizen. What Ideal Republics have fabled ours is to be.

411

Nor need we fear the boldest experiments which the moral sense of the best women conceive and advocate.

Yours truly
A. Bronson Alcott

Lucy Stone.

LETTER 67–17[1]

[to William T. Harris, St. Louis]

Concord Sep 17th 1867.

Dear Friend,

I return your copy of my M.S. with slight corrections and amendments. I regret the labor and pains bestowed to render it legible to the printer. But I can scarce hope more from your adepts than ours in this matter of reading bad M.S.S. You shall send me *"a proof,"* if you doubt about getting the text accurate, and can do so without delaying your day of publication unreasonably. I should like three or four copies of this third number, if you can afford to send them to me.

I send the names of two subscribers

> *Hon. Samuel E. Sewall, Boston*
> and
> *Mr. George P. Bradford,* Newport, R. Island

both thoughtful men and readers of free things.

You write heroically about the prospects and continuance of your Journal. I wish there were the like faith in Philosophy here at the East. Our scholars are ready to praise ability anywhere, but rather slow to believe it can come from the West. Your Journal surprises and provokes doubts whether it can maintain the promise of its first issues. I, of course, and Emerson of late, know your wealth and courage: so do Wasson, so Weiss. Cabot I have not met lately. But we hope to have him here next month with Wasson and Weiss, when I shall speak about yourself and Journal to get his thought.

Yesterday I was at "the Free Club" at Sargents. The attendance was large, the talk free and broad. Emerson read a paper of *Counsel,* very subtle and acceptable.

Morse is printing a little sketch of *Wendell Phillips,* in the October Radical.

I am talking about printing my Tablets at large. But find publishers full for the present.

Very truly yours
A Bronson Alcott

Wm. T. Harris.

---

[1] From a copy, in Alcott's hand, in the Alcott-Pratt Collection. The original is in the Alcott-Harris Collection in the Concord Free Public Library (see Appendix B).

LETTER 67–18

[to Cyrus A. Bartol, Boston]

Concord Sep. 18th 1867

Dear Friend,

You must let me thank you heartily for the strong words, now printed, spoken to the Divinity Students the other day.—In a sense honoring the speaker of July 38, as of July 67.[1] I take special pleasure in the added *Personality,* without which the spirit were but symbolized not identified, nor known experimentally.

That gathering last Monday! Let me not seem to forget or disparage the reading, and speech of others, if I tell you how deeply your Lyric utterance touched me, as it did *our friend,* and must all who listened to the inspiration and the ecstacy.

Pray excuse me for this warm expression of my interest in your words and yourself.

Most cordially,
A. Bronson Alcott.

Dr. Bartol.

[1] Emerson.

LETTER 67–19[1]

[to Cyrus A. Bartol, Boston]

Concord Octr 11th 1867.

Dear Sir,

I shall joyfully join your dinner party after our Club meeting on Monday. Emerson tells me he intends to avail himself of your invitation also. This morning's mail brings me a printed notice of our meeting and of your giving us an Essay.

Very cordially,
Yours
A. Bronson Alcott.

Dr. Bartol,

[1] MS. owned by the Fruitlands and Wayside Museums.

LETTER 67–20[1]

[to Mary E. Stearns, Medford, Mass.]

Concord October 23rd 1867.

Dear Mrs. Stearns,

I find in my Journal the following notes which I copy for your eye, hoping my words may find acceptance in your heart and thought also.

"Wednesday 10th. April. '67.

"Maj. Stearns is a national loss. But he leaves at a moment when his purposes for his country are being consummated in victories, which himself, more largely than known to any but himself, helped to win, such was the generosity of his services and his modesty in bestowing them. He was truly a noble man, and the noblest of the noble in his hospitalities to truth and merit, to the perceiving of which he had an instinctive sagacity that made him the natural prompter of the free spirit of his time. I imagine he was in communication, personally or by the pen, with a larger number of able and patriotic minds than any man in New-England, and commanded an influence as a private citizen second to none, taking as he did a leading part in most of the great reforms during the war, and following these into the period of reconstructing the country after its close. More than any man, he was the father of the Radical Republican Party, while at the same time the friend and counsellor of the advanced sentiment of which Phillips is the proper head. His services to the Country were constant and various. There are half a dozen passages in his life, any one of which would give a national fame to any man. And his acts of private munificence were not limited by his income, rich as he was and successful in a large business. He gave to objects overlooked by others: and more than any man I have known anticipated the future of his time. Practical to a downrightness that might seem bordering on roughness, he was yet in thought, the gentlest of Idealists; as delicately organized and tender as a woman, he had the candor and courage of a hero, suggesting in his tone and temper the attitude of the Martyr of Harper's Ferry. And to him is the country indebted mainly for the means which made the striking of that first stroke for its freedom effective. *Friday 14th* To Medford with Mrs. A. The services are simple and impressive. Portions of Scripture are read and prayers made. Emerson and Theophilus Parsons speak affectingly of the character and services of the deceased. We ride, Emerson, Parsons, myself and Mrs A. together to the family tomb at Mount Auburn. Mrs. Stearns and sons strow flowers upon the grave.

"Death is the one universal fact" said Parsons to me at the tomb; "Except Life", I added, and he assented.[2]

[1] MS. owned by the Fruitlands and Wayside Museums.
[2] The letter breaks off here.

LETTER 67-21

[to John T. Sargent, Boston]

Concord October 30th 1867

Dear Sir

Meeting Lord and Lady Amberley lately at Emersons, Lady A. expressed a wish to be present at a meeting of our Club. As they are to leave New England before the regular meeting next, I wish we might have an earlier sitting—say Monday,—for his convenience. Lord Amberley is the son of Lord Earl Russell and her ladyship is Lord Stanley's daughter. Both seem deeply interested in the Reforms of this Country and truly liberal in thought and spirit. As the Club represents the freest and broadest American Ideas—may we not say as much modestly?—I think persons of their social positions and sincerity, should not leave the Country without meeting with us. I trust yourself and Mr. Towne will agree with me, and we will send out invitations forthwith. Let Phillips be informed and secured as a star for the occasion.

If not convenient to have the meeting at your rooms Dr. Bartol, I am sure, will gladly open his.

As it will be necessary to learn whether the Amberleys can meet us on the _____please delay sending out invitations till you hear further from myself or Emerson.

Truly Yours
A. Bronson Alcott.

John T. Sargent.
Chestnut street

LETTER 67–22[1]

[to Mary E. Stearns, Medford, Mass.]

Concord Nov. 6th 1867.

Dear Mrs. Stearns,

May I hope that this note will find you so far freed from recent pressures, as to enjoy meeting a select company invited to meet Lord & Lady Amberley for free Conversations at Mr. Sargents on Thursday 14th. Nov. at 10 A.m. and bring Mr. Frank with you? Lord and Lady Amberley expressed the wish to know you for your own and Mr. Stearns' sake. And I thought you might enjoy meeting them at the Conversation. Emerson and Phillips are of the party. Mr Weiss and Mrs. Howe.

Pray excuse me if I intrude upon Chosen solitude by intimating this P.S. I really have forgotten, if I ever knew, the name of the person at the West for whom you obtained the Dials. And you must excuse me for thinking the name of *Stearns* has a feminine face and that a brave and noble one.

Truly Yours
A. Bronson Alcott

[1] MS. owned by the Fruitlands and Wayside Museums. A copy, in Alcott's hand, is in the Alcott-Pratt Collection.

LETTER 67–23[1]

[to William B. Rogers]

[Concord, November 6, 1867]

Dear Sir,

A select company are invited to meet Lord and Lady Amberley for free Conversation at the house of Mr. Sargent No. 13 Chestnut Street on Thursday Nov. 14th at 10" A.M.

415

Mr. Emerson and Mr Phillips are of the party. Mr Weiss will read a paper.

We hope yourself and Mrs Rogers are free to join us on that day.

Truly Yours,
A. Bronson Alcott.
Concord Nov. 6th
1867.

Prof Rogers.

¹ MS. owned by the Fruitlands and Wayside Museums.

LETTER 67–24

[to John Weiss]

Concord Nov 12th. 1867

Dear Sir,

We will leave you entirely free to read or not on Thursday. But cannot well spare you personally—speaking or silent. And shall expect you with Whittier at least of the persons you have invited—himself and yourself by all means, and others at your discretion. The company will be all the richer, nor less select, for your additions.

Yours truly,
A Bronson Alcott

Rev. John Weiss.

LETTER 67–25¹

[to William T. Harris, St. Louis]

Concord Novr. 15th 1867

Dear Friend,

Your last no. of the "Speculative" has been before me for a fortnight, and tis time that I wrote you a word about its contents. Certainly there is no abatement of thought, and the new contributors give freshness and variety of statement. Brockmeyer's papers on "Faust" promise much. Hedge's translation is good to have, so is Davidsons. Brinton is a new name to me. Dr. Hoffmanns Letter, I especially value, as showing—beside the important information it gives of the present state of philosophy in Germany—the interest there taken in thought with us. I trust the Correspondence will be continued as of international importance. Have you seen the notice of your Journal in the last no of the "North American"? I have not learned who wrote it.

Sanborn promises a notice in the "Commonwealth."

Yesterday, I met a select company gathered at Dr. Bartol's to give Lord and Lady Amberley—who have been staying at Emersons some days and are interested in American thought—some definite ideas of the religious views of

416

our most advanced Eastern thinkers. Weiss read a paper on "Method', sparkling throughout with thought and metaphor. I wish he may give it to you for your Journal. Next Monday he reads it before the Club, when it will be further discussed.

I met Senator Sumner lately and talked with him about your Journal. He expressed an interest in it, and to day I shall send him your prospectus.

Are there not rather more misprints in my "Genesis" than I am responsible for? Your text has been so correct hitherto that I am ashamed of being the first exception. Pray exclude me altogether, or let me have a reading of the proof sheets hereafter. My Book is delayed for the present. I am indebted to Mr Kroeger for several newspapers containing articles of his, which I have read with interest.

Very Sincerely Yours
A. Bronson Alcott

Wm. T. Harris

---

¹ From a copy, in Alcott's hand, in the Alcott-Pratt Collection. The original is in the Alcott-Harris Collection in the Concord Free Public Library (see Appendix B).

LETTER 67-26

[to Christopher Walton, London England]

Mr. Christopher Walton
    Editor of
"Law's Memorial,"
    24 Ludgate Street
        London
           England.

Concord, Mass, Nov 18th 1867

Mr. Christopher Walton.
Dear Sir,

I have lately had the pleasure of reading the copy of your "Cyclopedia of Pure Christian Theology and Theosophic Science," sent to our Harvard Library at Cambridge, and am desirous of learning from yourself, where a copy of the work may be obtained. My studies for many years have lain in the direction of the Mystic authors, Jacob Behmen being a favorite, and, as I judge, the master mind of these last centuries. I was fortunate, when in England in 1842, to find not only his works in Laws' edition, but most of the works of his disciples; Taylor, Pordage, ‖ Frances Lee ‖ Law, and others.

Your collection when completed will be a most valuable addition to our theological literature; and will interest the class of minds in this country with whom I am intimate. What renders my interest in your Collection the deeper just now, is the fact that some of the freest minds about Boston, have lately formed a Free Religious Club, which meets monthly for discussing the deepest questions in Religious philosophy and ‖ who ‖ would gladly read your contributions to this end. Mr Emerson, ‖ Dr. Hedge, ‖ Mesrs. Wasson and Weiss, scholars perhaps known to you by reputation, are members of the Club. Mr.

Emerson is my townman and near neighbor. We have also organized a Free Religious Association for diffusing a livelier faith in the divine life, among our people. I transmit herewith to your direction a pamphlet containing an account of their doings. Also a prospectus of *the Journal of Speculative Philosophy* edited by a young friend of mine and published at St. Louis, Missouri.

Very truly yours,
A. Bronson Alcott.

LETTER 67–27

[to Henry Sutton, England]

Concord, Mass. | Nov. 22nd 1867.

Mr. Henry Sutton.

Dear Sir,

If Personally a stranger to me yourself, your Books have long been familiar friends of mine, and I have only deferred telling you this by some secret persuasion of a new work of yours offering a happy occasion, and of excusing myself for the diffidence and delay. Now an additional motive prompts—as I have learned lately that an old friend, whose acquaintance I first made in '42. at Alcott House, Ham Common, is a brother of yours, by marriage, and I would like to learn something of his residence and welfare, that I may assure him of my remembrance and regard, through yourself.

I need not say that your Books—"*The Evangel of Love* and *Quinguenergia*," have interested me, especially the last named, finding as I do so much in its conception and working out akin to views and endeavors of my own; and commending itself, besides[,] to a large class of thoughtful minds here aiming at "*a new Practical Theology*," also. Very little as yet has been attempted in the way of organization. It is only lately that we have sought this, scattered as we are over New England, and tasked with professional interests. But we have formed, by way of becoming better acquainted with one another and comparing opinions and purposes, "*a Free Religious Fellowship*" meeting monthly and discussing in a genial manner, the prime questions of thought most concerning the attention of the time. Though composed largely of ministers, it is not confined to such, laymen and women are members, and we have found the meetings highly attractive and edifying. Lord and Lady Amberley now visiting in these parts, honored us with their company, at our last meeting and expressed much satisfaction in what they saw and heard. Besides these monthly discussions, we propose parlor Conversations and lectures in the various cities and towns where in any number of earnest persons can be gathered. Then we have a monthly magazine, now in its third Volume and a Journal of Speculative Philosophy circulating among the people. Some of our most advanced thinkers and ripest Scholars are members of the Association, speaking and writing as occasion offers. Mr. Emerson, Mr. Weiss, Mr Wasson, Dr Bartol and others.

If you care to look a little at us from a distance, you may find *at Trubner's & Co.'s in London*, some of the printed matter. I especially command to your notice "*The Radical*["] printed in Boston, and the Journal of Speculative Philosophy printed at St. Louis, Missouri.

It may interest you to know that Mr. Emerson is a near neighbor, and retains agreeable reccollections [sic] of yourself[.]

Be assured that should I visit England again I should seek you out eagerly, and that it would give me great pleasure to receive a line.

Very Sincerely Yours
A. Bronson Alcott

LETTER 67–28

[to Thomas Davidson, St. Louis]

Concord Novr. | 22nd 1867

Dear Sir,

Yours of the 19th has just reached me. And its contents are most gratifying. You are at the very Court and Academy of thought, and with the gifts and appetites to render yourself and associates ‖ happy and ‖ serviceable to the ends of good learning. How could you have been better placed? and more to your liking? or put your excellent gifts better to the service of the public? I am thinking of the accession alike to the circle at St. Louis, and contributors to the Journal, and please myself with the good fortune that sent you out there. Jove and Mercury atop of that Occidental Olympus, is good to think of.

And now if you will print *Plotinus* whether in Taylors' text, or your own translation, I, for one, shall be made glad that a Prince of philosophy speaks, as few of all time have spoken, to the few who are the fit audiance [sic]. I consider him the best text of metaphysical aptitude that can be put to any modern mind, and his style is perfection itself. If the *"Essay on the Essence of the Soul"* were not too long, I should say print that entire. But any thing of his is good. Pray give us a Chapter in your fourth No. If Harris' cares to venture my *Notes on Philosophers*, I will send them. There is too little of the Plotinus.

I send the Book by Express.

As to my being again in St. Louis during the winter, that, I imagine, is hardly practicable, ‖ either by me or Emerson ‖. The philosophers there have measured ‖ us both ‖ me fairly, and will hardly care for more of that sort.

I wrote a few days since to Mr. Harris, and shall write again soon.

Very Sincerely Yours,
A. Bronson Alcott.

Prof. Davidson.

LETTER 67–29

[to William T. Harris, St. Louis]

Concord Nov 26th 1867

Dear Friend,

I have made the emendations of the text of the Copy which you sent me, by which you will see for yourself how (with an exception or two) it stood in my copy now before me. You will see that in a few instances these affect the sense essentially, in others, are merely verbal and of no great importance. I take the blame mostly to myself. My M.S. puzzles printers and proof readers so [word] that I can hardly hope to have the text correct with every advantage of several readings of the proof sheets. But I shall gladly send more of the same, hoping you will be able to give me the reading of the proof before you print.

I have a paper on *"Ideas"* of about the same length as "the Genesis," and following that properly in order of publication. This I will send if you wish it for your first No. of the 2nd. Volume.

You encourage me to contribute by your flattering criticisms. I shall look with eagerness for your "Analytical Index.–" persuaded that, of my contemporaries, you best comprehend and appreciate my speculations in Philosophy. In fact, I begin to suspect that these are to travel West for readers.

I saw Cabot a moment lately, and asked him frankly about "Harris and Journal." "He must speak English and not German, and give us more of himself, less of Hegel."—I judge he believes profoundly in the Editor and liked all of yours that he had read, printed and written. "My paper on "Genesis was very good," but "nothing new," I imagine he would have added, but for courtesy.

I hope Weiss will give you his. It is good, and would give you another original contributor from the East. Hedge is good for translation, so is Cabot. Next month Wasson is to read a paper before our Club, which will doubtless be good for your pages also.

I learned with satisfaction of Hickock[?] and Seeley's[?] subscriptions. Hillard[?] is good for dollars[?], and Boston.

Davidson's scholarship and training are happy accessions to your society and Journal. I mailed 'The Plotinus" to your address through the ‖ mail ‖ P.O.

Let us take good hope seeing philosophy in the ascendent, and having an organ for its free diffusion.

To Kroeger and the rest, remembrances.

Truly Yours,
A. Bronson Alcott

Wm. T. Harris

[1] From a copy, in Alcott's hand, in the Alcott-Pratt Collection. The original is in the Alcott-Harris Collection in the Concord Free Public Library (see Appendix B).

LETTER 67–30

[to Caroline M. Severance]

Concord | Dec. 6th 1867

Dear Mrs Severance,

I shall be most happy to meet your townspeople in the several ways you name, and only await your advising me of the time

As far as at present advised I shall have nothing preengaged for Sunday next or the following. And all the better if Mr. Tiffany will be in his pulpit with me.

Yours sincerely
A. Bronson Alcott

Mrs Severance.

LETTER 67–31

[to Charles D. B. Mills, Syracuse]

Concord Dec 16 1867

Dear Sir,

I am heartily pleased to learn that you have something ready for printing about Pythagoras, and willing it should have the best chance of being read by appreciating readers. The number of these cannot be large, from the character of your subject, but select rather, and inclined to thought above the reading. For this reason, it seems to me that the Journal of Speculative Philosophy is the fittest place for printing. It has not a wide circulation, but is read by just the persons who would best appreciate your article. And Mr. Harris will gladly, I doubt not, print the whole at once. Moreover, I wish him, as the representative of Pure thought, to have the help and sympathy of its friends, and yours would be of weight with him and Journal. Next to this, *The Radical,* though less in sympathy with the kindly Samian, than the former. In neither case should you receive any other remuneration than that of seeing and reading in print. I think, besides, that we ‖ ough ‖ owe it to our thought to give it the best advantages, and not send it out begging admittance—at the doors of any *North American* or *Ch. Examiner* Editors, who have hitherto not proved themselves the better judges of that article, though assuming the jurisdiction of stamping at their mints the only genuine Coin for the Countries Currency. I wish I could persuade myself it were not mixed with much alloy, and were the pure metal it claims to be. One of the best papers in the *Spec. Journal* was refused admittance in terms that proved the scales for ascertaining the sterling values were wanting. Excellent papers read by Wasson and Weiss before our Radical Club are likely to find place in the *Spec.* after these have been read as lectures. Our Club is largely attended and doing good service in the way of interesting the younger ministers and students of Divinity.

It may interest you to know that one Alexandrian *Plotinus* is about clothing himself in an English dress. Prof. Davidson, who is now a teacher in one of the St. Louis schools is about undertaking it, giving the whole of Plotinus, and *Taylorized* those, he thinks. Davidson is a young Englishman highly educated, with an appetite for philosophy, and promises to be of great service to our St Louis friends.

Perhaps you will do me the favor to cast your Eyes over the *Genesis* paper in the last no. of the *Spec.* I have another on *Ideas* for the first no. of the 2nd. Volume.

At present I know of no engagements to take me long from home, and shall expect to see you with good advantages for Conversation when you come East. Mr Emerson is at the West, but expects to be at home early in January.

Cordially Yours

A. B. Alcott.

Bring the books when you come.

LETTER 67–32[1]

[to Louisa, Boston]

Concord, | Sunday MG. Dec 29th 67

Dear Louisa

Your Book pleases me. It takes the fancy and thought so agreeably and insinuates its moral so delicately, that the Lady Esop, so dutiful and knowing, never obtrudes as a pedantic Preacher or Goody, upon the simplicity and gaiety of the little ones.

That is the perfection of teaching. "not by force and dictation', as Plato says, 'but by gentleness accompanied with art and by every kind of invitation", and of the new Children's books that I have noticed of the new issues, I find yours the better in this art. And am sure the Mothers will find you out through the enthusiasm of your little readers; and you will have your double reward in appreciation and money.

Dickens does for one side of life, not the brightest nor best, but the ridiculous and false,—not perhaps the worst—and is a genial preacher of kindness and brotherly love. These the little ones have by birthright and you are helping them to keep it sweet and long. And what serves them serves their elders, too, by way of reviving their innocency and faith, if no more—which is the essence of the true religion alike in young and old.

I think, too, your parts in the Magazine[2] promise well, to make that a popular monthly.—I wish you to see in all this, the opening future that awaits you for reaching the public generally, in works that you are not permitted to forgo or long postpone.

I need not add my pleasure and pride in all this prospect.

Ever Your Father

and, at this writing, in his snug slippers, lazy and thankful.

[1] MS. in the Clifton Waller Barrett Library, University of Virginia.
[2] *Merry's Museum.* See Frank Luther Mott, *A History of American Magazines* (New York, 1930), I, 713–15.

LETTER 68–1

[to Mr. Fernald, Boston]

Concord Jan 7th 1868

Dear Sir,

I have lately recd. a letter from Mrs Penny of Topsham, England, in which she speaks of the works of St. Martin—portions of which her husband has translated from the French, and sent, (she writes) copies to you and Mr. Otis Clapp.

Can you let me have a look at them? My daughter will take them, and I will see them returned. And any information you can give concerning the translator, I shall be glad to have.

Next time I come into the City, let me have the pleasure of seeing you, and if you will name your hours, I will call then.

My daughter is fortunate in having found such good quarters under your roof.[1]

Mr. Fernald.

   6. Hayward Place

[1] The complimentary close and signature have been cut out.

LETTER 68–2[1]

[to Cyrus A. Bartol, Boston]

Concord Jan. 9th 1868.

Dear Friend,

   Can you see me some time soon, say some afternoon next week? I have some Communications to make which should have the benefit of your hospitable thought, and prompt [me] to the asking of this interview.

   Our Club is good, and becoming better at each meeting. And any more private Conversations than this favors, cannot but further its aims and inspire its discussions. I talked last evening with Emerson about our religious movement and find him interested and disposed to give his good thought and word.

   I believe he reads a Lecture soon at Cambridge following yours, about which I shall wish to hear from your own lips the more particularly. I, also, have a word that, in my own good opinion, claims expression in that connexion of thought. We have "a *Personal Theism*" to preach till men find their Pagan Polytheism, Atheism, Nihilism,—nought.

   Next Monday will suit me if it does yourself for our interview.[2]

Cordially
Yours
A. Bronson Alcott.

Dr. Bartol.

[1] MS. owned by the Fruitlands and Wayside Museums. A copy, in Alcott's hand, is in the Alcott-Pratt Collection.
[2] Bartol, in a letter of January 10, agreed to meet Alcott.

LETTER 68–3[1]

[to William T. Harris, St. Louis]

Concord Jan. 19th 1868

Dear Friend,

   Your Journal came yesterday and closes Vol. I. handsomely. I like your Preface. You dispose of criticisms ingeniously, and state the functions of the Philosophic editor with a masterly strength that should silence unbelievers in the possibilities of Original Thought and thinkers. Your paper on *"Philosophy Introductory"* establishes that fact beyond question. "The *Schopenhauer Doctrine of the Will*[2] strikes deep, too, and shows how largely the subtlest thought since Böhme is tinctured with his theosophic insights. And whose claims as an original thinker it becomes us Americans especially to recognize. I hope you will ‖ find ‖ find some one to take *"Baaders' account of him"* in hand forthwith along with *Hegel's.* If Davidson is not already too deep in *"Plotinus,"* set him upon a translation. What have you of more significance to offer your readers? Give us *that, without which,* thought either freezes or scorches,—the haze of the morning red with the twilight of evening's glow to temper speculation. "In wonder all philosophy begins, in wonder it ends," and the eras of thought open always out of this mystic realm of sun and shade—we trust our[?] for America *now.*

I must quote from a letter just recd. from an English student of Böhme in reply to one I wrote lately mentioning yourself and Journal.[3] She writes from "Topsham, Devonshire, Dec. 21th.—(The Mr. Walton—to whom my letter was addressed—is engaged in editing a *"Cyclopedia* of Pure Christian Theology and Theosophic Science" (Böhme being the Central Mind of his *Collection.)* Mrs Penny writes

"When your letter reached Mr. Walton he was staying a few days here, and he gave ‖ me and ‖ Mr. Penny and myself the pleasure of seeing it. It pleased us both very much to find that his book had awakened attention in Concord, as we think the studies which it would introduce more important than any others in in the world, and full of the deepest interest at every step in their progress. Mr Walton is now very much occupied, and before he left us he begged me to thank you for your letter, and to say that he should give himself the pleasuring of answering it as soon as he could command the leisure for doing so. I was much interested in your account of movements in America, and gladly undertook to give this message in order to make occasion for asking if you know any thing of the writings of *St. Martin.* He is an author whom we very much revere, not only as one of the most enlightened students of Böhme, but as one of the most profound and original thinkers that the world ever neglected. If you read much in *Baader* which I see named in *the Prospectus of your Journal,* you will find him frequently ‖ mentioning ‖ referring to St. Martin. I was glad to see that *"Baaders' works* were coming under the consideration of your Society, for as an exposition of Böhmes' doctrines, I find them very valuable. Mr. Walton had not before heard of the works of *Henry Sutton.* We shall now be on the lookout for them also, as[?] Mr. Penny has translated two of St. Martins works—[word] his "Correspondence with a Swiss friend during the French Revolution, and his *"Le Ministre de l'Homme Esprit."* copies of which he sent to Mr. Fernald of Boston."

The ‖ last ‖ "Correspondence" I have now by me and find good things in it. When I hear from Mr. Walton I will write further of this English school of Behmenists and hope to receive their publications for notice in your Journal, if you think best.

I write to *Sutton* also, sending *your prospectus,* but have as yet had nothing from him in reply. His "Quinquenergia" is a remarkable book and deserves notice also as the latest piece of English Mysticism.

We must put England as well as Germany in literary communication with us. I regret to learn about Stirling, and hope some of your Western Colleges and Libraries will rescue him from the Seas to Philosophy. Could you not contrive to find something for him at St. Louis? With him and Davidson, we might leave Carlyle, Mill & Co. to shift for themselves as they best can. I owe Davidson thanks and acknowledgments for letters and remembrances. His translations have greatly enriched your pages, and I am pleased to have the good accounts he gives me of his company and occupations. I will write to him soon, and shall be glad to hear often.

How soon must you have *my Paper* for printing in your next no.? It only needs more legible copying, and shall be sent forthwith if you wish it now. If you can find room for the whole it will please me best.—"The *Personality*" with "*The Ideas*" as the complement of my "*Pantheon*"—which will about double the matter of the "*Genesis*" *Paper*. If you have not room for the whole, print the "*Ideas*" first. There will follow, if you say so, the Chapters of "*Metamorphosis*" and "*Temperaments,*" for the coming numbers.—These embrace the *Speculative* Part of my Book, "the *Biographical Notes*" on Pythagoras, Plato, Plotinus, Plutarch, Behmen, Swedenborg, Goethe, Emerson, follow as an *Appendix. The Practical* part hardly rises to the dignity of philosophy. It is rather composed of Essays ‖ on Life, Nature, Books &c. ‖ for pleasant readings. I incline to give you the Speculative portion, if it prove to be freed sufficiently from the hue[s] of temperamental mysticism hardly acceptable to philosophy, ‖ as of its essence ‖ in form, but which some of us esteem its essence and soul.

Emerson returned with good hopes and a hearty acceptance of Harris and his friends. He speaks of the pleasure he had in your interview, and seemed more delighted than he was ready to express in Mr. Harris' appreciation of Mr. Alcott. He is taken more from his studies than formerly by multiplying literary and social obligations. Harvard College has made him one of its overseers and Boston is almost willing to adopt his fame.

On Wednesday next meets our Club when O. B. Frothingham reads a paper. I wish our Eastern minds could divest themselves of the egotism of their place of birth, and see themselves as others see who had not their misfortune of being born with Cambridge Eye-Glasses. But then you and I should take heed of our Connecticut squint, and be meek and lowly in our outlook at[?] the Grandeurs.

I was somewhat disappointed at not finding the *Analytical Index* which you promised of your Contents. But have to thank you for finding method in my paragraphs of Genesis. Write me at length soon.

Cordially Yours
A. Bronson Alcott.

Wm. T. Harris
I send the names of two good subscribers to the Speclv.
Samuel E. Sewall
J. B. Johnson
both of Boston.

[1] From a copy, in Alcott's hand, in the Alcott-Pratt Collection. The original is in the Alcott-Harris Collection in the Concord Free Public Library (see Appendix B).
[2] A translation by C. L. Bernays.
[3] See Letter 67-26.

[to William Russell, Lancaster, Mass.]

Concord Jan. 19th 1868

Dear Friend,

Your last dates Feb. 8th. last, and, for once, I anticipate you in our annual interchange of thought and social welfare. Not that I have much to communicate beside the facts of our domestic life, all of which I am happy of reporting as of the most pleasurable sort. Mrs A. enjoys fair health, and her children and grandchildrens' comforts and prospects. Anna and her boys Freddy and Johnny are very well—the mother devoted and the children beautiful alike in temper and person—all that fond parents could desire. They live now in Chelsea, having passed the summer with us and the Pratts. Her husband is in good business and a very worthy man. Louisa has taken a room in Boston for the winter. She writes for the Magazines and edits a Child's monthly also.[1] Her pen is sought far and wide and she finds it a source of considerable income, as well as a widening recognition of her merits as a writer. She has recovered from her illness of last winter, and enjoys a good share of health. May has Drawing Classes here, in Cambridge and Boston also, which occupy and interest her and are remunerative. She does a good deal of sketching in pencil and in sepia, which are very much admired for their delicacy of touch and selection. Mrs A. has the comfort of a faithful girl in housekeeping and we pass busy days with books and pen— she in constant correspondence with her world, and I with the human population of hers and the Ideal of mine besides. Once a month I meet the Club in Boston, have lectured once here before our Lyceum, and am [word] some Conversations of[?] Sunday afternoon in Boston soon. As opportunity offers I speak also in pulpits. The objects of the Club interest me and promise something for diffusing fresh life and light among the people. Next Wednesday O. B. Frothingham reads us a paper. Emerson, Wasson, Weiss, Bartol, Sam. Longfellow have read at former meetings.

Besides this, "*The Journal of Speculative Philosophy*, edited by my friend Harris, of St. Louis, has been a source of delight and hope for us here in America. It has reached its first Years' issue and opens with fair prospects for a second. I send you a number for your judgment of its merits. One of its contributors, Tom Davidson, is a country man of yours, was educated at Aberdeen, and has been Professor at the College in London, Canada. Mr. Harris, is a graduate of Yale and from Connecticut. By his invitation I have visited St. Louis more than once and met his friends there. He has drawn about him a circle of thoughtful and accomplished persons,—Professors, physicians, teachers, counsellors—gentlemen in high social and professional standing, formed a Philosophical Society which meets weekly, and contributes largely to his Journal, and is now Superintendent of the City Schools. Two years ago he made me a visit. If I am not greatly mistaken he is to make his mark on the metaphysical thought of his time. Had we fallen in with him 30 years ago, we should have had what we taught outside of ourselves but found not. With him, and his friends here at the East, we may leave Carlyle, Mill and Co. to shift as they best can. Have you read Walt. Whitmans' paper on Democracy in the Galaxy? If not and you are at leisure, try this new Columbus and his discovery in the "Atlantides". You know I too have something of the Caledonean love by descent, at least with yourself, but question sharply the morals of the Scotch Behemoth at whose sides Walt thrusts his ‖ fluked ‖ fork and so can see him sink without pity; much as we have admired his gambols once.

Emerson is just home from a lecturing tour out West. He is taken from his studies more than formerly by new literary obligations. Harvard College has made him one of its Overseers, and Boston is almost wishing to adopt his fame.

I shall be glad to hear of your studies, thoughts, and family. Mrs. Alcott and May send regards to yours along with mine.

Cordially Yours
A. Bronson Alcott.

Prof. Russell.

[1] " 'The Youth's Companion' pays $20 for two short tales each month." (Cheney, p. 193.)

[Letter to Walt Whitman, Washington; from Concord, January 19, 1868.]

LETTER 68–5[1]

[to Louisa, Boston]

Concord Feb. 19th '68

Dear Louisa,

After leaving you yesterday, I called at "Roberts Brothers," and found them ready to give their name and influence to my Book.[2] So I have about determined on giving them the sale instead of Spencer—whose name and means of advertizing have less weight among publishers. I think of giving the first sheets to the printer next Monday when I come in from West Newton.

I spoke of *The Story for the Girls*[3] which R. & Bs. asked you to write. And find that they expect it and would like to have it ready by September at longest. They want a book of 200 pages or more just as you choose. Mr. ‖ Nash ‖ [p. o.] Niles [p. in], the literary partner, spoke in terms of admiration of your literary ability, thinking most highly of your rising fame and prospects.

He obviously wishes to to [sic] become *your* publisher and *mine*.

Now I suppose you will come home soon and write your story.

My last visit to Boston apparently opens a brighter page for us personally and pecuniarily.

Your Father.

L.M.A.

[1] MS. in the Clifton Waller Barrett Library, University of Virginia.
[2] *Tablets.*
[3] *Little Women.*

LETTER 68–6

[to Caroline M. Severance]

Concord Feb 20th 1868.

Dear Mrs Severance,

The days you name for me suit very well. So we will say, March 7 & 8th. Meanwhile, you will have ascertained the prospects of your "Ladies' Club,"[1] about which I shall like to talk with you when I come.[2]

[1] The New England Woman's Club was organized on February 16, 1868, with Mrs. Severance, whose idea the club was, as president.
[2] The complimentary close and signature have been cut out.

LETTER 68–7[1]

[to William T. Harris, St. Louis]

Concord Feb 20th 1868

Dear Friend,

I have delayed writing, looking for ‖ something of ‖ [p. o.] word or proof sheets from you, and shall till I hear further of your disposition of the last. And the more eagerly as,—since I last wrote—a friend has offered to advance the money and take the risk of printing my Book. "Roberts Brothers" our best firm are wishing to give us their name and publish it. So I am about concluding the matter, and shall give my first sheets to the printers probably next week. The "Practical Part" comes before "the Speculative," and the printing will take till April, so as not to anticipate the paper you have.

I have lately met some interesting mystics in Boston, and will write further when I have fathomed them fairly.

Before *"the Free Religious Club,"*—which is doing good service, as you will read in this weeks "Commonwealth," there is now forming the *"Radical Religious Association,*" which I have met, and am to meet again next Monday Evening. This Association purposes building a Hall for Pure Theological Teaching, and promises to do good work in the way of Conversation and Lecture.

I regret to learn that Davidson has been sick and questions your climate, all seemed so fortunate for him and yourself. Remember me to him respectfully.

Enclosed are $4.00 subs[criptions] for your Journal from my friend *"A. C. Felton"*. He wishes Vol. 1 sent to his address 13 Brookline St. Boston—Vol. II, as the numbers appear, likewise.

Have just read Kroeger's pamphlets on "Government" &c.

Yours
A. B. Alcott

Wm. T. Harris

[1] From a copy, in Alcott's hand, in the Alcott-Pratt Collection. The original is in the Alcott-Harris Collection in the Concord Free Public Library (see Appendix B).

LETTER 68–8

[to Charles D. B. Mills, Syracuse]

Concord Feb. 27th 1868

Dear Friend,

"The Free Religious Club" meets at Rev. John T. Sargents' No. 13-Chestnut Street at 10 A.M. on Monday March 16th. Now suppose you plan to leave Syracuse early enough on Saturday the 14th to reach Concord on that day, spend Sunday the 15th with us, and go to Boston with us on Monday morning to "the Club." The train connects with the Worcester and Nashua at Worcester, and, at Groton Junction, with the Fitchburg which brings you to our Concord Station, where a Coach waits to convey you to our door late in the afternoon. If you have a Sunday train then you can reach Boston direct, and come to the Club at 10. Monday, at my invitation. But I hope you will come here on Saturday. Emerson tells me he is to be at home; and will be glad to see you; says he will write to you. Sanborn, too, will like to meet you here.

If your paper on "Pythagoras" has not gone to press, bring it with you. And "Jamblichus Life of Pythagoras" also.

Give us as much of the time as you can spare while you are East. My wife has her guest chamber ready for you, and my daughters will then be with us.

Cordially Yours

A. Bronson Alcott

C. D. B. Mills

LETTER 68–9

[to Thomas Davidson, St. Louis]

Concord Feb. 29th 1868.

Dear Sir,

I am glad to hear from yourself of your restoration to labor. And especially of your Translations of Lessings' Laocoön and the Plotinus. Both are the best of readings for the advanced thinkers of our time. Pray let us have them at the earliest practicable moment. The Laocoön is sure to Tempt our publishers, and it will not be difficult, I imagine, to find some one to bring out the Plotinus. Emerson has influence with Boston Houses and will delight to use it in your favor. He speaks hopefully of your literary purposes and prospects.

Your Greek Class must be something new at the West, as it would be here in Boston. Thank Miss Meedy for her Attic adventures for her sex, and Miss Brackett not less. Indeed your city outvies ours already in its Athenean instincts and studies alike in letters and philosophy.

I take great pleasure in Mr. Harris' ability and the success of his Journal. Both are a surprise to the scholars here, and attract much attention. He writes most hopefully about his Journal as if it were to be a Power in the land, as I am sure it is, and to win respect for us abroad.

Mr. Kroeger's "Fichte," I have not seen. I looked for it at "Williams," the other day, but they had none to show me. Kroeger has sent me his pamphlet on

"Government" which I have distributed to fit readers. I read your article in the Radical with interest.

My "Tablets" are in press. They may make a Volume of 300-pages, and appear sometime in April.

I am expecting Mills of Syracuse about the 15th March to pass a few days here. He has a paper on Pythagoras and takes kindly to the Antique thought. I have advised his giving his Pythagoras to the "Spec. Journal."

Wishing your recovery to health and letters

I am Truly Yours
A. Bronson Alcott

Prof Davidson
St. Louis

LETTER 68–10

[to Ellen A. Chandler, Framingham, Mass.][1]

Concord March 5th 1868.

Dear Miss Chandler,

I am to be at West Newton the coming Saturday and Sunday, and shall hope to ride out to Framingham on Monday unless Mr. Allen should detain me in his school that day. But I shall come unless something not now known to me prevents, either on Monday or Tuesday to pass the best part of the day; and if you care for it, an evening with yourself and friends.

Truly Yours,
A. Bronson Alcott.

Miss Chandler.

[1] Ellen A. Chandler was a teacher at the state teachers college in Framingham, a town twenty-one miles southwest of Boston and about twelve miles south of Concord.

LETTER 68–11

[to Charles Choate, Woburn, Mass.]

Concord April 1st 1868.

Dear Sir,

Mr. Sanborn tells me that you would like to open your parlors for some Conversations, and wait to learn when it will please me to meet your company. I write to say that I am to be in Boston next Monday evening, and if convenient to yourself will come out to Woburn on Tuesday for a Conversation on that Evening. A reply from yourself by Saturday next will be in time.

Yours respectfully,
A. Bronson Alcott

Charles Choate Esq.
Woburn

LETTER 68–12[1]

[to William T. Harris, St. Louis]

Concord April 2nd 1868.

Dear Friend,

Since sending you Mr. Waltons letter, I have received yours of March 12th & 25th and No. 1. of the second Volume of your "Journal." As to Walton's views and school, act your judgment about publishing. My opinion is, that Hegels' account of Behmen, with any historical additions of matter from Germany or England, would be best. You might dispose of the English mystics by printing the substance of Walton's letter, qualifying his phraseology a little to render it intelligible. I am about writing to him, and shall like to send him the last no. of your Journal if you will spare it. We shall like his Cyclopedia of mysticism, and if he sends the Book I will see that you have a sight of it if you wish.

Your last No. surpasses all former ones in breadth and variety. Your papers Americanize and make the thought their method ours. "The Introduction to Philosophy" will be an addition to philosophy and a Book for students everywhere. I see the Tribune has again noticed you with great respect, quoting from your "Statement of the Problem." What you have to say abo[ut] Rosencrantz and Peirce is good. I take Peirce to be the son of the Cambridge mathematics Professor, and perhaps defending as he best can the Professor's metaphysics, if not of the College.

My paper came without an error or misprint. The Book is in press and I have read the proofs of the First Essay—about 50 pages in type. It will take till May to complete it. I will try to send you advance sheets. We think of binding the Practical & Speculative Parts, each by itself, making two Vols of part of the Edition. It will make two Books of 200 pages each, perhaps more.

Your School Report is admirable, and will be noticed in the Commonwealth.

Kroegers', I have not yet seen. I shall look for your review of it in the Round Table next time I am in Boston.

Mills has been here; spoke twice in Boston to The Parker Fraternity, attended the Free Club, saw Emerson, and read me his paper on Pythagoras, which is to be printed, I think, in the Radical. Had you not Hegel's account, I should commend the paper to you, for the Speculative." It is excellent, in parts, and must be printed somewhere.

Next Monday Evening we have our Fourth meeting for discussing freedom of thought, at South End, in Boston.

It may be the basis of a Free Fellowship. I am one of three, to offer a platform of thought and action for the movement.

You do not speak of the ague in your last, but of busy works. I hope you are getting rid of that trouble.

I have to thank some one for a dozen of wine, sent me from St. Louis. Whether Hegelian or Kantian it is appetizing and tastes of friendships that I like to cherish.

Yours cordially
A. Bronson Alcott

Wm. T. Harris.

[1] From a copy, in Alcott's hand, in the Alcott-Pratt Collection. The original is in the Alcott-Harris Collection in the Concord Free Public Library (see Appendix B).

LETTER 68–13

[to Charles D. B. Mills, Syracuse]

Concord April 2nd. 1868.

Dear Friend,

Your note, informing me of your safe return, came duly to hand. We feared you were detained on the road by drifts and winds. We were glad to hear of Mr May's comfortable health.

I have just written to Mr. Harris about your paper on Pythagoras and purpose of printing it in the Radical. I doubt not that he would like to have it for his Journal, where I, for my part, should like to see it.

I was at another meeting for promoting free thought and speech, on Monday evening last, at South End in Boston, and am to meet the Association again next Monday evening, for finding the freest basis upon which free minds can unite for thought and work.

I send you Abbots' last words defining his present position.

I hoped to have had more time for conversation while you were here than we secured. But would not have missed hearing your admirable paper.

Remember me to Mrs. Mills and Mr May.

Truly Yours,
A. Bronson Alcott.

Chas. D. B. Mills,
    Syracuse.

LETTER 68–14

[to Martin Luther Holbrook]

Concord April 3rd 1868.

Dear Sir,

Accept my acknowledgments for the numbers of your Journal, which I find contains wholesome matter for all readers.

As to the paper you ask of me concerning "my experiences with food". I find myself just now so occupied with seeing a Book through the press that I shall not like to share any moment for preparing the account you desire.

I enclose, however, some sheets of my "Essay on the Garden," which you may think suitable for your pages. You shall print the whole, or part, or none as you judge best—making one or two articles—"*The Table Plants*" and the "*Rations.*" There are other portions of the text quite in the spirit of your Journal as "*The Orchard,*" "*Sweet Herbs*" "*Recreation*" &c. which, if you desire, may have place also.

My Book will be out sometime in May.

I shall be willing to receive any trifle in money that you deem just for any thing of mine you may print in your pages. And hope you will like my Book when it appears.

My remembrances to Mr. Locke if he is still in your city.

Respectfully,
A. Bronson Alcott

Dr. M. L. Holbrook

LETTER 68–15

[to Charles Choate, Woburn, Mass.]

Concord April 8th 1868.

Dear Sir,

I was in Boston yesterday and should have met yourself and friends as proposed, but for the forbidding storm which I supposed would ‖ have ‖ prevent any number from leaving home. Besides a cold caught on Sunday unfitted me for speaking freely. I trust another week will find things favorable for the Conversation: or it may be deferred till after the Club meeting at Dr. Bartols' on Monday the 20th. if you prefer to have it.

Yours respectfully,
A. Bronson Alcott.

Charles Choate Esq.

LETTER 68–16

[to Sidney H. Morse, Boston]

Concord April 10th 1868.

Dear Sir,

I think I might make a tour West sometime in June, were the necessary arrangements made before starting. The printing of my Book will detain me here till perhaps the middle of May, and I wish to attend the Anniversaries. After that, I might go West. And if you care to advise your friends at the several places you name of terms &c. the thing might be made practicable. Suppose they pledge $100 for a Sunday and three or four Conversations—say at Richmond, Indianapolis and Madison—that would insure travelling expenses and leave a little something to bring home. Then there are Cleaveland [sic], Toledo, Rochester, perhaps, and some other places for a word by the way.

I shall have no objection to any publicity you may charge[?] to give to the adventure in "the Radical" after the facts are ascertained.

The South End movement may become a central Point for Words and work. I include in my Idea, a Divinity School and Church neither reminding of Rome nor Jerusalem. And if those interested in the matter of organization consult me, I shall strive for the modern Temple for the modern Ideas and Doings.

The last No. of "the Radical" is excellent: Potter's paper a deeper touch than usual. Come up at any time, and we will see if we have anything for you. The "Montaigne" was all right—only it should have been longer. I hope Mills has sent you his paper on Pythagoras.

I have a letter from Davidson, who writes of coming East in July to print his translation of "Lessing's Laocoön." Kroeger is coming with him.

My hand to "our Clerk". Young men and women are our hope and strength.

Yours truly,
A. Bronson Alcott.

S. H. Morse.

LETTER 68–17

[to Ellen A. Chandler, Framingham, Mass.]

Concord April 10th 1868.

Dear Miss Chandler,

Your gracious response to my suggestion needs no modest apology from yourself. Tis "the great equality" that renders friendship possible and enjoyable. And why should we not attempt questions with the Wits, and compare notes? Rivers are brooks at their sources and flow together into the Ocean. May we not like other children pluck the flowers growing near the margins?

Goethe wrote

"On every height there lies repose."

And repose is the victory. What were life without this in its diadem? Are not all things excellent, admirable and is anything admirable that fails to inspire herois[m?] It only needs that we admire the excellent in itself worshipping it in Idea, not as Idol. Nor has any lived truly who fail to inspire worship from those who loved them best. You, who do yourself the justice of heroic daring in the realm of love and thought must come off the conqueror, and so may venture fearlessly where timid ones fear to tread. Master the masters. Don't aim at lower quarry. And such as yourself know the art of stooping to conquer nobly.

You speak of your delight at the last Symposium. It was a good meeting, and the better that youth and perception were there. Will you permit me to ask the pleasure of accompanying you again from Mrs. Parker's, (or any place you may name) to the next at Dr Bartol's on Monday the 20th. And will not your friend, Miss Tenny be free to come then? Mrs Cheney will read the paper.

You have given me pleasant hours, and delightful memories. Let me hope others are awaiting me alike in your presence and correspondence.

Cordially Yours,
A. Bronson Alcott.

Miss Ellen A. Chandler.

P.S. Your friend Miss Elliot seems to have found good company. Prof. Davidson writes "My Greek Class progresses most favorably. We are about starting a Shakespeare Class. We had an art meeting last Friday week at which several poems were discussed. Miss Brackett read a very able paper on "Tennyson's Maud." It will probably appear in the "Speculative Journal" by and by." &c.

A.B.A.

LETTER 68–18

[to Ellen A. Chandler, Framingham, Mass.]

Concord April 24th 1868

Dear Miss Chandler

I have just returned from Woburn having had an agreeable Conversation at Mr. Spragues an intelligent gentleman, who with Mrs S_____ have lately become interested in the Club and have attended the two last meetings. Mrs S. inquired about yourself and wishes to know you. I found the company very sensible and shall probably meet them again.

I am sure you must have agreeable memories of Monday's Reading and Conversation, and trust the pleasures of the afternoon added new charms and satisfactions.

Excuse me if I pushed personalities beyond the proprieties in my moments with your father at Jenek's and Palmers.

I enclose Davidson's paper, which I think you will read with interest also a photograph which my daughter May insists belongs to you.

Very Sincerely
Yours
A. Bronson Alcott.

LETTER 68–19

[to Walt Whitman, Washington, D.C.]

Concord April 28th 1868.

My dear Sir,

Your friendly note of the 26th has just come to hand, and yesterday came your noble paper on *Personalism*—for both of which attentions you have my thanks. I shall look for your vials of the aboriginal literature, fully believing that your thought is on the track of empire and sees the route to Personal Power for the nation as for the individual. ‖ Yet think of ‖ And never a people needed more the Cosmic thought to inspire and guide its action.

Yet think of the progress out of the twilight since your star dawned upon our hazy horizon!

Some friend has sent me from time to time appreciative notices of yourself, —knowing by some supreme instinct my hope in whatsoever promises expansion for our hemisphere.

You, too, kindly inform me of particulars about your present position and pursuits. I am interested in all you choose to communicate.

Emerson is just home from your city of steeples and stocks, but I have not spoken with him yet.

I know how fully he shares in my appreciation of yourself and poetry.

I ask your acceptance of the accompanying little sketch of "Emerson."

Truly Yours,
A. Bronson Alcott.

Walt Whitman.
Washington.

LETTER 68–20

[to Ellen A. Chandler, Framingham, Mass.]

Concord May 14th 1868

Dear Miss Chandler,

Shall I have the pleasure of calling for you again on Monday at Mrs. Parkers and accompanying you to the Club? I hope you will permit me, and without putting you to the trouble of writing meanwhile I will call there on Monday just before 10. You are a member of the Club and can come without invitation from any one. Please understand it so. Mr Weiss is to read a paper on Monday, and Mr Emerson sometime during Anniversary Week. If your enagagements permit I should like to see you in the City, thinking it will be agreeable to you to be there, as good subjects are to be discussed by good persons, and the opportunity will be rare for securing so much. Whether Mr. Johnson will be present I do not know. Lest you should have not been informed of the meeting most important to me I send you the Advertisement.

I find pleasure in your criticisms of Davidsons papers and especially in your admiring joy in [word] & music. I know it must be to those who have the soul of that sense quick and operative. I have heard so little that I can only feel the injustice I may have done myself in not cultivating it.

I will see if I can put you in the way of getting the Round Table if you still wish it. We will speak of it on Monday.

With the most pleasing impressions of yourself.

I am sincerely Yours
A. B. Alcott

LETTER 68–21

[to Mary E. Stearns, Medford, Mass.]

Concord May 26th 1868.

Dear Mrs. Stearns,

I was hasty it seems about the Club-meeting but thought I was simply seconding your wishes in proposing to hold our June sitting under your piazzas where, I am sure, the invited guests would have gladly met their kind hostess, to whose wishes as you will learn from Mr. Frank the day and hour of meeting were deferred. But if not yet, sometime,—may I venture to hope—such fellowship of thought and speech, may transpire under || your || her queenly hospitalities. Pray excuse me for venturing upon so much, without further consultation with you.

I wish you were equal to hear Mr. Emerson, reading on Thursday morning at Mr Sargents. And there are other promising matters to come off on Friday besides. Frank will of course attend and report to you. Whether there is the [word] "fire" for lighting the altar of a fresh faith for fresh hearts weary of the desecrated shrines and decaying suites[?] of the Churches, remains to be seen; nor are these treacherous clouds the most propitious omens of fair skies above.

Yours
A. Bronson Alcott.

LETTER 68–22

[to J. B. Johnson, Boston]

Concord June 13th 1868.

Dear Sir,

I shall gladly see you at my house on Wednesday and give as much of the day to conversation as you choose to take. You can reach here as early as half past 7 in the morning or an hour later. I wish the day may favor your purpose, and yourself be fairly repaid for your trouble in journeying so far expecting to carry away gold from any quarries in these parts. But come and take your luck good, or bad. The Country air will be remunerative at least[1]

J. B. Johnson.
    Boston.

[1] The complimentary close and signature have been cut out.

LETTER 68–23

[to Ellen A. Chandler, Framingham, Mass.]

Concord July 1st 1868.

Dear Miss Chandler,

"The Catalogue and Circular" came,—let me hope,—as a telegram of your coming after the Examinations. You have two months, I find, for recreating. Can you do better than venture into Concord atmosphere and see how it agrees with you? It will be most agreeable to me to serve you to such delights as are within my reach—Conversation, reading as you shall choose. Only let me have you for the moment for Ideas, when you prefer such entertainment. Then who knows how near a bright Wit and maiden may chance come to our gifted neighbor? Come and see. And when the ancients tire you can run to friends at the next door.

It would gratify me to ride over to your Examination but I may not promise so much.

Write if you have things to tell me, or ask.

Remembrances to our friends, and to Misses Tenney and Moore, particularly.

    With much esteem,
        Yours truly,
            A. Bronson Alcott

LETTER 68–24

[to Franklin B. Sanborn, Springfield, Mass.]

Concord July 1st 1868

Dear Friend,

You would have had an earlier reply to yours of the 21st, but that I wished to learn definitely when my book would be printed. Yesterday I was in Boston and find the printers want a fortnight at least for electrotyping and printing the sheets ready for binding. And the publishers advise delaying till September—the book-market is so dull at present. The book runs to 200 pages. I am to have proofs of title page and Contents to-morrow.

I fear it has too much of labor and quotation to please the critics and is too fragmentary and inconsequent to satisfy readers & thinkers.

You are very kind to propose giving it an early reading and review. And as you are not wont to overpraise, let me have the fair share of blame.

Conway shall have a copy as soon as it can be obtained.

I was disappointed in missing you at your leaving Concord. Tis not to the credit of our town, that with all its virtues and allurements it suffered the citizen to leave it, who, more than any, did most for its social improvement while residing with us.[1]

I wish I might hope to continue an intimacy every way so attractive by frequent correspondence.

Are you not coming this way during the summer?

Remember me to Mrs Sanborn and Tommy.

Cordially Yours
A. Bronson Alcott.

F. B. Sanborn
    Springfield
        Mass

---

[1] Sanborn had left Concord to become editor of the Springfield *Republican*.

LETTER 68–25[1]

[to William T. Harris, St. Louis]

Concord July 7th 1868

Dear Friend,

I have just read the last Proof Sheets of my Book, and hope to see it in covers by the first of August. There has been much delay in the printing, and now the market is so dull the publishers advise delaying its issue till September. As soon as the whole is struck off I will forward you advance sheets. I have reduced the matter to 200 pages.

Part I is popular.

Part II contains the Genesis and Pantheon with two added Chapters—*Instrumentalities* and *Metamorphosis*.

I fear the book has too much of labor and quotation to please the critics, and is too fragmentary and inconsequent to satisfy thinkers.

Your third No. of the *Journal* maintains its good reputation for strong thought and clear writing. For my reading "The *Phenomenology*" is most attractive. Let us have more of it. *"Comprehension"* has a deeper melody than meets the ear.

Mr. Emerson read me your letter of some weeks since, by which I learn of your Promotion to the Head Superintendence of the schools. I fear for your health. And have written to Davidson to persuade you to accompany him and

Kroeger East. Come and recruit here with us. You shall see Cabot, Weiss, Wasson, Abbot, Emerson, and other readers of philosophy.

Sanborn has gone to Springfield, Mass. to edit a newspaper.

Hoping to greet you soon at my threshold

I am yours faithfully,
A. Bronson Alcott

Wm. T. Harris

---

[1] From a copy, in Alcott's hand, in the Alcott-Pratt Collection. The original is in the Alcott-Harris Collection in the Concord Free Public Library (see Appendix B).

LETTER 68–26

[to Ellen A. Chandler, Framingham, Mass.]

Concord July 10th 1868.

Dear Miss Chandler,

The time you name for visiting Miss Moore finds me disengaged. You shall run over, morning, afternoon, or evening, as you feel disposed, and stay till the Ancient nods. I shall enjoy conversing, reading, and shall have you fast, as my study guest as long as you will consent to sit. Bring any papers of yours that I may hear, and tell me as much of your views and purposes as you feel free to impart. "Biography is almost the one thing needful, and man is perennially interesting to man; nay, if we look strictly to it, there is nothing else interesting." writes Carlyle.

Miss Moore has called, and tells me that you are coming on Tuesday next.

Very sincerely
Yours,
A. Bronson Alcott.

LETTER 68–27

[to John Weiss]

Concord July 28th 1868.

Dear Sir,

Mr Harris is to be at my house next Monday—(Aug 3rd) and may pass Tuesday in Concord. He wishes to see you before he leaves for St. Louis. When and where can you meet him? Will you ride up and see him here? or meet him at the Office of the Radical? in Boston? If he leaves for home on Friday, he fears he shall miss you. I hope you will not let him slip. Wasson he has seen, and young Peirce of Cambridge. Cabot he is to meet, and Abbot if possible. Emerson he sees here. And if you will come up on Monday or Tuesday we might have a social sitting. I hope you will think it worth the time and travel. Harris is a rare thinker for any time or country, and you should have a picture of his mind to carry with you.

Please write and name your terms of meeting.

Yours truly,
A. Bronson Alcott

Rev. John Weiss.

LETTER 68–28[1]

[to Franklin B. Sanborn, Springfield, Mass.]

Concord Aug 5th 1868.

Dear Friend

Your letter came to hand the morning after Mr. Harris left for St. Louis. He passed Sunday here, saw Emerson, went to Boston on Monday and met Cabot —Weiss at Watertown. Wasson he had met before he came to Concord. All who saw Harris seem favorably impressed by his attainments. Weiss writes me to day: "Mr. Harris has been here to my great pleasure. How splendidly posted up he is!" Emerson introduced him to Cabot and Agassiz, and he met young Peirce at Cambridge. He speaks hopefully of his Journal, read us letters from distinguished professors in Germany, Italy, and England, sympathising with his enterprize. He seemed overworked, but enthusiastic and adventurous as ever. Besides his Journal, he has the St Louis Schools on his shoulders.

Kroeger, Davidson and Miss Brackett have also been here for a day. Davidson has nearly completed his translation of "Lessing's Laocoön", and begun the "Plotinus." I am expecting him here again next week. He seems to have found his place at St Louis. Miss Chandler has been here on a visit to Miss Moore. We saw her often and pleasantly. Mr. Harris regretted that he missed seeing you. He returned by way of Montreal.

My Book is to be ready for the binders next week. I forward by Express to you at Springfield, advance sheets. You will find the errors marked to be corrected in the final proofs. To those marked, add *Boehme* and *Oken*, since marked. I hope to have bound copies by the first of September. How shall Conway's be sent to you? I shall wish to send copies to Wm. Channing, Walton and Penny. Shall you be sending a parcel soon?

We are all very well. Anna and her boys are here for the summer. Freddy deep in Pilgrims Progress and his spelling. Louisa is now at Gloucester, May is at Mount Desert with a Boston party.

Channing makes his Sunday visits, but hides his wanderings willfully, though he did own parenthetically to having seen you *somewhere* lately.

Will you not ride this way soon?

Kind regards to Mrs Sanborn and children.

Yours faithfully,
A. Bronson Alcott

Mr. Sanborn.

[1] MS. owned by the New York Public Library. A copy, in Alcott's hand, is in the Alcott-Pratt Collection.

LETTER 68–29

[to Franklin B. Sanborn, Springfield, Mass.]

Concord August 17th 1868.

Dear Friend,

"Roberts Brothers" have sent me six copies in sheets of my book for distributing to editors. As this is the final impression and shows the work as it is, I send a copy [to] your address to give you a fair sample. I add also a copy for Conway, to precede the bound copies which may not be ready for distribution till some time in September. If you are making up a parcel for him, include this, if you please with the promise of copies to be sent to him (when the book is published) for himself, Wm. Channing, Mat. Arnold and Charles Lane. I shall also wish to send copies to Christopher Walton and Mr. Penny, but may mail them direct to their address. Before then I hope to see you here.

I shall look for your notice of my book in the Republican, as touching the key-note for other friends to follow. and shall be very well content, if the book please and edify the few choice readers who owe its author good will and know how to excuse its literary blemishes: a popular fame, I do not expect. I will send more verses presently for "The Republican." Thanks for the numbers sent me the other day.

Sincerely Yours
A. Bronson Alcott

Mr. Sanborn.

LETTER 68–30

[to Ellen A. Chandler, Jamaica Plain? Mass.]

Concord August 23rd 1868.

Dear Miss Chandler,

Your welcome letter came to hand some days ago and is now before me.

Yes, the hours you passed here were pleasant to me, too; I only regret that you flew away so quickly. I am delighted with my pupils docility and could relish "talking" long on such charming terms. Now if I had a school of such, should I not have Vol. IInd of "A Record," to show? things remarkable to print and amaze elders with! Are we not all children when wisest?

I am pleased too at finding an adept at dipping into books, and should like to get a glimpse at her when she first takes up my Leaves. Suppose she were to write me how that happens—I mean when her Copy of "Tablets" comes to hand. 'Tis now in the binder's hands, and is promised next week. Where shall it be sent?

The lines from Quarles are
" 'Tis vain to flee till gentle mercy show
Her better eye. The further off we go
The swing of justice deals the mightier blow."

And

Please favor me with further extracts from your Commonplaces. And thus help me to enrich my papers on Plato and the rest. Sanborn has sent me his notice of "Tablets" in the Semi weekly issue of the Springfield Republican of last Wednesday. I wish I had another to send you.

Davidson and Harris have been here and gone. Harris and I came near finding you at Jamaica Plain, but his time was too short.

My niece Kate[?] May is here. She thinks admiringly of her good friends Miss Chandler and M[iss] Tenny. I find her gifted and ambitious, and to be cared for. She is to teach at West Newton.

Cordially Yours,
A. Bronson Alcott.

LETTER 68–31

[to Prof. Clarke, Oberlin, Ohio]

Concord Sep 4th 1868.

Dear Sir

Have you not confounded my name with Dr. Wm. A. Alcott's, who wrote voluminously on diet and domestic reform? It is true that we had much in common in regard to these subjects, but I have published my views by Conversations mostly, having written next to nothing.

I give you, however, the titles of books containing these in part, as reported by others:—

1/ *Record of a School*, exemplifying the General Principles of Spiritual Culture. Boston. 1835.

2/ *Record of Conversations on the Gospels* held in Mr. Alcott's School, unfolding the doctrine and discipline of Human Culture. Boston, 1836. 2 Vols.

3/ *Tablets*. a collection of Essays. Roberts Brothers, Boston. 1868. (just published)

Besides these, papers have appeared from time to time in *The Dial* 1841 to to 1845. in the *St. Louis Journal of Speculative Philosophy* 1867,'8. and *The Radical*.

The Record of a School and *Conversations on the Gospels,* have long been out of print. So has *the Dial.*

By John Greaves, I think you must mean *James P. Greaves* of England, who founded a School named *Alcott House* at Ham, in 1838. He published very little during his life time. His friends collected and published some of his writings under the title of *New Theosophic Revelations from his MS. Journals,* London, John Chapman 142 Strand. 1847. They published also a Periodical called the Healthian 1842–1844, a copy of which I will send you if you wish it.

Thanking you for your interest in the subjects of these volumes, and regretting I can serve you no better

I am
Yours truly,
A. Bronson Alcott.

Prof. Clark [sic].
   Oberlin
    Ohio.

LETTER 68–32

[to Ellen A. Chandler, Framingham, Mass.]

Concord Sep. 9th 1868.

Dear Miss Chandler,

I was yesterday in Boston and, after having an agreeable interview with Mr. Johnson, who spoke admiringly of yourself, returned to read your welcome note of the 6th. I left with the hope of finding my Book ready for distributing to the chosen friends who might value copies for the writer's sake, but learned that another week or more must pass before they would be ready. As I count a certain young lady among those, and now know that she will receive a copy, I shall send one according to her suggestion addressed to the care of J. A. White Esq.— wishing she may find it worthy of her acceptance; and willing to write me her thoughts as she reads from time to time. Who should better judge, or speak more frankly? I have plain copies at hand, but fancy the ornamental, (not yet ready) ‖ most becoming the receiver and ‖ more suitable as Gifts.

I wish the pages may prove "to be enjoyable, wholesome like nature, and flavored with the religion of wisdom."

You may be assured that I shall add my persuasives to yours to bring Mr. Emerson to Framingham. I need none to come myself.

Cordially Yours,
A. Bronson Alcott

Miss. Ellen A. Chandler.

LETTER 68–33[1]

[to Franklin B. Sanborn, Springfield, Mass.]

Concord Sep 9th 1868.

Dear Friend,

On returning yesterday from Boston I found yours of the 7th. I should have acknowledged your friendly notice of my Book at once, had I not expected to see you here. It was very acceptable and you have my thanks for it.

I have seen favorable notices also in the A. S. Standard[2] and the N. Y. Evening Post. Davidson will write a notice for the Round Table, and Weiss for the Radical. Advance sheets have been sent to Ripley of the N. Y. Tribune, and Towne of Chicago.

The book is to be published sometime this month. 800 copies are bound and ready when the market warrants the issue. 200 are to be put into finer binding with ornamental Title Page and portrait. These will hardly be ready before the first of October.

The copies for England shall be sent to your Room at the State House by Wednesday next if ready.

If you have reserved numbers of The Republican containing your notice of Tablets, I should like some of them, also of More's verses, if these have been inserted. I have looked over the files at the "Atheneum", but did not find them. The Republican derives a new interest now from your connection with it.

Mills paper on Pythagoras opens well. But the editors will not help free thought by printing papers like Egoity, Reason and Religion—as Wasson has told them in his criticism in the last Commonwealth. Mr. Emerson tells me he shall not go far West this season. I am not able yet to say whether I shall venture as far as St Louis. Mr Harris thought No. 3 of the Speculative Journal would be ready sometime this month. Cabot expressed great respect for Harris the other day when I met him for a moment at the Atheneum.

Channing continues his weekly visits as usual.

Next time you come to Concord to spend a night we shall claim you as our guest.

Anna and boys are still with us and expect to remain till October. They are a great joy to us all. Freddy is mastering the arts of spelling and Johnny of talking.

Louisa's book is printed and is to be published sometime in October. She has had a fortnight at Gloucester and May another at Mt. Desert. Anna and the boys were a week at Gloucester with Louisa.

My regards to Mrs. Sanborn and boys Tommy and—

Yours faithfully,
A. Bronson Alcott.

F. B. Sanborn
   Springfield.

---

¹ MS. owned by the New York Public Library. A copy, in Alcott's hand, is in the Alcott-Pratt Collection.
² *National Anti-Slavery Standard.*

LETTER 68–34

[to Prof. Clarke, Oberlin, Ohio]

Concord Sep. 14th 1868.

Dear Sir,

I mail to your address a parcel containing "The "Healthian," with a copy of "The Record of a School," and some other matters which may interest you, and in part answer your inquiries concerning thinkers and Teachers. I especially commend to your study the paper on "Pythagoras," and invite you to read the remainder of it when it appears in "the Radical." I consider him the father of the method of Conversation and the model Teacher for all time. You will read further about him in "The Tablets." Socrates and Plato taught thus chiefly—the latter, as you know, writing in that form. Christianity was first spoken from the lip to chosen disciples. It is the divinely-human way, and with its revival, we may hope for the rise of living thought and ascendancy of Personal virtue in communities.

I know of none "during the last third of the century," whose teachings have been purely conversational and Ideal.

Greaves and Coleridge in England, Pestalozzi in Switzerland are perhaps the purest examples, but the two last were writers also. And Emerson owes the best of his influence to the Conversational style of his writings and readings.

If you have not tried "Thoreau," please look into his attractive books.

I shall gladly serve you in ways most becoming to me. And if you come East shall hope to see you.

Truly Yours,
A. Bronson Alcott.

Prof Clarke

LETTER 68–35[1]

[to William T. Harris, St. Louis]

Concord Sep 22nd 1868.

Dear Friend,

Yours of the 17th. with appreciative views of my book, has just reached me. I had looked for a notice in "the Round Table, from Davidson, as he told me when here that he had the advanced sheets sent to "the Round Table, for that purpose. A review by yourself especially would have the force and authority of *thought* supported by philosophic method, and appearing just now while my book is undergoing the ordeal of public criticism would serve powerfully the interests of Pure Idealism, against which most of our scholars are setting their faces, and ready to drive a petty pen. I do not think the critic of the Nation of ‖ any ‖ much account unless it be to open an opportunity for ‖ some to ‖ discussing the whole subject, and showing the doctrine fully, which my few paragraphs poorly intimate—only "slip in says the critic in the Commonwealth in a provoking, by-the-way, taken[-]for-granted manner." But one good service it will effect, if no more,—provoking thought on the whole doctrine of Genesis, and set the mind astir on original problems which have slumbered so long. I wish you to believe me when I say, that of all American thinkers, I deem yourself best equipped by genius and study, to meet the demands of the occasion, doing the doctrine of my little book, the absolute justice. My style and manner may take care of themselves. The notice in The Commonwealth is perhaps just as to deficiencies ‖ of method and ability ‖ though I need to be convinced as yet.

200 copies of Tablets are now in the binders hands, having ornamental Title page and portrait. These ‖ will be ready ‖ are promised by the first of October. I have a notice of Kroegers', I suppose, printed in the St Louis Republican. The Boston Transcript, the A. Slavery Standard, and N. Y. Evening Post, have also noticed me favorable. Weiss has a notice printing, I understand in the Radical. Copies have been sent to the N.Y. Tribune, and Chicago Tribune; but I have seen nothing in these as yet. I sent to yourself and Kroeger bound copies by express some days ago.

Yours truly,
A. Bronson Alcott.

Wm. T. Harris.

---

[1] From a copy, in Alcott's hand, in the Alcott-Pratt Collection. The original is in the Alcott-Harris Collection in the Concord Free Public Library (see Appendix B).

LETTER 68–36

[to Ellen A. Chandler, Framingham, Mass.]

Concord, Sep 30th 1868

Dear Miss Chandler.

The delay of the photographer and binder is quite provoking. I was to have had my book a week ago, and still it has not come to hand, and we must wait for it still. Meanwhile I send you one of my School Reports, having just received a few copies from our Town Clerk. With yours is one also for Miss Moore in return for one borrowed of her some months since, but which Wendell Phillips begged and got. You may find suggestions useful in your Course of Teaching.

I hear the Radical Club is to meet at Mr. Sargents on the third Monday of October. Shall I have the pleasure of accompanying you as heretofore? Do not let me be an incumbrance upon the freedom of your steps. Since you are free to come without any one.

I wish you to retain || the || Sanborn's notice, if you care for it.

I hear whispers of your coming to pass a Sunday in Concord soon, when I shall have other notices to show you. I wish the visit may be.

Remembrances to your friends Miss Tenney and Miss Johnson.

Cordially Yours,
A. Bronson Alcott.

LETTER 68–37

[to Annie A. Preston]

Concord October 3rd 1868.

Dear Miss Preston,

Your note bearing date Sep. 7th, but reached me yesterday, having been misdirected to Concord, N.H.

I know of no one having better claims to my book than yourself. The delicacy of courage which dictated and made these known, commends itself to heart and head alike. An author has little of worth to print for his reader, who can be insensible to an appeal so true.

I have not a copy of Tablets bound at hand, but have a single one in sheets, which I forward herewith to your address.

Let me add, that it will interest me, if you will write frankly what you find in its leaves, after careful perusal. The criticism of young women is oftentimes of more weight than that of mere scholars. I shall be glad to know that any of my pages have been edifying to a seeker of wisdom like yourself.

Very truly
Yours
A. Bronson Alcott.

Miss Annie A. Preston.

LETTER 68–38[1]

[to Franklin B. Sanborn, Springfield, Mass.]

Concord October 6th 1868.

Dear Friend,

I write to acknowledge the receipt of "The SemiWeekly Republican," which has come regularly since your note of 23rd Sep. came to hand. "The two or three numbers", you spoke of as "waiting at the P.O. for me" the postmaster had *remailed* to Boston. If these contained notices or verses important for me to see, I should be sorry to lose them.

Robert's have not sent me as yet any copies of my book with the photographs. The Sun, I am informed, has done his part, but the binders delay theirs. I shall have some soon doubtless.

Harris writes (Sep. 17) "I have used all spare time for the last few days in reading "Tablets", and am qualified to pronounce the book a right rare book, full of reminiscences of our Primitive life in Paradise. I have tried to get time to work up a review for "the Round Table." I have many things to say of it, and shall get them into print eventually. I want to get time *to bite* that reviewer who writes for "the Nation" concerning the "Tablets" and "the Journal of Speculative Philosophy." I think he must live near Cambridge."

The publishers have sent me notices in "the New York Evening Mail", "the Boston Sunday Times" and "Watchman & Reflector,"[2] the last very favorable for a Religious Journal.

"Your Correspondent," has kindly notices and allusions concerning "Old Concord".

Do you know who wrote the "Tribute" to R. W. E. in the last Radical? He signs himself "H. H." and pays his Tribute most gracefully to the king.

The Radical Club meets on Monday the 19th of this month. Who reads, I have not learned, unless it falls to yourself.

Walt Whitman has sent me "The Broadway," containing verses of his, entitled

"Whispers of Heavenly Death"

The good Templars have had a Temperance meeting at the Town Hall, where Dr. Miner, Miss Hanniford and others made effective speeches.

We have not yet had the happiness to greet Mrs Sanborn and the children here. Mr Channing continues his Sunday afternoon and evening visits regularly.

Mrs Alcott is not quite as active as usual, but maintains her place as housekeeper. Louisa and May are still with us, but think of taking rooms in Boston, perhaps with Anna, who goes from us in a week or two. Louisa's book seems to be favorably received.[3]

I am in doubt about going West. There is talk of a Room for Sunday meetings in Boston. And I have almost concluded to venture a course of Evening Conversations there, to begin, perhaps about the first of November. I should like to talk out my world to a good company, as comment and elucidation of the theories implied mystically in my book—taking perhaps the topics of *Theism, Genesis,* Temperament, Marriage, Manners, Culture.

With remembrances to Mrs Sanborn and the boys. I remain

Sincerely Yours

A. Bronson Alcott

F. B. Sanborn.

[1] MS. owned by the New York Public Library. A copy, in Alcott's hand, is in the Alcott-Pratt Collection.

[2] A national Baptist periodical.

[3] *Little Women*, Part I.

LETTER 68–39

[to Henry Barnard, Hartford? Conn.?]

Concord October 27th 1868.

Dear Sir,

I write to inquire about Mr. Russell's paper on myself, which has not yet appeared in "The Journal of Education" for which it was written. As it was a friendly act on my friends part, and has lain waiting so long for insertion, I think you will agree with me that, unless you find a place for it at once, the paper should be returned to me, for use in some other ‖ Journal ‖ way. I might have it privately printed—or as an introduction to a new edition of "The Record of a School," which is talked about by a Boston bookseller. At any rate, you will not think me unreasonable ‖ in wishing ‖, after nearly half a centuries devotion to the interests of human culture, that I should become a little impatient at the slow recognition given to my labors in a Journal devoted to the cause of American Education especially.

Very truly

Yours

A. Bronson Alcott.

Henry Barnard.

LETTER 68–40

[to Ellen A. Chandler, Framingham, Mass.]

Concord Novr 1st 1868.

Dear Miss Chandler,

At last, I can show you the promised Book in fitting dress for your acceptance.

Be kind enough to receive it as a slight token of the regard for yourself inspired by our brief acquaintance, and with my hope that the perusal may in no wise diminish your respect for the writer.

Expecting to see you sometime during these autumn days, either with or without Mr. Emerson, (who assures me he shall take the earliest chance which his engagements permit for complying with your invitation,

I am
Very sincerely
Yours
A. Bronson Alcott

PS./

Mrs Alcott had purposed to have seen yourself and friends here this very day, but left unexpectedly to spend a few days with Anna at Maplewood.

LETTER 68–41[1]

[to William T. Harris, St. Louis]

Concord Novr 4th 1868.

Dear Friend,

Yesterday came "The Round Table" containing your masterly criticism. It is well worth waiting for. All the newspaper notices that I have seen were superficial, though mostly laudatory none so learned, discriminating and satisfactory as yours. Wasson disarmed his author to provoke a tilt with the ninny of "The Nation," and Ripley's criticism was only scholarly not philosophical.

I think we may accept your classification of the types of New England Idealism and take it as the true Key to its thought and methods. We shall get nothing like it either from East or West.

My Book is almost sold, only 100 copies in plain, and 200 in Illustrated remain on hand for Christmas and New Years. Ha[ve] you got yours?

I gave Kroeger's article (which you sent in your letter) to Slack. He hoped to find place for it in this week's "Commonwealth." If he does not Sanborn doubtless will. He takes good care of what is going on in the world of thought, and his paper "The Semi Weekly Republican," is for me the best newspaper we have in Massachusetts. I hope you see it. You will find notices of Emerson's late lectures. The one on "Transcendentalism" has awakened an interest in its history. I should like to see your criticism reprinted in some of our papers.

Morse is promoting courses of lectures at Worcester, Providence, and New Bedford in aid of The Radical. Emerson, Phillips, Weiss, Wasson and myself are to speak, if he succeeds.

I have thoughts of a course of Conversations in Boston after Emerson's lectures close and there is a movement for Sunday morning meetings ‖ in Boston ‖ there. Judge Robins of N. Have[n] has been here to propose lectures and Conversations in that city. If these engagements hold, I shall hardly go West till late in the winter. Meanwhile Morse is in correspondence about them.

I am looking for "The Speculative with interest.

Cordially Yours,
A. Bronson Alcott

Wm. T. Harris.

[1] From a copy, in Alcott's hand, in the Alcott-Pratt Collection. The original is in the Alcott-Harris Collection in the Concord Free Public Library (see Appendix B).

LETTER 68–42

[to Lucia M. Peabody, Boston]

Concord Novr. 5th. 1868.

Dear Miss Peabody,

I fear we must lose the pleasure of meeting your Society to morrow evening; as Mrs Alcott is from home, and I cannot conveniently be in the city to pass the night.

Will you return my thanks to the ladies for their kind invitation with the assurance that we shall gladly avail ourselves of any future opportunity that may offer of attending their meetings.

Most respectfully,
A. Bronson Alcott.

Miss L. M. Peabody
    Secy of N. E. Ladies' Club

LETTER 68–43

[to J. J. Locke, Greenfield, Mass.]

Concord Novr 9th 1868.

Dear Friend,

Your letter came too late for me to reply in time, as letters from here go first to Boston and are then distributed for outgoing mails. Besides, I could not have aided you in the way you proposed. You were invited to speak *your* thought, not anothers: any suggestions of mine must have put you out of that, at best. I doubt not you found fit words to speak and interested your audiance [*sic*]. It is a fit one f[or] free speaking like yours.

The matter of Sunday morning meetings stands just as we left it. I have spoken with Hallowell a word about them, and from what he said, infer that he might contribute something. Emerson will, and speak once or twice. I shall hope to see Weiss and Wasson at our next Club meeting, which comes regularly next Monday. You will be there of course, and we can consult further about it. If the Sunday meetings cannot be maintained, I shall perhaps try for some Conversations.

Morse and Marvin have courses of Lectures in prospect at Worcester, Providence and New Bedford in aid of The Radical. Emerson and myself, I understand, are to speak, with Phillips and others. At these places, I ‖ should probably ‖ might ‖ have ‖ have Conversations besides. A Course is talked about also in New Haven. But none of these engagements (if made) need ‖ not ‖ interfere with the Sunday Morning meetings and Conversations in Boston.

My book finds general favor with the reviewers. Harris has a fair ‖ review ‖ notice of it in "The Round Table," in which the Idealists Emerson, Alcott and Thoreau, are philosophically treated of.

Truly Yours,
A. Bronson Alcott.

J. J. Locke.

LETTER 68–44

[to Ellen A. Chandler, Framingham, Mass.]

Concord November 11th 1868.

Dear Miss Chandler,

I shall gladly accept your invitation of being your guest, and await your wishes as to the time of my visit. Thanksgiving week will be recess of School doubtless. Some Friday preceding or following will be convenient for me. Will you please name the day? Meanwhile am I not to meet you at the Woman's Convention in Boston next week? I missed you at the October Club and shall again at Mondays next. There was a lively report of it in the Antislavery Standard which I hope you saw. Weiss reads the next paper.

It may interest you to know that Mr Harris has written a criticism of my book for "The Round Table" of Oct. 31.st. I wish I had a duplicate of the paper for you. And if it chance not to fall under your eye, will bring it with me when I come. It is a masterly piece of criticism, treating our New-England Idealism worthily. We shall get nothing better East or West.

I hear of you at Emerson's lectures and am sure you are made happy and wise in his presence and hearing. I think I may be able to attend his last next Monday evening when I hope to get a glimpse of your face again.

Yours always

A. Bronson Alcott

Miss Ellen A. Chandler.
Framingham Normal School.

LETTER 68–45

[to Ellen A. Chandler, Framingham, Mass.]

Concord November 22nd 1868.

Dear Miss Chandler,

On returning yesterday from attending the Woman's Conventions, I found your note of the 17th. I am very sorry that you were unable to be there. The presence of so many noble men and women was victory already won for human freedom, and the proceedings, when you shall read the reports, I think will justify your hope that *these* would "be serious and simple and do some real good."

Mr Weiss spoke the substance of his Club paper and won hearty applause.

I hear Miss Stowe (who, as you will read, is President of "the N. E. Woman's Suffrage Association,") is to read the next paper. By rule, the Club meets on the 21st. Dec, when I hope you are free to attend. Higginson reads in January, I am told, and ‖ Frothingham ‖ Abbot in February.

I shall be on my way to Worcester (where I am to speak on Monday evening the 14th Dec) and shall gladly pass Friday (Saturday and Sunday if desired) with yourself and friends. If the minister of the Unitarian Church wishes, I will speak to his Congregation.[1] But *that* is perhaps not to be named beyond yourself and him.

I shall bring Mr Harris' Critique for you to see and read, and think you will agree with me in its being a masterly work. It was printed in three Nos. of "the Round Table of which, I infer, you have seen only the first.

I am glad to learn that Miss Tenney is better, and hope to see her when I come

Most truly

Yours,

A. Bronson Alcott

Miss Chandler.

¹ See Letter 68–49.

LETTER 68–46¹

[to William T. Harris, St. Louis]

Concord Novr. 22nd 1868.

Dear Friend,

I think your Critique of Tablets so ‖ deeply ‖ [p. o.] discriminating, and [p. in] ‖ profoundly ‖ so well considered, that I shall ask you to allow its insertion in a second edition, as an Introduction to the text and interpretation of its spirit and doctrine. I can hope for nothing from any quarter so good, and for which ‖ the ‖ slow readers will be more thankful. Any working out of the outline sketched for Book II. will of course add greatly to the value of the commentary, and sharpen the reader's insight. I thank you most heartily for this service rendered, not to my thought alone, but to the philosophical criticism of the country, and am sure of our scholars' profiting by the masterly example which you have given. I should like to have it come under Emerson's eye, between whom and myself not a word has yet been spoken concerning my Book. I only know that he has a copy obtained of the publishers.

I think of a Second Volume containing the Oracles, Orphic Sayings, and the Notes on Philosophers. If I am not drawn from my study to lecture and Converse, I ‖ purpose ‖ hope to compile this during the winter.

I am to give some Conversations in Boston—the first comes on Monday evening the 30th Nov. And I am to speak in a Lecture Course at Worcester on the 14th Dec., and meet the young Ladies of the Normal School at Framingham on the 11th preceding. If I should go West, I should probably leave by the 20th Dec. It looks now as if I might, and perhaps reach St. Louis sometime in January. I cannot ask of you to make any inquiries about Conversations in your city. But if any ‖ one ‖ of your friends feels disposed, shall like very well to meet such company as they may gather for me, and on their own terms. I might pass a fortnight in your city, and should enjoy meeting your teachers, if you thought it advisable. Remembrances to the Kroeger's, Davidson, & Miss Brackett.

Yours sincerely,

A. B. Alcott

Mr. Harris.

¹ From a copy, in Alcott's hand, in the Alcott-Pratt Collection. The original is in the Alcott-Harris Collection in the Concord Free Public Library (see Appendix B).

LETTER 68–47

[to Ellen A. Chandler, Framingham, Mass.]

Concord Novr 25th. 1868.

Dear Miss Chandler,

In my last note I omitted to write of my Conversation next Monday Evening at Mr. Sargents. I need not add how pleased I shall be to see you there with any of your friends who may honor me with their company. The Conversation is advertised for halfpast seven, but 8 O'clock usually comes before all are present.

Miss Moore tells me that you are to be at Framingham to-morrow and so I address you there.

Hoping your friend Miss Tenney is fast recovering and soon to be astir again, and asking you to offer her my sympathy and regards.

I am

Most truly

Yours

A. Bronson Alcott.

Miss Chandler.

LETTER 68–48

[to Carrie K. Sherman, New Bedford, Mass.]

Concord November 25th 1868.

Dear Madam,

But for various things which have occupied my time since the receipt of your note, you would have had an earlier response.

But you ask of me definitions of the undefinable, and I can only ask of you to distinguish finely *that* in yourself which differences yourself from other persons, and *that* which unites and makes them one with yourself also—makes you one with them indissolubly and forever. The unity is the Personality: the difference is the Individuality, which is the separable and perishable.

I do not see how I can make the distinction plainer by more words. It must be left to the culture of intuition and experience,—argument being of no avail in the matter. Only as One *is* it, can he *see* it. He must grow into and become One with The Person dwelling in every breast, and thus alone come to the comprehension of the saying:

"I and my father are one." i.e. Of that Personal Identity making all souls one with God.

For further possible quickenings of thought, let me refer you to my Book of "Tablets," and if you see "The Round Table," read a Review of it in Nos for Saturday Oct. 31st, and for November 7 & 14.

I very well remember the eager interest of the young lady at Haverhill in the Conversations there, and am gratified by the request the young wife

453

now makes, only wishing that I may not have darkened the matter by this scroll.

Very respectly [*sic*]
Yours,
A. Bronson Alcott.

LETTER 68–49

[to Ellen A. Chandler, Framingham, Mass.]

Maplewood Dec 1st. 1868

Dear Miss Chandler.

In your last note, you speak of Mr. Spaldings "thinking of making some arrangements so that he could ask me to speak in his Church on Sunday." I had in mind the simple arrangement only of taking some part in the Sunday Services— the reading of the Scripture, a hymn, and speaking in my way. And if he has a Sunday School it would please me to speak to the Children and teachers.

The Conversation on Monday evening was agreeable. It is proposed to have a series of six or more to be given at the Ladies Club Room, the time and terms to be advertised, ‖ and place of getting tickets, ‖ as these are to be public. Messrs. Morse and Morton are to make the arrangements and inform me by Saturday next. I shall delight to see you in the company and hope your duties will allow of your attendance.

You may address me here at Maplewood, Mass. where I am staying with my daughter Anna, for a ‖ month or so ‖ few days.

Very truly
Yours,
A. Bronson Alcott

Miss Ellen A. Chandler.

LETTER 68–50

[to Franklin B. Sanborn, Springfield, Mass.]

Maplewood Dec. 6th 1868.

Dear Friend,

Since I wrote last, Louisa and May have taken rooms in Boston, (No 17 Beacon Street) and Mrs Alcott has come to pass the winter here with Anna. We have closed our house in Concord for the time, and I am to be back and forth meanwhile, making Maplewood headquarters. Anna will enjoy her home all the more, and her mother be free from family cares which weary and worry her sadly. As we have a Post Office here, letters will find us, addressed to "Maplewood".

My tour West is deferred till after the Conversations. I am about beginning a course of Six at the Ladies' Club Room (probably the first on Wednesday Evening next). The subjects are to be advertised in to-morrows' papers. Your friend Morton and Mrs Moore of the Ladies Club, are doing the right thing in the matter of arrangements. I shall be most happy to see yourself and Mrs Sanborn honoring me by attendance.

I am to meet the Framingham Normal School next Friday evening, pass Sunday there with Miss Chandler, and speak in the Unitarian Church (probably) and again in the Course of Radical Lectures on Monday Evening the 14th at Worcester. Emerson follows Frothingham, to morrow Evening, Weiss, ‖ Wasson ‖ Phillips and Higginson follow me. The Lectures are in aid of "The Radical".

Harris writes that he is about printing Nos' 7 and 8 of "the Speculative" one after the other. He thinks "I am in danger of becoming famous in the sense that a member of Congress is, or that Pythagoras was in his time." I suggested the fitness of his Critical Notice for "the Round Table," for a Key to Tablets, and as an introduction to a new Edition. He writes: "If you should wish something of the kind, only more fully treating of the Speculative portion, perhaps I shall be able to give it to you. I don't know but that I shall write it for the Journal first."

I read your literary notes eagerly in the Semi Weekly Republican. You are obliging the Boston editors to borrow their freshest intelligence from a paper not to be had here at the news dealers.

I need not add that it will give me pleasure to hear from you often.

Most truly Yours.
A. Bronson Alcott

F. B. Sanborn.

LETTER 68–51

[to E. Bronson Cooke, Waterbury, Conn.]

Concord Dec 17th 1868.

Dear Sir,

Yours of the 14th came to hand. I certainly am honored, as is my daughter, by your friendly interest in us, and gladly send to you by Adam's Express, copies of "Tablets and "Little Women."

I am a weekly reader of your Journal and intend to be, while that and my eyes remain to me, to give local habitation[?] and name to the place of my nativity. My earliest reccollctions [sic] are associated with "the Green" and steeples, of Waterbury, when I used to ride behind my mother on Sundays to attend Church, and eat my dinner at Aunt Sue's. The steeples of the old Church and meeting house, were the first I ever saw. Wolcott meeting house had none. And I was confirmed by Bishop Brownell in the old Church at the same time with my father and William A. Alcott. The Green was then a frog pond, and we boys pulled flagroot to eat in Church. I rode sometimes to the old Mill atop of three bags of rye, and waited for my grist to be ground, and was curious about the Clock shops, having a mechanical turn of mind, though an Idealist then.

I read of your calamity at the time, and rejoice that you are so far recovered.

455

I take you to be older than I am, 69. But we have lived and are living in eventful times.—Yourself one of the Fathers of modern Waterbury.

Very truly Yours

A. Bronson Alcott

E. Bronson Cooke.

LETTER 68–52

[to Ellen A. Chandler, Framingham, Mass.]

Maplewood Dec 18th 1868.

Dear Miss Chandler,

Pleasant memories are with me of the days passed at Framingham with yourself and associates.—our evening Conversations and interviews especially. And I find they owe more than I knew to the charm of your presence and part in them. You are one of the few who converse and serve the delight which your company affords. I only wish—if I may write it—that you were nearer that I might partake the oftener.

Yesterday I had a half hour with Emerson, and learned that he is to read selections from English Poets to his class of ladies, beginning early in January. I enclose a note of Sanborn's concerning his Readings.

You may be sure of all I said about his wishing to visit the school, and *know you*, ‖ and to be assured of your potent magnetism ‖. Please ask him to name his day and secure him as your guest,—that is all. He spoke of writing to you. But wait not, write yourself and your importunity will please and prevail.

You will be ‖ pleased ‖ glad to learn that the Sunday meetings are to begin the first Sunday in January, (probably) at Horticultural Hall, the speakers to be Emerson, Alcott, Weiss, James, Johnson, Higginson, Wasson, Potter, Frothingham, Phillips, Abbot, Mrs Cheney and Mrs Howe (we hope) and perhaps others. The series extends through the months of January, February, March and April. Season Tickets $6. Single 50 cts. We have subscriptions already secured to make the meetings sure. I ‖ trust ‖ wish it may prove the possibility of a Church and of true worship.

My last Conversation I find gave much pleasure to a large and brilliant company. I only wished for a single young maiden. The next on "Woman," I learn is to be reported in full for the February "Radical." And I am to have the pleasure of your presence at the following one on "Plato".

Does your father go out of evenings? If he does, and cares for a treat bring him with you, at my invitation.

Miss Moore accompanies you of course.

I enclose Mr Harris' critique in the Round Table, with some other things that may interest you. The two sonnets are by Helen Hunt. When I find another of hers, printed in "The Independent", you shall have it. "The Evening with Alcott" is reported by Redpath, and "The Radical Club" by Kate Field. Morse and Marvin are purposing to print Davidson's translation of Lessing's "Laocoon".

Yours affectionately

A. Bronson Alcott

Miss Ellen A. Chandler.

PART SEVENTEEN

1869

LETTER 69–1

[to Ellen A. Chandler, Framingham, Mass.]

Maplewood Jan 6th 1869.

Dear Miss Chandler,

Though I have seen your face and caught some bright rays since I opened your last note, I will just now say how pleased I was to see you there, and to wonder by what deceiving star I lost an accent of your thought in the Conversation. Our Pegasus, I fear, ran a little wild and overbore when he should have won from the timid and hushful what these had to speak.

If you would only come to night, I think I should behave beautifully. But you insist that the Fates are forbidding, and I submit though "Beauty" suffer.

Pray excuse, if I write briefly, and enclose more verses for your Tablets.

The sonnet is exquisite. Whether I have before given you "An Hymn" I have forgotten.

"A happy new Year" from

Yours affectionately.
A. Bronson Alcott.

Miss Ellen A. Chandler.

LETTER 69–2

[to Ellen A. Chandler, Framingham, Mass.]

Maplewood Jan 15th 1869.

Dear Miss Chandler,

You are too much absorbed in the toils of your Annual Examination to dream even of matters outside, much less write. Oblige me then, if I obtrude my little note and its contents upon your thoughts for a moment just to advise you of matters and measures in which you take an interest.

The Sunday Afternoon meetings have been announced in the newspapers, which I trust have met your eye. If you must miss Mr Weiss tomorrow I hope you are free to attend some of the following Sundays. The speakers will be advertised from week to week, and you have your choice. Mr Emerson will not speak till sometime in February. Next Monday comes the Club, when Mr. Higginson reads. I imagine your Examination on Tuesday deprives us of your attendance. My thanks for "the Catalogue".

My Conversations closed last Wednesday. Three of the evenings were agreeable to me—that on Temperance & Descent, on Plato, and the last on *Theism* and Christianity. They have been well attended, and thought by my friends a great success. ‖ Three of them ‖ The one on Woman, Plato, and the last are reported at length and to appear in the Radical.

I am thinking of holding one more, at least, ‖ and if this promises fair, perhaps many. I shall advertise them ‖. They will be given at Horticultural Hall on Sunday evenings—the first on Sunday Jan 24th. at ½ past 7.

Enclosed are more papers for your Tablets, if you will.

Very affectionately Yours
A. Bronson Alcott.

LETTER 69–3[1]

[to William T. Harris, St. Louis]

Concord Jan 15th 1869.

Dear Friend,

No 3 of the Journal came to hand last Wednesday. It is full freighted with thoughtful matter giving fair assurance of its claim to long continuance. A few more numbers must give it a permanent place in our history, and these you promise its readers without question. I should like to see your "Introduction to Philosophy" the chosen text book in our schools and universities, that these might rightly name Philosophy as truly included in their list of studies. If professors were too stupid to teach in the right method, some of the bright students would comprehend and become philosophers in spite of their dull drill. Print it at once, and let them have the trial.

Your notice of my book is most gratifying to me. Of all others, yours alone has penetrated to the core of its thought, and fairly justified the text. Others have given their opinions merely, and though favorable for the most part, have little weight aside from the writers—nothing absolute in thought and method. For these reasons, I am the more desirous that your estimate should accompany the new edition, which will soon go to press. I shall gladly accept it as first written. But any revision or addition, by yourself, must render it the more profitable to the readers. 'Tis asking much of you, but all in the name of philosophy, our Common Friend.

My friends say the Conversations have been a great success, and beg for more. If I venture more, it will delay my visit till March into your neighborhood.

We have just advertised a series of Sunday meetings which promise well. I enclose our advertisement.—Higginson reads before the Radical Club next Monday, and Abbot in February.

Miss Chandler was at my Conversation on "Plato." She writes me often. I value her acquaintance above price. I am pleased to learn of Mr. Kroeger's literary success. His paper on "Leibnitz" in the North American I have not yet found time to read.

Am I so ill a correspondent that Prof. Davidson writes not lately. I heard he was going to N. York to edit "the Round Table." How can you spare him? or he you?

I take great pleasure in Miss Brackett's verses.

Please write at your first spare moment.

Most truly
Yours,
A. Bronson Alcott.

Wm. T. Harris.

---

[1] MS. owned by the New York Public Library. A copy, in Alcott's hand, is in the Alcott-Pratt Collection.

LETTER 69–4

[to Ellen A. Chandler, Framingham, Mass.]

Maplewood Jan 18th 1869.

Dear Miss Chandler,

I found your note awaiting my return from the Club on Monday where was Mr. Stone, to whose hands I committed mine of the same date. Of all our meetings, perhaps this gave most general delight. Col. Higginson's paper on the Greek Goddesses was chaste and classic. Every ear heard with eager satisfaction and the effect was charming. I wished you were of the happy group who listened to his portraits of the Girl, the maiden, the lover, the wife, mother, the consummate woman,—and a partaker in the discourse after the reading. Just what you would have said was not said by any of your sex—a misfortune that none of ours could arrest or parry. Had there been one Ideal Goddess to hold the conversation at the heights it invited.

"The Speculative Journal" has come to hand with verses to "the Ideal" by Miss Brackett. They are so good that I enclose a copy. The same number contains also a notice by Mr. Harris of Tablets which I send.

Mr. Weiss spoke to much acceptance on Sunday afternoon, to a good audiance [sic].

It would have given me pleasure to have been with you to day, but the memory of my recent visit must suffice for the present. I am to see you at the Anniversary Tables next week if not on Sunday afternoon or evening.

Yours most Cordially
A. Bronson Alcott.

Miss Ellen A Chandler.

LETTER 69–5[1]

[to Franklin B. Sanborn, Springfield, Mass.]

Maplewood Jan 18th 1869.

Dear Friend,

I have found the notice and enclose a copy. Being yourself present, you can temper any enthusiasm into which the writer may have risen on that moonlight night.

I was glad to see you yesterday, though but for the moment, in places where your face was formerly a bright part of the social scene. How chaste and classic were Higginson's Greek Divinities, the company so eager to hear and learn! What with the Club, Sunday Discourses, Emerson's Lectures and Readings, and the rest—the prospect seems hopeful. And though I hardly expect any one to share in my dreams, yet yesterday I fancied the sluggish and skeptical were touched with sensibility and kindlings of the East.

Your paper, with Warrington to aid you in reporting passing interests and events, (which the Boston Journals fail to see and note,) is the liveliest Chronicle of current New England Life that I read. I rode in to Weiss' Lecture last Sunday with Warrington, and we talked of the need of a Representative Journal to be printed here in Botson. Yourself, W——— and associates, and men of money and *principles* to sustain the undertaking—writing down that misnamed "Nation," which though printed in New York, reflects Boston and Cambridge politics and literature, disgracing when it is "proper" the free American thought.

Very truly
Yours
A. Bronson Alcott

[1]MS. owned by the New York Public Library. A copy, in Alcott's hand, is in the Alcott-Pratt Collection.

LETTER 69–6

[to Lucia M. Peabody, Boston]

Maplewood February 15th 1869.

Dear Miss Peabody,

Your note, enclosing an honorary member's Ticket, has just reached me here.

I am truly honored by the Directors of the New England Woman's Club in being thus admitted to its cordialities, and let me hope to its duties, also. It certainly will give me pleasure to attend its meetings occasionally, and to further in ways becoming me, the aims of an association having at heart what I regard one of the paramount interests of our time, as of all times—the dignity of woman.

Most respectfully
Yours
A. Bronson Alcott.

Miss L. M. Peabody
Sec. of New England Woman's Club.

LETTER 69-7

[to Thomas Davidson, St. Louis]

Maplewood, near Boston, | February 17th 1869.

Dear Friend,

My hearty acknowledgments for your sheet of scholarly gossip concerning your studies and friends at St. Louis. Most welcome what you write about your translations, which I am the more impatient to read, after my recent perusal of Grote's Plato. Of the NeoPlatonists, Proclus interests me less than ‖ Porphyry ‖ Plotinus whose ideas as far as I am informed are ‖ though less than Plotinus ‖ most akin to the Transcendental idealism of our time. Very few modern scholars can have read ‖ his ‖ Porphyrys *Sentences* in the Original and your translation will be surprising to them. ‖ He ‖ Plotinus seems, ‖ too ‖, the more lucid writer of the three and the one to introduce the Alexandrians to the modern reader. You are rendering high service to the advanced thinkers of our time, in setting before them in pure Saxon, the works of those great masters, thus assisting to revive the study of the purest philosophy the world has known, containing the germs of later thought, the ripest culture, beside which all else is but shallow pedantry, dealing with the emotions rather than intellect, superficially, not essentially. Yes, after the Greeks, nothing philosophical sweet, wholesome. Give us The *Sentences,* and all of him

"—who such things did see
Even in the tumult, that few can arrive of all named from
Philosophy to that high pitch, or to such scents dive."

The March Radical contains a full report of my Conversation on *Plato.* The last of the six given, on *Theism and Christianity* will appear in some following number. Better company would have made them more satisfactory. Besides these evenings, I have had three with the Divinity Students—thirty of them, and mostly Sympathising with the fresher thought.

Our Sunday Afternoon meetings have been well attended thus far. Abbot gave a thoughtful discourse on Free Religion and Christianity. Next comes Higginson on Immortality. Emerson, Frothingham, Johnson, Phillips, follow twelve lectures in all, and we hope the opening of future courses.

I am hesitating about venturing West, having been detained here thus late in the season and with the uncertainties of the long journey before. My chief attraction is St Louis, but I may postpone even that for the present.

I have read Mr. Kroegers "Leibnitz" with much pleasure. Even Cambridge condescends to notice St Louis philosoph[ers.]

My cordial remembrances to Miss Brackett, and your associates. May your Elisium everlast.

Very sincerely
Yours,
A Bronson Alcott.

Prof Davidson.

LETTER 69–8

[to Ellen A. Chandler, Framingham, Mass.]

Maplewood Feb. 25th 1869.

Dear Miss Chandler.

Chance favors friends when friends look for it. So our meeting fortunately and our Conversation last Monday was a happy accident, since pleasant words were spoken, and I brought away some very pleasant sealed ones—only a little more apologetic than seemed due, but very acceptable nevertheless. Let us write when we have things to say, and hold high silence when we have not. Nor will we question the silence or the speaking meanwhile. I shall like to send a word as the mood prompts. I certainly should not complain having Plato by me associated with the kindness that brought him to me, and with the knowledge that you are enjoying Emerson face to face on Saturdays.

What you write about "Little Women" and "Moods", very complimentary to Louisa, who will thank you for your good opinion of her stories—not as her mother and I think undeserved.

I hope to see you soon again at Emerson's Readings at the Woman's Club.

Very truly
Yours,
A. Bronson Alcott

Miss Chandler.

LETTER 69–9

[to John Langdon Sibley, Cambridge, Mass.]

Concord March 10th | 1869

Dear Sir,

I copy from my Genealogical Notes the facts which you ask concerning George Alcock.

"He was the eldest son of Dr John and grandson of Deacon George Alcock of Roxbury. Born March 25. 1655. he graduated at H. C. 1673. went to England, and died, 1676. at the house of his cousin, Benjamin Walker, in the parish of St. Katharines Free Church, als. Christ Church, London. Being the eldest son, he inherited the double portion of his father's property here in New England, which he left by will, dated at London ‖ March 12 ‖ 27 February. 1676, to his brothers John and Palsgrave, and to his married sisters Williams, Whitman, and Lamb, and to Elisabeth and Joanna, unmarried at the date of this instrument, also to his kinsman Benjamin Walker of London who appears came over and settled here after George's death.

"To the Church in Roxbury he gave the summe of five pounds, a like sum to the School in Roxbury, and to Peter Thacher of New England, Clerk, who was made one of his executors.

Sewall writes in his Diary, date "May 9 1676

Mr James ship arrived from London, wherein came Mr. Thacher, who brought news of ye death of George Alcock: he dyed of small pocks, March 12th. Mr Thacher and sister Davenport were here."

It appears that Mr Thacher was one ‖ of the signers of his ‖ of his executors, and present at ‖ its ‖ the approval of his will in London March 12. 1676.

The parchment in my possession is a formal testament, in Latin ‖ on parchment ‖, to his good behaviour, which he had probably asked to be sent to England, but is dated after his death. It is ‖ signed by ‖ dated Har. Coll in N. Eng. April 19th 1676. and signed by

        "Urianus Oakes Proess[?]
        Daniel Gookin
        Ammi - Rechamah Corlett Socii.
        Petrus Thacherus"

As you requested, I copy the Latin words, ‖ as you requested, ‖ in this document, preceding the word Quapropter—

/ ſomodum viſturum"—

comodum victurum, as I read from the similarity of the ſ to other words where c is necessary to the sense.

I have to apologise [*sic*] for not replying to your request at an earlier date. But have but just returned to my house in Concord.

                Yours Truly
                A. Bronson Alcott.

John Langdon Sibley Esq
    Lib. H.C.

LETTER 69–10

[to Mrs. H[?]. W. Sewall, Boston?]

              Concord March | 20th 1869.

Dear Mrs Sewall,

You shall convey my thanks to the ladies of your Committee for their confidence in the fitness of any words of mine for your Club, and assure them that I will speak on the day you name in your note. If the ladies will permit, it will please me best to converse without the embarrassment of written notes.

                Very truly
                Yours
                A. Bronson Alcott.

Mrs H[?]. W. Sewall
    Secy. of Art and Literature.

LETTER 69–11

[to James T[?]. Lee]

              Concord March 22nd 1869

My young friend,

Your letter does not surprise me, remembering as I do the boundless confidence of youth in elderly people, in those especially who have celebrity as wise and virtuous. I ‖ think ‖ consider this indeed the virtue of Youth and however I may think your confidence in this instance may be exaggerated by supposed excellencies with which you had endowed your sage, I respect and admire the heart that lends itself thus unreservedly to a Person on looking to him for light and guidance. So I think I may say you are no stranger to me, but one whom I may invite to my house for still better acquaintance face to face.

Now will you not meanwhile write and tell me so much of your past life as you modestly may, your associates, the books you enjoy, your hopes personally and socially. I will read with hope, and when we meet, perhaps a month hence, we shall be the better prepared to see what relations really exist between us.

Any young person pursuing wisdom and virtue, and willing to pay their full price, is a rare phenomenon in any time, in ours especially, and prophetic of better.

It is proper for me to add, that in one or two aspects, your fancy picture fails. I have a wife, and three daughters, one married, one an author, of whose "Little Women," you may have heard, and the youngest an artist. And that I am in my 69th year.

Very hopefully and
respectfully
Your friend
A. Bronson Alcott

Mr James T[?]. Lee.

LETTER 69–12[1]

[to Ellen A. Chandler, Framingham, Mass.]

[Concord, March 23, 1869]

'Tis much to have the company of Plato in these pinched times of ours.

Plato for thought,
Christ for action.

Happier for us were the two happily blended in life. O, for thought to float the mass of traditions off the minds of men and give them to action and ideas worthy of those masters of both! Now men run all to hands—nothing left for head or heart. Let us pray for new heads, as heretofore for new hearts, nor cease, though it were for a century.

[1] A portion of a letter, reprinted from Alcott, *Journals*, pp. 394–95.

LETTER 69–13[1]

[to Ellen A. Chandler, Framingham, Mass.]

Concord March 29th 1869

Dear Miss Chandler,

The picture you sent me the other day is the one I should have chosen, though the cloudy Luminary caressed the original a little coldly at the moment, and hid a trait or two that I could have wished had shone through more tellingly. 'Tis very pleasing, very acceptable, and you were very kind to send it to me.

And it happens that one of myself taken by the same artist in '54. and just copied, comes to hand. Will you accept of one as having less of age in it than the later ones.

Very cordially
Yours,
A. Bronson Alcott.

Miss Chandler.

---

[1] MS. owned by the Abernethy Library, Middlebury College. A copy, in Alcott's hand, is in the Alcott-Pratt Collection.

LETTER 69–14

[to Annie Adams Fields, Boston]

Concord April | 6th 1869.

Dear Mrs. Fields,

I am pleased to learn from your own writing that you find pleasure in my little Book. Mine, I say, very well aware how its best parts are not mine, and my plumes are borrowed,—I will not write stolen. Nor am I surprised that so familiar a reader as yourself of English Verse, should fail to recognize her favorite Cowley in my pages.

The lines alluded to in your note are so disguised by liberties taken with them, that "first[?] lines" mislead both eye and ear.—

You will find the originals in Cowley's Poem entitled "Destiny," and can see by reference my adaptions. May I hope the readers forgiveness for the presumption of tampering thus freely with the poets rhymes.

Very truly, Yours,
A Bronson Alcott.

LETTER 69–15

[to James T[?]. Lee]

Concord April | 6th 1869.

My Frank Young Friend,

Your every way gratifying letter of the 24th deserves an earlier acknowledgment. Yet I have not meanwhile been indifferent to its interesting contents, nor indisposed to court fuller accounts of your experiences and purposes. Be assured that you will not write too often nor too much about your interests, and plans for the future. All you have told of yourself is certainly greatly to your credit and augurs good things for your future. I like what you write concerning books and associates. Your religion too seems to be your own, rather American than Roman, and likely to adapt itself to your growth and duties. It is the fresh and loving heart that cares best for the good head and guides its ambitions to the best objects. Whether it prompts you to the studies suited to your abilities and calling, I am unable to judge, at least till I have the advantage of seeing you. Perhaps you have not yet found just what you are fitted for. I like your high aims, and think less of the special field in which these are carried into action. *Thought* is the ladder one must learn to mount if he would scale the heights of wisdom and virtue. The weak heads are as great impediments to progress as the wicked hearts. Philosophy and religion must walk abreast if we will achieve any thing ‖ good, or gratifying to the good. ‖ excellent; and a life is a failure that fails of finding in these its chief delights, in whatever pursuit it may be spent.

As to your coming to Concord—I think that matter will take care of itself when you come and see for yourself, what scope offers here for you. We cannot anticipate the issue. I wish to see you: you must see me, first. My daughters are busy about their tasks, and are to be absent more or less from home. I cultivate a garden during the season of outdoor work, but am much at my pen summer and winter. As to board, &c. that might chance to suit us and yourself. My wife is one of the old fashioned motherly sort, and my daughters are not without right notions of life.

I need not add that ‖ we ‖ I shall expect your picture.

Very kindly
Yours
A. Bronson Alcott

Mr. Lee.

LETTER 69–16

[to Ednah Dow Cheney, Jamaica Plain? Mass.]

Concord April 17th 1869

Dear Mrs Cheney,

I owe you an apology for witholding [*sic*] your MS and not forwarding something in reply to your request. My sole excuse is, that I hoped to do myself the pleasure of talking the Platonic matter over with you at your own house. There was so much suggested by the subject itself, and by your paper, that I felt how little I could do justice to it in a brief note, and how gratifying it would be to converse with you about it.

But I fear I shall not have that pleasure just yet and so write now to advise you of my seeming neglect. When I can leave home properly that pleasure shall be seized.

I am in doubt whether I can hear Miss Peabody's[1] paper on Monday at the Club; being detained at home just now unexpectedly. It will be sensible I am sure and suggestive.

We have to congratulate ourselves on the success of the Sunday Afternoon Lectures, and the Women's part especially.

> Most Truly
> Yours,
> A. Bronson Alcott.

Mrs E. D. Cheney

[1] Elizabeth Palmer Peabody, who was an active member of the Radical Club.

LETTER 69–17

[to Mrs. H[?]. W. Sewall, Boston?]

Concord April 19th 1869

Dear Mrs Sewall,

I had hoped to attend the Club meeting at Mr. Sargents to-day, but find my self this morning in unpresentable fix, and fear the like inflection will deprive me of the pleasure of meeting the Womans Club next Monday according to engagement. I regret it so happens, and hope it is not too late to find some one to address your Club on that day.

> Very Truly Yours
> A Bronson Alcott

LETTER 69–18[1]

[to Ellen A. Chandler, Framingham, Mass.]

Concord April 23rd 1869.

Dear Miss Chandler,

'Tis a long time from 8th April, yet your last dates thus far in the past, and you are without response from me. Nor had I chance last Monday to make my excuses in person as I intended. For what shall one do when some old ancestral sinner spots his physiognomy so mercilessly just at the moment when he would have all his native graces about him? I forgive, but how shall I forget for the weeks to come, since I am to lose the pleasure of meeting the amiables of the Women's Club next Monday as I had engaged to do.

Meanwhile what will you tell me about last Mondays meeting? Doubtless the paper was suggestive and the talk. But what shall I learn of these unless you sketch the picture, only do not leave one figure on the shade. It is a second disappointment, perhaps prefigures a third. But the May meetings are a month ahead yet. Meanwhile, too, my young Trojan has promised to visit me. If he prove the paragon my fancy paints, he remains for "all-time"—so he writes. Such faith is so strange one hails her with hope when she comes. He has sent his picture in advance. It is prepossessing in strength and manliness. We shall see when the original arrives.

Thanks again for the Plato's. I read at moments still, and hope to find time for Vol. IIId. after a little while.

Miss Moore made us a pleasant call, as fair and graceful as ever.

Last Sunday Hatham[?] the Walden Hermit took tea with us.—a sensible Saint in sylvan attire, and we liked him.

May is near, and the birds are here. Will you not fly into our neighborhood soon?

Very Cordially,
Yours,
A. Bronson Alcott.

Miss Chandler

---

[1] MS. owned by the Abernethy Library, Middlebury College.

LETTER 69–19

[to William Oldham,[1] Surrey, England]

Concord April 26th 1869.

My well remembered Friend,
        William Oldham,
Dear Sir,

Two letters of yours are before me. One is dated November 16th 1866. the other April 3rd of this Year. The first, I answered early in "67' and enclosed in one addressed to your brother-in-law. Henry Sutton, Nottingham England. This was returned to me sometime during the year "67. superscribed "not known in Nottingham." In the summer of "68. Miss Estlin made us a short call and informed me that you had removed from Gloucestershire into the neighborhood of the Howetts' near Esher, and that Mr Sutton was living at Manchester (I think) and editing a Temperance newspaper. By her I sent you a copy of my Book, (then hardly published) assured that in this way direct communication would be opened between us. Now your letter has come to hand giving account of yourself to date. I assure you that it gives me great pleasure to learn what you have communicated, and I trust you will continue to write often about yourself, and such friends of yours as I became acquainted with while in England.— Barmby, Barham, Gowland, and I shall be especially interested to learn about Charles Lane, of *Alcott House* and *Fruitlands* memories. It is perhaps my fault that I have heard nothing from him for many years. An occasional note by *Conway* or *Channing*, now and then, intimates that he is living in or about London, nothing more. Those old times and experiences have now grown *historical*, and begin to live again in memory, any thing about them, whether of persons, opinions, events, I gladly recover. How much pleasure it would afford me to see you and Lane again, and walk about the Ham grounds, where so many visions were cherished for human culture and improvement! *The Ham* and *Fruitlands Fellowships* will deserve a place in the history of these times. I trust you have the records of the first, and that Mr Lane has preserved his notes concerning the last, as it happens that, while I have full Journals of the years preceding my visit to England, and since leaving Fruitlands, very little remains of that eventful period of four years or so. I was so unfortunate as to write less and lose the little I did commit to paper. My life has since been rather rich and fruitful of satisfactions, and my Journals are ample. It is true that I have not *planted a Paradise outside,* as I once dreamed of doing, but rather cultivated the one already planted *inside,* and grown a little pleasant fruit, still good to taste and promising future crops of satisfactions. My family has grown up. The eldest *Anna.* is happily married, and has two bright boys, Louisa has grown into something of a popular author, Elisabeth passed from us a happy saint, and May, the youngest, gives herself to art with skill and enthusiasm. My wife is well, and for a woman of her age, 69, very active and capable. We have a pleasant place here, adjoining the one where we once lived, Hillside, which became Hawthorne's, and where he died, ‖ about ‖ in sight of Emerson's, and not far from Thoreau's home, while he was here. I cultivate a garden in its season, and converse more or less during the months in the cities. I have been far West several times, as far as St. Louis Missouri, where there is a Philosophical Society, and a Journal of Speculative Philosophy now in its third Volume—the only one of its kind in this country. Last winter I have given a course of Conversations in Boston. Mr Emerson has given a course of Readings there, and we have had a series of Sunday Afternoon meetings where addresses have been made by our best thinkers. We have also a monthly Club for Conversation, and a monthly Journal. I send my regards to your wife and brother in law, with kindest memories and affection to yourself.

A. Bronson Alcott.

(Wm. Oldham Surrey, England)

---

[1] Alcott met Oldham (1790–1879) on his visit to England in 1842. Oldham at that time was the "business" member of Alcott House. In 1837 Oldham had left his wife and children (first seeing they were well provided for) and about a year later had abandoned business for the "universal good." After some twenty-five years as a celibate he married (in 1862) Elizabeth Sarah Sutton, a sister of Henry Sutton. He wrote to Alcott February-September, 1870 describing the death of Charles Lane. A spiritualist, Oldham in that letter described his contacts with Lane immediately following the latter's death.

Letter 69–20

[to Christopher Walton, England]

Concord April 26th 1869.

Mr. Christopher Walton,
Dear Sir,

More than a year since I received a very full reply from yourself to a letter of mine, dated 22nd. November. "67. having meanwhile a letter from Mrs Penny acknowledging, at your request, the receipt of mine, and containing important information about St. Martins works translated by Mr. Penny, and which I have since read with interest, having borrowed the books of Mr. Fernald to whom they were sent by the translator. I have also looked through your Volumes of the Cyclopedia sent by yourself to the Harvard College Library, and read your notes, with my conviction deepened of the exceeding importance of giving to the world full accounts of the lives of Behmen's illustrious desciples. I hope nothing will defeat your purpose of doing this as you have intimated in your Prospectus. It is a kind of thought, with ‖ with ‖ which our advanced thinkers should be familiar in order to justify any claims to a real knowledge of spiritual things. I enclose a brief Sketch of Behmen lately printed in the Boston "Radical", calling attention as you will see, in a note, to your Prospectus. I wish I could add that any considerable number of our advanced thinkers had penetrated the core of the Mystery.

What little information you gave me of yourself makes me the more desirous of learning more. And I shall be thankful for any thing further concerning your present pursuits and purposes, especially of the progress of your *"Emblematic Illustrations,"* and those *fierce daily discussions* with your *Rationalist Opponent.* You may be sure, should I come to London, I should seek you out, and see how that argument was conducted.

I cannot promise any adequate return for your correspondence, but shall gladly communicate, from time to time, whatever seems most likely to interest you and your friends in the old country. My excuse for not making an earlier reply to your exceedingly full letter, is, that when it was received, I was about publishing a little book, which I thought might interest you, but which was delayed till autumn, and then came many engagements as you will see on reading the slips enclosed, which kept me very busy through the whole winter months, and have only just closed for the season. These will give you a hint at what is thought and doing here in Boston and its neighborhood. And I refer you to my book—the Speculative part more particularly, for my own Personal thoughts and experiences.

As to the Mr. *Sutton* of whom I spoke in my letter, I learn that he is now living at Manchester, editing a Temperance paper. I think he has espoused Swedenborgianism, which I consider a lapse out of Behmenism, but an advance on the current Sectarianism, and so good, if not *very good,* though here with in Boston it appears to be almost as sectarian as any. If you should fall in with a Mr. *William Oldham* now living at Little Ditton Hill, Surrey, about a mile from Hampton Court, and three miles from William Howetts' at Esher, "you might learn something more about Mr Sutton. Mr. Oldham is his brother in law, and in correspondence with me, having been long interested in spiritual things and once engaged in a school named *Alcott House* at Ham Common, conducted on spiritual principles. I believe he has since become a Spiritualist of the modern type, but is a good man, and knows a good deal about some of us here in Concord.—Among the papers enclosed is one respecting the Journal of Speculative Philosophy, Edited by Mr. Wm. T. Harris, and published at St. Louis, Missouri. Mr. Harris is one of our deepest thinkers, comprehending as wide a range, ‖ than ‖ as any American of his years, and likely to make his mark on the religious philosophy of his time. Portions of your letter I have sent him, and trust he will find a place for some notice of your views and purposes. If yourself, or Mr. Penny, would prepare an account of any movement in favor of Behmen in England, it would be a most valuable contribution to theosophic thought, and take its place in the Speculative Journal. You will see by his table of contents how comprehensive his range is, and yet that without Boêhme it is not inclusive. The papers on *Genesis* and *Pantheon* are contained in my book of *Tablets.* If you are interested to see the *"Journal"*, *Trubner and Co.* have copies, and also of the *"Radical"*.

I shall be greatly indebted to you for a copy of *the Cyclopedia* and any Behmenistic books which you may think will further our studies here. These will find the few who are able to read them with understanding and profit. Most of the speakers at the *Sunday afternoon meetings* would read and appreciate them.

Any parcel addressed to
> "A. Bronson Alcott.
> care of Roberts Brothers.
> Publishers,
> Boston."

will come to hand.

Oblige me by returning my acknowledgments and thanks to Mrs Penny for her very acceptable letter, and to Mr. Penny for the perusal of his translations of St. Martin lent me by Mr. Fernald, who is now preaching at the West. I may add that Mr. Emerson is active and increasing in wisdom and fame.

> Most truly
> Yours
> A. Bronson Alcott.

LETTER 69–21

[to Elizabeth Cady Stanton, New York City?]

Concord May 4th 1869.

Dear Mrs Stanton,

I recall with much satisfaction our short interview at Syracuse, and should gladly renew my acquaintance at your home in New York, with the added privilege of meeting the elect of your associates whose views and endeavors for promoting the equal advancement of the sexes and races have won so many of the friends of human civility and common rights every where to your side.—And your intimation of open parlors and thoughtful companies to fire them, offer additional attractions to a lover of Conversation like my self. I fear, however, that I must forego, for the present at least, these opportunities. And the loss is clearly mine—ours may I not almost say, if I am right in the persuasion that the slower sex are to be quickened and spurred forwards by the purer impulses and fairer ideals, in which yours instinctively share, and in which are conceived and nurtured into life that social state which our affections and advancing civilization alike predict. Woman complements and perfects man, and she is last taking her fit place abreast of him to perfect herself. You will not, I am sure, think me indifferent then to her welfare if I cherish the conviction that she is helping herself to secure her place in a better spirit and manner than any we can suggest or devise, and that it becomes us to take, rather than proffer ‖ our ‖ Consels [*sic*], readily waiting to learn her wishes and aims, as she has so long and so patiently deferred to us. Is it too much to hope that her practical ‖ skill ‖ sense and persuasive eloquence is to help us to give solid substance and abiding reality to our hearts early faith, restoring to a coming generation, if not to us, the lost paradise on Earth?

> With great regard
> Sincerely yours,
> A Bronson Alcott

LETTER 69–22

[to E. H. Heywood, Worcester, Mass.]

Concord May 7th 1869.

Dear Sir,

Your very flattering estimate of my little speech made at your Labor League Convention last January, half persuades me that I, too, may have words of practical significance to speak to the people, and, if able, I will endeavor to attend your coming Convention in Boston on the 26th of this month.

> Very truly Yours,
> A. Bronson Alcott.

LETTER 69–23

[to Daniel Ricketson, New Bedford, Mass.]

Concord May 8th 1869

Dear Friend,

I am late in acknowledgment of your Book of Verses.[1] It came to hand last Tuesday. || and || I have but just dipped into the leaves at intervals of gardening and family chores, and have yet to give to it the faithful reading which it invites and deserves. Were you here in my study,—and will you not be soon? I might speak the impression the fuller perusal makes on me, as I cannot hope to write it. Let me then name some of the pieces that touch me most tenderly as breathing the spirit and genius of the poet.

I find most for me in the second series:

"The Old Trammel," in the first calls up a *"homely"* picture in the old sense of the word—and "The gentle voice and quiet Eye," remind me of her who gave me birth and graced my home.

In the second series,

"Working at the Mill Betsy," breathes the kindly heart, and should be read at the coming Labor League Conventions. Then, "The Old Barn"

"The Winter's Evening,"

have the same homely charm of truth to Nature and simple things.

"My Quest" interests me as a piece of natural religion and wholesome independence of sects.

"In Memoriam, to H.D.T." and all you sing of him is touching, and from the deepest sympathy.

The Philosopher dancing[?], is memorable.

In the dearth of Pastoral verses, yours are significant. I wish they may prompt our young poets to treat of country life and its simple pleasures, as only Whittier and Channing have done before you. You remind me most of the first, and in the subdued melancholy of your verse, of Cowper: With more of cheer, I should say of Burns. I am looking for the poet who shall set an high example of singing New England things in the New England spirit,—shall be *Thoreau* in verse. And these verses of yours fairly entitle you to be linked with that fair name.

Channing was here last evening and carried away your book.

I need not add that I should be pleased to see you in Concord.

With kind regards to your family
Very truly yours
A Bronson Alcott

Danl. Ricketson.

[1] *The Autumn Sheaf.*

LETTER 69–24[1]

[to William T. Harris, St. Louis]

Concord May 12th | 1869.

Dear Friend,

Two numbers of the Journal have come to hand since I wrote you last, and your School Report. I have had two letters also from Mr Davidson. His studies and translations add new attractions to your Journal, and are specially interesting reading for me. Your Preface at the end of No 3. Vol. II. was so good for *the Radical* that I asked Morse to print the seven last paragraphs, and I hope will in the June number. Nothing better for his readers. The Kapila will mean more to me when I shall have the promised commentaries. Porphyrie's sentences come out timely. I am interested in every thing of the Alexandrian School and shall read whatever you print with pleasure. Davidson writes that he is translating *Parmenides* for your August issue.

I was glad to see your Art Essay on "The Last Judgment." It shows the value of philosophical studies for masterly criticism. I wish the North American may find any like it. Prof Matzers notice of your Journal will open the Eyes of your readers to the merits of American thought. It is clear that our Eastern scholars have ‖ nothing ‖ little to show that in skill and subteley [*sic*] can compare with the papers of the students of transcendental metaphysics at the West.

I have been compiling a book of Conversations given in various places during these last twenty years, and think of giving the MS. to Roberts Brothers for printing this autumn. They are wishing to get out a second edition of *The Tablets* also.

Next week come the Religious and Reform meetings in Boston. I am [in] doubt whether I shall attend them. Emerson is to read a paper to the Radical Club, and I believe Frothingham is to read one also. The Sunday Afternoon Meetings in Boston have proved a brilliant success and will doubtless be resumed in the coming autumn. Now if we had a weekly Journal our instrumentalities would be complete. And this will come presently.

Will you not come East again this summer. Come with time to compare thought with those of us, who do a little thinking.

I see Emerson but seldom lately.

Truly Yours
A. Bronson Alcott

Wm. T. Harris

[1] From a copy, in Alcott's hand, in the Alcott-Pratt Collection. The original is in the Alcott-Harris Collection in the Concord Free Public Library (see Appendix B).

LETTER 69–25[1]

[to Ellen A. Chandler, Framingham, Mass.]

Concord May 19th 1869.

Dear Miss Chandler,

Mr. Sanborn came up on Monday afternoon, fresh from the Club, and told us of the good Christian discussion that followed Emerson's reading. He thought he caught a glimpse of you there, but lost sight of you before he could speak to you. As he heard not a whisper from you during the discussion, we are left quite in the dark as to your creed—how largely mingled of Christian or Pagan pigments—and rather hoped—I, at least, do—that you have not curiously distinguished the tints, being so finely blended of the snow mixed with vermillion, that one might as properly enquire, *which was which?* on the cheek of your faith. I wait to learn what you will say of paper and comments, though I hear that Yerrington reported the whole for the Standard. But he cannot have done your part for me.

I failed again of attending.

Herewith find Mr. Edward King's "Concord" with Louisa's "Report" therefrom and thereof. King is of Sanborn's staff || of || in the Springfield Republican Office—has written a lively book, entitled, "My Paris," and is a bright youth of more than ordinary experience for his years.

If Louisa and I should take it into our heads to drive over to Framingham some fair day soon, what day of the week, will suit you best? She must not talk much, but would enjoy the ride, and, perhaps, a glance at the school.

I wish you would add another blossom to our Orchard.

Very truly
Yours,
A. Bronson Alcott.

Miss. Ellen A. Chandler

[1] MS. owned by the Abernethy Library, Middlebury College. A copy, in Alcott's hand, is in the Alcott-Pratt Collection.

LETTER 69–26[1]

[to Mary E. Stearns, Medford, Mass.]

Concord May 19th 1869.

Dear Mrs Stearns,

Think me not thoughtless of yourself all this meanwhile. Since I saw you last, at your own house, I have hardly been presentable,—have missed meeting the Radical Club for its three last sittings, and question whether I shall attend the anniversaries next week. As soon as I can properly leave my study and gardening, I purpose passing a day with you. And we shall think ourselves honored, as we shall be delighted, if you will guide your carriage wheels hitherward, any day. It is a long while since you have been in Concord. Will you not come and see how well Mrs Alcott is? And Louisa so hopefully healing those long standing hurts?—The very kindly reception her books have had from a growing public, proving a timely restorative.

We have read with interest Frank's letters in the Springfield Republican. Why should not the fruits of fair trees, bud and bear like fruits?

"In their good gifts, we hopeful see,
The fairer selves, we fain would be"?

Sanborn was here and spent a night lately. I hope you read his SemiWeekly sheet.

Let me thank you for your kind attentions to May, who is giving us much satisfaction by her enterprize and activity.

Very faithfully,
Yours
A. Bronson Alcott

Mrs. Mary E. Stearns.

[1] MS. owned by the Fruitlands and Wayside Museums. A copy, in Alcott's hand, is in the Alcott-Pratt Collection.

LETTER 69–27

[to Sidney H. Morse, Boston]

Concord May 20th 1869

Dear Sir,

I have read the M.S. and think it would be good reading for such of your readers as have not Margaret Fuller's writings at hand. And for those who have, this selection from them, and from her biographers, would serve to revive the memory of our best representative woman, of whom too much cannot be known by the friends of woman kind. For myself, I should like to see the paper printed (perhaps under a more appropriate title) in the Radical. I think the compiler has shown good judgment in her selections for illustrating Margaret's character and opinions.

What you write about the last Club, has shown darkly at times at some of the last meetings. Abbot and Phillips, perhaps mark its extremes. It is well these should come out distinctly. Huxley's God is by no means a lovely one: Jehovah grim as ‖ he was ‖ in Jewry even, were the more ‖ desirable ‖ companionable even. The Christian's amiable, almost human, but this covert theism, Positivism, nihilism, under any name sacred or scientific belongs not to thinkers and believers in a Pure Personal Mind.

Sanborn came up fresh from the Club and told us all about it. I hear that Yerrington's report of it is to appear in The Standard. Come up and let us talk over matters here at our leisure.

Very truly
Yours
A. Bronson Alcott.

Mr. S.H. Morse.

Letter 69–28[1]

[to Ellen A. Chandler, Framingham, Mass.]

Concord May 22nd 1869.

Dear Miss Chandler,

Here is Davidson's letter just come to hand.

Yes, there are many inducements to favor your calling and studies at St Louis. And you must judge whether you will forego the many you here enjoy at the East. I wish you could have both. But as this cannot be, I submit to your decision. I shall hope to have glimpses of you, whether East or West. "Westward the star of empire takes its way."

And it may be that New New England is for such as you. Freedom and a future it has at least. Nor could such a sequel as you describe follow the reading of a sage's paper, in any company gathered there to hear and discuss it. Morse wrote a dissenting note about the dispute, and Sanborn said the talk was much as you intimate in your note.

Certainly the opening for the study of Greek and German at St. Louis, is desirable, and the sympathy of the circle into which you would enter, would be an education. But I do not like to think of you so far away—rather hope some stroke of good fortune will yet bring you nearer, and even to Concord.

I question whether I shall go to any of the meetings in Boston next week. interested as I am in their objects and aims. Not that I am sick in the sense of your kind note, (yesterday received,) but of the sins you refer to therein. You feel much as I have when coming away from the last sittings which I attended.

I enclose also the first of King's papers on Concord.

Very cordially
Yours,
A Bronson Alcott

Miss Ellen A. Chandler

---

[1] MS. owned by the Abernethy Library, Middlebury College. A copy, in Alcott's hand, is in the Alcott-Pratt Collection.

LETTER 69–29

[to Thomas Davidson, St. Louis]

Concord May 28th 1869.

Dear Sir,

Yours came to hand, and I at once made your wishes known to Miss Chandler. She writes in reply—

"I would like the experience very much. The more I look at that side of the question, the more tempting it seems: but then it would be more from curiosity than inclination that I should go, if I went. I cannot "toil terribly" as my friends there seem to do. I have neither that sort of mental nor physical capacity. And with that element of desperate work taken out, their western life does not attract me. What should I do there in that circle without eyes? No. I am happy enough in my own New England, and find enough to do. My sphere is as large as I am, and it will grow as I grow. I would like to learn Greek and German, but the weakness of my eyes puts that quite out of question. After all they are only means.

"Yes there may be more freedom in The West," as you say, but after all the mind makes real freedom any where, and I am not much cramped by outside circumstances; the more I feel the bonds tighten, the more I must learn to get free of them. So I shall let the opportunity slip, hoping I am doing best. I thank Mr Davidson for his kindly mention of me to Mr. Harris."

I certainly wish Miss Chandler could have the advantages that your opening at the West offers. But, as you must perceive, desire rather to retain her here with us at the East.

With remembrances to all

Very truly
Yours
A. Bronson Alcott.

Prof Davidson.

[Letter to D. M. Wilson, Traveller Office, Boston; from Concord, between May 4 and June 4, 1869 (asking him to translate his notes of Alcott's lectures).]

LETTER 69–30[1]

[to Ellen A. Chandler, Framingham, Mass.]

Concord June 6th 1869.

Dear Miss Chandler,

The days of last week came and went without finding Miss Louisa in the mood for taking that ride to Framingham, as we had purposed. The two or three days of rain, 'tis true, left us but little choice. Whether the skies within and overhead shall be propitious for our ride during the coming week must be left to like chance to determine. I shall promote it by every persuasion of mine, with yours superadded, and we may be successful. We don't think Louisa is so much sick as worn by winter's cold and damp, which still persist in lingering out into genial June. Presently, she hopes to take to the mountains and snuff health and spirits, instead of this persistent capricious catarrh, now of six months irritation, cheating her out of temper and time, coveted for thought and creation. But these are coming at last, we trust, for her sake and New England girlhood generally.

As for myself, I am really seeable again, and fit to face a presence like yours, without shame, or diffidence, rather—if, indeed, I could be so rude ever, as to be deficient in that grace. Now, too, the anniversaries are past, and we have shared mind and manners alike. I am not sure but I might have adventured had I been presentable. The Club seems to have been attractive, ‖ and ‖ the Woman's meeting, and at Mr. Sargents—so was the Free Association as I learn from the reports.

I am almost tempted to ask *where* all that summer vacation of yours is to be passed. If a few days, at least, could fall into our neighborhood, *my* summer would promise fair and flowery.

I only glanced at Miss Moore when here last.

Ever yours cordially.
A. Bronson Alcott.

Miss Chandler

[1] MS. owned by the Abernethy Library, Middlebury College. A copy, in Alcott's hand, is in the Alcott-Pratt Collection.

LETTER 69–31[1]

[to William T. Harris, St. Louis]

Concord June 6th 1869.

Dear Friend,

I read Wasson's notice of your Journal in yesterday's Commonwealth with delight. I think it is about the first piece of righteous appreciation that has been volunteered by any one, and something that you must prize for its truth and honesty. Slowly, thoughtful minds are coming to see what you are purposing for thought, what you have done to invite your readers to partake of its values and advantages. I believe I wrote you my estimate of your masterly criticism of "the Last Judgment," and now Wasson writes his. Now I am desirous that you will publish your Introduction to Philosophy in solid form, as a sample of reasoned thought and true method. Let us have the *Organon* itself, that scholars and thinkers may quote, if not use, as authority, instead of parading some poor plodding mole of an Englishman's or Scotchman's improvement on Plato, Aristotle, Kant or Hegel. ‖ Baconized for practical uses. ‖ Is it not time that New Englishmen had done with that flitch of philosophy?

But I wished rather to tell you what good service you are doing for us Americans. Presently we shall suspect our depth of ignorance, finding how ignorant we are of our ignorance—that first requisite to knowledge itself.

Can't we find the way for concentrating the forces of thought in an Academy or College wherein young men and women may gain the uses and command of their gifts for the high ends of life and action. That were something to live for.

I have just taken your Round Table paper, omitting the first few paragraphs, for an "Introductory Critique," by William T. Harris" to my Tablets, 2nd Edition (when published)

Yours truly,
A. Bronson Alcott.

Wm. T. Harris

---

[1] From a copy, in Alcott's hand, in the Alcott-Pratt Collection. The original is in the Alcott-Harris Collection in the Concord Free Public Library (see Appendix B).

LETTER 69–32

[to Ellen A. Chandler, Framingham, Mass.]

Concord June 27th 1869.

Dear Miss Chandler,

As your "tumult and fright" are now past and leave you free to rest and dream, and

> "Feed this mind of ours
> In a wise passiveness."

Pray let nothing prevent your passing some days here with us. Louisa has gone to Canada for a month or so. But May is at home, and Mrs Alcott, hospitable as of old, to all friends, we shall enjoy our guest. Then here are wood and stream, Walden and Emerson. Any time most convenient to yourself will suit us—either before "The Fourth," or after, and if a Sunday came in the days chosen, we should be surer of Emerson.—May just comes in to say, she hopes it may be Thursday next, and your visit last over Sunday.

Have I now given you all of our attractions, and will you be flattered by them? I hold a wise silence as to chosen hours. Come and people these with your own pleasant self, with books and high discourse as the mood favors. I fancy we may have some delightful hours, and you shall be free to do just as you like—talk, or walk, or sit alone.

Concord is now in its loveliest attire, and unites with me in my invitation.

> "Did Nature e'er betray
> The heart that loved her?

Very cordially
Yours,
A. Bronson Alcott.

Miss Ellen A. Chandler.

LETTER 69–33[1]

[to Mary E. Stearns, Medford, Mass.]

Concord June 27th 1869.

Dear Mrs Stearns,

I have run up a long debt upon your patience and good will. Yet to show that I have not been thoughtless of you meanwhile, I enclose *a note written* more than a month ago. When May left home to spend a night with you but failed to reach Medford. Now she goes bent on seeing you there, and I on assuring you that I am not the less disposed to pass a day, and shall when nameless hindrances are overborne. My spring has been a very busy one here—all the days passed at home, having been but once to Boston since our return from Maplewood—not even to the Clubs and anniversaries. I imagine I am to sally forth again soon, and shall turn toward your house by a natural instinct. Now May passes a day with you and it seems to us that some fair fresh morning your strawberries and roses may consent to spare you long enough to ride to Concord as of old. Pray let May persuade you if I cannot. Mrs Alcott adds hers, and you are not insensible to her attractions as I have reason to know.

Very cordially
Yours
A. Bronson Alcott

Mrs Mary E. Stearns

---

[1] MS. owned by the Fruitlands and Wayside Museums.

LETTER 69–34[1]

[to Ellen A. Chandler, Framingham, Mass.]

Concord July 1st 1869.

Dear Miss Chandler,

No. the fates are propitious, if a little wilful, hoping to enhance their claims, doubtless, in taxing our patience meanwhile. But as soon after the 15th as convenient to yourself, we shall confide in your coming to Concord, and I, certainly, shall keep you as long as you will stay—what right has time to intrude impertinently in the matter, when so much that concerns him not in the least, is to be said or suggested?

Should any thing occur before that to make a later day more convenient to our housekeepers, you shall be informed in due season. I trust nothing will, and that, meanwhile, your Essay may speed fast and straight to the mark. Can you not bring the M.S. along with you?

Louisa writes from Canada where she is enjoying herself, though the weather is not yet all she had hoped.

Yours faithfully
and
Affectionately,
A. Bronson Alcott.

Miss Ellen A Chandler

¹ MS. owned by the Abernethy Library, Middlebury College. A copy, in Alcott's hand, is in the Alcott-Pratt Collection.

LETTER 69–35

[to Louisa, Rivière du Loup, Canada]

Concord July 4th 1869.

Dear Louisa,

We are in receipt of your three short notes—the last to Anna—and most glad to learn so favorable accounts of yourself and surroundings. I have read your picturesque description of friends and scenery, and can imagine you there very well content to be and remain during the pleasure season. You have the needed quiet—so very essential now—sensible companions in whom flows kindred blood, fresh scenery to stimulate fancy and restore jaded spirits. It is pleasant to think of you so happily placed and so contented. You will bring away health improved if not restored, spoils for romance, and the freed Genius, for future works. July and August are short time enough for all this.

We had the pleasure of seeing here, the other day, Mr. Fred Frothingham though he staid only long enough to describe the country about Riviere du Loup, and eat strawberries, being on his way to Cambridge and Commencement. He promised to come up again before he returned to Buffalo—will perhaps accompany your Uncle Samuel—who is expected some day this week. He preached in Cambridge, and Mr May preaches there to day.

May is having a visit from Amy Goodwin and playing off her mother's hospitalities on her Concord acquaintances generally, as she will doubtless write. I, too, am to have one little favor granted of that sort, on the 15th. when Miss Chandler is expected to pass a day or two.—

To-morrow is a great Temperance Celebration at Walden Pond—The celebrities are expected—Neal Dow, Dr. Miner &c.

I shall go to Boston—for the first time for ‖ three months ‖ 6 weeks on Tuesday or Wednesday next, and shall see Niles,¹ and Fuller. Proofs have been sent and returned as you desired.

Miss Waterman—now Mrs Lewis—from Chicago, and Severance, have just called and gone.

I am having uninterrupted days. My M.S. for the—book of "Conversations" is all ready for printing, and I shall take it to Niles on Tuesday. I think it deserves a reading. If found as attractive as Niles hoped, the book will go to press at once.

1869

The papers have sent you sick to Canada, and so "the Cost of an Idea" convalesces meanwhile they inform us.

If the mood prompts, address at least one letter to

Ever yours affectionately,
Papa.

Miss Louisa M Alcott
   Riviere du Loup, Canada East.

¹ Thomas Niles, editor for Roberts Brothers, Boston publishers.

LETTER 69–36¹

[to William T. Harris, St. Louis]

Concord July 24th 1869

Dear Friend,

I shall value any corrections, or additions which you make to the paper on Tablets. Omitting the first few paragraphs, I suggest beginning with

"Most people will be too busy" &c unless you choose to retain some parts, or substitute something original. We do not care to notice in any way "The Nation's" nonsense. I would send you the paper, had I a duplicate, and will ‖ now ‖ hereafter if you have preserved none. The second edition cannot appear till late in the year. I hear there is a favorable notice in the "Cincinnati Christian Quarterly" for July, but I have not seen it.

I enclose President Eliots advertisement of the new courses of Lectures to be given at Harvard College. Emerson, Cabot and Hedge have something to say, and their names present the College in a new light. You will perceive there are two vacan[cies] to be filled in the Philosophy course. Prof Fisher of Yale is named for the one, and Stirling ‖ has been written to ‖ for the other. Besides this, he is offered the Lowell Course, and the prospect of a professorship. He has been written to, and as he has cherished the hope of coming to this country, may avail of this opportunity. Your name has also been suggested, and Emerson I know is disposed to favor your claims to a place in the course. I wish it might be. Between Harris and Stirling we should stand the best chance of learning "the Secret of Hegel." I hope you will consider the matter. If not in this year's course, your turn should come in the next.

Henry James is advertised for a Book entitled "The Secret of Swedenborg. ‖ I am expecting the August number of your Journal now very soon. ‖

Kröeger's Translation of Fichte's Philosophy of Rights" I have *not* seen, nor "Philbrick's School Report." Philbrick has a Boston Board of School Committee men to humor, and a rather difficult place to keep. He fills it as well as any one could perhaps, and deserves praise. Next time I am in Boston, I shall try to see him. We must have a ‖ newspaper ‖ Journal for New-England, which is not pledged to please Boston. I am hoping to ‖ put ‖ see yourself and Sanborn sometime in the editorial charge of such an organ.

Miss Chandler has been my guest for the last week, and has but just gone. We have all been charmed with her beauty and brightness. She passed a day at Emerson's also while in Concord. Next time you come East we must visit

482

Framingham together, and see her in her School. Sanborn was here last Sunday. I hope you read his Semi Weekly Republican—the best paper we have in N. England.

Louisa is now in Canada, where she has been for the last month. Her *"Little Women,"* has been a great success, having reached its 20,000. copies. She has another book to appear next ‖ week ‖ month.[2]

By all means come East during the winter and stay awhile.

To all our friends remembrances.

Very truly Yours

A. Bronson Alcott.

Wm. T. Harris.

[1] From a copy, in Alcott's hand, in the Alcott-Pratt Collection. The original is in the Alcott-Harris Collection in the Concord Free Public Library (see Appendix B).

[2] *Camp and Fireside Stories (with Hospital Sketches).*

LETTER 69–37

[to Joseph Lyman, Jamaica Plain, Mass.]

Concord July 24th 1869

Mr. Lyman,

Dear Sir,

I must not commit these books to the obliging hands which brought them to me, without returning my thanks to yourself for the privilege of perusing them, with my excuse for retaining them so long from your library. But Plato is charming, and came to me in a charming manner. Besides I hoped from week to week to replace the volumes in the hands from which I received them. Now I do so. Yet cannot let our guest[1] leave my house without intimating to yourself and Mrs Lyman, the lively pleasure which her company and conversation have given us.

Truly Yours,

A. Bronson Alcott

Joseph Lyman Esq

Jamaica Plain.

[1] Ellen A. Chandler.

LETTER 69–38

[to Ellen A. Chandler, Jamaica Plain? Mass.]

[Concord, July 25, 1869]

To _____

My moments are not mine, thou art in sight
By day's employments and the dreams of night,

Nor dost one instant leave me free
Forgetful of thy world and thee.

Yet fair enchantress! 'tis not ‖ not ‖ thee, but thine
That charms me so: thy sibyl soul's outshine
But mocks my Senses, and reveals
My youth's fond promise that my age conceals.

July 25th 1869.

Concord.

LETTER 69–39[1]

[to William T. Harris, St. Louis]

Concord July 28th 1869.

Dear Friend,

I was yesterday in Boston to see publishers, and arrange for our Sunday Course of Lectures for the coming Season. We mean these to open in November and extend into the winter months. Our list includes most of last years, with your name and Mills' of Syracuse, and one or two others. We think the course will not be inclusive without your treatment from the standpoint of philosophy. Mr Morton,[2] our secretary, will write informing you of our wish, and asking for your subject and most convenient time to speak in the course. As you wrote of coming East this winter, we shall have additional claims on you. Pray let nothing interfere with your gratifying us, and more than any

Your friend
A. Bronson Alcott.

Mr Wm. T Harris.

[1] From a copy, in Alcott's hand, in the Alcott-Pratt Collection. The original is in the Alcott-Harris Collection in the Concord Free Public Library (see Appendix B).
[2] Edwin Morton.

LETTER 69–40

[to Ellen A. Chandler]

Concord August 1st 1869.

My Dear Miss Chandler,

Yes, " 'tis so much pleasanter to have a friend in one's study to talk with than to communicate by pen and ink." Yet even studies, I find, are not companionless after friends have talked in them and flown. Mine, at least, is peopled with pleasing memories of moments.

Not all mine, nor mine alone.
Though guest its threshold left so soon.

My Journal, too, is the richer for those days, and yours, ‖ you tell me ‖ I infer, opens with Concord. Well, I shall at least have ‖ won ‖ gained one desciple by commending the keeping of a Diary.

Emerson spoke praises again of his Sunday guest, as I met him yesterday on my way to the Post Office. I am beginning to be jealous,—shall I confess—lest he get the larger share, as he did on that walk on Friday evening. But we will be tender, and not break friendship over that gallantry.

I am pleased to learn that Mrs Leslie[1] has an "Emerson". I know not when I have enjoyed any words of a Naturalist like ‖ his ‖ her husband's Lowell Lectures. Would he not give one in the Sunday afternoon Course for the coming season? His name has been suggested, with that of Mr. Harris and the best of last winter's list.

Louisa returned on Thursday we hope refreshed and improved by her visit.

I enclose some slips to spare your eyes from the newspapers.

Yours affectionately
A Bronson Alcott.

Miss Ellen A. Chandler

---

[1] Susan Lyman Lesley. Her husband was J. Peter Lesley.

LETTER 69-41

[to Paulina W. Davis, Providence, R.I.]

Concord August 14th | 1869.

Dear Mrs Davis,

I am honored by your invitation to attend your National Convention at Newport on the 25 and 26th. It would afford me much pleasure and instruction to be present on an occasion that must bring together so many earnest advocates of human freedom, and upon a platform the broadest that human civilization has permitted since the lapse out of Eden.

But I fear to promise my self this happiness, and must leave the matter doubtful. Louisa is now recreating at Mount Desert. Should she return in season, and incline to accompany me, we may attend the Convention together. At any rate, we shall hope to visit Providence sometime during the coming autumn days, and avail ourselves of the pleasure of renewing our acquaintance with yourself and Mr. Davis, who is associated with an agreeable past, and whom, with yourself, I could wish to see oftener in Concord.

With much esteem,
Truly Yours,
A. Bronson Alcott.

Mrs Davis.

LETTER 69–42[1]

[to Julia Ward Howe, Newport, R.I.]

Concord August 22nd | 1869.

Dear Mrs Howe.

You invite my views on the subject of your proposed American Womans' Suffrage Association.

I am accustomed to defer to woman the questions that are properly hers. But as you ask, I venture a suggestion or two in reply to your request.

I take it for granted that the most advanced thinkers in England old and new, have conceded that woman's admission to full citizenship is the natural means of complementing our legislation, and thereby securing equality of rights to all members of the commonwealth. I think, too that most men have made up their minds to accept that reform, and regard the efforts of women to secure it with respect. Am I mistaken in my inference that men are as ready as women to promote it? Their attendance at the Conventions show no unwillingness to take part in the proceedings.

As to measures and instrumentalities for Furtherance, I value as ‖ most ‖ most efficient and readiest available

The Convention,

The Lecture,

The Press, and

The Conversation,

especially the last named, as being the simplest, the most natural, and in keeping with this humane reform. Consider the questions which woman's significance embosoms—questions not hitherto discussed with anything like the depth of insight now brought to bear upon them—questions, too, that court the protection of private treatment to be probed to their roots. The press cannot deal with them delicately; the pulpit touches them with reserve; while the lecture and Convention leave them also at a disadvantage before their mixed audiances [sic]. Surely the women cannot afford to overlook, much less dispense with, this graceful organ for diffusing information and the spirit of refinement that can soonest restore to the sexes, their personal rights in the family and the State. The closer the ties, the purer, that bind families together, the safer the countries' liberties. "Either Sex,' wrote Plato, without the other, is half itself." And Euripides: "Men need not try where women fail."—a compliment to woman's wit that man's discernment may gracefully accept, and gladly bestow. In all that refines and adorns mankind, it is universally admitted that she has led society—moulded it subtly ‖ after ‖ into her likeness. It were modest in man to inquire how far his failures in legislation as in character, came from excluding her counsels, and whether it does not especially become him, now that she claims her rightful place beside him, to accept joyfully her services in administering state affairs. Union is strength. It is the synonym of the American Idea. It is inclusive, and becomes the advocates of the largest liberty for all. It will be time enough to plead the measure of woman's deficiencies when those who have but the one advantage of preoccupancy of the field of legislation, shall have proved her services can be dispensed with with advantage to the Commonwealth. I trust your American Suffrage Association will be organized on the broadest principles and set its machinery in motion forthwith.

Very truly Yours,
A. Bronson Alcott.

Mrs Julia Ward Howe.
Newport.

¹ MS. owned by the New York Public Library. A copy, in Alcott's hand, is in the Alcott-Pratt Collection.

LETTER 69–43

[to Ellen A. Chandler, Framingham, Mass.]

Concord September 1st | 1869.

Dear Miss Chandler,

In a recent note, you speak of being unable to recall a passage from my Diary, which I read to you while you were here last. Here it is:

Landor's Biography.

"A more attractive volume I have not opened of late. There is a fascination in Landor's story. He seems to have been the victim of his temperament all his life long. I know not indeed when I have read a commentary so appalling as this life of his on the fate that breaks a noble mind on the wheel of its passions, precipitating it into the dungeons only to brighten its lights. His Genius was of impetuous wing, sure in its boldest flights, of surprising sweep and brilliancy. To him might be applied Coleridge's epithet of "myriad mindedness," so salient, so various, the sweep of thought. In dramatic power he reminds, indeed, more of Shakespeare than any modern writer: In his mastery of dialogue of Plato, in epic force of Eschylus. He seems to have been one of the Demigods of the Pagan Pantheon cast down out of place, out of time, restless even, and indignant at his fate.

"Heaven's exile straying from the orb of light. His stormful, wayward life illustrates in a manner scarcely less imposing than Napoleon's career, the recoiling fate in things. Of modern writers, he reminds me oftenest of Carlyle, whom fate scarcely less chains in its irons.—Of the four great minds of this century, Coleridge, Landor, Wordsworth—Carlyle alone survives and he appears to have done his work. Their greatness consists in their deliverance from the Scholasticism of their time, their clear perception of thought in its simplicity, and, together, they seem to have recovered for us, the light and learning of the Greeks and Romans. Goethe and Emerson come in for their share not less: It remains now for England, Germany, and America, to combine Occident and Orient into a consistent system, one with nature and the mind."—

I brought home from Boston on Monday "Henry Crabbe Robinson's Diary and Correspondence" just published by Fields and Osgood. Robinson was a friend of Landor's and gives much information of his times not before given to the public. The two books, Landor's and Robinson's should be read together.

By this time, I picture you as returned from the Alleghenies, and preparing for your School. When all is again organized for your term—then write a little word at your leisure.—Louisa and I think of a week's journey to Connecticut returning, perhaps, by way of Providence.

I must add my regret that I know not *when* I am to see you again,—*time* after all does trouble the absent, does it not? sometimes?

Affectionately
Yours,
A. Bronson Alcott.

Miss Chandler.

LETTER 69–44[1]

[to Franklin B. Sanborn, Springfield, Mass.]

Concord September 2nd | 1869.

Dear Friend,

Louisa and I think some of taking a journey to Wolcott, and if we do, shall take Springfield on our route. We may start next Monday. Whether Louisa will pause a train, I fear to enquire now, and must defer till we near Springfield. She is much improved in spirits, if not in physical vigor, and begins to think of resuming her pen again. Wolcott she has not seen since she was a child, and goes to picture the background of her new story. The "Little Women," have multiplied themselves surprisingly: her publishers now counting 23000 of them. The Hospital Sketches &c." are selling well. If health is restored she promises herself a busy winters' work. Her success has been a surprise, and very encouraging. The way to wide usefulness is fairly open to her: the celebrity she values little enough.

The bright incident in my summer has been Miss Chandlers' visit here for a week as our guest: we have enjoyed her company very much. She passed a Sunday at Emersons, and a day or two with her friend, Miss Moore. While here she read me a lively Essay of hers on "the Genius of Reading," which if she permits, I will send you when it appears in print.

There is an article by Harris in the August no. of his Journal,—"Elementary School Education" which I hope you will think deserves the publicity which your paper affords. He writes me that he intends coming East sometime during the winter. We hope to get a lecture from him in our Sunday Course. Most of last years' speakers are reengaged, with several new ones. Emerson declines. He is busied about his Harvard Course.

Landor and Crabb Robinson have been admirable summer reading.

Harris promises his revised Introduction to the new edition of Tablets, and Roberts Brothers have the M.S.S. "Conversations" in hand. The day for publication of these "Notes" and of "Tablets," is not determined.[2]

Concord failed of additional glory, so coveted, for Simmons, but this awaits him next trial.

Anna and the boys passed a fortnight with us lately. Mrs Alcott is very well and so is May. Come and spend another night with us when next in Boston. With kind regards to Mrs Sanborn and the children,

Most cordially

Yours

A. Bronson Alcott.

Mr. Sanborn.

[1] MS. owned by the New York Public Library. A copy, in Alcott's hand, is in the Alcott-Pratt Collection.

[2] The "Conversations" never was published; and the second edition of *Tablets* was to wait until 1879.

LETTER 69–45[1]

[to William T. Harris, St. Louis]

Concord September 2nd | 1869.

Dear Friend,

No II. for August has just come to hand, advanced sheets having come and been read as they arrived. This last is your most popular and readable issue. I have read carefully Kroëger's article on "Kant's System of Transcendentalism", and yours on "Elementary School Education." The "outlines of Hegel's Phenomenology" helps me to a clearer insight and comprehension of Hegel than any thing I before have read, and encourages me [word]. I shall look for more of it in coming nos. Weiss' verses are subtle and conceived in a philosophical spirit. Your article on "Elementary Education," should have a wider circulation than your Journal gives, and I have written to ask Sanborn to give it a place in his paper. It should go into the hands of College Professors, Superintendents of Schools and Teachers generally. What but superficiality and pretence can come of our present dismal drill and routine of studies?

I have not yet seen more than the advertisements in the London Journals of the Dialectical Club and their "Idealist," magazine. Emerson and Carlyle do stand for an Idea, and we shall be glad if any number of Englishmen, Old or New, can represent it in Club or Magazine.

In last weeks' "Semi Weekly N.Y. Tribune", I find a Letter of G Ripley's on "Herbert Spencer," whose guest *he* has been it seems, thinking you may not happen to see it, I send it enclosed. Ripley it seems is doing England for the Tribune, and is perhaps the best available man we have for that work. But alas! for us, when H. S. and his school of *Knownothingarians* lead the (so called) thinking of England. I fear New England is tinctured with it far more deeply than are aware. How far Emerson, Cabot, and Stirling (if he comes) have wit and weight to take out the stain remains to be seen.

I was glad to read Kroëgers' paper, and asked Emerson to read it carefully. He is very busy about his Harvard Lectures which come late in the course.

Our Sunday course opens in January with most of the last year's speakers reengaged, with some new ones. J. S. Dwight gives one on "Music as the Language and Medium of Religious Sentiment." We hope to have one from Lesley the naturalist. And yours we cannot forgo. Emerson is too busy, and declines.

The bright spot in my summer has been a week's visit from Miss Chandler, and Landor and Crabb Robinson have been admirable summer reading.

My "MS.S. Notes of Conversations" are in the publisher's hands, but the time for these and Tablets 2 Ed. to be published is not determined.

Louisa's "Little Women" is in its 23,000, and selling fast still. She and myself are thinking of a journey to Connecticut next week. She has not seen my native place since she was a child, and goes to get the picture for a background to her new story.

I shall be glad to hear from Mr Davidson on his return,

Very truly Yours,
A. Bronson Alcott

W. T. Harris.

[1] From a copy, in Alcott's hand, in the Alcott-Pratt Collection. The original, *dated September 3*, is in the Alcott-Harris Collection in the Concord Free Public Library (see Appendix B).

LETTER 69–46

[to J. N. Pardee, Southington, Conn.]

Concord September 3rd | 1869.

Mr Pardee,
Dear Sir,

Louisa and I think of visiting Wolcott, and may start next week, perhaps on Monday. But may not be able to take Southington on our route going or returning. If we can, we shall hope to find you there. At any rate, let us hope to see you in Concord when you are fairly established for your winters' studies at Cambridge. Call on your way out, if you find it most convenient

I trust you have had a profitable summer's work and learned much that will tell in your Divinity Course. Next to knowing is teaching, if teaching is not, indeed, the shortest way to knowing—the only one to *know what we know*. I owe to Bristol and Cheshire my initiation into the principles and methods of teaching, and this with no other teachers than my pupils and myself. Could I now begin a new career of practice, I see not wherein I could much better the one here first opened to me. Wolcott airs and scenery and simple people were negative forces, and so far harmless. I got all they had for me without effort, and have to thank Providence for being born out of harm's way, and coming to my calling with a simple heart and singleness of purpose, that, despite my ignorance, won for me some little success in life.

I have written late in answer to your full note of June 25th. but have been unusually busy this summer. My family are all well save Louisa whose health is improving we hope.

Yours truly.
A. Bronson Alcott

Mr J. N. Pardee.

LETTER 69–47[1]

[to Franklin B. Sanborn, Springfield, Mass.]

Dear Friend.   Concord September 8th | 1869

Thank you for your kind note of Saturday. We did not start for Connecticut on Monday, and shall not probably leave this week, Mrs Alcott having gone
to pass a few days with Anna, who is not quite as well as usual. But the trip to
Conn. is still in thought, and if time permits we shall hope to stop going out or
returning at Springfield for a train, perhaps for a night. Louisa's mood is imperative in the matter and cannot be foreseen.

Miss Chandler has sent me her Essay which I mail to you. Her Essay is
sensible and bright, and good for all to read. I should like to see whole, or in
part, in your Semi Weekly.

I also send you Abbots' Lecture. The call and doings of the Toledo Society
I think you have noticed. This, and the West Roxbury movements are significant of the undercurrent of free religious thought in New England and the West
especially. Our Sunday Evening's Lectures tell for Boston and the suburban
towns.

Most cordially
Yours
A. Bronson Alcott

Mr F. B. Sanborn.
P.S. The Pamphlets you may return to me.

[1] MS. owned by the New York Public Library.

LETTER 69–48

[to Fields, Osgood & Co., Boston]

Messrs Fields Osgood & Co.   Concord September 9th 1869.

I hasten to acknowledge the receipt of Mr May's book which came last
evening.[1] also to reply to your note of Sep. 1st. Much of the work the author
read to me in MS.—A book written in the spirit which characterizes this throughout, must commend itself to all right-minded readers, and will doubtless find such
all over the East and West, if not in the Middle states, and at the South.

As to the sale of any large number of copies here I cannot promise. Our
people are so near Boston, and read the advertisements so generally, that they
can obtain a book about as readily by ordering it of the publisher, as otherwise.
Still if you chose to send some copies on sale to the Postmaster, Mr. Whitcomb,
who retails school books and some others, it might fall under the notice of some
who might not see it elsewhere. The friends of Mr. May, living in our town,
will bespeak its reading.

A copy sent to the "Springfield Republican", would be sure of getting a good notice from Mr. Sanborn, once a resident here, and a friend of the authors.

Very respectfully
A. Bronson Alcott.

¹ Samuel J. May, *Some Recollections of Our Antislavery Conflict.*

LETTER 69–49

[to Caroline Sturgis Tappan]

Concord September, | 15[?]th 1869.

Dear Mrs Tappan,
Your son's tender tribute to your husband came to hand last evening. I have read it with great pleasure and have to thank you for it. Your husband is associated with some of the most interesting incidents of my life and times. He was a generous friend, and served me more than once in ways that showed his delicate humanity and kindness of heart. I must remain his debtor; the best return that I can as yet render being the respect which his admirable qualities of character inspired. I need not add how grateful is the testimony which he has left of his interest in our acquaintance. Virtues like his are imperishable. And you cannot ‖ have ‖ have enjoyed their fellowship so long without partaking of their beauty and immortality.
Your gift comes commended to me, besides, by happy memories of an acquaintance with yourself before I knew your husband.
I admire the simplicity with which your son has done his part.
When you come to Concord come with your children and see us. Mrs Alcott is now at Maplewood with Anna. Were she at home I am sure she would join me in her thanks and good wishes.

Very cordially
Yours,
A. Bronson Alcott.

LETTER 69–50¹

[to Ellen A. Chandler, Framingham, Mass.]

Concord September | 18th 1869.

Dear Miss Chandler,
Next to seeing is writing. And as I am denied the first pleasure, I take thankfully the second. Dr. Donne begins one of his letters to the Lady Goodyear thus charmingly:—
"Madam:
I am not come out England, if I remain in the noblest part of it —your mind. Yet I confess it is too much diminution to call your mind any part of England, or this world, since every part of your body deserves titles of higher dignity."

—I began with the intent of quoting no more, but the whole is so fine, so unlike any thing current now, that I am tempted to give it entire,—

"No Prince would be loath to die that were assured of so fair a tomb to preserve his memory: but I have a greater advantage than so. For, since there is a religion in friendship, and a death in absence, to make up an entire friend there must be a heaven too: and there can be no heaven so proportional to that religion and that death, as your favor. And I am the gladder that it is a heaven, than it were a Court or other high place of this world, because I am likelier to have a room there than here, and better cheap. Madam, my best treasure is time, and my best employment of that (next my thoughts of thankfulness for my Redeemer) is to study good wishes for you, in which I am by continual meditation, so learned that any creature, (except your own good Angel) when it would do you most good, might content to come and take instruction from

Your humble and
Affectionate Servant
J.D.

Amyens the
7 Febr year
1611."

How delicate the compliments and noble the sentiment with the fresh color of flattery that renders it rhetorically the more charming. I wish our New-England reserve had added any graces to the Old English frankness, and that I could feel at home in its stiff costume. But I cannot, and freely confess that I am more taken with compliments like Donne's, than the cold style and frosty sentiment of our time. Bettina may be too fanciful and extravagant, Goethe only somewhat too courtly, and less openhearted than were natural. Yet how much more graceful and attractive is that intimacy, than were it wrapped in the more decorous drapery of Boston manners.—Bashfulness is but a finer name for modesty—an accomplishment that nature loves to grace all his most charming things with. I wish my letter to blush beautifully, and court my friend's eyes as well as affections, by its coy diffidencies. Come to my heart kindly while standing at a distance; woo me by its glancing phrases, woo my friend, and teach us both how innocent is the pure heart, how sweet and precious Presence is—the serene heaven of Person how lovely.

So Donne to the Countess of Bedford:—

"Should I say I lived darker than were true,
Your radiation can all clouds subdue
But one, 'tis best light to contemplate you.

You for whose body God made better clay,
Or took soul's stuff, such as late decay,
Or such as needs small change at the last day.

This, as an amber drop enwraps a bee,
Coverings discover your quick soul, that we
May in your through-shine front our heart's thoughts see.

> You teach (though we learn not) a thing unknown
> To our hearts, the use of specular stone
> Through which all things within without are shown.
>
> Of such were temples: so, and such, you are;
> Being and seeming is your equal care,
> And Virtue's sum is to know and dare."

Wise moralist. Next time you come to ornament my study and me, we will open Donne. May that not be some one of these autumnal Saturday's with a Sunday forenoon in reserve? Come and listen; come and read the poets to me.

Your very excellent Essay—may I own it—is in Sanborn's keeping; only waiting a little for insertion in "The Republican." I meant to have surprised you rather with the sight of its reprint in this week's issue but must not longer delay its acknowledgment. It should have a wider circulation than Little Maine permits.

Those connubial rivers, of yours are not unhappily of New-England ancestry, though I rather like their wilder manners as does Bettina.—The more perhaps as a fancy take-off on its Charles—I had almost written Concord too, forgetting for the moment that Thoreau had fretted its lassitude, and Channing sung its patriotism.

> "_____ the English braves
> Flush with red jackets marched along the bank
> Of our slow river creeping to the sea.
> And said, doubt not, because the tide was slow,
> The rustics on its banks had hearts as slow."

I have to thank you for your very acceptable letter written since your return to your classes.

Louisa is much better and we still have our journey to Connecticut in prospect. May has just finished some pretty sketches of Concord scenery, which she may publish as "Concord Sketches."

Ever affectionately
Yours
A. Bronson Alcott.

Miss Ellen A. Chandler.

¹ MS. owned by the Abernethy Library, Middlebury College.

LETTER 69-51[1]

[to Ellen A. Chandler, Framingham, Mass.]

Concord October 3rd 1869.

Dear Miss Chandler,

Sundays are sweet sinners, so let me tell you how very gratifying your last Sunday's double sheet was. I wished, too, as I read of your return to your school, that I was in that "wonderful place" again, as at 25, with an associate of like "frame of mind" of my correspondent. It seemed as if something might be brought to pass worth speaking of out of School. For even then in my little school, I became persuaded that Ideas are the teacher's outfit, and felt "the poet and philosopher" budding forth from the stalk of my ignorance and inexperience. Rare gifts are requisite for touching susceptible youth to the finest issues. Even fair names and fine tones are charming influences. "Musical and pleasing," said the great teacher of Samos.

I shall like to hear more of the fair, bright-eyed Atalanta you have won to your assistance, and trust she is to compete more successfully against the bribe of the golden apples than her fabled namesake in the race.

Apropos of apples—here is today's Journal copied for you, with the added wish that you were here on the spot to select the sorts you best like.

"The last week has been sunny and Indian: only the maples along the brooksides suggesting thoughts of coming winter. The grapes hang temptingly in ripe clusters from the vines, and the apples redden the boughs. One is never satiated with sunshine: one tastes the three seasons under the ripened rinds of these fruits. Certainly the sun has done his best toward putting all spicy virtues into them, one sips Heaven's choicest juices distilled for his repast. Apples and grapes ripen at the same season. I imagine these were as they still are, God's Best and Onlys,—all others are but varieties. The berries are but grapes of the woods. Pears are Adam's apple tickled by man's art: as Peaches are Eve's,—these the only fruit that preserves most of Edens flavor and bloom. Pears plainly are gentlemen, peaches, ladies, less elegantly,—men and women.

It is remarkable, besides, that the apple and the grape have been tipples from Adam, first of gardeners, down to Noah, first of vintners, and his mellow descendents of our time. 'Tis the ever old-new-story, of clothed in other leaves, of tasting wantonly of divine delights. A sip of felicity is the most that mortals may safely take from any goblet.

I like best the witty Socrates way of telling the story.

"Some God, he says, more pitying than the rest, perceiving how all human pleasures and pains were intermingled, thought he could so mix as to confound them; but failing in this, he came as near to it as he could in advising eager mankind to sip but seldom, and from the brim,—thus permitting a taste of the unadulterated immortality which the chaste are here privileged to enjoy."

How much more gracefully told than in the Egyptian fable brought by dull Moses from King Phario's Court. So the Saxon Poet's version pleases more, though flavored rather too highly of King Solomon's.

> "Bring, bring me apples to assuage the fire
> That meanwhile scorches my consuming breast,
> Yet 'tis not every apple I desire,
> Nor that which pleases every palate best.
> 'Tis not the lasting Deusan I require
> Nor yet the red-cheeked Queening I request,
> Nor that which first-beshrewed the name of wife,
> Nor that whose beauty caused the golden strife.—
> No, no, give me an apple from the Tree of Life."

You shall call this, if you choose, The Hesperidean Leaf of the series.

Apple-picking is near at hand—a pretty Idyllic pastime still enjoyable. I have been these last days engaged in building an arbor under the pines on the hilltop overlooking the grape-trellis, and wherein it would please me to seat, (and proffer some clusters to,) the valued correspondent of whom one may dream pleasantly after she leaves his threshold.

Forgive these personal allusions, please, and write without wronging eyes or pupils, as the mood prompts—whether it chance to be semi-daily or centennially.

Very affectionately
Yours,
A. Bronson Alcott.

Miss Ellen A. Chandler

P.S. I enclose part of Sanborn's reprint of Harris article on Elementary Education, hoping some one of your friends will read it to you. Your Essay waits a little for room.

A.B.A.

---

[1] MS. owned by the Abernethy Library, Middlebury College.

LETTER 69–52

[to Ednah Dow Cheney, Jamaica Plain? Mass.]

Concord October 12th | 1869.

Dear Mrs Cheney,

If you will consider me as conditionally engaged to meet the N. E. Woman's Club at the time you name in your note, it would please me best. I should be sorry to disappoint the ladies a second time,[1] and fear to promise positively now. The opportunity is very inviting and I shall hope to avail my self of it. Meanwhile it would give me much pleasure to see you with advantages for conversation upon topics upon which thoughtful men and women are occupied as never before.

Louisa has thought of spending the winter in Italy. We have thought her improving, yet she is far from well, when, more than ever, health were an estate for her.

Very truly
Yours
A. Bronson Alcott.

Mrs Ednah D. Cheney.

[1] See Letter 69–17.

LETTER 69–53

[to Paulina W. Davis, Providence, R.I.]

Concord October 13th 1869.

Dear Mrs Davis.

Your kind invitation to attend your Woman's Convention next Tuesday and Wednesday, has just reached me. I wish it were convenient for me to do so, and that Louisa were disposed to accompany me. Though some better, she is far from well, and is thinking of spending the winter in Italy. But she has not fully determined whether to stay or go. Health and spirits were now an estate for her. Her book has found such surprising favor, and her publishers are so well disposed to print any thing which she might write.

You ask me to send you a word for woman. I wish I had ma[ny] good words for you. Such as I have were, however, better spoken than written by me, and in parlors rather than in Conventions, wherein I have, for the most part, hitherto, found myself ‖ rather ‖ out of place, and helpless as to furthering in the way of speech or resolution the good ends for which these were called. The Convention has a great work to perform, and women are using it admirably. Yet I please myself with the faith that they will not long forgo the still more effective instrumentality which the Conversation offers for discussing, under the freest advantages, the whole question of woman's relations, social and political. I offer this suggestion as the one that seems very important for the women to entertain, and which if carried into practice in our cities and towns, would in my judgment effect more than has been conceived by the friends of reform generally.

Regretting that I cannot serve you to something better

I am Very truly
Yours
A. Bronson Alcott

Mrs Paulina W. Davis

LETTER 69–54[1]

[to Ellen A. Chandler, Framingham, Mass.]

Concord October 19th 1869.

Dear Miss Chandler,

Shall I not have at least an hour or more of *You* during your stay in Concord? At any rate, let me have a glance and a word. I have not much to show for my Summer's work, but shall be pleased to make the best report of my days to you. Yet you must not permit me, (from courtesy) to intrude upon your pleasures.

Perhaps you will attend *our Church* on Sunday forenoon? That will be delightful, and very pious in you at least.

Louisa postpones her European journey till spring. I hope she will be in spirits to see you. May is very busy with her Classes, and *"Concord Sketches,"* most of which are photographed, and are really very beautiful. They will make a tasteful Gift Book, and discredit neither Concord nor the artist. Come and see how you like them.

> Very affectionately
> Yours.
> A. Bronson Alcott.

Miss Ellen A. Chandler.

¹ MS. owned by the Abernethy Library, Middlebury College. A copy, in Alcott's hand, is in the Alcott-Pratt Collection.

LETTER 69–55

[to Sidney H. Morse, Boston]

Concord October 19th 1869.

Dear Sir,

I have been too busy gathering my apples since your note came to hand, to look at my papers till to day. And now find nothing that you will desire for the "Radical." Something fit may, however, appear when I am free to look them over more carefully. My things do not take naturally a popular form suited for the general reader.

I am pleased to learn that you are to have something from Dr. Bartol, whose words always reward his readers. I hope his health is restored and that he will often contribute to your pages.

I had hoped to see you here during the summer, but you did not appear. I had a visit last week from two Divinity Students, who spoke well of their school and professors. Things move, and even old Cambridge has to lift its foot to a quicker step.

> Very Truly
> Yours
> A. Bronson Alcott.

S. H. Morse.

LETTER 69–56¹

[to Ellen A. Chandler, Framingham, Mass.]

Concord October 31st 1869

Dear Miss Chandler,

We close our house for the winter, to-morrow, and leave for Maplewood. I leave pleasant memories, and take pleasant ones with me, of your visits here, and look forwards to others when we shall return. Meanwhile, shall we not chance to come near in Boston, or elsewhere? I feel somewhat unwilling to date letters from any other place than *"Concord,"* but must consent to write Maplewood, or some other, for the four or five months to come.

I trust your adventurous voyage came to a happy end.

Cordially Yours,
A. Bronson Alcott.

Miss. Ellen A. Chandler.

¹ MS. owned by the Abernethy Library, Middlebury College. A copy, in Alcott's hand, is in the Alcott-Pratt Collection.

LETTER 69–57

[to William Henry Channing, Boston]

Concord October 31st 1869.

Dear Mr Channing,

I had hoped to return my thanks in person at your first Lecture, for your kindness in sending me tickets of admission. But I was unable and again on Friday last at your second. Next Friday Evening I shall hope to have that pleasure. Your subject is attractive, and one to which few of our time have given more thought, or can urge with a more fervid eloquence, than yourself. And it affords me great pleasure to know that you are again in Boston to press your theme at this auspicious moment.

Very cordially Yours
A Bronson Alcott.

LETTER 69–58

[to Franklin B. Sanborn, Springfield, Mass.]

Maplewood November 4th 1869

Dear Friend.

We closed our house on Tuesday last, and are here for the winter with Anna. Louisa and May have taken rooms at No. 43 Pinckney Street, where they purpose to pass the winter, though Louisa may go to Florida with her uncle Saml. J May, who thinks of visiting the Governor of that state, having married him lately to a young lady of Syracuse. Louisa is far from well, but hopes by abstinence from the hard work of the last years, to recover strength and spirits to resume her pen. May has been very busily engaged on her Book of *"Concord Sketches,"* which are to be published by Fields and Osgood, and are now in the hands of Smith the Photographer. There are 12 sketches, a vignette and tailpiece, with selected mottos from Emerson, Channing, Curtis, Thoreau, Ricketson, and Tablets.

Vignette—the one arched bridge.
1. *The monument*
   Hawthorne
2. *The Old Manse*
3. *The Wayside*

4. *Seat and walk*
   Emerson
5. *House*
6. *Summer House*
7 *Stairs inside of Summer House*
   Thoreau
8 *Hermitage at Walden Pond*
   Alcott
9 *House*
10 *Arbor*
11 *Woodland Estate*
12 *Concord River*
   TailPiece—Monument Street.

We think them spirited and picturesque and likely to please generally.

We had a pleasant visit the week before we left from Miss Chandler. Herself and Miss Moore rowed down the river from Framingham and back and injoyed their adventures highly.

Harris writes that he doubts whether he shall come East during the coming winter as he purposed some time ago. His last no. of his Journal is good. Read, if you have not, his article on *The True first Principle*. It is so short and comprehensive, that you might find place for it in the Republican," which you may mail hereafter to Maplewood.

I may take a turn West during the winter season, as far as St Louis. The Ladies of the N. E. Woman's Club have invited me to speak to them on the 29th of this month.

Mr Channing's Lectures are well attended I learn. I hope to hear him on Friday next on "China and the Chinese."

Mrs Alcott is very well and very happy here with Anna and her boys.

Remember me kindly to Mrs Sanborn and hers.

Very truly
Yours,
A Bronson Alcott

F. B. Sanborn.

LETTER 69–59[1]

[to William T. Harris, St. Louis]

Maplewood Novr 6th 1869.

Dear Friend,

We have closed our house in Concord and come to Maplewood, where Mrs Alcott will pass the winter with her daughter, Mrs Pratt. Louisa and May have taken rooms in Boston. I shall be here and there as opportunities open for me. A course of Conversations has been named in Buffalo, another in Toledo. Should these take effect, I might reach St. Louis. I can hardly hope for as busy a season here in Boston as the last, and should like very well to meet your circle again in St. Louis. On the 29th of this month, I am to meet the N. England Woman's Club," and hope to be ready to leave here directly after that. You are too busy with your official duties, to move in the matter. I remember you once named Mr. Kroeger. If you think the thing desirable and feasible, you may name it to him now. The summer has laid in a stock of strength that ought to serve me for some time to come. Just now, too, when a deeper interest in philosophical questions seems to be quickening the more thoughtful minds, I am the more desirous of mingling with mankind. Your last no. of *"the Speculative"* gave me much satisfaction. Your article *"The True First Principle"* contains the whole matter in a nut shell. I am delighted to know that a statement so comprehensively clear, and apprehensible, is written. Miss Chandler, who made me a visit lately, was charmed with it. I asked Emerson to read it carefully. James' "Secret of Swedenborg," proves to be no secret after all. James carries heavy clubs and mauls every thing he strikes at. I trust you have a word for him in preparation. He has never been fairly met by any master, and will enjoy a trial of weapons.

Remember me to your friends—in St. Louis.

Very truly Yours
A. Bronson Alcott.

* Little Women has reached its 30,000. And May has a Book of *"Concord Sketches"* in press of Fields Osgood & Co.

Wm. T. Harris,
St. Louis.

[1] From a copy, in Alcott's hand, in the Alcott-Pratt Collection. The original is in the Alcott-Harris Collection in the Concord Free Public Library (see Appendix B).

LETTER 69–60

[Ednah Dow Cheney, Jamaica Plain? Mass.]

Maplewood Novr 10th 1869.

Dear Mrs Cheney,

I was at the Womans' Club Room yesterday hoping to find you there, and say that, if still wished, I will venture now to promise a Conversation on the 29th. or at any day before that, if more convenient, as, after that date, I may leave for the West.

We have closed our house in Concord, and are now here with Anna as we were last winter. Louisa and May have taken rooms in Boston.

Very truly Yours
A. Bronson Alcott.

Mrs. E. D. Cheney.

LETTER 69–61[1]

[to Ellen A. Chandler, Framingham, Mass.]

Maplewood Nov. 14th 1869.

Dear Miss Chandler,

Lest I should miss meeting you at Louisa's room, (43 Pinckney Street) before

Friday next, when I purpose leaving for the West, I write a word just to say that in a country so wild and free something of interest cannot fail to prompt the pen to communication with those left at the East. I shall perhaps visit St. Louis and see your friends there. I cannot now speak of the extent of my journey, nor of the time of my return. The West has hitherto been unexpectedly hospitable to things that I entertain, and I may find it agreeable to pass the winter there. All the more will your words be welcomed in those Wilds, and the mails have a new interest as they arrive in the cities where I may chance to be staying at the time.

Mr. Channing is giving some interesting Lectures at the Lowell Institute. He sent me tickets. If you care to hear his next on Zoroaster, the Star-God of the East, come in on Friday evening and go with Louisa and May. He is a person whom you should see and hear once at least.

My Conversation at the Woman's Club Room is deferred till my return from the West. Mr. Channing may speak on the 29th. instead.

The Radical Club meets tomorrow at Dr. Bartols. Mr. Potter reads the paper. Mr Emerson, I hear is coming, and if I go, it will be to introduce Count Z_____ of Poland, to the company. He gave an interesting lecture on Poland, on Friday morning to the Woman's Club.

Very affectionately
Yours,
A. Bronson Alcott.

Miss Ellen A. Chandler.

---

¹ MS. owned by the Abernethy Library, Middlebury College.

LETTER 69–62

[to Franklin B. Sanborn, Springfield, Mass.]

Maplewood Novr. 15th 1869.

Dear Friend.

I have concluded to leave here on Friday of next week. 19th. (if possible,) and, if I knew you would be at home, might pass Friday night in Springfield. My wish is to reach Cleveland by the 24th. for the Suffrage Convention. I may pause for a train, or a day, at Syracuse and also at Buffalo. I may not be able to leave Boston till Monday morning; and so cannot stop long at any points on the way. You speak of leaving Springfield for the Convention on the 20th. which will be Saturday. If you should, we might go on together, at least a part of the way. Mr May may be going, and might join us at Syracuse if you had the Sunday to spare to spend with him and Mr Mills. I leave thus earlier than I first thought of doing, thinking I may find ‖ many ‖ persons at Cleveland, who may favor Conversations in their several places of residence, and may also find the way open for a tour for the whole winter season West. Besides, I shall like to attend the Convention and learn its temper and tendencies.

Address me at Cleveland where I may be for some days

Truly Yours

A. Bronson Alcott

Wm. T. Harris.[1]

[1] An error on Alcott's part. The letter was to Sanborn. "Cleveland" in the last sentence is probably also a carelessness.

[Letter to Louisa, Boston; from Cleveland, December 2, 1869.]

LETTER 69–63[1]

[to William T. Harris, St. Louis]

Cleveland, Ohio Decr. | 17th 1869.

Dear Friend.

I am to be here, or hereabouts, till after the holidays. Then I wish to go to Toledo, Detroit Ann Arbor and Chicago. But my route is not yet determined. At Elyria and Toledo I am engaged to give four Conversations, and to have four more here in addition to the five already given. I have been invited also to talk in ‖ Sydney, Dayton, and ‖ Bloomington, Ill. On my way to St. Louis, or returning from thence. I hope to pass a week in Cincinnati. When I shall come to St Louis will depend chiefly on the wishes and convenience of my friends there. I come without any pledges from them in any way, and shall accept gladly such hospitalities as they have opportunity and inclination to offer. I wish especially *to have as much of you,* as possible during my stay, which shall be longer or shorter, as yourself and friends may dictate.

I wish you would write, and tell me frankly how and when you are to be most at liberty to see me, and more than me, philosophy with me, personally and primitively. All the leisure at your command, I shall court, you may be sure. And in these fluent times, shall we not try a cast or two of Ideas which the times require?

I find it stimulating and invigorating, this eager and curious West. Unlike our East, which is mostly content with a dainty nibble at my things, the western people like a bold bait, and bite hard and ask for more of that sort.

If the hospitality thus far is continued to me as I go West, it must be spring, before I can well turn my face Eastward.

I go this afternoon to Elyria, an hours ride from here, to talk on "New England Authors."

Address me for the coming ten days at Toledo, Ohio, *care of* Israel Hall
Remembrances to friends at St. Louis.

Very truly
Yours
A. Bronson Alcott.

Wm. T. Harris.

---

¹ From a copy, in Alcott's hand, in the Alcott-Pratt Collection. The original is in the Alcott-Harris Collection in the Concord Free Public Library (see Appendix B).

LETTER 69–64

[to Thomas Kean, Buffalo]

Elyria, Ohio, Dec 25th 1869

Dear Sir,

I am to give a second course of Conversations in Cleveland beginning early
in January, and shall be in that city probably till the 10th. Should you have
any communications to make, or any enquiries, concerning some Conversations
in Buffalo, I shall be happy to hear from you, and to reply. I am to go from
Cleveland to Toledo, unless you arrange for me at Buffalo a course following the
one at Cleveland. This latter arrangement would, in some respects, suit me
better than one that should defer the matter till my return Eastward in February.
Still if the last, be preferable and more feasible, let the course come then. I
speak of finding a company in your city on the strength of your own and Mr
Frothingham's hopes.

I close a course here next Monday evening, and then go to Cleveland. Here
or there, I have had appreciative companies, and fair discourse.

Thanking you, for your kind interest in this matter, as for former attentions,

I am very respectfully
Yours
A. Bronson Alcott.

Mr. Thomas Kean.

ILLUSTRATIONS

Fruitlands, Alcott's "ideal community" dedicated to communal living, as it now appears. *(Courtesy Fruitlands Museums, Harvard, Massachusetts)*

1879.   1882.

CONCORD SCHOOL OF PHILOSOPHY.

FULL COURSE TICKET.

Admit..

To all the Classes and Lectures.

A. Bronson Alcott;

Dean of the Faculty.

Admission ticket, Concord School of Philosophy, founded by
Alcott, 1879.

Sketch by Alcott of "Hillside House," Concord, where the Alcott
family lived (see Letter 45–1) following the failure of the Fruitlands venture. *(Courtesy Concord Free Public Library)*

Mr. A. B. Alcott
June 1837.

Rev. R. Waldo Emerson,

Concord
Ms.

Holograph Letter 37–4 to Ralph Waldo Emerson. *(Courtesy Library of Congress)*

Boston June 6. 1837.

Dear Sir,

Not only on my own, but account of
Mr Fuller and friend, do I please myself with the hope of
hearing your good word, on occasion of a good purpose.
And yet, you must needs let special and local topics
slide into broad and general insight into things &
principles. Too much, the world suffers. Would you
believe it? I nestled last week foolishly, and scandalously
at these glorifying and glorified anniversaries. And
woe! to the world if it seek life or soundness from these
Quacks! Quackery! Poor sick, infirm, limited Humanity.
And these know nothing of the regimen that restores
sanity and soundness. Holiness! Holiness! the man of
Nazareth hath it; but not these. Now, dose! dosing!
and the Patient, special, half conscious of misplaced faith,
dies, faintly uttering "Physician heal thyself." Still
the same results; arms, legs, with sundry faculties
meant (or God worthiest) works at their service,

do flourish most lustrously in the light of Gods blessed Daytime, if perchance his kingdom shall be forestalled and taken by violence.

And Yet, I attended to some profit withal. too, to see the Straights of Humanity, as well as fullness, is somewhat. A Sage observer perceives, under all this hammer and word play, primal and irresistible instincts, which soever strive consciously or blindly, to compass the Possible. There yet lingers in all souls a belief in the possible perfectibility of outward and regular interests. And hence finite organs and instruments, are developed into some show, at least, of dexterity: the legs and arms work for somewhat. But open the eyes above them to perceive the occasions for securing the Inward and Divine, and then shall the infinite faculties be sharpened, and the soul use them worthily. Behold a Heaven! But the age of this age is holden; it apprehends not times, nor organs nor instruments, nor shall, till Some, Standing in its midst, preach the true Gospel of the Kingdom and restore it to light.

I intend accompanying you to Providence. I suppose you will reach Boston on Friday in season for the cars in the afternoon - 4 or 5 o'clock is the latest hour I believe. Please call on me at No 3. Temple Place if you pass that way before 1 P.M. or, should you wish, a word dropped at Munroe's would enable us to act in concert. Yet better: a word from your "Sanctum Sanctorum" at Concord, would shed light, meanwhile, whereby, I might discern the more vividly the aspects of "Psyche", with whom I am much in love - at this moment.

Most truly,

A. Bronson Alcott,

Holograph Letter 58–5 to A. R. Spofford. *(Courtesy Library of Congress)*

Concord 25th Jan, 1858.

Dear Sir,

I reached home on Saturday last to find my family comfortable; my daughter Elizabeth, though feeble very, still better than I expected to find her and hopeful of recovery.

Bradbury's company at Cleveland was very good and came to take the good parts for the three evenings.

This morning's mail brings me the "Cincinnati Daily Enquirer" newspaper containing the paragraphs on "Mr Alcott's Conversations." or Echoes of Emerson; and so rather good bad praises of them.

We crossed Walden Yesterday, Emerson, his children and myself, the ice being solid and supporting to the Idealist's feet as he glided across and struck into the woodpaths on the opposite shore. Last evening

I saw Thoreau, who is
trenchant and masterly
as ever. He had been reading
some papers in drawing
rooms to a good company
lately at Lynn.

I enclose the overplus
of money, with my thanks,
to yourself and friends for
their interest in our hasty
evening's performances. I
am to go to Lynn and New
Bedford presently.

The

The weather is mild and sunny
today, and the fields have
the air and port of Spring.

Very cordially
Yours,

A. Bronson Alcott.

J. R. Spofford Esq.

Cincinnati

Detroit February,
1st 1870.

Prof Tyler,

Dear Sir,

Being here for a
few days, and wishing to visit
your University before turning my
face eastward, I venture to
enclose my daughter's Photograph.
having heard her speak of the

upper side

Holograph Letter 70–2 to Moses Coit Tyler. *(Courtesy Cornell University Library)*

acquaintance which she made
with yourself while returning from
England a year or more since.

I also enclose a card or two
of Subjects for Conversations
which I have held in several
Cities West.   It would please
me to meet any companies wishing
such interviews in your City.

My engagements close here
next Friday evening.

If you care to advise me
in the particulars of your wishes,

and the opportunity were
fairly open for Conversation
in your Place. Where
address to the care of
"Louis T. Ives Esq. Detroit."
will find me.

Most respectfully.

A. Bronson Alcott.

PART EIGHTEEN

1870–1871

LETTER 70–1[1]

[to Benjamin B. Wiley, Chicago]

Cleveland, Ohio, Jan. 7th 1870.

Dear Sir,

  I am to be at Toledo sometime during this month to give some Conversations there, and might come to your city, if I knew that a company might be drawn together. My reception has been very flattering in this place, in Elyria, Tiffin, and I am to converse in Akron, and Sandusky City before I go to Toledo; at Detroit and Ann Arbor probably. Mrs Livermore and perhaps Mr. Collier, are away from Chicago. But I have supposed there are other persons, who might be disposed to promote a course of Conversations there.

  I enclose a card of our subjects here and at Elyria. But these may or may not be chosen in different places. For four Conversations the terms here have been two dollars, or fifty cents for a single evening.

  If you think favorably of having a course of Conversations in Chicago, and will drop me a line at Toledo, care of Israel Hall Esq. I shall feel greatly obliged.

Very Truly Yours,
A. Bronson Alcott.

B. B. Wiley Esq.

[1] MS. owned by the Fruitlands and Wayside Museums.

LETTER 70–2[1]

[to Moses Coit Tyler, Ann Arbor, Mich.]

Detroit February, | 1st 1870.

Prof Tyler,
Dear Sir,

  Being here for a few days, and wishing to visit your University before turning my face eastwards, I venture to enclose my daughter's photograph, having heard her speak of the agreeable acquaintance which she made with yourself while returning from England a year or more since. I also enclose a card or two of Subjects for Conversations which I have held in several Cities West. It would please me to meet any companies wishing such interviews in your City.

My engagements close here next Friday evening.

If you care to advise me in this particular of your wishes, and the opportunity were fairly open for Conversation in your place, letters addressed to the care of

"Louis T. Ives Esq. Detroit,"

will find me.

Most respectfully,
A. Bronson Alcott.

¹ MS. owned by the Cornell University Library. A copy, in Alcott's hand, is in the Alcott-Pratt Collection.

LETTER 70–3¹

[to William T. Harris, St. Louis]

Chicago, 22nd. February | 1870.

Dear Friend,

I am called East sooner than I had expected to be, and must forgo the pleasure of visiting your city for the present. My daughters, Louisa and May, embark for Italy early in March, and I hasten to see them set sail. Another season, I trust, will bring me West again and to St Louis, with fuller opportunity for Conversation than this has favored.

Meanwhile, much must transpire in the worlds of thought and affairs to interest and promote frequent correspondence between us. And may I not hope to see you in Concord during the summer?

My reception in the Cities West, has been most flattering and such as to lead me into these parts again. Here, especially, I am having most cordial acceptance. I spoke last Sunday evening in Laird Colliers' Church to a full audiance [sic], and meet Robert Collyers' friends to-morrow evening. To-night I have a Conversation on "Woman," I gave one last evening on "Concord Authors.'

Address me at Buffalo, care of Thomas Kean, Buffalo Courier, during the coming fortnight. I leave on Thursday for Detroit.

Remembrances to Friends in St. Louis.

Yours cordially,
A. Bronson Alcott

Mr Wm. T. Harris

¹ From a copy, in Alcott's hand, in the Alcott-Pratt Collection. The original is in the Alcott-Harris Collection in the Concord Free Public Library (see Appendix B).

LETTER 70-4

[to Charles D. B. Mills, Syracuse]

Maplewood March 20th 1870.

Dear Friend,

Yours with the money enclosed came to hand yesterday. I really do not recollect what the sum was which you put into my hands after the last Conversation, and will retain the $1.50. thanking you for your hearty interest in promoting the Conversations.

I reached Maplewood, where Mrs Alcott has spent the winter with Anna, on Wednesday, a week since, and found all well.

Louisa and May are to sail from New York in a Havre steamer for Brest, on the second of April. Louisa has recovered her voice, and though not free from some of her ails, is able to go abroad. May is well and full of hope and adventure.

I am well pleased with my Western tour and hope to renew it another season.

Regards to Mrs Mills and your son and daughter.

Yours sincerely
A. Bronson Alcott.

Chas. D. B. Mills,
Syracuse. N.Y.

LETTER 70-5[1]

[to William T. Harris, St. Louis]

Maplewood March 28th 1870.

Dear Friend,

I reached home on the 8th.[2] and have been interested since in assisting my daughters about preparing for their European tour. They sail on Saturday next from N. York. and may be gone a year or more.

In April, Mrs A. and myself return to Concord. I have not seen Emerson. He is busied I learn in preparing his lectures for the Cambridge Course. He begins to read in May. His course includes "The Natural History of the Mind." So we shall get his Metaphysic at last. Wm. Henry Channing is here. He is reading his Lectures (first given in the Lowell course) in parlors, and to great acceptance. He wishes to edit the Sacred Books of the Races. He may return to England, though preferring to remain here. Dwight spoke yesterday in the Sunday afternoon course on "Music, its relation to Culture and the Religious sentiment'. Channing follows next Sunday. The Radical Club continues its monthly sittings, I have attended none of these lately.

My winter's tour has been very gratifying. I have had good hearings and a better acceptance than I could have expected. The way seems opening for other seasons under better advantages. Mr. Ives of Detroit has taken upon himself the Agency to arrange a series of Conversations and Readings for me, from Syracuse to Chicago and from Chicago to St. Louis and Cincinnati. Emerson and Mrs Howe may be included in the arrangements. Besides Conversations and Parlor

Readings, Sunday Lectures, are included also. I spoke in several Churches—in Toledo, Detroit, Ann Arbor, Battle Creek, Chicago, Syracuse, and to good acceptance. Emerson and Mrs. Howe would have like opportunity if they choose to speak.

Your letter of the 15th reached me here. I hope you are getting some respite from the fight, and am sure you are to come out victorious. Have you had letters from Supt. Rickoff of Cleveland?—a thoughtful educator and ready to adopt improvements. Judge Pillars of Tiffin, Ohio, spoke of writing and subscribing for the Speculative." He is the most brilliant thinker that I encountered at the West. Ask Stallo about him.

Your January no. is one of your richest. Every article is excellent. Did you see Sanborn's notice in the Springfield Republican? He has also a notice of my Western tour—"Bronson Alcott at the West." If you do not see the Republican, I will send you, these notices.

Did I tell you that Prof. Hiram Corson of Annapolis, Md. had translated "Spinoza"? I see advertised ‖ a translation ‖ an edition of Berkeley's works. I did not find Abbot an Idealist. He seemed to be lingering in British Rationalism if not touched somewhat with Comte. But I think he will find his way out and come into clearness. I had better acceptance with other seekers than Unitarians, and found quite as much sympathy with the Orthodox as with the Latitudinarians—rather more. We shall never build a Church without *a God-Man* for its basis and Personality. Every religion has had its God-man, and only then can the God-head be revealed in His fullness to all mankind. Philosophy may take the man away, but must restore him at once to sense, as to thought, or philosophy fails and falsifies its high trusts. I look for the synthesis and ground that is to unify and found the Church of the future.

It was a great disappointment to turn homewards without seeing you and St. Louis. Come and see me as soon as you can run away from your cares and perplexities. Never was there more hope of a future than the one now before us!

Mr Kroeger has sent me his translation of Fichtes' Science of Knowledge. I must write my acknowledgement and regards. It is sometime since I had a word from Prof Davidson whose letters are always most acceptable. To him my remembrance, also, to Miss Brackett.

Very Sincerely
Yours
A. Bronson Alcott

Wm. T. Harris.

---

[1] From a copy, in Alcott's hand, in the Alcott-Pratt Collection. The original is in the Alcott-Harris Collection in the Concord Free Public Library (see Appendix B).

[2] According to the preceding Letter 70–4, Alcott reached Maplewood on Wednesday, March 9.

LETTER 70–6[1]

[to Ellen A. Chandler, Framingham, Mass.]

Maplewood March 29th 1870.

Dear Miss Chandler,

Your kind word of welcome was "welcome home" to me. And but for preoccupation of thoughts of seeing Louisa and May made ready to embark for Europe I should have written an earlier response. They passed last night here, and left this morning for 43 Pinckney St. They leave early Friday morning for New York to go aboard the steamer LaFayette, which sails for Brest on Saturday. I wish Louisa were in better health and spirits, but am consoled in the hope that she is under weigh to find them in a foreign climate. May takes both along with her, with happy expectations—the fulfilment of long cherished dreams.

When the girls are fairly afloat, I shall have the larger freedom to resume our pleasant correspondence. I have pleasant things to tell of my tour west. And shall like to listen to what you have to communicate during the four months that has passed since I had the happiness to speak with you. When shall I have a return of that pleasure? If I dared promise, I would say that I would visit you and your school at Framingham. But I must not.

We purpose returning to Concord about the first of May. Mr Emerson I have not yet seen since my return. I think of passing next Sunday in Concord.

My kind regards to Miss Moore.

Affectionately Yours
A. Bronson Alcott.

Miss Ellen A. Chandler.

[1] MS. owned by the Abernethy Library, Middlebury College. A copy, in Alcott's hand, is in the Alcott-Pratt Collection.

LETTER 70–7

[to J. N. Pardee, Cambridge, Mass.]

Maplewood April 1st 1870.

Dear Sir,

I shall be pleased to see you here, at my son-in-law Mr. Pratts,—where we shall be for the coming three or four weeks, and after that at our house in Concord. If you come out here, you will take the Saugus branch at the Eastern station, near the Fitchburg, in Boston. I am often in Boston and should be sorry to have you miss finding me at home. If you would drop a line advising me when you would come, I would be at home.

My tour West was one of pleasure and opens the way for future opportunities. The Western people have sharp appetites and bite eargerly instead of nibbling at the fruit you offer them.—I came home in better health and hope than I left last November.

I had to pass my sister again without seeing her,[1] but must take her house on my way out West next autumn.

Louisa and May left this morning for New York to take the Steamer for

Brest, which sails to-morrow. "The Old-Fashioned Girl" is published to-morrow—12,000 copies having been sold in advance and 4,000 more are printing.

I hear favorable reports by the Divinity School and hope to visit Cambridge presently. I was at Concord one day this week, and found Emerson busy with his University lectures.

When you come to see me, I shall have much to tell you about East and West.

Very truly
Yours,
A. Bronson Alcott

Mr. J. N. Pardee
    Divinity School
        Cambridge.

---

[1] Betsey Pardee, West Edmeston, N.Y.

LETTER 70–8

[to Charles Warren Stoddard, San Francisco]

Concord April 1st 1870.

Dear Sir,

On returning from a tour of four months at the West, I find yours of Feb. 24. with the pleasing verses enclosed. The Overland Monthly for April containing an article of yours has not reached me. I shall be pleased to read what you have written of the mistake of Missionaries in dealing with the instinctive faiths of the Islanders. Better leave them to their natural notions if we cannot quicken the instincts to spiritual intuitions. A God-Man seems essential to all races, and one with whom heart and head can come into sympathy, alike in feeling and thought. I have yet to learn of any race destitute of Theistic Ideas, and a moral sense.

I have not seen the Tablet, No. XV. as published in the Galaxy, to which you allude in your letter.

Be assured that whatever promotes a better acquaintance between East and West, I shall hail with pleasure and hope.

Very truly
Yours
A. Bronson Alcott.

Chas. Warren Stoddard,
    San. Francisco,
        Cal.

LETTER 70–9

[to Rowland Conner, Boston?]

Concord April 23rd 1870.

Dear Sir,

On returning from Plymouth, where I had past some days,[1] I find your note inviting me to open the Conversation at the May meeting of the Radical Club. I have many pleasant associations connected with the earlier discussions of the Club to draw me thither. But find that I must decline the invitation, as I am likely to be out of the State at the time of your meeting.

Very Respectfully
A. Bronson Alcott.

Rev. Rowland Conner,
    Secy.-Radical Club.

[1] With B. M. Watson.

LETTER 70–10[1]

[to Ellen A. Chandler, Framingham, Mass.]

Concord April 25th 1870.

Dear Miss Chandler,

Yes, come and see me soon, and welcome! The May-month is almost here; and if not to be found in field and wood, the buds may at least disclose to grace our interview. My study is ready to welcome our guest, and some six months' experiences supply themes for conversation. If it could happen of a Sunday, we could hold our Church apart and devoutly. So come and give me all the time you can spare from your friend, Miss Moore, while you stay. We shall miss the voyagers the less now safe in sunny France. They had a short passage of ten days from New York to Brest, and we are expecting letters by the return steamer, now nearly due. It will be good news when it comes.

I feel much as you write about the Horticultural Hall Sunday Lectures—not one of which have I heard. Nor have I been at the meetings of the Radical Club since my return from The West. Its earlier discussions were attractive and profitable, but the latter were not, and I have just declined an invitation to open the Conversation at the May meeting—the last of the season.

Mr. Emerson opens his University course of lectures this week. He is to give eighteen in all—three a week. They will be suggestive and edifying, and something new for Cambridge. I, too, am invited to meet the Divinity students at their Hall, and shall gladly, if the faculty countenance their request. So Cambridge and Concord may pledge faiths in all kindness, if not in sympathy entire.

Mrs Alcott and myself are sole occupants of our house just now, but we are expecting a housekeeper next week.

Affectionately Yours
A. Bronson Alcott.

Miss Ellen A. Chandler.

¹ MS. owned by the Abernethy Library, Middlebury College. A copy, in Alcott's hand, is in the Alcott-Pratt Collection.

LETTER 70–11

[to Benjamin Marston Watson, Plymouth, Mass.]

Concord May 1st 1870.

Dear Friend,

Your bale of bounties came safe to hand on Thursday and the trees are set fitly about lawn and hillside—a picture for time and the seasons to touch and complete.

The new pear and parcel were delivered to Emerson as you requested. I gave him the proper particulars as he inquired about them and the giver.

I retain very pleasant memories of my recent visit to Hillside, and must pass that way more than once before we climb[?].

When leisure permits Mrs A's flower seeds, and Mr A's sweet herbs

"That gladly cure our flesh because that they
Find their acquaintance there,"

may be sent to swell our debt of benefits.

Channing was here the first time since our return on Friday evening to tea and gossip. He was in a particularly pleasant mood, almost to "abandon," if the Tales[?] had permitted.

Faithfully Yours
A. Bronson Alcott.

Benjamin M. Watson,
Old Colony Nurseries

LETTER 70–12¹

[to William T. Harris, St. Louis]

Concord May 20th 1870.

Dear Friend,

The April No. of the Journal of Speculative Philosophy has come to hand since I wrote to you. I find good matter for thinkers in it. Your paper on "Immortality reached me in sheets. I have read it again with interest and profit. "The Philosophemes, Book Classification and translation of Hegel's Science of Rights, Morals and Religion also.² The No is an excellent one.

R. Randolph³ has sent me his writings for the last three or four years. With subtle merits, they do not specially interest me. I have written more than once and implied as much, but he persists in challenging my criticism.

Dr. Bernaze[?] came while I was in Boston. But I had an hour or two with him at the Hotel. Had we been fairly settled here, we should gladly offered hospitalities.

I have been wishing to call on Mr. Howison,[4] but have not found it convenient when in Boston. I hope to invite him here to spend a day soon.

We have good news from Louisa and May. They are spending this month in Brittany France. The "Old Fashioned Girl" is in its 30000.

Your inquiry about a house inspires the hope that you may be a neigbor of ours. 'Tis too much to hope for, "my cup would overflow."

There are half a dozen places here for sale, prices varying from $3000 to 7000. I think Hawthornes adjoining mine could be had for $3000, or 3500. There are about 20 acres and a house that he spent $2000 or more in repairing on his return from England eight years ago. There are eight acres of arable land in front, and the rest in wood, behind the house. My neighbor Moore offers $100 an acre for the eight adjoining his land, should the purchaser of the place wish to part with it.

There are several places in the village, some of them very desirable for a scholar—with a garden and orchard attached.

Come and look at them at once. There are so many things in prospect, that, with you here in Concord, I should live out my century.

Mrs Alcott desires me to say that *half of our house* is at your service should you choose to come and occupy with us.

Very cordially
Yours
A. Bronson Alcott

Wm. T. Harris.

---

[1] From a copy, in Alcott's hand, in the Alcott-Pratt Collection. The original is in the Alcott-Harris Collection in the Concord Free Public Library (see Appendix B).
[2] All by Harris. Alcott's "Philosophemes" did not appear until 1873.
[3] Richard Randolph, of Philadelphia.
[4] George Holmes Howison, who had recently moved from St. Louis.

LETTER 70-13

[to J. J. Locke, Greenfield? Mass.]

Concord June 4th 1870

Dear Friend,

I was in Boston yesterday and spoke to Dr. Smedley concerning yourself. He asks no fee for examinations, and will gladly meet calls after Monday next. I shall be at his rooms on Tuesday forenoon and again on Thursday. If you are able and inclined to submit to an examination on either of these days, or any day after, you will only need call and give your name, having perhaps to wait your turn, in his rooms.

After an examination you can better determine about being treated by him.

513

I should think Mr. Fulsom would assist, if Dr. Smedley speaks favorably of your case.

I will bring the most contributed by friends at Florence,[1] if Mr Hunt wishes me to speak there in July.

The Anniversaries were suggestive of sympathy and union.

Since I saw you my cold has been severe, but is softening.

Very truly
Yours
A. Bronson Alcott

J. J. Locke
Greenfield[?]

---

[1] In Massachusetts, a few miles northwest of Northampton. Alcott visited there several times at the invitation of Seth Hunt.

LETTER 70–14[1]

[to Ellen A. Chandler, Framingham, Mass.]

Concord June 6th 1870.

Dear Miss Chandler,

This delay in coming promises the longer stay when you are fairly here. A visitor who comes seldom should not fly away forthwith. And 'tis a comfort to catch one now and then who has a little leisure in her, and is deaf the while to the Engine's whistle. "Stay" is a charming word in friendship's vocabulary. And if one cannot stay in Conversation let him go and travel to the ends of the earth— if he is not there already. I like to take my friends leisurely and by sips, not at a hasty draught or two, as if they were froth and would evaporate forthwith.

If I know that you purposed coming next Saturday, I should not go to Boston, but be at home to get a sight and sip on Saturday evening. Sunday, I am to have you all the morning and as much longer as you will stay. But come when most convenient to yourself. I am to be at home every Sunday in the month, and free to see you. And June is the season for society and friend ship.

Louisa and May were still at Dinan in Brittany, where we last heard from them. They were enjoying the fine climate and picturesque scenery. Louisa was improving in health and spirits. Come, and let me read from her letters.

Very cordially
Yours
A. Bronson Alcott.

---

[1] MS. owned by the Abernethy Library, Middlebury College. A copy, in Alcott's hand, *dated June 5*, is in the Alcott-Pratt Collection.

LETTER 70–15

[to Mrs. Ely, Elyria, Ohio]

Concord June 10th 1870.

Dear Mrs Ely,

I am late in acknowledging yours dated May 15th. conveying to me intelligence of Mr Reddingtons' decease. The colds which I escaped mostly while journeying at the West, caught me here and I am just recovering from a severe influenza which leaves me without spirits to convey my sympathy to yourself and Mrs Reddington. Nor have I found words of much avail on occasions like this.

Mr Reddington's acquaintance was a great pleasure to me. He made a deep impression upon me by his singular probity and manliness. He seemed to be a missionary of light and freedom wherever he was. His magnetic influence over persons of different ages and dispositions was a constant surprise to me. I owe no small share of the favors I received in the cities and towns in his neighborhood, to his kindly introductions. Need I add that with all that is associated with Elyria of kindness and hospitality his absence must render the place no longer what it was to me. Elyria must feel his loss.

Mr Kenyon, too, has left you. I doubt not he finds a fairer field at St. Josephs, where I shall hope to find him on my tour West.

The same mail that brought yours brought me also a letter from Miss Della. She wrote in hope and spirits—in the enjoyment of opportunities long sought. I shall be passing Greenfield in July and hope to see her.

Louisa and May are now in Brittany, France, where they have been passing the last six weeks. They purpose going to the Italian Lakes and passing the winter in Rome. Louisas health is improving, and May is charmed with the country. Louisas "Old Fashioned Girl has met with unexpected favor, having reached its 30thooo.

Mrs Alcott and I have been here since the first of April. If you come East this season, we shall expect to see you here.

My journey West was most satisfactory. I now purpose leaving early in October for a tour perhaps to California. Be sure I shall pause at Elyria.

With cordial regards,
Very truly
Yours,
A. Bronson Alcott

LETTER 70–16

[to Fields, Osgood & Co., Boston]

Concord June 10th 1870.

Messrs Fields Osgood and Co.,

I find "Hawthorne's English NoteBooks" pleasant reading for these June days. We can never have too much of England from any lover of it. Mrs A. has also enjoyed his descriptive sketches of the Old Country—for which she has even his fondness—and writes with me in thanking you for the Books.

Few of his contemporaries have observed with finer eyes than did our American Romancer. His facts are better facts than most historian's, since he dealt with life and living things as only poets can.

I hope the Italian NoteBooks are to follow these soon.

Very truly Yours,
A. Bronson Alcott.

For Mr. Fields

LETTER 70–17

[to Mrs. Bagley, Lansing, Mich.]

Concord July 12th 1870

Dear Mrs. Bagley.

Your note reached on Saturday, and in reply I have to say the "The Conversations" have not gone to press, nor is it likely the book will be republished at present. Publishers here are disinclined to venture a new edition. ‖ at present. ‖ So we must wait. But I trust not long. I doubt not the book would find favor, especially at the West, where life is lived in a fresher spirit and new Ideas and methods are seized with avidity.

I have very pleasant recollections of my visit in your city—at your hospitable home particularly—and look forward with hope to a renewal of our interviews next autumn.

Mr Ives made us a short visit in May, but I was unable to enjoy his stay with us, as I wished. I am now partially restored, and hope to be able to leave for the West early in October.

I think it doubtful about Mr. Emerson finding the time for the Readings, as we hoped. Mrs Howe will like to do so, and Dr. Hedge said nothing would please him better. Messrs Weiss and Higginson would like to join us, also, and perhaps Mrs Cheney. Once set fairly on foot the adventure will not wait for speakers.

My daughters are enjoying themselves travelling abroad. When last heard from they were on their way to Switzerland and Italy. Louisa is regaining health and spirits and May adding sketches to her Portfolio.

Messrs Roberts and Brothers tell me they have answered your order for the books. I trust all is right.

My cordial remembrances to friends in your city—to your daughters particularly.

Truly Yours
A. Bronson Alcott.

LETTER 70–18

[to Louis T. Ives, Detroit]

Concord July 12th 1870.

Mr. Ives
Dear Sir,

I was very sorry to lose much of the pleasure of your visit here last May. But I am now beginning to be myself again, and hope to be in good plight for leaving in October for my proposed Western tour. It may chance to be as late as November before I may leave. We must not count for certainty upon Mr. Emerson. He may find time for some readings during the season. With Mrs Howe you are already in communication. Dr. Hedge of Brookline told me nothing would please him more than to give, and so would Higginson and Weiss. The three would interest and instruct any companies that might like to hear them. Wasson too would have good things to say and so would Mills of Syracuse

But perhaps it were best to experiment with two or three persons. The Adventure once fairly set on its feet, there will be no want of readers and speakers.[1]

I had a letter from Mrs Bagley last week, and have written her today.

Mrs Hosmer was here yesterday and brings good accounts of friends in Detroit. She tells me Mr. Mellen is coming East. I shall hope to see him in Concord, and if the way is open, preach for the benefit of our heathen.

My wife and I, both, owe letters to Mrs Leggett, and must write and tell her how large is our debt to her for all her kind inquiries about ourselves.

Louisa and May are enjoying themselves abroad. They are now on their route to Switzerland and Italy. Louisa's health and spirits are much improved.

I shall be glad to hear from you when you have any thing important to write. My kind remembrances to your wife and all in Elisabeth Street.

Truly Yours
A. Bronson Alcott.

[1] See Letter 70–5, par. 3.

LETTER 70–19

[to Robert Laird Collier, Chicago]

Concord July 21st 1870.

Dear Sir,

Yours inquiring about the Parlor Conversations is rec'd. Mr. Emerson tells me that he has also had a note from you making similar inquiries. From what he said, I infer that he finds himself too busily occupied in preparing his new course of Cambridge lectures to think of giving readings at the West.

I have thought of Weiss and Dr. Hedge, and Mrs Howe. All of them have expressed a wish to try the West. and all have things worth hearing. Weiss is sure to quicken the wits and charm any company.

Perhaps it were best to experiment with but two or three persons first. Once set fairly on its feet, the adventure will find speakers fast enough.

Mr. Louis T. Ives of Detroit has undertaken to make the necessary arrangements in the cities and towns along the great lines of road. You may find it advisable to communicate with him.

I hope to be ready to leave here early in November. It may be as late as January before I should reach Chicago. My topics can be named at a future date, if desired.

I am gratified to learn of your purpose of trying Conversations in place of lectures. Mr Mellen of Detroit, I hear, has found them very entertaining and instructive, and purposes resuming them in the autumn.

I have very pleasant recollections of my visit in your city.

Please accept my thanks for the hospitalities which yourself and friends there so liberally bestowed on me.

Very truly
Yours,
A. Bronson Alcott.

Rev. Rob. Laird Collier

LETTER 70–20

[to William T. Harris, St. Louis]

Concord July 29th 1870.

Dear Friend,

The newspaper containing the obituary of your little boy came to me last evening.[1] I had been expecting to hear from you for some weeks, and began to fear that you were ill yourself—broken down by your school labors—and was about writing when the news of your bereavement came.

A bright keen-eyed boy, I remember he was, and, like your surviving son, promising to make his mark. I trust his mother finds consolation in the thoughts which the event awakens, and is assured that time softens and heals like sorrows for present loss-*translation*, I should have written, to spheres of brighter activity.

You of course can meet the event with the manliness that the philosophy which you affect and have mastered, ensures. The death of children has something for heart and head to resolve, and no parent comes out of the experience without profit.

Will you take to studies as heretofore, or travel? Come this way if you leave St. Louis, and let us look into the philosophical future as far as we may. What lights are shining on that track? I am most desirous of seeing you, and the more that scope seems opening for activity here at the East also. I have purposes—dreams—(perhaps no more as yet)—about which I wish to speak with yourself specially, and here we can compare views at our leisure. Others are interested in yourself and your future. Emerson, Hedge, Prof Everett, should see you and learn your plans for the future.

Should you think of leaving St Louis, and purchasing a house in these parts, please fix your residence here in Concord. There are several places—Hawthornes for instance—on sale at reasonable prices. But whether you leave St Louis or not, come and see me. My wife, myself and housekeeper are sole occupants for the summer. The girls are now in Switzerland enjoying their travels. May has just had interesting adventures in the Pass of St. Bernard, and Louisa is gaining strength and spirits, her fame spreading almost world-wide, and golden showers falling into her lap from the sale of her books. They intend passing the winter in Italy and returning by way of England, if the war does not prevent.

Emerson is busy about next winter's University lectures, and you may as well have yours ready for reading in the same course. Hedge and Emerson—and Cabot will all favor your reading.

I purpose leaving for the West sometime in October. Mr Ives of Detroit has the matter in hand for Conversations in the chief cities. Has he written to you about it? If things prosper I may get as far as San Francisco.

I have just heard that "Tablets" has been translated into German.

With my sympathies and regards,

Affectionately Yours,

A. Bronson Alcott

Wm. T. Harris.

---

[1] The Harrises' six-year-old son, Ethan, had died on July 20. They earlier had lost an infant daughter.

LETTER 70–21

[to Seth Hunt, Northampton, Mass.]

Concord August 2nd | 1870.

Dear Sir,

It will give me pleasure to speak at Florence on the first Sunday in September as you propose, the proceeds more or less to be given to Mr. Locke. And if a subscription were started in time a little sum might perhaps be raised for his benefit. He is now under treatment of a Boston physician, who hopes to benefit, if not restore him to health and activity. Something has been raised by his friends here to pay his doctors' fee, and any thing added by his friends at Florence will be gratefully acknowledged by him.[1]

Very truly

Yours

A. Bronson Alcott.

Mr. Seth Hunt

[1] See Letter 70–13.

LETTER 70–22[1]

[to Ellen A. Chandler, Jamaica Plain? Mass.]

Concord Aug 16. | 1870

Dear Miss Chandler,

Excuse this delay in replying to yours of the 7th But I have been hoping meanwhile to be able to name the day when I might invite you to come and pass a few days with us. Mrs Alcott has been with Anna at Maplewood for a fortnight, and only returned to give our housekeeper another fortnight with her friends in Brookline. So the month is going fast and I am not to see you here as I had fondly hoped. Tis a disappointment for which the future is pledged to make ample amends.

Now can't you accompany me to Northampton on Saturday the 3rd September, taking the 11 train from Boston, and I joining you at our Concord Station at 12.m. That train takes us to Northampton at 5.p.m.—I go to Florence to speak on Sunday and return to Concord on Monday by the earliest train. I am to stay with Mr. Hunt in Northampton and ride over in his carriage on Sunday morning to Florence. It would give me much pleasure to have your **company** if you are free to leave home at that time, and inclined to see your friends at Northampton.

Your visit to Swampscott and the sea must have been very enjoyable—I have no knowledge of Miss Websters "Dramatic Sketches." The verses you quote are thoughtful and lead one to ask for more.

"What is a good letter?" you ask. Let Goethe tell us the mood in which such must be conceived and written:

"It may be owing to my mood at the time, but it seems to me that as well in writing as in treating of writings and actions, unless one write with a loving sympathy, a certain enthusiasm, the result is so defective as to have very little value. Pleasure, delight, sympathy in things and with persons all that is real, and that reproduces reality—all else is empty and vain."

The girls are enjoying their travels and adventures. They have been spending a month at Bex in Switzerland, and are now at Geneva. May has climbed the Alpine Pass to St. Bernard and writes a lively account of her adventures. Louisa's health is improving. The war they write is not likely to affect their plans of travelling.

Very cordially Yours
A. Bronson Alcott.

Miss Chandler.

---

[1] MS. owned by the Abernethy Library, Middlebury College. A copy, in Alcott's hand, is in the Alcott-Pratt Collection.

LETTER 70–23[1]

[to Louisa, Bex, Switzerland]

Concord [August] | 1870.

Dear Louisa.

Within you will find an exact copy of Mr. Sewall's Account as rendered to me on the 24th August 1870. I trust it will be clear to you, and you may see just what constitutes your property in stocks to date.

Of the $788. I have just drawn 200 for present needs, and shall draw more when I leave for the West in October. Of the $500 drawn in July, (from Roberts Brothers 6212.)[2] 300 was paid to *Mrs Stearns*, so that *we* have now had from Mr Sewall but 400 for our use, 175 of which is now in our hands. The dividends in all drawn since you left, (including mine) were 178.32. There will be another dividend due on your shares in October and December which John can draw for your mother, while I am away. Your stocks just invested will bring dividends too about the beginning of the year '71. About these you can inform your mother of your wishes.

My prospects are fair as to my Western tour. I ought not to return home without my $2000 at least, since I go advertised and and [*sic*] arrangements made for me in the cities and towns from Syracuse to Debuque [*sic*] and St Louis. and I may get as far as San Francisco. Mr. Mellen of Detroit has just been here full of inthusiasm [*sic*] about Conversations in Detroit and elsewhere. Saturday, I go to Florence to speak, and shall very likely see Sanborne [*sic*]. I am in much better plight than I have been for many years. My hearing is much improved, and I carry more weight of flesh, if not of thought, to my work. Last Monday I saw Niles. He has just returned from a pleasure trip, and taking orders for your books. They are all selling when nothing else is. He says *"Little Women and Old Fashioned Girl* will probaly [*sic*] reach the *1000* edition each by the end of the year, and I hear only praises from every tongue of their merits. Your $10.000 will soon double itself. and you may put another 10.000 into Mr. Sewall's hands by spring.

We are rejoicing in the accounts you write of your improved health and spirits. I pray these may continue as you journey from place to place. If Napoleon is dethroned, the war will be likely to come to a speedy end. and you can winter in Italy perhaps instead of England. Everybody inquires eagerly about you, and you are in the thoughts and affections of more persons than you imagine. Now get fairly well, and come home to

Your affectionate Father.

Love to May, much love.

[1] MS. in the Clifton Waller Barrett Library, University of Virginia. This is one of the few extant letters detailing financial affairs in the Alcott family. Evidence indicates that other letters on this subject were destroyed by Louisa. The financial statement accompanying Alcott's letter to Louisa appears on a separate manuscript page.

[2] The reference is to an attached financial statement:

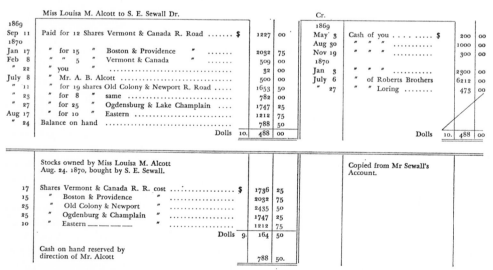

Miss Louisa M. Alcott to S. E. Sewall		Dr.				Cr.				
1869						**1869**				
Sep 11	Paid for 12 Shares Vermont & Canada R. Road .... $		1227	00		May 3	Cash of you . . . . $		200	00
1870						Aug 30	" " "		1000	00
Jan 17	" for 15 " Boston & Providence "		2032	75		Nov 19	" " "		300	00
Feb 8	" " 5 " Vermont & Canada "		509	00		**1870**				
" 22	" you "		32	00		Jan 3	" " "		2300	00
July 8	" Mr. A. B. Alcott		500	00		July 6	" of Roberts Brothers		6212	00
" 11	" for 19 shares Old Colony & Newport R. Road		1653	50		" 27	" " Loring		473	00
" 23	" for 8 " same		782	00						
" 27	" for 25 " Ogdensburg & Lake Champlain		1747	25						
Aug 17	" for 10 " Eastern		1212	75						
" 24	Balance on hand		788	50						
	Dolls	10.	488	00			Dolls	10.	488	00

Stocks owned by Miss Louisa M. Alcott Aug. 24. 1870, bought by S. E. Sewall.					Copied from Mr Sewall's Account.
17	Shares Vermont & Canada R. R. cost ...:............... $		1736	25	
15	" Boston & Providence "		2032	75	
25	" Old Colony & Newport "		2435	50	
25	" Ogdenburg & Champlain "		1747	25	
10	" Eastern _ _ _ _ _ "		1212	75	
	Dolls	9.	164	50	
Cash on hand reserved by direction of Mr. Alcott			788	50.	

The totals for the upper columns, seemingly, should be $10,484.75 and $10,485.00.

LETTER 70–24

[to Ellen A. Chandler, Framingham, Mass.]

Concord October 3rd 1870.

Dear Miss Chandler,

Come over on Monday the 10th and pass as much of the day with me as you can. We have to atone for our infrequent interviews during the last twelvemonth, and time flies relentlessly when friends meet. The shadow of an interview when you were last here, like the occasion, ‖ were ‖ was very enjoyable, yet tantalizing; one covets having his friends *solus* to find them and have them entirely.

I can hardly hope to meet you *so* again before I leave for the West.

The Radical Club has persuaded me to stay and open the Conversation on the 17th and should you care to favor the company with attendance, I may have that pleasure with the rest.

Now what shall I talk about? What do you say to this—*The Art and Method of Conversation.* But I shall see you before the meeting. It really seems good in you to ride so many miles. Yet I remember, the season has its attractions to reward your coming and going.

We have had late letters from the travellers. Louisa tells us she walked from Vevey to the Prison of Chillon, 12 miles, and felt refreshed by her jaunt.

Come and see if I can hear your whisper across my study

Affectionately Yours,
A. Bronson Alcott.

Miss Chandler.

LETTER 70–25[1]

[to William T. Harris, St. Louis]

Concord October 3rd 1870.

Dear Friend,

I hope to leave here for the West about the middle of October and, unless you think a later date would suit better, reach St Louis by about the second week in November. The Free Association advertise a Convention to be held at Cincinnati the last week in this month, and others (probably) during the first week in November following—these last at Toledo and Indianapolis. The National Unitarian Conference and Woman's Conventions are to be held in New York City on the 19 & 20th, 21. of this month, and I may take these meetings on my way West. I suppose I am to be in the principal cities—Chicago, Dubuque, Milwaukee, Detroit, Cleveland, Buffalo.—but the precise times are not fixed as yet. Mr. Ives of Detroit has taken that agency, but has not yet reported to me. I thought I would face Eastwards from St. Louis and have the season before me. But if you are purposing to come East in November as you intimated you might, I should arrange my tour otherwise. Please write forthwith and apprise me of your plans and wishes. I depend upon *seeing you at all events.*

The "Speculative" for July has not come to hand yet. But I saw a number at "the Boston Atheneum" on Saturday last. The "Plato" looked inviting. I am glad you are getting out your translation of "Hegels History of Philosophy," and trust you intend publishing it intire with your "Introduction.

I have seen "Niele's[?] Translation of Spinoza." It costs too much money, else I should put a copy in my library. But I can read it at the Atheneum. The "Aristotle's Physics" I have not—only the "Metaphysics and Ethics."

I shall bring with me "Chalmer's Translation of Lau-Tsze," the Chinese philosopher, just sent me by Wm. H. Channing. It contains remarkable things.

Towne has just sent me the First No. of his "Examiner." What with "Examiner "Index" and "Radical," the *Individualists* have organs for publishing their views. Have they a *philosophy* at the core of their thinking and printing?

Did you notice Hedge's paper on *Irving* in the last "Atlantic." If not look at it sometime.

I have been busied during the summer preparing a Volume entitled *"Concord* Days," which I hope to complete and perhaps publish in the spring. It embraces parts of the years 1869 and '70. including my tour West.

It seems as if the way were opening for the reign of Ideas in the Colleges. Emerson is busy on his Lectures for Harvard. Coming from the P. Office this morning he told me that Cutler[?] Prof of Eng. Literature had told him, he hoped to have Mr. Alcott meet his classes sometime during the winter. And Dr. Stearns, Dean of the Theological Faculty told me, the way was open for my meeting the students when they asked for it.

I am asked to open the next Radical Club on the 19th., and purpose to treat of *"the Art and Method of Conversation"* (Dialectic.)

Let me hear from you soon and I will write again before I leave for my Western tour.

Yours truly
A. Bronson Alcott.

Wm. T. Harris

[1] From a copy, in Alcott's hand, in the Alcott-Pratt Collection. The original is in the Alcott-Harris Collection in the Concord Free Public Library (see Appendix B).

LETTER 70–26

[to Louis T. Ives, Detroit]

Concord October 4th 1870

Mr Ives.
Dear Sir,

In your letter dated August 8th. you write of having mailed letters of enquiry about Conversations to various persons in the Western Cities, and that when their answers came to hand, you would inform me of their plans and wishes. As I am now restored to a sound condition, having recovered my hearing and health, I shall be leaving for the West within three weeks from this, if nothing unforeseen of arrangement on your part, shall not change my present purpose. It will be most convenient I think, for me to go by way of New York City, (where I may meet Mr. Mellen[1] at the Unitarian Conference,) and from thence to Cincinnati where the Free Religionists propose holding a Convention the last week in October. Being there, I could ride South to St. Louis very conveniently and from that City, face North and East, as any engagements in the cities might ‖ be found ‖ render it most practicable. I suppose I am to be at Chicago, Dubuque, Milwaukee; Detroit Toledo Cleavland [sic], and what further places I cannot say—on my way East of course, at Buffalo and Syracuse. Nothing definite is known by me about any of these places as to times. I go on the strength of last years acquaintance.

Mr Emerson tells me that he is to lecture at Buffalo and Toledo in January. He might easily ride up to your city and give you an evening or two. Mrs Howe tells me she can leave also for a fortnight or so.

Please write forthwith and give me any information you may have for us.

My kindest remembrance and regards to friends in Detroit

Yours truly
A.B. Alcott.

[1] W. R. G. Mellen of Detroit.

LETTER 70–27

[to Franklin B. Sanborn, Cincinnati]

Concord October 10th 1870

Dear Friend,

It will be as late as the 21 before I can conveniently leave Boston and perhaps not till the 24th. We hope to close our house here on Saturday next, but may not be able to do so.

On Monday the 17th I am to meet the Radical Club, and shall not wish to hurry West at once. Let me accommodate my coming to Springfield to your convenience for taking the trip to Connecticut. I have concluded to let slip the Unitarian Convention and so am free as to time.

We have good accounts from the travellers—now probably in Italy.

Yours truly
A. Bronson Alcott.

F. B. Sanborn
    at Cincinnati.

LETTER 70–28

[to Louis T. Ives, Detroit]

Concord October | 24th 1870.

Dear Sir,

I did not attend the Unitarian Convention, as I intended at the time I wrote you last, and so did not see Mr. Mellen, to learn any further particulars concerning the Conversations and Readings at Detroit or other places. I now purpose leaving here for Springfield to pass a day or two with Sanborn and, stopping at Syracuse and Buffalo, perhaps at Toledo, for making arrangements to meet companies if desired, reach Detroit about the middle of November, as you thought best for your friends there. Mr. Emerson, whom I saw yesterday, tells me he is to speak in Buffalo on the 17th. and (from what he implied rather than spake,) will visit Detroit if you can arrange for him about that time. We may be there *together* and have a Conversation perhaps. Mrs Howe I will try to see before I leave.

Perhaps you can persuade Mr Emerson to speak on Sunday, as well as lecture and converse.

Should you have further information to communicate please address to the care of "Rev. Saml. J. May, Syracuse N.Y."

I may be at the Free Religionist Convention in Toledo, advertised in the "Index," for November 7th and 8th.

Very truly
Yours
A. Bronson Alcott.

L. T. Ives Esq.

LETTER 70–29[1]

[to William T. Harris, St. Louis]

Concord October 24th | 1870.

Dear Friend,

I start next Wednesday for the West, and purpose reaching St. Louis about the first of December when you will have returned,—will you not?—from your New-England journey. I regret that I am not to be here to make sure of your meeting the persons you should see. But Emerson will introduce you. At the meeting of the Radical Club last Monday, you were invited to read a paper by the committee of Invitation. I hope you will. It may be spoken, if you prefer not to write your word, and the theme is left to yourself. You will edify and inspire the company.

In last Thursday's Tribune (N.Y.) is a sketch of the Conversation last Monday. It is very fairly reported as far as it goes. It is the first time I have met the Club for a twelvemonth.

I purpose being at Detroit about the 20th of November. Emerson is expected about the same time to lecture, and give a parlor Reading or two. He lectures also at Buffalo and Toledo. I hope you will not miss him.

Your July number of the Speculative is very attractive reading. I quoted what Hegel says of Plato's *tone* in his dialogues at the Club in illustration of the method of Discourse. Sanborn in "the Republican," and Wasson in the "Commonwealth" notice it favorably.

I have met Howison lately. He was at Monday's Club. When I return, I hope to see more of him with opportunities for conversation.

Will you not write me forthwith to the address of Rev Samuel J. May, Syracuse, N.Y. I shall see Mills there. Prospects at the West fair.

Very truly Yours
A. Bronson Alcott.

Wm. T. Harris.

---

[1] From a copy, in Alcott's hand, in the Alcott-Pratt Collection. The original is in the Alcott-Harris Collection in the Concord Free Public Library (see Appendix B).

LETTER 70–30

[to F. J. Russell, Waterbury, Conn.]

Concord October | 24th 1870.

Dear Sir,

Your kind invitation to share the hospitalities of your house when I should visit Waterbury, I have delayed answering till I could name the time of my visit. I now purpose leaving for Springfield next Wednesday to spend the night and possibly Thursday there with Mr. Sanborn, who wishes to accompany me to see scenes and people familiar to me during my earlier days. We shall hope to visit Wolcott together. And I to spend Sunday with yourself and congregation. Very pleasant it will be also to speak of times when as teacher and pupil we had fellowship in Germantown and Boston.

I shall hope to meet some of my mother's kindred in your flourishing city. And best of all make the acquaintance of your wife and children

Very truly
Yours
A. Bronson Alcott

Rev. F. J. Russell.

[Letter to Franklin B. Sanborn, Springfield, Mass.; from Concord, October 24, 1870. (Listed in a catalogue of the sale in 1918, by C. B. Libbie & Co., Boston, of "Autographs, Letters, and Manuscripts Left by the Late Frank B. Sanborn, Concord, Mass.")]

LETTER 70–31[1]

[to William T. Harris, St. Louis]

Detroit Novr 19th 1870

Dear Friend,

I am so far on my way to your city. The precise time when I shall reach you I cannot now foresee—probably about the first of December. Here I am giving a course of Conversations—four of these have been given and the last comes this evening. To morrow I speak in Mr. Mellen's Church, and on Monday evening have a Conversation on New England Authors in his Vestry. I purpose taking Ann Arbor, Battle Creek, Kalamazoo on my route to Chicago, stopping just to leave my Cards for Conversations (if desired) on my return homewards. I purpose coming direct from Chicago to St. Louis, only pausing perhaps at Springfield a train or two. I am to be at Dubuque by the middle of December, going from St. Louis, if that is the shortest route thither. Ten days or a fortnight I hope to have with you. If important please address the meanwhile to the care of Rev. Rob. Laird Collier, Chicago.

Thus far the hospitality of the West to me and mine has been most gratifying. And I come to your city with the assurance that one friend of freedom and philosophy has like sentiments in keeping for me. Indeed, I consider him the herald of freedom and philosophy in this Continental breadth and diffusiveness— East and West.

Most truly Yours
A. Bronson Alcott

Mr. W. T. Harris

[1] From a copy, in Alcott's hand, in the Alcott-Pratt Collection. The original is in the Alcott-Harris Collection in the Concord Free Public Library (see Appendix B).

LETTER 70–32

[to Mary Newbury Adams, Dubuque, Iowa]

St. Louis December | 1st 1870.

Dear Mrs Adams.

Mr. Harris has just put into my hands your kind note of enquiries about the time when you may look for my arrival in your city. My engagements here close on Saturday the 10th. and I purpose leaving for Dubuque on Sunday or Monday following stopping, possibly, for an evening at Bloomington on my way.

I am not apprized of the most direct route, but am told I can strike across, without passing through Chicago. The precise day of reaching you I cannot now define.

Be sure I shall seek you at once on my arrival.

With my thanks for your kind interest, and ‖ the ‖ pleasant anticipations of forming ‖ your ‖ an acquaintance with a friend of Mr. Bagleys.

> I am
> very Cordially Yours
> A. Bronson Alcott

Mrs Mary Newbury Adams
    Dubuque
      Iowa.

LETTER 70–33

[to Franklin B. Sanborn, Springfield, Mass.]

> St. Louis December | 3rd 1870.

Dear Friend,

Your parcel of "Republicans came to hand as directed, and I write hastily now to ask you to forward the next to me at Dubuque Iowa, where I expect to be on the 12th Dec. Please address to the care of "Mrs Mary Newbury Adams, Dubuque". I am to have a course of Conversations there, and, probably, meet the Round Table Club, an association of which I believe I spoke when I last saw you in Springfield.

At Detroit, I had a very agreeable company, besides the pleasure of addressing Mr Mellen's congregation on Sunday. I am to give four Conversations here and meet the Philosophical Society to morrow (Sunday.) Mr Harris has had a note from Cabot inquiring if he will lecture in the Cambridge Course. Prof. Eliot, wishing him to do so. He is too much occupied with his duties as School Superintendent and editing his Journal to promise just yet. I am passing days in the Schools, and find them excellent.

At Detroit I saw Mr Ives portrait of Emerson. It is the best likeness yet taken and the coloring is admirable. He asked, and I gave him several sittings. Emerson and Mrs Howe are invited to give lectures and readings in Detroit, and are likely to do so, during the lecture season, Emerson in January probably.

Mr. King is arranging for me on my return to Buffalo, and at the several towns on the route, I shall pause for Conversations.

News of John Pratt's decease reached me last Wednesday.[1] Mrs Alcott writes that she will remain with Anna till spring. Louisa and May were at Florence on the 30th October, about leaving for Rome. They write in the best of spirits.

> Very cordially Yours
> A. Bronson Alcott.

---

[1] Anna's husband, who died suddenly.

LETTER 70–34

[to Mrs. A. Bronson Alcott, Maplewood? Mass.]

Dubuque, Iowa, | December 16th 1870

My Dear,

I found not a moment to write from Bloomington, Ill., where I passed last Sunday and from whence I mailed to you my letter of the 9 written at St Louis.

At Bloomington I encountered the first rainy days of the season and the depths of this Egyptian mud from which there is no deliverance, and Day and Martin[?] are superfluities wherever it abounds. I spoke on Sunday in the Independent Church, had three Conversations, in the place, and visited the State Normal School at Normal, on Tuesday. My visit at St Louis was most gratifying.

Wednesday I reached this place, and am the guest of Mr. Austin Adams, who with his wife, are leading influences here and throughout the West. Mrs Adams is a sister of Mrs Bagley of Detroit, and *the representative woman of the West.*— a lady of culture and character, reminding me of Marg. Fuller. Herself and husband have drawn around them a circle of highly intelligent and earnest persons whom I met last evening and held a Conversation, the first of three or four which I am to give here[1]

[1] The letter breaks off at this point.

LETTER 71–1

[to Mary N. Adams, Dubuque, Iowa]

Davenport Jan 2nd 1871.

Dear Mrs Adams.

Finding letters at Chicago inviting me here, I came by the first train, reaching this place early this morning. I am to see Judge Dillon, Mr Searer[?], Mr French, presently, and arrange for some Conversations, three or more, as time favors. I am to return to Chicago next Tuesday and hold my first Conversation in the evening. Mr Collier makes all necessary preparations, and anticipates a successful course. I attended his Church yesterday (addressed his Sunday School, and dined with him. A second daughter was born about a month since,—"an original" I was told, as all babes doubtless are.

As you desired a word with your last words, seen rather than heard through the coach window on that cold evening, I write this hasty note, and to reassure you of the delightful memories of the hours spent in your hospitable home. It was a fortnight of satisfactions—ambrosial moments such as I have rarely enjoyed —a foretaste I fondly dream of the like another season. My "Social Ideal" has added charms heretofore mere dreams. Pray excuse my superlatives; they are not mischosen, but significant and real.

I trust you had the quiet Sunday you were anticipating, and shall take it most kindly if the letter to Mrs A. was written and despatched to Concord. I found nothing awaiting me at Chicago. Did I leave the letters you were wishing to copy behind in the haste of that last day? I do not find them with those you copied for me. If you find them, please mail to Mr. Colliers address, unless you think best to send them to me here, to the care of Judge Dillon.

Permit me to thank you again for your sisterly attentions while I was your guest. "The Comforter" promised to be sent, surely was *woman*.

I trust Mr Adams has returned safe to you and the children. I shall ever remember his kind attentions while his guest, and wise interest in my behalf.

Very Cordially
Your affectionate friend
A. Bronson Alcott.

Mrs Mary Newbury Adams.

LETTER 71–2

[to Mary N. Adams, Dubuque, Iowa]

Davenport Jan 7th 1871.

My Dear Mrs Adams,

Yours, with Mr Adam's Annabel's and your copy of Louisa's, reached me yesterday. My thanks for your interest in me and mine. Nor need you have any apprehensions that Davenporters, or others in these parts can steal my affections from the Dubuque circle. No, Dubuque still, though Davenport has its charms. I am already on the best of terms with excellent people, and have had several delightful evenings at the hospitable home of Ex-Mayor French whose guest I am while here. This evening I give my last Conversation at his house, and speak to morrow evening in the Unitarian Church. Yesterday, I dined with the Bishop and addressed the students at the College. Wednesday I spent at the soldiers Childrens House. Judge Dillon called on me early, and has been present with Mrs D. at two of my Conversations. I leave on Monday for Chicago to meet my company for Conversation on Tuesday evening.

By the same mail that brought me yours came letters from Anna and Louisa. Louisas is dated at Rome Nov. 20th. and is full of information. "The Pope, she writes, still sulks in the Vatican pretending to be a prisoner, which pretense deceives no one. He shuts up the Churches and galleries, forbids the usual fetes, and tries to make Rome sorry for his loss. But ungrateful Rome is too happy to be rid of him, and only laughs at his downfall which was such a dreadful downfall just after he had proclaimed himself infallible, that I hope he never will get up again. His cardinals are seldom seen but go about in close carriages looking very grim and plotting with all their crafty old evils how they may upset the King." &c.

The girls "are settled in a cozy little apartment in the Piazza Barbenini a gay square full of priests, peasants, soldiers, monks and strangers." Also the lovely fountain of the Triton before our windows. The rooms are a blaze of sunshine all day, and sunshine is health in [word] [.] May is taking lessons in water colors of Crowninshield an excellent artist and is happy, spending her morning in his studio, and her afternoons visiting galleries with me, or driving in the lovely Campagna. She takes Rome very calmly and has raptures over but few of the famous things. Her own tastes are so decided that the general opinion affects her very little, and we indulge in our naughty criticisms like a pair of Goths and Vandals as we are." I am tempted to send the original it is all so good.

Many thanks for writing to Mrs A. Nothing yet in the Davenport Gazette from "Quam[?]."

Love and kisses to the little poet and sister.

My regards to Mr Adams, and kind remembrances to friends in Dubuque.

With much esteem and
affection,
Truly your friend
A. Bronson Alcott.

Mrs. M. N. Adams

LETTER 71–3

[to Ellen A. Chandler, Framingham, Mass.]

Chicago January 20th 1871.

Dear Miss Chandler,

I redeem my pledge too late of writing from these cities and prairies of the West. My engagements have been unexpectedly numerous and agreeable, and promise a delightful success.

Yesterday I spent an hour with Mrs Davis at her ‖ elegant ‖ rooms on Wabash Avenue, and she and the Col. have honored me with their attendance at two of my Conversations. I was pleased to find her so companionable and happy. She told me that she heard frequently from you. This West is a country to be seen and known. I wish every New Englander could visit and expand in its free atmosphere. Every where I am entertained with a frankness and cordiality that adds a fresh significance to the word *hospitality*.

At St. Louis I met your friends Miss Eliot and Miss Brackett. My visit there was very agreeable. Mr. Harris gathered good companions for me, and I had several pleasant evenings. He makes good all my judgments concerning his character and genius. I know not another young man of like attainments and promise in the world of *Thought*.

At Dubuque I was the guest of a remarkable woman, Mrs Mary Newland [sic] Adams, who, more than any I have met, reminds me of Marg. Fuller. I was charmed and instructed by her wit and subtlety of genius. Mr. Emerson is now I believe in Detroit to give readings in the parlor of her sister, Mrs Bagley, and

Mrs Howe is expected to read sometime during the winter; so our parlor entertainments are travelling out of New England. Mr Ives of Detroit has painted the only head of Emerson that I find satisfactory.

I have picturesque letters from Louisa and May who are now in Rome where they are to spend four months. My dear Anna bears her loss like a saint, which she is. Gladly shall I return to Concord when my engagements here are over. Friends appear the more lovely when distant, and among those, *one* at least, not of my household. Will you write to me? If you will address to the care of Rev. Rob Laird Collier Chicago.

Affectionately Yours,
A. Bronson Alcott.

LETTER 71–4[1]

[to Ellen A. Chandler, Framingham, Mass.]

[Concord, March 5, 1871]

P.S. Your fragrant gift, my kind friend, comes to greet my arrival from the hospitable West. I did not need this to remind me of yourself and a charming past. Nor do I disparage the gift by intimating how much my pleasure would have been enhanced had the giver accompanied her gift. And now where and when am I to see you, and tell my story?

Cordially Yours
A.B.A.

[1] MS. owned by the Abernethy Library, Middlebury College. Alcott's postscript is to a letter written by Mrs. Alcott, dated March 5, 1871.

LETTER 71–5

[to Ellen A. Chandler, Framingham, Mass.]

Concord March 12th 1871.

Dear Miss Chandler,

Following my P.S. to Mrs A's note of Saturday last, please receive from me the accompanying book of Verses by H.H.[1] whose initials you will recognize and whose Genius you appreciate.

Let me add, moreover, that if the mails from the West have brought disappointment only, more than one epistle has been conceived, if not posted to your

532

address during the months that have elapsed since we met face to face. I would not have believed so long an interval could pass without some written salutation at least. Nor would there, had I not found such charming society in those Mississippi [sic] cities, permitting me scarce a moment's opportunity for solitude or pen all the days long and evening's late as well. You would think me painting "[word]," were I to attempt to tell you all, and be incredulous.

But when chance favors our meeting again I must picture to you "the Woman's Reading" Circle," the Gentleman's Round Table," at Dubuque, "Friends in Council" ‖ and ‖ the "Plato Club" at Jacksonville, "Philosophical Society" at St Louis, Literary Association," at Quincy—their members and themes of discourse. Life and thought are not the exclusive privileges of the East.

Louisa and May write from Rome, Feb. 20, that they purpose leaving for England about this time. They may return home sometime in May. Louisa's "Little ‖ Women ‖ Men" is nearly written, and she intends finishing the book before she leaves London and have it copyrighted there.

We are now settled in our house here, Anna and her boys to be future inmates of our household.

I am unable to hear Emerson at Horticultural Hall to day, where I might have met you doubtless.

Saturday's roses are still fragrant of the Roses of the Rosie afar[?].

Affectionately Your friend,
A. Bronson Alcott

Miss Ellen A. Chandler.

¹ Helen Hunt, *Verses by H. H.* (1870).

LETTER 71–6

[to Ednah Dow Cheney, Jamaica Plain, Mass.]

Concord May 7th 1871.

Dear Mrs Cheney,

Definitely on what day Louisa intends leaving London for Boston she has not informed us. It may be late in the month, but we shall look for her arrival by the middle of June. May thinks she may remain in England and pursue her art studies there. We shall look for something more definite by the next steamer.

Louisa was reading the proof sheets of her new book at her last writing, and both herself and sister were in the best of spirits. It is very kind in the ladies to desire bestowing their complements [sic] upon her on her arrival.

I cannot now be sure of meeting the May Clubs, having carpenters and masons to superintend, with planting besides. And I may add, the charming society of my little boys.

Very truly
Yours,
A. Bronson Alcott.

LETTER 71–7[1]

[to May, England]

[Concord, late May, 1871]

[letter fragment]

opportunities which you had coveted almost from a child. I know you are making the best use of them, and are grateful to those who have befriended you. We shall esteem you hereafter the more for your courage and perseverance in carrying your plans to such successful issues.

What you write about Mr. Ireland interests me. I think I did not meet him when in England, but Emerson has spoken his praises, and I believe, Carlyle also. Give him my regards if you meet him again, and express my regret at not having a single copy of my *"Emerson"* to send him. The hundred copies printed are all given away.—only our *family* copies remaining. Niles thinks the *"Record and Conversations"* may follow *"Little Men"* presently, and publish the Originals of the methods of teaching and discipline from which Louisa has drawn largely in her *Plumfield* story. Her

was to sail on the 25th. and is now fairly at sea. I shall try to meet her at the East Boston docks and bring her home at once.[2]

It seems as if you must feel lonely, now your kind friend Alice[3] and sister have left you among strangers. But I know your power of occupation, and trust you ‖ you ‖ are burying your loneliness in study and hardwork, and will shorten the days of absence from us. Your ride to Richmond and vicinity revives my visit there in 1842 when you were a baby. You were within sight of Ham Common and Alcott House. Alcott House on this side is in perfect order and awaits the occupancy of the expected guest, whom we all expect to greet at the gate in 10 days. Could there have been *two* instead of one. But I submit and think it best. —All are well and full of expectancy. Write often and tell us of the people and places you see.

Your affectionate
Father.

[1] MS. in the Clifton Waller Barrett Library, University of Virginia, a fragment on one sheet.
[2] Louisa sailed from England on May 25; the crossing took twelve days (see Cheney, p. 258).
[3] Alice Bartlett, who made the trip to Europe with Louisa and May. She had returned home on May 11 (see Cheney, p. 258).

LETTER 71–8[1]

[to William T. Harris, St. Louis]

Concord July 4th 1871.

Dear Friend,

I am pleased to learn that you purpose visiting us this month. Come directly to my house and give us all the time you can spare while in these parts.

How much we have to say, who shall tell! And Louisa is at home and will be curious to learn what you have to say of her Books after your recent readings. I hope besides to have you meet several persons who should know you better. Philosophy is hardly yet in the air of New England, and it will be salutary for our thinkers even to breathe a Western breeze when it chances to pass. I rejoice in what you write of the success of your Journal. Prof Porter, whom I met at the "Phi Beta" Anniversary last week spoke highly of it and its editor, saying that he should write you soon. His oration was in the right strain, and well received. I trust you will bring your April No.—

The Divinity Class are coming to see me soon. I wish it might be while you were here.

I returned from the West in the best of spirits, and have been busy since for the first month preparing for Louisas return, and after that arranging my M.S.S. for bindings. My Diaries, 17. Vols. are to be done next week. I have not been able to do much on *the Concord Days,*" but shall now set about it. "The *Plumfield School* described in '*Little* Men" has prompted Roberts Brothers to reprint *"the Record of a School,"* as an answer to readers who question whether such a school as Louisa has drawn were possible.

About something for your October Number, we will see when you come. What should you say to reprinting the best of the 'Orphic Sayings?" Copies of of "The Catalogue of School Report have come to hand.

Howison, whom I saw yesterday in Boston, promises to come and see me soon. Emerson is at home now. I have seen him but for a moment since his return from California. He is busy, I believe, in preparing his selected Poetry for the press.

What you say of my Western tour is most flattering. I had great satisfaction in it.

We have just heard of the death of my brother in law, Mr. May, and I leave this afternoon to attend his funeral on Thursday at Syracuse. If I knew the train which is to bring you East, I should be induced to linger about Syracuse and come on with you. Can't you address me there, anytime between this and the 12th?

With regards
Yours truly
A. B. Alcott

Wm. T. Harris.

---

[1] From a copy, in Alcott's hand, in the Alcott-Pratt Collection. The original is in the Alcott-Harris Collection in the Concord Free Public Library (see Appendix B).

[Letter to George H. Howison, Boston?; from Concord, July 13, 1871.]

LETTER 71–9

[to Joseph May, Newburyport? Mass.]

Concord July | 16th 1871.

My Dear Nephew,

I have tried in vain to recall the words spoken ‖ beside ‖ by your father's side on that memorable morning. It has been one of my infirmities from the beginning to speak the unreportable, and on this occasion especially. I should ‖ only ‖ mar the impression were I to seize only the words without embracing their spirit. And you must excuse me if I leave them as they fell on the ear of those who heard them. Believe me it was an unspeakable satisfaction to have spoken any thing worthy of the great and good man, whom it is your privilege to call by the tender name of Father.

Your aunt is silent but cheerful, and seems to be drawn all the more into the embraces of her household, by this event.

I shall look forward to the time when I may see you and yours at your own home.

My visit to Gerrit[?] Smith and the Sunday services in his Church were very gratifying.

With regards to your wife, believe me,

Yours affectionately
A. Bronson Alcott.

LETTER 71–10

[to Cyrus A. Bartol, Manchester, Mass.]

Concord July | 18th. 1871

Dear Sir

Mr Harris is with me, and will have Friday of next week in reserve for meeting some of our friends in these parts.

You spoke of inviting us to Manchester some time. Can't you do so on Friday the 28. Mr Harris expects Davidson and Howison by that time, and we should have the pleasure of meeting the St. Louis thinkers. Write me if you please.

Truly
A. Bronson Alcott

Dr. Bartol

LETTER 71–11

[to Cyrus A. Bartol, Manchester, Mass.]

Concord July 25 | 1871

Dear Sir

I am expecting Mr Harris to night, to spend tomorrow with me and I purpose accompanying him to Fitchburg on Thursday,[1] returning in the afternoon.

We hope to find Howison and Davidson there and bring them here to pass the night, and leave early on Friday for Boston in time for the train that takes to Beverly and Manchester. If I am posted aright we reach Manchester about 10 A.M. I hope Wasson, Weiss, Hedge (Cabot has sailed for Europe) will be with you, and others whom you may have invited.

Yours truly
A. Bronson *Alcott*

Dr. Bartol

[1] To attend the annual meeting of the American Institute of Instruction.

LETTER 71–12[1]

[to Ellen A. Chandler, Jamaica Plain? Mass.]

Concord August | 28th 1871.

My Dear Miss Chandler,

Yours of the 26th June I am ashamed to find has not been acknowledged. I fear that of March 17th has met with no better consideration.

I have to say in palliation of this inexcusable negligence on my part, that never has a season of late been so crowded with surprizes to the confusing of friendships and most things. Louisas return and the preparations for it, her frail health and capricious spirits since her arrival—many friends of hers and mine to be entertained, among these Mr Harris and Miss Brackett—Mr May's decease,[2] and my little boys—I need not add nor particularize, hardly apologize when I reflect that life is, for the most, apology itself.

And almost as I write comes the news of your loss. You wrote Mr Lyman was ill, and yourself devoted to his comfort. But I had not anticipated the event which withdraws him from you, and your kindly attentions. He must have been much to you, and the memories of the past summer be particularly precious. I had not the pleasure of knowing him further than what I saw of him when meeting him once with yourself in Boston. I have imagined there was a very tender attachment existing between him and yourself. Will this even affect your future prospects? Communicate whatsoever you may feel prompted to write. I shall regard it as an additional proof of your confidence, and trust it may renew a correspondence which has been every way so charming in times past. I hope Mrs Lyman finds consolations in this her bereavement.

Louisa is much better and about making a short visit to Leicester. On her return we hope to visit Connecticut together. How gladly would I visit you, if that might be.

With much love
and sympathy,
Your friend
A. Bronson Alcott

Miss Chandler

[1] MS. owned by the Abernethy Library, Middlebury College. A copy, in Alcott's hand, is in the Alcott-Pratt Collection.
[2] Samuel J. May died in July, 1871 (see Letter 71–8).

LETTER 71–13[1]

[to William T. Harris, St. Louis]

Concord September | 2nd 1871.

Dear Friend,

I looked for your address in the Report of the doings of the *National Teachers' Association,* and found only an allusion to it. You will publish it somewhere of course.

Mr Whipples report of your Paper read at Mr Sargents', you may have read noticed in *"The National Standard,* and "Springfield Republican."[2] I hope you will compile and publish in a Volume your Educational Lectures for the wider circulation which they deserve.—Miss Brackett, too, has good things for publication.

"The Record of a School,' is all printed, running to 300 pages. including Miss Peabody's qualifying Preface and Appendix. But the book stands upon sound principles, and may be left to itself safely.

I am hoping to have something fit to be named,
    "The Descent of Souls"
But question whether I can get it ready for your next No. of the Journal. *"The Quarrel"* may suggest and properly precede it.

I had purchased the set of *"The Dial"* for my library before your note reached me, and prefer to retain it. I had a set (wanting No 5) just bound having despaired of finding a full set at the bookstores. Burnham has been trying to get a full set for several years. I will spare the set, wanting No 5. I paid $20.00. for the full set, half calf. The imperfect set is also in half calf, and should be worth $16.00 at least. Unbound numbers cost $1.00. No's 5 and *14* can rarely be found.

We are now fairly in for autumn. Whether I shall go West I cannot now foresee.

Louisa is improving. She is now at Leicester on a short visit to her cousins the Mays. We hope to start together, Louisa and I, by the 15th. for Connecticut.

Your visit is memorable and promises propitious results.

My regards to Mrs *Harris* and *Theo,* regretting their call was so short and hurried. To Misses Brackett and Eliot also.

Truly Yours
A. Bronson Alcott.

Wm T. Harris.

---

[1] From a copy, in Alcott's hand, in the Alcott-Pratt Collection. The original is in the Alcott-Harris Collection in the Concord Free Public Library (see Appendix B).
[2] Harris had read a paper ("The Function of Education in Its Relation to Government, Society, and the Individual") at a meeting of the Radical Club on July 31.

LETTER 71–14

[to Mary N. Adams, Dubuque, Iowa]

Concord September | 8th 1871.

Dear Mrs Adams,

Louisa has been entertaining your kind invitation but fears she has neither strength nor spirits to venture so far. Last week she took winter quarters in Boston hoping to secure more privacy and a wider variety than our little village admits. We think she is benefitted by late treatment, being just now free from aches and pains of years standing. *I* do not give up our pretty plan of visiting you sometime, but must await *her* pleasure to bring it about beautifully. We had planned to visit Connecticut together about this time, but she declines.

Your sisters[1] visit was but a flurry and surprise, yet long enough to leave the most agreeable impressions—particularly on my wife and Anna.

My wife says,

"These western women are of the true type, and I freely forgive them for capitivating the affections of philosophers and poets who chance to share their hospitalities."

Mr. Emerson tells me that he has accepted invitations for Chicago and Quincy, and will come to Dubuque and Detroit if arrangements are made to economize his time and travel. I am hoping good things from his visits West, and glad that he has consented to make your acquaintance under the best advantages. You and Mr Adams will know what to do with him. One is better than two of a sort at once, so it will be soon enough for the other another season. Besides I cannot leave home yet. Perhaps Louisa may incline to prove all I tell her of those Missisipi [sic] cities by springtime.

Three letters of yours, yes, three, all written in full faith of swift response, yet all unanswered. Well, I confess myself the chief of princes[?], hopelessly such I fear. Yet not without a conscience. What shall one do, if he cant write when he d'ont? Moreover what can he expect if he dare the sibyls.

Miss Peckham's discourse came duly to hand, and was read with satisfaction. I found her very pleasant company when I met her at Toledo, and hope to see her in Concord when she visits the East. Perhaps she will be the first student to enter our *"New Academy,"* for which I have *four fellowships* already. East and West may take hands, joining Platonism with Christianity in good faith.

I hope during the winter to do a little for both.

Mrs Denman's[2] and Miss Chapin's visit from Quincy was very agreeable. Think of Miss Chapin at the head of the *Woman's University.*

Please remember me kindly to your friends in Dubuque.

With much regard to Mr. Adams,

Yours affectionately
A. Bronson Alcott.

[1] Mrs. Bagley.
[2] Sarah Denman of Quincy, Illinois, wife of Mathew B. Denman.

LETTER 71–15

[to George C. Young, Harrisburg, Pennsylvania?]

Concord September | 20th 1871.

Mr George C. Young
Dear Sir,
My cordial regards to the members of the "Harrisburg Radical Club," with my thanks for their honorary membership, and best wishes for its future usefulness and prosperity

Any reports of its sayings and doings from time to time will be received by me with pleasure.

Very respectfully
A. Bronson Alcott

LETTER 71–16[1]

[to William T. Harris, St. Louis]

Concord September | 20th 1871.

Dear Friend,
Have you noticed the paper on *Theism* in the July No. of the British Quarterly Review? I was yesterday in Boston and read it at the Athenaeum. Have we had any thing so hopeful for Philosophy lately in any of the British Journals? I read it with much satisfaction.

When we come to see that *Intuition is the primary postulate of thought*, many questions now perplexing and obscure, will be cleared up, and the lower and imperfect methods may take rank where they are available and belong.

I have threaded my *Lapse* sheets into something like satisfactory connexion. They grow luminous under the eye, and will do for printing presently—perhaps make an added chapter to the "*Tablets*" after you have used them.

If you can spare the time for the Introductory Critique, we may have occasion to use it soon, as only half-a-dozen copies of Tablets remain on the publisher's shelves.

"The Record of a School," is delayed by Miss Peabodies persisting in advertising Froebels methods in her Preface and Appendix. But we hope to compromise with her somehow, and have the book out by November certainly.

I doubt whether I shall leave home for any time during the winter.

Louisa is slowly gaining we hope, but it is a slow gain at best.

There are several competitors for my *Dials*, but I retain them till I hear from you.

Sincerely Yours,
A. Bronson Alcott

Wm. T. Harris.

[1] From a copy, in Alcott's hand, in the Alcott-Pratt Collection. The original is in the Alcott-Harris Collection in the Concord Free Public Library (see Appendix B).

LETTER 71–17[1]

[to Mr. Woods, Jacksonville, Ill.]

Concord Sepr 20th 1871.

Dear Sir

I very well remember the interesting visit to the Institution for the Deaf and Dumb, and other interviews with yourself, and with Mrs Wood, mentioned in your note of the 7th. I shall be most happy to promote your interests with the Boston Publishers. I was yesterday in Boston but failed in seeing Roberts Brothers. Next time I hope to be able to speak particularly of your wishes and doubt not they will esteem it a favor to have their publications noticed in your Journal. You are welcome to use my name as reference if it will serve you in the least.

"The Record of a School" has been delayed a little, but will appear probably in November.

I met at Fitchburg, your new Superintendent of Schools Mr. Harris, and am glad that he has fallen among a people so well disposed to further a liberal culture. I trust you see his brother's "Journal of Speculative Philosophy."

I owe my most cordial thanks to the good friends in your city who made my visit there so agreeable.

My remembrances to Dr. Jones and "The Plato Club," particularly.

Very truly

Yours,

A. Bronson Alcott.

[1] MS. owned by the Minneapolis Public Library.

LETTER 71–18

[to Anna C. Brackett, St. Louis]

Concord October 18th 1871.

Dear Miss Brackett,

I have you appreciative paper on Margaret Fuller, and wish it may find place in some of our magazines. Your strictures on Lowell's treatment of Margaret, if for nothing else, would exclude it from insertion in "The *Atlantic*", or "*Old and New,*" probably. Mr. Morse (in whose hands the paper now is) would like to publish it in "the *Radical*", and I delay returning it, hoping you will assent to his wishes. Mrs. Alcott read it, and thinks it the most satisfactory of the several attempts to do justice to the most remarkable woman of our time. At any rate, it should be published for the benefit of the many young women of our time.

When I learn your wishes I will comply with them. If you wish it returned I will return it. But you need not have sent the stamps. It is a complement [sic], as a pleasure, to have the opportunity of knowing what you are doing and thinking. I hope the "*Adonis,*" will appear in next no. of "*the Speculative*" It is a vein that should be worked with us. Read what Stedman writes in the last number of the Atlantic concerning "Tennison [sic] and Theocritus." The Pastoral and Idyllic, who has written unless it be Channing and Thoreau?—

541

You will see in "the Springfield Republican" of a week or two back a notice of Channings new Pastoral, entitled the "Wanderer." which is to appear this month published by *'Osgood and Co"*

Your "Athens" is charming.

Pray cultivate the Idealists to your hearts' content, and now that you have Prof. Davidson to inspire, the love of them and their lore, we may anticipate fair fruits.

I hope to hear from Mr Harris soon, and have a sight of the next No. of the "Speculative".

I question whether I shall leave my fireside for this season. Mr Emerson goes to Detroit, Dubuque, and Quincy. Another season will be ‖ time ‖ soon enough for me. Louisa is better, and has taken rooms in Boston for the winter. We expect May in November.

Regards to Miss Eliot.

Yours truly
A. Bronson Alcott.

Miss Anna Brackett

LETTER 71–19

[to Charles D. B. Mills, Syracuse]

Concord October | 30th 1871.

Dear Friend,

I am glad to hear of your purpose to devote yourself to *"The Word"*, and think you have fairly earned the privilege.

As to New England, I doubt not your utterances would be heard with pleasure and appreciation. I have thought of Florence as most likely to offer you a hearing and wish you may know more of that inquiring congregation, where Mrs Powell is now speaking

Mr Emerson, to whom I mentioned your purpose, suggested you writing to Mr. Hallowell, who has charge of some course of lectures in Boston, and would perhaps give you one of them. He thought they paid $50 a lecture.

You speak of Boston with some distrust, and I doubt not justly, though once heard there might affect your present judgment more favorably. Worcester is a free place and so is Lynn. Samuel Johnson could inform you about Lynn and Theodore Browne of Worcester.

When you come East take Concord on your way from Florence. I am to be at home probably all winter, and busy with some things which I should like to publish.

If you seek a publisher in Boston, Mr. Niles, of the firm of Roberts Brothers, is the man for you to consult. Louisa has found him most honorable and generous. He has in press a Book of Dr. Bartol's which must now be nearly ready for publication.

Mr Emerson, I believe, makes a short trip West in December. He is preparing a new volume of Essays for publication. Mr Channing has a volume of

Verses in press to which Emerson has written an Introduction. Louisa has taken winter quarters in Boston. She is much better, and begins to write again.

Anna and her boys are with us, and very well.

My regards to Mrs Mills and your children.

With much esteem,
Yours truly,
A. Bronson Alcott.

LETTER 71–20[1]

[to William T. Harris, St. Louis]

Concord Decr. | 4th 1871.

Dear Friend,

Yours was most welcome. And the "Speculative" attractive at sight. I have been too busy with my Concord Days," to open it but, for a hasty survey of its contents. The "Bion," is much to my taste, and let us have more in that vein. "The Quarrel" all right. Emerson spoke of the *Trendelenburg* as if he had read it carefully.[2] I was much gratified by your account of Dr. Jones[3] and his Plato Club. Jowett's translation makes us all his debtor. Presently scholars will begin to swear by Plato, as they have and still do by Shakespeare. I wish they may study him to better advantage than most have the in[?] "Book."

The Lapse paper I will take in hand again for a final revisal whenever you let me know the last date you can allow me.

As to the Introductory for Tablets, if you can have it ready by New Years, it would please me much. I believe the copies of Tablets are all gone from the publishers shelves; and shall try for the new edition, at once.

I shall be glad to spare my copy of 'the Dial," to yourself or any who may wish it. When I bought the perfect copy, I thought of your request. But when I had it in hand, felt I unwilling to spare it, since I questioned whether another would be found.

How far has Davidson done Plotinus? We cannot wait always. Emerson wants his translation of that and of the Laocoon. So do I. My regards and kind remembrance to him.

May returned a fortnight since very well. and Louisa is fast gaining strength and spirits. Continue your translation of Pedagogy[?], pray.

Yours
A.B.A.

Wm. T. Harris

---

[1] From a copy, in Alcott's hand, in the Alcott-Pratt Collection. The original, *dated December 7*, is in the Alcott-Harris Collection in the Concord Free Public Library (see Appendix B).

[2] Anna C. Brackett's "Bion's Threnody on Adonis"; Alcott's poem, "The Quarrel"; Thomas Davidson's translation of Trendelenburg, "The Logical Question in Hegel's System." All are in the *Journal of Speculative Philosophy,* V (October, 1871).

[3] Hiram K. Jones of Jacksonville, Illinois.

[to Franklin B. Sanborn, Springfield, Mass.]

Concord December | 16th 1871.

Dear Friend,

In the middle of setting a furnace came your full particular letter. And now that we are rejoicing in its genial warmth throughout our apartments we wonder how we endured the last winters spent here. It is a real luxury. And ‖ now ‖ with May for housekeeper, and my open fire place besides, I am tempted to forego my Western tour, altogether, for the home satisfactions:

"Go where I would, thou lucky Lar, stay here
Warm by a glittering chimney all the Year,

yet

I may leave for a month or so in the spring.

Mr Emerson has just returned from his short sally, and brings with him very pleasing memories of the Quincy and Dubuque companies. Dr. Jones of Jacksonville, the Platonist whom he met at Quincy, interested him, by his strong sense, his knowledge of Plato, his Plato Club. And Mrs Adams of Dubuque made a lively impression by her Western sense and sagacity. He gave Parlor readings and his discourse on Immortality, at both these cities. He remarked, "these companies are plainly the first fruits of Harris' labors." Yet Mrs Adam's is a friend of Abbots and sufficiently of the *"Free"* persuasion. Apropos of Harris, he writes that "Dr. Jones is keeping up his Plato Club and has just sent for a Jowetts Plato, which I have forwarded." Davidson writes, that he hopes "to place an Aristotle by the side of Jowett's Plato," adding, "This is rather an ambitious project, and of course must look for its accomplishment to the far future. I have already rendered into English the most of the Poetics and have made some advance in the Metaphysics.&c."

The six copies of Channing's Wanderer came from Osgood & Co. I have sent one to Miss Thoreau. Did I subscribe for them, and if so, who is to receive pay for them? Channing appears to be encouraged by his late recognition, though he "has not published any verses to speak of lately." Emerson has not spoken of his Poem since it was published. He called last evening to tell me of his Western tour, and was sorry to hear of the suspension of the "Record of a School" by Miss Peabody['s] whimseys, the Western friends wishing to have it, and the "Conversations."

Louisa is fixed in pleasant quarters in Boston. She is gaining in strength and spirits. Her new Holiday book is well received, 10,000 copies taken in advance of publication.

Anna and boys have gone to pass the winter at Pratt farm.

I regret the discontinuance of the Semi Weekly, and shall make the most of the Weekly which you propose sending. Enclosed is the money for payment of Mr. Russells. I do not know the price of subscription.

With regards to Mrs Sanborn and the children.

Yours faithfully
A. Bronson Alcott.

LETTER 71–22

[to Giles Badger Stebbins, Detroit?]

Concord Dec. 25 | 1871

Dear Sir

I regret that my engagements leave me little time to make the Selections from Boehme and others for which you wrote. Such as I had in my Common Place I have enclosed with some things of my own from which you shall choose any thing you deem suited to include in your book.[1]

I have but half of the Original Orphic Sayings. To your copying I send leaves of Tablets should you care to select from the Volume.

Your book comes at a fitting moment and will stimulate thought in the right direction

I regret there is not more of Boehme, but I have not all his works by me.

Very truly,

Yours;

A. Bronson Alcott

G. B. Stebbins.

[1] *Chapters from the Bible of the Ages* (1872).

LETTER 71–23[1]

[to Ellen A. Chandler, Boston?]

Concord December | 27th 1871.

Dear Miss Chandler

I am beginning to be covetous of my new Year's Gifts, the chief of which is seeing yourself with a day or two, if that may be, for Conversation. Now it need not arrive on that particular day in our Calendar, but at such time as may suit your convenience. May—who is now our housekeeper—wishes it may happen soon after the holidays. So I write to learn when you will oblige us, and the matter can be arranged with you. Can you come? If your engagements occupy other days, and you have a Sunday at your disposal, come on that day. You can leave here in time on Monday morning, to reach Boston by 9. and should Louisa happen to be with us then, she will accompany you.

She tells me she sees you sometimes at the Athaenum [*sic*], and has had the pleasure of a call or two at her room opposite. Now blush prettily when I tell you that she thinks you *"one of the few sensible young women who have a purpose and live deeper than appearances."* Did you never suspect that I thought so?

Come and tell me about your studies and teaching. And perhaps you will indulge me in some readings of M.S.S. in which I am now interested.—and let let [*sic*] me hope a bright day to my *"Concord Days."*[2]

I am spending this winter in my study, and shall enjoy an interview very much. It seems as if there were things to be spoken good to hear and speak under such attractions.

Affectionately
Yours
A. Bronson Alcott

Miss Chandler.

[1] MS. owned by the Abernethy Library, Middlebury College. A copy, in Alcott's hand, is in the Alcott-Pratt Collection.
[2] Alcott's *Concord Days* was published in 1872.

PART NINETEEN

1872

LETTER 72–1[1]

[to Thomas Davisdson, St. Louis]

Concord January, | 6th 1872

Dear Friend,

Your letter was a welcome surprise. Though a little disappointing in what you write about the Laocoon, and you tell me nothing about the Plotinus. Now if you will show us Aristotle's place in the world of thought by giving us a version of his works in *your* English, we will thank you, and try to see Plato all the more clearly than hitherto. It is some years since I read Aristotle, and was much taken with him. I am better acquainted with his Metaphysics than his Politics. His History of animals I remember interested me.

Your essay on "the Tragic" opens up an interesting field of thought. I think I agree with you in your distinctions between the Greek and English drama. Have we lost or gained by the Christian Individualism. If Jesus held the key to the mysteries of Fate, it does not appear that *Christian* thinkers, (if I may use the adjective) have mastered his idea, and I derive the greater satisfaction from the Greek solution.

The Ancients, it appears, accepted in good faith the sway of Fate, (or of Temperament, as we say) in their doctrine of Destinies, (hereby signifying that duplicity or polarity of forces operative in man's will, by which his Personal freedom is abridged or overridden.) Nor does it appear that they conceived deliverance possible from this dread Nemesis of existence: it was wrought into the substance of their tragedies, subjecting mind and matter alike, binding the Gods even in chains. If the modern thought professes to have freed itself from this Old Fatalism, it practically admits it nevertheless; Man's will gaining but slight advantage over the foes of the old tragedies. The Will, the entire Personality is still bound fast by the inexorable Powers, which his choices can neither propitiate nor overcome.

If Goethe treats the matter more freely and humanly, his dealing differs but in form from the Pagan dualism, man is the spoil of the demons after all. If Satan is suppressed for the moment, he is victorious at last.

Carlyle only renders it the more disastrous and dismaying, by all his wealth of thought, force of illustration, his formidable heroic figures. It is force reacting, pitted, against force throughout his embattled pages, himself a victim with them,

547

never victor, irritants all not quellers of the demon. Fate, Fate, his gospel forever. Freedom he seems never to have the possibility of achieving.

If Emerson is an improvement on Carlyle, it is by favor of temperament rather than thought: with him it is Individualism idealized, no more, and he hesitates to tread firmly the ground of Personality in the exercise of free Choices.

We look to St Louis for brighter light on these deep matters. Had Plato had Aristotle, had Hegel, the key? which? As thought made the world it should remember *how* it wrought, one would think, and show the method of Genesis to thinkers.

Jowett's Plato I have but glanced at at the bookstores. I shall be happy to find his translation as good as a German one. English scholars appear to have been incapable hitherto of divining the Greek mind.

Sanborn happened to be here a day or two after your essay came and took it to read, perhaps notice in the "Republican," which I trust you see sometimes at your reading room. I value the literary criticisms in it.

Emerson is now in Washington. He lectures there and in Baltimore. He speaks of his late visit at the West with much satisfaction—of Dr. Jones and his *Plato Club,* particularly.

I may make a short tour that way sometime in the spring. At present, I am trying to collect matter from my Diaries for a little book. The sheets look attractive and may find their way to the printing office sometime, under the title of *"Concord Days."*

I do not quite suit myself in the sheets selected for a contribution to "The Speculative" but shall try farther, if Mr. Harris inclines to favor me. I shall be glad to hear from him. Cabot whom I met the other day spoke in warm terms of him and of his Journal. Wasson intends spending a year or two in Germany. Bartol has a book in press and to appear this month.

Louisa is beginning to take up her pen again. She has taken rooms in Boston for the winter. Her books are meeting the general favor, and a wide sale.

The Year opens auspiciously. I shall hope to see you during its passage; with opportunity for conversation. Concord and St. Louis should cover the intermediate spaces.

Very truly Yours,
A. Bronson Alcott.

Thomas Davidson Esq.
　　　St. Louis.
Jan. 10th
　　P.S. I have read *"the Edmond* [sic] *Spencer* [sic]*"* in your review, with interest　　A.B.A.

---

[1] MS. owned by the Fruitlands and Wayside Museums. A copy (incorrectly *dated December 17*), in Alcott's hand, is in the Alcott-Pratt Collection.

LETTER 72-2

[to Franklin B. Sanborn, Springfield, Mass.]

Concord January | 19th 1872.

Dear Friend,

Enclosed is my subscription for the Republican sent to Mr. Russell. No matter about returning the bill receipted.

I read your notice of Davidson's Essay with pleasure. Pity that Davidson cannot devote his fine scholarship uninterruptedly to literary studies. Let us hope the march of Ideas will bring him the leisure presently, and Harvard be worthy of him.

Did you notice Hedges' and Childs' speeches in Wednesday's Advertiser on Woman's education, and compare them with Prof. Whites' of Cornell University?

I read Bowles on St. Louis. and his appreciation of Harris and Miss Brackett. New-England does not degenerate by migration plainly.

I shall be curious to read the Brahman's Treatise. Send it to Harris forth-with.

Emerson returned late on Wednesday evening just in time to hear Fields' lecture, and I passed the evening afterwards at his house where Fields and his wife passed the night. The lecture was a fine Lay sermon on *Cheerfulness*. and well received. Whatever Fields is not, certainly he is a good fellow and should recite his piece throughout N. England.

Emerson saw a good deal of Sumner, and met Walt Whitman.

Our winter is passing pleasantly, all of us much rejoicing in the tropical climate which we breathe.

Louisa improves steadily and promises to be herself again by spring.

All send regards to yourself and yours.

Affectionately
A. Bronson Alcott.

F. B. Sanborn.

LETTER 72-3

[to John H. Clifford, North Andover? Mass.]

Concord Jan. 30th 1872

Rev. Sir,

I shall be glad to give you a Sunday and an evening Conversation on your own terms, if it be nothing more than my expenses. Any thing more, if your people care to contribute, will be gladly received. But that matter shall be left altogether to you and them. If not so convenient for a Conversation on Sunday evening, I could remain over to Tuesday, and meet them on Monday evening.

Any Sunday coming soon will suit me.

Very respectfully,
A. Bronson Alcott.

Rev. John H. Clifford.

LETTER 72–4[1]

[to William T. Harris, St. Louis]

Concord February | 6th. 1872.

Dear Friend,

The last months have held me so intent on my "Concord Days," and in arranging my M.S.S. for binding, that I have taken little thought of other matters besides. If you had intimated a wish for my *"Lapse"* papers, I might have tried again for something to make good the title. Yet I fear the matter is not there to show for the spirit of the thing, and I await the call from *within* as much as from without to make the whole good alike to fact and idea.

I hope to send my M.S.S to the binder to-morrow, and to submit the sheets of "Concord Days" to Roberts Brothers in a week or two. You flatter me about my things while Emerson blames. Which am I to believe, and obey? What interests me so deeply, should I judge interest others, and so I rather believe my things deserve type and readers.

We had a good talk at Bartol's (private) lately on *"Influences"*, Emerson reading a paper, and Bartol, Hedge, Cabot, Weiss, giving their views. Had you been there the circle would have been full and round. Cabot spoke in his usual admiration of the Journal, and particularly of your School Syllabus &c. I wish we had a University waiting for a President. I should know the man to recommend. Emerson read me your recent letter about Stirling. Things are ripening.

Davidsons letter was good to get and answer.

I am expecting to go to North Andover to preach for a young Harvard divine settled there.

I send a photograph of my Temple School room.

Cordially Yours,

A. Bronson Alcott.

Wm. T. Harris.

---

[1] From a copy, in Alcott's hand, in the Alcott-Pratt Collection. The original is in the Alcott-Harris Collection in the Concord Free Public Library (see Appendix B).

LETTER 72–5

[to Joseph May, Newburyport, Mass.]

Concord February 28th | 1872.

My Dear Nephew,

I find I cannot conveniently leave home on Saturday as we talked, and must reserve my visit for warmer days, perhaps bring Louisa with me.

She ‖ has ‖ spent yesterday with us and appears to be daily improving in strength and spirits.

Your aunt is very well and desires her affectionate remembrance, hoping some day to greet you under her own roof in which I write.

With regard,

Yours

A. Bronson Alcott

LETTER 72–6[1]

[to Franklin B. Sanborn, Springfield, Mass.]

Concord March | 5th 1872.

Dear Friend,

Come up and spend a night when most convenient to yourself. I shall be at home and we shall all delight to entertain you. If you can come on Wednesday or Thursday evening May will be disengaged and can have the more time to give you. Anna and boys are passing these days at Pratt Farms, and we have a spare room or two for a guest.

Besides it is always a rare privilege to entertain the good under one's roof.

I suppose you must have heard that Madame Thoreau is passing from us. And with her departure much about Henry will be lost to us. I saw her last Friday and found her disposed for conversation but too far spent to indulge long.

Mrs Alcott is very well and will be glad to greet you.

Ever Yours

A. Bronson Alcott

F. B. Sanborn Esq.

[1] MS. owned by the Fruitlands and Wayside Museums.

LETTER 72–7

[to Cyrus A. Bartol, Boston]

Concord March | 7th 1872.

Dear Friend,

I wish I could tell you how your book[1] pleases and profits in perusal. All you say seems well said and timely. I am glad such a book is added to our religious literature, and am sure it must find many appreciative readers. What you say of Emerson, Parker, and Father Taylor is happily said, and your kindly notice of myself is most gratifying to me. Such a book is above criticism.

How much reason have we to rejoice in the time we are living in. And I take much pleasure in the part which you have played from the first. It is much to have maintained your freedom of thought, and held a place to speak freely your best during the long controversies of these years. Unto whom much is given, much is required. May you write other books as worthy to live as this last.

Had I had more time at command your welcome Volume would have had a fuller reading, and an earlier acknowledgment.

Ever Yours Cordially,
A. Bronson Alcott.

Dr. Bartol.

¹ *Radical Problems* (1872).

LETTER 72–8[1]

[to William T. Harris, St. Louis]

Concord March 11th | 1872

Dear Friend,

On looking over my sheets again carefully I do not find what answers in any large sense to my Idea of "The Lapse"; nothing that I am willing to have printed in your Journal under that title. Nor have I matter that falls naturally into a whole under any name. At best, all are but fragments, and these not fit for publishing as philosophy.

My book has taken up all my time, and absorbed some portions of what you saw when here of the Lapse papers. It is about ready for the press.

I hope you have not depended upon any thing from me for your next No. as no positive promise, I think, was made for an article.

Stirling's letter we read with much interest. Mr Emerson has returned it, I trust.

Your last letter was full of interesting matter.

Miss Brackett's prospectus commends her school to public favor. You must miss her and Miss Eliot from your teachers at St. Louis.[2]

I shall look with much hope for your school report.

Yours ever
A. Bronson Alcott

Wm. T. Harris

¹ From a copy, in Alcott's hand, in the Alcott-Pratt Collection. The original is in the Alcott-Harris Collection in the Concord Free Public Library (see Appendix B).
² Anna C. Brackett and Ida M. Eliot had left St. Louis to open a school in New York City.

LETTER 72–9[1]

[to Ellen A. Chandler, Framingham, Mass.]

Concord March | 13th 1872.

My Dear Miss Chandler,

I hope you are not waiting to be advised of our wish to have the pleasure of a Sunday's visit from you. I have been anticipating that promised study interview for weeks past, and shall picture till Presence shows the reality. Come now, at the first moment and tell me what you will, and indulge me in eye-beams and

Ideas in return.

You have not told me a word about your winter's duties and pleasures, nor have I interchanged mine with you. It seems as if a revival of our former frequent correspondence would be pleasant and have an added tint of freshness now. The sentiments obey laws of their own, and deal with time it may seem capriciously if measured by colder reason and current civilities. All the better for that. Good things are too good for all times. They make times and opportunities for their special pleasure and account.

I need not repeat what pleasant memories attend our acquaintance from the first, nor assure you of my wish to enjoy the like in the future.

About the "facts" of these past winter's days, we will speak at length when you come. And let us trust the thermometer will favor that speedily.

Ever affectionately,
A. Bronson Alcott

Miss Ellen A. Chandler

[1] MS. owned by the Abernethy Library, Middlebury College. A copy, in Alcott's hand, is in the Alcott-Pratt Collection.

LETTER 72–10[1]

[to Ellen A. Chandler, Framingham, Mass.]

Concord March 19th 1872

Dear Miss Chandler

Returning from Boston where I spent last night, I find your note saying you will pass Sunday with us. I shall look for you by the noon train, and hope the skies will favor your visit. May adds her request to mine that you will come, and I enclose her note.

If Mr. Emerson is at home and you incline we will take half an hour or so from our Sunday afternoon to call on him should the walking favor.

I had an agreeable morning at Dr. Bartols', young Gannett reading a good paper before the Radical Club.[2] Had I not supposed your hours preoccupied in your teaching I should have invited you to accompany me. The Club improves latterly and rewards for the hour. When you come we will discuss all things.

Till then, and always
Yours,
A. Bronson Alcott

Miss Chandler.

[1] MS. owned by the Abernethy Library, Middlebury College. A copy, in Alcott's hand, is in the Alcott-Pratt Collection.
[2] For a summary of W. C. Gannett's paper entitled "Looking at the Unseen," see Mary Fiske (Mrs. John T.) Sargent, ed., *Sketches and Reminiscences of the Radical Club of Chestnut Street, Boston* (Boston, 1880), pp. 67–72.

LETTER 72-11

[to Benjamin Marston Watson, Plymouth, Mass.]

Concord March 22nd 1872.

Dear Friend.

These continued cold days and a pre-engagement for next Sunday, must be my excuse for not meeting you at the Plymouth station on Saturday as you propose in your note. When summer days come, I promise myself the pleasure of renewing our old Themes—old and new—under your hospitable roof. If I can, Saturday following may favor us.

It happens besides that our annual Town meeting comes next Monday, and having some little stake in our town affairs, I desire to prove my loyalty.

When I come I will remember your request about bringing the books. I cannot promise another "Jar of Honey from Hybla,"[1] but may try your taste on a little ‖ gathered ‖ hived from our Concord flowers during these latter seasons

Very truly

Yours.

A. Bronson Alcott

B. M. Watson Esq.

[1] An ancient town in Sicily, famous for its honey.

LETTER 72-12[1]

[to Ellen A. Chandler, Framingham, Mass.]

Concord March 27th 1872.

Dear Miss Chandler,

I enclose Miss Brackett's Circular, forgotten while there was so much to be said and *read* in presence of my amiable guest, whose visit adds another pleasant memory to preceding ones, and which is but the forerunner of more in the future, let us fondly assume.

I heard that you found gallant company and escort from our station to your school-room.

Louisa comes up to-morrow to celebrate Freddy's birthday on Friday, and I may pass Sunday at Plymouth with the Watson's of rural fame.

Sanborn is at his pen again gossipping about us all editorially. Happily you have escaped this time, since he was not duly advised of your movements!

I had an evening with Emerson after our town meeting on Monday. He spoke of you with interest and regretted he was too busy to give you the time he wished. You did not tell me you were going to call on him specially, and so thinking May had *another* in her eye, and you were a party in the matter, I lost the pleasure of accompanying you, as I intended. You must have thought me uncivil, I fear, and had reason, after the implied understanding that you were to see him on Sunday.

For your kind patience with your imprisonment all Sunday forenoon, I can only offer the apology of loyal thanks. A good ear and face are fatal charmers.

Yours, affectionately,
A. Bronson Alcott.

Miss Chandler.

¹ MS. owned by the Abernethy Library, Middlebury College. A copy, in Alcott's hand, is in the Alcott-Pratt Collection.

LETTER 72–13

[to Ellen A. Chandler, Framingham, Mass.]

Concord April 6th | 1872.

Dear Miss Chandler,

Thinking Dr. Bartols lecture too characteristic of himself and of this theme for you not to see, I venture to enclose a copy taken from Mr Abbots Index, which hardly comes under your eye. I have seen nothing better in print.

Mr Harris writes that he purposes visiting New-England this month and hopes to pass Sunday the 22nd with me. On Monday 23rd the Club meets to hear a paper read by young Temple, a thoughtful divine and from whom profound things may be expected. If Mr Harris accompanies me, would you like to meet us at the Atheneum after your morning lessons are over, and dine with us at Parker House, or such place as you may prefer—, Louisa perhaps with us.

Affectionately,
A. Bronson Alcott.

LETTER 72–14¹

[to William T. Harris, St. Louis]

Concord April 9th 1872

Dear Friend,

Gladly shall I hail you at my door on Saturday the   [.]² Come and give me as much time as you can while here in these parts. We have many things to engage our thoughts, and, pray, allow yourself full time for your visit.

Your sheets of Report intimate in an intelligible manner the exceeding importance of moral education. Parents, Teachers, Professors, Statesmen, should read and profit thereby.

Davidson's "Western", promises good things also. I have just read the whole, and with good hope. When principles and Ideas are thus wisely treated and well, better times are coming for this long neglected interest of human culture. You seem to be quickening men and institutions for this good service. Come and tell me all about it.

My "Days" were given yesterday to the printer, and I am promised first proofs on Friday. So my book is fairly in hand. I am glad you are coming that I may have the benefit of your criticism in season.

Miss Chandler has lately paid me a Sunday's visit. She will like to see you while you are with us.

Yours Truly,
A. Bronson Alcott

Wm T. Harris.

---

¹ From a copy, in Alcott's hand, in the Alcott-Pratt Collection. The original, *dated April 7,* is in the Alcott-Harris Collection in the Concord Free Public Library (see Appendix B).
² The date has been left blank.

LETTER 72–15

[to Henry Terry, Waterbury? Conn.?]

Concord, Mass, April | 15th 1872.

Mr. Henry Terry.
Dear Sir,

I read in the last Waterbury American a notice of your Pamphlet on "American Clock-making".

Having worked when a boy of 14 at the shop of Silas Hoadley, first converted, I believe, by Mr. Ely Terry into a Clock Factory—the company being "Terry and Thomas," if I remember rightly, I am curious to learn what you can tell us of an interest that ‖ has ‖ has done so much to convert that section into a prosperous and intelligent community—though my native town of Wolcott may have profited less than most in this respect.

The clock cords and ivy pinions were in part furnished [by] my uncles and cousins from our hills and fields. and several of my cousins worked in the factories, or went south pedling the clocks—I had my turn with the rest.

Now you are a great and growing city: every drop of water in all the suburbs and neighboring towns, helps turn some mill wheel for the manufacture of useful and ornamental wares for the world's markets. If you make fast time, mankind must thank you if it has to bestir itself briskly to come up to the *striking.* I for one take pride in the fact that Progress starts so near my native hills.

I shall be much obliged if you will mail me a copy of your pamphlet, with price &c.

Very truly Yours,
A. Bronson Alcott

LETTER 72–16[1]

[to Ellen A. Chandler, Framingham, Mass.]

Concord May 5th 1872.

Dear Miss Chandler,

We were very sorry not to find you at any places where we sought, or hoped to see you. Mr. Harris came and spent a night, at two several times, with me. And I met him at Mrs Gov. Chaplins, at Dr. Bartols' and at the Woman's Club Rooms. His paper on Education was excellent and much praised. I tried to get a report for you but failed. You must come up for a day at your convenience, and we will make all delightfully historic.

You speak of "the lazy summer days and the rest and strength and beauty of the Hills." Have'nt we something that might do for hills to tempt you hither for a week's recreation when summer days come? Then you shall write "the attractive letters" you intimate, in the more attractive manner. I wish such a thing might be.

Now my book is fairly launched and partly in type to absorb the rest of this month at least. I have seen proof sheets to page 107. no farther.

I met the good Madame Kraige and her rosy daughter at the Woman's Club. The little saints should be kept such by such sweet faces as theirs.

Ever affectionately
A. Bronson Alcott

Miss Ellen A. Chandler.
P.S. Retain "Bartol" till you bring it yourself.

[1] MS. owned by the Abernethy Library, Middlebury College. A copy, in Alcott's hand, is in the Alcott-Pratt Collection.

LETTER 72–17

[to Mr. Hinckley]

Concord May, | 8th. 1872.

Mr. Hinckley.
Dear Sir.

I shall gladly meet your Club at the time you name in your note. My subject will be *"The Ideal Church'*. which may open a spirited Conversation let us hope.

Very truly
Yours,
A. Bronson Alcott.

LETTER 72–18

[to Thomas Davidson, St. Louis]

Concord June 19th 1872

Dear Sir,

I am glad to learn that you purpose spending your summer days so near and please my self in the ‖ pleasure ‖ hope of seeing you more than once at my house in Concord. I shall be at home after Monday of next week, and if you will advise me of the day when you will visit me, we shall not miss each other.

Hoping soon "to talk over the many things with you" here. I am

Very truly

Yours

A. Bronson Alcott

Mr. Thomas Davidson

LETTER 72–19

[to Celia Burleigh, Brooklyn, Conn.]

Concord June 30th 1872

Dear Mrs. Burleigh,

Accept my thanks for the book of Verses which I owe to your kindness. I find many sweet and noble lines in the Volume, and your tribute to the memory of a friend so near and dear to you as their author, is affecting.

It was not my happiness to know Mr. Burleigh save by connexion of the worthy family name which he bore. My brother-in-law Samuel J. May used to speak of him to me with affection, and it is plain that he filled a life with noble designs and good deeds.

With more leisure at command I hope to look further into his verses. And sometime ‖ come and s ‖ visit the spot where he found a friend (still continued) to make his life delightful.

Very truly Yours,

A. Bronson Alcott.

Mrs Celia Burleigh,
    Brooklyn, Conn.

LETTER 72–20

[to David H. Harris, Jacksonville, Ill.]

Concord July 4th 1872.

Dear Sir,

Accept my thanks for your gift of the photograph of "the Plato Club." It makes the existence of such a body very palpable and believable to such of my Eastern friends who may question the existence of such a Classic company out of New-England, and renders any accounts of mine creditable concerning the accomplishments of the West. Please give my respects to the members severally, and my hope of meeting the Club sometime during the coming Autumn.

Your brother[1] has been in these parts lately, but has not yet appeared in Concord. Mr. Amory, or Emery (which?)[2] from Quincy. Ill. was here yesterday, and gave us late accounts of friends at Quincy and Jacksonville.

Especially remember me to Dr. and Mrs Jones the Walcotts and Kings.[3] Mr. D. H. Harris

[1] William Torrey Harris.
[2] Samuel H. Emery.
[3] The complimentary close and signature have been cut out.

LETTER 72–21[1]

[to Ellen A. Chandler, Framingham, Mass.]

Concord July 10th 1872

Dear Miss Chandler,

I am strongly tempted to accompany Mrs Davis today, but the summer heats, with the uncertainties of making seasonable connections at West Concord to witness the exercises, seem too formidable and forbidding. But May requests me, since I cannot invite in person, to add her persuasions that you will come over with Mrs Davis on Thursday and spend Sunday with us. Come at once to your chamber under our roof—and so we shall have three days at least of enjoyment—myself the proper share!—Pray come and oblige us. Besides conversation, there is boating—the hammock, the arbor—and whatsoever frolic fancies[?], you gay ones may conceive.

Affectionately,
A. Bronson Alcott.

Miss Chandler
    Framingham

[1] MS. owned by the Abernethy Library, Middlebury College. A copy, in Alcott's hand, is in the Alcott-Pratt Collection.

LETTER 72–22

[to Charles D. B. Mills, Syracuse]

Concord July 11th 1872.

Dear Friend,

I was in Boston lately, and presented your wishes about your "Buddha" to Messr Roberts Brothers. Mr. Niles, the literary member of the house, and who determines these matters altogether;—says that he cannot predict the best for works of the class, yet he will read your M.S. when you have it ready, and give his decision about publishing.

He thinks Mr. Johnson takes all risks about publishing his book. Publishers are slow to venture where returns are so doubtful.

I shall be most happy to further your wishes with any of them, if my word can be of any service to you.

My book is nearly printed, running to near 300 pages, and the publishers hope to issue it sometime during *this* month.

My present purpose is to leave for the West sometime in October, so as to return before the New Year opens.

Mrs Adams from Dubuque has passed a day with us since Anniversary week,[1] and Mr. Emery of Quincy Ill. a scholar and student of philosophy, has been with us also.

Mr. Harris comes to attend the National Teachers' Association in August, and Davidson is now at Gloucester passing his summer, busy on Aristotle.

Our regards to yourself and yours

A. Bronson Alcott.

C. B. D. [*sic*] Mills.

[1] During her visit to Concord in June, Mrs. Adams started the cairn at Walden Pond as a monument to Thoreau (see Alcott, *Journals*, p. 426).

LETTER 72–23[1]

[to Ellen A. Chandler, Jamaica Plain? Mass.]

Concord July 15 1872.

Dear Miss Chandler,

We shall expect you by the 12 train on Saturday. If you do not come *then,* by one of the afternoon trains. 11 A.M. 2.35 and 4 P.M. are the hours from the Fitchburg Station for Concord. Come by the earliest if you can and with freedom to spend some days of next week. May particularly desires me to say that she "begs you will not hurry away," and my own claims are the less than indefinite? We expect Louisa will have returned from Gloucester and be with us by that time. And Mrs Davis will, of course, draw you from us to shorten your stay with *us.*

We regretted much to have lost *your day* at Framingham. But her babe's illness left her no choice, and the heats looked formidable to me. You must have had a delightful reunion. Come and make it better than it was in the telling.

I hope to have the last sheets of my *"Days"* to show you when you come,— your contributions to the text to surprize you. When one puts his correspondents into his book what shall be the penalty?

Affectionately
A. Bronson Alcott

Miss Ellen A Chandler

[1] MS. owned by the Abernethy Library, Middlebury College. A copy, in Alcott's hand, is in the Alcott-Pratt Collection.

LETTER 72-24[1]

[to Ellen A. Chandler]

Concord July 27th 1872.

Dear Miss Chandler.

Our Postmaster has found Miss Pratt's Circular—which I enclose.

Mr Emerson and family have taken quarters for the present at the Manse. The House is to be repaired, I believe, forthwith. The carpenter advises adding a mansard roof giving another story of rooms. He thinks the necessary repairs may all be covered by the Insurance, so the money loss will be inconsiderable.

But we shall never sit again *in the same rooms!*

Mr Emerson's papers he tells me are all safe, as far as he has examined, and unharmed. Those saved by yourself and Louisa were nearly all in the Attic of much value, most there having been destined to go to the rag-buyers.

Ellen returned this morning.

Only the most delightful memories abide of your too short visit which I hope you will repeat on your return from the mountains.

Affectionately
Yours
A. Bronson Alcott

Miss Chandler.

[1] MS. owned by the Abernethy Library, Middlebury College. A copy (incorrectly *dated July 2*), in Alcott's hand, is in the Alcott-Pratt Collection.

LETTER 72-25

[to Samuel A. Drake, Boston]

Concord August 26th | 1872.

Mr Drake,

Dear Sir,

Miss Fuller lived in Avon Place, north side, with her uncle, Henry Fuller, Esq. I am not aware that she had a school for young ladies in the city. She held Conversations for grown persons during the winter season. She taught in my School then held in the Masonic Temple, succeeding Miss Elisabeth Peabody. She went afterwards to Providence and taught in the school of Hiram Fuller. And from thence was invited to New York by Horace Greeley as a contributor to the "New York Tribune.' From thence she went abroad never to return. The dates of these movements you will be likely to find in Her "Memoirs" by Clarke, Channing and Emerson.[1]

Respectfully
Yours,
A. Bronson Alcott

Saml A. Drake

[1] *Memoirs of Margaret Fuller Ossoli* (1852).

1872

LETTER 72-26[1]

[to W. E. Eaton,[1] Boston]

Concord August | 31st 1872.

Dear Sir,

I must again repeat that I have too few facts concerning the character and educational services of the late Charles Brooks to warrant my promising any thing of importance for his "Memoir." I think I named Prof. Russell of Lancaster, Mass. as likelier to know more of his history in connection with education than any one surviving him. The last time I met Mr. Brooks he seemed to feel as if his services especially in promoting "Normal Schools" had not been duly appreciated by his countrymen. I have an impression that he felt himself the proper person for Secretary of the Board of Education, and was disappointed at not receiving an appointment to that office instead of Mr. Mann.

My brother in law, the late Saml J. May, was intimate with him, being settled at South Scituate while Mr. Brooks was at Hingham. But he is beyond our reach and Mr. George B. Emerson, who knew him perhaps better than any one, is abroad.

A man so active and able as was Mr Brooks should have ample justice done him by his friends.

Regretting that [I] have nothing more to offer,

I am,

very Respectfully,

A. Bronson Alcott.

[1] MS. in the Clifton Waller Barrett Library, University of Virginia. A copy, in Alcott's hand, is in the Alcott-Pratt Collection.
[2] Eaton was connected with an educational journal, the *Massachusetts Teacher*.

LETTER 72-27[1]

[to Ellen A. Chandler, Framingham, Mass.]

Concord September | 3rd 1872.

Dear Miss Chandler,

I have a moment to acknowledge the receipt of your kind favor of the 1st. and to tell you that Louisa and I leave early to-morrow morning for Connecticut, taking little Freddy with us. We make but a flying visit to the Old Homesteads in Wolcott, and its neighborhood, intending to return on Saturday following. Louisa has not seen the spot, since she was a mere child, and has, I suspect, designs on the place and people for a future story. You will be pleased to learn that she has recovered something of her former fire and freshness and is at her pen again at intervals.

May yesterday returned from her month's stay at at [*sic*] Clarke's Island, having enjoyed the boating, swimming, and like recreations by the seaside, brimmingly.

Your note gave me much pleasure, as every thing of yours, I need not assure you, always has and does.

Before I leave for the West, pray let me have a parting salute, if no more. Peaches are ripe now and blush to be tasted. Besides you are not unaware of their being a favorite fruit of mine.

Ever affectionately,
A. Bronson Alcott.

Miss Ellen A. Chandler.

[1] MS. owned by the Abernethy Library, Middlebury College. A copy, in Alcott's hand, is in the Alcott-Pratt Collection.

LETTER 72–28[1]

[to Ellen A. Chandler, Framingham, Mass.]

Concord Sep. 19th 1872.

Dear Miss Chandler,

My book is to be published on Saturday—day after to morrow.

Now shall I send your copy in the publisher's binding, or in sheets so that you may have it bound to match "The Tablets"?

In either choice, I will send you the Illustrated Title Page when I learn your wishes. This can readily be inserted by your own hands in either.

The covers are brown green and blue. Which of these, if you choose the bound copies?

It would add sweetly to the pleasure if I might put this little gift into your hands myself. But as that may not be, unless some happy chance were to bring you near, I must trust it to the mails instead.

I wish it may find as much favor in the eyes of the receiver, as her presence and conversation always brings the giver.

Yours affectionately,
A. Bronson Alcott.

Miss Ellen A. Chandler

[1] MS. owned by the Abernethy Library, Middlebury College. A copy, in Alcott's hand, is in the Alcott-Pratt Collection.

LETTER 72–29[1]

[to William T. Harris, St. Louis]

Concord September 19th 1872

Dear Friend,

My Book is printed and is to be published on Saturday,—day after to morrow. I was in Boston yesterday and learned that orders had been forwarded to the publishers for more than half of the edition of 1000 copies. Ripley has given it a notice in the Tribune, which, I doubt not, you may have seen. I expressed a copy to you by Adam's Express which should reach you with this. I shall be honored by any notice which you may find time to give it in *your* Journal, or elsewhere.

I purpose leaving for the West about the middle of October, taking Waterbury, New Haven, on my way: whether I come direct from thence to St. Louis, and go up the Misisippi [*sic*] cities to Dubuque, or proceed to that place, and come down the river to you, is not determined at present. Which will suit you and your friends best? I should like to give perhaps ten days or a fortnight to St. Louis, and at the best season.

Mrs Adams writes that she thinks I shall have as much as I can do in the cities and towns in her section—perhaps go as far as St. Paul. I can make arrangements as I go out for our more Eastern cities along the lines of travel. All looks most propitious at this time for a productive Winter's tour; for should I find unexpected favor, I might prolong my stay West till towards the Spring. This kind of service seems one that I can best perform for letters and Ideas, and is most agreeable to me. Perhaps I may be opening the way for the Institution for Culture that our time and people so much need, and which you have so ably set forth in your "Hoboken Essay,' which I have just read with great satisfaction. I trust I am looking in the right direction to yourself and followers for the initiation of the better education and Culture.

Sanborn has come to Concord probably to reside permanently. And I do not despair of your making our little town your home sometime. A new spirit is awakening here and only the [word] of things at the turn is wanting to make it a literary and philosophical centre for the future, as well as the present. So you see I am still not less a dreamer than of yore.

Louisa is now beginning to find her pen pleasant again.

Saturday Niles and Miller, the poet, are expected to come up ‖ to ‖ and dine with us. Emerson is at Nashon[2] with Mr. Forbes.[3] His house is undergoing repairs, and will be reopened he hopes by thanksgiving.

I read Ripleys notice of your Journal with pleasure and pride.

Truly Yours,
A. Bronson Alcott.

Wm. T. Harris
    St. Louis

[1] From a copy, in Alcott's hand, in the Alcott-Pratt Collection. The original is in the Alcott-Harris Collection in the Concord Free Public Library (see Appendix B).
[2] Na*u*shon Island, Massachusetts.
[3] Edith Emerson Forbes, Emerson's daughter.

LETTER 72–30

[to Ednah Dow Cheney, Jamaica Plain, Mass.]

Concord, October 3rd 1872.

Dear Mrs Cheney,

Your kind appreciation of my book is gratifying. Other friends too have signified their approval, and the public have taken the first edition from the publishers—a partial success at least, so the trade say.

As to the books about which you inquire for your nephew, perhaps Burnham, in School street, may have copies. Both have long been out of print, but lately inquiries have been made for them, and they may be republished. The Record of a School only waits Miss Peabody's approval to be published forthwith.

You inquire kindly whether I purpose going West. I do. And purpose to leave late in October; arrangements being made for meeting companies in the prinicipal cities. I may be absent for three months or more. If the Radical Club meets before I leave I shall hope to see you there.

Let me congratulate you on having the honor of giving the opening address of the Woman's Course of Lectures on English Literature.

Very truly
Yours.
A. Bronson Alcott.

Mrs Cheney.

LETTER 72–31

[to Mary N. Adams, Dubuque, Iowa]

Concord October 4th 1872

Dear Mrs Adams,

My book is published at last, and a copy of it, I trust, has reached you before this date. Shall I follow it soon after the 20th of this month, stopping along the route to arrange for Conversations on my return East? If so, I might reach Dubuque early in November to meet such engagements as await me in your neighborhood. Mr Harris writes that December (not earlier) will suit his friends best, at St. Louis. My stay may be longer or shorter, as circumstances shall determine. I will await your wishes in the matters.

Louisa leaves us to day for her winter quarters in Boston. She is in better spirits than when you were here, and begins to enjoy her pen with the former force and freshness. We made a short visit in September to the Old Homestead in Conn. taking Freddy with us. May is passing a fortnight at North Conway, but returns to resume her housekeeping. She is quite gay, and enjoys society beyond what our little village affords.

Anna and boys expect to spend the winter here. Having a warm furnace in the cellar, Mrs A. finds the house comfortable, and, with her girls and grandsons, consents to let me roam for a few months where she fancies people delight to entertain according to her notions of hospitality. She is enjoying a measure of leisure and spirits for reading and writing.

When one has a vigorous pen like hers at his elbow, can you wonder if he delegate writing to her sometimes?

Mr Emerson is now at the Manse, his family are still at Nashon [sic]. I think he may take his Thanksgiving dinner, with his English friends Tyndall and Froude, under his own roof.

Mr. Channing makes his weekly calls, and is very agreeable for the most part. He inquires often about you, and regrets not seeing more of you, while in these parts.

Mr. Sanborn is in pursuit of a house wishing to settle permanently in Concord. And Mr. Harris writes that "The Institution here must be."[1] Perhaps my winter's work may further it.

1872

The Radical Club meets on the 21st. I may leave soon after the session, taking Connecticut on my way West.

My family all desire their affectionate remembrance.

With great regard,
Truly Yours,
A. Bronson Alcott

Mrs. Mary Newbury Adams,
Dubuque, Iowa

¹ The Concord School of Philosophy, which became a reality in the summer of 1879.

LETTER 72–32

[to Mrs. M. D. Wolcott, Jacksonville, Ill.]

Concord October 4th | 1872

Dear Mrs Wolcott,

Enclosed you will find the Note of Introduction to Mr Dwight,¹ which I am happy to give, as well on your own as on your daughter's account,—well remembering the exceedingly hospitable reception which I received from yourself and Friends during my stay in your city.

Sometime during the present autumn or early in December, I hope to pass a few days with you again and enjoy another sitting or two with your Saturday's Symposeum [sic]—the like of which we cannot yet gather here in the East.

I sent your Plato—Dr. Jones—a few days since, a copy of my *"Concord Days,"* which I hope has come to hand by this time.

To him and to each of my friends in your circle, please offer my cherished affection and remembrance.

Rarely has it been my happiness to enjoy so much in any company as in the charmed circle in which I found myself embraced while in your city.

When next in Boston, I will call on Mr. Dwight and apprize him of your daughters wishes.

Most truly,
Yours,
A. Bronson Alcott

Mrs Wolcott.

¹ See the following Letter 72–33.

LETTER 72–33¹

[to John Sullivan Dwight, Boston]

Concord October, | 4th 1872

Dear Friend,

The bearer of this, Miss Wolcott of Jacksonville Ill. is desirous of enjoying the best opportunities for pursuing the study of Music that the city of Boston offers. She will be thankful for any information or assistance which you may render for enabling her to prosecute her studies advantageously. Miss Wolcott has given much attention to the study hitherto. She now wishes to perfect herself in the art of teaching it.

As an additional claim upon your kind attention, I may name the high character and attainments of her parents, whose hospitalities I have shared at their home in the West. And I may add, moreover,—what will not fail of having significance in your eyes, both are members of the *"Plato Club"* of that City

Very truly

Yours,

A. Bronson Alcott

John S. Dwight, Esq.
    Boston.

¹ MS. owned by the Dartmouth College Library.

LETTER 72–34

[to Samuel H. Emery, Quincy, Ill.]

Concord October, | 4th 1872.

Dear Sir,

Mr. Harris lately sent me Ripley's appreciative notice, in the N. Y. Tribune, of the July No. of the Journal of Speculative Philosophy, in which he makes most favorable mention of your article on *"the Parmenides of Plato"* and of the Philosophical Societies in Quincy and Jacksonville. I wish you may have seen it, if not, it is well worth looking up.

Sometime next month or in early December, I hope to visit Quincy again, and have opportunity for comparing notes, philosophical and literary with yourself and friends in your city.

Your short call upon us is remembered with much pleasure. It seemed another link for binding East and West together in the Chain of a nobler Idealism befitting our country and time.

Please give my cherished remembrances to all my friends in Quincy.

Very truly

Yours

A. Bronson Alcott

S. H. Emery, Jr

LETTER 72–35

[to Thomas Kean, Buffalo]

Concord October, | 4th 1872.

Dear Sir,

I shall be passing your city on my way to the Missisippi [*sic*] sometime about the last of this month, and will stop for a day or so, if you think it worth while, to arrange for some *Conversations* to be given either on my way West or return homewards. I shall hardly leave here till after the 20th. of this month, and if you care to consult your townspeople about the matter and report to me before that date, it may assist me in determining my plans for the winter's tour.

"My Concord Days" is published at last, and I directed my publishers to forward a copy to your office which I hope has come to hand before this date.

Very truly
Yours,
A. Bronson Alcott.

Thomas Kean Esq.
    Buffalo

LETTER 72–36

[to Mrs. Bagley, Detroit]

Concord October | 4th 1872.

Dear Mrs. Bagley,

I have just written to your sister, Mrs Adams,[1] that I purpose leaving for the Missisipi [sic] sometime about the last of this month, and shall take Detroit on my way out, of course. Whether I make any stay with you *then*, will depend upon your wishes altogether. I shall at least pause to call on my kind friends, and shall be happy to arrange for some Conversations before I return homewards.

Should any of them have any thing to communicate about the matter and it should reach me here before I leave home; ‖ and ‖ it would assist me in my plans for my winter's tour. If Mr. Ives is coming this way I hope he will arrive before the 20th. as I may visit Connecticut on my way West, and should otherwise fail to see him here in Concord.

My family are all very well, and retain delightful reccollections [sic] of your visit. We heard that Mr Bagley was in these parts during the summer, and hoped to have seen him in Concord.

Please remember me to all my friends in Detroit, especially to my hospitable hosts—hostess—the Leggetts.

Very truly,
Yours,
A. Bronson Alcott

Mrs Bagley.

[1] See Letter 72–31.

LETTER 72–37[1]

[to William T. Harris, St. Louis]

Dear Friend   Concord October 5th | 1872.

Your very acceptable letter of the 26th Sep. is received. What you say of my book is gratifying. And the notices that I have seen are very favorable. None are real criticisms, as one of yours would be, apprehensive of the Ideas out of which the text germinates and forms itself, but well meant and respectable. Besides these, I have received very gratifying letters from friends to whom I sent the book. You will gladly learn that it has already gone to a Second Edition, a good part of which is already sold. So I am to have some thing of a reading at any rate. I shall look for your notice with || something of || [p. o.] impatience, yet can afford to wait knowing the press of work you have at hand.[2]

I sent, directed to your care, a Copy of the "Days" to *Kroeger,* knowing you would find ways of getting it to him.

I have written to friends in most of the Western cities apprizing them of my purpose of leaving for the West soon after the 20th of this month. I shall make for Dubuque, as a centre for engagements in that section, which will perhaps occupy me, (if Mrs Adams plans prevail) through the month of November. I can then take the cities of Davenport, Quincy, Jacksonville, and Burlington on my way down the Missisipi [*sic*], reaching St Louis sometime, (I hope) as early in December as may be found practicable. I should like to give a fortnight at least to your city, and meet as many of your scholarly minds as can be reached properly.

All that I leave for you to determine for me. I think I could speak good words to your Teachers were they called under your auspices to hear, and converse, too, if you thought best.

I have written to Emery, and sent a book to *Dr. Jones.* Mrs Wolcott of the Plato Club has also written about their sittings.

I trust this winter's work will *tell* for us all.

Louisa has taken winter quarters in Boston, and taken up her pen, for a story. We had a short visit to Conn. from whence, I infer, she brought away spoils.

I have sent "Concord Days" to Miss Brackett, not knowing her No. She may not get it.

Regards to Davidson, with a copy of the same, by this mail, addressed to your care.

                                            Yours truly
                                            A. Bronson Alcott

Wm. T. Harris.

---

[1] From a copy, in Alcott's hand, in the Alcott-Pratt Collection. The original is in the Alcott-Harris Collection in the Concord Free Public Library (see Appendix B).

[2] Harris's notice of *Concord Days* appeared in the *Journal of Speculative Philosophy,* VI (October, 1872), 376–82.

LETTER 72–38

[to Sarah Denman, New Haven, Conn.]

Concord October 10th 1872

Dear Mrs Denman,

I am pleasantly surprised by your note, just received, and by the intimation that you still hold our little town in such high regard that you can think of "Wayside' as a possession. I shall be at home on Thursday next, and most happy to welcome you to my house, and hope you will remain as our guest till we can arrange, (if possible) the matter about which you inquire.

The present occupants have till next ‖ June ‖ March to determine whether they will remain longer. And I have the refusal of the place for you or any other purchaser, should they ‖ purchase, or ‖ leave.

I think a reasonable advance on the terms of the purchase would induce them to make the place over to any who should offer it.

Last week, I wrote to Mr Emery and Mrs Wolcott about my Western tour. When you come, we will talk further about it.

Most truly
Yours,
A. Bronson Alcott.

Mrs. Denman,
New Haven

LETTER 72–39

[to A. C. Felton, Lowell, Mass.][1]

Concord October | 10th 1872.

Dear Sir,

Your interest in myself and books,—one of which you were chiefly the means of putting in type—cannot be other than grateful to me. And the spirit in which you write commends itself to me.

I wish it were quite practicable for me to visit you before I leave for the West. I must be content rather to find you fairly released from legal bonds, and clothed in your own self-respect,—this temporary imprisonment perhaps classed with your blessings.

I shall hardly return before the New Year. Should my gains warrant, I may have it in my power to forward something from my receipts at the West. Really I know of no one to whom I could properly present your claims for pecuniary aid.

Truly Yours,
A. Bronson Alcott.

A. C. Felton.

[1] Felton had written from Lowell Jail asking Alcott to visit him.

LETTER 72–40

[to Anna C. Brackett, New York City]

Dear Miss Brackett.   Concord October 11th | 1872

I sent by mail addressed to you at New York City, a copy of "Concord Days." As I did not then know your number, the book may have missed you,—perhaps awaits your call at the Post Office. I have sent a copy to Mr. Harris who writes that he is meditating an extended notice of it. This I shall especially value when it appears. All the criticisms that I have seen, with one or two exceptions have been most favorable. The first edition is exhausted, and a second has mostly been taken by the booksellers. I shall be happy to learn your impressions after a full reading, if you find time to look into it. And please inform me if your copy comes to hand.

Mr. Harris has sent me part of your translation of the "Pedagogy." It promises well and is much needed in our superficial teaching.

I purpose leaving for the West about the first of November to be gone perhaps till New-Years. My engagements embrace the chief Missisippi [sic] cities. And I may reach Washington before I return.

I am expecting Mrs Denman of Quincy, Ill. on Thursday next. She wishes to buy ‖ Hillside ‖ Wayside, Hawthorne's place adjoining mine, for a Summer House for herself and friends. And Emery, *the Parmenidean,* may occupy it permanently, if she succeeds in purchasing it. With him, Harris, yourself, we might open our "Academy" modestly.

Louisa has taken quarters in Boston for the winter and resumed her pen.

With much regard,
Truly Yours,
A. Bronson Alcott

Miss A. C. Brackett
New York.

LETTER 72–41[1]

[to Ellen A. Chandler, Framingham, Mass.]

Dear Miss Chandler.   Concord October 17th | 1872.

I am to meet a select company of young ladies at Mrs Manning's 128 Beacon Street on Tuesday next at 11'30 A.M.

Miss Manning and her friend Miss Howe (a niece of Julia Ward) passed yesterday here with us, and arranged with May for the Conversation. The company is invited by the trio. The hour named for meeting was thought most convenient for most. It will give them much pleasure if your engagements permit your attendance.

Need I add that I shall be delighted to find you one of the circle? Certainly

I could not deny myself this opportunity of expressing my hope that either there, or at some other place I might see your face before leaving for the West.

Has Louisa informed you of her Winter quarters?

Affectionately
Yours,
A. Bronson Alcott.

Miss E. S. [*sic*] C.

¹ MS. owned by the Abernethy Library, Middlebury College. A copy, in Alcott's hand, is in the Alcott-Pratt Collection.

LETTER 72-42

[to Virginia Vaughan, Boston]

Concord October 17th | 1872.

Dear Miss Vaughan,

A select company of young ladies are to meet at Mrs Manning's 128 Beacon Street next Tuesday at 11"30 A.M.

Miss Manning, Miss Howe, (a niece of Julia Wards) and my daughter May, ask the favor of your attendance should your engagements permit.

It is to be a Conversation of mine; and I need not add my wish that you will favor us with your Company.

I shall be happy to call for you at about 11. and accompany you to Mrs Manning's.

Very truly
Yours
A. Bronson Alcott.

Miss Virginia Vaughan.

LETTER 72-43

[to Ellen A. Chandler, Framingham, Mass.]

Concord October 28th | 1872.

Dear Miss Chandler,

Thinking you might like to read some of the most flattering criticisms that have come to hand, I enclose one from "the Golden Age. Who writes it I am not informed.

Mr Harris has a short notice, he writes, for the next no. of his Journal. He appears to be dissatisfied with all the notices, and says;

"I have read that in "the Golden Age" and am glad to see the good will displayed there. I cannot like any of these criticisms, though, I must say frankly. They do not point out any thing when they praise it that is worth saying any thing about. They leave utterly unnoticed the best things, or else exhibit an entire want of understanding in this regard. They make frank concessions of faults that have no existence, and altogether their atmosphere as displayed in their remarks is so narrow and close, and so redolent of cheap radicalism and scepticism that it is not agreeable to sit down in their company even to a feast of "Concord Days". I shall get in a notice of Concord Days among my book Notices, and will try to be as just as I can.

I sent copy to Miss Brackett, but have not heard from her yet.

I think I may leave for the West sometime next week. If I should go to Plymouth to speak next Sunday, I shall wish to return through Boston on Monday the 4th. and will call at Louisa's room, No. 7 Allston Street (Mrs May's Boarding House,) hoping that your engagements will admit of your being there after the close of your School.

The Conversation at Mrs. Manning's was well attended, and passed pleasantly, the young ladies assured me. Sanborn alone was present to vary the company.

When will the busy schoolmistress find a little leisure from her duties to see and delight her friends?

Affectionately
Yours
A. Bronson Alcott

Miss Ellen Chandler

LETTER 72–44

[to Benjamin Marston Watson, Plymouth, Mass.]

Concord October 31st | 1872.

Dear Friend,

Your note has just come to hand with your kind invitation for Sunday the 9th. Novr. While it would have given me great pleasure to have sat beside your *parlor fire* during these November days, my engagements call me West before that date. I leave the day after the election, to be gone three months or more, visiting the principal Western cities. On my return I shall hope to pay you the visit which various circumstances seem to have prevented during the last twelvemonth.

I am pleased to learn that my Book interests my friends, especially yourself and household.

Very truly
Yours,
A. Bronson Alcott.

LETTER 72-45

[to J. B. Marvin, Washington, D.C.]

Concord Nover 1st. | 1872.

Dear Sir.

Your letter and friendly notice of my book came duly to hand. You have my thanks for your criticism—one of many in its praise.

As I purpose leaving for a three months' tour West soon after the Elections are over, I can hardly hope to visit Washington till sometime in February at least. Meanwhile should you find on inquiry sufficient interest felt by any persons in your city to warrant my coming you may address me at Concord.

As to terms, I cannot now specify any sum definitely—something more than to cover my travelling expenses would be desirable. If tickets of admission for three or four evenings were sold at, say $2.00. and the company numbered fifty persons, I should be justified, or you might take subscriptions for a given sum. But I leave the matter wholly to yourself.

As to topics. the time and company would best determine. I had a few pleasant words last week at the Unitarian Conference in Boston, with Mrs Johnson and Miss Donaldson by whom I sent a like message.

My regards to Mr Spofford whom I should like much to see.

Truly Yours.
A. Bronson Alcott.

J. B. Marvin
Washington City.
D. C.

LETTER 72-46

[to Celia Burleigh, Brooklyn, Conn.]

Concord November 1st | 1872

Dear Mrs Burleigh.

I find I have delayed so long my departure for the West that I must hasten forwards as fast as possible after the Elections of next week, and must forego, for the present, the agreeable visit to Brooklyn about which we spoke at the Unitarian Conference. But it will be my pleasure to renew my acquaintance with that place, and with yourself, at the earliest opportunity.

I expect to pass the next month or two in the Western Cities, where I find most delightful circles of earnest friends whom I greatly delight to meet.

On the whole I found much satisfaction in the recent Conference; and feel that a little while is to unite those who deemed themselves widely apart but the other day.

Very truly
Yours,
A. Bronson Alcott.

Celia Burleigh
Brooklyn, Conn.

LETTER 72-47

[to Charles D. B. Mills, Syracuse]

Dear Friend,
Concord November 1st | 1872.

I have written to Mr Morse to call at Roberts Brothers and take your M.S. On Monday next I am to be in Boston and will try to find Morse himself.

I purpose leaving for the West soon after the Elections are over, and hope to reach Syracuse by Saturday at least. In that case I should spend Sunday there and, perhaps, pass Westwards on Monday following, as I am to be in Dubuque as early in the month of November as possible after this delay in leaving home.

At the Unitarian Conference I saw Mr. Calthrop and Mr. Bragg of your city, with many friends from various States. On the whole, the Conference gave signs of life and progress. It needs but a little while to unite those who deemed themselves widely apart the other day.

Expecting to see you soon

I am
Very truly
Yours
A. Bronson Alcott

Chas. D. B. Mills.

LETTER 72-48[1]

[to Mary N. Adams, Dubuque, Iowa]

Dear Mrs Adams,
Concord November | 1st, 1872.

I purpose leaving for the West soon after the elections are over, and hope to reach Dubuque by the 16th. 'Tis later by a whole fortnight than I wished, but a freeman is unwilling to forego his suffrage in times like the present. I shall stop a train or two at Syracuse, Buffalo, Detroit, and Chicago, to arrange for Conversations on my return homewards. These are now fairly advertised in most of the western cities. Mr. Denman[2] from Quincy has paid us a short visit lately, and I have had letters from Mrs Wolcott of Jacksonville. At the Unitarian Convention held in Boston, I saw friends from Chicago, Davenport, Indianapolis, & Cleveland. Mrs Bagley has written me also. Thus every thing looks fair for a hearing at least. Should invitations thicken, I may prolong my stay into the new Year.

At the Conference I also met Mr. Taft of Humboldt College, who said he "must return to welcome us at his home in Springville." He certainly made a strong plea for his College and Dr Morrison added his. The Conference showed signs of life and progress. It needs but a little while for those who deemed themselves wide apart but the other day to find sympathy and friendly recognition.

Should you have anything to communicate before I reach your city, you shall address me at Detroit, where I shall pass a day with "the Governor" and his family on my way out.

Louisa has taken rooms in Boston for her winter quarters, and has a new book in press. Two editions of Concord Days are nearly sold and a third is proposed for the holidays.

Mr Emerson and Ellen sailed for England on the 23rd. to be gone till spring. Ellen wishes to see Egypt and they may go there before they return. Tyndall's lectures were fascinating. Froude and the other Englishmen I have not seen.

I am looking West with hope and interest, and shall soon, *(the Forces* permitting), be with you and yours.

Very truly
A. Bronson Alcott.

[1] MS. owned by the Iowa State Department of History and Archives, Des Moines, Iowa. The letter is framed with only pp. 2 and 3 showing. Consequently, the first part of the letter is copied from a typescript of p. 1, framed with the letter. There also appear to be two or three lines on p. 4. The letter is quoted in part in Hubert H. Hoeltje, "Some Iowa Lectures and Conversations of Amos Bronson Alcott," *Iowa Journal of History and Politics,* XXIX (July, 1931), 380. A copy, in Alcott's hand, is in the Alcott-Pratt Collection.

[2] The copy in the Alcott-Pratt Collection reads "Mrs Denman."

[Letter to Sidney H. Morse, Boston; from Concord, November? 1? 1872.]

Letter 72–49

[to Anna C. Brackett, New York City]

Concord November | 2nd 1872

Dear Miss Brackett,

Your letter has this morning come to hand with the gratifying intelligence of your success in N. York. I doubt not you are to realize your wishes in your School, and I know of none more deserving of the most sympathetic and enlightened patronage than yourself. We talk of education but how little there is deserving the name.

The books you inquire about are on the whole the best, for consulting about English Poetry of any I know. The title is:

"A complete Edition of the Poets of Great Britain by Robert Anderson M.D. London 1795 13 Vols. I think you will be most likely to find it at the Antique Bookstores. It should be in the great Libraries at any rate being a well known, and, I believe the most complete collection in print.

I start after the Elections for the West. expecting to reach St. Louis early in December. I had a note from Mr. Harris dated October 25th. in which he speaks of the early appearance of "the Journal of Spec. Phi." containing his notice of

"Concord Days," and not liking over much the praises thus far bestowed on the volume.

Very truly
Yours,
A. Bronson Alcott

Miss Anna C. Brackett
New York City.

LETTER 72-50[1]

[to William T. Harris, St. Louis]

Concord November | 7th 1872.

Dear Friend.

I leave to-morrow for Syracuse, expecting to reach Dubuque by the 15th. As neither the *Journal* nor the *Western* have yet come to hand, and I shall wish to see them as soon as published, you will oblige me if you will mail copies for me, to the care of Austin Adams Esqr. Dubuque, Iowa. I know they will keep me in Dubuque as long as they can, and if I shop for Conversations at Quincy and Jacksonville on my way down to St. Louis, the New Year will open before I reach you. I have been unable to leave earlier. And shall just pause going out at the intermediate places to arrange definitely about Conversations as I come East. Drop me a line at Dubuque with the Magazines.

"*Concord Days*" is finding readers and praises all round. Brooks and Calvert of Newport,[2] the last, about my sketch of *Goethe* specially. I believe the publishers intend to issue a third edition (corrected) for the holidays, the first and second being nearly sold.

Has Kroeger got his copy? Miss Brackett writes that she has hers, and that her School prospers. She deserves it beyond most teachers known to me.

Truly Yours,
A. Bronson Alcott.

Wm. T. Harris.

[1] From a copy, in Alcott's hand, in the Alcott-Pratt Collection. The original, *dated November 6,* is in the Alcott-Harris Collection in the Concord Free Public Library (see Appendix B).
[2] Charles Timothy Brooks and George Henry Calvert.

LETTER 72-51[1]

[to William T. Harris, St. Louis]

Dubuque November | 20th 1872.

Dear Friend,

My thanks for your Notice of "Concord Days." and for the literary sequel promised which, I doubt not will be equally satisfactory. When I see you, we will consider both together. The Boston fire, so calamitous to many, has left us,

Louisa and myself, I believe, unharmed. Her new book, she writes, is published today, an edition of 10 000 copies.[2]

I am to be here, and *hereabout,* for the ten days to come—going down the river next to Davenport, and hope to be in Quincy and Jacksonville by the middle of December, at least.

I am the guest of the Adams and find surprising company in Mrs Adams. Look at the Sibyls, and when I see you, I will tell you which of them survives in this wonderful woman.

I have three Conversations here, speak on Sunday in the Universalist Church, and meet the Round Table again. Next week attend a Teacher's Institute which meets here, and what else I know not. My reception is cordial and prospects hopeful.

Dr. Jones has written inviting me to Jacksonville, and I have invitations to Bloomington and Indianapolis.

If your Journals are out before Dec. 1st. mail copies to me here, care of Austin Adams Esq. Mrs Adams wishes much to know you, and she will personally some day not far distant.

Snider's criticisms are very remarkable papers.

Truly Yours
A. Bronson Alcott

Wm. T. Harris.

---

[1] From a copy, in Alcott's hand, in the Alcott-Pratt Collection. The original is in the Alcott-Harris Collection in the Concord Free Public Library (see Appendix B).
[2] *Shawl-Straps.*

LETTER 72-52[1]

[to Ezra M. Prince, Bloomington, Ill.]

Dubuque Iowa, | November 26th 1872

Dear Sir,

Your kindly note reached me here, forwarded from Concord, which place I left Nov. 8th. I have found most hospitable reception in this city—a wide variety of engagements, from unexpected quarters, and shall remember my visit with unalloyed satisfaction. I expect to leave here next Monday, for Fort Dodge, and by De Moins [*sic*] to Davenport and down the River to Burlington, Quincy, Jacksonville, St. Louis. On my way from thence to Chicago, it will give me much pleasure to meet my friends in Bloomington, and share the hospitalities of your home again. It must be sometime in January before I can reach your city. Any arrangements for Conversations, preaching, visiting the Schools, I shall be happy to be advised of in advance.

I may find words fit to be spoken to yourself and Mrs Prince in these hours of bereavement should I be so favored as to spend a few days with you. But time is the chief comforter and consoler for such afflictions and sorrows.

Remember me kindly to Mrs Prince and your children.

Very truly

Yours,

A. Bronson Alcott.

¹ MS. owned by the Cornell University Library.

LETTER 72–53

[to Austin Adams, Dubuque, Iowa]

Grinnell Dec. 20th 1872

Dear Sir,

I have wished to drop a line if it were but to express my acknowledgment of your own and Mrs Adams kindness in commending me to the persons whose names you gave in the towns along my route. Mr Allen, Miss Dendombe[?] and Richards, Mrs Twain, Mr Parsons all put me in the happiest communication with their friends and [word]folk, and I have had pleasant companies in all the places thus far visited.

At Des Moins [*sic*] I also dined with Mrs Savery.

I have been at Marshalltown and am here the guest of Prof[?] Mazour[?] of an Iowa College. I am to have a Conversation here; and leave probably on Monday for Iowa City where I may spend Christmas.

The West interests me by its energy and hospitality to the future.

Every where I hear yourself spoken of with great respect and think it a happy stroke of fortune that I have made the acquaintance of [a] person so influential in forming this growing Empire of the West.

To Mrs Adams and Yourself

much regard and affection

A.B.A.

Mr and Mrs Adams
Dubuque, Iowa
Dec

LETTER 72–54¹

[to Ellen A. Chandler, Framingham, Mass.]

Iowa City, Iowa, | December 30th 1872.

Dear Miss Chandler,

If distance enhances the romance of friendship, I must hasten to fulfill my promise, since here I face homewards, and from "the Iowa", or "pleasant land," of Indian tradition. A pleasant land and hospitable truly, open as their prairies, and serene as their skies. Everywhere, at Dubuque, Waterloo, Fort

Dodge, Des Moines, Marshalltown, Grinnell, here in Iowa City, the widest opportunities for meeting the best people—Parlors, halls, pulpits, school-rooms, regardless of sect or school, sex or circle. Really the enjoyment of such hospitalities alike to thought and person threatens to cast his own neighborhood into disrepute. Here at any rate is character, if less of culture, more of catholicity. The vigorous New England stock transplanted to the deeper[?] soil of these prairies, yields a fresher and riper fruit.

Some day, we will make a party of three or four, and see together this splendid state.

Very pleasant, my fellowships greatly enhanced, moreover, to be admitted into homes to find a daughter's name "a household word,"—her books better known even, than nearer home—her latest preceding me, and at every hearthside, on every platform I chance to mount, her story must be told, and gain in telling. Here at a Christmas Tree Festival, old and young, a roomfull [sic], must needs give three cheers after the telling, for the author of Little Women. Literally, Proud papa is everywhere promoted to the high places and honors on "Joe's [sic] account.

And, pray, how passes the holidays with yourself? One brief word, if no more, about there, many about yourself especially, whom amidst the many charming children of the prairies, I do not the less admire and remember.

I leave presently for Davenport, Iowa, where letters will find me if addressed to the care of

"George H. French Esq."

From thence I expect to take the River cities to St. Louis. It is my hope to write again, and again.

Very affectionately,
Your friend,
A. Bronson Alcott

Miss Ellen A. Chandler.

---

[1] MS. owned by the Abernethy Library, Middlebury College. The original, in Alcott's hand, is in the Alcott-Harris Collection in the Concord Free Public Library. For an account of Alcott's tour of Iowa in 1872–73, see Hubert Hoeltje, "Some Iowa Lectures and Conversations of Amos Bronson Alcott," *Iowa Journal of History and Politics*, XXIX (July, 1931), 379–90.

PART TWENTY

1873

LETTER 73–1[1]

[To William T. Harris, St. Louis]

Davenport, Iowa. | January 1st 1873.

Dear Friend,

Your parcels of "Journal of Education" and "The Western," I found await-ing me here. Thanks for both.

Your criticisms have thus far been most gratifying and this of "Concord Days", short as it is, dips deepest into the spirit, and draws forth the thought, as none that have come under ‖ the ‖ my eye thus far. Other papers in your Journals show to advantage the benefits of the studies to which you have turned the attention of Teachers and thinkers at the West.

I am to be here over Sunday, and then down the river. At Quincy I shall hope to write of further movements and doings. Great and greatly to be praised is *this* country, and the more *because it is run by young men.* What were progress without them. I shall have only good things to tell when I see you.

A happy New Year for philosophy and yourself.

Truly Yours
A Bronson Alcott

Wm. T. Harris,
St. Louis

[1] From a copy, in Alcott's hand, in the Alcott-Pratt Collection. The original is in the Al-cott-Harris Collection in the Concord Free Public Library (see Appendix B).

LETTER 73–2

[to Sarah Denman, Quincy, Ill.]

Davenport, Iowa. | January 3rd 1873.

Dear Mrs. Denman,

I am approaching your city more slowly than I intended, being detained in various cities, and drawn aside of the route planned for myself before I left the

East. At Dubuque I had invitations to Waterloo, Fort Dodge, Des Moines, Grinnell, Marshalltown, Iowa City, at which places I have had Conversations. I reached Davenport last Monday night. Here I am to have four Conversations and one or more at Moline. These will occupy most of the next week. I have no engagements as yet for Muscatine or Burlington. Mount Pleasant has been mentioned as a place for me to visit. Very likely I shall stop at these, one or all, on my way to Quincy. Precisely when I can reach your city, I cannot now foresee.

And should you have friends in any of them to whom you would be free to commend me, I shall be obliged to you for their names. Iowa has been exceedingly hospitable to me personally. I have found in all the cities which I have visited the kindest reception and every opportunity for meeting people that I could desire.

I shall be here till Wednesday the   [1] certainly. Should you have any thing to communicate, address to the care of George H. French, Esq. Davenport.

I remember with much pleasure my former visit to your city, and anticipate like satisfaction in store for my second. Meanwhile, I remain

Most truly

Yours,

A. Bronson Alcott

[1] The date has been left blank.

LETTER 73-3[1]

[to William T. Harris, St. Louis]

Muscatine, Iowa, | January 20th 1873.

Dear Friend

The appetite for philosophy in these Iowa cities is so strong, even to voracity, that such morsels as I am supposed to administer in parlors, pulpits, or platforms, keeps me longer in the several cities, than I had thought possible on setting my face from the East last November. Here I am in this little Missisipi [sic] river town, having come up the stream from Burlington to give them a Conversation and a Lecture. And they wish me to return and give them more of the like. I begin to see that I cannot satisfy the craving for fresher and fairer food in these places, and if I will return home in due season I must hasten forwards, leaving these opportunities thus proffered in the best of faith, for future use. Let us hope other and younger devotees are ripening for the good work.

I leave tomorrow morning for Burlington to meet company there in the evening. I may stop at Keokuk on my way to Quincy, which place I hope to reach next week certainly, and, giving them a week or so, then on to St. Louis. It must be February (sometime) before I reach your city. Meanwhile, you shall address me there, care of Mr. Emery.

My health thus far, with exception of a two weeks' cold, has been excellent. I am enjoying this intimacy with these Western communities, turning my winter to the best advantage both to myself, and I have cause to believe to those whom I meet—the children in the schools, particularly.

I hear favorable accounts from Concord. Louisa is busy upon her new story with improved health and spirits.

Expecting to see you face to face, presently.

I am truly

Yours,

A. Bronson Alcott.

Wm. T. Harris
    St. Louis.

[1] From a copy, in Alcott's hand, in the Alcott-Pratt Collection. The original is in the Alcott-Harris Collection in the Concord Free Public Library (see Appendix B).

[Letter to Mary N. Adams, Dubuque, Iowa; from Moline, Ill., received January 26, 1873 (noted in Mrs. Adams' Diary, owned by Mrs. Adele A. Bachman, South Orange, N.J.).]

LETTER 73-4

[to C. Bryan, Akron, Ohio]

Concord, February 26th | 1873.

Dear Sir.

On returning from a three months' tour at the West, spent chiefly in Iowa and Illinois, I find your letter of Dec. 14th 72. awaiting a reply.

It is gratifying to an author to learn that his books are read and prized by intelligent persons. What you write about mine, and your inquiry, is especially gratifying. But I must not attempt to answer your question in the limited space of a note. Many sheets were required for that. Perhaps *possessing, or not possessing a magnetic temperament,* contains the secret.

You inquire about Stirling. He has written but little besides the works you name. The next No. of the Journal of Speculative Philosophy will contain a paper of his on "Berkeley'.

I find readers of philosophy in most of the cities at the West. In Quincy. Ill. there is a "Plato Club." also at Jacksonville. I sometimes think there is more to be hoped of the West than of the East in *pure thinking.* I had a most hospitable hearing wherever I sojourned, and returned with full faith in the material and mental capabilities of the West. In all the chief cities are minds of promise.

I hope the *"shadow"* of which you wrote may be long and finally averted from your household.

Very truly

Yours,

A. Bronson Alcott.

C. Bryan Esq.
    Akron, Ohio

LETTER 73–5[1]

[to Mary N. Adams, Dubuque, Iowa]

Concord, February, | 27th 1873

Dear Mrs Adams,

In your last letter you wrote "I thought you were too busy to hear from me till your return to Concord. We have been exceedingly anxious to hear from you, and to hear the story of your sojourn through Iowa and at Quincy." No, not too busy to hear, but verily too engaged from day to day and from city to city to write at any length. Then I was summoned home from St Louis by the illness of my daughter Anna, and left suddenly to find her but just escaped from a severe attack of pneumonia. I am happy to write that she is much better though still feeble and shiftless. Louisa is hard at work on her new story, sixteen of the twenty chapters being finished. Mrs Alcott and May are quite well, and my boys also. Fortunately I reached home before the severe snow storm, to be useful here, though leaving behind many engagements unfulfilled. But Iowa, thanks to Mr. Adams and your kind considerate commendations held me for most of my tour. My story in fact began in Dubuque and ended at Quincy. For though I went down the river from thence to St Louis, and had a single evening's Conversation there before I left, there remained to take on my way homewards and complete my tour—Jacksonville, Bloomington, Galesburg, Chicago, Jackson, Lansing, Ann Arbor, Detroit, Sandusky, Cleveland, Buffalo, Rochester, Almira [sic], Syracuse. "As Mr. Alcott was about to make the tour of our State we felt a pride in having him start from Dubuque, as if it was his Iowa Home. And well you may. Every where attentions were showered upon me. Adams, the Adams' opened the doors of the best houses and admitted the stranger to the hospitable fellowship of the inmates. Dubuque for Iowa, and Quincy for Illinois! Good sense, good taste, advanced thought, refinement in both. What surprised me most and tells best, is the favor with which my "preachings" were received by almost every Sect in the several cities. Parlor, platform, School room. These were common enough, open of course for my teaching. I believe I may report having spoken in the pulpits of every sect admitting laymen. Nor were Episcopalians wanting in hospitality within the [word] of the Church. At Keokuk and Quincy, the young Unitarian ministers, Brown and Hosmer, were enthusiastic helpers. I spoke in their pulpits to full audiences [sic]. Why should not Pardee[2] exchange with them, and yourself and Mr. Adams make their acquaintance simply? Mr. Ijams of Iowa City did a brave thing in giving me his pulpit. I was sorry not to have seen more of Mr. Hammond. Mr Parsons may tell you, if he has not, about Judge Cole, and Mrs Savery, who (the lady) promised a *Fellowship* of $1000. for our *"Concord School*. Mrs Denman also, and Mrs Grimes of Burlington. I was her guest while in that city. and liked her exceedingly. In Quincy I met "the Plato Club," the Logic Club, "Friends in Council" and had a truly philosophic week of fellowship. Mr. Emery is "The Parmindean [sic]," and a most promising thinker. Thought appears to have been organized more fully in Quincy than in any Western city within my knowledge unless it be Jacksonville. I was disappointed while so near Dr. Jones and friends, not to have met them in their Plato Club and other sittings. The friends in Quincy had planned to meet me there last Saturday, and Mr. Harris purposed to accompany me thither from St. Louis. But good things are good to keep and season with the seasons. Another season we will see what will ripen. Even Louisa thinks she "must visit the West to thank it for its hospitalities to papa." A pretty feat certainly it were to belt this hemisphere with a sparkle of romance and of ideas!—What is the best season to see Iowa and cross to California, taking three months to do it?

I have had no time since my return to project spring or summer engagements. My "*Journal*" awaits digesting and putting in order. Whether my "notes" are worth editing and extending for a Book needs to be seen. The West is a most hopeful country in my eyes, and "*Western Days,*" as a complemental Volume of "*Concord Days*" were a pretty work to compile. You may be interested to learn that the latter has gone to a third edition, and this nearly exhausted. Louisa's ‖ has nearly finished her ‖ new story, entitled "Work," ‖ It ‖ is to be published in June, both here and in England. She receives $3000 from the Christian Union, and 75 from "the St. James Monthly (English)" besides her 25 cts a copy on the volume in Book form.

Mr. Emerson and Ellen we hear are returning to Italy, having visited Egypt. It is not every poet who sings the sphynx's [*sic*] song before beholding ‖ marbled ‖ the stone. His house is being finished for his reception on his return home this spring. Edward has returned and is to be married (they say) on his fathers and sisters return.

I dined with Dr. Bartol last Friday. He was very chatty, and had much to say in praise of Dubuque correspondents one of whom it seems had anticipated the best part of my story. He only needed to see the eight ladies Gift to confirm its truth. Some day you must entice him to your home, and confirm all that I tell of it and of Iowa.

To all my hospitable friends, pray give much love and delightful recollections of my visit. And to yourself Mr Adams and the children the larger measure. Mrs Alcott also desires thanks and remembrance.

P.S.
A. Bronson Alcott

/ My disappointment in not seeing your sister, Mrs Bagley, at Lansing is very great. I hope to have that pleasure nevertheless sometime.
A.B.A.

[1] MS. owned by Mrs. Adele A. Bachman, South Orange, N.J. Although dated February 27, the letter is postmarked February 26. A copy of a portion of the letter, in Alcott's hand, is in the Alcott-Pratt Collection.
[2] J. N. Pardee, now pastor of the First Universalist Church in Dubuque.

LETTER 73–6[1]

[to Ellen A. Chandler, Jamaica Plain? Mass.]
Concord, February | 27th 1873.
Dear Miss Chandler,

I was summoned from St. Louis by telegram announcing Anna's illness, and hastened home leaving many engagements unfulfilled. On reaching home I found Anna out of danger. She is now about the house again, though still feeble and shiftless. The rest of us are in usual health. I have had a delightful time, have made new acquaintances and renewed former ones, in those Western homes. I think I wrote you hastily, (was it from Davenport?) I certainly received a full letter in reply, for which many thanks. I wish you could visit the West and meet people in some circles as I have done. You must see and enjoy their free graceful hospitalities to appreciate fully any description. Shall I tell you, (and this without disparagement of the East) that I really feel lonely and misplaced here, shall I say, less at home, than in those sensible, sympathic circles? Will you believe it? I must find occasion to tell you all *somewhere,* and more livingly than by the pen. Will you find time and pleasure in seeing me at Louisa's room? And *when* shall it be? I purpose being in Boston early next week, and if you will name the day and hour, let me see you there. Will you? Little Johnny is passing some days with his aunt Louisa, and I am to bring him home on my return.

I hope you have had a happy, interesting winter, and escaped the prevailing distempers. All that and more you shall speak, if I may have the pleasure of listening.

My pen refuses writing all that the holder dictates, and only ventures modestly.

Yours affectionately,
A. Bronson Alcott

Miss Chandler.

[1] MS. owned by the Abernethy Library, Middlebury College. A copy, in Alcott's hand, is in the Alcott-Pratt Collection.

LETTER 73-7

[to Mrs. Perry, Keokuk, Iowa]

Concord, March. | 4th 1873.

Dear Mrs Perry,

I was summoned home suddenly by the illness of my eldest daughter, Mrs Pratt, leaving many of my engagements for Conversations unfulfilled. On arriving home I found my daughter recovering, and she is now out of danger. I had gone no farther than to St. Louis when called home. At Quincy I had a very charming week, and expected to go to Jacksonville from St. Louis. It is now so late in the season, and so far, that I must defer my visit West till another season, when I shall hope to meet my friends again in Keokuk.

I submitted the Letters to Mr. Sanborn, and you will find a paragraph concerning them in the Republican which I mail with this.

He says that as these have been published and are rather behind date, he will rather receive a fresh letter from your daughter from abroad, and if her sketches prove lively and good he will publish them in the Republican. As you will see he thinks well of the writer.

The weather here has been fearfully uncomfortable and the snow deeper than for many winters past.

Remember me to my friends in your city, and accept my thanks for the hospitalities of yourself and husband.

Very truly
Yours,
A. Bronson Alcott

LETTER 73-8

[to Christopher Walton, London, England]

Mr. Walton.   Concord, Mass. | March 10th 1873.

Dear Sir,

I send herewith a parcel, containing a copy of "Concord Days' and "Harris' Journal of Speculative Philosophy"—Two Numbers.

In "Concord Days" you will find a Chapter concerning *"Boehme,"* with a notice of yourself and "Cyclopedia." I trust you will not take it amiss that I have taken the liberty of publishing your letter as an advertisement of your interest in Boehme and his disciples.

In the Journals you will find a notice of my *book* by the editor. Also an article of mine entitled "Philosophemes"—the first of several which may follow. You may notice also a reference to Baader in a review at the end of the January Number. Mr. Harris would like to publish an article on *"Boehme's Theosophy"* prepared with care by some one acquainted fully with his ideas.

Mr Emerson, who is now abroad, and intending to pass a while in England, assured me before he left Concord last autumn, of his purpose of seeing you before his return. And Mr. George Bradford gave me an interesting account of his visiting you when he was in London. Is not some correspondence likely to promote the ends of philosophy on both sides of the Atlantic?

Be assured I shall be glad to hear from you of your present pursuits, and purposes for human regeneration.

I am, dear Sir,
very truly
Yours.
A. Bronson Alcott.

Mr. Christopher Walton,
    22. Ludgate Street,
        London

LETTER 73-9

[to Samuel Orcutt, Wolcott, Conn.]

                                      Concord, Mass. | March 11th 1873.

Dear Sir,

I am glad to learn that you are preparing a *History of Wolcott.* and wish I had materials that have not come into your hands to make it what you wish.

I know not how much space you can give to family genealogies—how much to biographical matters. And yet am unwilling that your book should lack any important matter that I can give to it.

It seems as if I could serve you best by making a visit to Wolcott when the snows are thawed and the landscape is open. I can tell you more, and more to your purpose, than I can write. And I can bring what matter I have for your selection and approval.

Our family had rather an important part in the early settlement of Spindle Hill John Alcock first taking up a large tract of land there in 1731. He was also one of the first members of the Church formed under Rev. Mr. Gillett.

I have the Alcock Genealogy more fully written out than is printed in the History of Waterbury.

Dr. Alcott's son Rev. William P. Alcott doubtless has materials for his fathers' biography.

But I must make a visit to my native town and compare notes with you and my townsfolk.

Very truly
Yours,
A. Bronson Alcott

Rev. Samuel Orcutt.
    Wolcott
      Conn.

LETTER 73–10[1]

[to Ellen A. Chandler, Jamaica Plain? Mass.]

Concord April 8th | 1873.

Dear Miss Chandler,

To-morrow evening, I meet the Divinity Students at Cambridge and purpose being at Louisa's rooms on Thursday. Shall I see you there sometime during the day? Any time between 12 and 4 P.M. will be convenient for me.

Hoping to find you disengaged, and with an hour for me at least, I wait in hope and affection

Truly Yours,
A. Bronson Alcott.

Miss Ellen A. Chandler

[1] MS. owned by the Abernethy Library, Middlebury College. A copy, in Alcott's hand, is in the Alcott-Pratt Collection.

LETTER 73–11

[to Kenningale Robert Cook, London, England]

Concord, Mass. | April 9th 1873.

Sir,

Since the receipt of yours dated March 3rd. and coming to hand on the

19th following, I have sought in vain at the bookstores for a copy of my book of *Conversations with Children on the Gospels*. The book has been out of print for many years. In fact, it was not published beyond the reading of the few friends of the School in which the Conversations were held, and cannot be obtained now unless by chance at the second hand bookstores. Nothing setting forth the Genius of childhood in its prime power and perfection has been thought of, much less attempted in literature, or culture.

Besides these volumes, a Record of the literary exercises and discipline of the same school was published at the time, a copy of which I mail to you with this note.[1]

Last autumn, I published a volume entitled *"Concord Days"*. This with *"Tablets,"* may be obtained through the English house of *"Sampson, Low*[?]*, Son, and Marston, Crown Buildings 188 Fleet Street, London"*—publishers of my daughter's works.

Mr. Thoreau was my townsman and near neighbor in Concord. He died in 1862. I am glad to learn that you have made his acquaintance. His works number 7 volumes. His M.S.S. have lately come into my possession, and contain matter for as many more.

I am gratified by your favorable impressions of myself and neighbor, and shall learn with pleasure whatever you may care to impart concerning your criticism for[?] children.

Yours truly
A. Bronson Alcott.

Kenningale Cook Esq.
London.

[1] Elizabeth Peabody's *Record of a School.*

LETTER 73–12

[to Orange Judd & Co., New York City]

Concord, Mass. | April 12th 1873.

Messrs Orange Judd & Co.

Can you furnish me with duplicates of the Hearth and Home containing the Cut and Sketch of my daughter Louisa, published about May or June, I believe) 1870? The compiler of "the Cyclopedia of American Literature[1] wishes to insert her name in a new edition of that work, and the historian of Wolcott Conn[2] (my native town) also desires a sketch for his work.

By sending me copies, (if you have them) you will much oblige,

Yours,
A Bronson Alcott

[1] Evert A. and George L. Duyckinck. But see Letter 73-15.
[2] Samuel Orcutt.

Letter 73–13[1]

[to William T. Harris, St. Louis]

Concord April | 14th 1873.

Dear Friend

I mailed to you a few days since a copy of the Literary World, and marked a paragraph therein relating to yourself. The World has started into respectability within the last two years, and begins to be esteemed as our best in Boston. The editor[2] was a schoolmate of Sanborn's at Exeter Academy N. Hampshire. I have only seen him lately, and happened to speak of you and of your Journal, when calling to subscribe for his. I hope his notice may not be disturbing to you.—He speaks, too, of me in like amiable mention. And now Sanborn gives his version of us both in his letter, dated at St. Louis. We might be far worse dealt with,—than by these complementary [*sic*] Journalists.

It was a sad errand for Sanborn. I did not venture to speak my fears about his brother on my return. He was at my Conversation with his wife, you may remember.

Sanborn tells me he had an hour with you. Did I tell you that I had been talking with the Harvard Divinity students? I have now had three evenings with them, and find them curious, but shall I say shallow. I am to meet them again, and may come closer than hitherto.

I called on Pres. Eliott[3] and intimated *possibilities* in your case. He seemed very desirous to have you connected with the College but *that Professor* stood in the way at present. I also met Prof. Everett.[4] Cambridge seems in a fair way to meet all demands, but slow and sure.

Louisa has finished her new Book, and hopes to see it out in June.

Emerson is expected home in May.

Very truly
Yours
A. Bronson Alcott

Wm. T. Harris.

[1] From a copy, in Alcott's hand, in the Alcott-Pratt Collection. The original is in the Alcott-Harris Collection in the Concord Free Public Library (see Appendix B).
[2] S. R. Crocker.
[3] Charles William Eliot.
[4] Charles Carroll Everett, Bussey Professor of Theology.

Letter 73–14

[to William P. Alcott, Greenwich, Conn.]

Concord April 21st | 1873.

Dear Sir

Revd. Samuel Orcutt of Wolcott, Conn., writes me that he is compiling a History of Wolcott, and wishes information concerning the engraved head of your father. He wishes to obtain the plate for impressions for his book. Any information which you may have to communicate concerning your father he will gladly receive. The book is to contain biographical Sketches, and genealogies of the families, especially of the first settlers.

The anniversary of the hundredth year of the founding of the Church is to be celebrated in September next—an occasion on which you will, I am sure, like to be present.

Should you find among your father's papers any thing for Mr. Orcutt he would know what proper use to make of it Any letters of mine, (for we began corresponding at the age 12 and 13.) I should gladly see and possess.—

My family are all well. Louisa has just finished a new book which is to be published in June.

I should like to learn of your mother's welfare, and of your own also and sisters. It was by accident that I learned your address lately.

Very truly
Yours,
A. Bronson Alcott.

Rev Wm. P. Alcott.
    Greenich [*sic*]
        Conn

LETTER 73–15

[to M. Laird Simons]

Concord April 25th 1873

Dear Sir.

Yours of April 9th. has just come to hand, through Roberts Brothers. Meanwhile, Mr. Drake had intimated your wishes to me, and I obtained from Messrs Orange Judd & Co. a copy of a notice of my daughter, Miss Louisa, printed in Hearth and Home for June, I think, of 1869. which I mailed to your address a few days since.

You will find in Appleton's Cyclopedia, a notice of myself prepared by Mr. Emerson, to which you may add, if you care to reedit, my book of "Tablets,' published in 1868 and "Concord Days" in 1873. ‖ I enclose photographs of myself and Miss Louisa ‖

To the list of books written by her, should be added Aunt Joe's [*sic*] Scrap Bag, "Shawlstraps—" and her novel just on the eve of publication, entitled "Work or Christie's Experience." In the Springfield Republican for April 11th. and The Literary World for April, you will find notices of my Tour at the West, from which you may gather some facts for such notice as you may care to insert of myself.

I enclose photographs of myself and Miss Louisa

Very truly Yours
A. Bronson Alcott.

M. Laird Simons Esq.

1873

LETTER 73–16

[to Mrs. Perry, Keokuk, Iowa]

Concord April 25th 1873.

Dear Mrs. Perry.

Soon after the receipt of your note, I handed your daughters letters to Mesrs. Roberts Brothers for perusal, hoping they might think them suited for publishing in a book as you desired. After retaining them meanwhile, they were yesterday returned with the remark that, however admirable as letters, they did not think it best to republish them now. And as you told me that you had duplicates, I retain those committed to me for the present.

One thing surely has been gained by this reading: Mr. Sanborn has made acquaintance with your daughter's Genius, and the Roberts will be ready to read any M.S.S. (foreign or domestic,) that she may commit to them hereafter. I think I wrote that Mr. Sanborn would gladly print any bright[?] letter of hers, should she choose to send him one from Germany, or wherever she may sojourn.

My daughter May left this morning for London where she purposes to pursue her ‖ art ‖ studies in the Art Galleries and probably visit the continent before she returns.

I sent you a notice of my *Western Tour* printed in the "Literary World," and also Mr. Sanborns' account of it in "the Springfield Republican" on reflection, I think I mailed the last to Mr. Brown.

Louisa has finished her story entitled *"Work"* which is to appear in June.

I retain pleasant memories of my friends in Keokuk, and hope to see them again another season

Very truly yours,
A Bronson Alcott

LETTER 73–17

[to D. Nicholson, New York City]

Concord, Mass. May 4 | 1873.

Dear Sir,

There were but 100 copies printed of the "Emerson" about which you inquire, and these were given to friends of his at home and abroad—Carlyle and Wm. H. Channing in England. I myself possess but a single copy, and cannot, I regret to say, "help you in the matter."

Very truly,
Yours,
A. Bronson Alcott

D. Nicholson Esq.
N.Y.

LETTER 73–18

[to Charles D. B. Mills, Syracuse]

Concord, Mass. | May 4th 1873.

Dear Friend,

I wish I could give you a full account of my Western tour within the space of my sheet. Let me say that it was very successful, and opens out a route for coming season in the states of Ohio, Michigan, Illinois, Iowa and Missouri. I shall probably leave again as early as October and expect to pass four or five months, perhaps going as far West as Omaha on the Missouri.

You need have no scruples about trenching on grounds where I have been. The world is wide and the West open to all who bring good seeds to sow. I shall be most happy to give you introductions to leading persons in all the cities where I have been. I shall hope to see you before you leave for the West, and then we can further the matter according to your wishes.

Sanborn has given an account of my tour, at some length and particularity in the Springfield Republican of April 11. I wish I had a copy to send you. The "Literary World" also has a notice, which I enclose.

I have met the Divinity students since my return, where I found your son. He expressed an interest in our Conversations, and in his studies. I shall hope to see him in Concord before he returns to Syracuse.

My family are all with me ‖ and very well, ‖ save May who sailed for England last Saturday intending to study in the Art Galleries, and probably go to the continent in autumn.

Mr Emerson is expected home about the first of June.

With kind remembrances to Mrs Mills and your daughter.

I am very truly

Yours

A. Bronson Alcott

C. D. B. Mills.

LETTER 73–19

[to Samuel Orcutt, Wolcott, Conn.]

Concord May 12th | 1873.

Dear Sir,

I enclose you this letter from Rev Wm. P. Alcott, thinking the information which it contains may forward your inquiries about his father's picture, which I hope you will be able to secure for your "History". Dr. Alcott was an honor to his family and native town, and should be perpetuated in picture if possible. The likeness is fair as I knew him.

I think I can furnish a few photographs of my daughter and of myself, if you desire them.

Just now, I am busy planting and spring work, but hope to be able to leave for Wolcott late in the month, if not before.

1873

I have a short sketch of Louisa, also of myself, which you may shorten if you like, or have not space for them.

Have you a sketch of Mr. Adin[?] Lewis—a man of some note in his day, and a benefactor to the schools of his native town?

Very truly Yours
A. Bronson Alcott

Rev. Samuel Orcutt

LETTER 73–20

[to Charles D. B. Mills, Syracuse]

Concord May 28th | 1873.

Dear Friend,

Of persons with whom it may be to your advantage to correspond with a view to lectures and Conversations, I name,

Mrs Mary Newbury Adams
Dubuque, Iowa

and from her and Mr. Adams you will get access to others occupying places of authority and social position throughout the state. They gave me letters of introduction, or prepared the way for a favorable reception from such in the chief cities which I visited. I found their names an open door for me wherever I went in Iowa. At Waterloo,

H. B. Allen, attorney.

At Fort Dodge, C. B. Richards, banker, also Mrs. Swain.

At Des Moins [sic] Hon. Galasha[?] Parsons, attorney. and Mrs Savery.

At Iowa City, Prof. W. G. Hammond and J. B. Edmunds.

At Davenport Rev. Mr. Seaver.

At Keokuk Rev. Mr. Brown and Dr Knowles.

At Burlington, Mrs Grimes.

at Mount Pleasant, Mr. C. C. Coles.

at Quincy, Ill. Mrs Denman and Samuel H. Emery Jr

At St Louis, Mo. Wm. T. Harris

at Bloomington, Ill. E. M. Prince. Esq.

at Chicago Rev Rob. Laird Collier and Rev. Mr. Wendte

Mrs Bagley at Detroit, and Rev. Mr. Forbush at Cleveland.

I shall be happy to have you use my name in any way that may serve you.

Truly Yours
A. Bronson Alcott

C. D. B. Mills
    Syracuse.

LETTER 73–21[1]

[to Ellen A. Chandler, Jamaica Plain, Mass.]

Concord, June 2nd | 1873.

Dear Miss Chandler,

Uncertain whether you see the Springfield Republican which chronicles the local news for us, especially, I enclose Sanborn's notice of Mr. Emerson's reception by his friends and townspeople on his return from Europe last Tuesday. Nothing could be more charming, and all the more that the whole was a surprise to him. It was beautiful to see with what modesty and sweetness he met and spoke to his admiring neighbors at his gate. Our little village became suddenly exalted and glorified thereby. Ellen's face beamed upon them, the type of bliss personified.[2]

Both appear in excellent health only browned by travel.

Emerson met many friends in England—Carlyle, Browning, Helps, Max Muller, Froude, Lord and Lady Amberly. He expresses himself greatly pleased with the perfect restoration of his house—says "it is the best in the world." All was finished to the front gates the day before his return.

I have had but a half hour with him yet. And now that he is come and the apple blossoms, what hinders my friend at the Plains from making her usual visit during the season of beauty and bloom? Nothing on our part but a house-keeper,—who don't come when she does, *then* for the expected pleasures!—

Louisa's story is done, and May writes from the London Art-Galleries delightedly.

Meanwhile and
affectionately Yours,
A. Bronson Alcott

Miss Ellen A. Chandler.

[1] MS. owned by the Abernethy Library, Middlebury College. A copy, in Alcott's hand, is in the Alcott-Pratt Collection.
[2] For a more detailed account of the festivities of May 27, see Alcott, *Journals*, pp. 432–34; and Ralph L. Rusk, *The Life of Ralph Waldo Emerson* (New York, 1949), pp. 479–80.

LETTER 73–22

[to Samuel Orcutt, Wolcott, Conn.]

Concord June 4th 1873.

Dear Sir,

I think I may leave here for Wolcott some day next week—by Thursday or Friday probably—and shall like to spend Sunday and attend meeting—not, I know, in the Old Meeting House as when a boy—but in the present one, and see the elders of the congregation mostly known by me from childhood, relations some of them by blood, if not by name. It is now many years since I have seen them gathered for Worship on Sunday. And times have changed, customs and manners.

I remember when the meeting house was full, crowded in pews and galleries, the population nearly 1000 and mostly attending—some even walking their two miles bare footed, carrying shoes and stockings and putting them on at the school house near, before they entered the meeting house. Then, the young people were numerous, filling all the galleries, and having the tithing man to oversee them. Old and young carried their heads of fennel and dill to chew *"in meeting time"*, the courtesy in the pews being to offer sprigs to any who had none. Sunday was a quiet day, the children reciting their catechism after meeting, having done the same on Saturday at the district school

I have heard nothing from Rev. William P. Alcott since I wrote you.

Should your engagements take you out of town on Sunday, I might not be in Wolcott till Monday or Tuesday following. I wish to learn the most you have to communicate about your "History." If you have not a copy of Bronson's History of Waterbury at hand, for reference, I can bring mine along with me.

I shall be glad to get a line from you before I leave home.

Very truly

Yours,

A. Bronson Alcott.

Rev. Samuel Orcutt

LETTER 73–23

[to D. Nicholson, New York City]

Concord June 7th 1873

Dear Sir

Yours of April 30th came duly to hand, and I mailed a note in answer to you on May 4th., which I here copy.

"There were but 100 copies printed of the *"Emerson,"* about which you inquire, and these were given to friends at home and abroad, to Carlyle & Mat Arnold W. H. Channing in England.

I myself possess but a single copy, and cannot, I regret to say, "help you in the matter."

I may add, however, that most of the Essay is contained in my "Concord Days," published by Roberts Brothers last September. The bust has not to my knowledge been copied elsewhere. ‖ And there ‖ It was not a photograph of Emerson's ‖ House ‖ Dwelling, but of his Summer House built by myself, in the work.

Truly Yours

A. Bronson Alcott

D. Nicholson
    N. Y. Tribune Buildg

LETTER 73-24[1]

[to Ellen A. Chandler, Jamaica Plain, Mass.]

Concord June 10th | 1873.

Dear Miss Chandler,

That is a charming complement [sic] of yours;—"Concord is a part of my life "and a very beautiful part, "a gracious possession forever."

Yes, verily, and so claims you personally, geographically, as *part of it*, for a few days now, summer days they shall be as best befitting

And so, on my return from a week's visit to Connecticut, you are to pay us your annual visit. Our housekeeper comes to day. Louisa is in good spirits her story fairly off her thoughts, and lovely June is ready to embrace and entertain her blushing daughters.

I write this in advance that you may be free to come, and not make other engagements meanwhile.

I sent you on Saturday a copy of "The Literary World" containing an extract from a letter of May's which I thought might interest you.

Affectionately,
A. Bronson Alcott.

Miss Ellen A. Chandler.

[1] MS. owned by the Abernethy Library, Middlebury College. A copy, in Alcott's hand, is in the Alcott-Pratt Collection.

LETTER 73-25

[to Ednah Dow Cheney, Jamaica Plain? Mass.]

Concord June 11th 1873.

Dear Mrs Cheney,

I leave for Connecticut tomorrow expecting to be gone from home ten days or more. As I shall pass Hartford going and returning, and you are to be at South Manchester, it would give great pleasure to see you there with your friends, the Cheney's whom I remember with satisfaction for their hospitality when visiting their busy village several years ago.

Should you care to communicate, a line addressed to the care of your kinsman, Mr Cheney, the silk merchant at Hartford, would find me on my return homewards.

I think we could arrange our Winter's tour West very pleasantly at Manchester.

Yes, the Free Religious meeting this year was most hopeful.

Yours truly,
A. Bronson Alcott.

[to Mrs. A. Bronson Alcott, Concord]

Bridgeport, Conn. | Sunday morning, June 21.[1] | 1873.

My Dear,

Thus far, a time of enjoyment with old friends, old places, and associations hallowed by youth, and antedating childhood. Wolcott generally, the ancestral estate of over a thousand acres on Spindle Hill, has been explored locally, the homesteads from the first to last settler and descendents—five generations—two of the houses, still standing a century old, and roads surveyed a century and half ago. Mr Orcutt and I have drawn an imaginary map and peopled the tract as it was, and is now; and some day of this week we are to have taken photographic views of several old homesteads for his history. He is a sensible stirring influence, and doing not a little to awaken the people from their ignorance and apathy. I am more than ever impressed by the commanding beauty and wide prospects of this hill region, its sweet air and cool water. Only a good boarding house is wanted to make it a chosen haunt of summer visitors. The scenery, the air—the fountain springs—these should ensure immortality. I wish the local names were as picturesque as the things indicated—Mad river, Lilly brook, Beaker hill, Kelberry swamp, Jack's rock.

I have staid mostly at James Alcott's who appears to be Mr. Orcutts main stay.—Louisa will recognize him and his wife, my first cousin. He took me to Church last Sunday, and both himself and wife have been as hospitable as they knew how to be during my visit.

On my way, I made a call on Dr. Barnard at Hartford, and Dr. Bushnell, the latter too unwell to see me, but I had an agreeable interview with Mrs. Bushnell and her daughter, both admirers of Louisa. I expect to see the Dr. on my return.

I came here last night from Waterbury and attend Church with Edward this forenoon. He is well and family, has an elegant house tastefully furnished, and in a prosperous business. Bridgeport is a city of about 25,000 inhabitants, the seat of the sewing machine interest. Last evening we had a ride in the park, along the shore of the Sound. It was a gay spectacle, Saturday being the gala day, hundreds of carriages, many costly "turnouts," footmen, a band of music, delicious seabreezes. Louisa would have found a fine subject for her descriptive pen. Barnam whose villa fronts the Park, was out with crowd in his carriage. A spectacle like this every Saturday must help the Sunday's piety and preaching, insensibly at least, and suggested as I rode in the crowd, what a beneficial influence it would have upon Old Concord. Even *you* would then praise it, for one virtue at least.

As I intimated I go to Church this forenoon, and return to Waterbury to morrow to attend the Consecration of St. John's on Tuesday. I purpose leaving for New Haven sometime during the week having a day or more in Wolcott for taking the photographs.

Last Sunday I spoke in Mr. Orcutts pulpit, and again on Tuesday evening, giving a lecture on "Rural Influences"—which was well attended.

Temple's letter, with Louisa's note reached me at Waterbury. I hope to reach home by Saturday next, but may be delayed longer in New Haven. If you write address me at New Haven.

Love to all

Ever Yours
A. B. A.

¹ Sunday was June 22.

LETTER 73–27¹

[to   ?   ]

Concord July 5th. 1873.

Dear Sir,

Your note came while I was in Connecticut. I am now returned and shall be glad to see you on any day you may name, only let me know when you are coming and bring your friend Taeker[?] with you. Mr Emerson, I doubt not, will see you.

You speak of spending the months of July and August in Princeton, and "making my face a part of your work."

Can you not come by Concord on your way there, and give me a part of a day at least? I have been [to] Boston seldom of late, and without time at command to call on you.

Very truly
Yours,
A. Bronson Alcott

¹ MS. owned by the Houghton Library, Harvard University.

LETTER 73–28¹

[to Ellen A. Chandler, Jamaica Plain, Mass.]

Concord July 6th | 1873.

Dear Miss Chandler,

Now my visit to Connecticut is past, and yours to Swampscot [sic], we shall expect you any day in Concord. Louisa is our housekeeper, and in spirits for entertaining guests—especially chosen ones. The season, too, is inviting. and you may "dawdle" delightfully in doors and out.

Come and renew past satisfactions, inspire fresh fellowship. Remember our acquaintance dates from '67. and has its future still. Need I remind you that your first espistle shows October '67. and your latest June '73? And that this writing is from

Yours affectionately,
A. Bronson Alcott.

Miss. Ellen A. Chandler.

¹ MS. owned by the Abernethy Library, Middlebury College. A copy, in Alcott's hand, is in the Alcott-Pratt Collection.

LETTER 73–29¹

[to Ellen A. Chandler]

Concord July 7th | 1873.

Dear Miss Chandler

Come up on Friday at farthest, if you cannot tomorrow, and spend Sunday with us, as Louisa wishes to go to Gloucester sometime during next week, and I fear your visit would lose its chief charm to yourself, were she absent the while.

These days are delightful, and befit good fellowship, in the country, especially in Concord.

Truly Yours,
A. Bronson Alcott.

Ellen A. Chandler.

¹ MS. owned by the Abernethy Library, Middlebury College.

LETTER 73–30

[to Samuel Orcutt, Wolcott, Conn.]

Concord August 5th. 1873.

Dear Sir,

Since returning from Connecticut, my wife has been seriously ill, so much so that we feared she could not recover. I am happy, however, to inform you that she is much better and we hope that she may be restored to health and herself again. In my anxiety, I have not had time for dwelling long on our Centennial, which bids fair to be all we have conceived, judging from present indications. Nothing but trouble at home, will prevent my being with you. I have some intimations from a friend that he has verses suitable for the occasion, and Mr. Sanborn, my neighbor, and literary editor of "the Springfield Republican" hopes to be able to accompany me, and report. We could not desire a more trustworthy reporter. I am not sure that Louisa can safely leave her mother even for a day, to be present. I trust you will not fail to call on Editor Cooke of the "Waterbury American", and give him the necessary details. He should be present to tell what he knows about Wolcott in his early days.

Mr. Bassett wrote, July 16th, that the photographs had not then been taken owing to unfavorable weather. James Alcott, he said, was to attend to the matter the first favorable day. I shall be glad to learn how the matter now stands.

My visit was every way satisfactory, and I look forward with pleasure to the 10 and 11th September.[1]

Very truly
Yours,
A. Bronson Alcott

Rev. Samuel Orcutt
    Wolcott

[1] The dates of the Wolcott Centennial Celebration.

LETTER 73-31[1]

[to Ellen A. Chandler, Jamaica Plain, Mass.]

Concord August 8th. 1873.

Dear Miss Chandler,

The delightful memories of your recent visit have been overshadowed by Mrs. Alcotts illness during the last three weeks. But I am able to inform you that she is now better, and we trust is to be restored to us and herself again. Yesterday she rode out, and enjoyed the novelty greatly. To day, she is reading and writing. Fortunate for us, Louisa is with us, and able to do all that could be done for the prostrate patient. May's happiness, too, added to soften our anxieties.

Your letter came in the midst of our troubles, and found me without heart or head to answer till hope and trust entered our doors again.

I hope you are having a summer of satisfactions, and may return to your chosen pursuits and duties with invigorated health, and the charming spirits with which you are wont to regale your friends.

Affectionately
Yours,
A. Bronson Alcott.

[1] MS. owned by the Abernethy Library, Middlebury College. A copy, in Alcott's hand, is in the Alcott-Pratt Collection.

LETTER 73-32[1]

[to Eliza Seaman Leggett, Detroit]

Concord, August 8th 1873

Dear Mrs. Leggett,

Your kind letter of the 4th has just come to hand, and been read by Mrs. Alcott. She desires me to thank you for your interest in us all, and to assure you that as soon as she finds herself able to put her thoughts upon paper, she will write to you personally. She has been very ill for the past three weeks, but is much better, and able to ride out. We hope she is to be restored to health and herself again. Fortunate for us that Louisa is well, and so helpful in our needs, and that Anna and the little men were also with us. Louisa's book is off her thoughts and finding favor with her many readers far and wide. We hear almost every week from May. In her last, dated July 18th she writes:

"Such an ideal trip as I am now enjoying seldom falls to the lot of common mortals. For what with Warwick, the first two days, Stratford upon Avon, the third, and Kenilworth today. My head fairly swims with the perfect delight of having a sympathetic party—two of whom paint with me, while a third reads aloud from Hawthorne's 'Old Home'—to enjoy all this in a more satisfactory [word?] than I could ever hoped to meet. Mr. Ives is truly delightful, and we have good times together. The ladies are most agreeable also."

She enclosed an ivy leaf from Shakespeare's garden, and a rose from Anna Hatheways, where she "got also an excellent sketch." All her letters are full of expressions of happiness.

"Does Mr. Alcott," you enquire, "now and then send a wish or a thought after his Western friends?"

Daily, my kind friend, and hopes to be with you and them in their various homes, if he can leave *his own* the coming season. It is my wish to leave early in October. My last tour was delightful and extended over a wide circuit. What you tell us of Mrs. Bagley's "Socials" is most hopeful. We look to Mrs. Bagley, Mrs. Adams and yourself for examples of what women can do for social culture. Mrs. Cheney hopes to visit the West, and may accompany me out, if she finds encouragement to leave New England.

Mr. Emerson is well. Mr. Channing's book on "Thoreau" is printed and awaits the favorable time for publication.[2] I expect to go to Conn. in September to attend the Centennial of my native town.

To Mrs. Bagley, Mrs. Robb, and their families, my kind remembrances with Mrs. Alcott's and my own to yourself and yours

A. Bronson Alcott

[1] MS. in the Burton Historical Collection, Detroit Public Library.
[2] William Ellery Channing, *Thoreau, the Poet Naturalist: With Memorial Verses* (1873).

LETTER 73–33

[to W. D. Gunning, Waltham, Mass.]

Concord August | 13th 1873.

Dear Sir,

It would give us much pleasure to welcome yourself and Mrs. Gunning, as you propose in your note. But Mrs. Alcott is just now quite unequal to see any one, especially strangers. Under any other circumstances I should consider myself wanting in civility, not to welcome yourself and Mrs G. hospitably within her "Old Homestead."

As to the Conversations at Waltham, of which you write. I shall gladly meet your company at any time most agreeable to them before the 10th of

September, when I expect to be absent from home for a few days. After that I shall be free again. Meanwhile I shall be glad to learn your wishes in regard to the matter.

I have not forgotten the pleasant call you made us some years since, and shall be happy to see and compare notes further as opportunity offers.

Very truly Yours
A. Bronson Alcott.

LETTER 73-34

[to William E. Channing]

[Concord, August 24, 1873]

Dear Mr. Channing.

I shall esteem it a favor to receive your verses. Come down some afternoon and bring them.

Mrs A. is now quite herself and will be very glad to renew her old interviews with you.

Yours.
A. Bronson Alcott

Sunday afternoon
   24th. August.
   '73.

LETTER 73-35

[to Samuel Orcutt, Wolcott, Conn.]

Concord August | 27th 1873.

Dear Sir,

I hope to start for Wolcott on Monday the 8th Septr. so as to have a day there before the 10th. If Mrs A's health warrants Louisa's leaving her at the time, she desires to accompany me.

I fear Mr. Sanborn's engagements may prevent his attending to report the proceedings. But fair reporters may be had perhaps from Waterbury. Editor Cooke should be present to tell, and report editorially in "the Waterbury American. He has important reminiscences, and takes a deep interest in every thing relating to Old Waterbury. Dr. Alcotts' son, I hope will attend and speak. And if Dr. Ives has a living representative we should hear from him also.

Mr. Channing has some verses which I have not yet seen, but which if appropriate would add to our variety. I expect to see them soon, and if he consents bring them.

Mr. Bassett wrote me, about the same date with your last, concerning the photographs. If not yet taken, the matter may rest till I come.

Mr. Sanborn has promised a fuller account of me for the History, if you wish more than you have in your hands.

603

I trust all things are maturing hopefully alike for the book and the "Celebration." May the days be auspicious, and our hilltop shine with worthy honors.

If you have any thing important to communicate please write before I leave.

Very truly

Yours,

A. Bronson Alcott.

Rev. Samuel Orcutt.

LETTER 73–36

[to George Barrell Emerson, Winthrop, Mass.]

Concord August | 30th 1873.

Dr. G. B. Emerson.

Dear Sir,

In partial compliance with your request, I have drawn upon my Journals and Memory, and herewith forward my notes, fearing that you will find meagre and disappointing. But they embrace nearly all that seemed suitable for your present purpose, and I wish you to use all or any part at your discretion. I enclose some notices which may also come into use for yours. "Barnard's Biographies' you have doubtless at hand for further reference.

As to The *Life*, I agree with you in thinking that, if conceived and compiled ably, it would be one of the most attractive and useful contributions to American educational literature.

I wish I could feel with yourself that the ability were mine to do any thing like justice to a work so inviting.

With much esteem

Truly Yours,

A. Bronson Alcott.

Dr. G. B. Emerson,
  Winthrop Mass.

LETTER 73–37

[to Elizabeth R. Fisher, Wakefield, Penn.]

Concord, September, | 6. 1873.

My Respected Friend.
  Miss Fisher,

I am pleased to learn that some friend of yours has done me the honor of sending my little book to so appreciative a reader as yourself. But I must leave you to guess who is the giver.

My remembrances of Germantown and Philadelphia friends especially of your father, are very pleasant. And yesterday we had a short call from, my young pupil, now a handsome a sensible gentleman, Mr. Owen Wister. Mrs. Alcott shared equally with myself the gratification of seeing him, and of inquiring about friends in Penn.

Mr. Russell, you doubtless have heard, died lately at Lancaster Mass. I attended his funeral. He had been able to be about till a few days before his decease. Mrs R. and her daughter remain at Lancaster. Frank is Assistant Rector of St. Johns Church, Waterbury Conn. and a very useful and accomplished clergy-man.

I hope sometime to visit Philadelphia and Germantown and renew acquaint-ance with such of my old friends as survive along with my former scholars.

My wife desires special remembrance.

Truly Yours,
A. Bronson Alcott.

LETTER 73-38[1]

[to William T. Harris, St. Louis]

Concord Sept. 6th. 1873

Dear Friend,

Roberts Brothers purpose to issue this autumn (without Miss Peabody's disclaimer) "The Record of a School." Some alteration in the stereotype plates may be necessary—of *the Preface* and *last chapters particularly*—The Printer has no impressions. Now, I wish you would mail to me, the bound sheets that I gave you. The portions published in *"the Western"*, are not essential. If de-tached[?] or soiled by your printer, send the rest. The Title, Preface and last chapters are what are wanted, for revision.

This appears to be the right manner of freeing *the experiment* from Miss Peabody's notions, and putting the work before the public on its true basis.

I leave for Wolcott tomorrow to attend a "Centennial Celebration". En-closed is a circular of the proposed proceedings.

We think of closing here for the winter about the first of October, and tak-ing quarters in Boston. If I can be spared, I purpose leaving for the West soon after our removal, and of taking St. Louis first, beginning there (if desired) and taking other places afterwards. If so, I might reach you late in October perhaps, with the hope of fulfilling last seasons' engagements.

"Channing's Thoreau" is just out. Read and see if it is not full of Genius. *"Method"* is not to be looked for.

Mrs Alcott is now quite comfortable. Louisa is very well—20,000 of *"Work"* sold. May is busy in the Art Galleries of London, writing pleasant letters home. Your humble servant, rather smart for an old youngster.

Truly Yours,
A. Bronson Alcott.

Wm. T. Harris

---

[1] From a copy, in Alcott's hand, in the Alcott-Pratt Collection. The original is in the Alcott-Harris Collection in the Concord Free Public Library (see Appendix B).

[to Samuel Orcutt, Wolcott, Conn.]

Concord, September | 18th 1873.

Dear Sir,

I shall gladly receive the Circulars for the Centenary Library, and will do my best to add to the subscriptions. If my name will serve you in the least, let me share the honor of having it added to the Library Committee. I think I can get subscriptions of books, if not of money, besides the works of the "Concord Authors" already promised. Their works alone will make a considerable library of 40 Vols. or more.

Allow me some little time to collect them.

It was a bright idea, and, by your account, is to be carried out forthwith.

"The Poem" is to be published in Sanborn's Report of the Proceedings compiled from various sources, and so comes into your hands for your History. I hope it will appear in this week's "Springfield Republican'.

Has any thing yet appeared in "the New York Tribune? I was told that a reporter was on the ground, the first day at least—and took full notes.

Mr. Belden has sent me reports published in Hartford papers. Mr Cooke promised a full report in this week's "American'.

We cannot sufficiently thank yourself and Townspeople for the pleasures and perfect success of "those two days on the Hill."

I hope to visit Wolcott again this autumn, and wish you would then let me take my books and M.S.S. I found new matter in my cousin Almon Alcotts garret—the papers of John Alcock and Capt. John, dating from 1731 to 1793.

Truly Yours,
A Bronson Alcott

Rev. Saml. Orcutt.

[to W. W. Belden, Bristol? Conn.]

Concord, Mass. | September 18th 1873

Dear Sir,

Your note with Reports of "the Centennial" has just reached me, for which receive my thanks. These are the first that I have seen. I was told that a "Tribune" reporter was present, but have not seen his report in The Tribune of last week or this.

I shall be further obliged if you will send me the Hartford reports you speak of, and any others that come within your reach.

"The days" were exceedingly interesting to me, as to all attendants, I believe, and I look forward with hope for the History which Mr. Orcutt is preparing. He has good materials and will, I doubt not, give us a good account of the mountain Town.

This Week's "Springfield Republican" will, probably, give a full report of the proceedings, including "the Poem", read by me.[1]

Your proposal for Conversations or Lectures in Bristol, will perhaps bring me soon into your parts again, and enable to Visit Wolcott also.

Possibly, my daughter Louisa ‖ might ‖ may then be able to accompany me.

Truly Yours,
A. Bronson Alcott.

Rev. W. W. Belden.

¹ Written by Channing.

LETTER 73–41

[to Ednah Dow Cheney]

Concord September | 19th 1873.

Dear Mrs Cheney.

So much uncertainty about my going West yet remains, that I cannot well arrange any thing definitely now. We have not determined whether we remain here through the winter or take quarters in Boston. If we stay here, I shall hardly leave for any length of time, on Mrs. Alcotts' account. Should we go to Boston, I might be spared perhaps for a short time. But as things now stand it is quite doubtful if I go West this season.

So you see that your plans may proceed quite irrespective of mine.

I will write, if you wish, to Mrs Adams, Mrs Bagley and Mr. Harris, if my letters will be of the least use to you. But Mrs Adams, Mrs Bagley and Mr. Harris, can open every door for you in Iowa, Michigan and Missouri.

Mrs Adams writes that Mr Adams will be at Desmoins [sic] during the month of October. But will be at home during November. But she will doubt-less inform you of the time when she wishes you to be in Dubuque.

Mrs Alcott is now quite comfortable. She rides out almost every day, and enjoys her grand children especially. Anna and the little boys have just returned from North Conway where they passed a month, much to their health and happiness.

I retain very pleasant reccollections [sic] of my late Visit to South Man-chester.

Louisa is now in the best of spirits. Her "Work" meets with surprising favor: 20,000 copies having been sold already. May writes from London gaily. She will probably remain till spring.

Very truly Yours,
A. Bronson Alcott

Mrs. Cheney.

LETTER 73-42

[to J. H. Temple, Nantucket, Mass.]

Concord September | 26th 1873.

Dear Friend,

I do not clearly make out by your note whether you wrote October 1st or 16th to come to Nantucket. If you will write the time on which you wish me to visit you I see nothing now to prevent my coming then, and I should like to be with you over Sunday.

We have about concluded to remain in Concord through the winter, and it is quite doubtful whether I go West this season.

I had a happy time at the Wolcott Centennial and shall mail an account of the proceedings with this.

Our Library is to be dedicated with an address by Emerson next Monday.

My family are all comfortably well. Mrs Alcott has been quite ill since you were here, as you have doubtless heard. She now rides out almost daily. We have pleasant Letters from May.

Truly Yours,
A. Bronson Alcott.

Rev. J H. Temple

LETTER 73-43

[to Samuel Orcutt, Wolcott, Conn.]

Concord September | 27th 1873.

Dear Sir.

Mr. Sanborn has omitted Channing's Verses in this week's Republican, wishing to have a correct impression—which, I hope, will appear in next week's issue. I enclose his account, entitled *"Alcott and Wolcott"* which you can use as you see fit. It was compiled from my *"Itinerary,"* and such reports of the Centennial as came to hand. I think you will find it mainly correct. My chief regret is that he could not be present to report at first hand.

Yesterday I mailed to your address a copy of Channings Poem corrected by himself, and as he wishes it to stand in your *History*.

I hear nothing as yet from Smith our photographer. We thought the negatives promised good impressions, and he was to send me some by mail. They have not come to hand. Should you be in Waterbury please inquire of Mr Bassett how the matter stands. At this rate, we shall not have our photographs till doomsday. I left $10. with Mr. Bassett to pay for them. If more is claimed, let me know.

Certainly our *Centenary* was a splendid success. We could have filled a *third* day delightfully.

I shall expect to hear about our Library soon.

Very truly
Yours
A. Bronson Alcott

Rev. Saml Orcutt.

LETTER 73-44

[to Thomas Ridgeway Gould, Boston?]

Concord October 1st. 1873

Dear Sir.

I am compelled, on consulting Louisa farther about the Bust, to postpone all further action on your part. My own pecuniary affairs are too precarious just now to warrant my taking so heavy a responsibility. And Louisa's income from R. Road stocks is too fluctuating to warrant so great a luxury—even for her father—; A delay in meeting our obligations to you, might be an inconvenience to yourself; ‖ also, ‖ and a source of discomfort to us. With your permission, we will therefore hope the future will be more propitious for all of us. A work of art from your skillful hands should be met by a generous as well as just compensation

Hoping still to prove myself a good subject under a more prolonged dispensation of your services

I am, greatly obliged.
Yours Truly,
A Bronson Alcott

P.S. I write this, lest I should fail to see you to day at the dedication.
A.B.A.

Mr. Gould.
Sculptor.

LETTER 73-45[1]

[to Ellen A. Chandler, Jamaica Plain? Mass.]

Concord October 3rd 1873.

Dear Miss Chandler,

We are wont to fancy that matters personally interesting to us, may please our friends also. And as you may not have noticed any thing in the newspapers concerning the "Wolcott Centennial Celebration," I enclose Sanborn's account published in last weeks' "Springfield Republican"—calling your attention specially to "Channing's "Poem." which was read by me on that occasion.

A corrected version of this will appear in "the Boston Daily Advertiser" of to-morrow morning.

The occasion was one of much interest and satisfaction to myself and townspeople.

I imagine you are returned to your Studies and Classes, where I like to think of you, next to seeing you here. Can't you ride up some Saturday and indulge us with that pleasure?

We have concluded to stay here through the coming winter, and I am to remain mostly at home, deferring my tour Westwards till spring at least.

Mrs Alcott is quite comfortable, riding out on pleasant days. We have happy accounts from May. Louisa is now very well, and Anna and my boys are with us, having had a month's recreation at Conway.

It would have enhanced my delight had I caught your face in the crowd of fine people who honored us at *the dedication of Our Concord Library* on Wednesday. The day was faultless and the services excellent. I trust you read them yesterday's Advertiser.

Come up and let me show you *"The Concord Alcove"*

Moreover—may I call some day next week, and take you to see a certain Head at Goulds' Studio, and learn your impressions about it?

I shall be in the city on Monday next, and will remember to ring at your school rooms, hoping to see you a moment.

Affectionately
Yours,
A. Bronson Alcott

Miss E. A. Chandler

[1] MS. owned by the Abernethy Library, Middlebury College. A copy, in Alcott's hand, is in the Alcott-Pratt Collection.

LETTER 73–46

[to J. H. Temple, Nantucket, Mass.]

Concord October 3rd 1873

Dear Sir.

Your note has just come to hand. I see nothing now to prevent my being with you on Thursday Oct 23rd. and you may advertize me for that, or the time fixed by yourself and friends. I can spend the following Sunday with you, if you wish, and meet your people in any way which may be thought best.

Meanwhile will you write and inform of the train from Boston which takes me to the Island.

I inclose a Springfield Republican's account of the Wolcott Celebration thinking you may be interested in biographical matter it contains. Can I bring any book from my Library

Truly Yours,
A. Bronson Alcott.

Rev. J. H. Temple.
   Nantucket

LETTER 73–47

[to H. F. Bassett, Waterbury, Conn.]

Concord October, 6th 1873.

Dear Sir,

I have heard nothing from Smith concerning the photographs. Has he failed again and hesitates about giving us the impressions? Or, is there some demur as to his pay? I shall like to know how the matter stands in his eyes, and will try to satisfy him about it.

Having waited so long I am getting impatient lest nothing should come of it after all our endeavours. At any rate, I should like to see what he has done.

I think it was arranged that the photographs, (mounted or not) should be sent to me. But none have come to hand. Were they misdirected? Sent by mail or by express?

Will you take time to inform me?

Last week I mailed to you a copy of The Springfield Republican containing Sanborns' article about the Wolcott Centenary. There were some misprints in Channings Poem, which are corrected in last Saturdays' Boston Daily Advertiser, a copy of which I will send you soon. We have concluded to pass the winter in Concord, so I shall hope to be in Waterbury again before spring.

Mr. Belden sent me his reports of the Centennial, and editor Cooke Elihu Burritts remarks.

> Regards to your family,
> Truly Yours,
> A. Bronson Alcott

H. F. Bassett
  Waterbury,
    Conn,

LETTER 73–48

[to Samuel Orcutt, Wolcott, Conn.]

Concord October 6th. 1873.

Dear Sir,

Saturday's Boston Daily Advertiser contained a corrected copy of Channings Poem, which I mail herein to your address. You will notice a misprint or two—the omission of *"are"* in the line—
"And prove how love and beauty yet *are* clear".
"This" for *"the"* in the line—
"This land is ours," &c

I enclose also another copy of Sanborn's article, thinking you might find it necessary to complete the whole if you wished to paste it on your page.

I am inviting subscriptions—of books as gifts mostly, and think I may have a choice collection for the Library. Emerson, Sanborn, Channing, owe it much good will; and Roberts Brothers will give of their books.

Saturday I wrote to Mr. Bassett[1] about the photographs.

I would send you my *"Itinerary" for June and September visits to Wolcott,* if I thought you would care to read and extract for *your History.* In these I wrote out many particulars which I may not have spoken at the Centennial or in Conversation with you. How forward is your work? If I should visit Wolcott in November or December would my notes be in time for your perusal? Sanborn promises a fuller sketch of me, if you wish it, and have room.

I think I may add also half a dozen subscribers to those already set to my name—6 copies more.—

Truly Yours,
A. Bronson Alcott

¹ See the preceding Letter 73–47, also dated October 6, a Monday.

LETTER 73–49

[to Philo Smith, Waterbury, Conn.]

Concord, October. | 13th 1873.

Dear Sir,

The photographs came to hand yesterday, and are an improvement on your first attempts. Mr. Bassett writes that you are paid for them according to our agreement. Now I wish you would send me three impressions of each of the following views, viz:—
House of Mrs Mable Alcott

> Dr. William's
> My father's
> Almon.
> James;

Fifteen pictures in all. I do not wish them mounted. When the History of Wolcott is ready, doubtless others will be wanted to be bound in the volume. These I want for my private collection. Send them by mail to my address:

A. Bronson Alcott,
Concord.
Mass

and oblige, yours,

A. Bronson Alcott.

I will send you the price on receipt of the pictures.
Mr. Smith,
  Photographer,
    Waterbury,
      Conn

LETTER 73–50

[to Samuel Orcutt, Wolcott, Conn.]

Concord October 14th | 1873.

Dear Sir,

Yours of the 13th has this morning come to hand.

I will see Sanborn about *the Sketches,* and put him in the way of furthering your wishes. He is better informed about the matter than any one else, and will like to prepare them.[1]

612

I hope this note will reach you in time to secure you from disappointment about visiting Concord. Yesterday it seemed practicable, and I wrote you to that effect. But it appears today that we are to close our house here in Concord next Wednesday or Thursday, in order to secure Winter Quarters for my family in Boston, and should be unable to offer you the hospitalities of a home, as we should gladly had ‖ it ‖ your visit been earlier. But I purpose leaving for Conn. soon after we are fairly fixed for the winter in the city. And we can consult about particulars of the History in Wolcott and Waterbury.

But I will write again soon.

Truly Yours,
A. Bronson Alcott.

Rev. Saml. Orcutt

---

[1] Sanborn wrote the material on the Alcotts which appeared in Samuel Orcutt, *History of the Town of Wolcott from 1731 to 1874.*

LETTER 73-51

[to H. F. Bassett, Waterbury, Conn.]

Concord October ‖ 14th 1873

Dear Sir,

The Photographs came to hand promptly and are really good for the price. I am obliged to you for the trouble you have taken about forwarding them. I have sent for some more. When the Wolcott History is ready doubtless others will wish copies for binding up in it. My brother from Fair Haven writes inquiring where he can get them.

We are just now about taking quarters in Boston for the Winter. When the family are fairly fixed I purpose making a visit to Connecticut—and to pass a few days in Waterbury. If desired I will speak then as we talked when I last saw you. I think I shall be along early in November.

Regards to yourself and family.

Truly Yours
A. Bronson Alcott

H. F. Bassett.

LETTER 73-52

[to J. H. Temple, Nantucket, Mass.]

Concord October 21st ‖ 1873.

Dear Sir,

We are now preparing to close our house here for the winter. And there are so many details to supervise and matters to dispatch, during this week and the next, that I must (though reluctantly) decline visiting Nantucket as was planned.

Then, as soon as my family is fixed in winter quarters in Boston, I must be off for Connecticut, and may go farther west to fulfil last season's engagements in various cities.

After all the West is, (for me at least) the fairest field for satisfactory work, and I am happy in having explored its opportunities and needs.

It is much for a people to know *what* are its wants, and *how* to supply these at the simplest cost.

My Card for this season's Conversations and Discourses is in the printers' hands. When done, I will forward a sample to you.

Truly Yours,
A. Bronson Alcott

Rev. J. H. Temple.

LETTER 73-53

[to Samuel Orcutt, Wolcott, Conn.]

Concord October | 22nd 1873.

Dear Sir,

I enclose a card for Conversations &c.

I now think of leaving for Waterbury and Wolcott the first week in November, and may stop for a lecture or Conversation, perhaps pass the Sunday, in Bristol. But I shall reach Wolcott as soon as I can, and ‖ think I shall ‖ hope to bring *"The Sketches* with me. Sanborn is now writing them and hopes to have them ready for me. He fears they will be too long for the Book. But is willing you should abridge, if you think best. They are of *myself,* at some length, of Louisa (with some additions to the one you have) of Mrs Alcott, May, and the mother of "the Little Men."—But you will not commit the mistake, I am sure, of having more of *"Alcott",* than is becoming.

I can spend a few days in Wolcott, and shall be glad to further your Book and the Library in any way that I can.

Truly Yours
A. Bronson Alcott.

Rev. Samuel Orcutt.

LETTER 73-54

[to Philo Smith, Waterbury, Conn.]

Concord October | 23rd 1873.

Dear Sir,

The Photographs came safely to hand this morning, and are very acceptable. I am pleased to learn that James Alcott likes them and has taken so many. I shall, doubtless, want some more—how many I cannot now say.

I shall be in Waterbury week after next, or about that time, and will then call and settle with you for these.

Yours truly,
A. Bronson Alcott.

Mr. Philo Smith.

LETTER 73-55

[to Mary N. Adams, Dubuque, Iowa]

Concord October | 27th. 1873.

Dear Mrs. Adams,

Our plans for the winter months being now determined definitely, I can write about my Winter's tour West. We had decided a month ago to remain here, but, as much on Louisa's account as her mothers concluded to close the house and take quarters in Boston—Louisa, her mother, Anna and the little men. So we leave here on Tuesday of next week,—my family for their rooms in Boston; I for Connecticut where I shall be for some weeks, and, if I find that I may safely leave the family, intend visiting the West and fulfilling last seasons engagements in various cities, with such others as may offer. I should not think of returning without seeing my friends in Dubuque. Mr. Adams and yourself particularly. About what time I may reach your city I cannot now say. I may go first to St. Louis and take the River cities along diverging at Jacksonville and other places as chance may favor. It may be New Years before I reach you. There are tempting opportunities on the way to detain me. Detroit, if I should take that place on my way to Chicago—Ann Arbor, Lansing, Jackson, but I shall probably take these on my return from Iowa eastwards.

I have forwarded my Cards for Conversations &c, to most cities where I have been formerly, and shall gladly visit them again if desired. As the seasons pass the interest in Parlor and pulpit teachings appears to deepen and spread, opening wider fields for itinerating. Mrs A. says, *"I have the largest Bishoprick of any Rt. Rev. in America"*. I am very happy to find myself in prime plight to visit it.

By Mr Ward who made us a short call last Wednesday, I sent "Channings Thoreau," and some Cards for Conversations. His stay was so short and I wished him to see our shows, that I had not a moment to write your name in the Book after our return from the monument &c. Mr Channing is here regularly on Tuesdays and Fridays. He will miss the family very much this winter. I hope you liked his Poem for the Wolcott Centennial—a copy of which I sent you with Mr. Sanborns account. The History of Wolcott is to be published about New Years.

I have not attended the Clubs nor anniversary meetings lately. "The Index" comes weekly informing us of the Free Religionist's attitude and teachings.[1] I have had as ready acceptance with Orthodox as "Unitarian liberals," and Free Religionists. The West is showing the wider hospitality and the East begins to profit by the example.

Mr Emerson declines lecturing this season, wishing to complete literary tasks left unfinished owing to his recent travels. I shall hope to meet Mrs Cheney somewhere on her route. She is the right representative woman for your section.

We have good accounts from May. She is enjoying her art studies and sends us sketches showing her improvement—sketches of Shakespear's birthplace, Kenilworth and copies of Turner's pictures in water colors.

Mrs Alcott is now quite well and pleased with the prospect of wintering in her native city. And Louisa hopes to take her Romance in hand of *"the Cost of an Idea."*

If you write address me at Waterbury, for the next month.

Sincerely Yours,
A Bronson Alcott

Mrs Mary N. Adams

---

¹ For a discussion of the *Index*, see Clarence F. Gohdes, *The Periodicals of American Transcendentalism* (Durham, 1931), pp. 229–54.

LETTER 73–56

[to Ellen A. Chandler]

Concord, October. | 1873.

Dear Miss Chandler,

The printer has set my topics in such winning types, that I cannot well resist sending you a sample. And to say, that we are to move into winter quarters in the City sometime next week. As we close our house here, and I am at liberty again to journey, as heretofore, I purpose leaving for Connecticut early in November, and may be drawn far West to fulfil last season's engagements—adding others, as chance may determine.

Concord is very dear to me. Yet I have learned to love the West, and can spend another winter very delightfully in those hospitable homes into which I have been privileged to enter—some of them more than once, and always leaving them wishing to repeat my visit.

If I am in Boston, and can take a friend's hand before I leave, I need not add, my pleasure will be full.

Very truly Yours,
A. Bronson Alcott

Miss Ellen A. Chandler.

LETTER 73–57¹

[to Franklin B. Sanborn, Concord]

Waterbury Nov. 18th 1873.

Dear Friend,

Your last portion of the Sketch reached me here, where I have been since Friday last. I return to Waterbury for a Conversation on Thursday evening next, having preached here last Sunday evening. I mail a report of my discourse herewith to you at Concord. I spoke at Florence and at Wolcott on preceding Sundays and shall (probably) speak in Mr. Anderson's pulpit, next Sunday. Here, a lecture is being arranged for some day of next week. I think of spending Thanksgiving at Bridgeport.

The History is to go to press at once. Mr. Orcutt has heard most of the Sketch, and will like to print the whole of it. I read all I have of it to my brother, (with whom I am staying) last evening, and we agreed that none should be omitted in the History. At any rate, it should be printed entire in some form. So you shall add as you like. What is written is fixed and sure to find *reason* for itself.

For your kindness in forwarding my letters from Concord P.O. take my thanks, as for the many favors received at your hands hitherto.

I have good news from Mrs A. and Louisa, and am very well, and happily engaged.

Today, snow fell and it has been wintry.

Remember me to Mrs S. and your boys all three.

Very truly
Yours,
A. Bronson Alcott.

Address me at Waterbury
F. B. Sanborn Esq
    Concord

[1] MS. in the Berg Collection, New York Public Library. A copy, in Alcott's hand, of a portion of the letter, is in the Alcott-Pratt Collection.

LETTER 73–58

[to Mrs. W. D. Gunning, Waltham, Mass.]

Boston, Nov 22nd. 1873.

Dear Mrs Gunning,

I returned yesterday from Connecticut, having deferred my tour farther Westwards owing to the financial embarrassments felt in those parts even more than with us in New England. This leaves me free to speak in your Sunday course at Waltham if you desire my services. At present I have no engagements for Sundays and shall gladly take my place in your course at such time as you may choose.

Yours truly,
A. Bronson Alcott

Address me at
    26 East Brookline Street,
    Boston

LETTER 73–59

[to Miss Haniford, New Haven, Conn.]

Boston December 3rd 1873.

Dear Miss Haniford,

Your copy of the Conversations came to hand yesterday, and you have my thanks for the favor. When Louisa's new story comes out, I shall send you a copy. The publishers speak of bringing it out about the 10 of this month.

I have many thanks also to offer to your mother and your friend of the household for their kind hospitalities during my late visit.

Please remember me to them and accept the regards of

Yours,
A. Bronson Alcott.

Miss Haniford,
New Haven,
Conn.

LETTER 73–60

[to Samuel Orcutt, Wolcott, Conn.]

Boston, December, | 26th 1873.

Dear Sir,

Mr Sanborn has finished his "Sketch,' and has written to you, he tells me. I now mail to you The M.S. and shall wish to see proof-sheets as these are struck off, before the final impression is taken. It would give me great pleasure, also, to read the final proofs, if you have duplicates and can forward them from time to time

The Sketch runs, as you will see, to 74 M.S. pages. You may like to separate by headings the notices of Misses Louisa and May.

As to printing and stitching copies in separate binding, I think I shall like 100 copies at least for private distribution. And for these I shall expect to pay the cost.

About illustrations, I know not what to report. Smiths' photographs, you say, are too large for binding in the History. I think favorably of heliotypes; and have consulted "Osgood & Co." here about price, &c. They will furnish these by the thousand at 8 cts apiece; and for 6 cts if several thousand are taken. The heliotypes which I have seen are almost as fine as engravings. And if Smith would forward *his negatives of Homesteads*[?] I should like to try a few impressions. The military papers can be taken from originals in my possession. A few superior pictures are more becoming than many poor ones. I shall await *your* wishes in the matter.

I am here in Boston with my family, and may leave for the West sometime in January. But this is undetermined. I shall be glad to hear further from you as the printing proceeds.

Sanborn has paid a tribute to his friend, that, if not too extended, seems fitting for your History. I hope the Sketch of Dr. William Alcott is worthy of him.

I am glad to learn that your printers have fairly set to work, and trust nothing will delay the work till it is finished.

You may enclose *"the choice papers,"* you named, and send them to me *here*—My address is

"*26 East Brookline Street
Boston*"
and I will keep you informed of future movements.

Very truly

Yours,

A. Bronson Alcott

Rev. Samuel Orcutt
Wolcott
Conn.

LETTER 73–61[1]

[to Franklin B. Sanborn, Concord]

Boston December, | 30th 1873.

My Dear Friend,

Very grateful are we all for the graceful manner in which you have sketched the family of Alcott. A happy new Year, many returns of such, to you and yours. A lifelong good will and good wishes were insufficient to repay our obligation for this and numerous acts of kindness.

Kindness and affection which we have received from your constant friendship.

Indulge us by accepting this slight token of the regards of your friends,

The Alcotts.

F. B. Sanborn
Concord.

[1] MS. owned by the Fruitlands and Wayside Museums. A copy, in Alcott's hand, is in the Alcott-Pratt Collection.

PART TWENTY-ONE

※

1874–1876

LETTER 74–1

[to Samuel Adams Drake, Boston]

Boston, January 17th | 1874.

Samuel A. Drake Esq.

Dear Sir,

I will gladly meet "The Historic Genealogical Society," on the day named in your note and occupy the time allowed with slight Sketches of Concord Authors. These must of necessity be very brief and imperfect. But I will do my best, and bespeak the indulgence of the Society for whatever shall be unsatisfactory.

Very truly
Yours,
A. Bronson Alcott.

LETTER 74–2

[to Samuel Orcutt, Wolcott, Conn.]

Boston January. | 17th 1874.

Dear Sir,

Osgood has just sent samples of his heliotypes, which I forward with this note.

They seem cheaper and more artistic than photographs. If you conclude to have some taken for your History, it will be necessary for you to send the glass negatives for the portraits and homesteads.

Impressions can be taken from any documents by Osgood, who can get negatives from them for his heliotypes. Did I leave John Alcox Commission and military orders with you? I do not find them with my other Wolcott collections. If you conclude to have heliotype illustrations, it will be necessary to forward Smith's glass negatives for the Wolcott homesteads, and Capt. John's military papers (if you have them) Negatives for portraits of myself and Louisa are here, and I will furnish a few impressions—also of the homesteads and documents, for the book.

The first form reached me last Friday and is an improvement on the former proofs. It reads well, and promises fair. I shall be glad to see the forms as fast as they come from the printers and pay the postage. Mr. Anderson's Introduction will add to the value of the Volume. You have interesting matter, besides your own text besides [*sic*].—Maxwell's and Channings Poems, and the biographies. It should be one of the best of Town Histories, as creditable to the town, as to yourself. I begin to look for its appearance with no little impatience.

Truly Yours,
A. Bronson Alcott.

Rev. Samuel Orcutt

LETTER 74-3

[to Theodore Tilton, New York City]

Boston January | 17th 1874.

Theodore Tilton Esq.
Dear Sir,

My subscription for *"The Golden Age"* expired with the year '73 and I wrote in December wishing the paper discontinued. It is still sent.

As much as I value its liberal American spirit, and have enjoyed its perusal, I must repeat my request for its discontinuance.

In these pinching times some of us must forego many desirable luxuries, if we will preserve our honesty and self-respect.

I return the two last numbers.

Very truly yours,
A. Bronson Alcott.

LETTER 74-4

[to William Channing Gannett, Boston]

Boston January | 22nd 1874.

Dear Sir,

You may consider me as ready to speak in the Sunday Afternoon course at such time as may be found most convenient or desirable My subject will be,—
"Modern Reformatory Ideas and Methods."

Thanking you for the opportunity,

I am
Truly Yours,
A. Bronson Alcott.

Rev. W. C. Gannett

LETTER 74–5

[to J. G. Brooks, Cambridge, Mass.]

Boston January | 22nd 1874.

Dear Sir.

Your arrangements for a Conversation next Tuesday evening at Mrs Mosher's, are very acceptable, and you may expect me there at the hour named—7½ or 8 o,clock.

Thanking you and Mrs Mosher for your interest in the matter,

I am

Truly Yours

A. Bronson Alcott.

Mr. J. G. Brooks.

LETTER 74–6

[to Charles Francis Richardson, New York City]

Boston January. | 26, 1874

Dear Sir,

I mail to your address "Notes of a Conversation held in Boston in 1850." If you find it suitable for printing in the Independent, please forward me a copy. If not suitable will you take charge of the M.S. and return by mail, as it is taken from a series, which I may think of publishing sometime in a Volume. I hope the M.S. will be found legible and not the worst for the typesetter to decipher.

My address for a month to come will be

26 East Brookline St.

Boston.

Truly Yours,

A. Bronson Alcott.

LETTER 74–7[1]

[to William T. Harris, St. Louis]

Boston, January 27. | 1874.

26 East Brookline

Street.

Dear Friend,

Your lecture delivered before the University Club reached me yesterday.[2] It is the most satisfactory thing of yours that I have happened to read. I wish you would think well enough of it to have some copies struck off for wider circulation than your St. Louis newspapers can give it. It should have ‖ a ‖ wider ‖ circulation ‖ advantages. Our Radical Clubs here need of just such ideas and where shall they get them, if not from yourself. Here are individualists, materialists, of the Spencer and Lewes type, labor-reformers, Darwinists, &c. all fumbling in the natural sphere for the solution of their doubts, all without any logical method, any hold of certainties to guide them to sure results. Your statements of the laws and order of thought, and the dialectic to guide, might arrest some of them, and turn their inquiries in a resulting order. Pray think of it, and if you do not print otherwise send me a few copies of the newspaper report. It is the same I think, with important additions delivered before the Chicago Phil Society, of which yourself or some one sent me a copy.

I am here spending the winter with my family, having been advised on account of the money pressure especially at the West, to defer my tour for this season. I made a short tour to Connecticut, and have been here in the city since Thanksgiving. I have had opportunities of meeting thoughtful companies, and have others in prospect. To night I meet students and others in Cambridge, and am to give Lecture presently in Boston on *Modern Reformatory Ideas and Methods* Last Sunday Johnson lectured at Horticultural Hall on *Transcendentalism as an element in thought and Progress.* It was good and listened to with attention by a large audiance [*sic*]. On the whole the best thing that has been said lately from the platform.

Emerson has not lectured yet this season. Our History of Wolcott is in press, and to contain among other biographies, a *sketch of myself,* by Sanborn. It will be published sometime in March. Let me hear from you soon.

> Affectionately Yours,
> A. Bronson Alcott.

Wm. T Harris

[1] From a copy, in Alcott's hand, in the Alcott-Pratt Collection. The original is in the Alcott-Harris Collection in the Concord Free Public Library (see Appendix B).
[2] "The Relation of Philosophy to Society, Art and Religion," delivered before the University Club of St. Louis (see Leidecker, *Yankee Teacher,* p. 398).

LETTER 74-8

[to Clarence D. Wyatt, Haverhill, Mass.]

Boston, January 30th | 1874.

Dear Sir

I think less of readings than of Conversations, and before one ventures to give counsel, he should know personally the one to whom it is proffered. I might suggest books to be studied, and methods of studying habits of life, and aims for future attainment, but these would be hazardous quite likely, unless the temperament and training were known.

If you think it worth while to come and see me, at No. 26 East Brookline Street, Boston, and will name the day, I will gladly meet you, and *'prescribe"* as the doctors say. Beyond that, it were perhaps of little profit to either of us to attempt any thing further.

Young people are wont to think wisdom and virtue can be administered like pills and powders by those whom they regard as elders in these attainments, but these are to be won by living and thinking alone, and after long efforts. They cost every thing beside.

Esteeming it an honor to be sought by young people, and wishing you faithful in your search and successful

I am truly
Yours
A. Bronson Alcott.

Mr. Clarence D. Wyatt.
    Haverhill
       Mass

LETTER 74–9

[to Albert F. Blaisdell, Provincetown, Mass.]

Boston January 30th | 1874.

Dear Sir,

A good selection from Coleridge should find favor with publishers and students of the best English thought. I for one should like much to have such to commend to young students particularly.

Coleridge has been to me the most suggestive and edifying of modern thinkers. His works embrace the whole field of life and literature and your selection would be an attractive introduction to them.

Suppose you forward to Roberts Brothers your M.SS. and get their views about publishing. I will speak to them if you wish me to, and further your wishes in the matter. At any rate, the design is excellent, and worth pursuing as a study for your own benefit if not for the public.

Very truly
Yours,
A. Bronson Alcott

A. F. Blaisdell,
    Provincetown,
       Mass.

LETTER 74–10[1]

[to William T. Harris, St. Louis]

Boston, February 7th | 1874.

Dear Friend,

Your *Introduction to Hegels' Philosophic Method[s?]* came duly to hand. I have studied it faithfully, and think I have thought it throughout with the aid of your *critical Exposition* of it. I wish it may find students, and help *methodize* our loose and inconsequent thinking. You have done a great work in doing this Exposition.

Sanborn has noticed your lecture before the University Club, as you may have seen. And Abbott speaks his praises in his *"Index"*, intimating his *differences*. Thinkers will sometime learn the difference between truths and opinions.—Of course you see "the *Index*" and *Republican*".

I wrote you lately and told you a little about my winter's doings. I have met a pleasant circle of students at Cambridge and expect to meet them again. Then I am to open the next Radical Club at Dr. Bartols', and speak in the Sunday series at Horticultural Hall. I have thoughts of trying for subjects, *"The Ages"*, at the Club, and *'Modern Reformatory Ideas and Methods"* in my Sunday Lecture. In this last I can speak of Western life and thought by way of illustration.

Do you still entertain the possibility of coming East to live? Harvard may be slow to find out and seat our American Hegel in its philosophical Chair. But there are those who think he should have the widest opportunities our country has to offer for teaching both by tongue and pen.

We think of returning to our house in Concord sometime next month.

Do you read the English Contemporary Review?

Most truly
Yours
A. Bronson Alcott

Wm. T. Harris.

---

¹ From a copy, in Alcott's hand, in the Alcott-Pratt Collection. The original is in the Alcott-Harris Collection in the Concord Free Public Library (see Appendix B).

LETTER 74–11

[to Samuel Orcutt, Wolcott, Conn.]

Boston February 14th | 1874.

Dear Sir.

The sheets of your history, lately sent, came duly to hand. As the story proceeds, the virtues and sacrifices of the early settlers stand out the more distinctly, and must excite the respect of their living descendants. Your method certainly has the merit of plain history, telling what is significant and important, omitting diffuse details. I notice a misprint or two but nothing of important [*sic*]. You will correct them of course in the final proofs.

I have been expecting to learn further about the illustrations, and will send you, if you wish, the papers which you named in your last letter. I trust you received the heliotypes. I have had no further communication with Osgood since, but shall if you desire further information.

The enclosed paper turned up last night on opening my Family Register.

It may be of no use, but I transmit it to you—with a few notes that may be found useful.

Sanborn tells me that he has heard from you, about the Sketch &c.

Address me as heretofore

26, Brookline Street, Boston.

Very truly

Yours

A. Bronson Alcott

Rev. Saml. Orcutt.

LETTER 74–12[1]

[to   ?   ]

[Concord? February? 1874?]

hope to be present at your next.

Miss May's address is

156 Torrington Square,

London/

W. C.

Very truly

yours

A. Bronson Alcott.

[1] The sheet preceding this fragment has been torn from the MS volume. The letter is positioned here as in the MS volume. May returned from England in March.

LETTER 74–13

[to Harriet N. Angel, Akron, Ohio]

Boston, February | 24th 1874.

Dear Miss Angel,

I am sorry that I have nothing of importance to communicate about *Brook Farm*. Mrss [*sic*] George Ripley and Charles A. Dana, were students of Townes, and the chiefs of the community. They are of course the best authorities to be consulted. I am not aware that either have published any account of their enterprize. If they have you will find it, probably, in Appletons new edition of the American Cyclopedia which they are editing.

There were brief papers published in the Dial, and in the Atlantic Monthly. Mr Emerson gave a lecture about it in Boston a year or two since, which was reported in the newspapers.

Neither Mr. Emerson nor Margaret Fuller were members Hawthorne was, George Wm. Curtiss John S. Dwight. Wm. Henry Channing was a transcient [*sic*] visitor only. It had nothing in common with Shakerism, except an attempt at equality in its economies. All were [word] some part in its industries.

You may have confounded Brook farm with Fruitlands—an effort of mine and an English friend, Charles Lane, to plant a society on Ideal grounds at Harvard, near the Shaker Family in that town. My daughter, Louisa, has given a burlesque sketch of it in a December number of the Independent, 1873. She may put it into a N England Romance sometime

I recall with pleasure my interview with yourself, and our departed friend, when I was in Akron.

With kind remembrances to Judge Bryon and yourself.

I am truly Yours
A. Bronson Alcott

Miss Harriet N. Angel,
  Akron, Ohio.

LETTER 74–14

[to Rowland Conner, Florence, Mass.]

Boston, February, | 24th 1874.

Dear Sir,

It will give me much satisfaction to attend the dedication of your New Hall on the 23rd and 24th of March next. I shall endeavour to be present on both days, and doubt not of our having an interesting and impressive service. Surely nothing of precedent or of formality need embarrass or dictate the proceedings of the day.

I anticipate livelier words, wider views, than have often been spoken from any platform—"*Cosmian*" in scope and significance truly. Let us have representative minds in all the wide varieties of thought and purpose to grace the occasion.

Very truly
Yours,
A. Bronson Alcott

Rev. Rowland Conner.
  Florence, Mass.

LETTER 74–15

[to Georgiana Davis, Boston]

Boston March 16th | 1874.

Dear Miss Davis,

Your favor is at hand. Please assure the Ladies of "The Moral Education Association', that I appreciate the honor done to me by their invitation to address them on the first of April. I shall gladly avail of the opportunity. My subject will be

"*Temperament and Descent*[?]."

Respectfully
Yours,
A. Bronson Alcott.

LETTER 74–16

[to Thomas M. Johnson, Osceola, Mo.]

Boston March 22nd. | 1874.

Dear Sir,

"The Autobiography of a Platonist," which you have in preparation, should be interesting to all students of *Ideas*. Whether there is a public for a literary venture of the kind I am not able to say; students of Plato, and of the Alexandrians, are rare. But a reaction appears to be setting in against the materialism of the Scientists. And Idealism must gain the ascendancy in due time. Your book appears to be on the winning side. And I shall be glad to see it in type.

At any rate, I shall be curious to learn more of its editor than his note informs me. The design appears to be excellent and worth pursuing as a study for your own benefit, if not for the public. I shall be glad to learn anything further which you may choose to communicate.

My address, after the first of April, will be Concord, Mass.

Very truly
Yours,
A. Bronson Alcott.

LETTER 74–17

[to Anna C. Brackett, New York City]

Concord April 7th 1874.

Dear Miss Brackett

I have to thank you for your Book.[1] Amidst the confusion of moving from our winter quarters in Boston to our house here, I have found moments to look into it, and see that you have spoken strong words for women and for the welfare of girls especially. I think we may well thank Dr. Clarke, too, for provoking so many women to speak their minds on the questions he so coarsely raised. It shows how much wiser women are than men about matters directly concerning women. I read his book with the feeling that it was written to the prejudices of Harvard College and of the profession. Science should be chastened to speak of the mysteries. I do not wonder the women visited his deservings upon him without stint. And your indignant protest brought the whole question up which has since set so many able pens busy about it. Men have said "no woman can think and write methodically. Well, how much more methodically did Milton or Locke treat the same subject in their famous essays? Is logic masculine only. And do men alone think? Your *Chapter on the* bill[?] I thought particularly good And the ideal philosophy that pervades your book gives it a superior tone. Mrs. Cheney's paper was characteristic and wise. Mrs Alcott has read the whole and commends it, and the reviews praise it, I see. She continues to enjoy her chamber and books. May has returned to relieve Louisa of the cares of housekeeping. We are all well.

I have had a busy winter in Boston and neighborhood. And meet to morrow *"Our Club"* composed chiefly of young persons—ministers, authors and teachers.[2] Mr. Emerson, Dr. Bartol, Howison, Mrs Cheney, are our elders.—Mr. Harris has sent advanced sheets of the April No of his Journal. Davidsons paper on *"the Conditions of Immortality"* from *Aristotle,* is specially suggestive.

I trust your school thrives.

> With much regard,
> Yours truly,
> A Bronson Alcott.

Miss. Anna C. Brackett
NYork.

[1] Anna C. Brackett, ed., *Education of American Girls: A Series of Essays* (New York, 1874).
[2] See Letter 74–21, par. 2.

LETTER 74–18

[to Mrs. Stone, Kalamazoo, Mich.]

Concord April 11th 1874.

Dear Mrs Stone,

You ask of me a word of encouragement to be read at the Annual Meeting of the Michigan State Suffrage Association to be held at Lansing, next May: "The Legislature', you inform me, 'having submitted an amendment to the Constitution for the enfranchisement of women to be voted on by the electors of the state, next November."

Now what shall I say? What that has not been said for furthering this reform of reforms? It seems the moderns are exhausted: the Hebrew and Christian Scriptures have been quoted and commented upon to the last syllable. I am tempted to try the novelty of a sentence or two from the Greek text. You Western people know a good thing when you hear one: nor are you too particular as to its authorship: taking it rather for its intrinsic significance than upon authority merely.

Take this, then, from Euripides: *"Men need not try where women fail."*

It is a noble tribute to the sex. The saying suggests the grave inquiry whether men have failed for want of womans counsels in political as in social legislation. Does any reasonable man question if there be not as many women having public gifts as there are men? Are not the proofs multiplying wherever women have opportunities opened for proving their fitness under conditions as favorable as these given to men? The womanly gifts and graces are as necessary in the conduct and complementing public duties and affairs, as in private household concerns. Where women—the best women, lead is it unsafe for any to follow? Woman will be womanly wherever placed. No condition can unsex the sexes. The ten commandments are safe in her keeping. Her vote will tell for the virtues, the [word], against the vices all. Plato gives her like share with men in his Ideal Cabinet,: admitting neither till they had contributed citizens to the republic; fining bachelors and denying them political privileges, *for this* reason. And all were to be educated from, and before, birth to be good citizens. He said:—

"Either sex, alone, was but half itself."

Socially we admit his assertion. And are just beginning to suspect that our republic needs to be complemented and rounded with womans counsels and administrations. Good republicans are asking if our legislation is unfixed and demoralized by the debauchery of party politics, private vices & the want of manly integrity, woman's honor.

Let our courtesy to woman be sincere; paid to her modesty as to her person; her intelligence as to her housekeeping; her refining influence in political as social circles. Where a husband would blush to take his wife and daughters, let him blush to be surprised by his sons.

Says

"Revere no god" says Sophocles, *'whom men adore by right* [?]."

And Euripides:

"Seek not thy fellow citizens to guide.
 Till thou can'st order well thine own fireside."

Women have their frailties as have men. But they have what men have not in like measure, the *divining power*. And they are divining their title to influence and sway in all relations—the highest, the lowest—asserting their right to hold with man the keys of empire. It is in the order of progress. They are stepping forth modestly from behind the scenes and taking their places abreast of man. Providentially, too, our civilization, our piety, our philosophy, literature, arts, all favor such advance; cry aloud for woman's agency to stem the current of corruption setting madly against our institutions. Does any observing man fail to perceive the signs of the time; discern what is in the air, the crisis approaching: who is the leader? Is it woman?

And if she who is nearest the ear of your chief magistrate shall prove to have won the victory for your state, the cause is royally won for states and kingdoms everywhere.

Mrs Alcott and Louisa join in hearty hopes for your success.

> I am, with great regard,
> truly Yours.
> A. Bronson Alcott.

P.S.

Be assured that, I retain pleasant memories of my stay in your hospitable home, and of the kindness of friends in Kalamazoo.—

> A.B.A.

LETTER 74–19

[to D. Coan, New York City]

Concord April | 14th 1874.

Dear Sir,

I can add little to the information you ask, concerning my pupils whose names you send me.

Samuel Tuckerman is the son of ‖ Augustin ‖ Gustavus Tuckerman of Boston, now deceased and cousin, I think, of the late Henry Tuckerman of New York. He is a Doctor of Music, I believe, and living in New York City.

Edmund Jackson is the son of the late Patrick Jackson of Boston. I have no further knowledge of him.

Samuel Rodman, was the son of Charles Morgan of New Bedford, and cousin of Charles Morgan of Philadelphia.[1] Father and son are both deceased.

Ellen, is the daughter of Mr. Perkins of Boston. I have no knowledge of her at present.

Lucia, is the daughter of the late Augustus Peabody of Boston. She taught a private school in Boston for many years with great success. She is one of the lately elected School Committee of Boston.

Nathan was the son of Mr Rice[,] merchant of Boston. Father and son are deceased.

Augustine is the son of Dr Shurtliff of Brookline. He is a physician settled in Brookline, and, like his father, a Swedenborgian.

Lemuel is the son of the late Chief Justice Shaw of Boston. He is a lawyer and living in Boston.

Josiah, is the son of Hon Josiah Quincy of Boston. He has written dramatic Verses and is devoted to literary pursuits.

George was the son of Mr Kuhn of Boston. He died young.

John B. is the son of Mr Belknap of Boston. I have no further knowledge of him.

Andrew Henshaw, son of Mr Henshaw of Boston.

Charles Morgan, son of Thomas Morgan of Philadelphia, and cousin of Samuel R. Morgan of New Bedford. He is an artist and lives abroad.

I wish I had further information for you.

Flattered by your interest in these pupils of mine, and in Ideas.

I am respectfully
Yours
A. Bronson Alcott

D. Coan.
New York.

---

[1] Alcott seems to have been careless here; see near the end of the letter.

LETTER 74–20

[to Samuel Orcutt, Wolcott, Conn.]

Concord April | 16th 1874.

Dear Sir,

You may send the proof sheets of Sanborn's Sketch direct to me here at Concord, and I will hand them after reading to Sanborn for his final corrections.

The missing sheets of the History have reached me, and I imagine others are on their way. The Civil portion becomes already very interesting. Your local information adds much to my knowledge of places and people.

Did not the early settler, Solomon Hotchkiss, probably pitch his tent, on the old blind road, now leading into the woods near the forks east of Kenias, and coming out at the Twitchell place? There is a decayed orchard at the turning of the path near this, which was, or may have been, the old route from John Alcock's to the Mill. Twitchell as you know named Alcocks daughter Deborah, and she after her husbands death, married *Walt Hotchkiss.* Titus Hotchkiss was owner of the place during my boyhood. Whether a descendent of Solomon or Walt, I am not informed. But you have done with both, perhaps. I think I could now locate several of the first settlers on Spindle Hill, and Clinton Hill which in my day was also called New Connecticut. I never heard it called *"New Canaan"* as printed

Yours truly,
A. Bronson Alcott.

Rev. Saml. Orcutt.

LETTER 74–21[1]

[to Mary N. Adams, Dubuque, Iowa]

Concord April 17th 1874.

Dear Mrs Adams,

Your long and very interesting letter came in the midst of the hurry of moving from our winter quarters in the City to our House in Concord. Now we are all settled for the summer. May returned from her year's absence just before we left Boston, and is now reinstated as mistress of the Mansion, at least for the summer. Louisa will be here, or in Boston, as the mood favors her movements. We had an agreeable winter in the city. Mrs. Alcott has been mostly well, and enjoyed the change from country to city life, meanwhile. She is now reinstated in her chamber above my study, and has as waiter and companion a Mrs. Lovejoy who formerly lived with us. She reads much, sews, as usual, and relinquishes household cares delightfully. Anna and her boys are now at *Pratt Farm,* near us. She lived next door to us during the winter in the city. The "little men" attended a private school near by, and made commendable progress in their studies. Our residence was on Brookline St facing St. James Hotel.— Thus, for our family geography and surroundings.

As to myself. I may add, that I have had a busy winter meeting people in the city and neighborhood. The *Clubs* have been active, and I have spoken before several Societies. I was lately at the dedication of *"Cosmian Hall"* at Florence, and sent you a report of the sayings and doings, if I remember rightly.— Just now, I am pleasing myself in forming a little Circle composed largely of young persons and a few elders, like Mr Emerson, Dr. Bartol, Mrs Cheney, and myself. We have had three sittings in Boston. Our May sitting we hope to have at my house in Concord. Mr. Emerson is to read a paper by way of opening Conversation. We meet monthly. We call it *"Our Club."* Our members are now about twenty. We do not wish to add many more. Only such are sought as can observe the fine laws of thought and method of sympathy. I wish it may prove the nucleus of an Ideal Fraternity, and a School for the rising Idealists. Do we not need such for correcting the tendency now so pronounced towards extreme Individualism? the denial of all Personality in Man, and hence ignoring Deity altogether?

It was my purpose last autumn to visit the West, and I set forth in November taking Connecticut on my way. While there, Mrs Cheney wrote me from St. Louis, advising me of the *money pressure* at the West, and hinting the prudence of postponing my tour till later in the season. So I returned and made the best of my disappointment in finding what was for me at the East. I live in hopes of visiting my many parishes in the various cities at the West another season. The West is shaping an Ideal Republic for us, and I find myself in a very congenial atmosphere in those parts. Here in New England we live more for the past, venture more cautiously into the future. Yet are perhaps doing our part, nevertheless, for freedom and fraternity.

In this connection it may interest you to learn that I have had several Conversations with students and others at Cambridge.[2] And in May, sometime, Mr Emerson and myself are to meet the Divinity Students at Divinity Hall with assent of the Professors. There are three or four very promising young men in the School: a son of Dr. Salter of Burlington, Iowa, also a Mr. Brooks and Mr. Wilson, from the West. All three are members of *"Our Club."* Samuel Longfellow, too, and Miss. Chandler.

I have just written to Mrs Stone of Kalamazoo, in response to her wish to have a word from me for the Suffrage Convention to be held at Lansing in May next. It will be an important gathering of earnest men and women, and must be specially significant to yourself and sister. If she who has the ear of ‖ your ‖ the Chief Magistrate has had her way with the Governor, then, I am sure, woman's freedom is politically achieved for your state and hers,—for all states and kingdoms.

That dream of yours, I must leave for the Sibyl's interpretation; flattered, as I confess I am, by the nocturnal compliment.

Your Chicago visit must have been very gratifying. What you tell me of Mills and Davidson is hopeful. I have just read with surprise Davidson's discourse on "Immortality" in the "Journal of Speculative Philosophy"—advanced sheets having been forwarded me by Harris. "The Record of a School." finds favor with readers and reviewers. The first edition of 1000 copies, the publishers inform me, has been disposed of. I hope he will venture *"The Conversations on the Gospels,"* next.

You are the most tantalizing of correspondents—both in quality and quantity; and have me largely in your debt, at best. If you accept the terms at this fearful cost, I certainly shall be content with the transaction.

I remember your children with pleasure.—To all my kind friends, please give my regards and thanks for their hospitalities in the past. They are too many to specify by name. Mr Emerson speaks of having received an interesting letter from you some time since. He tells me that he cannot answer letters now, and lectures but seldom.

With great regard for Mr Adams and yourself, Affectionately,

Your friend,

A. Bronson Alcott

Mrs. Mary N. Adams
    Dubuque.

¹ MS. owned by Mrs. Adele A. Bachman, South Orange, N.J. A copy, in Alcott's hand, is in the Alcott-Pratt Collection.
² At Mrs. Mosher's. She was also a member of "Our Club."

LETTER 74–22

[to J. G. Brooks, Cambridge, Mass.]

Concord May 5th 1874.

Dear Sir,

Our rule of admission to the Club hitherto has been by ticket *only*.

This morning I sent to yourself and Mr. Salter also to Mrs. Mosher, your tickets—for our May sitting. And, presuming on your discretion, I herewith enclose three more for your friends.

Whether they shall become members, depends upon themselves A little time will define more distinctly the terms of membership, and of matters pertaining thereto. Divinity students have special claims to consideration.

Mr. Emerson has not, or had not when I last spoke with him, learned the time fixed for meeting the students at Divinity Hall. He expressed much pleasure at having been invited.

I look forward with hope to this occasion, and to our meeting on the 13th.

Very truly,

Yours,

A. Bronson Alcott

Mr. J. G. Brooks,
    Divinity Hall,
        Cambridge:

LETTER 74–23¹

[to Ellen A. Chandler, Jamaica Plain? Mass.]

Concord May 5th 1874

Dear Miss Chandler,

I enclose your ticket to the next meeting of Our Club.

No: the Fates will not frown upon your attendance as hitherto. but admit you affectionately into Our Circle.

I have distributed forty tickets; to Mr. Emerson more than one, and enclose a duplicate for any chosen friend of yours whom you think will enjoy the interview, and possibly become a member.

Some little time will ‖ define ‖ fix definitely the terms of membership and matters pertaining thereto.

Mr Emerson has not named his theme, and we shall all enjoy the more the surprise when announced: or, still better—each one find the name and significance for himself. Surprise is one of the beauties of the poet's art, as of fine manners, and the charms of Conversation.

May has hardly smiled as yet: May-day lingers sullenly still as if threatening to delay and linger into June. Can it be waiting for our Schoolmistress' sallying forth into summer and its pleasures by mountain and stream? *Then,* we shall persuade her to try our fields and brook-sides, and learn whether former haunts have lost their charms for our summer guest. And would not Shakespeare entertain us for a summer's morning or two?[2] We will see.

So till Wednesday and Mr. Emerson, as always,

Affectionately Yours.
A. Bronson Alcott.

Miss. Ellen A. Chandler

---

[1] MS. owned by the Abernethy Library, Middlebury College. A copy, in Alcott's hand, is in the Alcott-Pratt Collection.
[2] A few days earlier, Alcott had read *Coriolanus* (see Alcott, *Journals*, p. 449).

LETTER 74–24

[to Ursula Wood Russell, Lancaster? Mass.]

Concord May, 6th 1874.

My Dear Friend,

Your generous gift with Mr. Russell's autograph,[1] and your own kind note accompanying it, came punctually to hand. Be assured, I shall prize the volume for its contents, but still more as a token of a friendship which must ever be memorable, associated as it will be with family ‖ friend-ships ‖ histories, and particularly with my friends' favorite studies. I may say that I owe to him my first taste of the sweets of literature and of philosophy. while the charms of his Conversations are among my most cherished memories.

Accept my hearty thanks for the book.

I can hardly add a word of sympathy to Mrs. Alcotts for you and yours in your recent sad bereavement. Bound as a family by the tenderest ties, the husband and fathers words and example like the good Vicars in Goldsmiths tale, do, I am sure allure "to the higher worlds, in which he has led the way."

We are all blessed with health and our share of satisfactions. Mrs. Alcott enjoys her books with frequent rides on pleasant days. May has returned and is our housekeeper with an assistant as companion for Mrs. Alcott. Louisa is luxuriating in the city for a month. Anna and her boys will spend the summer at Mr. Pratt's near us.

To yourself and daughters, much esteem and affection.

Your friend,
A. Bronson Alcott

Mrs Russell.

---

¹ William Russell had died August 16, 1873.

LETTER 74–25

[to Benjamin Marston Watson, Plymouth, Mass.]

Concord May 6th 1874.

My "Unforgotten" Friend,

Your generous gift of pair [sic] trees was enhanced in value as in fruitfulness by being delivered punctually by the hand of Mr. Emerson. They came late day before yesterday: were forgotten "in a night's dream only, and a waiting for a fructifying shower yesterday, and this day have been set by my own hands and those of our "Little Men," who have each adopted his, and associated his trees with the givers' name—"The Watson Present."

I am not sure as to the soil and aspect of my grounds for friendliness to this fruit—almost a human production, and paragon of all. But am sure of the amenities proper to Hillside being mingled in their "Genesis," and so promise myself a harvest in my day, with plenteous crops for the offshoots of our Family tree.

To Mrs Watson, and the young gentlemen and ladies now by courtesy as by grace of Culture and calling, my regards: with my thanks for this and former expressions of friendship from yourself.

Yours "unforgettingly,'
A Bronson Alcott

P.S:(in prose[?])

When you will come and see me, I will call again sometime at Hillside when you are "at home," and with leisure at command.

It is written *"my garden waits"* &c. in some page, I have read.

LETTER 74–26

[to Georgiana Davis, Boston]

Concord May 8th 1874.

Dear Miss Davis,

Yours of the 7th is receid. I am gratified to learn that my words spoken on a former occasion found favor with your Association. I shall gladly attend your Annual Meeting on the 28. at Wesleyan Hall, and comply with your request to address the meeting.

Thanking for this opportunity, to speak on the subject which your Association has taken so heartily in hand, and hoping to promote the same,

I am

Very Respectfully
Yours,
A. Bronson Alcott

Miss Georgiana Davis,
Sec. Moral Edn. Association.

LETTER 74–27

[to Samuel Orcutt, Wolcott, Conn.]

Concord, May 8 | 1874

Dear Sir

Concerning the Biography about which you inquire. I wish the same printed on tinted paper like the History; and without covers. I can have copies bound here as occasion may require. Can you favor me with the whole in sheets, before my decision is made about the title? I may wish to have John Alcock's struck off to accompany mine.

Somewhere it seems proper that the changes of the name should be explained in the History, perhaps at the foot of the page.

Some of my uncles continued ‖ continued ‖ to spell their names "*Alcock;*" others "*Alcox.*" John, the first settler, always wrote his "*Alcock,*" and all his ancestors did the same. About 1825 the name "*Alcott*" began to appear, as you suggest in your letter. I wrote it *Alcox*" till about that date. "*Newell,*" I think is right for the Military man.

We have now read and forwarded two mails of proof sheets of the biography.

Yours truly,
A. Bronson Alcott.

Rev. Samuel Olcott [*sic*]
Wolcott.

LETTER 74–28[1]

[to ?]

Concord May 12th 1874.

Dear Sir,

Yours is at hand. You may name my discourse "*a Lecture on Methods of Teaching*". This title will allow me to be discursive, and for Conversation to follow its delivery.

Truly Yours,
A. Bronson Alcott

[1] MS. in the Harris Collection of American Poetry and Plays, Brown University Library. A copy, in Alcott's hand, is in the Alcott-Pratt Collection.

LETTER 74–29

[to   ?   ]

Concord May 14th 1874.

Dear Sir,
   The books about which you inquire were published by Roberts Brothers of Boston, and may be obtained at their bookstore. *"Tablets,"* in one volume, was published in 1868. *Concord Days,"* one volume also, was published in 1873. The price is $1,50 the volume.

Yours respectfully
A. Bronson Alcott

LETTER 74–30

[to Elizabeth Palmer Peabody, Boston?]

Concord May 24th 1874.

Dear Miss Peabody,
   I had a kind note from Misses Garland and Weston, as from yourself, inviting me to attend the closing exercises of their Kindergarten Class, last Thursday. The rainstorm prevented my going to Boston as I intended on that day. Nor did I see Mr. Emerson or Ellen, and Louisa is staying in Boston.
   But you are sure of showing intelligent people in all ranks and relations of life, the fitness and beauty of Froebel's plans for educating the little ones into the pleasurable use of their hearts, hands and heads—combining play with instruction.
   If patience and persistency are to have their perfect rewards surely that satisfaction shall be yours.
   I have read your "Glimpses of Psychology," and esteem them divinations of the true method and spirit of touching the soul of childhood to its finest issues. When parents and the community generally, shall conceive the child to have had a divine as a human parentage, and that its life begins before its advent into bodily organs, we may hope to have something deserving the name of spiritual and intellectual education.
   I always refer in memory to the attempt which we made almost forty years ago at showing how this theory might be practically worked out on children coming to us under the best advantages then permitted by the state of education in Boston. And I think it was a charming success.
   I was glad to learn your high appreciation of 'Maurice.'
   Will you thank Misses Garland and Weston for their kind remembrance.

Your friend,
A. Bronson Alcott

Miss E. P. Peabody.

LETTER 74-31

[to Miss M. C. Pratt, Concord]

Dear Miss Pratt,   [Concord, June 8, 1874]

Very gladly shall I avail myself of the pleasure of presenting to the young Ladies of your graduating Class,[1] their diplomas on the evening of June 18th.

And, if desired, I will meet the young ladies of your school for a Conversation on any morning you may name, meanwhile—to morrow at 11. if you find that hour convenient.—

Very truly
Yours,
A. Bronson Alcott.

June 8th, 1874.

[1] Of the Wayside School in Concord.

LETTER 74-32

[to Jacob Batchelder, Lynn, Mass.]

Dear Sir,   Concord, June 10th | 1874.

Mr. Walton's address is *8. Ludgate Street, London."*

Should he favor your "Lynn Library" with a copy of his "Cyclopedia,'[1] we shall wish a like favor shown to ours in "Concord," of—[2]
Mr. Jacob Batchelder
      Lynn.

[1] See Letter 67-26.
[2] The following sheet, undoubtedly containing the remainder of the letter, has been torn out of the MS volume.

LETTER 74-33[1]

[to Louise Chandler Moulton, Boston]

Dear Mrs Moulton,   Concord June 16 | 1874.

Your pretty sketch of "A Day in Concord" is recd.

As you are plainly in love with our little village why will you not oblige us with the beauties of your pen, and favor the readers of the Tribune also, in giving a descriptive Sketch of our New Concord Library? We think it has not yet been celebrated according to its merits. And, on speaking with one of the directors, to day, he expressed the wish that you should visit it. That you may have some knowledge of its history, I enclose the Dedication Services.

And please take it kindly also, if I send a little sketch of Sanborn's, written for a History of Wolcott, Conn. soon to be published. Fancied you might be interested . . . some of its details. Need I add that Louisa and May were gratified by your complimentary Sketch. I need not add my pleasure in your writing wherever I find it.

Very truly
Yours,
A. Bronson Alcott.

¹ MS. owned by the Library of Congress. A copy, in Alcott's hand, is in the Alcott-Pratt Collection.

LETTER 74–34¹

[to William T. Harris, St. Louis]

Concord June 17th 1874.

Dear Friend,

Your School Report, forwarded to Williams and Co. Boston, I have at hand. I have all of your Reports and esteem them as models for School Superintendents. This last has special value and significance for the philosophical spirit in which it is written. Philosophy has not been hitherto a perceptible element in School Reports; nor in education itself, and we are far from appreciating its importance outside of Germany.

I have heard your name mentioned as a candidate for the Superintendent of the Boston Schools. The man who will do for these what you have done for those of St. Louis, will sway educational interests throughout New England.

I send you copies of the Dedication Services at the opening of our Concord Library, including Emerson's Address. Also Sanborn's Biographical Sketch of me, written for *"The History of Wolcott, Conn."* soon to be published.

Dr. Bartol read a striking paper on *"Shakespeare"* before "Our Club meeting" at my house, June 4th. There is a notice of it in last Saturdays *"Daily N.Y. Tribune."*

I miss No. 3. Vol. VII. of your Journal, or did you print but 3, Nos. in 1873?²

Truly Yours,
A. Bronson Alcott.

Wm. T. Harris.

¹ From a copy, in Alcott's hand, in the Alcott-Pratt Collection. The original is in the Alcott-Harris Collection in the Concord Free Public Library (see Appendix B).
² Four numbers *had* appeared.

LETTER 74-35[1]

[to Mary N. Adams, Dubuque, Iowa]

[Concord, June? 1874]

If I can obtain a copy, I will send you one.

I met Annabel also during Anniversary week in Boston at a lunch, where I saw also Gov. and Mrs Bagley for a few moments. I believe they are to return sometime during the summer, when we shall hope to see them in Concord.

Mrs Alcott has been quite comfortable since our return to our house. She rides out almost every day to see Anna and her boys. Louisa is with us now, and May is busy with her painting. The housekeeping goes smoothly—an[?] matter for scholars as for other members of a household.

I attended the Free Religious meeting during Anniversary week. It was an improvement on its predecessors in all respects.

I send you a copy of the Dedication Services at the opening of our Concord Library, including Mr. Emerson's Address: also, Sanborn's Biographical Sketch of me, written for Mr. Orcutt's History of Wolcott, Conn, soon to be published.

With great regard,
A. Bronson Alcott.

Mrs. M. N. Adams.

[1] The preceding sheet, undoubtedly containing the first two pages of this letter, has been torn out of the MS volume. The letter is positioned here as in the MS volume.

LETTER 74-36

[to Henry Wilson][1]

Concord July 14th 1874.

Hon. Henry Wilson,
Dear Sir,

Accept my thanks for Volume Second of your "History of the Rise and Fall of the Slave Power in America"

I have had time but to glance into its leaves, but doubt not that the same faithful portraitures which characterize your first Volume are found in this.

I read gladly of your improved health, and opportunities for still valuable services for freedom and fraternity.

I am,
Dear Sir,
Truly Yours,
A. Bronson Alcott.

Vice President Wilson

[1] Vice-President of the United States during Grant's second term. The book mentioned was part of a three-volume work (Boston, 1872–77).

LETTER 74-37

[to Henry S. Olcott,[1] New York City]

Concord July 21st 1874

Dear Sir,

In reply to your inquiries I have very little information to give you as to the difference in spelling our names, or the probable relationship between the New Haven and Hartford families. My ancestor Phillip Alcock one of the early settlers in New Haven, though not among the first, appears to have been the son of Thomas brother of George who came over in Winthrops company, and settled in Roxbury. As George married a sister of Rev. Thomas Hooker of Hartford, I infer that he came from Hookers' place of Residence in England though I have not been able to fix his place of nativity with certainty. Very likely the Thomas of Hartford was a relative of George and Thomas of Roxbury. Mr. Goodwins authority is questionable in the matter. Mrs. Savage I think did not trace the genealogy beyond Goodwin.

A History of Wolcott Conn is nearly through the press in which the Alcock genealogy will appear in full. I forward a sketch of myself, in which you may find nothing however[?] of a genealogical interest. I am sorry I have so little for you.

Very truly yours
A. Bronson Alcott

---

[1] Olcott had written asking whether his own name should properly be spelled "*A*lcott," and whether he and Bronson Alcott might be related.

LETTER 74-38

[to Thomas M. Johnson, Osceola, Mo.]

Concord, | July 26th 1874.

Dear Sir,

I have been hoping to have something of importance to communicate concerning Taylor, the Platonist. But have little to give in reply to your inquiries. On consulting Mr. Emerson, he tells me that all he learned while last in England, after many inquiries was, ‖ that ‖ that Taylor named his son *"Proclus."* Wordsworth nor the Professors at Oxford or Cambridge knew little or nothing of him, nor were his translations in the University Libraries.—to such depths of ignorance had the Scholars in England attained!

I owe to Taylor's Translations, my first readings in Greek Philosophy, and my love for his learned text leads me to prefer it still before any of the later versions. Taylor now[?] '*Thomas Stanley's History,"* appears to me to be the best authorities on matters relating to the Greek Philosophers and their works. I have often expressed the hope that some publisher would give us a reprint of Stanley's folio *History of Philosophy.* It does not treat of the Alexandrians to be sure, but it gives us the fathers of these. Maurice has an imperfect account of them in his Ancient History. But most of the translations and biographers that I have read were not idealists in the Platonic Sense and so fail of appreciating their authors' habit of thinking. Coleridge is the only Englishman besides Berkeley, who seemed fitted to do them justice.

Lest you should not have access to "the Encyclopedia Americana" edited by Francis Leiber and published in Boston in 1832, I copy for you the article on Taylor, from Vol. XII.

It is the most that I can now do for your literary venture.

Very truly

Yours,

A. Bronson Alcott.

Mr. Thomas M. Johnson.

LETTER 74–39

[to Thomas M. Johnson, Osceola, Mo.]

Concord August 2nd 1874.

Dear Sir,

Mr. Emerson has handed me the enclosed note of references, which may chance aid you in your quest of information concerning Thomas Taylor.

Probably no American has searched more fully and faithfully for what is preserved of this Platonic Briton, than Mr. Emerson.

I sincerely hope your purpose of giving us some fuller account of him, may be carried out by you, and that we may read here in New England with new admiration and hope, the fruits of your Western studies.

Very truly

Yours,

A. Bronson Alcott

Mr. Thomas M. Johnson.

LETTER 74–40

[to T. B. S. Rauncy[?], Battle Creek, Mich.]

Concord August 20th. | 1874.

Dear Sir,

Your friendly letter of the 6th came duly to hand, and revived pleasant memories of yourself and the many kind people whom I met when visiting your town. I certainly spent an agreeable week with you, and have indulged the hope of visiting your place again. If I go West this autumn, Battle Creek will be on my route, and I shall stop at least for a day, to call on you all. If desired make a longer stay. If I go, I expect to leave here probably about the first of October for a three months tour. Western people have been very ready to hear what I might have for them; and I entertain exceedingly favorable impressions of their hospitalities both mentally and bodily.

My Bishoprick now embraces a dozen states, extending from Western N. York to the Missouri and south to St. Louis.

643

As to your duties in regard to religious action, I have thought that where one could maintain his fidelity to his conscience, and remain in the Church, it were the better for him and the Church itself, which loses by every good man's withdrawal, and puts him at variance with what is good and ought to ‖ be ‖ survive, all reforms from within or without. But Conscience is imperative and each one must determine his action for himself. What opportunities might open outside for useful labor, in your case, I cannot say. Many of us now belong to ‖ to ‖ Churches of but one member only, and probably must content ourselves with this, till the wider sympathy pervades the hearts of professors of religion generally. A liberal Church is in formation, and is to be.

With regards to friends in Battle Creek,

I am,

Very truly Yours,

A. Bronson Alcott.

Mr. T. B. S. Rauncy[?]

LETTER 74–41

[to Edward Waldo Emerson,[1] Concord]

Concord September ‖ 14th 1874.

Dear Edward,

I believe you are one among the many admiring readers of Sir Walter Scott, and take pleasure in presenting you with the accompanying Phandos[?] edition of his Poetical Works.

In offering you this slight token of my regard, let me add my best wishes for the future welfare of yourself and yours on this joyful occasion of your wedding and settlement in your native town.

Very truly

Yours,

A. Bronson Alcott.

Dr. Edward W. Emerson.

---

[1] Emerson's son (1844–1930). He married Annie Keyes and "settled down in Concord as partner of Doctor Bartlett, the Emerson family doctor." (Rusk, *The Life of Ralph Waldo Emerson,* p. 483.)

[Letter to William T. Harris, St. Louis; from Concord, September 27, 1874 (see Appendix B).]

LETTER 74–42[1]

[to Ellen A. Chandler, Jamaica Plain? Mass.]

Fort Dodge, Iowa, | December 12th 1874.[2]

Dear Miss Chandler,

A poor postscript to my letters from these prairies were but a poor apology for the full letter of regard which I delight to forward to my admirable friend, whose acquaintance and correspondence has delighted and graced so many occasions in time past, and promises, let me believe, like satisfactions in future years.

I hurried away from home so unexpectedly that I failed of the parting call which I promised myself. And the more desired, for having been cheated out of yourself at *"Our Club Meeting,* at my house. The more in prospect! and a long stay when summer,—nay, when spring with its blossoms and birds comes again. I wish you may enjoy your Muses, meanwhile, and relate your fellowships when we shall meet.

I am finding much to admire, and little to dislike in these Western homes and schools. Strength and freshness, if not the learning and refinement common at the East. Less bookish and mannered, the people impress me favorably by their frankness and hospitality alike of behavior and to liberal ideas. May I add that even to such as myself, not a Sunday has past without an opportunity offered me to speak in some pulpit of some one or other religious persuasion, and I have done so—a liberality not common in N England. And "Conversations" follow with scarcely an interruption every evening. The schools, moreover, appear to be progressive, and school buildings the costliest structures even in the smallest towns. Of course, I am indulged in telling the pupils something of the author of "Little Women," in all. I am favored thus far with health and spirits for my work, and find the field attractive. It is fertile soil for sowing the seeds of an ideal culture.

The climate is delightful. The days have been sunny for the most part, || as || slight snows have fallen but were dissolved soon, and the air is clear and invigorating. Invalids from the East find it salutary and restorative for their common maladies.—I have happy news from Home, and by last letters accounts of the Birth day celebration. I trust you see Louisa sometimes. I grieve to learn that she is not yet freed from her ails.

I purpose passing the Holidays with the Adams' at Dubuque. It may be far into the winter season before I return to Concord.

I have written under pressure and hastily. I need not add my affection and deep regards for yourself.

My address till Christmas is to the care of *"Austin Adams, Dubuque,* Iowa. May I expect a little note from you? Meanwhile,

Cordially Yours,
A. Bronson Alcott.

Miss Chandler.

[1] MS. owned by the Abernethy Library, Middlebury College. A copy, in Alcott's hand, is in the Alcott-Pratt Collection.
[2] Alcott's extensive tour of 1874–75 had begun in October and lasted until April.

LETTER 75-1[1]

[to Louisa, Concord]

Milwaukee, Wisconsin, | February 4th 1875.

Dear Louisa.

Such an enthusiastic welcome and salute as your Head of the Little Women folk, received yesterday, from the Young Ladies College here. you would esteem sufficiently dramatic for a new play of the Alcott type.—150 girls all rising and raising hands at the Master's question. "How many have read Miss Alcotts Little Women," and then I need not tell what followed. After my little story of the famous lady was told in plain terms as the subject allowed scores of hands were stretched, arm over arm, by the gathered group, to take that of the "papa." And then as many autographs were inscribe[d] in Albums and little slips extemporized at the moment. What shall poor papa do but bear it gracefully and be himself[2]

[1] MS. in the Clifton Waller Barrett Library, University of Virginia.
[2] Only one sheet of the letter is in the collection, and that ends at this point.

LETTER 75-2[1]

[to Louisa, Concord]

Akron, Ohio | March 27th 1875.

Dear Louisa,

Having a few hours this morning to my self, I ran through the published chapters of your story in "St. Nicholas.'[2] Everyone praises and delights to tell me how much they like the wit and sense of the writer. So I read, and offer her my impressions, with the rest.

I infer you have in mind to show the absurdities of our modern modes of training the young.—Rose is to be subjected to various tests to prove her strength of character.—The aunts each of them trying their theory on their victim. The Uncle begins well. and opens up the sequel to the tale.

One thing in your stories I observe and admire—your sympathy with the lower and laboring class. The interview between Rose and Phebe over the audirons, is an example of this kind. You cannot urge this moral too strongly on your readers. There is still,—all professions to the contrary—a fearful prejudice concerning the dignity and duty of work, lurking it may be unsuspected in the dispositions of very good people which must be removed before any right relations can be established between the serving and the served. I think you are doing more than you are aware to break down this dispar[a]gement, by showing in unsuspected positions the morality and duty of serving. I wish I could find in the preaching of our time as wholesome teaching as your stories exemplify, as practical humane. And you have an audiance [sic] that no preacher, not all preachers combined, command. You have won the prize. I know something of its cost. But have you paid too dear for it? Millions are enjoying the fruits of your sacrifices.

In a few days I hope to see you, and fresher and hopefuller than for long years past.

Affectionately.
Your Father.

¹ MS. in the Clifton Waller Barrett Library, University of Virginia. Probably this is the letter as mailed to Louisa, and the MS. in the Alcott-Pratt Collection is a draft written the preceding day and kept by Alcott as a copy. The latter reads as follows:

Dear Louisa   Akron, Ohio, March | 26th. 1875.

While waiting for my evening's company, I have been running through the published Chapters of your story in the St. Nicholas. Why should not I praise and admire with the millions who read your tales? This opens well. Is it a satire on modern modes of training the young? Rose promises to be equal to the aunties, || and || the cousins, one and all. The Uncle too, and come out of the ordeal,—*herself*.

One trait in your stories I especially admire—your sympathy with the serving classes. The interview between Rose and Phebe over the andirons, is an example. You cannot urge this too strongly. There still lurks in the dispositions of very good people a prejudice, as cruel as it is ignoble, against useful service. I think you are doing far more than you are aware to break down this disparaging notion. I wish I could believe the preaching in all the pulpits of the land were as effective as your illustrious pen. And your audiance [*sic*]! Not all the preachers combined command the like.

"Who speaks to the eye," says Goethe, speaks to the mind entire." The novelist has the widest of publics. And are you aware that your books are more widely known and more eagerly read by young and old, than any storyteller of your day? Think of any writer who enjoys a like reputation!

Do you say, "well, what is that to me"? It may be nothing beyond the satisfaction that you have served your generation. Has the cost been too great? That you may not estimate. Millions are reaping the fruits of your sacrifices.

If your story fulfils the promise of its opening, it will be your best. Yet you may not expect for any the popularity of your "Little Women." That took the [torn] hearts of young and old. If you still question the assertion, you have but to journey into these parts to convince yourself of the place you hold in their affections.

In a few days, I hope to see you face to face, and find you free alike in fancy and limb.

Affectionately
Your Father.

Miss L. M. Alcott

² *Eight Cousins.*

LETTER 75-3

[to Hermann Krüsi, Oswego, N.Y.]

Concord, Mass. | April 8th 1875.

Dear Sir,

On returning lately from an extended Conversational tour through the Western States, I found your "Life of Pestalozzi",¹ and kind note. I have read the Life with much satisfaction. It adds interesting particulars which are not included in Bibers'—a work with which I have been familiar from the date of its publication.² Of the great educators of modern times, I owe most to the spirit and methods of Pestalozzi. Most of the improvements in education now become current may be traced to his quickening Ideas. And your fresher account of his services must awaken a livelier interest in him and his methods.

You honor me with some paragraphs of praise for my attempt to show in my Boston School particularly, the intuitive powers of children, by following out their thoughts on the deepest questions of life and duty. I have deemed my experiment every way deserving of more approval than it has yet obtained ‖ by ‖ [p. o.] from but the fewest of my contemporary educators.

It has been my intention when travelling West to visit Mr. Sheldon's School at Oswego. But I have been called home suddenly on more than one of my tours, and have that pleasure in prospect on some future opportunity.

I am happy to know that yourself, the gifted son of one of Pestalozzi's associates in his successive schools in Switzerland, has found encouragement for making the principles and methods of his master known to us in our republican country, and wish you every success whether in teaching or as an author.

I am, dear Sir,

Thankfully, and Very truly,

Yours—

A. Bronson Alcott

H. Krüsi

Oswego, NY.

---

[1] *Pestalozzi: His Life, Work, and Influence* (1875). Krüsi was the son of Hermann Krüsi, Pestalozzi's first associate.

[2] Edward Biber, *Henry Pestalozzi, and His Plan of Education* (1831).

LETTER 75–4

[to F. E. Anderson, Cambridge, Mass.]

Concord, April, ‖ 8th. 1875.

F. E. Anderson,

Sir,

On returning lately from an extended Conversational tour at the West, I find your note of November last, informing me of my being made an Honory [sic] Member of the Phi Beta Kappa Fraternity Chapter Alpha of Massachusetts.[1]

The honor thus conferred is as suprising [sic] to myself, as it is prized. To be associated with so distinguished a fraternity of scholars, and with our oldest university adds ‖ a ‖ dignity to any name. Certainly to one who has always considered himself very remotely entitled to either.

With thanks and proper acknowledgments for this unexpected privilege of fellowship

> I am, Sir,
> very respectfully
> Yours.
> A. Bronson Alcott

F. B [sic]. Anderson
  Corresponding Secretary
    of
  Phi Beta Kappa Fraternity,
    Harvard College.

---

[1] F. E. Anderson's letter to Alcott, as well as another copy of Alcott's reply, is reprinted in Alcott, *Journals*, p. 456.

LETTER 75–5

[to Benjamin Wells]

Concord April 29th 1875.

Dear Ben,

Yours of the 4th has been by me now for almost a month, and you have had no response. This long delay has not been from indifference to your writing, but chiefly to our almost entire absorption in preparing for and dismissing the Celebration of the 19th. Moreover, I but returned from my six months Tour at the West on the 1st of this month, and had to struggle with a six weeks cold, which, I am happy to find is now abated, and I have been about again during the last fortnight. Of our celebration you have doubtless read full accounts. Here in Concord, the day, despite the chill, passed off admirably, and the evening crowned the whole with life and gaiety. The Ball was largely attended: we all felt youthful and patriotic as became the occasion.

I was at Cambridge last Tuesday and dined with Sam. Longfellow, who spoke appreciatingly of yourself, anticipating good things of you in the future, regretting much your frail health. I wish you may learn how to use your forces for the furtherance of your future attainments.

I judge you are the victim of your thoughts, and wish there were any known regimen which you would practice faithfully for the cure of your mental malady. Perhaps you are finding this in your enthusiasm for the idyllic and rural.

"Who loves a garden still his Eden keeps—
Perennial pleasures plants, and wholesome harvests
      reaps"

I am pleased to find students of Virgil and Columella applying their ideas to rural affairs, and approving themselves alike to the soil and the soul of life and things.

You speak of melancholy. Would you cast out that demon, and see the last of him? Breathe country air, ventilate your studies, and come to the Book as to your breakfast and sweet nights sleep.

But I have neither space nor time for the rest. Come up and pass a day or two with us here and see what comes of it. You may dip into books, or into your friend as you choose.

> Yours truly,
> A. Bronson Alcott.

Benjamin Wells.

Letter 75–6[1]

[to   ?   ]

Concord May 7th. 1875.

Dear Madam,

Your note is just received.

I should be ashamed of myself to have your Convention sitting here, and myself remain silent—a listener merely to the stirring words, which, I am sure, w[il]l be spoken. But I must not promise a speech of argument or of persuasion at length. I may speak as the spirit moves. And you are at liberty to use my name, if it will be of the least use to further the ends of freedom and right.

I may not promise a very enthusiastic hearing by my neighbors at large, but am sure your words will have weight with some who have not given special attention to the subject hitherto.

History shows that no important reform has been won without the aid and countenance of women.

> Truly Yours,
> A. Bronson Alcott.

[1] MS. owned by the New York Public Library.

Letter 75–7

[to Samuel Longfellow, Cambridge, Mass.]

Concord May 11th 1875

Dear Sir,

I was yesterday in Boston, and left your umbrella at Colesworth's [sic] book store.

Here I found an antique Volume of Dr. Donne's Sermons. Donne never wrote a dull thing, and these were preached before the king. I fancied the worn calf-skin ‖ enclosed ‖ covered a dollars' worth of wit at least, and brought the book away.

This Colesworthy it seems deals in rhymes of his own as in other men's literary loves and, in doing up my parcel, added his Poem—Donne and Colesworthy in one envelope.

From what he said, it appeared that he is no stranger to yourself. I think I shall call at his shop again.

Mr. Emerson regretted that his engagement at Cambridge prevented having you to dine with him.

We shall hope to have another visit from you in June.

Truly Yours
A. Bronson Alcott

Saml. Longfellow.

LETTER 75–8

[to James Eddy, Providence, R.I.]

Concord May 25th | 1875.

Dear Sir,

I shall gladly renew our early acquaintance during my stay in Providence.

By some hidden association your name flashed into remembrance, the other day, and revived our fellowship at Mr. Newells', in Franklin Street, 40 years ago, and the discussions with Holbrook.[1]

How widely has our modern Lyceum drifted from his notion of its uses; Utilitarian that he was in the strictest sense, but a useful servant of his generation, and falling a victim at last to his enthusiasm for the rocks[?].

I purpose leaving Boston on Saturday by the 4. P.M. train, and shall seek you at the Providence Station, on my arrival.

Truly Yours,
A. Bronson Alcott

James Eddy, Esqr.
    Providence.

[1] Alcott, Eddy, and Josiah Holbrook had stayed at the same rooming house in Boston. For Holbrook's part in the Lyceum, see Carl Bode, *The American Lyceum* (New York, 1956).

LETTER 75–9[1]

[to John Sewall Pratt]

[Concord, June 24, 1875]

Grandpa Alcott
  To Johnny
    June 24th 1875.

A fine little sword
  For gallant Capt Jack,
As he marches down the hill
  His army at his back.

    No giants will it kill
      Since its only made for show;
    And the best way to fight,
      Is a kiss for a blow.

[1] MS. owned by the Houghton Library, Harvard University. The poem, addressed to John Pratt on his tenth birthday, is also quoted in Bonstelle and deForest, p. 156.

LETTER 75–10

[to Miss M. C. Pratt, Concord]

[Concord, June? 1875]

Dear Miss Pratt,

    I regret that an engagement in Boston for this evening deprives me of the pleasure of witnessing the closing exercises of your school.

    I have thought a happy chance that brings from year to year so many young women to meditate under the shades of Wayside. I wish they may have caught some hints of the scene of his Genius while treading the paths where he meditated his memorable tales.[1]

    Please express my best wishes to the young ladies for their welfare and use-fulness in the bright future which I am sure is theirs.
‖ and ‖ with health and prosperity for yourself[2]

[1] Hawthorne.
[2] The letter breaks off at this point. Probably only the complimentary close and signature are missing.

LETTER 75–11

[to   ?   ]

Concord June 1875

Dear Friend,

    I was glad to hear a word; but sorry to learn that you had been ill. I trust it is nothing serious. We cannot afford to have you crippled in ‖ in ‖ your good work so happily begun and so needful. As the years pass, new recruits will be needful to join in and continue it.

    I enclose the verses of Angelus Silesius. They were translated by Emmanuel Leherbe[?], a learned Swiss who was in these parts some years ago, but now deceased. I usually read the first Six verses, but all are characteristic.

    I am pleased to hear that you are purposing to publish your book of Essays. We need this Spiritual literature to qualify and complement so much now printed of an opposite character.

    Mr. Emerson is busy, I believe, preparing a new Volume for the press. And, I may publish my book of *Ideals* in the autumn.

    I am purposing to attend the literary anniversaries this week.

We have had a series of Sunday Evening Conversations at the houses of our neighbors lately. Thus far, they have been well attended and found much favor.

We, that is, my family are all very well. Louisa is passing the Summer with us. May is still our housekeeper. Mrs Alcott enjoys herself in reading and frequent rides Anna and her boys are at Mr. Pratts and well.

My regards to your family—all.

Truly Yours,
A. Bronson Alcott

LETTER 75-12

[to George S. Boatwell, Groton, Mass.]

Concord, July 6th | 1875.

Dear Sir,

Your note is at hand.

According to your kind invitation, I shall hope to pass Monday afternoon next, and Tuesday with you,—leaving Concord at 5 P.M. for Groton.

I wish the days may prove fair and friendly for our interview.

Very truly
Yours.
A. Bronson Alcott.

Hon. Geo. S. Boatwell.

/P.S. Meanwhile, I will press your wishes upon Miss Louisa, but fear unsuccessfully./

[Letter to P. N[?]. French; from Concord, July 9 or 16, 1875, inviting him to Concord.]

LETTER 75-13

[to Samuel Orcutt, Torrington, Conn.]

July 20th 1875.

Dear Sir,

I believe I am entitled to an additional copy of your History of Wolcott.

How shall I get it? I shall expect to pay the *expressing* at any rate either from Waterbury or Torrington, as you may direct.

I have had bound into my copy the photographs taken by the Waterbury man, with portraits of several of our name. It makes an elegant volume. I have also presented copies to our "*Concord Library*" and to "The New England Historic-Genealogical Society

I preached last Sunday at Newburyport, where I met our friend Rev. Mr. Belden, whom we remember as taking part in *our Centenary*. He is well pleased with his settlement and people. He gave good accounts of your Torrington settlement. I am glad if it is satisfactory to yourself and people. Any change were an improvement, in a social, as *pecuniary* way, upon your former one in Wolcott.

I trust your Torrington History speeds as well as the preaching.

I shall be glad to hear further about both. And should you visit, Mass, expect to see you in my own house at Concord.

Very truly
Yours,
A. Bronson Alcott

Rev. Saml. Orcutt.

LETTER 75-14[1]

[to William T. Harris, St. Louis]

Concord August 25th | 1875.

Dear Friend,

I have been hoping to see you enter my gate for some weeks past, but you do not appear, and I almost give you up for this season. And will consent to do so, if you will complete your several tasks meanwhile, and accomplish freedom from Nemesis. Davidson has been with me for a night, and yesterday Mrs. Baldwin was here. Emery made a short visit to New England but returned without coming to Concord. Just advise me by Postal Card when you approach that I may be at home to greet your arrival.

I have had a busy season since my return from the West. After copying out my *"Itinerary"*, I set about editing my Tablets" Vol. II. and have the MS. nearly ready for the press. I prefer my old title to any that occurs and the like arrangement into Book I. *Practical,* and Book II. *Speculative.* Under the heads of

I. 1/*Learning*   II.   *The Philosophemes.*
    2/*Discourse*   1/ *The Flight Downwards.*
    3/ *Creeds*   2/ *The Lapse.*
    4/ *Pursuits*   3/ *The Flight Upwards.*
    5/ *Nurture*

In arranging the *Philosophemes* for printing I have had to cut up more than one copy of the number containing || the || them, and this leaves my Volumes incomplete. I find No.   of Volume VIII. wanting, and should like two copies at least of No.   of the IX.

I find room for much revision and omission of the Philosophemes for putting them in condition for printing. Whether Roberts will venture to print this autumn is not determined, the book trade is by no means brisk just yet. Louisa's new story is printed and to appear in September. She is passing the summer at home, and May is also with us.

I am unusually well and Mrs. Alcott has enjoyed herself better than for some years.

The future of Philosophy looks propitious.

I am not purposing to leave Concord the coming season.

I give my Eleventh Conversation with our Villagers next Sunday evening.

Truly Yours,

A. Bronson Alcott

Wm. T. Harris

[1] From a copy, in Alcott's hand, in the Alcott-Pratt Collection. The original is in the Alcott-Harris Collection in the Concord Free Public Library (see Appendix B).

LETTER 75–15

[to Mrs. Dudley, Milwaukee? Wis.?]

Concord September 2nd. | 1875.

Dear Mrs Dudley,

I am late in replying to your kind note of August 22nd I am highly gratified to learn that you are to have access to the public in the way you name. A newspaper is a facile spokesman for thinkers in our time, and you (if I remember) are not unused to speak through its colums.

I cannot say "No" to your pressing request. Yet I do not find things as suitable as I could wish for presenting to you||r selection||. Still you may select from the accompanying parcel thoughts that may not be wholly misplaced in your colums. It is printed matter and so will spare you the trouble of copying for the printer. I thought sentences, if no more might serve to fill a spare space, at any rate. When I shall find more leisure than at present, I may write something more suitable.

My visit at your hospitable home remains a delightful memory. Nor am I without hope of straying into your State again sometime. Yes, and gladly enjoy a "long holiday" at your rural "Summer Home." And shall we not have the pleasure of returning your kind hospitalities here under our Elms? My wife and daughters will gladly receive you.

Louisa left us yesterday to pass a few weeks with her sister and the Little men on the Hampshire Hills.

To the Dr. and yourself,

my cordial regards,

A. Bronson Alcott.

LETTER 75–16

[to Samuel Orcutt, Torrington, Conn.]

Concord, September, | 17th 1875.

Dear Sir,

Thanks for the photograph of John Browns' Birth place. I took it, at first sight, to be the James Alcott House, and was undeceived only by the want of trees in the foreground. The resemblance, you may notice, is quite striking. It is the [2 words] type of the better class of houses built during the latter part of the last century. Channing and Sanborn tell me that they have also received copies of the picture. And Sanborn informs me that Channing has written verses on *Brown* for your History. He himself has not spoken about them, though he takes tea regularly with us every Wednesday.

On looking over my papers, I find matter that may serve you concerning Brown, particularly some notes of a Conversation of mine printed at the time in "the *Commonwealth*, then edited by Sanborn. I enclose them herein. As to your request to send you information concerning the Blakeslees of East Haven I find nothing in addition to what you have already, as I tore the leaves sent to you from my *"Itinerary"* and preserved no copy of them. I think those of the name who settled in Wolcott were relatives of Lydia Alcock who married and returned to North Haven from whence her mother Deborah Blakeslee came. The East Haven burying ground preserves the dates of the deaths of many of that name.

I am not expecting to visit Connecticut this season. I read that the Wolcott Church has settled a minister.

I shall be glad to hear further about your *historic* labors.

Truly Yours,
A. Bronson Alcott.

Rev. Saml. Orcutt

LETTER 75–17

[to Charles W. Fett[?], Ayer, Mass.]

Concord October 5th 1875

Dear Sir,

Your plan for an Industrial School appears both feasable [*sic*] and desirable, if you succeed in obtaining your boys to discipline and direct, as you wish. About the practical details in working it out. I have nothing to communicate. As I told you, when you were here. I have long since questioned the fitness of any considerable number of persons for Community life. A School is a possibility. Yet any separation from parents, for any long time, seems undesirable unless in case of their unfitness to have charge of their children. The family is *the unit* around which all social endeavors should organize, if we would succeed in educating men for the true ends of existence. And the cooperation of women in the practical working out is indispensable.

I do not see how you can hope for any success beyond what may be called a family boarding school; and this wholly independent of Shaker influences. If you write about the '*Shakers*' I shall be glad to read your report.

Miss Louisa is preparing for leaving home for New York My family are quite well the Little Men and their mother are now with us to pass the coming winter.

Truly Yours,
A. Bronson Alcott

Charles W. Fett[?]

Ayer

LETTER 75–18

[to Samuel May, Leicester, Mass.]

Concord, October. 7th. 1875.

Dear Sir.

The Biographical Sketch was written by Frank Sanborn, for Orcutts History of Wolcott Conn. published last year. As my ancestor John Alcock was one of the first settlers, and his descendants have been distinguished in the affairs of the town, a larger space was given to their biographies, Dr William and myself having place with others.

By some oversight of the printers the mistake as regards the date[?] Mr. Samuel J. May, was made, and not detected till it was too late for correction.

I wish nothing may delay the appearance in print of "the "May Family."

Did I tell you that their first settler, John May, was a member of Rev. John Eliots Church in Roxbury and of which my ancestor George Alcock was a deacon? They must have been neighbors. ‖ One of Deacon George's grandson's marrried ‖

My family are quite well. Mrs. Alcott enjoys herself with Anna and her boys, and a morning ride on fair days. May is our housekeeper. Louisa is preparing for a short visit to Mrs Wilkinson at Syracuse. Her new story is just out and favorably received.

Truly Yours,
A. Bronson Alcott.

Rev. Samuel May
Leicester

LETTER 75–19[1]

[to Mary N. Adams, Dubuque, Iowa]

[Concord, between October 7? and November 6? 1875]

"The Parlor and the Platform," opens a wide field for your Genius. The West is better prepared for such Parlor teachings than we are here.

You ask if I have seen "Taylors, Eleusinian and Bacchic Mysteries.' I have not seen the modern edition about which Mr. Johnson of Osceola Missouri, writes lately.[2] We cannot celebrate too enthusiastically the Ideal Philosophy in times like ours.

What you tell me of "the Philosophemes" is agreeably surprising. I hope to revise and edit them for a separate volume, thinking they may serve in texts for parlor and pulpit discourse.

You will miss 'the Wards" from your circle during their absence. I am expecting to hear of Mr. Adams promotion to the supreme bench. Will his new duties take you all with him to Des Moins [sic]. There is need of you both at the Capital if I judge rightly. I had less to praise than in other Iowan cities.

Louisa is now visiting her cousin Miss Wilkinson at Syracuse. She writes us lively letters about the Woman's Congress. From thence she goes to New York City to pass the winter (probably.) Her new story, 'the "Eight Cousins,' has gone to a third edition—10,000 copies having been disposed of since the date of publication. She is now quite well. May is with us now, and Anna and the Little Men, for the winter. Mrs Alcott is very comfortable, and enjoys her reading, and rides almost daily. I have occasional calls for Conversations and Sunday Services. I purpose passing the winter here in Concord.

Mr Emerson's new volume of Essays[3] is nearly through the press.

To all my friends in Dubuque pleasant remembrances.

Most truly Yours,
A. Bronson Alcott

Mrs M. N. Adams

[1] The sheet containing the first portion of this letter has been torn out of the MS volume. The letter is here positioned as in the MS volume.
[2] An edition of Thomas Taylor's work was published in New York in 1875.
[3] *Letters and Social Aims.*

LETTER 75–20

[to Georgiana Davis, Boston]

Concord November, | 6th 1875.

Dear Miss Davis,

Your note is at hand. And for any services which I can render your association I shall esteem it a pleasure and privilege to perform, whether in the way of counsel or of address.

Yours is a vital interest, underlying and embracing other reforms.

I wish it may enlist advocates especially of our sex to cooperate with yours for furthering personal purity in both.

Please let me know of your designs and doings from time to time.

And present my thanks to the association for this mark of its confidence.

I am
Very truly Yours,
A. Bronson Alcott.

Miss Georgiana Davis
   Secretary of Moral Education
   Society of Boston.

LETTER 75–21

[to Louisa, New York City]

Concord, November, | 17th 1875.

Dear Louisa,

You will read with interest the enclosed criticism, and take your share of credit for your creation of the *American Heroine"*. It seems one of the most discriminating of the many that have come to hand, and has the greater weight with Americans from the fact of being an Englishwoman's estimate. Sanborn tells me that Miss Macdonnel[?] is an author held in good repute, and Macmillians [sic] Magazine is, as you know, one of the most respectable of the London Journals.

But for your being so good a swimmer we might fear you would be fairly drenched and drowned in the floods of admiration showering upon you in the great metropolis. We read your accounts from week to week as they come to us with pleasure and pride.

I sent a note to your excellent companion Miss Holly, and esteem it a piece of good fortune that you are blessed with so fit an inmate and protector while in the broad city.

I am going to take tea with the Sanborns this evening. Vickey and little Frankey are passing the afternoon with Johnny. Freddy has gone to the Post office mounted on Sally proudly. May is in Boston today. She has pupils engaged, and is to meet them, I understand, twice a week.

Many good wishes attend you and all delights the city affords while you stay.

Your Father.

Miss. Louisa M. Alcott
New York City.

LETTER 75–22

[to A. H. Dooley, Terre Haute, Ind.]

Concord November | 24th 1875.

Dear Sir,

Yours came duly to hand, and I enclose in this a photograph of Thoreau taken from a crayon head of Rowse's, by Warren of Boston. It is the best we have. One was taken of him during his last days with us, but has the pallor of his disease and is disagreeable.

I am not surprised at finding yourself among the admiring readers of Thoreau's works at the West, where he finds the readier appreciation than in New-England.

I shall be glad to serve an enthusiast like yourself to any information about Thoreau not yet in your possession.

Have you seen "Channing's Memoir" of him printed by Roberts Brothers, Boston?

Very respectfully,
A. Bronson Alcott.

LETTER 75-23

[to Georgiana Davis, Boston]

Concord, November, | 24th. 1875.

Dear Miss Davis,

Yours has just come to hand.

Please present my Thanks to the Ladies of your Association for their renewed confidence, and assure them that I shall endeavor to attend their meeting in December, and will speak at their desire at their meeting in January.

My subject will be

'*Personal Purity.*"

If the ladies desire, and will inform me of your *Parlor meetings,* it would
give me pleasure to meet them, sometimes, whether in Boston or elsewhere.

Very truly Yours,
A. Bronson Alcott.

Miss Georgiana Davis
    Secy of M. E. A.

LETTER 75-24

[to A. B. Tuttle[?], Chicago]

Concord, November, | 24th 1875.

Dear Sir,

Your friendly letter of the 16, Novr. came duly to hand. I should have
forwarded an earlier reply to your inquiries had my plans for the Winter season
been fully determined. I find that I cannot well leave home for any length of
time during the early part of the season, and may not visit the West at all, certainly not earlier than February—much as it would please me to meet my kind
friends in those parts. You will have Mr. Mills and other wise men coming to
you as heretofore.

I read accounts of your designs and doings in "*The Liberal Worker* and the
Watertown Republican—both excellent for their free spirit and humanity.

Mr. Emerson has just ready a new volume of Essays for his numerous readers
here and abroad. Louisa is now in New-York City where she may pass the winter.
Her health is now much improved and we hope permanently established. Nothing would please me more than to have her travel at the West and enjoy the
hospitalities of her admirers throughout that section. Her *Eight* Cousins has
gone to a third edition, and finds general favor with her former readers and the
Journals.

I remember with pleasure the hospitalities shown me while in Chicago, and
at your home particularly. My regards to all of your household.

Very truly Yours
A. Bronson Alcott.

Mr. A. B. Tuttle[?]
    Chicago

LETTER 75-25

[to Mrs. C. L[?]. Cole, Mount Pleasant, Iowa]

Concord December | 2nd 1875.

Dear Mrs. Cole,

The accounts which you communicate of your social and intellectual recreations tell well for Mount Pleasant. And it is gratifying to learn that "the finely told history of *the Friends in Council*," proves so inspiring to your "Reading and Conversational Clubs.' I wish the Sketch may provoke similar associations || at || throughout the West.

As to the Wisconsin gentleman about whose generosities you inquire,—his proposition is to add $500 to a like sum contributed by any and every town within his County, having already established a library in his own place of residence. And I read that Mesrs Cole and Co bestow a like sum upon your proposed Library.

In a university town like yours, a Free Library, accessible to the students, seems almost indispensable. And knowing what yourself and friends have accomplished for public improvement, I cannot doubt of your success in this matter also.

It is but three years ago that we had like advantages in Concord. A private citizen gave $50,000. and a fine building. And now we have 10,000 volumes free to every inhabitant. The school children are its best patrons every family having access to the Library.

I know of no institution outside of the family and schools, more conducive to human culture than The Free Public Library.

I am passing pleasant days at home. Louisa purposes spending the winter in New-York City, where she now is. Her story *"The Eight Cousins"* meets with general acceptance at home and abroad. Her health appears to be permanently restored. I think it possible that she may visit the West next spring.

Mr Emerson's new volume of Essays is to be published soon.

With happy memories of many kind friends in your pleasant town,

I remain,

Truly Yours,

A. Bronson Alcott.

Mrs C. L[?]. Cole.

LETTER 75-26[1]

[to William T. Harris, St. Louis]

Concord December | 3rd 1875.

Dear Friend.

The city of Boston is about reorganizing its system of Public Schools, and a Superintendent is to be elected. I enclose || the || a list of the New-School Committee proposed for election. Perceiving your name mentioned as a Candidate for the office of Superintendent, I write to inquire whether you will serve, if elected, and if you will allow me to further your election by naming your extraordinary claims to that office to the proper electors. For myself, but far more for reforming our Boston School economies, I wish such a thing might be. And this office might presently open the way to Harvard College if you wished a professorship, &c. And how many other advantages I need not intimate.

Will you just dispatch a Postal Card on receipt of this in reply, Yes, or no.? The appointment is to be made soon.[2]

Truly Yours,
A. Bronson Alcott.

Wm. T. Harris

---

[1] From a copy, in Alcott's hand, in the Alcott-Pratt Collection. The original is in the Alcott-Harris Collection in the Concord Free Public Library (see Appendix B).

[2] Harris replied in a letter of December 8, which stated that he would not want the position, for under the present circumstances he would not be able to "reform" the Boston school system.

LETTER 75-27

[to Mary N. Adams, Dubuque, Iowa]

Concord December 26th | 1875.

Dear Mrs. Adams,

Your Holiday Gift was delivered in due season, and is preserved, "Laurel and Myrtle" in affectionate embrace with symbolic mottos in Mrs. A.s' Diary, where you and myself could have wished them for preservation. I infer that you are at home again from your lecture tour, pursuing your thoughts and your idols in the window. A year ago I found you far otherwise, yet with in spite of the shadow cast by your illness, my visit remains a delightful memory, especially those evenings in your parlors discussing "Ion" and other ideals. I deny myself a repetition of these delights for this season, being an important factor in our home circle during winter season. Nor am I without engagements to vary home studies and duties. I have calls for Sundays here and there, and Conversations. Early in January I am to speak to "The N. England Woman's Club" on "Transcendentalism', also to the "Woman's Moral Association." Here as at the West the women are taking the lead in primary reforms, as heretofore in times past.

When the holidays have passed I shall look for some account from yourself of your late labors in Iowa. I have read now and then a slight notice of them in the newspapers. And now that "the *Spectroscope*" has taken ‖ upon ‖ its range over the field, I shall doubtless be fully informed of what is doing in that section. Mrs Dudley is an interesting person, brave and gifted, and should make an excellent paper. Having made acquaintance with her and her contributors, I shall read the Spectroscope with interest. As yet I have seen nothing of yours in it. But, do you not know, that the whole is not told without your statement? Every year the Western thought becomes more and more significant, and this even in the lower plane of politics even.

Mr. Emerson's new Volume of Essays shows how important are his thoughts in shaping the new institutions. My Christmas Gift was a visit from him on Christmas Eve, and on Christmas day came yours. Louisa is passing the winter in New York City, and writes gaily of her pleasures in the metropolis. She is now in the best of health and spirits. Anna and boys are with us. May is our housekeeper having a Class in Boston. Mrs Alcott is in the midst of her family and its satisfactions. Our united regards to yourself and yours.

A. Bronson Alcott.

LETTER 75–28[1]

[to A. H. Dooley, Terre Haute, Ind.]

Concord December. | 29th 1875.

Dear Sir,

No full account of "The Brook Farm Community," has ever been published within my knowledge. There have [been] sketches of it from time to time given in the Magazines but no full account. The founder, Mr. George Ripley, of Boston, is now, and has been for many years past, the chief literary critic of The New York Tribune. He has never given his account of its origin and history.

Hepworth Dixon in his History of Communities in the United [States], entitled New America, published some years since,[2] doubtless included Brook Farm with others which he visited. But as I am not familiar with his work, I have nothing definite for you.

It was an attempt to organize favorable conditions for Self-Culture, but the members being mostly unaccustomed to farm labors, failed to make the experiment self-supporting and after continuing to increase its debts it fell to pieces at the end of six or seven years.

It appears that men and women are yet *too individual* to affiliate readily in any new social attempts, the family being the nearest approach to absolute association attained.

Henry Thoreau lived alone as you know, and thus [secured] in his way something like individual freedom. But think of a mate for him!

The Ideal Paradise is to come, but must first be embosomed fully in individual members.

Write to Miss Kate Stanton, Providence, Rhode Island, and ask her to send you her account of the French Familistree [sic] of Mon [sic] Eadie, a Guise.

Very truly

Yours,

A. Bronson Alcott.

---

[1] MS. owned by the New York Public Library. A copy, in Alcott's hand, is in the Alcott-Pratt Collection.

[2] In 1867.

LETTER 76–1

[to Ellen A. Chandler]

Concord January | 6th 1876.

Dear Miss Chandler,

Do you still attend the meetings of the Woman's Club?

If your interest in these continues, need I assure you that my pleasure will be brightened not a little at finding you at the Club Rooms next Monday Afternoon. The Ladies have honored me with an invitation to give them a talk on *"New England Transcendentalism."* Uncertain whether you are still a member, I enclose herein a Card of Admission to the meeting.

It was our wish to have seen you here during the Holidays, but this pleasure we were obliged to forego at last.

In part compensation for our disappointment, may I not have the satisfaction of adding a leaf at last, or more than one to our Volume? The last from your hand dates I perceive October 10th–1875.

What once was, why not again?

Affectionately,
Your Friend,[1]

Miss Ellen A. Chandler.

[1] The signature has been cut out.

LETTER 76–2

[to Mary Baker Glover,[1] Lynn, Mass.]

Concord January | 17th 1876.

Mrs Glover,

Accept my thanks for your remarkable volume entitled "Science and Health" which I have read with profound interest, and, let me add, the perusal has awakened an earnest desire to know more of yourself personally. The Sacred Truths which you announce and sustain by facts of the Immortal Life give to your work the seal of inspiration—reaffirm, in modern phrase, the Christian revelations. In times like ours, so sunk in sensualism, I hail with joy, any voice that speaks an assured word for God and Immortality. And my joy is heightened the more the words are of Woman's divinings.

But I should need more space than this paper allows, to speak as I would of yourself and Science.

May I then inquire if you would deem a visit from me an impertinence If not, and agreeable to you, will you please name the day when I may expect the pleasure of fuller interchange of views on these absorbing themes.

Very truly
Yours,
A. Bronson Alcott.

Mrs Mary Baker Glover.
Lynn

[1] Mary Baker Glover Eddy (1821–1910), founder of the Christian Science movement of which her book *Science and Health* (1875) has been the fundamental statement.

LETTER 76–3

[to Maria P. Wilson, Malden, Mass.]

Concord January 17th | 1876.

Dear Miss Wilson,

I shall gladly meet yourself and friends in the way you intimate in your note. I have at present no engagements for March, but may make a short tour at the West, and should prefer coming to Malden as soon as you can arrange for a Conversation.

Fifty cents admission has been the usual charge for an evening.

Your complimentary note and proffer of hospitalities are very agreeable to think of.

Very truly
Yours,
A. Bronson Alcott

Miss Maria P. Wilson

LETTER 76–4

[to E. H. Russell,[1] Worcester, Mass.]

Concord January | 18th 1876.

Mr. Russell,
Dear Sir,

Yours is at hand. I shall gladly comply with your invitation to meet your Class of young ladies, for some Conversations on the Principles and Methods of Teaching, and at such time as may be most convenient to yourself. I have no present engagements for the months of March or April.

Possibly, I may be leaving for a short tour at the West in April.

I really cannot name terms definitely, but shall thankfully receive any sum provided by the state for like services. I shall wish to spend a day, at least, in the school.

Very truly
Yours,
A. Bronson Alcott.

[1] Principal of the State Normal School at Worcester.

LETTER 76–5

[to G. M. Royce, Cambridge, Mass.]

Concord January, | 26th 1876.

Dear Sir,

Your note is at hand. Wednesday evening, February 2nd, will suit my convenience, and you may expect me then at your place of meeting. I am to take tea at Mrs Moshers' and shall join the Gentlemen of the Divinity || Students || School with hope for profitable discussion afterwards.

Truly Yours,
A. Bronson Alcott

Mr. G. M. Royce.
Divinity Hall,
Cambridge

LETTER 76–6

[to Lydia L. Patten, Carlisle, Mass.?]

Concord January | 27th 1876.

Dear Mrs Patten,

Since receiving your note I have selected from my Library, a few volumes that I thought might be acceptable and suited to find place on the shelves of your Carlisle Library. I wish these were more worthy of your acceptance.

Remembering with what greediness when a youth, I devoured every book that fell in my way in my obscure birth place I venture to offer these to your towns-folk. You will find a volume or two of my daughter Louisas, and one [of] my own among them. And I think the name of *Henry D. Thoreau,"* may be written in some of them.

I wish I had a copy of another book of mine entitled "Tablets" to include with the rest.

Will you inform me by what means the box containing them will best reach you

Truly Yours,
A. B. Alcott

LETTER 76–7

[to William Deutsch, St. Louis]

Concord January | 30th. 1876.

Dear Sir,

Your invitation to become a member of the St. Louis Society of Pedagogy is especially flattering. I know of no body of Educators who are doing more to diffuse the better views of Education far and wide. And in accepting an honorary membership: let me hope that I may render service worthy in some measure either by voice or pen. Yet I may not promise.

Please communicate my thankful acknowledgements to the Society for this distinguished complement [*sic*] of theirs.

And[1]

---

[1] The following sheet, undoubtedly containing the remainder of the letter, has been torn out of the MS volume.

LETTER 76–8

[to Mary Baker Glover, Lynn, Mass.]

Concord, January, | 30th. 1876.

Dear Mrs. Glover,

My visit left pleasant memories, and opens agreeable prospects. Faith, Hope and Charity are graces so rare in our modern life, that one comes within their presence with something of wonder and sweet surprize.

I certainly shall enjoy meeting your devoted circle; only let me know when and how I may be permitted that privilege. I wished to learn and have not undocile ears.

Last Sunday evening I met a pleasant circle at Mr. Emersons, and took occasion to speak of yourself, your science and disciples. Mrs. Emerson, it appeared, had heard of your book, and the company listened to what I had to tell with interest. In such ways, I shall best advertise yourself and your science.

Next Wednesday evening, I am to meet the Divinity Students at Cambridge for Conversation on divine Ideas and Methods. I think you may safely trust my commendations of your faith and methods to my auditors anywhere.

Hoping to meet you again for more intimate fellowship,

I am,

Cordially Yours,
A. Bronson Alcott.

LETTER 76–9

[to Mrs. A. M. Mosher, Cambridge, Mass.]

Concord February | 18th 1876.

Dear Mrs Mosher,

On returning last evening from three days' absence I find your note.

At present I have no engagement to prevent meeting yourself and friends (the Little Folks included) next Wednesday the 23rd.

Let me come out from Boston at 3. P.M. if the coaches serve, and meet your company as you may arrange for me.

If this suits your convenience please inform me in season

Truly Yours,
A. Bronson Alcott

Mrs. A. M. Mosher.
Cambridge

LETTER 76–10

[to Harrison Gray Otis Blake, Worcester, Mass.]

Concord March, | 8th 1876.

Dear Sir,

I am sorry that I have acquaintances to name in but three or four of the cities which you purpose visiting.

B. B. Wiley, banker, Chicago.

William T. Harris, St. Louis.

Rev. Mr. Wendte, Cincinnati, and

Rev. Dr. Furness, Philadelphia.

I know no one in Louisville, Omaha or San Francisco.

Nor do I recall the names of persons whom I met at the West specially interested in "Thoreau."

Mr. Harris I wish you to see, and through him, you will find those whom you will care to meet in that city: and Mr. Wiley will introduce you to the like in Chicago. I have not visited either Cincinnati or Philadelphia for several years, and know little about the liberal people in them.

I am pleased to learn of your purposed trip to the Far West. Every New Englander should see that portion of our Globe, as an important part of his culture. I am sure you will enjoy your sally, though I am not sure whether you are as good for the cars, as for your feet.

I am invited to pass a day or two in the Worcester Normal School sometime during this month, when I shall hope to see you further about your California expedition and other interesting matters.

Davidson's paper on "Aristotle" was a very learned piece of criticism, and above the range of most of his audiance [sic].

Very truly
Yours,
A. Bronson Alcott

Mr. H. G. O. Blake.

LETTER 76–11

[to George Bemner, Uxbridge, Mass.]

Concord March, 30th 1876.

Dear Sir,

I shall gladly visit your town at the time named in your note and pass a Sunday with you.

You may arrange for a lecture on Saturday evening the 15th. My subject will be

The Religious Tendencies and aspects of the time.

Very truly
Yours,
A. Bronson Alcott.

Rev. Geo. Bemner.

LETTER 76–12

[to Thomas Davidson, Cambridge, Mass.]

Concord April, | 8th 1876.

Dear Sir,

Our "Fortnightly Club" meets at my house on Friday evening April 21st. when the members will be most happy to hear your *"Aristotle,"* or should that paper have been sent to St. Louis, then the *Heraclitus."* We shall claim you as our guest while you remain in town, and hope you will spend Sunday with us.

Respectfully

A. Bronson Alcott

LETTER 76–13

[to Walt Whitman, Camden, N.J.]

Concord April 19th | 1876.

Dear Sir,

Last evening Mr Sanborn took tea with us and told us many interesting things about his recent call upon you.[1] He brought me your handsome books. It was with pleasure that I learned of the interest taken in this new edition of your writings.[2] I promise myself much satisfaction in renewing my acquaintance with your thoughts when I shall have more leisure for reading than this busy out-door season allows me.

I hear that your health is somewhat broken. I am sorry for this, yet am sure your spirit which has borne and braved your time so nobly and well, is superior to Fate. My visit to you with Thoreau remains a pleasant memory to me. He has withdrawn for a little while; but I shall cherish the hope of inter-changing words with you before we leave the scene of *"things"*.

My daughters wish to express their interest in your thoughts and welfare.

Sincerely Yours,

A. Bronson Alcott.

Mr. Walt Whitman)

PS. I shall mail to your address tomorrow a *"Post Office order"* for $10.00— the price of your books.

[1] See Gay Wilson Allen, *The Solitary Singer* (New York, 1955), p. 471.
[2] The sixth (Centennial) edition of *Leaves of Grass* (Camden, 1876), 2 vols.

LETTER 76-14

[to A. H. Dooley, Terre Haute, Ind.]

Concord, April, | 20th 1876.

Dear Sir,

Your letter is before me.

"The Philosophemes about which you inquire,[1] I design to publish in a volume which may go to press next autumn. The present is not a favorable time for issuing works of the philosophical type. I was willing these paragraphs should appear in *the rough* in the Journal of Speculative Philosophy.

O. B. Frothingham's *History of Transcendentalism in New England*[2] will favor the publication of works of thought and stimulate the American mind generally.

As to *Shelley,* he is less known and read than he deserves to be. One of the boldest and most independent young thinkers and writers of his time, he anticipated most of the questions now in the air of ours, and is especially stimulating to the young men and women, who seek independence. Had he lived, he would doubtless have qualified his early opinions and taken his place with the great names of English literature His mind would have deepened and sobered with age and experience. But the type of his thought was Ideal and of the highest. His mysticism would have been less || sensuous || fanciful and more spiritual. I may say religious.

Truly Yours
A. Bronson Alcott

[1] Alcott's "Philosophemes" had appeared in the *Journal of Speculative Philosophy,* VII (January, 1873), 46–48; IX (January, April, July, 1875), 1–16, 190–209, 245–63.
[2] See Letter 76–17.

LETTER 76-15

[to H. E. Robinson, Maryville, Mo.]

Concord April | 22nd 1876.

Dear Sir,

Your letter is at hand, and your inquiries concerning Thomas Taylors' translations well deserves a full reply, since so few of any time have cared much for his painstaking and valuable labors. Emerson was telling Davidson, the learned translator of Aristotles works (of which a Chapter will soon appear in Harris Journal of Speculative Philosophy) that when in England no one knew anything of *Taylor* personally.—and that he, Emerson, having first read Plato and Plotinus in Taylors translation still enjoyed it, though Taylor was not a *Grecian.* I have the like satisfaction and experience. Jowetts translation of Plato, is of course, the more accurate and modern. Of other Alexandrian writers, I know no other than Taylors translations. Having travelled rather extensively through several of the Western states, and aware of the interest in thought felt by many persons in the remote towns particularly, I am not surprised to learn of your favorite studies.

Have you made the acquaintance of Mr. Thomas M. Johnson of Osceola Missouri? His studies appear to be of like type with yours. And he contemplates translating many of the Alexandrian authors.

I am well pleased to add your name to the list of those who read and care for my books. The number is not so many as to render any accession indifferent to me.

I shall be pleased to hear from you again

Very truly
Yours
A. Bronson Alcott

Mr. H. E. Robinson.
　　Maryville
　　　Mo.

LETTER 76–16[1]

[to William T. Harris, St. Louis]

Concord May 8th | 1876.

Dear Friend,

Davidson was here lately and read at my house his paper on Heraclitus, and another in the village on Aristotle. I hoped to learn from him particulars about yourself; but he had next to nothing to tell me. Of course you are as ever very busy. But are we not to see you now soon. You are I learn to be at the *Centennial,*" and so cannot fail to come to Concord. I wish it may happen that you and our Jacksonville and Quincy friends might visit us at about the same time. *"Our Fortnightly Club."* would have high designs upon you and Dr. Jones. Concord has at last its Club and actually sits fortnightly.

Will you allow your name to stand for *"Secretary of the Board of Education?*[2] Mr White declines, and a new man is to be chosen—how soon I am not informed. I wish you were here, and at the Head of Education for the State of Massachusetts. If not yourself, then *Sanborn*. I know your name has been suggested by discriminating persons.

I have had a rather sleepy winter, but am now beginning to work a little, indoors and out. Niles has the *Philosophemes* but hesitates to publish just now. Emerson is to be at the Centennial I believe.

Louisa is with us now and quite well again.

Yours truly,
A. Bronson Alcott.

Wm. T. Harris

---

[1] From a copy, in Alcott's hand, in the Alcott-Pratt Collection. The original is in the Alcott-Harris Collection in the Concord Free Public Library (see Appendix B).
[2] See Letter 75–26.

LETTER 76–17

[to Octavius Brooks Frothingham, New York City]

Concord May 14th | 1876.

Dear Sir.

Your book[1] came duly to hand last Thursday, for which take my hearty thanks. I need not assure you of the hopeful sentiments with which I ‖ have ‖ anticipated its appearance, nor from the fitful glances which I have been able to give the volume amidst my spring planting, ‖ of ‖ question that my expectations ‖ being ‖ will be borne out on fuller perusal. closer study. It seems a fit moment in the tide of centuries to place before the mind some chronicle of the plastic ideas which molded so many[?] [word] the life[?] and [word] and institutions of a republic like ours, and whose vivifying agency is far from[?] spending itself upon the present or coming generation. While these [word] and inspire[?] the Idealist cannot [word] of [word] an admiring[?] and growing constancy. I ‖ must ‖ much commend the spirit in which you have shown the [word] debt to our great contemporary. How much ‖ greater ‖ more than they knew will your readers find they owe him, and, his companions in thought Marg Fuller, Parker and Ripley. And surely I may not complain of your partial estimate of any share ‖ in these ‖ of mine in such fruitful labors.

I cannot doubt of your book doing timely service[?], and wish you ‖ all ‖ every success in literary and social ‖ labors ‖ endeavors ‖ I hope to see ‖ with ‖ my ‖ these[?] eyes the Church may be not now visible[?], made

Very truly

Yours

A. Bronson Alcott

P.S. Shall I not have opportunity for comment and criticism during **Anniversary** week?

Rev. O. B. Frothingham

[1] *Transcendentalism in New England* (New York, 1876). For the material on Alcott, see "The Mystic," pp. 249–83.

LETTER 76–18

[to Mary J. Garland and Miss Weston, Boston]

[Concord, June 5, 1876]

Mr. Alcott's thanks for Miss Garland and Miss Weston's invitation to witness the Closing exercises of their Kindergarten Class on Wednesday next. He very much regrets that an engagement for that day will deprive him of that pleasure. Amidst all the improved instrumentalities of an Ideal culture for Children, he regards the Kindergarten of Froebel, as the most important, and wishes it every success every where.

Concord, June 5th.

1876

LETTER 76-19

[to **Edward C. Towne**, East Marshfield, Mass.]

Concord June 27th. 1876.

Dear Sir.

On returning from Boston, where I passed Sunday, I find your note requesting information about the first meetings of *"the Free Religious Club."*

I was not at the preliminary meeting held at Mr. Sargents, which called that of May 20th. when Saml. Longfellow read a paper on *"Sunday Services.* This was an interesting meeting, and fairly launched the Club. In June, I opened the discussion of the question—*"How to meet the case of Persons who do not attend Church?* and named the following means:—
By *Competent Teachers"*
Conversations
Clubs
Conventions
The Press. The conversation was earnest and with a face toward action in all directions." So I read (in my notes) Emerson attended and spoke in favor of concerted action, by voice, pen and type. He read in September following on *"Ethical Foundations".* This was a full meeting, and a lively discussion followed his reading.

In October, we met at Dr. Bartol's. He read a paper on *"Pure Theism"* Weiss read in November on the *"True Mental Method"* Lord Amberley attended this meeting.

In December, Wasson read on *"The Method of Thought"*

And Frothingham followed him in January, on *The Historical Position of Jesus."*

I find I have brief notes of the meetings of the Club almost up to this time, of all that I attended during the first three or four years of its sittings. These I shall be glad to show you when you make your purposed visit. There are *matters now in the air,* upon which sympathetic fellowship is needed to bring forth into fruit

Write me a few days before [you] come.

Cordially Yours,
A. Bronson Alcott

Rev. Edward C. Towne

LETTER 76-20

[to **Nicholas P. Gilman**, Bolton, Mass.]

Concord July 12th 1876.

Dear Sir.

On returning from Worcester yesterday afternoon I found your note awaiting me at the Post office.

The time you name Sunday August 13th. will suit me very well, and you may then expect me. I shall especially enjoy meeting Dr. Stone after an interval of many years. Mr Giles, too, is a resident still, I believe, of your town, and a relative of my wife.

Will you be kind enough to inform me of my best route to reach Bolton, and of the time of being at the proper stations on the way. I am not informed beyond the Lancaster station, if that is on my route.

Very truly
Yours
A. Bronson Alcott.

Rev. N. P. Gilman.

LETTER 76–21

[to Charles D. B. Mills, Syracuse]

Concord August 18th | 1876

Dear Friend,

I have owed you a reply to yours of July 28th. and shall still I fear, for any thing I may now communicate of interest or of importance in this late reply. I have been pleasantly occupied since I saw you last mostly about home, and answering occasional invitations to speak on Sundays and converse. The May Anniversaries I did not generally attend, only the Free Religious, whose doings were of less interest on the whole than usual. Frothingham's History of Transcendentalism", has added something of permanent value to our literature. The annals of that revival of religious life and thought, if no more. The book is well written and answers a popular need of the time.

I would gladly have attended the Labor League Convention, but the journey was not to be easily taken, and besides I must own with yourself "that with much in Radicalism I have no sympathy." I respect Mr. Abbot for his earnest enthusiasm and am sure of his doing a necessary work for his own and the coming time. Of such temper as his the Reformers are cast. And he is marshalling a fierce and formidable host to do his and their own work.

I shall hardly revisit the West during the coming Winter, much as it would please me to meet so many generous friends in those parts again. And much as I may value my own services, it is comforting to know that others are afield, yourself particularly, and serving so well the needs of that hospitable constituency. The World is yet, for the most part, Missionary Ground, and here also are ardent young disciples of Ideas ministering of what they have to give. Mr. Gannett, Chadwick, and of the elders Dr. Bartol and Sam. Longfellow. Next to the schooling gained in actual service, there needs a School for studies in the Philosophy of Life and Thought, and such *"Academy"* we must have sometime.

You ask if I have any facts not already published to give you about Emersons early life and training. I wish I had. But it is not easy to add to those, our sage is so modest and uncommunicative of his personal history. The public must wait a little, but who shall write that Biography does not yet appear. He is very busy with his editing new editions of his writings, and in fair condition, though Age has laid her hand upon him a little heavily of late.

I have been more in my garden this season than since "My Garden" took type, and enjoy excellent health and spirits for one of my years. Mrs Alcott is also quite well. She reads and rides out daily, resigning housekeeping to May, who is very efficient in that line. Louisa has passed the summer with us and has a new story ready for the press. Anna and boys passed the spring time with us, but are now recreating at Walpole N.H. Mr Harris made me a short visit in July, full of power and promise.

With kind regards to Mrs Mills.

Your friend,
A. Bronson Alcott.

C.D.B. Mills.

LETTER 76-22

[to Mary N. Adams, Dubuque, Iowa]

Dear Mrs. Adams.

Concord August 18/ | 1876/

Yes. your last dates June 15. and Mrs Ward's also, with two whole sheets and more dated Mexico City March 16th. and now at this postponed time you get a poor return, both of you for your kind letters of welcome intelligence about yourselves and others. I wish my duties were present always and not so often delayed as I fear—my kind correspondents have cause to remember, and how shall I return such amiable forbearance and possibly forgiveness for such negligence or worse, ingratitude? I can talk endless letters, but cannot write a seasonably short one. Yours and Mrs Ward's gave me much information, and Mrs Alcott had still more, like a prompt correspondent she replied at once, and doubtless filled her sheet with interesting particulars always at her pens tip, and gladly flowing therefrom.

As for myself, I have had productive days and months, have been in my garden more than on former seasons, since "my Garden" took type, and am in excellent health and keeping. The May Anniversaries were not specially attractive. I attended only 'the Free Religious,' whose doings were of less importance than usual. Frothingham's History of N. E. Transcendentalism has added something of permanent value to our literature—the annals of the revival of religious life and thought, if no more. I would have attended the Labor League Convention, but the Journey was not to be easily taken—though I may accompany Louisa to the Woman's Meeting in autumn. I respect Mr. Abbot's sanguine enthusiasm, his earnestness and courage, and am sure that he is to initiating necessary work for his day and coming times. Of such temper as his are reformers cast, and he is marshalling a formidable host to do his and their work.

I shall hardly revisit the West during the coming Winter. Mr Mills and others—yourself not least—are serving your constituents as only yourselves can. I hope to print a book of "Table Talk' sometime in the coming autumn. I have occasional calls for Sundays and for Conversations, here even in Concord. Mr Harris made me a short visit in July, full of power and promise.

Louisa has another story for autumn. Mr Emerson is busy editing the new

675

editions of his writings. Mrs Alcott reads and rides out almost daily. Anna and boys are recreating at Walpole N.H.

   With pleasant memories and regards

                                        Very cordially Yours,
                                        A.B.A.

LETTER 76–23

[to A. H. Dooley, Terre Haute, Ind.]

                                   Concord October | 26th 1876

Dear Sir

   My *"Table Talk"* went yesterday to press and will not appear till sometime in the new year, perhaps February.[1]

   Books of this type, are, as you intimate, the most suggestive and profitable reading. I wish mine may add to the list of such.—certainly the best of company for whetting the wits and setting the readers thoughts on fire.

   I add to your list "Luthers' Table Talk," "Bacon and Cowley's Essays. Emerson and Thoreau, may deserve their place also.

   I shall hardly visit the West during the coming lecture Season.

                                        Very truly
                                           Yours,
                                        A. Bronson Alcott.

A. H. Dooley

   [1] It was published in May, 1877.

LETTER 76–24

[to Anna C. Brackett, New York City]

                                   Concord, November, | 13th 1876.

Dear Miss Brackett,

   Accept my thanks for your book of Selected Poetry for Home and School[1] As I run my eye along the pretty pages, and find the choice pieces of the choice poets, from Chaucer to Emerson, I feel sure of your taste and discrimination in your selection. The schools and homes may not scruple to put the volume into the hands of their inmates. And surely it is time the select verses in our tongue were familiar to the students of the language, else why '*Mother*" it.

   You write hopefully of yourself and school. And when I am next in New-York, I shall hope to find you. Louisa speaks with pleasure of her visit a year since, and of yourself.

   She is just about sending forth a new book for the young folks,[2] who appear to like her stories wonderfully.

   May is now in Paris deep in Art studies.[3]

I am reading proof sheets of a book of Table Talk—which may appear about New Years.

It gives me pleasure always to learn of your pursuits and successes.

Very truly
Yours,
A. Bronson Alcott.

Miss. Brackett

[1] Anna C. Brackett and Ida M. Eliot, eds., *Silver Treasury of Poetry* (New York, 1876).
[2] *Rose in Bloom.*
[3] May had sailed on September 9, intending to spend a year in London or Paris. She died December 29, 1879, without returning home.

LETTER 76–25

[to Mrs. Dudley, Milwaukee, Wis.]

Concord December, | 7th 1876.

Dear Mrs Dudley

Your letter and the parcel came to hand yesterday. Welcome as these were, the better news brought of your becoming residents of New England, and perhaps neighbors of ours, was the more gratifying. Dr. Dudley seems an elected successor of Mr. Parker, and, if the Fraternity are aware of their prize—may do for them even more than their founder even conceived. I wish he may find full scope, and appreciation ‖ by them, and ‖ in the City he comes to enlighten.

I have had but a glance at your *"Spectroscope*.[1] enough however to perceive the busy world at the West ‖ which it ‖ whose spirit and doings it Chronicles.

I have pleasant memories of your visit, and we shall hope to see Dr. Dudley in Concord as soon as he can come to visit us after his arrival in Boston.

My household are now all well, and we have good news weekly from May now settled in Paris for the winter, and where she has the best advantages for pursuing her Art Studies.

I have not been in Boston since our visit there.

Give my respects to Dr. Dudley, whom I shall hope to ‖ meet ‖ greet soon at my door.

Cordially Yours
A. Bronson Alcott

[1] A short-lived journal published at Milwaukee (1875–76).

LETTER 76–26

[to S. H. Haskell, Newtonville, Mass.]

Concord December | 12th 1876.

Dear Sir,

Yours is at hand.[1] I wish I had what you ask of me to give you—counsel that should cure and restore. But this you may not hope from any one. The doctors differ so widely that their advice only distracts and discourages.

As a general statement it holds *that diseases of the body have their* rise in the soul, and a regimen for this should first be prescribed for the cure. Broken laws might be obeyed; and the steps retraced that led to the sufferings. Only so can health and vigor of body or mind be won—a slow process but the only safe and sure one to pursue.

Do not look primarily to any special diet or drug, but to correcting the habits—*whatever these are*—which mother your troubles. Salt or no salt may be equally salutary. Every one takes from his food different ingredients, in different proportions, (according to his temperament and tendencies) which chemistry is wholly incompetent to detect. As his tastes so is the man.

In general: continence, sobriety, temperance in diet, daily exercise in the open air, bathing, if strong enough and best in the morning, sleep and enough if one can get it, a cheerful spirit, a chosen task—these are the chief requisites for health and sanity both of mind and body. If one call in a physician, best trust to a Homeopath.[2]

[c]an hardly name any for consultation. Drs Jackson and Trall are extreme Vegetarians, and if one is not too far broken down, and has the faith in their regimen, offer perhaps the surest, though not a swift cure. No one can expect this Time and *Self-denial* are the only sure physicians.

This may be comfortless counsel, but is the best I have to offer. I am now 77 years of age, and have practiced for most of my life theories intimated herein.

Very truly

[1] Haskell had written October 11, telling Alcott that his nervous system had broken down, and asking advice.
[2] Some following material has been cut out along with the signature which was on the other side of the sheet.

LETTER 76–27[1]

[to Mary E. Stearns, Medford, Mass.]

[Concord? 1876?]

Monday 14th October.

To Medford and pass the night. Mrs. Stearns cherishes the hope of preparing her husbands' papers for the press. Perhaps more of the secret history of the reform movements of these last ten years originated with Maj. Stearns; were countenanced and carried into effect by his influence and money, than any man of his time. His life would be an important contribution to American history, political and social. He had the happiness of having a sympathising adviser in his wife; to whose prophetic insights and shrewd judgments of men and measures he owed some of his most brilliant successes. "The Stearns" were Phillips *Oracle.* They were in almost daily communication with him during the Kanzas troubles, and throughout the late war, up to the day of Maj. Stearns' death. It was Mrs. Stearns who sent Brackett the sculptor to model the bust of John Brown while imprisoned at Charlestown. To her, the hero owed largely the means by which he was enabled to strike that first blow for national emancipation. She was, in fact, the prompter of enterprizes, which forwarded by her husbands tact and energy, have become parts of the history of progress

Very Affectionately

Your friend.

A. Bronson Alcott

Mrs. Stearns

---

[1] MS. (probably just a portion of the letter) owned by the Fruitlands and Wayside Museums.

PART TWENTY-TWO

1877

[to Mary N. Adams, Dubuque, Iowa]

Concord January | 3rd 1877.

Dear Mrs. Adams,

Your welcome letter fragrant with flowers and affectionate remembrances reached us on New-Years Eve, and brought "glad tidings" of yourself and friends crowning and under the Bluffs of your Continental stream, where yourself particularly have the right of vision to abide.

What you write concerning your winter studies is specially significant. I wish the cities—even the metropolitan had learned to utilize and enjoy its gifts and opportunities as skilfully. That Birthday service was, I confess, rather surprizing, but since you have the Magian adoration and scent of frankincense inborn, and so must be forgiven for your Paganized Faith.

The best thing I have to communicate just now is the *Rev. Joseph Cook's Lectures* delivered to all Boston and suburbs on Monday noon, and have now reached 5 delivered and more to come.[1] Next Monday's is announced to be on *New England-transcendentalism.* And with the Genius and Scope of the Lecturer is likely to be the fairest estimate yet attempted—Frothinghams falling short in some important respects, as some of us think. Mr. Cook is a graduate of Yale, Harvard and Andover.[2] He has passed some years abroad, and brings home the deepest and broadest conclusions of German and English thinkers, with the ability to present them fairly and even eloquently. I have heard several of his lectures and met him socially, and think he is likely to do for us Americans what needs be done to complement and carry forwards, while deepening the best of our advanced thinking. Orthodox in the liberal sense, he has important advantages over the Radical wings, speaking *absolutely* as well as critically, while doing justice all round. I sent you one of his reports, and will forward his next. This is to be on *New England Transcendentalism.*

Next in interest, is the prospect of Dr Dudleys coming to speak to and perhaps take permanent charge of Parker's Fraternity people, who seem not to have advanced beyond, if not fallen away sadly from their devout leader. Dr. Dudley may restore and replace them upon safe and solid foundations. I was his guest for a whole week with Mills at Milwaukee, and found him a fund of wit and catholicity that gave good promise. Now if Boston will have him, and he will stay with us the new Pentucost [*sic*] *may* fall in spirit and word. Transcendental truth is plainly in the ascendant, and the new Century likely to bring in its advent.

Emerson is busy as ever. He is now preparing a paper for the March Magazine the New-Old-North American to be issued Bi monthly hereafter. Now May is gone, our Clubs are less lively and Concord without her, (I say this to you) falls into commonplace. She writes delightedly of her opportunities for studying Art in Paris from living models and with pleasant companions.

Louisa is passing the winter with us. Her new story has already run to 15000 copies sold, and her copyrights are remunerative. Anna and my boys are with us also.

Mrs Alcott is very well, rides out on pleasant days, and reads as if she still [*sic*] in *her teens*. Tithonus has his hold on myself still, and without the old melancholy. All send regards to yourself and family.

I venture to enclose the last proofs of the last printed chapter of my "Table Talk."

Yours affectionately
A. B. A.

[1] Flavius Josephus Cook (1838–1901). His very popular Monday noon lectures continued for twenty years.
[2] He left Yale before graduating, for reasons of health; was graduated from Harvard in 1865 and from the Andover Theological Seminary in 1868.

Letter 77–2

[to Theodore L. Pitt, Oneida, N.Y.]

Concord January | 19th 1877.

Dear Sir,

You have my thanks for the "Socialists,"[1] and for the appreciative Critique of the N. E. Transcendentalists, in which you appear to have a clearer vision of their aims and ideas than even the author of the Volume himself,—especially of the social and religious aspects of the movement.

The books you inquire about are not now to be obtained at the bookstores, excepting "the *Record of my School,*" and "*Concord Days.*" The Conversations with Children on the Gospels and Tablets have been asked for by numerous persons, (particularly at the West) and will be reprinted when my bookseller has confidence in the sale of them. Roberts Brothers of Boston have the Record of a School and Concord Days on sale at present.

I have read most of the proof-sheets of a new Volume entitled, "*Table Talk*" which is to appear sometime in the coming spring.

I am [p. in] indebted to someone for the "Socialist" which now comes to me regularly from week to week. I esteem it a privilege to be kept thus posted of Reforms and of their reception with the public. It is well to have hospitable ears, at least, for every new advent of truth the world over.

Truly Yours,
A. Bronson Alcott.

Mr. Theo. L. Pitt.

¹ The *American Socialist* (1876–79), of which Pitt was probably the editor, succeeded the *Circular* which for some years had been the organ of John Humphrey Noyes's perfectionist communities.

LETTER 77–3

[to Dr. Dudley, Boston]

Concord January | 19th 1877.

Dear Sir,

I was disappointed on finding you were not to be seen at your Hotel last Monday. But shall hope to be more fortunate when I am next in Boston. I may wish to hear Mr. Cook further on Theodore Parker next Monday, and shall then call—or, shall I not find you at the Lecture? Mr. Cook is saying noteworthy things from Monday to Monday, and his criticisms are not without deep significance.—on the whole the most so of any thing Boston has heard since Emerson spoke to its intellect. I trust you will not miss hearing what he may say of Parker, whose successor I wish his friends might find in yourself. But about this, and other current interests we must have time and opportunity for discussing fully.

Why will you not come and pass a day (and night) with us? Then we may do some justice to the *future* also. I wish that pleasure might be mine and ours. Will you write and say yes?

Emerson and Sanborn are neighbors you know and offer further inducements.

I have a gratifying note from Mrs. Dudley.

Very truly
Yours
A. Bronson Alcott

Rev. Dr. Dudley.

LETTER 77–4¹

[to William T. Harris, St. Louis]

Concord January | 1877.

Dear Friend,

I have inclosed the proof sheets of Chap VIII. of my book of *"Table Talk"*—which you will recognize as your notice of Mr. Alcott's Method &c—a glimpse of his standpoint of thinking. I wanted something to span across from *Practical* to *Speculative,* and this seemed just the || bridge || arch sprung by yourself for my readers crossing. I trust no scruple of yours will be interposed to withold [sic] the Chapter. I remembered your willingness to have your criticism of *Tablets* republished in a second edition of that work, and the printers were impatient for copy.

The book is now far on and I hope to read the proofs of the rest during February. Chap 1 of Book II *Method* is in type. *Person, Genesis, Temperament, Lapse, Destiny, Immortality,* follow, and close the Volume. I have used sparingly the Philosophemes, and please myself with the faith of having displayed *my world* more distinctly than hitherto.

Rev Joseph Cook is giving some rather important Lectures just now to full audiances [sic] in Boston—good for his *orthdox* listeners and helpful to *heterodox*. I send his last reported which I heard yesterday.

Dr. Dudley is speaking for a few Sundays or more to Parker's people. He is to be with me next week, and meet our "Fortnightly Club" here

Louisa has been very much flattered by an invitation to meet the contributors of "Johnson's Cyclopedia" at New York. Do you purpose joining the company? May writes from Paris—full of Art Ideas, and very busy at her studies

I am very well and the rest of us. Can you find a moment to write a line?

Yours truly,
A. Bronson Alcott.

Wm. T. Harris

---

¹ From a copy, in Alcott's hand, in the Alcott-Pratt Collection. The original, *dated January 23*, is in the Alcott-Harris Collection in the Concord Free Public Library (see Appendix B).

LETTER 77–5

[to Mrs. A. H. Spaulding, East Boston, Mass.]

Concord February, 9th | 1877.

Dear Mrs Spalding [sic],

Your arrangement for meeting your Home Club will suit me quite well. And I shall hope to find you at Mr. Cooks' Lecture on the Monday named in your note. (Feby. 26th). Perhaps your company would like to have my account of Transcendentalism in New England after listening (some of them at least) to Mr. Cook's version of it, as illustrated in Emerson and Parker, and the history of it, as given in Frothingham's Book, doubtless read by most. *"Idealism"* in general is always in favor with thoughtful people, and, just now, gaining the ears of the public again Mr. Frothingham of the contrary opinion notwithstanding. I shall be likely to speak on some of its aspects and prospects at any rate, name our theme whatever we may. Am I to give a lecture, or a parlor Conversation—which?

And may I not have a word further from you about your wishes?

Very truly
Yours,
A. Bronson Alcott.

LETTER 77–6[1]

[to Frank H. Bigelow, Washington, D.C.]

Concord, February, | 12th 1877.

Dear Sir,

Your confessions are not surprising. The present generation shares largely in your and like doubts—in material views of life, in indifferentism, infidelity— the result of ill-training, or worse no training mainly. Your letter shows that you are wishing to extricate your faith from the meshes of materialism, the web of sensationalism, and seeking to recover the freer, fresher motions of earlier days. Childhood's creed is the simplest and safest for all times. One cannot depart far from it without loss. Faith is the cradle in which all our faculties are kindly rocked, not to sleep, but to be succored till they gain sufficient confidence and strength to steady themselves: Yet may not declare their independence of their nurse's leadings, without disloyalty to truth and duty. Reason best follows in faith's footsteps. The heart has arguments of which the head is unacquainted. We walk by Faith rather than by sight, so far as we walk uprightly.—What were Christianity with its assurances of immortality without *Faith* as its basis? To what else shall revelation speak directly and gain response? What were the body bereft of Soul to animate and quicken every faculty of the Mind? Untwist this three-stranded cord binding these in one, and our Personality were but separated straggling cords threads of our present being. Death may dissolve the stuffs but only to prepare for twisting the threads anew of finer fibre. The heart refuses to entertain the abstract notion of non-being, extinction of our Personality. Even Reason finds *annihilation unthinkable,* and starts abashed at the spectre.

Yes: The Church of Christ opens and provides for the faithful. It nurtures, moreover the reason itself into loyalty Science and society are deepened and sweetened by its administrations. Not this Church specially, nor that, but the Church Universal, catholic, inclusive, by the piety quickening every faculty and dedicating all to life's varied duties. And how many there are outside of its walls, seeking for Gospel light, groping for guidance, awaiting the descent of the Spirit.

But I must send you my new book treating of such matters when it comes from the press.

As to books in general I find one is led by instinct to lay his hands upon the volume best suited to his needs. I think *Coleridge* is always most stimulating and profitable reading.

But I am come to the foot of my sheet, and have hardly opened the Book of Life for you—given an Index only.

I shall gladly hear further from you if you are prompted to write again.

Surely I remember the Studious schoolboy and his interest in the charming Dreamer's **Dream.**

Very truly
Yours,
A. Bronson Alcott.

[1] MS. owned by the Yale University Library. A copy, in Alcott's hand, is in the Alcott-Pratt Collection.

LETTER 77-7

[to Mrs. A. H. Spaulding, East Boston, Mass.]

Concord February | 21st 1877.

Dear Mrs Spaulding,

I shall gladly meet Mrs Stone and such friends as you may invite on the afternoon preceding the meeting of your Club. Good company is the best refreshment for speaking and I am not sufficiently aged[?] need [sic] sleep or rest under sweet Sunshine.

Mrs Stone I have known and shared her hospitalities more than once at her home in Michigan.

I shall seek you on Monday at Mr. Cook's Lecture and will accompany you to East Boston if you wish.

Very truly
Yours,
A. Bronson Alcott

Mrs. Spaulding

[Letter to Mary Baker Glover Eddy, Lynn, Mass.; from Concord, March 6, 1877.]

LETTER 77-8

[to Mr. Speare, Charlestown, Mass.]

Concord March | 26th 1877.

Dear Sir,

I shall gladly avail myself of your kind invitation to speak to your charge next Sunday. You may expect me to take tea with you on Saturday. And my daughter, Louisa, who will pass Saturday night in Boston, hopes to join me on Sunday in time for your morning Services at the Prison.

Very truly
Yours,
A. Bronson Alcott

Rev. Mr. Speare
Chaplain MS. Prison.

LETTER 77-9

[to May, Paris, France]

Concord April | 23rd 1877.

Dear May,

Red best represents your success at the Salon.[1] And so I begin this my note of salutation to you. It is an honor to yourself and to us all: the whole household joined in their Chorus at the happy news, as all have told, and I add mine to the vote. Your star is still in the ascendant and only yourself can dim its lustre. Every one to whom your success has been mentioned has taken pride in your honors. And the hopeful tone of your letters shows that you deserve them.

In your last, which came this morning I was gratified to find that you have received mine. If I have written seldom it is not for want of interest in yourself and studies. I hear, and read *carefully* all your letters as they come to hand from week to week, if less communicative I am not less thoughtful of you, than others of our household.

Just now all have their pens sharpened for congratulating you on your happiness and success. I trust you will continue to deserve both.

You speak of my *book*. It is promised early in May; and I shall mail to you an early copy. *Book* Ist may interest you. Mr Niles has good hopes of its success, and thinks coming during the month of Anniversaries is fortunate. Louisas new story in the "No *Name* Series" comes out to morrow. If you know its *"title,"* you are better in formed than I am. I am told by your mother that it surpasses its predecessors in power and brilliancy and—that the author will not be easily recognized by its readers.[2] Louisa, like yourself appears to be adding honors to her name, and what is far better giving pleasure (and nobler views of life) to her million readers and admirers.

You will wish to learn about your strawberries and rasperries [*sic*]. They are uncovered and Carney comes Thursday to help about stirring the ground about them. The Garden is ploughed, and soon to be planted. The orchard is to be sown with buckwheat. Your *orchard* is already green, and its blossoms with the buckwheat by the road will make a floral picture in June.

Mrs. Cheney made us a pleasant visit and read us a charming paper on *"Color."* To-day we rode out—your mother Louisa and myself—passing Anna's house, which looked homelike and tempting. Sanborn plants the garden for her, and shares the products. It seems a fortunate purchase and gives Anna and her boys a desirable home settles them in Concord at last; and leaves us ‖ a ‖ our Summer House, (if we choose), under the Elms.—

I have only mere commonplaces for you. And you are favored week by week with the particulars most interesting to you, by your mother and sisters.

Saturday I was in Boston to attend a *Kindergarten Festival* at Dr. Bartols' Church, taking a Note from Louisa to Miss Bartol concerning your *Salon* honors.

Every thing now moves happily [word] in parlors, study, and kitchen. And the furnishing of the Thoreau House occupies time and thoughts already[3] I wish every thing may suit your taste when you return—*Heaven* bless and keep you.

Your Father.

Miss May Alcott
    Paris

[1] May had submitted a still life to the Salon and it was accepted in April, 1877. Alcott wrote this letter of congratulations to his youngest daughter in red ink. The best account of May's activities in Europe is in Caroline Ticknor, *May Alcott: A Memoir* (Boston, 1928)—in which part of the present letter is quoted (p. 189).

[2] Of her book, *A Modern Mephistopheles*, Louisa wrote, in her Journal for January, February, 1877, "It has been simmering ever since I read Faust last year. Enjoyed doing it, being tired of providing moral pap for the young." In April she wrote, " 'M. M.' appears and causes much guessing. It is praised and criticized, and I enjoy the fun, especially when friends say, 'I know *you* didn't write it, for you can't hide your peculiar style.' " (Cheney, pp. 296, 297.)

[3] Anna, with help from Louisa, had bought the Thoreau house.

LETTER 77-10

[to A. H. Dooley, Terre Haute, Ind.]

Concord April | 28th 1877.

Dear Sir,

My Table Talk is promised early in May.

You ask my views of Mr. Cook. I have attended many of his Lectures, and think highly of his powers as a lecturer. He is awakening an interest in theological questions which have slumbered too long in our community, and our Boston pulpits are becoming active in consequence. Seven Sermons were aimed directly at his theology a few Sundays ago, and a course of lectures by Unitarian ministers to counteract his orthodox teachings, has just been announced. The first is to be given by James Freeman Clarke tomorrow (Sunday) evening.

I find much in common with his religious views, and think nothing has been done in Boston since Theodore Parkers preaching, so likely to be productive of good fruits for religion and philanthropy. In this favorable estimate of Mr. Cook's teachings, I am taken to account by many of the Radicals, of course.

Mr Cooks Lectures on Biology and Transcendentalism are to be published in the coming Autumn.

Yours Truly
A. Bronson Alcott.

Mr. A. H. Dooley

LETTER 77-11

[to Harrison Gray Otis Blake, Worcester, Mass.]

Concord May 4th | 1877.

Dear Friend,

An English correspondent of mine, Dr. Cook,[1] who has connection with the Dublin University Magazine, and an admirer of *Thoreau,* writes, inquiring if *something of his* is not available for publishing in that Journal—which, I believe has very good repute with Scholars. Now have you not something for him? or, if not, would you hesitate selecting from his papers in your possession a short article for him? I have consulted Emerson and Sanborn, and they agree that such contribution to an English Journal would help publish Thoreaus merits abroad and, perhaps, further the publication of his M.SS. at home.

Mr Niles, the leading man, in the firm of Roberts Brothers of Boston, offers to publish selection, and Emerson says he will help it, by any short introduction, to the public. Now if you will not prepare such, let Sanborn, and bring forth these M.SS. as may be found expedient and timely. A *book of Morals of Thoreau's* would be a stimulating volume.

Why will you not think favorable of the matter, and when I reply to Mr Cook offer him a sample of Henrys good things for his Journal.—

And would it not speed matters, if you would ride over here and pass a day or two with your old friends.

Very truly

Yours,

A Bronson Alcott

H. G. O. Blake
  Worcester
   Mass.

---

[1] Keningale Robert Cook of London; see Letter 77–21.

LETTER 77–12

[to Harrison Gray Otis Blake, Worcester, Mass.]

Concord May 15 | 1877.

Dear Sir

We shall expect you to dine, or, if you come in the afternoon to tea, and pass the night with us, Sanborn and Emerson (probably) will join us for the evening and we can consult about Thoreau's M.S.S..

I wish you may consent to compile a volume for the press forthwith. And we may arrange for the publication from time [sic] of the entire papers left by our gifted friend.

Can you not spend Sunday in Concord?

Very truly

Yours,

A. Bronson Alcott

H.G.O. Blake,
  Worcester

LETTER 77–13

[to Mary A. Brigham, W. Peterboro, N.H.]

Concord May 15th | 1877.

Dear Mrs Brigham,

I shall be pleased to visit your picturesque country in June and meet your Woman's Club. You shall name the time and the direct route for reaching your town, and you may forward tickets for the road, (if you choose); with any information concerning your wishes about my visit that you care to communicate.

Very truly

Yours

A. Bronson Alcott.

Mrs Mary A. Brigham.

LETTER 77–14[1]

[to William T. Harris, St. Louis]

Concord May, | 20th 1877.

Dear Friend,

I forward by mail a copy of my new book which is to be published ‖ on Thursday next ‖ next Monday. It has been too long in press, and the matter condensed meanwhile, and you may find it might have been further shortened and thus bettered. But I have neither the skill nor wit to render it more worthy of your acceptance. I shall value your criticism above all other that it may call forth, since I know of no thinker of my time or acquaintance, whom I judge better qualified to estimate its absolute merits, or point out its defects. I hope you are about getting some respite from your tasks and are purposing to spend days with us in New-England and particularly in Concord. Several new persons have risen above the horizon, since I saw you, and may prove shining lights in the future. Rev. *Joseph Cook* has been agitating the pool of our Athens, and set wide eddies abroad over the surface. I have found more in him than most of our type of thinking; and shall be curious to learn of your estimate. I hear that he was the pride of Yale, from whence he graduated about, I should think, your time. Have you any knowledge or recollections of him. Yesterday, Porter C. Bliss, editor of *"the Library Table,* was here Knowing him at Yale he spoke in admiring terms of his depth and brilliancy of Scholarship. He has drawn forth much comment from pulpit and press (I mean Mr. Cook); and addresses the Cambridge students in Appleton Chapel this evening. Bliss told me that your Journal was one of his text books.

May has been fortunate in having a picture of hers accepted at the Paris Salon, and writes with spirit and gaiety from that city of Art.

Next week I attend the May Anniversaries.—

Yours truly,

A. Bronson Alcott

Wm. T. Harris

---

[1] From a copy, in Alcott's hand, in the Alcott-Pratt Collection. The original is in the Alcott-Harris Collection in the Concord Free Public Library (see Appendix B).

LETTER 77–15

[to May, Paris, France]

Concord, May 20th | 1877.

Dear May,

Your picture and my book of Table Talk are now before me. The picture I consider a perfect likeness. It satisfies and delights as I become familiar with it from day to day. You may be pleased to have me tell you just where it stands against Book Table before the Western window in my study, the light falling upon the face from the front windows. Sanborn praised it yesterday (while taking tea with Blake) thinking it admirable. At first sight, the hat crowning it, seemed better omitted, but I am becoming pleased with it since it brings out the expression, and by contrast, harmonizes thus with the features. I shall be content to have you perpetuated in this fine presentment, and wish to express my thanks to your friend Miss Peckham[1] for the obligation that she has laid us all under by this work of her hand. Let me ask her acceptance of my book as some return for this beautiful gift. It is but a trifling acknowledgment. On her return to America I shall hope to welcome her to our home in Concord.

It must be a great satisfaction to have formed the acquaintance of the sisters and such comfortable quarters together in the City of Arts. And your accounts of your pursuits and pleasures from week to week, make our quietude here the more pleasurable by the stimulus of your gaieties abroad. "How well she writes," exclaims the matron in her cap, as she reads your letters, and we all respond, "Yes." I imagine artists as a class excel in this art of writing speaking as they do to *the eye*, that chiefest of artistic organs. We shall look for fuller illustrations of, this in your descriptions of the pictures at the Salon exhibition. What lucky star shone upon the fortunate position of your little gem in the collection! Names are fortunes and fames, say you. Yes, but character and genius gave them their place and power, and must perpetuate them. You are riding the wave bravely, and, I trust in your faithfulness to yourself, to keep your place and honor your name.

The Elms are out in leaflets and the orchard blossoming. I am told that having written my garden, I shall spoil its beauty and loveliness by planting a single seed this season. So instead of bean rows cornhills, the ground is sown with buckwheat for the bees to busy themselves with in honey time. And Sanborn plants instead in Anna's garden for us.

You may find passages that may please and entertain, possibly in my Table Talk. It is a neat book to the Eye at least. And if the reviewers accept it, I shall think myself not wholly out of date, and of existence.

Continue to keep us acquainted with your pleasures and purposes and sometimes address personally

Your proud father.

Miss May Alcott
    Paris

---

[1] Rose Peckham, who did the portrait of May. May and Rose Peckham and the latter's sister shared quarters in Paris.

Letter 77–16

[John White Chadwick, Brooklyn? N.Y.?]

Concord, May, 24th | 1877.

Dear Sir,

Your Postal Card is at hand.

In regard to the story about which you enquire I am in doubt whether it was a little fable of my own, or Mrs. Austin's "Story without an End."[1] (which I afterwards edited.) I have no recollection of having seen Miss Martineaus story, till I read it in her "Autobiography." I think it cannot be hers about which you enquire The little trifle of mine was published under the title of *"the Fountain"* in an annual—"the Gem", by Lilly Wait and Colman, booksellers in Boston in 1833—or thereabout. I have not a copy at hand.

And when are we to meet for more important discussions?

Very truly
Yours,
A. Bronson Alcott

Rev. J. W. Chadwick.

[1] Sarah Austin, trans. from the German of Friedrich Wilhelm Carové.

LETTER 77-17[1]

[to William T. Harris, St. Louis]

Concord June 6th | 1877.

Dear Friend

Your brief note informs me that you purpose visiting us early in July (probably) And I am now putting forward my earnest plea for your allowing yourself a wide margin for *Concord*. My house is spacious, and our *"Fortnightly Club"* will not willingly let you slip away without a word from you at least. So bring along a paper or two for Parlor reading. Then I am to have an Eternity and a day with my host besides.

Now Mills is here for the night and to-morrow. And Wm. Henry Channing is over from England and promises us a few days in July. Good luck should bring you here to us at the same time.

I spent last week in Boston attending the Anniversary meetings, heard Cook's closing lecture for this season. He has stirred the theological pools and done good service for metaphysical studies. May you meet him somewhere. He is now at New Haven, I believe, and is, I learn, soon to be married to a young lady of the city.[2] He has been most gracious to me during his lectures.

My book finds favor with reviewers thus far. Lest you should miss seeing Ripleys notice in last week's Tribune, I forward a copy enclosed.

How good *"Dogmatic Proofs of Immortality"* is in the last No. of the Speculative.[3] Who is the translator T. R. Vickroy?

Very truly
Yours
A Bronson Alcott

Wm. T. Harris.

[1] From a copy, in Alcott's hand, in the Alcott-Pratt Collection. The original is in the Alcott-Harris Collection in the Concord Free Public Library (see Appendix B).
[2] Georgiana Hemingway, with whom Alcott was to correspond beginning in the fall of 1877.
[3] XI (April, 1877), 177-97.

LETTER 77–18

[to Mary A. Brigham, W. Peterboro, N.H.]

Concord June 12 | 1877.

Dear Mrs. Brigham,

The time you name—Friday 22nd. for visiting your town, will suit me very well, and you may expect by the morning train, which leaves here at 8. AM. to find you or Mr. Jackson at Winchendon at 11." you tell me. I can meet your Club in the evening, pass Saturday and Sunday with you perhaps Monday, though I shall wish to return unless you have something for [me] on Monday. The Literary societies meet at Cambridge during the week.

Truly Yours,
A. Bronson Alcott.

P.S./ It will give me pleasure to speak in Mr. Jackson's desk if he wishes on Sunday.

LETTER 77–19[1]

[to William T. Harris, St. Louis]

Concord June | 30th 1877.

Dear Friend,

You wrote of visiting New England in July, (early in the month probably) I wish it might be convenient for you to come to us in Concord during the second week when W. H. Channing is to be with us and wishes much to meet you. He comes on Monday the 9th. and will stay, we hope three or four days. He is the guest of Emerson while here, and we shall claim you as ours for as long as you can stay in Concord. Mrs Emerson will open her parlors for an evening at least for a Conversation when we may feast on divine Philosophy,—Plato and the rest of your acquaintance. Please arrange to come then if possible—at any rate give me and Emerson a generous visit. You have missed him, when here for two seasons past.

I was at the "P.B.K."[2] on Thursday and had a scholarly day and dinner.

My book finds general favor with reviewers thus far. You will be amused on reading the "Atlantic Monthly's" estimate. But that Journal and the "Nation,' have forfeited the confidence of able scholars, and may be ignored.

Truly Yours
A. Bronson Alcott

Wm. T. Harris

[1] From a copy, in Alcott's hand, in the Alcott-Pratt Collection. The original is in the Alcott-Harris Collection in the Concord Free Public Library (see Appendix B).
[2] Phi Beta Kappa.

LETTER 77–20

[to E[?]. K. Whitaker, Washington, D.C.]

Concord July 2nd 1877.

Dear Sir

Your letter inquiring about the history of the Whitakers is at hand. I have given such attention as the time permitted during our Literary Anniversaries at Cambridge, and wish I had more definite information to forward to you.

I have found nothing reliable which is not found in our Concord History, concerning the name you bear. The town clerk, a very accurate person and familiar with our Records had no additional information to give me. Judge Hoar tells me that he has some dim recollections of a "Squire Whitaker," but nothing more. Our graveyards might perhaps assist in tracing the name remotely, had one time for the survey.

You will therefore have all accessible information at present in the following notes copied from our Concord History published in 183[?]5.

p. 387. *Whitaker*. Jonathan Whitaker was born before 1690. Son of John of Watertown. born 1664. Nathaniel and David married about 1700. and had large Families in the town. David died August 1791. aged 84. his wife died 1798. aged 90. Elisabeth ‖ born ‖ died January 1708—an aged woman.

pp. 276,77. In a document "concerning the disposal of town lands", dated November 12th 1772 the name of David Whitaker appears as signer with several others. This was probably "the Squire Whitaker dimly remembered by Judge Hoar.

In your visit to Mass. it might be satisfactory to you to consult fully our Records and graveyards.

My wife desires me to assure you of ‖ your ‖ her remembrance and former relation by marriage to her family.

Truly Yours
A. Bronson Alcott

LETTER 77–21[1]

[to Keningale Cook, London, England]

Concord July 6th 1877.

Dear Sir,

Your favor of last April has lain unacknowledged till I might make some suitable return for your interest in our deceased friend Mr. Thoreau—and, I may add in myself. I had besides the hope of forwarding passages from Mr. Thoreaus' M.S.S., and may do so eventually.

Mr. Thoreaus' sister, in whose care he left the MSS. has lately deceased. She left these to her brothers' friend—Mr. Blake of Worcester, who has them now in keeping. On mentioning to him your wish to publish extracts in your Dublin University Magazine he set about copying such, but, on second thought, preferred offering first to "The *Atlantic Monthly*. The Editor has them now in hand, but has not signified acceptance as yet. Mr. Blake authorizes me to forward them to you should he—the editor—decline their acceptance.

I write thus particularly in order to put the facts distinctly before you, and also to account, in part, for my delay in replying to your kind request.

I should be sorry to find my past silence, moreover, had been construed as indifference, on my part to your literary productions and pursuits. Your studies, letters, the articles in *"the Truth Seeker"* interested me, and I hoped you would favor me with the sight of your book on the Gospels when published.

I venture to forward herewith a little book of mine just published, and to beg your acceptance also of a biography of Mr. Thoreau, by his friend and townsman Wm. Ellery Channing.

Rev. Wm. Henry Channing is now visiting us. He wishes to make your acquaintance on his return to London next October. He is a cherished friend of ours, and will gladly give you the latest accounts of us.

I look with new interest into the Dublin University Magazine whenever I visit our Boston Athenaeum[;] the biographical papers are noteworthy[.] The tone of the Journal is excellent. I wish I may find something worthy of its pages to send you. Do you see Harris' Journal of Speculative Philosophy? The Editor is now visiting us.

I hear nothing further of your proposed book for Children.

Yours faithfully.

A. Bronson Alcott.

Keningale Cook L.L.D.

---

¹ MS. owned by the Fruitlands and Wayside Museums, pasted in a copy of *Table Talk* sent to Cook. A copy, in Alcott's hand, is in the Alcott-Pratt Collection.

LETTER 77–22

[to Keningale Cook, London, England]

[Concord, July 12, 1877]

Dr. Keningale Cook
    London.
Dear Sir,

I need but name the bearer of this Rev. Wm. H. Channing of England and America, to commend him to your cordial acquaintance and hospitalities.

Mr. Channing comes to you fresh from us. His too infrequent visits to our shores always stimulate and spiritualize those who are so fortunate as to meet him. And we return him to diffuse his sweetness and beauty to our neighbors over the seas.

Yours faithfully.

A. Bronson Alcott

Concord July 12th
    1877

[Letter to Rose Peckham, Paris, France; from Concord, July 12, 1877.]

LETTER 77-23[1]

[to May, Paris, France]

Concord July 26th | 1877.

Dear May,

Family birth days have been memorable heretofore in our Calendar. And though you are absent, we have your picture present to accost and ornament with garlands. Shall I tell you particulars? Artists have fine tastes and you shall see whether we have honored these in hanging your picture.

Anna's removal takes sundry things ornamental and useful from the rooms above and below—the boys book-case from my study with the rest. So my book case takes its place, and your picture, with Turners' portrait over it hangs there on The Wall instead, and the apostles beside it. The Table that stood under the West window now stands with flowers under your picture. The light falls from the South windows and brings out your best expression as we stand at the entry door. And my study table now faces the fair young lady as I write.—Not a single disparaging criticism as yet from the many, but approving from all. We are all delighted at having found its place, after many trials and discussions.

The last weeks have been varied by visits and Anna's preparations for, and removal to her New Home in The Village.

My good friend Wm. Henry Channing passed a fortnight in Concord, and I saw him almost daily. He comes again in August to preach for us. Then we shall probably have another Conversation at Emersons. We had a memorable evening, when Mr. Harris was here. He read a very suggestive paper on Michael Angelo's Fates.—the large painting being placed in sight. Mr. Channing spoke beautifully about the reading and picture, and Mr. Harris won the admiration of every one present. How his cousins and yourself would have enjoyed the evening with the rest of the company.

James Freeman Clarke preaches here next Sunday, and I am invited to another Conversation at Emerson's in the evening. So Concord gets a share of the fresh ideas now current.

Anna's new home promises to be most desirable. She is making it neat, tidy, convenient, for herself and boys and for us too when we choose to take quarters with her. She is very happy and hopeful in the prospect and possession.

Three of us linger awhile under the Elms. I trust Louisa will now get a taste of the quiet she covets for writing, with some slight relief from past cares and anxieties. She has not yet felt that she could join you in Paris. Why should she not when we have joined Anna in October?

We shall expect to see Miss Chandler here on her return.

You cannot appreciate fully our pleasure and pride in your successes, aims, and prospects. I trust Miss Peckham has received my letter of July 12th.

Your Father.

[1] Quoted in part in Ticknor, *May Alcott,* pp. 242–43.

[to Porter Cornelius Bliss, New York City]

Concord, August | 4th 1877.

Dear Sir,

I have read with pleasure your brief notice of my book of Table Talk in your Library Table. And have looked for following Nos. but none have reached me. Though not a subscriber, I fancied myself entitled to a reading as a future contributor. Yet it has occurred to me, that the M.S.S. which were put into your hands at my house, may have been found unsuitable, on further examination, for your Magazine. If for this, or any reason, you wish not to use them as proposed, please return them to me at Concord. and oblige

Yours truly,
A. Bronson Alcott.

Porter C. Bliss.
  Editor of Library Table.

[Letter to Mary Baker Glover Eddy, Lynn, Mass.; from Concord, August 21, 1877.]

[Letter to Mary Baker Glover Eddy, Lynn, Mass.; from Concord, September 14, 1877.]

LETTER 77–25

[to Mary N. Adams, Dubuque, Iowa]

Concord September 17th | 1877.

Dear Mrs. Adams.

Yours of July 23rd gave us interesting account of yourself and family about whom we are always happy to hear; of your literary studies and social entertainments also. I learn of few fellowships in Western cities more attractive than yours. I trust your summer recreations have been alike pleasurable and profitable.

I have but just returned from a short visit to my early home in Connecticut. It was shortened by my being called away by Mrs Alcott's illness. But I am happy to say that she is now comfortable though feeble: able to read a little and sleep without much disturbance. She had been unusually well during all summer, had rode out frequently, taken her usual lively interest in household and affairs generally. Especially concerned in Anna's purchase of "the *Thoreau house*" in the village and moving into it,—furnishing, &c. We can hardly hope that she can be to us all she has been in the past. Her chief satisfaction now is her correspondence with May, who writes weekly from Paris, where she purposes spending the coming winter. We are delighted with her success at the late Exhibition of pictures, having just received her "fruit piece," which was accepted by the commission of Artists and praised by all who have seen it. A fine portrait of her painted by a Miss Peckham of Providence, and her roommate in Paris, has also been sent us. May is so encouraged by her successes, that she writes of passing another year abroad. And now that Anna and her boys are fairly settled in a house of her own, Louisa feels a little more like indulging in literary work.— She having been our housekeeper during the summer mostly. Her new story *"Under the Lilacs"* (for which she is paid $3000. by Scribner) is to appear in November as a serial; and then published in Book form by Roberts Brothers. She is in better health than formerly, and has a future of possibilities awaiting her Genius.

Mr. Emerson is well, but not as active as formerly. Something of age seems apparent, particularly loss of recollection of common names.

Shall we not see you here in New England again. We now have Dr. Dudley and Joseph Cook to enlighten our community.

My book has found favor with the critics generally. I shall hardly get far from home during the coming autumn and winter. You will have Mr. Mills again doubtless. I have pleasant memories of kind friends in Dubuque. Regard to all, and to yourself and yours particularly.

> Your friend,
> A Bronson Alcott.

LETTER 77–26

[to Samuel Orcutt, Torrington? Conn.]

Concord September | 26th 1877

Dear Sir,

I forward to your address a copy of my *Table Talk*. and shall be pleased to learn that you find inspiration and profit in its perusal

I am glad to hear from yourself that your History of Torrington is so near publication. And wish, moreover, now that is off your mind, you would do like good work for Ancient Derby also[.] That is a tempting locality for the historian, for myself especially as a reader, since my maternal grandmother—Mary Chatfield—went from that place to Wolcott, as the bride of John Alcox, when Spindle Hill was mostly a mere Wilderness. Her family I find were among the first settlers of Old Derby, and still maintain their ancient standing[.] The architect of St. Johns Church Waterbury is, I am informed, a descendant.

I wish you may add its history to that of "Elihu Burritts of the Farmington Family of towns." Then I shall know most there is preserved of the local history of a large extent bordering upon Ancient Waterbury.

Mrs. Alcott is comfortable at present, but far from being restored to her former healthful condition.

I dined on Wednesday last in Boston with Rev. Joseph Cook. He begins his Monday Lectures for this season next Monday. His Lectures on Biology are advertised to appear next Saturday.

> Very truly,
> Yours,
> A. Bronson Alcott

Rev. Samuel Orcutt

LETTER 77–27

[to James Bintliff, Janesville, Wis.]

Concord September, | 27th 1877.

Dear Sir,

Yours is just at hand, and I forward to your address a photograph and a copy of my Table Talk. I am gratified that your association are sufficiently interested [in] "the Concord Group', and particularly in myself, to deem their works worthy of study.

The photograph is the latest and only impression of myself that I have at hand. I know of no earlier ones deserving of your ‖ possession, ‖ study.

Very truly

Yours,

A. Bronson Alcott

LETTER 77–28

[to Elihu Burritt, New Britain, Conn.]

Concord Mass. | September, | ‖ July, ‖ 27nd. 1877.

Dear Sir,

I have just read in The Waterbury American the announcement of the completion of your History of the Farmington Family of Towns. And as a portion of my native township formerly belonged to this family, I am desirous of possessing a copy of your Work. I am not informed whether it is yet published and for sale in the bookstores. And if you will inform me how I may obtain a copy, I shall be much obliged by your kindness.

These local histories are multiplying, and embrace the most attractive particulars of our National life.

Mr. Orcutts' of Wolcott, I regard as a good sample, and doubt not that yours, adds another.

I remember, moreover, that our birth places were not far distant, and that *our Connecticut* still holds a distinguished position in the National family of states.

Very truly

Yours,

A. Bronson Alcott.

Elihu Burritt Esqr.

New-Britain,

‖ Kensington, ‖

Conn.

LETTER 77–29

[to Francis Dyer, Wolcott, Conn.]

Dear Sir

Concord October, | 5th 1877.

I am sorry to have given you the trouble to inquire about my spectacles left carelessly in my haste in my chamber. They came properly to hand by mail, for which kindness you have my thanks.

As I had another pair at home I missed them only on my journey from Waterbury. My neglect in not acknowledging seasonably their reception, you will excuse on account of Mrs Alcott's illness. Though still with us we are expecting her departure for the new existen[ce] at any moment. She is very ready to depart, and with Christian expectations of nobler opportunities for service and reward.

My family are with me, save May who is now in London.
With much regard

Very truly Yours
A. Bronson Alcott

Rev. Francis Dyer
Wolcott, Conn

LETTER 77–30[1]

[to Georgiana Hemingway Cook, Boston]

Dear Mrs. Cook,

Concord October 5th | 1877.

The illness of my wife forbids my visiting the City to-day, to listen to Mr. Cook's Lecture, and if, you were disengaged, to see yourself again. I may be able to leave home next Monday.

Your husbands last Monday's Lecture is especially interesting, both for subtlety and novelty of treatment. I anticipate much satisfaction in this new course of his on the Holy of Holies.

Pray excuse me, if I reiterate my faith in the Lecturer's Genius, and anticipate a revival of spiritual life and studies from his Lectureship. Nothing since the descent of || of || the spirit in transcendental days has inspired like hopes in the future of religious thought, and Christian fellowship.

I have read the "Biology" with new interest, and wish it may find the perusal by thoughtful scholars and good Christians which its transparent treatment of Life and Immortality so eminently deserve.

Very truly
Yours,
A. Bronson Alcott.

[1] MS. owned by the Duke University Library.

LETTER 77–31

[to H. Powers, Manchester, N.H.]

Concord October, | 7th 1877.

Dear Sir,

It would give me much pleasure to attend your N. H. Unitarian Association which meets on the 16 & 17th of this month, and take part in its deliberations. Especially should I be interested in the phases of Faith which these will doubtless reveal. But the state of my wife's health does not allow me to promise my attendance at present. Thanking the Association for extending to me their kind invitation

I am very truly
Yours.
A. Bronson Alcott

Rev. H. Powers,
    Manchester

LETTER 77–32

[to Martin Luther Holbrook,[1] New York City]

Concord October. | 18th 1877

Dear Sir.

Half a century confined mostly to a Fruit and Bread diet, along with the dispositions and habits which this Christian regimen promotes, has confirmed me in the truth and beauty of the doctrines set forth so ably in your translation of Schlicklysen's treatise entitled Fruit and Bread, a Scientific Diet. It is a timely volume for the perusal of the general public, and especially for parents and reformers of all classes. Books like this treating of the whole Table of human increments are now particularly needed for instructing our people in the regimen for ensuring wholesome and vigorous habits of living and thinking. We suffer beyond measure for the want of a finer discrimination of the laws of vital as of spiritual chemistry, enabling us to tap the core of social and moral evils effectually. Your promised papers on Hygyene [sic] for farmers and mechanics will, I hope, reach the far wider and not less hungering community

You wish to know how I have trained my *Brain* to such fine thoughts as my books display? Your translation of Fruit and Bread furnishes the shortest reply to your question.—Yet I may add that a temperament inherited from a hardy and active ancestry doubtless was friendly to the formation of habits, which have given a charm to existence thus far, and if I prove faithful to the end, still promise a lengthened longevity. One would like to round off a busy century, and thus fulfil his earthly destiny.

As to my bill of fare, I add, moreover, that Fruits rank first and highest in the pyramid, Bread next, vegetables lowest and last, at its base. Flesh, if catering largely, especially to fair temperaments is essentially injurious, and dehumanizing. The less of it, the more readily, more genially, the body answers to the mind, the more ideal, spiritual, nor the less humane and practical.

Sobriety in all pleasures is the open path to the purest satisfactions this life can give, as it is the gateway to future beatitude.

You have my thanks for the gift of your book of Fruits and Bread.

Very truly

Yours.

A. Bronson Alcott

Dr. M. L. Holbrook.

[1] Editor of the *Herald of Health*.

LETTER 77–33[1]

[to Georgiana Hemingway Cook, Boston]

Concord October 26th | 1877.

Dear Mrs. Cook

I hope to be in the City next Monday, and hear Mr. Cook's Lecture. My friend Rev Wm. H. Channing is passing a few days with us in Concord, and wishes to hear the Mondays Lecture. I shall venture to bring him with me and trust to Mr. Cook's kindness for his taking a seat with me on the platform. And if Mr. Cook can give him a little time, after the lecture, he will esteem it a favor.

I shall be highly gratified to join Mr. Cook and yourself at the Belleview at. 2. PM, Monday, and hope to hear further concerning your wishes about the proposed "Conversations."

We had an edifying Conversation last evening at Emersons, and should Mr. Channing remain till November, we might anticipate the pleasure of his attendance at your Parlors.

I am expecting much profit from the perusal of Mr. Cooks Book on "Transcendentalism."

If our public are not stirred and illuminated by these Lectures and books of your husbands, we may postpone the descent of the spirit for a little while, at least.

Very truly Yours,

A. Bronson Alcott

Mrs. Cook.

[1] MS. owned by the Duke University Library. A copy, in Alcott's hand, is in the Alcott-Pratt Collection.

LETTER 77–34[1]

[to Georgiana Hemingway Cook, Boston]

Concord November | 2nd. Friday Morning. | [1877]

Dear Mrs. Cook,

I find I must not leave home for our Conversation next Monday evening.

701

But we will cherish the hope of meeting our Company at some time not far distant.

Mrs. Alcott is comfortable just now, but I may not dutifully leave her for a night.

I think I must have left the Independent's notice of Mr. Cook's book,—perhaps dropped it upon putting on my overcoat below.

How complacently some would play omniscience.—that saucy attempt in last week's Literary World—very harmless of course, and Mr. Cook has disposed of him and of his school satisfactorily. Yet his article is an insult to the intelligence of the Temple audiance [sic].

So Tyndall's lecture published in last week's Commonwealth.—has Mr. Cook happened to glance at it? Here are the lines of Coleridge's:—

"Forth from his dark and lonely hiding place,
(Portentous Sight.) the *owlet Atheism*
Sailing on obscure wings athwart the morn,[2]
Drops his blue fringed lids, and holds them close,
And hooting at the glorious Sun in Heaven,
Cries out—*"Where is it?"*—

Very truly
Yours
A. Bronson Alcott.

Mrs. Cook.
    Hotel Belleview.

---

[1] MS. owned by the Duke University Library. A copy, in Alcott's hand, is in the Alcott-Pratt Collection.
[2] Coleridge's line reads, "Sailing on obscene wings athwart the noon" ("Fears in Solitude," l. 83).

LETTER 77–35

[to   ?]

[Concord, November 10, 1877]

I have examined "Johnson's New Universal Cyclopedia;—a scientific and popular Treasury of Useful Knowledge," and think its extra ordinary merits fully justify its title. The authorities given for the several subjects treated in the work fairly warrent [sic] their accuracy. Comprised within four handy volumes ‖ the work ‖ [p. o.] it [p. in] is most convenient for use. As a dictionary of useful knowledge it seems indispensible: no library can be complete without a copy. For families, schools, and for general consultation, there is not, within my knowledge, any adequate substitute.

A. Bronson Alcott.

Concord, Novr. 10th
    1877.

LETTER 77–36[1]

[to May, London, England]

Concord November | 18th 1877.

Dear May,

Do you wonder why your punctual weekly mail has brought not a line lately from your Father? But you will note that the most important news comes in full detail from your faithful sisters. Nor can you be at loss to account for my silence when I tell you that they preferred informing you of family matters themselves, fearing that I might bring you home forthwith by my accounts. But now that I am *assured of your decision not to return at present,* I may write the more freely especially about your mother's condition and *future.* She suffers very little and sleeps by turns to wake for a bright word or smile, and soon relapses into the lethargic state again. It *cannot be long before she sleeps the sleep from which she will not awake to us.* You would not be sure of finding her with us should you sail at once! The dear patient is Patience itself: Every virtue that shone during her active life, now beams the more brightly during her weakness. Not many daughters have been blessed with a mother so unselfish and so noble! I shall hardly enjoy the old house again after her departure.

After many misgivings we ventured to bring her here to Anna's,[2] where she is now comfortable, and cared for by us and kind friends. She bore the ride better than we feared, and is thankful, most grateful, for the change. The house is a picture. Even your fine taste would hardly find occasion for criticism or change, though things are not yet in place fully. Your sisters will tell you fully about furniture, pictures, and the rest. My study is by no means roomy, but where Thoreau has sat and written, a humbler scholar will be content. I have invitations to speak at several places, in Boston and elsewhere, but decline: I must not be absent from home for a single night while your mother survives: nor hardly even for a day. My Table Talk is just advertised fully, and has been favorably noticed by the leading journals and newspapers. I wish to forward a copy to you by Mr. Channing when he returns, and shall give him your address. He has been much liked wherever he has spoken, and should not be permitted to return (from us) to the old Country.—

I am not indifferent, my daughter, to your social (possible) prospects, and trust entirely to your discretion should you be called to a decision so important to yourself, and family.

I read your letters faithfully, and am sure you have been very busy and very happy since you left us: Moreover, that you will have something to show testifying to your industry and talent when you return to us. Next spring will open new scenes and new prospects for us all.

Now a parting salute,

from

Your affectionate

Father.

Miss May Alcott.
London.

[1] A small section of this letter is quoted in Ticknor, *May Alcott,* p. 246.
[2] Mrs. Alcott had been moved (on November 14) to the Thoreau House, which Anna had bought in April.

LETTER 77-37

[to May, London, England]

Concord November | 25. 1877. | (Sunday evening.)

Dear May,

    This letter will prepare you for the next, which will doubtless apprize you of—your dear Mother's decease. For though she is semi-conscious at moments, and in a state of quiet rapture whispering to herself the happiness she enjoys she cannot survive many hours at most, and may have passed from us even before tomorrow mornings mail by which this goes to you. She does not suffer now, and has every attention that love and the tenderest nursing can give. Dr. Cooke has been most faithful, visiting her lately three times daily. And yesterday came Lizzy Wells and Louisa Greele, whom your mother was rejoiced to see beside her sick bed. Lizzy stays with her still, and may perhaps remain till the last sad rites are over.—

    Now don't distress yourself that you are not here at the last. You were advised to stay by all of us, even by your mother, and she inquired yesterday, if your Saturday letter had come. Your last was read to her. And before this reaches you, *mine of last week* has probably reached you. It has been a great comfort to your mothers last days that she passed them so comfortably in Anna's sunny chamber. And we all feel already much at home in our new quarters.

    All will be told you in our next.

    Anna adds her last accounts to mine

Sadly but affectionately,
Your Father.[1]

---

[1] Alcott's letter is followed by a note from Anna telling of Mrs. Alcott's death at 7:30 that evening.

LETTER 77-38

[to Richard Montague, Newton Center, Mass.][1]

Concord November | 29th 1877.

Dear Sir,

    It will give me great pleasure to see you and your friend Mr. Canfield, and if it will suit your convenience I will name Thursday of next week. I shall expect you to dine with me, and give much of the day as you can, for Conversation. Should a later day suit you better please inform me. Possibly I may chance to find you at Mr. Cooks Lecture on Monday.

Very truly
Yours,
A. Bronson Alcott.

---

[1] Addressed in care of G. E. Canfield, Cambridge, Mass.

LETTER 77-39

[to William H. Baldwin, Boston]

Dear Sir,

Concord November | 29 1877.

I can now leave home for an evening, and will gladly meet the Young Men's Christian Union next Thursday evening, unless you have provided another positively to open the Conversation. In that case I should hope to follow on some subsequent evening in your course on *"Practical Ethics"* than which no subject seems more suitable for the study of Young Men.

Very truly
Yours,
A. Bronson Alcott.

LETTER 77-40

[to Ellen A. Chandler]

Dear Miss Chandler,

Concord December | 2nd 1877.

I am not insensible to the sympathetic attentions of friends, and of yours especially—sisterly shall I call them for want of a more fitting epithet? And your kind note of the 29—the anniversary of Louisa's and my birthday,—with your flowerly tribute this morning—thanks for all, and for your kindness at this hour.

But for the fulfilment of her request the funeral on Wednesday would have included a wider circle of attendants—yourself along with other friends and acquaintances.

It was a beautiful day, and the services were touchingly beautiful and becoming. Rev. Mr. Foot of Kings Chapel, (where she worshipped during her girlhood, and where she was married,) read portions of Scripture and of the Burial Service, offered a simple prayer: Then Dr. Bartol spoke his characteristic eulogy, eloquent and fitting, and Mr. Garrison gave reminiscences of his first acquaintance with her and of her saintly brother. Friends from Boston, relatives and others, our friends and neighbors here, Mr and Mrs Emerson with the rest, attended the last rites.

As the dear dust had gone to its resting place on Tuesday afternoon nothing spectral haunted the fancy on the occasion.

And beautiful was the translation on Sunday eve—with smiling countenance whispering the raptures of her ascension, soul-conscious to the last.

Yesterday we rode to the Cemetery and spread flowers on her grave. Green be the spot as fragrant the memory of the Ascended!—

We are all at Annas, and not Alone.

Tenderly Yours
A. Bronson Alcott.

Miss Ellen A. Chandler.

LETTER 77–41

[to May, London, England]

Concord December | 9th 1877.

Dear May.

I may not let tomorrow's mail leave without its taking our sorrow, if not our consolation to you, and my assurances of love for your dutifulness to the dear departed while she was with us to read or hear read your full letters from week to week. Your last addressed to her and reaching us only a mail too late for her to hear read. Your grief will be deep and you will not be yourself at times but lost in remembrance of your dear mother's many virtues and the sense of your loss: These kind words that may not greet you more! But your *Art* may be your *solace* the while, and spare you many a sad reccollection [*sic*].

And then the beautiful close! the happy translation! Nothing could have been more characteristic more lovely! And the friends who honored her memory, the services so appropriate. Had you been with us, you would not have wished them otherwise. Dr. Bartol's eulogy was a noble tribute to her self, and the worth of the family from which she descended. And Mr. Garrison's reminiscences were most touching. It so happened that Mr. and Mrs. Emerson of our Concord friends sat by us, as perhaps Louisa or Anna has told you.

We are finding out the comforts of the new house, and are to add a furnace this week. Life of course runs differently here than it did under the Elms, but we are happily busied in putting things in order, and have our pleasures as well as pains meanwhile. Anna is ‖ now ‖ the *bond* and draws us all affectionately the mother of the family now. And how many of her mothers graces are hers!

I am having invitations to Converse and lecture, and gladly accept them. Next week I expect to open a course at the Belleview in Boston with a select company.

The boys are becoming learned and lovely, and if not for us, please come home to greet them. I do not like you saying England is to be your home.

Mr. Channing I trust will call upon you.

Affectionately
Your Father.

LETTER 77–42

[to May, London, England]

Concord December | 27th 1877.

Dear May.

Your last letter written directly on hearing of the event which we had anticipated for some days, and of which we had hoped to prepare you by our letters, seems to have reached you unexpectedly at last, and you are almost inconsolable on finding that you were not here as a witness of the last scene. Very grateful would your presence have been to us all—and especially to your mother—though she repeatedly insisted upon your not returning upon her account, and we did not write advising it—knowing that it would[1] nothing is wanting but the ‖ absence ‖ presence of the dear One who made the former house a Home for us all. These December days are autumnal, rather than wintry—the sun shines in at our windows lovingly as if to dissipate any sadness of ours.

I am invited to speak and Converse at several places. Last week I met a Choice company at the Belleview, and had a delightful evening—the first of a series of which I will tell you more hereafter. I was also at Westford and gave a lecture on "*N.E. Authors*" The boys are having their holidays Vacation. To day they are out skating.

I gave Miss Plummer a copy of "*Table Talk*" for Mrs Conway. I hope Mr. Channing has called upon you. I gave him your address. Write to me sometimes and let me write oftener.

Dear May,
From Your Father.

¹ Pages 2 and 3 of the letter are missing.

LETTER 77–43¹

[to Georgiana Hemingway Cook, Boston]

Dear Mrs Cook,   Concord December | 27th 1877

I forward herein some additional names of persons for taking places and parts in our Symposeum [*sic*] at our future sittings.

It was my intention to have put the list into your hands when at your rooms last Monday. If you choose to add to these the name of J. G. Whittier (whose present address I have not at hand) I am sure he would esteem his card of invitation a token of our respect, and might favor us with his company sometimes.

Very truly
Yours,
A. Bronson Alcott

Rev. John G. Brooks, Roxbury.
Rev. C. F. Dole, Jamaica Plain.
Rev. E. B. Willson, Salem.
Mr. Edward Horr ⎱
Mr. Albion Small ⎰
   Theological School
     Newton Centre
Rev. Mr. Brown, Brookline, Mass
Mrs A. H. Spaulding
   7 Princeton Street
     East Boston.

¹ MS. owned by the Duke University Library.

PART TWENTY-THREE

1878

LETTER 78–1[1]

[to Georgiana Hemingway Cook, Boston]

Concord January 1st. | 1878.

Dear Mrs Cook,

It will be most agreeable to me to meet our company on Monday evening the 14th after the Holidays are past, and, if the parlors shall not be overcrowded it would please me to have the full list of persons invited on that evening, at least. Some of them may find it inconvenient to attend, having previous engagements. And Mr. Cook and yourself doubtless wish to add to your former list. I judge as many as 60 or 70 may be comfortably seated.

Our topic for the evening will be

"Temperament."

The first evening appears to have been deemed a success and that is our best advertisement for future sittings

I have most of the ‖ twenty ‖ fifty tickets sent to me, and will return them to you when I next visit the City.

Very truly
Yours,
A. Bronson Alcott.

[1] MS. owned by the Duke University Library.

LETTER 78–2

[to J. S. Moulton, Westford, Mass.]

Concord January 8th | 1878

Dear Sir,

Yours of yesterday is at hand. And, if it suits yourself and friends, I will name Sunday January 20th. to be with you. It would please me to speak to your congregation in the forenoon, and meet, as you suggest, such company as may care for it, for a Conversation in the evening.

I shall wish to leave by an early train for Boston on Monday morning. You may expect me by the noon train from Concord.

Yours truly
A. Bronson Alcott.

Rev. Mr. Moulton

LETTER 78–3

[to Porter Cornelius Bliss, New York City]

Concord January | 8th 1878.

Dear Sir

Your Library Table comes fortnightly to me, and I look for some trace of the papers of mine put into your hands with the promise of their publication from yourself. As they have not appeared after so long an interval, I reasonably infer that you have deemed them unsuitable, or, at any rate, have deferred printing them, as promised. As I have other disposition for them, I must again request of you to return them to my address at Concord, Mass, unless you have unexpressed reasons for retaining them longer.[1]

Respectfully,
A. Bronson Alcott

Mr. Porter Bliss

[1] See Letter 77–24.

LETTER 78–4

[to Mr. Winchley, Littleton, Mass.]

Concord, January. | 25 1878.

Dear Sir,

Your Postal Card is at hand.

You may expect me by the late train, which reaches Littleton, (if I am rightly informed), in time for the Lecture. So I shall depend finding a Carriage at the Depot, to take me directly to the Hall, or to Mr. Smiths, if there is time.

Yours truly,
A. Bronson Alcott.

LETTER 78–5

[to Mary N. Adams, Dubuque, Iowa]

Concord January, | 27th 1878.

Dear Mrs Adams,

Our friends far and near have favored us with sympathetic letters, with loving appreciation of our ascended saint, for which we are especially grateful. I believe you were not left uninformed of her feeble bodily condition, and were perhaps not surprised at the event which withdrew her from us visibly. Nothing could have been more lovely than her departure. For the last weeks she was in the happiest frame of mind and wished the dissolution of the mortal coil that held her, though most of the time painlessly, in its bonds. She had been able to sit in her chair, enjoy her book, ride out often, during most of the autumn and took her usual interest in family matters, in her friends. A fortnight before she left us, she was removed to Anna's house on Main Street, where she was hoping, if spared to us, to pass the winter. A sunny Southern chamber was given her, and there she breathed her last. She hoped for sunnier skies than she left behind, but indulged in no scriptures besides her own significant speech. *"The power that brought me here will take the kindest care of me wherever I may be hereafter"* This is the substance of her faith and words. Wishing a private funeral, the remains were laid beside her child's in Sleepy Hollow, attended only by ourselves Anna, Louisa, my grandchildren and myself. This was on Monday. On the following Wednesday. Her friends and kindred assembled at Annas when Rev. Mr. Foote of King's Chapel (where she was accustomed to worship during her youth, and where she was married) read portions of the Church Burial Service, and was followed by Dr Bartol, who pronounced a fitting eulogy upon her many virtues. Mr. Garrison who had known her when living with her brother at Brooklyn, Conn. added his tribute to her memory. Mr. and Mrs. Emerson a few of our neighbors were with us, and the whole service was sweet and memorable

Life, of course, cannot be the same to us hereafter, but her unselfish noble life may shed a lustre of gladness upon the remaining days. Among the worthy women of her time she has a place hardly second to none for independent thinking and useful living.

Perhaps Louisa may sometime compile from her Journals and letters a memorial worthy of her character.

May was advised to remain abroad and is pursuing her art with enthusiasm in London: whither Louisa may join her next autumn. Anna and her boys are now settled in the Thoreau House on Main Street and I am passing the winter with her, and them, Louisa is also with us at present. We have closed the other House for the winter.

I am urged to make a short tour again at the West, and may venture later in the season. Dubuque is far away, and I may not get so far. I have opportunities for Conversing, and preaching here in N. E. have had two gatherings, largely of ministers at Joseph Cook's rooms in Boston, and enjoyed them highly. Dr. and Mrs Dudley, Dr Bartol, Dr Manning, Laird Collier, with many gentlemen, laymen and ladies, were of the company. I wish you had been one of the party. I am remarkably well and ever Yours affectionately

A. Bronson Alcott.

LETTER 78–6

[to Mrs. T. C. Higby, Austin, Texas]

Concord, Mass. | January 29th 1878.

Dear Mrs Higby,

But if you had written the name I knew you by as the least little bit of a tot, I should address you by that rather, instead of the one given as your present signature. Yes, I am that very teacher, and nephew of Dr. Tillotson Bronson, whom you clothed in the three cornered hat and knee breeches, whom every one loved and honored who knew him while living and lamented when he died. I was living and teaching in Cheshire when he died, and attended his funeral. And the school remains a delightful memory still—a model of which in my partiality there has been none such since—not even in its simple beauty and useful traits the more celebrated School in Boston which I taught afterwards. I have my School Journals of the Cheshire teaching, the names of all my Scholars, but I am unable to distinguish yours among these. Why will you not write and give me your family name? so that I can recall you in memory.

You speak of my daughter's Books. It is gratifying to know how far and wide her stories are read and prized by young and old alike, in this country and abroad. She is now a woman grown [and] may write more stories. Her mother was a noble woman of Boston birth, and has but lately left us at the age of 77. I am now 78. and in perfect health and have travelled almost to Texas several times, lecturing and conversing. My family consists of three daughters, the eldest married and has two sons. The youngest is an artist, now in London.

Now write me a full account of yourself and life at the West

> Your old teacher
> affectionately,
> A. Bronson Alcott

LETTER 78–7

[to Sarah Denman, Quincy, Ill.]

> Concord January | 29th 1878.

Dear Mrs Denman,

I have to thank yourself or some of my friends in your city, for the printed account of your Ladies Association, most fitly entitled, Friends in Counsel." I know of no Association of Ladies whose aims and Performance offer a finer model for imitation than yours, and retain pleasant recollections of my interviews with them, together and severally, during my visits in Quincy. How much the ladies owe to your assistance and counsels they are doubtless aware. And for your kind hospitalities when visiting your city, I am also deeply indebted.

I think I forwarded to your address, a newspaper containing a brief notice of Mrs Alcotts decease. You had the happiness of meeting her I believe more than once at our House in Concord, and she remembered your visit, and often spoke of it with pleasure.

And were we not promised another from you with our mutual friend Dr. Jones? Most gladly should we welcome you and him, now, even though the dear departed hostess were no longer here to salute you, and make glad the hospitalities of your stay.

Will you not write a line, my friend, informing us of your present welfare and that of our friends in Quincy.

> Cordially yours
> A. Bronson Alcott.

LETTER 78–8[1]

[to Eliza Seaman Leggett, Detroit]

Concord January | 29 1878

Dear Mrs. Leggett.

Our friends far and near have favored us with sympathetic letters full of loving appreciation of our ascended saint, and yours was specially acceptable. You were of those of whom she spoke with kind remembrance, and whom she would have gladly greeted at our threshold. She valued your letters, and remembered the hospitalities shown to her traveller at the fireside of friends at the Mill.[2] Mr. Ives, I think, was the only one of your family whom she had the pleasure of meeting (and entertaining at her home in Concord), and the only artist whom she permitted to take her picture.

I believe you were not left uninformed of her feeble bodily condition during the summer, and so were not unprepared to hear of the event which withdrew her from us visibly. She had been in a happy frame of mind, was able to sit in her chair, enjoy her book, ride out often, and took her usual interest in family affairs and her friends. A fortnight before she left us she was removed to Anna's house on Main Street in the village where she was hoping to pass the winter (if she should survive so long.) A sunny chamber was given her, and there she breathed her last. She hoped for sunnier skies even than she left behind, but indulged in no vague Scriptures merely trusting the good Power who brought her here would provide kindly for her wherever she might be hereafter. As she wished a private burial, the remains were laid beside her child's in Sleepy Hollow, followed only by ourselves—Anna, Louisa, her grandsons, and myself. On the following Wednesday, the kindred and friends assembled at Anna's when Rev. Mr. Foote of King's Chapel Boston (where she worshipped during her youth and where she was married) read portions of the Burial Service, and was followed by Dr. Bartol who spoke of her many virtues and unselfish life. Mr. and Mrs. Emerson, with a few of our neighbors were with us, and her old friend Mr. Garrison, added his tribute to her memory. Among the worthy women of her time she had a place hardly second to none for independent thinking useful living. I with Louisa may compile a memorial of her from her ample Journals and letters.

May was advised to remain abroad and is now in London pursuing her art with enthusiasm and success. Louisa may join her there in the coming Autumn. Anna and her boys are settled in the Thoreau house in the Village, and I am passing the winter there. Our other house is closed for the winter.

I am urged to make a short tour again at the West (and may venture later in the season, perhaps during March & April. I have appointments for conversing, preaching, and lecturing near home at present). Joseph Cook's Monday Lectures are stirring Boston just now Unitarian, Orthodox, Free Religionist, alike, and to good results I judge. I have met a select company at his Rooms in Boston, ministers, laymen, and ladies, and enjoyed the interview highly. Mr. Emerson reads a paper for Old South tomorrow on "*The Future of America*". Please remember me kindly to my friends in Detroit generally, and to your family especially.

Your friend.
A. Bronson Alcott

[1] From a typescript from a photostat in the Burton Historical Collection, Detroit Public Library.

[2] A note in the typescript: "Probably refers to the grist mill built on their neighbor's, Mr. William Cullen Bryant's, estate."

LETTER 78–9[1]

[to Joshua Young, Groton, Mass.]

Concord February | 6th 1878.

Dear Sir.

Your note is at hand. It will give me pleasure to comply with your request, and but for an engagement with Mr. Winchley to speak at Littleton on Sunday the 17th I could be with you then.

I have no engagement for Sunday next the 10th, nor for Sunday the 24th, and, if you wished could be with you on either of those days.

Thanking you for the privilege of meeting yourself and people

I am
Very truly Yours
A. Bronson Alcott.

[1] MS. owned by the Abernethy Library, Middlebury College. A copy, in Alcott's hand, is in the Alcott-Pratt Collection.

LETTER 78–10

[to Mr. and Mrs. A. J. Johnson, New York City]

Concord February | 16th 1878.

Mr. and Miss Alcott return their thanks to Mr and Mrs Johnson for their courtious [sic] invitation to the complimentary reception to be given by them to the editors and contributors of Johnsons Universal Cyclopedia on Wednesday evening February 20th. It would give them a rare pleasure to be present on an occasion which must gather together so many distinguished Scholars to celebrate one of the most important events in our literary history—the completion of an enterprise that ‖ institutes ‖ provides a Fireside Faculty for the diffusion of useful knowledge in every household, in every institution of learning in the Republic. Such a work confers imperishable honors alike upon its projector and its editors and contributors.

I may add that our ‖ little ‖ suburban town, already known for its love of liberty, civil and intellectual, has already added its many copies to its || families firesides and || Public Library and many firesides

Respectfully
A. Bronson Alcott

Mr. and Mrs A. J. Johnson
9 East 64th. St. New York.

LETTER 78–11

[to Hiram K. Jones, Jacksonville, Ill.]

Concord February | 22nd 1878.

Dear Friend,

I have lately received a letter from Mrs. Denman, in which she intimates that I may have the pleasure of seeing her in Concord. She also expresses the hope that yourself with other friends of hers and yours may accompany her. I need not assure you that myself and friends here in Concord will be most happy to greet you. Moreover, if my memory serves me faithfully we were promised a visit from you and them a year ago, or more. Now give your next vacation from your official duties, and recreate with us awhile here in New-England. Mr. Emerson is likely to be disengaged, and will take it amiss if you fail to see him, and we have attractions for you out of Concord. Though our Plato Clubs may be pale copies of yours, and our *Friends* less abler *Counsellers* [sic], than Mrs Denmans. Yet to our credit I may say, that the Lowell Plato Club, which I attended on Monday evening last, showed itself equal to the interpretation of the text of Sophocles and interesting conversation followed the reading.

I am finding unexpected access to parlors and pulpits in my neighborhood and enjoy the opportunities. Whether I shall extend my route out of New England later in the season remains undetermined. If assured of your visiting us in the summer, I should hardly think of it.

I remember your circle of Platonists with much satisfaction. And shall await your reply to my request, with no little solicitude.

Very cordially
Yours,
A. Bronson Alcott

Dr. H. K. Jones.

LETTER 78–12[1]

[to   ?   ]

Concord February | 22nd 1878

Dear Sir,

I am unable to enclose the autograph of William Ellery Channing, but forward herein those of Thoreau, and of Miss Alcott.

Respectfully,
A. Bronson Alcott.

[1] MS. owned by the Wellesley College Library.

LETTER 78–13

[to William S. Kennedy, Meadville, Pa.]

Concord March 4th | 1878.

Dear Sir.

The humanity of your views, touches me tenderly, and prompts the desire for fuller acquaintance than is possible by letters alone. Where so much is to be said upon a subject so vital as your note opens, one hesitates upon venturing a word even, when personal interviews are possible.

So, I think you must follow your impulse and visit us with a wide allowance of time for discussing this whole matter of the humane treatment of animals, the proper diet of mankind, with the subtle questions which the subject suggests.

Along with other reforms now in the air, this of a chaste human diet ranks most essential, and you may be its chosen advocate and Messias! Who knows?—

At any rate, I shall wish to know your views and aims better than it will be easy to learn them by letter.

I am almost, if not altogether, alone alike in theory and practice as regards the true diet for our race, and shall rejoice in any Sympathy of views which I may chance find, even in a single solitary contemporary.

Your questions are too many and too important, for me to attempt discussing in a single letter. And but for many engagements, your note would have been earlier acknowledged.

Let me hear from you farther and when you will visit Concord.

Very truly
Yours,
A. Bronson Alcott

Mr. Wm. S. Kennedy
Meadville, Pa.

LETTER 78–14

[to   ?   , Mt. Pleasant, Iowa]

Concord March | 7th 1878.

Dear Sir,

I am happy in contributing to the entertainment of your Conversational Club, the verses which you ask me to forward. They were written by the Revd. Wm. J. Fox an English Liberal Clergyman, reformer, and at one time, an influential member of Parliament. When in England I had the honor of dining at his house, and of visiting there, his friend Miss Flower Adams, author of the beautiful verses, now so often sung in our Churches.

"Nearer my God, to thee, &c.

Both poems first appeared in a selection made by Mr. Fox, for his Congregation. M. D. Conway now speaks to this Society.

I am pleased to learn that your Conversational Club still meets, and I trust prospers. My respects to its members.

Very truly
Yours,
A. Bronson Alcott.

"Make us a God," said man:
  Power first the voice obeyed.
  And soon a monstrous form
  The worshippers dismayed.
Uncouth and huge, by nations rude adored
With savage rites and sacrifice abhorred.

"Make us a God" said man.
  Art next the voice obeyed
  Lovely, serene, and grand
  Uprose the Athenean maid;
The perfect statue, Greece, with wreathed brows
Adores in festal rites and lyric vows.

"Make us a God," said man.
  Religion followed art,
  And answered: Look within,
  Find God in thine own heart,
His noblest image there and holiest shone
Silent revere—*and be thy self divine.*"

P.S.   Miss or Mrs. Lucy E. White of Mt. Pleasant also asks me to give the author's name. As I copy herein for your Club, I infer she will excuse me for not enclosing it to her address.   22nd 1878.

A.B.A.

LETTER 78–15

[to Miss Locke]

Concord March | 18th 1878.

Dear Miss Locke,

I shall gladly speak twice on Sunday if you wish, and will do so either on Sunday 24. or 30th as may be most convenient to your people. Will not your minister write and inform me of his preference. I shall wish him to take part in the Services, and hope to visit your mother also.

Very truly Yours,
A. Bronson Alcott

LETTER 78–16

[to A. J. Rich, Brookfield, Mass.]

Concord March | 22nd 1878.

Dear Sir,

Unless I hear from you meanwhile, wishing to withdraw your invitation to pass Sunday April 14th with you, I will consider myself engaged for that time.

Yet on condition that you take some part in the services both morning, and evening, if you have an evening meeting.

I like to read a Chapter one or more of the Hymns, and discourse as I may be prompted at the time.

On these conditions I shall be glad to serve you, and better than this, make your acquaintance. I have lately had several opportunities to speak on Sundays, and enjoy the *pulpiteering* very much.[1]

Rev. A. J. Rich.

[1] The complimentary close and signature have been cut out.

LETTER 78–17

[to Julius H. Ward, Roxbury, Mass.]

Concord March | 24th 1878.

Dear Sir,

I must own that your notice of the *Symposia* gave me pleasure, flattering as it is to my self. And your criticism of Phillips and Emerson is most satisfactory.

We ancients, as afortime [*sic*], look to those younger, (and possibly more hopeful of the future, as interested in the past), for discriminating appreciation.

Not being certain of finding you to morrow in the city, to speak my pleasure in yourself and Sunday enterprize, I write this brief note of acknowledgement.— adding that I look forwards with the hope that you may sometime find it pleasant to visit us in Concord.

Very cordially
Yours,[1]

Revd. Julius H. Ward.

[1] The signature has been cut out.

LETTER 78–18

[to May, London, England]

Concord April | 2nd 1878.

Yes, dear May, you have my benediction and my blessing.[1] And may you and yours, whom I shall hope to greet by your side when you please to offer him as yours to us, find the hopeful future all, and even more richly crowned with happiness than yourselves dare anticipate. Your pictures of delight in your friend, like all fair maidens at such sweet surprizes,—Your sketch of your beloved, I have read with pleasure and satisfaction. And we of this household all rejoice in your prospects—a blending of matrimony and Art, as you say.

Give my cordial regards to your Ernest, and my wish to have from him a word in his own hand writing by which I may come nearer to him than by yours even.

He has won a prize—(you may blush at the writing) which I doubt not he knows how to Treasure and keep. The only sadness intermingling with my joy, is that in becoming his, she seems to be less my own!—

Thus much, my dear May, at this fair moment, and much more hereafter from

Your affectionate
Father.

Miss May Alcott
    London.

---

[1] May had written from London on March 11, telling of her engagement to Ernest Nieriker. She wrote again from Havre, March 24, informing her family of her marriage two days earlier.

LETTER 78–19

[to James Eddy, Providence, R.I.]

Concord April | 5th. 1878.

Dear Friend,

Yours is just at hand. I shall gladly speak in your Chapel on Sunday next, and you may expect me by some of the Afternoon trains on Saturday.

A game at Bowles [sic] will be very acceptable in the evening, as you suggest, when we will measure our relative wits, whether, fed by beeves or otherwise.[1]

Very truly
Yours,
A. Bronson Alcott

James Eddy Esqr.

---

[1] Eddy, in his letter, had asked Alcott to bowl on Saturday evening, "if a vegetarian diet has left any strength in you."

LETTER 78–20

[to Hiram K. Jones, Jacksonville, Ill.]

Concord April | 5th. 1878.

Dear Friend,

I have made some inquiries concerning accommodations for friends, both at our Middlesex Hotel, and also at Private houses, and find such as I think would be found worthy of your acceptance.

My own house has been closed since last November, and I have passed the time since with my daughter in the Village. Louisa is also with me. I regret exceedingly that it is so, since it would have given me great pleasure to return in some measure the kind hospitalities of yourself and other friends who may honor us with their presence in our town. And how gladly would our absent Hostess have welcomed you inside of the now deserted threshold!—

I please myself with the hope that nothing adverse to your visit may happen meanwhile. And we shall hope to detain you long. New-England has some features novel to yourself, and we wish to prove also what the prairies of the West can produce

To Mrs Denman particularly, and friends in Quincy, as in Jacksonville, please convey my kind regards.

Cordially Yours,
A. Bronson Alcott.

Dr. Henry K. Jones.

LETTER 78–21

[to Daniel Ricketson, New Bedford, Mass.]

Concord April | 24th 1878.

Dear Friend,

On returning from Greenwood where I passed last Sunday, I find your most acceptable epistle, and wish I may return any fitting response for your kind sympathy, and appreciation of the departed.

Life can never be the same after a companion for half of one's existence here, has gone before him to felicities untold. Wordsworth's tribute might have all been addressed to my dear ascended partner,—I doubt not less to yours, of whom I have pleasant memories. The more incentives now, my friend, for work worthy of their virtues!

Fortunately I am blessed with perfect health, I might add—youthfulness of spirit—and will not disdain to round off my century, God and good angels willing it. 'Tis a fortunate time to live in and work nobly.

Since last November, I have been living with my daughters in the Thoreau House on Main Street. Sometime I hope to return to my old Home under the Elms. All of us are in good health, save Louisa who is resting from her labors a little. May has found a friend abroad, and is now happy with him at Havre. We have good accounts from the happy pair.

Yes! Thoreau's fame is on the ascendant. A braver person has hardly trodden our Globe in our day.

Channing I never meet now, seldom Hosmer.

Mr. Emerson is less abroad than formerly and pleads his old age when I meet him.

I need not add that we should like to see you again in Concord. To the Doctor and lady please give my kind remembrance.

Very truly
Yours,
A. Bronson Alcott

Mr. Daniel Ricketson.

LETTER 78–22

[to A. H. Dooley, Terre Haute, Ind.]

Concord April 28th | 1878.

Dear Sir,

You task me with questions far beyond the limits of my sheet to record, or my prescience to answer. And I may best refer you to Taylor's translation of Plotinus, for light, if the New-Testament, and your own Heart, needs assurance. I can hardly add any thing of importance to what I have implied in the last Chapters of my *Tablets* and *Table Talk*.

So long as the soul sins, it must *suffer*. And how many deaths and births it may undergo when disembodied from *this* fleshly coil, may be left to conjecture.

Yes, Mr Cook needs rest and has gone West to get it, after a month or more of lecturing in those parts. He is about the most significant phenomenon of our time—the herald of a better! His Books will be widely read and helpful to persons of religious persuasions. And he will improve upon himself as he thinks still more deeply.

You appreciate Thoreau, and with all his friends rejoice in his rising fame. He is one of the Immortals and cannot perish from human remembrance A young desciple of his named Walton Ricketson of New Bedford has moulded a bust of him. But this I have not seen. If it is worthy of him, it will find its place with other of his kind in our Town Library. Emerson and Hawthorne are already there,—Emerson, both in picture and in plaster.

We are expecting Dr. Henry Jones and friends of the Plato Clubs of Jacksonville and of Quincy, Ill. to visit us this summer. And some day may we not hope to see you here also.

Very truly
Yours,
A. Bronson Alcott.

Mr. A. H. Dooley.

LETTER 78–23

[to Georgiana Davis, Boston]

Concord May 3rd | 1878.

Dear Miss Davis,

I have always been ready to speak a word for Personal Purity whenever an opportunity has offered, and shall gladly avail myself of your invitation to speak at your Annual meeting[1] in Boston May 30th.

I have seldom found it convenient to attend the meetings of the Association from time to time, as I should gladly have done.

Truly Yours.

A. Bronson Alcott

P.S./I wish you may secure a word from Dr Bartol at your anual meeting.—

[1] Of the Moral Education Association.

LETTER 78–24

[to Ellen A. Chandler, Boston]

Concord May 6th | 1878.

Dear Miss Chandler,

I remember that I promised to inform you of May's address, when we should be apprised duly from herself as to her residence. By her last letter she informs us that she may be unsettled for a little while, and so we await to hear from her whence to direct. At the close of her last, she had left Havre and gone to Paris, where, or in its neighborhood, she should probably be, for the present. As you expressed a wish to write, (and she would be glad to hear from you I am sure,) we will forward your letter, if you will commit it to our keeping, in our next parcel.

I had hopes that our moving and spring fixings had all been done before this, and still hope our apple blossoms will not have faded, before you come to partake of their fragrance, and bring your own sunshine with you.

So I wait in patience for the pleasant word "Come" to be given by those who rule, and whose word may second my wishes.

Affectionately
Yours,
A. Bronson Alcott.

LETTER 78–25[1]

[to William T. Harris, St. Louis]

Concord May 6th 1878.

Dear Friend

You have been too deeply tasked lately to entertain correspondents at length, and so I have spared your feelings of obligation meanwhile. A long while it must be now since we have interchanged monosyllables even. And I merely forward a brief recognition now—adding my fears that you are overtasking yourself and defrauding your future of what it claims of you. I read on the Circular of the Social Science Association your name as one of the speakers at its coming meeting in Cincinnati. If not yet, I wish you may visit us during the summer, and if you can while Dr. Jones, Mrs Baldwin and Mrs. Denman are purposing to be with us in Concord. Your last visits have been so tantalizing by their hurry and preoccupancy that they gave me a shortlived pleasure, and I almost wished you had spared my disappointment A breath of leisure becomes the shallowest thinker, and even in our tasked Time, one may not cease to dream of finding a contemporary with a second to spare for high discourse. Am I to be the only one favored with an excuse of leisure?

Yet I must add I have been drawn abroad during the late season, and into pulpits, on platforms, of conflicting sects, and differing Schools of thought. Perhaps the most significant service that I have been permitted to render is ‖ my ‖ to the symposium of many minds at Mr. Cook's Rooms in Boston, of which you may have read newspaper reports from time to time.

Last evening, Emerson's Essay just published in the North American was read at our Fortnightly Club. His readers have his religious creed fully outwritten herein.

We are all well. I find myself apt for service. May writes from Paris of her happiness.

Very truly Yours
A. Bronson Alcott

Wm. T. Harris

¹ From a copy, in Alcott's hand, in the Alcott-Pratt Collection. The original is in the Alcott-Harris Collection in the Concord Free Public Library (see Appendix B).

LETTER 78–26

[to Mary N. Adams, Dubuque, Iowa]

Concord May 6th | 1878.

Dear Mrs. Adams,

I mail to your address a report of my last Conversation in Boston on Concord Authors. You will find nothing of importance in these notes, but they may show how persons of widely different views may meet for their hour, and leave with hospitable sentiments toward one another personally. I may add that I have found much satisfaction in these interviews, and think the five have been about the most significant service rendered by me lately to the advancement of free thought and good fellowship.

I have moreover been favored with frequent opportunities to speak in pulpits and on platforms during the season, and find a hearty response from religionists of all denominations. This is to me a happier fortune than were I favored with the acceptance of only one or two of the sects only. The *Good News* is for all of every name under Heaven.

Our Quincy and Jacksonville friends think of visiting us in July. Dr. and Mrs. Jones, Mr and Mrs Baldwin, Mrs Denman, and we hope Mr and Mrs

Emery may also come East, while *they* are here. And if you could join us, too, our measure would be full of satisfaction. I am with Anna in the village. My house is closed for the present, and so I lose the pleasure of welcoming my friends within doors, now that my departed wife no more presides there

You may have been advised of May's marriage to a Swiss gentleman named *Niericker* [*sic*]. They met in London, are now in Paris, and she writes happily of herself and of him. Louisa is now with us and free from literary tasks. Last evening Emerson's Essay on the Sovereignty of Ethics was read before our Fortnightly Club. Here we have his religious creed at last.

To all of your family and friends in Dubuque give my kind regards.

Your true friend,

A. Bronson Alcott.

LETTER 78-27

[to Sarah Denman, Quincy, Ill.]

Concord May 6th | 1878

Dear Mrs. Denman.

In your letter of last February, you speak of spending the summer in the East, and add: "I may call on you some day."

I beg it may be a long call and we will try to make it pleasant for you, and for your friends who may accompany you. Dr. Jones has since written that yourself Mr and Mrs Baldwin, Mrs Jones and myself at least think we shall spend a time at Concord say from the middle of July, and inquires about our public accommodations &c.

I have written him that these may be had both at Public and in Private Houses in our village. As I am now with my daughter in the village and my house is closed, I am to lose the pleasure of welcoming you within those once hospitable doors, as when my dear wife presided there. But we shall find pleasant quarters for you, and them, and hope you will lay your plans for a long summers' stay with us. We can sally forth from this centre, at our leisure, and here are pleasant wood paths and rural drives, and our people will wish to open their drawing rooms for our Guests. So let us hope that this proposed visit will not be let slip for another season.

You have doubtless heard of my daughter May's marriage to a Swiss Gentleman E‖ ugene ‖rnest Nieriker. She writes happily and is now passing the time with her new friend in Paris. Miss Louisa is with us, and is now free from literary tasks.

I enclose a report of my late Conversation in Boston upon Concord Authors. With kind regards to friends in Quincy. I am, dear Mrs Denman,

Truly Yours,

A. Bronson Alcott.

1878

LETTER 78–28

[to Julius H. Ward, Roxbury, Mass.]

Concord May 11th | 1878.

Dear Sir,
    Accept my thanks for your contribution to the New York Tribune. It is mainly satisfactory and gives the spirit of the last Symposeum [sic], in which you have taken so much interest. When you come to Concord we will dwell the more fully upon the significance of those interviews. And this shall be on any day of next week as you say in your note "in about a fortnight. I know of no thing now to take me away from home, but lest I should lose your visit, will you be kind enough to advise me of the day when you will come. Just now our appleblossoms are fragrant, and it seems the season for literature and friendship, let me add, for divinity and Emerson.

Very truly
Yours,
A. Bronson Alcott.

Rev. Julius H. Ward

LETTER 78–29

[to Ellen A. Chandler, Boston]

Concord June 3rd. 1878.

Dear Miss Chandler,
    Louisa and myself are purposing to attend the Commencement Exercises of the Boston University, at the Fremont Temple on Wednesday next, at 2. P.M. Having a spare ticket, I wish you might find it pleasant to accompany us, and if you will, I will call for you at your School at half past 1. and conduct you to The Temple.
    Hoping you can accompany us, I am

Most cordially
yours,
A. Bronson Alcott.

LETTER 78–30

[to Charles D. B. Mills, Syracuse]

Concord June 7th 1878

Dear Friend.
    I was gratified by your remembrance of me and mine, and particularly by the possession of the Photograph which is certainly a fairer likeness than the one

724

for which it is now substituted in my Album of distinguished friends. I thank you for it.

And when your friend, Rev. Mr. Stuart of Battle Creek presents himself, I shall be glad to entertain him both on his own and on your account. I have the most agreeable recollections of Battle Creek, where I have more than once been honored by the hospitable acceptance from its liberal minded citizens.

Let me add that I have had many opportunities lately for meeting favorably, both in parlors and pulpits, good people here in New England, and am at present in the best of health and hope.

I hear with much satisfaction of your wide acceptance at the West.

It is the seed time of thought and of pious faith, and I am happy to know that the sowers are in the field near and afar.

My daughter Mrs. Pratt has lately purchased the Thoreau House on Main street in the Village, where with Louisa and my grandsons, I have passed the time, since my dear wife passed into the Unseen.

Louisa is now resting a little from her literary labors, and my grandsons are fast passing into youth and manhood—very hopefully.

With kind remembrances to Mrs Mills.

> I am; very truly
> Yours,
> A. Bronson Alcott.

Cha's D. B. Mills.
Syracuse

LETTER 78-31

[to   ?   ]

[Concord, June 7, 1878]

I have given to Johnson's Universal Cyclopedia a general inspection, and find the contents very satisfactory. Much information is brought within convenient space for consultation, and for families and Schools I know of no compendium of knowledge so accessible. Since the work has come into my possession I find my grandsons now pursuing their studies at school almost daily consulting its pages. And many of the articles are upon subjects which have not heretofore found adequate treatment in works of this kind.

I may add that the canvasser for our town, Mr Reed, has done us a good service by distributing near forty copies of the work to subscribers here.[1]
Concord June
7. 1878.

---

[1] The complimentary close and signature have been cut out.

LETTER 78–32[1]

[to May, Meudon, France]

Concord June 8th 1878.

Dear May

For so I love to address you and this with no disparagement to your more euphonous *Madame!*

I write seldomer than if I had not the free perusal of your weekly epistles to your sisters. And these are so full of your happy experiences that I almost fear to intrude by a word of mine even. But now I have to forward along with my note something that may show my regard for yourself, as for the Art which was your earliest spouse, nor yet wholly forsaken in the newly found. And your husband may find in these sketches of your Concord Home and its haunts a more vivid picture than even you could frame in words. It was but yesterday that this number of *"the Art-Journal"* came to hand. I believe the sketch was taken since you left us. Nor was I at home at the time. And the description was written by Mr. Towle from such accounts as he could find of us: he never saw either of our Houses, Emersons or ours. It is picturesque, but you might have drawn a better one. Earnest [*sic*] and you may find the sketches good to show to your friends. This copy was given me by the publishers. And the single numbers are sold for 75 cents. So I shall have one for ourselves, and I have thought of nothing better to send you as a token of my love and remembrance.

As your sisters give their version of things, I will add a word of mine to theirs.

You must know then that I am kindly cared for at Anna's, and shall not be separated from her. And though life cannot even with her, ‖ cannot ‖ be what it was to me with your dear mother, much of happiness remains, and I trust years of activity for me still. I have many opportunities for meeting people and have had a pleasant winter and spring: the summer has also its promises of activity and enjoyment. Moreover Louisa and I have set about compiling from your mothers Diaries and Letters a Memoir of her Life, which Niles wishes to publish as soon as it is ready for the press. Your mother wrote much during some of the most eventful years of her life, and the Memoir may make a most edifying and instructive book. Sanborn will gladly assist us in its preparation.

Louisa is improving daily, and for your sake, dear May, I wish she may find you in your lovely nest, before the cold weather comes much as we shall be saddened by the change.

And let me add that I am sad at the thought of your being so far from us, and that I may not see you again on this side the seas or that. But then your happiness consoles me and I try to be resigned to the separation. How gladly should I greet you and your Ernest dear May. Assure him of my regards and my pride in so worthy a son.

Ever Your Father.

P.S.   I enclose a report for Ernest.

---

[1] The letter is quoted in part in Ticknor, *May Alcott*, p. 275.

[Letter to the editor of the *Herald*, Boston; from Concord, June 11? 1878.]

LETTER 78–33

[to Herbert H. Drake, Cambridge, Mass.]

Concord June 14th | 1878

Dear Sir

I have no engagement at this date for next Wednesday—the 19—and shall be happy to see yourself and friends in Concord[1]

Mr. Herbert H. Drake
   Divinity Hall.

[1] The complimentary close and signature have been cut out.

LETTER 78–34

[to George Zabriskie Gray,[1] Cambridge, Mass.]

Concord June 14th | 1878.

Rev. and dear Sir.

I have to thank you for the beautiful book which I hope to find leisure to peruse soon; and will just add now many pleasant memories of the day yourself and Dr. Zabriskie[2] passed with us.[3]

Dean G[ray]

[1] Dean of the Protestant Episcopal Theological School of Massachusetts.
[2] Gray's uncle.
[3] The complimentary close and signature have been cut out.

LETTER 78–35

[to Julius H. Ward, Roxbury, Mass.]

Concord June 14th | 1878.

Dear Sir,

Your friendly note has just come to hand, and on Tuesday came the Sunday Herald containing your very acceptable account of your visit here. We were well pleased with its fine tone and discretion, and thought it far the best yet given by the many pens set astir about our little village and its notabilities. To tell the whole frankly, I wrote at once to the editor of the Herald, enclosing my dollar, (having no scrip now) desiring him to send me a dozen copies, wishing to send them to friends at the West. They have not reached me yet. I shall hope to obtain some yet. I read your article on the World's University for women, surprised that I had known nothing of it before. I think the women are learning to help themselves without waiting for us to build piles of costly stones for their instruction.

You are very kind in your intentions to promote a visit to your home, and a meeting of your friends.

Cordially Yours.
A. Bronson Alcott.

Rev. Julius H. Ward.

LETTER 78–36

[to May, Meudon, France]

Concord June 30th 1878. | Sunday.

My dear May,

Your last letter mailed June 15th. (and put into my hand by loving Anna, before our breakfast,) affects me with joy, even to tears, at the details it gives of your happiness, of your delight especially in the visit of your mother and brother. Nothing could be more beautiful and characteristic. And all the talk at our breakfast Table was about you and your conquests. Anna, in her glee, even proposed that we should all take the next Steamer and come into being partakers of your satisfactions, so full, so fortunate, so romantic, and becoming our adventurer. We all took new accessions of pride along with our pleasure at the stroke of fair fortune which had befallen her, happier even than she had even dared to picture to herself.

Well: she deserves it all, and the long enjoyment of it. Tell Ernest his papa on this side of the Atlantic, was once too made supremely happy by the gift of hand and heart of the Lady whose daughter he now names *his beloved,* and clasps to his breast so affectionately. Yes, dear May, we are all delighted by your letter and the events which you describe so charmingly. I am not an indifferent reader, nor the worse correspondent if I write seldomer than your sisters. Yourself and Ernest are in my thoughts and prayers for your united happiness and prosperity.

It has been in my thought for some time to send Ernest copies of my books, and I have been seeking at the shops a copy of my Tablets to complete the set. I wish him to have the three volumes:

1/ *"Tablets"*
2/ *"Concord Days,"* and
3/ *"Table Talk."*

and also—   *"Record of my School."*

I have just recovered a copy of the Tablets, but it needs *new covers,* and shall forward the books when the set is ready. I need not add that I shall [be] pleased in his acceptance of them from the father of the author of *"Little Women"* and especially of one of them whom he calls by a very *tender name.* It will add to his satisfaction to learn that his son finds entertainment in their perusal. These, with the dozen volumes of that popular author, (and sister) may have place in some choice corner of your apartment, dear May. And by this time, I trust you have received "the *'Art-Journal'*" containing views of *"The Orchard* and *Emersons."*[1] Ernest will be pleased to see *The Homestead* of his Lady in old Concord.

I have to add that I am in perfect health and spirits, and delighted with the contents of every successive letter the mail brings us from Meudon and its lovers.

To both, as one,

A fathers' blessing,

A. Bronson Alcott.

¹ See Letter 78–32, par. 2.

LETTER 78–37

[to Sarah Denman, Quincy, Ill.]

Concord July 3rd 1878.

Dear Mrs. Denman

Louisa has made suitable enquiries about rooms in the Village, and finds near us at Mr. Geers on Main Street, a fine room looking out upon the river which with board can be had for $12.50 a week, or $25. for two. This seems the most desirable quarters of any in the village. The house is roomy, and Mr. Geer is a merchant going daily to the city

On the same street, and near Mr. Geers, is Mrs Jackson sister in law of Mrs Emerson who has a comfortable house and offers a chamber and board for two at $8. each a week. Either are good places. Mr and Mrs Emery passed a day here lately at the Hotel but did not commend it.

As to the road: Whether you leave by New Haven or Waterbury if you reach Springfield by 1. oclock, you can reach Concord about 6. PM. leaving the main Albany road at Worcester and connecting with the [word] at Ayer Junction.

Truly Yours,

A Bronson Alcott

Mrs. Sarah Denman

LETTER 78–38

[to May, Meudon, France]

Concord July 6th 1878

Dear May,

Mr. Bradford kindly calls to say, (and this, too, while I am reading your charming accounts of the visits of your new Kindred) that a niece or cousin of his sails this morning for Paris and will take a parcel to you—

I need not add how gladly I seize the chance to congratulate you on this auspicious year in which you were born into a new life of Love and Promise. Nor need I now consult my family Register for other dates of nativity. Love renders its votaries youthful and immortal.

And with this, your dear *Mother* presents you and yours with her picture— most happy in your happ[iness.] Doubt it not, as you doubt not the love that still lives in your remembrance of her.

As I have not seen this impression I cannot speak of its truthfulness.

But of your husbands picture, I can speak: It comes out beautifully under the glass. And certainly you have added new graces by your foreign alliance to the House of Alcott—so we all pronounce.

I am happy to learn—that your new friends all love and take pride in you and hope I may one day make the acquaintance of the House of Neirecker [*sic*], jointly and severally.

To Ernest and Yourself,
My love and blessing
Your Father.

Wednesday morning.

LETTER 78–39[1]

[to William T. Harris, St. Louis]

Concord July 25th 1878

Dear Friend,

Our friends from Jacksonville and Quincy[2] have passed a fortnight with us and taken our village by the wind of the spirit blowing as it listed. Dr Jones has surprized and illuminated us all. Almost every evening and every day opportunities have been extemporized for him and his party to meet our people socially and Platonically at my house, Emerson's, Sanborns Judge Hoars, and we should gladly prolong their stay with us. Concord has had another taste of the West, and finds it good and wholesome.

They leave to morrow, and I go with them as far as Birmingham, Conn. where Mrs. Denman has a sister residing—to be gone a fortnight or longer. I write hoping this will reach you in time to prevent my missing you on your Vacation tour North. I am anticipating a good visit with abundant leisure with you when you come to our town.

I am staying with Anna in the Thoreau House (now hers) where you shall be entertained as long as you can stay in Concord. Louisa is with us. Emerson is at home; and we shall have all the stronger appetites for you when you come to us again.

I wish you would advize me a little before your day of arrival that I may be sure to be at home. And if your engagements make it necessary for your coming soon, I will shorten my stay in Connecticut, or may [word] I meet you there on your way here?

Your friend,
A. Bronson Alcott

Wm. T. Harris.

---

[1] From a copy, in Alcott's hand, in the Alcott-Pratt Collection. The original is in the Alcott-Harris Collection in the Concord Free Public Library (see Appendix B).

[2] "Hiram K. Jones, accompanied by his wife, Mr. and Mrs. Elizur Wolcott, Mr. and Mrs. Mathew B. Denman (of Quincy), and two or three other 'Westerners.'" (Pochmann, *New England Transcendentalism and St. Louis Hegelianism*, p. 80.)

LETTER 78-40

[to Charles E. Upson, Wolcott, Conn.]

Concord August. | 12th 1878.

Dear Sir,

I regret exceedingly that I was informed too late to avail myself of the pleasure of speaking in Wolcott on the Sunday named in your note.[1] And am sorry if any misapprehension or disappointment followed. It has been a great pleasure hitherto, and esteemed a privilege by me, when visiting my birth-place to meet my towns folk in this public manner. And I wished, moreover, to make the acquaintance of their present minister in sacred things, who, I am told, if not a native, descends from the family which has honored Wolcott by its virtues and enterprize from its earliest settlement.

But I had spent the short time at several places, and left none for prolonging my stay in Connecticut. Otherwise I would have given an additional week to my visit. And I must defer seeing my relations, as I intended, both on Wolcott and Spindle Hill, till another visit, which I may make during the coming autumn. On both occasions when crossing the Hill, I had not the time to pause long.

Thanking you for the courtesy of your kind offer I am

Very truly Yours
A. Bronson Alcott

Rev. Charles E. Upson.

[1] August 4.

LETTER 78-41

[to Samuel Orcutt, Torrington? Conn.]

Concord August 12th | 1878.

Dear Sir.

I returned on Friday last from a fortnight's tour in Connecticut, during which I hoped to find you, and yet by some fatality I missed you, both at New Haven and Waterbury. And before I left Waterbury I mailed a Postal Card to your address at Wolcottville where I thought you might be at the time. I wished particularly to see you, and learn your future prospective literary tasks, as also to give orders for several copies of your Histories. Namely:—

From Dr. Henry K. Jones of Jacksonville, Illinois.

1 Copy of "History of Wolcott"

From Mrs. Sarah Denman of Birmingham, Conn. to the care of Mr Elmes of Birmingham.

1. copy of "History of Wolcott"
1 " of "History of Torrington."

These forwarded by mail with bill for the same, will be duly honored by payment.

I wish also

1. Copy of "History of Wolcott" in boards (if you have them) if not, bound, with your bill for the same, and for other copies, if I owe you for such.

It would have been better to have seen you and dispatched this business at once, but I was not so fortunate.

I was told that you purposed writing the History of Derby next. I wish you may. It is an old and respectable township, and there must be good material to work up.

My visit was delightful and would have been perfect had I met yourself.

Yours truly.

A. Bronson Alcott.

Rev. Samuel Orcutt.

LETTER 78–42[1]

[to William T. Harris, St. Louis]

Concord August 15th. 1878.

Dear Friend,

I returned last Friday from a fortnight's visit to Connecticut, and purpose being about home during the remainder of this month, at least, and shall hope to find you in Concord during this time, to give us several days for the ever-old-ever new things in which we have perennial interest. Dr. Jones and his friends have awakened an instinct, if no more, for philosophical studies in our villagers, and we shall expect from yourself an additional quickening when you join us. At any rate, I, for myself must bespeak the free opportunity for comparing Ideas and hopes with you, if we may gain some glimpse of new acquisitions, fresh faiths, and broader prospects, while you are present and vocal.

I think I am rejuvenating, and with a future before me for better and busier works than heretofore. It may be the dream of an ancient, but it is not the less for that possible and practicable.

Excuse the garrulity of your old friend and come and stop his mouth meanwhile with your weightier words.

A hint, if you please when you will arrive

Yours truly,

A. Bronson Alcott.

Wm. T. Harris.

[1] From a copy, in Alcott's hand, in the Alcott-Pratt Collection. The original is in the Alcott-Harris Collection in the Concord Free Public Library (see Appendix B).

LETTER 78–43

[to Sarah Denman, Birmingham, Conn.]

Concord August 17th 1878.

Dear Mrs. Denman,

I reached home just a week ago bringing with me most delightful memories of my Birmingham visit. It was a time of uninterrupted pleasures, and I must thank my host and hostess again and again for their kind hospitalities.

Dr. and Mrs. Jones left me at Bridgeport where I passed a night with my nephew. I had a refreshing bath and swim in the Sound with the "Scotch philosopher Dr. Anderson—and though I found his Divinity was quite liberal, I wished it were deepened and mellowed by Dr. Jone's Platonism. While here at the seaside Sanborns satisfactory notice of Dr. Jones reached us, and copies of it have been sent me in the Jacksonville, St. Louis and Chicago papers—thus giving it a wide and desirable circulation.

Yesterday came a letter from Mr. Orcutt informing me that he had sent his "History of Wolcott". to Dr. Jones, and would forward to your order *that* and the "History of Torrington".

I did not reach New Haven till Saturday, and left there on Tuesday morning for Waterbury, having a word with your brother at the Derby station just as the cars were about starting.

At Waterbury I had two days driving again to Wolcott and Plymouth renewing my associations with earlier days. I found all well at home.

I may visit Bridgeport again in September, and if I knew you were still at Birmingham I should be tempted to pause a train.

Our Concord circle have expressed much satisfaction in their late "invasion from the West."

I shall gladly hear from you again.

Most cordially
Yours,
A. Bronson Alcott

LETTER 78–44

[to Thomas M. Johnson, Mt. Olive, Mo.]

Concord August 17th | 1878

Dear Sir,

I am much gratified to learn by your letter (which reached Concord during a visit of mine to Connecticut) that you are still pursuing your philosophic studies, and promise a translation of Plotinus before long. If I remember rightly, we agreed when you did us the honor of visiting Concord, that, of the works of the New Platonists, those of Plotinus were most likely to interest the thinking public of our time. Taylor's translation of his select works is now difficult to obtain any where. My copy is lent most of the time and kept long.

I hope your biography of him will not long be delayed from us.

I have known of but one importation of his translations, and that not containing the whole of them. It was purchased I think, by some College at the West.

Lately we have had with us for a fortnight Dr. Jones and his friends from Jacksonville and Quincy Ill. visiting us. It was quite an invasion of platonism from the || West || prairies, and surprised our Concord circle powerfully If you see the St. Louis Globe of August 10th you will find an account of it by Sanborn of the Springfield Republican.

I think we may promise ourselves the uprise of the old Idealism to submerge the many shallow swimmers who are getting out beyond their depth both here and in the foreign seas of thought

I shall gladly hear from you from time to time of your studies and publications/

Truly Yours,
A. Bronson Alcott.

Thos. M. Johnson

LETTER 78–45

[to Louisa M. Fuller, Jacksonville? Ill.]

Concord August 20th | 1878

Dear Miss Fuller,

You have waited too long for some response to your note of regrets that you were not to be of the party from the West who visited us lately, and left such happy memories with us when they disappeared them selves. I may not attempt telling how much we were edified by their presence and wise words. Mr. Sanborn has spoken for them and their cause (which is ours not less) and I am glad to find the great central presses at the West have republished his report of their visit here.

You are fortunate in being one of the Circle, living in it, and tasting at the fountain Head. And sometime you will come yourself and see us here at the East—where Western fancy fixes the sun-rising!

I have just returned from a delightful fortnight's visit to Connecticut, accompanying part of our company thither. And yesterday came Dr. Jones letter, informing us of his return to Jacksonville on the last Saturdays gathering of your Plato Club; I can fancy how it drank off his lips delightedly his adventures in the Auroral country lately invaded by himself and party.

Yet westward the empire of *Ideas* takes its way. You are not less rich than ourselves are taken to be. You have an *Interpreter of the Orient* with you, as we have lately learned to our surprize and delight.

I wish I may have the pleasure of greeting you again personally and may sometime during the coming autumn.

Meantime, peace be with you, and always

Your Friend,
A. Bronson Alcott.

Miss. Louisa M. Fuller.

LETTER 78–46

[to Mary N. Adams, Dubuque, Iowa]

Concord August 21st | 1878.

Dear Mrs Adams,

I enclose herein Mr. Sanborn's notice of Dr. Jones and his party who have lately given us a fortnights' talk and interested all who cared to listen in our village. We are a little proud just now of Ideas and celebrate philosophy as never before since my residence in this little Athens. Certainly Dr. Jones is a very remarkable person and Sanborn's estimate of his interpretative Genius is well deserved.

Westward the empire of Ideas takes its way and just now finds there its freshest interpreter. He is a new star in our Ideal firmament.

I accompanied him, and his party (most of it) to Connecticut and passed a week there pleasantly, finding good people to meet and converse with. Now I am expecting Mr. Harris to visit us. He always interests and edifies his friends, and is a growing power in the philosophic world.

Mr. Jenk[?]. Jones from Janesville Wisconsin, called the other day full of enterprize and agitation. It is a hopeful sign to find so much activity astir at the West. I suspect you are doing the work there that we here at the East dream about only—so many Clubs and Associations all busy, means much.

I am very well and promise work still in the future. I am still living with Anna in the Village in Thoreau's last home with us.

Louisa is purposing to join her sister in Paris sometime during the present autumn.[1] She is fast recruiting from her late hard work, and resting. We have the happiest reports from May of her prospects and pursuits. Mr. Emerson is at home and about as usual.

Thoreau's Cairn has grown a good deal this summer—every visitor at Walden adding a stone. When will you come and see what you begun so happily for his memory?

To all my friends in Dubuque my regards and remembrance.

Your Friend,
A. Bronson Alcott.

[1] Louisa planned the trip for September, but at the last moment decided not to go (see Cheney p. 316).

LETTER 78–47

[to Francis Nicoll Zabriskie, New York City]

Concord August 31st | 1878

Dear Sir,

I have pleasure in thanking you for your excellent Address before the Alumni of the University of the City of New York, which I find has been noticed and applauded in some of our public Journals for your able advocacy of a cultivated Class—a great "Militia of Culture." I know not what other agency is to save us from anarchy and ignorance.

Your kind appreciation of our little village and its residents also demands my acknowledgements. When public visitors like yourself and your relative The Dean[1] find virtues[?] deserving tracts[?] of their respect, ‖ we ‖ in our people and our landscape, we naturally feel[?] a little proud of ourselves, but think we are worthy of their respect.

Very truly Yours
A. Bronson Alcott

Dr. Zabriskie.

[1] George Zabriskie Gray; see Letter 78–34.

LETTER 78-48

[to Thomas M. Johnson, Osceola? Mo.]

Concord September 24th | 1878

Dear Sir.

I am interested in your projected Journal of Idealism and Mysticism,[1] and wish you may find yourself warranted in starting an organ of such importance—I may add—necessity; just now most needful to satisfy the deeper instincts of many earnest devout souls both at home and over seas. As to pecuniary returns of your venture, I cannot judge. But I should hope it might pay its own costs at least after a little while—when those had once tasted it who most needed it.

Your heads[?] for the contents are representative and exhaustive.

I think much of republications of authors now little known, but whose thoughts must find acceptance with our religious and thinking public once brought to their notice. The religious element has always attached the liveliest significance to the mystic and Ideal in life and thought, and we have no Journal, or newspaper even, doing any justice to its force and power.

And biographical sketches of the great founders of these schools would form a most attractive feature of your magazine.

I should think you might publish your own sketches and translations in it, and thus prepare the way for their acceptance in book form.

I might find something also that you might deem suitable for its pages. I can think of no more suitable place for not a little matter now at hand, and awaiting an organ.

Let me hear from you further of the matter.

Very truly
Yours.
A. Bronson Alcott.

Mr. Thos. M. Johnson.

---

[1] Johnson edited the *Platonist*, a monthly journal, from 1881 to 1888. See Frank Luther Mott, *A History of American Magazines* (Cambridge, Mass., 1938), III, 89.

LETTER 78-49

[to Charles D. B. Mills, Syracuse]

Concord September | 30th, 1878.

Dear Friend,

Mr. Harris has written that he purposes visiting us sometime this fall, but he does not specify the day.

And, just now, I learn, by the newspapers, he is busy with *committee men* about the Schools. When he informs me (as he usually does a few days before his arrival) I will write you. And also apprize him of your wish to meet him. I am not [erased] sure of his route, coming or returning; but am sure of his wish to see you. We shall do our best to get "his best" while he is with us.

Dr. Jones and his party were a surprize to Concord even. And now it seems as if our *"Concord Summer Symposeum [sic]"* was made sure for coming seasons—

when we hope you will join us, with your parishioners, now so many and agile.

You and I, it seems, have fortunately laid hold of the keys and may turn the words of fellowship, *hemispherically,* East and West.

I am undecided about going West this season. If not, then a little duty done *here-about.* You, of course, have staff and wallet all ready for the pilgrimage.

We are all about, only Anna had a fall which confines her to her chamber,[1] but hopes to be downstairs soon. May writes often the happiest bride in all Paris.

Affectionate remembrances to all of yours and yourself.

A. Bronson Alcott

C B. D [*sic*] Mills.

---

[1] "Nan breaks her leg." (Cheney, p. 317.)

LETTER 78–50[1]

[to William T. Harris, St. Louis]

Concord October 5 | 1878.

Dear Friend,

I think I must have read the article on William Law in the Contemporary Review at the time it appeared (last December) but it made so slight an impression at the time, that I do not now recall a word of it He must be a knowing and ingeniously subtle minded thinker who should fathom Law's expository genius, a Behmenist moreover, to do any justice to him or the Arch-mystic of Germany.

Next time I am in Boston, I will try to remember to look at the article at the Atheneum.

Lately I have been with Louisa busily engaged in copying Letters and Diaries for a Memoir of Mrs. Alcott—and have been mostly at home all Summer, since my return from Conn.

We shall expect you to join us next August in our Concord Summer Symposeum [*sic*],[2] which is I think already [word] by Dr. Jones and party last summer.

Yesterday Cook opened his Lectures in Boston to a good and attentive audiance [*sic*]. He is now the best Voice crying in the Wilderness East and West. What has Thompson[3] done about his Journal of Mysticism and Idealism?

To day I cast my suffrage for good[?] and[?] a new[?] Justice in our state affairs[?].

Write me at once.

Wm. T. Harris. [p. in]

---

[1] From a copy, in Alcott's hand, in the Alcott-Pratt Collection. The original is in the Alcott-Harris Collection in the Concord Free Public Library (see Appendix B).

[2] As the result of the July visit of Alcott's "Western" friends, the Concord School of Philosophy was finally to become a reality.

[3] Thomas M. Johnson.

LETTER 78–51

[to Samuel Orcutt, New Haven, Conn.]

Concord November | 6th 1878.

Dear Sir

I regret that I cannot at this time forward to you the money due you for the Wolcott Histories,[1] and the more that I failed to find you and discharge my debt (even then too long delayed payment) But I have been feeling the pinch of the times, with others and find I must ask you to wait till I can give a lecture and find the money in my hands. I shall wish you then to forward me another copy of your History of Wolcott, and if you can afford to send two copies for $10. There will be no difficulty about mailing the money to you at New Haven. Write me again and inform me about that, and other historic matters that you may have in mind

As to religious instruction in the common schools during my attendance, besides reading in the New Testament daily and saying the Catechism on Saturdays, some of the school masters opened School with prayers. The Wolcott Bronsons—Clark and Irad always did, if I remember, and the latter seasoned his teachings with religious sentiments. We had a series of questions, I have reason to believe, prepared by Father[?] Deacon Isaac—like these—"Who was the meekest man," the strongest." &c

In my own teaching both at Bristol and Cheshire morning prayers were always made and I have reason to think my teachings were of the kind that may be named truly religious.

In Bristol West district many of the parents were Baptists and truly pious people.

I hope you will find Derby worth writing about

Truly Yours,

A. Bronson Alcott

Rev. Saml Orcutt

[1] Six dollars.

LETTER 78–52

[to Mrs. M. D. Wolcott, Jacksonville, Ill.]

Concord November 10th | 1878.

Dear Mrs Wolcott,

I am very sorry that my long silence should have caused you to question our confidence in yourself and friends. Be assured that no lasting injury came or can come from the matter in question. It never reached those (as far as I have learned) who might be disturbed by it—the Emerson's and Miss Peabody, and only one person—and she without influence—ever questioned me about, and I left her as ignorant of its author as she was before, only assuring her that Mrs. Wolcott was not the person.

All is right, and we shall take our friends even more cordially by the hand when they next honor us than at first, since they left such charming memories with us. And already our "Concord Summer Symposeum [sic] is beginning to be inquired about with Dr. Jones, Mr. Harris, Mr. Emery, as visitors and interpreters of the mystic texts. What opened so brilliantly is to be continued. Our Concord circle having once tasted of the nectar and ambrosia, asks eagerly for more. I must have a tenant at the Orchard, Plato taught in one (you remember) to entertain our guests, and the New Academy shall take form and name in philosophic annals.

Let me add, in palliation of my negligence, that untill [sic] within a few weeks, I had not given up the hope of visiting you this autumn, and so hoped to speak rather than write about *that* matter.

The Memoir has held me fast meantime and is now in Sanborns hands for criticism. Louisa is much improved in health and spirits and the Memoir will detain her with us till spring. May continues to write weekly, and is very happy with her husband and her Art. We are soon to have her portrait of her husband, and Madame at Baden writes charming letters in German and French to Anna, who translates them to us.

I have pleasant engagements for Lectures and Conversations, which, with the Memoir, well [word] along through the winter. In the spring, I may take a short tour as far as Jacksonville and Quincy.

Remember me kindly to my friends at both places and particularly to Dr. Jones and Mrs. Denman.

> Very cordially
> Yours,
> A. Bronson Alcott

LETTER 78-53

[to Arthur D. Bissell, Augustus D. Smith, Edgar S. Shumway, Amherst, Mass.]
Concord November, | 12th 1878.

Dear Sir,

You ask for my terms for one or more lectures.

For a single lecture you may pay me twenty dollars, and for three, if you wish them fifty dollars and travelling expenses.

I have wished to visit your town and its College particularly—and shall gladly avail myself of the opportunity should terms and time suit your convenience

I might speak for once on.—

> *"Concord Authors"*—

and leave subjects for other lectures to be determined after the first—the time, or times to be fixed accordingly.

Mr Emerson informs me that he will not lecture this season

> Respectfully,
> A. Bronson Alcott.

LETTER 78–54

[to May, Meudon, France]

Concord, | November 29th, 1878.

My dear May,

It was good in you to remember us at this season of memories—sad and joy-ful.

We had stowed our tribute of laurel and roses on the dear mound, recalled the last words, the sad rites, now hallowed by a twelve-month—when, on this anniversary of births, came your happy accounts to gladden us. Your letters have been a series of surprises from first to last, there seems to have been unin-terrupted satisfactions attending this friendship, nor has your Art been neglected meanwhile. And not your letters only, but your husband's have endeared him to his kindred Concord friends. It is gratifying to an author to find his thoughts are prized by his reader, and his writings valued. I trust the pleasure awaits me of taking my reader by the hand, and saluting him by a *more familiar name.—*

As your sisters letters inform you concerning what may interest you about home-matters, I may add a little about mine and myself.

I have been occupied during the last six months in copying *Letters* and *Diaries* for the *Memoirs*. It has been a great pleasure to live over the 70, and more years which these M.S.S. cover—50 of which were passed mostly with my-self,—and so bravely and beautifully given to duties, so devotedly, nobly lived!— Louisa will, I hope, have the pleasure of bringing you the book. I hope to take the first sheets to the printers next Monday. Mr Niles is waiting to put it to press.[1]

I think you will be pleased to learn of my engagements for December. I do not go West at present:

I am to give three lectures at Amherst College—the first—Dec. 6.
A lecture to the Divinity students at Cambridge — — — — — — — "9.
At Lunenburg — — — — — — — — — — — — — — — — — — "12.
Address the Young Men's Christian Association — — — — — — — "19.
Begin Conversations at the Hotel Belleview — — — — — — — — "23

And a Course of 6 conversations in Boston January 1879. I find myself in fair health on this my 79th birthday, and hope to enjoy a year of pleasure and *profit* in my chosen calling. I think I may assure you that Louisa is fairly re-stored to a good degree of health and *cheer*fulness.

I must not close without expressing our delight in the sweet letters your mother writes to Anna and Louisa. Pray give her my respects and thanks, with much love to Ernest.

Affectionately,
Your Father.

---

[1] The "Memoirs" of Mrs. Alcott was not published.

PART TWENTY-FOUR

1879

LETTER 79–1

[to A. H. Leppere, Florence, Mass.]

Concord January | 6th 1879.

Dear Sir.

Your letter contained just sentiments, and wise criticisms particularly concerning the Free Religious Movement and the Cosmians. Both are fast coming to their legitimate end, and must pass away into Nihilism.

I came near visiting Florence the other day, when at Amherst where I had pleasant intercourse with the students and Professors.

I am pleased to learn that you have [been] illuminating the Cosmian Atheism, of which I must think some of the neophytes have had more than enough. Burleigh made a good beginning, but hardly good enough to avert this dismal result.

As to your Essay, I shall wish to hear it, and it may chance that Sanborn may gather a party here for you.

I am to be at the Bayard Taylor Meeting on Friday of this week. Next Monday evening, the 13th—comes my second Conversation at Mr Cook's Parlors, on Tuesday 14th. I lecture at Westford. Besides these engagements, a course of Conversations is proposed to begin soon after the 15th. in Boston.

I shall be likely to be at home on Saturday the 11. and Sunday 12th. Will you not take Concord on your way to Boston,? and give me an hour or two in passing?

I have important matters in thought and shall be glad to see you.

I enclose Thomas W. Johnson's Prospectus of his Philosophical Quarterly—

Yours truly
A. Bronson Alcott

Mr. A. H. Leppere.

LETTER 79–2

[to Arthur D. Bissell, Augustus D. Smith, Edgar S. Shumway, Amherst, Mass.]
Concord January 21st | 1879.

Dear Sir,

Yours enclosing your note to Emerson is at hand, and yesterday I called on him, and Miss Ellen who makes his appointments, agreed to reply to your inquiries at once. She wishes him to read a paper to your company, but thought the time you named would not suit his convenience.

As to my next visit, the time you name, Friday February 7. suits and so for the Conversations on Saturday. But on Monday evening the 10th I am to hold a third Conversation at Mr. Cook's in Boston.

So I will wait for further instructions from your Committee
I have now only one engagement beside Friday the 31st in Boston.

Very truly
Yours
A. Bronson Alcott

LETTER 79–3[1]

[to William T. Harris, St. Louis]
Concord January 26 | 1879.

Dear Friend

I send you our Prospectus of the Concord Summer School of Philosophy and Literature.[2] As you will see we look to you for the teaching in Speculative Philosophy, and cannot afford to spare you from our Faculty. This prospectus has not yet been published, but awaits the acceptance of the Persons named before it is sent abroad and given to the public Journals.

I hope you will think favorable of our plan, and give your name and services. The fees for the term will, we have reason to believe, warrant the giving of $100. to each of the five Professors, and pay all other incidental expenses of the session.

This Idea has been a dream of mine for some years, and now seems quite practicable with our list of Professors named in the Prospectus, and Sanborn as Secretary. It is in *our* way, and from many quarters, is looked upon with much favor, particularly by students, and seekers for light, in all parts of the West.

I trust you will be able to visit us during the sessions and give us the services we ask. I know of no substitute for your department of thought Davidson is here and well disposed, and I write to Dr. Jones in full faith of securing his aid also. Concord should justify its fame.

Your Postal Card, and its joyous *Eureka* came to hand. Come and tell us *fully* of your discovery.

I am having many opportunities for Conversing, and enjoy them highly,—being in perfect health and hope.

Write at once, that we may issue our prospectus soon.

Yours fraternally,
A. Bronson Alcott.

Wm T Harris

[1] From a copy, in Alcott's hand, in the Alcott-Pratt Collection. The original is in the Alcott-Harris Collection in the Concord Free Public Library (see Appendix B).

[2] The prospectus reads as follows:

THE CONCORD SUMMER SCHOOL
of
Philosophy and Literature.

A Summer School for instruction by conference and conversation in literature and the higher philosophy, will open at the Orchard House of Mr. Alcott, in Concord, Massachusetts, on Tuesday, July 15, 1879, and continue for five weeks. The classes will be conducted by five Professors, who will each give ten Lectures or Conversations, between the hours of 9 and 11 A.M., and 3 and 5 P.M., each day of the week, except Sunday, being devoted to two sessions, and no more. Five days in the week will be occupied by the regular Professors, and the sixth by special Lecturers on related subjects.

The regular Professors will be,—

A. Bronson Alcott, of Concord, on Christian Theism.
William T. Harris, of St. Louis, on Speculative Philosophy.
H. K. Jones, of Jacksonville, Ill., on Platonic Philosophy.
David A. Wasson, of Medford, on Political Philosophy.
Mrs. Ednah D. Cheney, of Boston, on the History and Moral of Art.

The special Lecturers will be,—

F. B. Sanborn, of Concord, on Philanthropy and Social Science.
T. W. Higginson, of Cambridge, on Modern Literature.
Thomas Davidson, of Boston, on Greek Life and Literature.
George H. Howison, of Boston, on Philosophy from Leibnitz to Hegel;
and several others.

Mr. Alcott's class will meet in the forenoons of Tuesday and Thursday in each week; Dr. Jones's on Monday and Wednesday; Prof. Harris's in the forenoon of Friday and the afternoon of Thursday; Mr. Wasson's in the afternoons of Monday and Wednesday; Mrs. Cheney's in the afternoons of Tuesday and Friday. The special lecturers will meet their classes on Saturdays. Classes and exchanges will occasionally be made in this arrangement for the convenience of the instructors of the classes; and a more definite announcement of the order of the conversations and Lectures will be made before July 1.

The terms will be $3 for each of the courses of ten sessions; but each student will be required to pay at least $10 for the term, which will permit him to attend three of the regular courses and all the special lectures. The fees for all the courses, regular and special, will be $15, or $3 a week. Board may be obtained in the village at from $6 to $12 a week,—so that students may estimate their necessary expenses for the whole term at $50. In certain cases the fees for instruction will be remitted.

All students should be registered on or before June 1, 1879; at the office of the Secretary, in Boston. No preliminary examinations are required, and no limitation of age, sex, or residence in Concord will be prescribed; but it is recommended that persons under eighteen years should not present themselves as students, and that those who take all the courses should reside in the town during the term. The Concord Public Library of 14,000 volumes, will be open every day for the use of residents. Students coming and going daily during the term, may reach Concord from Boston by the Fitchburg Railroad, or the Middlesex Central; from Lowell, Andover, etc., by the Lowell & Framingham Railroad; from Southern Middlesex and Worcester Counties by the same road. The Orchard House stands on the Lexington road, east of Concord village, adjoining the Wayside estate, formerly the residence of Mr. Hawthorne.

Letters of inquiry may be addressed to,

A. BRONSON ALCOTT, Concord, Mass.,
Dean of the Faculty.
Or, F. B. SANBORN, Boston,
Secretary of the Faculty.

LETTER 79-4

[to Arthur D. Bissell, Augustus D. Smith, Edgar S. Shumway, Amherst, Mass.]
Concord January 27th | 1879.
Dear Sir,

Your arrangement for my Second lecture for Friday evening February 7th, allows me to fulfil engagements elsewhere meanwhile, and leave me to anticipate the pleasure of visiting your town afterwards with *Emerson.*

My subject for the lecture for the 7th will be *"Culture".*

I hope to bring for your consideration our *"Prospectus for the Concord Summer School of Philosophy and Literature.*

Very truly
Yours.
A. Bronson Alcott.

Mr. Arthur D. Bissell.
&c.

LETTER 79-5

[to   ?   ]
Concord February 20th | 1879.
Dear Sir.

I think you may find an answer to your inquiries in a pamphlet of Rev. Washington Gladden's entitled:—

"Was Bronson Alcott's School a type of God's Moral Government. A Review of Joseph's Cook's Theory of the Atonement." Published by Lockwood, Brooks and Co. 381 Washington Street, Boston, 1877. And if you care to look further, you will find the instance of Correction referred to by Mr. Cook, fully given in a book published by Roberts Brothers of Boston, entitled *"A Record of Mr. Alcott's School Exemplifying the Principles and Methods of Moral Culture. Third Edition, 1874."*

You will there find the spirit and principle in which punishment was administered, and its effects fairly stated. I shall be glad to find a justification of the Christian doctrine of the Atonement in these instances. The Atonement is a mystery not easily comprehended, but the mode of correction (and of punishment if you will) practiced in my school appears to shed some light into it. Pure *Christian Sympathy* is always *vicarious,* and works nowday [sic] in all our human and divine relations.

I shall be glad to hear further from you[1]

---

[1] The complimentary close and signature have been cut out.

LETTER 79–6

[to John H. Barrows, Lawrence, Mass.]

Concord February 20th 1879.

Dear Sir.

Yours of the 17th is at hand. I shall be glad to hear further from you concerning the proposed Conversations in your city. And in accordance with your request enclose the name of a subject or two for discussion when I shall have the pleasure of meeting your circle.

Concord Authors.
Books and Studies
Heredity, Spiritual and Human
The Atonement.

The former, as you will perceive, are *literary*. The latter, *Theological*. Other themes might be named but these are introductory and suggestive.

I am to be at Amherst on Wednesday of next week and Emerson speaks there on Friday, the 28.

Our last meeting at Mr Cooks was quite spirited and satisfacto[ry.][1]

Rev. John H. Barrows
    Lawrence
       Mass.

---

[1] The complimentary close and signature have been cut out.

LETTER 79–7[1]

[to Miss Brown]

Concord February 20th | 1879.

Dear Miss Brown,

I regret to learn of your illness: and trust you are now able to enjoy returning spirits and perusal of your favorite authors. Pray give yourself no anxiety beyond your recovery, and keep the *"Hours with the Mystics"* as long as you find pleasure and profit in the reading.

Yes, those were pleasant hours passed in my study to *another* as to yourself, and when you are disposed come again, and renew the pleasure.

Very truly
    Yours,
    A. Bronson Alcott

---

[1] MS. owned by the Houghton Library, Harvard University.

LETTER 79–8[1]

[to William T. Harris, St. Louis]

Concord February 21st 1879.

Dear Friend.

My letter of the 17th had hardly left, when yours of the 13th. came to hand, and yesterday came your *SchoolBooks.*[2]

I have looked with entire approbation into the series and am especially pleased with the method, and spirit of the selections. All the pieces are excellent in their tone, and adapted to the apprehension of the learners. Your heads entitled, *"For preparation"*—supply what has hitherto been altogether omitted in our school books. I trace your keen philosophical analysis in these preparatory notes, particularly in the lessons selected for the advanced Classes.

The whole series must attract the learner, stimulate and strengthen and refine alike the intellect and moral sentiments. The selections are fresh and chosen from a wider field than in former Readers. How the younger classes will brighten at the sight of the variety of pictures and lessons! The First Reader is a beauty. How can the little ones longer a [word] unwillingly to school."

There is Genius in the presentation of these books that should kindle enthusiasm both in pupils and Teachers.

I wish them the widest circulation throughout the states *north and south.*—

Our Prospectus will be ready for circulating soon. How many copies will you wish to distribute. We shall print a 1000. And may we look for a paragraph, if no more, of your approval, in your next issue of the *Journal?*

Truly Yours,

A. Bronson Alcott.

PS./My house is still unoccupied. If you leave St. Louis please come and take possession on your own terms. Our school does not open till July 21st. If you will not come Perhaps Emery may? Think of it.

A.B.A.

---

[1] From a copy, in Alcott's hand, in the Alcott-Pratt Collection. The original is in the Alcott-Harris Collection in the Concord Free Public Library (see Appendix B).
[2] Alcott's letter to Harris was probably dated February *15* (see Appendix B). For an account of Harris' editorship of *Appleton's School Readers,* see Kurt F. Leidecker, *Yankee Teacher: The Life of William Torrey Harris* (New York, 1946), pp. 335–39.

LETTER 79–9

[to Henry W. Rolfe, Amherst, Mass.]

Concord | March 4th 1879.

Dear Sir,

You are at full liberty, and have my thanks for wishing to publish in your "College Paper," some account of our *"Concord Summer School"*

Any thing you may have to say in its favor, will extend information more widely, and may add to the number of attendants

Mr. Emerson, whom I saw yesterday, regrets the disappointment, but hopes to read his Lecture to you soon.

Very truly
Yours,
A. Bronson Alcott

Mr. Henry W. Rolfe,
    Amherst College.

LETTER 79–10

[to Samuel Orcutt, New Haven? Conn.]

Concord, | March 4th 1879.

Dear Sir.

Your proposal to send me the incomplete copies of your History of Wolcott, is most gratifying and has my thanks. I shall find use for the sheets in my *"Gene-alogical Collections,"* if not in the *"Autobiography.* Every thing concerning Wolcott has a Household charm, and is treasured by me as a part of family history. And I was pleased to learn that Old Derby is to be done by the Historian of Wolcott also.

I have just returned from a two days' visit to Amherst and its collegians. The books may be sent by express as before.

I enclose a copy of our Prospectus of the Concord Summer School.[1]

Rev. Saml. Orcutt.

[1] The complimentary close and signature have been cut out.

LETTER 79–11

[to Mary N. Adams, Dubuque, Iowa]

Concord March 6th 1879.

Dear Mrs Adams,

With this comes the Prospectus of our Concord Summer School, in which yourself and our many friends throughout the West will take special interest— some of them, and may we not hope yourself will visit our Village during the Summer? Yes. *You* particularly, since our purposes and I trust our Methods are *yours,* as ours. I think we talked about this prospectively more than once under your roof, and foretold the like. Every thing looks propitious now, and we know not *what* may rise from the gathering—*what may not!* Come and *represent* the *hopes and Possibilities* of the wondrous West.

Meanwhile, it may interest you to learn that opportunities open on all sides and into all sects for speaking such words as I may have to speak. Last week at Amherst college where President, Professors and students lent gracious audience [*sic*]. Emerson goes there soon. And the evenings at Jos. Cook's, are *liberalizing* the attendants.

Louisa is with us. We have good news from May, who is still busy with brush and happy in her husband whose picture by herself, has lately come to us.

This is a poor return for your full letters. How can I write all? To Mr. Adams and the children and other friends kind remembrances

Your friend

A. Bronson Alcott

LETTER 79–12

[to Samuel H. Emery, Quincy, Ill.]

Concord March 6th 1879

Dear Sir.

I wrote you lately enclosing our Prospectus of the Concord Summer School, but suspecting misdirection of my letter, I now write again.

When you visited us last summer you thought of making Concord your place of residence, and intimated your removal here sometime during this spring or summer, and, if I remember rightly, thought you might like to occupy my House. It has been tenantless for a year and more, as I have not wished to rent it to such applicants as have been disposed to occupy it. Now it would please me much to learn that you still thought of coming to Concord, and also of taking my House. Will you write at once, and inform me of your plans and expectations We should like to find you and Mrs. Emery neighbors of ours, and host and hostess for the reception of our Classes during the Summer Sessions of our school.

Very truly

Yours,

A. Bronson Alcott.

LETTER 79–13[1]

[to A. H. Dooley?]

March 6th 1879.

Dear Sir,

I send you a copy of the Prospectus of our Summer School, and wish you and the Quincy friends may think well of it.

And may I indulge the hope that before the gathering in July, you will have made your home in our Village—if it may be—in The Orchard House itself?—It is still tenantless, and I should delight in finding yourself and yours the occupants. Can this be? And will you write at once of your wishes and expectations.

Mr. Emerson received the impression as I did, when you visited us last, that you purposed making Concord your place of residence.

Very truly,

Yours,

A. Bronson Alcott.

[1] MS. owned by the Houghton Library, Harvard University.

LETTER 79–14

[to Edgar S. Shumway, Amherst, Mass.]

Concord March. | 7th 1879.

Dear Sir,

Your questions are pertinent and profound.

Yes, the Soul is *I*.

And I is *Personal*.

Therefore *essential*, not a *property*.

I being Personal is *One;* not numerically, but essentially one and indivisible. The Soul is One therefore with God's Personality—since there is and can be but *One*. *One,* substantially. Good is essence, and in God the substance of all souls. Evil is insubstantial and the abusing of goods *Owning.* is to *One,* the good. The Evil cannot become One, but is many. The deuce—less *one.*

The one Personal, *owns* all. The sinner disowns himself. Yes. If God *should* sin he would *disperson* and undeify himself.

But Sin is *not* God in act and purpose, nor in essence, but the *deuced* will— the soul's abuse of its freedom to choose the Good. Hence Evil and Sin are consequences of mischoosing and *retribution.*

There may be less of *logic* than of Insight in these statements, but you and your roommates may detect the *flaws,* and find the substantial truth in them. I shall be glad to learn the result.

Very Truly
Yours.
A. Bronson Alcott.

LETTER 79–15[1]

[to Georgiana Hemingway Cook, Boston]

Concord March 7th | 1879.

Dear Mrs Cook,

I missed finding you when I last called, wishing to ask you to add the name of Rev. James Reed to your 'list of invitations.

Mr Reed is the (Swedenborgian) Minister of the New Church in Boston. He expressed a wish to attend the next Conversation on Monday evening—the 10th— I have not his address at hand.

Anticipating a happy evening, and brilliant discussion,

I am truly
Yours,
A. Bronson Alcott

[1] MS. owned by the Duke University Library.

LETTER 79–16

[to William Henry Channing, London, England]
Concord March 17th | 1879.

My dear Friend.

Without long apology for allowing the many months to pass since we parted so affectionately after our pleasant fellowship here in Concord and in Boston, I am happy in mailing to your address, along with this brief note, *Our "Prospectus of the Concord Summer School,"* which promises to be a success in the way of attendance at least, and we may hope of instruction. You will remember, my friend, our frequent conversations on this Academic project, and I certainly have very vivid recollections of your interest and hope in this, as in other instrumentalities for spiritual enlightenment. Dr. Jones visited us last summer with several ladies from the West and interested our Concord people deeply in his Platonic interpretations. Mr Cook has just closed another season's lectures and is to resume for a third in autumn. Our Conversations at his Rooms during last winter and a former course, have been largely attended, and I have every reason to please myself with the results. Extremes have met *sympathetically* if no nearer intellectually. I will find a Report of the last if I can and send you. Besides this opportunity, I have enjoyed my three visits to *Amherst,* where I met President Seelye and the students—a dozen of the latter purpose attending our Summer School. Emerson lectures at Amherst next Friday evening. We had a lively Conversation at his house last Sunday evening. I have been busy during the winter and am in perfect health, with a hopeful future of usefulness. Sanborn is active in the Philanthropies and his editing. I am just informed that Lathrop has purchased *Wayside* and will reside in Concord.

I am living with my daughters in the *Thoreau* House in the Village. Louisa is now with us, but may visit her sister now *Mrs Nieriker,* who is living near Paris, happy in her husband and her Art. Must I wait as long to hear from you and England? Your sympathetic letter of Jan 1878—was consoling!—Thanks
Yours ever—
A Bronson Alcott.

Rev. Wm. H. *Channing, London.*

LETTER 79–17

[to Mr. Hewes[?], Fitchburg, Mass.]
Concord, March 20th | 1879.

Dear Sir.

Your note is just at hand. I shall gladly meet your Literary Club, and, if you wish, speak in your pulpit on Sunday also. Will next Sunday suit you, or will that be too soon? One of your brethren, an orthodox minister, asked me to visit him and preach for him. I do not now recall his name It would please me to speak for both; but not in any other than a Christian sense—universality of spirit[?].

Very truly
Yours,
A. Bronson Alcott.

Rev Mr. Hewes[?]
Fitchburg.

LETTER 79–18

[to William Seymour Tyler, Amherst, Mass.]

Concord March | 22*nd* 1879.

Dear Sir.

Thank you heartily for your discriminating criticism on my Conversations with Children. I should do better now. And you will reccollect [sic] that these Conversations were held forty years ago, when I was but thirty seven years of age, and was under the bias of Unitarian divinity, from which I am now happy to believe I am fully freed. And the transcendental or mystical interpretations of Scripture would now be more in harmony with evengilical [sic] orthodoxy.

I was pleased to read in the Springfield Republican a most acceptable notice of Emerson and of his recent lecture in your town. I wish I knew who wrote it.

With most delightful remembran[ces] of my visit to your Collegiate seat and of your and Mrs. Tyler's hospitalities particularly,

I am,
Very truly
Yours.
A. Bronson Alcott.

LETTER 79–19

[to Mrs. Hayes, Boston]

Concord, March | 26th 1879.

Dear Mrs. Hayes,

Your note is at hand inviting me to meet your pupils and friends on the afternoon of Wednesday April 30th, next.

It will give me pleasure to comply with your request, and you may expect me at that time.[1]

---

[1] The complimentary close and signature have been cut out.

LETTER 79–20

[to Samuel Longfellow, Germantown, Penn.]

Concord March. | 27th 1879.

Dear Friend,

Your "Discourse' has just come to hand, for which you have my thanks. It revives delightful recollections of *our earliest Family Nest* since here[?] the doves flitted, and the babes made their advent—my daughters Anna and Louisa—with whom I now reside and have since the dear companion and Mother ascended. I remember the neighborhood and kind friends of that period. It is pleasant to know that you are with those who still dwell there.

I am gratified by your remembrance of myself. Sympathy is Sweet and a foretaste of unending friendship.

You may like to learn that Mr. Emerson is in his usual health. and that we have had opportunities of meeting the students of Amherst College

I enclose a Prospectus of our *"Concord Summer School"*

Truly Yours
A. Bronson Alcott.

LETTER 79–21

[to   ?   ]

Concord April 3rd 1879.

Dear Sir.

My acquaintance with Dr. Channing[1] was too brief to have much to report for your interesting anniversary of his birth. It began when he was in the height of his fame as a scholar and divine, and is remembered with much satisfaction. I had come from a neighboring state, then a young enthusiast, to take charge of an Infant School in Boston. Unitarianism was then in its prime, and he was its honored representative. He kindly invited me to his house, where during his stay in Boston, I passed many pleasant and profitable evenings in the discussion of questions then in the air—Education, Unitarianism, and Transcendentalism. Socialism Antislavery, in most of which his moderation and discretion served to temper my radical tendencies, and modify my extreme opinions, though at the time I might have thought him less sympathetic than I wished. He commanded my entire respect. I attended his Church in Federal Street, and owe to him, more than any other preacher, softened and rational impassions of the religious dogmas in which I had been educated. I think I may say that I became a Unitarian in the sense in which he then held that faith (though modified essentially since) by his teachings. His presence in the pulpit was always memorable, his words inspiring. His reading his Chosen Hymns, his prayers, were lyrical, eminently devotional, and his preaching apostolic. He often sat in the pulpit with, Dr Gannett,[2] and sometimes took no other part in the services but reading his favorite hymn and preaching. It was a great disappointment when he did neither. Some of his great Sermons were then being delivered, and the hush of attention, only interrupted by his *"I apprehend"* at the divisions of his theme, was marvellous to witness. His voice and countenance gave a sacred tone and devotion to his doctrine. Christianity was felt to be a revelation from the Father through his Son, the divine humanity kindred in essence and dignity with both. He was practical and ethical rather than mystic and metaphysical holding before his audiance [*sic*] the mirror of a divine life in that of their elder brother.

On returning from Philadelphia, where I had passed four years, I heard him less often, and saw him seldomer. He took a deep interest in my School for Moral and Spiritual Culture kept in the Old Masonic Temple, visited it more than once, and regretted deeply the circumstances which led to its close.

I remember visiting him more than once at his home in Newport, and, on one occasion attended Services there on Sunday in his little Church.

He died while I was in England.

These, dear Sir, are very brief and insignificant notes concerning our distinguished American ‖ scholar ‖ philanthropist and preacher who has adorned our literature and given a noble life to his country and Christendom.

Very truly
Yours,
A. Bronson Alcott.

[1] William Ellery Channing (1780–1842).
[2] Ezra Stiles Gannett.

LETTER 79–22[1]

[to   ?   ]

Concord April | 3rd 1879.

Dear Sir,

Your note is at hand. In reply, I may say that if next Monday evening will suit the convenience of yourself and friends, I will come and hold a Conversation in Mrs Mead's parlors.

My [subject] may be *"Concord Authors" "Heredity"*, or *Immortality"* as may be preferred.

I shall be satisfied with five dollars and expenses, though ten dollars would be what I have oftener received for an evening.

Very truly
Yours,
A. Bronson Alcott.

[1] MS. owned by the New York Public Library.

LETTER 79–23[1]

[to Keningale Robert Cook, London, England]

Concord Mass. | April 6th 1879.

Dear Sir,

I venture to forward to your address a "Prospectus of our Concord Summer School of Philosophy and Literature" and to assure you that I have looked at your *"Magazine"* whenever I have visited our Boston Atheneum, and read with interest your papers as these appeared. I have borne in mind meanwhile, your inquiries concerning Thoreau's unpublished writings, and, at one time, had the hope of sending you some Extracts for publication in your Magazine, but other place was preferred by those who had charge of his papers.

You were kind enough to ask for something of mine also. But I find nothing worthy of your acceptance.

I mentioned yourself and studies to my friend, Rev. Wm. H. Channing, (when he visited us last summer), and took the liberty of commending him to your acquaintance.

I need not assure you that I shall hear further from you with pleasure.

Very truly
Yours.
A. Bronson Alcott.

[1] MS. owned by the Fruitlands and Wayside Museums, and pasted in a presentation copy of Alcott's *Table Talk*.

LETTER 79–24

[to   ?]

Concord April 7th 1879.

Dear Sir,

Your proposition is very agreeable to me, and I shall gladly avail my self of Dr. Withrow's hospitalities to meet at his residence any company he may invite for the evening.

Next Monday evening, April 14 will suit my convenience, as I have engagements for an earlier date.

I may invite a few persons, meanwhile.

Very truly
Yours,
A. Bronson Alcott.

LETTER 79–25[1]

[to William T. Harris, St. Louis]

Concord April 7th | 1879

Dear Friend,

I am well pleased in finding your contributors to the Journal of Speculative

Philosophy venturing into the Mysteries of Theology so confidently. I think it a hopeful sign.

Mr Mead's[2] translation of Hegel's sketch of Jacob Boehme's Theosophy is an instance noteworthy. Our divinity students appear to relish a mystery. They seek and find in these, quickenings of the religious instincts. I find a mystic paradox sure to start a discussion in the best companies—whether these be named "Christian or Antichristian" I may add, moreover, that I have enjoyed unexpected opportunities lately for comparing the relative apprehension of these extremes. I must say, that between Head and Heart, I find my orthodox friends bridging these the safelier and surer.

At Cook's Dr. Channings *"Arianism"* bridged the chasm partly over, but Dr. Bartol and Higginson disclaimed their need of the passages. Heretofore the human race have felt the need, if history tells the truth. At Amherst the students so read the past[?] sanctioned by their professors. And both Emerson and myself were most generously entertained during our visits. Three of the senior graduates have already bespoken their rooms here for the Summer School, and others are expected.

Sunday before last I was at Fitchburg—preached morning and evening for the Unitarians, and between the services, for the orthodox. This is what I like—dealing *Universals* alike to both. Then I am invited to meet a select company of Rev. Dr. Withrow's friends at his residence in Boston. He is the pastor of Park Street Church, you may remember. I am also invited to converse at Lawrence, the orthodox minister inviting his friends. Besides, The Senior students in Harvard College wish me to meet their "Philosophical Club for discussing such questions as come up in their courses of study."—These opportunities are very gratifying. The Summer School promises well. Emery is expected here by the 20th April. He leaves Quincy, and I wish him to rent my house and receive our Classes during the sessions of the school. Letters of inquiry have come to hand from all parts of the country, largely from the West. Hundreds of Circulars have been distributed already.

Thanks for the sheets sent of your work and wishes. I do not relinquish the hope of your *anchoring* at last here in Concord—and as *my near neighbor.* Meanwhile

Truly Yours,
A. Bronson Alcott.

Wm. T. Harris.

[1] From a copy, in Alcott's hand, in the Alcott-Pratt Collection. The original is in the Alcott-Harris Collection in the Concord Free Public Library (see Appendix B).
[2] Edwin D. Mead, who lectured at the Concord School of Philosophy in 1881.

LETTER 79–26

[to   ?   ]

Concord April 9th 1879

Dear Sir,

On returning from Boston last evening, I find your note.

It would please me to find Rev. E. E. Hale and Dr. Miner present on Monday evening And I may add the names to your list, of

Mr. Frank B. Sanborn, Concord, Mass,
Dr. J. E. Brull and lady 269. Shawmut Avenue. and
Rev. Dr. Dudley and lady. 36. Worcester Square.
I am looking forward to having a pleasant and profitable evening.

I am, Revd Sir.
Very truly
Yours.
A. Bronson Alcott

LETTER 79–27

[to   ?   ]

Concord April 9th 1879.

Dear Sir,

The grounds behind my house slope gradually to the base of the hill, and are in shrubbery, with a number of maples and some other taller trees. The hill, as you see in the sketch is crowned with pines. If I remember, you had two photographs of the house and grounds and chose the one taken from the Eastern side. This I think we agreed was the better of the two.

I think I gave you information about the old door yard open to the road, and the door itself having the formidable knocker.

There were only the old elms then in front; and the lindens beyond the large butternut tree (seen still at the eastern end of the house) were planted along the lane by myself, as were most of the shrubbery on the grounds.

The woods should show boldly in your Sketch.[1]

[1] The remainder of the letter (probably just the complimentary close and signature) has been cut out.

LETTER 79–28[1]

[to   ?   ]

Concord April | 12th 1879.

Dear Sir,

Yours is just come to hand.

I am pleased to learn your interest in our proposed "Summer School", and flattered by your intention to visit us during the sessions.

It will give me pleasure to repeat my visit to your school at such time as may be most convenient to yourself. And I will await your naming the day.

Very truly
Yours,
A. Bronson Alcott.

[1] MS. owned by the New York Public Library.

LETTER 79–29

[to Marion Talbot, Boston]

Concord April 19th 1879.

Dear Miss Talbot,

Your note came to hand too late for me to meet your friends on Friday afternoon. I regretted this exceedingly. And hope the mischance may not deprive me of the pleasure of a future opportunity, and under more propitious Skies.

At present I have no engagements for next week, and shall gladly accept any invitation for any afternoon previous to Saturday.

It was my purpose to visit the University on Wednesday last but I was not in the City on that day.

Remembering with pleasure the kind hospitalities of your house lately.[1]

---

[1] The complimentary close and signature have been cut out.

LETTER 79–30

[to Miss Mitchell, Boston]

Concord April 24th 1879

Dear Miss Mitchell,

Yes, I should enjoy a little Symposium with your group of Babies, and shall be in the City next week some day, say Tuesday morning next—29th. And if you will drop me a line saying I may come then, about 10. A.m. or later if you wish—I will accommodate my visit to your convenience or, would you wish an earlier fresh morning hour?—

And it will add to the pleasure of the Colloquy, if the mothers will also be present.

I am to be at Mrs Hayes School 68. Chester Square on Wednesday April. 30th at 12½ P.M.[1]

---

[1] The complimentary close and signature have been cut out.

LETTER 79–31

[to Thomas M. Johnson?]

Concord April 24th | 1879.

Dear Sir,

I have distributed most of the Prospectus which you sent me, and have been looking for the appearance of No. I. of *"The Philosopher"*. I trust no impediment has arrested your purpose of publication. "The Philosopher" will fill a place in American Journalism becoming more and more obvious to observers of the undercurrent of philosophic thought both here and abroad.

The 'Journal of Speculative Philosophy" begins to touch upon pure mysticism in its April number, giving us a translation of Hegel's estimate of Boehme's Theosophy, and promising more. I have wished more than has appeared in former Numbers. There is hope for us when *Boehme* is studied in good earnest.

Mr. Harris writes that he will pass most of the coming month of July with us in Concord. Inquiries come daily to hand from all parts, particularly from the West, about our Summer School. Shall we not have No. I. of *"The Philosopher,'* if not the Editor, with us by that time?

The students at Harvard College have organized a "Philosophic Club,' and I am to meet them next Monday evening to consult about the problems of Philosophic thought now current at Cambridge and Concord.

I shall be glad to hear from you concerning your Journal, and your studies particularly.

Very truly
Yours,
A. Bronson Alcott.

LETTER 79–32[1]

[to May, Meudon, France]

Concord May 7th 1879.

My dear May.

Yes. Surely, my happy Child, you are to be congratulated, and again and again, on your success at the Salon, and in your husband's affections. I read your letter, announcing the acceptance of your picture, with pride, and almost wished, instead of the new name—euphonous as this is—the honor had been conferred upon

Miss May Alcott. But even dutiful daughters are honored when taking their husband's name, without loss of loyalty to their birth right. You are a successful member of our House, and I shall be content while you continue to honor it with your friendships and your Art in the future.

Were your picture here now in this crisis of the Slave Exodus I know not what new honors might await the artist on this side the Atlantic. The Negress might rival even Mrs. Stowe's Uncle Tom, as his counterpart—might couple your name with hers, and Louisa's whom we are informed are the only women authors much known on the continent. At any rate. I am happy in learning of your content to remain in France, taking life in a rational and right spirit. Nor do I yield the hope of seeing you here and welcoming you and yours to your old home and country.

I have space to add that Mr. and Mrs Emery from Quincy, Illinois, (just removed from thence, and wishing to settle in Concord), were here yesterday and will probably occupy The Orchard during the summer, and perhaps permanently. They are highly accomplished people, and will be ornaments of the place and town. The Summer School promises fairly. In the June number of *"Scribner,"* there will be a notice of it by Sanborn. Letters come almost daily from widely different places of inquiry about it. As I cannot recommend the Middlesex House, I am finding boardings and lodgings in private families. If no more than thirty apply we shall open the School.

I am in perfect health, very busy, having many engagements for Conversations, and am persuaded your dear Mother approves from her throne above us, and is the happier in her Heaven of bliss.

Your affectionate Father,
A.B.A.

P.S./

I value your letters, and have them all at hand in my family Volume.

[1] The first three paragraphs of this letter are quoted in Ticknor, *May Alcott*, pp. 288–89.

LETTER 79–33

[to Augustus D. Smith, Amherst, Mass.]

Concord May 9 | 1879.

Dear Sir,

Pleasant rooms in the village for your Fraternity can be secured for $1.50 and $2.00 each the week, as you may choose. And those—three of them, near the Orchard are still to be had on the former, that is $1.50. each. Shall I leave all further engagements for you to make on your arrival, or will you arrange before that time?

Mr. Emery from Quincy Illinois, has left the West, and will probably take possession of the Orchard House within a few days. He is a friend of Philosophy and of Mr. Harris, and will be an acquisition to our School.

My thanks to Prof. Tyler for his discriminating paper on Mr. Alcott in the "Christian Union".

Very truly Yours,
A Bronson Alcott.

LETTER 79–34

[to Marion Talbot, Boston]

Concord May 9th 1879

Dear Miss Talbot.

Most gladly shall I meet the members of the Gamma Delta and its invited friends and on the day named in your note. viz. Friday 16th May. and doubt not of our having a pleasant interview.

Half past one, P.M. will suit my convenience[1]

Miss Marion Talbot,
  66. Marlborough St
    Boston

[1] The complimentary close and signature have been cut out.

LETTER 79–35

[to Samuel H. Emery, Quincy, Ill.]

Concord May 12th | 1879

Dear Sir.

Your decision is very satisfactory, and the Orchard doors shall open to your entrance whenever you are pleased to occupy. My man has been busied to day in putting the walks in order, and when yourself and family arrive we can consult further about any desirable repairs to be made on the premises.

Very truly
Yours,
A. Bronson Alcott.

LETTER 79–36

[to Hiram K. Jones, Jacksonville, Ill.]

Concord May 13th | 1879.

Dear Friend,

Mr. Emery has arrived and visited us. I think you will be pleased to learn that he has taken "the Orchard" for the summer—and longer if he likes Concord well enough to stay with us. Nothing could have been more to my wishes than to secure him and Mrs. Emery as host and hostess for receiving our Summer classes. He takes possession before the School opens. Mr. Harris writes that he will spend most of July with us And we depend much upon him and yourself for the Absolute teaching. I hope you will give us all of the time assigned to the sittings. Mr. Emery tells me that Mrs Denman purposes to be with us again, and Mr. Block[?] from your city. Will not Mrs. Wolcott venture also, and tempt Mr. Wolcott along with her?

Inquiries come to hand from different and distant parts, concerning our School. It looks now as if we should have a full attendance.

I am having a wider range of opportunities than formerly for meeting people, and enjoy the variety. Philosophical and literary topics are taking on a profounder treatment, and interesting wider and more thoughtful circles. I think with yourself and Harris once here, and at work, the school of the future might be inaugurated—a thing I hope to see before retiring behind the scenes.

I shall hope to hear from you more definitely regarding your Summer plans. Regards to Mrs. Jones and friends in Jacksonville.

Truly Yours,
A. Bronson Alcott.

Dr. Jones.

LETTER 79–37

[to Robert D. Weeks, Newark, N.J.]

Concord May 13th 1879.

Dear Sir.

I have to thank you for your book,[1] which I have ‖ I have ‖ read with much interest and general acceptance of your views. It comes at a timely moment, when theological studies are reassuming their proper place and import in our Universities, and with thoughtful persons generally.—And moreover when there is pressing need of referring to Biblical Standards for stemming the tide of Anti christianity now setting so defiantly against the Revealed truths of religion and Absolute philosophy.

The general drift of your book is assuring and devout. You have suggestive texts and statements for the solution of Unitarian and Trinitarian. I value particularly your fine distinction between the terms Son of God, and God the Son. And what you say concerning Christ's Preexistence is particularly satisfactory. So are your views of what constitutes "The only Personal Trinity."

I am looking for a revisal of our current theology, and your book will further this most desirable end.

Should you have an impulse to write me, I should esteem it a favor, and have something more satisfactory to offer.

I venture to enclose a Circular of our Concord Summer School of Philosophy and Literature.

Very truly
Yours,
A. Bronson Alcott.

Mr. Robert D. Weeks.
Newark,
    N. Jersey

[1] *Jehova-Jesus: The Oneness of God: The True Trinity* (New York, 1876).

LETTER 79–38[1]

[to Mary N. Adams, Dubuque, Iowa]

Concord May 17 1879.

Dear Mrs. Adams

I am thinking that you will hardly be able to resist the attraction of our Summer School—the Scholars and the other excellent company expected here during the Sessions. Do not the "currents" tend hitherward and indicate the freight "elect" for us? and us only? I must hope so. Everything looks most propitious for an interesting and edifying time. Mr. Harris writes that he hopes to pass most of the month of July with us and Dr. Jones Mrs. Denman and others from many and different parts of the West are to pass more or less time here also.

I see not how this Era is to be fully represented without yourself nor will the West; We may not omit the mystic the Sibylline the Womanly. This is the

Era of Mediation between extremes geographically—ideally. *I* shall feel the *one* bereft of its *Unity* without this mediation

Though Mr. Emerson's name does not appear on our list he will doubtless take part in the teaching. His presence and favor were alone an inspiration Of the other speakers named I believe you are not unadvised. Others may fill the Saturdays not specially provided for. I even think our Sunday Service may indicate finer modes of praises and worship. Amherst College sends its delegation and other learned institutions.

My opportunities during the past winter for meeting persons of widely differing views and thus learning the [tendencies][2] and aims of the religiously inclined *particularly*. Extremes are meeting, surprising the many who fancied sympathy and fellowship impossible if not impious. It has been my privilege to reconcile and unite to eliminate the errors from the dogmas, creeds traditions of the sects and reveal the hidden truths; the human mind refuses to believe a lie and clings devoutly to the dogmas for the truth it [word—blank] I have been invited to speak in pulpits and gladly availed of the privilege hitherto hardly extended to me in New England. At the West you were more hospitable on this account I suppose it has been bruited abroad. I have lately read the report in the news papers that "Mr Alcott is become orthodox," and the West and the East is surprised at the charge, "Conversion" if you will. "Conversion" may be taken double. Certainly I should feel flattered by being taken into the folds of *any* religious body but would not be owned by any outside of the *Church Universal*.

My family are all well. May writes happily from Paris Another picture of hers has been accepted at the "Salon" Louisa may join her sometime in the autumn My own health is perfect. To all of your family my regards and remembrance

Faithfully yours,
A. Bronson Alcott.

Mrs. Mary Newbury Adams
Dubuque Iowa

[1] MS., a copy, in Mrs. Adams' hand, owned by Mrs. Adele A. Bachman, South Orange, N.J. Mrs. Adams apparently was unable to decipher two of the words in the letter—one of which is indicated by [word—blank]; the other has been interpolated (see *n.* 2, below). Her copy of the letter is followed by a note: "This was received May 21. The anniversary of the day I took dinner with him at 'Parkers' after Mr. Emerson's Lecture I had come from N.Y. to hear. M.N.A."

A copy, in Alcott's hand, is in the Alcott-Pratt Collection.

[2] Interpolated from the copy in the Alcott-Pratt Collection.

LETTER 79–39

[to Frank Wakeley Gunsaulus, Chillicothe, Ohio][1]

Concord, Mass. | May 18th 1879.

Dear Sir.

Your book reached me by last evening's mail, forwarded here from Boston by Houghton Osgood and Co. through whom I wish to express my thanks for the favor.

After reading title, table of contents, Preface and Introduction, I slept, and this morning returned with fresh appetite to the perusal of the whole Volume. My day has been given to it.—And I take my pen with a grateful sense of obligation to the author for the light and comfort his writing has given me.

Identified as I have been, and familiar with most of the persons named in the text, sympathizing at times with them in their views and aims, especially with *Emerson*—though less Pantheistic in tendency than most—I find myself at the age of 80, *overseeing,* I think, their past errors and short comings, and feeling in Sympathy and general agreement with the substance and drift of your excellent and timely Essay. And may I venture on the strength of this assurance to ask of you a fuller account of your personal experiences and pursuits than your text suggests, or is this presuming too far for a stranger to hope?

But I may not close my letter without adding that your book appears at this propitious period in our history—at a time when the gravest issues are rising into importance, and the ablest minds are needed to engage in their discussion. Deeper than all are the paramount questions of Theology. I find your book has touched these deeply and fairly, and trust it will awaken a livelier interest in the study of Christian theism—our sole stay against the flood of Errors now threatening us.

I venture to enclose a Circular of our "Concord Summer School of Philosophy and Literature, and to express the pleasure it would afford us to see you here during the sessions.

I am, dear Sir,
Very truly
Yours,
A. Bronson Alcott.

PS. Mr. Emerson has just called and taken your book for perusal—which, I trust, you will not take amiss.

A.B.A.

---

[1] This letter was probably addressed to Gunsaulus; see Letter 79–42.

LETTER 79–40

[to   ?   ]

Concord, Mass. | May 19th 1879.

Dear Sir,

Yesterday Mr. Emerson brought and read to me your interesting letter, in which you give full account of your ingenious discoveries, and less of your own biography than we wished.

We are neither of us practical gardeners at present, though I have dwelt in an Orchard for twenty years past, and celebrated rural pursuits in my books

We have a neighbor, however, who takes prizes at the Annual horticultural Fairs, and cultivates fruits extensively, and we agreed that to him your apple-bearing discovery should be commended.

Your account of yourself interests me particularly, and hoping your impressions of our town and its literature, may draw you in this direction, I venture to enclose a Circular of our Concord Summer School, and to assure you that we should be honored by your presence and attendance at the Sessions.

The stately photograph is most acceptable, and now ornaments my study mantel piece.

Very truly
Yours,
A. Bronson Alcott.

LETTER 79–41

[to Mr. and Mrs. Ward]

Concord May 24 | 1879.

Mr. and Mrs Ward have the congratulation of Mr. Alcott on the happy announcement of their daughter, Miss Belle's marriage. And could he make the dove's flight across the distance would be happy to witness that interesting ceremony. He remembers with pleasure the past New-Year's Reception at their hospitable home, and congratulates them, and the happy pair on their anticipated union. May it prove all that their most ardent hopes so fondly predict.[1]

[1] The letter is unsigned.

LETTER 79–42

[to Frank Wakeley Gunsaulus, Chillicothe, Ohio]

Concord May 27 | 1879.

Dear Sir.

Yours of the 25th is just received, and I shall hope to take you by the hand, and introduce you to the members of our Summer School at its opening in July next. You will have read in our "Circular' the terms of admission to all or any part of the courses of the lectures. And if you will give us one or more of yours, on some of the Saturdays assigned for special lecturers the gain will be mutual. Mr Sanborn has registered your name, as an attendant, and you can choose further for yourself as to the length of your visit with us and attendance at the school. Persons from all parts of the states are asking to have their names registered, and we hope the desired fifty may apply. Even with thirty we should open the lectures.

Board can be obtained at fair rates in private families in the village and farmhouses of the neighborhood.

As to using the extract from my letter in the way you name. You are at full liberty to do so—though the publication may excite some comment among my old associates. But this must come sooner or later, and your book[1] may happily furnish the apt occasion.

I shall look forward to meeting you with much pleasure.

Meanwhile, believe me,

Cordially Yours,

A. Bronson Alcott

---

[1] *The Metamorphosis of a Creed: An Essay in Present-Day Theology* (Chillicothe, Ohio, 1879). Gunsaulus (1850–1921) was to become an eminent Congregational clergyman.

LETTER 79–43[1]

[to William T. Harris, St. Louis]

Concord June 7th 1879.

Dear Friend.

Emery brought his goods yesterday and takes possession of the Orchard in a few days. He tells me that he has written and invited you to be his guest during our Summer Sessions of the School. And Dr. Jones will, I hope, be Sanborn's. What hinders our taking some flights during these summer days.

Ames writes that he found you in good condition, and hopeful of our adventure. Every thing promises fair now. Students are registering their names almost daily. Let us hope, if not [word] on fair[?] "the Orchard" may not misrepresent the Platonic Ideals with Dr. Jones and yourself to interpret and illustrate. I must try to do my subordinate part as best I may: and ‖ the ‖ our dream prove possibly *more than a dream.*—Emerson will smile upon us, and sometimes speak his good words and great.

You inquire if any of your Reports are wanting in my set. I find I have all of them in your chosen binding but Vol. 1870'71.

By some carelessness Part I. of my *Philosophemes,* has been mislaid or lost.— No 1 for January 1875. As I am wishing to have a separate copy of the series bound for reference, perhaps you can supply this number.

Howison tells me that he will be unable to favor us with his lectures. But Emery has much to say, and can supply the place doubtless.

Hoping to greet you soon, I am,

Very faithfully,

Yours.

A. Bronson Alcott

Wm. T. Harris.

---

[1] From a copy, in Alcott's hand, in the Alcott-Pratt Collection. The original is in the Alcott-Harris Collection in the Concord Free Public Library (see Appendix B).

LETTER 79–44

[to   ?   ]

Concord June 18th 1879.

Dear Sir.

In answer to your inquiries, I may say, that I have no consciousness of being "converted to Christianity by Rev. Joseph Cook," though I have listened to his Lectures and had Conversations in his rooms in Boston. I hold Mr. Cook in high estimation as a speaker who has stirred many minds to thinking on religious subjects East and West and wish him abundant acceptance wherever he speaks.

I may add, that I have aimed in my conversations and preaching to reconcile the different religious Sects, acting as a mediator rather, and that if I must be classed with any religious body, it may be with those who belong to the *"Church Universal* in distinction from the *"Church Individual."*

Yours truly.

A. Bronson Alcott

LETTER 79–45

[to Frank Wakeley Gunsaulus, Chillicothe, Ohio]

Concord June 22nd | 1879.

Dear Sir,

I am saddened at your account of yourself. And yet am unwilling to believe that you will be unable to be with us at our Summer Symposeum [*sic*]. Surely your prayers for restoration, your desire to be with us will not fail you, yourself and friend sent forward in due time.

If you are paying the forfeit for your painstaking labors, some portion should be remitted at this hour.

Just prepare meanwhile for taking up your couch, and for the cars, and come here and be made whole. Am I asking too much for your faith and coming strength?

The *picture* you name sending, has not yet come [to] hand,—the book has.—

Very truly

Yours,[1]

F. W. Gunsaulus

[1] The signature has been cut out.

LETTER 79–46

[to   ?   ]

Concord June 23rd | 1879.

Dear Sir,

Yours is not the first note of inquiry that has come to hand respecting my past and present religious views. Nor is it strange that after holding during the last winter months a series of Conversations at the Rooms of Rev. Joseph Cook in Boston, some influence should be attributed of his orthodoxy upon my present religious belief. I certainly hold Mr. Cook in high regard, and esteem him an agent in awakening an interest wherever he may speak, in a truly spiritual faith. I am not, however, aware of having been converted to orthodoxy, or drawn away from my former views by his teachings. I ought in candor to add, in answer to your inquiry, that while I sympathize less than formerly, with Unitarianism and other "isms", a Pantheist I have never been, nor has Transcendentalism at any time fully satisfied, though I have been classed with that school of thinkers. I have striven to reconcile the different religious beliefs with an underlying universal faith, and if I must be classed, prefer to belong to the *Church Universal,* not to any particular *Sectarian body* of Christians. Christ is the door at which it is safe to knock both for welcome admittance, and ‖ assured acceptance. ‖ "the peace that passeth understanding"

I am, Sir,

Very truly

Yours,

A. Bronson Alcott.

PS. I shall be pleased to hear further from you should you feel inclined to write *again.*

LETTER 79–47

[to Samuel Orcutt, New Haven? Conn.]

Concord June 27th 1879.

Dear Sir,

Certainly I am both honored and delighted in the descent of my grandmother *Mary Chatfield,* of whose family I had known less than of the *"Alcott's and Bronsons.* And the information given in your letter of her ancestry, explains some traits in my Father's character, (perhaps my own,) who, as you know, inherited the *maternal* name from his uncle Joseph of Derby, and transmitted it in that of my brother *"Chatfield".* I knew the family was highly respectable, and once visited the old Homestead on the Hill east of the Landing.

Of the *"Piersons"* I had only very general knowledge. I shall now take a personal interest in the family genealogy and History, connecte[d] as it is with Yale College and Connecticut Theology.

I find, on consulting *"Johnson's Cyclopedia,* that Abraham Pierson was born at Lynn, Mass, 1641. graduated at Harvard 1668. was ordained in 1672. at Newark N.J. as colleage [sic] to his Father, Revd. Abraham Pierson (1668,'72) was congregational pastor at Killingworth, Conn., 1694, 1707, and the first President of Yale College 1701–'07." I find also, there is a post village of the name of *Chatfield* in Minisota [sic], and another in Ohio.

You will learn more of the families in your researches, that will be interesting to me particularly, and I shall await the publication of your *"Derby History"* with much of eagerness and hope.

Of our *"Summer School"* we have the fairest prospects. Thirty names are now registered as students for the whole course of lectures, and our number will doubtless be full by the time the sessions open. We shall be pleased if you will visit us.

I have directed your letter to Rev. Dr. Clarke, Jamaica Plain, Roxbury, Mass, where he resides He should have important matter for your sketch of the Hull Family.[1]

I am always gratified in learning of yourself and labors.

Very truly

Yours,

A. Bronson Alcott.

[1] James Freeman Clarke's grandfather was General William Hull.

LETTER 79-48

[to   ?   ]

Concord June 27th 1879.

Dear Sir.

Thank you heartily for your "Sermon on the Perfection of the Bible".

There is need of celebrating its surpassing excellencies. For though it lies on our Tables, and is called an inspired Volume, I fear it is oftenest read but superficially, and its spirit but imperfectly apprehended. And this must follow while the minds of men are so faintly illuminated by "the Light that seeks to lighten every one that comes into the world."—

How much an interpreter is needed of these oracles of the spirit! *"Give me a boy. Said Dr. Nathaniel Taylor, "in Philosophy, and I care not who has him in Theology."*

It is out of the abundance of the Heart that the mouth speaks, and this *"Heart philosophy"* is the one thing needful to apprehend all mysteries.

We hope to do a little in the way of *interpretation* in our Summer School, which bids fair, thirty students having given their names, and more may be added before it opens. May we not hope to see you here, during its sessions?

Very truly

Yours,

A. Bronson Alcott.

LETTER 79-49

[to   ?   ]

Concord June 28th 1879.

Dear Sir,

I have examined my correspondence with Miss Muzzey, and find that her father was a Massachusetts man and married my first cousin, Miss Harriet Bronson daughter of Mr Amos Bronson, who settled at Springville Susquehannah

County, Penn. sometime about 1815. and that Miss Muzzey is now living in Brooklyn same county. and doubtless has information for your researches.

She writes her name

Annie L. Muzzey.

Very truly

Yours,

A. Bronson Alcott

LETTER 79–50

[to William Fairfield Warren,[1] Boston]

Concord June 28th | 1879.

Dear Sir,

I learn my misfortune in leaving the Table a moment too early—and thus the loss of your speech.—I was so impressed with the affectionate tribute paid by the assembled Scholars to Emerson, and his blushing reception of it, that I followed him soon after it had passed. But I have pleasant associations with the day and particularly with my conversation with yourself at the table and in the procession.

The Book of which I gave you some account,[2] I hope to bring my self some day of next week, and leave at your Beacon Street Rooms. I think you will find it interesting, and as the work of an author now but twenty three years of age promising, at least further services in the way of thought and criticism.[3]

Rev. Dr. Warren.

[1] President of Boston University.
[2] Gunsaulus' *Metamorphosis of a Creed.*
[3] The complimentary close and signature have been cut out.

LETTER 79–51

[to Miss Cleaver]

Concord July 6th 1879.

Dear Miss Cleaver,

I should be culpably indifferent to your earnest pleas for light and guidance did I not respond to your second inquiry—"What shall I do, or read? Am I only harboring foolish doubts, thinking foolishly on what may as well not be thought of?—or, should I try to continue in my thoughts, till I feel satisfaction and peace of mind?

or, drop it all and wait for further development when the soul is set free at last?

1. These are *not foolish* doubts, but cries of the spirit for help: and you cannot if you would set them at rest.

2. Yes! continue to strive for light. it may be waited for impatiently, but will come by persistent seeking and patient waiting.

3. You cannot drop it if you would. The *intellect has* duties to discharge as well as the heart—the head would have light to guide the affections, and the affections prompt the will to right actions. With every aid from *without*, the peace of Soul that frees and satisfies comes from *within*. One must seek to fathom the depths of his own soul to find the assistance that his prayers ask for.—Know himself, before he can apprehend the Self of Himself, God the Father, Nor is there *necessary anthropomorphism* in viewing Him in his *filial* relations to us— Personally not abstractly only thus is He brought home to our affections, and *apprehended* by the mind. *Comprehended* He is not fully by the most competent intelligence. Defining Him, confines and confuses. An element of mysticism clings to all our affections, and is essential to piety itself. You, being a Person, would address yourself to a Person, not an abstract thing, not to a Law alone. We do not address our friends, as *It*. but Personally as *Him* or *Her*. And for this reason *Pantheism* fails of answering the deepest religious needs of our souls. And Unitarianism in subordinating the Son to the *human* relations, fails to satisfy in not finding the divine A man-God is not a God-man. Hence Christianity supplies the Christ; and finds both God and Man—answers both to head and heart. to the threefoldness of our being—our affections, our reason, and our Will—the Holy Trinity within us, personally *incarnated* and a living Presence.

You mistake in writing me Revd. I am plain Mr.—though I sometimes speak in pulpits, and in those of all the sects, but *Romanists*.

If you desire to present your doubts or beliefs in further correspondence I shall gladly respond

Yours truly,
A. Bronson Alcott.

LETTER 79–52

[to Frank Wakeley Gunsaulus, Chillicothe, Ohio]

Concord July 7th 1879.

My dear Friend,

I hope by this time you are strengthening daily and recovering from your depression, so that we may hope to see you here—if not at the opening of our Summer School, before its close.[1] We cannot,—unless the good Disposer, orders otherwise—well dispense with your ‖ absence ‖ attendance *this*,—hardly less on your own account than ours. You are clearly due here on this significant gathering of persons with whom you would, most of any of your contemporaries delight to meet, and discuss the things that are so near your thoughts, and so precious. I shall expect you.

Meanwhile I enclose for your perusal a letter from my friend Miss *Elisabeth Peabody*, a lady, in some respects, as representative of the thoughts and experiences of the persons quoted from and criticised in your Book, as my self, if not better informed regarding them both in the past, and their present state of mind. You will see how she looks at your book and yourself. And you can hardly expect a more candid and discriminating account than hers. I wish you may find it not wholly unacceptable.

—I have sent your book to *Dr. William F. Warren, President of the Boston University,* for perusal, and (probably) for a notice. He is, as you may know, a learned man and catholic thinker, and likely to do you, and your Book, justice.

If you are able to write I shall enjoy a note, if no more from you.

Most cordially
Yours,
A. Bronson Alcott.

Mr. Gunsaulus.

---

[1] The first session of the Concord School of Philosophy opened July 15 and closed August 16. For a detailed account of that session, see Alcott, *Journals,* pp. 496–510. The best account of the School for all its ten summer sessions is Austin Warren, "The Concord School of Philosophy," *NEQ,* II (April, 1929), 199–233. The financial history of the School is given in Sanborn, *A. Bronson Alcott,* II, 532, *n.* 1.

Letter 79–53[1]

[to William Fairfield Warren, Wilbraham, Mass.]

Concord July 7th 1879.

Dear Sir,

I should have mailed the Book sooner to your address.[2] But Miss Elisabeth Peabody was so desirous of reading it on my account of its contents and the youth of its author, that I allowed her to take it for a few days. She now returns it, with saying that she intends writing to Mr. Gunsaulus her views of the book. She thinks Transcendentalism tends to Pantheism as the author implies, but questions the accuracy of his criticisms of the writers named by him. But she is much interested in him, and will doubtless write him a characteristic letter of her views, particularly of Dr. Channings religious opinions.

I mention this to show you the agreement of a thoughtful woman, and one who shared deeply in the transcendental movement, as in the Unitarian, and is a critical observer of the times.

I shall be happy to learn your views of the Book, from your Orthodox standpoint.

Very truly
Yours,
A. Bronson Alcott

Rev. Dr. Warren,
    at Wilbraham, Mass.

---

[1] MS. owned by the Boston University Libraries.
[2] See Letters 79–50 and 79–52.

[to Frank Wakeley Gunsaulus, Chillicothe, Ohio]

Concord August 6th 1879.

Dear Friend.

Mr. Harris has just left us for St. Louis, having given us ten lectures, and interested, not only his regular attendants, but many of our townspeople who flocked to hear him expound the Speculative philosophy. Our rooms at the Orchard House being too small, he gave his last but one in the Orthodox Vestry, Emerson, and others attending. He has won for Philosophy a new and lively interest, and for himself much respect for his genius and character. He was too much occupied while with us, to read your Book as he wished, and expressed a wish to possess a copy. I would suggest to you, if you think favorably, to forward a copy to him at St. Louis, and with the hope that he will review it. He of all others known by us, is the critic who can do it the justice it claims from some one of your contemporaries. It will not sleep, at any rate. But I wish to have Authority in its behalf.

Our School is assured Success, and I see not how we can refuse to open it another season. The lectures have all been most acceptable and well attended. We have yet another week to come before its close. I hoped to see you here. But it may be unsafe for you to come.

I shall be glad to hear from you again and again.

Very truly

Yours,

A. Bronson Alcott

Rev. F. W. Gunsaulus

[Letter to Chatfield Alcott, Oswego, N.Y.; from Concord, August 9, 1879.]

[to A. T. Frizelle, Sharon Center, Ohio]

Concord August 13th | 1879

Dear Sir.

No arrangement has yet been made for the publication of the Lectures and Conversations delivered at the School of Philosophy and Literature. Nor is it certain that the publication of the whole or part of them, will be arranged. Brief abstracts of some of them have been given in some of the newspapers. And possibly a pamphlet may be issued of the doings and prospects after the lectures close.

Very truly

Yours,

A. Bronson Alcott.

LETTER 79–56

[to William L., Wendell P., and Francis J. Garrison?]
For the "Tributes to Mr. Garrison".[2]

Concord, Mass. | Aug. 13, 1879.

Mr Alcott returns his thanks to the children of his illustrious friend, their Father, and wishes to add, that he esteems it one of the chiefest of privileges to have known him, enjoyed his friendship, and, in some humble manner, participated in the great labor of rescuing the Nation from dishonor, and restoring it to freedom and an unspotted name, among the governments of the earth.

He would, add, moreover, the regard in which Mrs. Alcott held this friend of her husband and hers, as of her sainted brother, who never could sufficiently express his affection for Mr. Garrison.

Few children in our time, have had a nobler example set them by a Father to live for the promotion of the happiness of others. May they, one and all, preserve his memory untarnished.

From their father's friend,
A. Bronson Alcott

[1] MS. owned by the Friends Historical Library of Swarthmore College.
[2] William Lloyd Garrison had died May 24, 1879.

LETTER 79–57

[to Elizabeth Thompson,[1] Concord]

Concord. August. | 14th 1879.

Dear Mrs. Thompson

Permit me to hand you a little book of mine, (now out of print) for occupying any spare moment of yours while at "the Wayside". I shall feel happier in knowing that my Book may speak when I am not permitted that pleasure. Hoping to meet you again, (though in a crowd) this evening,[2] allow me to subscribe myself.

Yours, affectionately,
A. Bronson Alcott.

Mrs. Elisabeth Thompson

[1] Mrs. Thompson, of New York City, later contributed $1,000 to the Concord School of Philosophy, from which was paid the cost of the Hillside Chapel, in which future lectures were held, on the grounds of Orchard House.
[2] At a party at Judge Hoar's (Alcott, *Journals*, p. 509).

LETTER 79–58

[to A. N. Alcott, Fredericksburg, Ohio]

Concord. September | 4th 1879.

Dear Sir.

Your letter giving the desired particulars of yourself, was gladly read, and confirms my persuasion of our kinship, though, not having your grandfather's name, I am unable to trace the relation accurately. My persuasion is that you descend from Mr. Daniel Alcott, the son of John, my great grandfather, and first settler of Wolcott, my native town in Connecticut.—Mr. Daniel Alcott moved from Wolcott early in this century. He went to Colebrook, Conn, and his children from thence to Saratoga, and his grandsons from those parts to places in the West. One of his granddaughters, named *"Marilda,"* married *"Oren Sage"* of Rochester, N.Y. and another, named *"Sylvia"*, married *"Lyman Ballard,"* of Attica, N.Y. another named *"Paulina"* married Mr. Havens of Pen Yan, N.Y. Of two sons, named, *Daniel and Amos,* I have no knowledge. Several of the name settled at Kalamazoo, Michigan. Others at Milwaukie [*sic*], Wisconsin. Others, of my generation, emigrated to New York and Ohio. Amongst some of these, I infer were your ancestors.—That you may have the possible key to these I send you a copy of the History of Wolcott, which contains a Genealogy of our Family, as far as this was known at the time of its compilation.

Your account of your present religious views interests me. and it [would] give me much pleasure to meet and compare notes mutually.

Our School proved a brilliant success, and will be opened again next Summer.

I looked on the map to find your present residence. I find you are not far from *"Medina"* where I have cousins named "Bronson", living and whom I sometimes visit. Have you seen Mr. Gunsaulus Book entitled, *"The Metamorphosis* of a Creed[?"] The author is, or was, lately living at Chillicothe, Ohio. I think you would find much sympathy with his views.

May I hope to hear from you further?

> Very truly Yours,
> A. Bronson Alcott

LETTER 79–59

[to Frank Wakeley Gunsaulus, Chillicothe? Ohio]

Concord September | 4th 1879.

Dear Sir./

I would not trouble you with many words, but am not a little anxious to learn of your welfare since you last wrote. You were then quite ill, and anxious about yourself, and troubled, moreover, about the usage of your fellow ministers. Your book, too, was an object of interest. I shall be gratified if I might learn from yourself (if able) something farther concerning these particulars.

I have taken a personal interest in yourself and in your Book, and shall await further information.

And you will take kindly, I am sure, what follows:—I forwarded a copy of your Book to Professor Tyler of Amherst College for his criticism. And he has just returned the book with his criticism, which I copy.—

I have read *through,* and some of it more than once "The Metamorphosis of a Creed," which you were so kind as to send to me by Mr. Shumway, and I now return it by mail.

It is not without its faults. Among them is a loose, wordy, and sometimes obscure style, and a still unsettled theology and philosophy. But it is a book of much learning, and power and rare interest. It seems to me, that the author establishes his propositions. His copious citations and numerous references, prove beyond dispute that the standard works of representative Unitarians are pervaded with the thought and spirit of Pantheism, this distinction between Transcendentalism and Idealism is perhaps hardly justified by usage. But it is convenient, and the difference between the *things* is important and well drawn.

I have lately read in the public Journals some account of *Rev. A. N. Alcotts* trial for heresy, and have had a letter from him (in answer to mine inquiring, chiefly, about his "Genealogy") in which he states his present theological views. As he dates from Fredericksburg Ohio, and your last from Chesterville, I find by consulting the map, that you must be almost near neighbors, and think you may have similar views, perhaps Sympathy, at least, in your relations to the Churches. I have just written, and named your book, believing, if you are not already known to each other, an acquaintance might be mutually profitable and agreeable.

I take *Mr. Alcott* to be a Kinsman of mine, and shall have an additional interest in his name and acquaintance.

The Summer School closed at the end of the five weeks' Session. It was a brilliant success, and we issue our Prospectus in a few days for next Summer's Session. I shall gladly forward a copy to you.

My health continues perfect, and hope infinite.—

May yours be restored, and yourself to good service in the *Church of Messias.*

Your friend

A. Bronson Alcott.

LETTER 79–60

[to Georgiana Hemingway Cook, Boston]

Concord September | 13th 1879

Dear Friend.

I have just returned from the Sessions of the Social Science Association at Saratoga and find your letter of the 9th. Yesterday I had consented to join a party for a round trip to Lake George, my chief pleasure in this excursion was the hope of finding you at Ticonderoga.

But as I was not sure of your being there, I concluded to return. We left last night at 12—and reached Concord to breakfast, having had a delightful time at the Springs, where I had not been before. Mr Sanborn and Miss Peabody accompanied me. The lectures and proceedings had much of interest, and the company I met also. Among other persons I made a charming acquaintance with Mrs Elisabeth Thompson of Philanthropic celebrity, a beautiful and lovely lady whom I wish yourself and Mr Cook to know.

I shall be at home on Friday the 19th, and gladly meet you at the station if I may learn the hour of your arrival.

I am gratified by your appreciation of our Summer School, and respond heartily to your estimate of its established Orthodoxy

Hoping to see, (and shall not Mr Cook accompany you) I defer further matters to our meeting

Most cordially
Yours,
A. Bronson Alcott

LETTER 79–61

[to Elizabeth Thompson, Saratoga, N.Y.]

Concord September | Sunday, 14th 1879.

Dear Mrs. Thompson.

You permitted me to write to you, a pleasure next to the enjoyment of your presence and conversation. I have thought a word now may add to your pleasure as you sit under the balconies, or even in the seclusion of your chamber. You have already so fully shared my heart's confidences that I can hardly hope to add a word or a sentiment more. Yet this I may assure you did bring a certain secret relief, to soften that formidable *"negative"*—the hope that you were to be sometimes *"not far away,"* and conversation forbidden forever. And I awoke this morning half reconciled to the fate that had saddened all the way from the last adieu at the Hotel. Excuse me, dear lady, if you have my confessions. To make these is a relief, and your compassionate heart has not yet learned to turn coldly from any pleas of sincere regard and affection.

I live in hope of seeing you here, and at "The Orchard,' where I know you enjoyed the riches of the summer's feast of wisdom.

Again let me add how charming are the memories of our brief acquaintance, and hopeful my anticipations of the future.

Affectionately,
A. B. A.

LETTER 79–62[1]

[to May, Meudon, France]

Concord September, | 24th 1879.

My Dear May.

Please accept from your Father the first rent-money yet received for the Orchard House since we left it nearly two years ago. It is but a trifle. But it takes to you not a little of affection, for yourself—and, may I not add—for the *Little One,* now at your bosom,[2] and the pledge of your love for the father, whom you have chosen for your friend and companion in your future Sojourn!—May every blessing await you and yours—

I read your last letter with delight at your present and prospective happiness. But I do not readily relinquish the hope of seeing you and yours and on this side of the seas. Such propitious fortunes have attended us these late years, that I am ready to believe impossibilities almost possible. Certainly we have abundant cause for gratitude and thankfulness for Heaven's benefits.

You will wish to have a word along with this little token, about the *"Orchard House"* itself It is not unlikely the Estate may be purchased and dedicated to a *"permanent School of Philosophy"* And possibly I my self may occupy it. This is among the possibilities of the future.

I have just returned from Andover, where I had the pleasure of addressing near 600 students professors and citizens of the town. It was a surprise and an honor. I will send you a report of it when it appears. These latter years are bestowing honors and rewards for the indifference of former ones.

Now dear May believe me in perfect health and spirits with pleasant prospects, and always

Your affectionate Father
A.B.A.

Regards to Ernest, and kiss—to his sister Sophia

---

[1] Quoted in part in Ticknor, *May Alcott*, p. 290.
[2] May's daughter, Louisa May Nieriker, was born November 8, 1879. See letter 79–78.

LETTER 79–63

[to Elizabeth Thompson]

Concord September | 27th 1879.

Dear Madam,

A choice way of hiding from pursuers! Just follow them and take covert under their every shadow!

I have just learned of your hiding place, having awaited the coming to hand of the *signal newspaper* in response to my note addressed to Saratoga soon after my return from that seat of pleasant memories.

Well, next to the Orchard itself, the present retreat is preferable to Lake George, New York or Washington cities, or Boston even.

And here I please my self in thinking my lady finds the best of company in herself, free from all impertinent pursuers, meanwhile.

So I submit to the humor, and, to please her love of letters, permit my pen to take liberties to lip denied.

Yet fancy "Budda [*sic*], Lord and Savior" may lighten her leisure even from far Asia.

Affectionately,
A. B. A.

LETTER 79–64

[to Miss Hyde]

Concord September | 30th 1879.

Dear Miss Hyde,

I remember my promise of visiting your School, and hope to repeat the pleasure of former visits on some fair day of next week. I happen to have engagements for all of this week.

Meanwhile the frosts will not have greatly deformed the landscape, but added fresh tints even to the maples, and the young ladies also.

Promising my self much pleasure in this visitation

I am

Very truly

Yours,

A. Bronson Alcott

LETTER 79–65[1]

[to   ?   ]

Concord, September, | 30 1879.

Dear Sir,

The book referred to by Mr. Sanborn must have been a Birth-day Gift privately printed in 1865. and the sketch of Emerson afterwards inserted in my Concord Days, which you write of having seen. Besides that I have published nothing about Emerson. Reporters of my Conversations on American Authors may have printed something from time to time, but nothing of any importance What Mr. Sanborn may have for you will be of value in preparing your Lectures. Emerson is a subject for book and lecture and I have found the West very appreciative of his Character and Genius

Our Concord School proved an unexpected success. We shall issue in a few days our Prospectus for next summer, and I will forward to you a copy.

Wishing you every success in your preaching and teaching, I am,

Very truly

Yours,

A. Bronson Alcott.

[1] MS. owned by the Fruitlands and Wayside Museums. An unsigned copy of most of the letter, in Alcott's hand, is in the Alcott-Pratt Collection.

LETTER 79–66

[to   ?   ]

Concord, | October 4th 1879.

Dear Madam,

I remember your frequently expressed wish to become a pupil of mine, while abiding in our neighborhood. Birds of passage must be charmed before they take wing for distant climes, fairer game. So I venture to bait your fancy on some leaves of mine—recent as you may perceive on perusal, and not less apposite, let me hope, to your present mood of thought and sentiment.

Our acquaintance has been too short and fitful to assure as faithfully. Let me believe that these Leaves may serve to deepen and confirm first impressions while they may amuse, entertain, possibly instruct our Visitor as she lingers during these deeply tinted autumnal days. I need not add they are for her eyes only.

Faithfully,
A. B. A.

LETTER 79-67[1]

[to William T. Harris, St. Louis]

Concord October 6th 1879.

Dear Friend,

Our Circulars for next summer's School of Philosophy are just issued, and I make haste to forward you a copy. I purpose following it soon, and to discuss future prospects and plans for the School and for yourself (if you will) at your own residence in St. Louis.

I cannot now determine accurately my route, nor the time of leaving Concord, but will apprize you when I have laid my plans more definitely. Meanwhile, and before I leave home, will you mail a Postal Card, saying that you approve or otherwise our arrangements for next Session of the School: and, besides, inform us if you are willing to give your name as one of the Incorporators of the School with Dr. Jones, Mrs Elisabeth Thompson, Mrs. Denman, Mr. Emery, Mr Sanborn and my self—*seven* in all.—We think it well to get it Incorporated, particularly if, as we now contemplate, having a Winter Session, of six months, and making the School a permanent Institution.—In order to make this assured, your residence here seems most important, certainly during a part of the year.—*Now,* to render this a feasible thing for you, I am authorised [*sic*] to say that Mrs Thompson, will pledge $500 towards your coming, and I offer you the occupancy of the Orchard, for any compensation that you may name—rather than miss your coming—free for the first year. Mrs Thompson is disposed to help us, and will even add another $500, if that sum shall be found necessary. She wishes much to see you meanwhile should you come on to New York during the winter. I shall avail my self of opportunities to speak of the School in my tour—see Dr. Jones, Mrs Denman, Mr Grimes, Mrs and Mr Adams of Dubuque, Gov. Bagley and others. The School *is to be,* and it seems as if you were essential to its existence.—I can add no more now, but wished to advize you of our plans in advance of my seeing you personally, and consulting further about them.

Very truly
Yours,
A Bronson Alcott

Wm. T. Harris.

---

[1] From a copy, in Alcott's hand, in the Alcott-Pratt Collection. The original is in the Alcott-Harris Collection in the Concord Free Public Library (see Appendix B).

LETTER 79–68

[to John Steinfort Kedney, Faribault, Minn.]

Concord October, | 6th. 1879.

Dear Sir./

I have deferred writing in reply to yours of last August till I could communicate definite information concerning next Summer's Session of the Concord School of Philosophy. Our Circulars have at last reached us from the printers, and I take pleasure in forwarding to you a Copy. We think our list of lecturers able and attractive. And at present, every indication for next Summer's Session is hopeful.

I purpose leaving Concord soon for a short tour West, and hope to reach your town and consult the future of our School, and of Philosophy generally, with yourself and friends at Faribault.

Meanwhile.

Most truly

Yours,

A. Bronson Alcott

Rev. Dr. Kedney

LETTER 79–69

[to Frank Wakeley Gunsaulus, Columbus, Ohio]

Concord, | October 6th. 1879.

Dear Friend,

Your full circumstantial letter has just come to hand and been read with sympathetic interest. It needs no apology on your part for your silence. Your illness and perplexities were sufficient, and besides I had heard of your settlement and successful labors at Columbus. Mr. Cook, (with whom I lately visited Andover) had confirmed all these best accounts of yourself.

And now, I have the pleasant prospect of seeing you soon, at your own home in Columbus, I purpose leaving here about the 20th of this month, and shall linger on my way—a few days in Connecticut, in Pennsylvania, visit my cousins at Medina, Ohio and then on to yourself. I have a relative living in your city, the widow of cousin, the late Dr. William A. Alcott. And I find the Rev. A. N. Alcott is not far away.

My tour West will take me to St. Louis and some of the Missisippi [sic] cities. I promise my self much pleasure in making your personal acquaintance, and learning more fully of your future plans and prospects.

I enclose this in a Circular of our next Summers Session of the Concord School of Philosophy.

Very cordially

Yours,

A. Bronson Alcott.

Rev. F. W. Gunsaulus.

LETTER 79-70

[to Horatio Nelson Powers, Bridgeport, Conn.]

Concord October | 11th. 1879.

Dear Sir/

Yours of 8th inst is at hand. Any evening most convenient for yourself and friends will suit me. I shall pass the Sunday preceding in Waterbury and can reach Bridgeport on Monday evening if you wish. But prefer that you should fix the time to suit yourselves.

From Bridgeport, I purpose going Westwards.

Very truly
Yours
A Bronson Alcott

Rev. Dr. Powers.

LETTER 79-71

[to Sarah Denman, Quincy, Ill.]

Concord, | October 14th 1879.

Dear Mrs Denman

I forward herewith a copy of our Circular for the next Summer's Session of our School of Philosophy, and hope to follow it about the last of this month for a tour as far as St. Louis, returning by way of Quincy and Jacksonville. I shall hope to see yourself and friends again in your homes and consult further on our School and matters in which we have a mutual interest. I cannot now determine the time when I may reach Quincy, nor the length of my Western Tour.

The prospects of the School are very encouraging. Already several names have been registered for next Summer's Session, and we have an attractive list of lecturers as you will see by the Circular. Then a lady, Mrs Elisabeth Thompson, has made us a donation of $1000 for promoting the objects of the School.

Mr. Harris writes that he may come to Concord to reside. The Emerys are already settled here for the present at least. They are now leaving the *Orchard House* for one, near us in the Village. And we hope Dr. Jones will yet consent to pass a longer time with us than during the Summer Sessions of the School.

Mrs. Lorenzo Bull made us a short visit, but I missed seeing her.

My family are well. May writes happily from Paris.

Hoping to meet you soon, I am,

Very faithfully
Yours,
A. Bronson Alcott

LETTER 79-72

[to A. N. Alcott, Fredericksburg, Ohio]

Concord, | October 14th 1879.

Dear Sir.

I forward to your address our Circular for next Summers' Session of our School of Philosophy, and purpose following it soon for a tour westwards as far as St. Louis. I wish to take Columbus on my route, and wish moreover, to see yourself at some point on the way. Perhaps you can ‖ inform ‖ advize me of my best route to Fredericksburg. Or, might I hope to meet you at Columbus? I would write and inform you of the time when I should be there. I should regret to miss seeing you, when so near your residence.

I leave here the last of next week, and expect to reach Columbus sometime in November, after visiting relatives in Pennsylvania and at Medina, Ohio. By the map, it seems as if I could take Fredericksburg on my way from Medina to Columbus. At any rate, I shall hope not to miss seeing you.

I shall be pleased to hear from you before I leave home

Truly Yours,[1]

Rev. A. N. Alcott
Fredericksburg

[1] The signature has been cut out.

LETTER 79-73

[to   ?   , Washington, D.C.]

Concord, | October 15th. 1879.

Dear Sir.

Your note requesting information concerning School desks, furniture &c. comes to hand just as I am about leaving for the West, and leaves me no time to do justice to the matter.

The most I can do now is to forward to you Dr. Alcott's Prize Essay on the Construction of School Houses, which is as much mine in its plan and details as his. The idea of the desks I believe, to be mine entirely, and first made and put into the Centre School House in Cheshire Conn, in 1826. We had both taught School in Bristol, Conn. before this date, and added backs to the rude benches, and introduced slates &c. for the younger classes.

If you have Russells American Journal of Education, at hand you may find an account of my Cheshire School, Vol. III. p.p. 26–34 and 86–94. In the latter is a drawing of my School-room. The side desks of which are I believe, the model of Dr. Alcott's.

His Essay was published some years later. I certainly had seen none of that pattern, and had these made at my own expense. The seats of the inner rows of desks were with backs and intended for those who used slates only. An account of the formation of my School in the Masonic Temple in Boston, 1835, is given in "Miss Peabody's Record of my School." I expect to find at Columbus, Ohio, where Dr. Alcotts widow is now residing important documents relating to our mutual improvements in Early Education. Should I find any thing of school furniture &c deserving of further notice, I shall gladly forward this to your address at Washington.

As I have no duplicate of Dr Alcott's Essay will you be careful and so return it to me at Concord, Mass.

Very Respectfully,
A. Bronson Alcott.

LETTER 79-74

[to Frank Wakeley Gunsaulus, Columbus, Ohio]

Concord, | October 15th 1879.

Dear Friend.

You may include my name in the list of lecturers, and for a single evening, if no more. I dare say I shall gladly avail of any services, in this way, that yourself and friends may care for. As to the time when I may reach Columbus, I cannot now foresee—probably by the middle of November; I wish it may be before.

Meanwhile, I am,

Faithfully
Yours,
A. Bronson Alcott.

LETTER 79-75

[to Horatio Nelson Powers, Bridgeport, Conn.]

Concord, October 15th 1879.

Dear Sir/

Tuesday evening, the 28th. will suit me very well for the Conversation.

I may reach Bridgeport on Monday sometime, but it may be not till Tuesday. But you may expect me without fail on Tuesday Evening.

I wish for our sakes we may have Olympian days and memorable evenings.

Yours truly,
A. Bronson Alcott.

Rev. Dr. H. N. Powers.

LETTER 79-76

[to William H. Channing, London, England]

Concord October | 16th. 1879.

My Dear Friend,

Your welcome letter August 4th with Mr. Arnold's charming Poem,[1] reached me a few days too late to be presented to the School of Philosophy, this having closed on the 20th of August, and with a success unexpected by every one. On reading your letter, your Sketch of the Author, and his Book I took them to my publishers Messrs. Roberts Brothers, and found the head of the House already disposed to publish the Poem. My copy went at once to the printers hands. And the American edition is just out, with your Sketch of the author, George Ripley's notice in the N.Y. Tribune and Dr. Holmes' (in part) in the International Review. Only the best things have been written as yet about the Poem, and only such deserve to be written. It is a charming Poem, treated in a tender spirit and with delicacy and power. It must make a lovely impression on the reader, chasten, and even serve to Christianize the faithless in Christianity. Its literary merits are surpassing. Knowing how good things are oftenest late in reaching him[2] I took the book to him yesterday with some account of its history. He of all its readers is the better Buddist [sic], our Budda [sic] if any one is. I am pleased to report him in fair health, and scarcely more *hesitant* than when you saw him last. He reads a lecture occasionally, and I meet him pleasantly at our P. Office. You will perceive we have his name in our list of lecturers for the Summer School of 1880. A copy of our Circular accompanies this letter.

You will not be surprised to learn that I am chiefly engaged in Promoting the success of the School, intending to plant it upon a solid foundation. We purpose having it incorporated as *"the Concord School of Philosophy."* Mr. Harris is expected to make his future residence here in *Concord* and issue his Journal as heretofore, but with *Concord* on its covers. He will probably occupy the *Orchard House.* Mr. Emery has occupied during the Summer. He is an important addition to our number. Dr. Jones will pass the summer with us, and, should the School become a permanency, remain during the Winter Sessions. A lady of wealth and philanthropy, Mrs Elisabeth Thompson, has passed the summer here and given the School a donation of *$1,000.* The Greave's Library, with additions is to be given also.

And further, I am now about leaving here for a tour through the Western States, and shall make the School the subject for lectures and Conversations with its many friends in those parts. The larger number of our Summer pupils came from the West.—

I am not, my friend, fully reconciled to your absence from us. Nor do I yet wholly relinquish yourself and your services for humanity to your British friends. We have prior and native claims upon you. Channing is the father of all of us who rightly claim the name of American, and philosopher. A Scholarship in the School of Philosophy should restore you to your country and *us.*

My family are all with me, except my daughter May, now Madam *Nieriker,* living in Paris, France.

Mr Coningale [sic] Cook editor of the University Magazine, London, writes that he wishes to make your acquaintance. Mr. Sanborn is still our most helpful associate.

I am in perfect health and hope to do some service in the future.

Every blessing attend you and yours, my dear and early Friend.

Faithfully yours,

A. Bronson Alcott

[1] Edwin Arnold's *The Light of Asia.*
[2] Emerson.

LETTER 79-77

[to ?]

Concord October | 17th 1879.

Dear Friend,

I have just received a pleasant letter from Mrs. Mitchell in which she speaks of her profitable interviews with yourself, her interest in the revival of literature and philosophy, and particularly of her hopes in our Concord Summer School. We were much pleased with her personally, and look forward to her return to us next Summer. The thoughtful West supplies us with our freshest and most promising pupils.

I have known this for some time, and should hardly have ventured upon our adventure of the Summer School without the assurance of this enthusiastic support.

I write now to forward to you Sanborns notice of Arnolds new Poem the Light of Asia which is written in your favorite vein of appreciation of the Oriental thought, and mystic piety. I am sure you will delight in the book. Budda's [sic] story is delightfully idealized, and brought most vividly before our Western mind. It must be good reading for Christians of all professions, and not less for the AntiChrists.

Do you take your tour West as early as this? If you should, I may chance to meet you again at some of your pauses on your route

I leave here on Friday next, and purpose to go as far as St Louis, and from thence up the Missisippi [sic] to Dubuque and return by my old route Eastwards.

We have primary work at heart and hand, and a future before us for good achievements.

Very truly Yours,
A. Bronson Alcott

LETTER 79-78

[to Ellen A. Chandler]

Concord October | 21st 1879

Dear Miss Chandler,

If not to see our friends often were the means of forgetting them, a charming friend of mine would have been oblivious by this time. Happily however time has no claims upon our affections, and place finds them as chance may fall out incidentally. I had hoped to have found you in the group of our Summer pupils, but another attraction drew you from us then. I wish it may suffice and another Summer Session find you with us. I have the best of reasons for believing Mr. Harris will then be a neighbor of ours, perhaps occupant of the Orchard House, and the School fairly inaugurated for another success.

That you may be assured in due time of our arrangements, I forward our Prospectus for 1880.

I must add, my regret at not seeing you again for a parting salute before leaving for the West on a short tour, next Friday morning.

Meanwhile, I am,

Faithfully Yours

A. Bronson Alcott

Miss. Ellen A. Chandler.

LETTER 79-79

[to May, Paris, France]

Concord November 27th 1879

Dear May,

I returned last evening from a month's tour at the West to learn of your joy in pressing a babe to your bosom, and feeling yourself its Mother. And my happiness is enlarged and deepened by the gift of a third grandchild, and a granddaughter to group with my grandsons'. Happy mother, and happy father of the dear little one! May it bless as now blesses both. And the name. *"Louisa May Nieriker"*, it sounds sweetly. I shall hear further from yourself and Ernest concerning this *Pride* of the House of Nieriker and Alcott Truly, I hoped it would be a girl, and am gratified. And the delightful letters of its now grandmother, would grace any family, any romance of real life.

How I wish I might take her by the hand and call her *"Sister."* Now, my dear daughter you have an added interest in your noble husband and yourself. Life becomes still the sweeter, and the more beautiful. New duties, new solicitudes. Believe that your ascended Mother smiles upon you and your babe from abode of bliss! Love never perishes. And your love for her is now made the lovelier in that of her grandchild, named after the sister she loved so dearly, and your own.

Louisa is now in Boston, but is to pass our *birth days*, the 29th in Concord, and happily I have returned to celebrate it with her, and the household.

I had a pleasant tour, saw our cousins at their homes, and this too, without any expense of health, or money beyond my receipts for actual services. But I cannot travel now as when younger. Every attention shown, makes hospitalities too burdensome to me, and I am only free and cosy in my own home.

Salute the babe for me and smile anew on your Ernest for his and God's blessing, on your love

Ever Your

Affectionate father.

P.S./

What shall I send my little granddaugh[ter] *"Louisa May"*?—

LETTER 79-80[1]

[to Georgiana Hemingway Cook, Boston]

Concord December | 3rd 1879.

Dear Madam

Mr. Harris has not arrived yet. He is expected sometime between the middle of this month and the New Year. I fear we shall lose the pleasure of a reading from him while he is on this visit to New England.

I was disappointed in not finding you at your rooms last Monday. I enjoyed my interview with Mr. Cook, and his Lecture particularly. We may thank the Father of Intellect and eloquence that his spirit has illuminated and touched the lips of our contemporary, with a prophet's fire, and a Christian's devotion.

I shall gladly meet our friends on the 15. and if you insist in honoring me, on that evening, will open the Conversation.

Truly I am blessed with many friends and the spirits to enjoy them cordially.

Very truly
Yours,
A. Bronson Alcott

Mrs Cook,
   17 Beacon Street.
     Boston.

---

[1] MS. owned by the Duke University Library. A copy, in Alcott's hand, is in the Alcott-Pratt Collection.

LETTER 79–81

[to ?]

Concord December | 10th 1879.

Dear Sir.

I have but lately returned from a month's tour at the West—no farther than Columbus and Cincinnati. By the date of your letter which I found awaiting my return, I find it may be too late for any matters that I might furnish for the use you might make of such, if I had them even for you,—which *I have not.* Doubtless there are such scattered along the leaves of my Diaries during many Years past, but I should hardly know *which* or *what* to select, if I undertook to do so. Nor could I find the *will* even were the time at command. My story can only be narrated superficially without free access to documents of which yourself may have had a mere glimpse. I am quite willing any one should write whatever is in the air, or from any facts accessible, and shall read with pleasure (as I have your paper on Concord and its people in the Chicago Standard,[1] sent by yourself to me) any account or criticism concerning Mr. Alcott—But am not curious, or in the least anxious, to place him or Mr. Emerson before the public as recent converts to Orthodoxy from Heterodoxy. *Time* will show where they are unmistakably And your account may assist doubtless.

I had a busy time at the West preaching twice every Sunday in Orthodox pulpits.

Yours truly,
A. B. Alcott

---

[1] A Baptist periodical—see Frank Luther Mott, *A History of American Magazines* (Cambridge, Mass., 1938), III, 72.

LETTER 79–82

[to Mrs. DuBois]   Concord December | 15. 1879

Dear Mrs. DuBois.

    Your papers reached me, and have been hastily perused. Like most things originating from your new world the contents are fresh, and full of promise, the future. I observe that the selections from ancient sources show select reading and fine taste.

    I am pleased to learn of my friends residence and pursuits. Yes, I am eighty years of age, and still find health and hope for future Services.

Your friend,
A. Bronson Alcott

LETTER 79–83

[to Miss Wilson, Indianapolis, Ind.]   Concord, Mass. | December 15th 1879.

Dear Miss Wilson,

    I remember your persuasive plea, and my promises, when I had the pleasure of greeting you at my friend Gunsaulus' in Columbus.

    Now, I was fairly on my way as far as Cincinnati and with Indianapolis in prospect. Here, to speak plainly, as along where I paused, it became apparent, that your Western hospitalities would soon pass beyond my power of acceptance: the temptations were too inviting, irresistable, for me to continue farther on my way, so I ran home in pure self-defence. It was a disappointment, since I had pleased my self with the hope of meeting many friends in many cities, and Indianapolis was so near, too.—

    Now, kind madam, you have my apology for not appearing at your threshold, No. 115. Pom[?] Street, Indianapolis, and I am left with the reccollection [sic] of pleasant glances bestowed on your correspondent at parting in Columbus.[1]

    [1] The complimentary close and signature have been cut out.

LETTER 79–84

[to Mr. Reid? Andover? Mass.?]
[Concord, December 17, 1879]

I take pleasure in commending the bearer of this,—Mr.   of Andover Mass, a graduate of Yale, a gentleman of rare social accomplishments and devout spirit, to the citizens of my native State.

    Mr. Reid[?] is canvassing the State for the House of Messrs D. Appleton and Company of New York, whose various publications are well known and too numerous to be here enumerated.

I wish, however, to invite the special attention of School Committees, Superintendents and Teachers, to their Series of School Readers lately prepared by Superintendents Harris, of St. Louis, Mo, and Rickoff of Cleveland Ohio.

These books are more nearly suited to the present needs of the Schools than any Class Books that have come within my knowledge, and are already widely adopted throughout the States, East and West. They are modern in design, beautifully illustrated, graded to the capacities of the classes, from the Primary to the High departments, and the Selections of lessons are made from the purest and most rational of our authors.

A. Bronson Alcott

Concord, December,
17th. 1879.

LETTER 79-85

[to Miss Cleaver]

Concord. December | 19th 1879.

Dear Miss Cleaver,

Your full revelation of your spiritual self under present surroundings interests me both in your present and future career. You see by my address in this note, that I am imagining you a single lady, and perhaps suffering from some tender experiences whose shadows still darken your future as they haunt your memories of the past. You think *discontent* is your *present bosom sin*.

Well, the poet says,

"And discontent is immortality' dissatisfaction with *one's self* of course rather than one's outward lot, or conditions. We would all have the roses without the prick of the thorns in plucking them. But few, if any, have or can, possess them on other conditions; such is the life mortal, and but the pains incident to the possession of the faith immortal and enduring.

Mr. Harris is expected here about this time. You will find a friend in him at least, of your *intellect* if not your *affections,* and it is a duty to espouse both, if we will attain the peace that passeth *understanding.*

Your friend,
A Bronson Alcott

LETTER 79-86

[to ?]

Concord December | 22nd. 1879.

Dear Sir.

Yours is received asking information concerning Vegetarian Societies. &c. about which I regret to say I have little to offer. Thirty years ago I had some correspondence with Foreign British Societies, but during the last Fifteen or twenty years have known nothing of them. And since the decease of my cousin, the late Dr. William A. Alcott, I think both the principles and practice which he advocated have faded mostly from the mind of men. The Rev. Mr. Metcalf of Philadelphia an advocate also of like reform, died soon after and with his decease, I lost all information about the little sect of Vegetarians with which he was associated.

I know of very few persons who have practiced for any time this truly humane and Christian regimen. And as I deem at the root of all reforms in morals and religion.

I myself have been freed from any dependence on the slaughter house for fifty years, and have not tasted of flesh nor had any temptation to taste meanwhile. I have just passed my 80 birth day, and returned from a tour at the West, speaking almost every evening while absent, and preaching sometimes twice of a Sunday. I am complimented by every one on my surprising youthfulness and vigor, and really find myself in perfect health. It may be that I am venturing too far on this to hope to round off my full century in 1900. But I fancy my work is better done than at any former period. I have only a slight deficiency in hearing from inherited tendencies to catarrh otherwise consider my self free from all bodily infirmities. I sleep soundly, take daily exercise, am in my study from 10 AM. till 4 PM. when not from home conversing or lecturing or preaching, though I am but lay preacher.

As to diet, my scale runs thus. Fruits largely, next grains in their variety (not pastries) then the greens, or herbs (as medicine) taken as food, last, the roots, and I allow a margin for milk butter and cheese; Spices of all kinds I never use, salt in the cooking. Only occasionally oysters or fish. For drink besides pure water, cocca [sic], chocolate. tea I seldom take nor coffee, nor fermented or distilled drinks. Bathing with the hand[?] morning and at night, sleep about eight hours, good books good company, and a chosen task complete my dietary.

Very truly Yours,
A Bronson Alcott

LETTER 79–87[1]

[to ?]

Concord December | 22nd 1879.

Dear Sir,

I am sorry if any words of mine have led you to distrust your power to treat Concord and its people intelligently and truly.[2] I simply meant to say, that it seemed unbecoming in me to furnish particulars for your pen to praise us. And as to the current newspaper criticisms concerning Mr Emerson Mr Cook and Mr Alcott I had no thought of implicating yourself in these. Time will settle such matters. Then I really had very little material that seemed likely to assist you in your purpose. Such as I have laid hands on I now forward to you with this note. Pray do not relinquish your purpose for any words of mine or qualify it in the least. I have every confidence in your ability and discretion and in your desire to set any portion of the public right about us. And shall like to place your account on the leaves of my Diary as I have your first paper.

I shall hardly leave home for any considerable distance this season, and had to run home from the profuse hospitalities pressed upon me at the West, in self-defence.

Mr. Cook is speaking with more than his former fervency and power this season.

Very truly
Yours,
A. Bronson Alcott

¹ Another copy of this letter, in Alcott's hand, is dated December 19.
² See Letter 79-81.

LETTER 79-88

[to Sarah Denman, Quincy, Ill.]

Concord December | 22nd 1879.

Dear Mrs. Denman

Your pleasant note is at hand, and my friend's best portraiture salutes me amiably whenever I glance at my study mantel piece. And when will "the *original*" favor us with her speaking presence personally, and long? Next Summer surely, she will make her promise good and fair.

We are already designing the new structure and the scite on the Orchard Hillside for this Philosophical Institute, and expecting Mr. Harris will visit us between this and the New Years. So ideas are in the bud awaiting for the spring time to put forth into blossom—sometime bear their fruits.

I am in perfect strength of such powers as have been given for active services and finding a wider range of sympathies than ever.

Mr. Cooks lectures are an improvement on former ones, and his utterances more fervent, and effective, I must think, for permanent good. Agitation is a blessing to the indifferent, the dull, the biogetted [*sic*], the superstitious, the skeptical, and he touches all of these phases of our time. "It is grist to our mill," as Goethe said.

Dr. Jones has not written lately.

Dear Lady,
Affectionately Yours,
A. Bronson Alcott.

LETTER 79-89

[to ?]

Concord December | 22nd 1879.

Dear Sir.

You ask some comment on your lines, entitled *"Thoreau."* As prose, your summary in connected sentences, I might think characteristic. But, as verse, allow me to say, nothing is added, and the ear disappointed the want of melody,

791

which neither the ideas, nor the lack of connexion fulfil. You have only given an Inventory of qualities Characteristic it is true, but neither in conception nor in expression properly poetic. And less than poet even in his prose your subject never was.

As you challenge my criticism, I frankly give it for what it is worth.

Try your pen at an Essay on Thoreau, in prose, and see if you are not better pleased yourself, than with this Catalogue.[1]

---

[1] The complimentary close and signature have been cut out.

LETTER 79–90

[to Ellen A. Chandler]

Concord December. | Christmas Eve [1879]

My dear Miss. Chandler,

Your sweet note, with its flowery greeting for the New Year, has this moment been read with delight, a sensation that always accompanies the recollection of yourself, the pleasures of past interviews,—I may add, at the sound of your name, the joy of your presence. Forgive me, if I am too presuming on your modesty, by my frank confessions. But I never take my pen to write to you without the illusion of being a youth, and only by a little, your senior in years. How unaccountable that is!

I was in town the other day, and with the intention of finding you for a word. But failed of reaching your haunt in time to enjoy that favor.—

Be sure I shall be happy to call after the holidays. And may these be to you, as they promise to my self, auspicious of future happiness.

Always affectionately

Yours,

A. Bronson Alcott

Miss. Ellen A. Chandler.

LETTER 79–91

[to Miss Cleaver]

Concord December, | 27th. 1879.

Dear Miss. Cleaver.

I regret that my use of the word "affection", should have led you to mistake my meaning.[1] You ask for *light*, but this is given *through* the affections, whose questions the *Intellect* cannot answer fully. And, as my friend is near you, I presumed he might assist you in their *solution*. Beyond that—nothing was implied in my letter. Then your inference arising from similarity of names. I am not the Rev. Mr. Alcott criticised in the scrap enclosed in your letter. I should doubtless agree with him as to *"The Will being the determining factor.* Yes:

our free choices deify or doom us, and we are *free* to choose, else there were neither merit nor demerit reward or punishment proper.

I traced your references in "Tablets," curiously. The *"dear 500,"* are not friends, only *acquaintances,* and then acquainted only externally: Souls only love. No bodies are *only bodies and soulless.* As to Temperament, and your being mostly molded of III. and IV.[2] I think that accounts for the *antagonism,* which your letters confess. Not conditions *external,* but internal, *temperamental,* vex and disturb us mostly. The "Peace that passeth all understanding". is but the reconciliation between the foes in one's own household—the Atonement between the Will and affections.

You need not tell me whether your complexion is fair or dark your eyes blue, or black. I can divine these without such information. Your verses are characteristic Ah! if the Will, *would* without the prompting of Must. But to most it is through the struggling kingdom of *Must,* that they enter that of *Peace.*

I am interested in your correspondence, and shall enjoy further continuance, if you incline to write.

Your friend,
A. Bronson Alcott.

[1] See Letter 79–85.
[2] I.e., III. The choleric or fiery; IV. The sanguine or ethereal *(Tablets,* p. 196, *n.).*

LETTER 79–92

[to Mrs. Brown]

Concord, December. | 30th 1879.

Dear Mrs. Brown,

Thanks for your kind remembrance. The beautiful book of Letters of your lamented husband came to hand on Christmas day, as if mirth and sadness had been intermingled in the memories of that Festival. For I remember your husband as a guest, whom our household delighted to greet and entertain for his cheerful and sprightly merriment and he was specially a charming companion to my dear wife who entered so heartily into his wholesome humor, and could herself contribute to his enjoyment hardly less.

His sudden decease was a sad surprise to us all. And, not only to yourself and family, but to the many friends to whom he was endeared for his manly, social qualities, must his absence from your circle, be felt as a sad bereavement. I must think his cheerful Faith, was the prelude to still more joyous delight in the new existence to which he was so suddenly summoned.

Allow me, dear lady, to proffer my sympathies to yourself and family, and to assure you that I remember with pleasure, the genial hospitalities bestowed by yourself under your kindly roof.

Truly,
Your Friend,
A. Bronson Alcott.

LETTER 79–93

[to Elizabeth Oakes Smith]

Concord, December | 30th 1879.—

Dear Madam,

Your open Letter addressed to my self in last week's Index,[1] with the Poem, were read with surprise. I may add, the perusal revived pleasant of pleasant [*sic*] interviews with yourself in years past. And you ask for replies to your several questions concerning the spirit and needs of Prayer.

May I not answer, in the affirmative to each and all of your questions, and this without specifying them? Have you not, in fact, answered them affirmatively yourself in the beautiful verses which you have inscribed to me?

The deep mystics and devout Saints of all times have borne like testimony to the duty and delights of Prayer. Sometimes silent, sometimes spoken. And if they, dwelling in the *"Presence"*, communing with the Highest, the Holiest, have thus borne testimony to the need of prayer, is it not likely that those less in the spirit, and distant, must feel the need of his Presence, and invoke his name for what they think they need? The human heart is fathomless, and not every devotee is wise in Plato's sense; asking only for what shall satisfy and fill its desires. It may overflow in shimmering accents, believing that the Father to whom it appeals will answer its pleadings according to its deservings. Prayer manifests itself according to Temperament, culture, custom, the sense of duty. It may marry itself to forms and Times. It may love the Hush of the spirit; it may delight in its overflow. Words may be impertinent: the soul prayerless in their attendance.

The forms of worship thus vary according to these conditions. The extremes are apparent in the Romanist and Quaker formulas of worship. Speaking for my self I could wish the ministers were allowed a wider liberty in our devotional services. If these were formal, liturgical, or left somewhat to Individual choice. ‖ as to time, need ‖ Let us pray, when we profess. And what more than all it were desirable to learn is, that spoken words, whether in private or public are not prayer, unless the heart indite and give them life.

Thanking you for this kind remembrance I am

Very truly

Your friend

A Bronson Alcott

[1] *Index*, X (December 25, 1879), 620–21.

LETTER 79–94[1]

[to Georgiana Hemingway Cook, Boston]

Concord, December, | 30th. 1879.

Dear Mrs. Cook.

The meeting of the Froebel Union has been postponed. So we shall not have Mr. Harris at any of our Conversations till a later date. He will not visit

New England at this time. When he does, I shall hope to make Mr. Cook and yourself acquainted with him. I am sure you will find in him much to interest and the acquaintance will be mutually agreeable.

Very truly

Yours

A. Bronson Alcott.

[1] MS. owned by the Duke University Library.

LETTER 79–95

[to Ellen A. Chandler]

Concord December | 31st 1879.

My dear Friend,

I obey an impulse of my heart in taking my pen to communicate the sad intelligence of our dear May's departure to other scenes.[1] This morning Mr Emerson brought with tearful countenance the telegram ammouncing the sad event—for particulars concerning the great change we await full accounts.

She leaves a Babe to console us under this unexpected bereavement. And has had two happy years of married delight. The bright, joyous spirit has gone to taste holier joys with the dear ones whom she has rejoined in the New Existence. Anna and Louisa are stricken with deep sorrow, but there wells from the heart's depths consolations and hopes to brighten the gloom.

Blessed are the dead, who ascend to prepare the way for their earthly survivors. Yes, they live the life immortal.

Your afflicted Friend.[2]

[1] May Alcott Nieriker died December 29, 1879. Her husband, Ernest, sent a telegram to Emerson as the best person to tell the Alcotts the unexpected news (see Cheney, p. 324).
[2] The signature has been cut out.

PART TWENTY-FIVE

1880

LETTER 80–1

[to Georgiana Hemingway Cook, Boston]

Concord January | 5th 1880.

Dear Mrs. Cook

Your request is gratefully acceptable. I will open the Conversation as you propose in your note just received. Please give me all the time that courtesy to others dictates. Immortality is a theme, whose grounds and issues are not readily divined and brought into the light of our common day. And I may be in the mood of reading the Verses, as you intimate.

I forward the names of some friends of mine to be added, if you please to your list of attendants.

Miss. Ellen A. Chandler,
83 Pinckney Street.
Mr. R. W. Emerson and
Miss Ellen Emerson, Concord.
Mrs. S. H. Emery and lady ″
Mr. Mc.Clure and sister ″
Mr Augustus D. Smith
Divinity School.
Cambridge.[1]

[1] The letter breaks off at this point. Probably only the complimentary close and signature are missing.

LETTER 80–2

[to Frank Wakeley Gunsaulus, Columbus, Ohio]

Concord January | 7th 1880.

My dear Friend,

Grief seems long, and loves to stay. And best so perhaps that we may learn this lesson fully.

796

You will read in the accompanying notice of Sanborn's the sad account. And, though we had forebodings of the event, yet, when on the last day of the year, the telegram came to us we were not prepared for the stroke. The full particulars have not yet reached us. Her babe survived as a sad memorial of her mother's history. It may come to us, and bear its mother's name. I have had only the departed in thought ever since, and found some relief in the verses which I send you with this note.

Your full letter comes in the midst of our sorrow. And it was of such friendly import, that for the moment I seemed to have found in the writer a brother, latest found and loveliest. Thanks for your kind intentions to me, and our friend philosophy. And when you are free tell me further of yourself and circle—to whom greetings for their love of yourself.

Presently, I shall be[?] more at rest, and may I not expect a word from you? The sisters are sorrowful but they have tasted of this cup before. And Time is a physician for the mourners

Love to your wife, your Sister, and to little "Joe[?]' particularly.

Your brother, and friend,
A. Bronson Alcott

Gunsaulus.

> Love loves to suffer, sacrifice,
> He suffers so, and [word] dies;
> His lessons thus he lowly learns,
> Thus bows his head, to heaven returns,
> Thus reassured, to Heaven returns,
> His head upon his breast he bends
> And reassured to Heaven ascends.

LETTER 80–3[1]

[to Mary E. Stearns, Medford, Mass.]

Concord January 14th | 1880.

Dear Mrs. Stearns.

Your kind Sympathetic note came to hand yesterday. Yes, the dear departed has gone to happier scenes and employments. She has left us a pledge of her human happiness in her babe which we hope to have as a member of our family in the spring. Full particulars of her last days have not yet reached us. Our sorrows are great, but time is medicinal and the heart is susceptible to human sympathies, as divine. May always spoke of your great regard and kindness. Please accept our united thanks for your kind remembrances at this time.

Always Yours,
A. Bronson Alcott.

[1] MS. in the Clifton Waller Barrett Library, University of Virginia. The letter is written on the back of the second leaf of a three-page printed poem:

LOVE'S MORROW.

I.
It was but yesterday
That all was bright and fair:
   Came over the sea,
   So merrily,
News from my darling there.
   Now over the sea
   Comes hither to me
   Knell of despair,—
"No more, no longer there!"

II.
Ah! gentle May,
Couldst thou not stay?
Why hurriest thou so swift away?
   No—not the same—
   Nor can it be—
   That lovely name—
   Ever again what once it was to me.
   It cannot, cannot be
   That lovely name to me.

III.
I cannot think her dead,
So lately, sweetly wed;
She who had tasted bliss,
A mother's virgin kiss,
Rich gifts conferred to bless
With costliest happiness.

IV.
Broken the golden band,
Severed the silken strand.
Ye sisters four!
Still to me two remain,
And two have gone before:
Our loss, her gain,—
And He who gave can all restore.
   And yet—Oh! why,
   My heart doth cry,
   Why take her thus away?

V.
I wake in tears and sorrow:
   Wearily I say,
"Come, come, fair morrow,
And chase my grief away!"
   Night-long I say,
"Haste, haste, fair morrow,
And bear my grief away!"
   All night long,
   My sad, sad song.

VI.
"Comes not the welcome morrow,"
   My boding heart doth say;
Still grief from grief doth borrow;
"My child is far away."
   Still as I pray
The deeper swells my sorrow.
Break, break! The risen day
Takes not my grief away.

VII.
Full well I know,
Joy's spring is fathomless,—
   Its fountains overflow
   To cheer and bless,
   And underneath our grief
   Wells forth and gives relief.
Transported May!
Thou couldst not stay;
Who gave, took thee away.

Come, child, and whisper peace to me,
Say, must I wait, or come to thee?
    I list to hear
      Thy message clear.
           VIII.
"Cease, cease new grief to borrow!"
Last night I heard her say;
"For sorrow hath no morrow,
'T is born of yesterday.
Translated thou shalt be,
My cloudless daylight see,
And bathe, as I, in fairest morrows endlessly."

                            A. BRONSON ALCOTT.

CONCORD, Jan. 4, 1880.

LETTER 80–4[1]

[to William Sloane Kennedy?]

                            Concord March 13th 1880.

Dear Sir.

You may expect me on Tuesday evening the 16th., according to your request. my subject, *Heredity*. I shall be in Cambridge sometime on Tuesday, and the guest, (probably) of Dean Gray, at the Parsonage.

                            Yours truly,
                            A. Bronson Alcott.

[1] MS. owned by the New York Public Library.

[Letter to William T. Harris, St. Louis; from Concord, March 22, 1880, quoted in part in Leidecker, *Yankee Teacher*, pp. 371–72. See Appendix B.]

LETTER 80–5

[to William T. Harris, St. Louis]

                          Concord March 30th | 1880.

Dear Friend.

Yours of the 24. has just come to hand, and your assurance of coming to Concord in June, gives us all much joy. The Orchard House is all ready for your occupancy, and the Chapel is to be completed before your arrival. With yourself we hope the "Journal of Speculative Philosophy", (as in some sort representative of the Concord School of thought) will also *date from Concord*.[1] This whole Idea of the School has suddenly budded and promises fruits, that not even the most extravagant fancy had dared in its fondest freaks. We are now looking for Wm. Henry Channing's arrival from London. He has written that he purposes to be with us during the Summer Session of the School, and will doubtless give us some lectures on Oriental Ideas. We shall stir up the memory of the public soon by an advertisement of the *Time* of its opening, and prospects.

Did I tell you that since January, I have been happily busied in writing some Verses, now numbering 800 lines entitled *"New Connecticut"*,[2] of which Sanborn thinks favorably. They are autobiographic, and for private eyes and ears. I have read them only to the Emerys.

Cook has done his work in Boston and gone West, leaving for Europe in the ‖ summer ‖ [p. o.] autumn [p. in].

I have your Reports in half calf from 1868.9. to 1878.9.

Please write when you find a moment for us.

Very truly Yours.
A. Bronson Alcott

Wm. T Harris

[1] Harris moved to Concord in May, 1880, and lived in Orchard House, which he purchased in 1884. He continued to edit the *Journal of Speculative Philosophy* which beginning in 1880 was published at New York City rather than at St. Louis.

[2] Privately printed in 1881.

LETTER 80–6

[to   ?   ]

Concord March | 30th 1880

Dear Madam,

You have my thanks for your little book entitled *"Vegetarianism, the Radical Cure for Intemperance."* I have to apologize for this late acknowledgment of it And wish now to add my word to the efficacy of a fruit diet in meliorating and ultimately extermining, (as far as lies within the essence of food) the appetite for sensual indulgences of every sort, and this too, when seemingly inveterated by long habit. I wish our time, and its tendencies in thought favored habits of chastity alike in thought and deed, and would pause to consider the effects of food, along with other Stimulants of the appetites and passions which are having such acceptance, and[?] havoc of health and virtue.

I have now been for more than fifty years an advocate of a pure diet, and have reached the age of 80. years. I consider my self in perfect health, and able to do my special work, better now than at any former period. This I owe largely to abstinence from flesh and intoxicating drinks.

Allow me to sympathize with you in your efforts at Personal Purity, and to express my hope of seeing you sometime in Concord for fuller opportunity.

Yours,
A. B. Alcott

LETTER 80–7

[to   ?   ]

Concord, April 3rd 1880.

Dear Madam.

You will find a Sketch of Miss Louisa (written by Mr. Sanborn of Concord) in "St. Nicholas" for December 1877. and of Miss [*sic*] May Nieriker (by him also) in the "Springfield Republican," for January, 1880, the precise date I do not recall. These Sketches contain all particulars in which the public have any special interest.

I add some printed Verses occasioned by the death of Miss May.

Very truly Yours,
A Bronson Alcott.

LETTER 80–8

[to Frank Wakeley Gunsaulus, Columbus, Ohio]

Concord April 3rd. 1880

Dear Friend.

I am wishing to learn further of your "Sunday Opera Utterances," about which I read some weeks since in one of your Columbus newspapers. It seemed a happy opportunity for you, and has doubtless proved its power for good influences by this time. Nothing is more needful, just now, than sincere words spoken in pulpits with fervor and power of conviction, and I am looking for the youthful spirit to speak these.

Yesterday came to see me Mr. Edwin D. Mead lately home from Germany, and who has just read some thoughtful lectures in Boston on "The Pioneers of German Religious Thought, the first of which I heard with satisfaction. He is likely to help us in this work of reformatory preaching.

Better still. Mr. Harris writes that he expects to become a resident of Concord in June next; and to give us his lectures in the Summer School Sessions. Our Chapel, the foundations of which are already laid is to be completed in May seating 200 persons, and we shall have means at hand for future uses beside. I hope nothing will interpose to prevent your attendance, and as many desciples as may accompany you. Everything bids fair for a full attendance[.]

I have been busied since January in writing verses of an earlier period of my life, and these, much to my surprise run to 800 lines!

Give my regards to all of our friends at Eastwood.

A line from you will be most acceptable.

Truly Yours,
A. Bronson Alcott.

LETTER 80–9

[to George Zabriskie Gray, Cambridge, Mass.]

Concord April 15th. 1880.

Dear Sir.

You have my thanks for the gift of the Book of Christian Ethics—which I have not yet found full leisure to read as I could wish. Its tone seems catholic, and truly Christian in doctrine, broad and deep in its divinity. I am glad to know of its author.

My late visit remains a pleasant memory, and Cambridge has quite a home aspect, now that I have shared the hospitalities of the Deanery.

I hope to forward to you in a few days; our Prospectus of the Concord Summer School of Philosophy, and my desire to see you here during the Summer.

With kind regards to my good hostess, and the children.

I am truly Yours,
A. Bronson Alcott.

Dean Gray.
Cambridge.

LETTER 80–10

[to J. P. Gulliver, Andover, Mass.]

Concord, April 15th. 1880.

Dear Sir.

Dr. Bartol in a recent interview with him expressed a wish to visit Andover. And this in company with myself. I need not add of the pleasure it would give me to accompany him, and, if opportunity were given us, to meet Professors and students in such manner as might be deemed proper, by yourself and Faculty of the Seminary, or should a more private interview be preferred, this would be very agreeable to us both.

I trust, dear Sir, you will excuse any liberty which this intimation of our[?] desire, may imply, and if convenient, address me a word in reply.

Let me add, how much satisfaction a second reading of your admirable Address has afforded me. In that devout tone, and Christian vision the student of matter and of spirit may be sure of the divine annointings.

Very truly Yours,
A. Bronson Alcott

Rev. Prof. Gulliver.

LETTER 80–11

[to Frank Wakeley Gunsaulus, Columbus, Ohio]

Concord April 24th 1880

Dear Friend

Your full particular letter has just come to hand. Yes, the treacherous mails are offenders, or blunderers, and both of us have been meanwhile left in "the dark." Is it too late to hope recovering your letters to me. I can ill afford to lose their contents. But how, after the long interval, I do not see. They the book and letters must be lodged in some P. Office. Perhaps will go to Washington, and from thence forwarded. Let us hope so at any rate.

Your letter was a surprise after so long suspense regarding yourself and friends at Columbus. I had heard by a newspaper sent me, by some one, of your Opera adventure, and am now delighted at your supurb [sic] success. As to the picture I had really forgotten the matter, and shall be glad to see a photograph of it, if you have one. Certainly I am honored by your interest in it. Along with your letter came one from Mrs. Cook informing me of Joseph Cook's visit to you, and much complementary [sic] account of my visit and preaching when with you. I hope Mr Channing will not pass you on his way to Cincinnati.

I have written since the year a Poem entitled New Connecticut, the homestead of my ancestors which I think of printing. We are sure of seeing you here in July. Our Chapel is to be finished early in June.

To all my friends, and yourself and family, regards and remembrances

A. B. Alcott.

LETTER 80–12[1]

[to Georgiana Hemingway Cook, New Haven? Conn.?]

Concord April 24th 1880.

Dear Mrs Cook,

I am highly pleased by your kind remembrance and pleasant letter just come to hand.

It was my intention to have seen yourself and Mr. Cook before you left Boston, but you had flown when I called at the Hotel Bellevue.

I am pleased to learn of Mr. Cook's visit at Columbus, and of his meeting my friend Gunsaulus—the annointed Preacher. With yours, came a letter from him, informing me of his superb success at the Opera House on Sunday afternoons.—

Next summer, we shall hear him at our "Orchard House Chapel."—In a few days, I shall hope to forward to you Circulars of the Summer Session.

Please convey to Mr. Cook when you write, my affectionate regards, and delight in his extensive usefulness.

Should I visit New Haven in the latter part of May next, I shall hope to find you at Fair Haven, where a brother of mine resides.

Very truly
Yours,
A. Bronson Alcott

Mrs. Georgie H. Cook.

<hr>

¹ MS. owned by the Duke University Library. A copy, in Alcott's hand, is in the Alcott-Pratt Collection.

<hr>

LETTER 80–13

[to C. Bryan, Akron, Ohio]

Concord April 24th 1880.

Dear Sir.

Can you find any satisfactory excuse for my neglecting to answer your note of inquiry about the origin and Ideas of our School of Philosophy? I can only say, that your note came to me while I was specially engaged in a matter of deep interest, and I put off a reply till it seemed likely the time had passed when this would serve your purpose.

Indeed our Ideas are yet too indefinite to find adequate formulating and may await the next Summer's Session to find such. I trust you will again favor, and honor us, by your attendance. In a few days I shall hope to forward to you our circular for the Summer Session.

A new Chapel is to be completed for the School on the grounds in May, and we are anticipating a full attendance.

Very truly
Yours,
A. Bronson Alcott.

<hr>

LETTER 80–14

[to Frank Wakeley Gunsaulus, Columbus, Ohio]

Concord May 5th 1880.

Dear Friend,

Yours of May 1st. is at hand. My Verses are in the hands of one of the editors of our Monthlies, and I await his decision about the printing. Being largely of a biographical texture, I hardly hope for his acceptance of them. The Poem runs to 800. lines, and includes 200 Verses of four lines. It is largely descriptive of the scenery of my native place and neighborhood, and would gain much in impression by good illustrations. If printed for private distribution these would hardly be given

I shall gladly hear from the publishers of the Ohio Trade and Home Journal, and particularly from yourself about your enterprizes.—When do you assume the editorship, &c.—It will please me to see the verses in print, and the fact of your interest in their circulation would be an inducement for having them appear at the West.

I shall expect to hear from you soon about the matter, and whatever you have to communicate about your own affairs.

Very truly, Yours,
A. Bronson Alcott

PS. I add a verse or two, if you care for them.

Death.

O, death! thou utterest deeper speech,
A tenderer, truer tone,
Than all our languages can reach,
Though all were *voiced* in one.

Thy glance is deep, and far beyond
All that our eyes can see:
Assures to fairest hopes and fond,
Their immortality.[1]

---

[1] Printed in Alcott's *Sonnets and Canzonets* (Boston, 1882), p. 83.

LETTER 80–15

[to Mrs. Mosher, Cambridge, Mass.]

Concord May 7th 1880.

Dear Mrs. Mosher,

My thanks for your note and Card inviting me to hear the Reading on the 15. I should enjoy being present but am just now overseeing the erection of our Summer Chapel at the Orchard House, and shall hardly be able to give the time. Please transmit my thanks to Miss Burg[?] for the complement [*sic*] of the Card.

I believe I was to inform you about the occupancy of the Orchard House for the Summer. Mr Harris is expected to come about the first of June, and may become a permanent occupant. But this will not, I hope deprive us of your company during the Session of the School. Mr Moore would like to rent a part of his house for the summer, and we need a convenient restaurant for our company.

Perhaps you would like to serve us.

Yours Truly
Yours
A Bronson Alcott

[to William T. Harris, St. Louis]

Concord May 11 1880.

Dear Friend,

I enclose to you a corrected copy of our Circular.

The carpenters have begun work on "The Chapel, and promise to complete it without delay. I am having the grounds put in order for their occupant, the house itself is, I believe, in good repair.

Applications for attending the School reach us almost daily. We may reasonably anticipate a full attendance. We are fortunate in our benefactor, Mrs Thompson, who is to be the guest of the Lothrops again and arrive here soon. Hardly less fortunate in having Wm. Channing with us.

We have bespoke of housekeepers in the village lodgings for our visitors. Now if you will just fix your residence here, the future of Philosophic thought will not depart to less worthy places. We will consent to let you rove widely if you will, meanwhile, but Concord to be your abiding home. Where else should Philosophy fix her seat, if not on her soil, in her embrace? Can I further your removal in any way not yet known by me?

Did I tell you that my young Divine, Gunsaulus, had become editor of a Columbus newspaper, and that the publishers offer to print and illustrate my Poem of *"New Connecticut?"* I am to read it next week to the Historic Genealogical Society of Boston. I have read it to our High School.

We are now in the midst of Appleblossoms and cheerful Springtime.

It will add to the charm of the season to have you and yours fairly embosomed within the Orchard and its precincts.

I am in perfect spirits and awaiting your arrival.

Yours fraternally
A. Bronson Alcott.

Prof. Wm. T. Harris.

P.S. Mrs. Mitchell has written me from St. Louis, and is to be with us again.—

---

[1] MS. owned by the Fruitlands and Wayside Museums. A copy, in Alcott's hand, is in the Alcott-Pratt Collection.

LETTER 80–17

[to Samuel Orcutt, New Haven? Conn.]

Concord May 12th. 1880.

Dear Sir.

I am pleased to learn that your History of Derby is so near being completed. And think it a piece of good fortune that a historian has cared to write about the towns from whence both my grandparents date their descent—*Capt. John Alcock and Mary Chatfield.*

In my Poem entitled, *"New Connecticut,"* are some verses that may interest yourself, if not your readers, concerning these persons, and the Scenery of the Naugatuck Valley.

I copy them for you:—
Of my grandfather, son of the first settler of Spindle Hill.

His eldest heir, of military port,
Won from his kinsmans hand a captain's sword;
Bold Trumbulls minute men, in field and fort,
Heard his commission and obeyed his word.

Of Derbys ancient stock his lady came,
The gentler virtues in her sweetly blent,
The matron of the Hill, a gracious name,
Grandchild of Yale's first chosen President.

Borne as a bride, through the deep, dark defile,
Behind her lord, on pillion seated high,
Mistress of his new mansion; she, the while,
Views gorge and river with admiring eye.

Bold scenery here, and wonderfully wild,
Oer the steep jagged rocks, the hemlocks lower,
Darkening the wave below; and high uppiled
On either side the Alpine summit's tower.

His upland district had received ‖ the ‖ its name
From many a spindle, busy wheel and quill,
Such household arts bestowed a local fame,
It bore the homely title, Spindle Hill.

Of the Naugatuck Valley, from Mount Jericho by Waterbury and through the Narrows.

Where the wild Naugatuck sweeps rushing by
Mount Jericho's ledge and thence along its shores,
Dashed heedless of the driftwoods eddying whirls
As by the cornfields green, it onward pours
And 'gainst the jutting rocks its current chafes and
            curls.

Now swollen by numerous streams the flooded bank
Sees Waterburys mills beside it rise,
Whose varied industry ‖ and ‖ in growing rank
Sheffield and English Birmingham outvies.

There quivering o'er its reed grown stagnant mire,
Hid neath steep hills, the ambitious village slept,
Hugged its white houses and its towering spire,
Round Abrigadors ledge, Mad River swept.

Nurse of fair business and mechanic art.
Whose fostering carefulness, unsparing hand,
Transformed the Vale into a bustling mart
Broidering with enterprizes the river's strand.

Defiant still it cleaves Rock Rimmons pile,
Mingling its wave with gallant Humphrey's name,
Friend of Mount Vernon's Chieftain, he, the while,
And warrior poet of provincial fame.

Vale of unpictured grandeur, dost await
The artists practiced pencil, eye and hand,
Thy peaks forth looking on "the Steady State",
Behold such stream by iron roadways spanned.

I shall bespeak a copy of your History as soon as published,
Truly Yours,
A. Bronson Alcott.

Rev. Samuel Orcutt

LETTER 80–18

[to Anna Russell, Lancaster, Mass.]

Concord May, 16th 1880.

Dear Anna,

On looking over letters received from your father,[1] during many years of our correspondence, I find the one enclosed as being most suitable to the use which you have in view. I could wish the promised biography of him might not long be delayed from the public. And am pleased to learn that meanwhile this tribute of remembrance and regard is to be preserved in your Library.

Lancaster can have *hardly* had in her list of citizens, one more widely useful than was your father. I esteem it as an happy circumstance of my lot in life to have so long and so early enjoyed his friendship, and to have been so intimately associated with him in some of the important reforms of human culture attempted in our time. To him, in my judgment, more than to another may be justly given the honor of having initiated most of the modern improvements in a more wholesome ‖ and efficient ‖ humane system of education. More than the public are aware is he their benefactor and friend.

I may add, that we are often reminded of the pleasant years when our family and yours were associated and sometimes dwellers under the same roof,—memories still cherished and dear.

We are all very well, and expecting in September the arrival of Mays child, Louisa May (then will be ten months old[)] from Baden, to become one of our family—the living memorial of the dear departed.—

We all join in much affection to yourself, sister, and your dear mother (whom I must come and see) when convenient to her and yourselves.

Affectionately Yours
A. Bronson Alcott

[1] William Russell.

LETTER 80–19[1]

[to Trustees of Boston University, Boston]

Concord May 28th 1880.

To the Trustees of Boston University
Gentlemen,

Thanking you for your invitation to attend the Exercises in Music Hall on Commencement Day, June 2nd., I shall hope to be present on that occasion

Respectfully,
A. Bronson Alcott.

[1] MS. owned by the Boston University Libraries.

LETTER 80–20

[to Frank Wakeley Gunsaulus, Columbus, Ohio]

Concord, Mass. | June 8th 1880.

Dear Friend,

My verses have been returned. As to your wish to publish them in your Journal I have thought that we might best arrange concerning the matter, while you are here attending our Summer School of Philosophy, and so defer till then.

Our Chapel is now finished, and Mr. Harris has just arrived with family and goods and taken possession of the Orchard House. I have almost daily applications for attendance from widely separated sections of country, and every thing promises a numerous attendance.

I hope nothing is to hinder your joining us for the whole Session, with as many of your friends as you may bring with you. The West is our feeder, and publisher to other parts of the country.

Very truly Yours
A Bronson Alcott

Rev. F. W. Gunsaulus

LETTER 80–21

[to Miss Ford]

Concord. June 15th 1880.

Dear Miss Ford,

If not detained by preparations for our Summer School, I shall hope to attend your Graduation Exercises on the 23rd inst.

Pleasant memories abide of former visits and prompt to renew themselves.

I hope the day may prove fair, and your pupils approve the excellence of your teaching

Very truly Yours
A. Bronson Alcott

LETTER 80–22

[to John Steinfort Kedney, Faribault, Minn.]

Concord June 26th 1880.

Dear Sir,

Yesterday I called at Mrs. OBrians and made inquiries concerning her summer accommodations. She has good rooms, and will be pleased to furnish every thing to make her guests comfortable. I spoke good words for yourself—will reserve a good room for you. Dr. and Mrs. Jones have engaged theirs. I think you will find hers a desirable house during your stay in town.

Prospects are most encouraging for the Summer Session of the School. Our Chapel is now completed, and adds to the attractions of spot [sic]. Mr. Harris has taken his residence at the Orchard House; with intention, of becoming a permanent occupant.

I trust we may be able to plant the seeds of a finer philosophical culture for our times.

Hoping to greet you soon, I am, dear sir,

Truly Yours,
A Bronson Alcott

LETTER 80–23

[to Mrs. John? B.? Tileston, Concord]

Concord June 28th 1880.

Dear Mrs. Tilleston [sic].

Mr. Channing writes that he wishes to pass Sunday the 11th July in Concord, and will, if convenient to yourself be your guest during the first days of the session of the Summer School at the Orchard House. He remembers your invitation given him some time since and will gladly accept your hospitalities at that time particularly.

Now will you inform me if his wishes comport with your conveniences, and I will write to him conveying them at Brooklyn, where he makes it his home, or if you prefer addressing him there yourself. Only I wish to learn your wishes meanwhile.

Truly Yours,
A Bronson Alcott

LETTER 80-24

[to Samuel Orcutt, New Haven? Conn.]

Concord June 30th 1880.

Dear Sir.

Your History of Derby came safely to hand, and has laid me under additional obligations to your patient industry in gathering and compiling in an accessible form the materials for your history of this ancient and respectable township. I have now read the whole with deep interest and find not a little of personal account The Book is hardly without its peer in literary execution and the printing is superb. Old Derby shines along the successive pages and has something to show for itself along its shores—of industry and thrift worthy all praise.

Now, please take New Haven for your next task. Its history awaits the pen of an enthusiast like yourself in local literature.

I am left uncertain about the descent of my grandmother Chatfield from President Pierson.[1] Yet from certain side lights appearing in your narrative, I judge she was of his family.

Now when I see you, we will discuss printing my Poem of New Connecticut in your next edition of the Wolcott History.

I shall endeavor to forward to you in a week or two the $5.00 for the Derby Book.

Can you not afford to visit us during the Session of our Summer School, and this free of tuition fees attending as my guest?

Very truly
Yours,
A. Bronson Alcott.

[1] Abraham Pierson, the first president of Yale College.

LETTER 80-25

[to John Bigelow?]

Concord July 5th 1880.

Dear Sir.

Accept my hearty thanks for the gift of your Compendium of Swedenborg's Writings.[1] I expect to find it helpful in my lectures on Mysticism to be given in the School of Philosophy.

I enclose a ticket of admission to the lectures, and hope you will favor us with your attendance and take part in the discussions.

It will be some return for your gift of the Book, and ensure juster appreciation of Swedenborgs teachings.

Very truly Yours,
A. Bronson Alcott.

---

[1] A second edition, revised, of Samuel M. Warren's *A Compendium of the Theological Writings of Swedenborg* (Philadephia, 1875) was published in 1879, with a biographical introduction by John Bigelow.

LETTER 80–26[1]

[to Benjamin Marston Watson, Plymouth, Mass.]

[Concord, August 21, 1880]

Yes, the school is a delight, and a realized dream of happy hours in days of sunshine. Life has been a surprise to me during these latter years, and I allow myself to anticipate yet happier surprises in the future still to be mine.

---

[1] This portion of a letter is quoted as it appears in Sanborn, *A. Bronson Alcott*, II, 530.

LETTER 80–27

[to Frank Wakeley Gunsaulus, Columbus, Ohio]

Concord, August 23rd. 1880.

My dear Friend

How am I to interpret your long silence, while I have written and forwarded, from time to time, newspaper accounts of what I thought might interest you in us, and in our Summer School particularly. That has closed, and neither yourself nor your friend Pres. Myers[?], have appeared with us. I have only just heard from a Mr. Randall of your city, that you are now settled over Dr. Hastings' Congregation, and that they and other friends of yours in the city, "feared to let you come to Concord, lest we should steal you away from them. Remember, I told them, they "might retain you for ten years unless you stole away of your own accord."—

Now if you will not come to us, I for one, must come to you sometime during the coming autumn, and perhaps bring Channing along also, or, will two at once be too many, and frighten away your parishioners from yourself, and growing usefulness? Channing thinks of remaining with us and speaking for the rising faith throughout the West. Eloquent as he is, and true to the *"Church universal"*—he will prove a minister for the Gospel of glad tidings to many a doubting soul while he speaks.

Your newspaper has not reached me lately. And how prospers the Volume of promised discourses? If you let me come to Columbus I shall bring my poem of "New Connecticut" along for your hearing and appreciation.

I shall wish to speak of "the Concord Summer School," of Concord Authors, preach if that is open to me, and meet the students at the Colleges and Schools.

I am perfectly well, and equal now to much work of this sort. Greet all my friends cordially, particularly of your household

Always yours,
A Bronson Alcott

LETTER 80–28

[to Edwin Doak Mead]

Concord September 7th | 1880.

Dear Sir.

I returned a few days since from a short stay at the Seaside and found your note awaiting me.

In compliance with your request, it gives me pleasure to commend yourself to the literary and philosophic public, as a gentleman, amply accomplished by studies at home and in Germany, to speak on questions in which our thoughtful people are interested with clearness and abundant information. In saying this, I am but expressing an opinion formed after hearing one of your lectures in your course delivered lately in Boston. Your topics are such as our lecture going public must be benefitted in listening to, and I wish you may find a wide range of opportunity for the hearing, during the coming season of literary and social entertainments.

Very truly
Yours,
A. Bronson Alcott

LETTER 80–29

[to ?]

Concord September 7th 1880.

Dear Sir,

You honor me by your note of invitation to attend the dedication of Margaret Fuller's Island at your "Oregon" in the distant Illinois: in which celebration of a noble ‖ lady, fame, a ‖ representative woman, and author of wide repute, your townsfolk confer a lasting honor on themselves and the spot they dedicate to her Genius.

Should I be travelling near your town, I should be unwilling to pass by your [word] Island, ‖ and ‖ without paying my respects to yourself and your neighbors in acknowledgment for your kind invitation

Believe me,
Truly yours, meanwhile
A. Bronson Alcott.

LETTER 80–30

[to Frank Wakeley Gunsaulus, Columbus, Ohio]

Concord, September | 11. 1880

Dear Friend

Your book came to hand soon after my letter was sealed and sent. And I have now read it with admiring interest. It confirms my former estimate of your right to stand in the Sacred place, and speak the words of God to your contemporaries. The whole volume breathes the fresh, wholesome breath of a truly Christian spirit, bracing, brave, and tenderly alive to the needs of souls in all states and conditions. I think the worlds business could be despatched the more quickly and [word] on such fare. I find no trace of narrow sectarianism or blind bigotry in your flowing sentences. They stir the blood quicken the affections, and bring the truth home to heart, head and hand. The preacher believes in his heart and inspires belief. The ancient truths are clothed with a freshness that renders them youthful and attractive And the preacher often rises into a stream of eloquence lyrical and sweetly human. There is a deal of practical humanity in these delightful utterances. Sermons I, III and IV. are touching tributes to the deeper sentiments, and the preachers affluence of illustration is shown to advantage in the VI and VII.

I wish the volume may find readers beyond the circle of Eastwood friends. The preachers are too few, in these latter days, who wake the heavenly melodies in the souls of their hearers.

This is a hasty estimate of the Volume, but a hearty and hopeful one

Columbus may well open its pulpits to the young preacher, and bless God that such Gifts have been theirs to secure.

I am hoping to be with you within the coming autumn.

Yours affectionately,

A. Bronson Alcott

LETTER 80–31

[to William Henry Channing]

Concord September. | 22nd 1880.

My dear Friend,

I forward to your address the accompanying Translation from the Greek of Plotinus, by Mr. Johnson, and take this chance of learning from yourself, of your future plans and prospects. I trust to your friendship for such frank account as you will give me. It is my hope, and most earnest desire that you will remain on this side, and accompany me on our projected tour of teaching at the West. Or, if you cannot accompany me at the start, arrange for our meeting at points, as may be found most convenient for us. I am wholly unadvized of your movements since you left us at Concord.

It is my purpose to leave here for Connecticut, with Sanborn, on the 12th October, passing a day at Northampton, thence on to Hartford, Cheshire, Waterbury, Wolcott (my native place), and by the 25th. I take my way Westwards, probably by Albany and Syracuse. May I not hope to hear from you soon about your own intended movements?

I think you must have been gratified with the friendly favor our Summer School has gained from the press and public generally. If the tides of life are thus rising, it behooves us to take advantage of the uplifting wave.

Pray let me hear from you, my best friend, forthwith.

Ever Yours,
A. Bronson Alcott.

LETTER 80–32

[to Mrs. Yale, Shelburne Falls, Mass.]

Concord September 24th | 1880.

Dear Madam,

I purpose leaving Concord about the middle of October, to pass a few days in Connecticut on my way. And if you still cherish your purpose regarding a call from my self, I shall gladly pause at your place, and meet such companies as you may gather for Conversation.

May I expect a note from you at your convenience?

Very truly
Yours,
A. Bronson Alcott.

Mrs. Yale,
Shelburne Falls
Mass

LETTER 80–33

[to Miss Sherwood, Rome, N.Y.]

Concord September | 29th 1880.

Dear Miss Sherwood

I purpose leaving here for Western parts about the middle of October, taking Connecticut on my way, and visiting a sister at West Edmeston, not far from Utica also. It may be as late as November before I shall be passing Rome, where it would give me pleasure to pause and meet your friends if you think it were desirable and chose to arrange a company for me. I prefer the Parlor Conversation but do not refuse the platform, and pulpit,

"Concord Authors",
"The Concord Summer School",

might be pleasing subjects for either Parlor or Platform Should the thought interest you, please write and advise me about the matter.

We have abundant proofs of the interest taken in our Summer School, as you have learned by your attendance and favorable newspaper reports.

Very truly,

Yours,

A. Bronson Alcott.

LETTER 80–34

[to ? , Batavia, Ill.]

Concord September, | 29th 1880.

Madam,

I remember the hasty words that passed in August last on our Public Square, and your invitation to visit Batavia, should I extend my route West as far as Chicago. I am about leaving here for those parts, and will write you should I find my self in Chicago any time during the coming autumn or winter. Meanwhile you may arrange companies for me, if you think such desirable.

"Concord Authors,"

"The Concord Summer School",

are subjects suitable alike for Parlor or Platform. And for the Pulpit the time and place will naturally suggest the theme.

May I hear from you before I leave home?

Very truly

Yours,

A. Bronson Alcott.

LETTER 80–35

[to Mary N. Adams, Dubuque, Iowa]

Concord September, | 29th 1880/

Dear Mrs. Adams,

I am about leaving here for Western parts, and, if not overborne by hospitalities and sent home too soon, I may journey again into your state and city. Yet I fear I may miss you, as I find you are advertised for the Woman's Congress to be held in Boston in October, a few days after my setting forth for my tour, taking Connecticut on my way. I should be sorry to miss seeing you here in Concord particularly. And hope you may reach New England before I leave it. How many interesting matters await our consideration! too many and important for enumeration, and can receive their due only in free conversation.

But should I miss you in New England may I not hope to find you in your home at the West? It will be late in this year before I should reach Iowa, and your home whether at Dubuque or Des Moins [sic].[1]

I hope to interest people in our Summer School of Philosophy, which has already won marked favor from the Public thus far and promises results of great significance in the future. The Parlor, Platform, and Pulpit are open to me wherever I journey. I am favored with health and spirits, I may add, unabated enthusiasm, for work, and this at an age when most of our race have done their best, and retired from the scene. I hope to see the fruits of former labor fully ripe and harvested, as the years pass.

Our little one has just come to us from over seas, a bright healthy child now of ten months, and bringing joy and hope with her.[2]

The family are purposing to pass the winter in Boston, closing the house here till spring. I may be at the West during the Season. Louisa is well and with her new charge very happy.

I shall hope to hear from you before I leave. I purpose starting about the middle of October.

To yours all very kind remembrances,

Affectionately,
A B. Alcott

[1] Austin Adams had been appointed to the Iowa Supreme Court on January 1, 1876.
[2] May's daughter, Louisa May Nieriker, arrived September 19. After Louisa's death in 1888, Ernest Nieriker took the girl to his home in Zurich, Switzerland.

LETTER 80–36

[to Mrs. Yale, Shelburne Falls, Mass.]

Concord October 6th 1880.

Dear Mrs Yale,

Your note has just reached me. The time you name for our "first meeting" comes on the day of an engagement in Connecticut. If you could defer till the 21st. Oct. I could reach you on that day conveniently and meet your company in the evening for a Conversation. I could pass Sunday with you, and speak if opportunity offered in one or more of your pulpits, and address the Sunday Schools. If a Second Conversation was desired this might come between these days.

The terms you name are by no means to be scorned. I wish rather it were in my way to render any services of mine free of charge.

Very truly Yours,
A. Bronson Alcott.

Mrs. Yale.

LETTER 80–37

[to   ?   ]

Concord, October 9th | 1880.

Dear Sir

Your note and Card of Lectures along with your printed Sermon, come to hand just as I am about starting for a Tour West, to be gone from New-England for some months. It would give me pleasure to serve you in the way you name.

But I have little influence in providing lecturers for the Boston Monday Lecture-ship, my name appearing in the list of the committee, by request of Mr. Cook chiefly.[1] Besides, you will permit me to suggest that from the tenor and tendency of your Sermon, the Committee would be more likely to favor views less original, and even, for Boston *less radical*. Mr. Cook's views were rather more than most of that Committee were ready to endorse, and yours would be looked upon with distrust by perhaps all of them. Boston is undergoing a change from Radical views to more Conservative and Christian-Unitarianism, Transcendentalism being hardly acceptable to the more devout minds.

Our School of Philosophy we hope has something of the mediatorial and reconciling tendency, bringing the extremes into sympathy, and deposing the Individualism that has been so current in times past.

I hardly expect to journey as far as Dakota. But if I should before my return, it would be my hope to find you, remembering your hospitalities in Quincy.

Very truly,

Yours,

A. Bronson Alcott

[1] A copy of the prospectus follows:

BOSTON MONDAY LECTURESHIP.

The undersigned Committee, in charge of the Boston Monday Lectureship, hereby authen-ticate and commend the Rev. T. R. Briggs, the bearer, as a canvasser on their behalf.

The Monday Lectureship has for five years addressed week day noon audiences of a size unparalleled in Boston, or in any other city of the United States or Europe.

The lectures, as reported in full, reach, weekly, in this country and Great Britain, a half million of readers.

The discussions of current events are quoted more widely than any English or American leading articles.

The Committee think it of great importance that the extraordinary opportunity of public usefulness which these facts point out should be occupied to the full, and not narrowed by any mercenary considerations.

The lecturer is in such demand elsewhere, and has been for three years, that he declines each season at least $5000 worth of invitations outside of Boston in order to speak here.

The Committee have sold reserved seats and taken contributions, and in this manner expect to raise half the sum required, and for the remainder they confidently appeal to all friends of Evangelical truth.

Hon. A. H. Rice, Ex-Gov. of Mass.	Prof. Edwards A. Park, LL.D., Andover Theol. Sem.
Hon. William Claflin, Ex-Gov. of Mass.	Rev. J. L. Withrow, D. D.
Rev. Z. Gray, D. D., Episcopal Theol. School, Cambridge.	A. Bronson Alcott.
Right Rev. Bishop Paddock	Russell Sturgis, Jr.
Prof. E. P. Gould, Newton Theol. Institution.	Right Rev. Bishop Foster.
Rev. William M. Baker, D. D.	Rev. A. J. Gordon, D. D.
Pres. Wm. F. Warren, D. D., Boston University.	Samuel Johnson.
Prof. L. T. Townsend, Boston University.	Prof. B. P. Bowne.
Rev. L. B. Bates, D. D.	Rev. M. R. Deming.
Prof. R. N. Horsford.	Prof. J. P. Gulliver, Andover Theol. Sem.
B. W. WILLIAMS, SEC. & TREAS.	HENRY F. DURANT, CHAIRMAN.

[Letter to Franklin B. Sanborn, Concord; from Albion, N.Y., November 27, 1880. (Listed in C. F. Libbie & Co. sale catalogue, April 23, 1918, "Autographs, Letters, and Manu-scripts Left by the Late Frank B. Sanborn.")]

PART TWENTY-SIX

1881–1884

[Letter to Franklin B. Sanborn, Concord; from Cincinnati, January 18, 1881. (Listed in C. F. Libbie & Co. sale catalogue.)]

LETTER 81–1[1]

[to Franklin B. Sanborn, Concord]

Burlington, Iowa | March 18th 1881—

Dear Friend,

Yours of March 8th and 9th reached me yesterday. Having now reached the Missisippi [*sic*], and soon to turn my face northward, visiting a few places in the interior of the state, I may begin to entertain the thought of returning homewards. My interest still continues unabated in the incidents of my journeyings, and to the cordial acceptance every where, that I shall hope to fulfil the promise of my tour though it extend almost into the summer sunshine.—

I talked with Mr. Harris about our next summer session of the School, and also with Dr. Jones: Mr. Harris recommended The Tablets as the text for my Conversations. And doubtless I might use this acceptably. Still I am disposed to leave the matter at present undetermined. And if you print our programs before my return it will be sufficient to give the title of *"Five Conversations on the philosophy of Life."*—My experience of last summer, inclines me to give myself the largest scope of treatment; Dr. Jones coincides with me in this respect: I find wherever I journey much interest expressed in next summers session, and we may expect a larger attendance than last year. Philosophy is a favorite, and no stranger, here in these prairies. the Colleges even offer criticisms on professors at the East.

I may remain here over Sunday and speak in Dr. Salters Church. I find Sunday's tasks very interesting. No Sunday as yet, since I left home, but has offered its pulpit. I am encouraged by the strength and spirits thus striving for such services.

I did not visit Quincy on learning that Mrs. Denman was ill.

Mr. Harris is now at St. Louis I believe. Every where he is spoken of with admiration, and high hopes regarding his future career.

Mr Gunsaulus writes that he will send me copies of my *"New* Connecticut" in a week or two. I hope you received a copy of his discourse on *"George Eliot."*

Have you copies of our *Program* at hand? I should like some for distribution. Address me to the Care of Mrs. C. T. Cole, Mount Pleasant, Iowa

Yours faithfully,

A. Bronson Alcott.

[1] MS. owned by the Fruitlands and Wayside Museums. Alcott's last and most extensive tour of the West began October 12, 1880, and ended May 14, 1881.

LETTER 81–2[1]

[to Franklin B. Sanborn, Concord]

Dubuque, Iowa | April 8th 1881.

My dear Friend,

Yours with the Circulars for the Summer School reached me here. The Circulars I was glad to have at hand, as I had distributed the last of a former envelope, and had none for eager applicants. From most of the cities and towns where I have spoken, I think we may count recruits for next summer's sessions. Philosophy is deemed a profitable possession here in these Prairies—something useful as well as ornamental, an occupant of the head as well as the bookshelf.

I am here for a few days the guest of Judge Adams and lady. The pulpit and parlor alike claim what I may have for them, and I am not reluctant to give them the best I have. I find attentive listeners and quick questioners respectively: less of tradition, broader views than has been my wont to encounter nearer the Atlantic shores.

I leave for Rockford, Ill. to morrow, where I am to speak on Sunday and Converse on following evenings. Many cities lie along my route eastward, and ready to arrest my passage. I find I must deny myself the pleasure, for want of time, of pausing in them all. The spring birds are already here. The snows dissolving, and ‖ the ‖ our pleasant Village dawns with the sunrise as I front eastward.

I hear nothing from Mr. Harris who hoped to return to Concord about this time from St. Louis.

Looking over my letters I find Mr. Myers' of College Hill. I wish he may have a chance to speak in our lecture course. I enclose his letter.

Cordially yours,

A. Bronson Alcott.

P.S. My host and hostess send their remembrance.

A.B.A.

[1] MS. owned by the Fruitlands and Wayside Museums.

LETTER 81–3

[to Mariette Wood, Rome, N.Y.]

Concord June 3rd 1881.

Dear Madam,

I remember with pleasure my visit to your charming little circle, and fear it will miss the Teacher's kindly influences should she desert her pleasant charges. But if she decides against them, I shall gladly give her the benefit, (should it prove such) of my endorsement of her fitness for the tasks of teaching Infants—than for which ‖ no ‖ finer gifts are requisite, and none so rare.

Very truly,
Yours,
A. Bronson Alcott

Mrs. Mariette Wood,
Rome, N. Y.

LETTER 81–4

[to John Amory Lowell,[1] Boston]

Concord June 15th 1881.

To the Trustee of the Lowell Institute.
Sir,

The learned book of the late Prof. Peirce entitled "Ideality in the Physical Sciences," came to hand yesterday. A time of uninterrupted leisure were necessary to do justice, by the most thoughtful mind, to the perusal of so profound a treatise. We esteem it an honor to our School of Philosophy that the illustrious author was pleased to read to us his first and second Chapters of the volume now printed.

It was while waiting for a third, that he passed into the Idealities about which he had so learnedly written.

With thanks for the Volume

I am, Sir,
Respectfully Yours,
A. Bronson Alcott

[1] The sole trustee of the Lowell Institute, John Amory Lowell died November 13, 1881. Probably his son Augustus did not succeed him as trustee until the father's death.

LETTER 81–5

[to ?]

Concord July 1st 1881.

Dear Friend.

I am the richer to day for your yesterday's Speech. It was a brave plea for brave scholarship, nobility of letters, The speaker knew his audiance [sic] and the occasion. An inspiring spectacle, the orator standing before the best scholarship, the best blood of New England and urging in his persuasive utterance, (Tempered with flashes of fire), faith in the instincts of the people—the impotence of learning alone,—for molding the character of republics. Courage in his case was not lost, nor popular eloquence. If our seer had ceased to speak, eloquence survives in a contemporary, sending his ideas beyond the circle of his readers, to be caught and converted into life by the mass of citizens.

Well, the days of listening have come, and with these have come the era of acceptance also, the proscribed, ‖ during ‖ for the quarter of the century past. Harvard Halls even will listen and applaud and provincial Boston blushes for once at the suggestion of its time-serving. "The Times" of this morning ventures polite things about the speech, and speaker, and this is praise and appreciation beyond its words.

I mailed to your address yesterday a copy of our Prospectus of the Summer School opening on the 11th. and shall be pleased to find you are willing to give us a look as a compliment to the Ideas which we hope to expound for the furtherance of virtuous living and brave thinking.

Truly Yours,
A. Bronson Alcott.

LETTER 81–6

[to Lilian Whiting, Boston?]

Concord July 5th 1881.

Dear Miss. Whiting

I fear the Conversation has slipped from our fingers, it has not reached me through the mail. I shall be sorry to lose it. It had been in my possession but a day, nor had Mr. Sanborn seen it as the reporter desired. Your pleas were too prevailing: I did not dream of learning that it appeared or portions of it in [the] Traveller.

Will you take the trouble to forward it to me at once.

Yours,
A. Bronson Alcott.

LETTER 81–7[1]

[to Anna Lydia Ward]

Concord, Mass. | August 1st. 1881.

Dear Miss Ward,

I write herein the particulars about which you ask information. I was born November 29th 1799 at Wolcott, New Haven County, State of Connecticut.

My autobiographical Poem will be published in a few days.[2] The notes, if not the verses, may interest you, and shall do myself the pleasure of forwarding a copy of the book to your address.

Respectfully,
A. Bronson Alcott.

P.S. Your Encyclopedia of Quotations must be a useful and attractive volume[3]

A.B.A.

[1] MS. in the Beecher Family Letters, Tanner Library, Illinois College, Jacksonville, Illinois.
[2] *New Connecticut.*
[3] *A Dictionary of Quotations in Prose* (1889).

LETTER 81–8

[to Lillian B. Smith Abbot]

Concord August 24th 1881.

Dear Madam,

I gladly give you my name, and testimony to your gift of Elocution, remembering your readings at the School of Oratory, and pleasant words which I had with you there. I am sure that any pupil of yours will be fortunate in having chosen you for teacher in this delightful accomplishment—one that I am happy in commending you to any wishing such aid.

Very truly
Yours,
A. Bronson Alcott.

Miss Lillian B. Smith,
    now Mrs Abbot

[Letter to Franklin B. Sanborn, Concord?; from Concord, September 2, 1881. (Listed in C. F. Libbie & Co. sale catalogue as a "Long letter giving notes upon 'Infancy.' ")]

LETTER 81–9

[to ?]

Concord September, | 19 1881.

Dear Sir,

Your Cyclopedia of Health and Longevity came safely by Express, and has found more than one reader in my household. Accept my thanks for the valuable gift along with very pleasant memories of the kind attentions given me by yourself and associates during my stay in your city. I read with sorrow of the decease of the venerable father whom I had the honor of meeting when I was with you.

Mr. Minner's call upon us was very agreeable to us, only too short. He gave us the last[?] accounts of the welfare of those who were so hospitable during my visit.

It may be worth adding to inform you that your patient is now fully repaired of any damages arising from his long tour at the West.

Very truly
Yours
A Bronson Alcott.

Letter 81–10

[to ?]

Concord September | 21st 1881

Dear Sir.

I forward to your address a copy of my little book, and am pleased to learn that you cared to possess a copy.

Mr. Walton I am informed by Rev. Wm. H. Channing, who knew him, died a year or more since, and his theosophic library and papers were, by Mr. Channings suggestion, given to one of the great London Institutions, I do not now remember the name now.

You are fortunate in having a copy of his Wm. Law, of whose Life and works I lately saw a copy in a Boston bookstore. It was an English print, and I shall put a copy in my library.

I shall be glad to hear from you and your studies often.

Truly Yours,
A. Bronson Alcott

Letter 81–11

[to ?]

Concord October 4th, 1881.

Dear Friend.

My thanks for your doomsday discourse which I had read and preserved in my Diary as a historic reference. I find a verse of mine read here on Memorial Day in Concord.

Let us believe[?] our Nation[?] begins a brave heroic life with this sacrifice.

Cordially
Yours,
A. Bronson Alcott.

LETTER 81–12[1]

[to Martin Kellogg Schermerhorn? Newport, R.I.]

Concord October | 17th 1881.

Dear Sir,

It would have been a great pleasure to me to have been with the friends of the good preacher to whose memory they dedicate a costly chapel.[2] But carpenters are a class whom one may not safely leave even for a day. I must, therefore, forego that pleasure, and ask the committee's acceptance of a verse or two, giving voice to what I might speak were I to be with you on Wednesday.

Very truly,

Yours,

A. Bronson Alcott.

---

[1] MS. owned by the Vassar College Library. Two copies, both in Alcott's hand, both dated October 16, are in the Alcott-Pratt Collection. This letter clearly precedes the following one.
[2] William Ellery Channing.

LETTER 81–13[1]

[to William T. Harris]

Concord October | 16th 1881—

Dear Friend

Yours is just at hand from Bloomington, where you must have done good work.

Your letter tells a most extravagant tale of Mr Alcotts orations at the West. I remember following on the trail of a certain Wm. T. Harris who left a streak of light wherever he sojourned, and was still blazing in that wilderness of trash, but consuming only such. I suppose we shall make a few clearings there, and prepare the ground for the culture of Ideas which the barrens in New England fail to produce.—

You ask about my work. Like Herbert I may say

> And now in age I hear[?] again
> After so many deaths, I live and write,
> I once more smell the dew and rain,
> And relish versing"

I have been on six months pedling tour to the Carolinas and Virginia, have been laid low with typhus, got up from a tussle with the Goblins and spectres horrible and walked all the way from Norfolk to Spindle Hill, stopping in New York a day to change homespun for broadcloth, to the amazement of the rustics who had known only what their own fields and looms had bestowed. Yes, The verses number now just 60, longer than part first of Pedler's Progress and there are sonnets and about the Lady, and the beginning of schools in Boston.

Best of all at the Memorial meeting here I read an ode to Garfield and the

Countries use to be made of that sacrifice. Moreover, and to close the list of work, "as you phrase it I have just sealed, for the Channing Memorial Services at Newport on Tuesday, a Sonnet to the Great Preacher to whom they then dedicate a costly Chapel—

The carpenters are now at work on the study and promise occupancy by Thanksgiving, when you shall report "the philosophers Progress" through the West and South—

These are stirring times for us, and work for all the wits[?] we have at command to animate and grow a new crop for the future.

Sanborn is here every few days and then away with the people. I think our skeptics, and sophists, and silly book worms will need step aside soon, lest they find themselves smothered and trodden in the mire of their nonsenses.

Your Journal has not yet reached me.

This is a long scribble but may serve for a sign of my

regard and affection.
A. Bronson Alcott

[1] From a copy, in Alcott's hand, in the Alcott-Pratt Collection. The original is in the Alcott-Harris Collection in the Concord Free Public Library (see Appendix B).

LETTER 81–14

[to George Willis Cooke, Dedham, Mass.]

Concord November 30th | 1881.

Dear Sir,

I wish you may gather sufficient information about the Dial contributors to complete your design.[1] And to the list of names mentioned in your note add J. Eliot Cabots, who may assist you. I gave you all the facts in my possession in my Conversation of which I find you have availed yourself in the text of your book —which I have just read with much satisfaction. It contains much that had not been printed, and you have said a good word for the School of the master.

I will think about the lecture.[2]

[1] An article published first as "The Dial: An Historical and Biographical Introduction, with a List of the Contributors," *Journal of Speculative Philosophy*, XIX (July, 1885), 225–65, 322–23; later as *An Historical and Biographical Introduction to Accompany the Dial as Reprinted in Numbers for the Rowfant Club* (Cleveland, 1902).
[2] The letter breaks off at this point.

LETTER 81–15[1]

[to Franklin B. Sanborn? Concord?]

[Concord] November 30th '81.

Dear Friend,

Many thanks for your sumptuous Gift Book of Illustrious Autographs.

The quondum [sic] Scribe may now revel amid the freaks of the quill during some generations past.

I need not add, the giver is valued beyond his gift, and that he is more to me than another in these ‖ days of several ‖ later Septenniads.

Again thanks, and an added stroke to the pages should the mood favor.

> Ever yours,
> affectionately,
> A. Bronson Alcott.

[1] MS. owned by the Fruitlands and Wayside Museums. A copy, in Alcott's hand, is in the Alcott-Pratt Collection.

LETTER 82–1[1]

[to Ellen A. Chandler]

[Concord, January 1, 1882]

Dear Miss Chandler,
and friend,

May I still fancy as aforetime[?] when the pen added to the pleasures of acquaintance. I venture this little New Years' remembrance, with good wishes, and many pleasant memories.—adding a verse or two.

> A.B.A.

[1] MS. owned by the Houghton Library, Harvard University. The letter is inserted on p. 3 of a copy of *New Connecticut*, which is inscribed:
> "A. Bronson Alcott
> to his friend
> Miss Chandler
> January 1 1882—"

LETTER 82–2[1]

[to Ellen A. Chandler]

Concord January 7th 1882.

Dear Miss Chandler,

Enclosed is a ticket of admission to the Woman's Club on Monday next. Not remembering whether you are a member, I send this, hoping to catch some of the former inspiration of your presence and interest, as I am then to read a Sonnet or two on that afternoon.

May I call for you at any place in the city?

> Yours affectionately,
> A. Bronson Alcott

Miss Ellen A. Chandler.

[1] MS. owned by the Abernethy Library, Middlebury College. A copy, in Alcott's hand, is in the Alcott-Pratt Collection.

LETTER 82-3[1]

[to Benjamin Marston Watson, Plymouth, Mass.]

[Concord, March 29, 1882]

These late months have flattered me with some sonnets addressed to friends, —one to a friend long cherished and held in remembrance, living in retirement at his rural Hillside. A copy will find you as soon as published.[2] The sonnets number many; and I am pleased with having sung, however lispingly, traits most apparent to me in the group of friends it has been my happy fortune to enjoy and love. I wish you would indulge me and your friends by looking at us here in our home. I shall be proud to introduce you to my new study and library.

[1] This portion of a letter is quoted as it appears in Sanborn, *A. Bronson Alcott*, II, 530.
[2] See A. Bronson Alcott, *Sonnets and Canzonets* (Boston, 1882).

LETTER 82-4

[to Ellen A. Chandler]

Concord May 23rd. 1882

My dear Miss Chandler,

I greet you on this auspicious union with a learned and excellent friend.[1] Suited, (as I have proofs enough), to your own learned tastes and aspirations.—A friend and relative also of my friend Watson of Plymouth, whose attractions of place and character, a Sonnet of mine celebrates. It has long been my hope, and is now made a reality, that you were to link your destiny with a noble Soul, and now it has come. May every kind star shine on your future. And may I be permitted to claim you as friend—I had written lover—not less, for this new friendship, and to still subscribe myself,

Affectionately, Yours,
A. Bronson Alcott.

[1] The reference is to Ellen Chandler's marriage to William Watson Goodwin, Eliot Professor of Greek at Harvard. He was a nephew of Benjamin Marston Watson.

LETTER 82-5[1]

[to O. Street]

Concord May 24th 1882

Dear Sir.

I am honored by the invitation of the Plato Club to meet with the members, and participate in its discussions, on Monday evening next, (the 29th) and shall esteem it a pleasure. Mrs. Richardsons kind hospitalities I have enjoyed and gratefully remember during my former visits to your city.

Very Truly Yours,
A. Bronson Alcott

Mr. O. Street,
    Pres. Plato Club

¹ MS. owned by the New York Public Library.

LETTER 82–6¹

[to   ?   ]

Concord June 8th. 1882

Dear Sir.

The family about which you make enquiry was named May. The young lady Kate. She is the daughter of Mr. Charles May who died some years ago at Lynn. His widow went to Dublyn [sic] N. Hampshire, where a son then lived, and where her daughter Kate found a husband named Robert Kirkpatrick. They are now living at Dillon, Montana.

Yours truly,
A. Bronson Alcott.

¹ MS. in the Charles Roberts Autograph Collection, Haverford College Library.

LETTER 82–7¹

[to Mary Russell Watson, Plymouth, Mass.]

[Concord, August 12, 1882]

I have a moment, before going to the Chapel this morning, to acknowledge your kind note advising me of Mr. Watson's illness. You do not say how ill he is; only your fears mingled with expressions of your funny patient's humors. I should infer that he would take that invading stranger in a jocose mood; and I take it as a hopeful sign. But will you not inform me if anything of the sadder transpires? The School closes this noon. When our invalid is on his feet again, and the School has been put behind a little, I shall like to greet the inmates of dear Hillside again.

¹ This portion of a letter is quoted as it appears in Sanborn, *A. Bronson Alcott*, II, 532.

LETTER 82–8[1]

[to ?]

Concord August, | 24th. 1882

My young friend.

I have not forgotten your letter and request. My autograph was written on the Cards, and mailed to your address. If you sent my portrait at the same time, I must have returned it. Lest it should have failed, I enclose one that I happen to have at hand. This may not be like the other but is a fair likeness of myself at the age of 82.

Yours truly,
A. Bronson Alcott

[1] MS. owned by the Historical Society of Pennsylvania.

LETTER 82–9[1]

[to ?]

Concord August 24th 1882

Dear Sir.

Your questions concerning the Christian Revelation and the Conscience deserve an explicit answer. Let me first say that any report of discussions on these, which you may read, is imperfect and, for want of connexion with the subject matter, misleading.

What I meant to say was that Christian Revelation gained so much the greater evidence when the soul's descent from God was implied in its prexistence [sic], since, being born out of him and then incarnated in a Babe, it must be older than the babes body, and, if this were admitted, there was a reasonable persuasion—if not certainty—that it would survive the decease of the body— thence an argument for its immortality. And I wished this *Spiritual* heredity were preached, in proof of the souls' immortality as a doctrine of Christianity. This would satisfy many who now grope for any evidence of their survival after the death of their body.

As to the Judgment following our wrong doing, this is sure. But no one can regain the state he lost by sinning, without help from strength above him. Every sin weakens him. Hence the Christian doctrine of atonement.

Conscience commands us to do what is right. But we are free to choose to do what we know to be wrong. Our sentence following the chosen wrong act, comes instantly, but the consequences are not done away with at once, and pass over into the future life even though we shall have repented and reformed. None can regain of himself what he has lost by a single sinful chosen deed. He may mistake, he may err in judgment, but this is not sinning. To choose the wrong and do the wrong, knowing it be wrong, and loving to do this, is *sin*. We were not free beings, in God's image, unless we could choose between the good and the evil. Conscience is the Voice of God's Spirit revealing to us our Duty.

Yours truly,
A Bronson Alcott

[1] MS. owned by the Library of the Chicago Historical Society.

LETTER 82-10[1]

[to John Burroughs, Riverby, West Park, N.Y.]

[Concord, October 11, 1882]

If the genuine Concord philosophy does not, as you intimate, flourish outside of Concord, its

> 'wine that never grew
> In the belly of the grape,'—

fair clusters, sunned under wise eyes, ripened in vineyards by the fertile banks of the Hudson, do flourish there, and find way to gladden some of the host here dwelling by sluggish Concord stream.

The crate came safely to hand yesterday. And that your generous gift shall not be selfishly appropriated and enjoyed, our friends and yours—Channing, Sanborn, and Harris—are to partake thereof this evening at our fortnightly Symposium, our Mystic Club.

> So if perchance we get heady.
> 'T will lighten us and steady,
> Check our hilarious flight,
> From soaring far from sight.

My thanks for your generous gift and your kind remembrance of me. Come yourself and see us.

Cordially yours
A. Bronson Alcott

[1] This letter is quoted as it appears in Clara Barrus, *The Life and Letters of John Burroughs* (Boston and New York, 1925), I, 248.

LETTER 82-11[1]

[to A. H. Dooley, Indianapolis, Ind.]

Concord, October 12th | 1882

Dear Sir,

I hoped to have seen you often when last in your city, not a mere street interview.

831

I will place your name in the list of subscribers for the Emerson, next time I am in Boston, and forward a copy, to your address with the autograph, when the book is published.[2]

Give my kind remembrances to Mr. Mc.Culluch and other friends in your city.

Yours truly,
A. Bronson Alcott.

---

[1] MS. owned by the Fruitlands and Wayside Museums.
[2] Alcott's *Ralph Waldo Emerson, Philosopher and Seer: An Estimate of His Character* (Boston, 1882). Emerson had died April 27, 1882.

LETTER 82–12[1]

[to ?]

Concord October 12th 1882.

Dear Sir,

The Card forwarded hither is at hand. But these impedimental agents Time and Space hold me bound within their confines. I wish the members of the "Emerson Society" may have a lively sitting this evening, and "Conduct" themselves in a Scholarly manner, becoming the theme and author. Success attend them in their studies and noble aims.

Cordially,
A. Bronson Alcott.

---

[1] MS. owned by the Minneapolis Public Library.

LETTER 82–13[1]

[to H.? F.? Bassett, Waterbury, Conn.]

Concord, October 13th 1882.

Mr. Bassett
   Librarian of Bronson Library
      Waterbury
         Conn.

Dear Sir,

I missed you, after we reached the Fair Grounds, and had no chance to put into your hand the fare for the horse and carriage that took us to Wolcott. I am ashamed at my carelessness in not giving it to you before I left you. And am not sure the sum I enclose is the price asked by the stable man. But the three dollars is most convenient to mail, and if this is not enough I will add the more. Was it $3. or 3.50?—

I had a pleasant journey, and saw most of the living—but how many are gone!

Thanks for your kind attentions

Truly Yours,
A. Bronson Alcott.[2]

[1] MS. owned by the Fruitlands and Wayside Museums.

[2] This is the last letter in the present collection that is written in Alcott's hand. On October 24, 1882, Alcott suffered a stroke from which he made little recovery. Although able to attend occasional lectures at the Concord School of Philosophy, he was unable to participate actively in any intellectual enterprises. His health slowly declined until his death on March 4, 1888, two days before Louisa's death.

LETTER 84–1[1]

[to Oliver Wendell Holmes]

Concord Dec 18th/84

Dear Mr Holmes.

Accept my thanks for your very valuable book. I like it very much, and shall greatly prize your kindness in sending it to me.

Faithfully Yours.
A. B. Alcott.

[1] MS. owned by the Library of Congress. The letter is *not* in Alcott's hand, but does bear his printed signature.

APPENDIX A

THE FOLLOWING LETTERS are quoted (mostly in part) in A. Bronson Alcott, *New Connecticut*, F. B. Sanborn, ed. (Boston, 1887). On p. 247 of that book, Sanborn has noted: "In copying his early correspondence for printing, Mr. Alcott has occasionally omitted and inserted matter, in order to give the story of the time more clearly. Any repetitions in these letters may thus be explained. In some cases the originals have been used by the editor."

To:

William A. Alcott; from Wolcott, Conn., May 29, 1817, pp. 172–73.

Anna and Joseph Alcox, Wolcott, Conn.; from Norfolk, Va., November 30, 1818, pp. 214–16.

Anna and Joseph Alcox, Wolcott, Conn.; from Norfolk, Va., February 14, 1819, pp. 216–18.

Anna and Joseph Alcox, Wolcott, Conn.; from Norfolk, Va., January 24, 1820, pp. 218–19. (See Letter 20-1.)

Anna and Joseph Alcox, Wolcott, Conn.; from Amos B. and Chatfield Alcox, Norfolk, Va., March 17, 1820, pp. 219–20.

William A. Alcott, Wolcott? Conn.; from Norfolk, Va., March 19, 1820, pp. 183–84, 220–21.

Anna and Joseph Alcox, Wolcott, Conn.; from Norfolk, Va., July 3, 1820, pp. 221–22.

Anna and Joseph Alcox, Wolcott, Conn.; from Abbeville? S.C., November? 1820, p. 189.

Anna and Joseph Alcox, Wolcott, Conn.; from Norfolk, Va., December 5, 1820, pp. 205–6.

Anna and Joseph Alcox, Wolcott, Conn.; from Norfolk, Va., April 3, 1821, pp. 225–26.

Chatfield Alcott, Wolcott, Conn.; from Warrenton, N.C., April 13, 1822, pp. 95–96.

Chatfield Alcott, Wolcott, Conn.; from Petersburg, Va., November 24, 1822, pp. 238–39.

William A. Alcott, Wolcott? Conn.; from Chowan County or Perquimans County, N.C., March, 1823, pp. 226–27.

Chatfield Alcott, Paris, N.Y.; from Cheshire, Conn., June 15, 1825, pp. 244–45. (See Letter 25-1.)

Anna and Joseph Alcox, Wolcott, Conn.; from Cheshire, Conn., November 1, 1825, p. 245.

William A. Alcott, New Haven, Conn.; from Cheshire, Conn., January 13, 1826, pp. 246–47.

APPENDIX B

LETTERS from Amos Bronson Alcott to William Torrey Harris in the Alcott-Harris Collection, Concord Free Public Library.

1857
Buffalo, N.Y., December 22

1858
Concord, Mass., November 15
Chicago, Ill., December 13

1863
Concord, Mass., June 4

1865
Concord, Mass., July 12
Concord, Mass., August 13
Concord, Mass., December 3

1866
Concord, Mass., January 15
Concord, Mass., February 2
Concord, Mass., April 17
Concord, Mass., June 3
Concord, Mass., June 17
Concord, Mass., July 15
Concord, Mass., September 13
Concord, Mass., November 18

1867
Concord, Mass., February 10
Concord, Mass., May 12
Concord, Mass., August 6
Concord, Mass., September 17
Concord, Mass., November 15
Concord, Mass., November 26

1868
Concord, Mass., January 19
Concord, Mass., February

Concord, Mass., February 20
Concord, Mass., February 26
Concord, Mass., March 4
Concord, Mass., April 2
Concord, Mass., July 7
Concord, Mass., July 12
Concord, Mass., September 22
Concord, Mass., November 4
Concord, Mass., November 22

1869
Concord, Mass., May 12
Concord, Mass., June 6
Concord, Mass., July 24
Concord, Mass., July 28
Concord, Mass., September 3
Maplewood, Mass., November 6
Cleveland, Ohio, December 17

1870
Elyria, Ohio, January 2
Ann Arbor, Mich., February 9
Chicago, Ill., February 22
Maplewood, Mass., March 28
Concord, Mass., May 20
Concord, Mass., October 3
Concord, Mass., October 24
Buffalo, N.Y., November 8
Detroit, Mich., November 19

1871
Concord, Mass., July 4
Concord, Mass., September 2
Concord, Mass., September 20

Concord, Mass., December 7

1872

Concord, Mass., February 6
Concord, Mass., March 11
Concord, Mass., April 7
Concord, Mass., May 17
Concord, Mass., July 5
Concord, Mass., September 19
Concord, Mass., October 5
Concord, Mass., October 10
Concord, Mass., November 6
Dubuque, Iowa, November 20
Des Moines, Iowa, December 14

1873

Davenport, Iowa, January 1
Muscatine, Iowa, January 20
Concord, Mass., February 19
Concord, Mass., April 14
Concord, Mass., September 6
Concord, Mass., October 22

1874

Boston, Mass., January 27
Boston, Mass., February 7
Concord, Mass., May 17
Concord, Mass., June 17
Concord, Mass., June 24
Concord, Mass., September 27
Quincy, Ill., November 6
Des Moines, Iowa, December 3
Fort Dodge, Iowa, December 11
Dubuque, Iowa, December 29

1875

Rockford, Ill., January 12
Janesville, Wis., January 19
Chicago, Ill., February 11

Chicago, Ill., February 17
Bloomington, Ill., March 1
Concord, Mass., April 6
Concord, Mass., August 25
Concord, Mass., November 6
Concord, Mass., December 3

1876

Concord, Mass., May 8

1877

Concord, Mass., January 23
Concord, Mass., May 20
Concord, Mass., June 6
Concord, Mass., June 30

1878

Concord, Mass., May 6
Concord, Mass., July 25
Concord, Mass., August 15
Concord, Mass., October 5

1879

Concord, Mass., January 26
Concord, Mass., February 15
Concord, Mass., February 21
Concord, Mass., April 7
Concord, Mass., April 18
Concord, Mass., May 13
Concord, Mass., June 7
Concord, Mass., October 6
Brooklyn, Conn., November 1

1880

Concord, Mass., March 22

1881

Columbus, Ohio, January 6
Concord, Mass., October 16

INDEX OF CORRESPONDENTS

Index of Correspondents

Bigelow?, John, 80–25
Bintliff, James, 77–27
Bissell, Arthur D., 78–53, 79–2, 79–4
Blaisdell, Albert F., 74–9
Blake, Harrison Gray Otis, 76–10, 77–11, 77–12
Bliss, Porter Cornelius, 77–24, 78–3
Boatwell, George S., 75–12
Boston *Herald,* Editor,—June 11? 1878
Boston University, Trustees of, 80–19
Brackett, Anna C., 71–18, 72–40, 72–49, 74–17, 76–24
Brigham, Mary A., 77–13, 77–18
Bronson Brothers, 55–1
Bronson, Hiram, 55–2
Bronson, Isaac, 59–14, 63–28
Bronson, Rebecca, 63–28
Bronson, Seymour, 64–4
—(?)September 23 or 24, 1859
Brooks, J. G., 74–5, 74–22
Brown, Miss, 79–7, 79–92
Bryan, C., 73–4, 80–13
Burleigh, Celia, 72–19, 72–46
Burritt, Elihu, 77–28
Burroughs, John, 82–9, 82–10

Calthrop, Mr.,—June 8, 1864
Chadwick, John White, 77–16
Chandler, Ellen A., 68–10, 68–17, 68–18, 68–20, 68–23, 68–26, 68–30, 68–32, 68–36, 68–40, 68–44, 68–45, 68–47, 68–49, 68–52, 69–1, 69–2, 69–4, 69–8, 69–12, 69–13, 69–18, 69–25, 69–28, 69–30, 69–32, 69–34, 69–38, 69–40, 69–43, 69–50, 69–51, 69–54, 69–56, 69–61, 70–6, 70–10, 70–14, 70–22, 70–24, 71–3, 71–4, 71–5, 71–12, 71–23, 72–9, 72–10, 72–12, 72–13, 72–16, 72–21, 72–23, 72–24, 72–27, 72–28, 72–41, 72–43, 72–54, 73–6, 73–10, 73–21, 73–24, 73–28, 73–29, 73–31, 73–45, 73–56, 74–23, 74–42, 76–1, 77–40, 78–24, 78–29, 79–78, 79–90, 79–95, 82–1, 82–2, 82–4
Channing, William Ellery (the Younger), 73–34
Channing, William Henry, 69–57, 79–16, 79–76, 80–31
Cheney, Ednah Dow Littlehale, 50–4, 51–2, 69–16, 69–52, 69–60, 71–6, 72–30, 73–25, 73–41
Choate, Charles, 68–11, 68–15
Clarke, Professor, 68–31, 68–34
Cleaver, Miss, 79–51, 79–85, 79–91
Clifford, John H., 72–3
Coan, D., 74–19

Cole, Mrs. C. L.?, 75–25
Collier, Robert Laird, 70–19
Concord, Town of, 63–7
Congregational Society, Fraternity of the Twenty-eighth, 64–7
Conner, Rowland, 70–9, 74–14
Cook, Georgiana Hemingway, 77–30, 77–33, 77–34, 77–43, 78–1, 79–15, 79–60, 79–80, 79–94, 80–1, 80–12
Cook, Kenningale Robert, 73–11, 77–21, 77–22, 79–23
Cooke, E. Bronson, 63–20, 63–27, 68–51
Cooke, George Willis, 81–14

Dana, Charles A., 58–8
Davidson, Thomas, 67–13, 67–28, 68–9, 69–7, 69–29, 72–1, 72–18, 76–12
Davis, Georgiana, 74–15, 74–26, 75–20, 75–23, 78–23
Davis, Paulina W., 69–41, 69–53
Davis, Thomas, 46–1, 62–8, 62–10
Denman, Sarah, 72–38, 73–2, 78–7, 78–27, 78–37, 78–43, 79–71, 79–88
Deutsch, William, 76–7
Dooley, A. H., 75–22, 75–28, 76–14, 76–23, 77–10, 78–22, 79–13?, 82–11
Drake, Herbert H., 78–33
Drake, Samuel Adams, 72–25, 74–1
DuBois, Mrs., 79–82
Dudley, Dr., 77–3
Dudley, Mrs., 75–15, 76–25
Dwight, John Sullivan, 72–33
Dyer, Francis, 77–29

Eaton, W. E., 72–26
Eddy, James, 75–8, 78–19
Eddy, Mary Baker Glover, 76–2, 76–8
—March 6, 1877; August 21, 1877; September 14, 1877
Ely, Mrs., 70–15
Emerson, Edward Waldo, 74–41
Emerson, George Barrell, 61–7, 73–36
Emerson, Lidian, 65–11
Emerson, Ralph Waldo, 37–2, 37–3, 37–4, 37–5, 37–7, 37–8, 37–9, 42–12
Emery, Samuel H., 72–34, 79–12, 79–35

Felton, A. C., 72–39
Fernald, W. M., 64–5, 68–1
Fett?, Charles W., 75–17
Fields, Annie Adams, 69–14

Fields, Osgood and Co., 69–48, 70–16
Fisher, Elizabeth R., 73–37
Ford, Miss, 80–21
Francis, Convers, 38–3
French, P. N. ?,—July 9 or 16, 1875
Frizelle, A. T., 79–55
Frothingham, Octavius Brooks, 76–17
Fuller, Louisa M., 78–45

Gage, Mrs. Francis D., 67–6
Gannett, William Channing, 74–4
Garland, Mary J., 76–18
Garrison, Francis J., 79–56
Garrison, Wendell P., 79–56
Garrison, William Lloyd, Jr., 63–1, 79–56
Gilman, Nicholas P., 76–20
Gould, Rebecca Sprogell, 64–14
Gould, Thomas Ridgeway, 73–44
Graham, Sylvester, 48–2
Gray, George Zabriskie, 78–34, 80–9
Gulliver, J. P., 80–10
Gunning, W. D., 73–33
Gunning, Mrs. W. D., 73–58
Gunsaulus, Frank Wakeley, 79–39, 79–42, 79–45, 79–52, 79–54, 79–59, 79–69, 79–74, 80–2, 80–8, 80–11, 80–14, 80–20, 80–27, 80–30

Hammond, E. L., 65–3
Haniford, Miss, 73–59
Harris, David H., 72–20
Harris, William Torrey, 57–38, 63–16, 65–17, 65–29, 66–2, 66–15, 66–17, 66–18, 67–7, 67–12, 67–15, 67–17, 67–25, 67–29, 68–3, 68–7, 68–12, 68–25, 68–35, 68–41, 68–46, 69–3, 69–24, 69–31, 69–36, 69–39, 69–45, 69–59, 69–63, 70–3, 70–5, 70–12, 70–20, 70–25, 70–29, 70–31, 71–8, 71–13, 71–16, 71–20, 72–4, 72–8, 72–14, 72–29, 72–37, 72–50, 72–51, 73–1, 73–3, 73–13, 73–38, 74–7, 74–10, 74–34, 75–14, 75–26, 76–16, 77–4, 77–14, 77–17, 77–19, 78–25, 78–39, 78–42, 78–50, 79–3, 79–8, 79–25, 79–43, 79–67, 80–5, 80–16, 81–13. (*See also* Appendix B.)
—April 17, 1866; September 27, 1874; March 22, 1880
Haskell, S. H., 76–26
Hayes, Mrs., 79–19
Hewes?, Mr., 79–17
Heywood, E. H., 69–22
Hickok, G. C., 64–20
Higby, Mrs. T. C., 78–6

840

GENERAL INDEX

The following index lists persons, publications, and organizations. It is necessarily selective, for Alcott mentions so many persons (frequently in almost catalogue fashion), that the shaping of an all-inclusive index would be an almost endless task. Hence, many persons and publications mentioned in the letters are not included in this General Index. Further, significant persons and publications which are mentioned with great frequency are listed with the notation passim: e.g., Ralph Waldo Emerson, William Torrey Harris, Samuel J. May, Samuel E. Sewall, Journal of Speculative Philosophy. Members of Alcott's immediate family are not listed in the General Index, since references to those persons occur throughout. However, references to publications by Alcott and members of his family are included.

The General Index should be used with the Index of Correspondents. Individual references to persons to whom Alcott wrote letters can be found in the Index of Correspondents, and those references are not repeated in the General Index.

Adams, Mary Newbury, 529, 531, 544, 560, 564, 578, 579, 594, 602, 607, 779, 820
Aesthetic Papers, 362
Agassiz, Louis, 192, 440
Alcott, A. Bronson, *Concord Days, passim; Conversations with Children on the Gospels, passim; Emerson*, 361–62, 364, 365, 366, 368, 369, 370, 371, 372–73, 374–75, 377, 592, 596; "Love's Morrow," 798–99; *New Connecticut*, xviii, 800, 806–8, 811, 820, 822, 827, 835; *Observations on the Principles and Methods of Infant Instruction*, 18; "Psyche," 28, 29n3; *Ralph Waldo Emerson, Philosopher and Seer*, 832; *Record of a School*, 44, 442, 448; *Sonnets and Canzonets*, 805, 828; *Table Talk, passim; Tablets, passim*
Alcott, Louisa May, *A Modern Mephistopheles*, 686; *An Old-Fashioned Girl*, 510, 513, 515, 521; *Aunt Jo's Scrap Bag*, 591; *Camp and Fireside Stories (with Hospital Sketches)*, 483, 488; "Cost of an Idea," 616, 618; *Eight Cousins*, 646, 657–58, 660, 661; *Flower Fables*, 191; *Hospital Sketches*, 343, 344n1, 348, 349, 391; *Little Men*, 533, 534, 535; *Little Women*, 462, 483, 488, 490, 501, 521, 646, 647; "Love and Self Love," 310, 318; *Moods*, 362, 363n1, 462; *Rose in Bloom*, 675, 676; *Shawl-Straps*, 578, 591; "The Modern Cinderella," 318; "Transcendental Wild Oats"(?), 627; "Under the Lilacs," 697; *Work*, 585, 591, 592, 595, 605, 607
Alcott, May, *Concord Sketches*, 494, 497, 501
Alcott, William Andrus, xix, 42, 43n5, 44, 79, 114, 130, 155, 162, 184, 191, 195, 289, 301, 302n1, 304, 328, 329, 442, 455, 588, 593, 619, 657, 780, 782
Alcott House (England), 48, 442, 468
Amberley, John Russell, Viscount, 414, 415, 416, 418, 595, 673
Amberley, Katharine Stanley Russell, Viscountess, 414, 415, 416, 418, 595
American Socialist, 681
Arnold, Edwin, *The Light of Asia*, 783–84, 785
Arnold, Matthew, 441, 596
Atlantic Monthly, 310, 313, 315, 318, 342, 370, 523, 541, 626, 692, 693

Barber, John Warner, *Connecticut Historical Collection*, 189n6
Barnard, Henry, 195, 249, 250, 280, 283, 299, 307, 321, 598
Bartol, Cyrus Augustus, 354, 403, 416, 418, 426, 434, 498, 502, 542, 548, 550, 555, 585, 625, 629, 633, 640, 673, 674, 686, 705, 706, 710, 721, 755, 802; *Radical Problems*, 551
Beecher, Henry Ward, 210, 211, 216, 226, 295, 296, 340
Bellows, Henry Whitney, 198, 199, 200, 201, 204, 207, 208, 210, 211, 212, 213, 214, 215, 216, 218, 219, 220, 226, 229, 231, 241
Biber, Edward, *Henry Pestalozzi, and His Plan of Education*, 647
Blake, Harrison Gray Otis, 191, 195, 299, 300, 693–94
Boatswain's Whistle, 359n1
Boston *Daily Advertiser*, 609, 610, 611
Bower, Samuel, 103, 104n5
Bowring, John, 64, 66, 68n3
Brackett, Anna C., 401, 410, 411, 434, 440, 452, 459, 461, 508, 531, 537, 549, 552, 554, 569, 573, 577; ed., *Education of American Girls: A Series of Essays*, 628; ed., *Silver Treasury of Poetry*, 676